THE INTERNATIONAL LAW OF MIGRANT SMUGGLING

Whether forced into relocation by fear of persecution, civil war, or humanitarian crisis, or pulled toward the prospect of better economic opportunities, more people are on the move than ever before. Opportunities for lawful entry into preferred destinations are decreasing rapidly, creating demand for a range of services that is increasingly being met by migrant smugglers: individuals or criminal groups who facilitate unauthorized entry into another country for profit.

This book, a companion volume to the award-winning *The International Law of Human Trafficking*, presents the first-ever comprehensive and in-depth analysis of the international law of migrant smuggling. The authors call on their direct experience of working with the United Nations to chart the development of new international laws and to link these specialist rules to other relevant areas of international law, including law of the sea, human rights law, and international refugee law. Through this analysis, the authors identify and explain the major legal obligations of States with respect to migrant smuggling, including those related to criminalization, interdiction and rescue at sea, protection, prevention, detention, and return.

Anne T. Gallagher AO is a lawyer, practitioner, teacher, and independent scholar with an established reputation in international affairs, particularly in human rights and the administration of criminal justice. She is a former United Nations Official (1992–2003) and was Special Adviser to Mary Robinson, the UN High Commissioner for Human Rights and former president of Ireland, from 1998 to 2002. In that capacity Dr. Gallagher participated directly in the development of the new international legal framework around transnational organized crime including the Migrant Smuggling Protocol. She continues to advise the United Nations and since 2003 has led a high-profile intergovernmental initiative that aims to strengthen legislative and criminal justice responses to human trafficking and related exploitation in South East Asia. According to the U.S. government, Dr. Gallagher is "the leading global authority on the international law on human trafficking." She is the author of many publications, including *The International Law of Human Trafficking*, which was awarded the 2011 American Society of International Law Certificate of Merit – Honorable Mention.

Fiona David is a Visiting Fellow at the Centre for International and Public Law at the Australian National University, where she teaches Transnational Criminal Law in the postgraduate program. As a lawyer and criminologist, she has nearly twenty years of experience working on migrant smuggling and human trafficking throughout Australia, Asia, and Africa, with organizations including the UN Office of Drugs and Crime and the International Organization for Migration, and on projects funded by AusAID, USAID, and the European Union. She was the principal Drafter of the UNODC *Model Law against the Smuggling of Migrants* and of the UNODC *Model Legislative Provisions against Organized Crime*. She is the Executive Director of Global Research at Walk Free Foundation, an international human rights organization.

The International Law of Migrant Smuggling

ANNE T. GALLAGHER AO

FIONA DAVID

CAMBRIDGE
UNIVERSITY PRESS

CAMBRIDGE
UNIVERSITY PRESS

32 Avenue of the Americas, New York NY 10013-2473, USA

Cambridge University Press is part of the University of Cambridge.

It furthers the University's mission by disseminating knowledge in the pursuit of education, learning and research at the highest international levels of excellence.

www.cambridge.org
Information on this title: www.cambridge.org/9781107015920

First published 2014

A catalogue record for this publication is available from the British Library

Library of Congress Cataloguing in Publication data
Gallagher, Anne T., author.
The international law of migrant smuggling / Anne T. Gallagher, Fiona David.
p. cm.
Includes bibliographical references and index.
ISBN 978-1-107-01592-0 (hardback)
1. Human trafficking. 2. Human trafficking – Prevention – International cooperation. 3. Human smuggling. 4. Emigration and immigration law. 5. Refugees – Legal status, laws, etc. 6. Human rights. I. David, Fiona, author. II. Title.
KZ7155.G357 2014
345′.0237–dc23 2013040596

ISBN 978-1-107-01592-0 Hardback

From the perspective of international law, any Government of a sovereign State, as a general rule if it deems necessary in its own interest, has the right to admit or not admit and to expel or not expel aliens who wish to enter or who reside in its territory, as well as to impose conditions on their entry or residence if it deems it necessary in the interest of its tranquility or domestic or international security, or of the health of its inhabitants.

Rolin-Jaquemyns, "The Right of Expulsion of Aliens," *Annuaire de l'Institut de droit international*, vol. X (1888–1889), Lausanne session, p. 235

What men, what monsters, what inhuman race,
What laws, what barbarous customs of the place,
Shut up a desert shore to drowning men,
And drive us to the cruel seas again?

Virgil, *Aenid I*, 539–540, Dryden's translation 1 (760–763), cited in Grotius, *The Freedom of the Seas* (1633)

Contents

Detailed Contents

UN Committee against Torture

UN Human Rights Committee

International Criminal Court

International Criminal Tribunal for the Former Yugoslavia

Table of Common Abbreviations

CEDAW	Convention on the Elimination of All Forms of Discrimination against Women
CERD	International Convention on the Elimination of All Forms of Racial Discrimination
CoE	Council of Europe
CPT	European Committee for the Prevention of Torture and Inhuman or Degrading Treatment or Punishment
CRC	Convention on the Rights of the Child
ECOSOC	(United Nations) Economic and Social Council
ECOWAS	Economic Community of West African States
EEZ	Exclusive Economic Zone
EU	European Union
Europol	European Police Office
Frontex	The European Agency for the Management of Operational Cooperation at the External Borders of the Member States of the European Union
HRC	Human Rights Committee
ICAO	International Civil Aviation Organization
ICC	International Criminal Court
ICCPR	International Covenant on Civil and Political Rights
ICESCR	International Covenant on Economic, Social and Cultural Rights
ICJ	International Court of Justice
ICTY	International Criminal Tribunal for the former Yugoslavia
IGO	International Governmental Organization
ILC	International Law Commission
IMO	International Maritime Organization
Interpol	International Criminal Police Organization
IOM	International Organization for Migration

MOU	Memorandum of Understanding
NATO	North Atlantic Treaty Organization
NGO	Non-governmental Organization
OAS	Organization of American States
OAU	Organization of African Unity
OHCHR	Office of the United Nations High Commissioner for Human Rights
OSCE	Organization for Security and Co-operation in Europe
SAARC	South Asian Association for Regional Cooperation
UDHR	Universal Declaration of Human Rights
UN	United Nations
UNHCR	United Nations High Commissioner for Refugees
UNICEF	United Nations Children's Fund
UNODC	United Nations Office on Drugs and Crime

Introduction

The term "migrant smuggling" refers to the unauthorized movement of individuals across national borders for the financial or other benefit of the smuggler. More simply, it can be understood as facilitating the breach of migration laws for profit. Although aspects of illegally facilitated migration are established criminal offenses in many countries, such practices were not the subject of international legal regulation until very recently. It was only in the late 1990s that the international community came together under the auspices of the United Nations to formulate a common understanding of what migrant smuggling is, and to adopt a treaty-based cooperation framework that would support a coherent response. The impetus for this development was readily apparent. Irregular migration[1] to key destination States, particularly the United States of America and parts of Europe, had grown sharply in the 1980s and 1990s. This was increasingly characterized by professionalization of migrant smuggling: a foreseeable and logical consequence of tighter immigration controls to the preferred destinations at a time when demand for such migration was rising rapidly. A focus on the facilitators of irregular migration, rather than just the migrants themselves, was widely viewed by destination States as a critical element in any effective response. The result of that process was a specialist legal regime comprising the Migrant Smuggling Protocol[2] and its parent instrument the

[1] Terminology around the issues addressed in this book is highly contested and international legal rules do not offer a clear way forward. The authors use the term "smuggled migrant" to refer to an individual whose entry or stay in a country is unlawful and has been facilitated by a third party for profit. When addressing the broader migration phenomenon of which migrant smuggling forms a part, the book eschews the pejorative and inaccurate "illegal migrant/migration" in favor of "irregular migrant/migration." Other terms in increasingly common use and generally equivalent accepted meaning are "undocumented migrant/migration" and "unauthorized migrant/migration."

[2] Protocol against the Smuggling of Migrants by Land, Sea and Air, supplementing the United Nations Convention against Transnational Organized Crime, 2241 UNTS 507, done Nov. 15, 2000, entered into force Jan. 28, 2004 [Migrant Smuggling Protocol].

United Nations Convention against Transnational Organized Crime.[3] In addition to defining smuggling, the Protocol and Convention detailed a range of obligations on States: from criminalizing migrant smuggling and related offenses to cooperating in the exchange of information, evidence, and intelligence.

The novelty of the issue contributed to a general perception that the regime around migrant smuggling established by the Organized Crime Convention and Migrant Smuggling Protocol was a complete or self-contained one. However, as this book will demonstrate, the relevant international legal framework is older and considerably broader; comprising a dense web of rights, obligations, and responsibilities drawn not just from the Protocol and Convention but also from the law of the sea, human rights law, and refugee law. Long-standing international principles establishing the rules of sovereignty and jurisdiction dictate the capacity of States to act against migrant smuggling. Equally distinguished principles place a range of limitations on that capacity. The secondary rules of international law are also vital: most particularly in attributing responsibility for internationally wrongful acts associated with migrant smuggling as well as with State responses.

It is this broader framework that is the focus of the present work, and the explicit purpose of the book is to set out the framework in a way that is as clear as its complexities, overlaps, and occasional inconsistencies allow. To date this has not yet been done. Scholarly legal writings on migrant smuggling have tended to focus solely on a single aspect of the Protocol,[4] or on the link between the Protocol and refugee law,[5] or on the link between migrant smuggling and human rights,[6] or migrant smuggling by sea.[7] Broader studies on various aspects of "international

[3] United Nations Convention against Transnational Organized Crime, 2225 UNTS 209, done Nov. 15, 2000, entered into force Sept. 29, 2003 [Organized Crime Convention].

[4] See, for example, A. Schloenhardt and H. Hickson, "Non-Criminalization of Smuggled Migrants: Rights, Obligations, and Australian Practice under Article 5 of the Protocol against the Smuggling of Migrants by Land, Sea, and Air," *International Journal of Refugee Law*, first published online Mar. 12, 2013; and T. Obokata, "The Legal Framework concerning the Smuggling of Migrants at Sea under the UN Protocol on the Smuggling of Migrants by Land, Sea and Air," in B. Ryan and V. Mitsilegas eds., *Extraterritorial Immigration Control: Legal Challenges* 151 (2010), at 151.

[5] See, for example, C. Brolan, "An Analysis of the Human Smuggling Trade and the *Protocol against the Smuggling of Migrants by Land, Air and Sea (2000)* from a Refugee Protection Perspective" (2002) 14(4) *International Journal of Refugee Law* 561; F. Crépeau, "The Fight against Migrant Smuggling: Migration Containment over Refugee Protection," in J. van Selm, K. Kamanga, J. Morrison, A. Nadig, S. Špoljar-Vržina, and L. van Willigen eds., *The Refugee Convention at Fifty: A View from Forced Migration Studies* 173 (2003) [Crépeau, "The Fight against Migrant Smuggling"]; and Z. Kasli, "Criminalising and Victimising the Migrant: Reflections on the UN Protocol and UNHCR's Position against Smuggling" (2011) 1(2) *Oxford Monitor of Forced Migration* 64.

[6] See, for example, T. Obokata, "Smuggling of Human Beings from a Human Rights Perspective: Obligations of Non-State and State Actors under International Human Rights Law" (2005) 17(2) *International Journal of Refugee Law* 394.

[7] See P. Mallia, *Migrant Smuggling by Sea: Combating a Current Threat to Maritime Security through the Creation of a Cooperative Framework* (2009).

migration law" tend to consider migrant smuggling incidentally, if at all.[8] Much stronger contributions to fleshing out important parts of the legal framework have in fact come from other sources: most particularly recent scholarship around extraterritorial immigration control,[9] and a considerably longer line of work on the irregular movement of asylum-seekers, including by sea.[10] The lack of a unified and comprehensive body of scholarship that seeks to describe and analyze the many legal dimensions of "migrant smuggling" is not on the whole surprising. The categorization is, in many senses an artificial one, and it is certainly much easier to consider a single angle on "migrant smuggling" or to examine the issue incidental to, or from the perspective of, a more established field of study. In attempting to fill the lacuna in the available literature the authors are acutely aware of the risks that inevitably accompany the generalist's efforts to synthesize rules and norms drawn from a wide range of well-trodden and carefully guarded specialist fields.

UNDERSTANDING THE ISSUES: SOME ILLUSTRATIVE CASE STUDIES

The nature of this book, a scholarly text focused squarely on capturing and analyzing the relevant legal rules, means that it is not particularly well served by a lengthy introduction that seeks to map the phenomenon of migrant smuggling. The reader may take advantage of data and analysis available elsewhere that amply describes how migrant smuggling happens as well as causes, manifestations, and trends.[11] In terms of scope it suffices at this point to note that current estimates place the

[8] See, for example, B. Opeskin, R. Perruchoud, and J. Redpath-Cross, eds., *Foundations of International Migration Law* (2013).

[9] See, for example, in B. Ryan and V. Mitsilegas eds., *Extraterritorial Immigration Control: Legal Challenges* (2010); M. den Heijer, *Europe and Extraterritorial Asylum* (2012); T. Gammeltoft-Hansen, *Access to Asylum: International Refugee Law and the Globalisation of Migration Control* (2011).

[10] See, for example, J. Pugash, "The Dilemma of the Sea Refugee: Rescue without Refuge" (1977) 18 *Harvard International Law Journal* 577; R. P. Schaffer, "The Singular Plight of Sea-Borne Refugees" (1978–1980) 8 *Australian Yearbook of International Law* 213; P. Monzini, "Migrant Smuggling via Maritime Routes" (*CeSPI – Centro Studi di Politica Internazionale*, 2004).

[11] See, for example, United Nations Office on Drugs and Crime, *Migrant Smuggling in Asia: A Thematic Review of Literature* (2012), for a systematic review of more than 100 primary research studies on migrant smuggling in relation to fourteen countries; United Nations Office on Drugs and Crime, *The Role of Organized Crime in the Smuggling of Migrants from West Africa to the European Union* (2011); United Nations Office on Drugs and Crime, *Issue Paper: Smuggling of Migrants by Sea* (2011); and United Nations Office on Drugs and Crime, *Issue Paper: Smuggling of Migrants by Air* (2010). See also A. Triandafyllidou and T. Maroukis, *Migrant Smuggling: Irregular Migration from Asia and Africa to Europe* (2012); and D. Kyle and R. Kozlowski eds., *Global Human Smuggling: Comparative Perspectives* (2nd ed. 2011). For a detailed study of migrant smuggling from the perspective of a single country of destination, see I. C. van Liempt, *Navigating Borders: Inside Perspectives on the Process of Human Smuggling into the Netherlands* (2007).

number of irregular migrants worldwide at up to thirty million[12] and that a substantial proportion of these persons can be expected to have used the services of smugglers at one or more points in their journey.

The following brief case studies have been selected with the broader purpose of the book in mind. They are not intended to provide a comprehensive, or even a representative overview of migrant smuggling. Their goal is much more modest: to illustrate how smuggling has occurred and continues to happen, to explain how it intersects with other forms of migration and other practices that have been separately criminalized such as torture, rape, or trafficking in persons, to allude to the range of legal issues that may arise in migrant smuggling cases, particularly refugee law, and to provide at least a preliminary insight into the attitudes and behaviors that both shape and reflect how migrant smuggling is considered and dealt with by States and the international community. The case studies are also an expository tool, referred to at appropriate points throughout the book to illustrate a particular finding, insight, or point of law.

The Golden Venture: Smuggling of Chinese Migrants into the United States

In 1993, a Chinese vessel, the *Golden Venture*, was deliberately run aground off the coast of New York. The 286 Chinese migrants crowded "like animals"[13] onboard who had each paid (or committed to pay after arrival) up to USD40,000 for a place on the vessel, were advised to jump into the sea and swim to shore. Ten died, of drowning or hypothermia, and most of the survivors were deported back to China.[14]

[12] International Organization for Migration, *World Migration Report* (2010) [IOM, *World Migration Report*], at 29. However, it is important to note that all available estimates around irregular migration, including those related to smuggling, are highly unreliable. For example, a European Union (EU) funded report noted in 2005 that the main EU database for irregular migration "is wholly inadequate to capture levels and trends in illegal migration processes and is therefore – in its current form – insufficient to guide European policy making on illegal migration": M. Jandl and A. Kraler, "Statistics on Refusals, Apprehensions and Removal: An Analysis of the CIREFI Data," in M. Poulain, N. Perrin, and A. Singleton eds., *THESIM: Towards Harmonized Statistics on European Migration* 271 (2006), at 285. The International Organization for Migration has also pointed out that "Data on stocks and flows of irregular migration, at the local, national, regional and global levels, vary widely and are usually imprecise. There is also a lack of comparable data, both over time and between locations. In the absence of an authoritative single source on irregular migrant numbers, analysis inevitably depends on widely fragmented sources, some of which are significantly out of date. Nevertheless, there is a general consensus that the number of irregular migrants has grown in recent years": IOM, *World Migration Report*, at 29.

[13] J. P. Fried, "Mastermind of *Golden Venture* Smuggling Ship Gets 20 Years," *New York Times*, Dec. 2, 1998, citing Judge Reena Raggi of the United States District Court of Brooklyn.

[14] A. J. Sein, "The Prosecution of Chinese Organized Crime Groups: The Sister Ping Case and Its Lessons" (2008) 11(2) *Trends in Organized Crime* 157, at 163. See also S. X. Zhang, *Chinese Human Smuggling Organizations: Families, Social Networks, and Cultural Imperatives* (2008), at 10, esp. note 3 [Zhang, *Chinese Human Smuggling Organizations*]. For further analysis of the incident see

Those who remained in the United States were detained for years. A few received asylum. Others were granted limited residency rights but formal regularization of their status has not occurred. More than twenty individuals were prosecuted for their involvement in the incident including "Sister Ping," the alleged mastermind of "a conglomerate built upon misery and greed" who had amassed over forty million dollars from migrant smuggling.[15] The political impact of the incident was considerable. In the context of a decade of surges of boat arrivals from near neighbors, this incident prompted the release of a presidential action plan to combat alien smuggling[16] and directly led to a significant increase in penalties for migrant smuggling in the United States.[17] It also highlighted the growing phenomenon of organized movement of migrants from China,[18] thereby feeding unease amongst affected States, who quickly began pushing for greater international legal cooperation on the issue: helping to lay the political ground for what was to become the United Nations Protocol against the Smuggling of Migrants by Land, Sea and Air.[19]

P. Radden Keefe, "The Snakehead: The Criminal Odyssey of Chinatown's Sister Ping," *The New Yorker*, Apr. 24, 2006 [Radden Keefe, "The Snakehead"].

15 Radden Keefe, "The Snakehead."

16 The White House, Washington (United States), "Memorandum: Presidential Decision Directive/NSC-9 on Alien Smuggling," June 18, 1993, available at www.fas.org/irp/offdocs/pdd/pdd-9.pdf (accessed May 12, 2013), also noted in "Measures to Combat Alien Smuggling: Report of the Secretary-General," UN Doc. A/49/350, Aug. 30, 1994, at para. 85.

17 See generally, R. A. Pedrozo, "International Initiatives to Combat Trafficking of Migrants by Sea," in J. N. Moore and M. H. Nordquist eds., *Current Maritime Issues and the International Maritime Organization* 53 (1999), at 55. Prior to the *Golden Venture* incident, migrant smugglers caught in the United States typically served between six to eighteen months in prison. The Violent Crime Control and Law Enforcement Act of 1994 increased the basic penalty for migrant smuggling to ten years imprisonment. Penalties of up to twenty years imprisonment were added for migrant smuggling involving injury or risk to life, and migrant smuggling resulting in death was made a capital offense. See also Zhang, *Chinese Human Smuggling Organizations*, at 136.

18 For example, in 1994 the United States reported to the United Nations "an alarming increase in the smuggling by sea of illegal immigrants from China during the last four years … interceptions … increased from fewer than two dozen persons in 1991 to over 3,000 [in the past several months]": "Measures to Combat Alien Smuggling: Report of the Secretary-General," UN Doc. A/49/350, Aug. 30, 1994, at para. 81. For an analysis of the various factors giving rise to the migrant smuggling trade from China, most particularly from Fujian province, see S. X. Zhang and M. S. Gaylord, "Bound for the Golden Mountain: The Social Organization of Chinese Alien Smuggling" (1996) 25(1) *Crime, Law, and Social Change* 1; Z. Liang and W. Ye, "From Fujian to New York: Understanding the New Chinese Immigration," in D. Kyle and R. Koslowski eds., *Global Human Smuggling: Comparative Perspectives* 187 (2001); Zhang, *Chinese Human Smuggling Organizations*; and J. Blatt, "Recent Trends in the Smuggling of Chinese into the United States" (2007) 15 *Willamette Journal of International Law and Dispute Resolution* 227. See also the contributions to P. J. Smith ed., *Human Smuggling: Chinese Migrant Trafficking and the Challenge to America's Immigration Tradition* (1997).

19 D. McClean, *Transnational Organized Crime: A Commentary on the UN Convention and Its Protocols* (2007), at 21–24; and D. Vlassis, "The Global Situation of Transnational Organized Crime, the Decision of the International Community to Develop an International Convention and the

Australia Refuses Entry to Vessel Carrying Rescued Smuggled Migrants

In August 2001, the Norwegian registered tanker the *MV Tampa*, traveling from Western Australia toward Singapore, was requested by Australian authorities to proceed to a vessel in distress. The vessel, located with Australian assistance, was found approximately 158 miles from Indonesia, and 85 miles north of Christmas Island, a territory of Australia. The 438 persons on board, mostly asylum-seekers from Afghanistan, were successfully rescued. The captain set course for the nearest suitable port in Indonesia but acceding to pressure from the rescued passengers, changed course and headed to Christmas Island. The vessel was instructed by Australian authorities to stop before it entered the Australian territorial sea and the Master of the vessel was threatened with prosecution for 'people-smuggling' offenses if he did not comply. Requests for medical and other assistance were not met for two days until a formal distress call was issued. The Master then entered Australian territorial waters without permission, stating that his vessel was unseaworthy for travel to Indonesia and that some passengers were in extreme medical distress. Australian military personnel boarded the vessel and denied disembarkation to the rescued passengers. The Master maintained the ship's position for five days, during which time only basic supplies and medical assistance were provided. The rescued persons were then moved on to an Australian military vessel and transferred to Nauru, an island country of Micronesia, which had agreed to process the rescuees at Australian expense. The Indonesian crew was transported to Christmas Island and charged with "people smuggling" offenses under Australian law. Within Australia, legal action was taken against the Australian government but the actions of the government were held to be constitutional. Within weeks legislation was introduced into the Commonwealth Parliament to retrospectively validate the actions of the government, to remove the right of court action, and to excise Christmas Island and other offshore territories from the full protection of Australian law. The incident also marked the introduction of the "Pacific Solution" whereby smuggled asylum-seekers who arrived by boat were transferred to detention centres on Nauru and Papua New Guinea, while their asylum claims were processed. At the international level the incident sparked a comprehensive review of laws and regulations around rescue at sea. The captain of the *MV Tampa* received Norway's highest civic award.[20]

Negotiation Process," in United Nations Asia and Far East Institute for the Prevention of Crime and the Treatment of Offenders, *Annual Report for 2000 and Resource Materials Series No. 59* 475 (2002).

20 The "*Tampa* incident" has been subject to intense examination and discussion. For forensic accounts of the broader political environment within which it played out, see D. Marr and M. Wilkinson, *Dark Victory* (2003); and P. Mares, *Borderline: Australia's Response to Refugees and Asylum Seekers*

Italy Turns Back Smuggled Migrants Intercepted on the High Seas

Between 2000 and 2012, the governments of Italy and Libya concluded a number of agreements, many of them in secret, aimed at controlling migrant smuggling into Italy.[21] Their focus was on "shared management" of migration flows and the "repatriation of migrants in an irregular situation."[22] The agreements envisaged joint maritime patrols to "be conducted in Libyan and international waters under the supervision of Libyan personnel and with participation by Italian crew members, and in Italian and international waters under the supervision of Italian personnel and with participation by the Libyan crew members."[23] The impact of the agreements and the joint patrols in particular has been substantial. For example, in May 2009, the Italian Interior Minister informed the Senate that the agreements with Libya had supported the recent high seas interception of 471 irregular migrants and their subsequent return to Libya.[24] One of these interceptions involved a flotilla of three vessels, intercepted on the High Seas on May 6, 2009, by Italian authorities. The Eritrean and Somali migrants on board were transferred onto Italian military ships and, within hours, handed over to Libyan authorities in the Port of Tripoli.[25] It was alleged that during the voyage the Italian authorities did not inform passengers of their real destination; took no steps to identify them; and confiscated all personal effects, including identity

in the Wake of the Tampa (2002). For an examination of the legal implications of the *Tampa* incident (which are considered further in Chapter 6), see D. Rothwell, "The Law of the Sea and the MV *Tampa* Incident: Reconciling Maritime Principles with Coastal State Sovereignty" (2002) 13(2) *Public Law Review* 118; P. Mathew, "Australian Refugee Protection in the Wakes of the *Tampa*" (2002) 96 *American Journal of International Law* 661; J. Hathaway, "Immigration Law Is Not Refugee Law," in *U.S. Committee for Refugees World Refugee Survey 2001*, June 2001, at 38–45; M. Crock, "In the Wake of the *Tampa*: Conflicting Visions of International Refugee Law in the Management of Refugee Flows" (2004) 12 *Pacific Rim Law and Policy Journal* 49; M. White, "*Tampa* Incident: Shipping, International and Maritime Legal Issues" (2004) 78 *Australian Law Journal* 101; and D. Guilfoyle, *Shipping Interdiction and the Law of the Sea* (2009), at 198–208.

21 These agreements, although not public, are discussed extensively in *Hirsi Jamaa and Others v. Italy*, (2012) 55 EHRR 21 (ECHR, Feb. 23, 2012) [*Hirsi Jamaa v. Italy*] and in Chapter 1, at Section 1.3.2.2.

22 Y. Maccanico, *The EU's Self-interested Response to Unrest in North Africa: The Meaning of Treaties and Readmission Agreements between Italy and North African States* (2012), at 4.

23 Cited in *Hirsi Jamaa v. Italy*, at para. 19.

24 Ibid. at para. 13.

25 This situation was the subject of an action in the European Court of Human Rights, brought by twenty-four Eritrean and Somali nationals from among that larger group of intercepted and returned migrants. The Court in this case was required to consider a number of questions including whether the actions of the Italian authorities amounted to a violation of the prohibition of *non-refoulement*, even though they took place outside the territory of Italy, and whether those same actions otherwise violated other provisions of the European Convention on Human Rights, including Article 3 (prohibition on torture and inhuman treatment); and Article 4 (prohibition on collective expulsion). See *Hirsi Jamaa v. Italy*.

documents.[26] Shortly after this incident the Italian government stated that in its view the return of migrants to the country from which they departed or through which they transited in this way was in full conformity with the Organized Crime Convention and the Migrant Smuggling Protocol.[27] The government further expressed the view that a State Party's ships may stop and board any vessel without nationality, if it is suspected of illegally transporting or smuggling migrants, and may return to a Requesting State those foreigners who left from that country.[28]

Smuggled Migrants Left to Die in the Mediterranean

In 2011, during the civil uprising in Libya, a small rubber boat departed Tripoli with seventy-two passengers bound for Italy. After two weeks at sea, the boat drifted back to Libya with only nine survivors. The Council of Europe subsequently reported that: "No one went to the aid of this boat, despite a distress call logged by the Italian Maritime Rescue Coordination Centre, which pinpointed the boat's position. There were also a number of alleged direct contacts between the boat in distress and other vessels, including a helicopter that dropped biscuits and water, but never returned, two fishing vessels, both of which refused to provide assistance, and a large military vessel which came into close contact with the boat, but ignored obvious distress signals."[29] The North Atlantic Treaty Organization (NATO), which reportedly had patrol boats in the area and would have been in a strong position to help identify those official vessels that made contact with the boat, refused to cooperate with Council of Europe investigators. No NATO Member State provided any information to help the investigation.[30]

[26] Ibid. at para. 11.

[27] Council of Europe, "Report to the Italian Government on the Visit to Italy Carried Out by the European Committee for the Prevention of Torture and Inhuman or Degrading Treatment or Punishment (CPT) from 27 to 31 July 2009," Doc. CPT/Inf (2010) 14, Apr. 28, 2010, at para. 15.

[28] Ibid. Italy provided substantial additional legal justifications for both the interceptions and returns in "Response of the Italian Government to the Report of the European Committee for the Prevention of Torture and Inhuman or Degrading Treatment or Punishment (CPT) on Its Visit to Italy from 27 to 31 July 2009," Doc. CPT/Inf (2010) 15, Apr. 28, 2010.

[29] Council of Europe, Parliamentary Assembly, *Lives Lost in the Mediterranean Sea: Who Is Responsible?* (Report of the Committee on Migration, Refugees and Displaced Persons, Doc. 12895, Apr. 5, 2012) [Council of Europe Parliamentary Assembly Report, *Lives Lost in the Mediterranean Sea*], at 1. For a forensic account of every aspect of the incident including a detailed mapping of all responses and copies of all available documentation, see C. Heller, L. Pezzani, and Situ Studio, *Report on the "Left-To-Die Boat"* (2012), available at www.forensic-architecture.org/publications/report-on-the-left-to-die-boat/ (accessed May 12, 2013).

[30] Council of Europe Parliamentary Assembly Report, *Lives Lost in the Mediterranean Sea*, at 14.

Exploitation and Torture of Smuggled Eritrean and Sudanese Migrants on the Sinai Peninsula

In late 2010, reports began to emerge about well-organized criminal smuggling networks operating in the Sinai, who are paid by Eritrean and Sudanese migrants, many of them asylum-seekers, for access to and passage through the Sinai Peninsula into Israel. Some migrants get through relatively unscathed. However, others are imprisoned for weeks or months until their relatives abroad pay large ransoms to secure their release. Those unable to pay are kept in captivity and forced to work off their debt. Severe violence including sexual violence is inflicted upon victims, some of whom are children. There has been little response from Egyptian authorities and very few exploiters have been arrested or prosecuted. Reports indicate complicity or active involvement on the part of Sudanese, Eritrean, and Egyptian officials and a failure of Egyptian authorities to investigate elements of the crime that are taking place in their territory.[31]

Deaths of Smuggled Migrants through Suffocation

United Kingdom 2000: Fifty-eight Chinese migrants were found dead in an air-tight lorry container of tomatoes at the port of Dover. They and the two survivors had each paid 20,000 British pounds to travel to the United Kingdom. After a joint investigation by United Kingdom and Dutch officials, the Dutch lorry driver was convicted of manslaughter and conspiracy to smuggle immigrants and jailed for fourteen years. Additional prosecutions were sought and secured in Hong Kong and the Netherlands.[32]

[31] For background information see F. Pleitgen, *Death in the Desert* (A CNN Freedom Project Documentary, Cable News Network, 2011), online video available at http://thecnnfreedomproject.blogs.cnn.com/2011/11/08/death-in-the-desert (accessed May 12, 2013); Human Rights Watch, *Egypt: End Sinai Nightmare for Migrants* (Sept. 5, 2012), available at www.hrw.org/news/2012/09/05/egypt-end-sinai-nightmare-migrants (accessed May 12, 2013); Ahmad Abu Draa, *African Migrant Smuggling Gangs Turn Sinai into Land of Torture*, Al-Masry Al-Youm (Egypt), (July 11, 2012) (English language translation by Nola Abboud, *Inside African Migrants' Perilous Journey to Israel* (July 19, 2012), available on Almonitor, at http://www.al-monitor.com/pulse/security/01/07/al-masri-al-yawm-african-migrant.html#ixzz2Ep5R2cwj (accessed May 12, 2013); B. Gittleson, "Inside Sinai's Torture Camps," *The Atlantic*, Nov. 14, 2012; and Physicians for Human Rights–Israel, *Hostages, Torture, and Rape in the Sinai Desert: A PHR-Israel Update about Recently Arriving Asylum Seekers* (Dec. 13, 2010), available at http://www.phr.org.il/default.asp?PageID=100&ItemID=953 (accessed May 12, 2013). For a more detailed review of the situation including an examination of the relationship between human trafficking and migrant smuggling, see M. van Reisen, M. Estefanos, and C. Rijken, *Human Trafficking in the Sinai: Refugees between Life and Death* (2012).

[32] See A. Brookes, "China Arrest in Dover Deaths Inquiry," *BBC News* (online), Jan. 27, 2001, available at http://news.bbc.co.uk/2/hi/asia-pacific/1139564.stm; "Driver Jailed over Immigrant Deaths," *BBC*

Thailand 2008: A group of 121 Myanmar migrants who had paid smugglers to transport them through Thailand in a seafood container lorry began to suffocate after the air-conditioning unit failed. They managed to alert the driver who refused to stop. Fifty-four migrants, mostly women, had died by the time the container was opened. No arrests were made, except of survivors who were quickly deported back to Myanmar.[33]

Tanzania 2012: In June 2012 a group of 113 migrants being smuggled through Tanzania to South Africa in a closed truck began to suffocate. By the time the driver stopped, forty-three migrants had died. The Deputy Home Affairs Minister was reported to have commented: "It is extremely sad and unfortunate that people die by using wrong and self-torturing means to illegally transport themselves to other destinations."[34] To date, no arrests have been made.

The United States–Mexico Border: Violence against, and Exploitation of, Smuggled Migrants

Mexican drug trafficking cartels are increasingly moving into the highly lucrative business of exploitative migrant smuggling. Security analysts have explained this shift as being caused, at least in part, by the "increased difficulty and danger involved in moving migrants over the Mexican border and into the United States."[35] The groups extort fees from migrants for safe passage across the border, and sometimes

News (online), Apr. 5, 2001, available at http://news.bbc.co.uk/2/hi/uk_news/1258240.stm; "14 years for Dover Tragedy Lorry Driver," *The Guardian* (online), Apr. 5, 2001, available atwww.guardian.co.uk/uk/2001/apr/05/immigration.immigrationandpublicservices; and on the Hong Kong coconspirator see "People Smuggler Gets Four Tears for Dover Migrant Deaths," *The Sun-Herald* (online), Feb. 9, 2003, available at www.smh.com.au/articles/2003/02/08/1044579986552.html (all articles in this note accessed May 12, 2013). For a broader contextual overview of the Israeli response, see T. Kritzman-Amir and T. Spijkerboer, "On the Morality and Legality of Borders: Border Policies and Asylum Seekers" (2013) 26 *Harvard Human Rights Journal* 1.

33 See I. MacKinnon, "54 Burmese Migrants Suffocate in Packed Lorry," *The Guardian* (online), Apr. 11, 2008, available at http://www.guardian.co.uk/world/2008/apr/11/burma.thailand (accessed May 12, 2013); Human Rights Watch, *From the Tiger to the Crocodile: Abuse of Migrant Workers in Thailand* (2010), at 90 and note 226. For a useful and detailed analysis of this case see E. Gjerdingen, "Suffocation Inside a Cold Storage Truck and Other Problems with Trafficking as 'Exploitation' and Smuggling as 'Choice' along the Thai-Burmese Border" (2009) 26 *Arizona Journal of International and Comparative Law* 699.

34 See S. Chhatbar (Associated Press), "43 Ethiopians, Somalis Suffocate in Truck Smuggle," *The Washington Times* (online), June 27, 2012, available at http://www.washingtontimes.com/news/2012/jun/27/43-ethiopians-somalis-suffocate-truck-smuggle/ (accessed May 12, 2013). See also "Migrants Suffocate to Death in Tanzania," *Al Jazeera English* (online), June 27, 2012, available at http://www.aljazeera.com/news/africa/2012/06/201262761257192287.html (accessed May 12, 2013).

35 See Stratfor, The Global Intelligence Files, WikiLeaks, Oct. 2011, available at http://wikileaks.org/gifiles/docs/161548_re-forcomment-cartels-and-human-smuggling-trafficking-.html (accessed May 12, 2013).

also force them into carrying narcotics. Smugglers have been known to rob, kidnap, and sometimes kill migrants on both sides of the border. The Mexican Human Rights Commission estimates that around 20,000 migrants are kidnapped for ransom each year.[36] In September 2010, *The Economist* reported on an incident that had taken place the previous month: "an 18-year-old Ecuadorean approached a military checkpoint in Tamaulipas, a northern state in Mexico. He had been shot in the neck and explained that he had just escaped a massacre. Mexican marines followed his directions to a barn a few miles away. There they found 72 men and women shot dead. The teenager told how the group, migrants from Central and South America, had been kidnapped on their way to the United States by bandits claiming to belong to the Zetas, a Mexican drug-trafficking gang. When they refused to work for the gangsters, they were executed. There were only two confirmed survivors."[37]

A NOTE ON THE POLITICS OF MIGRANT SMUGGLING: IRREGULAR MIGRATION AND ASYLUM

Although the legal landscape around migrant smuggling is the focus of this book, it would be misguided to consider that framework in isolation from the broader political and social forces that have impacted on its development and continue to shape the way in which migrant smuggling is identified and responded to. The following brief remarks, which aim to be introductory rather than comprehensive, address the place of "migrant smuggling" within the broader issue of irregular migration, as well as the link between asylum and migrant smuggling. In relation to the first it is important to acknowledge that powerful States of destination in particular have long been anxious about irregular migration. The involvement of facilitators, with its implication of increased efficiency in approaching and evading fortified borders, is widely viewed as presenting an additional and serious threat. Criminalization of irregular migration – of the migrants themselves – is one option. Although the inexorable creep of criminal law into migration control is evident in all Western States and many other parts of the world, criminalization of migrants may have limited impact and brings with it certain political and legal risks.[38] Criminalization of the

[36] Mexican Human Rights Commission, *Notebook on the Kidnapping of Migrants: Dimensions, Context and Testimonies* (2011), cited in S. Brodzinsky, "Migrant Kidnappings by Criminal Organizations 'Systematic' in Mexico," *In Sight Crime: Organized Crime in the Americas* (May 11, 2012), available at http://www.insightcrime.org/news-analysis/migrant-kidnappings-by-criminal-organizations-systematic-in-mexico (accessed May 12, 2013) (original report in Spanish).

[37] "No Safe Passage," *The Economist*, Sept. 9, 2010, available at http://www.economist.com/node/16994348 (accessed May 12, 2013).

[38] Generally on criminalization of migration and migrants see C. Dauvergne, *Making People Illegal: What Globalization Means for Migration and Law* (2008). See also Council of Europe, Commissioner for Human Rights, *Criminalisation of Migration in Europe: Human Rights Implications* (2010);

facilitation of such migration can be seen and sold quite differently: less an attack on individual migrants than on those who are profiting from their vulnerability and desperation.

Criminalization of smuggling also facilitates and helps rationalize new approaches to irregular migration. Commentators have noted the increasing prominence of bilateral less-than-treaty agreements, regulatory mechanisms, and operational structures aimed at externalizing migration management, a strategy that by "fostering a depoliticization and technicalization of governance, allows governors and migration control officials to 'avoid the judicial scrutiny that they face nationally' and to limit migrants' access to the judicial system."[39] More recent responses to migrant smuggling are almost inevitably *preventive* in the sense that they seek to ensure, by all possible means, that the migrants concerned do not enter the State of destination in the first place. A focus on the "crime" of migrant smuggling both justifies and explains the externalization of border controls. The explicit connection with transnational organized crime increases the likelihood that States will characterize smuggled migrants as criminals and migrant smuggling as a threat to public order and national security. This in turn does more than just "denigrate the compassionate response as folly,"[40] it also rationalizes the increased militarization of all aspects of border control – from surveillance to deterrence.

The politics of migrant smuggling are also, very much, the politics of asylum. In every part of the world, increasing numbers of asylum-seekers, including those with genuine claims to refugee status, are being transported by smugglers. Often, escape from persecution will only be possible with the help of smugglers. In the words of one refugee law scholar: "human smugglers play a critical role in assisting refugees to reach safety."[41] There can be no doubt that efforts to criminalize migrant smuggling have been largely driven by this reality and the fear of States that facilitated movement of asylum-seekers will lead to greatly increased movements from ever-distant points of origin.

L. Hales and L. Gelsthorpe, *The Criminalisation of Migrant Women* (Institute of Criminology, University of Cambridge, UK, Aug. 2012); B. Story, *Politics as Usual: The Criminalization of Asylum Seekers in the United States* (University of Oxford Refugee Studies Centre Working Paper No. 26, Sept. 2005).

39 M. Albahari, *Death and the Moral State: Making Borders and Sovereignty at the Southern Edges of Europe* (Centre for Comparative Immigration Studies, University of California, Working Paper 136, June 2006), at 21, citing G. Lahav and V. Guiraudon, "Comparative Perspectives on Border Control: Away from the Border and outside the State," in P. Andreas and T. Snider eds., *The Wall Around the West: State Borders and Immigration Controls in North America and Europe* (2000), at 59.

40 M. Crock and D. Ghezelbash, "Do Loose Lips Bring Ships? The Role of Policy, Politics and Human Rights in Managing Unauthorised Boat Arrivals" (2010) 19(2) *Griffith Law Review* 238 [Crock and Ghezelbash, "Do Loose Lips Bring Ships?"], at 239.

41 J. C. Hathaway, "Why Human Smuggling Is Vital," *National Post* (Canada), Sept. 13, 2010.

That fear is not without foundation. Asylum can only be sought once an individual is outside his or her own country, and countries that are easy for asylum-seekers to reach are often unable or unwilling to provide them with the protection and support they need.[42] Any measures intending to – or having the effect of – strengthening border controls are, ipso facto, detrimental to asylum-seekers because they close off the opportunity for such persons to reach a country in which they can claim and receive protection.[43] Particularly over the past decade, restrictions on entry to the preferred countries of asylum have become more onerous and appear increasingly directed toward exploiting this requirement to thwart the arrival of those who may claim asylum.[44] It is widely accepted that this development has had the effect of pushing into the hands of smugglers individuals who want or need to cross international borders. It follows that criminalizing smuggling will inevitably increase the human and financial costs of the migration services that are critical to the survival or well-being of many of the world's poor and persecuted. In short, truly effective international action against migrant smuggling will undoubtedly operate to disrupt, if not close off, a crucial avenue of escape for refugees, as well as for millions of economic migrants. At least in the case of refugees, such a result would seriously compromise the spirit, if not the letter, of international legal obligations with respect to protection.

These dangers are very real but the critical question for advocates and policy makers is whether they justify inaction on the issue of migrant smuggling. It is the position of the authors that although a focus on ending migrant smuggling certainly presents risks for asylum-seekers, so too does ignoring the very real harms that profit-driven facilitation of irregular migration inflicts on individuals, States, and the international community as a whole. It is our contention that the broader legal and systemic problems within the international protection system must be much more openly and honestly acknowledged. The likelihood that stronger border controls against smugglers will make it even harder for asylum-seekers to access protection serves to highlight the failings and inadequacies of the international system for refugee protection. To propose that States refrain from dealing with organized, profit-driven migrant smuggling because doing so will inevitably make access to asylum more

[42] See generally S. H. Legomsky, "Addressing Secondary Refugee Movements," in R. Cholewinski, R. Perruchoud, and E. MacDonald eds., *International Migration Law: Developing Paradigms and Key Challenges* 177 (2007), at 177–80.

[43] A. T. Gallagher, "Human Rights and Human Trafficking: Quagmire or Firm Ground? A Response to James Hathaway" (2009) 49(4) *Virginia Journal of International Law* 789, at 840–841, citing J. C. Hathaway, "The Human Rights Quagmire of 'Human Trafficking'" (2008) 49(1) *Virginia Journal of International Law* 1, at 35–39 and references contained therein.

[44] Ibid. at 841 and references contained therein.

difficult is to confuse the issue and to obscure its most obvious solutions – including reforms to national migration policies and the international refugee system itself.

THE STRUCTURE OF THE BOOK

The principal purpose of this book is to clarify, as precisely as possible, what States must do, what they may do, and what they are prevented from doing in relation to migrant smuggling. The task of clarifying obligations is important because, as the case studies set out previously so amply demonstrate, the emergence of new rules has not removed considerable uncertainty and disagreement. For those concerned with using international law to shape the behavior of States, normative precision is not a luxury but an operational necessity. States must understand exactly what international law requires of them if the international legal system is to have any hope of influencing and attaching consequences to their actions. A clear understanding of relevant rules is also essential for advocacy that purports to draw its authority from international law. Of course normative precision can be elusive, and it is just as important to show where the system has not yet reached, where it has fallen down, and where change is needed.

The book is divided into two parts. Part One sets out the broad legal framework around migrant smuggling comprising both primary and secondary rules. In short, what are States required to do or refrain from doing in this area, and under what circumstances will they be held legally responsible for violations of the primary rules? Part Two considers the application of this web of rules to specific situations, such as the requirement to criminalize migrant smuggling, and addresses smuggling by sea, prevention and international cooperation, protection and assistance to smuggled migrants, and detention and return of smuggled migrants.

The task set out for Part One, of establishing the parameters of the legal framework around migrant smuggling, requires consideration of a wide range of rules drawn from multiple areas of international law. The first two chapters set out the primary rules that establish the specific obligations of States: obligations that both prescribe certain conduct and, in different ways, set boundaries on the responses of States to migrant smuggling. Chapter 1 considers transnational criminal law, law of the sea, and laws around migration control. Although the principal focus is on rules of international application, consideration is also given to regimes that have developed at the regional level (most particularly within Europe). Chapter 2 is devoted to an examination of the relevant rules of human rights and refugee law, including the rights of smuggled migrants as aliens; the right to leave and return; the right to seek and receive asylum from persecution; the restrictions on expulsion and return; and the prohibition on arbitrary or inhumane detention.

Chapter 3 continues this analysis by exploring the applicable legal framework from a foundation level: specifically, those rules that delineate *which* State has capacity to take action and in *what* circumstances. The focus of this chapter is therefore on the legal competence of States, as well as limitations on that competence. The chapter first seeks to provide a high-level summary and clarification of those aspects of sovereignty and jurisdiction most relevant to migrant smuggling, including the special rules that apply in the maritime context. It then considers how the concept of jurisdiction operates under international human rights law and international refugee law: specifically, when and how do international human rights law and international refugee law apply extraterritorially to constrain State responses to migrant smuggling at the border, at sea, and in the territory of other States?

Chapter 4 turns to the secondary rules: specifically the question of whether, and under what circumstances, States will be held responsible for the many wrongs that are associated with smuggling. In one sense, issues of responsibility around State *responses* to migrant smuggling are relatively straightforward. In such situations, the act or omission can be linked directly to State institutions or State officials acting in their official capacity, and the question of attribution can usually be easily settled, even in cases where more than one State is involved. It then remains only to demonstrate that the act in question was indeed a breach of an international legal obligation in force for that State or those States. However, issues of responsibility become more complicated when they concern the harms that are associated with the smuggling process itself such as trafficking, violence, and exploitation. States may deny legal responsibility for such harms on the basis that the primary wrong (the smuggling) was committed by a private individual or entity and not by the State itself, and/or claim that they have done everything reasonably possible to avoid the harm. This is a problem because, as the International Law Commission has pointed out: "[a]s a general principle, the conduct of private persons or entities is not attributable to the State under international law."[45] How general is the general rule? Can implicated countries absolve themselves of any responsibility to these individuals on the basis that the conduct complained of is not directly attributable to the States themselves? Does the content of the primary rule itself (establishing the breach of the international legal obligation) have any bearing on whether a State can evade responsibility and its consequences? Chapter 4 engages with the elaborate and at times unsatisfying rules of State responsibility in seeking a response to these and other questions.

[45] International Law Commission, *Commentaries to the Draft Articles on Responsibility of States for Internationally Wrongful Acts*, in "Report of the International Law Commission on the Work of Its Fifty-Third Session," UN GAOR, 56th Sess, Supp. No. 10, UN Doc. A/56/10, at 59 (2001), at Art. 8, para. 1.

Part Two of this book focuses on identifying the specific obligations that flow from the relevant primary and secondary rules. As noted above, States must understand what is required of them before it becomes possible for these same requirements to influence their decision making. The process of identifying obligations must seek to answer – or at least address – the basic questions that are asked everywhere, everyday, in the context of real situations. For example: Are States obliged to criminalize migrant smuggling, as well as related offenses such as document fraud? If so, does international law include specific requirements with regard to criminalization, jurisdiction, and penalties? Under what circumstances may a State or group of States interdict a vessel carrying smuggled migrants? Under what circumstances must a State or the captain of a private vessel come to the aid of a smuggling vessel or migrants in distress at sea? How do rules of human rights and refugee law impact on interdiction as well as search and rescue? To what extent are States required or permitted to take action and cooperate with each other to prevent migrant smuggling – as well as the human rights and other abuses that often accompany smuggling? What obligations of protection and support are owed to smuggled migrants themselves, and under what circumstances may smuggled migrants be detained and forcibly returned? To what extent does the legal framework around assistance, detention, and return differentiate between different groups of smuggled migrants, including children, trafficked persons, those who are escaping persecution, and those who have suffered smuggling-related violence and exploitation? Specific legal obligations of States are identified and discussed under the following headings: obligations of criminalization, at Chapter 5; obligations related to smuggling by sea, at Chapter 6; obligations of prevention and international cooperation, at Chapter 7; obligations of protection, assistance and response, at Chapter 8; obligations related to detention of smuggled migrants, at Chapter 9; and obligations related to return of smuggled migrants, at Chapter 10.

The companion volume to this book, *The International Law of Human Trafficking*, provided a separate final chapter dealing with issues of compliance, implementation, and effectiveness.[46] The exercise has not been repeated here as that analysis of compliance theories and variables, as well as of the compliance machinery established around the transnational crime treaties[47] and international human rights law,

[46] A. T. Gallagher, *The International Law of Human Trafficking* (2010), ch. 9, esp. at 9.1. and 9.2.1.

[47] In relation to international compliance machinery, it remains to note the establishment of a new mechanism by States Parties to the Organized Crime Convention, the Working Group on the Smuggling of Migrants. Conference of Parties to the United Nations Convention on Transnational Organized Crime and its Protocols thereto, Resolution 5/3 (2010), "Implementation of the Protocol against the Smuggling of Migrants by Land, Sea and Air, supplementing the United Nations Convention against Transnational Organized Crime," UN Doc. CTOC/COP/2010/17, at 11, Dec. 2, 2010, at para. 9. At the time of this writing, the Working Group had held two meetings, at which aspects of criminalization, protection, prevention, and cooperation among States were considered.

is equally relevant to the subject of migrant smuggling. The book instead concludes with a brief epilogue that seeks to bring its various threads together with a view to the future. To what extent is the broader legal framework around migrant smuggling actually being recognized by States and intergovernmental organizations? What gaps and weaknesses around that framework have become most evident and how could they be remedied? How are broader trends in migration governance affecting the operation of the legal framework around migrant smuggling? How can the "complex, multi-level tapestry of diverse and contested institutions"[48] around global migration management be harnessed to ensure that responses to migrant smuggling are transparent and that international rules are recognized and respected by the many parties who exercise real power in this arena?

As with any work, both the selection of issues and the way in which they have been considered in this book have been informed by a number of personal convictions. These deserve to be clearly acknowledged at the outset. Foremost is the authors' understanding of migrant smuggling as being not just a form of organized criminal behavior but also the predictable outcome of certain global political and economic realities, most particularly the persistence of deep global economic inequalities, the prevalence of migration regimes that restrict the ability of individuals to secure legal access to preferred destinations and the consequent need for support in circumventing ever-increasing controls. Migration is one of the oldest strategies of human advancement and, as commentators have pointed out, it is unsurprising that that the modern Nation State, specifically liberal democracies, are not up to the task of stopping it.[49]

In acknowledging the inevitability of migrant smuggling, the authors also recognize the urgent need for States to respond to and prevent its worst excesses: the corruption and profiteering of individuals and criminal groups that, as shown through the case studies set out previously, result in suffering, exploitation, and death. States also need to acknowledge and take responsibility for their own contribution to smuggling-related harm. The risks to refugees inherent in efforts to strengthen borders from migrant smuggling are very real but, as noted above, we argue that these risks reside in the refugee regime itself, and the solution does not lie, as some commentators have suggested, in ignoring migrant smuggling. Critically, while supporting certain actions against migrant smuggling, we recognize inherent and demonstrable limitations on the capacity of States, both individually and collectively, to address this phenomenon effectively.[50] Migrant smuggling is, in fact, a textbook example of

48 A. Betts, "Introduction: Global Migration Governance," in A. Betts ed., *Global Migration Governance* 1 (2011), at 8.

49 On this aspect see C. Joppke, "Why Liberal States Accept Unwanted Immigration" (1998) 50 *World Politics* 266.

50 For a review of various policies and strategies against migrant smuggling from the perspective of impact and effectiveness, see Crock and Ghezelbash, "Do Loose Lips Bring Ships?"; C. Morehouse

the "wicked problem"[51]: one that is hard to define, keeps changing, and does not present a clear solution because of preexisting factors that are themselves highly resistant to change – in this case the very existence of States, gross inequalities among them, and strong motivations on the part of some to keep out others. We are in agreement with Crépeau, current UN Special Rapporteur on the Human Rights of Migrants, who writes:

> Smuggling is but a symptom that a demand for free movement of persons is mounting, as a companion to the free movement of goods, capital, and services. Treating these issues only through an escalation of repressive mechanisms ... will not lower the pressure ... it will only exacerbate the tensions, fuel international criminality and result in more rights violations for the migrants themselves, by the smugglers, as well as by our own national authorities.[52]

In other words, absent a fundamental change to global migration governance, smuggling will continue to be an important vehicle by which much irregular migration, whether forced or voluntary, happens. To deny this reality, and to develop laws and policies that seek to pretend otherwise, represents a willful disregard of both evidence and experience.

In terms of the ethics of migrant smuggling and responses to migrant smuggling, the authors turn to the international legal framework set out in this book for guidance. This framework is faulty and incomplete in parts but, when considered in its entirety, provides a strong foundation on which to build policies and practices that are both humane and pragmatic. The legal framework unambiguously affirms the right of States to control their borders, including placing restrictions on who may enter and under what conditions. Although international lawyers, as servants "not of

and M. Blomfield, *Irregular Migration in Europe* (Migration Policy Institute, Dec. 2011); European Parliament, Directorate-General for External Policies of the Union, *Analysis of the External Dimensions of the EU's Asylum and Immigration Policies: Summary and Recommendations for the European Parliament* (Aug. 6, 2006); S. Klepp, "A Contested Asylum System: The European Union between Refugee Protection and Border Control in the Mediterranean Sea" (2010) 12 *European Journal of Migration and Law* 1; C. Boswell, "The 'External Dimension' of EU Immigration and Asylum Policy" (2003) 79(3) *International Affairs* 619. On the impact of enforcement on the market for migrant smuggling see C. Gathmann, *The Effects of Enforcement on Illegal Markets: Evidence from Migrant Smuggling along the Southwestern Border* (Institute for the Study of Labor (IZA) Discussion Paper No. 1004, 2004). In the United States–Mexican border context, the demand for border smugglers was shown to be price elastic, with enforcement pressures causing facilitators to switch from heavily patrolled areas to more remote and dangerous crossing routes (see "When Less Is More: Border Enforcement and Undocumented Migration," Testimony of Douglas S. Massey before the Subcommittee on Immigration, Citizenship, Refugees, Border Security, and International Law Committee on the Judiciary U.S. House of Representatives, Apr. 20, 2007, esp. at 2–3).

[51] On the phenomenon of "wicked problems," see J. Conklin, *Dialogue Mapping: Building Shared Understanding of Wicked Problems* (2006).

[52] Crépeau, "The Fight against Migrant Smuggling," at 182.

power but of justice"[53] may rightly seek to work toward change, they cannot ignore or sideline the legal and political reality of State sovereignty in matters of immigration control. However it is also international law, as an expression of State will, that tempers the absolute nature of State sovereignty in critical ways, for example by refusing to criminalize the smuggled migrant and by prohibiting arbitrary and mass expulsion. It is international law, again as an expression of State will, that substantially restricts and carefully delineates the capacities of States to respond to migrant smuggling, largely through the recognition of fundamental human rights: the right of all persons to leave their own country and to return; the right to have their basic humanity respected; and the right to receive protection from persecution. In our view an approach to migrant smuggling that is firmly grounded in international law will not, of itself, deliver the solution to a problem that extends well beyond the scope and capacities of international law. Nevertheless, such an approach provides much-needed parameters and safeguards for the development of the national laws, policies, and actions that, in the end, determine much of what happens in the area of migration control. In that sense, it is this approach that provides the best – and perhaps the only – opportunity for ensuring an ethical and acceptable balancing of interests, rights, and obligations.

[53] P. Allott, "State Responsibility and the Unmaking of International Law" (1988) 29 *Harvard International Law Journal*, 1 at 24.

PART I

General Legal Framework

1

The Legal Framework: Transnational Criminal Law, Law of the Sea, and Migration Control

Until very recently, the issue of migrant smuggling was not directly the subject of any international legal framework. With the entry into force of the United Nations Convention against Transnational Organized Crime[1] (Organized Crime Convention), and the Protocol against the Smuggling of Migrants by Land, Sea and Air, supplementing that Convention[2] (Migrant Smuggling Protocol), the concept of migrant smuggling itself, and the framework governing responses to this issue has been considerably expanded and, in some respects, clarified. Nonetheless, it is necessary to emphasize that these instruments exist within a broader framework of rules, rights, and obligations that arise from multiple other branches of law. This chapter focuses on three areas that generate primary rules of direct application to the issue of migrant smuggling: transnational criminal law, law of the sea, and laws arising from regional/bilateral migration control agreements. Human rights and refugee law, the two other critical areas to generate primary rules of relevance to migrant smuggling, are of such central importance to this book and have such a crosscutting nature as to justify separate consideration in the following chapter.

It is appropriate at this point to make a brief observation on how the various sources of law and obligation are dealt with in the present chapter and the ones that follow. The usual starting point for any discussion on sources of international law is the Statute of the International Court of Justice, Article 38 of which sets out a catalogue of sources to be used in its decision making.[3] However, as Charlesworth

[1] United Nations Convention against Transnational Organized Crime, 2225 UNTS 209, done Nov. 15, 2000, entered into force Sept. 29, 2003 [Organized Crime Convention].

[2] Protocol against the Smuggling of Migrants by Land, Sea and Air, supplementing the United Nations Convention against Transnational Organized Crime, 2241 UNTS 507, done Nov. 15, 2000, entered into force Jan. 28, 2004 [Migrant Smuggling Protocol].

[3] "The Court, whose function is to decide in accordance with international law such disputes as are submitted to it, shall apply: a. international conventions, whether general or particular, establishing

Sections of this chapter draw on A. T. Gallagher, *The International Law of Human Trafficking* (2010) [Gallagher, *The International Law of Human Trafficking*] (chapter 2.2; 2.3.1.2; and 2.4).

has noted, the appeal of this list is also a trap: "it allows international lawyers to sidestep complex debates about the functions of international law and about the relative legitimacies of State consent."[4] Its formalism "obscures the fact that international law is generated by a multi-layered process of interactions, instruments, pressures and principles," with specialized areas of international law such as human rights (and indeed migrant smuggling), "differ[ing] in the priority that they accord to different sources and the approaches that they take to them."[5]

With these caveats in mind, the present work has sought to base its understanding of what the law *is* on a considered understanding of what States have sought to create and recognize as the law. This is in keeping with modern, positivist approaches to international law that accept the central place of consent in both the formation and continuing acceptance of international legal rules. In other words, States are bound by international laws because they choose to be: consent thereby legitimizes a rule as a rule. Consent to be bound is most clearly and unambiguously adduced from the purposeful decision of a State to enter into a treaty. However, other "traditional" sources of law recognized by the International Court of Justice – custom and general principles – are similarly dependent on the State making some kind of tangible commitment that serves to express its will. Although non-State actors play an important role in shaping international law, the task of identifying the source and nature of specific legal obligations is, in the view of the present authors, best served by an approach that accepts that international law is made, or recognized or accepted, through the will of States, and that "nothing becomes law for the international system from any other source."[6]

While recognizing the need to appreciate international law as a normative system and process, and not just a collection of rules,[7] this chapter and those that follow generally confine themselves to a survey and analysis of international legal rules that States have clearly consented to. In this book, the primary focus is on the complex web of international treaties that have developed over the past century to address issues that relate to the migrant smuggling phenomenon and, more particularly, to the response of States to that phenomenon. The present chapter also

rules expressly recognized by the contesting States; b. international custom, as evidence of a general practice accepted as law; c. the general principles of law recognized by civilized nations; d. subject to the provisions of Article 59, judicial decisions and the teachings of the most highly qualified publicists of the various nations, as subsidiary means for the determination of rules of law": Statute of the International Court of Justice, 961 UNTS 183, done June 26, 1945, entered into force Oct. 24, 1945 [ICJ Statute], at Art. 38(1).

4 H. Charlesworth, "Law-Making and Sources," in J. Crawford and M. Koskenniemi, eds., *The Cambridge Companion to International Law* 187 (2012), at 189.

5 Ibid.

6 L. Henkin, *International Law, Politics and Values* (1995) [Henkin, *International Law*], at 27.

7 R. Higgins, *Problems and Process: International Law and How We Use It* (1995), at 10.

provides a brief analysis of customary law as it relates to migrant smuggling, and of secondary and subsidiary sources of international law including general principles and judicial decisions. It concludes with an analysis of the rather elusive concept of "soft" law with a view to determining the nature of the contribution that this "category" of materials makes to the international legal framework around migrant smuggling.

1.1. MIGRANT SMUGGLING IN TRANSNATIONAL CRIMINAL LAW

1.1.1. *Historical Background and Context*

Given the level of contemporary political interest in migrant smuggling, its very recent emergence on the international political agenda is notable. A content review of resolutions and other working documents of the relevant international and regional agencies confirms that migrant smuggling (howsoever described) was simply not the subject of official discussions within these fora prior to the early 1990s.[8]

At the national level few States took an interest in the phenomenon of migrant smuggling until the late 1980s. One exception was the United States, whose concern about facilitated irregular migration is generally traced back to the mid-1960s, with the expiration, in 1964, of a guest worker program between Mexico and the United States, and the passage in 1965 of the *Immigration and Naturalization Act*, a law that provided the foundation for much of the United States' current migration system. Rosenblum and Brick describe the reforms as "a bad match for the structural forces that were already taking hold of the US migration system,"[9] including major economic and social changes in Mexico and Central America, a drastic reduction in the cost of long distance transportation, and a mismatch between supply and demand for low-cost labor in the United States. As a result:

> … the "illegal alien problem" became the defining issue for US policymakers within years of the 1965 reforms. Congress held 25 days of hearings on illegal immigration between 1971 and 1973, three presidents in a row convened task forces to

[8] The content review undertaken by the authors involved examining resolutions and documents of: the United Nations General Assembly, the United Nations Economic and Social Council, the Commission on Crime Prevention and Criminal Justice, the Council of Europe, and the G7/G8, for references to concepts equivalent to migrant smuggling, whether referred to as alien smuggling, irregular migration, illegal migrants, or other equivalents. One of the earliest, if not the earliest, reference to a term of this nature was in 1989, at an international conference on Indo-Chinese Refugees: "Documents: International Conference on Indo-Chinese Refugees (Geneva, 13 and 14 June 1989)" (1993) 5(4) *International Journal of Refugee Law* 617, which refers to "organized clandestine departures" (at 619).

[9] M. Rosenblum and K. Brick, *US Immigration Policy and Mexican/Central American Migration Flows: Then and Now* (2011), at 5.

study the problem, and spending on migration control (mostly Border Patrol personnel) increased five-fold between 1970 and 1985.[10]

United States' concern continued to grow throughout the 1970s and 1980s, with community and government anxieties increased by numerous high-profile waves of irregular migration from near neighbors. For example, between April and September 1980, 125,000 Cuban migrants arrived in the United States by boat.[11] That same year, 15,000 Haitians arrived in the same way.[12] By 1981, the "illegal alien" problem had been elevated to the highest levels: a Presidential Proclamation declared "illegal immigration" to be "a serious national problem detrimental to the interests of the United States" and promised that "the attempted entry of irregular migrants from the high seas to United States waters would be prevented by interdiction."[13] The bilateral agreements that followed this Proclamation are examined in Section 1.3.2.1.

In comparison with the situation in the United States, concern about migrant smuggling among major European countries of destination was much slower to emerge and to translate into specific action. This difference can be explained by economics as well as by history. For countries such as France and West Germany, a high demand for migrant labor acted as a strong counterweight to concerns over "illegals."[14] Until the mid-1970s, countries such as Italy and Spain had experienced at least a century of net emigration, and the political and social culture around migration, both regular and irregular, reflected this history. The situation changed slowly during the 1970s and 1980s, particularly for Italy.[15] By the late 1980s, the reunification

[10] Ibid. at 5–6 (citation omitted).

[11] D. Guilfoyle, *Shipping Interdiction and the Law of the Sea* (2009) [Guilfoyle, *Shipping Interdiction and the Law of the Sea*], at 192.

[12] A. Helton, "The United States Government Program of Intercepting and Forcibly Returning Haitian Boat People to Haiti: Policy Implications and Prospects" (1993) 10 *New York Law School Journal of Human Rights* 325, at 325 [Helton, "The United States Government Program of Intercepting and Forcibly Returning Haitian Boat People to Haiti"].

[13] Proclamation No. 4865, 46 Fed. Reg. 48,107 (1981), cited in ibid. at 326–327.

[14] J. Salt, "A Comparative Overview of International Trends and Types, 1950–80," (1989) 23(3) *International Migration Review* 431, at 452.

[15] Although the official records from Italy on migration are poor, those that are available confirm the rapid pace of change. For example, in 1986, some 20,000 migrants attempted to land on Italian shores and were refused entry. By 1993, this number had increased to 70,000: F. Fasani, *Undocumented Migration: Counting the Uncountable. Data and Trends across Europe* (Country Report: Italy) (2009) [Fasani, *Undocumented Migration*], at 112, Table 42. Those figures do not include migrants who were permitted to land. Between March and August 1991, some 40,000 fleeing Albanians were received into Italy: D. L. Zinn, "Adriatic Brethren or Black Sheep?: Migration in Italy and the Albanian Crisis, 1991" (1996) 3(3) *European Urban and Regional Studies* 241, at 241. Zinn notes that although initially greeted as "Adriatic brothers," the public mood of welcome shifted rapidly, and now-familiar distinctions began to be made between "political refugees" and "economic migrants" (ibid). It is relevant to note that the number of migrants landing on Italy's shores in the late 1980s and early 1990s, many of whom may have been smuggled, paled in comparison to the numbers entering Italy through regular means and overstaying. The Italian government held a series of amnesties in the 1980s and 1990s

of Germany and the collapse of the former Soviet Union had increased the pace of change dramatically, prompting a shift in national and regional policy around facilitated irregular migration described in more detail in Section 1.3.2.2.

The issue of migrant smuggling was brought sharply to international attention in 1993 when a Chinese vessel, the *Golden Venture*, was deliberately run aground off the coast of New York. The 286 Chinese migrants crowded "like animals"[16] onboard, who had each paid up to USD30,000 for a place on the vessel, were advised to jump into the sea and swim to shore, when the smaller landing vessel expected to transport them never arrived. Ten died, of drowning or hypothermia, and most of the survivors were deported back to China.[17] The *Golden Venture* incident promoted the release of a presidential action plan to combat alien smuggling[18] and directly led to a significant increase in penalties for migrant smuggling in the United States.[19] It also highlighted the growing phenomenon of organized movement of migrants from China,[20] thereby feeding unease among affected

aimed at regularizing this group, the first of which in 1980 received 5000 applications. This number rose to 113,349 in 1986–1988, and to 234,841 in 1990: Fasani, *Undocumented Migration*, at 64.

16 R. Fried, "Mastermind of *Golden Venture* Smuggling Ship Gets 20 Years," *New York Times*, December 2, 1998, citing Judge Reena Raggi of the United States District Court of Brooklyn.

17 A. J. Sein, "The Prosecution of Chinese Organized Crime Groups: The Sister Ping Case and Its Lessons" (2008) 11(2) *Trends in Organized Crime* 157, at 163. See also S. X. Zhang, *Chinese Human Smuggling Organizations: Families, Social Networks, and Cultural Imperatives* (2008) [Zhang, *Chinese Human Smuggling Organizations*], at 10, esp. n. 3.

18 Presidential Decision Directive/NSC-9 on Alien Smuggling, The White House, Washington, June 18, 1993, available at www.fas.org/irp/offdocs/pdd/pdd-9.pdf (accessed May 12, 2013); also noted in "Measures to Combat Alien Smuggling: Report of the Secretary-General," UN Doc. A/49/350, Aug. 30, 1994 [1994 UN Report on Alien Smuggling], at para. 85.

19 See generally, R. Pedrozo, "International Initiatives to Combat Trafficking of Migrants by Sea," in J. N. Moore and M. H. Nordquist, eds., *Current Maritime Issues and the International Maritime Organization* 53 (1999) [Pedrozo, "International Initiatives to Combat Trafficking of Migrants by Sea"], at 55. Prior to the *Golden Venture* incident, migrant smugglers caught in the United States typically served between six to eighteen months in prison. The Violent Crime Control and Law Enforcement Act of 1994 increased the basic penalty for migrant smuggling to ten years' imprisonment. Penalties of up to twenty years' imprisonment were envisaged for migrant smuggling involving injury or risk to life, and migrant smuggling resulting in death was made a capital offense. *Violent Crime Control and Law Enforcement Act of 1994* (Enrolled Bill [Final as Passed Both House and Senate] – ENR) H.R. 3355 (United States), at sec. 60024. See also Zhang, *Chinese Human Smuggling Organizations*, at 136.

20 For example, in 1994 the United States reported to the United Nations an "alarming increase in the smuggling by sea of illegal immigrants from China during the last four years … interceptions … increased from fewer than two dozen persons in 1991 to over 3,000 … [in the past several months]." 1994 UN Report on Alien Smuggling, para. 81. For an analysis of the various factors giving rise to the migrant smuggling trade from China, most particularly from the Fujian province, see S. X. Zhang and M. S. Gaylord, "Bound for the Golden Mountain: The Social Organization of Chinese Alien Smuggling" (1996) 25(1) *Crime, Law, and Social Change* 1; Z. Liang and W. Ye, "From Fujian to New York: Understanding the New Chinese Immigration," in D. Kyle and R. Koslowski eds., *Global Human Smuggling: Comparative Perspectives* 187 (2001); and Zhang, *Chinese Human Smuggling Organizations*. See also the contributions to P. J. Smith ed., *Human Smuggling: Chinese Migrant Trafficking and the Challenge to America's Immigration Tradition* (1997).

States, who quickly began pushing for greater international legal cooperation on the issue.[21]

Their advocacy found a receptive audience among the preferred destination countries of western and central Europe (most particularly Italy[22]), North America, and elsewhere that had experienced a significant increase in the number of "unauthorized arrivals."[23] There was growing evidence that criminal groups who were organized and sophisticated enough to exploit legislative, policy, and law enforcement weaknesses were facilitating much of this movement.[24] Deficiencies in international law were seen as particularly acute and detrimental: as summarized by advocates of a new treaty on the subject, there was no agreed definition of smuggling, no domestic obligation to criminalize smuggling, and no obligation to extradite or prosecute perpetrators,[25] resulting in a "legal lacuna under international law [that] is increasingly perceived as an obstacle to the effort of the international community to cope, in an efficient manner, with the phenomenon of smuggling of illegal migrants for criminal purposes."[26] The major receiving countries were quick to understand that the default position – a purely national approach to sanctioning those who facilitated such migration, supplemented by ad hoc and largely ineffective bilateral cooperation – played directly into the hands of smugglers and traffickers.[27]

21 D. McClean, *Transnational Organized Crime: A Commentary on the UN Convention and Its Protocols* (2007) [McClean, *Transnational Organized Crime*], at 21–24; D. Vlassis, "The Global Situation of Transnational Organized Crime, the Decision of the International Community to Develop an International Convention and the Negotiation Process," in United Nations Asia and Far East Institute for the Prevention of Crime and the Treatment of Offenders, *Annual Report for 2000 and Resource Materials Series No.* 59 475 (2002) [Vlassis, UNAFEI].

22 See further discussion at Section 1.3.2.2.

23 In addition to references at note 20 above, see generally F. David, Human Smuggling and Trafficking: An Overview of the Responses at the Federal Level – Australian Institute of Criminology Research and Public Policy Series No. 24 (2000) [David, *Human Smuggling and Trafficking*]; A. Schloenhardt, *Migrant Smuggling: Illegal Migration and Organised Crime in Australia and the Asia Pacific Region* (2003) [Schloenhardt, *Migrant Smuggling*]; S. X. Zhang and K. Chin, *The Characteristics of Chinese Human Smugglers: A Cross National Study* (2002) [Zhang and Chin, *Chinese Human Smugglers*]. See also the discussion of bilateral migration control agreements at Section 1.3.2; 1994 UN Report on Alien Smuggling.

24 David, *Human Smuggling and Trafficking*; Schloenhardt, *Migrant Smuggling*; Zhang and Chin, *Chinese Human Smugglers*; and 1994 UN Report on Alien Smuggling.

25 "Letter dated 16 September, 1997 from the Permanent Representative of Austria to the United Nations addressed to the Secretary-General," UN Doc. A/52/357, Sept. 17, 1997, at paras. 2–3 (transmitting a draft of the proposed convention) [Letter dated 16 September, 1997]. Also cited in McClean, *Transnational Organized Crime*, at 21–22.

26 Ibid.

27 See generally Vlassis, UNAFEI. See also A. Kirchener and L. Schiano di Pepe, "International Attempts to Conclude a Convention to Combat Illegal Migration" (1998) 10 *International Journal of Refugee Law* 662 [Kirchener and Schiano di Pepe, "International Attempts to Conclude a Convention to Combat Illegal Migration"]. See also the observation of the United States government in the 1994

The first truly international policy response to the phenomenon now known as migrant smuggling came from the International Maritime Organization (IMO). Within months of the *Golden Venture* incident, the United States government had submitted a draft resolution on "Enhancement of Safety of Life at Sea by the Prevention and Suppression of Alien Smuggling by Ship" to the IMO Assembly.[28] In its submission, the United States expressed its growing concern about the "serious safety and health issues associated with the growing problem of the smuggling of aliens by ship" and affirmed its belief that a resolution of the Assembly would "send a strong signal with respect to safety concerns and provide the framework to deter significantly the unsafe transport associated with alien smuggling operations."[29] On October 28–29, 1993, a drafting group, comprising seventeen countries as well as several international organizations[30] met to discuss the United States' proposal. A revised draft was quickly finalized, submitted to the IMO Assembly, and adopted on November 4, 1993. The resolution noted, with great concern, "incidents involving the smuggling of aliens on board ships and the serious problems associated with such activities for safety of life at sea" and called on Member States to: cooperate in suppressing unsafe practices associated with alien smuggling by sea; develop agreements and procedures to facilitate such cooperation; share information on ships believed to be engaged in such practices and either undertake or authorize inspection of their own ships suspected of being engaged in unsafe practices associated with migrant smuggling; and take "appropriate action" against stateless vessels engaged in alien smuggling.[31] This latter

UN Report on Alien Smuggling, at para. 79, that "Control of alien-smuggling is made more difficult in the United States by the fact that in a number of Central American countries, alien smuggling is not illegal and smugglers are often able to operate openly."

28 International Maritime Organization, Assembly, Draft Assembly Resolution on the Enhancement of Safety of Life at Sea by the Prevention and Suppression of Alien Smuggling by Ship submitted by the United States, A 18/11/3, 18th Session, Agenda Item 11, Sept. 3, 1993.

29 Ibid. at para. 4. Paragraph 2 of the Draft proposes that its purpose be to: reques[t] the co-operation of all Governments to increase efforts to detect ships being used to transport persons in an unsafe manner, to exchange information on such operations, to verify unsafe conditions through ship examinations, to assist in the humanitarian disposition of persons found on board ships being used for smuggling and to take actions, as appropriate, in accordance with national laws.

30 The following countries and organizations participated in the drafting group: Australia, Brazil, Canada, China, Cuba, Denmark, Finland, France, Germany, Greece, Japan, Mexico, Norway, Singapore, Tunisia, United Kingdom, United States, International Chamber of Shipping, International Shipping Federation. International Maritime Organization, Assembly, *Proposed draft Assembly resolution, Enhancement of Safety of Life at Sea by the Prevention and Suppression of Unsafe Practices associated with Alien Smuggling by Ship, submitted by the drafting group*, IMO Doc. A 18/C.2.WAT7/Rev.1, 18th Session, Committee II, Agenda Item 2, at para. 2.

31 International Maritime Organization, Assembly, *Enhancement of Safety of Life at Sea by the Prevention and Suppression of Unsafe Practices Associated with Alien Smuggling by Ships*, IMO Resolution A.773(18), Nov. 4, 1993.

provision would later form the basis of the obligations in Article 8 of the Migrant Smuggling Protocol.[32]

The United States did not limit its international diplomatic efforts to the International Maritime Organization. On the same day the draft IMO resolution was finalized, the United States introduced a similar resolution to the United Nations Commission on Crime Prevention and Criminal Justice, on the "Prevention of Alien Smuggling."[33] The resolution very quickly gained additional sponsors (Armenia, Cyprus, El Salvador, Greece, Guatemala, Mexico, and Romania).[34] Significantly, it also moved out of the relatively low profile Commission on Crime Prevention and Criminal Justice to the General Assembly. Shortly thereafter, the attention of the United Nations was officially engaged with the passing of a resolution in the General Assembly, in December 1993, on "prevention of smuggling of aliens."[35] The resolution expressed the Assembly's concern that "the activities of criminal organizations that profit illicitly by smuggling human beings and preying on the dignity and lives of migrants contribute to the complexity of the phenomenon of increasing international migration."[36] Significantly, it addressed many of the elements that are today found in the Migrant Smuggling Protocol; for example, noting the role of "international criminal groups" in convincing individuals to "migrate illegally," leading to the generation of "enormous profits."[37] This formulation of the problem to be addressed resonates strongly with the definition of "smuggling of migrants" now found in the Migrant Smuggling Protocol and discussed in detail at Section 1.1.3.1. However, the resolution also confirmed a link between smuggling and exploitation of migrants, which subsequently evaporated as the distinction between migrant smuggling and trafficking in persons emerged.[38] In addition to recognizing the danger of exploitation, the General Assembly also emphasized the importance of ensuring a focus on the root causes

32 The provisions of Article 8 are discussed further in Chapter 6.

33 "United States of America: Draft Resolution, Prevention of Alien Smuggling," UN Doc. A/C.3/48/L.9, Oct. 29, 1993.

34 See revised draft resolution, "Prevention of Alien Smuggling," UN Doc. A/C.3/48/L.9/Rev.2, Nov. 16, 1993.

35 UN General Assembly, "Prevention of the Smuggling of Aliens," GA Res. 48/102, UN GAOR, 48th sess, Agenda Item 10, UN Doc. A/RES/48/102, Mar. 8, 1994, adopted Dec. 20, 1993 [UNGA Res. 48/102].

36 Ibid. at Preamble.

37 Ibid.

38 "Noting that smugglers, particularly in the State of destination of the smuggling of aliens, often force migrants into forms of debt, bondage or servitude, often involving criminal activities, in order to pay for their passage": ibid. Note that the preamble also refers to the Supplementary Convention on the Abolition of Slavery, the Slave Trade, and Institutions and Practices Similar to Slavery (226 UNTS 3, done Apr. 30, 1956, entered into force Apr. 30, 1957), in the context of reaffirming the obligation on States to eliminate debt bondage: ibid.

of "smuggling of aliens," and the need to "provide humane treatment and protect the full human rights of migrants," while reaffirming that the "sovereignty and territorial integrity of all States must be respected, including their right to control their own borders."[39]

Critically, the General Assembly resolution provided the multilateral hook essential for justifying the elevation of migrant smuggling as an issue of common concern, by affirming that these practices have "transnational consequences," such that there is a "need for States to cooperate urgently at the bilateral and multilateral levels, as appropriate, to thwart these activities."[40] It called on States to take a set of actions to prevent "the practice of smuggling aliens," all of which are now found in the Migrant Smuggling Protocol, including the amendment of criminal laws if necessary, improving procedures to identify false travel documents, taking steps to ensure that carriers are not misused for smuggling aliens, cooperating with one another to prevent and respond to smuggling of migrants by sea, and cooperating with regard to the "socio-economic factors" involved in the "problem of the smuggling of aliens."[41] The General Assembly also made specific mention of the necessity of preserving legal migration and freedom of travel, the protection of refugees, and "strict observance of all the human rights of migrants."[42] Again, these are all matters that would ultimately be canvassed in the Migrant Smuggling Protocol.

The December 1993 General Assembly resolution added the issue of "smuggling of aliens" to the agenda of the annual meetings of the Commission on Crime Prevention and Criminal Justice. Over the following several years this resulted in a series of reports essentially summarizing the range of steps that States reported they were taking to combat migrant smuggling.[43] The first of these reports, issued by the General Assembly in August 1994, is useful for what it reveals about how the phenomenon of "alien smuggling" was understood by both the United Nations and its Member States. Taking language from a recently adopted resolution of the

39 Ibid.

40 Ibid.

41 Ibid.

42 Ibid.

43 1994 UN Report on Alien Smuggling; "International Cooperation in Combating Transnational Crime: Smuggling of Illegal Migrants – Measures to Combat the Smuggling of Migrants: Report of the Secretary-General (Addendum)," UN Doc. E/CN.15/1997/8/Add.1, Apr. 8, 1997; "International Cooperation in Combating Transnational Crime: Smuggling of Illegal Migrants – Measures to Combat the Smuggling of Illegal Migrants: Report of the Secretary-General," UN Doc E/CN.15/1997/8, Feb. 18, 1997; "Review of Priority Themes: Measures to Combat the Smuggling of Illegal Migrants: Report of the Secretary-General (Addendum)," UN Doc. E/CN.15/1996/4/Add.1, May 21, 1996; "Review of Priority Themes: Measures to Combat the Smuggling of Illegal Migrants: Report of the Secretary-General," UN Doc. E/CN.15/1996/4, Mar. 21, 1996.

Commission on Crime Prevention and Criminal Justice, the Secretary-General described the phenomenon as follows:

> Alien-smuggling involves the illegal movement of hundreds of thousands of persons from their countries of origin by criminal gangs, through various transit States to recipient countries for profit. Illegal immigrants endure dangers and inhumane treatment, lives are lost and there is great human suffering. This trade in human cargo often ends with the illegal immigrants' being forced into indentured servitude or criminal activities in order to repay the cost of their passage.[44]

The first sentence neatly encapsulates the current definition of migrant smuggling. However, the extract also makes clear that, in 1994, the international community considered "alien smuggling" to be a problem of human rights as well as a problem of migration control: a larger understanding of smuggling and its impact included practices and outcomes that are today associated with human trafficking, rather than smuggling. It was through the subsequent development of a separate definition of trafficking in persons that States were able to remove the exploitation aspect that was so central to earlier understandings of migrant smuggling. That shift served to focus both the definition and the proposed response to migrant smuggling on the *action* of smuggling itself rather than the *impact* of the crime on those who are smuggled. A review of these early reports indicates considerable confusion on the part of many States as to what constituted "alien smuggling." While several States reported action against the organized illegal movement of persons across national borders for profit, many others addressed only illegal entry into and departure from their territories.

Parallel developments in Europe fed into and strengthened these early international efforts. In 1993, European ministers responsible for migration affairs, meeting under the auspices of the Council of Europe, affirmed that "it should be a criminal offence to smuggle or to attempt to smuggle illegal migrants," and that "this should include the instigation, and the aiding and abetting of the offence."[45] They further declared that "particular consideration should be given to offences carried out for reward, and to offences carried out in an organized way," and that it should be possible to confiscate proceeds/instruments of crime.[46] These calls were echoed by a group of northern European States, at a conference organized by Sweden in early 1994.[47]

44 1994 UN Report on Alien Smuggling, para. 5.

45 Council of Europe, "Texts *adopted at the* European Conference on Uncontrolled Migration (Budapest, 15–16 February 1993)," Fifth Conference of European Ministers responsible for migration affairs (Athens, 18–19 November 1993), Doc. MMG–5 (93) 5, Oct. 19, 1993, at 3.

46 Ibid. at 3–4.

47 Conference on Uncontrolled Migration over the Baltic Sea, reported in 1994 UN Report on Alien Smuggling, para. 17.

States' interest in developing an international regulatory framework around migrant smuggling quickly gained momentum. In 1997 the government of Austria formally proposed the development of a new legal instrument to deal with the smuggling of migrants, focusing specifically on creation of a new criminal offense as well as measures related to investigation, prosecution, and extradition.[48] In its proposal, the Austrian government noted that this practice posed "a growing threat to the international community as a whole" and, given that it constituted a "very special form of organized crime," required a special convention.[49] The Italian government had, in the meantime, approached the International Maritime Organization with a proposal for the issuance of directives regarding "trafficking of migrants by sea"[50] and subsequently, for a "Multilateral Convention to Combat Illegal Migration by Sea."[51] Questions were raised about the Organization's competence to deal with this issue[52] and Italy subsequently decided to join forces with Austria in pushing for the development of a legal instrument against migrant smuggling within the context of the Crime Commission's work against transnational organized crime.[53] This goal was secured in late 1998 when the Ad Hoc Committee established to develop a convention on transnational organized crime was also mandated to discuss the elaboration of an international instrument on "illegal trafficking in, and transportation of migrants, including by sea."[54]

The perceived urgency of the issue is evident in the IMO Assembly issuing a circular, in December 1998, the strategic purpose of which was to "provide non-binding measures for the prevention and suppression of unsafe practices associated with the trafficking and transport of migrants by sea" pending entry into force of the international treaty.[55] Many of the provisions of the circular were eventually

48 "Letter dated 16 September, 1997." See further Kirchener and Schiano di Pepe, "International Attempts to Conclude a Convention to Combat Illegal Migration," at 670.

49 "Letter dated 16 September, 1997". See also Pedrozo, "International Initiatives to Combat Trafficking of Migrants by Sea," at 62–63.

50 Vlassis, UNAFEI, at 493.

51 International Maritime Organization, Legal Committee, *Proposed Multilateral Convention to Combat Illegal Migration by Sea*, IMO Doc. LEG 76/11/1, Aug. 1, 1997.

52 P. Mallia, *Migrant Smuggling by Sea: Combating a Current Threat to Maritime Security through the Creation of a Cooperative Framework* (2009) [Mallia, *Migrant Smuggling by Sea*], at 112, n. 4.

53 Vlassis, UNAFEI, at 493.

54 UN General Assembly, "Transnational Organized Crime," GA Res. 53/111, UN GAOR, 53rd sess, Agenda Item 101, UN Doc. A/RES/53/111, Jan. 20, 1999. Note that the Economic and Social Council had, already in 1998, determined that "an ad-hoc committee on the elaboration of a comprehensive international convention against transnational organized crime should hold discussions on the elaboration of an additional instrument against illegal trafficking in and transporting of migrants, including by sea": Pedrozo, "International Initiatives to Combat Trafficking of Migrants by Sea," at 64.

55 International Maritime Organization, Maritime Safety Committee, *Interim Measures for Combating Unsafe Practices Associated with the Traffic or Transport of Migrants by Sea*, IMO Doc. MSC/Circ.896, Dec. 16, 1998. The Interim Measures were revised in 2001. For an overview of the drafting process

reflected in that part of the Protocol dealing with smuggling by sea. However it is important to flag a substantial difference between these two instruments: the IMO circular focused squarely on migrant smuggling from a safety of life at sea perspective. The purpose and scope of the Protocol, including its smuggling by sea provisions, is considerably wider. That treaty, as well as its parent instrument, the Organized Crime Convention, is considered in detail in Section 1.1.2. The origins and principal features of the Protocol to Prevent, Suppress and Punish Trafficking in Persons, Especially Women and Children[56] (Trafficking Protocol) are also examined, in recognition of the "substantial overlap in the conduct involved in the two offences."[57]

1.1.2. *The Organized Crime Convention*

Proposals for an international treaty on transnational organized crime were first tabled at the World Ministerial Conference on Organized Transnational Crime in Naples, Italy, in November 1994.[58] Although not received enthusiastically by all States, the proposal was generally supported and, in late 1997, the UN General Assembly established an intergovernmental group of experts to prepare a preliminary draft.[59] Following receipt of the report of the group of experts,[60] the General Assembly decided to establish an open-ended, intergovernmental Ad Hoc Committee

during 1997–1998 see Pedrozo, "International Initiatives to Combat Trafficking of Migrants by Sea," at 57–62.

56 Protocol to Prevent, Suppress and Punish Trafficking in Persons, Especially Women and Children, supplementing the United Nations Convention against Transnational Organized Crime, 2237 UNTS 319, done Nov. 15, 2000, entered into force Dec. 25, 2003 [Trafficking Protocol].

57 United Nations Office on Drugs and Crime, Legislative Guides for the Implementation of the United Nations Convention against Transnational Organized Crime and the Protocols thereto, UN Sales No. E.05.V.2 (2004) [*Legislative Guide*], at 340 (para. 29).

58 On the history of United Nations engagement on this issue, and on developments leading up to the establishment of the Ad Hoc Committee, see United Nations Office on Drugs and Crime, Travaux Préparatoires *of the Negotiations for the Elaboration of the United Nations Convention against Transnational Organized Crime and the Protocols Thereto* (2006) [Travaux Préparatoires *for the Organized Crime Convention and Protocols*], at ix–xxvi. For a more informal analysis of this period, see D. Vlassis, "The UN Convention against Transnational Organized Crime," in M. R. Berdal and M. Serrano eds., *Transnational Organized Crime and International Security: Business as Usual?* 83 (2002) [Vlassis, "The UN Convention against Transnational Organized Crime"], at 85; and Vlassis, UNAFEI, at 492. See also McClean, *Transnational Organized Crime*, esp. at 2–7.

59 UN General Assembly, "Follow-Up to the Naples Political Declaration and Global Action Plan against Organized Transnational Crime," GA Res. 52/85, UN GAOR, 52nd sess, Agenda Item 103, UN Doc. A/RES/52/85, Jan. 30, 1998.

60 "Report of the Meeting of the Inter-Sessional Open-Ended Intergovernmental Group of Experts on the Elaboration of a Preliminary Draft of a Possible Comprehensive International Convention against

the negotiation process for all three instruments (including the Interpretative Notes) were released in 2006[76] and, in accordance with the Vienna Convention on the Law of Treaties, have been used by the authors as a secondary source in interpreting the text.[77] Two years earlier, the United Nations Office on Drugs and Crime issued a Legislative Guide to the Convention and its Protocols.[78] Although not intended to be authoritative or otherwise deliver a definitive legal interpretation of these instruments,[79] the Guide is nevertheless a helpful source of additional insight, particularly with regard to legislative implementation obligations.[80] Supplementary guidance has also been produced by the United Nations, including a Model Law against the Smuggling of Migrants;[81] and an International Framework for Action to Implement the Smuggling of Migrants Protocol[82]; these supplementary materials, although useful, cannot be considered on the same level as the above materials.

THE RELATIONSHIP BETWEEN THE CONVENTION AND ITS PROTOCOLS

The general rules governing the relationship between the Convention and its Protocols are set out in the Convention itself, with additional guidance provided by particular provisions of the Protocols. When read together, it is possible to identify four basic principles. First, as the Protocols were not intended to become stand-alone treaties, States must ratify the Convention before ratifying any of its

McClean also points out that in some cases the relevant Interpretative Note is not fully consistent with the text, thereby creating uncertainty in interpretation (ibid). The Interpretative Notes are contained in UN General Assembly, "Report of the Ad Hoc Committee on the Elaboration of a Convention against Transnational Organized Crime on the work of its first to eleventh sessions, Addendum: Interpretative notes for the official records (*travaux préparatoires*) of the negotiation of the United Nations Convention against Transnational Organized Crime and the Protocols thereto," UN Doc. A/55/383/Add.1, Nov. 3, 2000. All Interpretative Notes are also included in the Travaux Préparatoires *for the Organized Crime Convention and Protocols*. For ease of reference, throughout this book, references to Interpretative Notes have been given as references to the part of the *Travaux Préparatoires* in which they appear.

76 Travaux Préparatoires *for the Organized Crime Convention and Protocols*.

77 Vienna Convention on the Law of Treaties, 1155 UNTS 331, done May 23, 1969, entered into force Jan. 27, 1980 [Vienna Convention on the Law of Treaties], at Arts. 31–32.

78 United Nations Office on Drugs and Crime, Legislative Guides for the Implementation of the United Nations Convention against Transnational Organized Crime and the Protocols thereto, UN Sales No. E.05.V.2 (2004) [*Legislative Guide*].

79 Ibid. at xv–xvi.

80 Note that additional guidance has subsequently been provided by the United Nations in the form of draft model laws relating to both the Trafficking and Migrant Smuggling Protocols: United Nations Office on Drugs and Crime, *Model Law on Trafficking in Persons*, UN Sales No. E.09.V.11 (2009); United Nations Office on Drugs and Crime, *Model Law against the Smuggling of Migrants* (2010) [UNODC Model Law on Migrant Smuggling].

81 UNODC Model Law on Migrant Smuggling.

82 United Nations Office on Drugs and Crime, *International Framework for Action to Implement the Smuggling of Migrants Protocol* (2011).

Protocols.[83] A State Party to the Convention is not bound by a Protocol unless it also becomes a party to that Protocol.[84] Second, the Convention and its Protocols must be interpreted together, taking into account their stated purposes.[85] Third, the provisions of the Convention apply, *mutatis mutandis*, to the Protocols.[86] This means that in applying the Convention to the Protocols, modifications of interpretation or application should be made only when and to the extent that they are necessary.[87] Fourth, offenses established by the Protocols are to be regarded as offenses established by the Convention. As a result, the Convention's general provisions, for example on matters such as victim protection, law enforcement cooperation, mutual legal assistance, and extradition, are available and applicable to States in their implementation of the more specific and detailed provisions of the Protocols.[88]

The relationship between the Migrant Smuggling Protocol and the Trafficking Protocol is also highly relevant. This relationship, as well as important distinctions between the two instruments, is considered further at Section 1.1.4.

1.1.2.2. The Convention: Structure and Major Provisions

The Organized Crime Convention is essentially an instrument of international cooperation – its stated purpose being to promote interstate cooperation in order to combat transnational organized crime more effectively.[89] In this respect its goal is to enlarge the number of States taking effective measures against transnational crime

83 Organized Crime Convention, at Art. 37(2). See also *Legislative Guide*, at 253, 329. As the Legislative Guide points out, this provision ensures that in a case arising under one of the Protocols to which the States concerned are parties, all of the general provisions of the Convention (for example, relating to mutual legal assistance and protection of victims) will also be available and applicable.

84 Organized Crime Convention, at Art. 37(3).

85 Ibid. at Art. 37(4); Migrant Smuggling Protocol, at Art. 1(1); Trafficking Protocol, at Art. 1(1). See further *Legislative Guide*, at 253–255, 329–332.

86 Migrant Smuggling Protocol, at Art. 1(2); Trafficking Protocol, at Art. 1(2).

87 *Legislative Guide*, at 254, 330. The Interpretive Note on Article 1 of the Migrant Smuggling Protocol states that: "[t]his paragraph was adopted on the understanding that the words 'mutatis mutandis' meant 'with such modifications as circumstances require' or 'with the necessary modifications'. Provisions of the United Nations Convention Against Transnational Organized Crime that are applied to the Protocol under this Article would consequently be modified or interpreted so as to have the same essential meaning or effect in the Protocol as in the Convention": Travaux Préparatoires *for the Organized Crime Convention and Protocols*, at 457.

88 Migrant Smuggling Protocol, at Art. 1(3). See also *Legislative Guide*, at 254, 330–331. Note however that the Convention's victim protection provisions may not apply to those who have been smuggled. See further the discussion in Chapter 8.

89 Organized Crime Convention, at Art. 1. Note there is no preamble. McClean refers to the General Assembly resolution adopting the Convention ("United Nations Convention against Transnational Organized Crime," UN Doc. A/RES/55/25, Jan. 8, 2001) for additional insight into its purpose. McClean, *Transnational Organized Crime*, at 35–36.

and to forge and strengthen cross-border links.[90] More specifically, the Convention seeks to eliminate "safe havens" (where organized criminal activities or the concealment of evidence or profits can take place) by promoting the adoption, by States Parties, of basic minimum measures.[91]

Except where otherwise stated, there are three prerequisites for application of the Convention to a particular situation. First, the relevant offense must have some kind of transnational aspect.[92] Second, it must involve an organized criminal group.[93] Third, it must constitute a "serious crime."[94] As all three elements are defined very broadly, States are thereby able to use this instrument to address a wide range of contemporary criminal activity, including all aspects of migrant smuggling.[95] This is especially important in view of the fact that States may become party to the Convention without having to ratify any or all of the Protocols.[96] In short, even without the Protocol, the Convention itself provides a strong and broad platform for States to take action against migrant smuggling.

The core obligation of the Convention is that of criminalization. States Parties are required to criminalize a range of offenses, whether committed by individuals or corporate entities, including: participation in an organized criminal group[97];

90 *Legislative Guide*, at xvii–xviii.

91 United Nations Office for Drug Control and Crime Prevention, "Summary of the United Nations Protocol against Transnational Organized Crime and Protocols Thereto" (2000) *Trends in Organized Crime* 11.

92 Organized Crime Convention, at Art. 3(1). The Convention defines a transnational offense as one that is committed in more than one State; or committed in one State but substantially planned, directed, or controlled in another State; or committed in one State but involving an organized criminal group operating in more than one State; or committed in one State but having substantial effects on another State (Article 3(2)).

93 Ibid. at Art. 3(1). An organized criminal group is defined as "a structured group of three or more persons, existing for a period of time and acting in concert with the aim of committing one or more serious crimes or offences … in order to obtain, directly or indirectly, a financial or other material benefit": Organized Crime Convention, at Art. 2(a). An Interpretative Note confirms that "financial or other benefit" is to be understood broadly to include, for example, personal or sexual gratification: Travaux Préparatoires *for the Organized Crime Convention and Protocols*, at 17. See also ibid. at 12, 14–15. On the function and status of the Interpretative Notes to the Organized Crime Convention and Its Protocols, see McClean, *Transnational Organized Crime*, at 13.

94 Organized Crime Convention, at Art. 3(1)(b). "Serious crime" refers to conduct constituting a criminal offense punishable by a maximum deprivation of liberty of at least four years or a more serious penalty: ibid. at Art. 2(b). This definition is based on the results of a study of legislation in UN Member States contained in Ad Hoc Committee on the Elaboration of a Convention against Transnational Organized Crime, "Analytical Study on Serious Crime," UN Docs. A/AC.254/22, Nov. 30, 1999; A/AC.254/22/Add.1, Dec. 13, 1999; A/AC.254/22/Corr.1, Dec. 16, 1999.

95 For a trenchant critique of the breadth of these new international legal definitions, see V. Mitsilegas, "From National to Global, from Empirical to Legal: The Ambivalent Concept of Transnational Organized Crime," in M. E. Beare ed., *Critical Reflections on Transnational Organized Crime, Money Laundering and Corruption* 55 (2003). See also the introduction by M. E. Beare in the same volume.

96 Organized Crime Convention, at Art. 37(3).

97 Ibid. at Art. 5.

public sector corruption[98]; laundering of the proceeds of crime[99]; and obstruction of justice.[100] These offenses are also to be made subject to sanctions that take into account the gravity of the offense.[101] Critically, the obligation of criminalization stands independently of the transnational nature or the involvement of an organized criminal group.[102] In other words, these are not to be considered elements of the offense for criminalization purposes.[103]

A lack of communication and cooperation between national law enforcement authorities has been identified as one of the principal obstacles to effective action against transnational organized crime, including migrant smuggling. The Convention sets out a range of measures to be adopted by States Parties to enhance effective law enforcement in this area through, inter alia, improving information flows and enhancing coordination between relevant bodies.[104] The practical application of these provisions is likely to be enhanced by the inclusion of a detailed legal framework on mutual legal assistance in investigations, prosecutions, and judicial proceedings in relation to applicable offenses.[105] The relevant provisions constitute, in effect, a mini-treaty that can be used by States as the legal basis of a request for mutual legal assistance for a range of purposes including the taking of evidence, effecting service of judicial documents, executing searches, identifying the proceeds of crime, and producing information and documentation. States Parties are further encouraged to establish joint investigative bodies[106]; come to formal agreement on the use of special investigative techniques[107]; consider the transfer of criminal proceedings[108] and sentenced persons[109]; and they are required to facilitate extradition proceedings for applicable offenses.[110] National law enforcement structures are to

98 Ibid. at Art. 8. Corruption is not directly defined. Instead, States Parties are required to criminalize a range of conduct when committed intentionally, specifically "[t]he promise, offering or giving to a public official, directly or indirectly, of an undue advantage, for the official himself or herself or another person or entity, in order that the official act or refrain from acting in the exercise of his or her official duties" and "[t]he solicitation or acceptance by a public official, directly or indirectly, of an undue advantage for the official himself or herself or another person or entity, in order that the official act or refrain from acting in the exercise of his or her official duties": ibid.

99 Ibid. at Art. 6. "Proceeds of crime" is defined in Article 2(e): "... any property derived from or obtained, directly or indirectly, through the commission of an offence."

100 Ibid. at Art. 23.

101 Ibid. at Art. 11(1).

102 Ibid. at Art. 34. This provision does not apply to the extent that the Convention itself (at Article 5) would require the involvement of an organized criminal group: ibid.

103 Travaux Préparatoires *for the Organized Crime Convention and Protocols*, at 285.

104 Organized Crime Convention, at Art. 26.

105 Ibid. at Art. 18.

106 Ibid. at Art. 19.

107 Ibid. at Art. 20.

108 Ibid. at Art. 21.

109 Ibid. at Art. 17.

110 Ibid. at Art. 16.

be strengthened through education and training of relevant officials in order to prevent, detect, and control transnational organized crime.[111] States Parties are also to endeavor to take certain legal and financial steps to prevent transnational organized crime.[112] The reality that developing countries will require economic and technical assistance to fully implement the Convention's provisions is acknowledged in a detailed article that sets out a range of international cooperation measures, including the establishment of a dedicated United Nations funding mechanism.[113]

The Convention contains several important provisions on victims of transnational organized crime. States Parties are to take appropriate measures within their means to provide assistance and protection to victims – particularly in cases of threat of retaliation or intimidation.[114] Appropriate procedures to provide access to compensation and restitution are to be established[115] and, subject to their domestic laws, States Parties are to enable the views and concerns of victims to be presented and considered during criminal proceedings against offenders.[116] Appropriate measures are also to be taken to protect witnesses (including victims who are witnesses) from potential retaliation or intimidation.[117] The only other provision touching upon victims relates to the requirement that States Parties participate, as appropriate, in international projects to prevent transnational organized crime, "for example, by alleviating the circumstances that render socially marginalized groups vulnerable to the action of transnational organized crime."[118] The question of whether smuggled migrants are "victims" of transnational organized crime within the context of these provisions is an extremely important one and is considered further at Section 1.1.3.2.

The Convention establishes a Conference of the Parties to promote and review its implementation as well as to improve more generally the capacity of States Parties to combat transnational organized crime.[119] The Conference of Parties is envisaged to have a special role in facilitating several of the cooperative measures envisaged under the Convention, including: the provision of technical assistance, information exchange, and cooperation with IGOs and NGOs.[120] It is also responsible for periodic examination of the implementation of the Convention as well as making

111 Ibid. at Art. 29.

112 Ibid. at Art. 31.

113 Ibid. at Art. 30. See also Conference of the Parties to the United Nations Convention against Transnational Organized Crime, "Financial and budgetary matters: Note by the Secretariat," UN Doc. CTOC/COP/2012/13, June 27, 2012, at paras. 2–4, Annex I.

114 Organized Crime Convention, at Art. 25(1).

115 Ibid. at Art. 25(2).

116 Ibid. at Art. 25(3).

117 Ibid. at Art. 24.

118 Ibid. at Art. 31(7).

119 Ibid. at Art. 32(1).

120 Ibid. at Art. 32(3)(a)–(c).

recommendations to improve the Convention and its implementation[121] and for setting up any additional review mechanisms that may be required.[122] The nature and functioning of the Convention's implementation machinery (which extends to its Protocols) is subject to further consideration in the epilogue of this book.

1.1.3. *The Migrant Smuggling Protocol*

As noted previously the Migrant Smuggling Protocol is the principal international treaty dealing with the smuggling of migrants and is a central plank of the relevant international legal framework. This section considers the definition of migrant smuggling and the core features of the Protocol.

1.1.3.1. Definition of Migrant Smuggling

When the international community first came together to take concerted action against what is now known as migrant smuggling, there was still considerable confusion between the concepts of migrant smuggling and what is presently referred to as human trafficking. Right up to the late 1990s States, international organizations, and regional groupings were using a range of different terms interchangeably, such as "clandestine illegal migration,"[123] "alien smuggling,"[124] and even "trafficking of aliens"[125] to denote the problem of illegal or irregular migration that was facilitated by third parties for profit. The concept as it is currently understood nevertheless firmed up very quickly, in part as a response to the clarification of a distinction between migrant smuggling on the one hand and trafficking in persons on the other, which evolved through the drafting and conclusion of the Organized Crime Convention and its Protocols. As noted previously, this distinction also served to remove the "exploitation" element from the concept of migrant smuggling, thereby shifting the focus of the definition on to the *action* of migrant smuggling rather than its *impact* on those who are smuggled.

121 Ibid. at Art. 32(3)(d)–(e).

122 Ibid. at Art. 32(4). Vlassis observes that this latter provision was an indirect reference to the system of "peer review": Vlassis, "The UN Convention against Transnational Organized Crime," at 92.

123 See, for example, Council of Europe, "Conclusions," Fifth Conference of European Ministers Responsible for Migration Affairs, Athens, Nov. 18–19, 1993.

124 See, for example, International Maritime Organization, Enhancement of Safety of Life at Sea by the Prevention and Suppression of Unsafe Practices Associated with Alien Smuggling by Ships, IMO Resolution A.773(18), Nov. 4, 1993.

125 See, for example, J. Widgren, "Multilateral Cooperation to Combat Trafficking in Migrants and the Role of International Organizations," Discussion Paper submitted by Jonas Widgren, Director, International Centre for Migration Policy Development (ICMPD), Vienna, Austria, Eleventh IOM Seminar on Migration, Oct. 26–28, 1994, Geneva, at 3.

to offenses established under the Migrant Smuggling Protocol, it is not apparent that this restriction limits the scope of application of the Protocol in any way. All migrant smuggling by definition necessarily involves a transnational element, and the breadth of the Convention's concept of organized criminal group thereby operates to bring within the general operation of the Protocol almost every conceivable situation of migrant smuggling.[144] On the other hand, it is relevant to note that the transnational element may not necessarily be present in relation to other offenses established by the Protocol, such as facilitating illegal stay or production of fraudulent travel documents, both of which could easily be perpetrated within a single State.[145]

CRIMINAL LIABILITY OF SMUGGLED MIGRANTS

The question of criminal liability of smuggled migrants was a major point of discussion throughout the negotiations. Although there was general agreement from the outset that the Protocol should not be used to punish smuggled migrants, debate around the precise wording of the relevant provision underscored the apprehension felt by some delegations that the Protocol could potentially be used to grant immunity to irregular migrants, including those who had committed crimes such as the smuggling of other irregular migrants.[146] The final text confirms that migrants are not liable to criminal prosecution "for the fact of having been the object"[147] of the criminal offenses established by the Protocol. The Legislative Guide elaborates on the reasoning behind this provision: "[m]ere illegal entry may be a crime in some countries, but it is not recognized as a form of organized crime and is hence beyond the scope of the Convention and its Protocols."[148] In reality however, the impact of the noncriminalization clause is largely neutered by the operation of Article 6(4), discussed further below.

The concern of States that the Protocol could be used to grant immunity to irregular migrants was addressed by a provision preserving the rights of each State Party to take measures against persons whose conduct constitutes an offense under its domestic law.[149] As a practical matter therefore, the Protocol does nothing to

[144] Scholars have routinely misunderstood this aspect of the Organized Crime Convention and its Protocols. For example, in relation to the scope of application of the Trafficking Protocol, see Hathaway, "The Human Rights Quagmire of 'Human Trafficking'" ("... slavery or other forms of exploitation that occur entirely within the borders of one country without the involvement of outside parties are beyond the scope of the Trafficking Protocol": at 11.) For a detailed refutation of this claim, see Gallagher, "Human Rights and Human Trafficking: Quagmire or Firm Ground?" at 812.

[145] *Legislative Guide*, at 333 (para. 18).

[146] Travaux Préparatoires *for the Organized Crime Convention and Protocols*, at 482.

[147] Migrant Smuggling Protocol, at Art. 5.

[148] *Legislative Guide*, at 340 (para. 28).

[149] Migrant Smuggling Protocol, at Art. 6(4).

limit the capacity of States to criminalize acts such as illegal entry, illegal stay, and the possession of fraudulent travel documents. Offenses of this nature would not, however, necessarily be sufficient to trigger the broader operation of the Convention.

CRIMINALIZATION OF MIGRANT SMUGGLING AND RELATED CONDUCT

Criminalization is the heart of the Protocol: "serving not only to provide for the deterrence and punishment of the smuggling of migrants, but as the basis for the numerous forms of prevention, international cooperation, technical assistance and other measures."[150] The core obligation is to criminalize the smuggling of migrants when committed intentionally.[151] States Parties are further required to criminalize certain constituent or related elements of the crime of migrant smuggling:

- The intentional production of a fraudulent travel or identity document[152] for the purpose of enabling migrant smuggling;
- Procuring, providing, or possessing[153] such a document for the purpose of enabling migrant smuggling; and
- Using the above means or other illegal means (as defined under domestic law)[154] to enable a person to remain unlawfully within the State concerned[155] – including the procurement of legal residence by some illegal means, "even if the actual entry that preceded it was legal."[156]

150 *Legislative Guide*, at 349 (para. 55).

151 Migrant Smuggling Protocol, at Art. 6(1)(a). In accordance with Article 34(2) of the Convention, these corequisites (of transnationality and involvement of an organized criminal group) do not appear to apply to the obligation of criminalization except, as noted by the *Legislative Guide*, where the language of the criminalization requirement specifically incorporates one of these elements. *Legislative Guide*, at 333–334. But see discussion of ambiguity around application of Article 34(2) to Protocol offenses at notes 285 and 286 and accompanying text of this chapter, and Chapter 5, at Section 5.1.1.4.

152 Defined in the Protocol as "any travel or identity document: (i) That has been falsely made or altered in some material way by anyone other than a person or agency lawfully authorized to make or issue the travel or identity document on behalf of a State; or (ii) That has been improperly issued or obtained through misrepresentation, corruption or duress or in any other unlawful manner; or (iii) That is being used by a person other than the rightful holder": Migrant Smuggling Protocol, at Art. 3(c).

153 An Interpretative Note attached to Article 6 makes clear that the reference to "possession" does not extend to possession of a fraudulent travel or identity document by a migrant for purposes of enabling his or her smuggling. Travaux Préparatoires *for the Organized Crime Convention and Protocols*, at 489. The Legislative Guide confirms that "a migrant caught in possession of a fraudulent document would not generally fall within domestic offences adopted pursuant to paragraph 1 *(b)*, whereas a smuggler who possessed the same document for the purpose of enabling the smuggling of others would be within the same offence": *Legislative Guide*, at 349 (para. 54).

154 Travaux Préparatoires *for the Organized Crime Convention and Protocols*, at 489.

155 Migrant Smuggling Protocol, at Art. 6.1(b), 6.1(c).

156 *Legislative Guide*, at 341, n. 9.

States Parties are also obliged to criminalize attempting to commit such offenses[157]; participating as an accomplice in such offenses[158]; and organizing or directing others to commit such an offense.[159]

Article 6 of the Protocol introduces the concept of aggravated offenses. Broadly speaking, States Parties are required to recognize as aggravated smuggling offenses those that involve danger to the lives of migrants or that entail degrading or inhuman treatment, including exploitation.[160] Examples of smuggling involving danger to the lives of migrants are not difficult to find and may include the use of unsafe modes of transportation such as unseaworthy, overcrowded boats, or shipping containers. Degrading treatment could be expected to extend to treatment that has a highly negative impact on the well-being of the migrant while not endangering that person's life. The aggravating circumstance of exploitation raises several difficult questions. For example, at what point do the fees charged for the service of migrant smuggling and the way in which those fees are made payable become exploitative? Under what circumstances would exploitative migrant smuggling morph into, or overlap with, a trafficking offense?[161]

The consequence of characterizing an offense as "aggravated" will depend on the rules and conventions of the relevant legal system. As noted in the Legislative Guide, "this could take the form of either complete parallel offences, such as aggravated smuggling, or of provisions that require the courts to consider longer or more severe sentences" in situations where the basic offense has been established and the aggravating conditions are present.[162] However, as noted in the Model Law against the Smuggling of Migrants, what is important is that where the relevant circumstances are present, "offenders are subject to more severe penalties than they would be if these circumstances were not present."[163]

It is unclear what consequences, if any, are envisaged for the status of those persons who have been subjected to "aggravated" smuggling. As noted previously, the decision to characterize smuggled migrants not as victims but as "objects" of the process presumably excludes them from the victim support and protection provisions set out in Article 25 of the Organized Crime Convention, including access to

[157] "Subject to the basic concepts" of the legal system of the State: Migrant Smuggling Protocol, at Art. 6(2)(a). The *Legislative Guide* at 271–272 notes that this caveat was introduced to accommodate legal systems that do not recognize the criminal concept of "attempt."

[158] Smuggling Protocol, at Art. 6(2)(b).

[159] Ibid. at Art. 6(2)(c).

[160] Migrant Smuggling Protocol, at Art. 6(3). See further *Legislative Guide*, at 346–347; UNODC Model Law on Migrant Smuggling, at 41–45.

[161] This question is considered at several points in the book. See particularly Chapter 5, at Section 5.1.4.2.

[162] *Legislative Guide*, at 346 (para. 46).

[163] UNODC Model Law on Migrant Smuggling, at 40–41.

compensation and restitution.[164] However, it can be convincingly argued that persons who have been subjected to aggravated smuggling are indeed victims of crime within the Convention's Article 25 because of their status as victims of other crimes and/or of human rights violations, including, potentially inhuman or degrading treatment, or trafficking in persons.[165]

Apart from the requirement to establish aggravated offenses, the Protocol is silent on the issue of penalties. A provision that would require States Parties to make the commission of Article 6 offenses "liable to sanctions that take into account the grave nature of the offences" was quietly omitted from the final reading of the text.[166] Accordingly, the basic requirement of the Convention, that sanctions should take into account the gravity of the offense, will apply.[167]

The *mutatis mutandis* requirement extends to other mandatory provisions of the Convention, creating obligations on States Parties to take certain measures with respect to offenses established under the Protocol. These include obligations to:

- Criminalize the laundering of the proceeds of migrant smuggling[168];
- Ensure legal persons can be held liable for migrant smuggling offenses[169];
- Ensure migrant smuggling offenses are given broad jurisdictional application[170];

[164] See further Chapter 8, at Section 8.1.

[165] This is the approach taken in the Model Law against the Smuggling of Migrants, which recognizes that smuggled migrants would, in these circumstances, constitute victims of crime, and recommends national lawmakers consider including a provision allowing smuggled migrants who have been victimized in the smuggling process through aggravated smuggling be enabled to take civil or judicial proceedings to seek redress. It further recommends national lawmakers consider including a provision allowing smuggled migrants, who have been victimized in the smuggling process (including through aggravated smuggling), to be enabled to take civil or judicial proceedings. This was in recognition of the fact that smuggled migrants would in these circumstances constitute victims of crime. UNODC Model Law on Migrant Smuggling, at 69–70.

[166] The obligation to "impose penalties that take into account the grave nature of those offences" appeared in all drafts. Although noting the decision to omit this reference, the *Travaux Préparatoires* do not explain it: Travaux Préparatoires *for the Organized Crime Convention and Protocols*, at 363 (Trafficking Protocol) and 478–488 (Migrant Smuggling Protocol). It can be assumed that as such a provision was already included in the Convention (see the *Travaux Préparatoires*), its repetition in the Protocol was considered to be unnecessary.

[167] *Legislative Guide*, at 351 (para. 59) (referring to Article 11(1) of the Convention). See also Art. 10(4) (sanctions for legal persons to be effective, proportionate, and dissuasive); United Nations Office on Drugs and Crime, *Model Legislative Provisions against Organized Crime* (2012) [UNODC, *Model Legislative Provisions against Organized Crime*], at 47. But see McClean, *Transnational Organized Crime*, at 396 (noting a possible source of confusion on this point).

[168] Organized Crime Convention, at Art. 6.

[169] Ibid. at Art. 10. See further UNODC, Model Legislative Provisions against Organized Crime, at 50.

[170] Organized Crime Convention, at Art. 15. See further UNODC, *Model Legislative Provisions against Organized Crime*, at 25.

- Take appropriate measures to ensure that conditions of release for defendants do not jeopardize the ability to secure their presence at subsequent criminal proceedings[171];
- Establish a long statute of limitations period for migrant smuggling offenses[172];
- Provide, to the greatest extent possible, for the tracing, freezing, and confiscation of the proceeds of migrant smuggling in both domestic cases and in aid of other State Parties[173];
- Cooperate with other States Parties, in the investigation, prosecution, and judicial proceedings for migrant smuggling offenses, through joint investigations,[174] mutual legal assistance,[175] and extradition[176];
- Criminalize obstruction of justice[177];
- Protect victims and witnesses from potential retaliation or intimidation[178];
- Take appropriate measures to encourage those involved in migrant smuggling to cooperate with or assist national authorities[179]; and
- Provide for channels of communication and police-to-police cooperation in relation to the investigation of migrant smuggling offenses.[180]

ESTABLISHMENT OF JURISDICTION

A specific provision on jurisdiction, including a requirement to resolve competing claims of jurisdiction, was eventually dropped from the draft text of the Protocol without official explanation.[181] The obligations of States Parties with regard to

[171] Organized Crime Convention, at Art. 11(3). See further UNODC, *Model Legislative Provisions against Organized Crime*, at 108.

[172] Organized Crime Convention, at Art. 11(5). See further UNODC, *Model Legislative Provisions against Organized Crime*, at 101.

[173] Organized Crime Convention, at Arts. 12–14. See further United Nations Office on Drugs and Crime, Commonwealth Secretariat and International Monetary Fund, *Model Provisions on Money Laundering, Terrorist Financing, Preventive Measures and Proceeds of Crime (for common law legal systems)* (2009); United Nations Office on Drugs and Crime and International Monetary Fund, *Model Legislation on Money-Laundering and Financing of Terrorism* (for civil law systems) (2005).

[174] Organized Crime Convention, at Art. 19.

[175] Ibid. at Art. 18.

[176] Ibid. at Art. 16.

[177] Ibid. at Art. 23. See further UNODC, Model Legislative Provisions against Organized Crime, at 42–47.

[178] Organized Crime Convention, at Arts. 24–25. However, as noted previously, the extent to which the Convention's references to victims of transnational organized crime apply to smuggled migrants is unclear. See generally UNODC, *Model Legislative Provisions against Organized Crime*, at 111–119; and further discussion in Chapter 8.

[179] Organized Crime Convention, at Art. 26. For examples of measures that could be taken to this end, see the *Legislative Guide*, at 355, and UNODC, *Model Legislative Provisions against Organized Crime*, at 98–101.

[180] Organized Crime Convention, at Art. 27.

[181] Travaux Préparatoires *for the Organized Crime Convention and Protocols*, at 575–576.

establishment of criminal jurisdiction over migrant smuggling offenses and extradition of offenders are thereby to be found in the Organized Crime Convention and not in the Protocol itself.[182] The Convention requires States Parties to establish jurisdiction to investigate, prosecute, and punish all relevant offenses in certain specified circumstances, including: where the offense is committed within the territory of the State Party,[183] or on board a vessel flying its flag, or aircraft registered under the laws of that State Party.[184] The concept of "territory" necessarily includes the territorial sea of coastal States.[185]

The Convention encourages, but does not require, States Parties to establish jurisdiction in other circumstances, for example, when the offense is committed against[186] or by a national of a State.[187] In relation to certain specified offenses it further permits States to establish jurisdiction over such offenses that are committed outside their territory if committed "with a view to the commission of a serious crime within its territory."[188] In the case of migrant smuggling, for example, a State Party may legislate to establish jurisdiction over acts such as aiding, abetting, or organizing the commission of a serious crime involving an organized criminal group,[189] where those acts are done with a view to committing a crime of migrant smuggling within that State. An extension of jurisdiction in this way will have required the

182 Organized Crime Convention, at Art.15.

183 Ibid. at Art 15(1)(a).

184 Ibid. at Art. 15(1)(b). See further UNODC, *Model Legislative Provisions against Organized Crime*, at 25–29.

185 Organized Crime Convention, at Art. 15(1)(a); UNODC Model Law on Migrant Smuggling, at 22. For a discussion on rights and obligations attached to a coastal State's territorial sea, see Chapter 3, at Section 3.3.2.2 and Chapter 6, at Section 6.1.1.1.

186 There may be a question as to whether a State of nationality of a smuggled migrant would be able to assert jurisdiction on the basis of a crime having been committed "against" their national, given the reference to smuggled migrants in the Protocol not as victims but as objects of smuggling. However, in this regard, it is significant that the language of Article15(2)(a) makes no reference to "victims" but only refers to "offences committed against a national."

187 Organized Crime Convention, at Art. 15(2). See further UNODC Model Law on Migrant Smuggling, at 23–25.

188 Organized Crime Convention, at Art. 15(2)(c). See further UNODC Model Law on Migrant Smuggling, at 23–25.

189 Under the terms of Article 5(1) of the Organized Crime Convention, the original offenses could include "[a]greeing with one or more other persons to commit a serious crime for a purpose relating directly or indirectly to the obtaining of a financial or other material benefit" or of "[c]onduct by a person who, with knowledge of either the aim and general criminal activity of an organized criminal group or its intention to commit the crimes in question, takes an active part in: a. [c]riminal activities of the organized criminal group" or other activities of the organized criminal group in the knowledge that his or her participation will contribute to the achievement of the criminal aim; or "[o]rganizing, directing, aiding, abetting, facilitating or counselling the commission of serious crime involving an organized criminal group": ibid. Note that McClean questions whether the provisions of the Convention on jurisdiction can be so easily transposed to the Migrant Smuggling Protocol. McClean, *Transnational Organized Crime*, at 394.

State to have legislated for migrant smuggling or related acts to be punishable by a maximum deprivation of liberty of at least four years.[190]

The Convention requires States Parties to establish jurisdiction over nationals – irrespective of where the offense actually occurred – when the alleged offender is present in their territory and extradition is refused solely on the ground of nationality.[191] States Parties must treat offenses established under the Protocol as extraditable offenses under their relevant treaties and laws. Where extradition has been refused on the grounds of nationality, the State is required to submit the offenses to competent authorities for prosecution.[192] In other words, if domestic legislation prohibits extradition of a State's nationals, then that State Party is required to establish jurisdiction over migrant smuggling–related offenses committed by its nationals anywhere in the world.[193] States Parties are also permitted but not required to establish jurisdiction over offenses covered by the Convention (including the Protocol offenses) when the alleged (nonnational) offender is present in their territory and extradition is refused on any ground.[194]

In summary, and in addition to the general requirement to prosecute offenders for offenses committed within their territory, States Parties to the Convention and Migrant Smuggling Protocol are required to prosecute offenses of their nationals committed abroad *and/or* to make migrant smuggling an extraditable offense. The issue of jurisdiction is discussed further at various points later in the chapter in the context of international law of the sea and provisions relating to migrant smuggling by sea. See also the general discussion of jurisdiction in the context of "capacity to act" in Chapter 3.

MIGRANT SMUGGLING BY SEA

Reflecting the impetus behind its development, the Migrant Smuggling Protocol includes a detailed section on preventing and suppressing the smuggling of migrants by sea. This section of the Protocol is subject to detailed analysis in Chapter 6 in the context of a broader consideration of the relevant legal framework. The following analysis is therefore restricted to an overview of the major provisions as well as a brief examination of issues that emerged during the drafting process.

The Protocol does not seek to provide a new legal regime around smuggling by sea. Rather, its relevant provisions affirm core principles of the international law of the sea codified in the United Nations Convention on the Law of the Sea

190 Organized Crime Convention, at Art. 2(b).

191 Ibid. at Art 15(3). See further UNODC Model Law on Migrant Smuggling, at 23.

192 Organized Crime Convention, at Art. 16.

193 Ibid. at Art. 16(10).

194 Ibid. at Art. 15(4). See further UNODC Model Law on Migrant Smuggling, at 23.

(UNCLOS):[195] coastal States have extensive jurisdiction over national waters, subject only to certain exceptions such as innocent passage; ships have the nationality of the flag they are entitled to fly; a flag State has a duty to exercise its jurisdiction and control over ships flying its flag[196]; ships are subject to the exclusive jurisdiction of the flag State on the high seas[197]; there exists a universal right of visit over vessels without nationality; and States have a heavily circumscribed right of approach and visit in other situations. This reinforcement of existing rules is carried through to the key obligation contained in Article 7 of the Protocol: States Parties must cooperate in preventing and suppressing migrant smuggling by sea, "in accordance with the international law of the sea."[198] Existing rules are also reflected in Article 8, which establishes a cooperation regime intended to facilitate law enforcement action in relation to the smuggling of migrants involving the vessels of other States Parties.[199] These provisions reflect existing international legal rules that: (1) provide authority to flag States to take enforcement action with respect to their vessels – including those suspected of being engaged[200] in migrant smuggling[201]; (2) uphold the requirement of prior flag State consent with respect to such measures taken by another State; and (3) prevent any such measures from being taken in the territorial sea of another State, except with the permission or authorization of that State.[202]

The novelty and principal impact of the Protocol relates to situations where a State Party other than the flag State encounters a vessel suspected of being engaged in migrant smuggling that either (1) has the nationality of another State Party, or (2)

[195] United Nations Convention on the Law of the Sea, 1833 UNTS 3, done Dec. 10, 1982, entered into force Nov. 16, 1994 [UNCLOS].

[196] Ibid. at Art. 94.

[197] Ibid. at Art. 92(1).

[198] Migrant Smuggling Protocol, at Art. 7. The Interpretative Note attached to this Article confirms that: "the international law of the sea includes the United Nations Convention on the Law of the Sea as well as other relevant international instruments": Travaux Préparatoires *for the Organized Crime Convention and Protocols*, at 494. The *Travaux Préparatoires* further confirm the intention of the drafters to include both customary and conventional sources of law. Ibid. at 493.

[199] UNODC Model Law on Migrant Smuggling, at 83.

[200] "Engagement" in migrant smuggling is noted to extend to both direct and indirect engagement and thereby to cover not just vessels found to be carrying migrants but also other vessels ("mother ships") that transport smuggled migrants on open ocean voyages and may not be apprehended until after smuggled migrants have been transferred to smaller local vessels for the final stage of their journey. Travaux Préparatoires *for the Organized Crime Convention and Protocols*, at 506. The *Legislative Guide* confirms that the provisions explored in this part would not be applicable to vessels that had simply rescued migrants who were being smuggled by another vessel (at 386–387).

[201] Note the Organized Crime Convention requires flag States to establish jurisdiction when offenses have been committed on board a vessel flying their flag. Organized Crime Convention, at Art. 15.

[202] This restriction (which is noted in the *Travaux Préparatoires*) was not included in the text of the Protocol as it was considered by drafters to be well established in the law of the sea. Travaux Préparatoires *for the Organized Crime Convention and Protocols*, at 494.

is without nationality. However, once again, the Protocol does not really break new ground, rather extending and potentially rendering more effective actions that are already well within the law of the sea.[203] The relevant provisions can be summarized as follows:

- A State Party may request the assistance[204] of other States Parties in suppressing the use of a vessel suspected of engaging in migrant smuggling (where the vessel is flying that State's flag or claiming its registry or, while not flying that State's flag is, in reality, of the nationality of that State).[205]
- States Parties so requested are required to render such assistance "to the extent possible within their means."[206]
- A State Party may further notify another State Party that a vessel exercising its freedom of navigation rights[207] and flying the other State Party's flag, or apparently registered to that other State Party, is reasonably suspected of engaging in migrant smuggling, and may request confirmation of registry.[208] The Requested State must respond expeditiously to such a request.[209] Each State is required to designate an authority to receive and respond to such requests, and that designation is to be notified to all States Parties within one month via the UN Secretary-General.[210]
- In the above case, if registry is confirmed, the notifying State Party may request authorization from the flag State to *take appropriate measures* with regard to that vessel.[211]

[203] But see Chapter 6, at Section 6.1.1.3 for a more detailed discussion of whether certain provisions (such as those relating to action against stateless vessels on the high seas suspected of engaging in migrant smuggling) do indeed represent a departure from established rules.

[204] The nature and extent of "assistance" that may be requested or provided is not specified. Mallia cites the official Commentary to the United Nations Convention against Illicit Traffic in Narcotic Drugs and Psychotropic Substances (1582 UNTS 95, done Dec. 20, 1988, entered into force Nov. 11, 1990) in relation to the equivalent provision of the Drugs Convention as an indication of a potentially wide interpretation of forms of assistance that might include: "searching for the suspect vessel, preventing it from unloading or trans-shipping its cargo, facilitating the presence of the law enforcement officials of the flag State on board the pursuing vessel, and like matters": Mallia, *Migrant Smuggling by Sea*, at 122–123, citing United Nations, *Commentary on the United Nations Convention against Illicit Traffic in Narcotic Drugs and Psychotropic Substances* 1998, UN Doc. E/CN.7/590, Dec. 20, 1998, at para. 17(44).

[205] Migrant Smuggling Protocol, at Art. 8(1).

[206] Ibid.

[207] That is on the high seas or in the Exclusive Economic Zone and contiguous zone of another State that is not otherwise part of that State's territorial sea. UNCLOS, at Arts. 58(1), 87(1)(a), 90.

[208] Migrant Smuggling Protocol, at Art. 8(2).

[209] Ibid. at Art. 8(4).

[210] Ibid. at Art. 8(5). See further UNODC Model Law on Migrant Smuggling, at 86–87.

[211] Ibid.

- Among other things, "appropriate measures" that may be authorized by the flag State include authority to board and search the vessel.[212] If evidence of migrant smuggling is found, the flag State may further authorize the Requesting State to "take appropriate measures with respect to the vessel and persons and cargo on board."[213] No additional measures can be taken without express authorization of the flag State except on the basis of relevant agreements or "to relieve imminent danger to the lives of persons."[214] The flag State is further entitled to impose conditions on the measures to be taken,[215] and to be informed of the results of such measures.[216]
- A State Party that has reasonable grounds to suspect that a vessel without nationality on the high seas is engaged in the smuggling of migrants by sea may board and search that vessel.[217] If evidence of migrant smuggling is found, the State Party is required to take "appropriate measures in accordance with relevant domestic and international law."[218]

While acknowledging that the provision is not mandatory, the Legislative Guide appears to go considerably further than the text of the Protocol in encouraging States Parties to "establish their jurisdiction over vessels on the high seas flying the flag of another State party as well as over those without nationality, as this will ensure the proper functioning of the measures provided for under part II of the Protocol."[219] Significantly, the Protocol provision regarding jurisdiction on the high seas over foreign-flagged vessels differs sharply from the original Italian proposal, which conditioned such right of action on the existence of a link with the acting State: (1) if the vessel is "undoubtedly" bound for the State's coast, or (2) if it is "armed or governed or manned by its nationals."[220] In noting this departure from the original proposal, Mallia suggests that the provision as adopted potentially indicates a shift toward

212 Note however that "appropriate measures" are not specified. Mallia cites a provision of the Council of Europe Agreement on Illicit Traffic at Sea as an example of the nature and extent of measures that could be considered "appropriate" in the context of Article 8 of the Protocol. Mallia, *Migrant Smuggling by Sea*, at 123–125.

213 Migrant Smuggling Protocol, at Art. 8(2)(c).

214 Mallia, *Migrant Smuggling by Sea*, at 123–125. Note that the original wording of this provision referred to imminent danger "to the lives or safety of persons": Travaux Préparatoires *for the Organized Crime Convention and Protocols*, at 501, 503.

215 Migrant Smuggling Protocol, at Art. 8(5).

216 Ibid. at Art. 8(3).

217 Ibid. at Art. 8(7).

218 Ibid.

219 *Legislative Guide*, at 386 (para. 95), noting expressly though that this is "not a requirement under the Convention or the Protocol."

220 Cited in Mallia, *Migrant Smuggling by Sea*, at 114.

viewing migrant smuggling as a crime affecting the security of States generally, and thereby as an exception to the generally accepted rule that a State must be able to rely on some recognized basis of jurisdiction in order to exercise its enforcement jurisdiction in international waters.[221] A proposed territorial link, which would have authorized action where the vessel is entering the territorial waters of a State Party or reasonably suspected of being bound for the State Party's territorial waters, was similarly omitted.[222]

Drafters of the Protocol clearly recognized the risks associated with stopping and boarding vessels, as well as the related importance of upholding key principles of the law of the sea: specifically, the absolute priority of the flag State and freedom of navigation. The regime of cooperation is required to be consistent with the international law of the sea, including the critical obligation to render assistance to those in distress at sea.[223] Further, Article 9 of the Protocol reflects the very real humanitarian, operational, and commercial risks that may be involved in stopping, searching, and boarding vessels in the maritime environment, by subjecting measures taken by a State Party against smuggling of migrants at sea to detailed safeguards. For example, the flag State is expressly entitled to subject its authorization to conditions on the other State's exercise of jurisdiction.[224] Most critically, when carrying out such measures, States Parties are *required to ensure* the safety and humane treatment of all persons on board.[225] If suspicions about the vessel's involvement in migrant smuggling prove to be unfounded, then the State Party is required to compensate the vessel for any loss or damage.[226] Article 9 also requires the acting State to "take due account" of the rights, obligations, and exercise of jurisdiction of both coastal and flag States under existing international law.[227] It has been noted that the duty to "take due account" may not adequately reflect the very robust obligation of non-interference that is enshrined in the international law of the sea.[228]

221 Ibid.

222 Ibid. at 116.

223 UNCLOS, at Art. 98.

224 Migrant Smuggling Protocol, at Art. 8(5).

225 Ibid. at Art. 9(1) (emphasis added). As noted in the *Legislative Guide*, this obligation is of great practical importance, given the poor condition of vessels typically used by smugglers and the likelihood that boarding will take place far away from safe harbor conditions (at 365 (para. 70)). See also UNODC Model Law on Migrant Smuggling, at 91–96.

226 Migrant Smuggling Protocol, at Art. 9(2). This provision reflects Article 110(3) of UNCLOS.

227 Migrant Smuggling Protocol, at Art. 9(3).

228 Mallia, *Migrant Smuggling by Sea*, at 121. But see N. Klein, *Maritime Security and the Law of the Sea* (2011), at 127. Note that the savings clause in Article 19(1) of the Migrant Smuggling Protocol applies to the Convention on the Law of the Sea as well as to other preexisting international rights and obligations.

PREVENTION AND COOPERATION

Article 31 of the Organized Crime Convention contains a list of measures to be taken by States to prevent, inter alia, the smuggling of migrants.[229] The Protocol additionally requires the adoption of general measures to prevent migrant smuggling, with a particular focus on prevention through improved law enforcement. Great emphasis is given to the strengthening of border controls. In a set of provisions that are identical to those contained in the other two Protocols, States Parties are required to strengthen border controls to the extent possible and necessary to prevent and detect migrant smuggling.[230] They are also encouraged to establish and maintain direct channels of communication between each other as a way intensifying cooperation among border control agencies.[231] States Parties are to take steps to ensure both the *quality* and the *security* of travel documents[232] issued on their behalf and to cooperate in preventing their fraudulent use.[233] Specialized training aimed at preventing, combating, and eradicating migrant smuggling is to be provided or strengthened for immigration and other officials.[234]

The role of commercial carriers in preventing smuggling of migrants is addressed in the Protocol, by way of a requirement, "where appropriate, and without prejudice to applicable international conventions", that States Parties establish the obligation of commercial carriers to ascertain that all passengers have travel documents necessary for entry into the receiving State, and provide for sanctions in the event of violation of this obligation.[235] The Protocol does not require States to impose liability on commercial carriers who are involved in having transported undocumented/smuggled migrants but this possibility is certainly left open.[236] An Interpretative Note attached to this provision confirms the limits of obligations to be imposed on commercial carriers and also preserves general international legal obligations of States, including those related to refugees.[237]

[229] Organized Crime Convention, at Art. 31(7). See generally UNODC, *Model Legislative Provisions against Organized Crime*, at 1–18.

[230] Migrant Smuggling Protocol, at Art. 11(1).

[231] Ibid. at Art. 11(6).

[232] The *Travaux Préparatoires* confirm that the term "travel documents" includes: "any type of document required for entering or leaving a State under its domestic law and the term 'identity documents' includes any document commonly used to establish the identity of a person in a State under the laws or procedures of that State": Travaux Préparatoires *for the Organized Crime Convention and Protocols*, at 525.

[233] Migrant Smuggling Protocol, at Arts. 12–13.

[234] Ibid. at Art. 14.

[235] Ibid. at Arts. 11(2)–11(4).

[236] *Legislative Guide*, at 373 (para. 85).

[237] The *Travaux Préparatoires* confirm that: "[m]easures and sanctions applied in accordance with this paragraph should take into account other international obligations of the State party concerned. It

Little attention is given to prevention through addressing the factors that encourage or compel people to seek out the services of migrant smugglers. States Parties are instead subject to a vague and soft obligation of promoting or strengthening "development programmes and cooperation ... in order to combat the root socio-economic causes of the smuggling of migrants, such as poverty and underdevelopment."[238] A key preventative element is seen to be the dissemination of negative information aimed at discouraging potential migrants.[239] However even that obligation, although framed more sharply, is ultimately aspirational: States Parties are required to "increase public awareness of the fact that [migrant smuggling] ... is a criminal activity frequently perpetrated by organized criminal groups for profit and that it poses serious risks to the migrants concerned."[240]

Improved cooperation between countries on the issue of migrant smuggling is the raison d'être of the Protocol[241] and the obligation of cooperation is accordingly integrated into a range of provisions, including those related to the sharing of information[242] and, as noted later in the chapter, to the return of smuggled migrants.[243] Cross-border cooperation is also envisaged with respect to the strengthening of border controls and general law enforcement against migrant smuggling.[244] States Parties are encouraged to develop bilateral and regional agreements to further the purposes of the Protocol.[245] These specific provisions are supplemented by the Convention, which, as noted previously, includes detailed provisions on various forms of international cooperation including mutual legal assistance and extradition directed at the prevention and suppression of transnational organized crime.

should also be noted that this paragraph requires States parties to impose an obligation on commercial carriers only to ascertain whether or not passengers have the necessary documents in their possession and not to make any judgment or assessment of the validity or authenticity of the documents. It should further be noted that this paragraph does not unduly limit the discretion of States parties not to hold carriers liable for transporting undocumented refugees and that Article 19 preserves the general obligations of States parties under international law in this regard, making specific reference to the 1951 Convention and 1967 Protocol relating to the Status of Refugees. Article 11 was also adopted on the understanding that it would not be applied in such a way as to induce commercial carriers to impede unduly the movement of legitimate passengers": Travaux Préparatoires *for the Organized Crime Convention and Protocols*, at 521.

238 Migrant Smuggling Protocol, at Art. 15(3).

239 Ibid. at Art. 15(1)–(2). The Article cross-references Article 31 of the Convention that, inter alia, requires States Parties to "endeavour to promote public awareness regarding the existence, causes and gravity of and the threat posed by transnational organized crime."

240 Migrant Smuggling Protocol, at Art. 15(1).

241 Ibid. at Preamble.

242 Ibid. at Art. 10.

243 Ibid. at Art. 18.

244 Ibid. at Arts. 8, 11, 13–14.

245 Ibid. at Art. 17.

ASSISTANCE TO AND PROTECTION OF SMUGGLED MIGRANTS

A review of the Protocol's drafting history confirms that questions of assistance and protection for smuggled migrants were not addressed during the early stages of the negotiations. Nevertheless, as progress was made on the text, the potential impact of the Migrant Smuggling Protocol on human rights, including the rights of asylum-seekers and refugees, did become a point of discussion. For example, the *Travaux Préparatoires* note that in early 2000, the Group of Latin American and Caribbean States:

> were of the view that it was important to develop a legal instrument that would effectively target smugglers while protecting the rights of migrants. Therefore the protocol must take into account the relevant United Nations instruments on protection of migrants in connection with correcting social and economic imbalances ... it [is] important for the Migrants Protocol not to penalise migration ... or to convey an ambiguous message to the international community that would stimulate xenophobia, intolerance and racism. The negotiation process should take into account the causes of migration and the reasons for the increasing vulnerability of migrants. [246]

With only a few such exceptions, most participating States appeared reluctant to support the inclusion of strong human rights protections in the draft Protocol, and the suggestion of the Group of Latin American and Caribbean States in this regard did not gain significant traction within the drafting group. The informal group of intergovernmental agencies involved in the drafting process was much more active, persistently intervening to highlight potential risks, especially to the rights of asylum-seekers, posed by the new Protocol.[247] A major submission delivered by the group in February 2000 provides a useful summary of principal concerns, in particular with respect to the issue of asylum:[248]

> The Office [OHCHR], [UNHCR], UNICEF and IOM welcome the explicit references [in the draft text] to obligations of States Parties under the 1951 Convention

[246] "Progress Report of the Ad Hoc Committee on the Elaboration of a Convention against Transnational Organized Crime," UN Doc. A/AC.254/30-E/CN.15/2000/4, Mar. 29, 2000, at para. 18. See also "Informal note by the United Nations High Commissioner for Human Rights," UN Doc. A/AC.254/16, June 1, 1999 [HCHR Submission], at 4–8; and "Note by the Office of the United Nations High Commissioner for Human Rights, the Office of the United Nations High Commissioner for Refugees, the United Nations Children's Fund and the International Organization for Migration on the draft protocols concerning migrant smuggling and trafficking in persons," UN Doc. A/AC.254/27, Feb. 8, 2000 (and UN Doc. A.AC.254/27/Corr.1, Feb. 22, 2000, correcting the title of that document) [Inter-Agency Submission], at 15–22. Protection of the rights of smuggled migrants was finally included as one of the purposes of the Protocol: Migrant Smuggling Protocol, at Art. 2.

[247] See, for example, Inter-Agency Submission; HCHR Submission.

[248] Inter-Agency Submission, at paras. 16–18 (citations omitted). Note that the United Nations High Commissioner for Refugees (UNHCR) was originally left off the list of agencies preparing this submission. This was amended in the corrigendum.

Of course, differences between the two Protocols are equally substantive and, in the present context, much more significant. As the substantive obligations of the Trafficking Protocol have been dealt with in detail elsewhere by one of the present authors,[270] the following is restricted to a brief identification and analysis of the Protocol's major features, with special reference to the relationship, including distinctions and perceived and potential overlaps, between this instrument and the Migrant Smuggling Protocol.

1.1.4.1. Origins of the Trafficking Protocol

The origins of the Trafficking Protocol can be traced back to Argentina's interest in the issue of trafficking in minors and its dissatisfaction with the slow progress on negotiating an additional protocol to the Convention on the Rights of the Child[271] (CRC) to address child prostitution and child pornography.[272] Argentina was also concerned that a purely human rights perspective on this issue would be insufficient and accordingly lobbied strongly for trafficking to be dealt with as part of the broader international attack on transnational organized crime.[273] Argentina's proposal for a new convention against trafficking in minors was discussed at the 1997 session of the UN Commission on Crime Prevention and Criminal Justice.[274] Its timing was fortuitous. The powerful European institutions had recently decided to take the issue of trafficking seriously and were in the midst of developing their own detailed policies and responses.[275] The United States had also become active, with its president preparing to issue a detailed memorandum on measures to be taken by the government to combat violence against women and trafficking in women and girls.[276] A general awareness was also developing, among an influential group of States, of the need for a holistic approach where the crime control aspects of trafficking were addressed along with traditional human rights concerns.[277] Although Argentina's

[270] Gallagher, *The International Law of Human Trafficking*.

[271] Convention on the Rights of the Child, 1577 UNTS 3, done Nov. 20, 1989, entered into force Sept. 2, 1990 [CRC].

[272] Vlassis, UNAFEI, at 492.

[273] Ibid.

[274] "Strategies for Crime Prevention and Control, Particularly in Urban Areas and in the Context of Public Security: Measures to Prevent Trafficking in Children, Report of the Secretary-General," UN Doc. E/CN.15/1997/12, Feb. 28, 1997.

[275] On the early European response, see "Trafficking in Women and Girls: Note prepared by the Office of the High Commissioner for Human Rights and the ECE Secretariat," UN Doc. E/ECE/RW.2/2000/3, Dec. 1, 1999, esp. at 29–35.

[276] President W. J. Clinton, "Memorandum on Steps to Combat Violence against Women and Trafficking in Women and Girls," prepared for the secretary of state, the attorney general, the administrator of the Agency for International Development, the director of the United States Information Agency, Mar. 11, 1998, reprinted in (1998) 3(4) *Trends in Organized Crime* 20.

[277] See generally, Vlassis, UNAFEI.

original proposals related only to the trafficking of women and children, the Ad Hoc Committee eventually agreed this was unnecessarily restrictive and requested the General Assembly to modify its mandate accordingly.[278]

1.1.4.2. Overview and Comparison with the Smuggling Protocol

Under Article 2 of the Trafficking Protocol, the crime of human trafficking comprises three separate elements: an action (recruitment, transportation, transfer, harboring, or receipt of persons), a means (threat or use of force or other forms of coercion, abduction, fraud, deception, abuse of power, or abuse of a position of vulnerability, or the giving or receiving of payments or benefits to achieve the consent of a person having control over another person), and a purpose (exploitation) (Tables 1.2 and 1.3).[279] Exploitation is defined to include, at a minimum, exploitation of prostitution, other forms of sexual exploitation, forced labor or services, slavery or practices similar to slavery, servitude, or the removal of organs.[280] The definition includes a provision to the effect that the consent of a victim to the intended exploitation is irrelevant where any of these means have been used.[281] In other words, "[o]nce it is established that deception, force or other prohibited means were used, consent is irrelevant and cannot be used as a defence."[282]

The stated purpose of the Trafficking Protocol is threefold: first, to prevent and combat trafficking in persons, paying particular attention to the protection of women and children; second, to protect and assist victims of trafficking; and third, to promote and facilitate cooperation among States Parties to this end.[283] The structure of the Protocol generally follows this three-part approach. In terms of its scope of application, it is relevant to note that some commentators have misunderstood the Protocol as requiring States Parties to take action against trafficking only in respect to situations with a transnational element or involving an organized criminal group.[284] This interpretation does hold up indeed with respect to the interstate *cooperation* obligations of the Trafficking Protocol, but it fails to capture accurately the nature

[278] See "Draft Protocol to Combat International Trafficking in Women and Children, Supplementary to the United Nations Convention against Transnational Organized Crime: Proposal/Submitted by the United States of America," UN Doc. A/AC/254/4/Add.3, Nov. 25, 1998. See also Travaux Préparatoires *for the Organized Crime Convention and Protocols*, at 322; and "Progress Report of the Ad Hoc Committee on the Elaboration of a Convention against Transnational Organized Crime," UN Doc. A/AC.254/30-E/CN.15/2000/4, Mar. 29, 2000, at para. 34.

[279] Trafficking Protocol, at Art. 3.

[280] Ibid.

[281] Ibid. at Art. 3(b).

[282] *Legislative Guide*, at 270 (para. 37).

[283] Trafficking Protocol, at Art. 2.

[284] Hathaway, for example, asserts incorrectly that "slavery or other forms of exploitation that occur entirely within the borders of one country without the involvement of outside parties are beyond the scope of the Trafficking Protocol": Hathaway, "The Human Rights Quagmire of 'Human Trafficking,'" at 11.

TABLE 1.2 *Key elements of the international legal definition of trafficking in persons*

KEY ELEMENTS	
Action	Consisting of recruitment, transportation, transfer, harboring, or receipt of persons.
Means	Threat or use of force or other forms of coercion, abduction, fraud, deception, abuse of power or position of vulnerability, giving or receiving payments or benefits to achieve consent of a person having control over another.
Purpose	Exploitation (including, at a minimum, the exploitation of the prostitution of others, or other forms of sexual exploitation, forced labor or services, slavery or practices similar to slavery, servitude, or the removal of organs).

TABLE 1.3 *Key elements of the international legal definition of trafficking in children*

KEY ELEMENTS	
Action	Consisting of recruitment, transportation, transfer, harboring, or receipt of persons.
Purpose	Exploitation (including, at a minimum, the exploitation of the prostitution of others, or other forms of sexual exploitation, forced labor or services, slavery or practices similar to slavery, servitude, or the removal of organs).

of State Party obligations under the instrument as a whole. While the text of the relevant provisions is somewhat ambiguous and perhaps even contradictory,[285] there is solid support for the proposition that the provisions of both the Convention and the Protocol operate to require that the offense of trafficking be established in the domestic law of every State Party, independently of its transnational nature or the involvement of an organized criminal group.[286]

[285] See further Chapter 5, at Section 5.1.1.4.

[286] Organized Crime Convention, at Art. 34(2). See also Conference of the Parties to the United Nations Convention against Transnational Organized Crime, "Criminalization within the scope of the United Nations Convention against Transnational Organized Crime and the Protocols thereto: Note by the Secretariat," UN Doc. CTOC/COP/2008/4, Sept. 9, 2008, at para. 2 ("the offences need to be criminalized in domestic law independently of the transnational nature or the involvement of an organized criminal group"); *Legislative Guide*, at 276 (para. 45) ("transnationality is not required as an element of domestic offences") and also at 18–19, 275–76, 341; Travaux Préparatoires *for the Organized Crime Convention and Protocols*, at 285. On the matter of involvement of an organized criminal group, see also, for example, *Legislative Guide*, at 276 (para. 45) ("the involvement of an organized criminal group must not be required as a proof in a domestic prosecution").

CRIMINALIZATION, INVESTIGATION, AND PUNISHMENT OF TRAFFICKING

The obligation to criminalize trafficking when committed intentionally is contained in Article 5 and is a central and mandatory provision of that instrument.[287] Article 5 also obliges States Parties to criminalize attempting to commit such an offense,[288] participating as an accomplice in such an offense,[289] organizing or directing others to commit such an offense,[290] and obstruction of justice when carried out with respect to offenses established by the Protocol.[291] Importantly, the obligation extends only to "trafficking" as defined in that instrument and not to "related conduct."[292] In other words, it is the combination of constituent elements making up the crime of trafficking that are to be criminalized, not the elements themselves.[293] The obligation extends to both natural and legal persons although the liability for legal persons does not need to be "criminal."[294]

As with the Migrant Smuggling Protocol, the requirement that States Parties impose appropriate penalties for trafficking, accepted without question throughout the negotiation process, was quietly omitted from the final text.[295] Absent a specific provision on the subject, the relevant provisions of the Organized Crime Convention apply. In accordance with their obligations under that instrument, States Parties are required to ensure that sanctions adopted within domestic law take into account and be proportionate to the gravity of the offenses.[296] As with the Migrant Smuggling Protocol, the *mutatis mutandis* requirement extends to other mandatory provisions of the Convention, creating obligations on States Parties to take certain measures with respect to offenses established under the Trafficking Protocol.[297]

[287] *Legislative Guide*, at 269–270.

[288] "Subject to the basic concepts" of the legal system of the State: Trafficking Protocol, at Art. 5(2)(a). The *Legislative Guide* at 271–272 notes that this caveat was introduced to accommodate legal systems that do not recognize the criminal concept of "attempt."

[289] Trafficking Protocol, at Art. 5(2)(b).

[290] Ibid. at Art. 5(2)(c).

[291] Organized Crime Convention, at Art. 23.

[292] *Legislative Guide*, at 267–269. The Legislative Guide notes that this limitation is unique to the Trafficking Protocol. Both the Firearms Protocol and the Migrant Smuggling Protocol require criminalization of certain specified "related conduct."

[293] *Legislative Guide*, at 268–269. See further Chapter 5 for a detailed discussion of whether international law supports an obligation to criminalize component acts and related offenses.

[294] Organized Crime Convention, at Art. 10; *Legislative Guide*, at 270 (para. 36).

[295] The obligation to "impose penalties that take into account the grave nature of those offences" appeared in all drafts. Although noting the decision to omit this reference, the *Travaux Préparatoires* do not explain it: Travaux Préparatoires *for the Organized Crime Convention and Protocols*, at 363 (Trafficking Protocol) and 478–488 (Migrant Smuggling Protocol). It can be assumed that as such a provision was already included in the Organized Crime Convention (see the *Travaux Préparatoires*), its repetition in the Protocol was considered to be unnecessary.

[296] Organized Crime Convention, at Art. 11(1).

[297] See note 87 above, and accompanying text.

VICTIM PROTECTION AND SUPPORT

Part Two of the Trafficking Protocol, dealing with protection of the trafficked person, contains several important protective provisions.[298] Although rightly criticized for their conditional and qualified nature,[299] these provisions nevertheless go well beyond those accorded to smuggled migrants. Specifically, States Parties are required to:

- Protect the privacy and identity of trafficking victims in appropriate cases and to the extent possible under domestic law, including by making legal proceedings confidential to the extent that this is also possible under domestic law[300];
- Ensure that in appropriate cases, victims receive information on relevant court and administrative proceedings as well as assistance to enable their views to be presented and considered during criminal proceedings[301];
- Endeavor to provide for the physical safety of trafficking victims within their territory[302]; and
- Ensure that domestic law provides victims with the possibility of obtaining compensation.[303]

In terms of victim assistance and support, the relevant provision requires States Parties to "consider adopting legislative or other appropriate measures to provide for the physical, psychological and social recovery of victims of trafficking."[304] Special

[298] Further on victim protection and support, see Chapter 8.

[299] Inter-Agency Submission, at para. 7. For a useful summary of other interventions see the Travaux Préparatoires *for the Organized Crime Convention and Protocols*, at 368.

[300] Trafficking Protocol, at Art. 6(1). The *Legislative Guide*, at 283, notes that this may include courts being given authority to shield identities or otherwise protect the privacy of victims in appropriate cases. Reference should also be made to Article 24(2)(b) of the Organized Crime Convention, which provides for witnesses to be able to give evidence in safety.

[301] Trafficking Protocol, at Art. 6(2). Note that this is one of the few mandatory victim assistance provisions and should already have been implemented through legislation as required under Article 25(3) of the Organized Crime Convention. The *Legislative Guide*, at 284, notes a number of ways in which this provision could be given practical effect, including through provision of a right to submit a post-conviction, presentencing victim impact statement.

[302] Trafficking Protocol, at Art. 6(5). Note that this is a minimum standard that, in certain cases (such as in relation to witnesses), would be supplemented by additional requirements contained in Articles 24 and 25 of the Organized Crime Convention. See further *Legislative Guide*, at 285.

[303] Trafficking Protocol, at Art. 6(6). Note that the provision does not specify types of compensation. The *Legislative Guide* at 60 identifies a range of options including provisions allowing victims to sue offenders for civil damages, provisions allowing criminal courts to award criminal damages or compensation, and provisions establishing special funds or schemes for the benefit of victims of trafficking. In relation to the issue of compensation, it is relevant to note that a draft provision on the seizure, confiscation, and disposal of gains from trafficking was deleted following agreement that the corresponding Article of the Convention would apply *mutatis mutandis*. However the essence of the provision was lost in this move, and States Parties will now *not* be required to use the proceeds from seizure and confiscation to fund assistance and compensation for victims of trafficking.

[304] Trafficking Protocol, at Art. 6(3). The type of assistance set forth in this paragraph is applicable to both the receiving State and the State of origin of the victims of trafficking in persons, but only as regards

reference is made to the provision of housing, counseling, and information in a language the victim understands; medical, psychological, and material assistance; and employment, education, and training opportunities.[305]

The soft nature of these obligations means that a State Party will not be breaching either the letter or the spirit of the Convention if it decides, after proper consideration, to provide no material, medical, or other assistance whatsoever to any victim of trafficking within its territory. States also retain an implied right under the Convention to link the provision of such assistance to victims' willingness to cooperate with criminal justice agencies.

The characterization of *object/victim* is thereby a principal point of comparison between the Protocols on human trafficking and migrant smuggling. Those who have been trafficked are clearly identified as "victims": in this way confirming their automatic status, in international law, as victims of crime as well as victims of human rights violations.[306] In addition to provisions of protection and support in the Protocol itself, the broad victim protection provisions set out in Article 25 of the Organized Crime Convention are also automatically applicable. In contrast, beyond the rather ambiguous references to human rights and refugee law, examined previously, the Migrant Smuggling Protocol does not contain any substantive provisions relating to protection and support of those who have been smuggled. It deliberately withholds "victim" status from such persons, meaning there can be no automatic reference to the Convention's victim assistance protection provisions,[307] and possibly also from the general standards of obligation relating to victims of crime[308] – at least unless and until it can be shown that they are victims of another crime (such as sexual assault), or victims of trafficking and/or "aggravated smuggling."[309]

SPECIAL PROTECTIONS FOR TRAFFICKED CHILDREN

Despite the genesis of the Trafficking Protocol in this issue, the matter of child trafficking did not especially occupy delegations during the negotiations.[310] Early

victims who are in their respective territory. Paragraph 3 is applicable to the receiving State until the victim of trafficking in persons has returned to his or her State of origin, after which paragraph 3 will apply to the State of origin. The relevant Interpretative Note stipulates that "[t]he type of assistance set forth in this paragraph is applicable to both the receiving State and the State of origin but only as regards victims who are in their respective territory": Travaux Préparatoires *for the Organized Crime Convention and Protocols*, at 373.

305 Trafficking Protocol, at Art. 6(3). According to the *Legislative Guide*, the expected high cost of such measures, and the fact that their provision would be required of all States in which victims are found, precluded them from being made obligatory. *Legislative Guide*, at 288 (para. 62).

306 Further on the nature and consequences of that status, see Gallagher, *The International Law of Human Trafficking*, particularly chapters 5 and 6.

307 See particularly, Organized Crime Convention, at Art. 25.

308 See discussion in Chapter 8, at Section 8.1.

309 See further Chapter 5, at Section 5.1.4 and Chapter 8, at Section 8.2.

310 Further on special protections for trafficked children, see Chapter 8, at Section 8.2.2.6.

in the negotiations, the UN High Commissioner for Human Rights urged the Ad Hoc Committee to include special provisions to prevent trafficking in children and to protect child victims.[311] These calls were echoed in a separate submission by the Special Rapporteur on the Sale of Children, Child Prostitution and Child Pornography.[312] In February 2000, the Inter-Agency Group, alarmed at the lack of any progress on this issue, made the additional explicit recommendations on the issue.[313] Although the final version of the Protocol falls far short of this standard, it does contain several provisions aimed at ensuring relatively greater protection for trafficked children,[314] once again separating itself from the Migrant Smuggling Protocol, which contains only one brief and weak reference to "the special needs of women and children" in the context of protection and assistance.[315] The most significant of the Trafficking Protocol's provisions in respect of protection of children relates to the definition of trafficking in children itself – specifically, the omission of a means element.[316] In applying the Protocol's protection and assistance provisions, States Parties are required to take into account the special needs of child victims, including appropriate housing, education, and care.[317] The Legislative Guide has

[311] HCHR Submission, at 13–14.

[312] The Special Rapporteur proposed, inter alia, that the preamble should contain a paragraph recognizing the vulnerability of children as distinct and separate from circumstances attendant upon the vulnerability of women, as well as reference to the CRC. Travaux Préparatoires *for the Organized Crime Convention and Protocols*, at 324.

[313] "The Protocol should include an explicit acknowledgment of the fact that children have special rights under international law and, in particular in the light of the Convention on the Rights of the Child; that child victims of trafficking have special needs that must be recognized and met by States Parties; that States are obliged to take measures to prevent trafficking of children; and that in dealing with child victims of trafficking, the best interests of the child (including the specific right to physical and psychological recovery and social integration) are to be at all times paramount. Also important is clear recognition of the need to fight the impunity of those responsible for the trafficking, while at the same time ensuring that the child is not criminalized in any way. In that context, it should be noted that the overwhelming majority of States are already under such legal obligations through their ratification of the Convention on the Rights of the Child. Existing international law would also appear to require States to ensure, inter alia, that assistance and protection of child victims of trafficking is not made discretionary or otherwise dependent on the decision of national authorities. In accordance with Article 2 of the Convention, child victims of trafficking are entitled to the same protection as nationals of the receiving State in all matters, including those relating to protection of their privacy and physical and moral integrity": Inter-Agency Submission, at para. 6.

[314] The Protocol defines children as persons under the age of eighteen: Trafficking Protocol, at Art. 3(d).

[315] Migrant Smuggling Protocol, at Art. 16(4).

[316] See Section 1.1.4.

[317] Trafficking Protocol, at Art. 6(4). The provision requires consideration of "age, gender and special needs of victims of trafficking in persons, in particular the special needs of children." McClean points out that at one stage, this provision was limited to the special needs of children and that the widening of its scope of application to include considerations of both gender and special needs may have weakened its force. McClean, *Transnational Organized Crime*, at 340.

expanded on these provisions by providing examples of the kinds of steps that States could take to protect and assist child victims of trafficking.[318]

LEGAL STATUS AND REPATRIATION

The status of the victim in the receiving State was a critical issue in the negotiations.[319] Although NGOs and the Inter-Agency Group argued strongly for the inclusion of some kind of right of trafficked persons to remain in the receiving country, at least temporarily, this option was never seriously under consideration. According to the *Travaux Préparatoires*, "[m]ost delegations were concerned that the Protocol might inadvertently become a means of illicit migration if States Parties were obliged to adopt legislation permitting victims to remain in the countries to which they were trafficked."[320] States recognized, however, that in some cases there would be a legitimate need for victims to remain in their country of destination, for example, "for humanitarian purposes and to protect them from being victimized again by traffickers."[321] The final text provides that the State Party is to consider adopting legislative or other measures permitting victims of trafficking to remain in their territories temporarily or permanently in appropriate cases,[322] with appropriate consideration being given to humanitarian and compassionate factors.[323] No such provision was included in the Migrant Smuggling Protocol.

318 The Legislative Guide makes specific reference to the CRC and the principle of the best interests of the child enshrined therein. The Guide encourages States to ensure that even those whose age is uncertain are treated in accordance with the CRC until age is verified. It also sets out a list of possible measures that could be taken by States in order to assist and support victims of trafficking, including appointment of a guardian to protect the child's interests, ensuring no direct contact between the child and the suspected offender, providing shelter for children that guards against re-victimization, ensuring that those dealing with child victims are properly trained to understand their needs and rights, and considering the best interests of the child in relation to decisions about her or his repatriation. *Legislative Guide*, at 289–290.

319 Further on legal status and repatriation, see Chapter 8, at Section 8.2.2.

320 Travaux Préparatoires *for the Organized Crime Convention and Protocols*, at 380.

321 "Revised [seventh] draft Protocol to Prevent, Suppress and Punish Trafficking in Persons, Especially Women and Children, supplementing the United Nations Convention against Transnational Organized Crime," UN Doc. A/AC.254/4/Add.3/Rev.7, July 19, 2000, at n, 28.

322 Trafficking Protocol, at Art. 7(1). The *Travaux Préparatoires* confirm that delegations were in agreement that "it was not the intention of the paragraph to confer the right to remain, but that the decision whether or not to grant temporary or permanent residence was always at the discretion of the State party": Travaux Préparatoires *for the Organized Crime Convention and Protocols*, at 380, n. 8.

323 Trafficking Protocol, at Art. 7(2). The *Travaux Préparatoires* note that many delegations supported the view that the words "compassionate factors" referred to personal circumstances such as family situation, age, common-law marital relationship, and other factors that should be considered on an individual and case-by-case basis. "Humanitarian factors" were applicable to all persons, being the rights established in the human rights instruments. Travaux Préparatoires *for the Organized Crime Convention and Protocols*, at 380. McClean questions whether this is correct, pointing out that if human rights are applicable to all, "it is strange to find they are to be given merely 'appropriate consideration' in this context": McClean, *Transnational Organized Crime*, at 343.

Protocol is capable of modifying or extending certain rights and obligations of States under the international law of the sea. For example, the UNCLOS carefully specifies the circumstances under which a State's vessel may board a foreign vessel on the high seas. Although these circumstances do not include a suspicion that the foreign vessel is engaged in migrant smuggling, the Protocol could arguably operate to extend the right to board in this way.

Until the highly ambitious exercise of articulating a comprehensive law of the sea treaty was completed in 1982, the law of the sea (international maritime law) comprised a substantial body of customary law, built up over centuries, supplemented by a limited number of international treaties (including, most importantly, the four law of the sea conventions concluded in Geneva in 1958).[356] The core principles of international maritime law prior to the mid-twentieth century imposed a range of obligations on States aimed at ensuring the safety of international navigation as well as a recognition of particular rights, principles, and entitlements including:

- Freedom of navigation and freedom of the "open sea" (high seas);
- The right of "innocent passage";
- A right to exercise jurisdiction over vessels on the high seas in times of war (stemming from the laws of war);
- Right of coastal States to exercise sovereignty over a strip of waters (the maximum breadth of which had not yet been conclusively determined) immediately adjoining their coastlines (maritime belt, subsequently known as the "territorial sea");
- Right of a coastal State to pursue and apprehend a foreign vessel, even on to the high seas, when it had good reason to believe the vessel had infringed its laws while passing through that State's maritime belt (right of hot pursuit); and
- The principle that vessels have the nationality of the State whose flag they are entitled to fly.

Less settled were questions related to the extent of States' rights to exercise jurisdiction over foreign vessels on the high seas in relation to matters such as the slave

Law: Difficulties arising from the Diversification and Expansion of International Law," adopted by the International Law Commission at its 58th session, 2006, at para. 2(5).

[356] The Geneva Conventions formed the basis for the modern framework of the international law of the sea: Convention on the Territorial Sea and the Contiguous Zone, 516 UNTS 205, done Apr. 29, 1958, entered into force Sept. 10, 1964 [Territorial Sea Convention]; Convention on the High Seas, 450 UNTS 11, done Apr. 29, 1958, entered into force Sept. 30, 1962 [High Seas Convention]; Convention on Fishing and Conservation of the Living Resources of the High Seas, 559 UNTS 285, done Apr. 29, 1958, entered into force Mar. 20, 1966 [Fishing and Conservation Convention]; and the Convention on the Continental Shelf, 499 UNTS 311, done Apr. 29, 1958, entered into force June 10, 1964. Previous attempts to codify the international law of the sea had failed, including efforts by forty-four members of the League of Nations in 1930.

trade, or where there was serious suspicion that the vessel was a source of great danger to the sovereignty or security of the State. Up until the period immediately prior to the conclusion of UNCLOS, the practice of States in claiming different maritime zones varied widely. The conclusion and subsequent wide adoption of the 1982 United Nations Convention on the Law of the Sea has substantially clarified and refined the applicable rules.

1.2.1. *The United Nations Convention on the Law of the Sea*

In the years following the Second World War, conflicts between States arose in many areas of the law of the sea, most particularly in relation to the delineation of maritime boundaries. In 1957 the UN General Assembly decided to convene an international conference "to examine the law of the sea, taking account not only of the legal but also of the technical, biological, economic and political aspects of the problem, and to embody the results of its work in one or more international conventions or ... other instruments."[357] The First United Nations Conference on the Law of the Sea was held the following year and resulted in four separate conventions, which together provided a framework of rules governing the use of and rights to the high seas and the territorial sea. However, even the convening of a second conference did not resolve a number of important points that had been left unsettled, such as the breadth of the territorial sea. The situation was further complicated by the emergence of new contentious issues such as the rights of landlocked States; protection of the marine environment; and control over marine seabed resources beyond national jurisdiction, which developments in technology had rendered increasingly likely to be accessible.

In 1970 the General Assembly convened a Third United Nations Conference on the Law of the Sea, granting it a sweeping mandate to establish regimes of the high seas, coastal waters, seabed, and ocean floor; and to address issues including fishing and conservation of living resources on the high seas, marine scientific research, and preservation of the marine environment.[358] In 1982, after nine years of intensive negotiations attended by 151 States, the United Nations Convention on the Law of the Sea (UNCLOS), comprising 320 articles and nine annexes, was adopted. The

357 UN General Assembly, "International conference of plenipotentiaries to examine the law of the sea," GA Res. 1105, UN GAOR, 11th sess, 658th plen mtg, Supp. No 17, UN Doc. A/352, Feb. 21, 1957, at 54, para. 2.

358 UN General Assembly, "Reservation exclusively for peaceful purposes of the sea-bed and the ocean floor, and the subsoil thereof, underlying the high seas beyond the limits of present national jurisdiction and use of their resources in the interests of mankind, and convening of a conference on the law of the sea," GA Res. 2750(XXV)C, UN GAOR, 25th sess., 1933rd plen mtg, Supp. No. 28, UN Doc. A/8028, Dec. 17, 1970, at para. 2.

Convention affirmed the substance of core principles such as the obligation on States to exercise jurisdiction and control over ships flying their flag.[359] Other rights, obligations, and entitlements, including those most relevant to migrant smuggling, are fundamentally linked to the maritime zones and boundaries established by the Convention. As these zones and boundaries are considered in detail at Chapter 3, the following paragraphs summarize only their key aspects.

Territorial Sea: A coastal State's territorial sea is generally recognized as being the zone extending twelve nautical miles from its low-water baseline.[360] UNCLOS recognizes the sovereignty of States over its territorial sea,[361] although this does not mean that its municipal laws apply automatically.[362] A principal obstacle to the exercise of full jurisdiction by the coastal State within its territorial sea is the right of innocent passage, enjoyed by foreign vessels within that zone.[363] However, the coastal State may take necessary steps to prevent passage that is not innocent[364] (i.e., passage that is prejudicial to the peace, good order, or security of the coastal State).[365] Vessels exercising the right of passage are subject to local laws and regulations provided these conform to international law, including treaty obligations.[366] A coastal States should not exercise criminal jurisdiction on board a foreign ship passing through its territorial sea to arrest any person or conduct any investigation in connection with any crime committed on board the ship during its passage except: (1) if the consequences of the crime extend to the coastal State, (2) if the crime is of the kind to disturb the peace of the coastal State or the good order of the territorial sea, (c) if assistance of the coastal State has been requested by the master of the ship or by an accredited representative of the ship's flag State, or (4) if such measures are necessary for the suppression of drug trafficking.[367] Chapter 6 considers the application of these exceptions to a situation of migrant smuggling or suspected migrant smuggling. In relation to a crime committed *before* a foreign ship entered the territorial sea, the rules are even more restrictive: coastal States may not exercise criminal

359 UNCLOS, at Art. 94. See also Art. 99, requiring States to suppress the slave trade in relation to their own vessels.

360 Ibid. at Arts. 3–7.

361 Ibid. at Art. 2.

362 R. R. Churchill and A. V. Lowe, *The Law of the Sea* (3rd ed. 1999), at 75.

363 UNCLOS, at Art. 17.

364 Ibid. at Art. 25(1).

365 Ibid. at Art. 19(1). Article 19(2) sets out a list of acts that will be considered prejudicial to the peace, order, and security of the coastal State. These include "the loading or unloading of any commodity, currency or person contrary to the customs, fiscal, immigration or sanitary laws and regulations of the coastal State": ibid. at 19(1)(g). The issue of innocent passage with respect to vessels carrying rescued smuggled migrants to a place of safety is considered in Chapter 6, at notes 261–265 and accompanying text.

366 UNCLOS, at Arts. 21–22, 25(2).

367 Ibid. at Art. 27(1).

jurisdiction or undertake any criminal investigation on board such a foreign ship except in relation to enforcing certain aspects of its Exclusive Economic Zone jurisdiction or for purposes of marine environment protection.[368] A coastal State may authorize another State to exercise jurisdiction within its territorial sea and within the limits of the coastal State's own jurisdiction.[369] The nature and extent of the latter State's capacity to act is, within the limits set out previously, determined by the coastal State.

Contiguous Zone: Coastal States may assert a contiguous zone, which, if claimed, will extend no more than twenty-four miles from the baseline from which the breadth of the territorial sea is measured.[370] Within the contiguous zone, a coastal State may exercise the control necessary to prevent infringement of its customs, fiscal, immigration, and sanitary laws and regulations only, as well as to punish infringements of such laws and regulations committed within its territory or territorial sea.[371] As one commentator has noted, the preventive capacity applies only to *incoming* vessels in relation to which the coastal State anticipates an offense against its laws. Conversely, the punishment capacity can only apply to outgoing ships that have committed or been involved in the commission of an offense while within the jurisdiction of the coastal State.[372] The question of what constitutes necessary control is not fully settled. Brownlie characterizes the power of the coastal State in its contiguous zone as: "one of police and control, and transgressors cannot be visited with consequences amounting to reprisals or summary punishments."[373]

Exclusive Economic Zone: UNCLOS permits coastal States to claim an Exclusive Economic Zone (EEZ) extending up to 200 miles from the baseline of the territorial sea.[374] Within its EEZ, coastal States are granted a range of rights, principally related to exploration, exploitation, conservation, and management of natural resources and the marine environment.[375] Although a State's EEZ is not part of the high seas,[376]

368 Ibid. at Art. 27(5).

369 Ibid. at Art. 311(3): "Two or more States Parties may conclude agreements modifying or suspending the operation of provisions of this Convention, applicable solely to the relations between them, provided that such agreements do not relate to a provision derogation from which is incompatible with the effective execution of the object and purpose of this Convention..."

370 Ibid. at Art. 33(2).

371 Ibid. at Art. 33(1).

372 I. Brownlie, *Principles of Public International Law* (6th ed. 2003), at 196, citing G. Fitzmaurice, "Some Results of the Geneva Conference on the Law of the Sea," (1959) 8 *International & Comparative Law Quarterly* 73, at 113.

373 Ibid. at 195–196. See also D. P. O'Connell (I. Shearer ed.), *The International Law of the Sea*, vol. II (1984), at 1058.

374 UNCLOS, at Arts. 55, 57.

375 Ibid. at Art. 56.

376 Ibid. at Art. 86.

freedoms of the high seas apply.[377] In the context of migrant smuggling therefore, it is the legal regime of the high seas that must be considered.

High Seas: Under UNCLOS, the high seas encompass all those parts of the sea that are not included within the EEZ, territorial, or internal waters of a State.[378] The Convention affirms the customary principle of the freedom of the high seas, which is specified as comprising freedom of navigation, freedom of overflight, freedom to lay submarine cables and pipelines and to construct artificial islands, freedom of fishing, and freedom of scientific research.[379] It further confirms that, with only very narrow exceptions, flag States have exclusive jurisdiction over their vessels on the high seas.[380] The "right of visit," the most relevant exception to the general principle of freedom of the high seas, is considered in Chapter 6 in the context of a detailed discussion of powers of interception with respect to vessels carrying smuggled migrants. Irrespective of the justification, the act of boarding a foreign ship on the high seas is characterized as a privilege, and the Convention provides for strict liability in relation to any resulting loss or damage.[381] It is also relevant to note that the right to exercise freedom of the high seas could be compromised in a "hot pursuit": the pursuit of a foreign ship by a coastal State for suspected violations of the laws and regulations of that State, which commences within the territorial waters or contiguous zone of the coastal State and continues, uninterrupted, onto the high seas.[382] The right of hot pursuit ceases as soon as the ship pursued enters the territorial sea of its own State or of a third State.[383]

1.2.2. *Protection of Life at Sea Conventions*

It has been noted that the issue of protection of life at sea in the context of migrant smuggling gives rise to a tension between two well-established international legal principles: the obligation to render assistance to those in peril or lost at sea, and the fundamental right of States to control entry of nonnationals

[377] Ibid. at Art. 87. See also Art. 58.

[378] "or in the archipelagic waters of an archipelagic State": UNCLOS, at Art. 86.

[379] Ibid. at Art. 87. Note that several of these freedoms are subject to restriction. Freedom of fishing, for example, is subject to an obligation of cooperation with respect to conservation of the living resources of the high seas (Article 117).

[380] Ibid. at Art. 92(1). This provision codifies a well-established rule of customary international law, articulated by the Permanent Court of International Justice in the *SS Lotus Case*: "Vessels on the high seas are subject to no authority except that of the state whose flag they fly. In virtue of the principle of the freedom of the seas, that is to say, in the absence of any territorial sovereignty upon the high seas, no state may exercise any kind of jurisdiction over foreign vessels upon them": *SS Lotus (France v. Turkey) (Judgment)*, [1927] PCIJ Rep, Series A, No. 10, at 25.

[381] UNCLOS at Art. 110 (3).

[382] Ibid. at Art. 111(1).

[383] Ibid. at Art. 111(3).

into their territory.[384] The legal and political implications of this conflict are explored in Chapter 6. The following is a summary overview of the relevant legal framework.

The obligation to render assistance to those lost or in peril at sea is part of customary international law[385] and has been codified in many international agreements, including UNCLOS and two widely ratified treaties: the 1974 International Convention for the Safety of Life at Sea (SOLAS Convention),[386] and the 1979 International Convention on Maritime Search and Rescue (SAR Convention).[387]

UNCLOS imposes a duty on States Parties to require masters of their flagged vessels to assist and rescue any persons found at sea who are in danger of being lost or in some sort of distress.[388] The obligation on the master should extend to any action that "may reasonably be expected of him."[389] A similar obligation, to "proceed with all speed" to the assistance of all persons in distress at sea, is set out in the SOLAS Convention.[390]

The duty to render assistance is an absolute obligation – reflecting basic humanitarian principles that are part of the international law of the sea.[391] It extends to any persons regardless of their nationality or status or the place or circumstances in

384 M. den Heijer, *Europe and Extraterritorial Asylum* (2012) [den Heijer, *Europe and Extraterritorial Asylum*], at 230.

385 See generally M. Pallis, "Obligations of States towards Asylum Seekers at Sea: Interactions and Conflicts between Legal Regimes" (2002) 14 *International Journal of Refugee Law* 329, at 333–334; and B. H. Oxman, "Human Rights and the United Nations Convention on the Law of the Sea" (1998) 36 *Columbia Journal of Transnational Law* 399.

386 International Convention for the Safety of Life at Sea, 1974, as amended, 1184 UNTS 278, done Nov. 1, 1974, entered into force May 25, 1980 [SOLAS Convention].

387 International Convention on Maritime Search and Rescue, 1979, with annexes 1405 UNTS 97, done Apr. 27, 1979, entered into force June 22, 1985 [SAR Convention]. The SAR Convention was amended in 1998 by IMO Resolution MSC. 70(69) ("Amendments to the International Convention on Maritime Search and Rescue, 1979"), and again in 2004 by IMO Resolution MSC.155(78) ("Adoption of Amendments to the International Convention on Maritime Search and Rescue, 1979, as amended"). References to the SAR Convention are to the consolidated text.

388 This obligation is also set out in the SOLAS Convention (Annex, Chapter V, Regulation 33(1)) and the SAR Convention (Annex, chapter 2, para. 2.1.10). The SAR Convention defines distress as: "A situation wherein there is a reasonable certainty that a person, a vessel or other craft is threatened by grave and imminent danger and requires immediate assistance": SAR Convention, at Annex, chapter 1, para. 1.3.13. For further on what constitutes "distress," see generally den Heijer, *Europe and Extraterritorial Asylum*, at 232–233.

389 UNCLOS, at Art. 98(1)(b).

390 SOLAS Convention, at Annex, Chapter V, Regulation 33(1).

391 R. E. Fife, "The Duty to Render Assistance at Sea: Some Reflections after *Tampa*," in J. Petman and J. Klabbers eds., *Nordic Cosmopolitanism: Essays in International Law for Martti Koskenniemi* 469 (2003), at 475–477. Practical constraints are recognized in UNCLOS, in which a shipmaster's duty to render assistance is qualified "in so far as he can do so without serious danger to the ship, the crew or the passengers" and the duty of rescue in terms of "such action [as] may reasonably be expected of him": UNCLOS, at Art. 98(1). Thus, the practical implementation of the duty is left to the discretion

which they are found,[392] and thereby applies to smuggled migrants who find themselves in distress at sea. However the scope of this absolute duty to search, assist, and rescue – in relation to both the master of the rescuing vessel and the relevant coastal State – is not specified, and there is some disagreement, explored further in Chapter 6, as to what the duty actually entails.

An international review of the legal framework around rescue at sea was prompted by the *Tampa* incident, one of the case studies set out in the introduction to this book. The resulting amendments to the SAR and SOLAS Conventions, aimed at clarifying the nature and scope of relevant rights and obligations, were concluded in 2004, entering into force in 2006.[393]

The obligation to render assistance and rescue at sea is reinforced through requirements regarding search and rescue services. UNCLOS Article 98 requires every coastal State to "promote the establishment, operation and maintenance of an adequate and effective search and rescue service regarding safety on and over the sea."[394] Where circumstances so require, coastal States are to also enter into regional cooperation arrangements with neighboring States for this same purpose.[395] Obligations with respect to establishment of search and rescue services are detailed in both the SOLAS and SAR Conventions.[396] These instruments establish Search and Rescue Zones and confirm that Rescue Coordination Centers and other authorities involved in search and rescue should have sufficient authority and guidance to fulfill their duties and should be functioning in accordance with detailed international guidelines.

Although the developments outlined previously and explored in more detail in Chapter 6 have helped to clarify certain aspects of the international legal framework around safety of life at sea, a number of gaps and uncertainties remain. For example, the obligation to assist and rescue persons lost or in distress at sea does not appear to be supported by a correlative duty on the part of the involved State – or any other

of the shipmaster, taking into account all the circumstances: S. N. Nandan and S. Rosenne eds., *United Nations Convention on the Law of the Sea, 1982: A Commentary, Volume III* (1995), at 175.

392 SOLAS Convention, at Annex, Chapter V, Regulation 33(1); SAR Convention, at Annex, chapter 2, para. 2.1.10; International Maritime Organization, Maritime Safety Committee, *Adoption of Amendments to the International Convention on Maritime Search and Rescue, 1979, as amended*, IMO MSC Resolution MSC.155(78), adopted May 20, 2004, IMO Doc. MSC 78/26/Add.1 Annex 5, at preamble.

393 The 2004 amendments to SOLAS are in IMO Resolution MSC.153(78) ("Adoption of Amendments to the International Convention for the Safety of Life at Sea, 1974, as amended") and the 2004 amendments to SAR are in IMO Resolution MSC.155(78) ("Adoption of Amendments to the International Convention on Maritime Search and Rescue, 1979, as amended").

394 UNCLOS, at Art. 98(2).

395 Ibid.

396 SOLAS Convention, at Annex, Chapter V, Regulation 7; SAR Convention, at Annex, chapter 1, para. 1.3.3 and chapter 2.

State – to disembark persons rescued at sea. State practice in this area is conflicting. In 2009 the International Maritime Organization issued nonbinding guidelines that place primary responsibility for safe disembarkation on the coastal State in whose search and rescue zone the vessel is located.[397] However the Guidelines (and similar initiatives)[398] have not been universally accepted, and recent efforts to develop a binding regime for rescue operations and the disembarkation of migrants have failed.[399]

1.3. MIGRANT SMUGGLING AND REGIONAL/BILATERAL MIGRATION CONTROL TREATIES

Although the Migrant Smuggling Protocol remains the most comprehensive multilateral statement of obligations regarding migrant smuggling, the obligations in this treaty exist and operate within a broader web of regional treaties and bilateral instruments. With some recent exceptions, "migrant smuggling" is rarely specifically referred to, even in those agreements that postdate adoption of the Protocol. The criterion for inclusion of regional and bilateral instruments in the present section is therefore not their explicit reference to migrant smuggling but rather: (1) their general applicability to the facilitated movement of persons across a national border, in violation of national laws, for profit; and (2) their relevance to actions that are central to State responses to migrant smuggling such as interdiction and return. It is important to note that although not dealt with here, broader migration agreements, such as those dealing generally with readmission/repatriation of irregular migrants or with migrant access to labor markets, may also be relevant to establishing the international legal obligations of States in relation to the issue of migrant smuggling.

397 International Maritime Organization, Facilitation Committee, *Principles Relating to Administrative Procedures for Disembarking Persons Rescued at Sea*, IMO Doc. FAL.3/Circ.194, Jan. 22, 2009.

398 For example, International Maritime Organization, Maritime Safety Committee, *Guidelines on the Treatment of Persons Rescued at Sea*, IMO Resolution MSC.167(78), adopted May 10, 2004, IMO Doc. MSC.78/26/Add.2 Annex 34, esp. at para. 2.5; Council Decision of 26 April 2010 supplementing the Schengen Borders Code as regards the surveillance of the sea external borders in the context of operational cooperation coordinated by the European Agency for the Management of Operational Cooperation at the External Borders of the Member States of the European Union (2010/252/EU), OJ L 111/20, May 4, 2010 [EU Council Decision 2010/252/EU], to which Malta and Italy are opposed: V. Moreno-Lax, "The EU Regime on Interdiction, Search and Rescue, and Disembarkation: The Frontex Guidelines for Intervention at Sea" (2010) 25 *International Journal of Marine and Coastal Law* 621, at 627–628; and which, as discussed at note 505, has recently been annulled.

399 den Heijer, *Europe and Extraterritorial Asylum*, at 216; J. Coppens and E. Somers, "Towards New Rules on Disembarkation of Persons Rescued at Sea?" (2010) 25 *International Journal of Marine and Coastal Law* 377; and J. Coppens, "Disembarkation of Migrants Rescued at Sea: II" (2011) *De Lloyd (Antwerpen. Nederlandse ed.)* 55, at 55.

1.3.1. *Regional Instruments: Europe*

As noted previously, in comparison with the situation in the United States, concern about migrant smuggling among major European countries of destination was much slower to emerge and to translate into specific action. It was only from the late 1980s, with the reunification of Germany and the collapse of the former Soviet Union, that concern about irregular migration increased dramatically. From that point, the issue of irregular migration quickly became a high priority for EU Member States, providing considerable impetus for common policy grounding collective action at both bilateral and regional levels. That impetus, and the existence of structures to take it forward help to explain why this is the only region to have established legal rules around aspects of migrant smuggling. The instruments most directly relevant to the subject matter of this book are considered briefly later on in this section.[400]

Until the mid-1970s, there was almost no action on migration involving third-country nationals within the European Economic Community. However, by 1974, an expanded membership, economic recession, and national level decisions to stop labor recruitment from certain countries pushed the movement of migrant labor onto the European Economic Community agenda and clearly influenced the shape and direction of two critical European instruments, the Schengen Agreement, signed in 1985 among Germany, France, and the Benelux countries,[401] and the 1987 Single European Act.[402] Article 17 of the Convention Implementing the Schengen Agreement (Schengen Convention) established the basis for harmonization of State Party action against illegal migration.[403] Article 27(1) of the same instrument

[400] Note that the European legal framework around migrant smuggling potentially includes a much broader array of instruments such as those regulating return and cooperation in return. An example is the Directive 2008/115/EC of the European Parliament and of the Council of 16 December 2008 on common standards and procedures in Member States for returning illegally staying third-country nationals, OJ L 348/98, Dec. 24, 2008. This instrument and others are not addressed in the present chapter but are referred to at appropriate points throughout this book.

[401] Agreement between the Governments of the States of the Benelux Economic Union, the Federal Republic of Germany and the French Republic on the gradual abolition of checks at their common borders, OJ L 239/13, Sept. 22, 2000, done June 14, 1985, entered into force June 15, 1985 [Schengen Agreement].

[402] The Single European Act, OJ L 169, June 29, 1987, done Feb. 17, 1986, entered into force July 1, 1987. For a more detailed consideration of how concerns about irregular migration shaped the Schengen Agreement and the Single European Act, see G. Callovi, "Regulation of Immigration in 1993: Pieces of the European Community Jig-Saw Puzzle" (1992) 26(2) *International Migration Review* 353, at 358 [Callovi, "Regulation of Immigration in 1993"].

[403] "In regard to the movement of persons, the Parties shall endeavour to abolish the controls at the common frontiers and transfer them to their external frontiers. To that end, they shall endeavour to harmonise in advance, where necessary, the laws and administrative provisions concerning the prohibitions and restrictions which form the basis for the controls and to take complementary measures to safeguard security and combat illegal immigration by nationals of States that are not members of the European Communities": Convention Implementing the Schengen Agreement of 14 June 1985

addressed the subject of facilitated illegal migration (migrant smuggling) by requiring Contracting States to "impose appropriate penalties on any person who, for financial gain, assists or tries to assist an alien to enter or reside in the territory of one of the Contracting Parties in breach of that Contracting Party's law on the entry and residence of aliens."[404] If a Contracting State had information about such an infringement of the law of another Contracting State, it was required to inform that State.[405] If one State asked another to prosecute because of a breach of its laws, the former State was required to officially specify which provisions of its laws had been infringed.[406] Over the following decade, growing concern about "uncontrolled migration" was reflected in major legal and policy developments, not least the 1993 Treaty on the European Union.[407] 1993 also marked the first official reference, by a European institution, to the phenomenon "migrant smuggling."[408]

Article 27 of the Schengen Convention was subsequently repealed, to be extended and replaced by two Instruments both issued in November 2002: Council Directive 2002/90/EC defining the facilitation of unauthorized entry, transit, and residence[409]; and Council Framework Decision 2002/946 on the strengthening of the penal framework to prevent the facilitation of unauthorized entry, transit, and residence.[410]

between the Governments of the States of the Benelux Economic Union, the Federal Republic of Germany and the French Republic on the gradual abolition of checks at their common borders, OJ L 239/19, Sept. 22, 2000, done June 19, 1990, entered into force Sept. 1, 1993 [Schengen Convention].

404 Ibid.

405 Ibid. at Art. 27(2).

406 Ibid. at Art. 27(3).

407 See generally, C. J. Ulrich, "Alien-Smuggling and Uncontrolled Migration in Northern Europe and the Baltic Region" (HEUNI Paper No. 7, 1995), at 9. See also Callovi, "Regulation of Immigration in 1993."

408 Council of Europe, "Texts Adopted at the European Conference on Uncontrolled Migration," Fifth Conference of European Ministers Responsible for Migration Affairs, Athens, Nov. 18–19, 1993, at Recommendation 1(a).

409 Council Directive 2002/90/EC of 28 November 2002 defining the facilitation of unauthorised entry, transit and residence, OJ L 328/17, Dec. 5, 2002 [Council Directive 2002/90/EC]. See Article 288 of the Treaty of the European Union ("To exercise the Union's competences, the institutions shall adopt regulations, directives, decisions, recommendations and opinions... A directive shall be binding, as to the result to be achieved, upon each Member State to which it is addressed, but shall leave to the national authorities the choice of form and methods.") Consolidated versions of the Treaty on European Union and the Treaty on the Functioning of the European Union, OJ C 326/01, Oct. 26, 2012.

410 Council Framework Decision of 28 November 2002 on the strengthening of the penal framework to prevent the facilitation of unauthorised entry, transit and residence (2002/946/JHA), OJ L 328/1, Dec. 5, 2002 [Council Framework Decision 2002/946]. Although not considered a "treaty" in the usual sense, the adoption of the Framework Decision imposed specific obligations on Member States of the European Union as well as Candidate Countries to ensure that their laws and practices conform to its substantive provisions. They could, in effect, be viewed as obligations of result. See Treaty on European Union, OJ C 191, done Feb. 7, 1992, entered into force Nov. 1, 1993, at Art. 34(2)(b). Adopted as instruments of the third pillar, which was in place until December 1, 2009, Framework Decisions entered into force quickly without the requirement of formal ratification. They generally set out a restricted period for implementation. Member States are required to notify both the Council and the

A third instrument, a Directive on Short-Term Residency Permits,[411] is also relevant to the situation of persons who have been smuggled. These three instruments are briefly considered in the next sections.

1.3.1.1. The 2002 EU Directive and Framework Decision

On November 28, 2002, only months after it had first been proposed by the government of France, the European Union adopted Directive 2002/90, the principal purpose of which was to provide a common definition for the facilitation of unauthorized entry, transit, and residence into EU States.[412] The core provision of the Directive required Member States to impose effective, proportionate, and dissuasive sanctions on "any person who intentionally assists a person who is not a national of a Member State to enter, or transit across, the territory of a Member State in breach of the laws of the State concerned" and "any person who, for financial gain, intentionally assists a person who is not a national of a Member State to reside within the territory of a Member State in breach of the laws of the State concerned."[413] Member States are granted discretion to not impose sanctions in the first case if the aim of the facilitating behavior is "to provide humanitarian assistance to the person concerned."[414]

The provisions of the Directive are stricter than those of the Schengen Convention – requiring Member States to sanction facilitation of irregular entry even if this is not for financial gain. They are also considerably broader, requiring sanction for facilitating irregular stay as well as for accomplices and instigators.

The Directive is complemented by a Framework Decision, also initiated by France and adopted the same day, setting out minimum rules for penalties, liability of legal persons, and jurisdiction that go well beyond the brief reference to "appropriate penalties" in Article 27(1) of the Schengen Convention. The core obligations are as follows:

- Infringements defined in the Directive to be punishable by effective, proportionate, and dissuasive criminal penalties, which may entail extradition.[415]

Commission on measures taken to implement a Framework Decision. Such implementation is to be evaluated in an implementation report from the Commission that is later assessed by the Council. Although the Commission has no legal ability to enforce implementation of a Framework Decision, the European Court of Justice is entitled to interpret Framework Decisions via preliminary rulings.

411 Council Directive 2004/81/EC of 29 April 2004 on the residence permit issued to third-country nationals who are victims of trafficking in human beings or who have been the subject of an action to facilitate illegal immigration, who decide to cooperate with the competent authorities, OJ L 261, Aug. 6, 2004 [EU Council Directive on the residence permit].

412 Council Directive 2002/90/EC, at Recitation, para. 4.

413 Ibid. at Art. 1(1). Article 2 extends these provisions to persons who instigate, attempt, or are an accomplice in the specified infringements.

414 Ibid. at Art. 1(2).

415 Council Framework Decision 2002/946, at Art. 1(1).

- Criminal penalties may also be accompanied by confiscation of the means of transport used to commit the offense; a prohibition on practicing the occupational activity in the exercise of which the offense was committed, and deportation.[416]
- Provision to be made for offenses committed for financial gain to be punishable by custodial sentences with a maximum sentence of not less than eight years where they are committed: (i) as an activity of a criminal organization,[417] or (ii) while endangering the lives of the persons who are the subject of the offense.[418]
- Legal persons to be held liable for infringements under certain conditions and subject to specified penalties.[419]

The Framework Decision also sets out the jurisdictional scope of that instrument and the Directive. A Member State is required to exercise jurisdiction over infringements committed in whole or in part within its territory.[420] A Member State *may* exercise jurisdiction over infringements committed by one of its nationals, or for the benefit of a legal person established in its territory.[421] The principle of "extradite or prosecute" would apply in cases involving nationals of a Member State involved in the commission of offenses outside the territory of that State.[422]

The savings clause of the Framework Decision is narrow and rather oddly worded, stating that it "*shall apply without prejudice to the protection afforded refugees and asylum seekers in accordance with international law on refugees or other international instruments relating to human rights.*"[423] The formulation renders unclear the Framework Decision's commitment to international instruments related to human rights in respect of smuggled migrants who are not asylum-seekers or refugees. In practical terms it is unlikely States could argue away existing obligations on the basis that they were not specified in the savings clause, but the broader significance of the omission should not be underestimated.

[416] Ibid. at Art. 1(2).

[417] As defined in Article 1 of Joint Action of 21 December 1998 adopted by the Council on the basis of Article K.3 of the Treaty on European Union, on making it a criminal offence to participate in a criminal organisation in the Member States of the European Union (98/733/JHA), OJ L 351/1, Dec. 29, 1998. ("[A] criminal organisation shall mean a structured association, established over a period of time, of more than two persons, acting in concert with a view to committing offences which are punishable by deprivation of liberty or a detention order of a maximum of at least four years or a more serious penalty, whether such offences are an end in themselves or a means of obtaining material benefits and, where appropriate, of improperly influencing the operation of public authorities.")

[418] Council Framework Decision 2002/946, at Art. 1(3). But see Art. 1(4).

[419] Ibid. at Arts. 2–3.

[420] Ibid. at Art. 4(1)(a).

[421] Ibid. at Arts. 4(1)(b)–(c), 4(2).

[422] Ibid. at Art. 5.

[423] Ibid. at Art. 6 (emphasis added).

Member States were required to transpose both the Directive and the Framework Decision into national law by December 5, 2004,[424] at which time Article 27(1) of the 1990 Schengen Convention referred to previously would be repealed.[425] Both instruments remain in force despite changes within the legislative structure of the European Union. Since the entry into force of the Treaty of Lisbon, the Directive is subject to the jurisdiction of the Court of Justice.[426] The Framework Decision will be similarly subject to the jurisdiction of the Court from December 1, 2014.[427] However, the European Commission has indicated an intention to extend and perhaps merge the Directive and Framework Decision in the near future.[428] Official information on implementation of the two instruments is scarce, being limited to a 2006 report dealing only with operationalization of the Framework Decision.[429]

How do the Directive and Framework Decision fare in comparison with the Migrant Smuggling Protocol? Even leaving aside the complicated legal context of the European instruments, the comparison is generally not very favorable in their direction, both being seen to incorporate provisions that "rather than reinforcing the [Protocol], detract from it through a lack of clarity and precision."[430] This does not hold true on all points of comparison. The Framework Decision's provisions on sanctions, for example, are much more detailed than those set out in the Protocol. However, it is indeed possible to identify a number of key points of difference between the Protocol and the two EU instruments that appear to affirm the negative conclusion offered previously, including the following:

- The Protocol sets out a straightforward definition of migrant smuggling that clearly includes a profit element. The Framework Decision and Directive do not define migrant smuggling, do not take full account of the profit element,[431] and are directed broadly to "any person" assisting irregular migration.

424 Council Directive 2002/90/EC, at Art. 4(1); Framework Decision 2002/946, at Art. 9.

425 Council Directive 2002/90/EC, at Art. 5; Framework Decision 2002/946, at Art. 10.

426 It is reported that two cases have been brought to the Court against Member States failing to implement the Directive. S. Peers, E. Guild, and J. Tomkin eds., *EU Immigration and Asylum Law (Text and Commentary): Second Revised Edition*, Volume 1: Visa and Border Controls (2012), at 385 [Peers et al., *EU Immigration and Asylum Law*].

427 Ibid. at 386.

428 Ibid.

429 Commission of the European Communities, Report from the Commission based on Article 9 of the Council Framework Decision of 28 November 2002 on the strengthening of the penal framework to prevent the facilitation of unauthorised entry, transit and residence, COM(2006) 770 final, Dec. 6, 2006.

430 Peers et al., *EU Immigration and Asylum Law*, at 390.

431 This issue was raised by NGOs and UNHCR during the drafting process, to no avail. See European Council on Refugees and Exiles, *An Overview of Proposals Addressing Migrant Smuggling and Trafficking in Persons* (1991).

- The Protocol's criminalization provisions are much more detailed and explicit than those of the Directive.
- The savings clause of the Protocol is much more comprehensive than that contained in Article 6 of the Framework Decision, referring not just to refugee law but also to international human rights law as it would apply to all persons, not just refugees and asylum-seekers.
- The Protocol makes clear that smuggled migrants should not be subject to criminalization under its provisions. There is no equivalent provision in the Framework Decision or Directive.

It has been further argued that the Framework Decision and Directive do not sufficiently separate "migrant smuggling" from trafficking – despite the considerable work done by the European Union on the latter issue by 2002.[432] That claim is not on particularly firm ground when the Framework Decision on Trafficking, also adopted in 2002, is taken into account.[433]

Commentators have evidenced confusion over the scope of application of the EU instruments in comparison to that of the Protocol. Peers et al., for example, claim that the Migrant Smuggling Protocol is concerned only with the smuggling of persons from one State to another while the Directive and Framework Decision go beyond irregular entry in also attempting to cover activities such as irregular residence.[434] This reading is inaccurate as it focuses only on the Protocol's *definition* of migrant smuggling and fails to take into account the inclusion of related offenses that also require criminalization such as enabling illegal stay, and producing, procuring, or providing fraudulent travel documents for purposes of enabling migrant smuggling.[435] The common misunderstanding that the offense of migrant smuggling under the Protocol requires involvement of an organized criminal group is another source of confusion when comparing the regional and international legal frameworks.[436] As noted previously, this requirement applies only to operationalization of the Protocol *between* States Parties: the Organized Crime Convention is clear on the point that the offense of migrant smuggling in national laws should not require such an element.[437]

432 See further discussion in Chapter 5, at Section 5.2.

433 Council Framework Decision of 19 July 2002 on combating trafficking in human beings (2002/629/JHA), OJ L 203/1, Aug. 1, 2002. For a detailed analysis of that Framework Decision and its successor instrument, see Gallagher, *The International Law of Human Trafficking*, at 96–99, 103–110.

434 Peers et al., *EU Immigration and Asylum Law*, at 390.

435 Migrant Smuggling Protocol, at Arts. 6(1)(b)–(c).

436 It is on this mistaken basis that Ventrella, for example, concludes that the scope of Council Directive 2002/90/EC (requiring punishment of assisted irregular migration for financial gain whether a criminal organization is involved or not) is considerably wider than that of the Protocol. M. Ventrella, *The Control of People Smuggling and Trafficking in the EU: Experiences from the UK and Italy* (2010), at 45.

437 See notes 284 and 286 and accompanying text, above.

through interdiction,[466] one of the first bilateral agreements to address matters now commonly associated with migrant smuggling was concluded – between the United States of America and Haiti.[467] This agreement, which despite being in the form of an exchange of letters bears all the hallmarks of a treaty,[468] authorized United States government officials to exercise a right of visit over private Haitian vessels on the high seas, specifically: "Haiti permits the U.S. Coast Guard to board any Haitian flag vessel on the high seas or in Haitian territorial waters which the Coast Guard has reason to believe may be involved in the irregular carriage of passengers outbound from Haiti, to make inquiries concerning the status of those on board, to detain the vessel if it appears that an offense against United States immigration laws or appropriate Haitian laws has been or is being committed, and to return the vessel and the persons on board to Haiti."[469] The agreement further provided that the United States: "does not intend to return to Haiti any Haitian migrants whom the United States authorities determine to qualify for refugee status.[470] Supplementary Guidelines were developed to implement this provision, directing immigration officials on board Coast Guard interdiction vessels to monitor Coast Guard interviews of interdicted Haitians, and, in cases where indications of a claim to refugee status might arise, to conduct further investigations. Individuals found to have a bona-fide claim to asylum were to be brought to the United States for purposes of making such a claim.[471] Another provision, highly relevant in the present context, was an undertaking, by Haiti, to not prosecute for illegal departure "Haitians returned to Haiti who are not traffickers [sic]."[472] Over the following decade, this instrument provided the main legal basis for a large-scale interdiction program that drew strong criticism,

Italy and North African States (2012) [Maccanico, *The EU's Self-Interested Response*], available at www.statewatch.org/analyses/no-165-eu-north-africa.pdf (accessed May 12, 2013).

466 Proclamation No. 4865, 46 Fed. Reg. 48,107 (1981), cited in Helton, "The United States Government Program of Intercepting and Forcibly Returning Haitian Boat People to Haiti," at 326–327.

467 Exchange of Diplomatic Letters between E. H. Preeg, US Ambassador to Haiti, and E. Francisque, Haiti's Secretary of State for Foreign Affairs, TIAS No. 10241 (Sept. 23, 1981). Published as Agreement to Stop Clandestine Migration of Residents of Haiti to the United States, (1981) 20 ILM 1198, entered into force Sept. 23, 1981 [Agreement to Stop Clandestine Migration of Residents of Haiti to the United States]. Generally on the agreement and the interdiction program that followed, see D. A. Martin, "Interdiction, Intervention and the New Frontiers of Refugee Law and Policy" (1993) 33 *Virginia Journal of International Law* 473, esp. at 479–481; and S. H. Legomsky, "The USA and the Caribbean Interdiction Program" 18(3) (2006) *International Journal of Refugee Law* 677 [Legomsky, "The USA and the Caribbean Interdiction Program"].

468 Aust, *Modern Treaty Law and Practice*, esp. at 493–494, 496.

469 Summary as provided in Office of the Legal Adviser, United States Department of State, M. S. Pickering, S. J. Cummins and D. P. Stewart eds., *Digest of United States Practice in International Law* (1989–1990) [*Digest of US Practice in International Law*], at 48.

470 Agreement to Stop Clandestine Migration of Residents of Haiti to the United States, at 4.

471 *Digest of US Practice in International Law*, at 48–49.

472 Ibid. at 49.

most particularly for its negative impact on persons who appeared to be asylum-seekers.[473] Indeed, it has been reported that of the 21,800 Haitians interdicted between 1981 and 1990, only six were determined to have claims warranting a full asylum hearing.[474] In the early 1990s, political violence prompted a mass exodus of Haitians, and a further executive order from the United States president was issued authorizing the Coast Guard to intercept and return fleeing Haitians.[475] In a period of just six months, the United States Coast Guard interdicted 34,000 Haitians seeking to enter the United States by sea.[476] At this point the practice of considering asylum claims on board United States vessels was discontinued in favor of asylum-seekers being moved to Guantanamo Bay in Cuba for detention and processing.[477] A landmark Supreme Court case in 1993, examined in more detail in Chapter 6, affirmed that United States obligations under the Convention relating to the Status of Refugees[478] with respect to *non-refoulement* applied only to persons already admitted to United States territory, and did not extend to the high seas.[479] In 1994 the Haitian government formally terminated the agreement.[480]

During the 1990s, similar agreements were concluded by the United States with other Caribbean countries, including Cuba and the Dominican Republic. In the

473 Legomsky, "The USA and the Caribbean Interdiction Program," at 669–681. For a detailed critique of United States action in relation to Haitian asylum-seekers during this period, see H. Hongju Koh, "The 'Haiti Paradigm' in United States Human Rights Policy" (1994) 103 *Yale Law Journal* 2391 [Koh, "The 'Haiti Paradigm' in United States Human Rights Policy"].

474 Legomsky, "The USA and the Caribbean Interdiction Program," at 669–681.

475 Executive Order No. 12,807, 3 C.F.R. 303–04 (1993). The order includes authority "[t]o return the vessel and its passengers to the country from which it came, or to another country, when there is reason to believe that an offense is being committed against the United States immigration laws, or appropriate laws of a foreign country with which we have an arrangement to assist; provided, however, that the Attorney General, in his unreviewable discretion, may decide that a person who is a refugee will not be returned without his consent." See further Koh, "The 'Haiti Paradigm' in United States Human Rights Policy".

476 Guilfoyle, *Shipping Interdiction and the Law of the Sea*, at 190; and Legomsky, "The USA and the Caribbean Interdiction Program," at 679–681.

477 Legomsky, "The USA and the Caribbean Interdiction Program," at 680–682. See also Guilfoyle, *Shipping Interdiction and the Law of the Sea*, at 189–192.

478 Convention Relating to the Status of Refugees, 189 UNTS 137, done July 28, 1951, entered into force Apr. 22, 1954, as amended by the Protocol Relating to the Status of Refugees, 606 UNTS 267, done Jan. 31, 1967, entered into force Oct. 4, 1967.

479 *Sale, Acting Commissioner, Immigration and Naturalization Service, et al., Petitioners v. Haitian Centers Council, Inc., et al.*, 509 US 155 (US SC, June 21, 1993), at 155, 187. See further Chapter 3, Section 3.4.4.

480 G. W. Palmer, "Guarding the Coast: Alien Migrant Interdiction Operations at Sea" (1997) 29 *Connecticut Law Review* 1565, at 1577. See also E. Papastavridis, "Interception of Human Beings on the High Seas: A Contemporary Analysis under International Law" (2008) 36 *Syracuse Journal of International Law* 145 [Papastavridis, "Interception of Human Beings on the High Seas"], at 179. Note that subsequent United States practice raised questions about the extraterritorial application of the obligation of *non-refoulement*, discussed in Chapter 3, at Section 3.4.4.

case of Cuba, a series of accords concluded in 1995–1996 sought to stabilize an increasingly fragile situation involving mass exodus from Cuba and a growing inability on the part of the United States to cope.[481] The accords provided that Cuban migrants "rescued" and "intercepted" at sea would be returned to Cuba and receive instruction on legal means of immigration.[482] Cuba was required to refrain from any action against returned migrants for attempting to immigrate illegally and to "take effective measures in every way it can to prevent unsafe departures" in exchange for the United States agreeing to guarantee admission of at least 20,000 Cubans (in addition to an unlimited number of immediate relatives of United States citizens) each year.[483] Both parties further agreed to cooperate jointly to ensure "safe, legal, and orderly" migration, and that "all actions taken will be consistent with the parties' international obligations."[484] It is sobering to note that the success of interdictions made possible under these agreements has been reliably determined to have contributed to a significant increase in both demand for and availability of lucrative migrant smuggling operations between Cuba and the United States:

> Professional smugglers can provide vessels with the speed and maneuverability to outperform law enforcement resources. Boat captains have the expertise to navigate along both the Cuban and Florida coasts and are compensated handsomely for their willingness to take their chances against law enforcement on both sides of the Straits of Florida. Finally, professional smugglers can provide the necessary logistical coordination of the covert transit through an underground network collecting advance payment or financing of expensive fees from relatives in both Cuba and the United States.[485]

In 2003, following many years of interdicting Dominican Nationals seeking to reach Puerto Rico, the United States concluded a migration control agreement with the Dominican Republic.[486] This agreement refers directly to the Migrant Smuggling Protocol in relation to "the urgent need for international cooperation

[481] D. Brown, "Crooked Straits: Maritime Smuggling of Humans from Cuba to the United States" (2002) 33 *University of Miami Inter-American Law Review* 273 [Brown, "Crooked Straits"], at 275–276.

[482] Guilfoyle notes that the accords do not expressly provide the United States with permission to intercept Cuban vessels although such authorization appears to be tacit and has occurred over an extended period of time without protest. Guilfoyle, *Shipping Interdiction and the Law of the Sea*, at 194–195. See further discussion of interdiction in Chapter 6.

[483] Cuba–United States: Joint Statement on Normalization of Migration, Building on the Agreement of September 9, 1994, 35 ILM 327 (1996), done May 2, 1995.

[484] As cited in Brown, "Crooked Straits," at 276–277.

[485] Ibid.

[486] Agreement between the Government of the United States of America and the Government of the Dominican Republic Maritime Migration Law Enforcement, 2003 UST LEXIS 32, done May 20, 2003, entered into force May 20, 2003 [US–Dominican Republic Migration Agreement].

in suppressing the smugglings of migrants by sea."[487] It authorizes a range of actions aimed at preventing unsafe transport of migrants and migrant smuggling, including a right of the United States to board and search Dominican flagged vessels on the high seas and a right to detain suspect vessels in this maritime zone if evidence of migrant smuggling is found.[488] The agreement expands the jurisdiction of United States law enforcement action even further by way of a shiprider clause.[489] This provision, familiar to many bilateral drug control agreements, enables a Dominican official aboard a United States government vessel to authorize pursuit of a vessel into Dominican Republic waters and to enforce that country's laws therein.[490] Similar powers are granted to United States shipriders. It is the national shiprider who retains the right to board, search or seize the vessel and/or to request officials of the other State to do so.[491] The agreement obliges both countries to prosecute migrant smugglers and to confiscate vessels involved in migrant smuggling.[492] The parties further agree to take action against masters, officers, crewmembers, and other persons involved in the unsafe transport of persons by sea.[493]

1.3.2.2. Mediterranean Agreements

Many contemporary bilateral migrant smuggling control treaties have been concluded between EU Member States that are most directly affected by irregular migration from Asia and North Africa: specifically Malta, Spain, and Italy, and neighboring third countries. This reflects a shift in migration patterns away from the eastern land borders (in response to a closing of traditional entry points) to the Mediterranean basin and beyond – and a resulting redirection of European immigration control.

An early example is provided by an agreement concluded between Italy and Albania in 1997 as the strait between these two countries became part of the new EU border following Italy's entry into the Schengen Convention.[494] The agreement, which appears to have been inspired by the series of United States Presidential Orders authorizing the interception and return of Haitian asylum-seekers,[495]

[487] US–Dominican Republic Migration Agreement, at Preamble. The Protocol's definition of migrant smuggling is reproduced in Article 1.

[488] Ibid. at Art. 8.

[489] "Shiprider" is defined as "a law enforcement official of one Party authorized to embark on a law enforcement vessel or aircraft of the other Party": ibid. at Art. 1(14).

[490] Ibid. at Art. 4.

[491] Ibid. at Arts. 4–5.

[492] Ibid. at Art. 10(4).

[493] Ibid. at Art. 10(5).

[494] Italy signed the agreements on November 27, 1990.

[495] See references in I. Mann, "Dialectic of Transnationalism: Unauthorized Migration and Human Rights, 1993–2013" (2013) 54 *Harvard International Law Journal* 315, at n. 90.

took the form of an exchange of letters followed by an implementing protocol.[496] Its status as a treaty does not appear to be questioned.[497] The agreement generally followed the shiprider model explained previously, enabling Italy to secure on-the-spot authorization from Albania to interdict all Albanian vessels on the high seas suspected of migrant smuggling and vessels of any nationality found in Albanian territorial waters. Additional powers were granted to Italian warships to demand information from Albanian vessels and order them back to Albania if boarding was refused or if an inspection revealed evidence of migrant smuggling.[498]

The European Union has been pivotal in creating the broader policy environment within which bilateral cooperation between its Member States and critical third source or transit countries can occur.[499] In recent years the conclusion of bilateral agreements to deal with migrant smuggling in the Mediterranean and Atlantic has been prompted, at least in part, by the emergence of the EU External Borders Agency, Frontex, as the principal enforcement mechanism of the European Union's border control regime.[500] As commentators have noted, European law, including

496 Protocol between Italy and Albania to Prevent Certain Illegal Acts and Render Humanitarian Assistance to Those Leaving Albania, 2 April 1997 as cited in Guilfoyle, *Shipping Interdiction and the Law of the Sea*, at 210. Guilfoyle notes that only the Protocol, concluded a week after the exchange of letters, granted Italy authority to interdict. This became relevant following the sinking of an Albanian migrant smuggling vessel in international waters through collision with an Italian warship engaged in interdiction of that vessel. The sinking occurred after the exchange of letters but before the protocol authorizing such interdiction had been concluded. The question of State responsibility for the resulting harms was considered by the European Court of Human Rights in *Xhavara and Fifteen Others v. Italy and Albania*, Application No. 39473/98 (ECHR, Jan. 11, 2001), discussed in Chapter 3, at notes 329–330 and accompanying text, and Chapter 4, at Section 4.4.2.

497 See A. di Pascale, "Migration Control at Sea: The Italian Case," in B. Ryan and V. Mitsilegas eds., *Extraterritorial Immigration Control: Legal Challenges* 282 (2010) [di Pascale, "Migration Control at Sea: The Italian Case"], at 294. ("The agreement was adopted by a simplified procedure, where consent is expressed through the exchange of the instruments constituting the treaty.")

498 For a detailed consideration of the political context around these arrangements, see generally T. Perlmutter, "The Politics of Proximity: The Italian Response to the Albanian Crisis" (1998) 32 *International Migration Review* 203.

499 See generally T. Van Criekinge, *The EU–Africa Migration Partnership: A Case Study of the EU's Migration Dialogue with Ghana and Senegal* (EUI Migration Working Group, Mar. 2010).

500 The European Agency for the Management of Operational Cooperation at the External Borders of the Member States of the European Union (Frontex) was established by Council Regulation (EC) No 2007/2004 of 26 October 2004 (OJ L 349/1, Nov. 25, 2004) "with a view to improving the integrated management of the external borders of the Member States of the European Union" (Article 1). The Regulation acknowledges that responsibility for the control and surveillance of external borders lies with the Member States, mandating Frontex to "facilitate and render more effective the application of existing and future Community measures relating to the management of external borders. It shall do so by ensuring the coordination of Member States' actions in the implementation of those measures, thereby contributing to an efficient, high and uniform level of control on persons and surveillance of the external borders of the Member States" (Article 2).

the Schengen Borders Code,[501] does not empower Frontex to act beyond the external borders of the European Union.[502] Any Frontex operation on the high seas is governed by general rules of international law, including the important principle of exclusive flag State jurisdiction on the high seas.[503] However, Frontex operations in the territorial waters of a third State take place in that coastal State's sovereign domain and therefore, in addition to being governed by rules of international law, including human rights and refugee law,[504] require the coastal State's consent. These points were all made clear in a 2010 European Council decision that carefully detailed the rules under which Frontex operations were to take place.[505] It is relevant to cite the "General Principles" set out in that document:

> 1.1. Measures taken for the purpose of the surveillance operation shall be conducted in accordance with fundamental rights and in a way that does not put at risk the safety of the persons intercepted or rescued as well as of the participating units.

[501] Regulation (EC) No 562/2006 of the European Parliament and of the Council of 15 March 2006 establishing a Community Code on the rules governing the movement of persons across borders (Schengen Borders Code), OJ L 105/1, Apr. 13, 2006.

[502] See House of Lords (United Kingdom), European Union Committee, *Frontex: The EU External Borders Agency, Report with evidence* (9th Report of Session, 2007–08), at paras. 142–143 [House of Lords, *Frontex*].

[503] On this principle, see further Chapter 3, at Section 3.3.3.

[504] See Regulation (EU) No 1168/2011 of the European Parliament and of the Council of 25 October 2011 amending Council Regulation (EC) No 2007/2004 establishing a European Agency for the Management of Operational Cooperation at the External Borders of the Member States of the European Union, OJ L 304/1, Nov. 22, 2011, at recital 29 (a similar albeit less comprehensive provision was included in the initial regulation establishing Frontex, Council Regulation (EC) No 2007/2004 of 26 October 2004 (OJ L 349/1, Nov. 25, 2004), at recital 22); Council Decision 2010/252/EU, at Annex, Part I, paras. 1.2–1.4 (for a note on the status of this Decision, see note 505). For further discussion of Frontex and its obligations in international human rights and refugee law, see den Heijer, *Europe and Extraterritorial Asylum*, at 190–194, 212–213.

[505] EU Council Decision 2010/252/EU. Note that this decision was annulled by the European Court of Justice on September 5, 2012 for breach of the so-called comitology rule, on the basis that the decision constituted a major or essential development in the Schengen Border Code that only the European Parliament, not the Council of the European Union, was empowered to adopt: *European Parliament v. Council of the European Union* (Court of Justice of the European Union, C-355/10, Sept. 5, 2012) [*European Parliament*], at para. 84. The Court held that "the adoption of rules on the conferral of enforcement powers on border guards ... entails political choices falling within the responsibilities of the European Union legislature," and that, under the powers conferred by the decision, "the fundamental rights of the [intercepted] persons may be interfered with to such an extent that the involvement of the European Union legislature is required": *European Parliament*, at paras 76–77. Notwithstanding annulment, the decision is to maintain its effects on a provisional basis until the entry into force of replacement rules within a reasonable time: *European Parliament*, at para. 90; and see European Commission, Second biannual report on the functioning of the Schengen area 1 May 2012–31 October 2012, COM(2012) 686 final, Nov. 23, 2012, at para. 3.4, noting that the Commission intended to present a legislative proposal to replace Decision 2010/252/EU in early 2013. The Commission presented that proposal in April 2013: Proposal for a Regulation of the European Parliament and of the Council establishing rules for the surveillance of the external sea borders in

basis and authority in multilateral and (to a lesser extent) bilateral legal agreements. However, other sources of international legal rules – or avenues through which such rules can be identified – are also relevant, and these are considered briefly in the next sections.

1.4.1. *Customary Law,* Jus Cogens, *and Migrant Smuggling*

International customary law is defined as "evidence of a general practice accepted as law."[537] Such law is not written, although it may subsequently be "codified" into treaties. International legal doctrine asserts that a rule is customary if: (1) it reflects general and uniform State practice, and (2) that practice is accompanied by a subjective sense of legal obligation (*opinio juris*).[538] It is not necessary that all countries affirm a rule of customary international law for the norm to exist and to bind them.[539] All that is required is a general consensus that the rule in question is in fact an obligation and a sufficient level of conforming State practice, particularly from specially affected States.[540] In principle, custom and treaty law are equal in value. In the case of a conflict, a treaty rule (as *lex specialis*) would generally override the *lex generalis* of custom.[541]

While the legal definition of custom is well settled, its ephemeral nature has caused considerable difficulties in application. These difficulties are both conceptual

537 ICJ Statute, at Art. 38(1)(b).

538 "Not only must the acts concerned amount to a settled practice, but they must also be such, or be carried out in such a way, as to be evidence of a belief that this practice is rendered obligatory by the existence of a rule requiring it.... The States concerned must therefore feel that they are conforming to what amounts to a legal obligation": *North Sea Continental Shelf Cases (Federal Republic of Germany v. Denmark; Federal Republic of Germany v. Netherlands)*, [1969] ICJ Rep 3, at 44, para. 77. See also J. Crawford, *Brownlie's Principles of Public International Law* (8th ed. 2012), at 23–28.

539 Rather, the reverse is true: any State wishing not to be bound bears a heavy onus of proving it has persistently objected during and since the formation of the customary rule. States thus objecting to a norm of international customary law when it is being formed are not bound by it under the rule of the "persistent objector": "in principle, a State that indicates its dissent from a practice while the law is still in the process of development is not bound by that rule even after it matures": American Law Institute, *Restatement, Third: Foreign Relations Law of the United States* (1990), at 102. See also *Anglo–Norwegian Fisheries (United Kingdom v. Norway)*, [1951] ICJ Rep 116, at 131.

540 Although the nature and quality of the State practice needed remains controversial, the ICJ has indicated that it need not be uniform. In the *Nicaragua Case*, the Court held that: "[i]n order to deduce the existence of customary rules, the Court deems it sufficient that the conduct of States should in general be consistent with such a rule; and that instances of State conduct inconsistent with a given rule should generally have been treated as breaches of that rule, not as indications of the recognition of a new rule": *Military and Paramilitary Activities in and against Nicaragua (Nicaragua v. United States of America) (Merits)*, [1986] ICJ Rep 14 [*Nicaragua Case*], at para. 186.

541 International Law Commission, "Fragmentation of International Law: Difficulties Arising from the Diversification and Expansion of International Law," UN Doc. A/CN.4/L.682, Apr. 13, 2006, at Part C. But see also Part D (*lex posterior*).

(How does custom begin? Where does a sense of legal obligation come from before practice hardens into custom? How can States follow a rule from a sense of legal obligation without already having the required *opinio juris*? How should one distinguish between what States *believe* and what they say or do?) and operational (How much and what sort of practice is required to establish the first part of the custom test? How consistent should that practice be? What kind of evidence is required to establish *opinio juris*? What contribution do international organizations, international courts, and tribunals make to the development of customary international law?),[542] and have generally proved resistant to satisfactory resolution. In relation to the more practical concerns, Henkin observes that such questions have also never been definitively settled "because every 'piece' of customary law is different; develops in different circumstances, at a different rate of growth."[543]

Problems in the identification and application of custom have been exacerbated by the distinction commonly made between *traditional custom*, which is evolutionary, heavily reliant on State practice and best established through inductive reasoning; and what has been termed *modern custom*, which emphasizes *opinio juris* over State practice (or even collapses the two), is identified through a deductive process of reasoning that commences with a general statement of rules, and uses the multitude of sources commonly identified as "soft law," such that it can develop relatively quickly.[544] This opening up of the concept of customary international law has likely been a necessary aspect of the system's adaptation to a more complex operating environment.

However, some of the dangers discussed later on in the chapter with reference to soft law apply here, particularly the danger of a separation between *what is claimed to be law* and what States have bound themselves to through explicit or implicit consent.[545] In keeping with its generally conservative and consent-based approach to

[542] Henkin, *International Law*, at 29–31. See also A. D'Amato, *The Concept of Custom in International Law* (1971).

[543] Henkin, *International Law*, at 30.

[544] This separation (identified as two aspects of the same source of law rather than as opposing concepts) is carefully described and analyzed within the framework of a broader consideration of the theory of custom in A. E. Roberts, "Traditional and Modern Approaches to Customary International Law: A Reconciliation" (2001) 95 *American Journal of International Law* 757 [Roberts, "Traditional and Modern Approaches"]. In a view that has subsequently been criticized, Cheng goes so far as to posit the possibility of "instant custom," created through, for example, consensus indicated by the unanimous adoption of a UN resolution: B. Cheng, "United Nations Resolutions on Outer Space: 'Instant' International Customary Law?" (1965) 5 *Indian Journal of International Law* 23, at 35–40; and B. Cheng, "On the Nature and Sources of International Law," in B. Cheng ed., *International Law, Teaching and Practice* 201 (1982), at 222–229. See further N. Petersen, "Customary Law without Custom? Rules Principles, and the Role of State Practice in International Norm Creation" (2008) 23 *American University International Law Review* 275.

[545] See further J. Kelly, "The Twilight of Customary International Law" (2000) 40 *Virginia Journal of International Law* 449.

identification of obligations, this book largely restricts its consideration of customary norms to those that are already widely accepted to have met the required evidentiary threshold in practice.[546] In relation to the question of whether certain contemporary rules or norms not falling within that category may have moved toward or attained the status of customary law, the analysis is cautious, weighed in favor of traditional evidentiary sources of both practice and *opinio juris*, including treaties, national legislation, and decisions of international and regional courts. Provisions of multilateral treaties that have secured wide ratification, that have been effectively implemented through legislation and other positive measures, and that have also been applied by nonparties (especially when out of a sense of obligation), are identified as particularly strong evidence (and contributors to the development) of customary norms.[547] It is important to acknowledge that this conservative approach to custom is not one shared by many scholars working in fields related to the subject matter of this book. The debate around the customary legal status and scope of the obligation of *non-refoulement* in refugee law, considered in detail in the following chapter, is one example.

Despite the great codification project of the last century, the growing importance of treaties, and a range of objections to its legitimacy, integrity, and relevance,[548] custom continues to be recognized as an essential, independent source of international legal obligation. In the present context, customary international law is important for several reasons. First, not all States are party to the treaties of most relevance to the issue of migrant smuggling. The characterization of a particular rule as part of customary international law elevates that rule (and any resulting obligation) to one of universal applicability. For example, the obligation to rescue vessels or persons in distress on the high seas is widely considered to be a norm of customary international law, imposing obligations on all States, not just those that are party to the relevant international conventions. The conclusions in this book with respect to such obligations would therefore apply to all States. Another example is provided by the Vienna Convention on the Law of Treaties,[549] which largely codifies customary

[546] Of course, that threshold is itself highly contested. The International Court of Justice in the *Nicaragua Case*, for example, appeared to reverse the traditional test by emphasizing *opinio juris* (evidenced through United Nations resolutions) over State practice. See *Nicaragua Case*, as cited in Roberts, "Traditional and Modern Approaches," at 758–759.

[547] Note that even in such cases, treaties are themselves only a source of evidence of custom and/or *opinio juris*. As noted by the ICJ in the *Continental Shelf* case: "[i]t is of course axiomatic that the material of customary international law is to be looked for primarily in the actual practice and *opinio juris* of States, even though multilateral conventions may have an important role to play in recording and defining rules deriving from custom, or indeed in developing them": *Continental Shelf (Libyan Arab Jamahiriya v. Malta)*, [1985] ICJ Rep 13 [*Continental Shelf (Libyan Arab Jamahiriya v. Malta)*], at para. 27.

[548] See further Roberts, "Traditional and Modern Approaches," esp. at 759–761.

[549] Vienna Convention on the Law of Treaties, 1155 UNTS 331, done May 23, 1969, entered into force Jan. 27, 1980 [Vienna Convention on the Law of Treaties].

rules relating to the formation and interpretation of treaties. These customary rules operate to bind all States, not just those that are party to that Convention.[550] This becomes relevant at several points in the book, not least in relation to the question of whether certain bilateral agreements dealing with aspects of migrant smuggling are in fact treaties and how these agreements should be interpreted.[551]

In the areas of law examined in this book, custom can play an important role in shedding light on the actual content of codified rules. For example, custom is also an important constitutive element of the so-called secondary rules of international law – those rules that concern the circumstances under which a State is to be held responsible for a particular violation of international law – and the consequences of a finding of responsibility. It is therefore of particular relevance to the Chapter 4 discussion of State responsibility as it relates to responses to migrant smuggling.

International law also recognizes the existence of rules of *jus cogens*. A *jus cogens* rule is an established rule that is designated to be a "peremptory norm of general international law," one that is accepted and recognized by the international community of States as a whole as a norm from which no derogation is permitted and which can be modified only by a subsequent norm of general international law having the same character.[552] There is no definitive list of such peremptory norms, although there is strong evidence available to support the inclusion of rules outlawing aggression as well as prohibition on racial discrimination, apartheid, and genocide.[553] The prohibition on slavery and the slave trade, potentially relevant to certain manifestations of migrant smuggling, is also generally accepted to be a peremptory norm of international law.[554] Although *jus cogens* norms are clearly customary in nature,

550 See, for example, *Maritime Delimitation and Territorial Questions (Qatar v. Bahrain)*, [1995] ICJ Rep 6, at 18 (interpretation); *Fisheries Jurisdiction (United Kingdom v. Iceland) (Merits)*, [1974] ICJ Rep 3, at para. 36 (change of circumstances); *Legal Consequences for States of the Continued Presence of South Africa in Namibia (South West Africa) Notwithstanding Security Council Resolution 276 (Advisory Opinion)*, [1971] ICJ Rep 16, at para. 94 (material breach); *Gabcikovo–Nagymaros Project (Hungary v. Slovakia)*, [1997] ICJ Rep 7, at para. 99 (termination and suspension). As the International Law Commission has stated, "a codifying convention purporting to state existing rules of customary law may come to be regarded as the generally accepted formulation of the customary rules in question even by States not parties to the convention": Draft Articles on the Law of Treaties with Commentaries, adopted by the International Law Commission at its 18th session, 1966, in Yearbook of the International Law Commission, 1966, vol. II, UN Doc. A/6309/Rev.1, at 231.

551 See further Chapter 7, at Section 7.2.

552 Vienna Convention on the Law of Treaties, at Art. 53.

553 International Law Commission, "Fragmentation of International Law: Difficulties Arising from the Diversification and Expansion of International Law," UN Doc. A/CN.4/L.682, Apr. 13, 2006, at para. 374; International Law Commission, *Commentaries to the Draft Articles on Responsibility of States for Internationally Wrongful Acts*, in "Report of the International Law Commission on the Work of Its Fifty-third Session," UN GAOR, 56th Sess, Supp. No. 10, UN Doc. A/56/10, at 59 (2001), at Art. 15, para. 2.

554 See Gallagher, *The International Law of Human Trafficking*, at chapter 3.3.

their legitimacy derives less from the evidence of practice accompanied by *opinio juris* than from what Henkin has termed "authentic systemic consensus"[555] implicating the international system as a whole.

In addition, certain basic norms, arising either through custom or treaties, are considered to be universal in character and thereby in *effect*. Such norms (*erga omnes* norms) are owed to all States and give all States a legal interest in their protection. The right of all States to take action to protect an obligation *erga omnes* subsists irrespective of whether the State itself has suffered direct harm.[556] Although all norms of *jus cogens* will inevitably give rise to *erga omnes* obligations[557] (e.g., violation of a *jus cogens* rule gives rise to an obligation *erga omnes* to extradite or prosecute),[558] not all such obligations will necessarily meet the test of *jus cogens*.[559]

1.4.2. *Secondary and Subsidiary Sources of International Law*

Traditional statements of the sources of international law include general principles of law as a category that is secondary to both treaties and custom. This term is commonly understood to refer to principles that are consistent across the major legal systems of the world or, even further, "a proposition of law so fundamental that it will be found in virtually every legal system."[560] The nature of a "general principle of law" is that it could be applied by a State in a dispute with another State or by an international court or tribunal that is adjudicating such a dispute or otherwise pronouncing on a particular point of law, even if it is not part of a treaty or has not entered into international law as custom.[561] General principles are in accordance with the consensual view of international law because they cover matters basic or

555 Henkin, *International Law*, at 39.

556 The basis for this right was recognized by the International Court of Justice in *Barcelona Traction, Light and Power Company Limited (Second Phase) (Belgium v. Spain)*, [1970] ICJ Rep 3 [*Barcelona Traction Case*], at 32.

557 In the *Barcelona Traction Case*, ibid., the Court stated at 32 that "[s]uch obligations derive, for example, in contemporary international law, from the outlawing of acts of aggression, and of genocide, as also from the principles and rules concerning the basic rights of the human person, including protection from slavery and racial discrimination."

558 See generally, M. C. Bassiouni and E. M. Wise, *Aut Dedere Aut Judicare: The Duty to Extradite or Prosecute in International Law* (1995).

559 See generally, M. Byers, "Conceptualizing the Relationship between *Jus Cogens* and *Erga Omnes* Rules" (1997) 66 *Nordic Journal of International Law* 211. See also M. Ragazzi, *The Concept of International Obligations* Erga Omnes (2000), esp. at chapter 10. Ragazzi considers direct comparisons to be a category mistake as the concept of *jus cogens*, in his view, refers to *rules*, whereas the concept of *erga omnes* refers to *obligations*: at 193.

560 M. Janis, *An Introduction to International Law* (2003) [Janis, *An Introduction to International Law*], at 56.

561 See B. Cheng, *General Principles of Law as Applied by International Courts and Tribunals* (1987) [Cheng, *General Principles*], esp. at chapter 1, "Introduction." See also M. C. Bassiouni, "A Functional

fundamental to a legal order in relation to which States have already consented to be bound at the national level.

General principles of law have been viewed as an important element in the capacity of international law to grow and respond: in the words of Brierly, "an authoritative recognition of a dynamic element on international law, and of the creative function of the courts which may administer it."[562] Certainly the fact that this source of law requires recognition and acceptance but not necessarily State practice implies a capacity to infuse international law with norms that possess a "strong inherent" quality.[563] In practice however, its use has been much more pedestrian – being employed most often in situations where there is perceived to be a gap in the law that is not readily filled by available treaties and customary law. General principles invoked by international courts are usually of a procedural and administrative kind: part of the science or structure of "the law" and thereby part of international law because it is a system of law.[564] Examples include the principle of res judicata (once a matter has been definitely decided by a court, it cannot be decided again), good faith, judicial impartiality, legal certainty, and proportionality. The principal that "inferences of fact and circumstantial evidence" can be used to establish knowledge and legal responsibility was similarly recognized by the International Court of Justice as "admitted in all systems of law" and thereby part of international law.[565] General principles of law can also exist at the regional, rather than universal, level. For example, the right to remain silent when charged with a crime may well be a general principle of law in Europe and the Americas, as most countries in both regions recognize it in their legal system. However, it is unclear whether it would constitute a general principle of law internationally because many countries in other parts of the world do not specifically recognize it. Within the European system, the general principles of subsidiarity[566] and of fundamental rights[567] have special resonance for the interpretation and application of European law. General principles of law are

Approach to General Principles of International Law" (1990) 11 *Michigan Journal of International Law* 786.

[562] J. L. Brierly (H. Waldock ed.) *The Law of the Nations: An Introduction to the International Law of Peace* (6th ed. 1963), at 63.

[563] B. Simma and P. Alston, "The Sources of Human Rights Law: Custom, *Jus Cogens*, and General Principles" (1988–1989) 12 *Australian Yearbook of International Law* 82, at 102.

[564] Janis, *An Introduction to International Law*, at 41; and Henkin, *International Law*, at 32–33.

[565] *Corfu Channel (United Kingdom v. Albania)*, [1949] ICJ Rep 4, at 18.

[566] Legal basis of the principle of subsidiarity: "The second paragraph of Article 5 of the Treaty establishing the European Community (EC), in conjunction with the 12th recital of the preamble to and the second paragraph of Article 2 of the Treaty on European Union (TEU)."

[567] Treaty of Amsterdam amending the Treaty on European Union, the Treaties Establishing the European Communities and certain related acts, OJ C 340/1, done Oct. 2, 1997, entered into force May 1, 1999.

and suppression of unsafe practices associated with the trafficking or transport of migrants by sea. As noted previously, one particular circular, issued by the IMO Assembly in 1998, exercised substantial normative influence over the subsequent development of international legal rules relating to migrant smuggling by sea.[590] It is relevant to observe that the normatively framed "soft law" around the issue of migrant smuggling cited previously is generally very much focused on narrow, technical aspects of State responses. There is nothing to match the considerable and wide-ranging body of soft law that has developed around the issue of trafficking in persons and human rights.[591] There is, for example, no migrant-smuggling equivalent to the UN Principles and Guidelines on Human Rights and Human Trafficking,[592] or the UNHCR Guidelines on the application of the refugee convention to persons who have been trafficked,[593] or even the UNICEF Guidelines on protecting the rights of child victims of trafficking.[594]

The output of intergovernmental agencies may include instruments fitting the description of soft law. A relevant example that is used extensively in the present analysis of the international legal framework is the 2006 Legislative Guide to the Organized Crime Convention and its Protocols produced by the United Nations Office on Drugs and Crime. Regional consultative initiatives (on migrant smuggling as well as on migration issues more generally) have become increasingly important over the past decade[595] and are another important source of soft law. Outputs of the Bali Process on People Smuggling, Trafficking in Persons and Related Transnational Crime, for example, have included best practice guidelines and other materials that

Circ.896, Dec. 16, 1998, and Rev.1, June 12, 2001; and International Maritime Organization, Maritime Safety Committee, *Unsafe Practices Associated with the Trafficking or Transport of Migrants by Sea*, IMO Doc. MSC.3/Circ.13, July 31, 2007.

590 See note 55 above.

591 See further Gallagher, *The International Law of Human Trafficking*, at 138–143.

592 UN Economic and Social Council, Office of the United Nations High Commissioner on Human Rights, "Recommended Principles and Guidelines on Human Rights and Human Trafficking," UN Doc E/2002/68/Add.1, May 20, 2002. For information on the development of the Principles and Guidelines, and on how they have been used as a normative tool, see the introductory chapter to Office of the UN High Commissioner for Human Rights, *Commentary to the United Nations Recommended Principles and Guidelines on Human Rights and Human Trafficking* (2010).

593 UN High Commissioner for Refugees, *Guidelines on International Protection: The application of Article 1A(2) of the 1951 Convention and/or 1967 Protocol relating to the Status of Refugees to victims of trafficking and persons at risk of being trafficked*, UN Doc. HCR/GIP/06/07, Apr. 7, 2006.

594 United Nations Children's Fund, *Guidelines for the Protection of Child Victims of Trafficking* (Sept. 2006).

595 For a useful overview of the working methods and output of regional consultative mechanisms dealing with migration issues, including irregular migration and migrant smuggling, see R. Hansen, *An Assessment of Principal Regional Consultative Processes on Migration* (2010). See also C. Thouez and F. Channac, "Shaping International Migration Policy: The Role of Regional Consultative Processes" (2006) 29(2) *West European Politics* 370.

may well fit the designation of "soft law."[596] In addition, as noted previously, a proportion of bilateral agreements concluded to deal with aspects of irregular migration including migrant smuggling would appear to fall into the category of soft law, in the sense that they appear to have been deliberately framed so as to create less-than-treaty obligations.[597] The question of whether some of these instruments are "hard law disguised as soft" is as important to raise as it is difficult to answer, particularly given the environment of secrecy within which they are often negotiated and implemented.

Soft law relevant to migrant smuggling, most particularly of the "promotional-inspirational" variety, becomes considerably more abundant when one's sights are set more broadly. For example, the issue of irregular migration *writ large* has generated numerous instruments at the international and regional levels that would not be considered binding in international law.[598] Similarly, the legal framework around the rights of migrants is widely considered to include not just treaty-based norms but also an extensive body of soft law created through resolutions of key international bodies such as the UN General Assembly and Human Rights Council,[599] the

[596] The Bali Process was established in 2002 on the initiative of the government of Australia with cooperation from the government of Indonesia. Although ostensibly promoting cooperation on trafficking as well as migrant smuggling, it is the latter issue that provided the impetus for its creation and has, in practice, remained the clear focus of its efforts, despite official assertions to the contrary. See A. Gallagher, Submission to the Australian Parliamentary Inquiry into Slavery, Slavery-Like Conditions and People Trafficking (2013), available at http://works.bepress.com/anne_gallagher/23/ (accessed May 12, 2013), at paras. 19–20. The stated objectives of the Bali Process are: the development of more effective information and intelligence sharing; improved cooperation among regional law enforcement agencies to deter and combat people smuggling and trafficking networks; enhanced cooperation on border and visa systems to detect and prevent illegal movements; increased public awareness in order to discourage these activities and warn those susceptible; enhanced effectiveness of return as a strategy to deter people smuggling and trafficking through conclusion of appropriate arrangements; cooperation in verifying the identity and nationality of illegal migrants and trafficking victims; the enactment of national legislation to criminalize people smuggling and trafficking in persons; provision of appropriate protection and assistance to the victims of trafficking, particularly women and children; enhanced focus on tackling the root causes of illegal migration, including by increasing opportunities for legal migration between States; and assisting countries to adopt best practices in asylum management, in accordance with the principles of the Refugees Convention. See: www.baliprocess.net/index.asp?pageID=214583140 (accessed May 12, 2013). For an analysis of the Bali Process and its outputs, see A. Schloenhardt and J. H. Douglas, *Combatting Migrant Smuggling with Regional Diplomacy: An Examination of the Bali Process* (University of Queensland Research Paper, Feb. 2012).

[597] See Section 1.3.2.

[598] For a useful overview in a context relevant to the present study, see A. Betts, "Towards a Soft Law Framework for the Protection of Vulnerable Irregular Migrants" (2010) 22 *International Journal of Refugee Law* 209.

[599] For recent examples, see: UN General Assembly, "Protection of Migrants," GA Res. 66/172, UN GAOR, 66th sess, Agenda Item 69(b), UN Doc. A/Res/66/172, Mar. 29, 2012; and Human Rights Council, "Human Rights of Migrants," UN Doc. A/HRC/20/L.6, June 28, 2012.

Council of Europe,[600] and the United Nations High Commissioner for Refugees.[601] "Soft law" relevant to migrant smuggling may also include a range of instruments of broader scope and application. For example, international normative standards on the administration of criminal justice are highly pertinent to a consideration of many aspects of the response to migrant smuggling, most particularly to an examination of the rights of smuggled migrants and the obligations of States toward those persons. Additional relevant soft law standards address issues such as detention,[602] detention of children,[603] treatment of victims of crime,[604] and treatment of victims of gross human rights violations.[605]

What weight is to be given to soft law instruments in determining the existence and substantive content of a claimed right or an obligation? This question is a complicated one. Of primary concern, particularly to those of a more positivist-leaning bent, is the danger that actions or instruments never meant by States to create binding obligations are somehow construed in that way, to the general detriment of international law's legitimacy and impact. One commentator has charged that international legal scholars intent on finding "new legal materials" to expand their own fields of study have led the way in creating for soft law a power and influence that goes well beyond what is deserved.[606] In the contested and highly emotive field of migrant smuggling, a related danger is presented by the less-than-careful "scholar-activists": in particular those who have arrived at a particular policy position that is not well supported by "hard" international law and who then turn to soft law in order to bolster that position. It may be argued that certain efforts to expand the parameters of the obligation of *non-refoulement* within international refugee law, utilizing the writings of other commentators and nonlegal texts, is an instructive example.[607]

[600] For example, Council of Europe, Committee of Ministers, *Twenty Guidelines on Forced Return*, CM(2005)40 final, May 9, 2005; Council of Europe, Parliamentary Assembly, Resolution 1509 (2006) "Human Rights of Irregular Migrants," adopted June 27, 2006. Note that both these instruments attach themselves strongly to existing treaty obligations of Member States.

[601] For example, UN High Commissioner for Refugees, *Refugee Protection and Mixed Migration: A 10-Point Plan of Action* (2007).

[602] For example, UN General Assembly, "Body of Principles for the Protection of All Persons under Any Form of Detention or Imprisonment," adopted by GA Res. 43/173, UN Doc. A/RES/43/173 Annex, Dec. 9, 1988.

[603] For example, UN General Assembly, "United Nations Rules for the Protection of Juveniles Deprived of Their Liberty," adopted by GA Res. 45/113, UN Doc. A/RES/45/113 Annex, Dec. 14, 1990.

[604] For example, UN General Assembly, "Declaration of Basic Principles of Justice for Victims of Crime and Abuse of Power," adopted by GA Res. 40/34, UN Doc. A/RES/40/34 Annex, Nov. 29, 1985.

[605] For example, UN General Assembly, "Basic Principles and Guidelines on the Right to a Remedy and Reparation for Victims of Gross Violations of International Human Rights Law and Serious Violations of International Humanitarian Law," UN Doc. A/RES/60/147 Annex, Dec. 16, 2005.

[606] d'Aspremont, "Softness in International Law."

[607] See further Chapter 3, at Section 3.4.4.

Misuse or incorrect application of nontraditional sources of international law does not provide adequate justification for their outright rejection. It would be incorrect to state that the multitude of soft law instruments referred to previously are collectively irrelevant to determining the nature and substantive content of individual rights and State obligations in relation to migrant smuggling. There can be no doubt that in the present case, at least some soft law agreements "are not just failed treaties but can be a superior institutional choice"[608] with measurable legal effects. The most important of these instruments may directly contribute to the formation and recognition of customary law. They can, for example, provide examples or instances of both State practice and *opinio juris*. Soft law instruments in this field may also contribute to clarifying the nature and scope of a "soft" or even a "hard" legal norm. For example, the obligation of *non-refoulement* and other safeguards that apply in the context of migrant smuggling, has been rendered more precise through a range of instruments, of varying legal force, that specify the steps required by States to meet this obligation. In other cases, soft law instruments do not appear to have had this effect – underlining the importance of considering each right or obligation (or proposed right or obligation) and its associated authorities individually.

[608] Raustiala and Slaughter, "International Law, International Relations and Compliance," at 552.

2

The Legal Framework: Human Rights and Refugee Law

> While States are entitled to control their borders and regulate migration, they must do so in full compliance with their obligations as parties to the human rights treaties they have ratified or acceded to.[1]
>
> [W]e will decide who comes to this country and the circumstances in which they come.[2]

As noted in the previous chapter, the adoption of specialized legal rules around migrant smuggling is a relatively recent development. However, these rules did not emerge in a vacuum. Rather, they built on and added to a preexisting web of international laws that were relevant but not particular to migrant smuggling, including human rights and refugee law.

Human rights and refugee law are central to the issue of migrant smuggling in at least two important ways. First, these branches of law impose important limitations on how States can regulate and respond to migrant smuggling. For example, the right of all persons to leave any country, including their own, may operate to restrict the legal capacity of States to obstruct (or help other States obstruct) facilitated departure. The obligation of *non-refoulement* may prevent a State from returning a smuggled migrant to persecution. Second, human rights and refugee law confers certain legal entitlements on smuggled migrants that States and others are obliged to protect and respect. In some cases, the relevant entitlements are owed to smuggled migrants by virtue of their humanity: the right to life, for example, and the prohibition against discrimination or torture are universal and non-derogable, applying

1 UN Committee on the Elimination of Discrimination against Women, "General Recommendation No. 26 on Women Migrant Workers," UN Doc. CEDAW/C/2009/WP.1/R, Dec. 5, 2008 [CEDAW General Recommendation No. 26], at para. 3.

2 J. Howard (former prime minister of Australia), Policy Speech (Oct. 28, 2001), referring directly to the *Tampa* incident (on which see further Introduction and Chapter 6, at 6.2.1.3.)

Sections of this chapter draw on A. T. Gallagher, *The International Law of Human Trafficking* (2010) [Gallagher, *The International Law of Human Trafficking*] (chapters 3.1; 3.2.1; 3.5; and 5.2.3).

to all persons without distinction. Other rights may attach to a smuggled migrant by virtue of that person's status as a victim of trafficking, an asylum-seeker, a migrant worker, a woman, or a child.

While acknowledging the centrality of human rights law to the issue of migrant smuggling, it is also important not to overstate its reach or impact. As discussed in the previous chapter, States have been very careful to retain a long-held sovereign right to decide who can enter their territory and under what conditions. As one commentator has noted, what is *not* included in international texts is telling: despite claims of universalism in relation to human rights, the distinction between national and nonnationals is alive and well and "[t]he prerogatives of a nation-state when it comes to refusing access, residence, or naturalization to its territory have not been put into question."[3] The long-standing justifications for restricting rights – public order, public security, and public health and safety – have survived and flourished as legitimate defenses for withholding entitlements to certain groups and under certain circumstances. The characterization of migrant smuggling as a transnational organized crime that "bring[s] great harm to the States concerned"[4] dovetails very neatly with the traditional grounds on which rights are restricted.

The present chapter seeks to identify and explore the main legal issues that arise with respect to human rights in the context of migrant smuggling. In keeping with the general approach of the book the discussion is not directed toward propping up a particular policy position or outcome. Rather it seeks to ascertain, as clearly as possible, the extent to which international human rights law dictates, moderates, or otherwise impacts on how States may respond to migrant smuggling. The analysis is summary rather than exhaustive, seeking to provide a solid foundation for more detailed and specific examination of human rights in the context of particular issues such as prevention, cooperation, protection, detention, and return that are dealt with in subsequent chapters.

The chapter commences with an analysis of the *applicability* of international human rights law to smuggled migrants. In principle, human rights are universal, held by all persons by virtue of their humanity. However in practice the situation is more complex and States have long accorded a different level of treatment to nonnationals, a category to which smuggled migrants, by definition, belong. To what extent does the smuggled migrant's inevitable status as a noncitizen impact on the legal rights to which that person is entitled and the obligations of States to secure and protect those

3 V. Guiraudon and G. Lahav, "A Reappraisal of the State Sovereignty Debate: The Case of Migration Control" (2000) 33(2) *Comparative Political Studies* 163, at 168.

4 Protocol against the Smuggling of Migrants by Land, Sea and Air, supplementing the United Nations Convention against Transnational Organized Crime, 2241 UNTS 507, done Nov. 15, 2000, entered into force Jan. 28, 2004 [Migrant Smuggling Protocol], at Preamble.

rights? The issue of statelessness as it relates to migrant smuggling is also dealt with in the context of the broader question about the applicability of human rights. A further series of questions concern the relevance of human rights to the capacity of individuals to leave and return to a State. Most particularly, can States legitimately prevent individuals from leaving their own (or another) country? How do the rights to leave and return affect the way in which States may lawfully deal with smuggled migrants?

Although not always the case, many smuggled migrants will have fled persecution and human rights abuses in their country of origin. Accordingly, the specific rights of asylum-seekers and refugees are directly relevant to understanding the legal framework around migrant smuggling. The next section of this chapter considers the right to seek and receive asylum from persecution, focusing most particularly on the obligation of *non-refoulement*. Other issues related to the right to seek and receive asylum from persecution, including the obligation on States not to impose penalties for unlawful entry and the question of whether involvement in migrant smuggling can justify exclusion from protection, are also addressed.

Even where smuggled migrants are not refugees, specific human rights concerns may operate to limit their expulsion or return to their country of origin. The chapter considers additional, non–asylum-related restrictions on expulsion that are relevant to the situation of smuggled migrants: *non-refoulement* in relation to torture and other serious human rights violations, restrictions on expulsion of stateless persons, and restrictions on mass or collective expulsion. The section concludes with an overview of the protections to which persons subject to lawful expulsion or return are entitled.

In many parts of the world, smuggled migrants are increasingly subject to restrictions on their liberty, whether this is merely reporting obligations, administrative detention, or even imprisonment. The final section of the chapter examines the prohibition on arbitrary and inhumane detention and its implications for the treatment of smuggled migrants. Other, more specific human rights and human rights–related issues (such as the right to life in the context of access to emergency medical care) are not dealt with in any detail in this chapter but are considered at relevant points throughout the book.

The relevance of human rights and refugee law also depends, critically, on the scope of its application. There can be no disputing that the externalization of migration control – where various barriers and controls are put in place well before the prospective migrant ever gets near the territory of the State – has far-reaching implications for the regulation of migrant smuggling. Indeed, some commentators have observed that the development of extraterritorial immigration control practices can be motivated by a desire to *avoid* substantive legal and procedural guarantees.[5] Certainly the impact of those practices is almost invariably a weakening of those same guarantees. The question of whether human rights obligations extend beyond a State's territory (and if so, under what conditions and to what extent) is a central

5 B. Ryan and V. Mitsilegas, *Extraterritorial Immigration Control: Legal Challenges* (2010), at vii.

one for any study of migrant smuggling and is considered in detail in the following chapter in the context of a broader discussion on jurisdiction and capacity to act. Chapter 3 is also linked to the present one through its consideration of the extraterritorial application of the obligation of *non-refoulement*, a critical moderator of State action against migrant smuggling.

2.1. APPLICABILITY OF HUMAN RIGHTS LAW

Universality of international human rights law – the concept that human rights apply equally to all persons everywhere – is an important idea but not yet one that is fully reflected in the actions of the international community, the behavior of States, and the experience of many millions of people. This is not just a problem of perception: normative development has been uncomfortably one-sided, with international human rights law clearly limiting the obligations of States to certain places, groups of people, and situations. As Skogly notes, the concept of universalism is much more concerned with entitlement to, or *enjoyment* of human rights, than it is with obligation: "while all individuals everywhere are considered to have the same rights based on international law, the obligation-holders (normally States) do not have the same obligations with regard to individuals everywhere."[6] In short, the web of human rights obligations that moderate or constrain the actions of States are not applicable under all circumstances and in respect of all persons, and the duties that a State owes to a particular individual often depends on the nature of the relationship between the State and that individual. Geographical location, nationality, and citizenship are important determinants of both obligation and responsibility. The first of these elements is considered in Chapter 3, through that chapter's consideration of the relevance of territory to jurisdictional competence. The following section examines the applicability of human rights law from the perspective of nationality and citizenship, concepts that are highly relevant to a determination of both rights and obligations in the context of migrant smuggling.

2.1.1. *Smuggled Migrants as Noncitizens*

> [A]lthough the ideology of human rights does away with the concept of the state to concentrate on the equal value of all human beings, its practice relies on the way in which individuals are classified *in relation to a state*.[7]

6 S. Skogly, "Universal Human Rights without Universal Obligations?," in S. Joseph and A. McBeth eds., *Research Handbook on International Human Rights Law* (2010), at 71.

7 M-B. Dembour, "Human Rights Talk and Anthropological Ambivalence: The Particular Context of Universal Claims," in O. Harris ed., *Inside and Outside the Law: Anthropological Studies of Authority and Ambiguity* 14 (2006), at 26, cited in M. Albahari, *Death and the Moral State: Making Borders and*

the scope of its non-discrimination clause. The following paragraphs briefly consider this issue in relation to the human rights treaties that are of most relevance to smuggled migrants. The subsection concludes with a general finding on the applicability of international human rights law to noncitizens.

2.1.1.1. International Covenant on Civil and Political Rights

Does the fact that smuggled migrants are noncitizens affect their rights and entitlements under the International Covenant on Civil and Political Rights? Nowak observes that "[t]he principle of equality and the prohibition on discrimination runs like a red thread" throughout the International Covenant on Civil and Political Rights (ICCPR).[24] Article 2 extends application of this instrument to "all individuals within [the] territory [of the State Party] and subject to its jurisdiction ... without distinction of any kind such as race, colour, sex, language, religion, political or other opinion, national or social origin, property, birth or other status."[25] This provision is supplemented by an additional and broader non-discrimination clause at Article 26:

> All persons are equal before the law and are entitled without any discrimination to the equal protection of the law. In this respect, the law shall prohibit any discrimination and guarantee to all persons equal and effective protection against discrimination on any ground such as race, colour, sex, language, religion, political or other opinion, national or social origin, property, birth or other status.[26]

The Human Rights Committee has affirmed that:

> [T]he rights set forth in the Covenant apply to everyone, irrespective of reciprocity, and irrespective of his or her nationality or statelessness .... Thus, the general rule

24 M. Nowak, *U.N. Covenant on Civil and Political Rights: CCPR Commentary* (2nd revised ed. 2005) [Nowak, *CCPR Commentary*], at 600.

25 ICCPR, at Art. 2(1). Note that as with the UDHR, the list of prohibited grounds does not include nationality. The significance of this omission is generally played down, with one influential commentator arguing, unconvincingly, that "the list clearly is intended to be illustrative and not comprehensive" and, further, that nationality would anyway "appear to fall into the category of 'distinction of any kind'": R.B. Lillich, *The Human Rights of Aliens in Contemporary International Law* (1984), at 43, cited in Office of the United Nations High Commissioner for Human Rights, *The Rights of Non-Citizens* (2006) [OHCHR, *The Rights of Non-Citizens*], at 36.

26 ICCPR, at Art. 26. The Human Rights Committee has confirmed that this Article does not just duplicate the general affirmation of nondiscrimination set out in Article 2 but that it "prohibits discrimination in law or in fact in any field regulated and protected by public authorities ... the application of the principle of non-discrimination contained in article 26 is not limited to those rights which are provided for in the Covenant": UN Human Rights Committee, "General Comment No. 18: Non-discrimination," UN Doc. HRI/GEN/1/Rev.7, at 146, May 12, 2004, adopted Nov. 10, 1989, at para. 12.

> is that each one of the rights of the Covenant must be guaranteed without discrimination between citizens and aliens.[27]

In addition to explicitly confirming that guarantees of equality and non-discrimination extend to refugees and asylum-seekers,[28] the Human Rights Committee has further specified that:

> Aliens ... have an inherent right to life, protected by law, and may not be arbitrarily deprived of life. They may not be subjected to torture or to cruel, inhuman or degrading treatment or punishment; nor may they be held in slavery or servitude. Aliens have the full right to liberty and security of the person. If lawfully deprived of their liberty, they shall be treated with humanity and with respect for the inherent dignity of their person. Aliens may not be imprisoned for failure to fulfil a contractual obligation. They have the right to liberty of movement and free choice of residence; they shall be free to leave the country. Aliens shall be equal before the courts and tribunals, and shall be entitled to a fair and public hearing by a competent, independent and impartial tribunal established by law in the determination of any criminal charge or of rights and obligations in a suit at law. Aliens shall not be subject to retrospective penal legislation, and are entitled to recognition before the law. They may not be subjected to arbitrary or unlawful interference with their privacy, family, home or correspondence. They have the right to freedom of thought, conscience and religion, and the right to hold opinions and to express them. Aliens receive the benefit of the right of peaceful assembly and of freedom of association. They may marry when at marriageable age. Their children are entitled to those measures of protection required by their status as minors. In those cases where aliens constitute a minority within the meaning of article 27, they shall not be denied the right, in community with other members of their group, to

[27] UN Human Rights Committee, "General Comment No. 15: The Position of Aliens under the Covenant," UN Doc. HRI/GEN.1/Rev.7, at 140, May 12, 2004, adopted Apr. 11, 1986 [HRC General Comment No. 15], at paras. 1–2. The UN Special Rapporteur on the Rights of Non-Citizens noted that HRC General Comment No. 15 very much reflects the substance of the Declaration on the Human Rights of Individuals Who are not Nationals of the Country in which They Live: "The Rights of Non-Citizens: Preliminary Report of the Special Rapporteur, Mr David Weissbrodt," UN Doc. E/CN.4/Sub.2/2001/20, June 6, 2001, at para. 103. For an overview of the development of this Declaration as well as an examination of its contents, see Cholewinski, *Migrant Workers*, at 72–76. In the present context it is relevant to note that the Declaration specifically provides that nothing in it "shall be interpreted as legitimizing" any alien's illegal entry into and presence in a State, "nor shall any provision be interpreted as restricting the right of any State to promulgate law and regulations concerning the entry of aliens and the terms and conditions of their stay or to establish differences between nationals and aliens. However, such laws and regulations shall not be incompatible with the international legal obligations of that State, including those in the field of human rights": "Declaration on Human Rights of Non-Nationals," at Art. 2(1).

[28] UN Human Rights Committee, "General Comment No. 31: The Nature of the General Legal Obligation Imposed on States Parties to the Covenant," UN Doc. HRI/GEN.1/Rev.7, at 192, May 12, 2004, adopted Mar. 29, 2004 [HRC General Comment No. 31], at para. 10.

> enjoy their own culture, to profess and practise their own religion and to use their own language. Aliens are entitled to equal protection by the law. There shall be no discrimination between aliens and citizens in the application of these rights. These rights of aliens may be qualified only by such limitations as may be lawfully imposed under the Covenant.[29]

However the broader context of this apparently unambiguous position is also relevant. In the same General Comment the Committee affirmed that "once aliens are *allowed to enter the territory of a State party* they are entitled to the rights set out in the Covenant."[30] This caveat implies endorsement of some permissible restrictions on rights in respect of irregular migrants who have entered or seek to enter a State without authorization. Certainly, some of the rights in the ICCPR are not absolute in all circumstances, and States are permitted to limit these rights in certain circumstances. For example, the right of persons lawfully within the country to liberty of movement and residence may be subject to restrictions that are provided by law; necessary to secure national security, public order, public health or morals, or the rights or freedoms of others; and consistent with other rights recognized in the Covenant.[31] The right to freedom of thought, conscience, and religion[32]; the right to hold opinions without interference[33]; the right of peaceful assembly[34]; and the right to freedom of association[35] are similarly subject to lawful qualifications. Reference should also be made to Article 4(1) of the ICCPR, which permits derogations from certain, non-fundamental rights in times of public emergency that threaten the life of the nation, provided that such measures are strictly required by the exigencies of the situation and do not amount to discrimination "solely on the ground of race, colour, sex, language, religion or social origin." It is relevant to note that nationality and even national origin, as well as immigration status, are not included in this list of prohibited grounds. According to the *Travaux Préparatoires*, this omission reflected a general understanding of the fact that States will often find it necessary to discriminate against nationals of enemy States in times of national emergency.[36] In addition, and as explored further in Chapter 9 in the context of a consideration of the lawfulness of detention of smuggled migrants, the ICCPR restricts application

[29] HRC General Comment No. 15, at para. 7.

[30] HRC General Comment No. 15, at para. 6 (emphasis added).

[31] ICCPR, at Art. 12(3).

[32] Ibid. at Art. 18(3).

[33] Ibid. at Art. 19(3).

[34] Ibid. at Art. 21.

[35] Ibid. at Art. 22(2).

[36] Nowak, *CCPR Commentary*, at 99–100. Note that the word "solely" has been interpreted as confirming that emergency measures affecting a particular population group are permissible "as long as they do not intentionally target these population groups": ibid.

of the right to freedom of movement[37] and safeguards against arbitrary expulsion[38] to persons *lawfully* within the territory of the State Party.[39]

Within these restrictions, the Human Rights Committee has generally upheld the principle of equality of rights between citizens and noncitizens. The work of the Committee nevertheless reflects an assumption that differentiation based on citizenship can sometimes be reasonable and therefore not a breach of the Covenant's guarantee of equality and equal treatment.[40] However, the jurisprudence on this point is limited with the result that the parameters of reasonableness have not yet been clearly defined.[41]

2.1.1.2. International Covenant on Economic, Social, and Cultural Rights

Does the fact that smuggled migrants are noncitizens affect their rights and entitlements under the International Covenant on Economic, Social and Cultural Rights (ICESCR)? This instrument includes a nondiscrimination clause that is identical to that found in the ICCPR.[42] As with the ICCPR's clause, commentators are divided on the question of whether this provision would admit further grounds of discrimination such as nationality or citizenship.[43] In two important respects the ICESCR

37 ICCPR, at Art. 12(1).

38 Ibid. at Art. 13.

39 Note also that the right to participate in public affairs, to vote and hold office, and to have access to public service under Article 25 is restricted to "every citizen."

40 For a detailed analysis of this aspect of the work of the Human Rights Committee, see J. C. Hathaway, *The Rights of Refugees under International Law* (2005) [Hathaway, *The Rights of Refugees*], at 131–147.

41 Writing in 2005, Hathaway concludes that "[t]he present moment can thus be most accurately described as one of legal uncertainty on this point: until and unless the jurisprudence of the Human Rights Committee assesses the propriety of categorical differentiation based on citizenship across a broader range of issues, it will be difficult to know which forms of exclusion are likely to be found valid, and which are in breach of Art. 26": ibid. at 133. Hathaway is generally critical of the Committee's analysis of equality and nondiscrimination as these principles apply to nonnationals, describing it as formalistic and superficial, failing to grapple with a genuinely effects-based approach, and granting too wide a margin of appreciation to States: ibid. at 133–137, 150–151. For a detailed examination (and generally more optimistic) analysis of the Article 26 nondiscrimination clause in the context of refugee rights and complementary protection, see J. Pobjoy, "Treating Like Alike: The Principle of Non-discrimination as a Tool to Mandate the Equal Treatment of Refugees and Beneficiaries of Complementary Protection," (2010) 34(1) *Melbourne University Law Review* 181, at 203– 228.

42 "The States Parties to the present Covenant undertake to guarantee that the rights enunciated in the present Covenant will be exercised without discrimination of any kind as to race, colour, sex, language, religion, political or other opinion, national or social origin, property, birth or other status": ICESCR, at Art. 2(2).

43 See, for example, Cholewinski, *Migrant Workers*, at 57–58. The Committee on Economic, Social and Cultural Rights has said, in relation to the prohibition against discrimination, that it "encompasses all internationally prohibited grounds of discrimination": UN Committee on Economic, Social and Cultural Rights, "General Comment No. 13: The Right to Education," UN Doc. E/C.12/1999/10, Dec.

is weaker on noncitizen rights than the ICCPR. First, there is no specific extension of applicability of Covenant rights to all individuals within the territory or under the jurisdiction of the State Party. Second, developing countries are explicitly permitted to determine the extent to which they will guarantee the *economic* rights set forth in the Covenant to nonnationals.[44]

The Committee on Economic, Social and Cultural Rights (ICESCR Committee) has generally taken the view that the Covenant applies to all persons under the jurisdiction of the State Party, regardless of citizenship and status. In 2009 it explicitly affirmed that "[t]he Covenant rights apply to everyone including non-nationals, such as refugees, asylum-seekers, stateless persons, migrant workers and victims of international trafficking, regardless of legal status and documentation."[45] This general approach has support from the scholar/activist community,[46] and is strengthened by the fact that, apart from a general limitations clause,[47] specific restrictions

8, 1999 [CESCR General Comment No. 13], at para. 31. In a subsequent general comment on the right to health, the Committee also held that the Covenant proscribes "any discrimination … on the grounds of race, colour, sex, language, religion, political or other opinion, national or social origin, property, birth, physical or mental disability, health status (including HIV/AIDS), sexual orientation and civil, political, social or other status, which has the intention or effect of nullifying or impairing the equal enjoyment or exercise of the right to health": UN Committee on Economic, Social and Cultural Rights, "General Comment No. 14: The Right to the Highest Attainable Standard of Health," UN Doc. E/C.12/2000/4, Aug. 11, 2000, at para. 18. On the basis of the General Comment, the Special Rapporteur on the Rights of Non-Citizens has asserted that States Parties cannot discriminate against nonnationals with respect to the right to health if that discrimination intentionally or effectively nullifies or impairs their enjoyment to exercise of that right: "The Rights of Non-Citizens: Preliminary Report of the Special Rapporteur, Mr David Weissbrodt," UN Doc. E/CN.4/Sub.2/2001/20, June 6, 2001, at para. 60. Note that the Limburg Principles, developed by a group of experts and advocates in 1987 to clarify the nature of State obligations under the ICESCR and to guide its effective implementation, assert that the grounds of discrimination mentioned in Article 2(2) are not exhaustive: "The Limburg Principles on the Implementation of the International Covenant on Economic, Social and Cultural Rights," UN Doc. E/CN.4/1987/17, Annex, Jan. 8, 1987 [Limburg Principles], at para. 36.

44 "Developing countries, with due regard to human rights and their national economy, may determine to what extent they would guarantee the economic rights recognized in the present Covenant to non-nationals": ICESCR, at Art. 2(3). It can be argued that this provision implies an obligation on *developed* States Parties to guarantee provision of the relevant rights to nonnationals and on *all States* to guarantee provision of all noneconomic rights. For further on controversies and ambiguities surrounding this provision, see Cholewinski, *Migrant Workers*, at 58–60.

45 UN Committee on Economic, Social and Cultural Rights, "General Comment No. 20: Non-Discrimination in Economic, Social and Cultural Rights," UN Doc. E/C.12/GC/20, July 2, 2009 [CESCR General Comment No. 20], at para. 30.

46 See, for example, the NGO-developed Limburg Principles at para. 42: "As a general rule the Covenant applies equally to nationals and non-nationals."

47 ICESCR, Article 4, provides that "[t]he States Parties to the present Covenant recognize that, in the enjoyment of those rights provided by the State in conformity with the present Covenant, the State may subject such rights only to such limitations as are determined by law only in so far as this may be compatible with the nature of these rights and solely for the purpose of promoting the general welfare in a democratic society."

on the rights of aliens are limited to those discussed above. The language of certain Articles further reinforces this interpretation. In relation to the right to education, for example, the relevant Article refers to the right of "everyone."[48] The ICESCR Committee has also indicated that the principle of nondiscrimination in relation to access to educational institutions "extends to all persons of school age residing in the territory of a State party, including non-nationals, and irrespective of their legal status."[49] Another example of particular relevance to the present context is Article 6, establishing the right of "everyone" to "gain his living by work which he freely chooses or accepts."[50] The Special Rapporteur on the Rights of Non-Citizens has interpreted the Committee's General Comments on the right to health and the right to adequate housing as supportive of extending both rights to non-nationals.[51] These expansive interpretations receive confirmation in 2009 through the ICESCR Committee's General Comment No. 20 on Non-Discrimination, which states:

> The ground of nationality should not bar access to Covenant rights, e.g., all children within a State, including those with an undocumented status, have a right to receive education and access to adequate food and affordable health care. The Covenant rights apply to everyone including non-nationals, such as refugees, asylum-seekers, stateless persons, migrant workers and victims of international trafficking, regardless of legal status and documentation.[52]

However, this position is weakened somewhat by an accompanying footnote, which indicates that the statement is not to prejudice the application of Article 2(3) of ICESCR: "[d]eveloping countries, with due regard to human rights and their national economy, may determine to what extent they would guarantee the economic rights recognized in the present Covenant to non-nationals."[53]

Although repeatedly affirming in its General Comments the principle of equality, the ICESCR Committee has in practice demonstrated what one commentator identifies as a "flexible" approach in tailoring its views of State Party obligations depending on the legal status of the individual.[54] Judging from the practice of the ICESCR Committee in its Concluding Observations, it appears that those lawfully

[48] Ibid. at Art. 13.

[49] CESCR General Comment No. 13, at para. 34.

[50] ICESCR, at Art. 6.

[51] "The Rights of Non-Citizens: Preliminary Report of the Special Rapporteur, Mr David Weissbrodt," UN Doc. E/CN.4/Sub.2/2001/20, June 6, 2001, at 60–61. But see Cholewinski, *Migrant Workers*, at 61, arguing that the Committee's various pronouncements on the right to housing do not necessarily support a conclusion that this right applies to nonnationals.

[52] CESCR General Comment No. 20, at para. 30 (citations omitted).

[53] Ibid. at n. 22.

[54] M. M. Sepúlveda, *The Nature of the Obligations under the International Covenant on Economic, Social, and Cultural Rights* (2003) at 262.

within the territory of the State Party (including stateless persons, refugees, and asylum-seekers) are, for the most part, entitled to enjoy Covenant rights on an equal basis with citizens, and to a relatively greater extent than individuals illegally present.[55] This de facto categorical differentiation may operate to exclude from the protection of the ICESCR those individuals, including smuggled migrants, who have not entered or sought to enter the destination country lawfully and who are not able to make or sustain a claim for asylum. It is not yet apparent that this disadvantageous distinction based on legal status has been substantially altered following adoption of the ICESCR Committee's General Comment No. 20.

2.1.1.3. Convention on the Elimination of Racial Discrimination

Does the fact that smuggled migrants are noncitizens affect their rights and entitlements under the International Convention on the Elimination of All Forms of Racial Discrimination (CERD)[56]? This Convention contains the most unambiguous statement permitting differentiation between citizens and noncitizens. CERD qualifies its broad definition of racial discrimination[57] by declaring, in Article 1(2), that "[t]his Convention shall not apply to distinctions, exclusions, restrictions or preferences made by a State Party to this Convention between citizens and non-citizens."[58] Human rights advocates have typically minimized the significance of this clear distinction between citizens and noncitizens, pointing, for example, to the importance of interpreting these provisions in the light of the totality of international human rights law.[59] The relevant treaty body (the Committee on the Elimination of Racial Discrimination (Race Discrimination Committee)) has generally followed this line, noting that the troublesome provision is to be interpreted as merely providing "for

55 For a detailed and balanced consideration of the practice of the Committee with respect to the issue of noncitizens, see ibid., at 262–277. For a less nuanced view of the Committee's work in this area (which concludes by finding that "a compelling argument can be made that all non-nationals possess ICESCR rights"), see J. A. Dent, *Research Paper on the Social and Economic Rights of Non-Nationals in Europe* (European Council on Refugees and Exiles, 1998) [Dent, *Research Paper on the Social and Economic Rights of Non-Nationals in Europe*], at 3–4.

56 International Convention on the Elimination of All Forms of Racial Discrimination, 660 UNTS 195, done Dec. 21, 1965, entered into force Jan. 4, 1969 [CERD].

57 "[T]he term 'racial discrimination' shall mean any distinction, exclusion, restriction or preference based on race, colour, descent, or national or ethnic origin which has the purpose of effect of nullifying or impairing the recognition, enjoyment or exercise, on an equal footing, of human rights and fundamental freedoms in the political, economic, social, cultural or any other field of public life": ibid. at Art. 1(1).

58 Ibid. at Art. 1(2). Note that Article 1(3) provides that: "[n]othing in this Convention may be interpreted as affecting in any way the legal provisions of States Parties concerning nationality, citizenship or naturalization, provided that such provisions do not discriminate against any particular nationality."

59 OHCHR, *The Rights of Non-Citizens*, at 9.

the possibility of differentiating between citizens and non-citizens."[60] In its detailed General Comment on this issue, the Race Discrimination Committee confirmed its much earlier stance that Article 1(2):

> must be construed so as to avoid undermining the basic prohibition of discrimination; hence, it should not be interpreted to detract in any way from the rights and freedoms recognized and enunciated in particular in the Universal Declaration of Human Rights, the International Covenant on Civil and Political Rights and the International Covenant on Economic, Social and Cultural Rights.[61]

While recognizing limited exceptions, it affirms that "human rights are, in principle, to be enjoyed by all persons" and that "States parties are under an obligation to guarantee equality between citizens and non-citizens in the enjoyment of these rights to the extent recognized under international law."[62]

The Race Discrimination Committee has provided the following test for determining whether a particular measure that differentiates between persons on the basis of citizenship or immigration status cannot be justified as a special measure under Article 1(4):

> Under the Convention, differential treatment based on citizenship or immigration status will constitute discrimination if the criteria for such differentiation, judged in the light of the objectives and purposes of the Convention, are not applied pursuant to a legitimate aim, and are not proportional to the achievement of this aim.[63]

In its own deliberations, the Race Discrimination Committee has examined and pronounced on a wide range of situations involving discriminatory treatment of nonnationals, including migrant domestic workers as well as persons who have been smuggled and trafficked.[64] Since its adoption of a General Comment on the subject in 2004, in which States Parties were directed to report on discrimination against

[60] UN Committee on the Elimination of Racial Discrimination, "General Recommendation No. 30: Discrimination Against Non-Citizens," UN Doc. CERD/C/64/Misc.11/rev.3, Jan. 10, 2004 [CERD General Recommendation No. 30], at para. 1.

[61] Ibid. at para. 2. See also UN Committee on the Elimination of Racial Discrimination, "General Recommendation No. 1: States Parties' Obligations," UN Doc. HRI/GEN.1/Rev.7, at 198, May 12, 2004, adopted Feb. 25, 1972.

[62] CERD General Recommendation No. 30, at para. 3.

[63] Ibid. at para. 4.

[64] For a detailed but now dated overview of the Committee's consideration of the rights of nonnationals, see Cholewinski, *Migrant Workers*, at 62–64. See also the various reports of the Special Rapporteur on the Human Rights of Migrants ("The Rights of Non-Citizens: Preliminary Report of the Special Rapporteur, Mr David Weissbrodt," UN Doc. E/CN.4/Sub.2/2001/20, June 6, 2001; "The Rights of Non-Citizens: Progress Report of the Special Rapporteur, Mr David Weissbrodt," UN Doc. E/CN.4/Sub.2/2002/25, June 5, 2002; "The Rights of Non-Citizens: Final Report of the Special Rapporteur, Mr David Weissbrodt," UN Doc. E/CN.4/Sub.2/2003/23, May 26, 2003); and OHCHR, *The Rights of Non-Citizens*, esp. at 29–32.

nonnationals,[65] the Race Discrimination Committee has routinely addressed this issue in its consideration of States Parties' reports.[66]

2.1.1.4. Convention Against Torture and Other Cruel, Inhuman or Degrading Treatment or Punishment

The status of smuggled migrants as noncitizens in no way affects their rights and entitlements under the Convention against Torture and Other Cruel, Inhuman or Degrading Treatment or Punishment (Convention against Torture).[67] The Convention, which prohibits not just torture but also inhuman or degrading treatment or punishment,[68] is unequivocal on the point that the central prohibition and associated obligations apply equally to all persons, whether nationals or nonnationals: a State Party is required to "take effective legislative, administrative, judicial or other measures to prevent acts of torture in *any territory under its jurisdiction*."[69] A State Party is further required to establish jurisdiction over torture committed in any territory under its jurisdiction.[70] The Committee against Torture has reaffirmed the fact of its application to nonnationals on numerous occasions,[71] as well as its application outside the *territory* of the State Party.[72]

2.1.1.5. Convention on the Elimination of All Forms of Discrimination against Women

Does their status as noncitizens affect the rights and entitlements of women smuggled migrants under the Convention on the Elimination of All Forms of Discrimination

65 CERD General Recommendation No. 30, at para. 5. See also UN Committee on the Elimination of Racial Discrimination, "Guidelines for the CERD-Specific Document to be submitted by States Parties under Article 9, Paragraph 1, of the Convention," UN Doc. CERD/C/2007/1, June 13, 2008 (requiring under Articles 1, 3, and 5 reporting related to the situation of noncitizens).

66 See, for example, UN Committee on the Elimination of Racial Discrimination: "Concluding Observations: Israel" (advance unedited version), UN Doc. CERD/C/ISR/CO/14–16, Mar. 9, 2012; "Concluding Observations: Australia, UN Doc. CERD/C/AUS/CO/15–17, Sept. 13, 2010; "Concluding Observations: United Arab Emirates," UN Doc. CERD/C/ARE/CO/17, Sept. 21, 2009; "Concluding Observations: Russian Federation," UN Doc. CERD/C/RUS/CO/19, Sept. 22, 2008; "Concluding Observations: United States of America," UN Doc. CERD/C/USA/CO/6, May. 8, 2008; "Concluding Observations: Norway," UN Doc. CERD/C/NOR/CO/18, Oct. 19, 2006.

67 Convention against Torture and Other Cruel, Inhuman or Degrading Treatment or Punishment, 1465 UNTS 85, done Dec. 10, 1984, entered into force June 26, 1987 [Convention against Torture].

68 It is relevant to note that the concept of "inhuman or degrading treatment" is included in the Migrant Smuggling Protocol in the context of aggravated smuggling offenses. See further the discussion in Chapter 5, at 5.1.4.2.

69 Convention against Torture, at Art. 2(1) (emphasis added).

70 Ibid. at Art. 5(1)(a).

71 See M. Nowak and E. McArthur, *The United Nations Convention against Torture: A Commentary* (2008).

72 See further discussion in Chapter 3, at Section 3.4.4.

against Women (CEDAW)?[73] At the heart of this Convention is a broad prohibition on sex-based discrimination, the implications of which are considered at various points throughout this study. With respect to the application of this prohibition to nonnationals, the Convention is silent: while it does not specifically extend its application to all women within the territory or under the jurisdiction of a State Party, it also does not contain a CERD-type exclusionary clause. The Committee on the Elimination of Discrimination against Women (CEDAW Committee) has not directly addressed the issue through, for example, an explicit affirmation that nonnationals should receive the benefit of the rights guaranteed under CEDAW without discrimination. However, the CEDAW Committee does appear to base its own work on an assumption of broad applicability. It has, for example, repeatedly examined and expressed its concern for the situation of migrant women (vis-à-vis countries of destination) and other noncitizens, including migrant domestic workers, smuggled migrants, unaccompanied or undocumented female children, asylum-seekers, and refugees.[74] The CEDAW Committee has also affirmed that States Parties should ensure that foreign women are aware of their rights and have access to effective remedies when those rights are breached.[75]

[73] Convention on the Elimination of All Forms of Discrimination against Women, 1249 UNTS 13, done Dec. 18, 1979, entered into force Sept. 3, 1981.

[74] See, for example, UN Committee on the Elimination of Discrimination against Women: "Concluding Observations: New Zealand," (advance unedited version) UN Doc. CEDAW/C/NZL/CO/7, July 27, 2012 (migrant women, trafficking, and forced marriage); "Concluding Observations: Italy," UN Doc. CEDAW/C/ITA/CO/6, Aug. 2, 2011 (violence against women migrants, migrant prostitution); "Concluding Observations: Germany," UN Doc. CEDAW/C/DEU/CO/6, Feb. 12, 2009, at para. 34 (refugees and asylum-seekers); "Concluding Observations: Bahrain," UN Doc. CEDAW/C/BHR/CO/2, Nov. 14, 2008, at para. 30 (children of noncitizen parents) and 35 (migrant domestic workers); "Concluding Observations: Ecuador," UN Doc. CEDAW/C/ECU/CO/7, Nov. 7, 2008, at para. 26 (migrants, refugees, and asylum-seekers); "Concluding Observations: Belize," UN Doc. CEDAW/C/BLZ/CO/4, Aug. 10, 2007, at para. 33 (undocumented girl children); "Concluding Observations: Singapore," UN Doc. CEDAW/C/SGP/CO/3, Aug. 10, 2007, at paras. 21 (trafficked women and girls) and 23–24 (migrant domestic workers); "Concluding Observations: Greece," UN Doc. CEDAW/C/GRC/CO/6, Feb. 2, 2007, at paras. 31–32 (children of immigrant women); "Concluding Observations: Poland," UN Doc. CEDAW/C/POL/CO/6, Feb. 2, 2007, at para. 28 (refugees, asylum-seekers, and migrants); "Concluding Observations: China," UN Doc. CEDAW/C/CHN/CO/6, Aug. 25, 2006, at paras. 33 (refugees and asylum-seekers, and noting the precarious status and vulnerability of (presumably smuggled) North Korean women to abuse, trafficking, forced marriage, and virtual slavery) and 41 (migrant domestic workers); "Concluding Observations: The Former Yugoslav Republic of Macedonia," UN Doc. CEDAW/C/MKD/CO/3, Feb. 3, 2006, at para. 29 (refugees and asylum-seekers).

[75] See, for example, UN Committee on the Elimination of Discrimination against Women, "Concluding Comments: Germany," UN Doc. A/53/38 at 29, Aug. 17, 2000, at para. 318, cited in A. Byrnes, M. Herminia Graterol, and R. Chartres, "State Obligation and the Convention on the Elimination of All Forms of Discrimination against Women" (UNSW Law Research Paper No. 2007–48, July 19, 2007), at 56. Note however that such observations are rare, and the Committee's references to remedies are typically broad and formulaic.

Two General Recommendations of the CEDAW Committee touch directly on the application of this instrument to nonnationals. The first of these, adopted in 2008, concerned the rights of women migrant workers. In this context the Committee affirmed that "[w]hile States are entitled to control their borders and regulate migration, they must do so in full compliance with their obligations as parties to the human rights treaties they have ratified or acceded to."[76] General Recommendation 26 broadly affirms the applicability of a full range of Convention rights to women migrant workers but does not directly address the situation of nonnationals. This was remedied, at least in part, through General Recommendation No. 28 on the core obligations of States Parties under Article 2 of the Convention, released in 2010. The Recommendation confirms that Article 2 imposes on States Parties an obligation to pursue a policy of eliminating discrimination against women. That policy must, in the view of the Committee, "identify women within the jurisdiction of the State party (including non-citizen, migrant, refugee, asylum-seeking and stateless women) as the rights-bearers, with particular emphasis on the groups of women who are most marginalized and who may suffer from various forms of intersectional discrimination."[77] In a clumsily worded but otherwise clear paragraph, the Committee also affirms the application of the Convention's provisions to noncitizens:

> Although subject to international law, States primarily exercise territorial jurisdiction. The obligations of States parties apply, however, without discrimination both to citizens and non-citizens, including refugees, asylum-seekers, migrant workers and stateless persons, within their territory or effective control, even if not situated within the territory. States parties are responsible for all their actions affecting human rights, regardless of whether the affected persons are in their territory.[78]

2.1.1.6. Convention on the Rights of the Child

The Convention on the Rights of the Child (CRC) applies to all children within the jurisdiction of the State Party, without discrimination of any kind.[79] Accordingly, all child smuggled migrants within the jurisdiction of a State Party are entitled to

76 CEDAW General Recommendation No. 26, at para. 3.

77 UN Committee on the Elimination of Discrimination against Women, "General Recommendation No. 28 on the Core Obligations of States Parties under Article 2 of the Convention on the Elimination of All Forms of Discrimination against Women," UN Doc. CEDAW/C/GC/28, Dec. 16, 2010, at para. 26.

78 Ibid. at para. 12.

79 States Parties are required to "respect and ensure the rights set forth in the present Convention to each child within their jurisdiction without discrimination of any kind, irrespective of the child's or his or her parent's or legal guardian's race, colour, sex, language, religion, political or other opinion, national, ethnic or social origin, property, disability, birth or other status": CRC, at Art. 2(1).

the full protection of that instrument, irrespective of any other factor including their nationality or citizenship. The Committee on the Rights of the Child (CRC Committee), established to oversee implementation of this instrument, has explicitly affirmed that domestic implementation must ensure that the rights contained in the Convention protect all children, including noncitizens.[80] The CRC Committee routinely deals with issues affecting noncitizens, including refugees and asylum-seekers (who are very often smuggled), stateless persons, child migrant workers, and victims of trafficking.[81] The CRC Committee has also, through the mechanism of its General Comments, addressed the matter of unaccompanied children, identifying specific obligations toward this category of noncitizen vis-à-vis the destination State.[82] The CRC Committee is perhaps alone among the major human rights treaty bodies in specifically addressing the human rights implications of anti-migrant smuggling policies and practices, including those aimed at preventing the arrival of smuggled migrants.[83]

80 "[T]he enjoyment of rights stipulated in the Convention is not limited to children who are citizens of a State party and must therefore, if not explicitly stated otherwise in the Convention, also be available to all children – including asylum-seeking, refugee and migrant children – irrespective of their nationality, immigration status or statelessness": UN Committee on the Rights of the Child, "General Comment No. 6: Treatment of Unaccompanied and Separated Children Outside Their Country of Origin," UN Doc. CRC/GC/2005/6, Sept. 1, 2005 [CRC General Comment No. 6], at para. 12.

81 See, for example, UN Committee on the Rights of the Child: "Concluding Observations: Italy," UN Doc. CRC/C/ITA/CO3–4, Oct. 31, 2011, at paras. 63–66 (protection of unaccompanied children; rights of child asylum-seekers and others during "push-back" operations); "Concluding Observations: Spain," UN Doc. CRC/C/ESP/CO/3–4, Nov. 3, 2010, at paras. 57–60 (unaccompanied children; refugee and migrant children); "Concluding Observations: Chad," UN Doc. CRC/C/TCD/CO/2, Feb. 12, 2009, at paras. 40 (children of refugees and nomads), 71 (protection of refugee children from recruitment into military service), 73–74 (refugee children, including unaccompanied and separated children), and 77–78 (protection of refugee children from child labor); "Concluding Observations: Georgia," UN Doc. CRC/C/GEO/CO/3, June 23, 2008, at para. 59 (asylum-seeking and refugee children, including unaccompanied and separated children); "Concluding Observations: Jordan," UN Doc. CRC/C/JOR/CO/3, Sept. 29, 2007, at para. 80 (asylum-seeking and refugee children, particularly unaccompanied children); "Concluding Observations: Costa Rica," UN Doc. CRC/C/OPSC/CRI/CO/1, May 2, 2007, at para. 20 (migrant, smuggled, and trafficked children); "Concluding Observations: Latvia," UN Doc. CRC/C/LVA/CO/2, June 28, 2006, at para. 17 (identifying noncitizen, stateless, refugee, and minority group children as requiring special attention); "Concluding Observations: Mexico," UN Doc. CRC/C/MEX/CO/3, June 8, 2006, at paras. 60–61 (unaccompanied migrant and refugee children). For detailed additional references and analysis of the Committee's work in this area, see A. Gallagher, "Article 35," in P. Alston and J. Tobin, *The UN Convention on the Rights of the Child: A Commentary* (forthcoming 2014).

82 CRC General Comment No. 6.

83 See, for example, UN Committee on the Rights of the Child: "Concluding Observations: Italy," UN Doc. CRC/C/ITA/CO/3–4, Oct. 31, 2011, at para. 63: "The Committee welcomes the prohibition to expel or return persons under the age of 18 years and pregnant women under the immigration laws of the State party. It notes with concern, however, that children of foreign origin can be expelled from the country for reasons of public order and State security and that the State party, in implementing the 2009 interception policy of migrants ("push-back" policy), has returned children, including

2.1.1.7. Regional Human Rights Instruments

The level of variation found within the international human rights instruments with respect to nonnationals/noncitizens is reflected in the regional human rights instruments. The African Charter on Human and Peoples' Rights is perhaps the most inclusive, with almost every substantive right applying to "every individual" or "every human being," a broad nondiscrimination clause also referring to "every individual,"[84] and an open-ended list of grounds of prohibited discrimination.[85] The Charter's specific reference to "every citizen" in relation to the right to participate in government and public service[86] lends weight to the view that its other provisions apply to all persons, without distinction as to nationality or alienage. This position has been confirmed by the African Commission on Human and Peoples' Rights with respect to several key articles of the Charter.[87] The African Charter on the Rights and Welfare of the Child refers to "every child" being entitled to the enjoyment of the rights and freedoms recognized and guaranteed in that instrument.[88]

The American Convention on Human Rights guarantees almost every right contained in that instrument to "all persons subject to [the State Parties'] jurisdiction"[89] and confirms that "[f]or the purposes of this Convention, 'person' means every human being."[90] The Convention's nondiscrimination clause includes the

unaccompanied children, without examining the individual circumstances of each child or providing each child with a possibility to request asylum. The Committee is deeply concerned that some of the migrants pushed back have been identified as requiring international protection, in violation of the State party's non-refoulement obligations. It is further of serious concern to the Committee that the State party has detained children with their families when forcibly returning migrants, without the possibility to seek asylum."

84 "Every individual shall be entitled to the enjoyment of the rights and freedoms recognized and guaranteed in the present Charter without distinction of any kind such as race, ethnic group, color, sex, language, religion, political or any other opinion, national and social origin, fortune, birth or other status": African Charter on Human and Peoples' Rights, at Art. 2.

85 Ibid.

86 Ibid. at Art. 13.

87 See "The Rights of Non-Citizens: Progress Report of the Special Rapporteur, Mr David Weissbrodt: Addendum: Regional Activities," UN Doc. E/CN.4/Sub.2/2002/25/Add.2, June 3, 2002, at 2–22. The African Court on Human and Peoples' Rights, which became operational in 2006, is yet to directly pronounce on these issues.

88 African Charter on the Rights and Welfare of the Child, OAU Doc. CAB/LEG/24.9/49, done July 11, 1990, entered into force Nov. 29, 1999 [African Children's Charter], at Art. 3.

89 American Convention on Human Rights, at Art. 1. Article 22 of the Convention, dealing with freedom of movement, and residence, applies only to "[e]very person lawfully in the territory of a State Party." Article 23 guarantees the right to participation in government to "every citizen."

90 Ibid. at Art. 1(2). The inclusive nature of the American Convention is reinforced by the following paragraph of the preamble: "Recognizing that the essential rights of man are not derived from one's being a national of a certain State, but are based upon attributes of the human personality, and that they therefore justify international protection in the form of a Convention reinforcing or complementing the protection provided by the domestic law of the American States."

traditional grounds, extending to "any other social condition," a concept that does not appear to leave room for the inclusion of grounds such as national origin or alienage.[91]

The Convention for the Protection of Human Rights and Fundamental Freedoms (European Convention on Human Rights) contains a broad, open-ended nondiscrimination clause[92] and States Parties are required to "secure to everyone within their jurisdiction the rights and freedoms defined in [the Convention]."[93] The exclusion of "aliens" from the protection of the nondiscrimination clause with respect to one area[94] supports a contention that the remaining provisions of the Convention apply to all persons, not just nationals. The European Court of Human Rights has affirmed, on a number of occasions, the application of certain of the Convention's provisions to noncitizens – including third-country nationals.[95] The prohibition on inhuman treatment and the right to a family life have been repeatedly confirmed as applicable to all persons within Europe.[96] The situation may be less positive for socioeconomic rights, which suffer from relative neglect in the Convention itself as well as from the implicit tie with citizenship and nationality.[97] In this regard it is relevant to note that the European Social Charter makes a clear distinction between the entitlements of nonnationals lawfully present and those persons of an irregular status.[98] Within the Court itself there appears to be a strong and consistent push to

[91] "The States Parties to this Convention undertake to respect the rights and freedoms recognized herein and to ensure to all persons subject to their jurisdiction the free and full exercise of those rights and freedoms, without any discrimination for reasons of race, color, sex, language, religion, political or other opinion, national or social origin, economic status, birth, or any other social condition": ibid. at Art. 1. The term "social condition" is the only novel ground and its parameters are yet to be explored.

[92] "The enjoyment of the rights and freedoms set forth in this Convention shall be secured without discrimination on any ground such as sex, race, colour, language, religion, political or other opinion, national or social origin, association with a national minority, property, birth or other status": European Convention on Human Rights, at Art. 14.

[93] Ibid. at Art. 1.

[94] Ibid. at Art. 16, relating to the political activities of aliens.

[95] For a review of relevant case law, see generally H. Lambert, *The Position of Aliens in Relation to the European Convention on Human Rights*, Council of Europe (2007) [Lambert, *The Position of Aliens in Relation to the European Convention on Human Rights*].

[96] For an overview of relevant case law on the Article 8 right to protection of private and family life in the context of migration control and with a view to the impact on the status of irregular migrants in Europe, see D. Thym, "Respect for Private and Family Life under Article 8 ECHR in Immigration Cases: A Human Right to Regularize Illegal Stay?," (2008) 57 *International and Comparative Law Quarterly* 87.

[97] See R. O'Connell, "Only Partial Neglect? Developments in the Case-Law of the European Court on Human Rights on Socio-Economic Rights of Non-Nationals," in W. Benedek, W. Karl, A. Mijr, M. Nowak, and M. Kettermann eds., *European Yearbook on Human Rights* 2010 at 245 (2010).

[98] European Social Charter (revised), 2151 UNTS 277, ETS No. 163, done May 3, 1996, entered into force July 1, 1999, at Art. 19 and Appendix to the European Social Charter (Revised), "Scope of the Revised European Social Charter in terms of persons protected."

recognize the applicability of the Convention's principal provisions to all persons within the jurisdiction or effective control of States Parties.[99] However, European efforts to counter irregular migration, including through migrant smuggling, have repeatedly challenged judicial assertions of the Convention's broad applicability to nonnationals. These developments are considered at various points later on in the chapter (e.g., in relation to the prohibition on arbitrary expulsion) as well as in the following chapter in the context of an examination of the extraterritorial application of the European Convention on Human Rights and other human rights instruments.

2.1.1.8. Conclusion on Application of Human Rights to Smuggled Migrants Who Are Noncitizens

There is a general, in-principle and in-law consensus on the applicability of certain fundamental human rights to *all* persons, including smuggled migrants who are non-nationals or noncitizens. These rights include (but may well not be limited to) the right to life, liberty and security of person; liberty of movement including the right to return to one's own country; protection from inhuman treatment including *non-refoulement*; protection from arbitrary expulsion; freedom of thought, conscience, and religion; the right to privacy; the right to a family life; the right to recognition and equal protection before the law; the right not to be discriminated against on the basis of race, sex, language, religion, or other prohibited ground; and the right to health, education, and housing.[100] As noted in the introduction to this subsection, certain categories of noncitizens, such as stateless persons, migrant workers, asylum-seekers, refugees, trafficked persons, and children, will be entitled to additional status-related protection.[101] Beyond these fundamental rights, entitlements of noncitizens and obligations of States to them is highly uneven, typically depending on the terms of a particular treaty that is being or may be invoked. Most

[99] See generally, Lambert, *The Position of Aliens in Relation to the European Convention on Human Rights*. Lambert's review of relevant case law leads her to conclude that the Court "has been able to control states' freedom in the area of immigration, residence, and integration of aliens through a generous application of the principle of proportionality and a liberal interpretation of provisions" of the Convention. Ibid. at 22.

[100] This list is drawn on the analysis of the international and regional instruments considered previously as well as various reports of the Special Rapporteur on the Rights of Non-Citizens ("The Rights of Non-Citizens: Preliminary Report of the Special Rapporteur, Mr David Weissbrodt," UN Doc. E/CN.4/Sub.2/2001/20, June 6, 2001; "The Rights of Non-Citizens: Progress Report of the Special Rapporteur, Mr David Weissbrodt," UN Doc. E/CN.4/Sub.2/2002/25, June 5, 2002; "The Rights of Non-Citizens: Final Report of the Special Rapporteur, Mr David Weissbrodt," UN Doc. E/CN.4/Sub.2/2003/23, May 26, 2003); and from a distillation of the findings of those reports published in OHCHR, *The Rights of Non-Citizens*, esp. at 15–26.

[101] See further OHCHR, *The Rights of Non-Citizens*, at 28–34.

critically however, it is clear that, as a matter of international law, the fundamental rights likely to be of central relevance to smuggled migrants cannot be denied them solely on the basis of their status as aliens or noncitizens.

In deciding whether a category distinction between citizens and noncitizens is lawful, international human rights treaty bodies and regional courts have tended toward basing such decisions on considerations of reasonableness and proportionality.[102] This appears to accord with customary international law, under which substantive distinctions in treatment between nationals and nonnationals require a legitimate aim, objective justification, and reasonable proportionality between the distinction and its aims.[103] The previous analysis of treaty rules and practice confirms that a summary of the generally accepted approach advanced in 1983 is still applicable today:

> Distinctions are reasonable if they pursue a legitimate aim and have an objective justification, and a reasonable relationship of proportionality exists between the aim sought to be realized and the means employed. These criteria will usually be satisfied if the particular measures can reasonably be interpreted as being in the public interest as a whole and do not arbitrarily single out individuals or groups for invidious treatment.[104]

102 For example, the UN Human Rights Committee has stated that "[a] differentiation which is compatible with the provisions of the Covenant and is based on reasonable grounds does not amount to prohibited discrimination within the meaning of article 26": *Simunek et al v. Czech Republic*, UNHRC Comm. No. 516/1992, UN Doc. CCPR/C/54/D/516/1992, July 31, 1995, decided July 19, 1995, at para. 11.5. See also *Juridical Conditions and Rights of Undocumented Migrants*, Advisory Opinion OC=18/03, Inter-Am Ct. H.R. (ser. A) No. 18, Sept. 17, 2003, at para. 119: "States may not discriminate or tolerate discriminatory situations that prejudice migrants. However, the State may grant a distinct treatment to documented migrants with respect to undocumented migrants, or between migrants and nationals, provided that this differential treatment is reasonable, objective, proportionate and does not harm human rights. For example, distinctions may be made between migrants and nationals regarding ownership of some political rights."

103 Goodwin-Gill, for example, cites Judge Tanaka's dissenting judgment in the *South West Africa Cases* as support for the claim that the reasons for a distinction must first be relevant, and the measures subsequently adopted must be both reasonable and proportional: "[i]f individuals differ from one another ... their needs will be different, and accordingly, the content of the law may not be identical. Hence is derived the relativity of law to individual circumstances ... A different treatment comes into question only when and to the extent that it corresponds to the nature of the difference ... The issue is whether the difference exists ... Different treatment must not be given arbitrarily; it requires reasonableness, or must be in conformity with justice": *South West Africa Cases (Second Phase) (Ethiopia v. South Africa; Liberia v. South Africa)*, [1966] ICJ Rep 6, at 305, 313, cited in G. S. Goodwin-Gill, "Forced Migration and Human Rights" (Paper presented at the Expert Meeting on International Legal Norms and Migration, May 23–25, 2002). See McDougal et al., "The Protection of Aliens," at 444: although "[i]t is seldom seriously asserted that states cannot differentiate between nationals and aliens," such differentiation must "bear a reasonable relation to the differences in their obligations and loyalties."

104 J. A. Dent, *Research Paper on the Social and Economic Rights of Non-Nationals in Europe*, at 9, citing W. McKean, *Equality and Discrimination under International Law* (1983), at 287.

While affirming the protections available to non-nationals and noncitizens, it is important not to overstate their legal strength and political worth. The universality of human rights continues to be something of a legal fiction, most particularly for non-nationals and noncitizens who are within the State or seeking to enter it without authorization. States have studiously avoided locking themselves into a binding statement of rights of noncitizens and many continue to resist efforts aimed at formalizing obligations owed to this category of persons. A sobering example is provided by the long and troubled history of the United Nations Convention on the Rights of Migrant Workers, an instrument that has singularly failed to gain the support of those States that are most crucial to its effective realization.[105] Overall, progress in articulating and defending the rights of noncitizens within the broader human rights system has been incremental and somewhat one-sided, and continues to be hampered by the terms of some of the major treaties that permit differentiation under certain circumstances. It is also important to flag the high levels of discrepancy between entitlement and capacity to exercise that entitlement. Particularly in the case of irregular migrants, even when rights are theoretically available, they will often be practically inaccessible.

2.1.2. *Migrant Smuggling, Statelessness, and Human Rights*

International law defines a stateless person as anyone who is "not considered a national by any State under the operation of its law."[106] It has long been recognized that "the fact of not having a nationality or not enjoying in practice the protection of a State places stateless persons, *de jure* or *de facto*, in a position of inferiority incompatible with the respect of human rights."[107]

There are important links between statelessness and smuggling. Statelessness creates an obvious incentive for persons in this situation to use the services of migrant smugglers, as it is otherwise virtually impossible for them to access the travel documents necessary to move legally across borders. Statelessness also increases vulnerability to exploitative smuggling, and stateless people who are smuggled face unique difficulties, for example with regard to establishing their identity and accessing

[105] See further Gallagher, *The International Law of Human Trafficking*, at 168–176.

[106] Convention Relating to the Status of Stateless Persons, 360 UNTS 117, done Sept. 28, 1954, entered into force June 6, 1960 [Convention Relating to the Status of Stateless Persons], at Art. 1. For a useful examination of the various elements of this definition, see the Summary Conclusions of the United Nations High Commissioner for Refugees (UNHCR) Expert Meeting on the Concept of Stateless Persons under International Law ("Prato Conclusions"), 27–28 May 2010, esp. at part I, paras. 8–27.

[107] United Nations Department of Social Affairs, "A Study of Statelessness," Aug. 1949 (reedited by UNHCR, 1995), cited in H. Massey, "UNHCR and *De Facto* Statelessness," UNHCR Legal and Protection Policy Research Series (2010) [Massey, "UNHCR and *De Facto* Statelessness"], at 7.

protection and support. Smuggling can sometimes result in statelessness, for example, in relation to women who are smuggled abroad for marriage or other purposes and who in the process (often because of nationality laws that discriminate on the basis of sex) lose their nationality and/or that of their children.[108] Most common is a situation of de facto statelessness affecting smuggled migrants who, unable or unwilling to establish their nationality, languish in detention, often for long periods of time.[109]

The human rights and obligations identified previously as applicable to smuggled migrants who are noncitizens apply, as minimum standards, to stateless persons (whether stateless de jure or de facto). Stateless persons may also, under certain circumstances and in relation to certain areas, be entitled to additional or special rights.[110] The specialist framework around this issue, application of which is largely confined to de jure stateless persons, is established through two treaties: the Convention Relating to the Status of Stateless Persons (1954) and the Convention on the Reduction of Statelessness[111] (1961), and is reinforced by the major international

[108] Statelessness has not yet been subject to detailed examination from the perspective of migrant smuggling. For a discussion of such problems in the context of trafficking, see United States Department of State, "Trafficking in Persons Report" (2009), at 31; Vital Voices, "Stateless and Vulnerable to Human Trafficking in Thailand" (2007). For a review of issues of displacement and statelessness from a gender perspective, see UN Committee on the Elimination of Discrimination against Women, "Summary of background paper entitled 'Displacement, Statelessness and Questions of Gender Equality and the Convention on the Elimination of All Forms of Discrimination against Women'," UN Doc. CEDAW/C/2009/II/WP.3, July 1, 2009.

[109] UNHCR has defined de facto stateless persons as "persons outside the country of their nationality who are unable or, for valid reasons, are unwilling to avail themselves of the protection of that country. Protection in this sense refers to the right of diplomatic protection exercised by a State of nationality in order to remedy an internationally wrongful act against one of its nationals, as well as diplomatic and consular protection and assistance generally, including in relation to return to the State of nationality": Summary Conclusions of the UNHCR Expert Meeting on the Concept of Stateless Persons under International Law ("Prato Conclusions"), 27–28 May 2010, at part II, para. 2. With regard to undocumented migrants, UNHCR has noted: "Irregular migrants who are without identity documentation may or may not be unable or unwilling to avail themselves of the protection of the country of their nationality. As a rule there should have been a request for, and a refusal of, protection before it can be established that a person is *de facto* stateless. For example, Country A may make a finding that a particular individual is a national of Country B, and may seek to return that individual to Country B. Whether or not the individual is *de facto* stateless may depend on whether or not Country B is willing to cooperate in the process of identifying the individual's nationality and/or permit his or her return. Thus, prolonged non-cooperation including where the country of nationality does not respond to the host country's communications can also be considered as a refusal of protection in this context": ibid. at part II, para. 10. For further on the evolving concept of de facto statelessness and its limits, see Massey, "UNHCR and *De Facto* Statelessness."

[110] For a detailed consideration of these status-based rights, see D. Weissbrodt and C. Collins, "The Human Rights of Stateless Persons" (2006) 28 *Human Rights Quarterly* 245.

[111] Convention on the Reduction of Statelessness, 989 UNTS 175, done Aug. 30, 1961, entered into force Dec. 13, 1975 [Convention on the Reduction of Statelessness].

and regional human rights treaties.[112] International treaty law, and arguably also customary international law, prohibits States from depriving an individual of his or her nationality if this would result in statelessness.[113] States are also generally required to avoid actions that would result in statelessness.[114] This latter obligation should be viewed as extending to situations where statelessness arises through omission or neglect. In the context of human trafficking, for example, it has been asserted by UNHCR that this obligation would be violated: (1) when destination countries fail to undertake timely and effective identity checks in respect of irregular migrants, including those who have been trafficked, who are unable to prove their nationality through the usual means; and (2) when countries of origin fail to cooperate in such processes.[115]

2.2. RIGHT TO LEAVE AND RETURN

As flagged briefly in the introduction to this book, and discussed in detail in the following chapter, the sovereign power of a State to control the entry of nonnationals into its territory is well established in international law. A corollary to this power is, of course, the absence of a right of individuals to enter or reside in the territory of other States. Although international law recognizes the right of persons to leave any country, including their own, and to return to their country, it does not, aside from certain exceptions of limited applicability (but of central importance to the current discussion), recognize the existence of a corresponding right to enter or reside in a country other than one's own. Each of these rights, as well as the implications of their somewhat dichotomous relationship, is considered in detail later in the chapter.

2.2.1. *The Right to Leave*

Recognition of at least a qualified right to leave one's country can be traced back to the Magna Carta of 1215.[116] However, evolution of this right has been compromised

[112] For example, Article 7 of CRC and Article 24 of ICCPR effectively require the State to grant citizenship to children born in their territories who would otherwise be rendered stateless.

[113] Convention on the Reduction of Statelessness, at Art. 8(1).

[114] See generally, Convention on the Reduction of Statelessness.

[115] UN High Commissioner for Refugees, *Guidelines on International Protection: The Application of Article 1A(2) of the 1951 Convention and/or 1967 Protocol relating to the Status of Refugees to Victims of Trafficking and Persons at Risk of Being Trafficked*, UN Doc. HCR/GIP/06/07, Apr. 7, 2006, at paras. 41–43. Note that this position is somewhat at odds with the more conservative interpretation of obligations around statelessness set out in the Prato Conclusions cited at note 106 of this chapter.

[116] "In future, it shall be lawful for any man to leave and return to our kingdom unharmed and without fear, by land or water, and preserving his allegiance to us, except in time of war, for some short time, for the common benefit of the realm": chapter 42, cited in G. Cornelisse, *Immigration Detention and Human Rights* (2010) [Cornelisse, *Immigration Detention and Human Rights*], at 137.

and uneven. The restrictive emigration policies of colonial powers and, more recently, of the Union of Soviet Socialist Republics (USSR), China, and Cuba under communism illustrate the political obstacles to realization of an unfettered right to leave one's country.

Does international law permit a State to prevent citizens from leaving their own country? More particularly, is a State allowed (or even required) to prevent departure by irregular or unauthorized means, and can such departure be subject to prosecution or other sanction? These are not theoretical questions but ones with routine practical significance for numerous individuals. Many countries impose strict conditions on the exit of their citizens, and some explicitly criminalize unauthorized exit. In recent years, a number of countries have reacted to the growth in facilitated irregular migration by imposing a range of restrictions on – or interferences with – departure. States wishing to control entry of noncitizens into their territories can and often do demand, encourage, and even facilitate the imposition of such restrictions on departure by countries of origin and transit.[117] Some countries of destination have allegedly overseen or conducted more direct interventions aimed at preventing departure such as sabotaging vessels used to smuggle migrants.[118] More formal restrictions associated with destination-country efforts to prevent migrant smuggling from source or transit points include visa requirements and predeparture checks.[119] The interception of vessels is another common strategy to prevent or check departure.[120] Returning migrants have also been sanctioned for their unauthorized departure.[121]

Goodwin-Gill's position, that "it is not yet unlawful to move or to migrate, or to seek asylum, even if the criminalisation of 'irregular emigration' by sending states seems to be desired by the developed world"[122] is difficult to refute. However State practice appears to indicate that the right to leave falls somewhat short of a universally accepted norm, which, in the words of one commentator, is "neither enforced, nor taken seriously by those states unwilling to grant the right to leave to their citizens

117 See discussion of examples of bilateral instruments concluded for this purpose in Chapter 1, at Section 1.3.2.

118 For example, such allegations have been made against the Australian Federal Police in relation to that Agency's efforts to disrupt migrant smuggling operations in Indonesia. See C. Stewart, "Rocking the Boat," *The Weekend Australian*, Dec. 14, 2002, available at http://sievx.com/articles/challenging/20021214CameronStewart.html (accessed Nov. 18 2013). See also M. Grewcock, *Border Crimes: Australia's War on Illicit Migrants* (2009).

119 For a useful overview of State practice with respect to both visa requirements and pre-embarkation controls, see B. Ryan, "Extraterritorial Immigration Control: What Role for Legal Guarantees?," in B. Ryan and V. Mitsilegas eds., *Extraterritorial Immigration Control: Legal Challenges* 1 (2010), at 3–22.

120 See further the detailed discussion of interception at sea in Chapter 6.

121 For example, in Lao PDR. See A. T. Gallagher, "A Shadow Report on Human Trafficking in Lao PDR: The US Approach vs. International Law" (2006) 15 *Asian and Pacific Migration Journal* 525.

122 G. S. Goodwin-Gill, "The Right to Seek Asylum: Interception at Sea and the Principle of *Non-Refoulement*" (2011) 23(3) *International Journal of Refugee Law* 443, at 444.

and/or residents."[123] This is despite formal confirmation of its status as a separate entitlement as well as a core component of the broader right to freedom of movement. The Universal Declaration of Human Rights was the first instrument to affirm the existence of such a right, stating clearly that "[e]veryone has the right to leave any country."[124] Freedom to leave any country, including one's own, is also protected by the ICCPR,[125] CERD,[126] CRC,[127] the Migrant Workers Convention,[128] and all major regional human rights treaties.[129] In its implementation the right to leave has always been limited by practical realities relating to, for example, the individual's status as a minor or as a convicted criminal. The relevant instruments accommodate this reality by envisaging the possibility of lawful derogation in certain prescribed circumstances. The ICCPR, for example, does not permit restrictions on the right to leave "except those which are provided by law, are necessary to protect national security, public order (*ordre public*), public health or morals or the rights and freedoms of others, and are consistent with … other rights."[130] Accordingly, the lawfulness of any restriction on the right to leave is to be measured with reference to whether it is: (1) provided by law; (2) necessary on the basis of one or more stipulated grounds; and (3) consistent with other rights including, for example, the prohibition on discrimination.

As Hannum has noted, the right to leave is formulated in absolute terms, indicating that the appropriate point of departure is the widest possible scope of the freedom to move out of any country, including one's own.[131] A broad interpretation of the right to leave has been confirmed by the UN Human Rights Committee, the

[123] See, for example, D. Kochenov, "The Right to Leave any Country," in R. Plender ed., *International Migration Law* (forthcoming 2013), available at http://papers.ssrn.com/sol3/papers.cfm?abstract_id=1847769 (accessed May 12, 2013) [Kochenov, "The Right to Leave Any Country"], at 12.

[124] UDHR, at Art. 13(2). See also Article 29, which sets out applicable restrictions on this and other rights.

[125] ICCPR, at Art. 12(2).

[126] CERD, at Art. 5(d)(ii).

[127] CRC, at Art. 10(2).

[128] International Convention on the Protection of the Rights of All Migrant Workers and Members of Their Families, 2220 UNTS 3, done Dec. 18, 1990, entered into force July 1, 2003 [Migrant Workers Convention], at Art. 8(1).

[129] Protocol No. 4 to the Convention of 4 November 1950 for the Protection of Human Rights and Fundamental Freedoms, 1496 UNTS 263, done Sept. 16, 1963, entered into force May 2, 1968 [Protocol No. 4 to the European Convention on Human Rights], at Art. 2(2); American Convention on Human Rights, at Art. 22(2); African Charter on Human and Peoples' Rights, at Art. 12(2).

[130] ICCPR, at Art. 12(3). For generally equivalent provisions, see Protocol No. 4 to the European Convention on Human Rights, at Art. 2(3); American Convention on Human Rights, at Art. 22(3); African Charter on Human and Peoples' Rights, at Art. 12(2).

[131] H. Hannum, *The Right to Leave and Return in International Law and Practice* (1987) [Hannum, *The Right to Leave and Return*], at 19. This is confirmed in UN Human Rights Committee, "General Comment No. 27: Freedom of Movement," UN Doc. HRI/GEN/1/Rev.7, at 153, May 12, 2004, adopted Apr. 10, 1992 [HRC General Comment No. 27], at para. 13: "the relation between right and restriction, between norm and exception, must not be reversed."

only international body to have examined this right in any detail.[132] In its General Comment No. 27 on freedom of movement, adopted in 1999, the Committee confirmed the right to leave as essentially a right to travel.[133] From this perspective, an action such as the withholding or withdrawal of a vital travel document such as a passport without permissible justification would operate to violate the right to leave.[134] More broadly, General Comment No. 27 requires that any restrictions on the right to leave not impair the essence of the right.[135] Such restrictions must be proportionate, appropriate under the circumstances, and the "least intrusive instrument amongst those which might achieve the desired result."[136] Application of restrictions must "in any individual case, be based on clear legal grounds and meet the test of necessity and the requirements of proportionality."[137]

What of the link between State capacity or obligation to act against irregular migration, including through migrant smuggling, and the right to leave? At least one scholar has misunderstood the impact of the Migrant Smuggling Protocol, asserting in error that it "requires States to prevent migrants from leaving their territory by unauthorised or irregular means ... while criminal liability of smuggled migrants is excluded, this does not authorize migrants to leave their country by irregular means."[138] Referencing the legal regime established under the United Nations Convention against Transnational Organized Crime[139] and its Protocols, Harvey and Barnidge correctly conclude that:

> restrictions on the movement of the smuggled person will have to be justified within the terms of [ICCPR] article 12(3). The state must demonstrate that these

[132] Note also an earlier report on this subject requested by the UN Sub-Commission on Prevention of Discrimination and Protection of Minorities: J. D. Inglés, Special Rapporteur, "Study on Discrimination in Respect of the Right of Everyone to Leave Any Country, Including His Own, and to Return to His Country," UN Doc. E/CN.4/Sub.2/220/Rev.1, Jan. 1, 1963. Annex VI of this report sets out a number of principles attaching to the right to leave that, according to Kochenov, were used extensively in interpreting Article 12(2) of the ICCPR during the final decades of the twentieth century and formed the basis of General Comment 27, adopted by the Human Rights Committee in 1999. See further Kochenov, "The Right to Leave Any Country," at 10–12.

[133] HRC General Comment No. 27, at para. 9.

[134] See, for example, *Loubna El Ghar v. Socialist People's Libyan Arab Jamahiriya*, UNHRC Comm. No. 1107/2002, UN Doc. CCPR/C/82/D/1107/2002, Nov. 15, 2004, decided Mar. 29, 2004.

[135] HRC General Comment No. 27, at para. 13: "the relation between right and restriction, between norm and exception, must not be reversed."

[136] Ibid. at para. 14.

[137] Ibid. at para. 16.

[138] R. Perruchoud, "State Sovereignty and Freedom of Movement," in B. Opeskin, R. Perruchoud, and J. Redpath-Cross, *Foundations of International Migration Law* 123 (2012), at 139. Perruchoud adds: "It is yet to be determined whether implementation of the Smuggling Protocol will lead to a broad interpretation of the restrictions permitted by the ICCPR and hence to a further limitation of the right to leave, in the fight against irregular migration" (ibid.). For a detailed explanation of the scope of the Protocol in this regard see Chapter 5.

[139] United Nations Convention against Transnational Organized Crime, 2225 UNTS 209, done Nov. 15, 2000, entered into force Sept. 29, 2003 [Organized Crime Convention].

> restrictions meet the tests of legality and necessity, are consistent with the other provisions of the ICCPR, and come under one of the listed grounds. A state must be in a position to argue that any direct or indirect restrictions are for the purpose of tackling the pressing problem of smuggling and trafficking.[140]

The Human Rights Committee has acknowledged that externalization of immigration control can potentially violate the right to leave.[141] It is apparent that at least some of the common tactics used by States to restrict the departure of their citizens or nationals of a third State in the name of addressing smuggling will fail to meet the test mandated by that body. Such practices would include unreasonable restrictions on the issuing of passports and the requirement of special exit visas,[142] as well as the criminalization of irregular departure. Even if a State is able to argue that its emigration restrictions are based on a need to preserve public order or public morals through preventing smuggling, and that the measures taken are both necessary and in proportion to their stated aim, that same State must also be able to show that its restriction is nondiscriminatory in both intention and effect. Policies or practices that are directed toward or that disproportionately affect one group are unlikely to meet this standard.[143] It is also relevant to note that the requirement of necessity

[140] C. Harvey and R. P. Barnidge, Jr., "Human Rights, Free Movement and the Right to Leave in International Law" (2007) 19 *International Journal of Refugee Law* 1 [Harvey and Barnidge, "Human Rights, Free Movement and the Right to Leave in International Law"], at 14.

[141] See, for example, HRC General Comment No. 27, at para. 10: "The practice of States often shows that legal rules and administrative measures adversely affect the right to leave, in particular, a person's own country. It is therefore of the utmost importance that States parties report on all legal and practical restrictions on the right to leave which they apply both to nationals and to foreigners, in order to enable the Committee to assess the conformity of these rules and practices with article 12, paragraph 3. States Parties should also include information in their reports on measures that impose sanctions on international carriers which bring to their territory persons without required documents, where those measures affect the right to leave another country."

[142] For an overview of the jurisprudence of the UN Human Rights Committee on the issues of passports and exit visas, see generally: Hannum, *The Right to Leave and Return*; Harvey and Barnidge, "Human Rights, Free Movement and the Right to Leave in International Law." The UN Human Rights Committee has provided a list of practices and rules that will operate to obstruct the right to leave: "lack of access for applicants to the competent authorities and lack of information regarding requirements; the requirement to apply for special forms through which the proper application documents for the issuance of a passport can be obtained; the need for supportive statements from employers or family members; exact description of the travel route; issuance of passports only on payment of high fees substantially exceeding the cost of the service rendered by the administration; unreasonable delays in the issuance of travel documents; restrictions on family members travelling together; requirement of a repatriation deposit or a return ticket; requirement of an invitation from the State of destination or from people living there; harassment of applicants, for example by physical intimidation, arrest, loss of employment or expulsion of their children from school or university; refusal to issue a passport because the applicant is said to harm the good name of the country": HRC General Comment No. 27, at para. 17.

[143] For example, in the *European Roma Rights Centre Case*, the House of Lords found that the prescreening of potential migrants at the Prague airport by British immigration officials that led to Roma

and proportionality has an individual aspect to it, requiring that any interference with the right to leave one's country is justifiable and proportionate in the individual circumstances of a particular case.[144] In addition, as restrictions must be provided by law, extralegal measures such as passport confiscation by law enforcement officials would also be contrary to the right to leave. The penalizing of returning migrants for unauthorized departure in circumstances where the original restriction cannot be justified is another example of a practice unlikely to meet the test set out previously.

The right to leave can, in practice, be obstructed by another State – typically the country of expected destination. Common destination-country initiated obstructions include predeparture screening operations and carrier sanctions (that effectively also require additional screening at the point of departure) as well as more informal disruption measures. These mechanisms and practices are invariably implemented with the acquiescence of the country of origin. Their legality is to be judged with reference to the test outlined previously,[145] and it is reasonable to assume that the starting point is one in favor of the right: absent special circumstances justifiable with reference to interests of national security or public safety, for the maintenance of *ordre public*, for the prevention of crime,[146] for the protection of health or morals, or for the protection of the rights and freedoms of others, States can only lawfully encourage or facilitate restrictions that are nondiscriminatory, proportionate, and provided for by law.[147] In situations involving a violation of international law, responsibility for such violation would fall on the country of origin as well as the other involved State.[148]

Extraterritorial immigration control, even when undertaken in the territory of another State, will not always be viewed as interfering with the right to leave of persons in that latter State. For example, in the *Xhavara* case, discussed further in

migrants being treated with "more suspicion and subject to more intensive and intrusive questioning than non-Roma" and overwhelmingly more likely to be rejected was "inherently and systematically discriminatory and unlawful." *R (on the application of European Roma Rights Centre et al.) v. Immigration Officer at Prague Airport et al., ex parte European Roma Rights Centre et al.*, [2004] UKHL 55 (UK HL, Dec. 9, 2004) [*European Roma Rights Centre Case*], at para. 97 (Baroness Hale).

144 Cornelisse, *Immigration Detention and Human Rights*, at 155.

145 Note that the Human Rights Committee specifically referred to practices such as carrier sanctions in its General Comment 27 indicating that, at least in some cases, such immigration control measures will breach the right to leave another country. HRC General Comment No. 27, at para. 10.

146 Where States have criminalized migrant smuggling, it might be argued that a wide range of actions aimed at preventing the crime of migrant smuggling – including actions that effectively stop people from leaving their country – fall within the permissible derogations to the right to leave. However, such claims must be tested against the broader, accepted standards of legality, proportionality, and non-discrimination.

147 *European Roma Rights Centre Case*, at paras. 6, 98–104.

148 See discussion of State responsibility in Chapter 4.

Chapter 3,[149] the European Court of Human Rights held that the actions of Italy in stopping a boatload of irregular migrants in Albanian territory with the permission of the Albanian government did not violate the right of those migrants to leave Albania because it was directed, not at preventing their departure from Albania, but rather, their entry into Italian territory.[150] This decision has been criticized for failing to recognize that the obligations attached to the right to leave properly belong not just with the country of departure but with all States that are treaty-bound to respect that right, including, most particularly, those States exercising power and control beyond their territorial jurisdiction.[151]

2.2.2. *The Right to Return*

The international legal rules governing return of smuggled migrants are considered in detail in Chapter 10. At this point it is therefore only necessary to provide a brief overview of the right to return as a corollary of the right to leave. International law has traditionally recognized an obligation on a State to accept return of its nationals when demanded by another State on whose territory they are found.[152] Both this obligation and the rights to which it gives rise resided in the States concerned and not in the individual. It was only with the Universal Declaration of Human Rights that the international community expressly acknowledged that "[e]veryone has the right to ... return to his country."[153] The ICCPR confirms that "[n]o one shall be arbitrarily deprived of the right to enter his own country."[154] In interpreting this provision, the Human Rights Committee has held that "there are few, if any circumstances in which deprivation of the right to enter one's own country could be reasonable."[155] In relation to the term "own country," the Committee has affirmed that there are factors other than nationality that may establish close and enduring connections between a person and a country, including long-standing residence,

[149] See Chapter 3, at n. 329–330 and accompanying text.

[150] *Xhavara and Fifteen Others v. Italy and Albania*, Application No. 39473/98 (ECHR, Jan. 11, 2001) [*Xhavara and Fifteen Others v. Italy and Albania*], at judgment, para. 3.

[151] V. Moreno-Lax, "Must EU Borders Have Doors for Refugees? On the Compatibility of Schengen Visas and Carrier Sanctions with EU Member States' Obligations to Provide International Protection to Refugees" (2008) 10 *European Journal of Migration and Law* 315, at 353–354.

[152] Oppenheim, *International Law* (1955), at 645–646.

[153] UDHR, at Art. 13(2).

[154] ICCPR, at Art. 12(4).

[155] HRC General Comment No. 27, at para. 21. With reference to the concept of arbitrariness as used in this context, the Committee has further noted that it "is intended to emphasize that it applies to all State action, legislative, administrative and judicial; it guarantees that even interference provided for by law should be in accordance with the provisions, aims and objectives of the Covenant and should be, in any event, reasonable in the particular circumstances": ibid.

close personal and family ties, and intentions to remain, as well as to the absence of such ties elsewhere.[156]

The right to return to one's own country is also protected by CERD,[157] the Migrant Workers Convention,[158] and all major regional human rights treaties.[159] Other closely related (and sometimes overlapping) internationally recognized rules, such as the prohibition on exile[160] and on the expulsion of nationals,[161] provide further support for the right of all persons to return to their country. Academic discussion on the scope and substantive content of the right of return has tended to focus on particular situations involving entire populations, such as the Palestinians in relation to Israel and the Greek population of Turkish-occupied Cyprus.[162] As yet there has been little analysis of how this right may operate in respect of individuals whose presence in a country other than their own has been facilitated through practices such as smuggling.

2.3. RIGHT TO SEEK AND ENJOY ASYLUM FROM PERSECUTION

International law as it relates to refugees seeks to provide some measure of legal protection for persons who are forced to flee their countries of origin because of persecution for reasons of race, religion, nationality, membership of a particular social group, or political opinion.[163] The possibility that smuggled migrants may fall

[156] *Nystrom v. Australia*, UNHRC Comm. No. 1557/2007, UN Doc. CCPR/C/102/D/1557/2007, Sept. 1, 2011, decided July 18, 2011, at para. 7.4.

[157] CERD, at Art. 5(d)(ii).

[158] Migrant Workers Convention, at Art. 8(2).

[159] Protocol No. 4 to the European Convention on Human Rights, at Art. 3(2); American Convention on Human Rights, at Art. 22(5); African Charter on Human and Peoples' Rights, at Art. 12(2).

[160] See, for example, UDHR, at Art. 9: "[n]o one shall be subjected to arbitrary arrest, detention or exile."

[161] See further J.-M. Henckaerts, *Mass Expulsion in Modern Law and Practice* (1998), esp. at 78–82.

[162] See, for example, Y. Zilbershatz, "International Law and the Palestinian Right of Return to the State of Israel," in E. Benvenisti, C. Gans, and S. Hanafi eds., *Israel and the Palestinian Refugees* 191 (2007); J. M. Bracka, "Past the Point of No Return?: The Palestinian Right of Return in International Human Rights Law" (2005) 6 *Melbourne Journal of International Law* 272.

[163] The Refugee Convention, as amended by the Refugee Protocol, defines a refugee as anyone who, "owing to a well-founded fear of being persecuted for reasons of race, religion, nationality, membership of a particular social group or political opinion, is outside the country of his nationality and is unable, or owing to such fear, is unwilling to avail himself of the protection of that country; or who, not having a nationality and being outside the country of his former habitual residence as a result of such events, is unable, or, owing to such fear, is unwilling to return to it": Convention Relating to the Status of Refugees, 189 UNTS 137, done July 28, 1951, entered into force Apr. 22, 1954, as amended by the Protocol relating to the Status of Refugees, 606 UNTS 267, done Jan. 31, 1967, entered into force Oct. 4, 1967 [Refugee Convention], at Art. 1A(2). Note that certain of the regional refugee instruments may extend the category of persons to which this designation would apply. See further International Law Commission, "Second Report on the Expulsion of Aliens, by Mr. Maurice Kamto,

within the international legal definition of refugee is widely recognized,[164] as is the related possibility that action against irregular migration may impact on the ability of individuals to seek and receive asylum from persecution.[165] Note that the question of whether smuggling itself could ever be the basis of a claim for refugee status has not yet been explored and is not a focus of the current analysis.[166]

Although everyone has the right to *seek* and *enjoy* asylum from persecution,[167] the right to *receive* asylum is not absolute but predicated on a particular claim meeting the required international standards. In addition, as explored in detail in Section 2.3.1, international law operates to limit, but not to prohibit, the expulsion of refugees.

International refugee law has, over time, established the substantive content of the right to seek and enjoy asylum. It includes (but is not identical to) the principle of *non-refoulement*.[168] It further incorporates certain standards with regard to human rights of asylum-seekers, nondiscriminatory assessment and treatment, and non-penalization in case of illegal entry or presence. The right to seek and enjoy asylum from persecution also presupposes the existence of a capacity and willingness, on the part of the

Special Rapporteur," UN Doc. A/CN.4/573, July 20, 2006 [International Law Commission, "Second Report on the Expulsion of Aliens"], at paras. 57–71.

164 Not least by the Migrant Smuggling Protocol, which, at Article 19, makes specific reference to rights, obligations, and responsibilities arising under international refugee law.

165 See, for example, the judgment of the European Court of Human Rights in *Amuur v. France*, (1996) 22 EHRR 533 (ECHR, June 25, 1996), at para. 43 ("States' legitimate concern to foil the increasingly frequent attempts to get round immigration restrictions must not deprive asylum-seekers of the protection afforded by [the 1951 Convention and the European Convention]"). See further the references in the Introduction's discussion on this point, esp. notes 42–44.

166 Certainly the mere fact that a person has paid or otherwise been assisted in crossing a border illegally would not be sufficient to establish a valid claim for asylum. However, there may well be situations, particularly in relation to those involving "aggravated smuggling" or organized criminal groups, where the requirements for claiming refugee status or at least complementary protection can be satisfied. For a detailed analysis of this issue from the perspective of human trafficking (which, as noted in Chapter 1, at Section 1.1.3.2 and Chapter 5, at Section 5.1.4), is strongly related to the concept of "aggravated smuggling"), see Gallagher, *The International Law of Human Trafficking*, at 197–207.

167 UDHR, at Art. 14. See also the Charter of Fundamental Rights of the European Union, OJ C 364/1, Dec. 18, 2000, done Dec. 7, 2000, entered into force Dec. 1, 2009 with the Lisbon Treaty (Treaty of Lisbon amending the Treaty on European Union and the Treaty establishing the European Community, OJ C 306, done Dec. 13, 2007, entered into force Dec. 1, 2009) [Charter of Fundamental Rights of the European Union], at Art. 18 ("The right to asylum shall be guaranteed with due respect for the rules of the Geneva Convention of 28 July 1951 and the Protocol of 31 January 1967 relating to the status of refugees and in accordance with the Treaty establishing the European Community.).

168 Hathaway notes that the duty of *non-refoulement* can be distinguished from the right to asylum from persecution in some significant respects. Most important, the obligation prohibits only those measures that cause refugees to be returned to their persecutors. It says nothing about a duty on any State to *receive* refugees: "States parties may therefore deny entry to refugees so long as there is no real chance that their refusal will result in the return of the refugee to face the risk of being persecuted": Hathaway, *The Rights of Refugees*, at 301.

host State, to receive asylum-seekers and to provide the facilities necessary to ensure their claims are heard in an independent, fair, and efficient manner. Although the Convention relating to the Status of Refugees (Refugee Convention) does not mandate one particular approach, it appears self-evident that the legal and procedural framework should be sufficiently robust to ensure those who are entitled to refugee status actually receive it and that *non-refoulement* does not occur. According to the United Nations High Commissioner for Refugees (UNHCR), the "core procedural standards necessary to preserve the integrity of the asylum regime as both fair and efficient" include: access to guidance and advice on the procedure, access to legal counsel and interpreters, the opportunity to present evidence, a written record of the decision, and the opportunity to appeal against a negative decision.[169] Individual assessment is critical. As discussed at Section 2.4.3, deportation of groups of smuggled migrants without the benefit of individual assessment of their situation and attached risks, can, in addition to compromising their right to seek and receive asylum from persecution, also violate the prohibition on collective expulsion.[170]

The issues touched on in the following sections are central to the question of when smuggled migrants can be returned and under what conditions. Reference should therefore be made to Chapter 10, which considers in detail the rules and standards set out in this section from the perspective of return of smuggled migrants.

2.3.1. *The Obligation of* Non-refoulement *under Refugee Law*

International refugee law[171] prohibits a refugee being expelled or returned "in any manner whatsoever to the frontiers of territories where his life or freedom would be threatened on account of his race, religion, nationality, membership of a particular social group or political opinion."[172] This principle "establishes the refugee as the

[169] UN High Commissioner for Refugees, Global Consultations on International Protection, "Asylum Processes (Fair and Efficient Asylum Procedures)," UN Doc. EC/GC/01/12, May 31, 2001.

[170] See further discussion of collective expulsion in Chapter 10, at Section 10.2.2.

[171] Note that the obligation of *non-refoulement* also exists in international human rights law, attached, most prominently, to the prohibition on torture and inhuman and degrading treatment or punishment. See further Section 2.4.1 of this chapter.

[172] Refugee Convention, at Art. 33(1). Additional sources of the obligation of *non-refoulement* in the context of asylum include the OAU Convention Governing the Specific Aspects of Refugee Problems in Africa, 1001 UNTS 45, done Sept. 10, 1969, entered into force June 20, 1974, Article II(3); and Regulation (EC) No 562/2006 of the European Parliament and of the Council of 15 March 2006 establishing a Community Code on the rules governing the movement of persons across borders (Schengen Borders Code), OJ L 105/1, Apr. 13, 2006, at Preambular para. 20 (code to be applied: "in accordance with the Member States' obligations as regards international protection and non-refoulement"), and Article 13(1) (obligation to refuse entry to third-country nationals not fulfilling entry requirements "shall be without prejudice to the application of special provisions concerning the right of asylum and to international protection").

exception to the sovereign right of states to exercise migration control and reject foreigners at the borders."[173] Migrant smuggling is increasingly a part of the refugee experience, and *non-refoulement* in the context of international refugee law is accordingly of special relevance to any discussion of migrant smuggling.

The obligation of *non-refoulement* is widely, but not uniformly, recognized as a norm of customary international law – at least in the specific context of asylum from persecution.[174] Those advocating that *non-refoulement* is a norm of customary international law are also advocating its natural consequence: that all States, not just parties to the Refugee Convention, are required, as a matter of international law, to respect the obligation not to return those who are at risk of persecution.[175]

In terms of its scope of application, the obligation of *non-refoulement* is widely agreed to be applicable to all types of transfer or forms of forced removal of migrants, whether this is described as deportation, expulsion, extradition, informal transfer or rendition as well as nonadmission at borders. The obligation of *non-refoulement* is also viewed as applying, in respect of return, not just to the country of origin or habitual residence, but also to any other place where a person faces the same risks to life or freedom on one of the stipulated grounds. These and other aspects of the legal obligation of *non-refoulement* that are of particular relevance to the issue of migrant smuggling are considered in detail in Section 2.4.

Critically, the obligation of *non-refoulement* applies only to refugees who have left their country of origin. A State's protection obligations under the Refugee Convention do not come into operation with respect to a particular person as long

[173] T. Gammeltoft-Hansen, "Growing Barriers: International Refugee Law," in M. Gibney and S. Skogly eds., *Universal Human Rights and Extraterritorial Obligations* 55 (2010), at 58.

[174] See Office of the High Commissioner for Refugees, "The Principle of Non-Refoulement as a Norm of Customary International Law: Response to the Questions Posed to UNHCR by the Federal Constitutional Court of the Federal Republic of Germany in Cases 2 BvR 1938/93, 2 BvR 1953/93, 2 BvR 1954/93" (Jan. 31, 1994); Office of the High Commissioner for Refugees, "Summary Conclusions: The Principle of Non-Refoulement: Expert Roundtable organized by the UNHCR and the Lauterpacht Research Centre for International Law, University of Cambridge, UK, 9–10 July 2001," in E. Feller, V. Türk, and F. Nicholson eds., *Refugee Protection in International Law: UNHCR's Global Consultations on International Protection* 178 (2003); E. Lauterpacht and D. Bethlehem, "The Scope and Content of the Principle of *Non-Refoulement*: Opinion," also in E. Feller, V. Türk, and F. Nicholson eds., *Refugee Protection in International Law: UNHCR's Global Consultations on International Protection* 87 (2003) [Lauterpacht and Bethlehem, "The Scope and Content of the Principle of *Non-Refoulement*"]; N. Coleman, "Renewed Review of the Status of the Principle of Non-Refoulement as Customary International Law" (2003) 5 *European Journal of Migration and Law* 23; and "Declaration of States Parties to the 1951 Convention and/or its 1967 Protocol Relating to the Status of Refugees," UN Doc. HCR/MMSP/2001/09, Dec. 13, 2001, at para. 4. See also, however, Hathaway, *The Rights of Refugees*, at 363–370 (persuasively challenging the view that *non-refoulement* of refugees is an established principle of customary international law and lamenting, at 365, "the persistent overstatement of the reach of custom"). Hathaway expands on this position in J. C. Hathaway, "Leveraging Asylum" (2010) 45 *Texas International Law Journal* 503.

[175] See discussion of customary international law at Section 2.4.1 of this chapter.

as that person is still within the territory of his or her own State.[176] This is significant in the present context as certain actions to prevent illegal migration (including through migrant smuggling) can be initiated or conducted within the country of origin. Visa controls fall into this category of response, as do carrier sanctions. A State wishing to prevent asylum-seekers reaching their shores may take an even more direct approach, for example by instituting a system of predeparture screening by its immigration officers at airports in countries of origin. This was the situation in the *European Roma Rights Centre* case, decided by the House of Lords in 2004. In that case, the Court was called upon to consider, inter alia, whether the prohibition on *refoulement* applied to an operation by British officials at that Prague airport that had the apparent intention and clear effect of identifying and preventing the departure of asylum-seekers.[177] The Court affirmed that in order to qualify as a refugee, a foreign national must be outside his or her country of nationality.[178] The argument that the screening procedure was a breach of faith on the part of a State Party to the Refugee Convention because it prevented those seeking asylum from gaining international protection was rejected. Noting the clear language of the Refugee Convention's provision on *non-refoulement* (Article 33), the Court concluded: "there is no want of good faith if a State interprets a treaty as meaning what it says and declines to do anything greater than or different from what it has agreed to do."[179] This judgment appears to reflect the general consensus that immigration control measures aimed at or having the effect of preventing the departure of migrants including would-be refugees from their own countries may potentially compromise certain human rights (and be unlawful on that basis)[180] but do not violate the obligation of *non-refoulement*.

International law is clear on the point that the obligation of *non-refoulement* applies to "persons who may be subjected to persecution if returned to their country of origin *irrespective of whether or not they have been formally recognized as refugees*."[181] The right to seek and enjoy asylum from persecution presupposes the existence of a capacity and willingness, on the part of the host State, to receive asylum-seekers and to provide the facilities that are necessary to ensure their claims are heard in a fair and efficient manner.[182] State failures in this regard, as well as a refusal to consider

176 *European Roma Rights Centre Case*, at para. 14 (Lord Bingham).

177 Ibid.

178 Ibid. at para. 16 (Lord Bingham).

179 Ibid. at para. 19 (Lord Bingham).

180 See discussion of the *European Roma Rights Centre Case* in the context of the right to leave and the prohibition on discrimination, notes 176–179 and accompanying text above.

181 UN High Commissioner for Refugees Executive Committee Conclusion No. 6, "Non-Refoulement" (1977), at para. (c), cited in Hathaway, *The Rights of Refugees*, at 319, n. 193 (emphasis added).

182 See generally, G. Goodwin-Gill and J. McAdam, *The Refugee in International Law* (3rd ed. 2007) [Goodwin-Gill and McAdam, *The Refugee in International Law*], at ch. 3.

a claim for refugee status at all, will clearly place the asylum-seeker at risk of return and thereby compromise the obligation of *non-refoulement*. The question of what constitutes "fair and efficient" procedures for the reception and consideration of asylum claims is an important one, not least because it is a relevant consideration in determining whether *refoulement* has taken place. It is generally accepted that the required procedural safeguards include individualized assessment: "[i]n particular a denial of protection in the absence of a review of individual circumstances would be inconsistent with the prohibition of refoulement."[183]

Some contemporary responses to irregular migration and migrant smuggling are undertaken with the intention and/or effect of denying asylum-seekers[184] access to adequate assessment procedures and thereby to protection. The legal implications of these responses are examined at various points, most particularly in Chapter 6 (in relation to smuggling by sea), Chapter 9 (in relation to detention), and Chapter 10 (in relation to return).

2.3.2. *Obligation Not to Impose Penalties for Unlawful Entry*

Migrants who are in possession of valid documentation and permission to migrate have no need to use the services of those who organize the illegal crossing of borders for profit. It follows that smuggled migrants will inevitably be undocumented (or in possession of invalid documentation), and, given national criminalization trends, their entry into and/or stay in the country of destination will be unlawful. In many countries, undocumented migrants are not granted access to refugee determination procedures. Often, denial of access is not explicit, but rather a foreseeable

[183] Lauterpacht and Bethlehem, "The Scope and Content of the Principle of *Non-Refoulement*," at para. 100.

[184] The term "asylum-seeker" is generally used to refer to an individual whose refugee status is yet to be determined but whose claim to asylum entitles him or her to certain rights on the basis that he or she could be a refugee. UNHCR's Guidelines on Detention of Asylum-Seekers are stated to apply to "those whose claims are being considered within status determination procedures, as well as admissibility, pre-screening or other similar procedures. They also apply to those exercising their right to seek judicial review of their request for international protection": UN High Commissioner for Refugees, *Guidelines on the Applicable Criteria and Standards Relating to the Detention of Asylum-Seekers and Alternatives to Detention* (2012) [UNHCR Guidelines on Detention of Asylum-Seekers], at 10 (para. 9). But see International Law Commission, "Third Report on the Expulsion of Aliens, by Mr. Maurice Kamto, Special Rapporteur," UN Doc. A/CN.4/581, Apr. 19, 2007 [International Law Commission, "Third Report on the Expulsion of Aliens"], at paras. 58–59 (asserting that the two ideas of refuge and territorial asylum are different and disassociated in legal terms, and concluding, somewhat confusedly, that "(a) not all refugees are destined to become asylees; and (b) asylee status is determined by the national legislation of each state, unlike that of refugees, which is governed by international law ... Consequently, the rules applicable to the expulsion of the two categories of persons should be analysed separately, especially since there does not seem to be a rule for non-expulsion of asylees in international law").

and inevitable consequence of penalties imposed on all persons arriving without authorization. Summary deportation is an example of State responses to the generalized problem of irregular migration that have the effect of precluding assessment of potential asylum claims.[185] Sometimes, those who arrive without proper documentation are channeled into an inferior refugee determination procedure.[186] Smuggled migrants may also be subject to criminal prosecution or other penalties for the various means by which unlawful entry is secured, such as use of false documentation. Such legal action can operate to further obstruct their access to asylum determination procedures.[187]

Article 31(1) of the Refugee Convention specifically addresses the issue of penalties imposed for unlawful entry:

> The contracting States shall not impose penalties, on account of their illegal entry or presence, on refugees who, coming directly from a territory where their life or freedom was threatened in the sense of article 1 [of the Convention], enter or are present in their territory without authorization, provided they present themselves without delay to the authorities and show good cause for their illegal entry or presence.[188]

Obstructed or delayed access[189] to refugee determination procedures are undoubtedly penalties: a sanction for unlawful arrival or stay that would not be imposed on

[185] See, for example, Organization of American States, Inter-American Commission on Human Rights, *Report on Immigration in the United States: Detention and Due Process*, OEA/Ser.L/V/II. Doc. 78/10, Dec. 30, 2010, at paras. 99–108; "Report of the Special Rapporteur on the Human Rights of Migrants, Jorge Bustamante," UN Doc. A/65/222, Aug. 3, 2010, esp. at paras. 38–41; M. R. Pistone and J. J. Hoeffner, "Rules Are Made to Be Broken: How the Process of Expedited Removal Fails Asylum Seekers" (Villanova University School of Law Working Paper Series, Paper 49, 2006); B. Story, *Politics as Usual: The Criminalization of Asylum Seekers in the United States* (University of Oxford Refugee Studies Centre Working Paper No. 26, Sept. 2005), esp. at 12; C. Skulan, "Australia's Mandatory Detention of Unauthorized Asylum Seekers: History, Politics and Analysis under International Law" (2006) 21(1) *Georgetown Immigration Law Journal* 61, 73–76.

[186] See, for example, M. Price, *Rethinking Asylum: History, Purpose, and Limits* (2009), at 213–219, 223–224; Human Rights Watch, *Fast-Tracked Unfairness: Detention and Denial of Women Asylum Seekers in the UK* (2010), esp. at part V; Australian Human Rights Commission, *Face the Facts: Some Questions and Answers about Indigenous Peoples, Migrants and Refugees and Asylum Seekers* (2012), at 40–41.

[187] See, for example, Council of Europe, Commissioner for Human Rights, Criminalisation of Migration in Europe: Human Rights Implications, CommDH/Issue Paper (2010)1, Feb. 4, 2010, at 18–19; and "Report of the Special Rapporteur on the Human Rights of Migrants, Jorge Bustamante," UN Doc. A/65/222, Aug. 3, 2010, at paras. 40–41.

[188] Refugee Convention, at Art. 31(1). For further on this provision see also G. S. Goodwin-Gill, "Article 31 of the 1951 Convention Relating to the Status of Refugees: Non-penalization, Detention, and Protection," in E. Feller, V. Türk, and F. Nicholson eds., *Refugee Protection in International Law: UNHCR's Global Consultations on International Protection* 185 (2003) [Goodwin-Gill, "Article 31 of the Refugee Convention"], at 186–188; and Hathaway, *The Rights of Refugees*, at 406–412.

[189] For example, Australia's "no advantage" principle whereby asylum-seekers who arrive by boat are not to receive an "advantage" over refugees awaiting resettlement overseas. The principle derives from

asylum-seekers who arrived by regular means, such as properly documented arrivals by air or other transport who apply for asylum after having lawfully arrived. However, even where legal or procedural obstacles are not placed in the way of smuggled persons seeking asylum, such persons may still in reality be penalized for their mode of entry. In some countries, for example, asylum-seekers who are without required entry or stay documentation are automatically placed in immigration detention, for either a set period of time or until the refugee determination procedure is completed.[190] Although Article 31 would not preclude administrative detention, or provisional detention for the purposes of investigating the circumstances of entry or the identity of an asylum-seeker,[191] there are strong indications that, in practice, mandatory detention of asylum-seekers is often a punitive measure, also aimed at deterring would-be asylum-seekers from treading the same path.[192]

International law is clear on the point that asylum claims are to be considered on their substantive merits: the right to protection is located within the reasons for flight, not the mode of arrival. In other words, an individual cannot be denied refugee status – or, most important, the opportunity to make a claim for such status through fair assessment procedures – solely because of the way in which that person sought or secured entry into the country of destination. The Refugee Convention specifically envisages that at least some refugees will seek access to the country of refuge without permission and it explicitly extends protection from expulsion or *refoulement* to those persons. This means that delaying or withholding access to asylum determination procedures from those who have been smuggled to the country of refuge – including through automatic deportation – is not permitted.

a 2012 recommendation by a government-appointed expert panel on asylum-seekers. See Australian Government, Expert Panel on Asylum Seekers, Report of the Expert Panel on Asylum Seekers (August, 2012), at 14 (recommending that "Australian policymaking on asylum seeker issues" should be shaped, inter alia, by the "application of a 'no advantage' principle to ensure that no benefit is gained through circumventing regular migration arrangements.").

[190] See, for example, *Immigration Act* 1970 (Malta) (CAP. 217, Sept. 21, 1970), at Arts. 5, 10; *Migration Act* 1958 (Cth) (Australia), at ss. 177–178; and *Immigration Control and Refugee Recognition Act* (Japan) (Cabinet Order No. 319 of Oct. 4, 1951), at Arts. 24 and 39 (although these provisions ostensibly make detention discretionary, the Global Detention Project reports that the "Japanese government and Immigration Bureau apply the principle of *Zenken-Shuyo Shugi* (literal translation is 'detention of all violators,' which signifies mandatory detention) in practice": Global Detention Project, "Japan Detention Profile," Mar. 2013, available at www.globaldetentionproject.org/countries/asia-pacific/japan/introduction.html (accessed May 12, 2013)). See further the discussion on the prohibition on arbitrary detention at Section 2.5 of this chapter.

[191] Goodwin-Gill, "Article 31 of the Refugee Convention," at 194–196.

[192] See, for example, Organization of American States, Inter-American Commission on Human Rights, *Report on Immigration in the United States: Detention and Due Process*, OEA/Ser.L/V/II. Doc. 78/10, Dec. 30, 2010, at paras. 243–247; and "Report of the Special Rapporteur on the Human Rights of Migrants, François Crépeau," UN Doc. A/HRC/20/24, Apr. 2, 2012, esp. at para. 31.

The issue of penalties for unlawful arrival falling short of explicit denial of the opportunity to make a claim for refugee status is more complicated. Article 31(1) is conditional. It does not affect the legal capacity of a State to expel a refugee who unlawfully enters or is unlawfully present in that State – provided of course, that such expulsion does not violate the obligation of *non-refoulement*.[193] The provision does, however, "provide immunity for genuine refugees whose quest for asylum reasonably involved them in breaching the law."[194] Its strategic intention is clear: to encourage asylum-seekers who have entered clandestinely to seek to regularize their status as quickly as possible.[195] Protection against the penalty is granted only to those who do come forward without delay: smuggled asylum-seekers who fail to make themselves known to authorities in the country of refuge lose their initial immunity from penalization for unlawful entry. Importantly the asylum-seeker who has not had a chance to seek regularization of his or her status should not lose the protection of Article 31. This would apply to smuggled migrants who are intercepted in the territorial waters of their destination State, or who are intercepted just over the border. As Hathaway notes, "it would make no sense to deny [protection of Article 31] simply because apprehension by authorities was nearly immediate."[196]

One potential obstacle for smuggled migrants seeking the protection of Article 31 lies in the requirement that they are "coming directly from a territory where their life or freedom was threatened." The smuggling of asylum-seekers is often a very indirect process, involving multiple movements. For example, refugees from Afghanistan and Sri Lanka routinely make their way to Indonesia where arrangements are made to smuggle them to Australia. Refugees from Somalia may spend a great deal of time in countries of Northern Africa before being smuggled to Europe. If an asylum-seeker has found – or could have found – effective protection from persecution in the course of his or her journey to the eventual country of refuge then it is arguable that this requirement of "coming directly from a territory where their life or freedom is threatened" will not be satisfied. However, the immunity conferred by Article 31

[193] Goodwin-Gill, "Article 31 of the Refugee Convention," at 10; Hathaway, *The Rights of Refugees*, at 412–413.

[194] *R v. Uxbridge Magistrates' Court ex parte Adimi*, [1999] 4 All ER 520 (Eng. HC, July 29, 1999), per Justice Brown 523 (*R v. Uxbridge Magistrates' Court*), at 527, cited in Hathaway, *The Rights of Refugees*, at 388. Concurring with this opinion, Justice Newman added, at 537, that, in his view, "Apart from the current necessity to use false documents another current reality and advance, occurring since 1951, is the development of a readily accessible and worldwide network of air travel. As a result there is a choice of refuge beyond the first safe territory by land or sea. There have been distinctive and differing state responses to requests for asylum. Thus there exists a rational basis for exercising choice where to seek asylum. I am unable to accept that to recognise it is to legitimise forum shopping." This case concerned asylum-seekers who, entering the United Kingdom via other countries, had been prosecuted for using false passports.

[195] Hathaway, *The Rights of Refugees*, at 388.

[196] Ibid. at 391.

"involvement in an organized criminal group" as grounds for applying the "serious crimes" exclusion.[211]

UNHCR has advocated for a restrictive interpretation of "serious crime," stating that a serious crime, justifying refusal of protection, "must be a capital crime or a very grave punishable act."[212] In determining "seriousness," UNHCR holds that it is international, rather than national standards that are relevant.[213] However, scholars have generally preferred a more nuanced approach whereby the laws of the host country and its notions of serious criminality are also to be considered, along with the object and purpose of the Refugee Convention itself. In that regard, it is relevant to note that the crime of migrant smuggling can include conduct that varies widely in terms of both complicity and seriousness. This underscores the need to consider each fact situation individually, and to reject, as inconsistent with the object and purpose of the Refugee Convention, as well as the principle of proportionality, any blanket exclusion on all those involved in or convicted of a particular crime type, such as migrant smuggling.[214]

The exclusion clause considered previously applies only to serious crimes committed *outside the country of asylum*. The focus of that clause on fugitives from justice implies that the provision would only be triggered in respect of an individual

211 Rikhof, *The Criminal Refugee*. See also note 214 to this chapter.

212 UN High Commissioner for Refugees, *Handbook on Procedures and Criteria for Determining Refugee Status under the 1951 Convention and the 1967 Protocol Relating to the Status of Refugees*, UN Doc. HCR/IP/4/Eng/REV.1 (1979, reissued Jan. 2002), at para. 155. See also UN High Commissioner for Refugees, *UNHCR Statement on Article 1F of the 1951 Convention Issued in the context of the preliminary ruling references to the Court of Justice of the European Communities from the German Federal Administrative Court regarding the interpretation of Articles 12(2)(b) and (c) of the Qualification Directive* (July 2008) [UNHCR 2009 Statement on Article 1F of the Refugee Convention].

213 UN High Commissioner for Refugees, *Guidelines on International Protection: Application of the Exclusion Clauses: Article 1F of the 1951 Convention Relating to the Status of* Refugees, UN Doc. HCR/GIP/03/05, Sept. 4, 2003, at para. 14; and UN High Commissioner for Refugees, *Interpreting Article 1 of the 1951 Convention Relating to the Status of Refugees* (2001), at para. 45. Note that the existence of a widely ratified treaty on the subject of migrant smuggling that includes an obligation to criminalize migrant smuggling and related actions may be relevant to a determination of seriousness. On the question of exclusion from refugee status on the basis of being a terrorist or member of a terrorist organization, see UNHCR 2009 Statement on Article 1F of the Refugee Convention.

214 This issue was raised in an Australian case, decided in 2004. This case concerned a convicted smuggler whose claim for protection was refused on the basis that this conviction was for a serious crime within the meaning of Article 1F(b). Although the offense was clearly serious (carrying a maximum penalty of twenty years' imprisonment), the Tribunal disallowed application of the exclusion clause on the basis that the nature and circumstances of the applicant's involvement (e.g., he was not aware of the purpose of the journey until the smuggling vessel was already en route to Australia) did not reach the threshold of seriousness that would permit Australia to negate its obligations under the Convention. *SRCCCC and MIMIA* [2004] AATA 315 (Handley DP, Mar. 26, 2004), cited in Refugee Review Tribunal, A *Guide to Refugee Law in Australia* (2012), at 7–42. The question of whether or when more direct involvement would trigger the application of Article 1F has not been subsequently tested.

who had engaged in the crime of migrant smuggling previous to or during his or her flight from persecution. The legal situation may be different if the actual flight from persecution involves complicity in migrant smuggling and the country of refuge has criminalized migrant smuggling. In such a case, it could conceivably be argued that the country of refuge may not refuse to consider an application for asylum on the grounds provided by Article 1F(b) because the "serious crime" that provides the necessary trigger could not be considered to have been committed until arrival. The argument is however an artificial one and likely to be rejected by States as contrary to the broader purposes of the exclusion clause.

Even if the exclusion clause of Article 1F(b) is not applied to a particular migrant smuggler and he or she is indeed recognized as a refugee, the effectiveness of any protection secured through that recognition could potentially be compromised by additional exclusions set out in the Refugee Convention. For example, refugees who are lawfully within the country may be expelled (i.e., the host State is permitted to divest itself of its obligation of *non-refoulement*) on grounds of national security or public order.[215] In making a determination under this rule, States are required to present evidence of a credible and serious threat to the most basic interests of the State or its citizens.[216] For example, national security grounds are "not appropriate in local or isolated threats to law and order."[217] Similarly, concerns about damage to the State's reputation or its economic interests, or about encouraging unlawful/unwanted activity, would not be considered sufficient.[218] Commentators have pointed to the very serious consequences for the individual of *refoulement* as support for the proposition that "[t]he danger to the security of the country in contemplation in Article 33(2) must ... be taken to be very serious danger rather than danger of some lesser order."[219] This relationship between the seriousness of the consequences of *refoulement* and the seriousness of the danger posed was confirmed and explained by UNHCR in a 2006 Advisory Opinion, in which it stated that "[t]he threat to security exception to States' *non-refoulement* obligations, like any exception to human rights guarantees, must be interpreted restrictively and with full respect to the principle of proportionality. It must therefore be shown that the danger posed by the refugee is sufficient to justify *refoulement*."[220]

215 "The Contracting States shall not expel a refugee lawfully in their territory save on grounds of national security or public order": Refugee Convention, at Art. 32(1). Note that such an expulsion is subject to certain procedural requirements.

216 See the survey of national jurisprudence in Hathaway, *The Rights of Refugees*, at 264–266, 345–348.

217 UN High Commissioner for Refugees, *UNHCR Note on the Principle of* Non-Refoulement (1997) [UNHCR Note on the Principle of *Non-Refoulement*].

218 Hathaway, *The Rights of Refugees*, at 264–266, 345–348.

219 Lauterpacht and Bethlehem, "The Scope and Content of the Principle of *Non-Refoulement*," at para. 169.

220 UN High Commissioner for Refugees, *Advisory Opinion from the Office of the United Nations High Commissioner for Refugees (UNHCR) on the Scope of the National Security Exception in Article 33(2)*

States are also entitled to withhold protection from *refoulement* from criminally dangerous refugees: those who have been convicted of particularly serious crimes (in the country of refuge or elsewhere) *and* who are considered to be a danger to the country of asylum.[221] Commentators and national courts have considered the question of the relative weight of these various elements.[222] Although reaching different conclusions, all concur with UNHCR's view that the provision should be interpreted restrictively.[223] In relation to persons convicted of migrant smuggling offenses it is important to affirm that such a conviction is not, of itself, sufficient to authorize *refoulement* on this ground. The individual involved must also be shown to present a serious danger to the community. It is difficult to imagine a situation where involvement in migrant smuggling could constitute a "danger to the community" (as distinct from a danger to certain individuals) so as to support application of the exception to persons who have been or may in the future be engaged in migrant smuggling.

The International Law Commission (ILC), in its current draft articles on expulsion, has generally endorsed this standard, while explicitly proposing its extension to asylum-seekers:

> Draft article 6
>
> Prohibition of the expulsion of refugees
>
> 1. A State shall not expel a refugee lawfully in its territory save on grounds of national security or public order.

of the 1951 Convention Relating to the Status of Refugees (Jan. 6, 2006) [UNHCR Advisory Opinion on the Scope of the National Security Exception in Article 33(2)], at 1.

221 "The benefit of [the protection from *refoulement*] may not, however, be claimed by a refugee whom there are reasonable grounds for regarding as a danger to the security of the country in which he is, or who, having been convicted by a final judgment of a particularly serious crime, constitutes a danger to the community of that country": Refugee Convention, at Art. 33(2).

222 See, for example, Lauterpacht and Bethlehem, "The Scope and Content of the Principle of *Non-Refoulement*," at para. 111 (emphasizing that *refoulement* may be contemplated pursuant to this provision only in the most exceptional of circumstances (para. 136), and arguing that the critical factor is not the seriousness of any particular category of crime, but the question of whether the individual poses a danger to the community of the host country (para. 187)). See also Goodwin-Gill and McAdam's citation of the approach adopted by the Australian Federal Court in *A. v. Minister for Immigration and Multicultural Affairs* [1999] FCA 227 (Jan. 1, 1999). In that case, the majority expressed the view that a crime will not necessarily "be characterised as particularly serious or not particularly serious merely by reference to the nature of the crime." Instead, this characterization depends on the circumstances in which it was committed (paras. 4–5). Goodwin-Gill and McAdam argue that if this line of reasoning is accepted, it follows that it would be contrary to the Refugee Convention to legislate that specific crime types constitute "particularly serious" crimes for the purposes of the Refugee Convention, without consideration of the individual circumstances of each case: Goodwin-Gill and McAdam, *The Refugee in International Law*, at 239, referring to Australia: Migration Act 1958 (Cth), s. 91U; Canada: Immigration and Refugee Protection Act 2001, s. 36.

223 UNHCR Advisory Opinion on the Scope of the National Security Exception in Article 33(2)), at 1; and UNHCR Note on the Principle of *Non-Refoulement*.

> 2. Paragraph 1 shall also apply to any refugee unlawfully present in the territory of the State, who has applied for recognition of refugee status, while such application is pending.[224]

The question of whether smuggled asylum-seekers are able to benefit from the prohibition on expulsion of refugees (and indeed the prohibition on arbitrary expulsion of persons lawfully present) is considered in more detail in Chapter 10, at Section 10.2.1.2.

In conclusion, although migrant smuggling is being increasingly recognized as a serious crime against both national security and public order, it may still not reach the very high threshold set out previously in this discussion. Aggravated migrant smuggling involving reckless disregard for life, or elements of trafficking such as deception, coercion and exploitation, may indeed reach the required level of seriousness.[225] However, the test is a stringent one that focuses on the danger posed by the individual to the security and basic interests of the host State. Its scope of application is unlikely to extend, for example, to the mere possibility that a refugee present in the country (even if a convicted migrant smuggler) may become involved in future smuggling operations.

2.4. ADDITIONAL RESTRICTIONS ON EXPULSION AND RETURN OF SMUGGLED MIGRANTS

Restrictions on expulsion or return are not confined to asylum-seekers and refugees. In the context of migrant smuggling, a range of other issues that relate to the response of States must be addressed. Of great significance is the obligation of *non-refoulement* as it exists outside of international refugee law: What are the parameters of this obligation, and what is its relevance to the situation of smuggled migrants? In addition: Is the return of groups of smuggled migrants a violation of the prohibition on collective expulsion? What is the relevance of restrictions on expulsion of stateless persons to smuggled migrants? When expulsion is permitted under international law, what obligations does the expelling State owe to the concerned migrant? Does the conclusion of a "readmission agreement" with the country of origin or a "transit agreement" with a third State change the obligations of a State with respect to prohibited grounds of expulsion and protection of expelled migrants? These questions, which continue to arise at various points throughout this book, are considered in detail later in this chapter.

[224] International Law Commission, "Expulsion of Aliens: Texts of Draft Articles 1–32 Provisionally Adopted on First Reading by the Drafting Committee at the Sixty-Fourth Session of the International Law Commission," UN Doc. A/CN.4/L.797, May 24, 2012, at 2.

[225] See discussion of the concept of "aggravated smuggling" in the Migrant Smuggling Protocol, in Chapters 1 (Section 1.1.3.2) and 5 (Section 5.1.4).

2.4.1. Non-refoulement *in Relation to Torture and Other Serious Violations of Human Rights*

As a means of protection, the obligation of *non-refoulement* is much broader than asylum, being recognized as a fundamental principle of international human rights law. In this sense, it can potentially provide an alternative or additional ground for challenging the deportation, expulsion, or return of smuggled migrants. The principle is most widely associated with the prohibition on torture.[226] Under the Convention against Torture, States are prevented from returning or extraditing a person to another State where there are substantial grounds for believing that the individual in question would be subject to torture or other forms of ill-treatment.[227] Other specialist international human rights treaties as well as regional instruments affirm this rule.[228]

[226] Torture is defined as "any act by which severe pain or suffering, whether physical or mental, is intentionally inflicted on a person for such purposes as obtaining from him or a third person information or a confession, punishing him for an act he or a third person has committed or is suspected of having committed, or intimidating or coercing him or a third person, or for any reason based on discrimination of any kind, when such pain or suffering is inflicted by or at the instigation of or with the consent or acquiescence of a public official or other person acting in an official capacity": Convention against Torture, at Art. 1.

[227] Ibid. at Art. 3(1). See also Refugee Convention, at Art. 33; ICCPR, at Art. 7; CRC, at Art. 22. Note that the UN Special Rapporteur on Torture has recently linked torture and related harms to gender-based violence, including trafficking: "Report of the Special Rapporteur on Torture and Other Cruel, Inhuman or Degrading Treatment or Punishment, Manfred Nowak," UN Doc. A/HRC/7/3, Jan. 15, 2008, at paras. 44, 56–58.

[228] See, for example, American Convention on Human Rights, at Art. 22(8) ("In no case may an alien be deported or returned to a country, regardless of whether or not it is his country of origin, if in that country his right to life or personal freedom is in danger of being violated because of his race, nationality, religion, social status, or political opinions."); Inter-American Convention to Prevent and Punish Torture, 67 OASTS, done Dec. 9, 1985, entered into force, Feb. 28, 1987, reprinted in Basic Documents Pertaining to Human Rights in the Inter-American System, OAS/Ser.L/V/I.4 Rev. 9 (2003), at Art. 13 ("Extradition shall not be granted nor shall the person sought be returned when there are grounds to believe that his life is in danger, that he will be subjected to torture or to cruel, inhuman or degrading treatment, or that he will be tried by special or ad hoc courts in the requesting State."); International Convention for the Protection of All Persons from Enforced Disappearance, done Dec. 20, 2006, GA Res. 61/77, UN GAOR, 61st Sess, Agenda Item 68, UN Doc. A/Res/61/177, entered into force Dec. 23, 2010, at Art. 16 ("1. No State Party shall expel, return ('refouler'), surrender or extradite a person to another State where there are substantial grounds for believing that he or she would be in danger of being subjected to enforced disappearance. 2. For the purpose of determining whether there are such grounds, the competent authorities shall take into account all relevant considerations, including, where applicable, the existence in the State concerned of a consistent pattern of gross, flagrant or mass violations of human rights or of serious violations of international humanitarian law."); and the Charter of Fundamental Rights of the European Union, at Art. 19(2) ("No one may be removed, expelled or extradited to a State where there is a serious risk that he or she would be subjected to the death penalty, torture or other inhuman or degrading treatment or punishment.").

The obligation of *non-refoulement* as it exists in human rights law is widely asserted to be a fundamental component of the broader prohibition against torture and associated practices, rather than an additional element or separate requirement.[229] This is an important characterization because of its capacity to strengthen the normative weight of the obligation and broaden its applicability. As noted previously, the customary law status of the obligation of *non-refoulement* in the context of refugee law is disputed.[230] Although consensus is not universal, there is much less disagreement about the customary law status of the prohibition on torture.[231] If it is accepted that *non-refoulement* is a fundamental part of the prohibition on torture then it becomes binding on all States, irrespective of their adherence to the Convention against Torture or other human rights instruments. To the extent that the prohibition on torture is recognized as *jus cogens*: a peremptory rule of international law from which there can be no derogation (a concept discussed in Chapter 1 at Section 1.4.1); the obligation of *non-refoulement* in the context of torture is further strengthened.[232]

The prohibition on torture, inhuman and degrading treatment, or punishment contained in the European Convention on Human Rights (which does not specifically refer to the obligation of *non-refoulement*) has been interpreted, through a series of judgments, as prohibiting return in circumstances where an individual faces a real risk of torture, inhuman or degrading treatment, or punishment.[233] As

[229] For example, the UN Special Rapporteur on Torture has characterized the obligation as "an inherent part of the overall absolute and imperative nature of the prohibition of torture and other forms of ill-treatment." "Torture and other cruel, inhuman or degrading treatment or punishment, Note by the Secretary General," UN Doc. A/59/324, Sept. 1, 2004, at para. 28. See also Lauterpacht and Bethlehem, "The Scope and Content of the Principle of *Non-Refoulement*."

[230] See Chapter 1, at Section 1.4.1.

[231] On the prohibition of torture as a violation of customary law (and associated doctrinal difficulties in reconciling the requirements of *opinio juris* and State practice) within a more general discussion of theories of custom, see A. E. Roberts, "Traditional and Modern Approaches to Customary International Law" (2001) 95 *American Journal of International Law* 757. See also American Law Institute, *Restatement, Third: Foreign Relations Law of the United States* (1990), at paras. 102, 702 (recognizing torture and other cruel, inhuman, or degrading treatment or punishment as part of customary law). But see Hathaway, *The Rights of Refugees*, at 36–38 (provocatively arguing that of the traditional list of human rights commonly viewed as having acquired the status of customary international law, including the prohibition of torture, only race-based discrimination deserves this elevation because "formally codified racial disfranchisement is now virtually unknown" and *opinio juris* is both "explicit and powerful": ibid. at 36 (citation omitted).

[232] The usual citation to support the peremptory character of the prohibition on torture is *Filartiga v. Penalrala*, 630 F.2d 876 (2d Cir. 1980), where the Court held that State-sanctioned torture violates *jus cogens*. The International Law Commission has also included freedom from torture within its proposed list of peremptory norms. See International Law Commission, "Report of the International Law Commission," UN Doc. A/56/10, Supp. No. 10, 2001, at 208. For more generally on *jus cogens*, see Chapter 1, at Section 1.4.1.

[233] See, for example, *Soering v. United Kingdom*, (1989) 11 EHRR 439 (ECHR, July 7, 1989). In this case, the European Court of Human Rights found no express duty of *non-refoulement* under Article

a matter for international law. As the ILC's Special Rapporteur on the subject has observed:

> Expulsion does not fall within the scope of what some domestic laws call "governmental acts" which are not subject to any judicial review, because it involves the rules of human rights protection. Similarly, expulsion falls outside the ambit of what international law considers the exclusive jurisdiction of the State, which is not subject to international review.[251]

Irrespective of the legal status of the nonnationals concerned, States may not engage in collective (or "mass") expulsions, even when those expulsions do not violate the prohibition on *non-refoulement*.[252] The term "collective expulsion" refers to any measures compelling nonnationals, as a group, to leave a country or the territory of a country, except where such a measure is taken on the basis of a reasonable and objective examination of the particular case of each individual member of the group.[253] Collective expulsions are unequivocally prohibited in all major regional human rights treaties,[254] and regional courts and tribunals have repeatedly upheld the prohibition, including with respect to migrants who are not lawfully within the country concerned.[255] The Human Rights Committee has interpreted Article 13 of

[251] Ibid. at para. 209 (citations omitted).

[252] For a detailed, if dated, analysis of the general legal framework and associated practice around mass expulsion, see J. M. Henkaerts, *Mass Expulsion in Modern International Law and Practice* (1995).

[253] This definition and the status of the prohibition has been reiterated by the European Court of Human Rights in a number of cases. See, for example, *Andric v. Sweden* (1999) 28 EHRR CD218 (ECHR, Feb. 23, 1999), at para.1; *Sultani v. France*, Application No. 45223/05, [2007] ECHR 2007-IV (ECHR, Sept. 20. 2007); and *Čonka v. Belgium* (2002) 34 EHRR 54 (ECHR, Feb. 5 2002), at para. 56. It is also affirmed by the ILC Special Rapporteur on the Expulsion of Aliens; see International Law Commission, "Third Report on the Expulsion of Aliens," at para. 107. Note however that the territorial limitation of the definition has been challenged in the European Court of European Rights in *Hirsi Jamaa and Others v. Italy*, (2012) 55 EHRR 21 (ECHR, Feb. 23, 2012), examined further in Chapter 3 and Chapter 10.

[254] Protocol No. 4 to the European Convention on Human Rights, at Art. 4 ("Collective expulsion of aliens is prohibited."); American Convention on Human Rights, at Art. 22(9) ("The collective expulsion of aliens is prohibited."); African Charter on Human and Peoples' Rights, at Art. 12(5) ("The mass expulsion of non-nationals shall be prohibited" and "[m]ass expulsion shall be that which is aimed at national, racial, ethnic or religious groups"). Note that the ILC Special Rapporteur on the Expulsion of Aliens views the definition contained in the African Charter on Human and Peoples' Rights as unnecessarily restrictive, particularly in light of modern challenges to the prohibition of mass expulsion. See International Law Commission, "Third Report on the Expulsion of Aliens," at para. 108.

[255] On jurisprudence from the European Court of Human Rights, see Chapter 10, Section 10.2.2. The African Commission on Human and Peoples' Rights has identified violations of Article 12(5) of the African Charter in cases where large groups of migrants were expelled from the territory of a State Party and not provided an opportunity to challenge the decision on their deportation. As noted by the Office of the United Nations High Commissioner for Human Rights (OHCHR), the Commission has insisted that although the migrants concerned may be in the country illegally, the State Party's right to expel foreigners does not justify the manner employed to expel them. See *Rencontre Africaine*

the ICCPR as prohibiting arbitrary expulsion of persons lawfully present.[256] Several other international human rights treaty bodies have recognized the negative human rights implications of collective expulsions.[257]

In relation to the reach of the prohibition on collective expulsion, the ILC Special Rapporteur on the Expulsion of Aliens has concluded that:

> it seems reasonable to suggest that there is a general principle of international law on this matter that is "recognized by civilized nations" and prohibits collective expulsion. First of all, it would follow from the fact that if the admission of an alien is an individual right, the loss or denial of this right can only be by an individual act. Second, this rule against collective expulsion is enshrined in three regional human rights conventions that, among them, covers most States members of the international community.[258]

Chapter 10, which focuses on return of smuggled migrants, considers the circumstances under which the interception and/or return of a group of smuggled migrants would constitute collective expulsion and thereby violate the legal prohibition outlined in this section.

2.4.4. *Protection of Expelled and Returned Persons*

The previous discussion makes clear that although the long-held sovereign right of States to expel aliens has not been abolished, particularly with respect to those whose entry or presence is unauthorized or otherwise unlawful, it is severely constrained in a number of important ways. For example, in relation to those aliens *lawfully* present, international law requires that any expulsion not be arbitrary. Under the ICCPR and the European Convention on Human Rights, this requires, first and foremost, that the expulsion be in accordance with domestic law,[259] thereby limiting

pour la Défense des Droits de l'Homme v. Zambia, ACHPR Comm. No. 71/92 (African Commission on Human and Peoples' Rights, Aug. 2, 1996); and *Union Inter Africaine des Droits de l'Homme and Others v. Angola*, ACHPR Comm. No.159/96 (African Commission on Human and Peoples' Rights, Nov. 11, 1997), cited in Office of the United Nations High Commissioner for Human Rights, *Expulsion of Aliens in International Human Rights Law* (2006) [OHCHR, *Expulsion of Aliens in International Human Rights Law*], at 16.

256 HRC General Comment No. 15, at para. 10. The Committee has further indicated that the prohibition on collective expulsion extends beyond those lawfully within the country. See, for example, UN Human Rights Committee, "Concluding Observations: Dominican Republic," UN Doc. CCPR/CO/71/DOM, Apr. 26, 2001, at para. 16.

257 The Race Discrimination Committee, for example, has requested States Parties to "[e]nsure that non-citizens are not subject to collective expulsion, in particular in situations where there are insufficient guarantees that the personal circumstances of each of the persons concerned have been taken into account." CERD General Recommendation No. 30, at para. 26.

258 International Law Commission, "Third Report on the Expulsion of Aliens," at para. 115.

259 ICCPR, at Art. 13; Protocol No. 7 to the Convention of 4 November 1950 for the Protection of Human Rights and Fundamental Freedoms, 1525 UNTS 195, done Nov. 22, 1984, entered into force Nov. 1,

the grounds on which a valid expulsion may be based.[260] In addition, protection from arbitrariness requires that, barring compelling justification relating to national security and/or public order, aliens lawfully present be provided certain procedural guarantees. These include a right to submit reasons against the expulsion to a competent agency and a right to have the case reviewed in a proceeding where the individual concerned can be represented.[261]

Although the concept of arbitrariness can be argued to be of a more general application,[262] the procedural safeguards previously described are reserved for aliens lawfully present – they do not apply to migrants whose arrival or presence is unlawful including, ipso facto, those who have been smuggled. The only generalized exception to this rule relates to persons falling within the protection ambit of the Migrant Workers Convention.[263] However, as shown in Chapter 10, there are persuasive

1998, at Art. 1. See further discussion of the requirement of legality in the context of arbitrary expulsion in Chapter 10, at Section 10.2.1.

260 In addition to considering the ground of illegal entry, the ILC Special Rapporteur on Expulsion of Aliens has examined a number of common justifications for expulsion, including public order and public security, higher interests of the State, public health and morality, violations of law, ideological grounds and political activity, economic grounds, prevention and deterrence, and reprisals. See generally International Law Commission, "Sixth Report on the Expulsion of Aliens," at paras. 26–85.

261 See Nowak, *CCPR Commentary*, at 296–301. The ICCPR Article 13 procedural requirements relating to expulsion were examined by the ICJ in *Ahmadou Sadio Diallo (Republic of Guinea v. Democratic Republic of the Congo)*, [2010] ICJ Rep 639 [*Ahmadou Sadio Diallo Case*]. See further Chapter 10, at Section 10.4.1.

262 The Human Rights Committee, for example, has applied this concept in considering the lawfulness of expulsion involving persons not lawfully present. In *Winata v Australia*, the Committee affirmed that although "there is significant scope for States parties to enforce their immigration policy and to require departure of unlawfully present persons," that discretion is "not unlimited and may come to be exercised arbitrarily in certain circumstances." In this particular case, involving long-term irregular immigrants, the Committee held that "it is incumbent on the State party to demonstrate additional factors justifying the removal ... that go beyond a simple enforcement of its immigration laws *in order to avoid a characterization of arbitrariness*" (emphasis added). *Winata v. Australia*, UNHRC Comm. No. 930/2000, UN Doc. CCPR/C/72/D/930/2000, Aug. 16, 2001, decided July 26, 2001, at para. 7.3.

263 In addition to prohibiting collective expulsion, Article 22 of that instrument provides for extensive procedural protections in the case of expulsion as follows: 1. ... Each case of expulsion shall be examined and decided individually. 2. Migrant workers and members of their families may be expelled from the territory of a State Party only in pursuance of a decision taken by the competent authority in accordance with law. 3. The decision shall be communicated to them in a language they understand. Upon their request where not otherwise mandatory, the decision shall be communicated to them in writing and, save in exceptional circumstances on account of national security, the reasons for the decision likewise stated. The persons concerned shall be informed of these rights before or at the latest at the time the decision is rendered. 4. Except where a final decision is pronounced by a judicial authority, the person concerned shall have the right to submit the reason he or she should not be expelled and to have his or her case reviewed by the competent authority, unless compelling reasons of national security require otherwise. Pending such review, the person concerned shall have the right to seek a stay of the decision of expulsion. 5. If a decision of expulsion that has already been executed is subsequently annulled, the person concerned shall have the right to seek compensation according to law and the earlier decision shall not be used to prevent him or her from re-entering the State concerned. 6. In

grounds for arguing that smuggled asylum-seekers also fall within the category of "lawfully present" for the period during which their claims are being assessed.[264] In addition, it is relevant to reiterate that international human rights law and refugee law have evolved to place certain limitations on the freedom of a State to expel persons, irrespective of their legal status within that country, if such expulsion would expose such persons to serious violations of human rights. The most important protections in this regard have already been noted and extensively discussed. For example, the obligation of *non-refoulement* requires that the expelling State ensure an asylum-seeker is not returned to face persecution, or indeed that any person is not returned to face violations of the right to life, torture, or other inhuman treatment. The right to seek and receive asylum requires that those in need of protection are identified as such and dealt with appropriately. As discussed previously, the obligation to avoid mass expulsion is linked to the provision of certain procedural requirements, including individual assessment. The capacity of the State to expel certain other categories of persons, such as victims of trafficking and unaccompanied children, is also legally constrained.[265] States may also not discriminate in the expulsion of smuggled migrants or, in the words of the ILC Special Rapporteur on the subject, they may not apply the rights in question in a discriminatory fashion.[266] An expulsion order that was directed solely at smuggled migrants of a particular national or ethnic origin for example, would, in principle, violate the prohibition on discrimination.

The ultimate lawfulness of any expulsion, whether involving an alien lawfully present or not, is inextricably linked to *how* that expulsion takes place. In other

case of expulsion, the person concerned shall have a reasonable opportunity before or after departure to settle any claims for wages and other entitlements due to him or her and any pending liabilities. 7. Without prejudice to the execution of a decision of expulsion, a migrant worker or a member of his or her family who is subject to such a decision may seek entry into a State other than his or her State of origin. 8. In case of expulsion of a migrant worker or a member of his or her family the costs of expulsion shall not be borne by him or her. The person concerned may be required to pay his or her own travel costs. 9. Expulsion from the State of employment shall not in itself prejudice any rights of a migrant worker or a member of his or her family acquired in accordance with the law of that State, including the right to receive wages and other entitlements due to him or her.

Note also Article 23 which provides that, provides that, in the case of expulsion, the person concerned shall be informed without delay of his or her right to have recourse to the protection and assistance of the consular or diplomatic authorities of the State of origin, and that the authorities of the expelling State shall facilitate the exercise of such right.

264 See further Chapter 10, at Section 10.2.1.2.

265 See further the discussion in Chapter 8, at Section 8.2.

266 International Law Commission, "Fifth Report on the Expulsion of Aliens," at para. 155. The Rapporteur has proposed a draft article on the subject as follows: "*Draft article 14: Obligation not to discriminate.* 1. The State shall exercise its right of expulsion with regard to the persons concerned without discrimination of any kind, on grounds such as race, colour, sex, language, religion, political or other opinion, national or social origin, property, birth or other status. 2. Such non-discrimination shall also apply to the enjoyment, by a person being expelled, of the rights and freedoms provided for in international human rights law and in the legislation of the expelling State": ibid. at para. 156.

words, even if a particular expulsion is, in principle, legally justified, its legality could be compromised by the manner in which that expulsion is carried out.[267] Most important, a State that is legally entitled, in principle, to expel a smuggled migrant is nevertheless required to ensure that the relevant and important rights of that person are protected and respected during the expulsion process.[268] As a practical matter, this means that any expulsion must be executed in a manner that does not breach the basic rights or dignity of the individual involved. As the ILC Special Rapporteur on the Expulsion of Aliens has affirmed, "[p]ersons being expelled, for whatever reason, remain human beings who, as such, must continue to enjoy all their fundamental rights."[269] He continues:

> Persons whom a State has decided to expel must be protected, particularly as such persons are made vulnerable by their status as aliens and by the prospect of their expulsion. They are guaranteed this protection under international law and under the law of the expelling State, regardless of their legal status and of the conditions under which they entered the territory of that State, whether as legal or illegal aliens.[270]

Several of the rights and obligations most relevant to the conduct of expulsions involving smuggled migrants are briefly considered later in this chapter. Subsequent chapters provide a more detailed and practice-based examination of these matters, including the specific issue of pre-deportation detention, examined in detail in Chapter 9.

2.4.4.1. Use of Force in the Conduct of Expulsions

Expulsion of smuggled migrants commonly involves forced removal of persons from the territory of the State or from an area within which the State is exercising control

[267] "An otherwise lawful deportation order may be rendered illegal if it is carried out in an unjust or harsh manner. Physical force which would cause or would be likely to cause bodily harm or injury should not be used in executing the order": L. Sohn and T. Buergenthal eds., *The Movement of Persons across Borders*, Studies in Transnational Legal Policy, vol. 23, at 96, cited in International Law Commission, "Sixth Report on the Expulsion of Aliens," at n. 560.

[268] The ILC Special Rapporteur on the Expulsion of Aliens has proposed that it is "fundamental" rights that must be protected during expulsion, noting that it is "unrealistic to require that a person being expelled be able to benefit from all the human rights guaranteed by international instruments and by the domestic law of the expelling State": International Law Commission, "Fifth Report on the Expulsion of Aliens," at para. 17. A considerable portion of this report is devoted to analyzing the concept and substantive content of the concept of fundamental rights.

[269] International Law Commission, "Fifth Report on the Expulsion of Aliens," at para. 10.

[270] Ibid. The rapporteur subsequently proposes a draft article setting out the *general obligation to respect the human rights of persons being expelled* as follows: "Any person who has been or is being expelled is entitled to respect for his or her fundamental rights and all other rights the implementation of which is required by his or her specific circumstances": ibid. at para. 50.

over those migrants. The basic rights to which these persons are entitled is not affected by their circumstances or legal status, and the expelling State will inevitably be responsible for any violations of the right to life, the right to dignity, and the security of the person, and the prohibition on torture, inhuman or degrading treatment, or punishment occasioned by that expulsion.[271] An interdiction and "turn-back" of a migrant smuggling vessel on the high seas will incur responsibility of the acting State for any resulting human rights violation.[272] Legal responsibility of the State for violations is not affected by the expulsion being conducted by or through a third party, such as a private contractor or a multinational border control team.[273]

International courts and tribunals have repeatedly noted the importance of ensuring that migrants who are being returned against their will are protected from physical harm although there is limited jurisprudence available to support a fleshing out of this very general obligation. Most recently, in its first-ever consideration of the issue of expulsion of aliens, the International Court of Justice emphasized that the rights of persons being expelled must be protected and upheld: "[t]here is no doubt (…) that the prohibition of inhuman and degrading treatment is among the rules of general international law which are binding on all States in all circumstances, even apart from any treaty commitments."[274] The European Court of Human Rights has affirmed that methods of deportation (expulsion) must not violate the prohibition on torture, inhuman or degrading treatment, or punishment.[275] In considering the liability of a State Party for injury and death that occurred in the course of an interception at sea, the Court noted that States Parties are bound to respect the lives of all those falling within their jurisdiction.[276] The Court recalled its observation in *Osman v. United Kingdom*[277] that Article 2 requires States not only to restrain from causing death but also to take measures to protect the lives of individuals within their jurisdiction.[278]

[271] "Calvo maintained that when a government expels a foreigner in a harsh inconsiderate manner (*'avec des formes blessantes'*) the latter's State of nationality has a right to base a claim on the expulsion as a violation of international law": R. Plender, *International Migration Law* (2nd revised ed. 1988), at 469–471 (quoting *Dictionnaire de droit international public et privé*). "[A] State engages international responsibility if it expels an alien … in an unnecessarily injurious manner": ibid. at 459, cited in International Law Commission, "Sixth Report on the Expulsion of Aliens," at n. 562. See further discussion on State responsibility in Chapter 4.

[272] See discussion of interdiction at sea in Chapter 6. See also discussion of extraterritorial application of human rights obligations in Chapter 3.

[273] See discussion on attribution of legal responsibility in Chapter 4, at Section 4.2.1.

[274] *Ahmadou Sadio Diallo Case*, at para. 87.

[275] *Alzery v. Sweden*, Application No. 10786/04 (Decision of Admissibility), [2004] ECHR 2004IV- (ECHR, Oct. 26, 2004).

[276] *Xhavara and Fifteen Others v. Italy and Albania*, at judgment, para. 1.

[277] Ibid., referring to *Osman v. The United Kingdom*, (2000) 29 EHRR 245 (ECHR, Oct. 28, 1998), at para. 115.

[278] *Xhavara and Fifteen Others v. Italy and Albania*, at judgment, para. 1.

The Human Rights Committee and the Committee against Torture have both repeatedly expressed concern over violations of the right to life and the prohibition on torture, inhuman or degrading treatment, or punishment in the context of forced return of asylum-seekers.[279] The supervisory body established under the European Convention for the Prevention of Torture and Inhuman or Degrading Treatment or Punishment[280] has been much more detailed and specific, addressing and rejecting a range of practices associated with forced removal, including physical assault as a form of persuasion or punishment.[281]

[279] When examining the State report of Belgium, the Human Rights Committee noted that certain techniques of restraint used in the forced removal of aliens (e.g., placing a cushion over the face of a recalcitrant deportee to prevent shouting and biting) entailed a risk to life. It noted that the case of a Nigerian national who died in such a manner illustrates the need to reexamine the whole procedure of forcible deportations. UN Human Rights Committee, "Concluding Observations: Belgium," UN Doc. CCPR/CO/81/BEL, Aug. 12, 2004, at para. 15. See also UN Committee against Torture, "Conclusions and Recommendations: Spain," UN Doc. CAT/C/CR/29/3, Dec. 23, 2002, at para. 11(c) (Committee against Torture expressing its concern about "cases of ill-treatment during enforced expulsion from the country, particularly in the case of unaccompanied minors").

[280] European Convention for the Prevention of Torture and Inhuman or Degrading Treatment or Punishment, ETS 126, 26.XI.1987, done Nov. 26, 1987, entered into force Feb. 1, 1989 (as amended by Protocols No. 1 (ETS No. 151) and No. 2 (ETS No. 152), which entered into force on March 1, 2002).

[281] "[I]t is entirely unacceptable for persons subject to a deportation order to be physically assaulted as a form of persuasion to board a means of transport or as a punishment for not having done so. The CPT [European Committee for the Prevention of Torture and Inhuman or Degrading Treatment or Punishment] welcomes the fact that this rule is reflected in many of the relevant instructions in the countries visited. For instance, some instructions which the CPT examined prohibit the use of means of restraint designed to punish the foreigner for resisting or which cause unnecessary pain.

"[T]he force and the means of restraint used should be no more than is reasonably necessary. The CPT welcomes the fact that in some countries the use of force and means of restraint during deportation procedures is reviewed in detail, in the light of the principles of lawfulness, proportionality and appropriateness.

"[...] The CPT has made it clear that the use of force and/or means of restraint capable of causing positional asphyxia should be avoided whenever possible and that any such use in exceptional circumstances must be the subject of guidelines designed to reduce to a minimum the risks to the health of the person concerned.

"In addition to the avoidance of the risks of positional asphyxia referred to above, the CPT has systemically recommended an absolute ban on the use of means likely to obstruct the airways (nose and/or mouth) partially or wholly. [...] It notes that this practice is now expressly prohibited in many States Parties and invites States which have not already done so to introduce binding provisions in this respect without further delay.

"It is essential that, in the event of a flight emergency while the plane is airborne, the rescue of the person being deported is not impeded. Consequently, it must be possible to remove immediately any means restricting the freedom of movement of the deportee, upon an order from the crew.

"[...] In the CPT's opinion, security considerations can never serve to justify escort staff wearing masks during deportation operations. This practice is highly undesirable, since it could make it very difficult to ascertain who is responsible in the event of allegations of ill-treatment.

"The CPT also has very serious reservations about the use of incapacitating or irritant gases to bring recalcitrant detainees under control in order to remove them from their cells and transfer them to the aircraft.

The relative strength of the prohibition against torture, inhuman or degrading treatment, or punishment, combined with the widespread acknowledgment of its application to all persons, irrespective of legal status or any other consideration,[282] supports the proposal of the International Law Commission for the articulation of a specific obligation, of all States, to protect persons subject to expulsion from torture and cruel, inhuman and degrading treatment, or punishment.[283] Application of this standard to the specific issue of migrant smuggling is affirmed by its inclusion in the Migrant Smuggling Protocol, which requires States Parties, in implementing this instrument, to take, consistent with its obligations under international law:

> ... all appropriate measures, including legislation if necessary, to preserve and protect the rights of [smuggled migrants] as accorded under applicable international law, in particular the right to life and the right not to be subjected to torture or other cruel, inhuman or degrading treatment or punishment.[284]

"[T]he importance has been highlighted of allowing immigration detainees to undergo a medical examination before the decision to deport them is implemented. This precaution is particularly necessary when the use of force and/or special measures is envisaged.

"Operations involving the deportation of immigration detainees must be preceded by measures to help the persons concerned to organize their return, particularly on the family, work and psychological fronts.

"Similarly, all persons who have been the subject of an abortive deportation operation must undergo a medical examination as soon as they are returned to detention.

"The importance of establishing internal and external monitoring systems in an area as sensitive as deportation operations by air cannot be overemphasized": European Committee for the Prevention of Torture and Inhuman or Degrading Treatment or Punishment, 13th General Report on the CPT's activities, CPT/Inf (2003) 35, cited in International Law Commission, "Sixth Report on the Expulsion of Aliens," at para. 234.

282 See, for example, HRC General Comment No. 15, at para. 7 ("Aliens ... must not be subjected to torture or to cruel, inhuman or degrading treatment or punishment"). See also "Declaration on Human Rights of Non-Nationals," at Art. 6 ("No alien shall be subjected to torture or to cruel, inhuman or degrading treatment or punishment").

283 "*Draft article 11: Obligation to protect persons being expelled from torture and cruel, inhuman or degrading treatment.* 1. A State may not, in its territory, subject a person being expelled to torture or to cruel, inhuman or degrading treatment.": International Law Commission, "Fifth Report on the Expulsion of Aliens," at para. 120. Note that the Rapporteur proposes special and additional consideration for the treatment of child aliens subject to expulsion. ("*Draft article 12: Specific case of the protection of children being expelled.* 1. A child being expelled shall be considered, treated and protected as a child, irrespective of his or her immigration status": ibid. at para. 127.

284 Migrant Smuggling Protocol, at Art. 16(1). An Interpretative Note confirms that the listing of certain rights in this paragraph was intended to emphasize the need to protect those rights in the case of smuggled migrants, but that the provision should not be interpreted as excluding or derogating from any other rights not listed. Interpretative Notes, included in United Nations Office on Drugs and Crime, Travaux Préparatoires *of the Negotiations for the Elaboration of the United Nations Convention against Transnational Organized Crime and the Protocols Thereto* (2006), at 541. The subsequent Note declares that Article 16(1) should not be understood as imposing new or additional obligations on States "beyond those contained in existing international instruments and customary international law": ibid.

2.5.1. No Arbitrary Detention

The international legal standard in relation to liberty and the prohibition on arbitrary detention is set out in Article 9(1) of the ICCPR:

> Everyone has the right to liberty and security of person. No one shall be subjected to arbitrary arrest or detention. No one shall be deprived of his liberty except on such grounds and in accordance with such procedures as are established by law.[298]

Similar provisions can be found in other international[299] and all major regional human rights treaties,[300] and it is evident that the standard applies to all persons, irrespective of their immigration status or other distinction.[301] In determining its scope and applicability, it is important to note that the right to liberty is not absolute. International law recognizes that States retain the ability to use measures that deprive people of their liberty, and this includes detention for unlawful entry or stay. Deprivation of liberty only becomes problematic in legal terms when it is unlawful and arbitrary.[302] States should make sure that they define precisely those cases in which deprivation of liberty is permissible. The principle of *legality* is violated if someone is detained on grounds that are not clearly established in a domestic law or are contrary to such law.[303] It can also be argued that this principle is violated if detention breaches international human rights standards, for example by operating to prevent a smuggled asylum-seeker from applying for refugee status.[304]

The *prohibition on arbitrariness* represents a second, additional requirement for States in relation to deprivation of liberty. In other words, it is not enough that the national law permits detention of smuggled migrants. That law must itself not be

[298] ICCPR, at Art. 9(1).

[299] See, for example, Migrant Workers Convention, at Art. 16(4) ("Migrant Workers and members of their families shall not be subjected individually or collectively to arbitrary arrest or detention; they shall not be deprived of their liberty except on such grounds and in accordance with such procedures as are established by law.").

[300] European Convention on Human Rights, at Art. 5(1); African Charter on Human and Peoples' Rights, at Art. 6; American Convention on Human Rights, at Art. 7.

[301] See, for example, "Declaration on Human Rights of Non-Nationals," at Art. 5 ("Aliens shall enjoy, in accordance with domestic law and subject to the relevant international obligations of the State in which they are present, in particular the following rights: (a) The right to life and security of person; no alien shall be subjected to arbitrary arrest or detention; no alien shall be deprived of his or her liberty except on such grounds and in accordance with such procedures as are established by law").

[302] Nowak, *CCPR Commentary*, at 211. See also UN Human Rights Committee, "General Comment No. 8: Right to Liberty and Security of Persons," UN Doc. HRI/GEN/1/Rev.7 at 130, May 12, 2004, adopted June 30, 1982.

[303] Nowak, *CCPR Commentary*, at 224; Y. Dinstein, "Right to Life, Physical Integrity, and Liberty," in L. Henkin ed., *The International Bill of Rights: The Covenant on Civil and Political Rights* 114 (1981), at 130.

[304] See further Chapter 9.

arbitrary and its application must not take place arbitrarily.[305] The word "arbitrary" refers to elements of injustice, unpredictability, unreasonableness, capriciousness, and lack of proportionality, as well as failures with respect to the common law principle of due process of law.[306] The Human Rights Committee has confirmed that detention of persons seeking asylum is not, per se, arbitrary.[307] However, the Committee has further stipulated that the prohibition on arbitrariness requires legally authorized detention to be reasonable and necessary in all of the circumstances of the case, and to be a proportionate means to achieve a legitimate aim.[308]

Deprivation of liberty provided by law must not be "manifestly disproportional, unjust or unpredictable."[309] The manner in which a decision is taken to deprive someone of his or her liberty must be capable of being deemed appropriate and proportionate in view of the circumstances of the case.[310] Importantly, a detention situation that was originally not arbitrary might become arbitrary if it continues over time without proper justification.[311] Regional human rights courts have confirmed that indefinite detention, particularly that which can be characterized as disproportionate or discriminatory (e.g., between nationals and nonnationals), violates the fundamental right to protection from arbitrary detention.[312]

Finally, States are required, under international law, to ensure that necessary procedural guarantees are in place to identify and respond to situations of unlawful or

[305] Nowak, *CCPR Commentary*, at 224–228; S. Joseph, J. Schultz, and M. Castan, *The International Covenant on Civil and Political Rights: Cases, Materials and Commentary* (2004) [Joseph et al., *The ICCPR*], at 308. In the *Chahal* case, the European Court of Human Rights confirmed that the requirement of "lawfulness" refers not just to conformity to national law, but also requires "that any deprivation of liberty should be in keeping with the purpose of Article 5, namely to protect the individual from arbitrariness." *Chahal v. The United Kingdom*, (1997) 23 EHRR 413 (ECHR, Nov. 15, 1996), at para. 118.

[306] Nowak, *CCPR Commentary*, at 225; Joseph et al., *The ICCPR*, at 156, 308–309. See also UN Human Rights Committee, "General Comment No. 16: The Right to Respect of Privacy, Family, Home and Correspondence, and Protection of Honour and Reputation," UN Doc. HRI/GEN/1/Rev.7 at 142, May 12, 2004, adopted Apr. 8, 1988, at para. 4: "[t]he introduction of the concept of arbitrariness is intended to guarantee that even interference provided for by law should be in accordance with the provisions, aims and objectives of the Covenant and should be, in any event, reasonable in the particular circumstances."

[307] *A. v. Australia*, UNHRC Comm. No. 560/1993, UN Doc. CCPR/C/59/D/560/1993, Apr. 30, 1997, decided Apr. 3, 1997 [*A. v. Australia*], at para. 9.3 ("there is no basis for the … claim that it is per se arbitrary to detain individuals requesting asylum").

[308] Ibid. at para. 9.2; *Hugo van Alphen v. The Netherlands*, UNHRC Comm. No. 305/1988, UN Doc. CCPR/C/39/D/305/1988, Aug. 15, 1990, decided July 23, 1990 [*Hugo van Alphen v. The Netherlands*], at para. 5.8.

[309] Nowak, *CCPR Commentary*, at 225.

[310] Ibid.

[311] Ibid. at 226.

[312] See, for example, *A. and Others v. United Kingdom*, (2009) 49 EHRR 29 (ECHR, Feb. 19, 2009), finding a violation of Article 5 of the European Convention on Human Rights.

arbitrary deprivation of liberty. The ICCPR specifies several of these procedural guarantees:

> Anyone who is deprived of his liberty by arrest or detention shall be entitled to take proceedings before a court, in order that the court may decide without delay on the lawfulness of his detention and order his release if the detention is not lawful[313];

and "[a]nyone who has been the victim of unlawful arrest or detention shall have an enforceable right to compensation."[314] Other international and regional instruments provide similar guarantees.[315]

Do different considerations or standards apply to the detention of smuggled asylum-seekers? The Human Rights Committee has examined a number of communications involving the administrative detention of asylum-seekers who have arrived unlawfully on to the territory of a State Party. The Committee has confirmed that:

> the fact of illegal entry may indicate a need for investigation and there may be other factors particular to the individual, such as the likelihood of absconding and lack of cooperation, which may justify detention for a period. *Without such factors detention may be considered arbitrary, even if entry was illegal.*[316]

The Committee has further confirmed that the procedural requirements in Article 9(2) of the ICCPR apply to administrative detention, including for purposes of immigration control, noting that any decisions to keep a person in detention should be open to "periodical review" so as to "reassess the necessity of detention," and that detention "should not continue beyond the period for which a State party can provide appropriate justification."[317] Further, according to the Committee, States should show that "there were no less invasive means of achieving the same ends."[318]

313 ICCPR, at Art. 9(4).

314 Ibid. at Art. 9(5).

315 Migrant Workers Convention, at Art. 16(8) (Migrant workers and members of their families who are under any form of detention must "be entitled to take proceedings before a court, in order that that court may decide without delay on the lawfulness of their detention and order their release if the detention is not lawful."); European Convention on Human Rights, at Arts. 5(1)–(4); American Convention on Human Rights, at Art. 7; and African Charter on Human and Peoples' Rights, at Art. 6.

316 A. *v. Australia*, at para. 9.4 (emphasis added).

317 *Danyal Shafiq v. Australia*, UNHRC Comm. No. 1324/2004, UN Doc. CCPR/C/88/D/1324/2004, Nov. 13, 2006, decided Oct. 31, 2006, at para. 7.2. See also A. *v. Australia*, at para. 9.4; *Bakhtiyari v. Australia*, UNHRC Comm. No. 1069/2002, UN Doc. CCPR/C/79/1069/2002, Nov. 6, 2003, decided Oct. 29, 2003, at para. 9.2.

318 *Shams and Others v. Australia*, UNHRC Comm. Nos. 1255, 1256, 1259, 1260, 1266, 1268, 1270, 1288/2004, UN Doc. CCPR/C/90/D/1255,1256,1259,1260,1266,1268,1270&1288/2004, Sept. 11, 2007, decided July 20, 2007, at para. 7.2. See also C. *v. Australia*, UNHRC Comm. No. 900/1999, UN Doc. CCPR/C/76/D/900/1999, Nov. 13, 2002, decided Oct. 28, 2002, at para. 8.2.

It is relevant at this point to recall that the capacity of States to penalize asylum-seekers for the fact of their unlawful arrival, including through detention, is constrained by Article 31 of the Refugee Convention. The same Article states that restrictions on the movement of refugees shall be limited to only those that "are necessary," and that "such restrictions shall only be applied until their status in the country is regularized or they obtain admission into another country."[319] In line with this provision, UNHCR goes somewhat beyond the position of the Human Rights Committee in asserting that "detention of asylum-seekers should normally be avoided and be a measure of last resort."[320] According to UNHCR, the grounds that would justify detaining an asylum-seeker are limited to the following: (1) to protect public order (including to prevent absconding, for initial identification/verification purposes, and to record the elements on which the claim for asylum is based); (2) to protect public health (must be justifiable in an individual's case); and (3) to protect national security (and even in such case it must be necessary, proportionate to the threat, nondiscriminatory, and subject to judicial oversight).[321] Detention of asylum-seekers for other purposes, for example, as part of a policy to deter future asylum-seekers, or as a punitive or disciplinary measure for illegal entry or presence in the country, is asserted to be contrary to international law.[322] UNHCR concludes that, for detention of asylum-seekers to be lawful and not arbitrary:

> ...any detention needs to be necessary in the individual case, reasonable in all the circumstances and proportionate to a legitimate purpose ... Further, failure to consider less coercive or intrusive means could also render detention arbitrary.[323]

In summary, it is apparent that the detention of smuggled migrants could, in certain cases, amount to unlawful deprivation of liberty and violate the prohibition on arbitrary detention. The likelihood of detention being characterized as unlawful or arbitrary is particularly high if it can be shown that such detention is not specifically provided for in law or is imposed contrary to law; is provided for or imposed in a discriminatory manner; is imposed for a prolonged, unspecified, or indefinite period; is unjust, unpredictable, and/or disproportionate; or is not subject to judicial or administrative review to confirm its legality and that it continues to be necessary in the circumstances, with the possibility for release where no grounds for

[319] Refugee Convention, at Art. 31(2).
[320] UNHCR Guidelines on Detention of Asylum-Seekers, at introductory para. 2.
[321] Ibid. at Guideline 4.1.
[322] Ibid.
[323] Ibid. at 15 (para. 18), citing *Hugo van Alphen v. The Netherlands* and *A. v. Australia*.

its continuation exist. These substantive and procedural requirements are subject to further, practical consideration in the specific context of migrant smuggling as discussed in Chapter 9.

2.5.2. *Conditions of Detention*

It is not sufficient for States to satisfy the requirement that detention of smuggled migrants be both lawful and nonarbitrary. International law requires that all persons, including smuggled migrants, who are lawfully and nonarbitrarily deprived of their liberty be treated with humanity and with respect for the inherent dignity of their person.[324] This raises one of the most critical and urgent issues facing many smuggled migrants. As noted by the ILC Special Rapporteur on the Expulsion of Aliens:

> The conditions in which aliens are detained prior to expulsion are among the most criticized aspects of State practice with respect to expulsion. It is generally during this phase of expulsion that some of the worst violations of an alien's rights occur.[325]

Establishing that States owe a "positive obligation" of care[326] toward those who are so completely within the State's power is only the first step. The task of determining the substantive content of the obligation to ensure that detainees are treated with humanity and respect for their dignity requires consideration of a range of different human rights. For example, the prohibition on discrimination is closely linked to the obligation to ensure that smuggled migrants who are detained are treated with humanity and respect for their dignity.[327] International and regional human rights bodies have also repeatedly observed the link between the obligation to ensure that detainees are treated with humanity and respect for their dignity, and the prohibi-

[324] ICCPR, Article 10(1). The Human Rights Committee has affirmed that this obligation applies to any person "deprived of liberty under the laws and authority of the State." UN Human Rights Committee, "General Comment No. 21: Humane Treatment of Persons Deprived of Their Liberty," UN Doc. HRI/GEN/1/Rev.7, at 153, May 12, 2004, adopted Apr. 10, 1992 [HRC General Comment No. 21], at para. 2. On application to aliens, see HRC General Comment No. 15, at para. 7. See also Migrant Workers Convention, at Art. 17(1) ("Migrant workers and members of their families who are deprived of their liberty shall be treated with humanity and with respect for the inherent dignity of the human person and for their cultural identity").

[325] International Law Commission, "Sixth Report on the Expulsion of Aliens," at para. 213.

[326] HRC General Comment No. 21, at para. 3.

[327] See, for example, CERD General Recommendation No. 30, at para. 19. (States should: "Ensure the security of non-citizens, in particular with regard to arbitrary detention, as well as ensure that conditions in centres for refugees and asylum-seekers meet international standards").

tion on torture and inhuman or degrading treatment or punishment.[328] As noted by the European Court of Human Rights:

> [T]he measures which deprive an individual of his or her freedom inevitably involve suffering and humiliation. This is a situation that cannot be avoided and that is not, in and of itself, a violation of [the prohibition on torture and cruel, inhuman or degrading treatment or punishment]. Nevertheless, this article requires a State to ensure that the conditions in which a person is detained are compatible with respect for human dignity, that detention arrangements do not cause distress or hardship to a degree that exceeds the inevitable level of suffering inherent in such a measure, and that, in terms of the practical aspects of confinement, an individual's health and well-being are provided for adequately.[329]

The Refugee Convention does not stipulate conditions of detention for asylum-seekers. However, UNHCR has affirmed, on many occasions, the common standard of humane detention identified previously.[330] UNHCR's Guidelines on Detention of Asylum-Seekers seek to flesh out the various elements or standards that reflect current international legal standards relating to the detention of asylum-seekers.[331] For this purpose it utilizes and affirms the applicability of jurisprudence generated by international human rights bodies,[332] as well as soft law instruments such as the UN

[328] See, for example, "Report of the Special Rapporteur on the Human Rights of Migrants, François Crépeau," UN Doc. A/HRC/20/24, Apr. 2, 2012, at paras. 32, 44, 46; *M.S.S. v. Belgium and Greece*, (2011) 53 EHRR 2 (ECHR, Jan. 21, 2011), esp. at paras. 230–234; Human Rights Watch, *The EU's Dirty Hands: Frontex Involvement in Ill-Treatment of Migrant Detainees in Greece* (2011), at 29–36; and UN Committee against Torture, "Conclusions and Recommendations: Ukraine," UN Doc. CAT/C/UKR/CO/5, Aug. 3, 2007, at para 20 (noting "the poor and overcrowded conditions of detention for asylum-seekers"). Note however Nowak's point that conditions of detention may violate the ICCPR Article 10 requirement for detainees to be treated with humanity, without necessarily violating the Article 7 prohibition on inhuman treatment: Nowak, *CCPR Commentary*, at 245.

[329] *Tabesh v. Greece*, Application No. 8256/07, [2009] ECHR 2224 (ECHR, Nov. 26, 2009), at para. 36, cited International Law Commission, "Sixth Report on the Expulsion of Aliens," at para. 221.

[330] See, for example, UN High Commissioner for Refugees Executive Committee, *Conclusion No. 93 – Conclusion on the Reception of Asylum-Seekers in the Context of Individual Asylum Systems*, Oct. 8, 2002.

[331] UNHCR Guidelines on Detention of Asylum-Seekers, at introductory para. 1. Guideline 8 is specific to conditions of detention.

[332] See, for example, UN Committee on the Elimination of Racial Discrimination, "Concluding Observations: South Africa," UN Doc. CERD/C/ZAF/CO/3, Oct. 19, 2006, at para. 23 (detained non-citizens to be protected from extortion and ill-treatment by public officials as well as given access to information about their rights and available legal remedies); UN Committee on Migrant Workers, "Concluding Observations: Mexico," UN Doc. CMW/C/MEX/CO/1, Dec. 20, 2006, at paras. 28, 34 (opportunity to lodge complaints of violations; right of consular access); UN Human Rights Committee, "Concluding Observations: Poland," UN Doc. CCPR/C/POL/CO/6, Nov. 15, 2010, at paras. 17–18 (overcrowding, inadequate healthcare, inadequate access to information on asylum-seeker rights); and UN Human Rights Committee, "Draft Concluding Observations: Belgium," UN Doc. CCPR/C/BEL/CO/5, Nov. 16, 2010, at para. 20 (excessive use of force against detained foreign nationals).

Body of Principles for the Protection of all Persons under Any Form of Detention or Imprisonment.[333] Taken together, these standards are asserted to require the initial screening of all asylum-seekers to identify trauma or torture victims for purposes of treatment as well as segregation of facilities (men from women, children from nonrelative adults, asylum-seekers from convicted criminals or prisoners on remand). They also require that detained asylum-seekers be provided with the opportunity to:

- Make regular contact and receive (where possible, private) visits from friends, relatives, religious, social, and legal counsel.
- Receive appropriate medical treatment, and psychological counseling where appropriate.
- Conduct some form of physical exercise.
- Practice their religion and to receive a diet in keeping with their religion.
- Access basic necessities (i.e. beds, shower facilities, basic toiletries, etc.).
- Continue further education or vocational training.
- Make complaints about their treatment.[334]

Additional considerations apply in relation to detained persons with special vulnerabilities, including women, elderly persons, children, and those with a disability.[335] Other substantive entitlements identified by international human rights bodies as relevant to asylum-seekers and other irregular migrants in detention include access to legal advice and information, access to consular assistance, and access to remedies for violations.[336]

2.5.3. *Detention of Smuggled Children*

Children make up a significant proportion of smuggled migrants[337] and they run similar risks to adults of being detained by national authorities in the country of destination (or elsewhere). International legal rules on the detention of children are very exacting and are governed by the overriding principle of respect for the child's best interests, as discussed previously. The strictness of rules around detention of children reflects an acknowledgment of the fact that detained children are highly vulnerable to abuse, victimization, and the violation of their rights. Under

333 UN General Assembly, "Body of Principles for the Protection of All Persons under Any Form of Detention or Imprisonment," adopted by GA Res. 43/173, UN Doc. A/RES/43/173, Annex, Dec. 9, 1988.

334 UNHCR Guidelines on Detention of Asylum-Seekers, at Guideline 8.

335 Ibid. at Guidelines 6–8.

336 See note 331 above. For additional references, see Hathaway, *The Rights of Refugees*, at 435–439.

337 United Nations Office on Drugs and Crime, *Smuggling of Migrants: A Global Review and Annotated Bibliography of Recent Publications* (2011), at 39. See also J. Bhabha and M. Crock, *Seeking Asylum Alone: A Comparative Study* (2007), at 32.

the provisions of the CRC, no child is to be deprived of his or her liberty unlawfully or arbitrarily.[338] This prohibition extends beyond penal detention to include deprivation of liberty on the basis of the child's welfare, health, and protection. It is therefore directly relevant to the situation of smuggled children who are detained in welfare facilities and shelters as well as in immigration detention.[339] International law requires any form of juvenile detention to be in conformity with the law, used only as a measure of last resort, and imposed for the shortest appropriate period of time.[340]

UNHCR has clearly stated that child asylum-seekers, including of course those who have been smuggled, should not generally be detained.[341] Under relevant UNHCR Guidelines, child asylum-seekers should be released into the care of family members who already have residency within the asylum country. Where this is not possible, alternative care arrangements providing adequate accommodation and appropriate supervision should be made available.[342] All appropriate alternatives to detention should be considered in the case of children accompanying their parents, and children and their primary caregivers should not be detained unless this is the only means of maintaining family unity. If these alternatives are not able to be applied and States do detain children, this should, in accordance with Article 37 of the CRC, be as a measure of last resort, and for the shortest possible period of time.[343] The Committee on the Rights of the Child has affirmed

[338] CRC, at Art. 37(b).

[339] The "UN Rules for the Protection of Juveniles Deprived of Their Liberty," at paragraph 11(b), define a deprivation of liberty as any form of detention or imprisonment or the placement of a person in a public or private custodial setting from which a person under the age of eighteen is not permitted to leave at will, by order of any judicial, administrative, or other public authority: UN General Assembly, "United Nations Rules for the Protection of Juveniles Deprived of Their Liberty," adopted by GA Res. 45/113, UN Doc. A/RES/45/113, Dec. 14, 1990.

[340] CRC, at Art. 37(b); "UN Rules for the Protection of Juveniles Deprived of Their Liberty," at para. 2; CRC General Comment No. 6, at para. 61. See also UN Committee on the Rights of the Child: "Concluding Observations: The Netherlands," UN Doc. CRC/C/15/Add.227, Feb. 26, 2004, at para. 54; "Concluding Observations: Canada," UN Doc. CRC/C/15/Add.215, Oct. 27, 2003, at para. 47.

[341] See UN High Commissioner for Refugees, *Refugee Children: Guidelines on Protection and Care* (1994), at chapter 7, part IV ("Detention"); *UNHCR's Guidelines on Policies and Procedures in Dealing with Unaccompanied Children Seeking Asylum* (Feb. 1997), at Guideline 7.6; and UNHCR Guidelines on Detention of Asylum-Seekers, at Guideline 9.2.

[342] See UN High Commissioner for Refugees, *Refugee Children: Guidelines on Protection and Care* (1994), at ch. 7, part IV ("Detention"); *UNHCR's Guidelines on Policies and Procedures in Dealing with Unaccompanied Children Seeking Asylum* (Feb. 1997), at Guideline 7.7; and UNHCR Guidelines on Detention of Asylum-Seekers, at Guideline 9.2.

[343] UN High Commissioner for Refugees: *Refugee Children: Guidelines on Protection and Care* (1994), at chapter 7, part IV ("Detention"); *UNHCR's Guidelines on Policies and Procedures in Dealing with Unaccompanied Children Seeking Asylum* (Feb. 1997), at Guideline 7.7; UN High Commissioner for Refugees, Executive Committee, *Conclusion on Children at Risk*, Doc. No. 107 (LVIII) – 2007, Feb. 22, 2007, at (b); and UNHCR Guidelines on Detention of Asylum-Seekers, at Guideline 9.1.

the importance of not detaining children caught up in counter-smuggling "push-back" operations.[344]

In addition to stipulating the circumstances under which a child can be detained, international law also imposes conditions on the conduct of such detention. Once again, the overriding principle is respect for the best interests of the child, including respect for his or her humanity and human dignity.[345] Additional and more detailed rules concern the separation of children detainees from adults[346]; the right of the detained child to maintain contact with his or her family through correspondence and visits[347]; the right of the detained child to prompt access to legal and other appropriate assistance[348]; and the right of the detained child to challenge the legality of the deprivation of his or her liberty before a court or other competent, independent and impartial authority, and to a prompt decision on any such action.[349] Detained children are further entitled to support for their physical and psychological recovery and social reintegration in an environment that fosters the health, self-respect, and dignity of the child.[350] International law also provides that each case involving a child deprived of his or her liberty should be handled expeditiously without any unnecessary delay.[351] These provisions appear to confirm the need to ensure that decisions impacting on the welfare and well-being of smuggled children are made on a case-by-case basis and with a view to ensuring the best interests of that individual child.

344 UN Committee on the Rights of the Child, "Concluding Observations: Italy," UN Doc. CRC/C/ITA/CO/3–4, Oct. 31, 2011, at para. 63 ("The Committee is deeply concerned that some of the migrants pushed back have been identified as requiring international protection, in violation of the State party's non-refoulement obligations. It is further of serious concern to the Committee that the State party has detained children with their families when forcibly returning migrants, without the possibility to seek asylum.").

345 CRC, at Art. 37(c). For an example of application of this principle in the context of smuggled child asylum-seekers, see UN Committee on the Rights of the Child, "Concluding Observations: Australia," UN Doc. CRC/C/15/Add.268, Oct. 20, 2005, at para. 64.

346 CRC, at Art. 37(c); "UN Rules for the Protection of Juveniles Deprived of Their Liberty," at para. 29; CRC General Comment No. 6, at para. 63.

347 CRC, at Art. 37(c); "UN Rules for the Protection of Juveniles Deprived of Their Liberty," at para. 29; CRC General Comment No. 6, at para. 63.

348 CRC Optional Protocol, at Art. 8; United Nations Children's Fund, *Guidelines for the Protection of Child Victims of Trafficking* (Sept. 2006) [UNICEF Guidelines], at Guidelines 4.2, 7.1, 9.2.1, 10.1, 10.2; CRC General Comment No. 6, at para. 63.

349 CRC, at Art. 37(d).

350 Ibid. at Art. 39; CRC Optional Protocol, at Art. 8; UNICEF Guidelines, at Guidelines 7.1, 7.2.

351 CRC Optional Protocol, at Art. 8.1(g); UNICEF Guidelines, at Guideline 8.

3

Acting against Migrant Smuggling: Capacities and Limitations

> There is no more important way to avoid conflict than by providing clear norms as to which state can exercise authority over whom, and in what circumstances. Without that allocation of competences, all is rancour and chaos.[1]

The allocation of competence – or capacity to act – is crucial to the operation of international law. The reverse side of that – limitations on capacity to act – is similarly determinative. The previous chapters set out the primary rules that establish the specific obligations of States: obligations that both prescribe certain conduct and, in different ways, set boundaries on the responses of States to migrant smuggling. The present chapter explores the applicable legal framework from a foundation level: the basis and scope of States' capacity to act under the principles of State sovereignty and jurisdiction. Just as the State remains the foundation on which international law is based, these keystone principles, by delineating the capacity of States to act, establish the parameters for what is and is not permissible in public international law.

It is a basic premise of this book that States have established for themselves a legitimate interest in preventing, responding to, and prosecuting migrant smuggling. However, securing that interest is not an automatic right or privilege. It is subject to a range of rules: most important, those that delineate *which* State has capacity to take action and in *what* circumstances. The international legal concepts of sovereignty and jurisdiction, examined in detail in Sections 3.1 and 3.2, provide the structure within which such questions may be answered. Of course, international law is not just about determining who can do what and when. Its task is also to ensure that, to the extent it is possible and appropriate, the State with the relatively greater *capacity* to take action (in terms of resources, access

[1] R. Higgins, *Problems and Process: International Law and How We Use It* (1995), at 56.

The authors acknowledge the important contribution of Angela Ha to the shaping of this chapter, most particularly Part 1.

to offenders, victims, evidence, etc.) coincides with the State with the strongest *claim* to take action as a matter of legitimate interest. Establishing this harmonization between capacity in fact and capacity in law requires a complex range of cooperative arrangements – from extradition treaties, to shiprider agreements and other bilateral or multilateral arrangements – whereby States may delegate to other States their own capacity to act.

The focus of this chapter is therefore essentially on the legal competence of States, as well as limitations on that competence. Capacity to act is a theme that runs through all major questions associated with migrant smuggling. It takes on particular importance in the context of criminalization – determining when a State is entitled to prescribe and enforce laws criminalizing conduct – but is also relevant to determining the circumstances under which human rights and refugee law obligations of States arise. The purpose of this chapter is twofold: (1) to provide a high-level summary and clarification of those aspects of sovereignty and jurisdiction most relevant to migrant smuggling, and (2) to provide a much more detailed analysis of one specific question: To what extent do international rules of fundamental importance to migrant smuggling – human rights and refugee law – bind States in relation to their extraterritorial actions?

The key questions considered in this chapter include the following:

- What is the relationship between State sovereignty and immigration control?
- How does international law differentiate between the capacity of a State to prescribe rules and to enforce them? On what bases may a State prescribe and enforce rules?
- When, and on what bases, is a State entitled to prescribe and enforce rules in respect of migrant smuggling?
- When is a State entitled to prescribe and enforce rules relating to migrant smuggling activity outside its territory? What happens when more than one State is entitled to act?
- When and under what circumstances is a State entitled to act in respect of migrant smuggling activities at sea? How does the capacity of a coastal State change depending on the proximity of a suspect vessel to its coastline? What capacity do coastal States, flag States of suspect vessels, and third States have to intervene in respect of migrant smuggling at sea? What actions may be taken with respect to vessels on the high seas, and what capacity do coastal States have to pursue and arrest a suspect vessel that seeks to evade arrest by fleeing to the high seas?
- How does the concept of jurisdiction operate under international human rights law and international refugee law? Specifically: When and how do international human rights law and international refugee law apply extraterritorially to

constrain State responses to migrant smuggling at the border, at sea, and in the territory of other States?

The chapter begins with a brief overview of State sovereignty, the starting point of any discussion about legal capacity to act. It then considers jurisdiction in international law: the principles that set out when and for what reasons a State is entitled to make rules regulating conduct and to take steps to enforce those rules. Capacity to act in the maritime context is critical to an assessment of the legal framework around migrant smuggling, and the very specific jurisdictional regime established under the law of the sea is subject to separate consideration, which in turn provides the framework for a more detailed discussion of smuggling by sea in Chapter 6. The remainder of the chapter is devoted to an examination of the operational scope of what are essentially limitations on the capacity to act: specifically the question of extraterritorial jurisdiction in the context of international human rights law and international refugee law.

PART 1: CAPACITY TO ACT

3.1. BASIC PRINCIPLES OF STATE SOVEREIGNTY

> Two cheers then, for sovereignty, understood as the defeasible but protected status in the international system, carrying with it the presumption of full governmental authority over a polity and territory. Reports of the death of sovereignty are much exaggerated.[2]

State sovereignty is not so much a rule of international law as its starting point, "the basic constitutional doctrine of the law of nations"[3] that both explains and legitimizes the inherent governing power of each State. This includes the power to relinquish authority to others.[4]

In as far as international law is premised on the concept of the State, it is necessarily based on the foundation of State sovereignty.[5] As the Permanent Court of

[2] J. Crawford, "Sovereignty as a Legal Value," in J. Crawford and M. Koskenniemi eds., *The Cambridge Companion to International Law* 117 (2012) [Crawford, "Sovereignty as a Legal Value"], at 132.

[3] J. Crawford, *Brownlie's Principles of Public International Law* (8th ed. 2012) [Crawford, *Brownlie's Principles of Public International Law*], at 448.

[4] "… [N]ot only is the state free to exercise its sovereignty; the protection of interests practically requires it. It can enter into a variety of political relations involving association with other states. It can decide to 'pool' sovereignty through regional institutions such as the European Union – assuming they are available to it. Or it can enter into specific substantive arrangements with other states and organizations. Short of full-scale integration in another state, its sovereignty survives such exercises of it, reflecting the continued identity of the territorial community to which its government should be (and sometimes is) accountable": Crawford, "Sovereignty as a Legal Value," at 132.

[5] M. N. Shaw, *International Law* (6th ed. 2008) [Shaw, *International Law*], at 487.

International Justice stated in the *Island of Palmas* arbitration, "sovereignty in the relations between States signifies independence [which] in regard to a portion of the globe is the right to exercise therein, to the exclusion of any other State, the functions of a State."[6] Sovereignty, therefore, may be thought of as a broad and normative concept almost synonymous with Statehood, encompassing the "totality of international rights and duties recognized by international law" as inherent in the notion of Statehood.[7]

The claim that sovereignty is the necessary "point of departure in settling most questions that concern international relations"[8] is certainly true of the issue of migrant smuggling. Threats (or perceptions of threats) to sovereignty were the primary impetus and justification for development of a legal regime against transnational organized crime, including the practice of migrant smuggling. The sovereign right of States to control their own borders is routinely invoked as both explanation and justification for action against illegal migration and migrant smuggling.[9] States also invoke sovereignty as a shield against responses to crimes such as migrant smuggling that could be considered an unjustifiable interference in their internal affairs.[10]

6 *Island of Palmas Case (Netherlands v. United States)*, (1949) 2 UNRIAA 829 (Permanent Court of Arbitration, Apr. 4, 1928) [*Island of Palmas Case*], at 838.

7 *Reparation for Injuries Suffered in the Service of the United Nations (Advisory Opinion)*, [1949] ICJ Rep 174, at 180, cited in J. Crawford, *The Creation of States in International Law* (2nd ed. 2006) [Crawford, *The Creation of States*], at 32. On broader concepts of sovereignty, see T. Gammeltoft-Hansen and R. Adler-Nissen, "An Introduction to Sovereignty Games," in R. Adler-Nissen and T Gammeltoft-Hansen eds., *Sovereignty Games: Instrumentalizing State Sovereignty in Europe and Beyond* 1 (2008), at 3: "sovereignty appears to be a multifaceted technical concept… In legal terms, sovereignty sets out the material and geographical scope of a polity's authority and thereby the mutual exclusive claims in a world inhabited by a plurality of states; in political terms, sovereignty signifies the supremacy and inviolability of a state's institutions… As a legal-political concept, sovereignty in this sense transgresses any simply definition, but it may best be described along the continuum of its different guises. These include sovereignty as a *competence*, a set of legal rights toward both the peers and the subjects of the polity; sovereignty as *power or control*, whether envisaged in political, economic, or symbolical terms; sovereignty as *legitimacy*, especially since the rise of debates on popular sovereignty; and sovereignty as *personality, entailing a certain number of duties and obligations for those claiming it*." (emphases added).

8 *Island of Palmas Case*, at 838.

9 See, for example, the independent report on smuggling of asylum-seekers into Australia: Australian Government, Report of the Expert Panel on Asylum Seekers, August 2012, Attachment 2, at 77 ("People smuggling is a global and a regional problem. To facilitate and profit from irregular migration, networks need to transcend international borders, undermining state sovereignty and security in addition to risking the safety of irregular migrants").

10 See United Nations Convention against Transnational Organized Crime, 2225 UNTS 209, done Nov. 15, 2000, entered into force Sept. 29, 2003 [Organized Crime Convention], at Art. 4 ("1. States Parties shall carry out their obligations under this Convention in a manner consistent with the principles of sovereign equality and territorial integrity of States and that of non-intervention in the domestic affairs of other States. 2. Nothing in this Convention entitles a State Party to undertake in the territory of another State the exercise of jurisdiction and performance of functions that are reserved exclusively for the authorities of that other State by its domestic law.").

A full and nuanced understanding of sovereignty, including its implications and limitations, is essential to understanding how and to what extent migrant smuggling can be monitored, governed, and controlled by international law.

The following section outlines key aspects of sovereignty, and briefly sets out their implications for a study of migrant smuggling.

3.1.1. *Sovereign Equality and Noninterference*

International cooperation and international law are both founded on the basic concepts of State sovereignty and equality, which are enshrined in the Charter of the United Nations itself.[11] The legal concept of formal sovereign equality is further elaborated in the United Nations Declaration on Friendly Relations:

> All States enjoy sovereign equality. They have equal rights and duties and are equal members of the international community, notwithstanding differences of an economic, social, political or other nature. In particular, sovereign equality includes the following elements: (a) States are juridically equal; (b) each State enjoys the rights inherent in full sovereignty; (c) each State has the duty to respect the personality of other States; (d) the territorial integrity and political independence of the State are inviolable; (e) each State has the right freely to choose and develop its political, social, economic and cultural systems; (f) each State has the duty to comply fully and in good faith with its international obligations and to live in peace with other States.[12]

Sovereign equality, in this sense, may be regarded as an *external manifestation* of sovereignty. It operates defensively as a shield against external interference. The principle of noninterference[13] by one State in the internal affairs of another is the logical consequence of both sovereign equality and territorial sovereignty, whereby each State must be regarded as having full powers to govern within its territory to

11 Charter of the United Nations, 1 UNTS 16, done June 26, 1945, entered into force Oct. 24, 1945, at Art. 2(1).

12 UN General Assembly, "Declaration on Principles of International Law concerning Friendly Relations and Co-operation among States in accordance with the Charter of the United Nations," GA Res. 2625 UN GAOR, 25th sess, 1883rd plen mtg, Supp. No. 18, UN Doc. A/5217, adopted Oct 24. 1970 [Declaration on Friendly Relations].

13 See further *Military and Paramilitary Activities in and against Nicaragua (Nicaragua v. United States of America) (Merits)*, [1986] ICJ Rep 14 [*Nicaragua Case*], at para. 202 ("The principle of non-intervention involves the right of every sovereign State to conduct its affairs without outside interference ... It has ... been presented as a corollary of the principle of the sovereign equality of States."); and Declaration on Friendly Relations ("No State or group of States has the right to intervene, directly or indirectly, for any reason whatever, in the internal or external affairs of any other State.... Every State has an inalienable right to choose its political, economic, social and cultural systems, without interference in any form by another State").

the exclusion of all other States.[14] Sovereign equality and noninterference further provide the basis for modern positivist approaches to international law, which recognize the consent of States to be bound by a rule as essential to that rule's legitimacy. The consent of affected States is therefore the critical criterion for any expansion or contraction of a State's existing legal capacity to act.

Formal equality both dictates and preserves such basic practices as international lawmaking, the functions of international legal institutions, and the principles of dispute settlement in international law. However, its relevance in practice should not be overstated.[15] The *principle* of formal equality cannot – and does not – override major inequalities in the practical ability of different States to take action, bear duties, and enforce rights in international law. In some areas, such as environmental law and trade law, this has given rise to the notion of a "'duality of norms' – that is, the idea that in some fields it is unfair or unrealistic to impose the same legal obligations on every State."[16] As discussed in Chapter 6, this is arguably also the case with respect to many aspects of migrant smuggling–related law enforcement at sea, in which coercive rights and duties have been unevenly assigned, often by treaty, from States with limited resources or capacity to a small number of States with greater resources at their disposal and thus far greater capacity to exercise maritime power.

3.1.2. *Territorial Sovereignty*

In contrast to sovereign equality (characterized earlier in this chapter as an external expression of sovereignty vis-à-vis other States), territorial sovereignty pertains

14 The findings of Arbitrator Huber in *Island of Palmas Case*, although confined to territorial sovereignty, are instructive: "Territorial sovereignty ... involves the exclusive right to display the activities of a State. This right has as corollary a duty: the obligation to protect within the territory the rights of other States, in particular their right to integrity and inviolability ... Without manifesting its territorial sovereignty in a manner corresponding to circumstances, the State cannot fulfill this duty. Territory sovereignty cannot limit itself to its negative side, i.e., to excluding the activities of other States; for it serves to divide between nations the space upon which human activities are employed, in order to assure them at all points the minimum of protection of which international law is the guardian": at 839.

15 See A. V. Lowe, *International Law* (2007) [Lowe, *International Law*], at 114 (referring to sovereign equality as "a prominent element of the catechism of international lawyers, fundamental and unshakeable in theory but baseless and with few meaningful consequences in practice.").

16 In Lowe's view, this imbalance inevitably arises in the practical application of certain areas of law: "One might say that in cases where differential obligations are imposed the law still applies equally, in as much as each State is equally bound by the rules that apply to it, and it is simply the range of applicable rules that varies from State to State. That is, of course, true, but only at a level of abstraction that conceals the practical reality, which is that *in certain fields the principle of sovereign equality has been departed from because it has appeared to States to be in the interests of justice and the efficient promotion of global interests* to do so": ibid. at 116 (emphasis added).

generally to the *internal* manifestation of sovereignty.[17] Put simply, it refers not to "ownership of but [rather] *governing power with respect to* territory"[18]; or, in the words of arbitrator Huber in the *Island of Palmas* arbitration, to the "exclusive competence of the State in regard to its own territory ... the right to exercise therein, to the exclusion of any other State, the functions of a State."[19] Territorial sovereignty is the natural consequence of two fundamental criteria for statehood: a defined territory[20] and government.[21] It expresses as a normative principle of international law: the requirement that each State possesses exclusive and effective competence to regulate affairs within its territory. Insofar as effective government constitutes the most widely accepted and understood criterion of modern Statehood (in turn the basis of international law), territorial sovereignty has been said to constitute both "an essential foundation of international relations,"[22] and "a fundamental axiom" of international law.[23]

Territorial sovereignty goes hand in hand with territorial jurisdiction, the primary basis for jurisdiction in international law. This latter concept is discussed further at Section 3.2.2.1 of this chapter.

3.1.3. *The Reserved Domain of Domestic Jurisdiction*

The natural consequence of sovereign equality and noninterference is internal sovereignty: that is, exclusivity of power within the reserved domain (*domaine réservé*) of a State's domestic jurisdiction. Internal sovereignty is the basis for legislative power and the authority of each national legal system to govern within the State. Internal sovereignty is exclusive, marking out an area that is beyond the reach of international law.

The concept of a "reserved domain" is vague and circular and has not escaped criticism on these grounds.[24] Certainly it is evident that within the contemporary international legal environment, domestic jurisdiction or the reserved domain should not be considered static or stand-alone concepts. Rather, as the Permanent Court of International Justice recognized in the *Nationality Decrees* decision, they are

[17] C. Parry, J. Grant, and C. Barker eds., *Parry and Grant Encyclopaedic Dictionary of International Law* (3rd ed. 2009), at 598. On a more nuanced view, see Arbitrator Huber's findings in the *Island of Palmas Case* decision, at note 14 above.

[18] Crawford, *The Creation of States*, at 56 (emphasis added).

[19] *Island of Palmas Case*, at 838.

[20] Convention on Rights and Duties of States adopted by the Seventh International Conference of American States, 165 LNTS 20, done Dec. 26, 1933, entered into force Dec. 26, 1934 at Art. 1(b).

[21] Ibid. at Art. 1(c).

[22] *Corfu Channel (United Kingdom v. Albania) (Merits)*, [1949] ICJ Rep 4, at 35.

[23] Shaw, *International Law*, at 487–488, citing D. P. O'Connell, *International Law*, vol. 1 (2nd ed. 1970), at 403.

[24] Crawford, *Brownlie's Principles of Public International Law*, at 453–455.

relative: having meaning only with reference to what is regulated, at any given time, by the consent-based rules of public international law.[25] The granting of nationality and immigration control has traditionally been cited as being archetypally within the reserved domain of States.[26] The continual affirmation of this position through instruments such as the Migrant Smuggling Protocol[27] indicate that it is an enduring one. However, a central premise of the present book is that the entitlement of a State to control the entry of aliens into its territory must be filtered through the lens of international rules that the State has in one way or another agreed to. The way in which a State regulates immigration and polices its borders is therefore *not* entirely outside the reach of international law.[28]

As international law matures and expands in scope, it has become widely accepted that "no subject is irrevocably fixed within the reserved domain."[29] International

25 "The question whether a certain matter is or is not solely within the jurisdiction of a State is an essentially relative question; it depends upon the development of international relations": *Nationality Decrees in Tunis and Morocco*, [1923] PCIJ Rep, Series B, No. 4, at 24. See similarly *Aegean Sea Continental Shelf (Greece v. Turkey) (Jurisdiction)*, [1978] ICJ Rep 3, at para. 77: "it hardly seems conceivable that in such a convention [the 1928 General Act for the Pacific Settlement of International Disputes] terms like 'domestic jurisdiction' and 'territorial status' were intended to have a fixed content regardless of the subsequent evolution of international law."

26 I. Brownlie, *Principles of Public International Law* (7th ed. 2008) [Brownlie, *Principles of Public International Law*], at 293, citing C. Rousseau, "L'Indépendance de l'État dans l'Ordre International" (1948) 73(2) *Recueil des Cours* 167, at 239–46; and G. Cornelisse, *Immigration Detention and Human Rights: Rethinking Territorial Sovereignty* (2010), at 161–163, noting that although the development of the international human right to leave curtails the domestic jurisdiction of States over *emigration*, it remains commonly accepted that *immigration* lies within the reserved domain of domestic jurisdiction. Shaw, *International Law*, at 647: "State functions which are regarded as beyond the reach of international legal control and within the exclusive sphere of state management include the setting of conditions for the grant of nationality and the elaboration of the circumstances in which aliens may enter the country." See further G. Goodwin-Gill, *International Law and the Movement of Persons between States* (1978) [Goodwin-Gill, *International Law and the Movement of Persons*], at 51–58, noting that "[q]uestions of immigration, of the entry and expulsion of aliens, fall easily within traditional conceptions of domestic jurisdiction" (at 51, but see note 288 in this chapter); *Nottebohm*, finding that it is "for every sovereign State, to settle by its own legislation the rules relating to the acquisition of its nationality, and to confer that nationality by naturalization granted by its own organs in accordance with that legislation": *Nottebohm (Liechtenstein v. Guatemala)*, [1955] ICJ Rep 4, at 20; and the 1930 Convention on Certain Questions in Relation to the Conflict of Nationality Laws, 179 LNTS 89, done Apr. 12, 1930, entered into force July 1, 1937: "It is for each State to determine under its own law who are its nationals.": at Art. 1.

27 Protocol against the Smuggling of Migrants by Land, Sea and Air, supplementing the United Nations Convention against Transnational Organized Crime, 2241 UNTS 507, done Nov. 15, 2000, entered into force Jan. 28, 2004 [Migrant Smuggling Protocol].

28 See further Goodwin-Gill, *International Law and the Movement of Persons*, at 51–58: "Issues arising from the exercise of powers of exclusion and expulsion are commonly affected by matters such as nationality and human rights. For this reason, any claimed presumption that such powers are sealed within the reserved domain requires close scrutiny." (at 58).

29 Brownlie, *Principles of Public International Law*, at 293.

human rights law has been joined by areas as diverse as environmental protection,[30] trade,[31] and disaster management[32] in being recognized as suitable subjects of international cooperation and regulation through new and often very complex international legal frameworks. Although migration law is still considered by some to be "the last bastion of sovereignty,"[33] the "problem" of migrant smuggling has not escaped this evolution.

3.2. PRINCIPLES OF JURISDICTION IN GENERAL INTERNATIONAL LAW

In spite of its centrality to the operation of international law, the topic of jurisdiction is, like sovereignty, complex, ambiguous, and not well understood.[34] The present section seeks to cut through some of the ambiguities and complexities in briefly considering the principles of law relating to jurisdiction, with a specific focus on their relevance for the international legal regulation of migrant smuggling. It should be noted at the outset that this discussion is concerned solely with jurisdiction in the

30 See, for example, P. W. Birnie, A. E. Boyle, and C. Redgwell, *International Law and the Environment* (2009), at 128–130, regarding the designation of the environment as a "common concern."

31 See, for example, J. P. Trachtmann, "The International Economic Law Revolution" (1996) 17(1) *University of Pennsylvania Journal of International Economic Law* 33, at 36: "international economic law is the leading engine for revising the *domaine réservé* of traditional public international law, the unquestioned margin of deference accorded the state."

32 See the International Law Commission's ongoing work on the Draft Articles on the Protection of Persons in the Event of Disasters: Reports on the Protection of Persons in the Event of Disasters by the Special Rapporteur, Mr. Eduardo Valencia-Ospina, "Preliminary Report," UN Doc. A/CN.4/598, May 5, 2008, "Second Report," UN Doc. A/CN.4/615, May 7, 2009, "Third Report," A/CN.4/629, Mar. 31, 2010, "Fourth Report," UN Doc. ACN.4/643, May 11, 2011, "Fifth Report," A/CN.4/652, Apr. 9, 2012; Reports of the drafting committee, "Texts of Draft Articles 1, 2, 3, 4 and 5 as Provisionally Adopted by the Drafting Committee," UN Doc. A/CN.4/L.758, July, 24, 2009, "Texts and Titles of Draft Articles 6, 7, 8 and 9 Provisionally Adopted by the Drafting Committee on 6, 7 and 8 July 2010," UN Doc. A/CN.4/L.776, July 14, 2010, "Texts and titles of Draft Articles 10 and 11 Provisionally Adopted by the Drafting Committee on 19 July 2011," UN Doc. A/CN.4/L.794, July 20, 2011, "Texts and Titles of Draft Articles 5 bis, 12, 13, 14 and 15, Provisionally Adopted by the Drafting Committee from 5 to 11 July 2012," UN Doc. A/CN.4/L.812, July 12, 2012; and International Law Commission, "Protection of Persons in the Event of Disasters, Memorandum by the Secretariat," UN Doc. A/CN.4/590, Dec. 11, 2007.

33 C. Dauvergne, *Making People Illegal: What Globalisation Means for Migration Law* (2008), at 169.

34 It has been remarked, for example, that "[j]urisdiction, as a topic of international law, has a less solid and universal basis than is often supposed": A. Lowe and C. Staker, "Jurisdiction," in M. D. Evans ed., *International Law* 313 (3rd ed. 2010) [Lowe and Staker, "Jurisdiction"], at 315, and also at 338: "Curiously, there is no satisfactory modern monograph on jurisdiction." See also C. Ryngaert, *Jurisdiction in International Law* (2008) [Ryngaert, *Jurisdiction in International* Law], at 6: "The law of jurisdiction is doubtless one of the most essential as well as controversial fields of international law," and at 5: "While international lawyers often employ the term 'jurisdiction', and most of them have an inkling of what it means, defining jurisdiction is hardly self-evident," citing B. George, "Extraterritorial Application of Penal Legislation" (1966) 64 *Michigan Law Review* 609, at 621: "One of the most difficult words in the legal lexicon to define is the term 'jurisdiction'."

sense of *State capacity to act.* It does not consider jurisdiction in the context of the authority of international bodies, such as courts, to decide what the law is.

The discussion is in five parts. The first part considers the meaning of the term "jurisdiction" and the differences between prescriptive and enforcement jurisdiction. The second part outlines the various bases on which prescriptive jurisdiction – that is, jurisdiction to regulate by prescribing laws or other rules – can be exercised. These bases or "heads" of jurisdiction form the crux of any discussion of jurisdiction, as they provide a principled framework for the difficult but necessary exercise of *allocating* competence: that is, determining the extent of jurisdiction by setting out when and why a particular State will be entitled to regulate certain conduct or events. All but the first of these grounds (territory) is concerned with allocation of *extraterritorial* jurisdiction. The third part focuses on the relatively straightforward issue of when a State has enforcement jurisdiction – jurisdiction to compel compliance with its rules. The fourth part examines the recent and significant trend, highly relevant to the issue of migrant smuggling, of establishing "quasi-universal" jurisdiction through treaty law for transnational crimes. The final part considers how claims of jurisdiction made concurrently by two or more States may be resolved.

3.2.1. *Understanding Jurisdiction*

In the context of international law, jurisdiction is essentially a byword for *competence* – "the extent of each State's right to regulate conduct or the consequences of events."[35] In this sense, jurisdiction, literally the *juris dictum* or the speaking of the law, refers to the parameters of a State's ability to create and regulate its particular public order through any exercise of State powers.[36] Jurisdiction, like sovereignty, may be considered an attribute of Statehood (as a manifestation of State sovereignty through the judicial, legislative, and executive branches of its government) as well as a natural extension of the reserved domain and its attendant principle of noninterference.[37] This does not mean, however, that jurisdiction is an inward-looking or State-centric concept. The question of competence arises whenever a State purports to regulate any conduct that is not exclusively domestic, either because no obvious domestic link exists or because the conduct affects the interests of several States,

35 R. Jennings and A. Watts eds., *Oppenheim's International Law: Volume I, Peace* (9th ed. 1992) [*Oppenheim's International Law: Volume I, Peace (9th ed.)*], at 456.

36 Lowe and Staker, "Jurisdiction," at 313–314.

37 Crawford, *Brownlie's Principles of Public International Law*, at 456. See further Ryngaert, *Jurisdiction in International* Law, at 5–6: "What is certain is that jurisdiction somehow relates to sovereignty. … As [the international law of jurisdiction] ensures that States, especially powerful States, do not assert jurisdiction over affairs which are the domain of other States, it is closely related to the customary international law principles of non-intervention and sovereign equality of States."

each of which may stake a claim of jurisdiction. In international law, whether a State has such competence in a particular situation will be determined exclusively by the rules of jurisdiction.[38] In other words, jurisdiction as a matter of international law is essentially about establishing a framework for avoiding conflict between States in situations of overlapping or concurrent claims of competence, and ensuring that "vacuums of jurisdiction"[39] are dealt with appropriately.

Jurisdiction in international law generally refers to two different types of competence: (1) competence to make laws and regulations governing a matter (*prescriptive* jurisdiction); and (2) competence to compel compliance with those rules, including through recourse to punitive or coercive measures (*enforcement* jurisdiction).[40] The distinction between prescriptive and enforcement jurisdiction is critical because the powers to prescribe laws and to enforce them are not always coextensive.[41] Because prescriptive and enforcement jurisdiction operate in fundamentally different ways, very different tests apply to justify their application. For prescriptive jurisdiction, the test is a multifaceted one, and multiple alternative principles may be invoked. For enforcement jurisdiction, the test is a straightforward but stringent one of territoriality. These principles and their associated tests of application are examined in the next sections.

3.2.2. *Prescriptive Jurisdiction over the Crime of Migrant Smuggling*

In this context, prescriptive jurisdiction is concerned with establishing when a State may prescribe acts as criminal under its own law. This area of international law is dynamic and contested. That can be explained, at least in part, by the fact that there are very few impediments to a State declaring it has prescriptive jurisdiction over an issue. Although there is frequently a practical limit on how many States may

38 F. A. Mann, "The Doctrine of Jurisdiction in International Law," in *Hague Recueil des cours*, vol. 111 (1964) [Mann, "The Doctrine of Jurisdiction"], at 9–13.

39 B. Simma and A. T. Müller, "Exercise and the Limits of Jurisdiction," in J. Crawford and M. Koskenniemi eds., *The Cambridge Companion to International Law*, 134 (2012) [Simma and Müller, "Exercise and the Limits of Jurisdiction"], at 138.

40 There is potentially a third category of "adjudicative jurisdiction," referring to the competence of a State's courts to determine a contested issue between parties in cases referred to them, which has been identified, for example, in the American Law Institute's *Restatement (Third) of the Foreign Relations Law of the United States* and the Council of Europe's *Model Plan for the Classification of Documents concerning State Practice in the Field of Public International Law* (June 12, 1997) (Part Eight, subsection III). However, this book adopts the view of Lowe and Staker that the adjudicative competence of courts to determine and enforce the law is simply the judicial aspect of prescriptive and enforcement jurisdiction respectively. See further Lowe and Staker, "Jurisdiction," at 315–317; and Shaw, *International Law*, at 645–646.

41 M. C. Bassiouni, "The History of Universal Jurisdiction and Its Place in International Law," in S. Macedo ed., *Universal Jurisdiction: National Courts and the Prosecution of Serious Crimes under International Law* 39 (2004) [Bassiouni, "The History of Universal Jurisdiction"], at 40.

exercise enforcement jurisdiction (the taking of coercive action) over a particular act or offender, there is no such practical limit on how many States may proclaim identical, overlapping, or even inconsistent rules to govern a certain matter (the reconciliation of which is considered in Chapter 3, Section 3.2.5). If assertion of jurisdiction is not available on the basis of territoriality, international law recognizes four alternative bases for claiming prescriptive jurisdiction over a matter or situation.

3.2.2.1. Territoriality

Territoriality is the most important and most straightforward basis for assertions of jurisdiction in international law, a direct consequence of sovereignty that vests in each State an entitlement to regulate acts and events taking place in its territory.[42] Within the area comprising its "territory," a State enjoys "plenary" jurisdiction, that is, presumptively unlimited and all-encompassing powers to prescribe (and enforce) rules.

It is important to note that the reach of territoriality applies also to a State's territorial sea, extending no more than twelve nautical miles from its coast, and to the airspace above its land and sea territory. Restricted territorial jurisdiction is also recognized in respect of other areas such as a State's Exclusive Economic Zone (EEZ), where it may exercise territorial powers in respect of certain functions such as exploitation of natural resources and conservation of the marine environment.[43] In addition, the concept of the "flag State" serves to extend territorial jurisdiction into areas where a State may otherwise have no or limited jurisdictional competence. For purposes of determining jurisdiction at international law, official vessels including ships and aircraft are most accurately considered as the subjects of nationality jurisdiction, considered further at Section 3.2.2.2, though in practice their regulation by States may (by reason of official immunity) resemble the exercise of territoriality jurisdiction.[44]

The principle that the State in which a crime has been committed may exercise jurisdiction within the territory of the State presents few problems. However, more

[42] Lowe and Staker, "Jurisdiction," at 320; Ryngaert, *Jurisdiction in International* Law, at 42. See also Ryngaert, *Jurisdiction in International Law*, at 29: "The primacy of territorial jurisdiction is usually premised on the principle of sovereign equality of States and the principle of non-intervention (or non-interference)"; and Shaw, *International Law*, at 652–653: "The territorial basis for the exercise of jurisdiction reflects one aspect of the sovereignty exercisable by a state in its territorial home, and is the indispensable foundation for the application of the series of legal rights that a state possesses. That a country should be able to legislate with regard to activities within its territory and to prosecute for offences committed upon its soil is a logical manifestation of a world order of independent states …" (citation omitted).

[43] See further discussion of maritime zones at Section 3.3.2 in this chapter.

[44] Lowe and Staker, "Jurisdiction," at 322.

complex issues arise when different components of an offense occur in different locations. Migrant smuggling provides a quintessential example: the acquiring or preparation of fraudulent travel or identity documents may take place in the State of origin or a transit State; the actual facilitation of illegal cross-border entry may take place in two or more States; and enabling and facilitating the illegal residence of a smuggled migrant takes place in the destination State.

International law accommodates these situations by recognizing a division of territorial jurisdiction into "subjective" and "objective" variants,[45] sometimes distinguished as "conduct" and "result."[46] Subjective territoriality creates jurisdiction over crimes that are initiated within the territory of the State, but completed outside its territory ("conduct"). Objective territoriality enables jurisdiction to be asserted "when any essential constituent element of a crime is consummated on the [asserting] State's territory" (result).[47] As Crawford notes, the cumulative effect of the two bases is that "whenever the constituent elements of a crime occur across an interstate boundary, both States have jurisdiction."[48] This issue is considered further in Chapter 5 in the context of criminalization of migrant smuggling offenses.

3.2.2.2. Extraterritorial Jurisdiction: Nationality/Passive Personality

The second universally accepted ground for establishing jurisdiction – in this instance for extraterritorial acts – is nationality. International law permits a State to exercise prescriptive jurisdiction over the conduct of its nationals, wherever that conduct may occur, solely on the basis of nationality.[49] Historically, sovereigns asserted "nationality" jurisdiction over their subjects on the basis of allegiance, long before consolidating sovereign control over territory.[50] However, as the territorial State rose in prominence to become the basic unit of modern international relations and the subject and object of international law, territorial jurisdiction eclipsed nationality as the most prominent basis for jurisdiction.[51]

45 Ibid. at 321–322; and Ryngaert, *Jurisdiction in International* Law, at 76.

46 Simma and Müller, "Exercise and the Limits of Jurisdiction," at 140–141.

47 Crawford, *Brownlie's Principles of Public International Law*, at 458.

48 Ibid. at 459.

49 G. Triggs, *International Law: Contemporary Principles and Practices* (2nd ed. 2011) [Triggs, *International Law*], at 436.

50 Lowe and Staker, "Jurisdiction," at 323. See also Ryngaert, *Jurisdiction in International Law*, at 44: "In the ancient world, composed of communities rather than territories, allegiances based on religion, race, or nationality prevailed over those based on territoriality."

51 "[T]he advent of the European territorial State as the paradigmatic unit of the international legal order has long since given territorial jurisdiction pre-eminence. Jurisdiction based on nationality is used relatively infrequently": Lowe and Staker, "Jurisdiction," at 323. See also Ryngaert, *Jurisdiction in International* Law, at 47: "from the seventeenth century on, a century that witnessed the rise of the

Today, prescriptive jurisdiction based on nationality is generally only exercised to prevent and punish the commission of particularly serious offenses such as child sex offenses, terrorism and, most recently, certain offenses created through transnational criminal law such as those relating to corruption and drug trafficking as well as offenses established under the Organized Crime Convention and its Protocols. In all these situations it is the nationality of the suspect or offender that is relevant to the establishment of jurisdiction. The Organized Crime Convention for example, permits a State Party to exercise its jurisdiction in respect of migrant smuggling offenses when the offense is committed either against one of its nationals[52] (as in the case of aggravated migrant smuggling endangering life or safety[53]) or committed by one of its nationals.[54] The provision is optional and explicitly made subject to the Convention's overarching provisions related to protection of the sovereignty of other States.[55] It has nevertheless provided a basis for criminalization in a number of States.[56]

Nationality may also provide a "necessary criterion" of jurisdiction where territoriality is inappropriate or impossible to assert. As territoriality is inapplicable on the high seas and its superjacent airspace, the principle of flag State jurisdiction over ships and aircraft is another important variety of nationality jurisdiction[57] of particular relevance to the present study. It is relevant to note at this point that international law recognizes three very different types of nationals: (1) citizens[58]; (2) corporations

modern and fully sovereign nation State in the aftermath of the Westphalian Peace (1648), … the pre-eminence of the principle of territoriality in public international law became gradually entrenched in Europe."

[52] Organized Crime Convention, at Art. 15(2)(a). This case is sometimes referred to as the "passive personality principle" of jurisdiction and is a variant of the nationality grounds.

[53] Migrant Smuggling Protocol, at Art 6(3).

[54] Organized Crime Convention, at Art. 15(2)(b). Note that the link between the Convention and the Migrant Smuggling Protocol means that these provisions are applicable to such offenses when they are conducted in the course of migrant smuggling.

[55] Organized Crime Convention, Article 15(2), is expressed as being subject to Article 4, which provides that "States Parties shall carry out their obligations under this Convention in a manner consistent with the principles of sovereign equality and territorial integrity of States and that of non-intervention in the domestic affairs of other States" and that "Nothing in this Convention entitles a State Party to undertake in the territory of another State the exercise of jurisdiction and performance of functions that are reserved exclusively for the authorities of that other State by its domestic law."

[56] For example, the New Zealand Crimes Act 1961 as amended provides for extraterritorial jurisdiction in respect of migrant smuggling, human trafficking, money laundering, and participation in organized criminal groups where either the person to be charged or the person in respect of whom the offense is alleged to have been committed is a New Zealand citizen: Crimes Act 1961 (New Zealand), at Section 7A.

[57] "This is sometimes treated as a kind of quasi-territorial jurisdiction; but it is better to regard it is a quasi-national jurisdiction in order to resist the temptation to regard ships and aircraft as pieces of floating or flying territory of the State, which they are not": Lowe, *International Law*, at 175.

[58] Application of principles of jurisdiction to individual nationals is largely unproblematic – apart from issues that may arise when an individual holds dual nationality, or when it is alleged that some

and legal persons – typically but not always ascribed the nationality of their seat of incorporation[59]; and (3) ships and aircraft, which are considered as nationals of the State under whose flag they sail or fly.[60]

The centuries-old jurisdictional basis of "passive personality" is a variant on the nationality basis. It holds that a State is entitled to exercise jurisdiction over offenses in situations where the victim of those offenses is one of its nationals. Thus, in contrast to the nationality principle, which is based on the nationality of the *offender*, the principle of passive personality looks to the nationality of the *victim*. Contemporary claims of jurisdiction on the basis of passive personality are invariably based on treaty provisions that expressly provide for jurisdiction in cases where the victim is a national of the State. As noted above, the Organized Crime Convention provides one such example,[61] although it is essential to note in this context that persons who are subject to migrant smuggling may not fall within the category of "victim."[62] It is also important to acknowledge that, as with diplomatic protection,[63] any exercise of passive personality jurisdiction requires a large measure of political will on the part of the involved States. In the case of "victims" of a migrant smuggling–related crime, the fact that such persons are often nationals of States that have been unwilling or unable to offer them even the most basic protections should be considered.

requisite element of good faith or genuine connection is lacking. See Lowe and Staker, "Jurisdiction," at 324–325. See further Triggs, *International Law*, at 438–439.

59 *Barcelona Traction, Light and Power Company Limited (Second Phase) (Belgium v. Spain)*, [1970] ICJ Rep 3, at 42. See further Crawford, *Brownlie's Principles of Public International Law*, at 509–533.

60 Note that particular rules have evolved regarding matters such as the grant of nationality to ships and vessels and restraints on the exercise of territorially based jurisdiction where ships or aircraft flying the flag of one State are present in the ports and territorial waters of another. These rules and principles are essential to the study of migrant smuggling at sea, and are considered further at Section 3.3 in this chapter.

61 Organized Crime Convention, at Art. 15(2)(a).

62 See Chapter 1, esp. at notes 137–140 and accompanying text, and Chapter 8, at Section 8.1.

63 Where a State espouses the claim of its citizen who has been injured by another State and takes diplomatic action on his or her behalf against the offending State. For example, in *Diallo*, the Republic of Guinea brought an application before the International Court of Justice concerning "violations of [Guinean national] Mr. Diallo's individual rights alleged by Guinea to have resulted from the arrest, detention and expulsion measures taken against him": *Ahmadou Sadio Diallo (Republic of Guinea v. Democratic Republic of the Congo)*, [2010] ICJ Rep 639, at para. 43; similarly, in the *LaGrand Case*, Germany successfully brought a claim that the United States had violated the individual rights accorded to German nationals the LaGrand brothers under the Vienna Convention on Consular Assistance: *LaGrand (Germany v. Untied States of America)*, [2001] ICJ Rep 466. Note that diplomatic protection (as distinct from passive personality jurisdiction) could also arise, at least in theory, in other situations: for example, the arrest and detention of a crew-member of a vessel used for migrant smuggling with the State of origin alleging that the individual was in fact a victim of trafficking or was a child (and, in either case, not being provided the rights attached to that status).

3.2.2.3. Extraterritorial Jurisdiction: Protective Principle

International law has long recognized that "certain interests of states are so essential that acts directed against them qualify as sufficiently close to prompt those states' jurisdiction."[64] In the context of the present discussion, that recognition translates into the right of a State to assert prescriptive jurisdiction over certain offenses committed outside its territory by nonnationals that threaten "its essential security interests."[65] The question of what constitutes a State's essential security interests is an important one for the present discussion and is discussed below.

The protective principle as a basis of jurisdiction has a long history in international law, recognizing that "states required the competence to punish foreign conduct that frustrated [their] sovereign right to internal peace."[66] Although its existence is relatively well established,[67] the parameters of the principle are unclear, "beyond a vague sense of gravity."[68] Some scholars assert that State practice in the exercise of protective jurisdiction has, on the whole, been cautious and confined to relatively narrow circumstances in which the State's essential interests genuinely do appear to be threatened.[69] Others are much less sanguine, arguing that its "vague formulation ... has enabled states to use the concept as a pretext for regulating extraterritorial conduct that bears no meaningful connection to their own national security."[70]

The scope of offenses asserted by States as offending their "essential security interests" is unclear. Representative examples include economic offenses such as counterfeiting currency, treason, and – significantly for the purposes of this book – illegal immigration.[71] A 1948 case decided in the United Kingdom Privy Council, *Molvan*, is generally cited as the authority for upholding the protective principle as a basis of

64 Simma and Müller, "Exercise and the Limits of Jurisdiction," at 143.

65 Lowe, *International Law*, at 176. See, for example, *Arrest Warrant of 11 April 2000 (Democratic Republic of the Congo v. Belgium)*, [2002] ICJ Rep 3 [*Arrest Warrant Case*], at para. 4 (Separate Opinion of Judge Guillaume): jurisdiction may be asserted "if the crime threatens [the State's] internal or external security"; and Separate Opinion of Judge Rezek, at para. 4: "the principle of the *defence of certain legal interests* to which the State attaches particular value: the life and physical integrity of the sovereign, the national heritage, good governance" (emphasis in original).

66 N. Bialostozky, "Protective Jurisdiction as a Circumstance Precluding Wrongfulness" (2012) [Bialostozky, "Protective Jurisdiction"], available at http://papers.ssrn.com/sol3/papers.cfm?abstract_id=2143686 (accessed May 12, 2013), at 4 and references contained therein.

67 Shaw, *International Law*, at 667.

68 Crawford, *Brownlie's Principles of Public International Law*, at 462.

69 Triggs, *International Law*, at 442. See also Lowe and Staker, "Jurisdiction," at 326 ("The rationale of the protective principle is clearly linked to the protection of vital State interests. Accordingly, while the category is not closed, the potential for its expansion is limited.... The pressure to expand the use of this principle, and the danger of unshackling it from the protection of truly *vital* interests and of permitting its use for the convenient advancement of important interests, is clear").

70 Bialostozky, "Protective Jurisdiction," at 1.

71 Crawford, *Brownlie's Principles of Public International Law*, at 462; Triggs, *International Law*, at 442; and Lowe and Staker, "Jurisdiction," at 326.

jurisdiction, in this case, for preventing the unlawful invasion of territory by a vessel carrying "illegal immigrants."[72] More recently, the United States has asserted protective jurisdiction over aliens on the high seas in the context of preventing drug trafficking.[73] The protective principle has also been invoked as supporting the exercise of jurisdiction in the context of environmental injury and large-scale damage to a State's economic interests.[74]

[72] The vessel "Asya" had been intercepted on the high seas and escorted to a Palestinian port after it was found to be carrying illegal immigrants destined for Palestine. The vessel was forfeited to the government of Palestine after its owner, a foreigner, was found to have abetted an act of illegal immigration – notwithstanding that the abetment took place entirely outside Palestinian territory. Noting that the penalty was "so expedient, if not essential, for the purpose of preventing an unlawful invasion of its territory," the Privy Council held that international law had not been breached. The Privy Council rejected the contention that "crime is local" (as stated in *MacLeod v. Attorney-General for New South Wales*, [1891] AC 455, a case overturning a conviction of bigamy where the act of a second marriage had taken place outside New South Wales (Australia)), finding that no principle of international law was violated by a criminal law that "penalizes persons of whatever nationality and wherever resident, who abet or are deemed to abet an offence against its laws": *Naim Molvan, Owner of Motor Vessel "Asya" v. Attorney-General for Palestine* [1948] AC 351, at 371, 370. It should be noted, however, that the Privy Council's decision largely turned on the presumptive statelessness of the vessel, which was flying a Zionist flag at the time of seizure. As for enforcement jurisdiction, the judgment confirms that acts of enforcement may only be taken against persons or vessels present within the territory of the State. See further Section 3.2.3 in this chapter.

[73] See the various cases concerning the Maritime Drug Law Enforcement Act 1986, 46 U.S.C. § 1903 (United States). In *United States v. Suerte*, the defendant was a Philippine national and the captain of a Maltese-flagged vessel arrested by the United States, with Maltese consent, on the high seas in connection with cocaine trafficking from Venezuela to Europe. In determining that the exercise of jurisdiction was not unlawful, the United States Fifth Circuit Court of Appeals noted that the United States Congress had found that "trafficking in controlled substances aboard vessels … presents a specific threat to the security and societal well-being of the United States" (*United States v. Suerte*, 291 F.3d 366 (5th Cir., 2002), at 377, citing 46 USC App § 1902). See *also United States v. Sinisterra*, No. 06–15824, 2007 WL 1695698 (11th Cir. 2007), at 3 ("Congress, under the 'protective principle' of international law, may assert extraterritorial jurisdiction over vessels in the high seas that are engaged in conduct that has a potentially adverse effect and is generally recognized as a crime by nations that have reasonably developed legal systems"); and *United States v. Bravo*, 489 F.3d 1 (1st Cir. 2007), at 7 ("The extra-territorial jurisdiction authorized in the [Maritime Drug Law Enforcement Act] is consistent with the 'protective principle' of international law"). Other decisions appear to push the limits of the protective principle under international law: *United States v. Martinez-Hidalgo*, 993 F.2d 1052 (3d Cir. 1993), at 1056 ("we see nothing fundamentally unfair in applying [the Maritime Drug Law Enforcement Act] exactly as Congress intended – *extraterritorially without regard for a nexus between the defendant's conduct and the United States*" (emphasis added)); *United States v. Gonzalez*, 776 F.2d 931 (11th Cir. 1985), at 939–940 ("the protective principle does not require that there be proof of an actual or intended effect inside the United States"). Bennett correctly notes that "these justifications are likely incorrect if the vessels are not destined for the United States": A. Bennett, "That Sinking Feeling: Stateless Ships, Universal Jurisdiction and the Drug Trafficking Vessel Interdiction Act" (2012) 37(2) *Yale Journal of International Law* 433, at 443, n. 71. See also S. Murphy, "Extraterritorial Application of U.S. Law to Crimes on Foreign Vessels" (2003) 97 *American Journal of International Law* 183.

[74] See generally Bialostozky, "Protective Jurisdiction as a Circumstance Precluding Wrongfulness."

In the case of migrant smuggling, clearly articulated examples of State practice regarding assertion of protective jurisdiction are relatively rare. First, it is not always easy to distinguish protective jurisdiction from assertions of objective territorial jurisdiction. That is, depending on the legislative definition of the crime, it may be possible to justify assertions of jurisdiction over otherwise extraterritorial acts of migrant smuggling on the basis that they form part of an activity – illegal immigration – to be completed within the State's territory (objective territoriality).[75] This possibility is reflected in the Organized Crime Convention, which allows a State to establish jurisdiction over specified criminal acts related to migrant smuggling "committed outside its territory with a view to the commission of" another offense within the territory of the State: arguably an exercise of objective territoriality jurisdiction.[76] Second, although there is ample modern State practice of seeking treaty-based consent to board, escort, and arrest vessels suspected of illegal immigration on the high seas (which may suggest that the protective principle of prescriptive jurisdiction would *not* be accepted as a rule of customary international law in the context of migrant smuggling),[77] this is far from conclusive: the practice of seeking prior consent is arguably more directly attributable to the principle of exclusive flag State jurisdiction on the high seas, discussed further at Section 3.3.3.

3.2.2.4. Extraterritorial Jurisdiction: Universal Jurisdiction

Universal jurisdiction refers to the capacity of a State to assert jurisdiction over a small number of very serious offenses purely on the basis of the nature of the crime committed, even if no link of territoriality, nationality, or vital interests is established. All States have jurisdiction over such crimes, regardless of where the offense was committed or any other connection with that State.[78]

[75] See further notes 47–48 above and the accompanying text. For example, although in the wake of the *Tampa* incident, the Australian government publicly invoked the right to "decide who comes to this country and the circumstances in which they come," such a statement may be read for the purposes of jurisdiction under international law to be either an invocation of protective jurisdiction or territoriality jurisdiction (the vessel having entered the territorial sea), or both. J. Howard, prime minister of Australia (Policy Speech, Oct. 28, 2001), referring directly to the *Tampa* incident. See further Chapter 6, at Section 6.2.1.3 regarding the *Tampa* incident and Section 3.3.2 of this chapter regarding territoriality jurisdiction in the territorial sea.

[76] Organized Crime Convention, at Art. 15(2)(c).

[77] The current rules around interdiction at sea are considered further at Chapter 6 in this book.

[78] D. Guilfoyle, *Shipping Interdiction and the Law of the Sea* (2009) [Guilfoyle, *Shipping Interdiction and the Law of the Sea*], at 43, citing *Oppenheim's International Law: Volume I, Peace (9th ed.)*, at 469–70 and others; Triggs, *International Law*, at 444. Note however that, consistent with the territorial basis for enforcement jurisdiction, some physical access to the accused or their property is still necessary to enforce jurisdiction. "The *exercise* of universal jurisdiction requires the presence of the alleged offender in the territory of the prosecuting State or on board a vessel flying its flag or an aircraft which is registered under its laws, or other lawful forms of control over the alleged offender": Institute

The list of offenses generally recognized as attracting universal jurisdiction is short and can be divided into two.[79] The first part of the list comprises crimes that are considered so heinous as to be "of concern to the international community as a whole"[80] and to thereby establish a nexus with all States: war crimes, crimes against humanity, genocide, and slavery. In the second part of the list is piracy, which typically takes place outside the territorial jurisdiction of any State. As a practical matter, granting all States jurisdiction over piracy has long been considered necessary in its suppression.[81]

Efforts have periodically been made, by States and others, to expand the list of offenses attracting universal jurisdiction to include, for example, gross human rights violations, environmental crimes, apartheid, and drug trafficking.[82] Commentators have however pointed out the danger of political manipulation and the potential for conflict in such expansionist efforts.[83] When considering the scope of the concept of universal jurisdiction it is also important to consider how customary law develops. A crime does not become subject to universal jurisdiction simply because it is

of International Law, "Seventeenth Commission: Universal Criminal Jurisdiction with regard to the Crime of Genocide, Crimes against Humanity and War Crimes," Resolution adopted Aug. 26, 2005, at para. 3(b) (emphasis added).

79 For further on this division see Simma and Müller, "Exercise and the Limits of Jurisdiction," at 144–145; Lowe and Staker, "Jurisdiction," at 326–327.

80 Rome Statute of the International Criminal Court, 2187 UNTS 3, done July 17, 1998, entered into force July 1, 2002, at Art. 5.

81 Ibid.

82 For example, crimes such as narcotics trafficking, apartheid, mercenary fighting, and certain environmental offenses had been included in the 1991 draft of the Draft Code of Crimes against the Peace and Security of Mankind, but were ultimately omitted from the final version adopted by the International Law Commission in 1996: Shaw, *International Law*, at 671, citing the Draft Code provisionally adopted in 1991 (see "Report of the International Law Commission on the Work of Its Forty-Third Session," UN Doc. A/46/10, Sep. 10, 1991) and "Report of the International Law Commission on the Work of Its Forty-Eighth Session," UN Doc. A/51/10, Jan. 1, 1996, at 9. For an analysis of the draft Code, including its significance as a source of authority for "international crimes" such as genocide, war crimes, and slavery, see J. Allain and J. R. Jones, "A Patchwork of Norms: Commentary on the 1996 Draft Code of Crimes against the Peace and Security of Mankind" (1994) *European Journal of International Law* 100; and T. McCormack and G. Simpson, "The International Law Commission's Draft Code of Crimes against the Peace and Security of Mankind: An Appraisal of the Substantive Provisions" (1994) 5 *Criminal Law Forum* 1.

83 As stated by Bassiouni, "[w]hile there is no doubt that it is a useful and, at times, necessary instrument of international criminal justice, it is also attended by various dangers. If used in a politically motivated manner or simply to vex and harass leaders of other States, universal jurisdiction could disrupt world order and deprive individuals of their basic rights. Even with the best of intentions, universal jurisdiction could be used imprudently, creating unnecessary frictions between States and abuses of legal processes. For these reasons and more, the exercise of universal jurisdiction ought generally to be reserved for the most serious international crimes, such as genocide, crimes against humanity, and war crimes, though there may be other international crimes for which universal jurisdiction is provided for by an applicable treaty, as in the case of terrorism": Bassiouni, "The History of Universal Jurisdiction," at 39–40.

law set out at Sections 3.2.2 and 3.2.3 above will apply and it may be necessary to resolve any conflicts or objections through ad hoc arrangements or consent.

The expansion of jurisdiction through consent (treaty-based or otherwise) takes on particular importance in regulating activities at sea, including activities related to migrant smuggling. The law of the sea sets out a complex regime of jurisdictional zones and espouses a general principle of exclusive flag State jurisdiction on the high seas, such that the State in which a vessel is registered and whose flag it flies is generally the only State permitted to exercise enforcement powers over the activities on board. At the same time, the physical nature of the seas and the significant maritime resources required to effectively patrol its vast spaces limits the capacity of any one State, particularly those without significant maritime power, to control the activities of its flag ships at sea. Major source and transit countries of smuggled migrants frequently lack the resources (and perhaps also the political will) required to effectively patrol migrant smuggling in their coastal waters. Although the Migrant Smuggling Protocol itself does not amend the jurisdictional rules, which exist under the law of the sea and which are discussed further in Section 3.3, it does oblige States to cooperate in order to render the existing regime of jurisdiction under the law of the sea more effective.[103] Under the Protocol, States Parties are also to consider concluding bilateral or regional agreements or understandings to prevent and combat smuggling and to enhance the provisions of the Protocol.[104] A large number of treaties, memoranda of understanding, and ad hoc arrangements have developed whereby smaller flag States or coastal States grant consent to other States to intercept vessels engaged in transnational crimes such as migrant smuggling, drug trafficking, and illegal arms trading. Examples include: arrangements permitting one State to intervene in the territorial waters; provisions deeming silence after notification to constitute consent for interception; and "shiprider" arrangements for joint operations, in which the coastal or flag State retains a level of control by means of placing an official on board the vessel of the intercepting State to authorize interceptions. Further on the operation of such arrangements in certain regions, see the discussion of bilateral migration treaties in Chapter 1, at Section 1.3. A detailed discussion of jurisdiction at sea and multilateral arrangements for interception is contained at Section 3.3, and Chapter 6, at Section 6.1.1.

103 X. Hinrichs, "Measures against Smuggling of Migrants at Sea: A Law of the Sea Related Perspective" (2003) 36(2) *Revue Belge de Droit International* 413, at 450–451. For example, in their capacity as flag States, States Parties are obliged to respond expeditiously to any requests by another State Party of confirmation of a ship's registry or for authorization to exercise jurisdiction, and to designate an authority or where necessary authorities to receive and respond to such requests: Migrant Smuggling Protocol, at Arts. 8(4), 8(6). On other obligations of cooperation generally under the Migrant Smuggling Protocol, see Chapter 1, at Section 1.1.3.2.

104 Migrant Smuggling Protocol, at Art. 17.

3.2.5. *Concurrent or Overlapping Jurisdiction*

The many different possible bases for prescriptive jurisdiction mean that a single transnational criminal act will frequently be subject to multiple claims of jurisdiction. So long as the prescriptive jurisdiction being exercised by States is overlapping but not inconsistent, this may be desirable for eliminating gaps in the international legal response to transnational crimes such as migrant smuggling. In fact, a tendency to "err on the side of caution and over-jurisdictionalise"[105] may be seen as a response to the international community's fear of jurisdictional black holes within which criminals, including migrant smugglers, can operate with impunity.

Because prescriptive jurisdiction is a declaratory power only, conflict is not inevitable where States declare similar or consistent rules to govern transnational conduct. Problems will likely only arise when States enact divergent or inconsistent criminal laws in respect of the same (extraterritorial or transnational) conduct, such that one could not obey the laws of one State without falling foul of the laws of another. In relation to transnational crimes, careful definition of crimes and harmonization of domestic laws should be considered best practice, as it facilitates clarity, compliance, and international criminal cooperation. Treaties and other sources of international law are indispensible in the process of definition and harmonization.

The issue of overlapping jurisdiction is most likely to arise as a problem at the enforcement stage. Even where the criminal laws of different States have been harmonized, both practical and legal considerations (such as the widely accepted prohibition against "double jeopardy")[106] dictate that only one State should prosecute. The rules around allocation of capacity where more than one State seeks to enforce jurisdiction are flexible, and generally take into account both practical considerations of capacity (who has the offender, the evidence, and the will to prosecute?) and an assessment of interest or connection.[107] For example, the State that

[105] Simma and Müller, "Exercise and the Limits of Jurisdiction," at 148.

[106] International Covenant on Civil and Political Rights, 999 UNTS 171, done Dec. 16, 1996, entered into force Mar. 23, 1976 [ICCPR], at Art. 14(7).

[107] See, for example, American Law Institute, *Restatement (Third) of the Foreign Relations Law of the United States* (1990), at § 403(3): "each state has an obligation to evaluate its own as well as the other state's interest in exercising jurisdiction, in light of all the relevant factors [listed at § 403(2)]; a state should defer to the other state if that state's interest is clearly greater." Note also that a similar provision was included in the draft text of the Migrant Smuggling Protocol but did not survive the negotiations: "[i]f more than one State Party intends to resume jurisdiction over an alleged offender . . ., the States Parties concerned shall consult each other with a view to renouncing jurisdiction in order to render possible proceedings in the territory of the State Party most directly affected by the commission of the smuggling of migrants." This was omitted from the final text without official explanation: United Nations Office on Drugs and Crime, Travaux Préparatoires *of the Negotiations for the Elaboration of the United Nations Convention against Transnational Organized Crime and the Protocols Thereto* (2006), at 575–576.

has apprehended the offender, and thus the State in whose territory the offender is present, will typically be the State best placed to prosecute. "The priority of a jurisdictional interest is, however, a political as much as a legal problem," such that "which state proceeds first is usually a matter of negotiation."[108]

Extradition in the case of migrant smuggling is dealt with in the context of a broader discussion of international cooperation in Chapter 7. It suffices for present purposes to make some brief observations. First, the State requesting extradition must itself be able to show a jurisdictional link to the offender or the offense in question. As the International Court of Justice recently noted in the context of the Convention against Torture: "[t]he State in whose territory the suspect is present does indeed have the option of extraditing him to a country which has made such a request, but on the condition that it is to a State which has jurisdiction in some capacity, pursuant to Article 5 of the Convention,[109] to prosecute and try him."[110] Extradition law also recognizes a "double criminality" requirement: the conduct in question must be criminalized under the laws of both the Requesting and the Requested State. This helps to explain the importance placed by States engaged in fighting migrant smuggling on the development of common definitions and offenses.

3.3. PRINCIPLES OF JURISDICTION AT SEA

As noted in Chapter 1, it was the phenomenon of migrant smuggling by sea that provided much of the impetus for development of the Migrant Smuggling Protocol. Although it is well established that land-based smuggling is much more significant in terms of numbers, the relatively higher visibility and higher risks associated with smuggling by sea have likely elevated its significance in terms of both international and national policy. Chapter 6 provides a detailed explanation and analysis of the relevant legal framework around smuggling by sea. The purpose of the present section is limited to describing the jurisdictional rules that underlie that framework:

[108] Boister, *An Introduction to Transnational Criminal Law*, at 153.

[109] "1. Each State Party shall take such measures as may be necessary to establish its jurisdiction over the offences referred to in article 4 in the following cases: (a). When the offences are committed in any territory under its jurisdiction or on board a ship or aircraft registered in that State; (b) When the alleged offender is a national of that State; (c). When the victim was a national of that State if that State considers it appropriate. 2. Each State Party shall likewise take such measures as may be necessary to establish its jurisdiction over such offences in cases where the alleged offender is present in any territory under its jurisdiction and it does not extradite him pursuant to article 8 to any of the States mentioned in Paragraph 1 of this article": Convention against Torture and Other Cruel, Inhuman or Degrading Treatment or Punishment, 1465 UNTS 85, done Dec. 10, 1984, entered into force June 26, 1987 [Convention against Torture], at Art. 5.

[110] *Questions Relating to the Obligation to Prosecute or Extradite (Belgium v. Senegal) (Judgment)* (not yet reported) (ICJ, July 20, 2012), at para. 120.

specifically, to delineate, as carefully as possible, the capacities of States in relation to different parts of the world oceans. After a brief introduction to the key treaties, the section sets out the various maritime zones of jurisdiction. It then considers the basic principles of jurisdiction that govern vessels, navigation, and interception.

The twin concepts of sovereignty and jurisdiction, considered in the first part of the chapter, are central to this discussion. Although the ocean is, in reality, a single, interconnected space, the law of the sea divides that space into multiple jurisdictional zones.[111] That division reflects a tension between the assertion of sovereignty (for example by coastal States over their territorial waters) and resistance to it (for example, the principle that States must be free to act in areas beyond the sovereignty of other States).[112] These two opposing principles have dominated the development of the law of the sea, and underpin the gradual evolution of its key features: coastal State powers within various coastal maritime zones; the long-standing fundamental freedoms of the high seas[113]; and international responses to contemporary issues as diverse as pollution, hazardous cargoes, nuclear proliferation, and migrant smuggling. Jurisdiction at sea is characterized by "varying scales of competence of coastal States and shipping States over things, persons and events," giving rise to potentially overlapping and creeping regimes.[114] These factors ensure that there is no simple answer to the question of capacity to act in the context of responses to migrant smuggling by sea: such capacity can only be ascertained through a careful dissection of the relevant rules and their equally careful application to specific fact situations.

3.3.1. *Key Treaties*

The law of the sea comprises a mixture of both custom and treaties. However, two sets of instruments are of central importance, justifying their separate introduction: the 1958 Geneva Conventions and the 1982 United Nations Convention on the Law of the Sea (UNCLOS).

111 "It may be said that the history of the law of the sea is that of the division of the ocean": Y. Tanaka, "Zonal and Integrated Management Approaches to Ocean Governance: Reflections on a Dual Approach in International Law of the Sea" (2004) 19(4) *International Journal of Marine and Coastal Law* 483, at 483.

112 Ibid. at 484. See also S. Scott, "The LOS Convention as a Constitutional Regime for the Oceans," in A. Oude Elferink ed., *Stability and Change in the Law of the Sea: The Role of the LOS Convention* 9 (2006) [Scott, "The LOS Convention as a Constitutional Regime for the Oceans"], at 25: "The most basic source of international maritime conflict has traditionally been the interests of coastal States versus those of States protecting their merchant, fishing and naval fleets in terms of freedom of the seas, although the same States could be active in both."

113 There are four recognized freedoms of the sea: freedom of navigation (the most important), freedom of fishing, freedom to lay submarine cables and pipelines, and freedom of overflight over the high seas: see High Seas Convention, at Art. 2; UNCLOS, at Art. 87.

114 D. P. O'Connell (I. Shearer ed.), *The International Law of the Sea*, vol. II (1984), at 732.

Until the entry into force of UNCLOS in 1994, the main treaties were the four, relatively short treaties, all concluded in 1958 (the Geneva Conventions): the Convention on the Territorial Sea and the Contiguous Zone (Territorial Sea Convention),[115] the Convention on the Continental Shelf,[116] the High Seas Convention,[117] and the Convention on Fishing and Conservation of Living Resources of the High Seas.[118] The High Seas Convention was expressly intended "to codify the rules of international law relating to the high seas," and said to be "generally declaratory of established principles of international law,"[119] such that its rules are binding upon party and nonparty States alike. No such declaration was made in respect of the other three conventions, which represented a mixture of custom and progressive development.[120] Many provisions of the Territorial Sea Convention as well as the High Seas Convention were subsequently reproduced in UNCLOS with little substantive change.

The UNCLOS Convention, hailed as "a constitution for the oceans,"[121] emerged from decades of negotiation involving most of the world's States.[122] With 320 articles and 9 annexes, UNCLOS represents a comprehensive "package deal" establishing the legal order of the oceans[123] – the whole of which must be accepted by parties, as

115 Convention on the Territorial Sea and the Contiguous Zone, 516 UNTS 205, done Apr. 29, 1958, entered into force Sept. 10, 1964 [Territorial Sea Convention].

116 Convention on the Continental Shelf, 499 UNTS 311, done Apr. 29, 1958, entered into force June 10, 1964.

117 Convention on the High Seas, 450 UNTS 11, done Apr. 29, 1958, entered into force Sept. 30, 1962 [High Seas Convention].

118 Convention on Fishing and Conservation of the Living Resources of the High Seas, 559 UNTS 285, done Apr. 29, 1958, entered into force Mar. 20, 1966.

119 High Seas Convention, at Preamble.

120 For example, the International Court of Justice in *North Sea Continental Shelf Cases (Federal Republic of Germany v. Denmark; Federal Republic of Germany v. Netherlands)*, [1969] ICJ Rep 3, specifically found that the equidistance rule of delimitation contained in Article 6 of the Territorial Seas Convention had not yet entered into custom.

121 See the statement of President Koh at the conclusion of the drafting conference, arguing that that drafters had achieved "our fundamental objective of producing a comprehensive constitution for the oceans which will stand the test of time": T. Koh, "A Constitution for the Oceans," *The Law of the Sea: Official Text of the UN Convention on the Law of the Sea*, UN Sales No. E.83.V.5 (1983) [Koh, "A Constitution for the Oceans"], at xxxiii. See also Scott, "The LOS Convention as a Constitutional Regime for the Oceans"; J. Harrison, *Making the Law of the Sea: A Study in the Development of International Law* (2011) [Harrison, *Making the Law of the Sea*], at 48–51: "for a large part, it has created a universal legal framework for the regulation of the oceans" (at 51).

122 For an overview of the negotiation process, see D. Rothwell and T. Stephens, *The International Law of the Sea* (2010) [Rothwell and Stephens, *The International Law of the Sea*], at 6–14; and Harrison, *Making the Law of the Sea*, at 31–48. This consensus-based negotiation basis arguably contributed to the development of customary international law: see Harrison, *Making the Law of the Sea*, at 53–55.

123 UNCLOS, at Preamble, noting "the desire to settle … all issues relating to the law of the sea," … "conscious that the problems of ocean space are closely interrelated and need to be considered as a whole," and "establishing, through this Convention, … a legal order for the seas and oceans."

reservations are expressly forbidden.[124] Substantial parts of UNCLOS codified existing custom and reproduce existing rules from the 1958 Conventions, such as those on the territorial and high seas.[125] UNCLOS also included important innovations that departed from the existing law, including significant changes to customary rules on innocent passage[126] and the introduction of entirely new concepts including the EEZ,[127] transit passage through straits,[128] and archipelagic waters,[129] some of which have subsequently been recognized as having entered into custom.[130]

3.3.2. *Zones of Maritime Jurisdiction*

The different maritime zones (Figure 3.1) delineate the extent, if any, of a coastal State's jurisdiction – and thereby its capacity to act against migrant smuggling – over its offshore waters. Each zone is characterized by its own specific legal regime, with varying levels of coastal State jurisdiction and foreign rights of navigation.

3.3.2.1. Internal Waters

As a general rule, each maritime zone is measured from the coastal State's baseline. The baseline is generally taken to be "the low-water line along the coast as marked on large-scale charts officially recognized by the coastal State."[131] The rules for constructing baselines also make particular exceptions to enclose internal waters in respect of, for example, bays, river mouths, nearby islands, fringing reefs, and deeply indented or island-fringed coastlines.[132] "Archipelagic" States – a term defined accordingly to strict criteria in Article 47 of UNCLOS – are subject to both

124 Article 309. As stated by President Koh at the closing ceremony of the drafting conference, "[a]lthough the Convention consists of a series of compromises, they form an integral whole. This is why the Convention does not provide for reservations. It is therefore not permissible for States to pick what they like and disregard what they do not like. In international law, as in domestic law, rights and duties go hand in hand. It is therefore legally impermissible to claim rights under the Convention without being willing to assume the correlative duties": Koh, "A Constitution for the Oceans," at xxxvi.

125 Harrison, *Making the Law of the Sea*, at 53, citing the United Kingdom statement at the closing ceremony of the drafting conference: "many of the Convention's provisions are a restatement or codification of existing conventional or customary international law and state practice."

126 UNCLOS, at Art. 19.

127 Ibid. at Arts. 55–75.

128 Ibid. at Arts. 37–44.

129 Ibid. at Art. 49.

130 For example, innocent passage (*Nicaragua Case*, at para. 111); the Exclusive Economic Zone (*Delimitation of the Maritime Boundary in the Gulf of Maine Area (Canada v. United States of America)*, [1984] ICJ Rep 246, at para. 294).

131 UNCLOS, at Art. 5.

132 See R. R. Churchill and A. V. Lowe, *The Law of the Sea* (3rd ed. 1999) [Churchill and Lowe, *The Law of the Sea*], at 31–52.

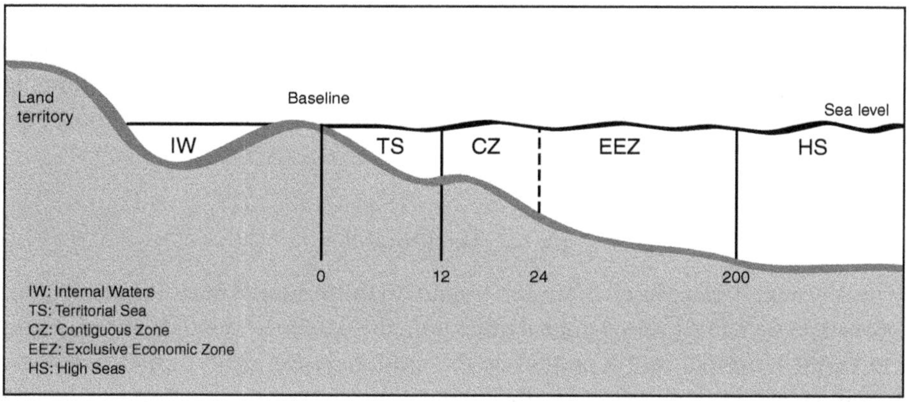

FIGURE 3.1 Maritime Zones under the United Nations Convention on the law of the sea.

the usual rules for measuring internal waters as well as an additional special regime of archipelagic baselines from which different maritime zones are measured.[133]

The internal waters refer to those waters that lie landward of the baseline.[134] These include bays, gulfs, estuaries, and ports.[135] Internal waters are not so much a maritime zone per se and have not traditionally been viewed as a subject of international concern.[136] Rather, internal waters are largely assimilated to the territory of the State, and the State enjoys full territorial sovereignty over its internal waters, encompassing both prescriptive and enforcement jurisdiction.[137] Foreign vessels enjoy no right to enter internal waters under customary international law,[138] and the regime of innocent passage described in the following section does not apply. If a foreign vessel enters internal waters, the coastal State is entitled to exercise, based on the principle

[133] Archipelagic baselines enclose "archipelagic waters," which "are neither internal waters nor territorial sea, although they bear a number of resemblances to the latter": Churchill and Lowe, *The Law of the Sea*, at 125. See generally ibid. at 118–130.

[134] D. P. O'Connell (I. Shearer ed.), *The International Law of the Sea*, vol. I (1982) [O'Connell, *The International Law of the Sea* (Vol. 1)], at 338; Churchill and Lowe, *The Law of the Sea*, at 60.

[135] O'Connell, *The International Law of the Sea* (Vol. 1), at 338.

[136] Rothwell and Stephens, *The International Law of the Sea*, at 52.

[137] O'Connell, *The International Law of the Sea* (Vol. 1), at 338; M. Evans, "The Law of the Sea," in M. D. Evans ed., *International Law* 651 (3rd ed. 2010) [Evans, "The Law of the Sea"], at 658; Churchill and Lowe, *The Law of the Sea*, at 61; Rothwell and Stephens, *The International Law of the Sea*, at 54.

[138] Evans, "The Law of the Sea," at 658; Churchill and Lowe, *The Law of the Sea*, at 61. The sole exception(s) are first, cases of distress (which is more accurately not a permissive ground but rather a circumstance precluding wrongfulness under the rules of State responsibility, examined further in Chapter 4), and second, where straight baselines have been drawn under the new treaty rules of the Territorial Sea Convention or UNCLOS, in which case a right of innocent passage persists in the newly enclosed internal waters: UNCLOS, at Art. 8(2). See also Territorial Sea Convention, at Art. 5(2).

of territoriality, the full extent of both its prescriptive and enforcement jurisdiction. Out of comity,[139] States have generally declined to regulate matters strictly internal to the ship, rather leaving these to the jurisdiction of the authorities of the flag State.[140] However, in respect of a range of concerns, from environmental protection to the rights of seafarers, this traditional deference appears to be eroding.

3.3.2.2. Territorial Sea

The sovereignty of a coastal State also extends to the territorial sea,[141] an adjacent belt of sea not exceeding twelve nautical miles from the baseline.[142] Unlike other maritime zones, the territorial sea "appertains to the territorial sovereignty of the coastal state and thus belongs to it automatically."[143] States are not required to assert sovereignty over their territorial sea in order to enjoy it. Conversely, as the International Court of Justice has affirmed, territorial waters may not be disclaimed by the coastal State:

> International law does not say to a State: "You are entitled to claim territorial waters if you want them." No maritime State can refuse them. . . . The possession of this territory is not optional, not dependent upon the will of the State, but compulsory.[144]

Within the territorial sea, coastal States enjoy sovereignty and thus full jurisdictional powers[145] subject to important limitations in UNCLOS and "to other rules of international law."[146]

Within the territorial sea, coastal States have rights and duties inherent in sovereignty. However, also in the territorial sea, foreign vessels have privileges, particularly associated with the right of innocent passage.[147] The right of coastal States to exercise either prescriptive or enforcement jurisdiction in the territorial sea must be reconciled with the right of innocent foreign vessels to undertake "continuous and

[139] Under the doctrine of international comity States should apply foreign law or limit domestic jurisdiction out of respect for foreign sovereignty. L. Oppenheim (H. Lauterpacht ed.), *International Law: A Treatise* (1955), at 34, n. 1.

[140] Churchill and Lowe, *The Law of the Sea*, at 66. For further on the concept of flag State jurisdiction, see Chapter 6, at Section 6.1.1.3.

[141] UNCLOS, at Art. 2.

[142] Ibid. at Art. 3.

[143] Shaw, *International Law*, at 569. See further Churchill and Lowe, *The Law of the Sea*, at 80–81.

[144] *Anglo-Norwegian Fisheries (United Kingdom v. Norway)*, [1951] ICJ Rep 116, at 131, per McNair J. (dissenting), at 160.

[145] O'Connell, *The International Law of the Sea* (Vol. 1), at 744; Evans, "The Law of the Sea," at 658; and Rothwell and Stephens, *The International Law of the Sea*, at 73: "The extent of coastal state sovereignty and jurisdiction over the territorial sea is vast and even taking into account the limitations imposed by [UNCLOS] in relation to innocent passage, relatively unfettered with respect to core areas of state interest."

[146] UNCLOS, at Art. 2(3).

[147] Crawford, *Brownlie's Principles of Public International Law*, at 260.

expeditious"[148] navigation through a coastal State's territorial sea, as discussed further in this section. Beyond a fairly wide interpretation of the extent to which innocent passage must be protected, coastal States arguably retain full or plenary prescriptive jurisdiction to make laws and regulations in respect of conduct in their territorial seas.[149] In particular, coastal States are free to make laws and regulations in respect of non-innocent conduct or passage by foreign vessels in their territorial seas.[150] The scope of the coastal State's enforcement jurisdiction in the territorial sea is similarly wide, except in respect of crimes committed before the ship entered the territorial sea, where that ship is merely passing through without entering internal waters,[151] and subject to having due regard to the interests of navigation[152] and comity.

The following sections consider, in turn: first, the regime of innocent passage protected by international law; second, the rights of coastal States to regulate innocent passage (and other aspects of the coastal State's prescriptive jurisdiction over foreign vessels in the territorial sea); and, third, the question of enforcement jurisdiction over foreign vessels in the territorial sea.

INNOCENT PASSAGE

Ships of all States, whether coastal or landlocked, enjoy the right of innocent passage through the territorial seas of coastal States.[153] This right of innocent passage constitutes the major constraint on the coastal State's jurisdiction over its territorial waters, because, as discussed further below in the section titled "The Right to Passage," coastal States are prohibited from exercising jurisdiction in a manner that would unreasonably inhibit innocent passage. The precise definition of what is and is not innocent passage is therefore crucial.

Under UNCLOS, "passage" refers to:

1. … navigation through the territorial sea for the purpose of:
   a. traversing that sea without entering internal waters or calling at a roadstead or port facility outside territorial waters; or
   b. proceeding to or from internal waters or a call at such roadstead or port facility.

[148] See UNCLOS, at Art. 18.

[149] Although, as discussed at Chapter 6, Section 6.1.1.1, this proposition is not without controversy.

[150] "It is … well established in State practice that ships not engaged in innocent passage, whether because they are not passing, or are passing but are not innocent, are subject to all coastal State laws. Beyond this, it seems a legitimate inference that States retain the right to extend any other legislation apart from that dealing with navigation and so on, to foreign ships in their waters, but that they will normally be expected, as a matter of comity, to refrain from doing so": Churchill and Lowe, *The Law of the Sea*, at 95.

[151] UNCLOS, at Art. 27(5).

[152] Ibid. at Art. 27(4).

[153] Ibid. at Art. 17. See also Evans, "The Law of the Sea," at 661.

2. Passage shall be continuous and expeditious. However, passage includes stopping and anchoring, but only in so far as the same are incidental to ordinary navigation or are rendered necessary by *force majeure* or distress or for the purpose of rendering assistance to persons, ships or aircraft in danger or distress.[154]

Passage thus refers to navigating continuously and expeditiously through the territorial sea, with exceptions only for conduct incidental to such navigation or as a result of *force majeure* and similar circumstances. Any vessel that is "hovering," "cruising," or "loitering" in the territorial sea would not be engaged in "passage" and thus would fall outside the regime of innocent passage, regardless of whether its conduct was otherwise "innocent."[155]

Regarding the criterion of "innocence," passage is innocent "so long as it is not prejudicial to the peace, good order or security of the coastal State."[156] Although this appears to be a relatively open-ended definition, the parameters are further refined by Article 19(2) of UNCLOS, which provides that passage of a foreign ship cannot be considered "innocent" if it engages in one or more of a large number of specified activities[157] in the territorial sea, as well as:

- any threat or use of force against the sovereignty or territorial integrity of the coastal State[158];
- the loading or unloading of any person contrary to the immigration laws and regulations of the coastal State.[159]

In fact, the final paragraph of Article 19(2) states that *any* activity not having a direct bearing on passage is deemed to be prejudicial to the coastal State and therefore non-innocent for the purposes of the coastal State's right of jurisdiction.[160]

The reference in the chapeau of Article 19(2) of UNCLOS to "engag[ing] in any of the following activities" indicates that some "activity" is indeed required, such that mere passage, without more, would not amount to prejudice to the State.[161] Thus, the

154 UNCLOS, at Art. 18. See also Territorial Sea Convention, at Art. 14(2)–(3).
155 Churchill and Lowe, *The Law of the Sea*, at 82; and Evans, "The Law of the Sea," at 661.
156 UNCLOS, at Art. 19(1). See also Territorial Sea Convention, Art 14(4).
157 Other activities specified as non-innocent under Article 19(2) include weapons practice; spying; propaganda; launching or taking on board any aircraft or military device; loading or unloading any person or goods contrary to customs, fiscal, immigration, or sanitary regulations; willful and serious pollution; fishing; research or surveying; and interference with coastal communications other facilities.
158 UNCLOS, at Art. 19(2)(a).
159 Ibid. at Art. 19(2)(g).
160 See also R. Barnes, "The International Law of the Sea and Migration Control," in B. Ryan and R. Mitsilegas, *Extraterritorial Immigration Control: Legal Challenges* 103 (2010), at 123 [Barnes, "The International Law of the Sea and Migration Control"].
161 Churchill and Lowe, *The Law of the Sea*, at 85.

mere carriage of smuggled migrants by a vessel passing through the territorial waters, destined for a third State, would not, of itself, render that passage non-innocent.[162] This notwithstanding, the carriage of smuggled migrants may arguably be regulated not because it renders passage non-innocent under Article 19 but because the coastal State retains a general criminal jurisdiction over the territorial sea.[163]

In 1989, the United States of America and the Union of Soviet Socialist Republics issued a Uniform Interpretation of Norms of International Law Governing Innocent Passage, in which they proclaimed that "Article 19 of [UNCLOS] sets out in paragraph 2 an exhaustive list of activities that would render passage not innocent. A ship passing through the territorial sea that does not engage in any of those activities is in innocent passage."[164] This position however, must be understood in the context of two principal maritime powers who had not, at that time, ratified UNCLOS.[165] It has been suggested that this statement, along with other subsequent practice by UNCLOS States Parties,[166] appears to support the view that the treaty rule in Article 19(2) should be viewed as an exhaustive list of non-innocent conduct for the purposes of the innocent passage regime and, further, as representing a rule of

162 There may be a relevant parallel here with the position regarding a vessel carrying materiel for weapons of mass destruction (WMD) destined for and intended for use against (distant) third States. Guilfoyle convincingly argues that, even though the UN Security Council has designated the proliferation of WMDs as a threat to international peace and security (see, for example, UN Security Council, "Note [on the Summit Meeting of the Security Council held Jan. 31, 1992] by the President of the Security Council," UN Doc. S/23500, Jan. 31, 1992, at 4; UN Security Council Resolution 1540, UN SCOR, 4956th mtg, UN Doc. S/RES/1540, Apr. 28, 2004, at Preamble), mere carriage of WMD materiel through the territorial sea would not render passage non-innocent: "it is the external acts of a vessel engaged in innocent passage, not its internal economy, which may prejudice a coastal state's security. It is hard to see that a latent threat in the vessel's hold, destined elsewhere, has any 'external' manifestation capable of affecting the character of passage": Guilfoyle, *Shipping Interdiction and the Law of the Sea*, at 242. *Contra* the position of the European Commission suggesting that, for members of the European Community, there may be an obligation for a coastal Member State to intervene if a vessel passing through its territorial waters intends to smuggle migrants to another Member State; such an obligation allegedly "flowing from the Community's policies on the crossing of external borders and the establishment of an area without internal frontiers": Commission Staff Working Document, "Study on the International Law Instruments in Relation to Illegal Immigration by Sea," SEC (2007) 691, May 15, 2007, at para. 2.1.3; a position that "would appear to depart textually from the language of UNCLOS": M. den Heijer, *Europe and Extraterritorial Asylum* (2012) [den Heijer, *Europe and Extraterritorial Asylum*], at 219.

163 See Chapter 6, at Section 6.1.1.1.

164 Union of Soviet Socialist Republics – United States of America, Joint Statement with Attached Uniform Interpretation of Rules of International Law Governing Innocent Passage, Sept. 23, 1989, 28 International Legal Materials 1444 (1989), at para. 3. See further V. Lowe, "Uniform Interpretation of the Rules of International Law Governing Innocent Passage" (1991) 6 *International Journal of Estuarine and Coastal Law* 73.

165 The Russian Federation ratified UNCLOS March 12, 1997. The United States remains a nonparty.

166 Including protests where States have adopted legislation at variance with Article 19: Churchill and Lowe, *The Law of the Sea*, at 86–87.

custom.[167] However, it does not appear that sufficient State practice has amassed to ascertain conclusively whether the list in Article 19(2) should be construed as exhaustive.[168]

THE RIGHT TO PREVENT PASSAGE

A coastal State is entitled, under international treaty law, to "take the necessary steps in its territorial sea to prevent passage which is not innocent"[169] and similarly, under custom, to exclude hovering vessels and those otherwise not engaged in passage.[170] Although not expressly mentioned, the taking of "necessary steps" should be interpreted as including a right to escort the vessel to the high seas.[171] In the case of ships proceeding to internal waters, the coastal State also has the right to take the necessary steps to prevent any breach of the conditions to which admission of those ships to internal waters or such a call is subject.[172]

These UNCLOS rules have important implications for the jurisdiction of coastal States over vessels engaged in migrant smuggling.[173] A Commission of the European Communities study of the international law instruments in relation to "illegal immigration by sea" summarized its view of the situation as follows:

> A ship which has the intention to disembark passengers in contravention of the coastal states immigration laws cannot benefit from this right [of innocent passage]. The coastal state has the right to escort such a ship to the high seas or proceed with arrests.[174]

[167] Ibid. See also M. Nordquist ed., *United Nations Convention on the Law of the Sea 1982: A Commentary*, Vol. 2 (1985), at 177–178: "This formal interpretation by two principal maritime Powers – which are also among the largest coastal States – ... will influence the practice of States and the interpretation of a provision which previously might have been regarded as ambiguous on the essential point of whether or not paragraph 2 was exhaustive."

[168] Nordquist notes that although Article 19(2)(l) was criticized during the drafting process as conferring on Article 19 an "open-ended" character, attempts to change it were rejected. See also Barnes, "The International Law of the Sea and Migration Control," at 123.

[169] UNCLOS, at Art. 25(1). See also Territorial Sea Convention, at Art. 16(1).

[170] Churchill and Lowe, *The Law of the Sea*, at 87.

[171] Barnes, "The International Law of the Sea and Migration Control," at 124.

[172] UNCLOS, at Art. 25(2).

[173] For a more detailed discussion with specific reference to migrant smuggling by sea, see Chapter 6.

[174] Commission Staff Working Document, "Study on the International Law Instruments in Relation to Illegal Immigration by Sea," SEC (2007) 691, May 15, 2007, at para. 2.1.2. "In the same situation and in a Community context it could be regarded as an obligation for Member State X to intervene if a ship making use of the right of innocent passage in its territorial waters has the intention to disembark illegal immigrants in Member State Y. Such an obligation, while not explicitly established, should be considered as flowing from the Community's policies on the crossing of external borders and the establishment of an area without internal frontiers": ibid. at para. 2.1.3. For further in relation to the right to intercept migrant smuggling vessels at sea, see Chapter 6.

anticipatory power of prevention, however, it falls short of any power of arrest, being limited to such actions as "inspections and warnings."[202]

3.3.2.4. Exclusive Economic Zone

The Exclusive Economic Zone (EEZ) has relatively little significance for the issue of migrant smuggling. Like the contiguous zone, the EEZ is optional and must be specifically claimed by coastal States.[203] It was specially created under UNCLOS, but has since been recognized by the International Court of Justice as having entered into customary law.[204]

The EEZ refers to a resource-related functional zone[205] up to 200 nautical miles seaward of the coastal State's baseline,[206] in which the coastal State enjoys certain sovereign rights over resources, but not sovereignty as such.[207] The rights allocated to coastal States are expressed as "sovereign rights for the purpose of exploring and exploiting, conserving and managing the natural resources, whether living or non-living" of the superjacent water column, the seabed, and its subsoil, and other economic activities such as the production of energy from water, currents, and winds.[208] The coastal State also enjoys exclusive jurisdiction with regard to the establishment, use, and regulation of artificial islands, installations, and structures[209]; marine scientific research[210]; and the protection and preservation of the marine environment,[211] including certain powers to control pollution.[212] Finally and residually, UNCLOS provides that the coastal State enjoys within the EEZ all "other rights and duties provided for in this Convention,"[213] which appears to refer, in particular, to those rights enjoyed within the coterminous or overlapping contiguous zone and the right of hot pursuit (discussed further in Chapter 6).[214] Otherwise, subject to the limited rights of the coastal State, ships within the EEZ are entitled to high seas freedoms.

202 I. Shearer, "Problems of Jurisdiction and Law Enforcement against Delinquent Vessels" (1986) 35 *International and Comparative Law Quarterly* 320, at 330.
203 Churchill and Lowe, *The Law of the Sea*, at 161.
204 "[T]he institution of the exclusive economic zone ... is shown by the practice of states to have become a part of customary law": *Continental Shelf (Libyan Arab Jamahiriya v. Malta)*, [1985] ICJ Rep 13, at 33. See also *Continental Shelf (Tunisia v. Libyan Arab Jamahiriya)*, [1982] ICJ Rep 18, at 74.
205 Churchill and Lowe, *The Law of the Sea*, at 166.
206 UNCLOS, at Art. 57.
207 Ibid. at Art. 56(1)(a).
208 Ibid.
209 Ibid. at Arts. 56(1)(b)(i), 60.
210 Ibid. at Art. 56(1)(b)(ii).
211 Ibid. at Art. 56(1)(b)(iii).
212 Ibid. at Arts. 210(5), 211(5)–(6), 216, 220, 234.
213 Ibid. at Art. 56(1)(c).
214 Churchill and Lowe, *The Law of the Sea*, at 169.

3.3.2.5. High Seas

Unlike the maritime zones of jurisdiction previously considered, over all of which the coastal State exercises some form of jurisdiction or control, the high seas specify an area beyond the jurisdiction or control of any one State. Indeed, the relevant treaty provisions define the high seas in the negative: in the High Seas Convention as "all parts of the sea that are not included in the territorial sea or in the internal waters of a State,"[215] and under UNCLOS as "all parts of the sea that are not included in the EEZ, in the territorial sea or in the internal waters of a State, or in the archipelagic waters of an archipelagic State."[216]

It is a rule of customary international law, codified in the High Seas Convention and UNCLOS, that the high seas are open to all States and that no State may acquire sovereignty over any part of them.[217] The High Seas Convention, which asserted itself as "generally declaratory of established principles of international law,"[218] proclaimed four freedoms of the high seas: freedom of navigation, freedom of fishing, freedom to lay submarine cables and pipelines, and freedom of overflight.[219] Each of these freedoms, and "others which are recognized by the general principles of international law",[220] are enjoyed by all States, and each State, whether coastal or landlocked, has the right to sail ships under its flag on the high seas.[221] Having been recognized as a part of customary international law in the High Seas Convention, each of these freedoms was repeated in UNCLOS.[222]

The basic principle relating to jurisdiction on the high seas is that the flag State alone is entitled to exercise prescriptive and enforcement jurisdiction over its ship.[223] Accordingly, a State may not exercise jurisdiction on the high seas in respect of a vessel carrying smuggled migrants, even if destined for its territory, unless the State: (1) has sought and received the consent of the flag State to take action; or (2) is able to establish one of the limited exceptions for intervention, discussed further in the following section such as where the vessel is stateless or engaging in piracy, the slave trade, or unauthorized broadcasting.[224]

215 High Seas Convention, at Art. 1.
216 UNCLOS, at Art. 86.
217 High Seas Convention, at Art. 2; UNCLOS, at Arts. 87, 89; Churchill and Lowe, *The Law of the Sea*, at 204.
218 High Seas Convention, at Art. 2.
219 Ibid. at Art. 2(1)–(4).
220 Ibid. at Art. 2.
221 Ibid. at Arts. 2–4.
222 UNCLOS, at Art. 87.
223 Shaw, *International Law*, at 614.
224 UNCLOS, at Art. 110; High Seas Convention, at Art. 22.

law, those efforts have largely been unsuccessful.[252] However, it is important to recognize that the concept of slavery is indeed evolving and may well accommodate (presently, or at some point in the future) egregious forms of exploitation that involve the clear exercise of powers attached to the right of ownership.[253] As discussed further in Chapter 6, the possibility that vessels engaged in transporting migrants for profit may also be engaged in conduct that could be characterized as slave trading should not be discounted.

Ultimately, even evidence of involvement in slave trading provides only a very limited exception to the principle of flag State jurisdiction on the high seas. Both UNCLOS and the High Seas Convention grant State vessels the right to board vessels suspected of the slave trade only, but it is the flag State alone that is entitled and indeed obliged to prosecute and punish offenders.[254] The long-standing customary principle of exclusive flag State jurisdiction in cases of slavery was recognized in the 1817 case of *Le Louis*, in which the United Kingdom High Court of Admiralty held that a British cruiser had unlawfully captured a French vessel engaging in the slave trade on the high seas, on the basis the flag State alone was entitled to prosecute slave trading on board its vessels on the high seas.[255]

3.3.3.3. Hot Pursuit

The right of hot pursuit is another, highly relevant exception to the exclusive jurisdiction of flag States on the high seas. Subject to strict conditions, a right of hot pursuit arises where a vessel has violated the laws of the coastal State within the territory, territorial waters, the contiguous zone, or the EEZ of that State and seeks to flee to the high seas. The right of hot pursuit has long been recognized in custom,[256] and was codified and extended to new jurisdictional zones in the High Seas Convention and in UNCLOS.

145, at 164–178; E. Papastavridis, "'Fortress Europe' and FRONTEX: Within or without International Law?" (2010) 79 *Nordic Journal of International law* 75, at 85.

[252] See Gallagher, *The International Law of Human Trafficking*, at 177–191.

[253] Ibid. at 190.

[254] UNCLOS, at Art. 110; High Seas Convention, at Art. 22. Under UNCLOS Article 99, and High Seas Convention Article 13, each State is obliged to take measures to prevent and punish the transport of slaves on board ships authorized to fly its flag. See further Shaw, *International Law*, at 616; and N. Klein, *Maritime Security and the Law of the Sea* (2011) [Klein, *Maritime Security and the Law of the Sea*], at 122. Similarly, in respect of drug trafficking, UNCLOS provides only for a duty of cooperation to suppress drug trafficking, explicitly affirming the exclusive jurisdiction of flag States by noting that these States "may request the co-operation of other States to suppress such traffic" without imposing any obligation to do so: UNCLOS, at Art. 108.

[255] *Le Louis* (1817) 165 Eng. Rep. 1464, cited in Klein, *Maritime Security and the Law of the Sea*, at 122.

[256] See, for example, *SS "I'm Alone" (Canada v. United States)* (1935) 3 UNRIAA 1609.

Under Article 111 of UNCLOS and Article 23 of the High Seas Convention, where the coastal State has good reason to believe that the foreign vessel has violated its laws, a warship or other official ship or aircraft authorized by the coastal State is entitled to pursue the vessel to the high seas and seize it.[257] Pursuit may only be commenced after giving a visual or auditory signal to stop, given at a distance close enough to be seen or heard by the foreign ship.[258]

Pursuit must be commenced when the foreign ship (or one of its boats) is in the territorial sea, contiguous zone, or EEZ of the State, where there is good reason to suspect a breach of coastal State laws and regulations applicable in the relevant zone.[259]

In establishing presence within a relevant zone, both UNCLOS and the High Seas Convention recognize the doctrine of constructive presence. This means that the treaties look to the location of "the foreign ship *or one of its boats*,"[260] or "the ship pursued *or one of its boats or other craft working as a team and using the ship pursued as a mother ship*."[261] This is an important clarification because it allows the coastal State to pursue and arrest a "mother ship" on the basis that this vessel sends or meets a boat within a jurisdictional zone of the coastal State, even if the mother ship itself "hovers" outside the relevant jurisdictional zone or remains at all times on the high seas.[262] For example, in the United Kingdom case of *R v. Mills*, the Court accepted that the United Kingdom could exercise hot pursuit to pursue and arrest on the high seas the *Poseidon*, a foreign ship that smuggled cannabis into the United Kingdom

[257] UNCLOS, at Art. 111(1); High Seas Convention, at Art. 23(1).

[258] UNCLOS, at Art. 111(4); High Seas Convention, at Art. 23(3).

[259] "If the foreign ship is within a contiguous zone, as defined in article 33, the pursuit may only be undertaken if there has been a violation of the rights for the protection of which the zone was established": UNCLOS, at Art. 111(1). See also High Seas Convention, at Art. 23(1). The same applies for the Exclusive Economic Zone: UNCLOS, at Art. 111(2).

[260] UNCLOS, at Art. 111(1) (emphasis added); High Seas Convention, at Art. 23(1) (emphasis added).

[261] UNCLOS, at Art. 111(4) (emphasis added). "Hot pursuit is not deemed to have begun unless the pursuing ship has satisfied itself by such practicable means as may be necessary that the ship pursued *or one of its boats or other craft working as a team and using the ship pursued as a mother ship* is within the limits of the territorial sea, or, as the case may be, within the contiguous zone or the exclusive economic zone": UNCLOS, at Art. 111(4) (emphasis added). See similarly High Seas Convention, at Art. 23(3).

[262] "When a foreign ship outside territorial waters sends boats into territorial waters which commit offences there, the mother ship renders herself liable to seizure by reason of these vicarious operations": A. McNair, *International Law Opinions*, Vol. 1 (1956), at 245. See also *R v. Mills*, which accepted the lawfulness of hot pursuit to arrest a mother ship in circumstances where "[a]t the time when the authority to arrest the *Poseidon* was received she was in International Waters and had never entered the territorial waters of any state": *R v. Mills and Others* (unreported) (Croydon Crown Court, 1995) [*R v. Mills*], at 4 (Judge Devonshire), cited in W. C. Gilmore, "Hot Pursuit: The Case of *R v. Mills and Others*" (1995) 44 *International and Comparative Law Quarterly* 949 [Gilmore, "Hot Pursuit: The Case of *R v. Mills*"], at 951–952.

by transferring its cargo on the high seas to a British trawler that subsequently landed on a British beach.[263]

Pursuit must be "hot," that is, continuous and uninterrupted; the right of hot pursuit ceases as soon as pursuit is interrupted (for example, because the pursuing vessel loses sight of the foreign ship or is recalled).[264] The right of pursuit ceases as soon as the foreign vessel enters the territorial sea of its flag State or any third State.[265]

PART 2: EXTRATERRITORIAL JURISDICTION AND LIMITATIONS ON CAPACITY TO ACT

As noted in the introduction to this chapter, establishing the competence of States to act is not just a matter to be resolved through analysis of the concepts of jurisdiction and sovereignty. It also requires a careful consideration of the limitations, placed by international law, on that capacity. In the context of migrant smuggling, the previous analysis confirmed that limitations derive from general rules of jurisdictional competence as well as from various sources of primary obligation such as the law of the sea. However, additional relevant and critical limitations are those considered in Chapter 2: the rules of international human rights and refugee law.

Much State action against migrant smuggling takes place outside the territorial jurisdiction of the acting State. The trend toward increased "internationalization" and "extraterritorialization" of migration control has been extensively and compellingly documented.[266] This raises questions regarding limitations on capacity to act, specifically: To what extent do the human rights obligations imposed on States vis-à-vis persons located and actions taking place within their territory apply with respect to persons located and actions taking place outside the territory of the State? The following section seeks to answer that basic but important question in relation to human rights norms generally, as well in respect of the human rights and refugee law obligation of *non-refoulement*.

[263] *R v. Mills* (Judge Devonshire). Other aspects of the case have been criticized as going beyond the international law of the sea. See Gilmore, "Hot Pursuit: The Case of *R v. Mills*."

[264] In *R v. Mills*, ships of the United Kingdom task force continuously shadowed the *Poseidon* from the time that it transferred cannabis to the British trawler to the time that it was arrested: Gilmore, "Hot Pursuit: The Case of *R v. Mills*, at 951. In contrast, in *M/V Saiga (No. 2)*, the International Tribunal for the Law of the Sea held that the arrest of a vessel was unlawful for several reasons, including interruption of pursuit: "the small patrol boat P35 that was sent out on 26 October 1997 on a northward course to search for the *Saiga* was recalled when information was received that the *Saiga* had changed course. This recall constituted a clear interruption of any pursuit, whatever legal basis might have existed for its commencement in the first place": at para. 147.

[265] UNCLOS, at Art. 111(3); High Seas Convention, at Art. 23(2).

[266] See references in Chapter 1, at Section 1.3.

It is relevant to note an important terminological point on the matter of jurisdiction. As "jurisdiction" was used in the first part of this chapter, the weight of its meaning related specifically to *capacity* to act. However, in the context of extraterritorial application of human rights and refugee law, considerations of "jurisdiction" generally refer to the question of whether a state is under an *obligation* to act or to refrain from acting. The issue of extraterritorial application of human rights and refugee law may also raise questions of State responsibility for internationally wrongful acts or omissions. Reference should therefore also be made to Chapter 4.

3.4. EXTRATERRITORIAL APPLICATION OF HUMAN RIGHTS OBLIGATIONS

In modern immigration control, States are increasingly taking actions in the name of preventing irregular migration outside of their territory and long before the migrant ever reaches the frontier. Accordingly, the question arises whether States – taking action to control migration outside of their territory – owe human rights obligations to persons they encounter as part of this action and whether those same rules thereby limit the capacity of States to act in these circumstances.

The central question to be asked is whether, and under what circumstances, a State that is party to a particular human rights treaty owes legal obligations under that treaty to a person who is not within the territory of that State (the same question can of course be asked vis-à-vis obligations that arise through customary law or another recognized source). It should be noted at the outset that this is a complex and unsettled area of international law, characterized by conflicting and often unclear jurisprudence.[267] Arguably, it is only in very recent times that the relevant principles of extraterritorial human rights law have begun to coalesce into something potentially capable of providing a firm foundation for analysis of specific issues and situations. The following section explains these principles and traces their development from early jurisprudential debates to the present state of the law.

3.4.1. *International Instruments and Jurisprudence*

Taking the accepted approach to treaty interpretation that favors the "ordinary meaning" consistent with "object and purpose,"[268] it would appear, at first glance, that

[267] For useful analyses of the broader issues as well as of the practice of international and regional human rights bodies, see M. Gondek, *The Reach of Human Rights in a Globalising World: Extraterritorial Application of Human Rights Treaties* (2009) and K. da Costa, *The Extraterritorial Application of Selected Human Rights Treaties* (2012).

[268] Vienna Convention on the Law of Treaties, at Art. 31(1). For a discussion of this general rule of treaty interpretation including "the perils of 'ordinary meaning,'" see J. C. Hathaway, *The Rights of Refugees under International Law* (2005) [Hathaway, *The Rights of Refugees*], at 49–53.

Until recently, the most authoritative Court ruling on this issue was the 2001 *Banković* case.[313] In this case the Court was required to decide whether the victims of the 1999 aerial bombardment of Belgrade[314] by Member States outside the area of their effective overall control were nevertheless within their "jurisdiction" for purposes of the triggering obligations under the Convention. Stating that the European Convention would apply extraterritorially only in "exceptional circumstances"[315] the Court found that this did not extend to the mere fact of a State having infringed on the rights of an individual in another country.[316] In other words, in contrast to the *Alejandre* decision of its American counterpart, control over airspace and a capacity to inflict harm were not sufficient to establish the necessary jurisdictional link. In justifying its narrow reading of the Convention's jurisdiction clause, the Court cited its essentially regional nature and further concluded that:

> from the standpoint of public international law, the jurisdictional competence of a State is primarily territorial. While international law does not exclude a State's exercise of jurisdiction extra-territorially, the suggested bases of such jurisdiction (including nationality, flag, diplomatic and consular relations, effect, protection, passive personality and universality) are, as a general rule, defined and limited by the sovereign territorial rights of the other relevant States.[317]

In addition, the Court rejected as inappropriate the notion that jurisdiction could be "divided and tailored in accordance with the particular circumstances of the extra-territorial act in question."[318]

The decision in *Banković*, although perhaps explicable from a policy perspective,[319] was greeted with widespread dismay and a rejection of the legal grounds on

[313] *Banković and Others v. Belgium and Others*, (2007) 44 EHRR SE5 (ECHR, Dec. 12, 2001) [*Banković v. Belgium*].

[314] Belgrade at the time was part of the Federal Republic of Yugoslavia, which was not party to the European Convention on Human Rights.

[315] *Banković v. Belgium*, at para. 72. Specifically, when the "State, through the effective control of the relevant territory and its inhabitants abroad as a consequence of military occupation or through the consent, invitation or acquiescence of the Government of that territory, exercises all or some of the public powers normally to be exercised by that Government": ibid. at para. 69. Other exceptional circumstances cited by the Court were "cases involving the activities of [a State's] diplomatic or consular agents abroad and on board craft vessels registered in, or flying the flag of, that State": ibid. at para. 71.

[316] Ibid. at para. 73.

[317] Ibid. at para. 57.

[318] Ibid. at para. 73. It has been noted that "[a] conceptualization of jurisdiction as unitary and exclusive clearly informs the reasoning": C. Costello, "Courting Access to Asylum in Europe: Recent Supranational Jurisprudence Explored" (2012) 12(2) *Human Rights Law Review* 287, at 296.

[319] See Milanovic, "*Al-Skeini* and *Al-Jedda* in Strasbourg" (explaining the various factors pushing the Court to come up with a legal justification for making the extraterritorial application of the European Convention on Human Rights exceptional).

which it was based, particularly among those who saw the European Convention on Human Rights as an important constraint on hostilities conducted by States Parties to the Convention outside the region.[320] A particular concern was the Court's focus on the *legality* of the extraterritorial action: its strict equation of "jurisdiction" with "authority to act" meant that a State might profit from the very illegality of its conduct (being beyond the limits of jurisdiction in international law) to avoid triggering its human rights obligations vis-à-vis those affected by its unlawful acts.[321]

Although the *Banković* test was applied in a number of subsequent cases,[322] more recent decisions of the Court appear to indicate a shift away from the strict *Banković* standard of effective control over *territory* and toward recognition of the exercise of power and authority over *individuals* as sufficient to establish jurisdiction.[323]

[320] See, for example, K. Altiparmak, "*Bankovic*: An Obstacle to the Application of the European Convention on Human Rights in Iraq?" (2004) 9(2) *Journal of Conflict and Security Law* 213; E. Roxstrom, M. Gibney, and T. Einarsen, "The NATO Bombing Case: (*Banković et al. v. Belgium et al.*) and the Limits of Western Human Rights Protection" (2005) 23 *Boston University International Law Journal* 55 [Roxtrom et al., "The NATO Bombing Case"] (concluding that the decision "evinces a vision of human rights that, ultimately, is inimical to the very purpose of human rights" (at 56)). See also R. Lawson, "Life after *Bankovic*: On the Extraterritorial Application of the European Convention of Human Rights," in F. Coomans and M. Kamminga eds., *Extraterritorial Application of Human Rights Treaties* 83 (2004) [Lawson, "Life after *Bankovic*"]; M. O'Boyle, "The European Convention of Human Rights and Extraterritorial Jurisdiction: A Comment on 'Life after *Bankovic*,'" in F. Coomans and M. Kamminga eds., *Extraterritorial Application of Human Rights Treaties* 125 (2004); and O. Ben-Naftali and Y. Shany, "Living in Denial: The Application of Human Rights in the Occupied Territories" (2004) 37 *Israel Law Review* 17 [Ben-Naftali and Shany, "Living in Denial"], at 80–83.

[321] On this point, see further King, "The Extraterritorial Human Rights Obligations of States," at 533, 538.

[322] For example: *Al-Saadoon and Mufdhi v. The United Kingdom*, (Decision on Admissibility) (2009) 49 EHRR SE11 (ECHR, June 30, 2009) (violations of the European Convention on Human Rights in British-occupied Iraq: the case fitted the "exceptional circumstances" exceptions to territorial jurisdiction established by the court in *Banković*, with the United Kingdom being found to have exercised "total and exclusive" de facto control over detention facilities and thereby jurisdiction over the applicants for the duration of their detention).

[323] In the 2004 *Ilaşcu* case, for example, concerning acts of Russian forces within separatist Transdniestria in Moldovan territory, the Court affirmed that although "jurisdiction is presumed to be exercised normally through the State's territory," "in exceptional circumstances the acts of [States Parties] performed outside their territory, or which produce effects there, may amount to exercise by them of their jurisdiction within the meaning of Article 1 of the Convention." (*Ilaşcu and Others v. Moldova and Russia*, (2005) 40 EHRR 46 (ECHR, July 8, 2004), at paras. 312, 314.). In the *Issa* case, concerning a Turkish incursion into northern Iraq, the Court reverted to the "effective overall control standard" of earlier cases, adding that "a State may also be held accountable for violation of the Convention rights and freedoms of persons who are in the territory of another State but who are found to be under the former State's authority and control through its agents operating – whether lawfully or unlawfully – in the latter State." (*Issa and Others v. Turkey*, (2005) 41 EHRR 27 (ECHR, Mar. 30, 2005), at para. 71.). Significantly (and inconsistently with its decision in *Banković*), the Court added that: "[a]ccountability in such situations stems from the fact that Article 1 of the Convention cannot be interpreted so as to allow a State party to perpetrate violations of the Convention on the territory of another State, which it could not perpetrate on its own territory": ibid.

The shift was decisively confirmed by two cases decided in 2011.[324] The most relevant of these to the present discussion is *Al Skeini v. United Kingdom*, a case brought by relatives of persons alleged to be under United Kingdom jurisdiction when they were killed, and in relation to which it was alleged there had been no effective investigation into the deaths, in breach of Article 2 of the European Convention on Human Rights. The Court in this case rejected two propositions that its own previous judgments had helped to establish: first, that the Convention applied only in the juridical and geographical space created by States Parties; and second, that extraterritorial jurisdiction would apply only in situations where the State has "control" over an *area* outside its territory. While affirming the *Banković* finding that Article 1 of the Convention is a primarily territorial limitation, the Court nevertheless found that the obligations of the Convention applied to British soldiers who were exercising public powers in Iraq, stating that "[w]hat is decisive in such cases is the *exercise of physical power and control over the person in question*."[325] Whenever jurisdiction is so established, "the State is under an obligation under Article 1 to secure to that individual the rights and freedoms under Section 1 of the Convention that are relevant to the situation of that individual."[326]

Banković confirmed that one of several exceptions to the general rule limiting application of the Convention to the territory of State Parties is in relation to "the activities ... on board ... vessels registered in, or flying the flag of, that State."[327] The principle that flag State jurisdiction can give rise to responsibility under the Convention (and that the Convention can apply on the high seas)[328] has been affirmed in several subsequent cases. The 2001 *Xhavara* case concerned a collision between an Italian coast guard vessel and a boat flying an Albanian flag that was carrying potential (presumably smuggled) migrants, many of whom drowned as a result of the collision.[329] The incident happened in the context of a bilateral agreement between Albania and Italy that permitted the latter to intercept vessels flying the Albanian flag that were suspected of carrying irregular migrants. Although ultimately finding the case inadmissible because of a failure to exhaust local remedies, the Court did consider that Italy, as flag State of the patrol vessel, had exercised jurisdiction and had discharged

[324] *Al-Skeini and Others v. United Kingdom*, (2011) 53 EHRR 18 (ECHR, July 7, 2011) [*Al-Skeini v. United Kingdom*]; and *Al-Jedda v. United Kingdom*, (2011) 53 EHRR 23 (ECHR, July 7, 2011).

[325] *Al-Skeini v. United Kingdom*, at para. 136 (emphasis added). Milanovic notes that the reliance of the Court on the fact that the occupying forces were using "public powers" limits the impact of the judgment on fact situations such as that found in the *Banković* case: Milanovic, "*Al-Skeini* and *Al-Jedda* in Strasbourg," at 128.

[326] *Al-Skeini v. United Kingdom*, at para. 137.

[327] *Banković v. Belgium*, at para. 71.

[328] For a discussion of this aspect of the judgment, see E. Papastavridis, "Piracy off Somalia: The 'Emperors and the Thieves of the Oceans' in the 21st Century," in A. Abass ed., *Protecting Human Security in Africa* 122 (2010), at 146–147.

[329] *Xhavara and Fifteen Others v. Italy and Albania*, Application No. 39473/98 (ECHR, Jan. 11, 2001).

its responsibilities under the Convention by initiating manslaughter proceedings against the patrol vessel captain.[330] Implicit in this finding is that Italy, as flag State of the patrol vessel, would have been responsible for any human rights violations caused by that vessel to persons on board the Albanian-flagged boat. It is notable however that neither Italy nor Albania raised the issue of jurisdiction.

The *Medvedyev* case[331] concerned the high-seas interception, by the French Navy, of a Cambodia-registered cargo boat, suspected of transporting large quantities of narcotics for distribution in Europe. French military officials boarded and rerouted the vessel after confining the crew. The Court acknowledged that "the special nature of the marine environment" was relevant but "cannot justify an area outside the law where ships' crews are covered by no legal system capable of affording them enjoyment of the rights and guarantees protected by the Convention which the States have undertaken to secure to everyone within their jurisdiction."[332] It found that France had exercised full, exclusive, and continuous control over the vessel and its crew and, accordingly, that the applicants had been under the jurisdiction of France from the time of interception.[333] In an examination of the merits of the case, the Court found that arrest procedures had violated the applicant's rights under the European Convention on Human Rights.[334]

In April 2012, the Grand Chamber of the European Court of Human Rights[335] issued its judgment in *Hirsi Jamaa v. Italy*, a case concerning the high seas interception and push-back to Libya of smuggled Somali and Eritrean nationals by the Italian coast guard.[336] The actions took place within the framework of agreements reached between Libya and Italy that were examined in detail in Chapter 1. The Court held that Italy's actions violated fundamental rights including the prohibition on torture and inhuman or degrading treatment or punishment and the prohibition on collective expulsion of nonnationals – despite the relevant actions occurring outside Italy's territory.

3.4.3. *Preliminary Conclusions about Extraterritorial Application of Human Rights Law*

The previous overview confirms that the international legal position with respect to the extraterritorial application of human rights law is both shifting and unclear,

330 For further on this, see Lawson, "Life after *Bankovic*," at 99–100.
331 *Medvedyev and Others v. France*, (2010) 51 EHRR 39 (ECHR Mar. 29, 2010).
332 Ibid. at para. 81.
333 Ibid. at para. 50.
334 Ibid. at para. 63.
335 The Grand Chamber "shall accept the request if the case raises a serious question affecting the interpretation or application of the Convention or the protocols thereto, or a serious issue of general importance." European Convention on Human Rights, at Art. 43.
336 *Hirsi Jamaa and Others v. Italy*, (2012) 55 EHRR 21 (ECHR, Feb. 23, 2012).

complicated by State practice that remains far from uniform.[337] It is necessary to acknowledge that international human rights law was developed to regulate the conduct of States within their own borders. The jurisdictional clauses found in most of the major human rights treaties confirms that obligations were generally not foreseen to extend beyond the territory of the State. However, this position is increasingly at odds with a world in which States can and readily do assert power outside their borders or otherwise engage in conduct that has extraterritorial effect. In addition to the present focus of migration control, the areas of military intervention, military occupation, counterterrorism, and drug control are just a few of many contemporary examples. As commentators have noted, efforts to exclude extraterritorial activity from the purview of human rights are contrary to basic ideas about the rule of law and universal justice, creating a double standard that damages the legitimacy of human rights and undermines its core institutions.[338]

As with any other treaty, human rights instruments must be read according to the ordinary meaning of the text. However other considerations are also relevant and, in the context of extraterritorial application of human rights obligations, international courts, human rights bodies, and commentators have demonstrated an increasing willingness to interpret treaty obligations in a manner that pays particular regard to the humanitarian "object and purpose" of these treaties. This is certainly the case with the ICCPR where the interpretation of jurisdiction by both the Human Rights Committee and the International Court of Justice represents a substantial widening of the Covenant's initially accepted scope. In the European context, the European Court has accepted that the human rights obligations of a State should not depend on the physical location of the individual in question (within or outside its territory) but should rather be commensurate with the extent to which that person is under the power, authority, and control of that State. The greater the degree of power, authority, and control, the more likely the State is under human rights obligations and the wider the scope of those obligations.[339] The nature of the obligation in question is also relevant to determining the scope of application of a particular human rights instrument or a specific provision: for example, violations of the right to life and the prohibition on torture may more easily trigger a wider scope of obligation than would be the case with less "fundamental" rights.[340] In a similar way, very onerous obligations may be more difficult to trigger than, for example, prohibitions on arbitrary decision making. This approach calls for the scope of obligations owed by

[337] For a useful overview of State Practice in the United States, United Kingdom, and Canada, see Hathaway et al., "Human Rights Abroad," esp. at 393–404.

[338] See Roxtrom et al., "The NATO Bombing Case."

[339] *Al-Skeini v. United Kingdom*, esp. at 136–137.

[340] See M. Nowak, "Obligations of States to Prevent and Prohibit Torture in an Extraterritorial Perspective," in M. Gibney and S. Skogly eds., *Universal Human Rights and Extraterritorial Obligations* 11 (2010).

States extraterritorially to be determined according to the level of control or power exercised by the State[341] and taking into account the State's capacity to respect or fulfill the particular right in question.[342]

3.4.4. *Extraterritorial Application of the Obligation of* Non-refoulement

As explained in the previous chapter,[343] international human rights law prohibits States from extraditing, deporting, expelling, or otherwise removing a person from their territory where there are substantial grounds for believing that there is a risk of serious human rights violations, most particularly torture and violations of the right to life, in the destination State.[344] To the extent that *non-refoulement* is part of international human rights law, the various tests put forward by international judicial and human rights bodies and considered previously would be relevant to the scope of application of that obligation. In the context of the international human rights law obligation of *non-refoulement* to torture, ill-treatment, or the death penalty, international human rights bodies have recognized that extraterritorial jurisdiction, where established, entails an obligation not to *refoule* persons to face torture, ill-treatment, or execution – even if, in practice, that "return" is only a handover to the local State authorities in whose territory the State conducting the return has been acting

341 Ben-Naftali and Shany argue that "the scope of obligations introduced by human rights conventions change in light of the circumstances and intensity of the interaction between the state and the protected individuals": Ben-Naftali and Shany, "Living in Denial," at 82. This would justify a highly fact-based analysis, such that the level of human rights obligations owed would be likely to differ depending on whether, for example, the factual context was one of decisive physical control (e.g., through detention of a person or seizure of a vessel), or violations occurring during temporary military incursions into foreign territory. Note that this approach, although compelling in principle, runs a risk of conflating the preliminary question of jurisdiction with substantive questions of responsibility and the discharge of obligations to a standard of due diligence (see further the discussion of due diligence in Chapter 4, at Section 4.3.3)

342 For example, Ben-Naftali and Shany note that although Inter-American jurisprudence recognizes the obligation of consular officers abroad not to arbitrarily refuse to issue new passports to citizens living abroad (citing, inter alia, *Samuel Lichtensztejn v. Uruguay*, UNHRC Comm. No. 77/1980, UN Doc. CCPR/C/18/D/77/1980, Mar. 31, 1983, decided Mar. 31, 1983, at para. 6.1: "The issue of a passport to a Uruguayan citizen is clearly a matter within the jurisdiction of the Uruguayan authorities and [the applicant] is 'subject to the jurisdiction' of Uruguay for that purpose"), it would be unreasonable to suggest those consular officers are also obliged to secure socioeconomic rights such as the right to food or health services: Ben-Naftali and Shany, "Living in Denial," at 74.

343 See Chapter 2, at Section 2.4.

344 See, for example, Convention against Torture, at Art. 3. The Human Rights Committee has read an obligation of *non-refoulement* into Article 7 of the ICCPR. UN Human Rights Committee, "General Comment No. 20: Replaces General Comment 7 concerning Prohibition of Torture and Cruel Treatment or Punishment (Art. 7)," UN Doc. HRI/GEN/1/Rev.7, May 12, 2004, at 150, adopted Oct. 3, 1992, at para. 9 ("States parties must not expose individuals to the danger of torture or cruel, inhuman or degrading treatment or punishment upon return to another country by way of their extradition, expulsion or *refoulement*").

extraterritorially.[345] For example, if extraterritorial application of the Convention against Torture is recognized as being triggered by de facto control over a vessel or individual on the high seas, then this would apply as much to the *non-refoulement* obligation of that instrument as it would to the central prohibition on torture.

Arising under a different set of treaty obligations, the extraterritorial application of the obligation of *non-refoulement* under refugee law must be considered separately to *non-refoulement* under human rights law. As noted previously, early controversies over the geographical scope of the obligation of *non-refoulement* focused on the question of whether the obligation extended to asylum-seekers rejected *at the border* – before they had entered the host State. This issue was soon settled in favor of the principle applying "both at the border and within the territory of a State."[346] Although there has been some disagreement on the question of State powers and obligations within its territorial sea,[347] it is generally accepted that in the context of the obligation of *non-refoulement*, the notion of "territory" includes the territorial sea.[348]

345 *Al-Saadoon and Mufdhi v. United Kingdom* (2010) (Decision on Merits) 51 EHRR 9 (ECHR, Mar. 2, 2010). The European Court, having established extraterritorial jurisdiction on the basis of the United Kingdom's detention of two Iraqi individuals in British-run military detention facilities in Iraq, held that the United Kingdom had violated the obligation of *non-refoulement* by transferring the men to Iraqi authorities in whose hands they faced "a real risk of being sentenced to death and executed": ibid. at para. 143. The Court rejected the United Kingdom's argument that it was obliged to respect Iraqi sovereignty and transfer the detainees, both Iraqi nationals held in Iraqi territory, to the custody of Iraqi courts when requested: ibid. at para. 138. Similarly, in *Munaf*, the Human Rights Committee confirmed the extraterritorial application of *non-refoulement* to torture or execution by considering whether Romania, by allowing the applicant (an Iraqi-American dual national) to leave the Romanian embassy in Baghdad, exercised jurisdiction over him in a way that exposed him to torture or the death penalty: UN Human Rights Committee, *Munaf v. Romania*, at para. 14.2. Romania ultimately prevailed on the basis that the risk to the applicant was not sufficiently foreseeable: ibid. at paras. 14.4–14.5. See also E. Lauterpacht and D. Bethlehem, "The Scope and Content of the Principle of *Non-Refoulement*: Opinion," in E. Feller, V. Türk, and F. Nicholson eds., *Refugee Protection in International Law: UNHCR's Global Consultations on International Protection* 87 (2003) [Lauterpacht and Bethlehem, "The Scope and Content of *Non-Refoulement*"], at para. 114, arguing that where an individual takes refuge in a diplomatic mission within his or her national State, the State providing refuge is subject to an obligation of *non-refoulement* under international refugee law.

346 See the various UNHCR Executive Committee conclusions cited in Mallia, *Migrant Smuggling by Sea*, at 85; and Hathaway, *The Rights of Refugees*, at 315–317 (stating his view that the obligation of *non-refoulement* always included nonadmission at the frontier as well as ejection from the State).

347 See further Chapter 6, at Section 6.1.1.1.

348 Mallia acknowledges that the powers and obligations of a State with respect to its territorial sea are not beyond dispute. However, she concludes that this ambivalence does not extend to the question of whether the obligation of *non-refoulement* is applicable: "there cannot be any argument to defend the failure to process any asylum claims made by people on the vessel while it is in the territorial waters of a State. In other words, while under the law of the sea regime a State may turn back vessels at the borders of its territorial sea and also order a vessel to leave the territorial sea ... once a claim for asylum is made within the territorial sea, the coastal State is obliged to arrange for the processing of

For as long as the encounter between host country and asylum-seeker took place on the frontier or within the territory of the former, the jurisdictional scope of the principle was not a matter of particular concern. Today however, the externalization of migration control means that the asylum-seeker will typically encounter representatives of the host State before even reaching its frontiers – perhaps at a foreign airport, within the territorial seas of a third State, or on the high seas. Very often, the purpose of such encounters is to push the asylum-seeker back to where he or she came from, or to another country altogether. The central questions that this raises has been well phrased by Gammeltoft-Hansen: (1) To what extent can the protection normally afforded to asylum-seekers and refugees be extended to situations where States engage in migration control outside their territories?, and (2) How are protection obligations distributed when extraterritorial migration control is operated within the territory of another State?[349]

There is a clear basis in the Convention against Torture, and abundant case law and other materials confirming the extraterritorial application of the prohibition on *refoulement* in connection with torture. However the situation vis-à-vis refugee law is not as clear. The Refugee Convention[350] itself is not particularly helpful on this point. Unlike the majority of human rights treaties, the Convention does not contain a clause specifying the scope of its application either generally or with specific reference to *non-refoulement*. Individual rights are granted or withheld depending on the status of the individual in question. All refugees, whether arriving through authorized or nonauthorized means, and whether inside or seeking entry to the territory of a State Party, are granted the basic protections of the Convention, including nondiscrimination, access to courts, education, and prohibition of *refoulement*. However, many additional rights, including those of an economic and social nature, are reserved for those who are pre-authorized to enter and reside ("lawfully staying") in the State Party. These additional rights would not, at least initially, be available to "refugees unlawfully in the country of refuge"[351]: persons with a valid claim for asylum whose arrival or stay is in breach of national migration control laws. The rights accorded to a refugee are, in short, relative to his or her relationship to the host State, with *physical presence* in the State appearing as an expected minimum prerequisite.

such claim in order to ensure that it does not violate the *non-refoulement* obligation": Mallia, *Migrant Smuggling by Sea*, at 86.

349 T. Gammeltoft-Hansen, "Growing Barriers: International Refugee Law," in M. Gibney and S. Skogly eds., *Universal Human Rights and Extraterritorial Obligations* 55 (2010) [Gammeltoft-Hansen, "Growing Barriers: International Refugee Law"], at 55.

350 Convention Relating to the Status of Refugees, 189 UNTS 137, done July 28, 1951, entered into force Apr. 22, 1954, as amended by the Protocol Relating to the Status of Refugees, 606 UNTS 267, done Jan. 31, 1967, entered into force Oct. 4, 1967 [Refugee Convention].

351 Ibid. at Art. 31.

The lack of clarity regarding the scope of application of the Refugee Convention's protection provisions, along with somewhat inconsistent jurisprudence on this issue (both discussed in this section) appears to have helped to bolster a restrictive interpretation that generally favors the intentions of those States engaging in extraterritorial migration control. However, commentators seeking a different conclusion have pointed to the fact that, as *non-refoulement* is also a principle of human rights law, there are solid grounds for reading this specialized obligation in light of the more positive developments that have occurred in that other sphere. According to Klug and Howe for example, "the complementarity and mutually reinforcing nature of international human rights law and international refugee law speak strongly in favor of delineating the same territorial scope for all expressions of the *non-refoulement* principle, whether developed under refugee or human rights law."[352] Conversely, it is possible to point to some essential differences between the two spheres that affect the nature and substantive content of obligations. Most critically, human rights law is fundamentally concerned with how States treat their own citizens, whereas international refugee law requires States to extend protections to persons who are, by definition, nonnationals. The previous chapter provides ample evidence of the extent to which the rights of nonnationals are compromised in international law and of the continuing reluctance of States to extend substantive rights to this larger group to which smuggled migrants and asylum-seekers both belong.[353] Another important distinction relates to focus and objective. Human rights law generally seeks to prevent violations and oblige States to implement their obligations. Refugee law by contrast, is reactive, accepting the fact of human rights violations being committed by States and attempting to deal with the results.[354]

Irrespective of one's views on the level of correlation between the human rights obligation of *non-refoulement* and the obligation under refugee law, the fact that the question of extraterritorial application remains unsettled with respect to human rights is, of itself, sufficient to justify a separate analysis of the extraterritorial scope of the obligation under refugee law. The task is not a straightforward one, as illustrated by the widely different conclusions reached by different entities weighing up the same body of evidence and authority.

The United States Supreme Court was one of the first national courts to consider the extraterritorial scope of the *non-refoulement* obligation in the Refugee Convention. In the 1993 *Sale* case, the Court was called on to decide whether the

[352] A. Klug and T. Howe, "The Concept of State Jurisdiction and the Applicability of the *Non-refoulement* Principle to Extraterritorial Interception Measures," in B. Ryan and R. Mitsilegas eds., *Extraterritorial Immigration Control: Legal Challenges* 69 (2010), at 71–72.

[353] See further Chapter 2, at Section 2.1.1.

[354] See further the discussion in Gammeltoft-Hansen, "Growing Barriers: International Refugee Law," esp. at 57–58.

principle of *non-refoulement* applied to Haitian asylum-seekers intercepted on the high seas by United States Coast Guard officials.[355] The Court concluded that the obligation of *non-refoulement* applied to those "on the threshold of initial entry"[356] and not to "aliens interdicted on the high seas."[357] In short, the obligation did not and was never intended to apply to persons beyond the territory of the United States. In reaching this decision the Court considered the meaning of the terms "expel," "return" ("a defensive act of resistance or exclusion at a border"[358]), and "*refouler*," as well as the implication of their juxtaposition. It also found that the drafting history of the relevant provision confirmed the right of *non-refoulement* as applying only to aliens "on the threshold of initial entry."[359] In considering the implications of the second paragraph of Article 33, which preserves the right of States to return a refugee "whom there are reasonable grounds for regarding as a danger to the security of the country *in which he is*,"[360] the Court reasoned that if *non-refoulement* obligations were applied to refugees on the high seas, this would create an anomaly whereby those persons could not be returned, even if they were considered a danger, as they were not *in* any country.[361]

The Court noted the humanitarian objective of the Convention but concluded that:

> The drafters of the Convention and the parties to the [Refugee] Protocol ... may not have contemplated that any nation would gather fleeing refugees and return them to the one country they had desperately sought to escape; such actions may even violate the spirit of Article 33; but a treaty cannot impose uncontemplated extraterritorial obligations on those who ratify it through no more than its general humanitarian intent. Because the text of article 33 cannot reasonably be read to say anything at all about a nation's actions toward aliens outside its own territory, it does not prohibit such actions.[362]

[355] *Sale, Acting Commissioner, Immigration and Naturalization Service, et al., Petitioners v. Haitian Centers Council, Inc., et al.*, 509 US 155 (US SC, Jun. 21, 1993) [*Sale v. Haitian Centers Council*].

[356] Ibid. at 187.

[357] Ibid. at 187.

[358] Ibid. at 192.

[359] Ibid. at 187.

[360] Refugee Convention, at Art. 33(2) (emphasis added).

[361] For a critical review of the Court's analysis on this point see UN High Commissioner for Refugees, *Advisory Opinion on the Extraterritorial Application of Non-refoulement Obligations under the 1951 Convention Relating to the Status of Refugees and Its 1967 Protocol* (Jan. 26, 2007) [UNHCR *Advisory Opinion on Extraterritorial Application of Non-Refoulement Obligations*], at paras. 28–29 and accompanying notes; Gammeltoft-Hansen, "Growing Barriers: International Refugee Law," at 60–61; and Hathaway, *The Rights of Refugees*, at 337–339. For a very detailed analysis of the case including of Justice Blackmun's dissenting opinion, which embodies many of the substantive arguments advanced by scholars, see M. Gibney, *Global Refugee Crisis: A Reference Handbook* (2nd ed. 2010), at 52–61.

[362] *Sale v. Haitian Centers Council*, at 183.

In his sole dissenting opinion, Justice Blackmun rejected the majority view that the language and drafting history of Article 33 supported a rejection of extraterritorial application. For him, the notion that a country can "[go] forth to seize aliens who are not at its borders and return them to persecution"[363] was inconceivable: "vulnerable refugees shall not be returned. The language is clear, and the command is straightforward; that should be the end of the enquiry."[364] As one commentator noted, the majority and dissent in the case "disagreed so fundamentally on each and every legal aspect of the *refoulement* issue that it is hard to believe that both opinions were addressing the same problem."[365]

The main elements of the *Sale* judgment were roundly rejected by the Inter-American Commission on Human Rights[366] and, a decade later, by the United Nations High Commissioner for Refugees (UNHCR) in its 2007 Advisory Opinion on this subject. UNHCR argued that the accepted approach to treaty interpretation – ordinary meaning, object and purpose, and drafting history – all supported a conclusion that the obligation not to return a refugee or asylum-seeker to a country where he or she would be at risk of persecution or other serious harm applies "wherever a state exercises jurisdiction, including at the frontier, on the high seas or on the territory of another State."[367] For UNHCR, the "overriding humanitarian object and purpose of the Convention"[368] is particularly relevant: an escape clause that would allow States to neatly avoid their obligation of *non-refoulement* by moving their refugee reception operations offshore would not be in keeping with the spirit of the refugee protection regime. The UNHCR opinion has been cited many times, including by international organizations, to support application of the principle of *non-refoulement* to interceptions of irregular migrants, including asylum-seekers, on the high seas.[369] However others, including the United States government, have been highly critical of that opinion. The United States government has advanced its own interpretation of the Convention's object, purpose, and drafting history, as well as a conservative view of what constitutes "practice," to support a contention that

[363] Ibid. at 197.
[364] Ibid. at 190.
[365] R. L. Newmark, "*Non-refoulement* Run Afoul: The Questionable Legality of Extraterritorial Repatriation Programs" (1993) 71 *Washington University Law Quarterly* 833, at 858.
[366] *Haitian Centre for Human Rights et al. v. United States*, Case No. 10.675, Report No. 51/96, Inter-AmCHR Doc. OEA/Ser.L/V/II.95 Doc. 7 rev (Inter-Am. Comm. H.R., Mar. 13, 1997).
[367] UNHCR *Advisory Opinion on Extraterritorial Application of Non-refoulement Obligations*, at para. 24.
[368] Ibid. at para. 30.
[369] See, for example, Council of Europe, Parliamentary Assembly, *The Interception and Rescue at Sea of Asylum Seekers, Refugees and Irregular Migrants* (Report of the Committee on Migration, Refugees and Population, June 1, 2011), esp. at paras. 8–9, 30–32.

"Article 33 applies only with respect to aliens who are inside a Contracting State's territory."[370]

Scholars of international refugee law have conducted detailed textual and historical analyses of Article 33. Their reading of the drafters' intent and the object and purpose of the Convention as a whole ("to prohibit *return in any manner whatsoever* of refugees to countries where they may face persecution"[371]) is very different to that of the *Sale* court and indeed to that of the United States government cited previously, as is their interpretation of the meaning of the key words "return" and "*refouler.*" In contrast to other provisions in the Refugee Convention "which condition the rights and benefits accorded to refugees on degrees of presence and lawful residence,"[372] commentators have noted that Article 33 makes no reference to geography or legal presence, but rather:

> prohibits the return of refugees "*in any manner whatsoever*" to the frontiers of territories where they may be persecuted ... regardless of whether the relevant action [of return] occurs "beyond the national territory of the State in question, at border posts or other points of entry, in international zones, at transit points, etc."[373]

There is very little scholarly support for the argument in *Sale* that only a territorial-based understanding of the obligation of *non-refoulement* would make sense of the exception set out in Article 33(2). The conclusions of scholars almost uniformly support UNHCR's position that the arguments adopted in *Sale* are "simply not compelling"[374] and that Article 33(1) is indeed applicable extraterritorially.[375]

370 See United States, Department of State, *Observations of the United States on the Advisory Opinion of the UN High Commissioner for Refugees on the Extraterritorial Application of Non-refoulement Obligations under the 1951 Convention Relating to the Status of Refugees and Its 1967 Protocol*, Dec. 28, 2007 (citation omitted).

371 G. Goodwin-Gill and J. McAdam, *The Refugee in International Law* (3rd ed. 2007) [Goodwin-Gill and McAdam, *The Refugee in International Law*], at 248 (emphasis in original).

372 Ibid. at 246.

373 Ibid. at 246 (emphasis in original), citing Lauterpacht and Bethlehem, "The Scope and Content of *Non-refoulement*", at para. 67, and noting that *non-refoulement* also applies extraterritorially where an individual has taken refuge in a diplomatic mission within his or her national State. It is important to acknowledge however, that the extract reflects a conclusion reached by Lauterpacht and Bethlehem on the basis of expanding notions of jurisdiction in international human rights law. For reasons set out previously, it is suggested that the parallels with international refugee law on this point are far from exact.

374 Hathaway, *The Rights of Refugees*, at 340.

375 See, for example, H. Koh, "The 'Haiti Paradigm' in United States Human Rights Policy" (2004) 103 *Yale Law Journal* 2391; Goodwin-Gill and McAdam, *The Refugee in International Law*, at 247–248; Hathaway, *The Rights of Refugees*, at 336–339; Gammeltoft-Hansen, "Growing Barriers: International Refugee Law"; and T. Gammeltoft-Hansen, "The Externalisation of European Migration Control and the Reach of International Refugee Law," in E. Guild and P. Minderhoud eds., *The First Decade of EU Migration and Asylum Law* (anniversary volume of the *European Journal of Migration*) 273 (2011) [Gammeltoft-Hansen, "The Externalisation of European Migration Control"], esp. at 280–285.

Despite its scholarly strength and persuasive logic, this consensus view among commentators and UNHCR is worryingly one-sided, and consequentially fragile. The text and drafting history of Article 33 are undeniably ambiguous, and the United States government is not alone among States in expressing support for a restrictive view of the scope of Article 33(1).[376] *Sale's* narrow interpretation has also been affirmed in a number of domestic decisions, most notably by the UK House of Lords in the *European Rights Centre Roma* case.[377] As observed recently by an Australian Federal Court judge, "the judgment of the final appellate courts in the US, the UK and Australia, spanning over eleven years is a considerable barrier to the acceptance of the views of the expert scholars and UNHCR."[378] In this context it is essential to reiterate that domestic judicial decisions and scholarly writings are only subsidiary means for determining international law,[379] and State practice remains ambiguous at best.[380] What is clear is the lack of strong evidence for State consent to an understanding of the obligation of *non-refoulement* that extends to asylum-seekers who are not at the borders or physically within the territory of the State.

The practices triggering the question of extraterritorial application of *non-refoulement* obligations under the Refugee Convention are relatively new, and their legal implications are still being explored and tested. The Refugee Convention envisaged granting rights and imposing obligations with a view to the treatment of persons already within the territory of Contracting States, "not in relation to people who came knocking on their doors from outside."[381] Its drafters clearly did not contemplate States being routinely engaged in offshore migration control. The concept of organized criminal groups providing a transportation service for migrants and refugees was undoubtedly even more remote to those engaged in crafting the language of Article 33. As States, courts, and human rights bodies are forced to confront the

376 For example, Fisher-Lescano et al. report that the German Federal Ministry of the Interior has stated that "state practice and predominant legal opinion are that the principle of non-refoulement in the Geneva Refugee Convention does not apply on the high seas to persons alleging persecution, since the high seas are extraterritorial," A. Fisher-Lescano, T. Lohr, and T. Tohidipur, "Border Controls at Sea: Requirements under International Human Rights and Refugee Law" (2009) 21(2) *International Journal of Refugee Law* 256, at 265.

377 *R (on the application of European Roma Rights Centre et al.) v. Immigration Officer at Prague Airport et al., ex parte European Roma Rights Centre et al.*, [2004] UKHL 55 (UK HL, Dec. 9, 2004), esp. at paras. 27, 65–71. See also the decision of the Australian High Court in *Applicant A v. Minister for Immigration and Ethnic Affairs* (1997) 190 CLR 225 (Aus. HC, Feb. 24, 1997), esp. at paras. 273–274.

378 Justice A. North, "Extraterritorial Effect of Non-refoulement," address to the International Association of Refugee Law Judges World Conference, Bled, Slovenia, 7–9 September 2011, available at www3.austlii.edu.au/au/journals/FedJSchol/2011/19.html (accessed May 12, 2013).

379 Statute of the International Court of Justice, 961 UNTS 183, done June 26, 1945, entered into force Oct. 24, 1945, at Art. 38(1)(d).

380 See further discussion of interdiction at sea in Chapter 6.

381 I. Shearer, "Book Reviews: D. Weissbrodt, *The Human Rights of Non-citizens*," (2010) 22(1) *International Journal of Refugee Law* 140, at 142.

realities of extraterritorial immigration control, it can be expected that the understanding of the scope of the obligation of *non-refoulement* will evolve to better reflect these new realities. The previous section confirmed that such a shift is already underway within international human rights law: in that sphere the move toward acceptance of the extraterritorial application of human rights obligations is slow but apparently inexorable. In critical areas such as the right to life and the prohibition on torture, progress toward acceptance of an expanded scope of application is even more marked. The arguments that have been advanced for expanding the *ratione loci* of human rights: most particularly, that *control* and *authority* over individuals or territory, not mere geography, is ultimately what really matters, will become increasingly difficult to reject in the context of refugee protection. As one commentator has remarked, even the most parsimonious interpretation of Article 33 would subject the obligation of *non-refoulement* to the general proposition that States are responsible for the human rights of persons "subject to or within their jurisdiction."[382] Scrutiny of foundational legal concepts such as jurisdiction and responsibility in light of radically new migration control practices is likely to further narrow the space within which a restrictive reading of the scope of the obligation of *non-refoulement* can be credibly defended.

3.5. SUMMARY OF THE KEY PRINCIPLES OF SOVEREIGNTY AND JURISDICTION RELEVANT TO MIGRANT SMUGGLING

The task of the present chapter has been to explore the relationship of principles of sovereignty and jurisdiction to the capacity of States to act, particularly in response to migrant smuggling. The key points are summarized in this section.

Capacity to Act

First, the principle of State sovereignty is a basic starting point in considering the legal aspects of migrant smuggling. This principle confers on States the capacity to regulate affairs within their territory, including wide powers in respect of controlling immigration (and thereby acting to prevent and respond to migrant smuggling). However, this is subject to an important caveat: although immigration has traditionally been considered to be exclusively a matter for domestic jurisdiction, it is today increasingly subject to the influence of international law and, in particular, of international human rights law and refugee law.

Second, the concept of jurisdiction – competence to act – includes *prescriptive* jurisdiction (competence to prescribe laws and other rules, for example criminalizing

[382] Gammeltoft-Hansen, "The Externalisation of European Migration Control," at 285.

claims of violations of international law: for example, intergovernmental commissions and human rights treaty bodies. Responsibility claims can also be "domesticated" and brought before national courts.[2] A finding of responsibility can, in short, be used in many ways, by different mechanisms and different parties, to enforce, encourage, and facilitate compliance with international law.

While States will generally be compelled to accept legal responsibility for their *responses* to migrant smuggling, they may reject responsibility for the act of migrant smuggling and its consequences: pointing to the actions of organized criminals, to other States in not securing their borders, or even the smuggled migrants themselves, rather than actions or omissions of the State itself. In some instances, such a rejection of responsibility will be legally justifiable. However, there are many situations of migrant smuggling in which States can indeed be found to be legally responsible. At the level of practice, questions of State responsibility in the present context are most likely to arise with reference to State *responses* to migrant smuggling, or State responsibility for particularly egregious forms of smuggling involving death or serious injury to the migrants.

A list of questions that address State responsibility in migrant smuggling provides a useful overview of the key issues:

- When and under what circumstances are States responsible to other States for migrant smuggling that occurs within their borders or jurisdiction? For example: can States be held legally responsible for failing to prevent migrant smuggling?
- When and under what circumstances can States be held responsible for migrant smuggling by private parties, which involves exploitation and other harms?
- When and under what circumstances can a State be held responsible for violations of international law that occur in the course of a migrant smuggling response undertaken by its agents or officials? Can responsibility be avoided or modified if, for example, the relevant act occurs outside the territory of the State, the relevant actors are not State agents or officials but rather private parties (such as companies to whom migration control functions have been outsourced), or one State has consented to another acting on its behalf?
- How is responsibility allocated in the context of joint operations between two or more States? Are the rules in that situation the same as those that would apply in the context of operations carried out by intergovernmental organizations?

[2] J. Crawford and S. Olleson, "The Nature and Forms of International Responsibility," in M. D. Evans ed., *International Law* 451 (2006) [Crawford and Olleson, "The Nature and Forms of International Responsibility"], at 456.

- When and under what circumstances can a State be held responsible for violations of international law that occur in the course of a migrant smuggling response conducted by another State?

The present section commences with a brief overview of the rules of State responsibility and their origin, before examining the two specific requirements of responsibility: attribution and breach of obligation. Issues around responsibility for responses to smuggling or other aspects of smuggling-related harm originating in the conduct of private persons or entities is subject to separate and detailed consideration, as is the issue of responsibility for violations that occur in the context of joint operations and operations carried out by international organizations on behalf of States. The chapter then summarizes the consequences of a finding of responsibility, rules relating to invocation of responsibility, and countermeasures. The section concludes with a summary of the key principles of responsibility relevant to migrant smuggling.

4.1. INTERNATIONAL LAW AND RESPONSIBILITY

The terms "international responsibility" and "State responsibility" "cover[] the relations which arise under international law from the internationally wrongful act of a State."[3] The "secondary rules" of State responsibility operate to require the State to make reparations for a failure to comply with an international legal obligation.

The question of State responsibility for violation of international rules has been considered by international courts and tribunals on numerous occasions and has generated substantial State practice. Formal codification efforts culminated with the finalization of a set of principles ("Articles") for consideration by the United Nations and its Member States.[4] At some point it was expected that this process would eventually result in a multilateral treaty.[5] However, the passing of more than

3 International Law Commission, *Draft Articles on Responsibility of States for Internationally Wrongful Acts*, in "Report of the International Law Commission on the Work of Its Fifty-Third Session," UN GAOR, 56th Sess, Supp. No. 10, UN Doc. A/56/10, at 43 (2001) (referred to in this chapter as "ILC Draft Articles"), at Art. 1, para. 5.

4 The official text of the *Commentaries* to the ILC Draft Articles appear in the 2001 report of the ILC, see ibid., at 59, and are referred to in this chapter as "ILC Commentary." The notes and references in this chapter are to the Articles and Commentary as set out in J. Crawford ed., *The International Law Commission's Articles on State Responsibility: Introduction, Text, and Commentaries* (2002) [Crawford, *The ILC's Articles on State Responsibility*].

5 The complete text of the Articles was adopted by the ILC at its fifty-third session in 2001 and subsequently referred to the UN General Assembly for its consideration. In its recommendation to the UN General Assembly, the ILC proposed a two-stage approach for taking its work forward: some form of endorsement or taking note of the Articles, followed by the possible conversion of the Articles into a multilateral convention at a later stage. See International Law Commission, "Summary Record of the 2675th Meeting," UN Doc. A/CN.4/SR.2675, May 11, 2001, at 66–67, paras. 61–62.

therefore the acts and omissions of individuals that must be examined. When is an individual acting in his or her private capacity, and when is she or he acting for or on behalf of the State? For example, in the context of migrant smuggling, is a guard in a privately run detention center who assaults a detainee acting in his or her private or public capacity? Are these actions attributable to the State that has engaged the contractor running the detention center? Attribution is a central conundrum of State responsibility and an issue that is addressed in considerable detail by the ILC in Chapter II of its Articles.

Can a particular act or omission be attributed to more than one State? This question is highly relevant in the present context: States are increasingly coordinating their control efforts against migrant smuggling through, for example, joint border patrols and operations against vessels or vehicles suspected of illegally transporting migrants. The general principle is that States can indeed be individually responsible for actions or omissions in which they were involved with another State or group of States.[29] Note that the present section is concerned with whether conduct can be attributed to *a* State; the different question of *which* State is to be held responsible (for example in the context of joint operations) is subject to separate examination at Section 4.4.[30]

Attribution can generally be established without difficulty when the conduct in question is clearly that of an organ of the State. The ILC formulates its principle on this point as follows:

> The conduct of any State organ shall be considered an act of that State under international law, whether the organ exercises legislative, executive, judicial or other functions, whatever position it holds in the organization of the State, and whatever its character as an organ of the central government or of a territorial unit of the State.[31]

That the conduct of any organ of the State will be regarded as an act of that State is a well-established rule of international law and one affirmed by the ICJ to be "of

[29] ILC Draft Articles, at Art. 47(1): "Where several States are responsible for the same internationally wrongful act, the responsibility of each State may be invoked in relation to that act." See also the ILC Commentary on this provision, which notes that the principle of independent responsibility expressed in this Article reflects the position under general international law, absent an agreement to the contrary between the States concerned: ILC Commentary, at Art. 47, para. 3. See further ILC Draft Article 19, which makes clear that "attribution of international responsibility to an assisting, directing or coercing State does not preclude the responsibility of the assisted, directed or coerced State". ILC Commentary, at Art. 19, para. 1.

[30] See further Sections 4.4 and 4.7.1 of this chapter.

[31] ILC Draft Articles, at Art. 4.

a customary character."[32] Accordingly, actions of a State's immigration service, for example, and actions of the officials in that service, will clearly be the actions of the State. Article 4 has been framed very broadly and clearly indicates that any entity or authority exercising public powers in the State is considered as an organ of that State for the purposes of attributing responsibility.[33] This would suggest that attribution could flow from the actions of a private security contractor involved in immigration detention to the State who contracted that provider. In addition, Article 4 supports the contention that no distinction is to be made between the acts of "superior" and "subordinate" officials[34] (provided, of course, that both are acting in their official capacity), a refinement of the general principle of attribution of responsibility for individuals' conduct or that of their subordinates, which has been strengthened considerably by the decisions of international criminal tribunals.[35] Attribution is not

32 *Difference Relating to Immunity from Legal Process of a Special Rapporteur of the Commission on Human Rights (Advisory Opinion)*, [1999] ICJ Rep 62, at 87, para. 62, cited in ILC Commentary, at Art. 4, para. 6.

33 Note paragraph 2 of ILC Draft Article 4: "[a]n organ includes any person or entity which has that status in accordance with the internal law of the State." The ILC Commentary notes that the use of the word "includes" denies the State any opportunity of avoiding responsibility for the conduct of a body that is, in reality, an organ of that State by denying it that status under its own law: ILC Commentary, at Art. 4, para. 6.

34 ILC Commentary, at Art. 4, para. 7.

35 See, for example, *Prosecutor v. Bemba*, Case ICC-01/05–01/08, ICC Pre-Trial Chamber II, June 15, 2009 (command responsibility, preferring the standard enunciated by the International Criminal Tribunal for the former Yugoslavia (ICTY) Trial Chamber in *Blaskic*); *Prosecutor v. Brima et al.*, Case SCSL-04–16-T, SCSL Trial Chamber, June 20, 2007; *Prosecutor v. Naletilic and Martinovic*, Case IT-98–24-A, ICTY Appeals Chamber, May 3, 2006 (command responsibility and failure to prevent or punish); *Prosecutor v. Hadzihasanovic*, Case IT-01–47-T, ICTY Trial Chamber, Mar. 15, 2006 (command responsibility and failure to punish); *Prosecutor v. Halilovic*, Case IT-01–48-T, ICTY Trial Chamber, Nov. 16, 2005 (command responsibility as imposing criminal liability for a superior's "failure to act when under a duty to do so," at para. 38); *Prosecutor v. Kajelijeli*, Case ICTR-98–44A-A, ICTR Appeals Chamber, May 23, 2005 (command responsibility and the superior-subordinate relationship); *Prosecutor v. Ntagerura et al.*, Case ICTR-99–46-T, ICTR Trial Chamber, Feb. 25, 2004; *Prosecutor v. Baglishema*, Case ICTR-95–1A-A, ICTR Appeals Chamber, July 3, 2002 (command responsibility and the superior-subordinate relationship); *Prosecutor v. Krnojelac*, Case IT-97–25-T, ICTY Trial Chamber, Mar. 15, 2002 (superior authority); *Prosecutor v. Kvocka et al.*, Case IT-98–30/1, ICTY Trial Chamber, Nov. 2, 2001 (superior authority); *Prosecutor v. Kordic and Cerkez*, Case IT-95–14–2, ICTY Trial Chamber, Feb. 21, 2001 (command responsibility); *Prosecutor v. Delalic et al.*, Case IT-96–21-A, ICTY Appeals Chamber, Feb. 20, 2001 (command responsibility); *Prosecutor v. Blaskic*, Case IT-95–14-T, ICTY Trial Chamber, Mar. 3, 2000 (command responsibility); *Prosecutor v. Aleksovski*, Case IT-95–14/1-T, ICTY Trial Chamber, June 25, 1999 (authority – de jure or de facto – of the defendant); *Prosecutor v. Kayishema and Ruzindana*, Case ICTR-95–1-T, ICTR Trial Chamber, May 21, 1999 (command responsibility and mens rea); *Prosecutor v. Delalic et al.*, Case IT-96–21-T, ICTY Trial Chamber, Nov. 16, 1998 (command responsibility); and *Prosecutor v. Erdemovic*, Case IT-96–22-T, ICTY Trial Chamber, May 31, 1996. See also J. Dungel, "Command Responsibility in International Criminal Tribunals" (Paper presented at the National Consultative Summit on Extrajudicial Killings and Enforced Disappearances: Searching for Solutions, July 16–17, 2007), available at http://sc.judiciary.gov.ph/publications/summit/Summit%20 Papers/Dungel%20-%20Command%20Responsibility%20in%20ICT.pdf (accessed May 12, 2013).

compromised even in the case of gross incompetence on the part of the offending State organ and even if the conduct has been disowned by other organs of the State.[36]

Some State organs almost invariably act only in their public capacity. In other words, they do not have a potential private capacity in the same way that other State entities may. A determination of responsibility involving such a State entity is not likely to be overly complicated. A law or executive order mandating the interception and forced return of vessels on the high seas suspected of carrying smuggled migrants, or a judicial decision upholding the mandatory detention of all smuggled migrants, would both be readily identified as acts of the State that are subject to international legal scrutiny. The acts of an official vessel involved in the interception or turn back of ships carrying asylum-seekers would be similarly identified as acts of the State, which, if in breach of an international obligation, would give rise to responsibility. A State will, of course, be responsible for its legislative and other omissions as well as its acts. A legal and administrative system that failed to provide a fair trial to alleged migrant smugglers; a right of access to habeas corpus; or a right of access to remedies for those smuggled migrants who have suffered a violation of their human rights would, for example, directly implicate the State concerned. Subject to a finding that the act or omission itself constituted a breach of an international obligation of that State (such as the obligation of *non-refoulement*, the right to a fair trial, the prohibition on torture, or the right of access to remedies), the international responsibility of the State would be directly engaged in relation to these situations.

For some acts or omissions, it will not be readily apparent whether the person who undertakes them is part of a State organ who acts with the capacity of that organ and thereby on behalf of that State. In making such a determination, the ILC Commentary clearly indicates that the central question will be whether the individual concerned is acting in an apparently official capacity or under color of authority.[37] Importantly, "[i]t is irrelevant for this purpose that the person concerned may have had ulterior or improper motives or may be abusing public power."[38] That the act in question was unauthorized or ultra vires is also irrelevant in determining whether it is to be characterized as an act of the State.[39] These are both relevant considerations in the present context. States could, for example, defend themselves against allegations of public sector involvement in

36 ILC Commentary, at Art. 7, para. 2.

37 Ibid. at Art. 4, para. 13.

38 Ibid.

39 Ibid. See also ILC Draft Articles, at Art. 7 (note that the Article 7 provision applies both to organs of the State and to "a person or entity empowered to exercise elements of the governmental authority").

migrant smuggling by pointing out that such involvement is contrary to national law and policy. However, under the rules of attribution, a national prohibition against behavior prohibited by international law is insufficient for the State to avoid its international legal responsibility. Two cases mentioned in the ILC's Commentary serve to confirm the rule that conduct "carried out by persons cloaked by governmental authority"[40] is attributable to the State. In the *Caire* case, a French national was killed by two Mexican officials who had tried to rob him. The Commission held:

> that the two officers, even if they are deemed to have acted outside their competence … and even if their superiors countermanded an order, have involved the responsibility of the State, since they acted under the cover of their status as officers and used means placed at their disposal on account of that status.[41]

In the *Velásquez Rodríguez* case, the Inter-American Court of Human Rights stated that a determination as to whether a breach of the American Convention on Human Rights[42] had occurred did not depend on whether provisions of internal law had been contravened or authority exceeded:

> [U]nder international law a State is responsible for the acts of its agents undertaken in their official capacity and for their omissions, even when those agents act outside the sphere of their authority or violate internal law.[43]

The task then becomes one of distinguishing, not between authorized and unauthorized conduct, but between "official" conduct and "private" conduct. Some situations will be relatively straightforward. For example, it has been reliably reported that State coastal patrol agencies have ignored vessels carrying smuggled migrants that are obviously in severe distress.[44] In addition to violating international legal

40 *Petrolane Inc. v. Islamic Republic of Iran*, (1991) 27 Iran-USCTR 64 (Iran–US Claims Tribunal, Aug. 14, 1991), at 92, cited in ILC Commentary, at Art. 7, para. 7.

41 *Caire (France v. Mexico)*, (1952) 5 UNRIAA 516 (French–Mexican Claims Commission, June 7, 1929), at 531, cited in ILC Commentary, at Art. 7, para. 5.

42 American Convention on Human Rights, 1144 UNTS 123, done Nov. 22, 1969, entered into force July 18, 1978 [American Convention on Human Rights].

43 *Velásquez Rodríguez v. Honduras*, Inter-Am Ct. H.R. (ser. C) No. 4, July 29, 1988 [*Velásquez Rodríguez Case*], at para. 170, cited in ILC Commentary, at Art. 7, para. 6.

44 See, for example, the "left-to-die" case study set out in the introduction to this book. In that case, an independent report found that "No one went to the aid of this boat, despite a distress call logged by the Italian Maritime Rescue Coordination Centre, which pinpointed the boat's position. There were also a number of alleged direct contacts between the boat in distress and other vessels, including a helicopter that dropped biscuits and water, but never returned, two fishing vessels, both of which refused to provide assistance, and a large military vessel which came into close contact with the boat, but ignored obvious distress signals." Council of Europe, Parliamentary Assembly, *Lives Lost in the Mediterranean Sea: Who Is Responsible?* (Report of the Committee on Migration, Refugees and

standards relating to, for example, safety of life at sea[45] and the right to life, such practices are likely to be contrary to domestic law with the result that the individuals involved are exceeding their lawful authority. However, in this example, it is their official position that enables the conduct. In this situation, the attribution of this conduct to the State and a consequential finding of responsibility against that State should therefore not be particularly difficult. The apparent lack of any such a finding in this case points to problems in the enforcement of the relevant legal framework but not necessarily to a problem with the scope and relevance of the applicable rules.

Further complications with respect to attribution arise when the acts or omissions in question appear to be those of private individuals who also happen to be agents of the State. What is the situation, for example, in respect of an individual law enforcement official who profits directly from organizing or facilitating migrant smuggling or from channeling smuggled migrants into forced or exploitative labor? The ILC notes that attribution will not extend to conduct that is "so removed from the scope of . . . official functions that it should be assimilated to that of private individuals, not attributable to the State."[46] It suggests, with oblique reference to the due diligence test discussed at 4.3.3. below,[47] that:

> The problem of drawing the line between unauthorized but still "official" conduct, on the one hand, and "private" conduct on the other, may be avoided if the conduct complained of is systematic or recurrent, such that the State knew or ought to have known of it and should have taken steps to prevent it.[48]

In all cases a distinction will need to be made between unauthorized conduct that is nevertheless undertaken with apparent authority, and unauthorized conduct that is purely private. Apparent authority could be inferred in the above example by showing that it is the official position of that individual that gives him or her the knowledge and protection to act in this way. In other words, the conduct was only possible because of the individual's official position and use of apparent authority. Although such a finding would appear to point to a presumption in favor of such conduct being attributable to the State, more evidence may be required to satisfy the standard set by the ILC – for example, the use of official vehicles to transport smuggled migrants, use of law enforcement "authority" to compel smuggled migrants in some

Displaced Persons) Doc. 12895, Apr. 5, 2012 [Council of Europe Parliamentary Assembly Report, *Lives Lost in the Mediterranean Sea*], at 1.

45 See discussion in Chapter 1, at Section 1.2 and Chapter 6, at Section 6.3.

46 ILC Commentary, at Art. 7, para. 7.

47 See Section 4.3.3 of this chapter.

48 ILC Commentary, at Art. 7, para. 8.

way, use of police intelligence to avoid detection, or the use of law enforcement colleagues to provide "protection."[49]

Increasingly, individuals and entities that are not "organs" of the State are nevertheless empowered to exercise elements of governmental authority. Examples include private security firms contracted by States to exercise public powers of detention and even to engage in border control activities, including surveillance and interception. Commercial carriers are routinely empowered – and mandated – to exercise certain immigration control functions, and private transport companies are contracted to manage forced removals.[50]

As a general rule, the "privatization" of core governmental functions including detention and immigration control does not permit States to avoid legal responsibility under international law. The ILC Draft Articles are clear on the point that the conduct of persons or entities so empowered will be attributable to the State provided that the person or entity is acting in that capacity in the particular instance.[51] If the actions of a private entity attributable to the State breach international obligations, then the State's international responsibility will be engaged. Violations of the rights of smuggled migrants in privately managed immigration detention facilities can accordingly be attributable to the State. Excessive use of force by a privately contracted transport company in the course of a forced removal could, in the same way, be attributable to the State ordering that removal.

Is it possible for conduct outside the official structure of the State by individuals or groups not specifically empowered to exercise State functions to nevertheless be attributable to that State?[52] The ILC Draft Articles envisage this possibility if the person or group of persons "is in fact acting on the instructions of, or under

49 On this point, note Lawson's observation that "the police official does not perform an act of his State if, when off duty and out of personal motives, he kills his wife and her lover; nor would his conduct be attributed to the State if he used the gun supplied to him by the State for the performance of his official duties": R. Lawson, "Out of Control: State Responsibility and Human Rights: Will the ILC's Definition of the 'Act of State' Meet the Challenges of the 21st Century?," in M. Castermans-Holleman, R. van Hoof, and J. Smith eds., *The Role of the Nation-State in the 21st Century: Human Rights, International Organisations and Foreign Policy: Essays in Honour of Peter Baehr* 91 (1998) [Lawson, "Out of Control: State Responsibility and Human Rights"], at 97.

50 On the extensive involvement of private companies in border control, see B. Hayes, *NeoConOpticon: The EU Security-Industrial Complex* (2009), at 12. See also M. Flynn and C. Cannon, *The Privatization of Immigration Detention: Towards a Global View* (Global Detention Project Working Paper, 2009); and T. Gammeltoft-Hansen, *Access to Asylum: International Refugee Law and the Globalisation of Migration Control* (2011) [Gammeltoft-Hansen, *Access to Asylum*], chapter 5, "The Privatization of Migration Control and State Responsibility," at 158–208.

51 ILC Draft Articles, at Art. 5.

52 The distinct question of State responsibility arising out of (but without attribution of) purely private conduct (for example, because of a failure to prevent or punish private harm) is discussed at Section 4.3.

the direction or control of, that State in carrying out the conduct."[53] As den Heijer notes, in this third and most controversial basis of attribution: "it is not the quality of being an 'agent' of the state that is decisive for establishing state responsibility, but the factual relationship between the state and the conduct complained of."[54] An example of such a factual relationship relevant to the present context may involve private persons being recruited by the State to engage in migrant smuggling interception – or indeed to perform auxiliary border control activities outside the formal State structure.[55] Another example may relate to a private fishing vessel whose capacity to come to the rescue of a migrant smuggling vessel in distress is curtailed by a legislative prohibition or other act of the State.

The question in both cases becomes whether such entities are acting under the *instructions*, *direction*, or *control* of their State. Only one of these three elements is required and must relate to the conduct in question.[56] Judicial consideration of this issue has focused particularly on the level of direction or control that is required to establish attribution. In considering whether the violative conduct of the contras in Nicaragua was attributable to the United States, the ICJ held that the dependency of the contras on the United States was insufficient. It was necessary to prove that the United States, in fact, exercised "effective control" to the point that it was apparent the contras were acting on its behalf.[57] The Appeals Chamber of the International Criminal Tribunal for the former Yugoslavia (ICTY) (in considering the question of attribution in the context of individual criminal responsibility rather than State responsibility) rejected the "effective control" test on the basis that it was contrary to the very logic of State responsibility and inconsistent with State and judicial practice. It concluded that the degree of control required for attribution varied according to the factual circumstances, and that "overall control" was the preferred test.[58] The ICJ subsequently rejected the ICTY standard, affirming, in its *Bosnian Genocide* judgment, the stricter "complete" and "effective" control tests first articulated in the

[53] ILC Draft Articles, at Art. 8.

[54] M. den Heijer, *Europe and Extraterritorial Asylum* (2012) [den Heijer, *Europe and Extraterritorial Asylum*], at 67.

[55] For example, sections 40 (entitled "Searches: contracting out") and 41 of the United Kingdom *Immigration, Asylum and Nationality Act 2006* provide explicitly for the use of private contractors in border control activities both at the United Kingdom's territorial borders and under its juxtaposed controls scheme. Gammeltoft-Hansen, *Access to Asylum*, at 182.

[56] ILC Commentary, at Art. 8, para. 7.

[57] *Nicaragua Case*, at 62, 64–65, cited in ILC Commentary, at Art. 8, para. 4.

[58] *Prosecutor v. Tadić*, Case IT-94-1-A, ICTY Appeals Chamber, July 15, 1999, at para. 117, cited in ILC Commentary, at Art. 8, para. 5. Note that this lower threshold of control required for attribution appeared to be accepted by the European Court of Human Rights, which subsequently decided that the question was whether the entity in question was operating "under the effective authority or at least under the decisive influence" of the State: *Ilaşcu and Others v. Moldova and Russia*, (2005) 40 EHRR 46 (ECHR, July 8, 2004), at para. 392.

Nicaragua case.[59] In rejecting the ICTY test of overall control, the ICJ expressed concern that such a test would have the effect of "broadening the scope of State responsibility well beyond the fundamental principle governing the law of international responsibility."[60]

The *Bosnian Genocide* judgment was widely criticized as setting too high a threshold for attribution of responsibility. Critics focused on the unreasonableness of the result,[61] as well as apparent deficiencies in the Court's interpretation and application of the relevant law, including of the ICTY judgment.[62] Others affirmed the judgment as a reasonable application of the current customary norm.[63] Certainly, in relation to both practice and doctrine, this aspect of State responsibility appears to be in flux as those responsible for the interpretation and application of international law are confronted with new situations and new challenges that strain traditional doctrines of attribution. There is some evidence that, at least in relation to State practice, the threshold is being lowered as States find the traditional "effective control" or even "overall control" tests "insufficient to address the threats posed by global criminals and the States that harbor them."[64] In potentially uncomfortable partnership are

59 *Bosnian Genocide Case*, at paras. 399–407. Generally on the judgment as it relates to the issue of State responsibility, see M. Milanovic, "State Responsibility for Genocide: A Follow-Up," (2007) 18 *European Journal of International Law* 669 [Milanovic, "State Responsibility for Genocide: A Follow-Up"].

60 *Bosnian Genocide Case*, at para. 406 ("It must next be noted that the 'overall control' test has the major drawback of broadening the scope of State responsibility well beyond the fundamental principle governing the law of international responsibility: a State is responsible only for its own conduct, that is to say the conduct of persons acting, on whatever basis, on its behalf. That is true of acts carried out by its official organs, and also by persons or entities which are not formally recognized as official organs under internal law but which must nevertheless be equated with State organs because they are in a relationship of complete dependence on the State. Apart from these cases, a State's responsibility can be incurred for acts committed by persons or groups of persons – neither State organs nor to be equated with such organs – only if, assuming those acts to be internationally wrongful, they are attributable to it under the rule of customary international law reflected in Article 8 cited above (paragraph 398). This is so where an organ of the State gave the instructions or provided the direction pursuant to which the perpetrators of the wrongful act acted or where it exercised effective control over the action during which the wrong was committed. In this regard the 'overall control' test is unsuitable, for it stretches too far, almost to breaking point, the connection which must exist between the conduct of a State's organs and its international responsibility."). Note the ICJ rejected application of the ICTY's test on several other grounds. See further Milanovic, "State Responsibility for Genocide: A Follow-Up."

61 See, for example, Gibney ("if extraterritorial state responsibility could not be established in this particular case, it is difficult to imagine under what circumstances it could ever be established"): M. Gibney, "Genocide and State Responsibility" (2007) 7 *Human Rights Law Review* 760, at 771, cited in McCorquodale, "Impact on State Responsibility," at 244.

62 See A. Cassese, "The *Nicaragua* and *Tadić* Tests Revisited in Light of the ICJ Judgment on Genocide in Bosnia" (2007) 18(4) *European Journal of International Law* 649.

63 Milanovic, "State Responsibility for Genocide: A Follow-Up."

64 A-M. Slaughter and W. Burke-White, "An International Constitutional Moment" (2002) 43 *Harvard International Law Journal* 1, at 20, cited in D. Jinks, "State Responsibility for the Acts of Private Armed Groups" (2003) 4 *Chicago Journal of International Law* 83, at 90.

human rights advocates arguing for the recognition of an exceptional (lower) test of control under international human rights law in relation to prospectively problematic non-State entities such as private military contractors.[65]

The ILC Draft Articles envisage several additional bases for attribution: when the conduct is of an insurrectional or other movement that becomes the new government of a State, or that succeeds in establishing a new State[66]; when elements of governmental authority are exercised in the absence of such authority and in circumstances such as to call for the exercise of those elements of authority[67]; and when the State acknowledges and adopts otherwise non-attributable conduct as the State's own.[68] These additional bases of attribution serve to confirm both the nature and the limits of the general rules. In relation to the conduct of private persons or entities (discussed in more detail at Section 4.3 of this chapter), attribution relies on the existence of a special circumstance linking apparently private behavior to the State itself. In other words, in order to establish attribution for the conduct of non-State entities, it is necessary to show the existence of a link between that entity and the State. The link establishing attribution can manifest itself in the public nature of the act. It can also rely upon a range of other factors including control, authorization, approval, awareness, or support. Outside of these situations, and absent specific undertakings or guarantees, the State will not be responsible for the conduct of private persons or entities.[69] The identified situations are therefore not exceptions but additional refinements of the long-standing rule of international law attributing responsibility to the State for the conduct of its organs and representatives. In the words of Vattel:

> if the nation, or its ruler, approve and ratify the act of the citizen, it takes upon itself the act, and may then be regarded by the injured party as the real author of the affront of which the citizen was perhaps only the instrument.[70]

65 See, for example, McCorquodale, "Impact on State Responsibility," esp. at 245–246. McCorquodale cites the ICJ judgment in *Armed Activities on the Territory of the Congo (Democratic Republic of the Congo v. Uganda)*, [2005] ICJ Rep 168, as indicative of a different and lower threshold of control in relation to international human rights law: ibid. at 245. For further on this issue, see C. Hoppe, "Passing the Buck: State Responsibility for Private Military Companies" (2008) 19(5) *European Journal of International Law* 989.

66 ILC Draft Articles, at Art. 10.

67 Ibid. at Art. 9

68 Ibid. at Art. 11.

69 However, the State may incur responsibility because of a concomitant failure to prevent or punish the harmful conduct of private persons or entities. This is a distinct basis of responsibility not based on the attribution of that private person's conduct to the State. See further in Section 4.3 of this chapter.

70 E. de Vattel, *The Law of Nations: Book III* (reprinted 1974), at 136, cited in G. Townsend, "State Responsibility for Acts of De-Facto Agents" (1997) 14 *Arizona Journal of International and Comparative Law* 635, at 636.

4.2.2. Requirement of a Breach of Obligation

As noted previously, the second mandatory condition for an internationally wrongful act of a State is that the conduct attributable to the State constitutes a breach of an international obligation of that State (the "primary rule"). The ILC has emphasized the importance of distinguishing between the question of attribution and the characterization of conduct as internationally wrongful: "[t]o show that conduct is attributable to the State says nothing, as such, about the legality or otherwise of that conduct."[71] Conduct attributable to a State that does not constitute a breach of an international obligation of that State will not be characterized as an internationally wrongful act and will not thereby engage its responsibility. In the same way, a breach of an international obligation owed by that State that cannot be attributed to the State will not be considered an act of that State and will therefore also fail to engage that State's responsibility under international law.

It is therefore only when these two elements – conduct attributable to the State, and conduct constituting a breach of that State's obligation – have both been established that the standard for establishing international legal responsibility of the State will have been satisfied. The only possible way for a State to escape a finding of responsibility when these two elements are present is for it to successfully claim the existence of "special circumstances precluding wrongfulness."[72] Such a claim may operate to preclude responsibility for the period during which the special circumstance exists, while not affecting the underlying obligation.[73] The scope of recognized situations is narrow and, in practice, the successful establishment of these special circumstances is relatively rare. A potential example in the present context could involve a State citing the special circumstance of "necessity" in the case of "mass influx to justify an attenuated form of asylum determination or the imposition of restrictions on the freedom of movement of non-nationals – measures that would

[71] ILC Commentary, at Part One, Chapter II, para. 4.

[72] The law of State responsibility recognizes that certain circumstances will operate to preclude a State from responsibility for its otherwise unlawful acts or omissions. The ILC Draft Articles identify six such circumstances as being presently recognized under general international law: consent (Article 20), self-defense (Article 21); countermeasures (Article 22); *force majeure* (Article 23); distress (Article 24); and necessity (Article 25).

[73] Circumstances precluding wrongfulness do not annul or otherwise terminate the obligation in question. Rather, they provide a justification for non-performance of an obligation, a justification that continues for as long as the applicable circumstance continues: ILC Commentary, at Part One, Chapter V, paras. 2–3. The duty to comply with the obligation in question will revive once the circumstance precluding wrongfulness ceases to exist. Importantly, none of these circumstances will operate to preclude the wrongfulness of a State with respect to a peremptory norm of international law: ILC Draft Articles, at Art. 26. The work of the ILC on this particular aspect of State responsibility has attracted some controversy and criticism. See, for example, Allott, "State Responsibility and the Unmaking of International Law."

otherwise not be in conformity with that State's international obligations.[74] In the context of international human rights law, these "special circumstances precluding wrongfulness" under the secondary rules of State responsibility are paralleled at the primary level by provisions in a number of international human rights treaties permitting the restriction of certain rights if necessary to protect, for example, national security and public health, as well as, exceptionally, derogation from certain rights on strict grounds in times of public emergency.[75] Note however that the status and authority of the "necessity" justification for otherwise unlawful action has been challenged on both legal and practical grounds.[76]

How should one determine whether a particular act or omission constitutes a breach of an international obligation of the State concerned? It is at this point that reference must be made to the underlying primary rule as "[t]here is no such thing as a breach of an international obligation in the abstract."[77] Under ILC Draft Article 12, "[t]here is a breach of an international obligation by a State when an act of that State is not in conformity with what is required of it by that obligation, regardless of its origin or character."[78] Accordingly, absent special considerations relating, for example, to circumstances precluding wrongfulness, the question of whether and when there has been a breach of an obligation will depend on "the precise terms of the obligation, its interpretation and application, taking into account its object and purpose and the facts of the case."[79] In other words, the exact nature of the obligations (and therefore the nature of any possible breach) can only be ascertained with reference to the primary rule, which could reside in a treaty, in customary international law, or in any other accepted source of international legal obligation – or indeed, in a combination of sources.

As the ILC has indicated and as the first two chapters of this book confirm, the possible range of conduct proscribed (or prescribed) by an international obligation is extremely wide. Transnational criminal law, as it applies to migrant smuggling for example, may require the State to pass new legislation or to modify or repeal existing legislation. It may require the State to cooperate with another State in specified areas or to provide specified services. The law of the sea may also oblige States to pass legislation, for example requiring masters of ships flying their flag to go to the aid of persons lost or in distress at sea. International human rights law may require

74 The special circumstance precluding wrongfulness of necessity is recognized in Article 25 of the ILC Draft Articles. This example does not imply an assumption that the "circumstances precluding wrongfulness" could be successfully asserted in this situation.

75 See discussion of the national security exception in Chapter 10, at Section 10.2.1.1.

76 See, for example, Sloane, "On the Use and Abuse of Necessity in the Law of State Responsibility."

77 ILC Commentary, at Part One, Chapter III, para. 2.

78 ILC Draft Articles, at Art. 12.

79 ILC Commentary, at Art. 12, para. 1.

the State to refrain from certain actions and from intruding into certain spheres. Many human rights treaties go beyond a negative obligation of noninterference in requiring States Parties to take positive steps – to "respect and ensure,"[80] toward "realization,"[81] to "secure,"[82] to "prohibit and bring to an end,"[83] and to "pursue by all appropriate means."[84] The general formulation requires States Parties to secure rights for everyone within their own territory or subject to their jurisdiction.[85] Additionally, as explored in Chapter 3, States have repeatedly been held responsible, under the major international and regional human rights treaties, for acts and omissions that produce effects outside their territory. In that regard, it is relevant to note that the secondary rules of State responsibility do not distinguish between wrongful acts committed within the territory of a State and those committed extraterritorially.[86] Human rights and other laws may operate to impose on States Parties certain obligations with respect to the conduct of non-State actors, even in cases where the conduct of the non-State actor is not attributable to the State. An example in the present case may involve the State taking certain action to prevent and respond effectively to private violence against migrants of the kind cited in the case study "The United States–Mexico Border: violence against, and exploitation of, smuggled migrants," set out in the introduction to this book. In relation to these cases – and indeed every other case – "it is by comparing the conduct in fact engaged in by the State with the conduct legally prescribed by the international obligation that one can determine whether or not there is a breach of that obligation."[87]

It is well settled that an act of a State does not constitute a breach of an international obligation unless the State is bound by the obligation at the time the act in question occurs.[88] It follows that conduct that presently amounts to a breach but

80 International Covenant on Civil and Political Rights, 999 UNTS 171, done Dec. 16, 1996, entered into force Mar. 3, 1976 [ICCPR], at Art. 2; American Convention on Human Rights, at Art. 1(1).

81 ICCPR, at Art. 1(3); American Convention on Human Rights, at Art. 26; Convention on the Elimination of All Forms of Discrimination against Women, 1249 UNTS 13, done De. 13, 1979, entered into force Sept. 3, 1981 [CEDAW], at Art. 2(a).

82 Convention for the Protection of Human Rights and Fundamental Freedoms, 213 UNTS 222, done Nov. 4, 1950, entered into force Sept. 3, 1953 [European Convention on Human Rights], at Art. 1.

83 International Convention on the Elimination of All Forms of Racial Discrimination, 660 UNTS 195, done Dec. 21, 1965, entered into force Jan. 4, 1969 [CERD], at Art. 2(1).

84 CEDAW, at Art. 2.

85 See further the discussion on the rights of noncitizens in Chapter 3.

86 "[T]he acts or omissions of organs of the State are attributable to the State as a possible source of responsibility regardless of whether they have been perpetrated in national or in foreign territory": "Report of the International Law Commission on the Work of Its Twenty-Seventh Session," *Yearbook of the International Law Commission*, vol. II (1975), at 84, cited in den Heijer, *Europe and Extraterritorial Asylum*, at 59–60.

87 ILC Commentary, at Art. 12, para. 2.

88 ILC Draft Articles, at Art. 13. The ILC Commentary on Article 13 (at paragraph 1) notes that this provision reflects the general principle of intertemporal law as stated in the *Island of Palmas* case: "[a] juridical fact must be appreciated in the light of the law contemporary with it, and not of the

that did not at the time of its occurrence will not engage the responsibility of the relevant State. The principle of no retrospective assumption of responsibility is particularly important in relation to a "new" area of international legal regulation such as migrant smuggling. The obligation to criminalize migrant smuggling, for example, explored in detail in Chapter 5, is relatively recent. A State would not be held responsible for failing to criminalize migrant smuggling unless and until that obligation came into existence for that State (through, for example, ratification or accession to the Migrant Smuggling Protocol[89]). However, as previous chapters have confirmed, the legal framework around migrant smuggling is much wider than the obligation of criminalization. For example, to the extent that migrant smuggling–related conduct of the State or its agents involved breaches of human rights, the State would be responsible for violations of international legal obligations that are already in force. Similarly, if the prohibition on *exploitative migrant smuggling* were considered to be part of the general peremptory norm prohibiting slavery and the slave trade,[90] then it could be argued that all States have been obliged to eliminate such smuggling for as long as this interpretation of the prohibition on slavery has existed. These examples serve to underlie the importance of establishing, with as much precision as possible, the substantive content of the primary rule.

In terms of identifying when a wrongful act begins or ends, the rules are also clear. A breach by way of an act that is noncontinuing in nature is deemed to have occurred at the time the relevant act takes place, irrespective of whether and for how long the effects of that act are felt.[91] A single act of inhumane treatment (for example, failing to rescue a smuggled asylum-seeker in distress), even if it has ongoing negative effects for the victim, would fall into this category of noncontinuing breach. In contrast, a breach by way of an act that has a continuing character extends for as long as the nonconforming act continues.[92] For example, the prohibitions on *non-*

law in force at the time when a dispute in regard to it arises or falls to be settled" ((*Netherlands v. United States*), (1949) 2 UNRIAA 829 (Permanent Court of Arbitration, Apr. 4, 1928), at 845). The Commentary provides a relevant example on this point: in the mid-nineteenth century, a mixed arbitration tribunal was called upon to decide whether British action to seize American vessels engaged in the slave trade and to free slaves belonging to American nationals was unlawful. Certain of these acts were held to have taken place at a time when the slave trade was considered lawful. Accordingly, the British authorities were held to have breached the international legal obligation to protect and respect the property of foreign nationals. It was only the later incidents that were held to have occurred at a time when the slave trade had been "prohibited by all civilized nations." The responsibility of Great Britain was therefore not engaged by the later incidents. ILC Commentary, at Art. 13, para. 2.

89 Protocol against the Smuggling of Migrants by Land, Sea and Air, supplementing the United Nations Convention against Transnational Organized Crime, 2241 UNTS 507, done Nov. 15, 2000, entered into force Jan. 28, 2004 [Migrant Smuggling Protocol].

90 See further Chapter 3, Section 3.3.3.2.

91 ILC Draft Articles, at Art. 14(1).

92 Ibid. at Art. 14(2).

refoulement and on inhuman treatment may be violated through legislation mandating interdiction and turn-back at sea without consideration of protection claims.[93] The breach in question begins with the passing of that act and continues for as long as it remains in force. In the case of an obligation to prevent the occurrence of a given event (for example, the obligation on States to prevent violence against nonnationals), the State is generally in breach for however long it remains not in conformity with that obligation.[94]

Many of the core international obligations relevant to migrant smuggling, such as the prohibition on discrimination, the obligation of *non-refoulement*, and the obligation to rescue those in distress at sea could be breached by a composite act, involving "some aggregate of conduct and not individual acts as such."[95] Under these circumstances, the actual breach will occur at the time when the particular act or omission occurs, which, when taken together with other acts or omissions, is sufficient to constitute the wrongful act.[96] In such cases, the rules of State responsibility serve to identify the "breach" as having commenced from the first of the acts or omissions in the series of acts constituting the wrongful conduct.[97] Expedited removal for example, will not, of itself, constitute a breach of a primary obligation unless and until other acts or omissions, such as excessive use of force or failure to consider protection claims, also occur. For the purposes of State responsibility, the breach occurs at the "threshold" point at which the contents of the obligation are satisfied with reference to the conduct of the State. Once this threshold is crossed, the time of commission extends, in the words of the ILC: "over the whole period during which any of the acts was committed."[98]

Unlike traditional doctrines, the modern laws of State responsibility do not identify damage as an essential aspect of an internationally wrongful act giving rise to State responsibility. In other words, it is the violation of the obligation and not the resulting damage that constitutes the inherent legal injury and therefore entails responsibility.[99] In a similar vein, the question of "fault," generally understood as an intention to harm, will be irrelevant to a determination of responsibility for an internationally wrongful act, absent a specific requirement of such an element in the primary obligation.[100] As explored later on in the chapter, this is the case even with respect to the question of State responsibility for private acts, where the absence

93 See further Chapter 6.
94 ILC Draft Articles, at Art. 14(3).
95 ILC Commentary, at Art. 15, para. 2.
96 ILC Draft Articles, at Art. 15(1).
97 Ibid. at Art. 15(2).
98 ILC Commentary, at Art. 15, para. 3.
99 Ibid. at Art. 2, para. 9. See further T. Meron, *The Humanization of International Law* (2006), at 252–253.
100 ILC Commentary, at Art. 2, para. 10. For an analysis of the ILC's position on "fault," see A. Gattini, "Smoking/No Smoking: Some Remarks on the Current Place of Fault in the ILC Draft Articles on

of fault on the part of State organs or officials is not, of itself, sufficient to avoid a finding of responsibility.

4.3. STATE RESPONSIBILITY FOR BREACH OF OBLIGATIONS ORIGINATING IN THE CONDUCT OF PRIVATE PERSONS OR ENTITIES

The previous section outlined the basic principles of attribution applicable to State responsibility as these are generally recognized in international law and as they have been codified by the ILC. In the context of migrant smuggling, it was shown that certain acts committed by the State (which may relate to smuggling itself or to a State's response to smuggling) that are in breach of its international legal obligations entail the international responsibility of that State. The notion of "act of State" will be extended, in certain situations, to cover acts committed by non-State entities that are under the control of the State or that are adopted or otherwise claimed by the State. As discussed previously, this would include the actions of private entities engaged by the State to participate in migration control activities, such as private contractors involved in undertaking border patrols or managing detention centers.[101] The scope of the rules of State responsibility is thereby sufficiently broad to encompass most aspects of a State's *response* to migrant smuggling.

The same cannot be said with respect to State responsibility and the actual process of migrant smuggling itself. In the absence of some official authority or link (such as complicity of officials), the actual process of migrant smuggling cannot be readily attributed to a State. This raises questions about whether a State could in fact be held responsible under the international rules of responsibility with respect to smuggled migrants who suffocate in a container, or who drown at sea on overcrowded vessels, or who are placed in debt bondage. Can responsibility of a State be invoked in relation to vessels flying its flag that fail to rescue migrants in distress?

Although a link may indeed be made, for example, between failure of State policy and the actions of migrant smugglers, in law, the starting position is not particularly promising: "[a]s a general principle, the conduct of private persons or entities is not attributable to the State under international law."[102] In other words, absent the

State Responsibility" (1999) 10(2) *European Journal of International Law* 397. See also J. Crawford, "Revising the Draft Articles on State Responsibility" (1999) 10(2) *European Journal of International Law* 435 [Crawford, "Revising the Draft Articles on State Responsibility"], esp. at 438.

[101] On the privatization of detention centres, see generally M. Flynn and C. Cannon, *The Privatization of Immigration Detention: Towards a Global View* (Global Detention Project Working Paper, 2009).

[102] ILC Commentary, at Art. 8, para.1. See also the Commentary to Article 11, at paragraph 2: "[t]he general principle, drawn from State practice and international judicial decisions, is that the conduct of a person or group of persons not acting on behalf of the State is not considered as an act of the State

existence of carefully defined special circumstances as outlined earlier in this chapter, private action will be considered as such and will not implicate the responsibility of the State.

4.3.1. *Implications of the General Rule of Non-attribution of Private Conduct*

As shown previously, in many situations of harm that occur in the context of migrant smuggling, direct State involvement is either not present or unable to be conclusively established. This is particularly the case with the actual *process* of smuggling, which is typically controlled and conducted by individual entrepreneurs and loosely organized criminal groups. Individual State officials undoubtedly facilitate this trade through their inaction, inertia, and occasional active involvement. However, any smuggling-related harms – in terms of both the process and the end result – are very much a direct consequence of actions taken by private entities, and States of origin or transit rarely take steps to adopt the conduct of these groups as their own.

How do these realities square with the general principle of non-attribution for acts of private persons? Can countries of origin, transit, and destination for smuggled migrants simply exempt themselves from any responsibility to each other (in relation, for example, to an obligation to prevent smuggling), to these individuals (in relation, for example, to an obligation to protect from harm) – and to the international community as a whole – on the basis that the conduct complained of is not directly attributable to them? If this were indeed the case, international rules on State responsibility would appear to offer very little scope for securing the accountability of States for the full range of harms associated with migrant smuggling – most of the harms of migrant smuggling would simply be outside the scope of international law. Such a result would appear to run counter to the apparent intentions behind specialized instruments such as the Migrant Smuggling Protocol as well as to the international legal order's greater purpose of securing accountability and justice for individuals whose rights and freedoms have been denied. It also fails to recognize the actual and potential capacity of States to structure their internal order (including through regulation and control of private conduct) in a way that can either facilitate or obstruct migrant smuggling and the various harms and human rights abuses with which it is very often associated.

The issue of State responsibility for the acts of private persons has become an immensely important one in recent years as the near-exclusive power of the State in many different areas is eroded in favor of private individuals and entities, including

under international law. This conclusion holds irrespective of the circumstances in which the private person acts and of the interests affected by the person's conduct."

business corporations, criminal organizations, rebel groups, and terrorists who act in pursuit of their own private agendas. These entities clearly have the capacity to engage in acts that compromise not just human rights but also laws relating to organized crime, the conduct of warfare, maintenance of international peace and security, migration control, trade, and environmental protection. It is therefore important to consider in more detail the circumstances under which States will be held responsible for how they act in respect of such acts and/or their consequences.

This is not a separate discussion invoking new or previously unexplored rules. Rather, it is a more careful consideration of the two conditions of responsibility explored in the previous section and summarized in this section: existence of a breach of obligation, and attribution of that breach to the State.

4.3.2. *Moving Beyond the General Rule: State Responsibility to Prevent, Protect, and Respond in Relation to Migrant Smuggling*

Although not departing from the general principle of non-attribution of private conduct, the ILC has acknowledged that the rules governing attribution have a cumulative effect "such that a State may be responsible for the effects of the conduct of private parties, if it failed to take necessary measures to prevent those effects."[103] This concession reflects a discernible movement toward a more nuanced conception of State responsibility. Particularly in the area of human rights, there is growing acceptance that the State will be responsible, not only if it abrogates human rights in the traditional sense (sometimes referred to as *direct responsibility* arising out of *vertical application* of legal obligations) but also if it fails to adequately protect those within its jurisdiction from the actions of others that result in a violation of rights (sometimes referred to as *indirect responsibility* arising out of *horizontal application* of legal obligations).[104] In other

[103] ILC Commentary, at Part One, Chapter II, para. 4. An example drawn from the *Tehran Hostages Case* is used to illustrate this point: the seizing of the American Embassy in Tehran by private individuals did not immediately engage the international legal responsibility of the State of Iran. It was only after the government failed to assert control over the situation that the conduct of the private individuals became attributable to the State itself. It was therefore Iran's failure "to take appropriate steps" to protect the Embassy that "by itself constituted [a] clear and serious violation": *United States Diplomatic and Consular Staff in Tehran (United States of America v. Iran)*, [1980] ICJ Rep 3 [*Tehran Hostages Case*], at para. 61, 67. The Court noted that the Iranian authorities were aware of their obligations to protect consular and diplomatic staff and premises and that they had the means at their disposal but "completely failed to comply with these obligations": ibid. at para. 68.

[104] The seminal text in relation to indirect/horizontal application of international human rights law remains A. Clapham, *Human Rights in the Private Sphere* (1996). For a more recent exploration of these same themes including a considered analysis of the major objections to an expansion of international human rights law to include non-State actors, see A. Clapham, *Human Rights Obligations of Non-State Actors* (2006).

words, the State can incur international responsibility for a private act in the case of an action or omission of the State's own organs "where [these organs] are guilty of not having done everything within their power to prevent the injurious act of the private individual or to punish it suitably if it has occurred despite everything."[105] Therefore, in the present context, the fact that the State was not the cause of the initial harm (exploitation of or violence against smuggled migrants, for example, or failure of a private vessel registered to that State to rescue another vessel in distress) may not, of itself, be sufficient to absolve the State from responsibility for that harm and resulting consequences if it could have taken steps to prevent them. Importantly, the finding of indirect responsibility is made on the basis of the State's own omissions (attributable to it) and does not require the separate attribution of private conduct to the State under the principles discussed at in Section 4.1 of this chapter.

The secondary rules of State responsibility only envisage the *possibility* of State responsibility for private harm. Whether such responsibility exists in a particular case will invariably be a matter for the applicable primary rules. An example is provided by the *Bosnian Genocide* case. The actual commission of genocide was ultimately not attributable to Serbia under the standard of attribution adopted by the ICJ. However, the Court found that Serbia was nevertheless responsible for breaching its specific treaty obligation to *prevent* genocide.[106] International human rights law provides many similar examples of "positive obligations" whereby the State is required to do more than merely abstain from committing violations. These are commonly identified as obligations to *protect*, to *respect*, to *fulfill*, language that appears in transnational criminal law as well as in human rights treaties.[107]

[105] Lawson, "Out of Control: State Responsibility and Human Rights," at 96. This position echoes that taken by Jiménez de Arechaga, writing in 1978: "[t]he basis of State responsibility for acts of private individuals is not complicity with the perpetrator but solely failure of the State to perform its international duty of preventing the unlawful act or, failing that, to arrest the offender and bring him to justice." E. Jiménez de Arechaga, "International Responsibility," in M. Sorensen ed., *Manual of Public International Law* 531 (1968) [Jiménez de Arechaga, "International Responsibility"], at 560.

[106] *Bosnian Genocide Case*. See also A. Gattini, "Breach of the Obligation to Prevent and Reparation Thereof in the ICJ's Genocide Judgment" (2007) 18(4) *European Journal of International Law* 695.

[107] See, for example, Migrant Smuggling Protocol, at Art. 16(1) ("In implementing this Protocol, each State Party shall take, consistent with its obligations under international law, all appropriate measures, including legislation if necessary, to *preserve* and *protect* the rights of persons who have been the object of conduct set forth in article 6 of this Protocol…"); and Art. 7, ("State Parties shall cooperate to the fullest extent possible to *prevent* and *suppress* the smuggling of migrants by sea …" (emphasis added)); ICCPR, at Art. 6(1) ("Every human being has the inherent right to life. This right shall be *protected* by law" (emphasis added)); European Convention on Human Rights, at Art. 1 ("The High Contracting Parties shall *secure* to everyone within their jurisdiction the rights and freedoms defined in Section I of this Convention" (emphasis added)); American Convention on Human Rights, at Art. 1 ("The States Parties to this Convention undertake to *respect* the rights and freedoms recognized herein and to *ensure* to all persons subject to their jurisdiction the free and full exercise of those rights and freedoms." (emphases added)); African Charter on Human and Peoples' Rights, 1520 UNTS 217,

This three-level typology of a State's obligations under international human rights law is now widely accepted[108] although it is important to acknowledge that its application will differ depending on the nature and substantive content of the particular right or obligation under consideration. Generally however, a failure on the part of the State to protect (including from private interference), respect, or fulfill its human rights obligations – owed to every person within its jurisdiction[109] – is something that is directly attributable to the State and, therefore, sufficient to trigger its international legal responsibility. In this connection it is relevant to note that many of the most important human rights, including the right to life, the prohibition on torture and cruel and inhuman treatment, the prohibition on discrimination, the right to education, and the right to privacy can only be properly implemented by imposing duties on private individuals. Regional human rights courts in particular have been instrumental in confirming that a State may be held responsible *for its own acts* if it has encouraged individuals to engage in acts contrary to human rights,[110] if it has failed to "secure" specified rights and freedoms in its domestic law,[111] or if it has failed to take "reasonable and appropriate measures" of protection.[112]

Can a State be held responsible under international law for omissions such as failure to prosecute exploitation of smuggled migrants or failure to control criminal groups known to engage in migrant smuggling? For example, could Egypt be held responsible for taking no action to stop the abuse and torture of smuggled migrants in the Sinai, documented in the Introduction to this book? From the perspective of the law of State responsibility there is certainly no obstacle to such a finding, provided the relevant primary rule supports the existence of an obligation to that effect.[113] International tribunals have previously recognized State inaction in the

done June 27, 1981, entered into force Oct. 21, 1986 [African Charter], at Art. 18(3) ("The State shall *ensure* the elimination of every discrimination against women and also ensure the protection of the rights of the woman and the child." (emphasis added); Convention on the Rights of Persons with Disabilities, 2515 UNTS 3, done Dec. 13, 2006, entered into force May 3, 2008, at Art. 1 ("The purpose of the present Convention is to promote, *protect* and *ensure* the full and equal enjoyment of all human rights and fundamental freedoms by all persons with disabilities, and to promote respect for their inherent dignity" (emphasis added)). See Chapter 8 for a detailed examination of this provision.

108 Note also proposals for a fourth level of obligation "to promote." See for example A. Eide, "Economic, Social and Cultural Rights as Human Rights," in A. Eide, C. Krause, and A. Rosas eds., *Economic, Social, and Cultural Rights: A Textbook* 21 (1995).

109 On the specific concept of international human rights law and the obligation of *non-refoulement*, see Chapter 3, Section 3.4.4.

110 See, for example, *Lopez Ostra v. Spain*, (1995) 20 EHRR 277 (ECHR, Dec. 9, 1994).

111 See, for example, *X and Y v. the Netherlands*, (1986) 8 EHRR 235 (ECHR, Mar. 26, 1985).

112 See, for example, *Platform "Ärtze Für das Leben" v. Austria*, (1991) 13 EHRR 204 (ECHR, June 21, 1988).

113 See, as an example from a related field, the first European Court of Human Rights decision to engage directly with trafficking in persons-related wrongs, *Rantsev v. Cyprus and Russia*, which concerned a Russian national and probable victim of trafficking who died in Cyprus after falling from the

face of certain private conduct (i.e., failure to protect) as evidence of complicity and therefore as invoking that State's responsibility.[114] A failure on the part of the State to prosecute private wrongs has also, on a number of occasions, led to findings of responsibility.[115]

4.3.3. *Identifying Violations Giving Rise to Responsibility: The Due Diligence Standard*

What measure is to be used in judging whether a State has taken adequate steps to meet its obligations – for example, to protect established rights from private interference, and to respond to such interferences when they have occurred? Once again, this is not a test for the secondary rules of State responsibility. Whether a breach has occurred must be determined with reference to the primary rule. As discussed further in this section, a primary rule requiring States to "respect," "ensure," or "secure" human rights will impose a different standard with regard to protection from private interference than one requiring the State to refrain from certain conduct.

Despite differences in the nature of the primary obligations, the standard most commonly cited in the human rights context is that of "due diligence." Under this standard, a State is obliged to exercise a measure of care in preventing and responding to the acts of private entities that interfere with established rights. Due diligence is "an obligation to deploy adequate means, to exercise best possible efforts, to do the utmost, to obtain th[e] result."[116] Failure to prevent an anticipated abuse or violation

apartment of her employer's associate. Although her death itself and her likely exploitation as a "cabaret artiste" were not attributed to Cyprus or Russia, both States were held, by the European Court of Human Rights, to have violated related human rights obligations, for example through failure to regulate employment and through inaction in the face of private conduct. Specifically, the Court held that Article 4 of the European Convention on Human Rights required Member States to "put in place adequate measures regulating businesses often used as a cover for human trafficking": *Rantsev v. Cyprus and Russia*, (2010) 51 EHRR 1 (ECHR, Jan. 7, 2010) [*Rantsev v. Cyprus and Russia*], at para. 285. Further violations identified by the Court included failure to carry out an effective investigation into the death (including securing the relevant evidence from overseas as well as domestically, and investigating whether there had been any trafficking-related corruption); and the maintenance of a regime of artiste visas that did not afford protection against trafficking. Ibid. at paras. 293, 309.

[114] *Zafiro Case (Great Britain v. United States)*, (1955) 6 UNRIAA 160 (Great Britain–United States Arbitral Tribunal, Nov. 30, 1925) (concerning liability for injuries inflicted by civilian crew of a naval ship under circumstances in which State officials had not adopted effective measures to prevent), cited in R. J. Cook, "State Responsibility for Violations of Women's Human Rights" (1994) 7 *Harvard Human Rights Journal* 125 [Cook, "State Responsibility for Violations of Women's Human Rights"], at 145.

[115] *Janes Case (United States v. Mexico)*, (1951) 4 UNRIAA 82 (Mexican–United States General Claims Commission, Nov. 16, 1926), at 87 (concerning liability for failure to prosecute), cited in Cook, "State Responsibility for Violations of Women's Human Rights," at 145. See also *Velásquez Rodríguez Case*.

[116] *Responsibilities and Obligations of States Sponsoring Persons and Entities with Respect to Activities in the Area (Advisory Opinion)*, (2011) ITLOS Case No. 17 (Feb. 1, 2011), at para. 110.

by a private individual or entity will therefore invoke the responsibility of the State. In the same vein, legal responsibility will arise when the State fails to remedy abuses or violations of international law – not only because access to remedies is of itself an established right,[117] but also because the failure of the State to provide remedies in cases involving non-State interference with rights is a breach of the standard of due diligence. In other words, the State could have made the situation better for the victim but failed to do so.

The "due diligence" standard has a long history in the law of State responsibility for injury to aliens[118] and is a central doctrine of a number of areas of international law, including international environmental law.[119] It entered international human rights law through a landmark decision of the Inter-American Court of Human Rights in 1988. In the *Velásquez Rodríguez* case,[120] the Court found that the disappearance of the complainant had been carried out by State officials. However, more importantly for the present discussion, the Court further held that "even had that fact not been proven," the State would have been liable for its lack of due diligence in preventing or punishing the violative conduct of putatively private actors.[121] The Court confirmed that responsibility is incurred when:

> a violation of ... rights ... has occurred with the support or the acquiescence of the government, [or when] the State has allowed the act to take place without taking measures to prevent it or to punish those responsible.[122]

In this case, liability derived from a breach, by the State, of the rule contained in Article 1 of the American Convention on Human Rights requiring States Parties to "*respect*" the rights guaranteed by the Convention and to "*ensure*" their full and free exercise to all persons.[123] In a judgment with implications for the international and regional human rights treaties that also impose on States an obligation to "protect" or "ensure" human rights for persons within their territories or under their jurisdictions, the Court held that States are required "to organize the governmental

[117] See further Chapter 8, at Section 8.3.2.

[118] M. N. Shaw, *International Law* (5th ed. 2003) [Shaw, *International Law*], at 721–724; D. Shelton, "Private Violations, Public Wrongs and the Responsibilities of States" (1989) 13(1) *Fordham International Law Journal* 1 [Shelton, "Private Violations, Public Wrongs"], at 21–23.

[119] On the development and application of the doctrine of due diligence in international environmental law, see P. Birnie, A. Boyle, and C. Redgwell, *International Law and the Environment* (2009), at chapter 3, section 4(2).

[120] Note that the most relevant aspects of the *Velásquez Rodríguez* judgment for the present study are also reflected in another case that was considered by the Court in 1989: *Godínez Cruz v. Honduras*, Inter-Am Ct. H.R. (ser. C) No. 5, Jan. 20, 1989. Both judgments are analyzed in detail in Shelton, "Private Violations, Public Wrongs."

[121] *Velásquez Rodríguez Case*, at para. 182.

[122] Ibid. at para. 173.

[123] American Convention on Human Rights, at Art. 1(1).

apparatus and, in general, all the structures through which public power is exercised, so that they are capable of juridically ensuring the free and full enjoyment of human rights."[124]

In addition to preventing violation of protected rights, the State must also attempt to investigate and punish such violations, restore the right violated, and provide appropriate compensation for resulting damages.[125] These heads of responsibility would apply even when the State itself was not the immediate agent of harm. For example, a State could be legally responsible for its lack of due diligence in preventing or responding appropriately to a violation.[126] A State could also incur responsibility by failing to seriously investigate private abuses of rights – thereby aiding in their commission.[127] The doctrine to emerge from *Velásquez Rodríguez* with respect to State responsibility for the acts of private entities is usefully summarized in the following extract from the judgment:

> The State has [under Article 1 of the American Convention] a legal duty to take reasonable steps to prevent human rights violations and to use the means at its disposal to carry out a serious investigation of violations committed within its jurisdiction, to identify those responsible, to impose the appropriate punishment and to ensure the victim adequate compensation.[128]

While acknowledging the importance of *Velásquez Rodríguez*, it is essential to emphasize that the decision does not mitigate the general rule governing the non-attribution of private conduct to States. The Court explicitly affirmed that the State is responsible only for those human rights violations that can ultimately be attributed to the act or omission of a public authority under the rules of international law.[129] In this sense, the due diligence standard actually *affirms* that a State will not be responsible for purely private harm.[130] In cases where responsibility for the

[124] *Velásquez Rodríguez Case*, at para. 166.
[125] Ibid. at para. 177.
[126] Ibid. at para. 172.
[127] Ibid. at para. 166.
[128] Ibid. at para. 174.
[129] Ibid. at para. 164.
[130] Shelton, "Private Violations, Public Wrongs," at 22, citing F. V. Garcia-Amador, L. Sohn, and R. Baxter, *Recent Codification of the Law of State Responsibility for Injuries to Aliens* (1974), at 28. Shelton points to an important and contextually relevant arbitral decision under the law of State responsibility for injuries to aliens in support of this point: "[t]he mere fact that an alien has suffered at the hands of private persons an aggression, which could have been averted by the presence of a sufficient police force on the spot, does not make a government liable for damages under international law. There must be shown special circumstances from which the responsibility of the authorities arises: either their behavior in connection with the particular occurrence, or a general failure to comply with their duty to maintain order, to prevent crimes or to … punish criminals," citing W.A. *Noyes Case (Panama v. United States)*, (1955) 6 UNRIAA 308 (United States–Panama General Claims Commission, May 22, 1933).

initial act does not fall on the State, responsibility can still be imputed because of a subsequent failure on the part of the State to exercise "due diligence" in preventing, responding to, or remedying abuses committed by private persons or entities.[131] Whether such imputation is possible depends on the relevant primary rules and the facts of the case. As ILC Rapporteur Crawford has noted, "different primary rules of international law impose different standards, ranging from 'due diligence' to 'strict liability' … all of those standards are capable of giving rise to responsibility in the event of a breach."[132] In other words, there must be an obligation, within the primary rule, for the State to prevent, respond, or remedy abuses, and the facts must be able to show that the State has failed to discharge that obligation.

Since this decision, there has been increasing indication that due diligence is becoming the accepted benchmark against which certain types of legal obligations, in particular human rights obligations, are to be interpreted.[133] In *Osman v. UK*,[134] the European Court of Human Rights found that the State could be held responsible for a failure of its police forces to respond to harassment that ultimately resulted in death (although the United Kingdom was not found to be responsible in this case). In *Akkoç v. Turkey*, the European Court of Human Rights, in the context of the right to life, explained that the State's primary duty is "to secure the right to life by putting into place effective criminal-law provisions to deter the commission of offences … [and] law-enforcement machinery for the prevention, suppression and punishment of breaches."[135] The Court continued (citing *Osman v. UK*) that this duty may extend in appropriate circumstances "to a positive obligation on the authorities to take preventive operational measures to protect an individual whose life is at risk from the criminal acts of another individual."[136] The African Commission on Human and Peoples' Rights has similarly explained that:

> the State is obliged to protect right-holders against other subjects by legislation and provision of effective remedies … Protection generally entails the creation and maintenance of an atmosphere or framework by an effective interplay of laws and regulations so that individuals will be able to freely realize their rights and freedoms.[137]

[131] *Velásquez Rodríguez Case*, at para. 172.

[132] See Crawford, "Revising the Draft Articles on State Responsibility," at 438.

[133] It is in the context of violence against women that the due diligence standard has been most often affirmed by the international community as an appropriate measure of State obligation with respect to the conduct of private entities. For a detailed examination of relevant law and jurisprudence, see Gallagher, *The International Law of Human Trafficking*, at 244–247.

[134] *Osman v. The United Kingdom*, (2000) 29 EHRR 245 (ECHR, Oct. 28, 1998) [*Osman v. UK*].

[135] *Akkoç v. Turkey*, (2002) 34 EHRR 51 (ECHR, Oct. 10, 2000), at para. 77.

[136] Ibid.

[137] *Social and Economic Rights Action Center and Center for Economic and Social Rights v. Nigeria*, Case No. ACHPR Comm. No. 155/96 (African Commission on Human and Peoples' Rights, May 27, 2002), at para. 46.

How does "due diligence" apply in practice? The *Velásquez Rodríguez* case was ultimately concerned with a situation in which the State was tolerating apparently private actions that violated human rights as opposed to merely failing to act (in this case, enacting appropriate protective legislation). Inferring such "toleration" or the absence of due diligence in the context of migrant smuggling will rarely be straightforward. Can "toleration" leading to responsibility be inferred from systematic and otherwise inexplicable failure to apprehend and prosecute known or suspected smugglers who are also involved in the exploitation of their victims? Can it be inferred from the absence of any legislative, administrative, or social measures to protect migrants? What is the situation with regard to claims that the State is *unable* (as opposed to unwilling) to protect its citizens and others within its territory from harms associated with migrant smuggling?

The due diligence standard provides a starting point but it by no means delivers an authoritative response to such questions. This is not just because of the impact of the primary rules (and their general lack of precision) but also because of an absence of clarity on the point of whether diligence should be assessed with reference to the capacities of the State or whether an international standard should be used. Should due diligence be analyzed in relation to "means at the disposal of the State"?[138] Would a more appropriate test be whether the breach could have been prevented by reasonable diligence on the part of the State?[139] Is the question of foreseeability (or feasibility of action) relevant? Is the character and importance of the norm in question relevant to determining the standard of care required? These questions cannot be answered in the abstract but must be addressed with reference to the norm in question and the particular facts and circumstances of the case. Ultimately, a decision is likely to come down to an assessment of whether, under the circumstances of the particular case, the State is taking its obligations seriously.[140] In applying the due diligence standard to specific obligations, the present study gives consideration

[138] *Tehran Hostages Case*, at paras. 63, 68.

[139] Shelton, for example, argues that due diligence requires "reasonable measures of prevention that a well-administered government could be expected to exercise under similar circumstances": Shelton, "Private Violations, Public Wrongs," at 23.

[140] Writing on the subject of domestic violence, the UN Special Rapporteur on Violence against Women, Its Causes and Consequences, has proposed a seriousness test for deciding whether a State has met the due diligence standard: "the test is whether the State undertakes its duties seriously … If statistics illustrate that existing laws are ineffective in protecting women from violence, States must find other complementary mechanisms to prevent domestic violence. Thus, if education, dismantling of institutional violence, demystifying domestic violence, training of State personnel, the funding of shelters and other direct services for victim-survivors and the systematic documentation of all incidents of domestic violence are found to be effective tools in preventing domestic violence and protecting women's human rights, all become obligations in which the State must exercise due diligence in carrying out." "Report of the Special Rapporteur on Violence against Women, Its Causes and Consequences, Ms. Radhika Coomaraswamy," UN Doc. E/CN.4/1996/53, Feb. 5, 1996, at paras. 37, 141.

to each of these aspects while focusing, most particularly, on the *ability of the State to influence an alternative, more positive outcome.*

4.3.4. *Conclusion: The Primacy of the Primary Rules*

Acts of private persons, such as criminals involved in migrant smuggling, or even State officials who are complicit in smuggling but acting in their private capacity, cannot generally be attributed to States – so their acts or omissions will not generally engage State responsibility. The development of stricter standards of State responsibility in certain areas of international law (for example, environmental protection) may have led to a modified application of this general rule in certain circumstances (such as human rights), but not to its abandonment.[141]

In the specific context of human rights, the State may incur international responsibility in relation to private acts if it can be shown that the State's own organs have omitted to respond appropriately to such acts in terms of both preventing their occurrence and dealing with their consequences. In other words, the State's responsibility under such circumstances derives not from its involvement in or complicity with the original act (which could, if established, constitute an additional head of responsibility) but from the breach of consequential, independent legal obligations. The level of obligation (for example, to prevent and respond) will ultimately depend on the relevant primary rule. However, a finding of responsibility will generally depend upon establishing that the State has failed to secure recognized rights and freedoms in its domestic law or failed to take what, in the context of the European Convention on Human Rights, have been termed "reasonable and appropriate" measures of protection.[142]

In the case of migrant smuggling, a State may, for example, refuse to accept responsibility for the acts of organized criminal groups taking place within its jurisdiction on the basis of the "private" nature of the acts. It may also reject responsibility on the grounds of its inability to exercise effective control over the presence, power, and influence of such groups. Neither claim will be a defense if a primary rule can be shown to have been breached; that the State did not reasonably use

[141] Note that there is some disagreement as to the nature and extent of this modification. Shelton, for example, identifies the due diligence standard as being an *exception* to the general rules of State responsibility: Shelton, "Private Violations, Public Wrongs," at 22. Crawford, however, is emphatic on the point that such refinements relate only to the primary rule and therefore leave intact the validity of the general principle: Crawford, "Revising the Draft Articles on State Responsibility," at 438, 441.

[142] See Lawson, "Out of Control: State Responsibility and Human Rights," at 105. In Lawson's view, the State can only incur international responsibility for a private act in the case of an action or omission of the State's own organs "where they are guilty of not having done everything within their power to prevent the injurious act of the private individual or to punish it suitably if it has occurred despite everything": ibid. at 96.

whatever means it had available to *prevent* the breach in question; and, if prevention was not possible, to respond appropriately to it. A determination on this point will depend heavily on the facts of a particular case and the nature of the obligations in question. In the present case, a relevant example of such an obligation is provided by Article 16(1) of the Migrant Smuggling Protocol:

> In implementing this Protocol, each State Party shall take, consistent with its obligations under international law, all appropriate measures, including legislation if necessary, to preserve and protect the rights of persons who have been the object of conduct set forth in article 6 of this Protocol as accorded under applicable international law, in particular the right to life and the right not to be subjected to torture or other cruel, inhuman or degrading treatment or punishment.

In relation to the specific issue of human rights violations, a determination will also turn on the facts and the obligations in question.[143] In this particular context, the increasingly accepted standard of "due diligence" renders it unlikely that States will be able to avoid responsibility for the acts of private persons or entities when the State's ability to influence an alternative outcome can be established.

International human rights law has accepted the notion that the State is required, under certain circumstances, to guarantee rights as opposed to simply refraining from intervening.[144] In other words, the effective enjoyment of human rights will often require positive actions by the State including, but not limited to, the provision of a legal infrastructure through which human rights can be secured and violations redressed. This does not mean, however, that developments in international human rights law (for example, with regard to making the State responsible if laws authorize a certain action that results in violations, or if it fails to provide proper safeguards against abuses of rights by private persons) have resulted in substantive change to the general law of attribution.[145] The specific requirements for responsibility vary from one primary rule to another.[146] Ultimately, it is these rules that will be determinative: "if the State acts or fails to act, its responsibility is potentially engaged and remaining questions are left to be resolved by the interpretation and application of the relevant primary rules."[147] Accordingly, if the test in a particular case is deemed to be one of

[143] In his examination of State responsibility under the European Convention on Human Rights, Lawson proposes a presumption along the following lines: "a State is bound to secure the relevant rights and freedoms throughout its territory. The presumption is rebuttable: in exceptional circumstances the State may be able to demonstrate that it has no means whatsoever to secure specific rights and freedoms ... to all persons in its territory." Ibid. at 114.

[144] Crawford, "Revising the Draft Articles on State Responsibility," at 439.

[145] This is the position taken by the ILC Special Rapporteur on State Responsibility. See ibid. at 439–440. Crawford also rejects the idea that such developments have created any *lex specialis* in the field of human rights: ibid.

[146] Ibid. at 438.

[147] Ibid. at 440.

would be clearly attributable to the host Member State.[164] However, as he points out, this attribution is a consequence of the specific model of cooperation and does not mean the State providing the guest officer would be able to avoid its own obligations under human rights law, including the obligation to prevent violations.[165]

4.4.3. *Joint Conduct and the Implication of One State in the Act of Another State*

As noted previously, it is not at all certain that other common models of cooperation around the issue of migrant smuggling – such as the practice of stationing destination country border officials at departure points in countries of origin or transit for irregular/smuggled migrants – would fall within Article 6 (attributing responsibility solely to the "receiving" State). In relation to this example, the organ placed at the disposal of the receiving State will invariably be present with the conditional consent of that State but will not necessarily be assumed to be within that State's control and authority such that its actions can and should be attributed directly to the State. Similarly, in relation to many shiprider agreements,[166] where "guest" officials of one State are placed on a vessel flagged to another State, the relevant officials are generally not operating under their host's command structure but rather each remains within his or her State's own control and command – and indeed it is this status that underlies the rationale of the shiprider model. As the ILC Commentary makes clear, draft Article 6 "is not concerned with ordinary situations of interstate cooperation or collaboration, pursuant to treaty or otherwise."[167]

What are the rules of responsibility with respect to cooperation or collaboration between States that falls short of one State placing an organ under the complete authority and control of the other? In other words, how is responsibility to be attributed when multiple States – or indeed joint organs of multiple States that do not have the character of an international organization[168] – are engaged in a wrongful act? Dominicé usefully distinguishes two different sets of circumstances where the responsibility of multiple States may be engaged: first, circumstances where the internationally wrongful act is attributable to multiple States, and second, circumstances

[164] den Heijer, *Europe and Extraterritorial Asylum*, at 255–256.

[165] Ibid.

[166] See further Chapter 1, at notes 489–493 and accompanying text.

[167] See *Xhavara and Fifteen Others v. Italy and* Albania, cited in ILC Commentary, at Art. 6, para. 2, n. 130.

[168] Den Heijer argues, with reference to the ILC Commentary, that in this context, an organ can be labeled as a common organ only if its acts can be attributed to more than one State in accordance with existing attribution rules. den Heijer, *Europe and Extraterritorial Asylum*, at 88–89. On the separate question of when international organizations may themselves be held responsible for wrongful acts, see Section 4.7.1 in this chapter.

where one State is *implicated in the unlawful act of another State*.[169] This distinction, although a fine one, is more than merely academic.

The first situation is one of joint conduct, and will generally involve circumstances in which two or more States take joint action together. This may occur in the case of joint operations, such as military action or maritime patrol, undertaken by multiple States.[170] Joint conduct may also occur where multiple States take action together through a joint organ. The starting point in such situations is the overarching principle of independent responsibility outlined previously – that each State is responsible for its own internationally wrongful conduct.[171] In the context of a joint operation therefore, each State involved will be jointly and separately responsible for any internationally wrongful acts that occur over the course of that operation. Although analogies to municipal law are often imperfect, the ICJ appeared willing to accept, in the case of *Certain Phosphate Lands in Nauru*, that joint and several responsibility is recognized, at least in principle, in international law.[172] Of course, as noted by den Heijer, there is a threshold for considering collaborative conduct as "joint" for purposes of establishing multiple responsibility: conduct "can only be designated as 'joint' when the activity complained of was carried out in accordance with the instructions of all states involved and … all responsible states had it in their power to prevent the alleged misconduct."[173] A similar analysis also applies in the case of multiple State responsibility where different States have breached distinct obligations through different conduct, which breaches jointly contribute to the same injury.[174]

The second situation, where one State is implicated in the wrongful act of another State, is slightly different. In this case, the analysis of responsibility is predicated on some contribution by the first State to the wrongful act of the other State, falling short of "coauthoring" the act. In other words, a finding of responsibility may take place without attributing to the first State the wrongful act of the second State.

[169] C. Dominicé, "Attribution of Conduct to Multiple States and the Implication of a State in the Act of Another State," in J. Crawford, A. Pellet, and S. Olleson eds., *The Law of International Responsibility* 281 (2010), at 281.

[170] Joint military action was at issue in the North Atlantic Treaty Organization (NATO) cases before the International Court of Justice of *Legality of Use of Force*, in which Yugoslavia filed a claim against ten Member States of NATO: see, for example, *Legality of Use of Force (Yugoslavia v. Spain)*, Request for the Indication of Provisional Measures, [1999] ICJ Rep 761; *Legality of Use of Force (Yugoslavia v. United States of America)*, Request for the Indication of Provisional Measures, [1999] ICJ Rep 916.

[171] ILC Draft Articles, at Art. 47.

[172] *Certain Phosphate Lands in Nauru (Nauru v. Australia)*, [1992] ICJ Rep 240, at 283–285 (Separate Opinion of Judge Shahabuddeen). The case ultimately did not proceed to a determination of merits.

[173] den Heijer, *Europe and Extraterritorial Asylum*, at 89.

[174] This was the situation in the *Corfu Channel Case*, in which Albania through its failure to warn the United Kingdom was held responsible for injury caused to it by Yugoslav-laid mines: *Corfu Channel Case*, at 4. This would also be the case where the exploitation of a smuggled migrant has been enabled by different omissions on the part of the State of origin/transit and the State of destination. See, for example, the case of *Rantsev v Cyprus and Russia* (concerning the exploitation of a trafficking victim).

Three examples of "derived responsibility" or "exceptions to the principle of independent responsibility"[175] are recognized in the ILC Draft Articles: (1) cases where one State provides *aid or assistance* to another State with a view to assisting the latter State to commit an internationally wrongful act (Article 16); (2) cases where one State exercises *direction or control* over the commission of an internationally wrongful act by another State (Article 17), and (3) cases where one State deliberately *coerces* another State into committing an internationally wrongful act (Article 18). The following paragraphs examine the rules that govern State responsibility by implication in the acts of another, with a particular focus on the first exception that may be more commonly relevant to conduct related to migrant smuggling.

ILC Draft Article 16 is generally accepted to be declaratory of customary international law[176] as it relates to *complicity* of one State in the unlawful act of another. The article provides that a State that aids or assists another State in the commission of an internationally wrongful act is responsible for doing so: (1) if the first State was aware of the circumstances making the conduct of the assisting State internationally wrongful, (2) if the aid or assistance is given with a view to facilitating the commission of the wrongful act and actually does so facilitate.; and (3) if that act would be wrongful if it had been committed by the first State.[177] This previously obscure provision of the international law of State responsibility has attracted significant attention over the past decade, to the point where "the possible responsibility for complicity is one of the most important and difficult issues which arise in the daily work of government legal departments."[178]

Certainly questions of complicity are highly relevant in the context of responses to migrant smuggling. The provision of aid and assistance by States (typically States of destination) to other States (typically States of origin or transit) to prevent irregular migration is widespread and in fact, is sanctioned under the cooperation regime established by the Migrant Smuggling Protocol. It follows that many smuggling-related situations could potentially fall within this exception to independent responsibility. State A may provide State B with unmarked marine vessels that it knows will be used to interdict smuggled migrants in a way that is unlawful (for example, because such interdiction does not respect the jurisdiction of a third State or because it violates prohibitions relating to the use of force).[179] State A may return

[175] ILC Commentary, at Part One, Chapter IV, para. 8.

[176] For a thorough review of the evidence for the existence of such a customary rule, see H. P. Aust, *Complicity and the Law of State Responsibility* (2011) [Aust, *Complicity and the Law of State Responsibility*], at 419.

[177] ILC Draft Articles, at Art. 16.

[178] G. Nolte, Foreword to Aust, *Complicity and the Law of State Responsibility*, at ix.

[179] This example is based on the bilateral cooperation agreement signed by the Italian Minister of the Interior and the Libyan Minister of Foreign Affairs on December 29, 2007, examined in detail in

smuggled migrants to State B with knowledge that State B will subsequently violate the prohibition of *non-refoulement*. In relation to both these examples, State B, as the one directly involved in the commission of the internationally wrongful act, will be primarily responsible. State A will be legally responsible "to the extent that its own conduct has caused or contributed to the internationally wrongful act."[180] This standard of causation is a lower one than in the case of genuinely "joint" conduct, where two or more States are authors of the same act: unlike in the case of joint conduct,[181] under Article 16 "[t]here is no requirement that the aid or assistance should have been essential to the performance of the internationally wrongful act; it is sufficient if it contributed significantly."[182] A finding of responsibility for aid and assistance will however ultimately depend on whether the three conditions set out earlier in the section are fulfilled. In relation to the return of smuggled migrants for example, responsibility of the returning State (State A) would be engaged if: State A was *aware* that the smuggled migrants would be subject to *refoulement* by State B, that State A *intended* this outcome,[183] that the *refoulement* did indeed take place, and that State A itself would have been in violation of its international obligations if State A itself had directly engaged in the *refoulement* of the smuggled migrants.

Despite its apparent connection to much cooperative action around migrant smuggling, the application of Article 16 is unlikely to be straightforward in practice.[184] The lack of jurisprudence and scholarly consensus around what constitutes "complicity" or "aid and assistance" in the context of State responsibility is one problem.[185] The ILC Commentary makes clear that a determination of responsibility under this head will depend on the facts and circumstances of the case: that these need to be "carefully examined to determine whether the aiding State by its aid was aware of and intended to facilitate the commission of the internationally wrongful conduct."[186] Certainly the facts and circumstances must support a substantial (i.e.,

Chapter 1 at Section 1.3.2.2. See also Chapter 6, Section 6.4 (a note on attribution of responsibility for unlawful acts in responding to smuggling by sea).

180 ILC Commentary, at Art. 16, para. 1.

181 See note 168 above and the accompanying text.

182 ILC Commentary, Art. 16, para. 5.

183 On the subjective element of intent in this context, see Aust, *Complicity and the Law of State Responsibility*, at 420.

184 The requirement of specific intention, in particular, has been criticized for threatening to "make the whole construction of complicity unworkable": B. Graefrath, "Complicity in the Law of International Responsibility" (1996) 29 *Revue Belge de Droit International* 370, at 375.

185 For a detailed and careful examination of this issue with reference to ILC Draft Article 16, see Aust, *Complicity and the Law of State Responsibility*, at chapter 5. More generally see V. Lowe, "Responsibility for the Conduct of Other States" (2002) 101 *Japanese Journal of International Law* 1; and G. Nolte and H. P. Aust, "Equivocal Helpers – Complicit States, Mixed Messages and International Law" (2009) 58 *International and Comparative Law Quarterly* 1.

186 ILC Commentary, at Art. 16, para. 9.

determine what is required in terms of restitution. Actions to secure restitution in a case of migrant smuggling may include the removal of a State's vessel from the territory of another State; the release of an individual from unlawful detention; rescindment of a return order or, conversely, safe return to one's place of residence.[233] Restitution for a failure of protection may be more difficult if the failure has already resulted in harm, such as persecution, that cannot be reversed. In such cases, other means of reparation may be required. Rehabilitation, an accepted form of reparation in human rights law,[234] can be considered an aspect of restitution to the extent that it seeks to ensure that the person who has suffered a gross violation of human rights has his or her status and position "restored" in the eyes of the law as well as of the wider community. Victims of serious violations of human rights associated with migrant smuggling, such as exploitation, serious physical injury, or danger to life, will inevitably require a range of support services, including medical and psychological care, and legal and social assistance. The rehabilitation element of reparation would impose an obligation on the offending State to provide such services.

Compensation, the second form of reparation, is payable for damage caused by an internationally wrongful act to the extent that "such damage is not made good by restitution."[235] Its function is to "address the *actual losses* incurred as a result of the internationally wrongful act."[236] Compensation covers "any financially assessable damage,"[237] including nonmaterial damage but not extending to punitive or "moral damage," in the sense of "affront or injury caused by a violation of rights not associated with actual damage" (which is more properly the subject of satisfaction).[238] "Moral damage," in this context, is not to be confused with nonmaterial damage such as loss of loved ones, injury to feelings, pain and suffering, loss of social position, or injury to reputation, which may be difficult to quantify but is no less than material injury for the purposes of the law of State responsibility.[239] Although restitution retains its primacy as a legal principle, compensation appears to be the most frequently sought form of reparation.[240] The way in which compensation is to work in a particular situation will depend on a range of factors,

[233] These examples are drawn from the "Principles and Guidelines on the Right to a Remedy and Reparation," at para. 19.

[234] Ibid. at paras. 18, 21.

[235] ILC Draft Articles, at Art. 36(1).

[236] ILC Commentary, at Art. 36, para. 4 (emphasis added).

[237] ILC Draft Articles, at Art. 36(2).

[238] ILC Commentary, at Art. 36, para. 1.

[239] Ibid. at Art. 36, para. 16, citing *Lusitania (Germany v. United States)*, (1956) 7 UNRIAA 32 (United States–Germany Mixed Claims Commission, Nov. 1, 1923).

[240] Ibid. at Art. 36, paras. 2–3.

including the relevant primary rule[241] and "concern to reach an equitable and acceptable outcome."[242]

Satisfaction, the final internationally recognized form of reparation, is an exceptional remedy for injuries in relation to which it is not possible to fully restore the situation that existed previous to the breach and for which compensation will not be an adequate remedy. The obligation of satisfaction is exceptional in the sense that it will exist for the responsible State only "insofar as [the injury] cannot be made good by restitution or compensation."[243] Satisfaction, which must be proportionate to the injury,[244] can take various forms depending on the circumstances of a particular case, but may include "an acknowledgement of the breach, an expression of regret, a formal apology or another appropriate modality."[245] The ILC Commentary also gives the examples of due inquiry into how the wrongful situation arose, a compensation fund for victims, and disciplinary or penal action against the individuals whose conduct caused the internationally wrongful act.[246] Reparation through satisfaction may be especially appropriate in the context of a multifaceted breach of international law such as those associated with migrant smuggling, particularly where violations of individuals' human rights have also occurred. Note that the issue of remedies in the specific context of migrant smuggling is considered in further detail in Chapter 8.

Can a State avoid liability for the full weight of reparations owing for an internationally wrongful act by pointing to contributing factors or other causes falling outside its sphere of control? In the present context it is relevant to mention that migrant smuggling related harms are often caused by a combination of factors, not all of which can necessarily be ascribed to a single State. For example, the failure of a State of origin to prevent individuals from being smuggled by known exploiters in the first place can be argued to be a concurrent cause of the harm they may suffer through exploitation and ill-treatment in transit. This reality, however, would be

241 For example, both the Migrant Smuggling Protocol and UNCLOS provide for compensation for loss or damage sustained through measures taken against a suspect vessel where those measures subsequently prove to be unfounded. Migrant Smuggling Protocol, at Art. 9(2); United Nations Convention on the Law of the Sea, 1833 UNTS 3, done Dec. 10, 1982, entered into force Nov. 16, 1994 [UNCLOS], at Art. 110(3).

242 ILC Commentary, at Art. 36, para. 7. For examples of the types of damage that may be compensable and methods of quantification see ibid. at paras. 8–34. For a detailed discussion of compensation in the area of international human rights law including the practice of human rights courts and other bodies, see Shelton, *Remedies in International Human Rights Law*, esp. at chapter 8.

243 ILC Draft Articles, at Art. 37(1). See ILC Commentary, at Art. 37, para. 1.

244 ILC Draft Articles, at Art. 37(3).

245 ILC Draft Articles, at Art. 37(2). See further ILC Commentary, at Art. 37, para. 5. The issue of appropriateness was raised by the International Court of Justice in the *LaGrand Case* in which it held that "an apology would not suffice in cases where the individuals concerned have been subjected to prolonged detention or convicted and sentenced to severe penalties" following a failure of consular notification: *LaGrand (Germany v. United States of America)*, [2001] ICJ Rep 466, at para. 125.

246 ILC Commentary, at Art. 37, para. 5.

insufficient to reduce or attenuate the obligation of reparation owed in a particular case by either State.[247]

In any case where more than one State is jointly responsible for the injury, the primary interest should be that of ensuring proper reparation is made to the injured party, thereby guaranteeing the effectiveness of the norms breached. The interests of the responsible State in providing no more reparation than is necessary are of secondary importance only.[248] In practice, the injured State is generally entitled to bring a claim for full reparation against any one of the jointly responsible States, in line with any procedural requirements and provided that the injured State does not recover, by way of compensation, more than the damage it has suffered.[249] Questions of contribution by other responsible States toward that reparation may also arise, but are strictly a matter for the responsible States and will not affect the right of the injured State to seek full reparation from the responsible State of its choice.

As shown by the ICJ in the *Tehran Hostages* case, a State that is held responsible for an international wrong also cannot lessen its obligation of reparation by pointing to concurrent causes on the part of a private party – such as an organized criminal group.[250] As stated by the ILC in its Commentary:

> unless some part of the injury can be shown to be severable in causal terms from that attributed to the responsible State, the latter is held responsible for all the consequences, not being too remote, of its wrongful conduct.[251]

[247] In the *Corfu Channel Case*, for example, the United Kingdom recovered the full amount of its damage claim against Albania based on its wrongful failure to warn of the presence of mines, even though the mines had been laid by a third State: *Corfu Channel Case*, at 250, cited in ILC Commentary, at Art. 31, para. 12. The ILC Draft Articles further note that its Articles 16–18 on the responsibility of a State in connection with the act of another are "without prejudice to the international responsibility, under other provisions of these articles, of the State which commits the act in question": at Art. 19 (which thereby "preserves the responsibility of the State which has committed the internationally wrongful act, albeit with the aid or assistance, under the direction and control or subject to the coercion of another State": ILC Commentary, at Art. 19, para 1). See, similarly, Article 47 on the independent responsibility of States where more than one State is responsible for the same internationally wrongful act. It has been stated that "even if the commentary does not say so, article 47 is relevant also in the case of aid or assistance to the State in committing the wrongful act": Orakhelashvili, "Division of Reparation between Responsible Entitles," at 658. Note that a different analysis applies where a State has aided or assisted in the wrongful conduct of another State (as distinct from being a joint coauthor of the injury), in which case the level of reparation owed will likely be determined on a case-by-case basis depending on factors such as the level of complicity and participation: Orakhelashvili, "Division of Reparation between Responsible Entitles," at 658–659.

[248] Orakhelashvili, "Division of Reparation between Responsible Entitles," at 647–648.

[249] ILC Draft Articles, at Art. 47.

[250] *Tehran Hostages Case*, at 29–32, cited in ILC Commentary, at Art. 31, para. 12.

[251] ILC Commentary, at Art. 31, para. 13.

4.5.2. *Consequences Attached to Serious Breaches of Peremptory Norms*

Is there one uniform set of consequences attached to breaches of international legal rules, or do the consequences vary according to the severity of the breach and/or the relative importance of the primary rule that has been violated? The question of a qualitative distinction between different breaches of international law has occupied international courts, tribunals, and commentators for many years. The ILC, along with much of the international legal community, has long acknowledged the existence of a hierarchy of norms "ensuing from the recognition by the international community of the pre-eminence of certain common interests and values and the consequent necessity of surrounding them with maximum legal protection."[252] The related identification, by the ICJ, of legal obligations *erga omnes* (those that, by virtue of the importance of the rights involved, are owed to the international community as a whole),[253] provides further evidence of the existence of a special class of norms.[254]

Although acceptance of this "entrenched legal phenomenon"[255] may be widespread, considerable divisions arose with respect to the way in which the notion of a normative hierarchy could be incorporated into the ILC's work on State responsibility. After much debate, the ILC abandoned its attempt to forge a distinction through

[252] G. Abi-Saab, "The Uses of Article 19" (1999) 10(2) *European Journal of International Law* 339 [Abi-Saab, "The Uses of Article 19"], at 339.

[253] The basis for this doctrine is a statement of the International Court of Justice in the *Barcelona Traction Case*: "an essential distinction should be drawn between the obligations of a State towards the international community as a whole, and those arising vis-à-vis another State in the field of diplomatic protection. By their very nature the former are the concern of all States. In view of the importance of the rights involved, all States can be held to have a legal interest in their protection; they are obligations *erga omnes* ... Such obligations derive, for example, in contemporary international law, from the outlawing of acts of aggression, and of genocide, as also from the principles and rules concerning the basic rights of the human person, including protection from slavery and racial discrimination. Some of the corresponding rights of protection have entered into the body of general international law ... others are conferred by international instruments of a universal or quasi-universal character": *Barcelona Traction, Light and Power Company Limited (Second Phase) (Belgium v. Spain)*, [1970] ICJ Rep 3 [*Barcelona Traction Case*], at paras. 33–34.

[254] The relationship between peremptory norms and obligations *erga omnes* (i.e., whether they are different concepts or two aspects of a single idea) is not completely clear. The ILC Commentary identifies a substantive overlap and notes that all examples given by the ICJ of obligations owed to the international community as a whole involve obligations arising under peremptory norms of international law: ILC Commentary, at Part Two, Introduction, paras. 2–7. Cassese, while noting that opinions remain divided on the matter, concludes that "based on State practice, the better view is that the two categories inextricably coincide: every peremptory norm imposes obligation *erga omnes* and, vice-versa, every obligation *erga omnes* proper is laid down in a peremptory norm" and indeed that "it appears that in fact – from the point of view of State responsibility – the distinction between the two categories ... is without merit": A. Cassese, "The Character of the Violated Obligation," in J. Crawford, A. Pellet, and S. Olleson eds., *The Law of International Responsibility* 415 (2010), at 417.

[255] Abi-Saab, "The Uses of Article 19," at 340.

the creation of two different categories of wrongs: "international crimes of State" (most serious) and "internationally wrongful acts" or "international delicts" (relatively less serious). In their final version, the ILC Draft Articles omit all reference to "international crimes of State" and instead focus on serious violations of peremptory norms of international law. Such violations are to be identified using the general rules of responsibility but attract a special regime of consequences, which is described further in Section 4.6 and which involves not just the responsible State but all other States as well. Violations of peremptory norms of international law also impact on rules regarding entitlement to invoke responsibility. This issue is considered in the following section.

The notion of a peremptory norm of international law was codified in the Vienna Convention on the Law of Treaties as one that is:

> recognised by the international community of States as a whole as a norm from which no derogation is permitted and which can be modified only by a subsequent norm of general international law having the same character.[256]

These "stringent" criteria[257] have served to ensure that very few norms can be conclusively claimed as peremptory. The ILC Commentary notes that those widely accepted and recognized as such "include the prohibitions of aggression, genocide, slavery, racial discrimination, crimes against humanity and torture as well as, more recently, the right to self-determination."[258] In establishing the possible relevance to migrant smuggling it should be noted that there are numerous examples of State officials being responsible – directly and indirectly – for smuggled migrants being subjected to inhuman treatment potentially rising to the level of torture. Also, it is not beyond the bounds of possibility that forceful migrant smuggling control measures instituted by one State could be perceived by another State as an act of aggression. For example, if a State were to sail its armed vessels into the territorial

[256] Vienna Convention on the Law of Treaties, at Art. 53. Note that this concept is also included in the Vienna Convention on the Law of Treaties between States and International Organizations or between International Organizations, done Mar. 21 1986, not yet in force, UN Doc. A/CONF.129/15, reprinted in (1986) 25 ILM 543, at Art. 53 (Vienna Convention on the Law of Treaties between States and International Organizations or between International Organizations).

[257] ILC Commentary, at Art. 26, para. 5.

[258] Ibid. citing the ICJ in *East Timor (Portugal v. Australia)*, [1995] ICJ Rep 90, at 102, para. 29. The commentary adds that "[s]o far, relatively few peremptory norms have been recognized as such. But various tribunals, national and international, have affirmed the idea of peremptory norms in contexts not limited to the validity of treaties": ibid. It cites the decisions of the ICTY in *Prosecutor v. Furundzija*, Case IT-95–17/1-T, ICTY Trial Chamber, Dec. 10, 1998, and of the English House of Lords in *R v. Bow Street Metropolitan Stipendiary Magistrate, ex parte Pinochet Ugarte (No. 3)*, [1999] 2 All ER 97, esp. at 108–109, 114–115 (per Lord Browne-Wilkinson). See further *Legality of the Threat or Use of Nuclear Weapons (Advisory Opinion)*, [1996] ICJ Rep 226, at 257, para. 79. See also ILC Commentary, at Art. 40, paras. 4–5.

waters of another State, without the latter State's permission, intending to forcibly offload boatloads of smuggled migrants, this could well be interpreted as an act of aggression. A similar interpretation could be applied to a State's military forces firing across the border at nationals of a neighboring State who were attempting to cross. In addition, the transportation of slaves through migrant smuggling cannot be ruled out as a contemporary (or future) possibility.[259] It is therefore relevant to briefly consider the responsibility regime established in the ILC Draft Articles for breaches of such peremptory norms.

Under the ILC State responsibility regime, serious breaches of peremptory norms of international law give rise to particular consequences above and beyond those attaching to other breaches of international obligations. In particular, States are under a positive obligation to cooperate in order to end, through lawful means, any serious breach.[260] In addition, States are under a "duty of abstention"[261] that requires, first, that they do not recognize as lawful any situation created by such a breach, and, second, that they not render aid or assistance in maintaining this situation.[262]

The scope of application of this special responsibility regime is highly restricted. For a particular situation to qualify, there must, as noted previously, have been "a serious breach by a State of an obligation arising under a peremptory norm of general international law."[263] To be considered as "serious" the breach in question must involve "a gross or systematic failure by the responsible State to fulfill its obligation."[264] According to the ILC Commentary, a violation would have to be carried out in an organized and deliberate way to be regarded as systematic,[265] and an isolated violation of a peremptory norm would be unlikely to qualify on this point. The term "gross" refers to the intensity of the violation or of its effects: "it denotes violations of a flagrant nature, amounting to a direct and outright assault on the values protected by the rule."[266] Factors that could go toward establishing the seriousness of the breach include intent, the scope and number of individual violations, and the gravity of their consequences for victims.[267] On this basis, application of the ILC's special responsibility regime to situations of migrant smuggling and State

[259] See further Chapter 3, Section 3.3.3.2.

[260] ILC Draft Articles, at Art. 41(1). The ILC Commentary notes that the question as to whether general international law prescribes a positive duty of cooperation under such circumstances is not yet settled. This provision may therefore reflect the progressive development of international law. ILC Commentary, at Art. 41, para. 3.

[261] ILC Commentary, at Art. 41, para. 4.

[262] ILC Draft Articles, at Art. 41(2).

[263] Ibid. at Art. 40(1).

[264] Ibid. at Art. 40(2).

[265] ILC Commentary, at Art. 40, para. 8.

[266] Ibid.

[267] Ibid.

responses to migrant smuggling is likely to be fraught with legal and practical difficulty. Although the definition of "act of aggression" has yet to be clearly delineated in international law,[268] it fundamentally implies the use of armed force by one State against another: a threshold that has not yet been reached in the context of State responses to migrant smuggling. In the case of smuggling allegedly involving slaves it will first be necessary to establish that the circumstances of the particular case justify its characterization as one of slavery or the slave trade or otherwise as a crime against humanity for which the State in question is legally responsible. This would involve reference to the primary obligation as well as application of rules of attribution, as explored at Section 4.2.1. It is only following such a finding that the additional hurdle of "seriousness" must be overcome by showing that the breach involved a gross or systematic failure by the State to fulfill its obligation to prevent the conduct identified as violative of a peremptory norm.

4.6. INVOCATION OF RESPONSIBILITY

The term "invocation" refers to the taking of "measures of a relatively formal character" by one State against another State, such as the raising of a claim or the commencement of proceedings in an international court or tribunal.[269] Rules relating to invocation of responsibility thereby govern how State responsibility is actually administered in practice. Although State responsibility will exist independently of its invocation by another State, it is important, as a practical matter, to be able to identify what States actually faced with a breach of an international obligation are able to do in terms of securing cessation and/or reparation from the offending State.[270]

The questions surrounding implementation of State responsibility are particularly complex in those areas of law of most relevance to the present study (including human rights law and transnational criminal law), where the post-breach

[268] The Statute of the International Criminal Court identifies the crime of aggression as one of the core crimes under the Court's jurisdiction. However it was not until 2010 that amendments defining the crime of aggression were adopted. In that context, States agreed that an "act of aggression" is "the use of armed force by a State against the sovereignty, territorial integrity or political independence of another State, or in any other manner inconsistent with the Charter of the United Nations": Amendments on the Crime of Aggression to the Rome Statute of the International Criminal Court, Resolution RC/Res.6 of the Review Conference of the Rome Statute: The Crime of Aggression, done June 11, 2010.

[269] ILC Commentary, at Art. 42, para. 2. Mere protest or other "informal" diplomatic contacts do not amount to an invocation of responsibility unless they also include a specific claim (e.g., for restitution). The definition of "invocation" has been criticized as being too narrow: see E. Brown Weiss, "Invoking State Responsibility in the Twenty-First Century" (2002) 96 *American Journal of International Law* 798 [Brown Weiss, "Invoking State Responsibility in the Twenty-First Century"], at 800.

[270] ILC Commentary, at Part Three, Introduction.

relationship will most commonly be one between the offending State and the other parties to the agreement in question. The opposing party will be extended to include the international community as a whole when the breach relates to rights that are recognized to be of a fundamental nature.[271] In human rights law particularly there is also another possibility: that a non-State entity, namely the aggrieved individual or even an interested nongovernment organization, could invoke responsibility and thereby claim reparation for injury.[272] This is possible because of the peculiar nature of this branch of law: the primary obligation in human rights treaties is, in fact, owed to the individual and not to his or her State. Those human rights treaties with an individual complaints procedure have taken this theoretical possibility to its logical conclusion by permitting an aggrieved individual to bypass the State completely and to invoke responsibility on his or her own account. Whether and to what extent non-State entities can invoke responsibility of a State will depend on the content of the relevant primary rule.[273] The following paragraphs will examine the general international legal rules governing invocation of responsibility *between States* before considering the very particular regime created under international human rights treaties.

4.6.1. *General Rules Governing Invocation of Responsibility*

General rules of international law provide that only an "injured State" can invoke responsibility on its own account.[274] Under the ILC regime, a State is entitled, as an injured State, to invoke the responsibility of another State (and is entitled to resort to all stipulated means of redress) if the obligation breached is owed:

- To that State individually[275] (i.e., if the invoking State has an individual right to the performance of the relevant obligation[276]); or
- To a group of States including that State or to the international community as a whole, *providing* that the breach specially affects that State *or* that it is "of such a character as radically to change the position of all the other States to which the obligation is owed with respect to the further performance of the obligation."[277]

[271] See notes 253–254 above and accompanying text.
[272] This possibility is acknowledged in Article 33 of the ILC Draft Articles. See also ILC Commentary, at Art. 33, paras. 1–4.
[273] See Chapter 2 of this book.
[274] See further J. Crawford ed., *The International Law Commission's Articles on State Responsibility: Introduction, Text, and Commentaries* (2002) [Crawford, *The ILC's Articles on State Responsibility*], at 54–260.
[275] ILC Draft Articles, at Art. 42(a).
[276] ILC Commentary, at Art. 42, para. 5.
[277] ILC Draft Articles, at Art. 42(b).

According to the ILC Commentary, to be "specially affected" and thereby considered as injured for the purposes of entitlement to invoke responsibility, the State in question must be able to show that it has been affected by the breach "in a way which distinguishes it from the generality of other States to which the obligation is owed."[278] Situations in which the breach of a collective obligation is of a nature to radically affect every other State to which the obligation is owed are most likely to arise under regimes created through treaties that establish interdependent obligations for all States Parties.[279] Such situations would not occur in the context of human rights treaties, which "do not operate in an all-or-nothing way."[280]

Invocation of responsibility by a State against another State in the context of migrant smuggling could involve both types of obligations. Certainly it is possible to envisage a situation whereby an injured State could claim breach of an obligation owed to it individually – for example, through violation of a bilateral agreement governing matters such as allocation of responsibility for interception and disembarkation of smuggled migrants. In the context of collective obligations, a State seeking to invoke responsibility of other States on its own account will normally be required to establish its status as "injured" by showing that it has been "specially affected" by the breach in question.[281] In addition to the legal difficulties there are likely to be practical obstacles: individuals who have felt the need to engage migrant smugglers (or indeed, whose rights are affected by anti-smuggling activities of other States) are very likely to lack the effective protection of their State.

There may well be situations in which more than one State is "injured" by an internationally wrongful act. In such cases, international law is clear on the point that each of the States injured by this act has an independent and severable right to invoke the responsibility of the offending State.[282] As noted previously, a similar rule applies in situations whereby several States are responsible for the same wrongful act. An example relevant to the present context would be a joint operation against

[278] ILC Commentary, at Art. 42, para. 12, giving the example of the collective obligation to prevent, reduce, and control marine pollution under Article 194 of the UNCLOS, the breach of which may specially affect one or several coastal States.

[279] For example, a disarmament treaty or a treaty establishing a military or nuclear-free zone. See further ILC Commentary, at Art. 42, paras. 5, 13–15.

[280] Crawford, *The ILC's Articles on State Responsibility*, at 41. The same can be said of transnational criminal law treaties such as the Organized Crime Convention and its Protocols: United Nations Convention against Transnational Organized Crime, 2225 UNTS 209, done Nov. 15, 2000, entered into force Sept. 29, 2003; and the Trafficking Protocol, Migrant Smuggling Protocol, and Protocol against the Illicit Manufacturing of and Trafficking in Firearms, Their Parts and Components and Ammunition, supplementing the United Nations Convention against Transnational Organized Crime, 2326 UNTS 208, done May 31, 2001, entered into force July 3, 2005.

[281] ILC Commentary, at Art. 48, para. 10.

[282] ILC Draft Articles, at Art. 46. On the practice of international courts and tribunals on this point, see ILC Commentary, at Art. 46, paras. 1–4.

migrant smuggling that led to violation of another State's sovereignty or of the rights of the migrants involved. Further, a claim against one State would not operate to prejudice any right of future action by one injured State against the other responsible State(s).[283]

Can a State that has not been "injured" by a breach of international legal obligation under the terms previously detailed still invoke the responsibility of another State? This is an essential question in realizing State responsibility for human rights violations – particularly in relation to violations committed by a State against its own citizens or against persons who are without the effective protection of their State of nationality. International law appears to be moving to a point whereby direct "injury" is not always an essential precondition to launching a claim. ILC Draft Article 48 (aspects of which are argued to be progressive development and not codification of an established rule[284]) has been described as an attempt to balance the traditional bilateralism of the law of State responsibility with the rise of collective interests.[285] Article 48 foresees a situation whereby a State that is not permitted to invoke responsibility on its own account may nevertheless invoke responsibility in its capacity as a member of a group to which the obligation is owed or as a member of the international community as a whole. More precisely, responsibility can be invoked by a noninjured State in one of two situations. In the first situation, the obligation whose breach gives rise to the international responsibility must have been owed to a group of which the invoking State belongs, and the obligation must have been established for the collective interest.[286] The nature of an obligation falling within this first category must be such as to "transcend the sphere of bilateral relations of the States parties"[287] and would include, for example, regional systems for the protection of human rights such as have been established in Europe, the Americas, and Africa.[288]

In the second situation, the relevant obligation must be one that is owed to the international community as a whole.[289] The ILC Commentary attached to this Article confirms that this particular provision is intended to give effect to the concept of obligations *erga omnes*, explained at Section 4.5.2 of this chapter.

[283] ILC Draft Articles, at Art. 47(2)(b), provided that the total sum of compensation sought does not exceed the damage suffered: ibid. at Art. 47(2)(a).

[284] Brown Weiss, "Invoking State Responsibility in the Twenty-First Century," at 803–815.

[285] I. Scobbie, "The Invocation of Responsibility for the Breach of 'Obligations under Peremptory Norms of General International Law'" (2002) 13(5) *European Journal of International Law* 1201, at 1204.

[286] ILC Draft Articles, at Art. 48(1).

[287] ILC Commentary, at Art. 48, para. 7.

[288] Ibid.

[289] ILC Draft Articles, at Art. 48(2). On the term "international community as a whole," see ILC Commentary, at Art. 48, para. 7; and Brown Weiss, "Invoking State Responsibility in the Twenty-First Century," at 804.

The relevance of the provision lies in the fact that at least some of the legal obligations identified in the previous chapters as being potentially relevant to migrant smuggling, such as the prohibition on torture, can be characterized as obligations *erga omnes*.[290] Importantly, the full spectrum of remedies is available only to injured States. The claimant State under Article 48, not having been injured in its own right, is not entitled to claim compensation on its own behalf (and apparently not entitled to engage in countermeasures).[291] The emphasis is accordingly on cessation of the wrongful act; guarantees of noncontinuation as appropriate; and, in the interests of those injured or of the beneficiaries of the obligation, performance of the obligation of reparation.[292] Beyond that, the availability of reparation will depend on a range of factors most easily ascertained with reference to the primary rule and the individual circumstances of the case.

In terms of procedural requirements, international law provides guidance on the modalities to be observed regarding the making and recognition of claims involving State responsibility, which are the same whether or not the claim is being made by an "injured" State.[293] For example, the invoking State is required to give notice of its claim.[294] Such notice may specify the conduct that the responsible State is to take in order to cease the wrongful act as well as the form of reparation it is seeking.[295] General international law also requires the injured State to fulfill any applicable rule relating to nationality of claims[296] as well as, in applicable cases, the customary rule requiring exhaustion of local remedies.[297] Most claims involving violations of

[290] The court in the *Barcelona Traction Case* identified obligations *erga omnes* as deriving, for example, "from the principles and rules concerning basic rights of the human person, including protection from slavery and racial discrimination": at para. 34. Brown Weiss notes that this category of obligations is likely to grow, especially in relation to human rights and environmental protection. She argues that, through Article 48, the ILC "sets the stage for states to invoke state responsibility for the breach of any obligation owed to the international community": Brown Weiss, "Invoking State Responsibility in the Twenty-First Century," at 804.

[291] ILC Draft Article 54 preserves the right of States invoking responsibility under Article 48 to take "lawful measures" to ensure cessation of the violation and reparation in the interest of the State and beneficiaries of the obligation breached.

[292] ILC Draft Articles, at Arts. 48(2), 54.

[293] ILC Draft Article 48(3) extends application of the procedural provisions contained in Articles 43 (notice of claim), 44 (admissibility of claims), and 45 (loss of the right to invoke responsibility) to invocation of responsibility by a noninjured State entitled to do so under paragraph 1 of Article 48.

[294] ILC Draft Articles, at Art. 43(1); Vienna Convention on the Law of Treaties, at Art. 65.

[295] ILC Draft Articles, at Art. 43(2); Vienna Convention on the Law of Treaties, at Art. 65.

[296] ILC Draft Articles, at Art. 44(a): "Admissibility of claims: The responsibility of a State may not be invoked if: (*a*) the claim is not brought in accordance with any applicable rule relating to the nationality of claims; (*b*) the claim is one to which the rule of exhaustion of local remedies applies and any available and effective local remedy has not been exhausted." The rule of nationality is most strongly associated with cases of diplomatic protection.

[297] Ibid. at Art. 44(b). Note that the ILC Commentary identifies this rule as one of customary international law: ILC Commentary, at Art. 44, para. 4. The exhaustion of local remedies rule was

international human rights law will be subject to this latter rule whereby the claim itself will be rendered inadmissible if available and effective local remedies have not been exhausted.[298] An injured State can also lose its right to invoke a claim through waiver or acquiescence.[299]

4.6.2. *Rules Governing Invocation of Responsibility for Violations of Human Rights Norms*

The ILC provisions on invocation of responsibility "operate in a residual way"[300] and do not affect the international legal rights of individuals and non-State entities under particular treaty regimes. Customary rules governing a particular area of law can also play an important role in determining applicable rules with respect to invocation. In the area of human rights, custom as well as international and regional human rights treaties have together created a set of rules that express the special nature of human rights and that both reflect and differ from the generally applicable rules set out in the previous section. Concordance between the general rules and

an important aspect of the law of State responsibility for injury to aliens. An alien alleging breach of an international obligation was obliged to exhaust all remedies available in the host country before his or her State of nationality could take over the claim. See further Shaw, *International Law*, at 730–733. On the application of this rule in the specific context of contemporary international human rights law, see S. D'Ascoli and K. M. Scherr, "The Rule of Prior Exhaustion of Local Remedies in the International Law Doctrine and Its Application in the Specific Context of Human Rights Protection," European University Institute Working Paper LAW No. 2007/02 (Feb. 19, 2007) [D'Ascoli and Scherr, "The Rule of Prior Exhaustion of Local Remedies in the International Law Doctrine and Its Application in the Specific Context of Human Rights Protection"].

298 See, for example, the American Convention on Human Rights, at Art. 46(1)(a); European Convention on Human Rights, at Art. 35; African Charter, at Arts. 50, 56(5)–(6); CERD, at Arts. 11(3), 14(7)(a); ICCPR, at Art. 41(1)(c); Optional Protocol to the International Covenant on Civil and Political Rights, 999 UNTS 171, done Dec. 16, 1966, entered into force Mar. 23, 1976 [ICCPR First Optional Protocol], at Art. 5(2)(b); Convention against Torture and Other Cruel, Inhuman or Degrading Treatment or Punishment, 1465 UNTS 85, done Dec. 10, 1984, entered into force June 26, 1987 [Convention against Torture], at Art. 21(1)(c); and Optional Protocol to the Convention on the Elimination of All Forms of Discrimination against Women, 2131 UNTS 83, done Oct. 6, 1999, entered into force Dec. 22, 2000 [CEDAW Optional Protocol], at Art. 4(1). Note that customary law does not require the claimant to satisfy this requirement if local remedies can be shown to be unavailable or otherwise ineffective: *Robert E. Brown Case (United States v. Great Britain)*, (1955) 6 UNRIAA 120 (Great Britain–United States Arbitral Tribunal, Nov. 23, 1923). Brownlie states that "[t]he best test appears to be that an effective remedy must be available 'as a matter of reasonable possibility'": I. Brownlie, *Principles of Public International Law* (7th ed. 2008), at 495. In most cases, the treaty provisions referred to previously specifically exclude the application of the exhaustion of local remedies rule in cases where their exhaustion is unreasonably prolonged, ineffective, or otherwise unavailable. See further Shaw, *International Law*; and D'Ascoli and Scherr, "The Rule of Prior Exhaustion of Local Remedies in the International Law Doctrine and Its Application in the Specific Context of Human Rights Protection."

299 ILC Draft Articles, at Art. 45; Vienna Convention on the Law of Treaties, at Art. 45.

300 ILC Commentary, at Art. 55, para. 2.

the special regime is high. Human rights law recognizes, for example, the concept of certain internationally wrongful acts offending the international system and international society as a whole; "[a]s such, they injure the 'legal' interest of each and every party to a human rights treaty and, with respect to customary human rights, of all States."[301] The ILC rules that extend a right of invocation to noninjured States are in accordance with international human rights law, which does not require a connection of nationality between the "victim" and the invoking State:

> Unless a treaty provision otherwise provides or implies, a claim alleging violation of human rights may therefore be submitted by one State against another even if the individual victim possesses the nationality of the defendant State and not of the complaining State.[302]

Most of the major international and regional human rights treaties, as well as labor rights conventions, create and regulate systems for the submission and consideration of complaints by one State Party against another.[303] The right to challenge violations is vested in all States Parties, irrespective of the nationality of the victim and of any material injury to the claimant State. Although such provisions would appear to offer an important avenue for securing State responsibility for violations of human rights, including in the context of migrant smuggling, they are very rarely used.[304]

[301] Meron, *Human Rights and Humanitarian Norms as Customary Law*, at 148. See further the discussion of obligations *erga omnes* at notes 285 and 290, above, and the accompanying text.

[302] Meron, *Human Rights and Humanitarian Norms as Customary Law*, at 196, citing American Law Institute, *Restatement (Third) of the Foreign Relations Law of the United States* (1987), at § 703(2).

[303] See, for example, European Convention on Human Rights, at Arts. 24, 48 (compulsory jurisdiction of the European Court over interstate complaints); ICCPR, at Art. 41 (jurisdiction of the Human Rights Committee over interstate complaints dependent on special acceptance); Convention against Torture, at Art. 21 (jurisdiction of the Committee against Torture over interstate complaints dependent on special acceptance); American Convention on Human Rights, at Art. 45 (jurisdiction of the Inter-American Court of Human Rights dependent on special acceptance); African Charter, at Art. 49 (right of States Parties to refer violations by other States Parties to the African Commission on Human and Peoples' Rights); and the Protocol to the African Charter on Human and Peoples' Rights on the Establishment of the African Court on Human and Peoples' Rights, OAU Doc. OAU/LEG/EXP/AFCHPR/PROT(III), done June 9, 1998, entered into force Jan. 25, 2004, at Art. 5 (permitting both States Parties that have lodged complaints with the Commission and those that have had complaints lodged against them to refer these cases to the Court).

[304] For a discussion of why interstate complaints are so rare, see P. H. Kooijmans, "Interstate Dispute Settlement in the Field of Human Rights," in M. Brus, A. S. Muller, and S. Wiermers eds., *The United Nations Decade of International Law: Reflections on International Dispute Settlement* 87 (1991); S. Leckie, "The Interstate Complaint Procedure in International Human Rights Law: Hopeful Prospects or Wishful Thinking?" (1988) 10 *Human Rights Quarterly* 249; and generally, M. T. Kamminga, *Inter-State Accountability for Violations of Human Rights* (1992) (describing the formal interstate complaints procedures under most human rights treaties as "a dead letter," at 47). A useful discussion of international State responsibility, the right to a remedy, and the rarity of interstate complaints in the context of "the uniqueness of human rights cases" can be found in Shelton, *Remedies in International Human Rights Law*, at 47–49.

Of much more practical significance are the provisions contained in or attached to many international and regional human rights treaties that provide for the possibility of *individuals* alleging violations of human rights by States Parties and seeking remedies on their own behalf.[305] It is relevant to note that, at least at the international level, such procedures almost never form an integral part of the central treaty but require a separate adherence by States Parties prepared to subject themselves to invocation of legal responsibility in this way. Individual complaints procedures have proved to be useful mechanisms for fleshing out the substance of specific human rights provisions and even, on occasion, for prompting legislative and administrative changes that result in a substantial improvement in the protection of rights. It is important not to overstate the influence and remedial value of these procedures. Relatively low and skewed ratification rates means that they do not offer a secure or consistent avenue for securing accountability and redress in relation to specific cases or situations. However it is important to note that the human rights implications of State responses to migrant smuggling have indeed been examined on occasion by various human rights bodies, most significantly by the UN Human Rights Committee and by the European Court of Human Rights.[306]

The rules governing invocation of responsibility for violations of human rights norms are permissive. States *may* invoke the responsibility of others under certain circumstances. However, they do not appear to be under an obligation to do so. Some have argued that this represents an overly narrow a reading of both obligations and responsibilities, particularly with regard to international human rights law. Henkin, for example, asserts that "[e]very State Party [to the major human rights instruments] has a right, and has also assumed responsibility, to seek compliance by other States for *their* undertakings under such treaties,"[307] and that "every State is responsible to seek compliance by all other States with their obligations under the customary international law of human rights."[308] Although such an interpretation

305 ICCPR First Optional Protocol; CEDAW Optional Protocol; Optional Protocol to the International Covenant on Economic, Social and Cultural Rights, UN Doc. A/63/435, done Dec. 10, 2008, not yet in force; Convention against Torture, at Art. 22; CERD, at Art. 14; American Convention on Human Rights, at Art. 90; European Convention on Human Rights, at Art. 25; African Charter, at Arts. 55–56.

306 See, for example, *Hirsi Jamaa and Others v. Italy*, (2012) 55 EHRR 21 (ECHR, Feb. 23, 2012); *Xhavara and Fifteen Others v. Italy and Albania*, Application No. 39473/98 (ECHR, Jan. 11, 2001); *A. v. Australia*, UNHRC Comm. No. 560/1993, UN Doc. CCPR/C/59/D/560/1993, Apr. 30, 1997, decided Apr. 3, 1997; *C. v. Australia*, UNHRC Comm. No. 900/1999, UN Doc. CCPR/C/76/D/900/1999, Nov. 13, 2002, decided Oct. 28, 2002; and *Omar Sharif Baban et al. v. Australia*, UNHRC Comm. No. 1014/2001, CCPR/C/78/D/1014/2001, Sept. 18, 2003, decided Aug. 6, 2003.

307 L. Henkin, "Interstate Responsibility for Compliance with Human Rights Obligations," in L. C. Vohrah et al. eds., *Man's Inhumanity to Man: Essays on International Law in Honour of Antonio Cassese* 383 (2003), at 383.

308 Ibid.

the legal responsibilities of international organizations has thereby become a matter of pressing concern.[328] It is important to acknowledge that this is not just a matter of holding international organizations to account. It is critical to address the danger that States may use the organizational veil to shield themselves from incurring legal responsibility for internationally wrongful acts.[329]

The responsibility of intergovernmental organizations for internationally wrongful acts is of high significance in the context of migrant smuggling – as is the danger, identified previously, of States potentially avoiding responsibility through use of an organizational shield. As noted, a number of major international organizations are deeply involved in the response to migrant smuggling. The actions of some have been subject to intense criticism. NATO, for example, has been accused of failing to take steps to protect smuggled migrants in distress.[330] Frontex, the European Union's external border enforcement agency,[331] has been accused of both complicity and direct involvement in inhuman and degrading treatment against migrants, violations of the right to leave, discrimination, violation of the right to protection of personal data, and violations of the principle of *non-refoulement*.[332] It has also been accused of violating the territorial sovereignty of a third State in the course of

[328] E. Suzuki and S. Nanwani, "Responsibility of International Organizations: The Accountability Mechanisms of Multilateral Development Banks" (2006) 27 *Michigan Journal of International Law* 177, at 180.

[329] A. Stumer, "Liability of Member States for Acts of International Organizations: Reconsidering the Policy Objections" (2007) 48 *Harvard International Law Journal* 553.

[330] See Council of Europe Parliamentary Assembly Report, *Lives Lost in the Mediterranean Sea*; and C. Heller, L. Pezzani and Situ Studio, *Report on the "Left-To-Die Boat"* (2012), available at www.forensic-architecture.org/publications/report-on-the-left-to-die-boat/ (accessed May 12, 2013).

[331] The European Agency for the Management of Operational Cooperation at the External Borders of the Member States of the European Union (Frontex) was established by European Council Regulation (EC) 2007/2004 to support Member State implementation of EU border control rules. For both patrol and incident response, Frontex deploys Rapid Border Intervention Teams (RABAT) drawn from a pool of law enforcement officials provided by participating EU Member States. RABAT engage in patrols and also respond to specific migration incidents that have included interception of vessels carrying smuggled migrants. Council Regulation (EC) No 2007/2004 of 26 October 2004 establishing a European Agency for the Management of Operational Cooperation at the External Borders of the Member States of the European Union, OJ L 349/1, Nov. 25, 2004; as amended by Regulation (EC) No 863/2007 of the European Parliament and of the Council of 11 July 2007 establishing a mechanism for the creation of Rapid Border Intervention Teams and amending Council Regulation (EC) No 2007/2004 as regards that mechanism and regulating the tasks and powers of guest officers, OJ L 199/30, July 31, 2007, and Regulation (EU) No 1168/2011 of the European Parliament and of the Council of 25 October 2011 amending Council Regulation (EC) No 2007/2004 establishing a European Agency for the Management of Operational Cooperation at the External Borders of the Member States of the European Union, OJ L 304/1, Nov. 22, 2011. See further the agency website: www.frontex.europa.eu/.

[332] See, for example, Human Rights Watch, *The EU's Dirty Hands: Frontex Involvement in Ill-Treatment of Migrant Detainees in Greece* (2011). See also Keller et al., *Frontex Agency: Which Guarantees for Human Rights?*

a patrol aimed at combating illegal immigration.[333] Frontex activities are officially characterized as "joint operations," which, according to the above analysis, should implicate the responsibility of involved Member States. However, the question of whether Frontex, or its parent organization, the European Union, incurs separate legal responsibility for such violations is a separate and important one. The following brief overview of the current state of the law seeks to provide general guidance.

It can be convincingly argued that, in the real world, international organizations act only when and because their Members (States) cause them to act. Within this framework of analysis, international organizations do not have any real autonomy and thereby, are not the appropriate subjects of international legal responsibility. However, the legal situation is more complicated. International law has traditionally recognized the separate international legal personality of intergovernmental organizations (conferred by States), including their capacity to enter into and become bound by treaties.[334] International organizations are, in the words of the ICJ, "bound by any obligations incumbent upon them under general rules of international law, under their constitutions or under international agreements to which they are parties."[335] A critical aspect of their legal personality is the capacity of international organizations to be legally responsible for the acts and omissions that violate international law and that can be attributed to them under the secondary rules that govern such responsibility. Importantly, attribution of conduct necessary to establish an internationally wrongful act has been recognized by the ICJ as extending beyond employees of the organization to include the actions of contractors or agents who have been recruited to carry out or help carry out one of the functions of the organization.[336] It would also appear, controversially, to cover the conduct of State organs (such as border patrol or military units) placed at the disposal of the organization and under its "effective control."[337]

333 The accusation, made by Turkey, was denied by Frontex. See C. Deliso, "Safeguarding Europe's Southern Borders: Interview with Klaus Roesler, Director of Operations Division, Frontex," (Sept. 23, 2011) available at www.balkanalysis.com/greece/2011/09/23/safeguarding-europe's-southern-borders-interview-with-klaus-roesler-director-of-operations-division-frontex/ (accessed May 12, 2013).

334 See generally, P. Klein and P. Sands eds., *Bowett's Law of International Institutions* (2009), esp. at Part III, "Legal Personality." See also the Vienna Convention on the Law of Treaties between States and International Organizations or between International Organizations.

335 *Interpretation of the Agreement of 25 March 1951 between the WHO and Egypt (Advisory Opinion)*, [1980] ICJ Rep 73, at 89–90, para. 37.

336 *Reparation for Injuries Case*, at 177. This position is reflected in Article 4(2) of the ILC Draft Articles on Responsibility of International Organizations provisionally adopted so far by the Commission with commentaries thereto, in "Report of the International Law Commission on the Work of Its Fifty-Sixth Session," UNGAOR, 56th Sess., Supp. No. 10, UN Doc. A/59/10, at 100 (2004), at 103–109.

337 ILC, *Draft Articles on the Responsibility of International Organizations*, at Art. 7. This issue was considered by the European Court of Human Rights in a recent and highly controversial judgment in which it held that the actions of armed forces of States acting under UN Security Council authorization

The ILC Draft Articles on the Responsibility of International Organizations,[338] adopted in 2011 after a decade of controversial and at times convoluted debate,[339] generally reinforce these positions. Critically, they affirm the primacy of the primary rules: irrespective of attribution, international organizations will only be held responsible for breaches of rules to which they themselves are bound. In ascertaining the responsibility of an international organization for migrant smuggling–related harms, it is therefore necessary to first establish which of the relevant primary rules bind that organization. International organizations are generally not bound by most of the rules of particular relevance to migrant smuggling, including human rights, refugee law, and transnational criminal law. However, there are important exceptions, most particularly in the European context. The European Union, for example, has received the legal basis for eventual accession to the European Convention on Human Rights.[340]

in Kosovo were attributable to the UN and not to the States themselves or to NATO (to whom the UN had delegated operational command). The decisive question for the Court was whether "the UNSC [United Nations Security Council] retained *ultimate authority and control* so that operational command only was delegated": *Behrami and Behrami v. France; Saramati v. France, Germany and Norway*, (2007) 45 EHRR 10 (ECHR, May 2, 2007), para. 133 (emphasis added). The ILC Rapporteur Gaja noted at the time that a different conclusion would have been reached had the Court applied then ILC Draft Article 5 (final Article 7), which used the test of "effective control"; he also concluded that "as a matter of policy, the approach taken by the European Court of Human Rights is unconvincing. It would lead to attributing to the United Nations conduct which the organization has not specifically authorized and of which it may have little knowledge or no knowledge at all": G. Gaja, Special Rapporteur, "Seventh Report on Responsibility of International Organizations," UN Doc A/CN.4/610, Mar. 27, 2009, at paras. 26, 30. See further K. M. Larsen, "Attribution of Conduct in Peace Operations: The 'Ultimate Authority and Control' Test" (2008) 19(3) *European Journal of International Law* 509; M. Milanović and T. Papić, "As Bad as It Gets: The European Court of Human Rights' *Behrami and Saramati* Decision and General International Law" (2009) 58 *International and Comparative Law Quarterly* 267; and A. Sari, "Jurisdiction and International Responsibility in Peace Support Operations: The *Behrami* and *Saramati* Cases" (2008) 8 *Human Rights Law Review* 151.

338 The articles define "international organization" as "an organization established by a treaty or other instrument governed by international law and possessing its own international legal personality" (Article 2(a)). Note that the articles also address the responsibility of States for internationally wrongful acts in connection with the conduct of an international organization (Article 1(2)).

339 For a careful and insightful critique of the challenges faced and the limitations of the draft articles, see J. d'Aspremont, "The Articles on the Responsibility of International Organizations: Magnifying the Fissures in the Law of International Responsibility" (2012) 9 *International Organizations Law Review* 15.

340 The European Union's accession to the European Convention on Human Rights is required under Article 6 of the Lisbon Treaty (Treaty of Lisbon amending the Treaty on European Union and the Treaty establishing the European Community, OJ C 306, done Dec. 13, 2007, entered into force Dec. 1, 2009) and foreseen by Article 59 of the Convention as amended by Protocol No. 14 (Protocol No. 14 to the Convention of 4 November 1950 for the Protection of Human Rights and Fundamental Freedoms, ETS 194, amending the control system of the Convention, done May 13, 2004, entered into force June 1, 2010). For a comprehensive examination of the background to this initiative, the key issues, and the legal framework for accession, see X. Groussot, T. Lock, and L. Pech, "EU Accession to

In terms of the secondary rules of responsibility, the Articles reiterate familiar notions of international legal responsibility: first, that responsibility is the consequence of an internationally wrongful act; and second, that responsibility requires the relevant act or omission to be: (1) attributable to the organization, and (2) a breach of an international obligation of that organization in force at the relevant time.[341] Its central position is that every internationally wrongful act of an international organization entails the international legal responsibility of that organization. Substantive provisions of particular significance to the present discussion include the following:

- The conduct of an organ or agent of the organization, performing the functions of the organ or agent, shall be attributable to the organization[342];
- Such conduct shall be attributable even if the organ or agent exceeds their official authority or acts outside instructions provided they are acting in an official capacity and within the overall functions of the organization[343];
- The conduct of an *organ of a State* or an organ or agent of an international organization that is placed at the disposal of another international organization will be attributable to the latter organization if it exercises effective control over that conduct.[344]

A separate chapter of the draft articles deals with responsibility of international organizations in connection with the actions of a State or of another international organization.[345] These generally ascribe responsibility to international organizations for aiding and assisting or coercing a State in the commission of an internationally wrongful act.[346] Finally, another separate part of the draft articles also deals with the responsibility of Member States in connection with the act of an international organization, as discussed previously.

How do these principles of responsibility of international organizations apply in respect of the real-life examples cited earlier in the chapter? The situation of Frontex provides a useful lens through which to briefly examine several issues in connection with attribution of wrongful conduct to international organizations in the context of migrant smuggling. As noted in Chapter 1, Frontex has been designated the principal enforcement mechanism of the European Union's border control regime.

the European Convention on Human Rights: A Legal Assessment of the Draft Accession Agreement of 14th October 2011," (Foundation Robert Schuman, European Issues No. 218, Nov. 7, 2011).

341 ILC, *Draft Articles on the Responsibility of International Organizations*, at Arts. 4, 11.

342 Ibid. at Art. 6.

343 Ibid. at Art. 8.

344 Ibid. at Art. 7 (emphasis added).

345 Chapter IV: Responsibility of an international organization in connection with the act of a State or another international organization.

346 ILC, *Draft Articles on the Responsibility of International Organizations*. at Arts. 14–16.

Pending European Union accession to the European Convention on Human Rights, the matter of relevant primary rules governing Frontex operations remains to be definitively settled. Nevertheless, Frontex's obligation to act within international law, including human rights and refugee law, has been explicitly acknowledged, most recently in a 2010 Decision of the EU Council[347] (subsequently annulled on separate grounds as exceeding the jurisdiction of the Council[348]), and further in an EU Parliamentary Regulation (October 2011).[349] Critically, the question of whether Frontex is itself an international organization, distinct from the European Union and with its own "legal personality" capable of giving rise to responsibility in the first place, is not settled. Its legal basis, including capacity to act, is similarly ambiguous. As noted in Chapter 1, the relevant regulatory framework stresses the Agency's coordination and facilitation function, emphasizing the point that "responsibility for the control and surveillance of external borders lies with the Member States."[350] However, as Baldaccini has noted, "Frontex's mandate and governance structure, and its practice, suggest otherwise."[351] Certainly the 2011 EU Regulation makes clear that there has been a substantial delegation of powers from Member States to the agency. Frontex is in fact vested with authority to make decisions and take substantial initiative[352] – potential indicia of the "effective control" criteria required under

347 Council Decision of 26 April 2010 supplementing the Schengen Borders Code as regards the surveillance of the sea external borders in the context of operational cooperation coordinated by the European Agency for the Management of Operational Cooperation at the External Borders of the Member States of the European Union (2010/252/EU), OJ L 111/20, May 5, 2010.

348 See Chapter 1, note 505.

349 Regulation (EU) No 1168/2011 of the European Parliament and of the Council of 25 October 2011 amending Council Regulation (EC) No 2007/2004 establishing a European Agency for the Management of Operational Cooperation at the External Borders of the Member States of the European Union, OJ L 304/1, Nov. 22, 2011 [EU Regulation 1168/2011].

350 Ibid. at Art. 1(2).

351 A. Baldaccini, "Extraterritorial Border Controls in the EU: The Role of Frontex in Operations at Sea," in B. Ryan and V. Mitsilegas eds., *Extraterritorial Immigration Control: Legal Challenges* 229 (2010), at 230.

352 Revised Article 3 of EU Regulation 1168/2011, for example, dealing with joint operations and pilot projects at the external borders States, in part, that: "1. The Agency shall *evaluate, approve and coordinate proposals for joint operations and pilot projects* made by Member States, including the requests of Member States related to circumstances requiring increased technical and operational assistance, especially in cases of specific and disproportionate pressures. The Agency may itself *initiate and carry out joint operations and pilot projects* in cooperation with the Member States concerned and in agreement with the host Member States. It may also *decide to put its technical equipment at the disposal of Member States* participating in the joint operations or pilot projects … 1a. The Agency *may terminate*, after informing the Member State concerned, joint operations and pilot projects if the conditions to conduct those joint operations or pilot projects are no longer fulfilled… 1b. The Agency shall *constitute a pool of border guards called European Border Guard Teams* … for possible deployment during joint operations and pilot projects referred to in paragraph 1. It *shall decide on the deployment of human resources and technical equipment* in accordance with Articles 3a and 7… 4. The Agency *shall finance or co-finance the joint operations and pilot projects* referred to in paragraph 1, with grants from its budget in accordance with the financial rules applicable to the Agency…" (emphases added).

the ILC Draft Articles (on Responsibility of States for Internationally Wrongful Acts). It would not be difficult to argue that wrongful acts occurring in the course of taking such initiatives or implementing such decisions are indeed attributable to Frontex (or its parent organization), as well as (separately and independently) to any Member States involved in the commission of the wrongful act, under the principles set out in this chapter.

4.7.2. *Legal Responsibilities of Private Persons and Private Entities*

International law is not, of course, just for and about States and the organizations they establish to advance their collective interests. International human rights law, for example, is based on an acceptance of the idea that individuals have legal personality. They are holders of legal entitlements that can, in some cases, be directly enforced against States by those same individuals. International law has also come some way toward recognizing that it is persons, not abstract entities, who break rules and violate rights. The concept of individual criminal liability, first recognized at Nuremburg and more recently institutionalized in international law through the Statute of the International Criminal Court,[353] is perhaps the best example of such recognition. International criminal law unambiguously recognizes that individuals can be held legally responsible for a range of internationally wrongful acts, including war crimes and crimes against humanity.[354] Beyond international criminal law, international responsibility in relation to individuals remains undeveloped.[355] A similar situation exists with respect to armed opposition groups.[356] However, even under international criminal law, the nature of this responsibility and the way in which it may be invoked remains uncertain.

Beyond this narrow field, discussion of the law as it stands too often morphs into discussion of the law as it could or perhaps should be. Corporations, for example, do indeed have certain limited rights and duties under contemporary human rights law in areas such as foreign investment and environmental damage[357] and, in some

[353] Rome Statute of the International Criminal Court, 2187 UNTS 3, done July 17, 1998, entered into force July 1, 2002.

[354] A related example is the requirement that those committing genocide be punished "whether they are constitutionally responsible rulers, public officials or private individuals": Convention on the Prevention and Punishment of the Crime of Genocide, 78 UNTS 227, Dec. 9, 1948, entered into force Jan. 12, 1951, at Art. 4.

[355] Crawford and Olleson, "The Nature and Forms of International Responsibility," at 453.

[356] Members of such groups are of course subject to international criminal responsibility. The group itself may, under certain circumstances, also be held responsible for violations of relevant humanitarian law and human rights norms. See generally A. Clapham, *Human Rights Obligations of Non-State Actors* (2006), at chapter 7.

[357] D. Kinley and J. Tadaki, "From Talk to Walk: The Emergence of Human Rights Responsibilities for Corporations at International Law," (2004) 44 *Virginia Journal of International Law* 931, at 946–947.

cases, are even empowered to enforce their rights against others.[358] The arguments for anything more substantial rest largely on the shifting and unstable sands of soft accountability processes that can only optimistically be characterized as "law." For present purposes, it is apparent that private corporations are not directly liable under international law for breaches of international standards relating to migrant smuggling (for example, harms inflicted on smuggled migrants during forced repatriations). The possibility of invoking international legal responsibility against organized criminal groups involved in migrant smuggling appears to be even more remote. Although sobering, this verdict serves to highlight the value of utilizing and extending existing methods for securing accountability for the actions of non-State entities, for example through criminal actions and civil suits in national courts.

A realistic assessment of the current situation should not operate to lessen the impetus toward expanding the reach of international law to include private actors and to hold such actors accountable for violations. In certain areas of migrant smuggling, as in other areas of international law, the impunity that non-State actors continue to enjoy operates to undermine the effectiveness of international legal regulation and denies justice to many.

4.8. SUMMARY OF KEY PRINCIPLES OF STATE RESPONSIBILITY RELEVANT TO MIGRANT SMUGGLING

The task of the present chapter has been to explore the relationship between migrant smuggling – including State responses to migrant smuggling – and the legal responsibility of States. The analysis set out in the chapter has provided some important insights and a few preliminary conclusions.

First, international legal responsibility requires that the act or omission be attributable to the State. The key principles of attribution are as follows:

- The "official" (even if unauthorized) conduct of a State organ or of a State official who violates established primary rules will be attributable to the State.
- Whether an act or omission of a government official is determined to be "official" or private depends on whether the conduct in question was carried out by persons acting with apparent governmental authority.
- A legislative, executive, or judicial act will most easily be directly attributable to the State because of the inevitably "official" nature of such acts.
- An act of a government plane or ship (such as a coast guard vessel) under the command of an officer commissioned by that State will be attributable to that State.

358 Ibid. at 947.

- Examples of other acts potentially attributable to the State (subject to the requirement set out in the second point above) could include: direct involvement of public officials in migrant smuggling, substantial involvement and/or effective control by public officials or entities over organized criminal groups implicated in migrant smuggling, and corruption of the judicial process through bribery.
- States will generally not be held responsible for the conduct of private entities absent a special circumstance (indicating control and/or approval) linking apparent private behavior to the State itself.

Second, in addition to being attributable to the State, the act or omission must *also* constitute a breach of an international obligation of the State.

- The question of whether there has been a breach of an obligation depends on the content and interpretation of the primary rules.
- In areas of law significant to migrant smuggling, including human rights law, refugee law, and transnational criminal law, the relevant primary obligation may extend beyond negative obligations of noninterference to include positive obligations such as legislative reform, provision of remedies, and protection from non-State interference.
- Breaches of obligation may involve composite acts and omissions, the combined result of which constitutes the breach.
- Breaches of obligation may be attributable to two or more States in circumstances of joint conduct such as joint operations against migrant smuggling.

Third, despite the general rule of non-attribution of private conduct, the primacy of the primary rule means that there will be some circumstances under which the State can be held responsible for violations that relate to situations of migrant smuggling originating in the conduct of private persons or entities.

- In cases where responsibility for the initial act does not fall on the State, responsibility could still be imputed through a concomitant or subsequent failure on the part of the State to prevent, respond to, or remedy abuses committed by private persons or entities. Whether responsibility can be imputed in this way in a particular case will always depend on the content of the relevant primary rule.
- Human rights treaties often impose a general obligation on States to, for example, "respect" and "ensure" the rights identified in that instrument. In such cases, States are required to guarantee rights as opposed to merely refraining from interfering with their enjoyment. This will usually require at least some action on the part of the State Party to prevent and respond to non-State interference with established rights.

- The standard of "due diligence" is becoming the accepted benchmark against which State actions to prevent or respond to violations originating in the acts of third parties are to be judged. An assessment of whether a State has met such a standard will depend, once again, on the content of the original obligation as well as the facts and circumstances of the case.
- States will generally not be able to avoid responsibility for the harmful acts of private persons against smuggled migrants when a State's ability to influence an alternative, more positive outcome (judged against the primary rule) can be established. In such cases, the source of responsibility is not the act itself but the failure of the State to take measures of prevention or response in accordance with the required standard.

Fourth, in certain circumstances, multiple States or entities including international organizations may incur responsibility.

- States that have either jointly undertaken a wrongful act, including by acting through a joint organ, or jointly caused a single injury, will each be jointly and independently responsible for the totality of the injury caused.
- Subject to meeting certain stringent criteria, a State may also incur responsibility through implication in the unlawful act of another State: by giving aid or assistance to, exercising direction and control over, or coercing that State to commit the unlawful act.
- International organizations may incur international legal responsibility for wrongful acts on a similar basis to States: if the relevant act or omission is (i) attributable to the organization; and (ii) a breach of an international obligation of that organization in force at the relevant time.
- In respect of the wrongful acts of international organizations, it is important to recall that attribution to and the responsibility of an international organization will not automatically exclude separate responsibility on the part of any Member State involved in carrying out the act in question.

Fifth, a finding of State responsibility carries with it certain consequences. International law dictates consequences for breach and invocation of responsibility. These apply in all cases to the extent they have not been displaced by a regime created under a specific system or treaty.

- The immediate and automatic consequence of a finding of responsibility is an obligation of cessation. The second, automatic obligation on the offending State is to make full reparation for injury caused by the internationally wrongful act.
- International law recognizes a range of elements within the concept of reparations, namely restitution, compensation, and satisfaction. Sub-elements of

these categories, particularly appropriate for responding to human rights violations, include rehabilitation and guarantees of non-repetition.

- International law generally recognizes only the right of an "injured" State to invoke responsibility on its own account. However, direct injury is not always an essential precondition to launching a claim, especially in relation to collective obligations owed to a group of States or to the international community as a whole.
- In cases where joint responsibility is borne by multiple States, the injured State is entitled to claim for the entirety of its injury against any of the responsible States.
- Rules governing invocation of responsibility for violations of international human rights law differ significantly from those that apply to breaches of international law more generally. In both treaty law and custom, there is usually no damage requirement and no requirement for a connection of nationality between the "victim" and the invoking State. Most of the major human rights treaties have developed their own invocation procedures, which, in at least several cases, provide for the possibility of individuals alleging violations of human rights and seeking reparation.

Writing about State responsibility almost half a century ago, García-Amador described it as "[o]ne of the most vast and complex [areas] of international law – it would be difficult to find a topic beset with greater confusion and uncertainty."[359] Although the finalization of the International Law Commission's work has gone some way toward improving this situation, it remains true that these abstract rules of uneven authority are, as noted in the introduction to this book, "devilishly difficult to apply."[360] It is unsurprising that State responsibility remains an area where angels (and international lawyers) fear to tread. The challenges must, however, be faced head-on. State responsibility (and increasingly, responsibility of international organizations) is the heart and soul of international law. Without these secondary rules, the substance and impact of the primary rules would be lost. The inverse is also true. The task of determining responsibility and its consequences in a specific situation can only be undertaken with reference to the primary rules, which are, after all, the original source of obligation. The practical implications of this relationship between the primary rules relating to migrant smuggling and those governing responsibility for their breach are explored in detail in the following chapters.

[359] F. V. García-Amador, "First Report on International Responsibility," UN Doc. A/CN.4/SER.A/1956/Add.1, reprinted in *Yearbook of the International Law Commission*, vol. II (1956) 173, at 175, cited in Allott, "State Responsibility and the Unmaking of International Law," at 4.

[360] Caron, "The ILC Articles on State Responsibility: The Paradoxical Relationship between Form and Authority," at 872.

PART II

Specific Rules and Obligations

5

Criminalization of Migrant Smuggling

Although States have long applied administrative sanctions to unauthorized border crossings, the establishment of a web of standardized criminal offenses to the specific practice of facilitating another person's unauthorized migration for profit is a very recent innovation. As noted in the introduction to this book, the increased focus on criminalization of irregular migration generally – and migrant smuggling in particular – has generated very different responses, hailed by some as a success of State cooperation over organized criminal groups, and by others as a dangerous development for migrants and their rights. The resulting tension, a thread that runs throughout the book, is particularly relevant to the substance of the present chapter. It is against this complex background that the international legal obligations of criminalization with respect to migrant smuggling set out in the chapter should be considered.

It is important to acknowledge at the outset that the sources of direct legal obligation in this area are narrow and highly specific: at the international level resting on the Organized Crime Convention[1] and the Migrant Smuggling Protocol,[2] and at the regional level, on a single European Union Directive[3] and accompanying Framework Decision.[4] Customary international law does not recognize any criminalization-related obligations with regard to migrant smuggling. Accordingly, although other aspects of the legal framework discussed in previous chapters may

1 United Nations Convention against Transnational Organized Crime, 2225 UNTS 209, done Nov. 15, 2000, entered into force Sept. 29, 2003 [Organized Crime Convention].

2 Protocol against the Smuggling of Migrants by Land, Sea and Air, supplementing the United Nations Convention against Transnational Organized Crime, 2241 UNTS 507, done Nov. 15, 2000, entered into force Jan. 28, 2004 [Migrant Smuggling Protocol].

3 Council Directive 2002/90/EC of 28 November 2002 defining the facilitation of unauthorised entry, transit and residence, OJ L 328/17, Dec. 5, 2002 [Council Directive 2002/90/EC].

4 Council Framework Decision of 28 November 2002 on the strengthening of the penal framework to prevent the facilitation of unauthorised entry, transit and residence, (2002/946/JHA), OJ L 328/1, Dec. 5, 2002 [Council Framework Decision 2002/946].

well apply, it would be very difficult to argue that States not party to those treaties are under any legal compulsion to enact legislation criminalizing migrant smuggling or related conduct. However, the absence of a customary obligation is not relevant for most States: the Organized Crime Convention and Migrant Smuggling Protocol have both been widely ratified,[5] and, with limited exceptions, the relevant European instruments bind all EU Member States.

The present chapter focuses on analyzing the scope and substantive content of the criminalization provisions of the directly relevant treaties, drawing on other instruments and sources of obligation where relevant. It commences with a detailed examination of the criminalization obligations of the Migrant Smuggling Protocol, identifying both the conduct to be criminalized and the elements of the offense. Equally important is the conduct that *may not* be criminalized. The requirement that the Protocol not be used to criminalize migrants for the fact of having been smuggled is subject to separate and detailed examination. Although the act of "migrant smuggling" is a central focus of the Protocol, the obligation of criminalization extends to related offenses including document fraud, enabling illegal residence, and "aggravated migrant smuggling." The elements and implications of each of these offenses are also considered. As explained in Chapter 1, the Organized Crime Convention sets out a number of criminalization obligations that apply to migrant smuggling while also establishing the rules around jurisdiction, penalties, and the treatment of witnesses. Each of these aspects is examined in detail. The chapter then turns to obligations of criminalization that have been developed within the European system. It concludes with a note on the rights of suspects and the right to a fair trial: matters that are not dealt with in the key specialist instruments but that nevertheless comprise an important part of the relevant legal framework.

5.1. CRIMINALIZATION OBLIGATIONS UNDER THE MIGRANT SMUGGLING PROTOCOL

The Migrant Smuggling Protocol is one component of a broader prohibition regime that has developed around transnational organized crime. Similar prohibition regimes exist in relation to matters such as slavery, terrorism, and the global drug trade, principally with the intention of standardizing cooperation among governments with the goal of minimizing or eliminating safe havens "from which certain crimes can be committed and to which criminals can flee to escape prosecution and punishment."[6] Some commentators have questioned

[5] 179 and 138 States respectively as at Oct. 2013.

[6] E. A. Nadelmann, "Global Prohibition Regimes: The Evolution of Norms in International Society" (1990) 44(4) *International Organization* 479, at 481.

the appropriateness of establishing a "*transnational* duty to criminalize simple smuggling," noting that smuggling is "more of an affront to particularized sovereign interests than a threat to the general well being."[7] However, this description of the obligation to criminalize migrant smuggling misstates the nature of transnational crime control regimes. Such regimes do not create individual penal responsibility or indeed, any particular "duty" under international law. Rather, crime suppression conventions such as the Organized Crime Convention and Migrant Smuggling Protocol, treaties entered into on the basis of consent, "impose obligations on State Parties to enact and enforce certain municipal offenses."[8] The source of the obligation is international but the enforcement is undertaken at the national level through domestic law.

A fundamental purpose of the Migrant Smuggling Protocol is to promote closer alignment of national laws on migrant smuggling. It seeks to achieve this through providing common definitions of key terms, such as "smuggling of migrants" and "illegal entry," and by requiring States Parties to enact and enforce, in their own legal systems, laws that criminalize certain specified conduct. As noted in the Legislative Guide to the Protocol:

> [...] the criminalization requirements are central both to the Protocol and the Convention, serving not only to provide for the deterrence and punishment of the smuggling of migrants, but as the basis for the numerous forms of prevention, international cooperation, technical assistance and other measures set out in the instruments.[9]

The facilitation of international cooperation is another important purpose of the Protocol. States that implement their criminalization obligations in national law will readily meet the dual criminality requirements that arise under various international cooperation regimes, including for mutual legal assistance, extradition, and recovery of the proceeds of crime. Note that this aspect of the international legal framework is considered in detail in Chapter 7.

[7] J. C. Hathaway, "The Human Rights Quagmire of 'Human Trafficking'" (2008) 49(1) *Virginia Journal of International Law* 1, at 6 (emphasis in original), asserting at 5 that "most smuggling has historically been a consensual and relatively benign market-based response" to immigration laws. "Importantly, the Smuggling Protocol – unlike the Trafficking Protocol – does not limit the duty to criminalize to forms of dealing likely to lead to exploitation": ibid. at 27.

[8] N. Boister, "Transnational Criminal Law?" (2003) 14 *European Journal of International Law* 953, at 962. For a detailed analysis of the structure and function of transnational criminal law see N. Boister, *An Introduction to Transnational Criminal Law* (2012), esp. at Part A.

[9] United Nations Office on Drugs and Crime, Legislative Guides for the Implementation of the United Nations Convention against Transnational Organized Crime and the Protocols thereto, UN Sales No. E.05.V.2 (2004) [*Legislative Guide*], at 349 (para. 55).

5.1.1. *Conduct to be Criminalized and Key Aspects of the Criminalization Obligation*

The Migrant Smuggling Protocol requires States Parties to criminalize a range of conduct, each part of which is related to the central concept of "smuggling of migrants." The key operative provision in this regard is Article 6 of the Protocol, which provides that States Parties "shall adopt such legislative and other measures as may be necessary to establish as criminal offences, when committed intentionally and in order to obtain directly or indirectly a financial or material benefit," the following conduct:

- smuggling of migrants (Article 6(1)(a));
- producing, procuring, providing, or possessing fraudulent travel or identity documents when done for the purpose of enabling smuggling of migrants (Article 6(1)(b));
- enabling a person who is not a national or a permanent resident to remain in the State concerned without complying with the necessary requirements for legally remaining in the State, and by using illegal means (Article 6(1)(c));
- organizing or directing any of the above crimes (Article 6(2)(c));
- attempting to commit any of the above offenses, subject to the basic concepts of the State Party's legal system (Article 6(2)(a));
- participating as an accomplice in any of the above offenses, subject to the basic concepts of the State Party's legal system (Article 6(2)(b)); and
- aggravated forms of the above offenses, involving conduct that endangers or is likely to endanger the lives or safety of the migrants concerned, or that entails inhuman or degrading treatment, including for exploitation of such migrants (Article 6(3)).

As explained in Chapter 1, the legal framework around migrant smuggling comprises rules of varying strength.[10] It is relevant to note that Article 6 uses the language of "shall." Accordingly, States Parties to the Protocol are *required* to establish as criminal offenses the specific conduct nominated in that article, when committed intentionally and in order to obtain, directly or indirectly, a financial or other material benefit.

5.1.1.1. No Criminalization of Migrants

The requirement to criminalize migrant smuggling and related conduct established under Article 6 must be considered alongside the operation of Article 5, which

[10] See Chapter 1, at Section 1.4.3.

provides that migrants shall not become liable to criminal prosecution under the Protocol for the fact of having been the object of conduct set forth in Article 6. The clear intention was to ensure that any offense provisions developed to give effect to the Protocol aim to target migrant *smugglers*, and not persons being smuggled. This is confirmed by the Legislative Guide:

> [It was] the intention of the drafters that the sanctions established in accordance with the Protocol should apply to the smuggling of migrants by organized criminal groups and not to mere migration or migrants, even in cases where it involves entry or residence that is illegal under the laws of the State concerned ... Mere illegal entry may be a crime in some countries, but it is not recognized as a form of organized crime and is hence beyond the scope of the Convention and its Protocols. Procuring the illegal entry or illegal residence of migrants by an organized criminal group (a term that includes an element of financial or other material benefit), on the other hand, has been recognized as a serious form of transnational organized crime and is therefore the primary focus of the Protocol.[11]

In relation to offenses created in accordance with the Migrant Smuggling Protocol, States Parties are accordingly required to ensure that migrants are not liable to criminal prosecution for these offenses, provided that their only involvement was being the "object" of the smuggling process. This provision does not operate to completely shield smuggled migrants from prosecution: in particular, States are not prevented from prosecuting smuggled migrants for the full range of non–smuggling related criminal offences. Also, if a smuggled migrant otherwise meets the elements of a Protocol offense (for example, by facilitating the illegal entry of other smuggled migrants as well as themselves for profit), then nothing in the Protocol prevents their prosecution by a State Party.

5.1.1.2. Preservation of National Immigration Laws

Article 5 must, in turn, be reconciled with the operation of Article 6(4), which provides that "Nothing in this Protocol shall prevent a State Party from taking measures against a person whose conduct constitutes an offence under its domestic law." Although Article 6(4) preserves the right of States to implement domestic criminal laws generally, criminal laws related to migration are likely to be most relevant. The interaction between Articles 5 and 6(4) is described in the Legislative Guide as follows:

> Generally, the purpose of the Protocol is to prevent and combat the smuggling of migrants as a form of transnational organized crime, while at the same time not

[11] *Legislative Guide*, at 340 (para. 28).

> criminalizing mere migration, even if illegal under other elements of national law. This is reflected both in article 5 and article 6, paragraph 4, as noted above, and in the fact that the offences that might otherwise be applicable to mere migrants, and especially the document-related offenses established by article 6, paragraph 1(b), have been formulated to reduce or eliminate such application. Thus, for example, a migrant caught in possession of a fraudulent document would not generally fall within domestic offences adopted pursuant to paragraph 1(b), whereas a smuggler who possessed the same document for the purpose of enabling the smuggling of others would be within the same offense.[12]

Although this explanation provides some insight it does not fully address the reality that, through Article 6(4), States have carefully preserved their right to enact national laws criminalizing migration-related offenses. In other words, there is nothing in the Protocol to prevent States Parties from enacting or retaining national laws that, for example, criminalize illegal entry or residence, including by the migrants themselves. Similarly, States may enact laws criminalizing the possession of fraudulent travel documents and apply those laws to smuggled migrants. However, offenses of this nature are outside of the scope of the Protocol and also outside the scope of the Organized Crime Convention. Accordingly, their enactment could never be justified under the terms of the Protocol and States Parties do not owe each other any obligation to cooperate in suppressing such offenses. Similarly, the international cooperation provisions of the Organized Crime Convention would not be activated by a request relating to mere illegal entry, as, absent other factors, such conduct would not fall within the definition of offenses established in accordance with the Convention.[13]

5.1.1.3. Preservation of Human Rights and Refugee Law

The requirement to criminalize migrant smuggling must also be considered alongside Article 19 of the Protocol, which operates to preserve both international human rights and refugee law, specifically referencing the obligation of *non-refoulement*. As noted at various points in this book, asylum-seekers and refugees are frequently required to use the services of smugglers to flee persecution, serious human rights violations, and conflict. Article 19 operates to affirm that asylum claims should not be jeopardized by the fact of the claimant having been smuggled. In this regard reference should be made to Article 31(1) of the 1951 Convention relating to the Status

[12] Ibid. at 349 (para. 54).

[13] See further Migrant Smuggling Protocol, Article 1(3), read with Articles 16(1) and 18(1) of the Organized Crime Convention.

of Refugees[14] (Refugee Convention), which provides that refugees should not be penalized for illegal entry or presence, provided such persons are "coming directly from a territory where their life or freedom was threatened" and "provided they present themselves without delay to the authorities and show good cause for their illegal entry or presence."

Of course, this protection operates to the benefit of the refugee, not the smuggler (assuming the smuggler is not a refugee). In addition, the fact that the smuggled migrant may be a refugee in no way impacts on the smuggler's liability, assuming the smuggling has involved financial or material benefit to the smuggler. There are situations where smugglers deliberately abuse or misuse the asylum process (for example, by lodging fraudulent asylum claims) as part of their modus operandi of enabling illegal entry, transit, or residence. The smugglers in this situation are not protected by Article 31 of the Refugee Convention, and their actions would likely fall within the scope of the Migrant Smuggling Protocol (for example, procuring or providing a fraudulently obtained travel document to enable illegal entry or residence).[15] Note that the non-penalization provision of the Refugee Convention is subject to separate and detailed analysis in Chapter 2, at Section 2.3.2.

5.1.1.4. Offenses to be Transnational and Involve an Organized Criminal Group

The obligation to criminalize the conduct specified in Article 6 of the Protocol should be read in conjunction with Article 34(2) of the Organized Crime Convention, which in essence provides that all substantive offenses under the Convention (specifically, those relating to participation in an organized criminal group, money laundering offenses, corruption offenses, and obstruction of justice) are to be established in the domestic law of each State Party "independently of the transnational nature or the involvement of an organized criminal group."[16] There is no specific provision in either the Convention or the Protocol to extend the application of this provision to other offenses created under the Protocol such as migrant smuggling and enabling illegal residence. This potentially supports an argument[17] that Article 4 of

[14] Convention Relating to the Status of Refugees, 189 UNTS 137, done July 28, 1951, entered into force Apr. 22, 1954, as amended by the Protocol Relating to the Status of Refugees, 606 UNTS 267, done Jan. 31, 1967, entered into force Oct. 4, 1967 [Refugee Convention].

[15] See Chapter 2, at Section 2.3.3 (esp. note 198).

[16] Further on the scope of the Convention including the definitions of "organized criminal group," "serious crime," and "transnational offense," see Chapter 1, at notes 92–94.

[17] See T. Obokata, "The Legal Framework Concerning the Smuggling of Migrants at Sea under the UN Protocol on the Smuggling of Migrants by Land, Sea and Air," in B. Ryan and M. Mitsilegas eds., *Extraterritorial Migration Control: Legal Challenges* 151 (2010), at 153. ("smuggling facilitated by friends or relatives, or by agents who are not part of an organized criminal group, are excluded

the Migrant Smuggling Protocol, which explicitly affirms its scope of application as being "prevention, investigation and prosecution of [migrant smuggling offenses] *where the offences are transnational in nature and involve an organized criminal group*,"[18] does *not* require States Parties to establish the relevant offenses in their national law "independently of the transnational nature or the involvement of an organized criminal group."[19]

This interpretation presents some problems, particularly when considered against the object and purpose of the Protocol. Certainly the intention of the drafters was to focus on migrant smuggling undertaken by organized criminal groups, to the exclusion of those operating for reasons such as family reunification or humanitarian reasons.[20] However it is certainly conceivable that smuggling of the kind intended to be covered by the Protocol, involving serious criminality, could indeed be perpetrated by one person acting alone. In addition, although it is clear that smuggling offenses themselves will necessarily have a transnational element, this is not always the case for certain other offenses established under the Protocol such as enabling illegal residence and producing fraudulent travel or identity documents for purposes of enabling smuggling. A requirement that States Parties incorporate transnationality as an element of such offenses could present a significant obstruction to anti-smuggling efforts. It is this reasoning that appears to underlie the position of the Legislative Guide on the matter.[21] The Guide does not address the ambiguities in Article 34(2). Rather it emphatically asserts that:

> while States parties should have to establish some degree of transnationality and organized crime with respect to most aspects of the Protocol, their prosecutors should not have to prove either element in order to obtain a conviction for smuggling of migrants or any other offence established in accordance with the Convention or

from the current legal framework"). For reasons set out later in the chapter it is submitted that the first part of this assertion is incorrect. With respect to family and friends, the statement is also incorrect. As explained at Section 5.1.2 the critical factor is not the relationship between the smuggler and the smuggled but whether the facilitated movement was for purposes of financial or material gain.

[18] Emphasis added. See also the Preamble to the Protocol, which expresses concern about "the significant increase in the activities of organized criminal groups in smuggling of migrants."

[19] Organized Crime Convention, at Art. 34(2).

[20] Absent a requirement of the involvement of an organized criminal group, it is possible that at least some "humanitarian" smugglers would come within national laws on migrant smuggling. For example, an uncle who procures the illegal entry of his nephew so that he can come and work in the uncle's shop – giving the uncle access to unpaid labor – would appear to meet the definition of migrant smuggling. The uncle has procured the illegal entry of another person who is not a national, and he did this for his own financial benefit. Given the breadth of the definition of "organized criminal group," including this as an element of migrant smuggling is not a complete guarantee of excluding "humanitarian smugglers," but it would certainly more clearly exclude some.

[21] See *Legislative Guide*, at 333 (para. 20).

5.1.3. *Criminalization of Offenses Related to Migrant Smuggling*

The Migrant Smuggling Protocol requires States Parties to criminalize a range of conduct that both supports and is integral to the smuggling process. These offenses are considered in the next subsections.

5.1.3.1. Document Offenses

Although some migrant smuggling is perpetrated through clandestine border crossings that obviate the need for documentation, many smuggled migrants enter the destination country through the use of fraudulent travel and identity documents. The term "fraudulent," when used in this context, includes "legitimate" documents that were acquired through fraudulent or other illegal means such as theft, as well as altered and entirely fabricated documents. Research has uncovered a vast range of services attached to the production and utilization of fraudulent travel and identity documents, ranging from simple theft and sale of passports to travel schemes that involve falsifying entire corporate records, in order to allow the record holders to enter other countries on fraudulently obtained business visas.[33] The United Nations has reported that many document services attached to migrant smuggling are beyond the scope of individual operators, requiring the capital and levels of organization that are typical of large and highly organized criminal groups.[34] It has been further noted that a substantial portion of identity-related crime is associated with migrant smuggling offenses.[35]

States Parties to the Protocol are required to criminalize the acts of producing, procuring, providing, or possessing a fraudulent travel or identity document, when committed for the purpose of enabling smuggling of migrants.[36] In common with other Article 6 offenses, the document offenses are intended to operate with a focus on the smugglers, not the smuggled migrants. This is brought out in the elements of the offense (Table 5.2).

The physical element required by Article 6(1)(b)(i) concerns the *production* of a fraudulent travel or identity document, and those required by Article 6(1)(b)(ii) concern the *procurement, provision, or possession* of such a document. As noted in the

[33] For a review of the market as it exists in Asia, see United Nations Office on Drugs and Crime, *Migrant Smuggling in Asia: A Thematic Review of Literature* (2012) [UNODC, *Migrant Smuggling in Asia*].

[34] Conference of the Parties to the United Nations Convention against Transnational Organized Crime, "Criminalization within the scope of the United Nations Convention against Transnational Organized Crime and the Protocols thereto: Note by the Secretariat," UN Doc. CTOC/COP/2008/4, Sept. 9, 2008, at 4.

[35] Ibid.

[36] Migrant Smuggling Protocol, at Art. 6(1)(b).

TABLE 5.2 *Elements of the document offenses in Article 6(1)(b) of the Migrant Smuggling Protocol*

	Physical element	Corresponding fault element
(1)	Produce a fraudulent travel or identity document (conduct).	a) Conduct must be intentional (voluntarily, through willed conduct); b) Conduct must be undertaken for the purpose of enabling smuggling of migrants; and c) Conduct must be done in order to obtain financial or other material benefit.
(2)	Procure, provide, or possess a fraudulent travel or identity document (conduct).	a) Conduct must be undertaken for the purpose of enabling smuggling of migrants; b) Conduct must be intentional (voluntarily, through willed conduct); and c) Conduct must be done in order to obtain financial or other material benefit.

Legislative Guide, there are in fact three fault elements that attach to the physical conduct in each of these offenses:

> ... [T]here must have been the intention to produce, procure, provide or possess the document, with the added intention or purpose of obtaining a financial or other material benefit. In the case of the document offenses, however, there must also have been the intention or purpose of enabling the smuggling of migrants. This is an additional safeguard against criminalizing those who smuggle themselves...[37]

The three fault elements that are required for the offense of production of fraudulent travel or identity documents are therefore: (1) that the conduct is undertaken intentionally (i.e., voluntarily and through willed conduct), (2) that the conduct is undertaken for the purpose of enabling the smuggling of migrants, and (3) that the conduct is undertaken in order to obtain a financial or other material benefit. The drafting history of the Protocol confirms the conclusion of the Legislative Guide that the three fault elements were intended to exclude situations where migrants themselves were found in possession of fraudulent travel or identity documents, in circumstances where the document was for their own personal use.[38] Of course, this protection is not unlimited. For example, a smuggled migrant may be found in possession of 300 passports, one of which he or she intended for personal use and the

[37] *Legislative Guide*, at 344 (para. 41).

[38] The relevant Interpretative Note stipulates that Article 6(1)(b) "... was adopted on the understanding that subparagraph (ii) would only apply when the possession in question was for the purpose of smuggling migrants as set forth in subparagraph *(a)*. Thus, a migrant who possessed a fraudulent document to enable his or her own smuggling would not be included": Travaux Préparatoires *for the Organized Crime Convention and Protocols*, at 489.

TABLE 5.3 *Elements of the offense of enabling illegal residence in Article 6(1)(c) of the Migrant Smuggling Protocol*

	Physical element	Corresponding fault element
(1)	Enabling a person to remain in a State without complying with the necessary requirements for legally remaining in the State (result).	a) Intentional (voluntary, willed act); b) In order to obtain, directly or indirectly, a financial or other material benefit.
(2)	The person is not a national or permanent resident (circumstance).	No fault element required.
(3)	By means of producing, procuring, providing, or possessing a fraudulent travel or identity document, or any other illegal means (conduct).	a) Intentional (voluntary, willed act); b) In order to obtain, directly or indirectly, a financial or other material benefit.

clearly compromise the overall efficacy of the Protocol as a tool to combat migrant smuggling.

States Parties to the Protocol are required to criminalize attempting to commit smuggling of migrants, document offenses, and enabling illegal residence.[47] This obligation of States Parties is expressed as being "[s]ubject to the basic concepts of its legal system,"[48] an acknowledgment that not all legal systems recognize the concept of attempting to commit a criminal act. The Legislative Guide explains further:

> Of those States that do criminalize attempts, most require that some fairly substantial course of conduct be established before there can be a conviction. In some cases one or more positive acts must be established, while in others prosecutors must establish that the accused has done everything possible to complete the offence, which failed for other reasons. The fact that the offence subsequently turns out to have been impossible (e.g. cases where the person being smuggled was deceased, non-existent or a law enforcement officer) is generally not considered a defence in cases of attempt.[49]

The Interpretative Notes attached to this provision affirm that references to attempts are "understood in some countries to include both acts perpetrated in preparation for a criminal offence and those carried out in an unsuccessful attempt to commit the offence."[50] Both forms of "attempt" would thereby be covered by the Protocol to the extent they are reflected in the national legal system.

the Gulf of Aden (2008), at 4. See also the discussion of the *Golden Venture* in the Introduction, and notes 51 and 52 below.

47 Migrant Smuggling Protocol, at Art. 6(2)(a).

48 Ibid.

49 *Legislative Guide*, at 347 (para. 51).

50 Travaux Préparatoires *for the Organized Crime Convention and Protocols*, at 489.

In some legal systems, attempts attract the same penalty as the completed offense. However, in other systems, it is usual for attempts to attract a lower penalty than the completed offense. It is important to consider the practical results of these traditions, in light of the modern modus operandi of smuggling:

> For example, in many contexts, a strong coastguard presence will mean that smuggled migrants seeking to illegally enter a country by sea are rarely successful in achieving that illegal entry. Rather, the modus operandi of the smugglers is to take the migrants within sight of land and then dump the migrants into the sea knowing (or hoping) that they will be able to swim to shore or be rescued by the coastguard. Accordingly, the coastguard will seek to proactively intervene in these situations to avoid loss of human life.[51]

A related example involves smugglers disabling their vessel in order to encourage coastal States to rescue stranded passengers.[52] It would run counter to the purpose of the Protocol if migrant smugglers, in this scenario, were able to avoid the most serious penalties by claiming they had merely *attempted* smuggling, rather than *succeeded* in completing the offense. There is nothing in the Protocol that requires States to differentiate between attempts and completed conduct. Instead, States are simply required to ensure that attempts are criminalized along with completed conduct. Given the potential for situations such as the ones described earlier in this paragraph, there may be practical benefits from a law enforcement and prosecution perspective to covering the entire smuggling process (from preparation, to attempt, to completed conduct) under one offense provision that allows for discretion in sentencing. This would also avoid the gaps that may follow efforts to break the smuggling process down into each and every one of its component parts.

5.1.3.4. Accomplices, and Organizing or Directing

The migrant smuggling process can involve multiple offenders, each of whom plays a different but interrelated role. For example, in the context of organized smuggling of Chinese migrants to the United States, Zhang and Chin have noted that migrant smuggling is typically perpetrated not by an organized hierarchy of offenders, but by a network of individuals, each of whom has his or her own contacts and networks.[53]

51 UNODC Model Law on Migrant Smuggling, at 29.

52 See, for example, the discussion of the prosecutions of Mohamed Tanir and Beny in relation to the sabotage of SIEV (Suspected Illegal Entry Vessel) 36 in Australian waters in 2009, in A. Schloenhardt and C. Martin, "Prosecution and Punishment of People Smugglers in Australia 2008–2011" (2012) 40 *Federal Law Review* 111, [Schloenhardt and Martin, "Prosecution and Punishment of People Smugglers in Australia 2008–2011"], at 117–118.

53 S. X. Zhang and K. Chin, *Characteristics of Chinese Human Smugglers* (US Department of Justice, Office of Justice Programs, National Institute of Justice, 2004), cited in UNODC, *Migrant Smuggling in Asia*, at 48–49.

Similarly, in the West African context, smuggled migrants may rely on any number of service providers along their route, including transport touts, professional transporters, and higher-level brokers.[54] Although the level of complicity of each involved person is likely very different, all play a critical role in the final result that is the smuggling process and, very often, the exploitation of the smuggled migrant.

States Parties are required to criminalize participating as an accomplice to the three main offenses established by the Protocol: smuggling of migrants; producing a fraudulent travel or identity document for the purpose of enabling smuggling of migrants; and enabling illegal residence.[55] States Parties are also required to criminalize participating as an accomplice in procuring, providing, or possessing a fraudulent travel or identity document for the purpose of enabling the smuggling of migrants.[56] However, this latter obligation is expressed as being subject to the basic concepts of the State's legal system. The Legislative Guide explains that this approach sought to address concerns about the potentially broad reach of these offenses, including

> ... concerns in some systems about overly broad legislation and whether one could be made an accomplice to offences such as possession. There were also concerns about viability in view of some of the defined meanings of "fraudulent document" and whether one could, for example, be an accomplice to the possession of a document that only becomes a "fraudulent document" when actually used by a person to whom it was not issued ...[57]

The existence of varying levels of culpability among persons involved in migrant smuggling is clear. For example, the person who receives direct and substantial financial rewards through sending multiple boatloads of smuggled migrants from Indonesia to Australia is unlikely to be one of those who crews the boat and is arrested on or before arrival.[58] This reality underscores the importance of ensuring

54 United Nations Office on Drugs and Crime, The Role of Organized Crime in the Smuggling of Migrants from West Africa to the European Union (2011), at 33.

55 Migrant Smuggling Protocol, at Art. 6(2)(b).

56 Ibid.

57 *Legislative Guide*, at 348 (para. 52).

58 This is underscored by the fact that in the context of smuggling by sea from Indonesia to Australia, poor fisherman, often children, are recruited to crew the boats for these dangerous journeys. "Between 1 September 2008 and 22 November 2011, 180 young Indonesians who said that they were children arrived in Australia, having worked as crew on boats bringing asylum seekers to Australia": Australian Human Rights Commission, *An Age of Uncertainty: Inquiry into the Treatment of Individuals Suspected of People Smuggling Offences Who Say That They Are Children* (July 2012), [Australian Human Rights Commission, *An Age of Uncertainty*], at 18. For a comprehensive analysis of migrant smuggling prosecutions in Australian between 2008 and 2011, see Schloenhardt and Martin, "Prosecution and Punishment of People Smugglers in Australia 2008–2011". See also *John Curtis v. Mohamad Sidik and Koa Najar* [1999] NTSC 135 (Supreme Court of the Northern Territory, Australia, Dec. 6, 1999), in which the Court noted that the proper response to the use of children on vessels was not to punish the children, but to more severely punish those responsible for putting the children in this situation (at para. 24).

TABLE 5.4 *Elements of the offenses in Article 6(2) of the Migrant Smuggling Protocol*

Physical element	Corresponding fault element
Attempt (smuggling of migrants, document offenses, enabling illegal residence).	None specified. As per primary offense.
Participate as an accomplice (smuggling of migrants, document offenses, enabling illegal residence).	None specified. As per primary offense.
Organize or direct (smuggling of migrants, document offenses, enabling illegal residence).	None specified. As per primary offense.

that criminal laws cover organizers, including those who seek to direct criminal conduct from a safe distance. Article 6(2) of the Protocol requires States to criminalize organizing or directing other persons to engage in the three main offenses established by that instrument: smuggling of migrants; producing, procuring, providing, or possessing a fraudulent travel or identity document for the purpose of enabling smuggling of migrants; and enabling illegal residence.[59] It is important to note that some of the requirements in Article 6(2) operate in parallel with other criminalization requirements that exist under the Convention.[60] For example, there may be an overlap between the requirement to criminalize organizing or directing others to engage in smuggling-related crimes, and the requirement under Article 5 of the Convention to criminalize participation in an organized criminal group. Further, as a practical matter, the requirements under Article 6 of the Convention to criminalize money laundering and under Article 8 of the Convention to criminalize corruption may pick up many situations where criminals are effectively acting as accomplices to migrant smuggling activities.

The elements of the offenses required by Article 6(2) are drawn primarily from the offenses themselves (smuggling of migrants, document offenses, enabling illegal residence), with the additional requirement of a physical element of conduct demonstrating attempt, participating as an accomplice, or organizing or directing one of these offenses. Article 6(2) does not require that any particular fault element be attached to this conduct. Accordingly, the fault element would be as required by the primary offenses themselves (smuggling of migrants, document offenses, enabling illegal residence) (Table 5.4).

5.1.4. *Circumstances of Aggravation*

Article 6 of the Protocol introduces the concept of aggravated offenses. Broadly speaking, States Parties are required to ensure that smuggling offenses that involve

[59] Migrant Smuggling Protocol, at Art. 6(2)(c).
[60] *Legislative Guide*, at 344 (para. 41).

danger to the lives of migrants or that entail degrading treatment or exploitation attract higher penalties. The scope and substantive content of this obligation is examined below in the next subsections.

5.1.4.1. Obligation to Establish Aggravated Offenses

States Parties to the Protocol are required to ensure that when the primary offenses (smuggling of migrants, producing a fraudulent travel document, or enabling illegal residence) occur in circumstances that either endanger, or are likely to endanger, the lives or safety of the migrants concerned, or that entail inhuman or degrading treatment, including for exploitation of such migrants, this will constitute a circumstance of aggravation for sentencing purposes.[61] The requirement to establish equivalent circumstances of aggravation for participating as an accomplice, and organizing or directing one of the primary offenses, operates subject to the basic concepts of States Parties' legal systems.[62] The manner in which States Parties are to meet this obligation is not specified in the Protocol. States could simply specify that these circumstances constitute circumstances of aggravation for the primary offenses, or they could operate as separate, distinct offenses attracting a higher penalty than the primary offenses (Table 5.5).

5.1.4.2. Meaning of "Inhuman or Degrading Treatment, Including for Exploitation"

The reference to circumstances that endanger, or are likely to endanger, the lives or safety of the migrants concerned, is self-explanatory. It might involve, for example, situations where migrant smuggling involves transporting migrants hidden in shipping containers, or in other confined and dangerous situations without adequate ventilation, food, or water. As discussed in the Introduction, such practices are a common feature of many migrant smuggling situations. The transportation of smuggled migrants across inhospitable terrain or in vessels that are inadequately equipped for the journey are additional, common examples of smuggling practices that inevitably endanger lives and safety.

The reference to circumstances that entail "inhuman or degrading treatment, including for exploitation," requires more careful consideration. The Universal Declaration of Human Rights proclaims that "[n]o one shall be subjected to torture

61 Migrant Smuggling Protocol, at Art. 6(3).

62 Ibid.

TABLE 5.5 *Elements of the requirements in Article 6(3) of the Migrant Smuggling Protocol*

Physical element	Corresponding fault element
(Smuggling of migrants, producing a fraudulent travel document, or enabling illegal residence) in circumstances that endanger, or are likely to endanger, the lives or safety of the migrants concerned.	None specified. As per primary offense.
(Smuggling of migrants, producing a fraudulent travel document, or enabling illegal residence) in circumstances that entail inhuman or degrading treatment, including for exploitation of such migrants.	None specified. As per primary offense.
Participating as an accomplice to (smuggling of migrants, producing a fraudulent travel document, or enabling illegal residence) in circumstances that endanger, or are likely to endanger, the lives or safety of the migrants concerned.	None specified. As per primary offense.
Participating as an accomplice to (smuggling of migrants, producing a fraudulent travel document, or enabling illegal residence) in circumstances that entail inhuman or degrading treatment, including for exploitation of such migrants.	None specified. As per primary offense.
Organizing or directing (smuggling of migrants, producing a fraudulent travel document, or enabling illegal residence) in circumstances that endanger, or are likely to endanger, the lives or safety of the migrants concerned.	None specified. As per primary offense.
Organizing or directing (smuggling of migrants, producing a fraudulent travel document, or enabling illegal residence) in circumstances that entail inhuman or degrading treatment, including for exploitation of such migrants.	None specified. As per primary offense.

or to cruel, inhuman or degrading treatment or punishment."[63] This principle is now well enshrined in international treaty law, being a central and non-derogable provision of major international and regional human rights instruments,[64] and, despite

[63] Universal Declaration of Human Rights, adopted by UNGA Res. 217A (III), UN GAOR, 3rd sess, 183rd plen mtg, UN Doc. A/810 at 71, Dec. 10, 1948 [UDHR], at Art. 5.

[64] See International Covenant on Civil and Political Rights, 999 UNTS 171, done Dec. 16, 1966, entered into force Mar. 23, 1976 [ICCPR], at Art. 7; Convention against Torture and Other Cruel, Inhuman or Degrading Treatment or Punishment, 1465 UNTS 85, done Dec. 10, 1984, entered into force June 26, 1987 [Convention against Torture], at Art. 16; Rome Statute of the International Criminal Court, 2187 UNTS 3, done July 17, 1998, entered into force July 1, 2002 [ICC Statute], at Art. 7(1)(k); International Convention on the Protection of the Rights of All Migrant Workers and Members of Their Families, UN Doc. A/Res/45/158, done Dec. 18, 1990, entered into force July 1, 2003, at Art. 10; Convention for the Protection of Human Rights and Fundamental Freedoms, 213 UNTS 222, done

inconsistent State practice, the prohibition on torture is widely recognized to be a rule of customary international law.[65] Its elevated status is well described through the following extract from the judgment of the International Criminal Tribunal for the former Yugoslavia (ICTY) in the *Furundzija* case:

> [T]he prohibition of torture laid down in human rights treaties enshrines an absolute right, which can never be derogated from, not even in time of emergency ... This is linked to the fact ... that the prohibition on torture is a peremptory norm or *jus cogens*.... This prohibition is so extensive that States are even barred by international law from expelling, returning or extraditing a person to another State where there are substantial grounds for believing that the person would be in danger of being subjected to torture.[66]

Its fundamental and customary status means that while States Parties to specific instruments prohibiting torture will be under particular obligations vis-à-vis those instruments, all States are bound by the essence of the international legal prohibition.[67]

The jurisprudence of international courts, tribunals, and treaty bodies has helped to flesh out the substantive content of the obligation on States with respect to the prohibition against torture and related conduct. One of the most important developments has been the recognition that States are under an obligation to prevent and respond to torture and related conduct irrespective of whether the perpetrators are

Nov. 4, 1950, entered into force Sept. 3, 1953 [European Convention on Human Rights], at Art. 3; American Convention on Human Rights, 1144 UNTS 123, done Nov. 22, 1969, entered into force July 18, 1978 [American Convention on Human Rights], at Art. 5; African Charter on Human and Peoples' Rights, 1520 UNTS 217, done June 27, 1981, entered into force Oct. 21, 1986 [African Charter], at Art. 5.

65 See American Law Institute, *Restatement (Third) of the Foreign Relations Law of the United States* § 102(2) (1987), at para. 702. The customary legal status of the prohibition on torture and cruel, inhuman, or degrading treatment has also been recognized as part of international humanitarian law, binding on all parties to an internal or international armed conflict. For a careful discussion of the customary status of the prohibition in the context of international humanitarian law. see J-M. Henckaerts and L. Doswald-Beck, *Customary International Humanitarian Law* (2006), at ch. 32, Rule 90. See further the discussion in Chapter 2, at Section 2.4.1.

66 *Prosecutor v. Furundzija*, Case IT-95–17/1-T, ICTY Trial Chamber, Dec. 10, 1988, at para. 144 (citations omitted). See also UN Human Rights Committee, "General Comment No. 24: Issues relating to reservations made upon ratification or accession to the Covenant or the Optional Protocols thereto, or in relation to declarations under article 41 of the Covenant," UN Doc. CCPR/C/21/Rev.1/Add.6, Nov. 11, adopted Nov. 2, 1994, at para. 10: "...some non-derogable rights, which in any event cannot be reserved because of their status as peremptory norms, are also of this character – the prohibition of torture and arbitrary deprivation of life are examples."

67 See further E. de Wet, "The Prohibition of Torture as an International Norm of *Jus Cogens* and Its Implications for National and Customary Law" (2004) 15 *European Journal of International Law* 97; A. Baldaccini, "The EU Directive on Return: Principles and Protests" (2010) 28(4) *Refugee Survey Quarterly* 114, at 120; and on State practice, O. A. Hathaway, "The Promise and Limits of the International Law of Torture," in S. Levinson ed., *Torture: A Collection* 199 (2004).

public officials or private persons.[68] In the present context, this means that all States are required to prevent and respond to acts of torture, cruel, inhuman or degrading treatment or punishment committed against any persons under their jurisdiction or control,[69] including those who have been or are being smuggled. In the context of State responsibility, the analysis in Chapter 4 confirms that responsibility of States will be engaged in relation to such acts committed by non-State or private actors when State authorities or others acting in an official capacity know or have reasonable grounds to believe that these acts are taking place, and do not exercise due diligence to "prevent, investigate, prosecute and punish" those committing them.[70]

The Migrant Smuggling Protocol builds on this long tradition of prohibiting torture and inhuman and degrading treatment, by requiring States Parties to take legislative measures to ensure that persons involved in smuggling of migrants – where this also involves inhuman or degrading treatment of the migrants concerned – are subject to a higher degree of punishment than persons who merely engage in smuggling of migrants without ill-treatment.[71]

While the concept of "torture" benefits from an agreed international legal definition,[72] the other terms that form part of the prohibition and that are in fact much more central to the issue at hand, including "inhuman and degrading treatment," are not defined in the Migrant Smuggling Protocol or indeed, in any other international treaty. Pronouncements by the Human Rights Committee suggest that

68 See, for example, UN Human Rights Committee, "General Comment No. 20: Replaces General Comment 7 concerning Prohibition of Torture and Cruel Treatment or Punishment," UN Doc. HRI/GEN/1/Rev.7, at 150, May 12, 2004, adopted Oct. 3, 1992 [HRC General Comment No. 20], at para. 2: "It is the duty of the State party to afford everyone protection through legislative and other measures as may be necessary against the acts prohibited by article 7, whether inflicted by people acting in their official capacity, outside their official capacity or in a private capacity." The UN Special Rapporteur on Torture has affirmed that the definition of torture in the Convention against Torture "clearly extends State obligations into the private sphere and should be interpreted to include State failure to protect persons within its jurisdiction from torture and ill-treatment committed by private individuals": "Report of the Special Rapporteur on Torture and Other Cruel, Inhuman or Degrading Treatment or Punishment, Manfred Nowak," UN Doc. A/HRC/7/3, Jan. 15, 2008 [Nowak, "Report of the Special Rapporteur on Torture (2008)"], at para. 31.

69 See discussion in Chapter 2, esp. at Section 2.4, and Chapter 3, at Part 2, on the scope of human rights obligations.

70 See further Chapter 4, at Section 4.3.3.

71 Migrant Smuggling Protocol, at Art. 6(3)(b).

72 The Convention against Torture at Article 1 provides the following definition: "For the purposes of this Convention, the term 'torture' means any act by which severe pain or suffering, whether physical or mental, is intentionally inflicted on a person for such purposes as obtaining from him or a third person information or a confession, punishing him for an act he or a third person has committed or is suspected of having committed, or intimidating or coercing him or a third person, or for any reason based on discrimination of any kind, when such pain or suffering is inflicted by or at the instigation of or with the consent or acquiescence of a public official or other person acting in an official capacity. It does not include pain or suffering arising only from, inherent in or incidental to lawful sanctions."

decisions about what constitutes "inhuman and degrading treatment" must be made on a case-by-case basis.[73] The severity of treatment and its purpose have both been identified as relevant, particularly when it comes to distinguishing cruel or inhuman and degrading treatment from torture.[74]

Despite this lack of firm guidance, it is nevertheless possible to identify some of the characteristics of treatment that has been said to be "inhuman or degrading." First, it is clear that "inhuman or degrading treatment" includes not only acts that cause physical suffering, but also acts that cause mental suffering to the victim.[75] Second, "inhuman or degrading treatment" covers a range of treatment that causes physical or mental suffering but that cannot be defined as "torture" because it lacks one of the requisite elements. As Nowak has noted, "torture" is defined in the Convention against Torture as involving acts of public officials, which intentionally inflict severe physical or mental pain or suffering, in order to fulfill a certain purpose, such as the extortion of information or confessions;[76] "[o]ther actions or omissions are not considered to be torture but rather, depending on the kind, purpose and severity, cruel, inhuman or degrading treatment; in these cases, a certain minimum of pain or suffering is imposed, but one or several of the essential elements of the term torture are lacking: intent, fulfilment of a certain purpose and/or intensity of the severe pain."[77] Third, treatment must meet

73 See HRC General Comment No. 20, at para. 4: "The Covenant does not contain any definition of the concepts covered by article 7, nor does the Committee consider it necessary to draw up a list of prohibited acts or to establish sharp distinctions between the different kinds of punishment or treatment; the distinctions depend on the nature, purpose and severity of the treatment applied."

74 On the relative severity aspect, see, for example, *Aktas v. Turkey*, (2004) 38 EHRR 18 (ECHR, Apr. 24, 2003), at para. 313: "In determining whether a particular form of ill-treatment should be qualified as torture, consideration must be given to the distinction, embodied in Art.3, between this notion and that of inhuman or degrading treatment. As noted in previous cases, it appears that it was the intention that the Convention should, by means of this distinction, attach a special stigma to deliberate inhuman treatment causing very serious and cruel suffering [citation omitted]. In addition to the severity of the treatment, there is a purposive element, as recognised in the United Nations Convention against Torture or Other Cruel, Inhuman or Degrading Treatment or Punishment, which came into force on 26 June 1987, which defines torture in terms of the intentional infliction of severe pain or suffering with the aim, inter alia, of obtaining information, inflicting punishment or intimidating [citation omitted]."

75 HRC General Comment No. 20, at para. 5. See also the American Convention on Human Rights, at Art. 5(1), which refers specifically to the right of every person to have his or her "physical, mental, and moral integrity respected."

76 M. Nowak, *U.N. Covenant on Civil and Political Rights: CCPR Commentary* (2nd revised ed. 2005) [Nowak, *CCPR Commentary*], at 161. The European Court of Human Rights has also sought in *Ireland v. United Kingdom*, (1979–80) 2 EHRR 25, (ECHR, Jan. 18, 1978) [*Ireland v. United Kingdom*] to draw a line between "torture" and "cruel, inhuman and degrading treatment," with torture being at the upper end of the spectrum of ill-treatment.

77 Nowak, *CCPR Commentary*, at 161. Nowak gives the example of an Austrian prisoner, forgotten by the authorities, who was left for twenty days without food or water, fearing he would slowly starve to death. In view of the severe physical and mental pain this inflicted, this is considered to be an example of inhuman or cruel treatment. However, as there was no active undertaking, intent, or purposefulness, this was not torture. Ibid.

a certain level of *severity* before it can constitute "inhuman or degrading treatment." Dating back to a landmark case in 1979 on interrogation techniques put into practice by the United Kingdom on suspects in Northern Ireland, the European Court of Human Rights has consistently held that treatment is *inhuman* where it was premeditated, was applied for hours at a stretch, and caused either actual bodily injury or intense physical and mental suffering. Treatment has been held to be *degrading* because it was such as to arouse in the victims feelings of fear, anguish, and inferiority capable of humiliating and debasing them.[78] It is also relevant to note that in the context of crimes against humanity, the Rome Statute of the International Criminal Court refers to listed crimes including slavery, torture, and murder, along with other "inhumane acts" of a similar character to those listed in the Statute "intentionally causing great suffering, or serious injury to body or to mental or physical health."[79]

The language of Article 6(3)(b) of the Migrant Smuggling Protocol is unique in that it includes "inhuman and degrading treatment, *including exploitation*"[80] as a circumstance of aggravation. The Interpretative Notes to the Protocol state that "[t]he words 'inhuman or degrading treatment' in subparagraph *(b)* were intended, without prejudice to the scope and application of the trafficking in persons protocol, to include certain forms of exploitation."[81] At the very least, this suggests that the concept of "inhuman and degrading treatment" is intended to include the specific forms of "exploitation" that are listed in the Trafficking Protocol (the prostitution of others and other forms of sexual exploitation, forced labor, slavery and slavery-like practices, servitude, and the removal of organs).[82] As noted in the Model Law against the Smuggling of Migrants, this has significant potential implications for the national legal framework, particularly with respect to possible overlap between this circumstance of aggravation and existing national laws on trafficking in persons:

> It should be noted that the presence of exploitation in what would otherwise be a smuggling case may make the trafficking offence applicable if the State party concerned has ratified and implemented the Trafficking in Persons Protocol. For example, it is very difficult to conceive of a situation where a migrant has been smuggled for the purpose of forced labour or slavery, without there also having been some element of deception or coercion in the process (the "means" element of the trafficking definition). This would bring the conduct squarely within the definition of "trafficking in persons" contained in the Trafficking in Persons Protocol.[83]

78 This line of reasoning originated in *Ireland v. United Kingdom*. For a recent example of its application, see *Yordanov v. Bulgaria*, Application No. 56856/00, [2006] ECHR 2006–V (ECHR, Nov. 10, 2006).

79 ICC Statute, at Art. 7.

80 Emphasis added.

81 Travaux Préparatoires *for the Organized Crime Convention and Protocols*, at 489.

82 Trafficking Protocol, at Art. 3(a).

83 UNODC Model Law on Migrant Smuggling, at 43–44.

A contextual reading of the reference to "exploitation" suggests that "inhuman or degrading treatment, *including* exploitation" was intended to have a broader coverage than just the forms of exploitation covered by the Trafficking Protocol. Certainly it is possible to cite numerous examples where smuggled migrants are treated in a way that is "inhuman or degrading" but that would not amount to "exploitation," as it is defined in the Trafficking Protocol. This might include, for example, situations where migrants are subjected to actions intended to arouse feelings of fear, anguish, and inferiority in the course of the smuggling process or after arriving at their destination. It is also possible to conceive of situations where the treatment of a smuggled migrant is "exploitative" – in the sense that it is abusive and for the gain of another – but not of the same nature as "exploitation" referenced in the trafficking definition. Examples offered in the UNODC Model Law against the Smuggling of Migrants include slum landlords who charge smuggled migrants exorbitant rates for substandard accommodation, or persons who take smuggled migrants who have become stranded to a water source but only in return for their money and possessions.[84]

Whether it is most appropriate to describe a particular situation as either aggravated migrant smuggling or trafficking in persons will depend on the facts of each individual case. However, it is worth reiterating that the elements of the offense of aggravated migrant smuggling are potentially different from the elements of the offense of trafficking in persons. In aggravated migrant smuggling, it is necessary to prove that the smuggling or related crime occurred *in circumstances* that included "inhuman or degrading treatment, including for exploitation." This is a physical element of the crime (a circumstance). In contrast, under the human trafficking offenses enacted in accordance with the Trafficking Protocol, it is necessary to prove that the *suspect intended to subject the victim to exploitation*. This is a mental element (intention). In some instances, it may be easier for the prosecution to prove the existence of a circumstance than it is to prove the suspect had the necessary intention to exploit at the requisite time. In other words, in some situations, it may be easier to prosecute a case of aggravated smuggling than of trafficking in persons (Table 5.6).[85]

"Inhuman and degrading treatment" can have a significant gender dimension, for example, in situations where female migrants are being subjected to sexual violence in the smuggling process.[86] This aspect of the relevant international legal

84 Ibid. at 53.

85 Note that a decision in this regard would need to factor in other considerations such as the status of the individual involved and the rights and entitlements that attach to that status. For example, many States now provide legislatively mandated protection and assistance to persons who have been identified as "victims of trafficking" that may not be available to those subject to aggravated forms of smuggling.

86 A relevant example is provided through a study on migrant workers in Thailand, in which a young Cambodian factory worker describes elements of her smuggling experience as follows: "A Cambodian

TABLE 5.6 *Differences in the elements of aggravated smuggling and trafficking in persons*

Offense	Physical element	Mental element
Aggravated smuggling	(Primary offense occurs) in circumstances that involve inhuman or degrading treatment, including for exploitation.	None specified. Refer to the mental elements for the primary offense.
Trafficking in persons	a) Recruit, transfer, harbor, or receive (conduct); b) through use of force, threat, deception, or coercion (conduct).	Undertake the conduct for the purpose of exploiting the victim (intention).

prohibition is being increasingly recognized, as are its implications for the nature of the obligation on States with regard to preventing and responding to such inhuman and degrading treatment.[87]

It is difficult to develop a list of circumstances that would comprehensively cover all the possible variants of conduct that might constitute "inhuman and degrading treatment, including exploitation" and many such circumstances would also constitute other offenses in national criminal laws, whether kidnapping, extortion, assault, or torture. However, the following are suggested as relevant examples, bearing in mind the range of exploitative conduct that is perpetrated against smuggled migrants.

- Subjecting or exposing smuggled migrants to very poor, or harsh conditions of travel, that do not risk their physical safety (a circumstance falling under Article 6(3)(a) of the Migrant Smuggling Protocol), but are nevertheless inhuman or degrading.
- Subjecting or exposing smuggled migrants to conditions of life, travel, housing, or work that are incompatible with human dignity. This might include for example: depriving smuggled migrants of food, water, or medical treatment for extended periods of time; confining smuggled migrants without light, in

broker brought me from home to work here. There were altogether 25 women in the group. I didn't know any of them. We all had to stay in a small hut in a forest for three days. One of the women was raped in the hut and another man wanted to rape me while I was sleeping. Both of us could not do anything. We were alone and nobody cared to help. Everyone just wanted to get out of the forest and get jobs" (Global Alliance against Traffic in Women, *Women, Mobility and Reproductive Health: The Assessment of the Circumstances of Mobility and Reproductive Health Needs among Women Migrant Workers in Thailand* (Apr. 2007), at 76.

87 See, for example, Nowak, "Report of the Special Rapporteur on Torture (2008)," at chapters II and III.

cramped, unsanitary conditions for extended periods of time; or subjecting smuggled migrants to treatment that is intended to humiliate them such as requiring them to remove their clothing against their will.

- Subjecting or exposing smuggled migrants to (actual or threatened) physical or sexual violence that would cause severe suffering, pain, or injury, including actual or threatened violence aimed at extorting money.
- Smuggling practices that involve exploitation of a nature included in the trafficking-in-persons definition, such as the prostitution of others and other forms of sexual exploitation; forced labor;[88] slavery[89]; and slavery-like practices,[90] such as debt bondage, serfdom, and servile marriage; exploitation of children (for example, using children as accomplices or participants in criminal conduct); servitude, or coerced labor[91]; and removal of organs.

The existence of any such circumstances should be sufficient to establish a particular situation of migrant smuggling as "aggravated" within the terms of the Protocol. However, there is another important dimension, which has already been briefly referred to and which is explored in greater detail in subsequent chapters: the fact that migrant smuggling involves inhuman or degrading treatment or exploitation is sufficient to trigger specific obligations on concerned States; including obligations of prevention[92] and protection.[93] Failure to discharge such obligations to the necessary level of due diligence (for example, through failure to come to the aid of

[88] The terminology of *forced labor or services* derives from the International Labour Organization (ILO) Convention on Forced Labour (Convention concerning Forced and Compulsory Labour, 39 UNTS 55, ILO No. 29, done Jun. 28, 1930, entered into force, May 1, 1932). The elements of forced labor or services include (1) work or service that is exacted under menace of penalty and (2) this work or service is undertaken involuntarily (Article 2). According to the ILO, forced labor or services is not the same as situations merely involving low wages or poor working conditions, or lack of choice because of economic necessity. It represents a severe violation of human rights, and restriction of freedom. International Labour Organization, *A Global Alliance against Forced Labour: Global Report under the Follow-Up to the ILO Declaration on Fundamental Principles and Rights at Work, Report of the Director General* (2005), at 5.

[89] The term "slavery" has a long legal history. In several treaties, one of the defining features of slavery is the exercise of any or all of the powers attaching to the right of ownership of a person: See, for example, Convention to Suppress the Slave Trade and Slavery, 60 LNTS 253, done Sept. 25, 1926, entered into force Mar. 9, 1927, at Art. 1; ICC Statute, at Art. 7(2)(c); European Convention on Human Rights, at Art. 4.

[90] Slavery-like practices are defined in the Supplementary Convention on the Abolition of Slavery, the Slave Trade, and Institutions and Practices Similar to Slavery, 226 UNTS 3, done Apr. 30 1956, entered into force Apr. 30, 1957 [Supplementary Slavery Convention], at Art. 1.

[91] In the Supplementary Slavery Convention, a person of "servile status" includes a person who is a victim of debt bondage, serfdom, or the institutions of service marriage or child exploitation, described in that Convention in Article 7(b). The concept of "servitude" is also found in international human rights instruments, namely the ICCPR (Article 8) and UDHR (Article 4).

[92] See further Chapter 7, at Section 7.1.2.5.

[93] See further Chapter 8.

migrants in distress), will, as demonstrated in Chapter 4, trigger the international legal responsibility of the implicated State.

5.1.5. *Criminalization and Related Obligations under the Organized Crime Convention*

As detailed in Chapter 1, the criminalization obligations in the Protocol exist as part of the broader framework of obligations created by the Organized Crime Convention. A number of the obligations in the Convention are of direct relevance to the obligation to criminalize migrant smuggling. Specifically applicable are the provisions on:

- Proportionate sanctions (Article 11);
- Ensuring the liability of legal persons such as companies and associations (Article 10);
- Confiscation and seizure of proceeds of crime and property, equipment, and other instrumentalities used in the commission of smuggling offenses (Article 12);
- Disposal of confiscated proceeds of crime or property (Article 14);
- Jurisdiction (Article 15);
- International cooperation through mutual legal assistance, including for recovery of proceeds of crime, and extradition (Articles 13, 16, and 18);
- Protection of witnesses (Article 24);
- Assistance to and protection of victims of crime, including compensation (Article 25).

The international cooperation aspects of the Convention are explored in Chapter 7. The following section explores those aspects of the Convention relating to sanctions, jurisdiction, legal persons, protection of witnesses, and assistance to and protection of victims of crime.

5.1.5.1. Proportionate Sanctions

As discussed in the Introduction to this book, the issue of migrant smuggling at the national level is often controversial and highly politicized. These sensitivities are frequently visible around discussions of how migrant smugglers should be punished for their actions. Recent legislative trends toward very high sanctions against migrant smugglers, such as mandatory penalties of ten or even twenty years' imprisonment, have reflected these sentiments, as well as the reality that some forms of smuggling involve extremely serious criminality causing injury, death, or severe exploitation.[94] However, it is essential to acknowledge that the term "migrant smuggling" is defined very broadly, capturing a wide range of practices with highly different levels of severity and culpability.[95] The criminal culpability of a person who opportunistically transports one or two people on his or her motorcycle across a border is – and should be considered to be – very different to that of a highly organized criminal entrepreneur who directs a business transporting migrants in shipping containers from China to the United States. It is also essential to recognize that, in common with many other forms of organized crime, those smugglers who come into contact with national criminal justice agencies are often at the lowest end of the criminal hierarchy. In the context of smuggling by sea for example, the United Nations Office on Drugs and Crime has explained that:

> Sometimes the "captain" is an experienced fisherman or seafarer who has been recruited by the smuggler specifically for his skills; the smugglers may even have tested his capabilities before the journey is undertaken. In regions where fishermen are recruited by smugglers for [their] seafaring skills and their knowledge of particular waters and land masses, the smuggler will sometimes offer the fisherman more money to transport a group of migrants than he could possibly make otherwise. Persons who are tempted into accepting such an offer may or may not know of the risk they incur and the illegality of what they are being asked to

94 See, for example, a discussion of the Australian mandatory sentencing regime in Schloenhardt and Martin, "Prosecution and Punishment of People Smugglers in Australia 2008–2011." Section 233B of the Migration Act 1958 (Cth) (Australia) establishes an aggravated offense of people smuggling involving danger of death or serious harm, to which is attached a mandatory penalty of "imprisonment for 20 years or 2,000 penalty units or both." Amendments to the Act in 2013 removed "exploitation" as an element of an aggravated offense. The Act also creates, under section 233C, a separate aggravated people-smuggling offense that involves bringing to Australia five or more noncitizens who have "no lawful right to come to Australia." The offense carries a mandatory five-year jail sentence with a three-year non-parole period for first-time offenders. Until late August 2012, crew and organizers were uniformly charged with this offense – and mandatorily sentenced to five years in jail – regardless of their individual level of culpability and indeed of any consideration as to whether persons found to have a valid claim to asylum should rightly be identified as having "no lawful right to come to Australia." The Commonwealth Attorney-General issued a Direction on August 27, 2012, to enable crew to be charged with a lesser offense that does not carry a mandatory sentence, but the mandatory sentencing laws remain in place and, accordingly, the Direction can be revoked at any time. Most people ultimately charged with people smuggling offenses in Australia are detained for three to six months without charge for any offense, and without access to legal advice or review of the lawfulness of their detention. See also A. Trotter and M. Garozzo, "Mandatory Sentencing for People Smuggling: Issues of Law and Policy" (2012) 36 *Melbourne University Law Review* 553. For analysis of the human rights implications of the mandatory sentencing and indefinite pre-charge detention laws, see the Individual Communication to the UN Human Rights Committee filed in October 2012 by the University of New South Wales Human Rights Clinic on behalf of Indonesian migrant smuggler Mr. Nasir, available at www.law.unsw.edu.au/sites/law.unsw.edu.au/files/docs/hrc-communication-final-no_appendix.pdf (accessed May 12, 2013).

95 UNODC, *Migrant Smuggling in Asia*, at 36.

do, but it is clear that the smugglers pass the risk of prosecution on to those they recruit.[96]

The Organized Crime Convention requires States Parties to make the commission of Convention and Protocol offenses "liable to sanctions that take into account the gravity of that offence."[97] The Legislative Guide elaborates, stating that it is "necessary to ensure that the prosecution, treatment and sanctioning of offenders around the world is [...] comparatively symmetric and consistent with the harm they have caused and with the benefits they have derived from their criminal activities."[98] Although the Convention is silent on the issue of precisely what sanctions are appropriate, it is clear that the intention was to ensure that penalties are sufficient to outweigh the benefits of involvement in migrant smuggling.[99] In that regard it should be noted that inappropriately light sentences that do not reflect the harm caused or the benefits derived will likely compromise the criminal justice task and thereby the broader purposes of the Protocol. Very light sentences may also impede the effectiveness of international cooperation procedures, where these rely on a statutory minimum.

However, extremely heavy penalties are equally, if not more problematic. Of particular concern are legislatively mandated minimum penalties that, particularly if set very high, do not satisfy the test of sanctions that "take into account the gravity" of the offense because they remove the measure of judicial discretion necessary for its proper application.[100] Provision for the death penalty in smuggling cases would be extremely difficult to ever justify, not just from a human rights perspective[101] but also because of the nature of the offenses involved, including the highly varying levels of complicity inherent in smuggling cases. Such draconian penalties would also negatively impact on the overall effectiveness of the Protocol by introducing obstacles to effective international cooperation.[102]

5.1.5.2. Legal Persons

Those involved in migrant smuggling may seek to avoid prosecution through disguising their operations under the cover of a legitimate business or other activity. For example, the line between legal and illegal travel and labor recruitment agencies

[96] United Nations Office on Drugs and Crime, *Issue Paper: Smuggling of Migrants by Sea* (2011), at 30.

[97] Organized Crime Convention, at Art. 11(1), read with the Migrant Smuggling Protocol, at Art. 1(3).

[98] *Legislative Guide*, at 130 (para. 261).

[99] Ibid. at 130 (para. 262).

[100] See note 94 in this chapter. For a consideration of this issue from the perspective of trafficking in persons, see A. T. Gallagher, *The International Law of Human Trafficking* (2010), at 395.

[101] See generally, W. Schabas, *The Abolition of the Death Penalty in International Law* (2002); and Nowak, *CCPR Commentary*, at 133–153.

[102] For discussion of cooperation obligations under the Migrant Smuggling Protocol see Chapter 7.

on Short-Term Residency Permits[131] introduced in Chapter 1. Under this instrument, EU States have discretion to grant short-term residency permits to "[persons] who have been the subject of an illegal action to facilitate migrant smuggling" in exchange for cooperation with police or judicial authorities. To date, very few States have taken up the option of providing a reflection period to smuggled migrants, despite its readily apparent value in relation to the prosecution of smugglers.

Smuggled migrants who are cooperating with criminal justice agencies may also need protection from retaliation. This is recognized in the Organized Crime Convention, which requires States Parties to "take appropriate measures within [their] means to provide effective protection from potential retaliation or intimidation for witnesses" (and their relatives and others close to them as appropriate) who give evidence in criminal proceedings for Convention offenses.[132] The Convention envisages a range of measures that may give effect to this obligation, all of which are to be without prejudice to the rights of defendants, including their right to due process. These include establishing procedures for physical protection of such persons (including possible relocation to another State) and providing evidentiary rules to permit testimony to be given in a manner that ensures their safety.[133]

Various materials are available to guide States on implementing their obligation to protect witnesses of organized criminal activity, including migrant smuggling. One example is provided by the United Nations Good Practices for the Protection of Witnesses in Criminal Proceedings Involving Organized Crime. This document explicitly recognizes that the ability of a witness to give testimony in a judicial setting and to cooperate with law enforcement without fear of intimidation or reprisal is essential to maintaining the rule of law.[134] It affirms that the concept of witness protection encompasses a range of possibilities, from simple and inexpensive measures to more formal witness protection programs.[135] The Organized Crime Convention

[131] Council Directive 2004/81/EC of 29 April 2004 on the residence permit issued to third-country nationals who are victims of trafficking in human beings or who have been the subject of an action to facilitate illegal immigration, who decide to cooperate with the competent authorities, OJ L 261, Aug. 6, 2004.

[132] Organized Crime Convention, at Art. 24(1).

[133] Ibid.

[134] United Nations Office on Drugs and Crime, *Good Practices for the Protection of Witnesses in Criminal Proceedings Involving Organized Crime* (2008), at 1.

[135] "Protection may be as simple as providing a police escort to the courtroom, offering temporary residence in a safe house or using modern communications technology (such as videoconferencing) for testimony. There are other cases, though, where cooperation by a witness is critical to successful prosecution but the reach and strength of the threatening criminal group is so powerful that extraordinary measures are required to ensure the witness's safety. In such cases, resettlement of the witness under a new identity in a new, undisclosed place of residence in the same country or even abroad may be the only viable alternative." Ibid. at 1.

itself provides two examples of such measures: the first, formal witness protection programs that focus on providing physical protection, and the second, evidentiary rules that permit witnesses to give evidence safely.[136] There are many other strategies that may be useful beyond this, and the Model Legislative Provisions against Organized Crime provide examples of legislative strategies that could be used, including a focus on both the safety and judicial protection of witnesses.[137] Any such measures should, as recognized in the Organized Crime Convention, be without prejudice to the rights of defendants, including their right to due process.[138]

5.2. CRIMINALIZATION OBLIGATIONS: THE EUROPEAN UNION

The Migrant Smuggling Protocol is the only global instrument mandating the criminalization of migrant smuggling. However, this is an issue around which European States and their organizations have also been very active. As detailed in Chapter 1, Article 27(1) of the Schengen Convention[139] required States Parties to "impose appropriate penalties on any person who, for financial gain, assists or tries to assist an alien to enter or reside in the territory of one of the Contracting Parties in breach of that Contracting Party's law on the entry and residence of aliens." It should be noted that the purpose element of this provision referred only to "financial gain," in contrast with the Protocol's broader concept of "financial or other material benefit." Article 27(1) was repealed as of 2004 by a 2002 EU Council Directive[140] and associated Framework Decision[141] that eliminated the requirement of material gain altogether, as discussed in the next section. Both instruments have been the subject of substantial criticism from refugee and human rights advocates.[142]

136 Organized Crime Convention, at Art. 24(2).

137 UNODC, *Model Legislative Provisions against Organized Crime*, at 112–113.

138 Organized Crime Convention, at Art. 24(2).

139 Convention Implementing the Schengen Agreement of 14 June 1985 between the Governments of the States of the Benelux Economic Union, the Federal Republic of Germany and the French Republic on the gradual abolition of checks at their common borders, OJ L 239/19, Sept. 22, 2000, done June 19, 1990, entered into force Sept. 1, 1993 [Schengen Convention].

140 Council Directive 2002/90/EC of 28 November 2002 defining the facilitation of unauthorised entry, transit and residence, OJ L 328/17, Dec. 5, 2002 [Council Directive 2002/90/EC], at Art. 5.

141 Council Framework Decision of 28 November 2002 on the strengthening of the penal framework to prevent the facilitation of unauthorised entry, transit and residence (2002/946/JHA), OJ L 328/1, Dec. 5, 2002 [Council Framework Decision 2002/946].

142 See, for example, Statewatch News Online, "EU: An Area of Expulsion, Carrier Sanctions and Criminalisation: French Presidency Crackdown on Aiding Asylum-Seekers," Statewatch (online), Oct. 2000, available at www.statewatch.org/news/oct00/05frimm.htm (accessed May 12, 2013); R. Cholewinski, "European Union Policy on Irregular Migration: Human Rights Lost?" in B. Bogusz, R. Cholewinski, A. Cygan, and E. Szyszczak eds., *Irregular Migration and Human Rights: Theoretical, European and International Perspectives* (2004), at 174–175.

5.2.1. 2002 EU Directive on Facilitation of Unauthorized Entry, Transit, and Residence

Since the adoption of the Schengen Convention, the European Union has continued to further narrow and tighten its laws and sanctions on "illegal migration."[143] A review of developments in this broader area is outside the confines of the present chapter.[144] The present section focuses attention squarely on the criminalization aspect of two key EU instruments dealing with migrant smuggling that were introduced in Chapter 1: a Directive, and Framework Decision, both adopted in 2002.[145]

The, principal purpose of the EU Directive on Facilitation of Unauthorized Entry, Transit and Residence[146] is to provide a common definition for the facilitation of unauthorized entry, transit, and residence into EU States. At the time of its adoption, the Directive represented a marked shift away from the Schengen focus on facilitating irregular entry or residence for profit, and toward what might be described as mere facilitated illegal entry or transit. Article 1 requires States to impose "effective and proportionate sanctions and dissuasive sanctions"[147] on the following:

(a) any person who intentionally assists a person who is not a national of a Member State to enter, or transit across, the territory of a Member State in breach of the laws of the State concerned on the entry or transit of aliens;

[143] "Illegal migration" is the terminology used in Article 79 of the Treaty on the Functioning of the European Union, OJ C 326/47, Oct. 26, 2012, done Feb. 7, 1992, entered into force Nov. 1, 1993. Note however that later instruments such as the Directive 2008/115/EC of the European Parliament and of the Council of 16 December 2008 on common standards and procedures in Member States for returning illegally staying third-country nationals, OJ L 348/98, Dec. 24, 2008, avoids the term. For further on terminology see C. Morehouse and M. Blomfield, *Irregular Migration in Europe* (Migration Policy Institute, Dec. 2011), at 4–6.

[144] For the text of all European and EU Member State legislation related to immigration and asylum, see www.eurasylum.org/Portal/DesktopDefault.aspx?tabindex=10&tabid=7 (accessed May 12, 2013). The body of literature around EU law and practice in this area is substantial and growing. See, for example, S. Peers, E. Guild, and J. Tomkin eds., *EU Immigration and Asylum Law (Text and Commentary): Second Revised Edition*, Volume 1: Visa and Border Controls (2012) [Peers et al., *EU Immigration and Asylum Law (Text and Commentary)*]; S. Peers, *EU Justice and Home Affairs Law* (3rd ed. 2011) [Peers, *EU Justice and Home Affairs Law*]; and S. S. Juss ed., *The Ashgate Research Companion to Migration Law, Theory and Policy* (2013), esp. at part 1. In relation to the specific issue of criminalization, see R. Cholewinski, "The Criminalisation of Migration in EU Law and Policy," in A. Baldaccini, E. Guild, and H. Toner eds., *Whose Freedom, Security and Justice? EU Immigration and Asylum Law and Policy* (2007); and E. Guild, "Criminalisation of Migration in Europe: Human Rights Implications" (Issue Paper, Council of Europe, Commissioner for Human Rights, 2010).

[145] The institutional authority and arrangements around both instruments are complex and have shifted as a result of the entry into force of the Treaty of Lisbon. For further detail see Peers, *EU Justice and Home Affairs Law*, at 535–538.

[146] Council Directive 2002/90/EC, at Recitation para. 4.

[147] Ibid. at Art. 3.

(b) any person who, for financial gain, intentionally assists a person who is not a national of a Member State to reside within the territory of a Member State in breach of the laws of the State concerned on the residence of aliens.

The Directive adopts a circuitous approach to smuggling cases that are of a humanitarian nature. Rather than excluding such cases from the conduct to be subject to sanction, Member States "may decide not to impose sanctions with regard to the behaviour defined in paragraph 1(a) by applying its national law and practice for cases where the aim of the behaviour is to provide humanitarian assistance to the person concerned."[148] There is no requirement that sanctions not be imposed, leaving Member States free to impose sanctions in these circumstances. In short, the capacity of any Member State to sanction humanitarian smuggling is fully preserved, as is its capacity to sanction smuggling that is not otherwise profit based, such as smuggling aimed at family reunification. It is relevant to note that a Directive adopted in 2009 providing for minimum standards on sanctions and measures against employers of illegally staying third-country nationals stipulates that assistance to migrants in order to lodge complaints against employers must not be considered to be facilitation of unlawful residence for purposes of the 2002 Directive.[149]

Unlike the Migrant Smuggling Protocol, the EU Directive 2002/90/EC makes no reference to the protection of refugees or asylum-seekers. This is despite a concerted campaign by the UN High Commissioner for Refugees (UNHCR) and refugee advocates to ensure that the proposed EU measure did not interfere with "the basic human right of individuals to seek and enjoy in other countries asylum from persecution."[150] Proposals for a savings clause similar to that set out in Article 19 of the Migrant Smuggling Protocol were unsuccessful.[151]

[148] Ibid. at Art. 1(2).

[149] Directive 2009/52/EC of the European Parliament and of the Council of 18 June 2009 providing for minimum standards on sanctions and measures against employers of illegally staying third-country nationals, OJ L 168/24, June 30, 2009, at Art. 13(3).

[150] UN High Commissioner for Refugees, "UNHCR Comments on the French Presidency Proposals for a Council Directive and Council Framework Decision on Preventing the Facilitation of Unauthorised Entry and Residence," Sept. 22, 2000, at para. 5. UNHCR summarized the risks as follows: "The lack of proper or adequate documentation on the part of asylum-seekers cannot in itself justify refusal to admit to a State's territory or summary exclusion from asylum proceedings. The 1951 Convention also provides in Article 31(1) that States shall not impose penalties, on account of their illegal entry or presence, on refugees who present themselves without delay to the authorities and who show good reasons for their illegal entry and presence." Ibid. at para. 6.

[151] UNHCR recommended the inclusion of the following savings clause: "Nothing in this Directive/Framework Decision shall affect the protection afforded to refugees and asylum-seekers under international refugee law and international human rights law, in particular the compliance of Member States with their obligations under Articles 31 and 33 of the 1951 Convention relating to the Status of Refugees." Ibid. at para. 7.

5.2.1.1. Assisting Illegal Entry or Transit

The EU Directive 2002/90/EC requires the imposition of sanctions on intentionally assisting a person who is not a national of a Member State to enter, or transit across, the territory of a Member State in breach of laws of the State concerning the entry or transit of aliens.[152] The elements of the offense are different from the elements of smuggling of migrants, as prescribed in the Migrant Smuggling Protocol (Table 5.7).

As discussed previously, the relevant provisions of the Migrant Smuggling Protocol focus primarily on conduct involving assisted illegal entry or residence, when undertaken for profit or benefit.[153] In contrast, the Directive focuses on both entry and *transit*.[154] Further, unlike the Migrant Smuggling Protocol, there is no requirement in the Directive that the person involved in assisting illegal entry or transit sought to secure any financial or other material benefit.[155] Accordingly, the mere act of assisting another person to illegally enter or transit a Member State is sufficient to establish the offense. As a result, the scope of the EU Directive is far broader than the scope of the Protocol, and would potentially cover many of the "humanitarian" situations that the drafters of the Protocol so carefully sought to avoid capturing.

5.2.1.2. Assisting Illegal Residence for Financial Gain

The Directive further requires States to impose sanctions on any person who, for financial gain, intentionally assists a person who is not a national of a Member State to reside within the territory of a Member State in breach of the laws of the State concerned on the residence of aliens.[156] The elements of this offense are roughly comparable to the elements of the corresponding article in the Migrant Smuggling Protocol on enabling illegal residence (Table 5.8).[157]

5.2.1.3. Instigation, Participation and Attempts

As with the Migrant Smuggling Protocol, the Directive requires States to "take the measures necessary to ensure that the sanctions" are also applicable to the instigator

[152] Council Directive 2002/90/EC, at Art. 1(1)(a).

[153] Migrant Smuggling Protocol, at Art. 6.

[154] Council Directive 2002/90/EC, at Art. 1(1)(a).

[155] For a discussion of the origins of this approach in French domestic law, see J. Vernier, "French Criminal and Administrative Law concerning Smuggling of Migrants and Trafficking in Human Beings: Punishing Trafficked People for Their Protection?" in E. Guild and P. Minderhoud eds., *Immigration and Criminal Law in the European Union: The Legal Measures and Social Consequences of Criminal Law in Member States on Trafficking and Smuggling in Human Beings* 7 (2006).

[156] Council Directive 2002/90/EC, at Art. 1(1)(b).

[157] Migrant Smuggling Protocol, at Art. 6(1)(c).

TABLE 5.7 *Elements of assisting illegal entry or transit under EU Directive 2002/90/EC, Article 1(a)*

Physical element	Corresponding fault element
Assist a person who is not a national of a Member State to enter or transit across territory of a Member State in breach of laws on entry or transit of aliens (conduct).	Intention.

TABLE 5.8 *Elements of assisting illegal residence for financial gain under EU Directive 2002/90/EC, Article 1(b)*

Physical element	Corresponding fault element
Assist a person who is not a national of a Member State to reside within territory of Member State in breach of laws concerning residence of aliens (conduct).	a) Conduct is intentional; b) Conduct is undertaken for financial gain.

of an offense under Article 1, an accomplice in such an offense, and attempts to commit such offenses.[158] Given the breadth of the principal offenses, this provision would likely extend to cover, as "accomplices," many "non-professional" facilitators, such as family members who assist other family members to irregularly migrate. Once again, this is a result that was carefully avoided by the drafters of the Migrant Smuggling Protocol.

5.2.2. 2002 EU Framework Decision on Facilitation of Unauthorized Entry, Transit, and Residence

The Directive is accompanied by a Framework Decision (Council Framework Decision 2002/946), adopted the same day, setting out minimum rules for penalties, liability of legal persons, and jurisdiction. The Framework Decision provides that infringements defined in the Directive shall be punishable by "effective, proportionate and dissuasive criminal penalties," which may include extradition.[159] Criminal penalties may also be accompanied by confiscation of the means of transport used to commit the offense, a prohibition on practicing the occupational activity in the exercise of which the offense was committed, and deportation.[160] The Framework

[158] Council Directive 2002/90/EC, at Art. 2.
[159] Council Framework Decision 2002/946, at Art. 1(1).
[160] Ibid. at Art. 1(2).

Decision recognizes the concept of aggravated offenses: the offenses of unauthorized entry and transit (not residence) are to be punishable by custodial sentences with a maximum sentence of not less than eight years when they are committed for financial gain and: (1) as an activity of a criminal organization,[161] or (2) while endangering the lives of the persons who are the subject of the offense.[162] Member States may reduce the maximum penalty to at least six years if necessary to preserve the coherence of national penalty systems.[163] Legal persons are to be held liable for infringements under certain conditions and subject to specified penalties.[164]

The Framework Decision also sets out the jurisdictional scope of that instrument and of the Directive. A Member State is required to exercise jurisdiction over infringements committed in whole or in part within its territory.[165] A Member State *may* exercise jurisdiction over infringements committed by one of its nationals, or for the benefit of a legal person established in its territory.[166] The principle of "extradite or prosecute" would apply in cases involving nationals of a Member State involved in the commission of offenses outside the territory of that State.[167]

As noted in Chapter 1, the Framework Decision contains an important savings clause. This provides that its provisions are to apply "without prejudice to the protection afforded refugees and asylum-seekers in accordance with international law on refugees or other international instruments relating to human rights."[168] The formulation is narrow. For example, it does not appear to extend to smuggled migrants who are not asylum-seekers or refugees but who may have a claim for protection under international human rights law.[169]

Member States were required to transpose both the Directive and the Framework Decision into national law by December 5, 2004,[170] at which time Article 27(1) of the 1990 Schengen Convention referred to previously was repealed.[171] Since the entry

[161] As defined in Article 1 of Joint Action of 21 December 1998 adopted by the Council on the basis of Article K.3 of the Treaty on European Union, on making it a criminal offence to participate in a criminal organisation in the Member States of the European Union (98/733/JHA), OJ L 351/1, Dec. 29, 1998. ("[A] criminal organisation shall mean a structured association, established over a period of time, of more than two persons, acting in concert with a view to committing offences which are punishable by deprivation of liberty or a detention order of a maximum of at least four years or a more serious penalty, whether such offences are an end in themselves or a means of obtaining material benefits and, where appropriate, of improperly influencing the operation of public authorities.")

[162] Council Framework Decision 2002/946, at Art. 1(3).

[163] Ibid. at Art. 1(4)

[164] Ibid. at Arts. 2–3.

[165] Ibid. at Art. 4(1)(a).

[166] Ibid. at Arts. 4(1)(b)–(c), 4(2).

[167] Ibid. at Art. 5.

[168] Ibid. at Art. 6.

[169] See further discussion of international protection obligations in Chapter 8.

[170] Council Directive 2002/90/EC, at Art. 4(1); Council Framework Decision 2002/946, at Art. 9.

[171] Council Directive 2002/90/EC, at Art. 5; Council Framework Decision 2002/946, at Art. 10.

into force of the Treaty of Lisbon,[172] the Directive is subject to the jurisdiction of the European Court of Justice.[173] The Framework Decision will be similarly subject to the jurisdiction of the Court from December 1, 2014.[174] However, the European Commission has indicated an intention to extend and perhaps merge the Directive and Framework Decision in the near future.[175] Official information on implementation of the two instruments is scarce, being limited to a 2006 report dealing only with operationalization of the Framework Decision.[176]

5.3. A NOTE ON THE RIGHTS OF SUSPECTS AND THE RIGHT TO A FAIR TRIAL

The danger that suspects' rights will be trampled on in efforts to combat migrant smuggling is not a remote one. The call from an Australian prime minister for migrant smugglers to "rot in jail" and "rot in hell"[177] may well have been politically motivated hyperbole. However, it usefully reflects and underscores the seriousness with which States are approaching the issue of migrant smuggling and the gradual but apparently inexorable shifting of the issue onto the national security agenda. One of the most immediate and obvious dangers is that, as has happened in the area of terrorism, the temptation to compromise the rights of individuals suspected of certain crimes will prove difficult to resist.[178] In some countries, the identification

[172] Treaty of Lisbon amending the Treaty on European Union and the Treaty establishing the European Community, OJ C 306/1, done Dec. 13, 2007, entered into force Dec. 1, 2009.

[173] The operation of the Directive was considered by the Court of Justice in *Minh Khoa Vo* (Court of Justice of the European Union, C-83/12 PPU, Apr. 10, 2012).

[174] Peers et al., *EU Immigration and Asylum Law (Text and Commentary)*, at 385.

[175] Ibid.

[176] Commission of the European Communities, Report from the Commission based on Article 9 of the Council Framework Decision of 28 November 2002 on the strengthening of the penal framework to prevent the facilitation of unauthorised entry, transit and residence, COM(2006) 770 final, Dec. 6, 2006.

[177] In 2009, responding to a fatal blast on board a smuggling vessel, the then Australian prime minister Kevin Rudd stated: "people smugglers are the vilest form of human life. They trade on the tragedy of others and that's why they should rot in jail and in my own view, rot in hell." Quoted in E. Rogers, "Rudd Wants People Smugglers to 'Rot in Hell,'" ABC News, Apr. 17, 2009, available at www.abc.net.au/news/2009–04–17/rudd-wants-people-smugglers-to-rot-in-hell/1653814 (accessed May 12, 2013).

[178] UN Human Rights Council, "Report of the Special Rapporteur on the Promotion and Protection of Human Rights and Fundamental Freedoms while Countering Terrorism, Martin Scheinin" UN Doc. A/HRC/4/26, Jan. 29, 2007; "Report of the United Nations High Commissioner for Human Rights on the Protection of Human Rights and Fundamental Freedoms while Countering Terrorism," UN Doc. A/HRC/4/88, Mar. 9, 2007 (specifically addressing the procedural obligations of States toward terrorism suspects, the principle of *non-refoulement*, and the human rights aspects of individual sanctions implemented against terrorism suspects by States). Generally on the relevance of international law to actions against terrorism, see H. Duffy, *The "War on Terror" and the Framework of International Law* (2005).

of migrant smuggling as a threat to national security and the linking of migrant smuggling to other security threats including terrorism could well be used to justify application of a different set of rights and entitlements for suspects.[179]

Many of the countries that are leading the push for prosecution of smuggled migrants have relatively robust criminal justice systems that include appropriate human rights protections. It can reasonably be expected that even in face of political pressure to deliver convictions, these criminal justice systems should be able to provide justice without compromising rights. However, that cannot be taken for granted, and States must be aware that their treatment of migrant smugglers – both suspects and persons convicted of smuggling-related offenses – is itself regulated by established rules of international law. Risks to the rights of suspects will be especially acute in countries with weak or dysfunctional criminal justice systems where rules of evidence and procedure already fall short of international standards. As has occurred in relation to trafficking in persons,[180] these countries may be subject to intense pressure from other States to arrest and prosecute migrant smugglers. It is submitted that such pressure should not be exerted where the State seeking cooperation is aware, or should be aware, that persons subject to prosecution are unlikely to receive a fair trial. States providing such support may in fact be held responsible under international law for violations of human rights that are encouraged or facilitated in this way.[181]

As already noted, international law imposes certain obligations on States with respect to their treatment of individuals suspected (and indeed convicted) of any offenses, including offenses related to migrant smuggling. As with any other crime, States are required to ensure that their pursuit of suspected smugglers is never at the expense of the international rules governing human rights and the administration of justice. The relevant rules can usefully be summarized as follows: all persons charged with criminal offenses, including migrant smuggling, are entitled to specific substantive rights. These include the right to equality before courts and tribunals (i.e., to the same treatment irrespective of factors such as their nationality or the crime they are charged with); the right to be presumed innocent; the right to a fair and impartial hearing; the right to be tried within a reasonable time period; the right to be tried by a competent, independent, and impartial court or tribunal; and the

[179] See, for example, Human Smuggling and Anti-Trafficking Center (United States), A *Report to Congress as Required by Section 7202(d) of the Intelligence Reform and Terrorism Prevention Act of 2004* (2005) (affirming at iii the joint position of the United States' Departments of State and Homeland Security that "Human smuggling, trafficking in persons, and clandestine terrorist travel are transnational issues that threaten national security").

[180] See A. T. Gallagher, "Improving the Effectiveness of the International Law of Human Trafficking: A Vision for the Future of the US Trafficking in Persons Reports" (2011) 12 *Human Rights Review* 381.

[181] See further Chapter 4, at Section 4.4 for discussion of State responsibility in the context of joint operations and other forms of interstate cooperation.

right to have a conviction and sentence reviewed by a higher court or tribunal.[182] The right to be subject to penalties that are proportionate to the gravity of the offense and to the offender's role in the smuggling situation is also, as noted at Section 5.1.5.1 of this chapter, absolutely crucial. None of these rights may be abrogated for any reason, including for considerations of national security or public order.

It has been reported that organizers of migrant smuggling will sometimes deliberately recruit males under the age of eighteen years to assist in the smuggling process. Indonesian children, for example, have ended up in Australian prisons charged with, or convicted of, smuggling offenses.[183] It may well be that the recruitment of children is a deliberate strategy to avoid or minimize the force of the criminal justice response. In such cases, the prosecuting State may be reluctant to feed into this strategy by allowing children involved in smuggling operations to be returned without penalty. Although such sentiments are understandable, they cannot justify a violation of the relevant international legal rules. A critical, initial obligation of States is to actively identify children among persons who have been apprehended for involvement in migrant smuggling. Failure to quickly and accurately identify such children will inevitably lead to a failure to respect and protect the special and additional rights to which those children are entitled. It should thereby be considered a breach of the State's obligations under international law.

In terms of the rights owed to such children, the core rules can be found in the Convention on the Rights of the Child.[184] This instrument confirms that a child in conflict with the law has the right to a standard and form of treatment that promotes the child's sense of dignity and worth, that takes the child's age into account, and that aims at his or her reintegration into society. It also affirms that children in conflict with the law are entitled to the substantive and procedural guarantees aimed at ensuring a fair hearing, full protection of their right to privacy, and the provision of legal or other assistance for their defense.[185] Judicial proceedings and institutional placements shall be avoided wherever possible.[186] As discussed in detail in Chapter 9 (Section 9.4.3) children accused or convicted of migrant smuggling offenses are also entitled to special protection with regard to their detention.[187]

[182] These rights are set out in the UDHR (Article 10) and the ICCPR (Article14). With only minor differences they are also reflected in regional human rights treaties. See the African Charter (Article 7), the European Convention on Human Rights (Article 6), and the American Convention on Human Rights (Article 8).

[183] See Australian Human Rights Commission, *An Age of Uncertainty*.

[184] Convention on the Rights of the Child, 1577 UNTS 3, done Nov. 20, 1989, entered into force Sept. 2, 1990.

[185] Ibid. at Art. 40(2).

[186] Ibid. at Art. 40(3)–(4).

[187] See further Chapter 9, at Section 9.4.3.

A State that fails to observe international legal rules on the administration of criminal justice in relation to any person suspected, charged with, or convicted of a migrant smuggling offense commits an internationally wrongful act for which it is legally responsible. Such failures also risk compromising the integrity and reputation of the criminal justice response and can lead to an erosion of community support for the investigation and prosecution of smugglers.

5.4. CONCLUSIONS ON OBLIGATIONS RELATED TO CRIMINALIZATION

Criminalization of migrant smuggling is central to the specialist legal regime that has been established around this issue. However, as customary international law does not recognize specific obligations in this area, it is only those States participating in the specialist treaty regime that are legally obliged to criminalize migrant smuggling. Other international laws may impose obligations on States to take action in respect of certain matters: for example to respond effectively to smuggling involving inhumane treatment or punishment. In addition, international law requires that relevant rules of human rights and refugee law, including the obligation of *non-refoulement*, are to be preserved in relation to all aspects of criminalization including the treatment of suspects and persons convicted of smuggling offenses.

States Parties to the Migrant Smuggling Protocol are obliged to criminalize migrant smuggling and attempted migrant smuggling, ensuring higher penalties are attached to smuggling offenses that involve danger to the lives of migrants or that entail degrading treatment or exploitation. States Parties are also required to criminalize a range of related conduct including enabling unlawful residence and document fraud. States Parties are further bound by obligations arising from the Organized Crime Convention relating to matters such as sanctions; ensuring the liability of legal persons; confiscation, seizure, and disposal of proceeds of crime; jurisdiction; international cooperation; and witness protection. The Protocol's savings clause with respect to human rights and refugee law is applicable in respect of these criminalization provisions.

The Migrant Smuggling Protocol may not be used to criminalize migrants for the fact of having been smuggled, although States are not prevented from prosecuting smuggled migrants for the full range of non–smuggling-related criminal offenses. Laws criminalizing smuggled migrants – for example in relation to unlawful entry or possession of fraudulent travel documents for personal use – could not be justified under the terms of the Protocol, and States Parties do not owe each other any obligation to cooperate in suppressing such offenses.

The only other treaty-based sources of obligation with respect to criminalizing migrant smuggling are the 2002 EU Directive on Facilitation of Unauthorized

Entry, Transit and Residence and its associated Framework Decision. These instruments generally follow the structure and range of offenses established under the Migrant Smuggling Protocol. However, their potential reach is greater, principally because the relevant obligations extend to conduct assisting illegal entry, transit, and residence irrespective of whether such conduct was undertaken for the purpose of financial gain.

6

Migrant Smuggling by Sea: Interdiction and Rescue

Migrants, including asylum-seekers and refugees, have long turned to the sea to escape brutal regimes, humanitarian crises, hunger, poverty, and unemployment. At times, and particularly in connection with conflict, the scale of these human movements has been remarkable, with literally hundreds of thousands of people from one country or region using the sea to seek refuge.[1] During periods of extreme crisis, there is no doubt that passage by sea provides a vital escape valve.[2]

1 On the mass migration of Indo-Chinese refugees by sea during the 1970s, see J. Pugash, "The Dilemma of the Sea Refugee: Rescue without Refuge" (1977) 18 *Harvard International Law Journal* 577 [Pugash, "The Dilemma of the Sea Refugee"]. Another example is provided by the wave of migration from the Caribbean to the United States in the early 1980s: between April and September 1980, 125,000 Cuban migrants arrived in the United States by boat. (D. Guilfoyle, *Shipping Interdiction and the Law of the Sea* (2009) [Guilfoyle, *Shipping Interdiction and the Law of the Sea*], at 192). That same year, 15,000 Haitians arrived in the same way. (A. Helton, "The United States Government Program of Intercepting and Forcibly Returning Haitian Boat People to Haiti: Policy Implications and Prospects" (1993) 10 *New York Law School Journal of Human Rights* 325, at 325). Migration by sea from North Africa to southern Europe provides a much more recent example. See further references in Chapter 1, at Section 1.1. More recently, it was reported that during 2012 "[a] record 107,500 [Ethiopian and Somali] refugees and migrants made the dangerous journey from the Horn of Africa to Yemen": UN High Commissioner for Refugees, "Record Number of African Refugees and Migrants Cross the Gulf of Aden in 2012" (*Briefing Notes*, Jan. 15, 2013), available at www.unhcr.org/50f5633c9.html (accessed May 12, 2013). The UN High Commissioner for Refugees (UNHCR) reports that the boats are often packed beyond capacity and that smugglers will sometimes force passengers to swim to shore in order to avoid detection, often with tragic consequences (ibid). Arriving migrants who are met by smugglers and traffickers offering to facilitate the next part of their journey through Yemen to other Gulf States are at high risk of exploitation, violence, and sexual abuse. See Medecins Sans Frontieres, *No Choice: Somali and Ethiopian Refugees, Asylum Seekers and Migrants Crossing the Gulf of Aden* (2008); Human Rights Watch, *Hostile Shores: Abuse and Refoulement of Asylum Seekers and Refugees in Yemen* (2009); and A. Soucy, *Mixed Migration from the Horn of Africa to Yemen: Protection Risks and Challenges* (Danish Refugee Council, 2011).

2 See for example, J-J. F. Espenilla, "Injustice Ignored: A Case Study of the Irregular Sea Migration of the Rohingyan Boat People" (2010) 8(1) *Asia Europe Journal* 45 (discussing clandestine movements by sea of Rohingya refugees from camps in Bangladesh).

Even outside conflict-related movements, smuggling by sea may be the cheapest, or perhaps the only option available to individuals who are forced or wish to move. It may also be just one part of a multistage journey that includes smuggling by air and across land borders. Sea travel for smuggled migrants is often dangerous, typically involving lengthy journeys onboard overcrowded and barely seaworthy vessels, such as converted fishing boats, ill-equipped for the conditions of the journey and the physical needs of their many passengers. Although the data around smuggling-related fatalities is incomplete, available information appears to confirm that smuggling by sea carries with it a particularly high risk of death through drowning, suffocation, dehydration, starvation, and violence.[3] Smuggling by sea also places considerable strain on the search and rescue services of involved coastal States.[4]

Responses to migrant smuggling at sea take place in a complex and challenging legal landscape, comprised of cumulative rules and obligations imposed under the law of the sea, international human rights law, refugee law, and transnational criminal law. Conceptually, there are broadly two ways in which States respond to migrant smuggling at sea. First, consistent with State sovereignty and the prerogative of border control, coastal States are *entitled* under certain circumstances to intercept or interdict vessels engaged in migrant smuggling at sea in order to prevent unauthorized migrants from entering their territory. Such law enforcement actions must take place in accordance with the law of the sea and other rules of international law, and within the bounds of any multilateral or bilateral agreement for interdiction of migrant smuggling at sea. Second, independently of interdiction, the law of the sea also *obliges* shipmasters and States to render assistance/rescue to any persons in distress at sea, including to smuggled migrants and migrant smugglers. The obligations of assistance under the law of the sea, including the obligations of search and

[3] See case studies detailed in the Introduction. See also M. K. Li, M. A. Beck, Q. Shi and R. C. Harruff, "Unexpected Hazard of Illegal Immigration: Outbreak of Viral Myocarditis Exacerbated by Confinement and Deprivation in a Shipboard Cargo Container" (2004) 25(2) *American Journal of Forensic Medicine and Pathology* 117. Observatories that record the number of deaths of migrants by sea include the *Border Crossing Observatory*, based at Monash University (Australia), which has maintained a record of all known deaths associated with Australia's borders since January 1, 2000: "The Australian Border Deaths Database" (the most recent publication records (Jan. 1, 2000 – Apr. 2013) are available at http://artsonline.monash.edu.au/thebordercrossingobservatory/publications/the-australian-border-deaths-database/ (accessed May 12, 2013)). See also L. Weber and S. Pickering, *Globalization and Borders: Death at the Global Frontier* (2011).

[4] For example, in just three days, March 26 to 28, 2011, Italian authorities were engaged in maritime incidents involving approximately 4300 people: over 2200 were assisted at sea, and approximately 2000 were rescued in distress situations. Council of Europe, Parliamentary Assembly, *Lives Lost in the Mediterranean Sea: Who Is Responsible?* (Report of the Committee on Migration, Refugees and Displaced Persons, Doc. 12895, Apr. 5, 2012) [Council of Europe Parliamentary Assembly Report, *Lives Lost in the Mediterranean Sea*].

rescue, are motivated purely by humanitarian considerations and apply at all times in respect of any persons in distress at sea.

From an international legal perspective, the issue of smuggling by sea presents some particular complications that may not arise (or will arise in a different way) in respect of smuggling over land borders or by air. Some of these challenges relate to the nature of the space itself. The sheer size of the seas is a practical challenge. Coastal States require considerable personnel and resources, such as patrol vessels and aircraft, to regulate their adjacent sea expanses effectively. The isolated nature of operations at sea also renders difficult the effective discharge and monitoring of law enforcement operations as well as of States' search and rescue obligations under the law of the sea and obligations under human rights and refugee law. The core of many legal complexities is jurisdiction. As explained in Chapter 1, the oceans of the world are divided up into zones, to which are attached different rights and responsibilities. Deciding which State has the capacity to act in a particular migrant smuggling situation at sea, and establishing the correct limits on that capacity, is often very difficult. The allocation of responsibilities – toward smuggled refugees for example, or toward smuggled migrants in distress, is similarly challenging. This process of identifying capacities and allocating responsibilities is an age-old problem of international law, but the well-established rules were not developed with practices such as migrant smuggling in mind. It is only in very recent years that such responses have begun to be subject to international legal scrutiny.

This chapter seeks to critically examine the international legal framework that addresses these issues – the capacity of States to respond to migrant smuggling by sea, limits on that capacity, and the intersecting question of legal obligations toward smuggled migrants under a number of applicable legal regimes: the law of the sea, international human rights law, refugee law, and transnational criminal law (which both reiterates and reinforces many existing rules in this area). The chapter commences with a consideration of the rules that govern law enforcement at sea, most particularly the interdictions at sea that have become a central plank of the anti-smuggling response of many States. The term "interdiction" is now commonly used to describe all aspects of what Guilfoyle identifies as a two-step process: "first, the boarding, inspection, and search of a ship at sea suspected of prohibited conduct; second, where such suspicions prove justified, taking measures including any combination of arresting the vessel, arresting persons aboard or seizing cargo."[5] The rules applicable to a particular situation will be determined by a range of factors, including where the interdiction takes place; the status of the vessel; the status of the interdicting authority; and, of course, the conduct and outcome of the interdiction itself. Further, in the context of migrant smuggling, maritime law enforcement operations

5 Guilfoyle, *Shipping Interdiction and the Law of the Sea*, at 4.

have gone beyond the steps involved in interdiction noted by Guilfoyle, and have for example, extended to other actions such as towing a vessel to another regulatory zone (for example, from the territorial waters of the coastal State to the high seas), or returning it to the point of embarkation. An important question to be addressed is therefore if and when these so-called push backs constitute a legitimate form of law enforcement action.

Independently of interdiction, the law of the sea also calls on States and their shipmasters to render assistance to any persons in distress at sea, including to smuggled migrants and migrant smugglers alike. Although there is a clear conceptual difference between rescue and interdiction, in practice the lines between the two are often blurred. In responding to migrant smuggling at sea and in justifying measures taken, States have frequently invoked maritime safety and the grave dangers to life arising from migrant smuggling at sea.[6] In addition to securing political support for interdictions, characterizing an interdiction as a rescue operation may enable States to evade certain obligations.[7] In practice, rescue operations may coincide with, or transform into, operations to interdict or otherwise divert migrant smuggling vessels. In the face of this factual confusion and overlap, the difference between interdiction and rescue must be emphasized: interdiction and rescue operate in fundamentally different ways, and the legal framework governing rescue at sea does not apply to interception operations that have no search and rescue component.[8] At the same time, the right of States to regulate migration, including through interdiction, in no way displaces the duty of States and shipmasters to provide assistance to persons in distress at sea.[9]

The second part of the chapter accordingly considers the legal framework around the duty to render assistance and to establish search and rescue services. What is the

6 As discussed later in the chapter, the Protocol against the Smuggling of Migrants by Land, Sea and Air, supplementing the United Nations Convention against Transnational Organized Crime, 2241 UNTS 507, done Nov. 15, 2000, entered into force Jan. 28, 2004 [Migrant Smuggling Protocol], originated, at least in part, in an International Maritime Organization (IMO) Assembly resolution largely focused on maritime safety: *Enhancement of Safety of Life at Sea by the Prevention and Suppression of Unsafe Practices Associated with Alien Smuggling by Ships*, IMO Resolution A.773(18), Nov. 4, 1993.

7 Giuffré notes that EU States generally prefer to deem their activities on the high seas as "rescue" missions rather than "interceptions" as the former do not fall under the Schengen Border Code and thereby do not trigger the Article 7 obligation either to handle asylum requests or to proceed with a minimum check of migrants' identities. M. Giuffré, "State Responsibility Beyond Borders: What Legal Basis for Italy's Push-Backs to Libya?" (2013) 24 *International Journal of Refugee Law* 692 [Giuffré, "State Responsibility Beyond Borders"], at 707.

8 UN High Commissioner for Refugees, "Expert Meeting on Refugees and Asylum-Seekers in Distress at Sea – How Best to Respond? Djibouti, 8–10 November 2011" (2012) 24(2) *International Journal of Refugee Law* 485.

9 R. Barnes, "The International Law of the Sea and Migration Control," in B. Ryan and V. Mitsilegas eds., *Extraterritorial Immigration Control: Legal Challenges* 103 (2010) [Barnes, "The International Law of the Sea and Migration Control"], at 134.

duty of shipmasters and of coastal States? Which State is responsible for disembarkation of persons interdicted and/or rescued at sea? Is a coastal State ever entitled to deny disembarkation? What is the situation if no State will admit the rescued migrants? Is the rescuing State obliged to take the rescued migrants back to its territory?

The third and final part of the chapter considers the ways in which human rights and refugee law apply to migrant smuggling by sea. This analysis reflects the reality of mixed migration; specifically the fact that alongside migrants to whom no protection obligations are owed, many persons intercepted and/or rescued at sea will be seeking asylum from persecution. How do States that are engaged in interceptions and rescues discharge their obligations to such persons? More generally, what rights are owed to migrants at sea who are the subject of either a law enforcement or rescue operation? What corresponding obligations are imposed on the States undertaking such operations?

This chapter weaves together, reinforces, and extends several other parts of the book. Of particular relevance is Chapter 3, Part 1 (capacity to act), which provides a detailed description and analysis of the relevant principles of jurisdiction as well as a substantive section on principles of jurisdiction at sea. The discussion in Chapter 3, at Section 3.4 on extraterritorial application of human rights and refugee law obligations is also highly relevant. Reference should further be made to the discussion of rescue of migrants in distress in Chapter 7, at Section 7.1.2.5, and to Chapters 9 and 10, which deal with detention and return of smuggled migrants respectively.

6.1. INTERDICTION AT SEA

There is no international legal definition of the term "interdiction at sea" (and its commonly employed synonym "interception") although the two-step process outlined previously provides a useful overview of the various actions that may come under such headings. Certainly in the context of migrant smuggling, these "vague and ambiguous"[10] concepts are widely taken to refer to a range of different measures aimed at either preventing a vessel from commencing a journey, or more commonly, taking control of a vessel so as to disrupt or prevent its intended journey.[11] As a

[10] M. Tondini, "The Legality of Intercepting Boat People under Search and Rescue and Border Control Operations with Reference to Recent Italian Interventions in the Mediterranean Sea and the ECtHR Decision in the *Hirsi* Case" (2012) 18 *The Journal of International Maritime Law* 59 [Tondini, "The Legality of Intercepting Boat People"], at 59.

[11] UNHCR, for example, has referred to "interception" as "one of the measures employed by States to: i. prevent embarkation of persons on an international journey; ii. prevent further onward international travel by persons who have commenced their journey; or iii. assert control of vessels where there are reasonable grounds to believe that the vessel is transporting persons contrary to international or

practical matter, it is useful to understand interdiction as the maritime equivalent of the exercise of coercive law enforcement powers on land. Just as law enforcement officials may seek to stop, search, and arrest a person or seize property on land, in the maritime context, a State might seek to stop, board, and search a vessel, and undertake the arrest of persons, the vessel itself, or cargo.[12] Two of the case studies set out in the Introduction to this book (*Australia Refuses Entry to Vessel Carrying Rescued Smuggled Migrants*[13] and *Italy Turns Back Smuggled Migrants Intercepted on the High Seas*[14]) involved interdiction.

Many of the international legal issues relevant to interdiction revolve around the issue of jurisdiction, "the extent of each state's right to regulate conduct or the consequences of events."[15] As explained previously in this book, jurisdiction in international law generally refers to two different types of competence: (1) competence to make laws and regulations governing a matter (*prescriptive* jurisdiction); and (2) competence to compel compliance with those rules, including through recourse to punitive or coercive measures (*enforcement* jurisdiction).[16] In strictly legal terms, interdiction is an exercise by the State of its *enforcement jurisdiction*. In other words, the State is taking specific actions to compel compliance with the laws it has prescribed. The rules around enforcement jurisdiction have been explored in detail in Chapter 3 in the context of a broader discussion of capacity to act, and it is therefore only necessary to provide a summary of the relevant points prior to their more practical application in this chapter. In brief, international law recognizes that enforcement jurisdiction is about the exercise of coercive powers. States are accordingly given much wider latitude to prescribe rules than to actually enforce them. The relevant rule of customary law has two aspects: (1) a State *may* exercise enforcement jurisdiction within its own territory but not outside it, and (2) a State *must not* exercise enforcement jurisdiction in the territory of another State without its permission.[17] States may expand their capacity to enforce the rules they have prescribed – and the capacity of other States to do so – through consent (generally treaty-based). The allocation of jurisdictional competence between States in this way is a marked feature of global prohibition regimes such as those that apply to drug trafficking and to migrant smuggling.

national maritime law": UN High Commissioner for Refugees Executive Committee, *Conclusion on Protection Safeguards in Interception Measures*, Doc. No. 97 (LIV) – 2003, Oct. 10, 2003.

12 Guilfoyle, *Shipping Interdiction and the Law of the Sea*, at 9.

13 See Introduction, at note 20 and accompanying text.

14 See Introduction, at notes 21–28 and accompanying text.

15 R. Jennings and A. Watts eds., *Oppenheim's International Law: Volume I, Peace* (9th ed. 1992), [Jennings and Watts, *Oppenheim's International Law: Volume 1, Peace*, 9th ed.], at 456.

16 See further Chapter 3, at Section 3.2.

17 See references in Chapter 3, at note 93.

Although enforcement jurisdiction on land is relatively straightforward, in the maritime context it is complicated by a number of different factors. As has been explained in detail in Chapter 3, the law of the sea sets out a complex regime of jurisdictional zones, each with its own jurisdictional rules.[18] A significant portion of the world's oceans does not lie within the jurisdictional reach of a single State. In considering the legal implications of a particular maritime interdiction it is therefore critical to ask: In what maritime zone is the interdiction occurring? What are the relevant rules on exercise of enforcement jurisdiction in that zone? What consent-based arrangements are in place, and to what extent do they modify those rules? What is the nationality of the interdicting vessel and of the vessel subject to interdiction?

Any authority to interdict – whether based on established rules of jurisdiction or on a specific treaty that operates to modify those rules – is subject to a range of other rules that will prescribe the parameters of that authority. Where a specific agreement applies, the relevant parameters will generally be determined with reference to that agreement. For example, a treaty providing consent to exercise authority may be limited to boarding, or it may extend as far as seizure. The provisions of relevant instruments discussed at Sections 6.1.1.3 and 6.1.2, including the United Nations Convention on the Law of the Sea[19] (UNCLOS), certainly presuppose that use of force may be required to effect a certain action. However, the question of whether an interdiction may involve the use of force, and limits on the use of permissible force, is not easily answered. As explained at Section 6.3.3, the issue is closely connected to the protection of life and safety under international human rights law. There are of course many other human rights considerations that arise in the context of interdiction, ranging from the right to privacy to the prohibition on arbitrary detention. In the context of criminal enforcement, proper compliance with the rules of jurisdiction and human rights will also often be critical to ensuring the effectiveness of subsequent criminal proceedings. These are discussed in Chapters 2 and 3, and at relevant points throughout this chapter.

6.1.1. *Power to Interdict under the Law of the Sea*

The law of the sea recognizes a range of maritime zones, to which are attached different jurisdictional rules and entitlements that impact directly on the question of when and under what circumstances international law will recognize a State's power to interdict a vessel carrying smuggled migrants. The preeminence of this

[18] See Chapter 3, at Section 3.3.

[19] United Nations Convention on the Law of the Sea, 1833 UNTS 3, done Dec. 10, 1982, entered into force Nov. 16, 1994 [UNCLOS].

regime is both reiterated and reinforced by the Migrant Smuggling Protocol.[20] It is therefore appropriate to initially consider the question of power to interdict with reference to those different zones and the rules and principles of jurisdiction that apply to them. Note that Chapter 3 contains a detailed description of each maritime zone and its relevant rules. The following discussion summarizes that information before going on to consider how these rules apply to situations of interdiction.

6.1.1.1. Interdiction in Internal Waters and the Territorial Sea

The sovereignty of a coastal State extends to its internal waters.[21] For all practical purposes, internal waters have the same legal status as the land territory of Nation States. Vessels seeking to enter a State's internal waters are required to secure the same sorts of permissions as would be needed by a vessel or individual seeking to enter the country through other channels, such as by land or air, unless there are circumstances of *force majeure* or distress.[22] Accordingly, a State can exercise the full extent of its law enforcement powers against a migrant smuggling vessel in its internal waters, much as it could any other foreign person or vessel within its sovereign territory.

The sovereignty of a coastal State also extends to the territorial sea,[23] an adjacent belt of sea not exceeding twelve nautical miles from its baseline.[24] Within the territorial sea, coastal States enjoy sovereignty and thus full jurisdictional powers[25] subject to important limitations in UNCLOS discussed in this subsection, as well as to "other rules of international law."[26] There is no automatic application of national law to the territorial sea: the scope of application depends on the law itself.[27]

[20] Migrant Smuggling Protocol, at Arts. 7, 9(3).

[21] UNCLOS, at Art. 2.

[22] Rothwell argues that the right of a ship in distress to enter internal waters such as ports and harbors arises from customary international law, and is reflected by the right of vessels to stop and anchor in territorial waters, where rendered necessary by *force majeure* or distress, as per Article 18(2) of UNCLOS: D. Rothwell, "The Law of the Sea and the MV *Tampa* Incident: Reconciling Maritime Principles with Coastal State Sovereignty" (2002) 13(2) *Public Law Review* 118 [Rothwell, "The Law of the Sea and the MV *Tampa* Incident"], at 123–124.

[23] UNCLOS, at Art. 2.

[24] Ibid. at Art. 3.

[25] D. P. O'Connell (I. Shearer ed.), *The International Law of the Sea*, vol. 1 (1982), at 744; M. Evans, "The Law of the Sea," in M. Evans ed., *International Law* 651 (3rd ed. 2010), at 658; and D. Rothwell and T. Stephens, *The International Law of the Sea* (2010), at 73: "The extent of coastal state sovereignty and jurisdiction over the territorial sea is vast and even taking into account the limitations imposed by [UNCLOS] in relation to innocent passage, relatively unfettered with respect to core areas of state interest."

[26] UNCLOS, at Art. 2(3).

[27] R. R. Churchill and A. V. Lowe, *The Law of the Sea* (3rd ed. 1999) [Churchill and Lowe, *The Law of the Sea*], at 75.

Accordingly, many States have national laws that clearly specify that criminal laws apply to conduct committed in the territorial sea.[28] Vessels in the territorial sea are thereby subject to the national laws of the State, including criminal and immigration laws, much as any person traveling through the State's land territory.

Although State sovereignty over the territorial sea provides coastal States with wide prescriptive and enforcement powers, this is subject to the right of innocent passage – as well as to other soft and hard law restrictions on the exercise of coastal State jurisdiction. The right of innocent passage, which has a solid basis in customary law and is enshrined in the relevant law of the sea instruments,[29] recognizes that vessels frequently need to transit through the territorial waters of coastal States in the course of longer journeys. The competence of a coastal State to prescribe and enforce laws and regulations in its territorial sea is circumscribed by the obligation to respect the right of other States' ships to innocent passage.[30]

The meaning and limits of "innocent passage" are relevant to whether coastal States can nonetheless exercise both prescriptive and law enforcement jurisdiction in the territorial sea. First, it is relevant to consider whether a vessel carrying smuggled migrants is engaged in innocent passage. "Innocence" in this context refers to process as well as intent and outcome. In relation to the process, passage must be continuous and expeditious. It may include stopping and anchoring, but only insofar as this is incidental to ordinary navigation, or is rendered necessary by *force majeure* or distress or for the purpose of rendering assistance to persons, ships, or aircraft in danger or distress.[31] In relation to intent and outcome, passage is innocent "so long as it is not prejudicial to the peace, good order or security of the coastal State."[32] Passage will not be considered "innocent" if the vessel engages in one or more of a range of specified activities, of which the most relevant to migrant smuggling is the loading or unloading of any person contrary to the immigration laws and regulations of the coastal State.[33] Accordingly, the right of innocent passage does

[28] See, for example, section 15 B of Australia's Acts Interpretation Act 1901 (Cth).

[29] See UNCLOS, at Arts. 17–20; and Convention on the Territorial Sea and the Contiguous Zone, 516 UNTS 205, done Apr. 29, 1958, entered into force Sept. 10, 1964 [Territorial Sea Convention], at Arts. 14–20.

[30] UNCLOS, at Arts. 17, 21.

[31] Ibid. at Art. 18. See also Territorial Sea Convention, at Art. 14(3).

[32] UNCLOS, at Art. 19(1). See also Territorial Sea Convention, at Art. 14(4).

[33] UNCLOS, at Art. 19(2)(g). Note that another exception (Article 19(2)(a)) extends to "any threat or use of force against the sovereignty, territorial integrity or political independence of the coastal State." It is highly unlikely that migrant smuggling activities would fall within this exception. See M. H. Nordquist, S. Rosenne, and S. N. Nandan, *United Nations Convention on the Law of the Sea 1982: A Commentary*, vol. 3 (1995) [Nordquist et al., *United Nations Convention on the Law of the Sea 1982: A Commentary*], at 175 ("Paragraph 2(a) states the fundamental rule of international law embodied in Article 2, paragraph 4, of the United Nations Charter.").

not prevent a coastal State from prescribing and enforcing laws regulating entry and exit, many of which will have direct relevance to migrant smuggling.

Do coastal States have the capacity to regulate and enforce laws regarding mere passage of vessels through coastal waters, where these vessels are carrying prospective smuggled migrants destined for another State? Arguably, a coastal State could prescribe and seek to enforce national laws to the effect that it is an offense to undertake passage through the territorial sea intending to breach the immigration laws of another State. Laws of this nature may become more common as an increasing number of States criminalize migrant smuggling, and as the norm of interstate cooperation to prevent migrant smuggling strengthens. The question remains however, whether laws of this nature would constitute an interference with the right of innocent passage. The answer depends on how innocent passage is understood, and the parameters of the concept as it applies to migrant smuggling through the territorial sea are still evolving. As has been explained previously, the UNCLOS reference in the chapeau of the relevant article to "engag[ing] in any of the following activities" indicates that some "activity" is indeed required, such that mere passage, without more, would not amount to prejudice to the State.[34] This interpretation supports the view that the mere passage of a vessel carrying smuggled migrants through the territorial waters of one State, destined for a third State, would not, of itself, render that passage non-innocent.[35] However that position is not universally accepted by States and intergovernmental organizations. For example, in a review of the relevant law, the European Commission has expressed the view that:

> [I]t could be regarded as an obligation for Member State X to intervene if a ship making use of the right of innocent passage in its territorial waters has the intention to disembark illegal immigrants in Member State Y. Such an obligation, while not explicitly established, should be considered as flowing from the Community's policies on the crossing of external borders and the establishment of an area without internal frontiers.[36]

On this view, coastal States are not only *permitted* to take action against transiting smuggling vessels, they are *obliged* to do so. However, this interpretation is likely of narrow application, resting as it does on existing frameworks of cooperation that are not replicated outside the European Community.

How may coastal States respond to the non-innocent passage of a migrant smuggling vessel? International law permits a coastal State to "take the necessary steps in

[34] Churchill and Lowe, *The Law of the Sea*, at 85. See further Chapter 3, at Section 3.3.2.2.

[35] See further the analogy with a vessel carrying materiel for weapons of mass destruction destined for and intended for use against (distant) third States at Chapter 3, note 162.

[36] European Commission, Staff Working Document, "Study on the International Law Instruments in Relation to Illegal Immigration by Sea," SEC(2007) 691, May 15, 2007, at para. 2.1.3.

its territorial sea to prevent passage which is not innocent."[37] The term "necessary steps" is not defined or otherwise explained. However, in the case of a vessel that has the intention to disembark passengers in contravention of the coastal State's immigration laws, it is generally agreed that the coastal State has "the right to escort such a ship to the high seas or proceed with arrests."[38] In the case of vessels that are proceeding to internal waters, the coastal State also has the right to take the necessary steps to prevent any breach of the conditions to which admission of those ships to internal waters is subject.[39] Accordingly, in this situation, coastal States have the right to take actions to enforce criminal and immigration laws, just as they would at airports, land borders, or ports. In summary, a vessel that is passing through the territorial sea, but intending to disembark smuggled migrants in that coastal State contrary to the immigration laws of that State, is clearly not engaged in innocent passage.[40] Accordingly, the coastal State has the right to take law enforcement action against the vessel in question and any passengers and crew.

Irrespective of whether passage is innocent or not, States retain full capacity to enforce their criminal law in respect of crimes committed on passing ships in a number of specified situations: if the consequences of the crime extend to the coastal State, if the crime is of a kind to disturb the peace of the country or the good order of the territorial sea, if the master of the vessel or its flag State has requested the coastal State to assist, if the measures are necessary to suppress drug trafficking,[41] or if the foreign ship is passing through the territorial sea after leaving the coastal State's internal waters.[42] As noted in Chapter 3, the carriage of smuggled migrants to be disembarked in the coastal State would clearly fall within the first of these listed circumstances and arguably the second as well.[43] In relation to the first exception, this would clearly permit interdiction of a ship in territorial waters when it has, for example, previously entered internal waters and disembarked smuggled migrants before attempting to leave.

There are some restrictions on the capacity of a coastal State to enforce national laws on vessels merely passing through the territorial sea. Article 27(1) of UNCLOS

37 UNCLOS, at Art. 25(1). See also Territorial Sea Convention, at Art. 16(1). Note that customary rules would further permit the coastal State to take enforcement action against hovering vessels and those otherwise not engaged in passage: Churchill and Lowe, *The Law of the Sea*, at 87.

38 European Commission, Staff Working Document, "Study on the International Law Instruments in Relation to Illegal Immigration by Sea," SEC(2007) 691, May 15, 2007, at para. 2.1.2. See also Barnes, "The International Law of the Sea and Migration Control," at 124.

39 UNCLOS, at Art. 25(2).

40 Ibid. at Art. 19(2)(g).

41 Ibid. at Art. 27(1).

42 Ibid. at Art. 27(2).

43 P. Mallia, *Migrant Smuggling by Sea: Combating a Current Threat to Maritime Security through the Creation of a Cooperative Framework* (2009) [Mallia, *Migrant Smuggling by Sea*], at 51.

provides that the criminal jurisdiction of the coastal State "*should not* be exercised on board a foreign ship *passing through* the territorial sea to arrest any person or to conduct any investigation in connection with *any crime committed on board the ship during its passage*,"[44] It is important to note the language of the relevant treaty obligations: that criminal jurisdiction "should not" be exercised. This hortative or "soft *negotium*"[45] phrasing was deliberately chosen to replace the original, harder proposal of "may not." The result is that "although States were expected, as a matter of comity, not to enforce their laws in respect of crimes committed on passing ships [except in the circumstances listed in the provision and discussed in this subsection], they nonetheless retained the ultimate legal right to do so if they wish." [46] In other words, the provision preserves the coastal State's right to take law enforcement action on board a foreign vessel in the territorial sea, even if the consequences of those actions do not extend to the coastal State.

When, and in what circumstances, could States in good faith ignore the rule set out in Article 27(1) of UNCLOS? One example is provided by the practice of States in the counter-proliferation of weapons of mass destruction (WMD). Because of their global impact, the interception of WMD materiel being transported by sea has recently been the subject of a UN Security Council resolution, obliging UN Member States to "adopt and enforce appropriate effective laws which prohibit any non-State actor to ... transport [or] transfer" WMD materiel and to "[d]evelop and maintain appropriate effective border controls and law enforcement efforts to ... combat ... the illicit trafficking and brokering in such items."[47] Although it appears that mere carriage of WMD materiel through the territorial sea (destined for a third State) may not, of itself, render passage non-innocent,[48] jurisdiction may nevertheless

44 Emphases added.

45 See Chapter 1, at Section 1.4.3.

46 Churchill and Lowe explain in relation to Article 17 of the Territorial Sea Convention (the precursor to Article 27 of UNCLOS): "The United States proposed an amendment with the specific purpose of reasserting the full jurisdiction of the coastal State by replacing the mandatory requirement that States 'may not' exercise jurisdiction except in the stated circumstances with the exhortatory suggestion that they 'should not' do so. This was accepted, with the result that although States should, as a matter of comity, not enforce their laws in respect of crimes committed on passing ships unless the consequences extend to the coastal State, or disturb the peace of the country or the good order of the territorial sea, or coastal State intervention is requested by the flag State ... they nonetheless retain the ultimate legal right to do so if they wish. ... Enforcement jurisdiction is excluded in law in only one case: where the crime was committed before the ship entered the territorial sea and the ship is merely passing through the sea without entering internal waters": R. R. Churchill and A. V. Lowe, *The Law of the Sea* (2nd ed. 1988), at 81. See also I. A. Shearer, "Problems of Jurisdiction and Law Enforcement against Delinquent Vessels" (1986) 35 *International and Comparative Law Quarterly* 320 [Shearer, "Problems of Jurisdiction and Law Enforcement against Delinquent Vessels"], at 327.

47 UN Security Council, Resolution 1540, UN Doc. A/RES/1540 (2004), Apr. 28, 2004, at paras. 2, 3(c).

48 On the basis that none of the terms of Article 19, which gives a strict definition of innocent and non-innocent passage, has been breached. See further D. Guilfoyle, "Maritime Interdiction of Weapons of

be exercised under the rules of UNCLOS, consistent with the inherent power of the coastal State to exercise jurisdiction in its territorial sea. As Guilfoyle concludes:

> Article 27 ... reflects the restraint exercised in state practice as a matter of comity rather than strict obligation. Thus, states have criminal jurisdiction over ships within their territorial sea, which they generally should not exercise for purposes outside Article 27, but, nonetheless, may. In the context of WMD shipments passing through the territorial sea, it is exactly that capacity to act which becomes an obligation to act under the terms of Resolution 1540.[49]

There is no UN Security Council resolution on migrant smuggling as there is for WMD, so it is difficult to justify applying the same analysis to the interdiction of vessels carrying smuggled migrants destined for other States. However, the view that regional obligations to prevent migrant smuggling do in fact result in an obligation of coastal States to prevent such transit is reflected in the European Commission discussion paper considered previously[50] and could well be proposed with respect to the broader international obligation of prevention captured in the Migrant Smuggling Protocol.

The right of coastal States to interdict foreign vessels in their territorial sea is also subject to an important restriction aimed at promoting respect for the "internal economy" of foreign vessels. Article 27(5) of UNCLOS provides that, except for certain resource or environmental crimes, States "may not" exercise jurisdiction in respect of *any* crimes committed *prior* to entering the territorial sea "if the ship, proceeding from a foreign port, is only passing through the territorial sea without entering internal waters." Thus, as concluded in Chapter 3, unless requested to do so by the flag State of the vessel in question, the coastal State would not be competent to arrest or prosecute a transiting vessel, in respect of any migrant-smuggling crimes committed and completed prior to entering the coastal State's territorial waters, simply because the coastal State is aware that the ship had previously disembarked smuggled migrants in another country. The critical distinction is whether the offense in question is completed or still continuing; where the offense is one of a continuous nature (such as the carrying of smuggled migrants), the coastal

Mass Destruction" (2007) 12(1) *Journal of Conflict & Security Law* 1, [Guilfoyle, "Maritime Interdiction of Weapons of Mass Destruction"], at 17: "the reference in article 19(2) of UNCLOS to 'passage shall take place' coupled with the list of acts not regarded as 'innocent', indicates a focus on the character of the passage itself. The assumption is that it is the external acts of a vessel engaged in innocent passage, not its internal economy, which may prejudice a coastal sate's security. It is hard to see that a latent threat in the vessel's hold, destined elsewhere, has any 'external' manifestation capable of affecting the character of passage."

49 Ibid.

50 European Commission, Staff Working Document, "Study on the International Law Instruments in Relation to Illegal Immigration by Sea," SEC(2007) 691, May 15, 2007.

State "should not," but nevertheless remains entitled to exercise criminal jurisdiction under Article 27(1).

What is the situation when a State acts in the territorial waters of another State, with that State's consent? The law of the sea does not prevent a coastal State from entering into an agreement that would grant another State the right to exercise the coastal State's own de jure jurisdictional authority within the coastal State's territorial waters.[51] In other words, through agreement, a State may effectively transfer or share its rights of enforcement jurisdiction with another State. As introduced in Chapter 1, this is a common occurrence in the area of migrant smuggling, with many States entering into bilateral agreements for joint cooperation in the conduct of surveillance patrols and interdictions. The coastal State retains the right to determine the conditions under which such "cooperation" will occur. The exercise of jurisdiction by or with a third State cannot exceed the powers that the coastal State itself would be entitled to exercise should it be acting alone and, as discussed in Chapter 4, delegation or assignment of authority by the coastal State will not generally operate to absolve that State of international legal responsibility for wrongful acts occasioned though the use of such delegated authority. Cooperation agreements and joint patrols raise a number of other issues, and these are considered further in this chapter at Section 6.1.2.

6.1.1.2. Interdiction in the Contiguous Zone and the Exclusive Economic Zone

Each coastal State is entitled to claim as a contiguous zone the area of sea extending seaward from the baseline of the coastal State, up to twenty-four nautical miles.[52] Jurisdiction within this zone is not conferred automatically but must be claimed. For coastal States that claim a full contiguous zone, this area will thereby extend twelve nautical miles from the outer limits of their territorial sea. Within that zone, ships enjoy high seas freedoms. However, the coastal State "may exercise the control necessary," in the contiguous zone, to prevent and punish infringements of certain types of laws and regulations that have occurred or are anticipated to occur within its territory or territorial sea, including those related to immigration.[53] The enforcement jurisdiction permitted coastal States in the contiguous

[51] Council of Europe, Parliamentary Assembly, Report of the Committee on Migration, Refugees and Population, *The Interception and Rescue at Sea of Asylum Seekers, Refugees and Irregular Migrants*, Doc. 12628, June 1, 2011, at para. 24.

[52] UNCLOS, at Art. 33.

[53] Ibid. at Art. 33(1)(a)–(b). The other types of laws and regulations with which the contiguous zone is concerned are customs, fiscal, and sanitary laws and regulations: ibid.

zone is accordingly very narrow, relating to conduct committed or anticipated in the territorial sea.[54] Importantly, this means that no enforcement jurisdiction is permissible in respect of vessels merely transiting the contiguous zone, without any intention to enter the territorial sea.[55] Further, as discussed previously, the scope of enforcement jurisdiction differs according to whether the vessel is inbound or outbound. The terms of UNCLOS do not support any prescriptive jurisdiction in the contiguous zone itself.[56]

The narrow scope of a State's jurisdiction in its contiguous zone has been confirmed by the International Tribunal for the Law of the Sea in the *M/V Saiga* arbitration, which noted that "the power of the coastal State to punish infringement of the stated laws (committed outside the territorial areas or within the contiguous zone) is not generally permissible in relation to vessels merely located in the contiguous zone and *not proven to have some relevant connection with territorial areas*."[57] International law therefore does not support a coastal State's exercising enforcement jurisdiction over a vessel in its contiguous zone where the vessel is carrying migrants intended for disembarkation in another coastal State, even if the disembarkation would breach that coastal State's migration laws. For such jurisdiction to arise, some further arrangement such as flag State consent would be necessary to permit such interdiction.

What is the situation with respect to a migrant smuggling vessel in the contiguous zone that is seeking to enter the territorial sea of the coastal State? International law of the sea clearly supports a power on the part of the coastal State to prevent, in the contiguous zone, an anticipated offense against the stipulated categories of offenses taking place within its territory or territorial waters. However, this anticipatory power of prevention may not be sufficient to justify anything but a very limited interdiction in the contiguous zone. For example, although it may well support actions such as "inspections and warnings," it is unlikely to extend to more serious measures such as boarding, arrest of individuals, or other assumptions of control over the vessel.[58] Similarly, in contrast to push-back operations in which a coastal State removes an offending vessel from its territorial waters, it is unlikely that push-backs to the high seas (as distinct from the prevention of entry into territorial

54 See further Chapter 3, at note 196.

55 One exception to this is in relation to hovering mother ships from which smaller vessels depart to enter the territorial sea, under the doctrine of constructive presence. See Chapter 3, at Section 3.3.3.3.

56 Churchill and Lowe, *The Law of the Sea*, at 137.

57 *M/V Saiga (No. 2) (St Vincent and the Grenadines v. Guinea)*, International Tribunal for the Law of the Sea Case No. 2, July 1, 1999, [1999] ITLOS Rep 10 [*M/V Saiga (No. 2)*], at para. 15 (Separate Opinion of Judge Laing) (emphasis added).

58 Shearer, "Problems of Jurisdiction and Law Enforcement against Delinquent Vessels," at 330.

waters) would be permitted in respect of anticipated offenses in the contiguous zone. In other words, a coastal State may not take enforcement action beyond such preventive measures against a migrant smuggling vessel within its contiguous zone unless and until the vessel enters its territorial zone. Some conflicting State practice should nevertheless be noted. The European Union, for example, has been ambiguous on this point by making no apparent distinction between the territorial sea and contiguous zones with respect to interceptions carried out through Frontex.[59]

Coastal States' powers are significantly greater with respect to "outgoing" migrant smuggling vessels: those that have recently left the territorial sea and are passing through the contiguous zone – for example, after having disembarked their human cargo. In relation to outgoing ships, the coastal State's powers extend to "punishment"[60] as a power that would very likely support the lawfulness of interdiction.

In relation to vessels without nationality in the contiguous zone, the capacity of a coastal State authority to interdict will, at a minimum, equate to the capacity to interdict on the high seas. Reference should therefore be made to the discussion of action against stateless vessels on the high seas, while noting that coastal States may well argue additional enforcement authority over migrant smuggling vessels without nationality within their contiguous zone.

The Exclusive Economic Zone (EEZ) is a resource-related zone adjacent to the territorial sea, up to 200 nautical miles from the baseline.[61] States enjoy certain sovereign rights (but not sovereignty) over resources in that zone.[62] For migrant smuggling purposes, it is relevant to note that coastal States are entitled to extend certain protections and controls for resource-related installations such as oil and rigs.[63] However, these are fairly limited. Otherwise within this zone, ships are entitled to high seas freedoms.

59 See Council Decision of 26 April 2010 supplementing the Schengen Borders Code as regards the surveillance of the sea external borders in the context of operational cooperation coordinated by the European Agency for the Management of Operational Cooperation at the External Borders of the Member States of the European Union (2010/252/EU), OJ L 111/20, May 5, 2010. Rule 2.5.1. of the attached operational rule for Frontex is entitled "Territorial waters and contiguous zone." It provides that any interdiction or related action in the territorial waters or contiguous zone of a Member State that does not participate in the operation shall be conducted in accordance with the authorization of the coastal State (at Annex, Part I, para. 2.5.1.2). See also M. den Heijer, *Europe and Extraterritorial Asylum* (2012) [den Heijer, *Europe and Extraterritorial Asylum*], at 220.

60 G. Fitzmaurice, "Some Results of the Geneva Conference on the Law of the Sea" (1959) 8(1) *International and Comparative Law Quarterly* 73, at 114.

61 UNCLOS, at Art. 57.

62 Ibid. at Art. 56.

63 Ibid. at Art. 60.

6.1.1.3. Interdiction on the High Seas

Unlike the maritime zones of jurisdiction previously considered, over all of which the coastal State exercises some form of jurisdiction or control, the high seas are beyond the jurisdiction or control of any one State. Indeed, the relevant treaty provisions define the high seas in the negative in the High Seas Convention as "all parts of the sea that are not included in the territorial sea or in the internal waters of a State"[64]; and under UNCLOS as "all parts of the sea that are not included in the exclusive economic zone, in the territorial sea or in the internal waters of a State, or in the archipelagic waters of an archipelagic State." [65] The high seas are open to all States, whether coastal or landlocked.[66]

THE PRINCIPLES OF FREEDOM OF NAVIGATION AND FLAG STATE JURISDICTION

International treaty law codifies the well-established rule of customary international law that the high seas are open to all States and that no State may acquire sovereignty over any part of them.[67] The High Seas Convention, which asserted itself as "generally declaratory of established principles of international law,"[68] proclaimed four freedoms of the high seas: freedom of navigation, freedom of fishing, freedom to lay submarine cables and pipelines, and freedom of overflight.[69] Each of these freedoms, along with "others which are recognized by the general principles of international law,"[70] are enjoyed by all States, and each State, whether coastal or landlocked, has the right to sail ships under its flag on the high seas.[71] Having been recognized as a part of customary international law in the High Seas Convention, each of these freedoms was repeated in UNCLOS.[72]

The long-standing customary principle of exclusive flag State jurisdiction on the high seas was clearly articulated by the Permanent Court of International Justice in the *Lotus* decision:

> [V]essels on the high seas are subject to no authority except that of the State whose flag they fly. In virtue of the principle of the freedom of the seas, that is to say, the

[64] Convention on the High Seas, 450 UNTS 11, done Apr. 29, 1958, entered into force Sept. 30, 1962 [High Seas Convention], at Art. 1.

[65] UNCLOS, at Art. 86.

[66] Ibid. at Art. 87.

[67] High Seas Convention, at Art. 2; UNCLOS, at Arts. 87, 89; and Churchill and Lowe, *The Law of the Sea*, at 204.

[68] High Seas Convention, at Preamble.

[69] Ibid. at Art. 2(1)–(4).

[70] Ibid. at Art. 2.

[71] Ibid. at Arts. 2–4.

[72] UNCLOS, at Arts. 87–90.

absence of any territorial sovereignty upon the high seas, no State may exercise any kind of jurisdiction over foreign vessels upon them.[73]

The principle is enshrined in both UNCLOS and the High Seas Convention, which state that "Ships shall sail under the flag of one State only and, save in exceptional cases expressly provided for in international treaties or in this Convention, shall be subject to its exclusive jurisdiction on the high seas."[74] Accordingly, States are prevented from exercising enforcement jurisdiction on the high seas in respect of a vessel carrying smuggled migrants, even if destined for the State's territory, unless the situation falls within one of several recognized exceptions:

- *Consent of the flag State:* As an exercise of their sovereignty, States have the capacity to give their consent to law enforcement action either in relation to specific instances or as a form of "standing" consent in advance, for their flagged vessels. Further, States can give their consent for a foreign State to take certain actions (such as boarding), while withholding consent for other actions, such as the arrest of the vessel and its crew. Specific agreements in this regard have been concluded between States relating to the interdiction of vessels carrying irregular migrants, and these are discussed further Section 6.1.3.
- *Status and activity exceptions:* These relate either to the status of the vessel (that it is stateless or effectively stateless[75]) or the actions in which it is involved (the international crimes of piracy,[76] slave trading,[77] or unauthorized broadcasting[78]).
- *Hot pursuit:* Situations in which the vessel is engaged in an activity already subject to coastal State enforcement jurisdiction and may thereby be pursued

[73] *SS Lotus (France v. Turkey) (Judgment)*, [1927] PCIJ Rep, Series A, No. 10, at 25.

[74] UNCLOS, at Art. 92(1). See also High Seas Convention, at Art. 6(1).

[75] UNCLOS, at Art. 110(1)(d). Note also that "[a] ship which sails under the flags of two or more States, using them according to convenience … may be assimilated to a ship without nationality" (Article 92(2)). A similar provision allows a State vessel to intervene where "though flying a foreign flag or refusing to show its flag, the ship is, in reality, of the same nationality as the warship" (Article 110(1)(e)).

[76] Ibid. at Art. 105 ("On the high seas, or in any other place outside the jurisdiction of any State, every State may seize a pirate ship or aircraft, or a ship or aircraft taken by piracy and under the control of pirates, and arrest the persons and seize the property on board. The courts of the State which carried out the seizure may decide upon the penalties to be imposed, and may also determine the action to be taken with regard to the ships, aircraft or property, subject to the rights of third parties acting in good faith."). See also High Seas Convention, at Art. 19.

[77] UNCLOS, at Art. 110(1)(b); High Seas Convention, at Art. 22(1)(b). See also UNCLOS, at Art. 99; and High Seas Convention, at Art. 13.

[78] UNCLOS, at Arts. 109–110. "On the high seas, a State having jurisdiction in accordance with paragraph 3 may, in conformity with article 110, arrest any person or ship engaged in unauthorized broadcasting and seize the broadcasting apparatus": ibid. at Art. 109(4).

to and on the high seas under the rules of hot pursuit. Each of the exceptions is considered in detail at Section 6.1.1.4.

In relation to the status and activity exceptions, the right to exercise jurisdiction under these limited circumstances is, at least initially, limited to a "right of visit."[79] This entails a right of approach vested in a warship or other State vessel[80] in order "to verify the ship's right to fly its flag. To this end, it may send a boat under the command of an officer to the suspected ship. If suspicion remains after the documents have been checked, it may proceed to a further examination on board the ship, which must be carried out with all possible consideration."[81]

The law of the sea clearly characterizes the right of visit as an exception to the general principle of the freedom of the high seas, and the limits on its scope are in keeping with its exceptional nature. The right is therefore to be exercised cautiously. International law imposes an obligation on the State exercising the right of visit to compensate the boarded vessel for any loss or damage if suspicions prove unfounded, and provided that the ship boarded has not committed any act justifying those suspicions.[82]

INTERDICTION ON THE HIGH SEAS: STATELESS VESSELS

The rules governing stateless vessels on the high seas are critical to a consideration of the legal framework around migrant smuggling interdictions – for the simple reason that the vast majority of migrant smuggling vessels are unregistered or improperly registered.[83] As such they are considered without nationality – or "stateless."

UNCLOS grants official vessels on the high seas an express right of visit (a right to board and inspect) over stateless vessels.[84] However, the Convention does not specify what actions, if any, may be taken by the State beyond boarding and inspecting such vessels. It does not, for example, clearly grant criminal enforcement jurisdiction to boarding/inspecting States except in the context of two specific international crimes: piracy[85] and unauthorized broadcasting.[86] As discussed further at Section

79 Generally on the right of visit, see M. D. Fink, "The Right of Visit for Warships: Some Challenges in Applying the Law of Maritime Interdiction on the High Seas," (2010) 49 *Revue de droit militaire et de droit de la guerre* 7.

80 The provisions of Article 110 apply to warships as well as "to any other duly authorized ships or aircraft clearly marked and identifiable as being on government service": UNCLOS, at Art. 110(5).

81 Ibid. at Art. 110(2); High Seas Convention, at Art. 22(2).

82 UNCLOS, at Art. 110(3); High Seas Convention, at Art. 22(3).

83 See UN General Assembly, "Oceans and the Law of the Sea: Report of the Secretary-General," UN Doc. A/53/456, Oct. 5, 1998, at para. 135; and European Commission, Staff Working Document, "Study on the International Law Instruments in Relation to Illegal Immigration by Sea," SEC(2007) 691, May 15, 2007, at para. 1.5.

84 UNCLOS, at Art. 110(1)(d).

85 Ibid. at Art. 105.

86 Ibid. at Art. 109.

6.1.2, this ambiguity is continued in the Migrant Smuggling Protocol, which affirms the right of boarding and inspection with respect to suspected migrant smuggling and authorizes the boarding State to take "appropriate measures in accordance with relevant domestic and international law" if those suspicions are confirmed.[87]

As noted in Chapter 3, there is strong support among some States for the position that stateless vessels may be subject to universal enforcement action (i.e., that a "stateless vessel may be seized by any state as it enjoys the protection of none").[88] The United States Court of Appeals has affirmed this position, famously asserting that "vessels without nationality are international pariahs. They have no internationally recognized rights to move freely on the high seas."[89] EU Member States have made similar assertions in justifying exercise of jurisdictional authority during interdiction activities carried out on the high seas off the Canary Islands and in the central Mediterranean.[90] The European Council has been even more specific:

> The flagless ships generally used in practice for the irregular transportation of migrants cannot invoke freedom of navigation in the high seas. Any country can intervene against such ships and can prevent them from passage, proceed to arrest or escort the flagless ship to a port.[91]

On another view that is widely endorsed by scholars, enforcement action such as interdiction is not permitted without some further jurisdictional nexus or permissive rule (such as in cases of suspected slave trading, piracy, or unauthorized broadcasting).[92] Absent a specific jurisdictional nexus, any interdiction would be limited to actions recognized under the right of visit (boarding and inspection), except where a right to seizure derives from another treaty or obligation.[93]

The difference between these two positions is substantial. In relation to situations of migrant smuggling, the practical results are almost diametrically opposed. Under

87 Migrant Smuggling Protocol, at Art. 8(7).

88 Guilfoyle, *Shipping Interdiction and the Law of the Sea*, at 17. See also E. Papastavridis, "The Right of Visit on the High Seas in a Theoretical Perspective: *Mare Liberum* versus *Mare Clausum* Revisited" (2011) 24(01) *Leiden Journal of International Law* 45, at 65.

89 *United States v. Marino-Garcia and Others*, 679 F.2d 1373 (11th Circ. 1982); ILDC 687 (US 1982), July 9, 1982, cited in N. Boister, *An Introduction to Transnational Criminal Law* (2012), at 177.

90 Council of Europe, Parliamentary Assembly, Report of the Committee on Migration, Refugees and Population, *The Interception and Rescue at Sea of Asylum Seekers, Refugees and Irregular Migrants*, Doc. 12628, June 1, 2011, at para. 25.

91 European Commission, Staff Working Document, "Study on the International Law Instruments in Relation to Illegal Immigration by Sea," SEC(2007) 691, May 15, 2007, at para. 2.2.2.

92 Churchill and Lowe, *The Law of the Sea*, at 214; Guilfoyle, *Shipping Interdiction and the Law of the* Sea, at 17; and Mallia, *Migrant Smuggling by Sea*, at 69.

93 V. Moreno-Lax, "Seeking Asylum in the Mediterranean: Against a Fragmentary Reading of EU Member States' Obligations Accruing at Sea" (2011) 23(2) *International Journal of Refugee Law* 174, at 186.

the first view, any State has full legal authority to stop, search, and take control of a migrant smuggling vessel without nationality while it is on the high seas. Under the second view, States are *prevented* from exercising any enforcement authority over such vessels *unless* they are able to show that the vessel is engaged in a prohibited activity (that does not include migrant smuggling), or they are otherwise able to establish a nexus with that vessel based on an existing right or obligation.

Of course, as Churchill and Lowe have pointed out, there is a practical flaw to the conclusion that States are prevented from interdicting stateless vessels on the high seas: put simply, the lack of nationality of the vessel means that no State is likely to protest such assertion of jurisdiction.[94] However a more substantive objection to the assertion that States are prevented from exercising jurisdiction over stateless vessels on the high seas lies in the nature of international law itself. International law has long held that nationality is a prerequisite for enjoyment of the protection of the law, and that a ship without nationality loses this protection, thereby falling within the full jurisdictional power of the boarding State.[95] There is no strong evidence available that this foundational assumption is under any kind of serious threat.

INTERDICTION ON THE HIGH SEAS: INTERNATIONAL CRIMES

Could smuggling of migrants ever fall within one of the established exceptions to high seas freedoms relating to criminal conduct? This question becomes particularly important if one accepts a more conservative interpretation of the current international legal rules that does not recognize statelessness of the vessel as automatically conferring enforcement jurisdiction on all States beyond a "right of visit."

The list of established offense exceptions specified in UNCLOS is very brief, and the only one that could realistically be relevant to the situation of migrant smuggling is "slave trading."[96] There is certainly no inherent incompatibility between the two practices. Whereas slave trading involves individuals being transported and traded for purposes of exploitation, and migrant smuggling involves illegal cross-border movement for profit, each can involve elements of the other. In other words, provided they are being moved across a border without authorization, all slaves transported by sea are, by definition, also being smuggled. Conversely, persons who are being smuggled could also potentially be victims of the slave trade. However the

94 Churchill and Lowe, *The Law of the Sea*, at 172.

95 This view is expressed in Oppenheim's International Law: "In the interest of order on the open sea, a vessel not sailing under the maritime flag of a State enjoys no protection whatsoever, for the freedom of navigation on the open sea is freedom for such vessels only as sail under the flag of a State": Jennings and Watts, *Oppenheim's International Law: Volume 1, Peace*, 9th ed., at 546. For a further consideration of scholarly opinion and State practice in this area, see den Heijer, *Europe and Extraterritorial Asylum*, at 224–226.

96 UNCLOS, at Arts. 99, 110.

association is by no means automatic, or even very likely. As noted in Chapter 3, at Section 3.3.3.2, there have been substantial efforts in recent years to include under the rubric of slavery a range of highly exploitative practices that take away personal freedom and involve serious exploitation.[97] Discussion in this book on the concept of "exploitative smuggling" has confirmed that at least a proportion of persons being smuggled are victims or potential victims of what many civil society advocates, public officials, and international organizations would term "modern slavery."[98] This campaign has had significant impact at the level of public awareness and advocacy but its effect on international law has been much more muted.[99] While avoiding the temptation to expand the definition of slavery beyond what is correct and appropriate, it is nevertheless important to recognize that the concept is indeed evolving and may well accommodate (presently, or at some point in the future) egregious forms of exploitation that involve the clear exercise of powers attached to the right of ownership.[100] The *possibility* certainly exists that vessels engaged in transporting migrants for profit may also be engaged in conduct that could be characterized as slave trading. In the 2012 *Hirsi Jamaa* case, the Italian government cited the UNCLOS provision on slave trading as one basis for its claim that a push-back operation on the high seas was in accordance with international law of the sea.[101] It is critical to note that while rejecting that claim, the Court did not reject the assertion that such smuggling could indeed rise to the level of slave trading.[102]

Even in the face of evidence of slave trading, the principle of flag-State jurisdiction on the high seas is preserved. Official vessels encountering vessels on the high

[97] See E. Papastavridis, "Interception of Human Beings on the High Seas: A Contemporary Analysis under International Law" (2009) 36 *Syracuse Journal of International Law and Commerce* 146, at 163–178; and E. Papastavridis, "'Fortress Europe' and FRONTEX: Within or without International Law?" (2010) 79 *Nordic Journal of International law* 75, at 85. See also the extensive citations in A. T. Gallagher, *The International Law of Human Trafficking* (2010) [Gallagher, *The International Law of Human Trafficking*], at 177–191.

[98] See further the case study on the exploitation of smuggled Eritrean migrants on the Sinai Peninsula in the Introduction. See also Chapter 5 at Section 5.1.4 for a discussion of legal principles relevant to addressing aggravated smuggling.

[99] See Gallagher, *The International Law of Human Trafficking*, at 177–191.

[100] Ibid. at 190.

[101] *Hirsi Jamaa and Others v. Italy*, (2012) 55 EHRR 21 (ECHR, Feb. 23, 2012) [*Hirsi Jamaa v. Italy*], at 79 (concurring opinion of Judge Pinto de Albuquerque).

[102] In respect of Italy's justification for turn-back on this and other grounds (including the applicability of the Migrant Smuggling Protocol) Judge Pinto de Albuquerque held: "None of these provisions can reasonably be invoked in order to justify an exception to the *non-refoulement* obligation and, consequently, to the prohibition of collective expulsion. Only a misconstruction of these norms, which aim to secure the protection of especially vulnerable persons (victims of trafficking, illegal migrants, persons in danger or in distress on the high seas) could justify the exposure of these persons to an additional risk of ill-treatment by delivering them to those countries from where they have fled": ibid. at 80.

seas that they suspect of engaging in the slave trade are granted a right of visit; that is, they are permitted to board the vessel.[103] However, the law of the sea confers no additional entitlements, and certainly not the broad enforcement jurisdiction that would permit a State to arrest persons or otherwise take control of a vessel. It is only the flag State that is entitled (in fact, obliged) to prosecute and punish the transport of slaves on ships authorized to fly its flag.[104] UNCLOS is silent on the legal position with respect to vessels without nationality suspected of carrying slaves. However the right of visit that exists with respect to stateless vessels means that there is no additional advantage to be gained in terms of jurisdictional authority to interdict by asserting that a vessel without nationality suspected of engaging in migrant smuggling may also be engaged in slave trading. Nevertheless, this is not the end of the matter, and it is important to consider the broader international legal framework. For example, it has often been argued that slavery and the slave trade are – or should be – crimes attracting "universal jurisdiction," and thereby capable of being prosecuted by any State irrespective of the existence of any territorial or other jurisdictional nexus.[105] But the historical evidence for slavery as a crime of universal jurisdiction is not particularly strong.[106] A further complication for a State wishing to invoke such a justi-

[103] UNCLOS, at Art. 110(1)(b).

[104] Ibid. at Art. 110; High Seas Convention, at Art. 22. Under UNCLOS Article 99, and High Seas Convention Article 13, each State is obliged to take measures to prevent and punish the transport of slaves on board ships authorized to fly its flag. See further M. N Shaw, *International Law* (6th ed. 2008), at 616; and N. Klein, *Maritime Security and the Law of the Sea* (2011) [Klein, *Maritime Security and the Law of the Sea*], at 122. Similarly, in respect of drug trafficking, UNCLOS provides only for a duty of cooperation to suppress drug trafficking, explicitly affirming the exclusive jurisdiction of flag States by noting that these States "may request the cooperation of other States to suppress such traffic," without imposing any obligation to do so: UNCLOS, at Art. 108. The customary principle of exclusive flag State jurisdiction in cases of slavery was recognized in the 1817 case of *Le Louis*, in which the United Kingdom High Court of Admiralty held that a British cruiser had unlawfully captured a French vessel engaging in the slave trade on the high seas, on the basis that the flag State alone was entitled to prosecute slave trading on board its vessels on the high seas. *Le Louis* (1817) 165 Eng. Rep. 1464, cited in Klein, *Maritime Security and the Law of the Sea*, at 122.

[105] "Where a state has universal jurisdiction, it may punish conduct although the state has no links of territoriality or nationality with the offender or victim": *Beanal v. Freeport-McMoRan, Inc.*, 969 F. Supp. 362, 361 (E.D. La. 1997), referring to American Law Institute, *Restatement (Third) of Foreign Relations Law of the United States* (1987), at § 404. See further Chapter 3, at Section 3.2.2.4.

[106] As Kontorovich has noted, "historical evidence does not support [the view of slavery as an offense attracting universal jurisdiction]. At most, international treaties on slave trading created 'delegated jurisdiction' whereby several nations conveyed to one another the right to exercise some of their jurisdictional powers with respect to a particular offense, effectively making each state an agent of the others": E. Kontorovich, "The Piracy Analogy: Modern Universal Jurisdiction's Hollow Foundations" (2004) 45 *Harvard International Law Journal* 183, at 193 (citations omitted). Kontorovich further asserts that "[n]o state practice supports universal jurisdiction over slave trading," and that this misconception around this issue arose through a confusion with consent-based arrangements between a small group of states in relation to efforts to end the transatlantic slave trade: ibid. at 193–194.

fication for an interdiction lies in its being required to establish a situation of slavery or slave trading, still a legally difficult undertaking with an uncertain outcome.

It becomes even more important therefore, to consider whether the categories of crime falling within the terms of the law of the sea exception have been – or could be– expanded to include migrant smuggling itself. Certainly there is some indication that the established categories are not considered immutable. For example, the United States has also asserted jurisdiction in respect of both flagged and stateless vessels engaged in drug trafficking and driftnet fishing.[107] This opens up the possibility of a similar assertion being made with respect to migrant smuggling. Given the political stakes and the slow but relentless expansion of extraterritorial migration control, such a development should be anticipated. This issue is considered further at Section 6.1.2 in the context of a discussion on the impact of the Migrant Smuggling Protocol on the law of the sea.

6.1.1.4. Interdiction and the Doctrine of Hot Pursuit

The issue of hot pursuit may also be relevant in the context of interdictions related to migrant smuggling. Hot pursuit is essentially a law enforcement activity, and the right of hot pursuit permits a coastal State to extend its law enforcement jurisdiction beyond "standard" enforcement jurisdiction (such as the territorial sea, or the contiguous zone in respect of outgoing vessels suspected of having committed a certain type of offense) by commencing and maintaining an uninterrupted pursuit of a fleeing vessel. The right arises where a vessel has violated the laws of the coastal State within the territory, territorial waters, the contiguous zone, or the EEZ of that State and is seeking to flee to the high seas. The right of hot pursuit is an important customary principle of international law. Under both the High Seas Convention (Article 23) and UNCLOS (Article 111), where the coastal State has good reason to believe that the foreign vessel has violated the State's laws, a warship or other official ship or aircraft authorized by the coastal State is entitled to pursue the vessel to the high seas and seize it.[108]

[107] Maritime Drug Law Enforcement Act 1986, 46 U.S.C. § 1903 (United States), cited in Churchill and Lowe, *The Law of the Sea*, at 214, n. 24; "Announcement from the United States Department of State to Enforce Moratorium on Driftnet Fishing, 8 March 1993" (1993) 23 *Law of the Sea Bulletin* 107; and Drug Trafficking Vessel Interdiction Act 2008, 18 U.S.C. § 2285 (United States) (criminalizing the operation of submersible and semisubmersible vessels without nationality, outside of any one country's territorial sea and with the intent to evade detection). See further A. Bennett, "That Sinking Feeling: Stateless Ships, Universal Jurisdiction and the Drug Trafficking Vessel Interdiction Act" (2012) 37(2) *Yale Journal of International Law* 433.

[108] UNCLOS, at Art. 111(1); High Seas Convention, at Art. 23(1). For a contemporary examination of the doctrine of hot pursuit, see R. Walker, "International Law of the Sea: Applying the Doctrine of Hot Pursuit in the 21st Century" (2011) 17 *Auckland University Law Review* 194.

The rules regarding how a pursuit is to be conducted are very specific. These were previously outlined in Chapter 3, at Section 3.3.3.3 and are summarized now with particular reference to situations involving smuggling at sea.

- Pursuit may only be commenced after giving a visual or auditory signal to stop, given at a distance close enough to be seen or heard by the foreign ship.[109]
- Pursuit must be commenced when the foreign ship (or one of its boats) is in the territorial sea, contiguous zone, or EEZ of the State, where there is good reason to suspect a breach of coastal State laws and regulations applicable in the relevant zone.[110] Thus, hot pursuit may be commenced to pursue a migrant smuggling vessel in the contiguous zone that violated immigration laws within the territorial sea or territory of the coastal State.[111] In contrast, no right of hot pursuit arises if the same vessel has left the contiguous zone and is in the EEZ when spotted by the coastal State, because the coastal State enjoys no jurisdiction in the EEZ in respect of immigration.[112]
- It is not necessary for the pursuing ship or aircraft to be in the same jurisdictional zone as the target vessel when pursuit is commenced.
- Under the doctrine of constructive presence, a coastal State may pursue and arrest a "mother ship" on the basis that this vessel sends or meets a boat within a relevant jurisdictional zone of the coastal State, even if the mother ship itself "hovers" outside the relevant jurisdictional zone or remains at all times on the high seas.[113]

109 UNCLOS, at Art. 111(4); High Seas Convention, at Art. 23(3).

110 "If the foreign ship is within a contiguous zone, as defined in article 33, the pursuit may only be undertaken if there has been a violation of the rights for the protection of which the zone was established": UNCLOS, at Art. 111(1). See also High Seas Convention, at Art. 23(1). The same applies for the Exclusive Economic Zone: UNCLOS, at Art. 111(2).

111 In the contiguous zone, the coastal State may exercise the control necessary to punish infringement of immigration laws and regulations within its territory or territorial sea: UNCLOS, at Art. 33.

112 See Chapter 3, at Section 3.3.3.3. See also, for example, the *M/V Saiga (No. 2)* case, in which the International Tribunal for the Law of the Sea held that hot pursuit had not been lawfully exercised. In that decision, Guinea commenced pursuit of a St. Vincent and Grenadines vessel in the Exclusive Economic Zone (EEZ) on the basis that it had supplied gas to fishing vessels in the EEZ in breach of Guinean customs laws. However, the Tribunal rejected this argument on the basis that the coastal State only has jurisdiction to apply its customs laws and regulations in the EEZ to artificial islands, installations, and structures (UNCLOS, Article 60(2)), and not in respect of any other parts of the EEZ: at para. 127.

113 UNCLOS, at Art. 111(1), 111(4). See also A. D. McNair, *International Law Opinions*, vol. 1 (1956), at 245: "When a foreign ship outside territorial waters sends boats into territorial waters which commit offences there, the mother ship renders herself liable to seizure by reason of these vicarious operations."; and *R v. Mills*, which accepted the lawfulness of hot pursuit to arrest a mother ship in circumstances where "[a]t the time when the authority to arrest the *Poseidon* was received she was in International Waters and had never entered the territorial waters of any state": *R v. Mills and others* (unreported) (Croydon Crown Court, 1995) [*R v. Mills*], at 4 (Judge Devonshire), cited in W. C.

- Pursuit must be "hot," that is, continuous and uninterrupted, and the right of hot pursuit ceases as soon as pursuit is interrupted: for example, because the pursuing vessel loses sight of the foreign ship or is recalled.[114] Regarding the continuity of pursuit, the relevant treaties expressly provide that pursuit commenced by an aircraft may be transferred to a ship or other aircraft of the State if the aircraft itself is unable to arrest the ship. In that case, the aircraft that commenced hot pursuit by giving the order to stop "must itself actively pursue the ship until a ship or another aircraft of the coastal State, summoned by the aircraft, arrives to take over the pursuit."[115]
- Hot pursuit also ceases as soon as the foreign vessel enters the territorial sea of its flag State or any third State.[116]

In the leading decision on hot pursuit, the International Tribunal for the Law of the Sea has affirmed that "the conditions for the exercise of the right of hot pursuit under article 111 of the Convention are cumulative; each of them has to be satisfied for the pursuit to be legitimate under the Convention."[117] The Tribunal also affirmed that in arresting any vessel, general international law "which is applicable by virtue of article 293 of the Convention, requires that the use of force must be avoided as far as possible and, where force is unavoidable, it must not go beyond what is reasonable and necessary in the circumstances."[118] As is the case for the right of visit, the State must compensate a vessel for any loss or damage caused by stopping or arresting the vessel outside the territorial sea in circumstances that do not justify hot pursuit.[119]

6.1.1.5. General Rules on the Use of Force during Interdictions

In the context of interdictions, questions related to the use of force – indeed to human rights issues more generally – will typically arise in relation to vessels without

Gilmore, "Hot Pursuit: The Case of R v. Mills and Others" (1995) 44 *International and Comparative Law Quarterly* 949 [Gilmore, "Hot Pursuit: The Case of *R v. Mills*"], at 951–952.

114 In *R v. Mills*, ships of the United Kingdom task force continuously shadowed the *Poseidon* from the time that it transferred cannabis to the British trawler to the time that it was arrested: Gilmore, "Hot Pursuit: The Case of *R v. Mills*, at 951. In contrast, in *M/V Saiga (No. 2)*, the International Tribunal for the Law of the Sea held that the arrest of a vessel was unlawful for several reasons, including interruption of the pursuit: "[T]he small patrol boat P35 that was sent out on 26 October 1997 on a northward course to search for the *Saiga* was recalled when information was received that the *Saiga* had changed course. This recall constituted a clear interruption of any pursuit, whatever legal basis might have existed for its commencement in the first place": at para. 147.

115 UNCLOS, at Art. 111(6); High Seas Convention, at Art. 23(5).

116 UNCLOS, at Art. 111(3); High Seas Convention, at Art. 23(2).

117 *M/V Saiga (No. 2)*, at para. 146.

118 Ibid. at para. 155.

119 UNCLOS, at Art. 111(8); High Seas Convention, at Art. 23(7).

nationality encountered on the high seas. Although the key issues are considered in detail later in the chapter in the context of human rights protections during interdictions, their importance warrants separate consideration with a view to extracting and highlighting the key rules under the law of the sea that apply to all enforcement actions.

A number of UNCLOS provisions examined previously, for example Article 110 authorizing stopping and boarding for the purpose of exercising the right of visit, imply or even require coercive action. However, UNCLOS itself does not contain specific provisions that regulate the use of force. Nonetheless, the International Tribunal on the Law of the Sea has confirmed that international law contains very specific rules on when and how force may be used in such circumstances. In the *M/V Saiga* judgment, the Tribunal affirmed previous international decisions in concluding that:

> [International law] requires that the use of force must be avoided as far as possible and, where force is inevitable, it must not go beyond what is reasonable and necessary in the circumstances. Considerations of humanity must apply in the law of the sea as they do in other areas.[120]

The Tribunal further asserted that as a matter of basic principle, government officials engaged in an authorized interdiction should "avoid the use of force except when and to the degree necessary to ensure [their own] safety ... and where ... obstructed in the execution of their duties. The degree of force used shall not exceed that reasonably required in the circumstances."[121]

The Tribunal further affirmed that "normal practice" required a series of escalating actions aimed at stopping the vessel and that "[i]t is only after the appropriate actions fail that the pursuing vessel may, as a last resort, use force. Even then, appropriate warning must be issued ... and all efforts should be made to ensure that life is not endangered."[122] A subsequent arbitral award relating to a dispute between Guyana and Suriname affirmed this aspect of the *M/V Saiga* judgment in "accept[ing] the argument that in international law force may be used in law enforcement activities provided that such force is unavoidable, reasonable and necessary."[123]

[120] *M/V Saiga (No. 2)*, at para. 155.

[121] Ibid. at para. 156. The Tribunal cites the UN Fish Stocks Agreement, which permits certain non-flag States to board and inspect fishing vessels on the high seas. The possibility of the use of force after boarding is envisaged in Article 22(1)(f), which states that the inspecting State shall "avoid the use of force except when and to the degree necessary to ensure the safety of the inspectors and where the inspectors are obstructed in the execution of their duties": Agreement for the Implementation of the Provisions of the United Nations Convention on the Law of the Sea of 10 December 1982 relating to the Conservation and Management of Straddling Fish Stocks and Highly Migratory Fish Stocks, UN Doc. A/CONF.164/37, Sept. 8, 1995.

[122] *M/V Saiga (No. 2)*, at para 156.

[123] *Guyana v. Suriname*, (2008) 47(2) ILM 166 (Award of Sept. 17, 2007), at para. 455.

Guilfoyle perceptively points out that such conclusions on the use of force during interdictions – that it must be "a measure of last resort" for example, or "reasonable and necessary in the circumstances" – are not of great practical use to those charged with making decisions about interventions.[124] However, it is necessary to recognize that in this area, as in many others covered by the present book, States have refrained from developing and attaching themselves to highly specific rules. Guilfoyle's ultimate conclusion, that the use of force by States when intercepting vessels, must be: (1) a measure of last resort; (2i) proportional to the objective in sight; and (3) the minimum reasonably necessary[125] appears to be reflective of the generally accepted standard and as good a guide as any for evaluating the conduct of States in relation to interdiction of vessels carrying smuggled migrants.

6.1.2. *Impact of the Migrant Smuggling Protocol*

As previously explained, the Migrant Smuggling Protocol does not itself create a new legal framework for the interdicting vessels engaged in migrant smuggling. However, in relation to State Party efforts to prevent and suppress the smuggling of migrants by sea, the Protocol both restates and requires consistency with the international law of the sea. In addition, the Protocol sets out a cooperative framework, which operates within the confines of the existing international law of the sea rules. Thus, it is the international law of the sea that provides the basic legal framework governing enforcement action over vessels engaged in migrant smuggling. Although UNCLOS establishes the fundamental rules in this area, it contains no provisions specific to migrant smuggling.[126] As discussed previously, the only crimes that are specifically referred to in that Convention in the context of justifying enforcement action are slavery, piracy, illicit traffic in psychotropic substances, and unauthorized broadcasting from the high seas.[127] The Convention does however affirm that its jurisdictional rules may be modified by agreement between States.[128] The Migrant Smuggling Protocol itself is an example of this kind of agreement and, in promoting bilateral and multilateral cooperation between States to prevent migrant smuggling by sea,[129] appears to encourage such modification. The present section will therefore

[124] Guilfoyle, *Shipping Interdiction and the Law of the Sea*, at 271 (citations omitted).

[125] Ibid. at 280–282. See also D. Guilfoyle, "Human Rights Issues and Non-flag State Boarding of Suspect Ships in International Waters," in C. R. Symmons ed., *Selected Contemporary Issues in the Law of the Sea* 83 (2011).

[126] See further X. Hinrichs, "Measures against Smuggling of Migrants at Sea: A Law of the Sea Related Perspective" (2003) 36(2) *Revue Belge de Droit International* 413 [Hinrichs, "Measures against Smuggling of Migrants at Sea"], at 415.

[127] UNCLOS, at Arts. 99–101, 108–109.

[128] Ibid. at Art. 311.

[129] Migrant Smuggling Protocol, at Art. 7.

examine the operation of this instrument in the context of the international law of the sea, focusing particularly on the way in which its provisions modify or otherwise impact on generally applicable rules.

As Chapter 1 explained, the origins of the Migrant Smuggling Protocol can be traced back to a flurry of activity around smuggling by sea within the International Maritime Organization (IMO) and subsequently the United Nations, led largely by the United States and Italy and reflecting concerns about the serious risks associated with smuggling by sea. The Protocol's core provisions draw heavily on a draft initially submitted to the IMO by Italy in 1997 but without much of the detail of that original proposal.[130] In both substance and format it also draws heavily on the 1988 United Nations Convention against Illicit Traffic in Narcotic Drugs and Psychotropic Substances[131] (Drug Control Convention) as well as work undertaken by the IMO prior to and during the period of time the Convention and Protocols were being negotiated – most particularly the 1998 IMO Circular on combating unsafe practices associated with the trafficking or transport of migrants by sea.[132]

Building on the existing regulatory framework codified in UNCLOS, the Migrant Smuggling Protocol gives shape to a cooperative regime that States Parties can use to seek consent from, or give consent to, other States Parties to take actions against their flagged vessels beyond the limits of the territorial sea, where the smuggling of migrants is involved. It is important to reiterate that the regime established by the Migrant Smuggling Protocol does not alter the underlying legal framework provided by the international law of the sea.[133] Rather, it reflects and relies upon core principles of the international law of the sea explored in detail in the previous section: vessels have the nationality of the flag they are entitled to fly, a flag State has a duty to exercise its jurisdiction and control over vessels flying its flag, vessels are subject to the exclusive jurisdiction of the flag State on the high seas, there exists a universal right of visit over vessels without nationality, and the right of approach and visit in other situations is heavily circumscribed. Flag States are already free under the international law of the sea to authorize another State to exercise some or all of its powers

[130] Mallia, *Migrant Smuggling by Sea*, at 112–116.

[131] United Nations Convention against Illicit Traffic in Narcotic Drugs and Psychotropic Substances, 1582 UNTS 95, done Dec. 20, 1988, entered into force Nov. 11, 1990 [Drug Control Convention], esp. at Art. 17.

[132] International Maritime Organization, Maritime Safety Committee, *Interim Measures for Combating Unsafe Practices Associated with the Trafficking or Transport of Migrants by Sea*, IMO Doc. MSC/Circ.896, Dec. 16, 1998. For a detailed analysis of the Circular as well as its drafting history, see R. A. Pedrozo, "International Initiatives to Combat Trafficking of Migrants by Sea," in J. N. Moore and M. H. Nordquist eds., *Current Maritime Issues and the International Maritime Organization* 53 (1999), esp. at 55–62.

[133] Migrant Smuggling Protocol, Article 7, refers to cooperation "in accordance with the international law of the sea." For a further detailed discussion of the Migrant Smuggling Protocol's intersection and operation vis-à-vis UNCLOS, see Hinrichs, "Measures against Smuggling of Migrants at Sea," at 413.

on board a ship flying its flag, whether for migrant smuggling or drugs. However, the obligations in the Migrant Smuggling Protocol, like the equivalent provisions in the Drug Control Convention, create a specific mechanism through which cooperation with appropriate safeguards can occur.[134] In this way, the Protocol is intended to facilitate and render more efficient cooperation than is already legally possible, while ensuring relevant safeguards are in place.[135] As discussed further below,[136] the only potential deviation from established rules lies in the Protocol's recognition of a right of action with respect to stateless vessels on the high seas suspected of engaging in migrant smuggling: a provision that arguably extends the scope of action permitted to States beyond what is permitted under the UNCLOS right of visit.[137]

Although not displacing the general law of the sea, the maritime cooperation aspects of the Migrant Smuggling Protocol reflect the clear intention of States, evident in the drafting history of the Organized Crime Convention[138] and the Protocol, to expand the capacity of individual States Parties to act against certain crimes being committed outside their own borders. As detailed further in Chapter 1, States Parties are required to establish jurisdiction to investigate, prosecute, and punish all relevant offenses in certain specified circumstances, including where the offense is committed within the territory of the State Party,[139] on board a vessel flying its flag, or on an aircraft registered under the laws of that State Party.[140] The concept of "territory" necessarily includes the territorial sea of coastal States.[141] The Organized Crime Convention encourages, but does not require, States Parties to establish jurisdiction in other circumstances – for example, when the offense is committed against[142] or by a national of a State.[143] In relation to certain specified offenses it further permits

[134] Migrant Smuggling Protocol, at Art. 9.

[135] T. Treves, "Human Rights and the Law of Sea," (2010) 28(1) *Berkeley Journal of International Law* 1 [Treves, "Human Rights and the Law of the Sea"], at 10.

[136] At notes 169–173 and accompanying text.

[137] Ibid.

[138] United Nations Convention against Transnational Organized Crime, 2225 UNTS 209, done Nov. 15, 2000, entered into force Sept. 29, 2003 [Organized Crime Convention].

[139] Ibid. at Art. 15(1)(a).

[140] Ibid. at Art. 15(1)(b). See further United Nations Office on Drugs and Crime, *Model Legislative Provisions against Organized Crime* (2012), at 25–29.

[141] Organized Crime Convention, at Art. 15(1)(a); United Nations Office on Drugs and Crime, *Model Law against the Smuggling of Migrants* (2010) [UNODC Model Law on Migrant Smuggling], at 22.

[142] There may be some question as to whether a State of nationality of a smuggled migrant would be able to assert jurisdiction on the basis of a crime having been committed "against" their national, given the reference to smuggled migrants in the Protocol not as victims but as objects of smuggling. However, in this regard, it is significant that the language of Article 15(2)(a) makes no reference to "victims" but refers only to "offences committed against a national." Logically, this would appear to include smuggled migrants, whether described as "objects" or "victims."

[143] Organized Crime Convention, at Art. 15(2). See further UNODC Model Law on Migrant Smuggling, at 23–25.

States to establish jurisdiction over such offenses that are committed outside their territory if committed "with a view to the commission of a serious crime within its territory."[144] In the case of migrant smuggling, for example, a State Party may legislate to establish jurisdiction over acts such as aiding, abetting, or organizing the commission of a serious crime involving an organized criminal group,[145] where those acts are done with a view to committing a crime of migrant smuggling within that State. An extension of jurisdiction in this way will have required the State to have legislated for migrant smuggling or related acts to be punishable by a maximum deprivation of liberty of at least four years.[146]

The central obligation, contained in Article 7 of the Migrant Smuggling Protocol, is for States Parties to cooperate in preventing and suppressing migrant smuggling by sea "in accordance with the international law of the sea."[147] Article 8 establishes a cooperation regime intended to facilitate law enforcement action in relation to the smuggling of migrants involving the vessels of other States Parties.[148] These provisions reflect existing international legal rules that: (1) recognize the authority of flag States to take action with respect to their vessels suspected of being engaged[149] in

144 Organized Crime Convention, at Art. 15(2)(c). See further UNODC Model Law on Migrant Smuggling, at 23–25.

145 Under the terms of Article 5(1) of the Organized Crime Convention, the original offenses could include "[a]greeing with one or more other persons to commit a serious crime for a purpose relating directly or indirectly to the obtaining of a financial or other material benefit" or of "[c]onduct by a person who, with knowledge of either the aim and general criminal activity of an organized criminal group or its intention to commit the crimes in question, takes an active part in: a. [c]riminal activities of the organized criminal group" or other activities of the organized criminal group in the knowledge that his or her participation will contribute to the achievement of the criminal aim; or "[o]rganizing, directing, aiding, abetting, facilitating or counselling the commission of serious crime involving an organized criminal group." Note that McClean questions whether the provisions of the Convention on jurisdiction can be so easily transposed to the Migrant Smuggling Protocol. D. McClean, *Transnational Organized Crime: A Commentary on the UN Convention and Its Protocols* (2007) [McClean, *Transnational Organized Crime*], at 394.

146 Organized Crime Convention, at Art. 2(b).

147 Migrant Smuggling Protocol, at Art. 7. The Interpretative Note attached to this Article confirms that "the international law of the sea includes the United Nations Convention on the Law of the Sea as well as other relevant international instruments": cited in United Nations Office on Drugs and Crime, Travaux Préparatoires *of the Negotiations for the Elaboration of the United Nations Convention against Transnational Organized Crime and the Protocols Thereto* (2006) [Travaux Préparatoires *for the Organized Crime Convention and Protocols*], at 494. The *Travaux Préparatoires* further confirm the intention of the drafters to include both customary and conventional sources of law. Ibid. at 493.

148 UNODC Model Law on Migrant Smuggling, at 83.

149 "Engagement" in migrant smuggling is noted to extend to both direct and indirect engagement and thereby to cover not just vessels found to be carrying migrants but also other vessels ("mother ships") that transport smuggled migrants on open ocean voyages and may not be apprehended until after smuggled migrants have been transferred to smaller local vessels for the final stage of their journey. Travaux Préparatoires *for the Organized Crime Convention and Protocols*, at 506. The Legislative Guide confirms that the provisions explored in this part would not be applicable to vessels that had simply rescued migrants who were being smuggled by another vessel. United Nations Office on Drugs

migrant smuggling[150]; (2) uphold the requirement of prior flag State consent with respect to such measures taken by another State; and (3) prevent any such measures from being taken in the territorial sea of another State, except with the permission or authorization of that State.[151]

The substance of the Protocol's section on smuggling by sea is therefore concerned with articulating the rules to apply in situations where a State Party other than the flag State encounters a vessel suspected of being engaged in migrant smuggling that either (1) has the nationality of a State Party, or (2) is without nationality. The term "vessel" is defined to include any type of watercraft capable of being used as a means of transportation.[152] Accordingly, the scope of the cooperation obligation would presumably extend to rubber dinghies and other small craft, commonly used in smuggling by sea. Under the Protocol, States Parties are required to designate what is effectively a central authority to receive and respond to requests for assistance, thereby creating the administrative machinery necessary to expedite cooperation.[153]

With regard to vessels suspected of being engaged in smuggling that are flagged to another State Party, the regime does not provide a State Party seeking to act with any automatic or preexisting enforcement powers. Rather, it relies on cooperation: from the State Party seeking to act in requesting permission from the flag State Party, and from the flag State Party in responding promptly and providing the State seeking to act with permission to take enforcement action.

The relevant provisions are as follows:

- A State Party may request the assistance[154] of other States Parties in suppressing the use of a vessel suspected of engaging in migrant smuggling (where the

and Crime, *Legislative Guides for the Implementation of the United Nations Convention against Transnational Organized Crime and the Protocols thereto*, UN Sales No. E.05.V.2 (2004) [*Legislative Guide*], at 386–387.

150 Note the Organized Crime Convention requires flag States to establish jurisdiction when offenses have been committed on board a vessel flying their flag (Article 15).

151 This restriction (which is noted in the *Travaux Préparatoires*) was not included in the text of the Protocol as it was considered by drafters to be well established in the law of the sea. Travaux Préparatoires *for the Organized Crime Convention and Protocols*, at 494.

152 The Migrant Smuggling Protocol, Article 3(d) defines a "vessel" as "any type of water craft, including non-displacement craft and seaplanes, used or capable of being used as a means of transportation on water, except a warship, naval auxiliary or other vessel owned or operated by a Government and used, for the time being, only on government non-commercial service."

153 Migrant Smuggling Protocol, at Art. 8(6).

154 The nature and extent of "assistance" that may be requested or provided is not specified. Mallia cites the official Commentary to the Drug Control Convention in relation to the equivalent provision of the Convention as an indication of a potentially wide interpretation of forms of assistance that might include "searching for the suspect vessel, preventing it from unloading or trans-shipping its cargo, facilitating the presence of the law enforcement officials of the flag State on board the pursuing vessel, and like matters": Mallia, *Migrant Smuggling by Sea*, at 122–123, citing United Nations, *Commentary*

vessel is flying that State's flag or claiming its registry or, while not flying that State's flag but in reality of the nationality of that State),[155] irrespective of the maritime zone in which that vessel is located.

- States Parties so requested are required to render such assistance "to the extent possible within their means."[156]
- A State Party may further notify another State Party that a vessel exercising its freedom of navigation rights (i.e., located beyond the limits of the territorial sea of any State)[157] and flying the other State Party's flag, or apparently registered to that other State Party, is reasonably suspected of engaging in migrant smuggling, and the State Party may request confirmation of registry.[158] The Requested State must respond expeditiously to such a request.[159] Each State is required to designate an authority to receive and respond to such requests, and that designation is to be notified to all States Parties within one month via the UN Secretary-General.[160]
- In the above case, if registry is confirmed, the notifying State Party may request authorization from the flag State to *take appropriate measures* with regard to that vessel.[161] The Protocol does not oblige flag States to authorize any course of action but it provides that flag States "may" authorize, among other things: boarding and searching of the vessel.
- If evidence of migrant smuggling is found, the flag State may further authorize the Requesting State to "take appropriate measures with respect to the vessel and persons and cargo on board."[162] No additional measures can be taken without express authorization of the flag State except on the basis of relevant agreements or "to relieve imminent danger to the lives of persons."[163] The flag State

on the United Nations Convention against Illicit Traffic in Narcotic Drugs and Psychotropic Substances 1998, UN Doc. E/CN.7/590, Dec. 20, 1998, at para. 17(44).

155 Migrant Smuggling Protocol, at Art. 8(1).

156 Ibid. This anticipates there may be situations where no assistance is possible, with an assessment of means left to the Requested State. The nature, type, and extent of "assistance" that might be provided by the Requested State remains undefined, and therefore would depend on the States involved agreeing on the terms of any assistance. Key issues to be agreed upon include whether the request for assistance extends to searching or boarding the vessel, or arresting the persons onboard. See further Hinrichs, "Measures against Smuggling of Migrants at Sea," at 431.

157 That is, on the high seas or in the exclusive economic zone and contiguous zone of another State that is not otherwise part of that State's territorial sea. UNCLOS, at Arts. 58(1), 87(1)(a), 90.

158 Migrant Smuggling Protocol, at Art. 8(2).

159 Ibid. at Art. 8(4).

160 Ibid. at Art. 8(5). See further UNODC Model Law on Migrant Smuggling, at 86–87.

161 Migrant Smuggling Protocol, at Art. 8(6).

162 Ibid. at Art. 8(2)(c).

163 Ibid. at Art. 8(5). See also Mallia, *Migrant Smuggling by Sea*, at 123–125. Note that the original wording of this provision referred to imminent danger "to the lives or safety of persons": Travaux Préparatoires *for the Organized Crime Convention and Protocols*, at 501, 503.

is further entitled to impose conditions on the measures to be taken,[164] and to be informed of the results of such measures.[165]

Several important concepts including "reasonable grounds" and "appropriate measures" are not defined. The term "reasonable grounds" echoes the language used to justify a right of visit under UNCLOS, and has been interpreted by one commentator, somewhat ambiguously, to mean more than a "mere" suspicion that migrant smuggling is occurring through the vessel.[166] Certainly it is apparent that States would be prevented from using the relevant provision as a pretext for randomly intercepting vessels. Beyond this, it is unclear what constraint the requirement to establish "reasonable grounds" would actually exert in practice.

The question of what constitutes "appropriate measures" that may be authorized by the flag State is potentially more significant. The Protocol is silent on this point, leaving open the question of whether this would include – or indeed extend beyond – an authority to board and search the vessel.[167] It is therefore left to the Requested and Requesting State to determine and agree in advance on the extent of the authorization. Consistent with the law of the sea, the Protocol provides that flag States granting such authorizations can make them subject to conditions, including but not limited to conditions relating to responsibility and the extent of measures to be taken.[168] For example, the flag State might authorize the Requesting State to board the vessel and then to seek further instructions before taking any action; or it may authorize not only boarding but also seizure of the vessel and arrest of any persons on board involved in smuggling activity. This question of "appropriate measures" is considered further at Section 6.5 with respect to migrant-smuggling vessels without nationality.

A largely unremarked (and occasionally misunderstood)[169] but potentially far-reaching provision permits a State Party to board and search a vessel where it

[164] Migrant Smuggling Protocol, at Art. 8(5).

[165] Ibid. at Art. 8(3).

[166] Hinrichs, "Measures against Smuggling of Migrants at Sea," at 431.

[167] "Appropriate measures" are not specified. Mallia cites a provision of the Council of Europe Agreement on Illicit Traffic at Sea as an example of the nature and extent of measures that could be considered "appropriate" in the context of Article 8 of the Protocol. Mallia, *Migrant Smuggling by Sea*, at 123–125.

[168] Migrant Smuggling Protocol, at Art. 8(5).

[169] Obokata, for example, links Article 8(5) ("... A State Party shall take no additional measures without the express authorization of the flag State, except those necessary to relieve imminent danger to the lives of persons or those which derive from relevant bilateral or multilateral agreements") with this provision to propose that human rights obligations may "allow States to board a vessel for early detention [sic] or timely provision of protection, if its nationality is unclear." T. Obokata, "The Legal Framework concerning the Smuggling of Migrants at Sea under the UN Protocol on the Smuggling of Migrants by Land, Sea and Air" in B. Ryan and M. Mitsilegas eds., *Extraterritorial Migration Control: Legal Challenges* 151 (2010), at 160.

has reasonable grounds to suspect that the vessel is without nationality (or can be assimilated to a vessel without nationality) and is engaged in the smuggling of migrants by sea.[170] Although this part of the provision merely restates Article 110 of UNCLOS, the remainder asserts that if evidence of migrant smuggling is found, the State Party "shall take appropriate measures in accordance with relevant domestic and international law."[171] That language is considerably broader than the corresponding law of the sea provision. The right of visit under UNCLOS arises where a vessel is on the high seas, and there are reasonable grounds for suspecting that the ship is engaged in piracy, slave trade, or unauthorized broadcasting, or is without nationality. Article 8(7) effectively extends the right of visit to include situations where a State Party has "reasonable grounds to suspect that a vessel is engaged in the smuggling of migrants by sea," provided it is also without nationality or can be assimilated to a ship without nationality. The right of visit under UNCLOS permits fairly limited "examination on board the ship"[172] (in contrast with the "appropriate measures" provision in the Migrant Smuggling Protocol). "Appropriate measures" in the Protocol are not specified but commentators have referred to similar provisions in the UN drug control regime to suggest that it would include a right to seize the ship, to place the crew under arrest, and to instigate prosecution.[173]

Does the Migrant Smuggling Protocol limit or otherwise affect the actions that intercepting States may take against smuggled migrants themselves? One commentator so argues, as "Article 5 of the UN Migrant Smuggling Protocol prohibits the criminalization of migrants who have been the object of migrant smuggling," States are thereby prevented from using the Protocol to subject smuggled migrants themselves to arrest, detention, or forcible escort to their territory.[174] This position misstates the relevant provision of the Protocol, which certainly prevents the Protocol from being used as a basis for criminalizing smuggled migrants *for the fact of having been smuggled*, but which explicitly affirms that *nothing* in the Protocol limits the existing rights of States Parties to take action against those whose conduct constitutes an offense under their national law.[175] In other words, if the smuggled migrants

[170] Migrant Smuggling Protocol, at Art. 8(7).

[171] Ibid.

[172] UNCLOS Article 110(2) provides that: "In the cases provided for in paragraph 1, the warship may proceed to verify the ship's right to fly its flag. To this end, it may send a boat under the command of an officer to the suspected ship. If suspicion remains after the documents have been checked, it may proceed to a further examination on board the ship, which must be carried out with all possible consideration."

[173] den Heijer, *Europe and Extraterritorial Asylum*, at 229, n. 100.

[174] Ibid. at 229.

[175] Migrant Smuggling Protocol, at Art. 6(4).

in question have committed another offense under national law (such as attempted illegal entry), they could nonetheless be arrested, without breaching Article 5 of the Migrant Smuggling Protocol.

It is clear from the language of the Protocol that the need to seek consent for law enforcement operations in no way impacts on the obligation to preserve life at sea, discussed in more detail at Section 6.3.3.1. The Protocol provides that States Parties shall take no additional measures without the express authorization of the flag State, "except those necessary to relieve imminent danger to the lives of persons or those which derive from relevant bilateral or multilateral agreements."[176] The Protocol further requires States Parties to ensure the safe and humane treatment of all persons on board a vessel during law enforcement cooperative activities at sea.[177] This obligation has particular relevance to situations where vessels are intercepted at sea as part of border measures undertaken to suppress the smuggling of migrants. There are safety implications, not only in terms of the immediate need to ensure the physical safety of all persons (including the smuggled migrants) on board any intercepted vessel, but also with regard to ensuring that any persons at risk of harm (for example, from organized criminals) or who express a desire to seek international protection (either under human rights or refugee law) are referred to the appropriate expert authorities.

Consistent with an equivalent UNCLOS provision on the right of visit,[178] the Protocol obliges States Parties to ensure compensation is provided to the vessel when "grounds for measures taken ... prove to be unfounded ... provided that the vessel has not committed any act justifying the measures taken."[179] For example, a vessel that was knowingly anchored near a mother ship may, by this action, have given reasonable grounds to suspect it was involved in the activities of that mother ship, even if this proved to be incorrect. As a further example, a vessel that failed to stop when requested to do so by an authorized officer, without a reasonable excuse may also forfeit any entitlement to compensation.

The obligations in the Protocol regarding cooperation at sea are to be interpreted in light of human rights and refugee law.[180] These obligations are discussed in detail at Section 6.3 of this chapter., and more generally, in Chapters 3 and 7.

176 Ibid. at Art. 8(5).

177 Ibid. at Art. 9(1)(a).

178 UNCLOS, at Art. 110(3) ("If the suspicions prove to be unfounded, and provided that the ship boarded has not committed any act justifying them, it shall be compensated for any loss or damage that may have been sustained").

179 Migrant Smuggling Protocol, at Art. 9(2).

180 Ibid. at Art. 19.

6.1.3. A Note on Regional and Bilateral Arrangements for Interdiction

As detailed in Chapter 1, bilateral agreements aimed at controlling aspects of migrant smuggling have been in existence since at least the 1980s and are becoming an increasingly common means of facilitating joint operations and extending the jurisdiction of States, particularly in relation to the interception of suspect vessels on the high seas or in the territorial waters of another State. That chapter identified and explored the key features of these agreements: their potentially ambiguous legal status, their sometimes secret character, and their asymmetric distribution of costs and benefits.[181] The purpose of this section is to briefly consider the nature and scope of such arrangements with specific reference to their provisions on interception at sea. Of particular relevance to the present discussion is the question of how these arrangements modify or otherwise affect the regime established by the law of the sea and the Migrant Smuggling Protocol. Further reference should be made to Chapter 1, which, in addition to providing a more generalized examination of bilateral arrangements and practice in Europe and North America, also introduces the operations and legal issues around the single regional body that is involved in interdictions at sea: the European Border Agency for the Management of Operational Cooperation at the External Borders of the Member States of the European Union (known as "Frontex").[182]

It should be noted at the outset that bilateral and regional arrangements are widely considered by States to be key to a more effective and coordinated response to organized criminal activity with a transnational dimension such as migrant smuggling. States are, in fact, being actively encouraged to allocate jurisdictional competence among themselves in order to facilitate cooperation, increase accountability, and reduce "safe harbors" of impunity for such crimes.[183] For example the Migrant Smuggling Protocol explicitly requires States Parties to "consider the conclusion of bilateral or regional agreements or operational arrangements or understandings aimed at: (a) Establishing the most appropriate and effective measures to prevent and combat [migrant smuggling and related offenses]; or (b) Enhancing the provisions of [the] Protocol among themselves."[184] As discussed elsewhere,[185] European policy is similarly encouraging of such agreements and their effective implementation.

[181] At Section 1.3.

[182] See further Chapter 1, at Section 1.3.2.2.

[183] See, for example, *Legislative Guide*, at 104 (para. 210): "The main concern in the international community is that no serious crimes go unpunished and that all parts of the crime are punished wherever they took place. Jurisdictional gaps that enable fugitives to find safe havens need to be reduced or eliminated."

[184] Migrant Smuggling Protocol, at Art. 17. Note that a similar provision was originally included in the Protocol's chapter on smuggling by sea. McClean, *Transnational Organized Crime*, at 430.

[185] See further Chapter 1, at Section 1.3.1.

The piecemeal and highly differentiated nature of existing arrangements makes categorization and analysis difficult. It is nevertheless useful at this introductory point to provide a brief and somewhat provisional overview of the types of arrangements that have been concluded between States and at the regional level to support interdiction of irregular migrants at sea.

Shiprider arrangements: are a means of bringing together the State with an interest in preventing smuggling (and generally superior resources to do so) with the State that has the necessary enforcement jurisdiction, in a manner that seeks to preserve the latter's position as decision maker and responsible agent. Such arrangements take many forms, and indeed many operations designated as "joint patrols" are in fact a variation on the shiprider model. Typically however, such arrangements will enable an official of the State of origin/embarkation (State A) to be placed aboard an official vessel of the State seeking to prevent irregular migration into its territory (State B). The official from State A is able to authorize an interdiction of a migrant smuggling vessel within the territorial waters of State A, enforcing the laws of State A. Shiprider agreements can also be used to enable State B to facilitate enforcement action against vessels flagged to State A encountered in any maritime zone, including on the high seas.

Joint patrols: States may agree to engage in interdiction through joint action where both parties are in control of the interdicting vessel. An example is provided by a 2007 agreement concluded between Italy and Libya, considered in more detail in Chapter 1. Under the terms of that agreement, Italy and Libya undertook to jointly organize maritime patrols using vessels made available on a temporary basis by Italy. Mixed crews were to be present on ships, made up of Libyan personnel and Italian police officers. Italian police officers were to provide training, guidance, and technical assistance on the use and handling of the ships. Surveillance, and search and rescue operations were to be conducted in the departure and transit areas of vessels used to transport clandestine immigrants, both in Libyan territorial waters and in international waters, and were to be in compliance with the international conventions in force and in accordance with the operational arrangements to be decided by the two countries.[186] Spain has entered into similar arrangements with a number of African States, including Morocco, Mauritania, and Senegal.[187]

Joint patrols through a coordinating mechanism: Frontex operates to assist EU Member States with implementation of the operational aspects of border control,[188]

[186] *Hirsi Jamaa v. Italy*, at para. 19.

[187] See further P. G. Andrade, "Extraterritorial Strategies to Tackle Irregular Migration by Sea," in B. Ryan and V. Mitsilegas eds., *Extraterritorial Immigration Control: Legal Challenges* 311 (2010).

[188] Frontex was established by Council Regulation (EC) No 2007/2004 of 26 October 2004 establishing a European Agency for the Management of Operational Cooperation at the External Borders of the Member States of the European Union, OJ L 349/1, Nov. 25, 2004. This was amended by Regulation

principally the planning and execution of joint surveillance and interdiction operations at sea. As discussed in Chapter 1, the legal basis for Frontex operations is not completely clear. However the agency has repeatedly asserted that, as a purely technical actor with coordinating responsibilities, it does not operate independently. Consent for its involvement in interdictions in the territorial waters of third countries is provided through agreement between one or more EU Member States and the State within whose jurisdiction the interdiction operation takes place.[189] Joint patrols coordinated through Frontex typically involve multiple EU Member States.

Coastal/flag State consent: a coastal or flag State may dispense with the shiprider and joint patrol options and permit another State to directly engage in interdictions in areas where that State has jurisdiction. A coastal State may, for example, agree to an official vessel from another State entering its territorial waters and interdicting vessels seeking to smuggle migrants through that maritime zone. A flag State may consent to other States' interdicting its vessels where migrant smuggling is suspected. Under the Migrant Smuggling Protocol, a State that is requested by another State for assistance in suppressing the use of a vessel in migrant smuggling is required to render such assistance "to the extent possible within [its] means."[190] As demonstrated by a number of agreements reached between countries of Europe and North Arica, a coastal State may further consent to migrant smuggling vessels (whether flagged or not) intercepted by other States on the high seas being returned to the coastal State for disembarkation.

Whatever particular form they take, bilateral and regional arrangements for interdiction raise common legal issues. Most relevant for the present discussion are questions of control and responsibility. Specifically, if two or more States are involved in an interdiction at sea, how is responsibility for a resulting internationally wrongful

(EC) No 863/2007 of the European Parliament and of the Council of 11 July 2007 establishing a mechanism for the creation of Rapid Border Intervention Teams and amending Council Regulation (EC) No 2007/2004 as regards that mechanism and regulating the tasks and powers of guest officers, OJ L 199/30, July 31, 2007; and again by Regulation (EU) No 1168/2011 of the European Parliament and of the Council of 25 October 2011 amending Council Regulation (EC) No 2007/2004 establishing a European Agency for the Management of Operational Cooperation at the External Borders of the Member States of the European Union, OJ L 304/1, Nov. 22, 2011.

[189] House of Lords (United Kingdom), European Union Committee, *Frontex: The EU External Borders Agency, Report with Evidence* (9th Report of Session 2007–08), at paras. 142–143. The report cautions that even with such agreement "there is some doubt as to whether the mandate of Frontex stretches so far" (at para. 146). The legal status of bilateral agreements concluded in the context of Frontex operations is also unclear. For example, in the context of Italy, di Pascale refers to "bilateral cooperation between ministries of Home Affairs of the countries concerned": A. di Pascale, "Migration Control at Sea: The Italian Case," in B. Ryan and V. Mitsilegas eds., *Extraterritorial Immigration Control: Legal Challenges* 282 (2010), at 291. See also V. Moreno-Lax, "The EU Regime on Interdiction, Search and Rescue, and Disembarkation: The Frontex Guidelines for Intervention at Sea," (2010) 25(4) *International Journal of Marine and Coastal Law* 621.

[190] Migrant Smuggling Protocol, at Art. 8(1).

act to be allocated? Can responsibility (either full or shared) be attributed to an international agency involved in coordinating the interdiction? What constraints, if any, does international law place on a State granting consent to another State to exercise enforcement jurisdiction on its behalf? These questions have been considered in detail in Chapter 3, at Section 3.2.4, and it is necessary at this point only to reiterate the conclusions of that analysis:

- States are permitted, indeed encouraged under international law, to share jurisdictional competence among themselves in seeking to deal more effectively with migrant smuggling;
- States may give consent to other States to assume or share enforcement jurisdiction over a migrant smuggling vessel to the extent that the consenting State possesses the enforcement jurisdiction it grants to another.
- A State that consents to another State assuming or sharing enforcement jurisdiction over a migrant smuggling vessel may nevertheless be held responsible for unlawful acts that result from the exercise of enforcement jurisdiction.
- In the case of shiprider arrangements and joint patrols involving the maritime interdiction of migrant-smuggling vessels, the involved States are jointly responsible for internationally wrongful acts that occur during or as the result of such interdiction.

These principles of joint or shared responsibility are borne out in the human rights jurisprudence on interdictions at sea, in which the involvement of a third State in the interdiction, for example under the terms of a bilateral treaty, has never been accepted as a basis for absolving the respondent State of responsibility.[191] Bilateral and regional agreements for interdiction are examined further at Section 6.3 of this chapter in the context of a consideration of human rights and refugee law obligations around interdiction.

191 For example, the complainants in *Hirsi Jamaa v. Italy* brought a successful claim against Italy, notwithstanding that the violations took place during interdiction operations by Italian vessels that had been transferred to Libya and were manned by joint Italian-Libyan crews, and over which Libya retained formal authority on board. It has been argued elsewhere that responsibility for any human rights violations occurring during those operations would fall on Libya: T. Gammeltoft-Hansen and T. E. Aalberts, "Sovereignty at Sea: The Law and Politics of Saving Lives in the *Mare Liberum*," DIIS Working Paper 2010:18 [Gammeltoft-Hansen and Aalberts, "Sovereignty at Sea"], at 18–19. Notably, Italy did not appear to specifically plead Libyan responsibility as a defense or mitigating factor in its submissions in the *Hirsi Jamaa* case, although the judgment noted, at paragraph 129, that "Italy cannot evade its own responsibility by relying on its obligations arising out of bilateral agreements with Libya. Even if it were to be assumed that those agreements made express provision for the return to Libya of migrants intercepted on the high seas, the Contracting States' responsibility continues even after their having entered into treaty commitments subsequent to the entry into force of the Convention or its Protocols in respect of these States."

6.2. SEARCH, RESCUE, AND DISEMBARKATION

The case study "Smuggled Migrants Left to Die in the Mediterranean" set out in the Introduction to this book provides just one example of States and private parties failing to discharge their duty to go to the assistance of vessels and persons in distress at sea: a duty that extends to smuggled migrants. For merchant vessels, the reasons for this failure are sometimes purely commercial: the rescue of a vessel in distress will inevitably incur costly delays and other impositions that are unlikely to ever be compensated, particularly in relation to rescues involving smuggled irregular migrants.[192] Concerns about the safety of the rescuing vessel may also be a consideration. Other concerns, relating much more directly to the growing regulation and criminalization of irregular migration, were revealed through a Council of Europe Parliamentary Commission investigation into the "left to die" incident.[193] Those going to the rescue of smuggled migrants will often be unable to establish an agreed point of disembarkation with States reluctant to bear the burden of processing and repatriation, and may be tied up in lengthy negotiations with coastal States for weeks or even months. Merchant vessels in particular fear being criminalized by States for carrying and/or disembarking irregular migrants. For State vessels, a failure to rescue migrants in distress will often relate to a desire to avoid bringing rescued migrants within their effective control – and thereby their sphere of legal responsibility, particularly under the rules of refugee law and international human rights law. In short, a failure to rescue can be a way of avoiding the problem of assessing asylum claims, separating refugees from "economic migrants," and organizing return.

Despite serious problems in implementation, the international legal framework around rescue is relatively straightforward. International law has long required

[192] UNHCR reported that "In May 2007 … a group of 27 Africans were rescued by the Italian Navy after they had spent three days and nights clinging to tuna pens dragged by a Maltese fishing boat, the *Budafel*. The boat's captain told the media he refused to divert his ship to disembark the men because he was afraid of losing his valuable catch of tuna." W. Spindler, "Between the Devil and the Deep Blue Sea: Anti-immigration Policies, Reckless Smugglers and Cold Commercial Calculations May Be Endangering Lives at Sea," (2007) 148(4) *Refugees*, available at www.unhcr.org/refmag/148/index.html (accessed May 12, 2013). The issue is long-standing. In 1983, the UNHCR's Executive Committee reported that "[a]ccording to available statistics, significantly fewer Indo-Chinese refugees are currently being rescued at sea than in previous years, both in absolute numbers and as a proportion of total boat arrivals. … Shipowners and masters of vessels have stated that they again anticipated financial losses due to delays encountered in picking up and disembarking refugees," particularly under commercial "time charter" arrangements. In response, the UNHCR introduced a scheme to reimburse rescuing shipowners for costs related to the care of refugees rescued at sea and incurred in connection with disembarkation, although reimbursement was capped at a mere US$5 per refugee and US$5,000 per ship. UN High Commissioner for Refugees, *Problems Related to the Rescue of Asylum-Seekers in Distress at Sea*, EC/SCP/30, Sept. 1, 1983.

[193] Council of Europe Parliamentary Assembly Report, *Lives Lost in the Mediterranean Sea*, at 4 (para. 13.4), 18 (para. 104).

States and their shipmasters to render assistance to any person or vessel in distress at sea.[194] This obligation, which applies to all States through a combination of customary and treaty law, operates at all times and in all maritime zones. It extends to all persons and vessels regardless of nationality, legal status, or any other difference. Obligations relating to search and rescue are of a humanitarian nature and, as a matter of law are distinct from the legal framework governing interception outlined earlier in this chapter. However, as noted previously, this distinction does not always play out in practice. Many interdiction operations against vessels carrying irregular migrants are characterized by involved States as search and rescue operations.[195] Irrespective of how they are understood or described, the rescue of migrants or vessels in distress will often involve or morph into interception, and vice versa. In relation to both types of operations, legally complex questions commonly arise as to where persons interdicted and/or rescued are to be taken and disembarked. The key dilemma in this regard is a variation of one that has arisen regularly throughout this book: in this case a conflict between an obligation to rescue on the one hand, and the right of States to regulate the entry of persons into their territory on the other. In practice, this has meant that rescuing vessels may face very serious challenges in disembarking rescued persons taken on board. The most striking recent example of this is the 2001 *Tampa* incident, described in the Introduction to this book and discussed in further detail at Section 6.2.1.3 of this chapter.

This section provides an overview of the rules around search, rescue, and disembarkation with specific reference to the situation of migrant smuggling and the practice of States and intergovernmental bodies in the context of migration control. Key questions include the following:

[194] There is no clear definition of what constitutes "distress" under this legal framework, although in relation to vessels there appears to be agreement that the distress must involve an element of real danger to the ship, its cargo, and crew. For a useful review of relevant national case law on this point see A. P. Morrison, *Places of Refuge for Ships in Distress: Problems and Methods of Resolution* (2012), at 76–77. On the concept of "person in distress," see Section 6.2.1.4 of this chapter.

[195] For example, the official United States Coast Guard webpage entitled "Alien Migrant Interdiction" states that: "*Primarily*, the Coast Guard maintains its humanitarian responsibility to prevent the loss of life at sea, since the majority of migrant vessels are dangerously overloaded, unseaworthy or otherwise unsafe" (emphasis added), available at www.uscg.mil/hq/cg5/cg531/amio/amio.asp (accessed May 12, 2013). Similarly, in the case of *Hirsi Jamaa v. Italy*, the respondent State argued that the "vessels carrying the applicants had been intercepted in the context of the rescue on the high seas of persons in distress ... and could in no circumstances be described as a maritime police operation. The Italian ships had confined themselves to intervening to assist the three vessels in distress and ensuring the safety of the persons on board. They had then accompanied the intercepted migrants to Libya in accordance with [bilateral agreements]" (at para. 65).

- What is the duty of shipmasters (of both official and private vessels) to render assistance? What is the source of this duty? When does it arise, and how is it qualified?
- What are the search and rescue obligations of States? When do they arise, and how do they differ from the obligations on shipmasters?
- Which State is responsible for disembarkation of persons interdicted and/or rescued at sea? Is a coastal State ever obliged to permit, or entitled to deny disembarkation?

The section draws on previous discussions, most particularly the examination of State responsibility in Chapter 4 and the consideration of extraterritorial application of human rights and refugee law in Chapter 3.

6.2.1. Obligations regarding Persons or Vessels in Distress

The relevant legal framework around maritime rescue of persons or vessels in distress comprises UNCLOS and two widely ratified treaties: the much-amended 1974 International Convention for the Safety of Life at Sea (SOLAS Convention),[196] and the 1979 International Convention on Maritime Search and Rescue (SAR Convention).[197] The framework also includes several additional treaties related to maritime traffic[198] and salvage,[199] as well as resolutions and other instruments of international organizations, most particularly the International Maritime Organization.[200] As with the issue of interdiction, international human rights and

[196] International Convention for the Safety of Life at Sea, 1974, as amended, 1184 UNTS 278, done Nov. 1, 1974, entered into force May 25, 1980 [SOLAS Convention].

[197] International Convention on Maritime Search and Rescue, 1979, with annexes 1405 UNTS 97, done Apr. 27, 1979, entered into force June 22, 1985 [SAR Convention]. The SAR Convention was amended in 1998 by IMO Resolution MSC. 70(69) ("Amendments to the International Convention on Maritime Search and Rescue, 1979"), and again in 2004 by IMO Resolution MSC.155(78) ("Adoption of Amendments to the International Convention on Maritime Search and Rescue, 1979, as amended"). References to the SAR Convention are to the consolidated text.

[198] Convention on Facilitation of International Maritime Traffic, 1965, 591 UNTS 8564, done Apr. 9, 1965, entered into force Mar. 5, 1967, in particular Section 6.C, Standards 6.8–6.10.

[199] International Convention on Salvage, 1989, 1953 UNTS 165, done Apr. 28, 1989, entered into force July 14, 1996, at Art. 10 [International Convention on Salvage].

[200] International Maritime Organization: Assembly, *Enhancement of Safety of Life at Sea by the Prevention and Suppression of Unsafe Practices Associated with Alien Smuggling by Ships*, IMO Resolution A.773(18), Nov. 4, 1993; Assembly, *Guidelines on the Allocation of Responsibilities to Seek the Successful Resolution of Stowaway Cases*, IMO Resolution A.871(20), Nov. 27, 1997; Assembly, *Combating Unsafe Practices Associated with the Trafficking or Transport of Migrants by Sea*, IMO Resolution A.867(20), Nov. 27, 1997; and Maritime Safety Committee, *Interim Measures for Combating Unsafe Practices Associated with the Trafficking or Transport of Migrants by Sea*, IMO Doc. MSC/Circ.896/Rev.1, June 12, 2001.

refugee law, considered further at 6.3 below, are also part of the legal framework around rescue of vessels and migrants in distress.

A critical issue in this regard is the concept of distress: specifically, the question of what constitutes: (1) a distress signal; (2) a person in distress; or (3) a vessel in distress, thereby triggering the legal framework of assistance or rescue at sea. This aspect is subject to detailed consideration under Section 6.2.1.4 of this chapter (issues of concern related to rescue and disembarkation of smuggled migrants).

6.2.1.1. Obligation of Shipmasters to Render Assistance

It is privately owned and operated vessels, not designated search and rescue vessels, that are playing the frontline role in search and rescue efforts. As the IMO has acknowledged:

> [i]t is impossible to arrange SAR [search and rescue] services that depend totally upon dedicated shore-based rescue units to provide timely assistance to all persons in distress at sea. Shipmasters have certain duties that must be carried out in order to provide for safety of life at sea, preserve the integrity of global SAR services of which they are part, and to comply with humanitarian and legal obligations.[201]

The obligation of shipmasters to render assistance to those in distress or danger at sea is rooted in long-standing maritime tradition[202] that was first enshrined in legal form in 1910.[203] It has been widely recognized as a principle of customary international law, binding on all States.[204] Whereas the capacity of individual States to interdict vessels engaged in migrant smuggling hinges on the existence of some form of jurisdiction (flag State, coastal State) or consent of the flag State, these issues are irrelevant in the context of the duty to render assistance to persons in distress.

[201] International Maritime Organization, Maritime Safety Committee, *Guidelines on the Treatment of Persons Rescued at Sea*, IMO Resolution MSC.167(78), adopted May 10, 2004, IMO Doc. MSC 78/26/Add.2 Annex 34 [IMO Guidelines on the Treatment of Persons Rescued at Sea], at para. 5.1.

[202] See B. H. Oxman, "Human Rights and the United Nations Convention on the Law of the Sea" (1998) 36 *Columbia Journal of Transnational Law* 399 [Oxman, "Human Rights and UNCLOS"], at 414.

[203] Convention for the Unification of Certain Rules of Law Respecting Assistance and Salvage at Sea, 212 CTS 187; USTS 576, 37 Stat. 1658; UKTS No. 4 (1913) Cd. 6677, done Sept. 23, 1910, entered into force Mar. 1, 1912 (Article 11: "Every master is bound, so far as he can do so without serious danger to his vessel, her crew and her passengers, to render assistance to everybody, even though an enemy, found at sea in danger of being lost.").

[204] See generally M. Pallis, "Obligations of States towards Asylum Seekers at Sea: Interactions and Conflicts between Legal Regimes" (2002) 14 *International Journal of Refugee Law* 329, at 333–334; and Oxman, "Human Rights and UNCLOS." Fife argues that the obligation reflects "elementary considerations of humanity as a general principle of law and therefore as a source of law in its own right. R. E. Fife, "The Duty to Render Assistance at Sea: Some Reflections after *Tampa*," in J. Petman and J. Klabbers eds., *Nordic Cosmopolitanism: Essays in International law for Martti Koskenniemi* 469 (2003) [Fife, "The Duty to Render Assistance at Sea"], at 470–471, 482.

Rather, the duty is one that "exists throughout the ocean, whether in the territorial sea, in straits used for international navigation, in archipelagic waters, in the exclusive economic zone or on the high seas. Assistance is to be given to any person, ship or aircraft in distress."[205] The framework of legal obligation, set out in Article 95 of UNCLOS, provides that there is a *positive obligation* on flag States to require the master of every ship flying its flag "in so far as he can do so without serious danger to the ship, the crew or the passengers":

(a) to render assistance to any person found at sea in danger of being lost;
(b) to proceed with all possible speed to the rescue of persons in distress, if informed of their need of assistance, insofar as such action may reasonably be expected of him;
(c) after a collision, to render assistance to the other ship, its crew, and its passengers and, where possible, to inform the other ship of the name of his own ship, its port of registry, and the nearest port at which it will call.

The terms of this provision contemplate distinct circumstances in which assistance must be given: both to persons "found at sea" by a chance encounter, and to persons "in distress" of whom the shipmaster becomes aware, for example by means of a distress call or under a procedure established under the SOLAS or SAR Conventions, and in cases of collision.

The same obligation is contained in the High Seas Convention, which remains in force for those States Parties that are not party to UNCLOS.[206] This obligation is not limited to coastal States and draws no distinction between shipmasters of private, military, or commercial vessels. As such, it applies to all shipmasters, irrespective of the nature of their vessel or reason for being in the area.[207]

The UNCLOS obligation for shipmasters to render assistance is given more operational detail in the SOLAS Convention and the 1989 International Convention on Salvage.[208] The SOLAS Convention, which unlike UNCLOS is addressed directly to shipmasters, requires that:

> The master of a ship at sea which is in a position to be able to provide assistance, on receiving information from any source that persons are in distress at sea, is bound to

[205] Nordquist et al., *United Nations Convention on the Law of the Sea 1982: A Commentary*, at 177.

[206] High Seas Convention, at Art. 12.

[207] See Council of Europe Parliamentary Assembly Report, *Lives Lost in the Mediterranean Sea*, at 12 (para. 55).

[208] The interaction between the "umbrella" convention that is UNCLOS, and the operational regulations promulgated by the IMO, are discussed in International Maritime Organization, *Implications of the United Nations Convention on the Law of the Sea for the International Maritime Organization, Study by the Secretariat of the International Maritime Organization (IMO)*, IMO Doc. LEG/MISC.7, Jan. 19, 2012. With regard to the duty to assist, see in particular pages 37–39.

> proceed with all speed to their assistance, if possible informing them or the search and rescue service that the ship is doing so...[209]

Similarly, the International Convention on Salvage provides that shipmasters are duty bound to render assistance to any person in danger of being lost at sea.[210] The question of whether these provisions impose a direct obligation on shipmasters (rather than on States to ensure the masters of their vessels comply with the obligation) is disputed.[211] The IMO Guidelines appear to accept the existence of an independent obligation on shipmasters:

> Shipmasters have certain duties that must be carried out in order to provide for safety of life at sea, preserve the integrity of global SAR services of which they are part, and to comply with humanitarian and legal obligations. In this regard, shipmasters should ... understand and heed obligations under international law to assist persons in distress at sea ... do everything possible, within the capabilities and limitations of the ship, to treat the survivors humanely and to meet their immediate needs.[212]

However, the more practical view is that "[a]lthough at first sight the treaties refer to the masters of ships and appear to create obligations for them, the binding element is on States parties."[213] Obligations under international law, with the exception of specialized fields such as international criminal law, are addressed to States and generally not to private individuals. Nevertheless, the obligation upon States to subject their shipmasters to a duty to render assistance ultimately achieves a similar result, in that an obligation does exist albeit under the domestic law of States Parties and not under international law itself.

209 SOLAS Convention, at Chapter V, Regulation 33 (previously regulation 10 but renumbered as a result of amendments in 2000). Note that the word "information" replaced the word "signal" as a result of the 2004 amendments to the Convention. See further International Maritime Organization, *Implications of the United Nations Convention on the Law of the Sea for the International Maritime Organization, Study by the Secretariat of the International Maritime Organization (IMO)*, IMO Doc. LEG/MISC.7, Jan. 19, 2012, at 37–38.

210 International Convention on Salvage, at Art. 10.

211 See A. Zimmermann, ed., J. Dörschner, and F. Machts assistant eds., *The 1951 Convention Relating to the Status of Refugees and Its 1967 Protocol* (2011), at 824–825.

212 IMO Guidelines on the Treatment of Persons Rescued at Sea, at para 5.1.

213 M. Pallis, "Obligations of States towards Asylum Seekers at Sea: Interactions and Conflicts between Legal Regimes" (2002) 14 *International Journal of Refugee Law* 329, at 332, n. 13, citing M. Simonnet, *La Convention Sur la Haute Mer* (1966), ch. IX: "[O]n a vu que, respectueuse de la souveraineté de Etats, [the High Seas Convention] a le plus souvent edicte des regles s'imposant non pas directement aux navires, mais imposant aux Etats d'astreindre les navires battant leur pavilion a observer telle ou telle prescription" [roughly: we have seen that, in deference to the sovereignty of States, the High Seas Convention most often pronounces rules that are not direct obligations on ships, but that oblige States to compel ships flying their flag to observe such or such rule].

International law does not provide clear guidance on how these obligations are to be operationalized.[214] For example, are States required to enact and enforce legislation criminalizing shipmasters that fail to assist? A number of States have enacted laws imposing criminal and/or civil liability on shipmasters for failing to render assistance to those who are in distress at sea,[215] and it could be convincingly argued that such legislative provision is an essential element of ensuring the effective implementation of the obligation.[216] However, the practice is far from universal, and States of destination for smuggled migrants, as well as major shipping States, may well resist attempts to compel them to legislate in this way.

International law also refrains from stipulating the nature and scope of assistance to be provided in individual situations, although it appears clear that the duty on shipmasters is to render assistance, not necessarily to rescue, except in situations where rescue is both necessary and feasible. In relation to the first criteria, it is certainly possible to envisage a situation in which an encountered vessel has run out of fuel or provisions and requests only refueling or reprovisioning, not "rescue."[217] As detailed previously, the obligation is subject to practical contingencies of safety and reasonableness. Although the relevant rules contain specific directions as to what must be done and in what manner, shipmasters ultimately retain a considerable flexibility in deciding the nature and extent of their response.[218] It has been asserted that this "calculated ambiguity"[219] provides the necessary flexibility for rescuers to fulfill their obligations with due regard to the safety of their own ship and crew as

[214] But note the more detailed guidance provided in standards-based international resource materials such as the International Aeronautical and Maritime Search and Rescue Manual (IAMSAR Manual). Volume III of this resource is intended to be carried onboard all ships, to help with performance of search and rescue functions. IMO Guidelines on the Treatment of Persons Rescued at Sea, at para. 4.5.

[215] For example, Article 1158 of the *Italian Code of Navigation* imposes a duty of rescue and provides for the imprisonment of the master of a national or foreign ship who does not come to the rescue of a person or vessel in distress. See V. D. Fina's commentary (Italy) in T. McCormack ed., "Correspondents Reports: A Guide to State Practice in the Field of International Humanitarian Law" (2010) 13 *Yearbook of International Humanitarian Law* 449, at 545–546. See further Pugash, "The Dilemma of the Sea Refugee," at 578–582.

[216] See recommendation in Council of Europe Parliamentary Assembly Report, *Lives Lost in the Mediterranean Sea*, at 4 (para. 13.4.4).

[217] Note that the requirement of necessity prevents this criteria from being used to justify the provision of interim and insufficient assistance such as food and water drops to vessels in distress. See also *Smuggled Migrants Left to Die in the Mediterranean*, in the Introduction to this book.

[218] Nordquist et al., *United Nations Convention on the Law of the Sea 1982: A Commentary*, at 175. See also D. G. Wilson, "Interdiction on the High Seas: The Role and Authority of a Master in the Boarding and Searching of His Ship by Foreign Warships" (2008) 55 *Naval Law Review* 157.

[219] F. J. Kenney and V. Tasikas, "The *Tampa* Incident: IMO Perspectives and Responses on the Treatment of Persons Rescued at Sea" (2003) 12(1) *Pacific Rim Law and Policy Journal* 143 [Kenney and Tasikas, "The *Tampa* Incident"], at 151.

well as the particular needs of the situation,[220] and that the discretion of the shipmaster in this respect is preserved.[221] However, the lack of specificity has also caused conflict, leading to a clarification of certain rules contained in the SOLAS and SAR Conventions detailed further at Section 6.2.1.3. These include an affirmation that the obligation of assistance and rescue extends to any persons regardless of their nationality or status or the circumstances in which they are found.[222] As noted previously, this extends the obligation to cover all possible situations in which smuggled migrants may be in distress at sea, irrespective of where they are found, how they are found, or the nature and origin of their distress.

6.2.1.2. Search and Rescue Obligations of Coastal States

The obligation on shipmasters to render assistance and rescue at sea is supplemented by requirements on coastal and port States, codified in the same instruments, regarding search and rescue services. UNCLOS Article 98 requires every coastal State to "promote the establishment, operation and maintenance of an adequate and effective search and rescue service regarding safety on and over the sea and, where circumstances so require, by way of mutual regional arrangements cooperate with neighbouring States for this purpose."[223]

Obligations with respect to establishment of search and rescue services are detailed in both the SOLAS and SAR Conventions.[224] The SOLAS Convention is primarily concerned with establishing minimum safety standards for ships engaged in international voyages. However it also obliges Contracting Governments to:

> Ensure that necessary arrangements are made for distress communication and coordination in their area of responsibility and for the rescue of persons in distress at sea around its coasts. These arrangements shall include the establishment, operation and maintenance of such search and rescue facilities as are deemed practicable and necessary.[225]

The SOLAS Convention does not detail how these requirements are to operate in practice. The 1979 SAR Convention was developed with the aim of establishing an internationally agreed search and rescue plan that would cover the world's oceans.

[220] See, for example, S. Cacciaguidi-Fahy, "The Law of the Sea and Human Rights," in S. R. Silverburg ed., *International Law: Contemporary Issues and Future Developments* (2011).

[221] Nordquist et al., *United Nations Convention on the Law of the Sea 1982: A Commentary*, at 175.

[222] SOLAS Convention, at Annex, Chapter V, Regulation 33(1); SAR Convention, at Annex, chapter 2, para. 2.1.10.

[223] UNCLOS, at Art. 98(2).

[224] SOLAS Convention, at Annex, Chapter V, Regulation 7; SAR Convention, at Annex, chapter 1, para. 1.3.3 and chapter 2.

[225] SOLAS Convention, at Chapter V, Regulation 7(1).

The Convention foreshadowed the establishment of Search and Rescue Regions by agreement[226] as well as the establishment of national Rescue Coordination Centers that would be responsible for search and rescue operations within these zones. The location of the rescue operation determines which State's Rescue Coordination Center is responsible for coordination of the rescue operation. The State responsible for the Search and Rescue Region where assistance is rendered is also assigned primary responsibility for the delivery of the intercepted migrants to a "place of safety."

The Technical Annex of the Convention was substantially revised in 1998 to clarify responsibilities of governments and promote greater regional cooperation in search and rescue. Further revisions undertaken in 2004 dealt with rescue at sea and are subject to detailed consideration at Section 6.2.1.3. The Convention requires States Parties to "ensure that necessary arrangements are made" for the provision of "adequate search and rescue services" for persons in distress at sea "round their coasts."[227] States Parties are required to "arrange that their search and rescue services are able to give prompt response to distress calls."[228] The Convention provides that:

> On receiving information that a person is in distress at sea in an area within which a Party provides for the overall co-ordination of search and rescue operations, the responsible authorities of that Party shall take urgent steps to provide the most appropriate assistance available.[229]

Provisional search and rescue plans have been developed in line with the requirements of the Convention in most of the thirteen designated regions. However, division of Search and Rescue Zones and obligations between States has been a major source of controversy.[230] Plans are yet to be completed for certain critical regions, including, most notably, the Mediterranean, which is the site of so many maritime disasters involving smuggled migrants.[231]

[226] SAR Convention, at Annex, Rule 2.1.4. After its entry into force, the world's oceans were divided into thirteen such regions: International Maritime Organization, *Implications of the United Nations Convention on the Law of the Sea for the International Maritime Organization, Study by the Secretariat of the International Maritime Organization (IMO)*, IMO Doc. LEG/MISC.6, Sept. 10, 2008, at 39.

[227] SAR Convention, at Annex, Rule 2.1.1

[228] Ibid. at Rule 2.1.8.

[229] Ibid. at Rule 2.1.9.

[230] See generally, T. Gammeltoft-Hansen, *Access to Asylum: International Refugee Law and the Globalisation of Migration Control* (2011), at 140–145. For an example of a specific dispute (and its tragic consequences), see "Ministry Rejects Maroni's Claims on Migrants Boat Rescue," *Times of Malta* online, Apr. 7, 2011, available at www.timesofmalta.com/articles/view/20110407/local/ministry-rejects-maronis-claims-on-migrants-boat-rescue.358773 (accessed May 12, 2013). See also S. Klepp, "A Double Bind: Malta and the Rescue of Unwanted Migrants at Sea, a Legal Anthropological Perspective on the Humanitarian Law of the Sea" (2011) 23 *International Journal of Refugee Law* 538.

[231] According to the IMO, by 2012, provisional search and rescue plans have been developed but not yet completed for the Western South Atlantic, Eastern North Pacific, Eastern South Pacific, and

6.2.1.3. Amendments to the Rules around Rescue and Disembarkation

As noted previously, the well-established customary and conventional duty to rescue persons in distress at sea is seriously undermined by the lack of an equally rigorous obligation with respect to the disembarkation of persons rescued at sea. In short, a State may refuse to accept the disembarkation of rescued persons or impose obligations on that disembarkation.[232] The dilemma caused by this anomaly in the legal framework is not new. Writing in the 1970s about the Indo-Chinese refugee situation Pugash observed:

> It is well settled that the master of a ship is duty-bound to rescue anyone in danger of being lost at sea. It is equally well settled that a sovereign State is under no duty to admit unwanted alien settled that a sovereign State is under no duty to admit unwanted alien. The plight of the Vietnam refugee draws the two principles into the Catch 22 of the law of the sea. The shipmaster of a freighter in waters off Indochina is obligated to rescue Vietnamese sea refugees, but no nation is bound to take the refugees once they have been rescued.[233]

A number of high profile maritime incidents around the turn of the twenty-first century highlighted the risk to the search and rescue regime occasioned by a lack of willingness of coastal States to permit entry into their territorial waters and ports of ships and persons in distress. The August 2001 *Tampa* incident, the details of which were outlined in the Introduction to this book, laid bare the ambiguities and consequent frailties of the international legal framework around rescue of migrants in distress at sea and, most particularly, exposed the lack of clear rules around disembarkation of such persons.[234] In this case the shipmaster, by any measure, amply fulfilled his obligation to render assistance by saving 433 men, women, and children from a sinking vessel and seeking to provide them with shelter, sustenance, and medical care. The vessel was located in Indonesia's exclusive economic zone but was within Australia's Search and Rescue Zone, and the request to assist the vessel had been made by the Australian authorities. Although the *Tampa* initially headed toward Indonesia after the rescue, it turned toward Christmas Island under threats by

Mediterranean and Black Seas regions: International Maritime Organization, *Implications of the United Nations Convention on the Law of the Sea for the International Maritime Organization, Study by the Secretariat of the International Maritime Organization (IMO)*, IMO Doc. LEG/MISC.7, Jan. 19, 2012, at 38. For a discussion of migrant smuggling by sea, see United Nations Office on Drugs and Crime, *Issue Paper: Smuggling of Migrants by Sea* (2011), P. Monzini, *Migrant Smuggling via Maritime Routes (CeSPI – Centro Studi di Politica Internazionale*, 2004).

[232] G. Goodwin-Gill and J. McAdam, *The Refugee in International Law* (3rd ed. 2007) [Goodwin-Gill and McAdam, *The Refugee in International Law*], at 278.

[233] Pugash, "The Dilemma of the Sea Refugee," at 578.

[234] See further Rothwell, "The Law of the Sea and the MV *Tampa* Incident."

several rescued migrants to commit suicide if the captain did not change course.[235] Having loaded the 433 survivors on board his ship, which was licensed to carry no more than 50 persons,[236] the captain was denied entry to Australian territorial waters to disembark the rescued migrants.[237] This was notwithstanding communications by the captain to Australian authorities indicating that the medical situation on board was critical and that several rescued persons were at risk of death,[238] and the issuing of repeated distress signals by the *Tampa* itself. Among several justifications offered during the incident and afterward, Australia argued that the "rescue" was complete once the migrants had boarded the *Tampa*.[239] In a subsequent trial statement, the Australian government stated that Special Air Service officers had boarded the vessel, including:

> SAS [Special Air Service] medical personnel whose purpose was to render medical and humanitarian assistance in response to a distress signal. Part of the purpose was to provide security for the crew. Another part of the purpose was to deal with any medical emergencies and *thus remove the basis for the distress signal and facilitate the departure of the ship from Australian Waters*.[240]

This, and similar incidents, created considerable concern that the obligation to rescue would be undermined by the practical difficulties that shipmasters might face if they would, having rescued smuggled migrants, be unable to disembark them in a timely manner. Writing in 2002 shortly after the *Tampa* incident, Rothwell echoed the conclusion reached by a number of commentators before him, that:

[235] *Victorian Council for Civil Liberties Incorporated v. Minister for Immigration and Multicultural Affairs* [2001] FCA 1297 [*Victorian Council for Civil Liberties Incorporated v. Minister for Immigration and Multicultural Affairs*], at para. 18.

[236] Ibid. at para 15.

[237] See further Rothwell, "The Law of the Sea and the MV *Tampa* Incident."

[238] "As discussed at approx 11.30 today the medical situation on board is critical. *If it is not addressed immediately people will die shortly*. At this time, four people on board are unconscious, 1 broken leg and 3 women are pregnant. Additionally diarrhoea is severe and a number of people are in a dangerously dehydrated condition. The ship has now run out of the relevant medical supplies and has no way of feeding these people.... If the situation is not resolved soon more drastic action, may have to be taken to prevent loss of life": Communication by Captain Rinnan's solicitor to Ms. Godwin, First Assistant Secretary, Defence Task Force, Department of Immigration and Multicultural Affairs, August 27, 2001, cited in *Victorian Council for Civil Liberties Incorporated v. Minister for Immigration and Multicultural Affairs*, at para. 22 (emphasis in original). The captain also contacted the Royal Flying Doctor Service to report that several rescuees were unconscious, one had a broken leg, and that two pregnant women were suffering pains: ibid. at para. 23.

[239] The MV *Tampa* incident: Communication by the Government of Australia, IMO Circular Letter No. 2345, Oct. 15, 2001, at 2.

[240] Statement of agreed facts in *Victorian Council for Civil Liberties Incorporated v. Minister for Immigration and Multicultural Affairs*, at para 35 (emphasis added).

> While international law creates clear obligations on coastal states to coordinate [maritime search and rescue] operations and for ships to go to the aid of persons and other ships in distress, it remains unclear as to who has responsibility for the rescued persons after the actual rescue has taken place.[241]

Within months of *Tampa*, the IMO Assembly adopted a resolution authorizing a comprehensive review of safety measures and procedures for the treatment of persons rescued at sea.[242] The outcome of this review was a set of substantial amendments to Chapter V of the SOLAS Convention and to Chapters 2, 3, and 4 of the Annex to the SAR Convention,[243] adopted by the IMO Maritime Safety Committee in 2004, entering into force in 2006.[244] The amendments aimed to clarify the nature and scope of relevant rights and obligations and, more specifically, "to help ensure that persons in distress are assisted, while minimizing the inconvenience to assisting ships and ensuring the continued integrity of SAR [search and rescue] services."[245] They further sought to ensure that "the obligation of the ship master to render assistance is complemented by a corresponding obligation of States to co-operate in rescue situations, thereby relieving the master of the responsibility to care for survivors, and allowing individuals who are rescued at sea in such circumstances to be delivered promptly to a place of safety."[246] Their major provisions include:

[241] Rothwell, "The Law of the Sea and the MV *Tampa* Incident," at 120.

[242] International Maritime Organization, Assembly, *Review of Safety Measures and Procedures for the Treatment of Persons Rescued at Sea*, IMO Resolution A.920(22), adopted Nov. 29, 2001, IMO Doc. A 22/Res.920, Jan. 22, 2002. The resolution called for a review of the major international conventions and related IMO instruments "for the purpose of identifying any existing gaps, inconsistencies, ambiguities, vagueness or other inadequacies and, in the light of such review, to take action as appropriate, so that: survivors of distress incidents are given assistance regardless of nationality or status or of the circumstances in which they are found; ships which have retrieved persons in distress at sea are able to deliver the survivors to a place of safety; and survivors, regardless of nationality or status, including undocumented migrants, asylum seekers, refugees and stowaways, are treated while on board in the manner prescribed in the relevant IMO instruments and in accordance with relevant international agreements and long-standing humanitarian maritime traditions" (at para. 1).

[243] The amendments are set out in International Maritime Organization, Maritime Safety Committee, *Report of the Maritime Safety Committee on Its Seventy-Eighth Session*, IMO Docs. MSC 78/26/Add.1 and MSC 78/26/Add.2, June 4, 2004. The two amendments of particular relevance in this chapter are: International Maritime Organization, Maritime Safety Committee, *Adoption of Amendments to the International Convention for the Safety of Life at Sea, 1974, as Amended*, IMO MSC Resolution MSC.153(78), May 20, 2004 [IMO Res. MSC.153(78) (SOLAS)]; and International Maritime Organization, Maritime Safety Committee, *Adoption of Amendments to the International Convention on Maritime Search and Rescue, 1979, as amended*, IMO MSC Resolution MSC.155(78), May 20, 2004 [IMO Res. MSC.155(78) (SAR)].

[244] IMO Res. MSC.153(78) (SOLAS), at para. 3; IMO Res. MSC.155(78) (SAR), at para. 3.

[245] IMO Guidelines on the Treatment of Persons Rescued at Sea, at para. 2.3.

[246] International Maritime Organization and Office of the UN High Commissioner for Refugees, *Rescue at Sea: A Guide to Principles and Practice as Applied to Migrants and Refugees* (2006), at 2.

- A definition of search and rescue services[247] and clarification of the meaning of "persons in distress";[248]
- A clarification that the existing obligation under the SOLAS Convention to provide assistance applies to any persons in distress "regardless of the nationality or status of such persons or the circumstances in which they are found"[249];
- A requirement of States Parties to cooperate and coordinate with each other to ensure that masters of ships providing assistance by embarking persons in distress at sea are released from their obligations with minimum further deviation from the ship's intended voyage, provided that this "does not further endanger the safety of life at sea";[250]
- A requirement of States Parties to cooperate and coordinate with each other to assist the ship's master in delivering persons rescued at sea to a place of safety,[251] taking into account the circumstances of the case[252]; with the country that has coordinated the search and rescue operation exercising "primary responsibility for ensuring such co-ordination and co-operation occurs";[253]
- A requirement that shipmasters who have embarked persons in distress at sea shall treat them with humanity, within the capabilities and limits of the ship; and

[247] "Search and rescue service" means "[t]he performance of distress monitoring, communication, coordination and search and rescue functions, including provision of medical advice, initial medical assistance, or medical evacuation, through the use of public and private resources including cooperating aircraft, vessels and other craft and installations"; "search" as "[a]n operation, normally coordinated by a rescue coordination centre or rescue sub-centre, using available personnel and facilities to locate persons in distress"; and "rescue" as "[a]n operation to retrieve persons in distress, provide for their initial medical or other needs, and deliver them to a place of safety." International Maritime Organization, Maritime Safety Committee, *Amendments to the International Convention on Maritime Search and Rescue of 27 April 1979*, concluded London, May 18, 1998, Annex, paras. 1.3.1–1.3.3. See also IMO Res. MSC.153(78) (SOLAS), at Annex, Chapter V, Regulation 2.

[248] "Distress phase" means "a situation wherein there is a reasonable certainty that a person, a vessel or other craft is threatened by grave and imminent danger and requires immediate assistance": SAR Convention, at Annex, chapter 1, para. 1.3.13. Further, "persons in distress" includes "persons in need of assistance who have found refuge on a coast in a remote location within an ocean area inaccessible to any rescue facility other than as provided for in the annex [to the SAR Convention]": IMO Res. MSC.155(78) (SAR)), at Annex, chapter 2, para. 2.1.

[249] IMO Res. MSC.153(78) (SOLAS), at Annex, Regulation 33, para. 3.

[250] Ibid. at Annex, Regulation 33, para. 4; IMO Res. MSC.155(78) (SAR), at Annex, chapter 3, para. 3.1.

[251] On the concept of "a place of safety" see notes 258–265 in this chapter and accompanying text.

[252] The IMO Guidelines on the Treatment of Persons Rescued at Sea explain that "[t]hese circumstances may include factors such as the situation on board the assisting ship, on scene conditions, medical needs, and availability of transportation or other rescue units. Each case is unique, and selection of a place of safety may need to account for a variety of important factors" (at para. 6.15).

[253] IMO Res. MSC.153(78) (SOLAS), at Annex, Regulation 33, para. 4; IMO Res. MSC.155(78) (SAR), at Annex, chapter 3, para. 3.1. For further discussion of the uncertainties surrounding interpretation of this provision see note 257.

- An affirmation of a shipmaster's discretion in the context of search and rescue: "[t]he owner, the charterer, the company operating the ship . . ., or any other person shall not prevent or restrict the master of the ship from taking or executing any decision which, in the master's professional judgment, is necessary for safety of life at sea and protection of the marine environment."[254]

With regard to responsibility for disembarking persons rescued at sea, the amendments provide that:

> The Contracting Government responsible for the search and rescue region in which such assistance is rendered shall exercise primary responsibility for ensuring such co-ordination and co-operation occurs, so that survivors assisted are disembarked from the assisting ship and *delivered to a place of safety*, taking into account the particular circumstances of the case and guidelines developed by the Organization. In these cases, the relevant Contracting Government shall arrange for such disembarkation to be effected as soon as reasonably practicable.[255]

It is important to point out the limits of this obligation. Contracting Governments responsible for the Search and Rescue Region in which the event occurs are certainly not expressly obliged to accept disembarkation of rescued persons: their responsibility is limited to leading coordination and cooperation efforts aimed at delivering such persons to a place of safety.[256] However, it is not yet clear whether this primary responsibility may have implications under the rules of international human rights law – for example, protracted confinement to a vessel under deteriorating conditions may raise issues under international human rights law or even, in certain circumstances, compel a State with primary responsibility to accept disembarkation.[257]

[254] IMO Res. MSC.153(78) (SOLAS), at Annex, Regulation 34–1.

[255] Ibid. at Annex, Regulation 33, para. 4 (emphasis added).

[256] Gammeltoft-Hansen and Aalberts have written that "[u]nder the 2004 amendments the state within whose SAR zone rescue takes place has the responsibility for 'coordinating' that persons rescued are disembarked at a place of safety. The dominant interpretation is that this entails allowing disembarkation at the state's own ports unless disembarkation can be arranged elsewhere. Yet, the language is clearly a compromise and a number of States still resist that the new amendments entail a hard obligation to allow disembarkation": Gammeltoft-Hansen and Aalberts, "Sovereignty at Sea," at 17, n. 26. Indeed, it is doubtful whether that "dominant interpretation" is correct – or indeed is even dominant except among scholars. Principles adopted by the IMO Facilitation Committee in 2009 contained only a soft law exhortation that "[i]f disembarkation from the rescuing ship cannot be arranged swiftly elsewhere, the Government responsible for the SAR area should accept the disembarkation of the persons rescued": International Maritime Organization, Facilitation Committee, *Principles Relating to the Administrative Procedures for Disembarking Persons Rescued at Sea*, IMO Doc. FAL.3/Circ.194, Jan. 22, 2009, at Principle 2.3. Subsequent proposals to amend the SOLAS and SAR Conventions to incorporate the principles failed. For a detailed discussion, see J. Coppens and E. Somers, "Towards New Rules on Disembarkation of Persons Rescued at Sea?" (2010) 25 *International Journal of Marine and Coastal Law* 377.

[257] Even though no State is strictly obliged to accept disembarkation (see discussion at Section 6.2.1.4 of this chapter, "Disembarkation"), obligations under international human rights law may compel the

The amendments to the SOLAS and SAR Conventions were complemented by a set of Guidelines on the Treatment of Persons Rescued at Sea, also adopted by the IMO in 2004.[258] These Guidelines aim at supporting the effective implementation of the amendments, specifically "with regard to humanitarian obligations and obligations under the relevant international law relating to treatment of persons rescued at sea."[259] In substance, they confirm and explain the rationale and substantive content of the legal framework, providing additional explanation of key concepts and setting out procedures for shipmasters and States to follow in order to ensure that the core objectives of the rescue at sea framework can be secured with minimal burden to ships engaged in retrieving persons in distress at sea. One section of the Guidelines explains, in considerable detail, the highly relevant concept of "a place of safety":

> A place of safety (as referred to in the Annex to the 1979 SAR Convention, paragraph 1.3.2) is a location where rescue operations are considered to terminate. It is also a place where the survivors' safety of life is no longer threatened and where their basic human needs (such as food, shelter and medical needs) can be met. Further, it is a place from which transportation arrangements can be made for the survivors' next or final destination.[260]

According to the Guidelines, an assisting ship should *not* be considered a place of safety, simply on the basis that, as argued by Australia in the *Tampa* incident, the survivors are no longer in immediate danger once on board. The Guidelines note that an assisting ship may not have the necessary facilities and equipment to properly care for survivors without endangering its own safety:

> Even if the ship is capable of safely accommodating the survivors and may serve as a temporary place of safety, it should be relieved of this responsibility as soon as alternative arrangements can be made. A place of safety may be on land, or it may be aboard a rescue unit or other suitable vessel or facility at sea that

State with "ultimate" or "primary" responsibility for the migrants to ensure disembarkation occurs within a reasonable period of time (e.g., very protracted refusal of disembarkation may give rise to human rights violations by a State if the rescuees' conditions on board the vessel are deteriorating). There are serious problems with designating one State as "primarily" responsible given that the State so designated is often unable or unwilling to comply or does not accept that it has primary responsibility. The designation also facilitates avoidance of responsibility by other implicated States that are able to refer to the designated State's primary responsibility. See further Gammeltoft-Hansen and Aalberts, "Sovereignty at Sea," at 15, in relation to the "Budafel tuna pen incident" ("By reference to Libya's primary responsibility under the SAR rules, Malta's disavowed its own responsibility for disembarkation on the basis of maritime customary law").

[258] International Maritime Organization, Maritime Safety Committee, *Guidelines on the Treatment of Persons Rescued at Sea*, IMO Resolution MSC.167(78), adopted May 10, 2004, IMO Doc. MSC 78/26/Add.2 Annex 34 [IMO Guidelines on the Treatment of Persons Rescued at Sea].

[259] Ibid. at para. 1.1.

[260] Ibid. at para. 6.12.

can serve as a place of safety until the survivors are disembarked to their next destination.[261]

The Guidelines further provide that States should cooperate with each other with regard to providing suitable places of safety for survivors after considering relevant factors and risks.[262] They explicitly affirm that a relevant consideration in the case of asylum-seekers and refugees recovered at sea is "[t]he need to avoid disembarkation in territories where the lives and freedoms of those alleging a well-founded fear of persecution would be threatened."[263] This aspect of the concept of safety has been taken up in a 2011 Council of Europe Resolution, which notes that the concept of "place of safety" continues to be interpreted differently and calls on Member States to interpret a "place of safety" to mean "a place which can meet the immediate needs of those disembarked and in no way jeopardises their fundamental rights, since the notion of 'safety' extends beyond mere protection from physical danger and must also take into account the fundamental rights dimension of the proposed place of disembarkation."[264] The essence of these provisions has been reiterated in the Principles relating to Administrative Procedures for Disembarking Persons Rescued at Sea,[265] adopted by the IMO in 2009.

6.2.1.4. Issues of Concern Related to Rescue and Disembarkation of Smuggled Migrants

Few of the ambiguities and operational challenges around search and rescue were fully resolved through the 2004 amendments to the SOLAS and SAR Conventions and the adoption of the accompanying IMO Guidelines. The following paragraphs briefly consider those matters that are of most significance to the issue of migrant smuggling by sea.

Distress: When is a vessel or an individual in "distress" and therefore within the legal framework of assistance or rescue at sea? The SAR Convention defines "distress phase" as "[a] situation wherein there is a reasonable certainty that a vessel or a person is threatened by grave or imminent danger and requires immediate

[261] Ibid. at paras. 6.13–6.14.
[262] Ibid. at para. 6.16.
[263] Ibid. at para. 6.17.
[264] Council of Europe, Parliamentary Assembly, Resolution 1821(2011) on The interception and rescue at sea of asylum seekers, refugees and irregular migrants, adopted June 21, 2011, at para. 9.5.
[265] International Maritime Organization, Facilitation Committee, *Principles Relating to Administrative Procedures for Disembarking Persons Rescued at Sea*, IMO Doc. FAL.3/Circ.194, Jan. 22, 2009.

rendering humanitarian assistance by rescuing people in distress at sea does not constitute a crime of aiding illegal immigration."[288] Finally, it should be noted that the clarification in the IMO Guidelines on the Treatment of Persons Rescued at Sea, that a rescue operation is not considered to terminate until persons are delivered to a "place of safety,"[289] arguably extends the mantle of what constitutes a "rescue operation" up until the point of disembarkation, whether this is on to land or some other suitable facility.[290] It remains to be seen whether the crew of a rescuing vessel that, finding itself in distress following a rescue, disembarks rescued persons in breach of instructions from the coastal State, would be able to avoid prosecution under domestic laws by relying on their obligation to render humanitarian assistance or from the fact of the rescuing vessel's own distress.[291]

Deliberate Sabotage of Vessel and Use of Force against Rescuers: States have reported that the crew and/or passengers of some migrant smuggling vessels have deliberately incapacitated the vessel in order to trigger a search and recue and that force or the threat of force has been used "to "persuade" masters and crews of rescuing ships to transport survivors to a particular destination."[292] Although such conduct may well contribute to a hardening of State attitudes with regard to search, rescue, and disembarkation, it does not alter the basic international legal obligations.[293] For example, in the *Tampa* incident, the duress exerted upon the captain by certain survivors' threats to commit suicide unless the *Tampa* changed course for Australia in no way vitiated the *Tampa*'s subsequent distress signals when anchored just outside Australian territorial waters. The concept of distress appears to be a

288 Ibid. at 546.

289 IMO Guidelines on the Treatment of Persons Rescued at Sea, at para. 6.12.

290 Ibid. at paras. 6.13–6.14.

291 On the legal situation of vessels in distress entering a port or internal waters, see "The Enterprise" in J. B. Moore, *History and Digest of the International Arbitrations in which the United States Has Been a Party*, vol. 4 (1898), at 4363: "The reason for this rule is obvious. It would be a manifest injustice to punish foreigners for a breach of certain laws, unintentionally committed by them, and by reason of circumstances over which they had no control." Cited in D. P. O'Connell (I. Shearer ed.), *The International Law of the Sea*, vol. 1 (1982), at 857, n. 29; and Rothwell, "The Law of the Sea and the MV *Tampa* Incident," at 124, n. 37.

292 See Australian Department for Transport and Regional Services, *Guidelines for Commercial Shipping Rescuing Persons at Sea in or Adjacent to the Australian Search and Rescue Region* (June 2005). Note that reports around the *Tampa* incident appear to confirm that the captain's original plan to return the rescued migrants to Indonesia was thwarted by protests from a group of rescued migrants who threatened self harm if they were not taken to a Western country. See references in note 20 in the Introduction to this book. See also Kenney and Tasikas, "The *Tampa* Incident." For a separate example see "Asylum-Seekers Sabotaged SIEV 36 off Ashmore Reef, Coroner Finds," *The Australian*, Mar. 17, 2010, available at www.theaustralian.com.au/news/asylum-seekers-sabotaged-siev-36-off-ashmore-reef-coroner-finds/story-e6frg6n6–1225841839976 (accessed May 12, 2013).

293 See generally D. J. Devine, "Ships in Distress – A Judicial Contribution from the South Atlantic" (1996) 20(3) *Marine Policy* 229, at 231–232.

purely factual one: not dependent on a consideration of how that situation arose or who was responsible. Given the humanitarian nature of rescue and assistance obligations, it is difficult to see how the cause of distress could operate to diminish the necessity and obligation to assist. Even in cases of deliberate sabotage or threats of violence, rescue and assistance obligations must be considered to apply in full force, tempered only by the shipmaster's discretion to determine the feasibility of assistance. Provided that jurisdictional requirements are met (for example, flag State consent or location within the coastal State's territorial sea), there would be nothing to prevent subsequent disciplinary or criminal proceedings under national law being taken against rescued persons in respect of any wrongful acts.

Human Rights and Refugee Law Obligations: It is essential to emphasize that, as with interdiction, the legal framework around search and rescue and disembarkation also includes human rights and refugee law. The extent to which these areas of law, most particularly the obligation of *non-refoulement*, affect obligations around search and rescue, and constrain the right of States to deny disembarkation, are considered in detail in the following section.

6.3. HUMAN RIGHTS AND REFUGEE LAW DURING INTERDICTION AND RESCUE

The capacity of States to act against migrant smuggling by sea is determined, not just by the rules set out previously, but also by the requirements of international human rights and refugee law. In this area of the smuggling response as in all others, it is not defensible for States to carve out a legal or policy regime that is isolated from these broader obligations: to adopt what one scholar has accurately termed a "fragmentary reading" of maritime obligations,[294] for example by characterizing migration control operations either as "rescues" or interdictions, depending on which legal regime offers the most legal flexibility.[295] This is recognized, most explicitly, in the

[294] V. Moreno-Lax, "Seeking Asylum in the Mediterranean: Against a Fragmentary Reading of EU Member States' Obligations Accruing at Sea" (2011) 23(2) *International Journal of Refugee Law* 174.

[295] As noted previously, this approach has been adopted by a number of States in an apparent effort to alter the nature of their legal obligations to rescued/interdicted migrants. Fischer-Lescano et al. argue persuasively that States "cannot circumvent refugee law and human rights requirements by declaring border control measures – that is, the interception, turning back, redirecting etc. of refugee boats – to be rescue measures. In the case of both rescue at sea and border control measures *vis à vis* migrants who are not in distress at sea, the following procedures are required: transfer of the protection seekers and migrants to a safe place on EU territory; conduct of proceedings in order to examine the asylum application; legal review of the decision": A. Fischer-Lescano, T. Löhr, and T. Tohidipur, "Border Controls at Sea: Requirements under International Human Rights and Refugee Law" (2009) 21(2) *International Journal of Refugee Law* 256 [Fischer-Lescano et al., "Border Controls at Sea"], at 291. The European Court of Human Rights, in *Hirsi Jamaa v. Italy*, affirmed that "the rules for the rescue of persons at sea and those governing the fight against people trafficking [and presumably also migrant

Migrant Smuggling Protocol, which affirms that *all* actions taken under that instrument must be in conformity with existing human rights rules, including the prohibition on discrimination and *non-refoulement*,[296] and which further stipulates that measures taken in respect of vessels suspected of engaging in migrant smuggling are to be "in accordance with national and international law."[297] The law of the sea also rejects fragmentation, explicitly recognizing the continued application of existing, nonconflicting rules.[298] As Treves succinctly concludes: "Rules of the Law of the Sea are sometimes inspired by human rights considerations and may or must be interpreted in light of such considerations. The application of rules on human rights may require the consideration of rules of the Law of the Sea."[299]

However, application of that broader legal framework in the context of smuggling by sea is rarely straightforward and often fraught. Although common human rights and refugee law principles apply to rescues and border control interdictions, there are also important distinctions that can complicate an assessment of lawfulness in relation to certain actions.[300] Particularly problematic in the present context are questions related to the extraterritorial application of the relevant rules: which rights and obligations apply to whom, and in which maritime zone? At what point are smuggled migrants considered to be under the jurisdiction of a particular State, and what are the consequences of that for the migrant's rights and the State's obligations? Can a State legitimately avoid or minimize its human rights and refugee law obligations by shifting the encounter with a smuggled migrant to international waters or the territorial waters of another State? At what point is the right to seek asylum activated, and what factors trigger a corresponding obligation on the part of a State engaged in responding to migrant smuggling? Other questions that arise when considering State responses to migrant smuggling are less about what Guilfoyle has identified as the threshold issues and more about substantive rules, such as the prohibition on disproportionate use of force and inhuman treatment; the prohibition of arbitrary detention and arbitrary expulsion; and, critically, the obligation of *non-refoulement* under both human rights and refugee law.

The legal framework within which many of these issues are to be considered has already been explained and discussed in considerable detail. Reference should

smuggling] impose on States the obligation to fulfil the obligations arising out of international refugee law, including the '*non-refoulement*' principle" (at para. 134).

296 Migrant Smuggling Protocol, at Art. 19.

297 Ibid. at Art. 8(7). See discussion of this provision at Section 6.1.2 of this chapter.

298 UNCLOS, at Art. 293 (permitting the application of other rules of international law not incompatible with the Convention).

299 Treves, "Human Rights and the Law of the Sea," at 12.

300 For example, Tondini points out that "[c]arrying out a SAR intervention entails limits ... to the use of force by naval officers, which are much narrower than those applicable to a border control operation": Tondini, "The Legality of Intercepting Boat People," at 60.

particularly be made to Chapter 2 (substantive rights), Chapter 3 (extraterritorial application of human rights and refugee law), and Chapter 4 (State responsibility for wrongful acts). The present section draws out the key points of that previous analysis while considering, in more detail, and with reference to specific issues and questions, how it applies to the very particular situation of smuggling by sea.

6.3.1. *Application of Human Rights Law at Sea*

Application of human rights law will generally be straightforward when a response to migrant smuggling at sea (whether interdiction or rescue or both) occurs wholly within the territory of a State or on a vessel that is flagged to that State. As discussed previously, States exercise full sovereign authority and jurisdiction within their territory, including internal waters and the territorial sea. The practice of "excision," whereby certain parts of a State such as airport transit areas or offshore islands[301] are deemed to be outside the State's territory for purposes of national migration law, may have domestic legal implications but does not affect the State's international legal obligations at all. In relation to interceptions, rescues, or other encounters with migrant-smuggling vessels within a State's internal waters or territorial sea, there is no substantial difference in the application of the law: human rights and refugee law to which that State is bound will apply in exactly the same way as it would if the event were entirely contained within a State's land borders.[302] It remains only to

[301] Australia's excision policy is well described by Fischer-Lescano et al.: "... Australia adopted a law in 2001 whereby various islands within the 12 mile zone are defined as outside the 'migration zone' within the meaning of the Migration Act of 1954. Pursuant to this legislation, Australia's Migration Act obligations do not apply on the islands concerned. The Act is also the vehicle for implementing the Refugee Convention in Australia. Thus, the obligations arising from it are also rescinded. Individuals disembarking on the islands concerned are indeed questioned as 'offshore entry persons' by the UNHCR or Australian officials on regional islands and asked about their reasons for fleeing. But they are exposed to a malfunctioning asylum system and have access neither to legal protection nor to government information centres": Fischer-Lescano et al., "Border Controls at Sea," at 262. See further M. Crock and D. Ghezelbash, "Do Loose Lips Bring Ships? The Role of Policy, Politics and Human Rights in Managing Unauthorised Boat Arrivals" (2010) 19(2) *Griffith Law Review* 238, at 264–265. UNHCR is emphatic that "[d]omestic law is not determinative of the existence of jurisdiction as a matter of fact under international law," citing the Vienna Convention on the Law of Treaties (1155 UNTS 331, done May 23, 1969, entered into force Jan. 27, 1980), Article 27 (providing that a State may not invoke the provisions of its internal law as a justification for its failure to perform a treaty), and Article 3 of the International Law Commission's Draft Articles on the Responsibility of States for Internationally Wrongful Acts. UN High Commissioner for Refugees, *Maritime Interception Operations and the Processing of International Protection Claims: Legal Standards and Policy Considerations with Respect to Extraterritorial Processing* (Protection Policy Paper, Nov. 2010) [UNHCR Protection Policy Paper: Maritime Interception Operations], at 4, n. 10.

[302] In relation to the obligation of *non-refoulement* see: UN High Commissioner for Refugees Executive Committee, *Conclusion on Protection Safeguards in Interception Measures*, Doc. No. 97 (LIV) – 2003, Oct. 10, 2003, at para. (a)(i): "The State within whose sovereign territory, or territorial waters,

consider whether an obligation has in fact been breached and whether that breach can be attributed to the State in question. Once these two tests are satisfied then an internationally wrongful act, incurring that State's legal responsibility, will be established.

A much more difficult set of issues arise when the response occurs outside the territory of the State – in its EEZ for example, on the high seas, or in the territorial waters of another State. The central question to be asked at this point has already been addressed in Chapter 2: whether, and under what circumstances a State that is party to a particular human rights treaty (or under a customary law obligation) owes legal obligations under that treaty (or customary rule) to a person who is not within the territory of that State. In many respects this is the critical issue for the international law of migrant smuggling. Commentators have identified the growing shift toward extraterritorial immigration control as motivated largely by a desire to avoid the substantive and procedural guarantees to which migrants, including those who have been smuggled, are entitled.[303] Even if this does not hold true for all smuggling-related interventions at sea, it is clearly essential to examine whether States are indeed able to shift or minimize their obligations in this way and, if so, under what circumstances. The following paragraphs summarize those parts of the more extensive analysis of extraterritorial application of human rights and refugee law obligations set out in Chapter 3 that are most relevant to the issue of smuggling by sea.

International human rights treaties generally specify their scope of application as extending to every person within their territory and/or under their jurisdiction.[304] The notion of being under the jurisdiction of a State has been interpreted by the Human Rights Committee in connection with the International Covenant on Civil and Political Rights (ICCPR) as meaning that a State Party must respect and ensure the rights laid down in the Covenant to anyone within its de facto jurisdiction, that is, persons who are "within *the power or effective control* of that State Party, even if not situated within the territory of the State Party."[305] It further

interception takes place has the primary responsibility for addressing any protection needs of intercepted persons."

303 See generally B. Ryan, "Extraterritorial Immigration Control: What Role for Legal Guarantees?," in B. Ryan and V. Mitsilegas eds., *Extraterritorial Immigration Control: Legal Challenges* 1 (2010).

304 See, for example, International Covenant on Civil and Political Rights, 999 UNTS 171, done Dec. 16, 1996, entered into force Mar. 23, 1976 [ICCPR], at Art. 2(1); Convention for the Protection of Human Rights and Fundamental Freedoms, 213 UNTS 222, done Nov. 4, 1950, entered into force Sept. 3, 1953 [European Convention on Human Rights], at Art. 1; American Convention on Human Rights, 1144 UNTS 123, done Nov. 22, 1969, entered into force July 18, 1978, at Art. 1; Convention against Torture and Other Cruel, Inhuman or Degrading Treatment or Punishment, 1465 UNTS 85, done Dec. 10, 1984, entered into force June 26, 1987, at Art. 2.

305 UN Human Rights Committee, "General Comment No. 31: The Nature of the General Legal Obligation Imposed on States Parties to the Covenant," UN Doc. HRI/GEN.1/Rev.7, at 192, May 12, 2004, adopted Mar. 29, 2004, at para. 10 (emphasis added).

confirmed that "enjoyment of Covenant rights is not limited to citizens of States Parties but must also be available to all individuals, regardless of nationality or statelessness, such as asylum seekers, refugees, migrant workers and other persons, who may find themselves in the territory or subject to the jurisdiction of the State Party."[306] This latter principle is applicable "to those within the power or effective control of the forces of a State Party acting outside its territory, regardless of the circumstances in which such power or effective control was obtained."[307] A similar line of reasoning has been followed by the Committee against Torture, which has refined the test of the Human Rights Committee to identify both "factual" and "effective" control as triggers for application of the Convention against Torture outside the territory of a State Party.[308] In one relevant case involving irregular migrants rescued at sea by Spain and taken to Mauritania for processing, the Committee found that Spain had exercised control over the migrants from the time of their rescue right through to their detention in Mauritania, and that Spain consequently incurred responsibility for their protection under the Convention.[309]

Although not explicitly adopting the "power and control" test, the International Court of Justice has generally affirmed that provisions of human rights treaties will apply to actions of a State outside its territory even where the terms of the treaty do not envisage such extraterritorial application.[310] In relation to the ICCPR, the Court noted that:

> [W]hile the jurisdiction of States is primarily territorial, it may sometimes be exercised outside the national territory. Considering the object and purpose of the International Covenant on Civil and Political Rights, it would seem natural that,

306 Ibid.

307 Ibid.

308 UN Committee against Torture, "General Comment No. 2: Implementation of Article 2 by States Parties," UN Doc. CAT/C/GC/2, Jan. 24, 2008, at para. 16. See further Chapter 3 at Section 3.4.1. Note the Committee's further statement that "The Committee considers that the scope of 'territory' under article 2 must also include situations where a State party exercises, directly or indirectly, de facto or de jure control over persons in detention" (ibid.).

309 *J.H.A v. Spain*, UNCAT Comm. No. 323/2007, UN Doc. CAT/C/41/D/323/2007, Nov. 21, 2008, decided Nov. 10, 2008, at para. 8.2 (also referred to as the *Marine I* case). For a more detailed consideration of this case and its implications for the issue of extraterritorial application of human rights law in the context of maritime interdiction and rescue, see K. Wouters and M. den Heijer, "The *Marine I* Case: A Comment" (2010) 22(1) *International Journal of Refugee Law* 1.

310 *Legal Consequences of the Construction of a Wall in the Occupied Palestinian Territory (Advisory Opinion)*, [2004] ICJ Rep 136 [*Israeli Wall Advisory Opinion*], at para. 111. See also *Armed Activities on the Territory of the Congo (Democratic Republic of the Congo v. Uganda)*, [2005] ICJ Rep 168, at para. 216; and *Application of the International Convention on the Elimination of All Forms of Racial Discrimination (Georgia v. Russian Federation) (Provisional Measures)*, [2008] ICJ Rep 353, at para. 109. For further on these cases see Chapter 3, at Section 3.4.1.

even when such is the case, States Parties to the Covenant should be bound to comply with its provisions.[311]

At the regional level, the most substantial jurisprudence has emerged from consideration of the scope of application of the European Convention on Human Rights. The analysis in Chapter 3 confirmed that the starting point is an acceptance of the essentially territorial nature of this instrument and a corresponding reluctance to interpret the Convention as being applicable to all State Party conduct everywhere. The focus has accordingly been on establishing the parameters of exceptions. Although earlier cases of the European Court of Human Rights emphasized effective control over *territory*,[312] later judgments have moved toward recognition of the exercise of power and authority over *individuals* as sufficient to establish jurisdiction.[313] Several cases, involving scenarios of relevance to the issue of smuggling by sea, deserve brief mention. The 2008 *Xhavara* case concerned a fatal high seas collision between an Italian coast guard vessel that was seeking to intercept an Albanian flagged boat carrying irregular migrants.[314] Although not being required to pronounce directly on the point, the Court's judgment appeared to confirm the responsibility of Italy, as flag State of the patrol vessel, for any violations of the European Convention on Human Rights caused by its actions. In the 2010 *Medvedyev* case (high seas boarding and rerouting by a French naval vessel of a Cambodia-registered cargo vessel suspected of transporting narcotics), the Court affirmed "the special nature of the marine environment" but stated that this "cannot justify an area outside the law where ships' crews are covered by no legal system capable of affording them enjoyment of the rights and guarantees protected by the Convention which the States have undertaken to secure to everyone within their jurisdiction..."[315] It found that France had exercised full, exclusive, and continuous control over the vessel and its crew and, accordingly, that the applicants had been under the jurisdiction of France from the time of interception.[316] In an examination of the merits of the case, the

[311] *Israeli Wall Advisory Opinion*, at para. 109. This position was reiterated by the Court and extended to other core human rights treaties in the ICJ's *Armed Activities on the Territory of the Congo* case, at paras. 216–220.

[312] Most famously *Banković and Others v. Belgium and Others*, (2007) 44 EHRR SE5 (ECHR, Dec. 12, 2001). For further analysis of this case and references to the extensive and largely critical literature, see Chapter 3 at notes 313–318 and accompanying text.

[313] Most recently by the European Court of Human Rights in *Al-Skeini and Others v. United Kingdom*, (2011) 53 EHRR 18 (ECHR, July 7, 2011); and *Al-Jedda v. United Kingdom*, (2011) 53 EHRR 23 (ECHR, July 7, 2011). For earlier examples of the same approach see *Ilaşcu and Others v. Moldova and Russia*, (2005) 40 EHRR 46 (ECHR, July 8, 2004), at paras. 312, 314; and *Issa and Others v. Turkey*, (2005) 41 EHRR 27 (ECHR, Mar. 30, 2005), at para. 71.

[314] *Xhavara and Fifteen Others v. Italy and Albania*, Application No. 39473/98 (ECHR, Jan. 11, 2001) (Admissibility) (only available in French).

[315] *Medvedyev and Others v. France*, (2010) 51 EHRR 39 (ECHR, Mar. 29, 2010), at para. 81.

[316] Ibid. at para. 67.

Court found that the arrests constituted unlawful detention and were thus in breach of Article 5 of the Convention.[317] In the 2012 case of *Hirsi Jamaa v. Italy* (high seas interception and push-back to Libya of smuggled Somali and Eritrean nationals by the Italian coast guard), the Court found that Italy had exercised both de jure and de facto jurisdiction over the applicant, specifically stating its view that:

> [T]he removal of aliens carried out in the context of interceptions on the high seas by the authorities of a State in the exercise of their sovereign authority, the effect of which is to prevent migrants from reaching the borders of the State or even to push them back to another State, constitutes an exercise of jurisdiction...[318]

The Court held that Italy's actions violated fundamental rights, including the prohibition on torture and inhuman or degrading treatment or punishment and the prohibition of collective expulsion of nonnationals – despite the relevant actions occurring outside Italy's territory. Critically, the fact that this was billed as a search and rescue operation, that the Italian authorities had not boarded the vessels, and that they had not used weapons, did not affect the Court's judgment on the point of jurisdiction and extraterritorial application of the European Convention on Human Rights.[319] The ruling does indeed appear to be, in the words of one commentator, "a resounding endorsement of the responsibility of States for their migration control activities at sea."[320]

Certainly, a few cases from a single regional court should not be considered sufficient to settle such complicated matters definitively, and for all States: the analysis in Chapter 3 confirmed that the international legal position with respect to the extraterritorial application of human rights law is yet to be conclusively determined. Further, the language of many human rights treaties on this point is ambiguous, and State practice is inconsistent. Nevertheless, the situation does appear to be evolving in a decided direction. International and regional judicial and human rights institutions in particular appear united in rejecting the possibility of a physical or juridical lacuna: a space in which States Parties to human rights treaties may violate with impunity the rules that govern their conduct at home. It is reasonable to argue for the conclusion that appears to follow logically from that position: that extraterritorial human rights obligations will arise "when a State exercises control, power,

[317] Ibid. at paras. 102–103.

[318] *Hirsi Jamaa v. Italy*, at para. 180.

[319] Ibid. at para. 79 ("Italy cannot circumvent its 'jurisdiction' under the Convention by describing the events at issue as rescue operations on the high seas. In particular, the Court cannot subscribe to the Government's argument that Italy was not responsible for the fate of the applicants on account of the allegedly minimal control exercised by the authorities over the parties concerned at the material time.").

[320] C. Costello, "Courting Access to Asylum in Europe: Recent Supranational Jurisprudence Explored" (2012) 12 *Human Rights Law Review* 287 [Costello, "Courting Access to Asylum in Europe"], at 300.

or authority over people or situations located outside its sovereign territory in a way that could have an impact on the enjoyment of human rights by those people or in such situations."[321] There can be little doubt that interdiction or rescue of a migrant smuggling vessel on the high seas or in the territory of another State, which involves conduct such as boarding the vessel, altering its course, or detaining persons on board fall within this "power, control or authority" test.

Unfortunately, this leaves unanswered the question of whether States owe extraterritorial human rights obligations to smuggled migrants at sea who are *not* interdicted or rescued. The "left to die" case study in the Introduction to this book concerned a situation in which it appears that several States were aware of a migrant smuggling vessel in serious distress and failed to act. Certainly at no time was the vessel under the "power, authority or control" of any of those States. Accordingly, although such States may be found to have failed to exercise their search and rescue responsibilities under the law of the sea, it is much less clear whether those same States could be held to account for failure to discharge their human rights obligations extraterritorially.

6.3.2. *Application of Refugee Law at Sea*

The question of extraterritorial application of the obligation of *non-refoulement* in the context of human rights law is addressed by the general principles of jurisdiction set out in Chapter 3 and outlined previously. In brief, once a State is found to be exercising power, control, or authority (i.e., jurisdiction) over an individual or situation, then the State will be obliged not to return persons to face torture, ill-treatment, or execution.[322] In this context "return" would include the transfer of an individual to the local State authorities in whose territory the State conducting the return has been acting extraterritorially.[323]

Determining the scope of the obligation of *non-refoulement* under refugee law is a different and much more difficult endeavor, not least because of the Refugee Convention's[324] lack of clarity regarding its scope of application of the relevant provision. The analysis in Chapter 3 canvassed the inconsistent jurisprudence, doctrinal

[321] O. De Schutter, A. Eide, A. Khalfan, M. Orellana, M. Salomon, and I. Seiderman, "Commentary to the Maastricht Principles on Extraterritorial Obligations of States in the Area of Economic, Social and Cultural Rights" (2012) 34 *Human Rights Quarterly* 1084, at 1090.

[322] See discussion of the prohibition on torture and the related obligation of *non-refoulement* in Chapter 2 at Section 2.4.1.

[323] See discussion of this point at Chapter 3 note 345 and accompanying text.

[324] Convention Relating to the Status of Refugees, 189 UNTS 137, done July 28, 1951, entered into force Apr. 22, 1954, as amended by the Protocol relating to the Status of Refugees, 606 UNTS 267, done Jan. 31, 1967, entered into force Oct. 4, 1967 [Refugee Convention].

disagreements, and ambiguous State practice that both reflect and perpetuate an unhelpful division. On one side lies the United Nations High Commissioner for Refugees (UNHCR) and a large number of commentators who assert, using a range of sources including the drafting history of the relevant provision and the object and purpose of the Convention, that the obligation not to return a refugee or asylum-seeker to a country where he or she would be at risk of persecution or other serious harm applies "wherever a State exercises jurisdiction, including at the frontier, on the high seas or on the territory of another State."[325] On the other side lie the views of a number of destination States and a thin but generally consistent body of jurisprudence, which, if taken together, lend support to the argument that States have *not* consented to an understanding of the obligation of *non-refoulement* that extends its application to asylum-seekers who are not at the borders or physically within the territory of the State.[326]

Although a detailed analysis of regional legal systems is outside the scope of this book,[327] some important variations in the scope of the obligation of *non-refoulement* under European law and policy deserve to be mentioned. The inclusion of a right to asylum in the Charter of Fundamental Rights of the European Union,[328] as well as the reiteration of an obligation of *non-refoulement* in a range of instruments touching on extraterritorial migration control such as the Schengen Borders Code[329] and the later Frontex rules,[330] provide some indication that the jurisdictional scope of

325 UN High Commissioner for Refugees, *Advisory Opinion on the Extraterritorial Application of Non-refoulement Obligations under the 1951 Convention Relating to the Status of Refugees and Its 1967 Protocol* (Jan. 26, 2007) [UNHCR Advisory Opinion on the Extraterritorial Application of Non-refoulement Obligations], at para. 24. See also G. Goodwin-Gill, "The Right to Seek Asylum: Interception at Sea and the Principle of Non-refoulement" (2011) 23(3) *International Journal of Refugee Law* 443.

326 See further Chapter 3, notes 355–365 and accompanying text.

327 Further on this aspect in relation to Europe see V. Moreno-Lax, "(Extraterritorial) Entry Controls and (Extraterritorial) Non-refoulement in EU Law," in M. Maes, M.-C. Foblets, and P. De Bruycker eds., *External Dimensions of EU Migration and Asylum Law and Policy/Dimensions Externes du Droit et de la Politique d'Immigration et d'Asile de l'UE* (2011). See also Costello, "Courting Access to Asylum in Europe," esp. at 307–310.

328 Charter of Fundamental Rights of the European Union, OJ C 364/1, Dec. 18, 2000, done Dec. 7, 2000, entered into force Dec. 1, 2009 with the Lisbon Treaty (Treaty of Lisbon amending the Treaty on European Union and the Treaty establishing the European Community, OJ C 306, done Dec. 13, 2007, entered into force Dec. 1, 2009), at Art. 18: "The right to asylum shall be guaranteed with due respect for the rules of the Geneva Convention of 28 July 1951 and the Protocol of 31 January 1967 relating to the status of refugees and in accordance with the Treaty establishing the European Community."

329 Regulation (EC) No 562/2006 of the European Parliament and of the Council of 15 March 2006 establishing a Community Code on the rules governing the movement of persons across borders (Schengen Borders Code), OJ L 105/1, Apr. 13, 2006, at Art. 3: "[the regulation is] without prejudice to … the rights of refugees and persons requesting international protection, in particular as regards *non-refoulement*."

330 Regulation (EC) No. 2007/2004 of 26 October 2004 establishing a European Agency for the Management of Operational Cooperation at the External Borders of the Member States of the European Union, OJ L 349/1, Nov. 25, 2004 (as amended by Regulation (EU) No 1168/2011 of the European Parliament and of the

Jamaa v. Italy strongly affirmed the continuing responsibility of the State of jurisdiction for the human rights of intercepted or smuggled migrants and the impossibility of transferring the relevant obligations to a State that is manifestly incapable or unwilling to provide the necessary standard of international protection.[378]

The misgivings that have been expressed by UNHCR and many commentators about extraterritorial processing of asylum claims are clearly well-founded. However, it is important to acknowledge that the use of procedures such as third-country processing in respect of smuggled migrants rescued or intercepted at sea are not ipso facto unlawful. Any assessment of lawfulness must necessarily involve a consideration of whether the procedure or action in question risks or does in fact result in a violation of the obligation of *non-refoulement*. Inevitably, this will require an assessment of the structure and practice of specific arrangements and the specific circumstances of individual situations.

indirect *refoulement*" in Greece, and that the Afghani applicant's asylum claim would not have been seriously examined by the Greek authorities). In *Plaintiff M70/2011 and Plaintiff M106/2011 v. Minister for Immigration and Citizenship* (2011) 244 CLR 144 (Aus. HC, Aug. 31, 2011), the Australian High Court was called to rule on the legitimacy of the transfer of the applicants (smuggled asylum-seekers) from Australia to Malaysia. That case, although primarily concerned with interpreting domestic law, also drew on international law principles in that interpretation. The Court was called upon to determine whether a "refugee swap" deal between the two countries was in compliance with Australia's domestic law, most particularly the requirement in section 198(3)A of the Migration Act 1958 (Cth) that the relevant country provided access to effective refugee determination procedures and "protection" to both asylum-seekers and refugees. It found that, although scrutiny of Malaysia's practices in relation to asylum-seekers and refugees was relevant and desirable, this could not "replace the requirement that the country has obliged itself, through its laws, to provide the necessary recognition and protection" (at para. 245, per Justice Kiefel). In its joint judgment, the Court concluded: "Where, as in the present case, it is agreed that Malaysia: first, does not recognise the status of refugee in its domestic law and does not undertake any activities related to the reception, registration, documentation and status determination of asylum seekers and refugees; secondly, is not party to the Refugees Convention or the Refugees Protocol; and, thirdly, has made no legally binding arrangement with Australia obliging it to accord the protections required by those instruments; it was not open to the Minister to conclude that Malaysia provides the access or protections referred to in s 198A(3)(i)–(iii)" (at para. 135). For additional background and analysis, including of the Court's extension of the identified obligations beyond *non-refoulement*, see S. Dehm, "Sovereignty, Protection and the Limits to Regional Refugee Status Determination Arrangements" (2012) 28 *Merkourios: Utrecht Journal of International and European law* 53.

378 *Hirsi Jamaa v. Italy*, at para. 129 ("[T]he Court observes that Italy cannot evade its own responsibility by relying on its obligations arising out of bilateral agreements with Libya. Even if it were to be assumed that those agreements made express provision for the return to Libya of migrants intercepted on the high seas, the Contracting States' responsibility continues even after their having entered into treaty commitments subsequent to the entry into force of the Convention or its Protocols in respect of these States"). Note that the Court in this case found two violations of Article 3 of the European Convention on Human Rights (prohibition on "torture or inhuman or degrading treatment or punishment") on account of the fact that the applicants were at risk of ill-treatment in Libya (paragraph 138) and at risk of arbitrary repatriation and the threat of subsequent violations of Article 3 occurring in Somalia and Eritrea (paragraph 158).

6.4. A NOTE ON ATTRIBUTION OF RESPONSIBILITY FOR UNLAWFUL ACTS IN RESPONDING TO SMUGGLING BY SEA

The rules of State responsibility that were set out in detail in Chapter 4 have particular relevance to the issue of smuggling by sea. As explained previously, responsibility under international law is established through a two-step process: first, whether the act or omission is attributable to the State under international law;[379] and second, whether the act or omission constitutes a breach of an international obligation of the State[380] in force at the relevant time. It is necessary for both tests to be satisfied: conduct attributable to a State that does not constitute a breach of an international obligation of that State will not be characterized as an internationally wrongful act and will not thereby engage its responsibility. In the same way, a breach of an international obligation owed by that State that cannot be attributed to the State will not be considered an act of that State and will therefore also fail to engage that State's responsibility under international law.

The analysis in this chapter has been primarily concerned with establishing the scope of the relevant primary rules: specifically, the circumstances under which a State is bound by a particular obligation regarding, for example, rescue at sea or the treatment of intercepted migrants. In most cases, the second part of the equation, attribution of conduct, will be uncomplicated. The actions or omissions of an official vessel such as a warship or coast guard vessel with respect to an interdiction or rescue is directly attributed to the State, as is the conduct of officials on board such vessels. Provided that the State is bound by the relevant primary rule, then it will be responsible for any wrongful acts committed by its vessels or officials. It is important to note that the secondary rules of State responsibility do not distinguish between wrongful acts committed within the territory of a State and those committed extraterritorially: once it is established that the State was under the relevant obligation at the time the wrongful act occurred (determined with reference to the primary rule) and that the act can be attributed to the State, then the fact that the conduct took place outside its territory is immaterial to establishing responsibility.[381]

However, not all actions related to smuggling at sea are this straightforward, and complications can certainly arise with respect to attribution of conduct. The key question will generally concern how responsibility should be attributed when

379 ILC Draft Articles, at Art. 2(a).

380 Ibid. at Art. 2(b).

381 "[T]he acts or omissions of organs of the State are attributable to the State as a possible source of responsibility regardless of whether they have been perpetrated in national or in foreign territory": "Report of the International Law Commission on the Work of Its Twenty-Seventh Session," *Yearbook of the International Law Commission*, Vol. II (1975), at 84, cited in den Heijer, *Europe and Extraterritorial Asylum*, at 17.

one or more States are in some way involved in an enforcement action against a migrant smuggling vessel. For example, one State may authorize another to take enforcement action in its own territorial waters or against vessels flying its flag. Two States may jointly engage in an interdiction on the high seas or in the territorial sea of one of the States or a third State. A further complication will arise when an international organization directs or controls an operation that gives rise to an unlawful act. In relation to such situations, the conclusions reached in Chapter 4 deserve to be reiterated:

Independent Responsibility: International law recognizes the principle of independent responsibility. In essence this means that the responsibility of one State is not diminished by the fact that one or more other States are also responsible for that same wrongful act.[382] Questions of joint responsibility – and of whether two or more States are to be held responsible for the same wrongful act – are not settled by the Draft Articles on Responsibility of States for Internationally Wrongful Acts but will depend on the facts and the primary rules applicable to the State concerned.[383] In principle however, provided both States are bound by the rule that has been breached by the joint conduct, then the breach will be independently attributable to each involved State.[384]

Placing an Organ or Official of a State at the Disposal of Another State: State A may place its officials on board a vessel of State B for purposes of authorizing State B to interdict a migrant smuggling vessel located in the territory of State A. The analysis in Chapter 4 confirmed that provided such an arrangement is for the purposes of State A or even for joint purposes, State A remains responsible for the conduct of its organ or official.[385] It is only in the very rare instance when the organ or official is truly placed at the disposal of State B (i.e., "with the consent, under the authority of *and* for the purposes of the receiving State" as well as "under its exclusive direction

[382] ILC Draft Articles, at Art. 47(1): "Where several States are responsible for the same internationally wrongful act, the responsibility of each State may be invoked [by the injured State] in relation to that act."

[383] ILC Draft Articles (commentary), at 125 (para. 6).

[384] Guiffre provides the example of a series of high seas interceptions of asylum-seekers in 2009 to illustrate the point: "[the] refugees ... were transferred to Italian vessels, shipped to Libya, and handed over to Libyan authorities. Thus, the wrongful act – consisting of subjecting returned persons to inhuman treatments and *refoulement* to countries of origin – could be attributed to both Italy and Libya." Giuffré, "State Responsibility Beyond Borders," at 723. She cites, as another example of independent responsibility, the 2010 interdictions by Libyan vessels of individuals within Maltese search and rescue waters and subsequent diversion of the migrants to Libya: "If it was proved that the 2010 return programmes failed to bring rescued people to a place of safety, Malta – which in its SAR region has primary responsibility toward people in distress – would be liable regardless of whether these actions were carried out by officials of the transit country (Libya) acting on behalf of the potential destination state" (at 724).

[385] See discussion of *Xhavara* case in Chapter 3 at note 329 and accompanying text.

and control, rather than on instructions from the sending State"[386]) that its conduct will be attributable to State B alone.[387]

Involvement of Multiple States in a Wrongful Act: The principle of independent responsibility means that each State involved in a genuinely joint operation[388] against smuggling by sea (including through a joint organ) will be jointly and separately responsible for any internationally wrongful acts that occur over the course of that operation. That responsibility can be attributed to more than one State will not materially affect the responsibility of individual States.[389] The only material difference may lie in the substantive content of the relevant primary rule to which different participating States are bound.

Complicity in the Wrongful Act of Another State: Outside a genuinely joint action, a State may nevertheless be found complicit in the unlawful act of another State through aiding and assisting that State,[390] through directing or controlling it,[391] or through coercion.[392] Any potential case of responsibility through complicity in the context of migrant smuggling by sea is likely to relate to the first of these forms of conduct. An example could involve one State (State A) providing vessels to another State (State B) that are subsequently used for unlawful actions. However, the threshold is set very high. For State A to be held complicit in internationally wrongful acts committed by State B it would be necessary to establish that State A was *aware* the vessels it provided would be used in the commission of an internationally wrongful act; that it *intended* the vessels to be used in this way, and they actually *were* so used by State B; and that the wrongful act would have been wrongful if it was directly attributable to State A (i.e., if State A was bound by the obligation violated by State B).[393] As the State directly involved in the commission of the internationally wrongful act, State B will be primarily responsible. State A will be legally responsible "to the extent that its own conduct has caused or contributed to the internationally wrongful act."[394]

386 ILC Draft Articles (commentary), at 44 (para. 2) (emphasis added).

387 See further den Heijer's discussion of the "guest officer" model used by Frontex, in den Heijer, *Europe and Extraterritorial Asylum*, at 181–182, 255–256.

388 Note den Heijer's observation that conduct "can only be designated as 'joint' when the activity complained of was carried out in accordance with the instructions of all states involved and that all responsible states had it in their power to prevent the alleged misconduct": Ibid. at 89.

389 ILC Draft Articles, at Art. 47 (and commentary, at 124 (para. 1)).

390 Ibid. at Art. 16.

391 Ibid. at Art. 17.

392 Ibid. at Art. 18.

393 Ibid. at Art. 16 (and commentary, at 66 (para. 3)).

394 Ibid. (commentary), at 66 (para. 1). The difficulties of assessing complicity in an internationally wrongful act, and the ways in which these may be addressed, have been considered in detail in Chapter 4, at Section 4.4. For an optimistic consideration of whether cooperation between Italy and

Operations Associated with International Organizations: States will generally be responsible for their own actions under the rules set out previously in circumstances where an action against migrant smuggling by sea takes place under the auspices of an international agency such as Frontex. Even where conduct can be attributed to the organization (a separate issue, examined in detail at Chapter 4, Section 4.7.1) the participating State will not be released from responsibility on this basis.

Further reference should be made to Chapter 4 for a consideration of the consequences attached to a finding of responsibility and invocation of responsibility.

6.5. CONCLUSIONS ON OBLIGATIONS RELATED TO INTERDICTION AND RESCUE

Although reiterated and reinforced by the Migrant Smuggling Protocol, it is the international law of the sea that provides the basic legal framework governing enforcement action over vessels engaged in migrant smuggling. The relevant rules grant coastal States a wide degree of latitude to take law enforcement action in their national waters against foreign vessels engaged in migrant smuggling to or from that State. For example a coastal State will generally be able to take law enforcement action both within its territorial sea and its contiguous zone against foreign flagged vessels and vessels without nationality where this is necessary to prevent breaches of the coastal State's immigration laws.[395] Action may also be taken against a foreign vessel by a coastal State in its territorial sea or contiguous zone through the exercise of the right of hot pursuit, where suspected breaches of national law are involved.[396] In respect of flagged vessels, the consent of the flag State is not required in these situations. However, the capacity of States to unilaterally exercise law enforcement jurisdiction in international waters is far more limited. On the high seas, vessels are generally subject to the exclusive jurisdiction of the flag State.[397] With the exceptions of the right of visit and stateless vessels,[398] most law enforcement actions will require the consent of the flag State of the target vessel. The scope of enforcement jurisdiction that may be exercised in respect of a stateless vessel is not entirely clear and remains to be definitively settled.[399]

The jurisdictional rules set out earlier in the chapter may be modified by consent, and bilateral and multilateral efforts to address migrant smuggling have been

Libya on irregular migration would constitute responsibility through complicity, see Giuffré, "State Responsibility Beyond Borders," at 725–732.

395 UNCLOS, at Arts. 19(2)(g), 21, 25, 33(1).

396 Ibid. at Arts. 33, 111.

397 Ibid. at Art. 92.

398 Ibid. at Art. 110.

399 See further Chapter 3, at Section 3.3.3.1.

directed to that end. Although not substantially altering the underlying legal framework, the Migrant Smuggling Protocol has created a specific mechanism through which cooperation around migrant smuggling by sea can occur, thereby facilitating and rendering more efficient cooperation that is already legally possible under the general rules set out previously. In one key area, vessels without nationality suspected of carrying smuggled migrants, the Protocol's requirements go beyond those set out in the law of the sea. States Parties that have reasonable grounds to suspect a vessel without nationality is engaged in the smuggling of migrants by sea is empowered to board and search that vessel and, if evidence of migrant smuggling is found, required to take (unspecified): "appropriate measures in accordance with relevant domestic and international law."[400]

The law of the sea, as reiterated by the Migrant Smuggling Protocol, also requires States and their shipmasters to render assistance to any person or vessel in distress at sea. This obligation operates at all times and in all maritime zones. It extends to all persons and vessels regardless of nationality, legal status, or any other difference. The obligation is subject to practical contingencies of safety and reasonableness, and the scope of required assistance should be commensurate with the nature and severity of the distress. Port and coastal States are further required to establish search and rescue services aimed at coordinating the rescue of persons in distress at sea around their coasts. Amendments to the legal framework that entered into force in 2004 affirmed a number of additional obligations on port and coastal States, including a duty to ensure that masters of ships providing assistance to persons in distress at sea are relieved from their responsibilities as soon as practicable and that the involved States cooperate with the ship's master in delivering persons rescued at sea to a place of safety. The amendments further clarified that the State in whose search and rescue region the assistance is rendered is to take primary responsibility for ensuring such coordination and cooperation occurs, so that survivors assisted are disembarked from the assisting ship and delivered to a place of safety. Although adding a measure of substance to the relevant obligations the amendments have not resolved uncertainty and disagreement around whether and when coastal States may deny disembarkation of rescued smuggled migrants.

Irrespective of the jurisdictional grounds for an interception and the maritime zone within which the interdiction takes place, the use of force by States when interdicting vessels carrying smuggled migrants must be a measure of last resort. It must further be proportionate to the objective and be the minimum reasonably necessary to achieve that purpose. It must not cause unnecessary harm. Recent developments appear to confirm that interdicting States will generally be held responsible under international law for violations of human rights that occur in relation to vessels or

[400] Migrant Smuggling Protocol, at Art. 8(7).

persons that are in some way or another under their authority or control, even if the relevant action or omission occurs outside the territorial jurisdiction of that State. The rules relating to right to life, arbitrary detention, inhumane and degrading treatment, and collective expulsion are particularly relevant to situations of interdiction and will bind all States engaged in interdiction irrespective of the purpose, circumstances, or location of the interdiction. Within Europe, recent jurisprudence has confirmed the extraterritorial application of the obligation of *non-refoulement*, most particularly in the context of extraterritorial immigration control. The scope of the obligation at the international level is less certain although apparently moving in a similar direction. Although interception of smuggled migrants on the high seas does not, of itself, violate the prohibition on *refoulement*, such actions may not result in asylum-seekers and refugees being denied access to international protection, or result in persons in need of international protection being returned to a situation in which they are at risk of persecution or serious violations of human rights.

7

Prevention and International Cooperation to Combat Migrant Smuggling

The concept of "prevention" can be used in the migrant smuggling context in very different ways, and it is perhaps wise to avoid the lure of neat classification that some have succumbed to.[1] However, a meaningful discussion does require certain parameters, and for the purposes of this chapter the following working definition of prevention, drawn from the more broadly applicable UN Guidelines on Prevention of Crime, is offered:

> "[C]rime Prevention" comprises strategies and measures that seek to reduce the risk of crimes occurring, and their potential harmful effects on individuals and society, including fear of crime, by intervening to influence their multiple causes.[2]

Even within these parameters, the notion of "prevention" remains very broad. In the present context, the scope of preventative measures could conceivably extend across the full range of legal, policy, and practical responses examined in this and other chapters. For example, while criminal laws enable offenders to be punished, they also operate to deter potential offenders. More effective border controls could

[1] See, for example, United Nations Office on Drugs and Crime, *Toolkit to Combat Smuggling of Migrants* (2010) [UNODC, *Toolkit to Combat Smuggling of Migrants*], Tool 9: Prevention of the Smuggling of Migrants, at 6–7 (proposing a demand-supply classification of prevention efforts).

[2] UN Economic and Social Council, "Guidelines for the Prevention of Crime," ECOSOC Res. 2002/13, Annex, July 24, 2002 [ECOSOC Guidelines for the Prevention of Crime], at para. 3. Crime prevention is defined in the European regional context as follows: "Crime prevention covers all measures that are intended to reduce or otherwise contribute to reducing crime and citizens' feeling of insecurity, both quantitatively and qualitatively, either through directly deterring criminal activities or through policies and interventions designed to reduce the potential for crime and the causes of crime. It includes work by government, competent authorities, criminal justice agencies, local authorities, and the specialist associations they have set up in Europe, the private and voluntary sectors, researchers and the public, supported by the media": Council Decision of 28 May 2001 setting up a European crime prevention network (2001/427/JHA), OJ L 153/1, Jun. 8, 2001, at Art. 1(3).

Sections of this chapter draw on A.T. Gallagher, *The International Law of Human Trafficking* (2010) [Gallagher, *The International Law of Human Trafficking*] (chapters 7.5; 8.1 and 8.3).

be considered a major plank in a State's prevention strategy, as could an information campaign designed to discourage potential migrants from seeking the services of smugglers – or potential smugglers from being involved in criminal activities. Joint patrols – interceptions at sea and the full suite of extraterritorial migration control measures that are now common responses to migrant smuggling – can be, and often are, characterized as "prevention." International cooperation, from joint investigations to mutual legal assistance, is a central preventive strategy within the international legal framework and for many States. Efforts aimed at preventing migrant smuggling can of course extend beyond border control and criminal justice responses, to a focus on causal factors such as conflict and poverty or the mismatch between the availability of regular migration places and demand by persons who wish to or are being forced to move. Another important but often less visible aspect of this issue relates to prevention of exploitation and abuse in the migrant smuggling process itself.

The present chapter is divided into two parts. The first part is concerned with the scope and substantive content of the international legal obligation of prevention as it relates to migrant smuggling: what States are required to do and what constraints international law places on States with respect to their actions aimed at preventing migrant smuggling. It commences with an analysis of the general obligation of prevention within transnational criminal law. This is followed by a review of the more specific prevention obligations articulated in specialist instruments, most particularly the Migrant Smuggling Protocol,[3] regarding: (1) awareness-raising and addressing root causes; (2) strengthened border controls, including measures to encourage or compel carriers to prevent migrant smuggling; (3) security and control of documents; and (4) training and technical cooperation. Consideration is then given to the obligation to prevent smuggling-related harms: obligations that arise primarily through human rights law but are reinforced through specific obligations in the Migrant Smuggling Protocol. The first part of the chapter concludes with a brief consideration of migrant smuggling–related corruption in the context of prevention with a view to discerning the scope and content of State obligations in this area.

The second part of this chapter provides an in-depth consideration of one specific tool of prevention that is central to the legal and policy framework around migrant smuggling: international cooperation. The analysis considers the various mechanisms that exist to facilitate international cooperation, including informal cooperation, joint investigations, and transfer of suspects, as well as the mechanisms of mutual legal assistance and extradition.

[3] Protocol against the Smuggling of Migrants by Land, Sea and Air, supplementing the United Nations Convention against Transnational Organized Crime, 2241 UNTS 507, done Nov. 15, 2000, entered into force Jan. 28, 2004 [Migrant Smuggling Protocol].

7.1. PREVENTION IN RELATION TO MIGRANT SMUGGLING

"Prevention" in its narrowest sense, refers simply to efforts aimed at stopping an event or situation from occurring. It is perhaps unsurprising therefore, that in many States, prevention efforts are conceptualized restrictively, and are limited to erecting barriers (legal, administrative, physical) either at the border or before the border, that operate to stop future acts of migrant smuggling from occurring. However, as with any form of crime prevention, a considered approach to preventing migrant smuggling must seek to do more than simply stop criminals in their tracks: it must address the *causes* of crime.[4] Accordingly, dealing with public sector complicity in migrant smuggling may be a legitimate prevention strategy, as may be efforts to address poverty, inequality, violence, or other triggers for individuals to seek out the services of smugglers. Migrant smuggling is a complex social and economic process: in any given situation, there is unlikely to be a single cause but rather multiple causative factors that operate cumulatively. In fact, given the complexity of the drivers of migrant smuggling, the list of potential prevention measures will be as wide-ranging as the factors that are found to cause or contribute to migrant smuggling in the first place.[5]

In relation to all such measures, the primary focus of this present part is on establishing their legal basis and, more generally, the substantive content and parameters of the relevant obligation: What prevention obligations exist in international law? What constraints does international law place on State actions aimed at preventing migrant smuggling? To what extent does the obligation of prevention extend beyond prevention of migrant smuggling to include prevention of the human rights violations that may be associated with the smuggling process such as inhuman or degrading modes of transportation, violence, and exploitation? In regard to the latter

4 As Ekblom and Tilley note: "There are many possible causes of criminal events. Some causes are remote – such as abuse in childhood producing sexual and violent assaults in later life, or structural and technological change introducing completely new opportunities for crime. Others are closer to hand – the presence of a motivated offender in a suitable situation for committing a crime. It is these *immediate* (or "proximal") *circumstances* surrounding the criminal event – the offender in the situation – which form the final point at which all the diverse structural, social, ecological and psychological causes of the criminal event converge" (emphasis in original). P. Ekblom and N. Tilley, "Going Equipped: Criminology, Crime Prevention and the Resourceful Offender" (2000) 40(3) *British Journal of Criminology* 376, at 378–379.

5 For example, Carling and Harnández-Carretero discuss eight different types of policy interventions aimed to address "unauthorised migration," including: detection and apprehension of migrants; post-arrival processing; repatriation; pre-border surveillance and control; awareness campaigns in countries of origin; prevention of illegal employment; employment creation in countries of origin; and programs for legal migration. J. Carling and M. Hernández-Carretero, "Protecting Europe and Protecting Migrants? Strategies for Managing Unauthorised Migration from Africa" (2011) 13 *British Journal of Politics and International Relations* 42 [Carling and Hernández-Carretero, "Protecting Europe and Protecting Migrants?"].

question it is important to reiterate the conclusion reached in Chapter 4 that in this context, States are under a positive obligation to act with due diligence in preventing acts of private persons that result in violations of human rights.[6] The same principles of obligation and responsibility apply to States with respect to preventing the exploitation and abuse of smuggled migrants.

In relation to all prevention laws, policies, and activities, irrespective of their particular focus or scope, States are under an independent obligation to avoid violation of established rights. This obligation is affirmed in international treaty law, for example, through the savings clause in the Migrant Smuggling Protocol.[7] Violation of any established right or obligation in the course of any prevention activity – from unlawful incursion into the territory of a third State during an interception, to the establishment of immigration controls that violate the prohibition of non-discrimination – will trigger that State's international legal responsibility.

7.1.1. *General Prevention Obligations in Transnational Criminal Law*

The discussion of State responsibility in Chapter 4 confirmed that States bear international responsibility for preventing the occurrence of internationally wrongful acts: in the words of the International Law Commission, the State is required to take "all reasonable or necessary measures to prevent a given event from occurring..."[8] As explained in that chapter, a decision on what is "reasonable or necessary" in a particular situation will require consideration of the facts of the case and surrounding circumstances, including the capacities of the State, as well as of the relevant primary rules.

It can be persuasively argued that without serious efforts being applied to the prevention of migrant smuggling, States of preferred destination are destined to a perpetual cycle of stricter migration controls, higher fences, and increasingly harsh criminalization of migration in an effort to keep out those persons or groups they do not wish to admit. It is significant then, that the stated purpose of the Organized Crime Convention is to promote cooperation to *prevent* and combat transnational organized crime *more effectively*,[9] and that the purpose of the Migrant Smuggling

6 See Chapter 4, at Section 4.3.3.

7 Migrant Smuggling Protocol, at Art. 19.

8 "[B]ut without warranting that the event will not occur": International Law Commission (ILC), *Commentaries to the Draft Articles on Responsibility of States for Internationally Wrongful Acts*, in "Report of the International Law Commission on the Work of Its Fifty-Third Session," UN GAOR, 56th Sess, Supp. No. 10, UN Doc. A/56/10, at 59 (2001) [Commentary to the ILC Draft Articles on State Responsibility], at Art. 14, para. 14.

9 United Nations Convention against Transnational Organized Crime, 2225 UNTS 209, done Nov. 15, 2000, entered into force Sept. 29, 2003 [Organized Crime Convention], at Art. 1. See also Article 3, on scope of application.

Protocol is to *prevent* and combat migrant smuggling, as well as to promote cooperation among States Parties to that end, while protecting the rights of smuggled migrants.[10] Commitments or references to the importance of prevention of migrant smuggling are found in some regional treaties and soft law instruments.[11] At least for those States that are party to one or more of the relevant specialist treaties, migrant smuggling itself may be the "internationally wrongful act" act that States are required to take measures to prevent. Other internationally wrongful acts, such as violations of human rights through inhuman treatment, or violation of rescue obligations through failure of flagged vessels to come to the aid of migrants in distress, may also be involved. In these latter cases the same principles of responsibility will apply: a State will be held liable for such internationally wrongful acts, even if not directly implicated in the original harm, to the extent that it failed to take reasonable measures to prevent that act from occurring.

The Organized Crime Convention provides much of the basic framework for responding to transnational crime once it has occurred, through: (1) a focus on criminalization of consistent core offenses (participation in an organized criminal group,

[10] Migrant Smuggling Protocol, at Art. 2.

[11] Article 3(2) of the Treaty on European Union provides that: "The Union shall offer its citizens an area of freedom, security and justice without internal frontiers, in which the free movement of persons is ensured in conjunction with appropriate measures with respect to external border controls, asylum, immigration and the prevention and combating of crime": Treaty on European Union, OJ C 326/13, Oct. 26, 2012, done Feb. 7, 1992, entered into force Nov. 1, 1993. Article 79 of the Treaty on the Functioning of the European Union refers more specifically to the prevention of immigration-related crime: "The Union shall develop a common immigration policy aimed at ensuring, at all stages, the efficient management of migration flows, fair treatment of third-country nationals residing legally in Member States, and the prevention of, and enhanced measures to combat, illegal immigration and trafficking in human beings." Article 84 refers to the establishment of crime prevention functions more broadly. Treaty on the Functioning of the European Union, OJ C 326/47, Oct. 26, 2012, done Feb. 7, 1992, entered into force Nov. 1, 1993 [Treaty on the Functioning of the European Union]. Key elements of the plan to combat irregular migration are articulated in the Proposal for a Comprehensive Plan to Combat Illegal Immigration and Trafficking of Human Beings in the European Union (2002/C, 142/02), OJ C 142/23, June 14, 2002 (in this chapter the Plan is referred to as the EU Comprehensive Plan to Combat Illegal Immigration and Trafficking of Human Beings; the heading "Proposal" is misleading as the plan was adopted by the Justice and Home Affairs Council of February 28, 2002). The Organization of American States does not have a treaty on this issue but has adopted the Hemispheric Plan of Action against Transnational Organized Crime (OAS Doc. OEA/Ser.G, CP/RES. 908 (1567/06), adopted by the Permanent Council Oct. 25, 2006), one of the purposes of which is to "[p]revent and combat transnational organized crime, in full observance of human rights, using as a frame of reference the Palermo Convention and the three additional Protocols thereto" (at para. 1). There is no specific reference to migrant smuggling in the 1997 ASEAN Declaration on Transnational Crime (adopted Dec. 20, 1997, 1st ASEAN Conference on Transnational Crime, Manila, Philippines), which emphasizes "combating" of such crimes rather than prevention. The Joint Africa–EU Declaration on Migration and Development (Tripoli, Nov. 22–23, 2006) explicitly links the challenges of "illegal or irregular migration" to the challenges posed by conflict, poverty, and underdevelopment.

money laundering, corruption, and obstruction of justice); (2) the development of responses to these crimes, ensuring companies and other legal persons do not escape criminal justice; and (3) international cooperation between law enforcement and prosecution services. However, the Convention also includes a broad obligation specific to "prevention" of transnational organized crime.[12]

Although used extensively throughout the Convention, the term "prevention" is not defined and the scope of the corresponding obligations is accordingly highly uncertain. The early drafting history of the Convention provides some support for the argument that prevention should be understood broadly, in line with the UN Economic and Social Council (ECOSOC) Guidelines for the Prevention of Crime definition set out earlier in the chapter.[13] This is the position taken by the UN Office on Drugs and Crime (UNODC) Model Legislative Provisions against Organized Crime[14] with regard to the core prevention provision of the Convention.[15] The Model Legislative Provisions propose that crime prevention in the context of implementation of Convention obligations encompass a wide range of approaches, including those that focus on reducing the risk of victimization[16] (through decreasing risk

[12] Organized Crime Convention, at Art. 31.

[13] For example, early discussions within the drafting group for the Convention confirmed that it "should include specific provisions on prevention and not be restricted to the suppression of crime." Prevention was understood broadly to include "taking measures designed to reduce legal, social, administrative or technical opportunities exploited by criminal organizations," and measures to increase the transparency of financial institutions. It was also noted that prevention depended on an evidence base, so the group recommended inclusion of provisions on collection and exchange of data and information to inform prevention efforts. "Report of the Meeting of the Inter-Sessional Open-Ended Intergovernmental Group of Experts on the Elaboration of a Preliminary Draft of a Possible Comprehensive International Convention against Organized Transnational Crime (Warsaw, Feb. 2–6, 1998)," UN Doc. E/CN.15/1998/5, Feb. 18, 1998, in particular paragraph 61 and Article 22 of the proposed draft instrument.

[14] United Nations Office on Drugs and Crime, *Model Legislative Provisions against Organized Crime* (2012) [UNODC, *Model Legislative Provisions against Organized Crime*].

[15] The Model Legislative Provisions assert that the term "prevention" in Article 31 of the Convention should be understood broadly as referring to "crime prevention" in the sense this term has been defined by paragraph 6 of the ECOSOC Guidelines for the Prevention of Crime (at 17). Crime prevention is defined in the European regional context as follows: "Crime prevention covers all measures that are intended to reduce or otherwise contribute to reducing crime and citizens' feeling of insecurity, both quantitatively and qualitatively, either through directly deterring criminal activities or through policies and interventions designed to reduce the potential for crime and the causes of crime. It includes work by government, competent authorities, criminal justice agencies, local authorities, and the specialist associations they have set up in Europe, the private and voluntary sectors, researchers and the public, supported by the media": Council Decision of 28 May 2001 setting up a European crime prevention network (2001/427/JHA), OJ L 153/1, June 8, 2001, at Art. 1(3).

[16] Note that this aspect presents some difficulty in the present context because the status of "victim of crime" is prima facie withheld from smuggled migrants who have not themselves been subject to exploitation, human trafficking, or other serious abuse. See discussion on protection obligations in Chapter 8, at Section 8.1.

factors and increasing protective factors), reducing the attractiveness of offending (through, for example, increasing the social and material costs of being involved in crime while also reducing the benefits), and reducing opportunities for offending.[17] Significantly the Guidelines clearly affirm the link between crime prevention, the rule of law, and human rights: "The rule of law and those human rights which are recognized in international instruments to which Member States are parties must be respected in all aspects of crime prevention. A culture of lawfulness should be actively promoted in crime prevention."[18]

The principal prevention obligations of the Organized Crime Convention are set out in a single article that addresses a wide range of themes. States Parties are required to "endeavour to develop and evaluate national projects and to establish and promote best practices and policies aimed at the prevention of transnational organized crime."[19] They are further required to "endeavour," in accordance with the fundamental principles of their national law, to "reduce … opportunities for organized criminal groups to participate in lawful markets with proceeds of crime, through appropriate legislative, administrative or other measures."[20] A list of such measures provides some indication of the breadth of the Convention's concept of prevention:

- Strengthening of cooperation between criminal justice agencies and private entities;

[17] ECOSOC Guidelines for the Prevention of Crime, at para. 6. The Guidelines identify eight principles as fundamental to effective crime prevention, which can be summarized as follows: (1) Government leadership. All levels of government should play a leadership role in developing effective and humane crime prevention strategies, and in creating and maintaining institutional frameworks for their implementation and review; (2) Socioeconomic development and inclusion. Crime prevention considerations should be integrated into all relevant social and economic policies and programs, including those addressing unemployment, education, health, housing and urban planning, poverty, social marginalization and exclusion; (3) Cooperation and partnership. These should be an integral part of crime prevention, given the wide-ranging causes of crime and the skills and responsibilities needed to address them; (4) Sustainability and accountability. Crime prevention requires adequate resources, including funding for structures and activities, in order to be sustained; (5) Knowledge base. Crime prevention strategies and policies should be based on a broad, multidisciplinary foundation of knowledge about crime problems, their multiple causes, and promising and proven practices; (6) Human rights, rule of law, and a culture of lawfulness. The human rights recognized in international legal instruments to which States are parties must be recognized and respected in all aspects of crime prevention; (7) Interdependency. National crime prevention diagnoses and strategies should take account of the links between local criminal problems and transnational organized crime. (8) Differentiation. Crime prevention strategies should, when appropriate, pay due regard to the different needs of men and women and consider the special needs of vulnerable members of society. See further United Nations Office on Drugs and Crime, *Handbook on the Crime Prevention Guidelines: Making Them Work* (2010).

[18] ECOSOC Guidelines for the Prevention of Crime, at para. 12.

[19] Organized Crime Convention, at Art. 31(1).

[20] Ibid. at Art. 31(2).

Although paragraphs (1) and (2) of Article 15 in the Protocol are limited to a focus on information campaigns and public awareness, the obligation in paragraph (3) is far broader, potentially covering a wide range of prevention initiatives at the local, national, and international levels focused on the causes of smuggling. States Parties are required to "promote or strengthen, as appropriate, development programmes and cooperation at the national, regional and international levels, taking into account the socio-economic realities of migration and paying special attention to economically and socially depressed areas, in order to combat the root socio-economic causes of the smuggling of migrants, such as poverty and underdevelopment."[44] The breadth of Article 15(3) should not be mistaken for strength. Although the provision is made mandatory through the word "shall," the caveat of "as appropriate" operates as a strong modifier. In short, the provision is "largely aspirational"[45] and relies on States to give it substance. Its significance may, however, lie in the recognition "that a root cause of smuggling is the desire of people to migrate away from conditions such as poverty or oppression in search of better lives."[46]

International and regional policy on migrant smuggling supports the need for States to address the conditions that lead to migrant smuggling by providing improved avenues for safe and legal migration and by action against employers who engage smuggled migrants.[47] These areas of focus are arguably an important component of the obligation to address "root causes," under the Protocol.[48] However, as

44 Migrant Smuggling Protocol, at Art. 15(3). Note that the preamble to the Protocol also acknowledges the link between migration and development, referring to General Assembly Resolution 54/212 of December 22, 1999 on strengthening international cooperation and development, in order to address the root causes of migration, and to maximize the benefits of international migration to those concerned (UN General Assembly, "International Migration and Development," UN Doc. A/RES/54/212, Feb. 1, 2000).

45 McClean, *Transnational Organized Crime*, at 425.

46 *Legislative Guide*, at 372 (para. 82).

47 Global Commission on International Migration, *Migration in an Interconnected World: New Directions for Action* (Report of the Global Commission on International Migration, Oct. 2, 2005), at 80. See also the UN Development Programme's 2009 Human Development Report, which states that migration policy reform may include "[o]pening up existing entry channels so that more people can emigrate; ensuring basic rights for migrants; lowering the cost of migration; finding solutions that benefit both destination communities and the migrants they receive; making it easier for people to move within their own countries; and including migration in national development strategies – all have important and complementary contributions to make to human development": United Nations Development Programme, *Overcoming Barriers: Human Mobility and Development* (Human Development Report, 2009), Overview, at 4.

48 For a reiteration of this position see, for example, the Co-Chair's statement from the Fourth Bali Regional Ministerial Conference on People Smuggling, Trafficking in Persons and Related Transnational Crime (Indonesia, Mar. 29–30, 2011), available at www.unodc.org/documents/southeastasiaandpacific//2011/11/som/Bali_process_FINAL_Ministerial_Co-chairs_statement_BRMC_IV-1.pdf (accessed May 12, 2013), which includes a "non-binding regional framework," in which Ministers agree that: "[a]rrangements should seek to address root causes of irregular movement and promote population stabilisation wherever possible" (at para. 19(iv)).

with the Protocol, it is difficult to discern, from those texts, any sense of legal obligation on the part of States to take such measures. Certainly, addressing root causes through provision of improved avenues for safe and legal migration is rarely part of the practice or rhetoric of migrant smuggling prevention in any major country of destination.

In Europe there has been some recent action toward addressing employers who engage irregular workers, including those who have been smuggled, principally through a 2009 Directive of the European Parliament on sanctions and measures against employers of illegally staying third-country nationals.[49] This initiative seeks to prevent irregular migration (and its facilitation) through addressing the "pull" factor of employment. Under the Directive, Member States are required to create an offense of employing illegally staying, third-country nationals. This is to be considered a more serious offense when accompanied by "particularly exploitative working conditions" or human trafficking.[50] Infringements are to be subject to effective, proportionate, and dissuasive sanctions, including financial sanctions in relation to each illegally employed person, and payment of the costs of returning illegally employed persons. One innovative aspect of the Directive is its focus on ensuring even "illegal" workers can claim unpaid wages, including taxes and social security payments, through legal mechanisms,[51] an important factor in ensuring employers do not simply avoid paying "illegal" workers through denouncing them to the authorities.[52] Significantly, in order to minimize potential disputes regarding the amount of remuneration owing, employers are presumed to have employed the third-country national for a minimum of three months' duration for wages as specified in applicable awards or agreements.[53]

The Directive also requires the establishment of a complaints mechanism whereby third-country nationals can lodge complaints directly or through designated third

49 Directive 2009/52/EC of the European Parliament and of the Council of 18 June 2009 providing for minimum standards on sanctions and measures against employers of illegally staying third-country nationals, OJ L 168/24, June 30, 2009 [Directive 2009/52/EC].

50 Ibid. at Art. 9(c)–(d). The term "particularly exploitative working conditions" is defined to include: "working conditions, including those resulting from gender based or other discrimination, where there is a striking disproportion compared with the terms of employment of legally employed workers which, for example, affects workers' health or safety, and which offends human dignity": at Art. 2(i).

51 Ibid. at Art. 6.

52 F. David, *Labour Trafficking* (Australian Institute of Criminology, Research and Public Policy Series 108, 2010), at 51.

53 Directive 2009/52/EC, at Art. 6(3). The issue of subcontracting is also addressed, as the contractor of which the employer is a direct subcontractor can be held liable to payment of sanctions and back payments (Article 8). For a discussion of the operation of this Directive in practice, see further E. Dewhurst, "The Right of Irregular Immigrants to Outstanding Remuneration under the EU Sanctions Directive: Rethinking Domestic Labour Policy in a Globalised World" (2011) 13(4) *European Journal of Migration and Law* 389.

parties such as trade unions.[54] When providing assistance to lodge complaints, these third parties are protected from possible sanction for facilitating unauthorized residence.[55] To supplement the complaints mechanism, Member States are free to grant residence permits of limited duration, linked to the length of relevant national proceedings, to third-country nationals who have been subjected to particularly exploitative working conditions or who were illegally employed minors and who cooperate in criminal proceedings against the employer.[56] Although most EU States have taken steps to transpose the Directive into national law it has not been uniformly accepted[57] and it is too early to make any assessment of the Directive's impact on migrant smuggling patterns and trends.

7.1.2.2. Border Control Measures Including Carrier Sanctions

The concept of "border control" is frequently referred to in treaties and policy instruments on migrant smuggling and migration issues generally but typically not defined.[58] Although border control can be understood narrowly to mean checks undertaken at the physical border, recent State practice suggests the concept has expanded to encompass a number of measures that are undertaken before the border, at the border, and even after entry. A broadening of the concept of border control is clearly linked to the growing externalization of such controls, which now involve not only the country of destination but also countries of origin and transit, as well as private industry partners.[59]

54 Directive 2009/52/EC, at Art. 13(1).

55 Ibid. at Art. 13(3).

56 Ibid. at Art. 13(4). See also the Council Directive 2004/81/EC of 29 April 2004 on the residence permit issued to third-country nationals who are victims of trafficking in human beings or who have been the subject of an action to facilitate illegal immigration, who decide to cooperate with the competent authorities, OJ L 261, Aug. 6, 2004. See further Chapter 1, at Section 1.3.1.2.

57 For example, the United Kingdom has opted out of the Directive, citing its creation of additional and unnecessary costs and administrative burdens on employers and an overly broad definition of "employer." The UK government also objected to provisions granting rights of back payment to illegally staying workers on the basis that they "would be difficult to administer and would send the wrong message by rewarding breaches of immigration legislation." UK Home Office, Written Statement to Parliament, *EU Directive on Sanctions against Employers of Illegally Staying Third-Country Nationals* (delivered on May 24, 2011).

58 In one rare example of such a definition, the EU Directive on Passenger Data defines "border control" for the purposes of that Directive as "a check carried out at a border in response exclusively to an intention to cross that border, regardless of any other consideration": Council Directive 2004/82/EC of 29 April 2004 on the obligation of carriers to communicate passenger data, OJ L 261/24, Aug. 6, 2004, at Art. 2(c).

59 See generally C. Rodier, "Analysis of the External Dimension of the European Union's Asylum and Immigration Policies – Summary and Recommendations for the European Parliament," Doc. No.DGExPo/B/PolDep/ETUDE/2006_11 (June 8, 2006), at 6–7. See also the discussion of agreements "linked to" readmission, in J-P. Cassarino, "Dealing with Unbalanced Reciprocities: Cooperation on

BORDER CONTROL IN THE CONTEXT OF MIGRANT SMUGGLING

As noted in the Introduction to this book, a singular focus on border control presents a particular and apparently unresolvable dilemma: although more effective border controls are in one sense necessary to prevent migrant smuggling, they will inevitably lead (or at least contribute) to a greater reliance, by migrants, on those who are able to evade such controls and thereby facilitate their irregular migration.[60] In short, border controls are part of the solution to migrant smuggling but they are also, inevitably, a fundamental part of the problem. The international legal framework reflects this tension but does not resolve or even address it. The international policy response has been equally unsatisfactory, noting the need for "holistic" or "comprehensive" approaches, without adequately acknowledging the disproportionate legal and policy weight attached to law enforcement and border control measures in comparison with prevention strategies that focus on causal factors.[61]

Another dilemma is presented by the readily observable phenomenon of migrant smugglers simply shifting their modus operandi in response to changes in migration policies or the redirection of law enforcement resources.[62] This results in what has been described as increased professionalization,[63] and an "arms race,"[64] generating

Readmission and Implications," in J-P. Cassarino ed., *Unbalanced Reciprocities: Cooperation on Readmission in the Euro-Mediterranean Area* 1 (Middle East Institute Special Edition *Viewpoints*, 2010). The author notes that these agreements, pioneered by France, Greece, Italy, and Spain, often reflect a three-pronged focus on "1) the fight against unauthorized migration, including the issue of readmission, 2) the reinforced control of borders, including *ad hoc* technical assistance, and 3) the joint management of labor migration with third countries of origin, including enhanced development aid," with the focus heavily weighted in favor of the first two points: at 9–10.

60 This dilemma has been recognized by the United Nations: "Where people have no choice but to leave, strong border controls can have no deterrent impact but will only make it more difficult for them to move, possibly fueling demand for smuggling services to circumvent border controls in ways that may risk lives and safety": UNODC, *Framework for Action*, at 43. See also United Nations Office on Drugs and Crime, *Smuggling of Migrants: A Global Review and Annotated Bibliography of Recent Publications* (2011), at 30.

61 See, for example, CTOC, "Challenges and Good Practices in the Prevention of the Smuggling of Migrants," at para. 9: "Where people are forced to leave their homes, strong border controls can have no deterrent impact but conversely can increase demand for smuggling services to circumvent obstacles to migration. Good practice is to ensure that immediate prevention measures such as strengthened border control are complemented by longer-term efforts to dismantle the criminal organizations behind smuggling of migrants, and to address the root causes of demand for smuggling services." See also UNODC, *Framework for Action*, at 15–16.

62 P. Monzini, "Sea Border Crossings: The Organisation of Irregular Migration to Italy" (2007) 12 *Mediterranean Politics* 163, at 180.

63 P. Monzini, F. Pastore, and G. Sciortino, "Human Smuggling to/through Italy" (Research Project, *The Human Smuggling and Trafficking in Migrants: Types, Origins and Dynamics in a Comparative and Interdisciplinary Perspective*, April 2004), at 59.

64 F. Heckmann, "Illegal Migration: What Can We Know and What Can We Explain? The Case of Germany," in A. Portes and J. DeWind eds., *Rethinking Migration: New Theoretical and Empirical Perspectives* (2007), at 303.

predictable and ever-escalating responses from both sides. States of destination will typically respond to a change in the actual or perceived level of migrant smuggling threat through measures such as "an increase in material and technological resources; changes in legislation and administrative rules; and cooperation with other states and training of their personnel."[65] Smugglers, on the other hand, will respond to law enforcement or other pressures through "changes of routes; increase in technological sophistication; professionalization and specialization; increase of juridical sophistication; development of marketing strategies such as more systematic recruitment and improvement of "services"; guaranteed smuggling and special fees for certain groups; and attempts to corrupt state officials." [66]

It has also been noted that implementation of the obligation to strengthen border controls to prevent migrant smuggling is typically undifferentiated:

> Often the focus of border controls is on preventing and detecting irregular migration rather than on preventing and detecting smuggling of migrants. The result can be that a situation of smuggling of migrants is dealt with as a migration issue rather than as a criminal issue, representing a lost opportunity to investigate the organized crime groups facilitating irregular movements.[67]

BORDER CONTROL OBLIGATIONS IN THE MIGRANT SMUGGLING PROTOCOL

Border control is central to the Migrant Smuggling Protocol, and relevant provisions are integrated throughout its text. The key provision establishes an obligation on States, without prejudice to international commitments in relation to the free movement of people, to "strengthen, to the extent possible, such border controls as may be necessary to prevent and detect the smuggling of migrants."[68] The term "border control" is not defined, and the general requirement in Article 11(1), that States take steps necessary to strengthen their border controls to prevent and detect migrant smuggling, is extremely vague. Although the obligation is made subject to "international commitments in relation to the free movement of people,"[69] no guidance is provided, in the Protocol or elsewhere, or indeed since its adoption, on how this caveat is to operate. These various factors conspire to make it extremely difficult to establish the basic parameters of the substantive content of the obligation, except perhaps by recourse to the factual question of what kind of "border controls" effectively "prevent and detect" migrant smuggling.

65 Ibid.
66 Ibid.
67 CTOC, "Challenges and Good Practices in the Prevention of the Smuggling of Migrants," at para. 11.
68 Migrant Smuggling Protocol, at Art. 11(1).
69 Ibid.

The *limitations* on State action to engage in border control are much clearer. As United Nations agencies pointed out during the drafting process, the legitimate interest of States in strengthening border controls may not impinge upon the internationally recognized human rights of individuals. Most particularly, such controls must "not limit the right of individuals to seek and enjoy in other countries asylum from persecution as provided for under the Convention relating to the Status of Refugees."[70] The Protocol's savings clause provides separate confirmation that its "border control" provisions are to be read as subject to the obligations arising from human rights and refugee law, and obligations to rescue persons in distress at sea.[71]

LIABILITY OF COMMERCIAL CARRIERS FOR MIGRANT SMUGGLING

State-imposed obligations on commercial carriers to engage in document checks of their passengers date back to the early 1900s.[72] Carrier sanctions have been an important part of the response to irregular migration in Europe and North America since the 1980s.[73] For example, by 1987, the then five Schengen States (Belgium, Denmark, Italy, Germany, and the United Kingdom) had all introduced this concept into their national laws.[74] In 1988, the relevant annex to the Convention on International Civil Aviation (Chicago Convention)[75] was amended to provide that States were not to sanction carriers in the event that passengers are found inadmissible unless there is evidence to suggest that the carrier in question was negligent in taking precautions to verify that the passenger has complied with the documentary requirements for entry into the receiving State.[76] In 1990, the Schengen Implementation Convention

[70] UN General Assembly, "Note by the Office of the United Nations High Commissioner for Human Rights, the United Nations Children's Fund and the International Organization for Migration on the draft protocols concerning migrant smuggling and trafficking in persons," UN Doc. A/AC.254/27, Feb. 8, 2000, at para. 7.

[71] Migrant Smuggling Protocol, at Art. 19.

[72] See generally J. Gilboy, "Implications of 'Third-Party' Involvement in Enforcement: The INS, Illegal Travelers, and International Airlines" (1997) 31 *Law and Society Review* 505, at 507. See also S. Scholten and P. Minderhoud, "Regulating Immigration Control: Carrier Sanctions in the Netherlands" (2008) 10(2) *European Journal of Migration and Law* 123 [Scholten and Minderhoud, "Regulating Immigration Control"], at 123–124.

[73] For a comprehensive overview of these early regimes, see E. Feller, "Carrier Sanctions and International Law" (1989) 1 *International Journal of Refugee Law* 48.

[74] UN High Commissioner for Refugees, *UNHCR Position: Visa Requirements and Carrier Sanctions* (1995). The United Kingdom legislation has been subject to considerable review and critique, most particularly with respect to its impact on the rights of refugees. See, for example, A. Ruff, "The Immigration (Carriers Liability) Act 1987: Its Implications for Refugees and Airlines" (1989) 1 *International Journal of Refugee Law* 481; and F. Nicholson, "Implementation of the Immigration (Carriers' Liability) Act 1987: Privatising Immigration Functions at the Expense of International Obligations?" (1997) 46 *International Comparative Law Quarterly* 586.

[75] Convention on Civil Aviation, 15 UNTS 295, done Dec. 7, 1944, entered into force Apr. 4, 1947.

[76] Ibid. at Annex 9–Facilitation (12th ed. 2005, up to and including Amendment 21 (2009)).

provided for carrier sanctions without allowing exemption for lack of evidence of negligence.[77]

In the international context, the early drafts of what became Article 11 of the Migrant Smuggling Protocol focused solely on establishing the obligation of carriers to detect and prevent migrant smuggling.[78] At the time of drafting, carrier sanctions were, as noted previously, already well established in Europe and had been introduced to international treaty law through the 1988 United Nations Drug Control Convention.[79] At one of its later sessions, the drafting committee decided that it was necessary to ensure consistency between the articles in the Trafficking and Migrant Smuggling Protocols.[80] As a result, text was added to the draft migrant smuggling protocol to extend the scope of Article 11 beyond carrier sanctions to include obligations relating to strengthening of border controls to prevent and detect the smuggling of migrants,[81] measures that permit the denial of entry or revocation of visas of

77 Convention Implementing the Schengen Agreement of 14 June 1985 between the Governments of the States of the Benelux Economic Union, the Federal Republic of Germany and the French Republic on the gradual abolition of checks at their common borders, OJ L 239/19, Sept. 22, 2000, done June 19, 1990, entered into force Sept. 1, 1993 [Schengen Convention]. Under this Agreement States Parties are agreed (subject to their obligations under the Refugee Convention (Convention Relating to the Status of Refugees, 189 UNTS 137, done July 28, 1951, entered into force April 22, 1954)) to impose a set of obligations on commercial carriers with regard to document checks and the return of irregular migrants. States Parties further agreed to oblige carriers to take all necessary measures to ensure that aliens to be carried into their territory were in possession of necessary travel documents (Article 26(1)(b)), and to impose penalties on carriers who transport aliens without necessary travel documents to their territories (Article 26(2)). This was reinforced by a further requirement: that States oblige carriers to take responsibility for returning any aliens found to have been transported on their vessels without the necessary documentation (Article 26(1)(a)). Together, these measures created a strong financial incentive for commercial carriers to check documentation before disembarkation. Carrier sanctions have more recently been adopted into European Law through the integration of the Schengen *Acquis* (Agreement) into the framework of the European Union (Treaty of Amsterdam amending the Treaty on European Union, the Treaties Establishing the European Communities and certain related acts, OJ C 340/1, done Oct. 2, 1997, entered into force May 1, 1999); Protocol (No 19) on the Schengen *Acquis* integrated into the framework of the European Union, OJ C 326/290, done May 5, 2008, entered into force Dec. 1, 2009; and further extended through a Council Directive on this issue: Council Directive 2001/51/EC of 28 June 2001 supplementing the provisions of Article 26 of the Convention implementing the Schengen Agreement of 14 June 1985, OJ L 187/45, July 10, 2001.

78 Travaux Préparatoires *for the Organized Crime Convention and Protocols*, at 519.

79 United Nations Convention against Illicit Traffic in Narcotic Drugs and Psychotropic, 1582 UNTS 95, done Dec. 20, 1988, entered into force Nov. 11, 1990 [1988 Drug Control Convention], at Art. 15.

80 Travaux Préparatoires *for the Organized Crime Convention and Protocols*, at 520.

81 Migrant Smuggling Protocol, at Art. 11(1). An identical obligation is found in the Protocol to Prevent, Suppress and Punish Trafficking in Persons, Especially Women and Children, supplementing the United Nations Convention against Transnational Organized Crime, 2237 UNTS 319, done Nov. 15, 2000, entered into force Dec. 25, 2003 [Trafficking Protocol], at Art. 11(1).

persons implicated in the commission of smuggling offenses,[82] and strengthening of cooperation among border agencies.[83]

Under the Migrant Smuggling Protocol, States Parties are to adopt "legislative or other appropriate measures to prevent, to the extent possible, means of transport operated by commercial carriers" from being used in the commission of smuggling offenses.[84] Although "commercial carrier" is not defined, the term can be understood to refer to a legal or natural person who engages in the transportation of goods or people for commercial gain.[85] As noted in the relevant Interpretative Note, this provision "requires States Parties to impose an obligation on commercial carriers only to ascertain whether or not passengers have the necessary documents in their possession and not to make any judgement or assessment of the validity or authenticity of the documents."[86] States are further obliged to take the measures necessary to provide for "sanctions" where carriers fail to meet the obligation to check documentation.[87] The Legislative Guide affirms that while the basic obligation to be placed on carriers is "to ascertain basic possession of whatever documents may be needed to enter the State of destination," there is to be no obligation placed on carriers "to assess the authenticity or validity of the documents or whether they have been validly issued to the person who possesses them."[88] The obligation is, in other words, "to attach liability to the carriers for not having checked the documents as required."[89] States remain free to impose liability on carriers for transporting undocumented migrants, but the Protocol does not impose any requirement to that effect. The Protocol does not require States to impose liability on carriers for transporting undocumented migrants – although it does not operate to prevent the imposition of such liability.

In Europe, efforts have continued since 2000 to further sharpen the requirements on carriers to contribute to border control, initially introduced through the

82 Migrant Smuggling Protocol, at Art. 11(5).

83 Ibid. at Art. 11(6).

84 Ibid. at Art. 11(2).

85 This definition appears in the United Nations Office on Drugs and Crime, *Model Law against the Smuggling of Migrants* (2010) [UNODC Model Law on Migrant Smuggling] at 12–13, drawing on definitions of "commercial carrier" found in the 1988 Drug Control Convention ("'Commercial carrier' means any person or any public, private or other entity engaged in transporting persons, goods or mails for remuneration, hire or any other benefit" (Article 1(d)), and the Schengen Convention ("carrier: shall mean any natural or legal person whose occupation it is to provide passenger transport by air, sea or land" (Article 1)).

86 Interpretative Note on Article 11, as included in the Travaux Préparatoires *for the Organized Crime Convention and Protocols*, at 521.

87 Migrant Smuggling Protocol, at Art. 11(4). See also Trafficking Protocol, at Art. 11(4). As noted in the UNODC Model Law on Migrant Smuggling (at 58), there are several ways to fulfill this obligation: the establishment of criminal offenses is one option but in many countries, it may be more appropriate to address this issue through civil regulatory laws.

88 *Legislative Guide*, at 298, para. 75.

89 Ibid.

Schengen Implementation Convention. In 2001, the European Union agreed to a Directive, the aim of which was to supplement the Schengen Convention regime by providing for consistent "dissuasive, proportionate and effective" penalties across the Union.[90] The Directive further obliges States to ensure that carriers are liable not just for sanctions for breach of obligations, but also for actually returning third-country nationals refused entry, either through facilitating their return, or meeting the cost of their return or the cost of their stay and return.[91]

In 2004, the European Union passed a further Directive requiring air carriers to provide advance notice of passenger data.[92] The stated purpose of the Directive is to improve border control and combat illegal immigration but the Directive also permits Member States to use the advance passenger data for law enforcement purposes to a certain extent, under certain conditions.[93] As with the carrier sanctions regime, Member States are required to impose "dissuasive, proportionate and effective" penalties on air carriers, that, as a result of fault, have not transmitted data or have transmitted incomplete or false data. In 2007, the European Commission submitted a proposal that would see a further expansion of obligations on carriers with regard to passenger data, through requiring passenger name record data (PNR data)[94] for law enforcement purposes. After the proposal lapsed, it was resubmitted

[90] Council Directive 2001/51/EC of 28 June 2001 supplementing the provisions of Article 26 of the Convention implementing the Schengen Agreement of 14 June 1985, OJ L 187/45, July 10, 2001. Article 4(1) of the Directive provides that carrier sanction penalties, in addition to being dissuasive, effective, and proportionate, should be set as follows: "(a) either the maximum amount of the applicable financial penalties is not less than EUR 5000 or equivalent national currency at the rate of exchange published in the Official Journal on 10 August 2001, for each person carried, or (b) the minimum amount of these penalties is not less than EUR 3000 or equivalent national currency at the rate of exchange published in the Official Journal on 10 August 2001, for each person carried, or (c) the maximum amount of the penalty imposed as a lump sum for each infringement is not less that EUR 500000 or equivalent national currency at the rate of exchange published in the Official Journal on 10 August 2001, irrespective of the number of persons carried."

[91] Ibid. at Art. 3.

[92] Council Directive 2004/82/EC of 29 April 2004 on the obligation of carriers to communicate passenger data, OJ L 261/24, Aug. 6, 2004. As a result of Article 3, the information required to be transmitted to the competent authorities is: the number and type of travel document used, nationality, full names, the date of birth, the border crossing point of entry into the territory of the Member States, code of transport, departure and arrival time of the transportation, total number of passengers carried on that transport, the initial point of embarkation.

[93] The transposition of the Directive into European Union law is discussed in E. Canetta, S. Korpelainen, C. Mortera, L. Robson, V. Minkova and K. Damianakis, "Evaluation on the Implementation and Functioning of the Obligation of Carriers to Communicate Passenger Data Set Up by Directive 2004/82" (Final Report for Directorate-General for Home Affairs, 2012).

[94] Passenger Name Record (PNR) data is unverified data provided by passengers, and collected by carriers on their reservations and departures control systems, for commercial purposes. It includes information such as travel dates, itinerary, contact details, travel agent details, means of payment used (including credit card details), seat numbers, and baggage information.

in 2011.[95] Although this proposal has yet to result in a Directive, the European Parliament has already moved to conclude bilateral agreements to exchange PNR data, including with the United States and Australia.[96]

The issue of carrier sanctions is a vexed one. Although not prima facie contrary to international law, it is undeniable that such mechanisms can and often do lead to violations of important international legal rules. The main issue in this regard relates to asylum-seekers and refugees. In practice, the operation of carrier sanctions actually works against access to international protection, as it is asylum-seekers who are most likely to lack the documentation required for a carrier to avoid penalty. There is little doubt that States have used the carrier sanctions beyond their accepted purpose of migration control to actively prevent the physical arrival of refugees into their territory and thereby to thwart applications for protection. This tactic has generally been very successful for reasons explained by the United Nations High Commissioner for Refugees:

> Forcing carriers to verify visas and other travel documentation helps to shift the burden of determining the need for protection to those whose motivation is to avoid monetary penalties on their corporate employer, rather than to provide protection to individuals. In so doing, it contributes to placing this very important responsibility in the hands of those (a) unauthorized to make asylum determinations on behalf of States (b) thoroughly untrained in the nuances and procedures of refugee and asylum principles, and (c) motivated by economic rather than humanitarian considerations. Inquiry into whether the absence of valid documentation may evidence the need for immediate protection of the traveller is never reached.[97]

[95] European Commission, Proposal for a Directive of the European Parliament and of the Council on the use of Passenger Name Record data for the prevention, detection, investigation and prosecution of terrorist offences and serious crime, COM(2011) 32 final, Feb. 2, 2011 [2011 Proposal for a Directive on the use of PNR data]. Under this proposal, PNR data, including credit card information, is to be collected in relation to terrorist offenses and serious crime. The proposal provides that the definition of serious transnational crime should be taken from Article 2 of Council Framework Decision 2002/584/JHA (Council Framework Decision of 13 June 2002 on the European Arrest Warrant and the surrender procedures between Member States (2002/584/JHA), OJ L 190/1, July 18, 2002) and the UN Organized Crime Convention. The Framework Decision on the European Arrest Warrant does not define "serious crime" but lists a number of crimes covered by the Decision, including facilitation of unauthorized entry. Serious crime is defined in Article 2(b) of the Organized Crime Convention as "conduct constituting an offence punishable by a maximum deprivation of liberty of at least four years or a more serious penalty." See further 2011 Proposal for a Directive on the use of PNR data, at Draft Art. 2.

[96] Agreement between the United States of America and the European Union on the use and transfer of Passenger Name Records to the United States Department of Homeland Security (done Sept. 29, 2011), OJ L 215/5, Nov. 8, 2012; Agreement between the European Union and Australia on the processing and transfer of Passenger Name Record (PNR) data by air carriers to the Australian Customs and Border Protection Service (done Dec. 14, 2011), OJ L 186/4, July 14, 2012.

[97] UN High Commissioner for Refugees, *UNHCR Position on Conventions Recently Concluded in Europe (Dublin and Schengen Conventions)* (Aug. 16, 1991, 3 European Series 2, at 385).

State practice with respect to carrier sanctions and persons who are seeking asylum or who may be refugees is not settled one way or another. In some countries, national law provides for carriers to be exempt from sanctions in relation to situations where an asylum claim is made or deemed admissible. In other countries sanctions will be imposed on a carrier irrespective of whether the improperly documented migrant was found to be a refugee.[98] Although the Migrant Smuggling Protocol does not deal with this issue directly, an Interpretative Note attached to the relevant article affirms that the obligation on States Parties to impose carrier sanctions "does not unduly limit the discretion of States parties not to hold carriers liable for transporting undocumented refugees."[99] In other words, States Parties are not *prevented* from exempting commercial carriers from sanction if their undocumented or improperly documented passengers are indeed refugees.[100] The Interpretative Note also makes reference to the savings clause of the Protocol that explicitly preserves the general obligations of States Parties under international law, including through specific reference to the Refugee Convention.[101] This is taken up by the Model Law on Migrant Smuggling, which proposes a specific exemption for carrier liability, in situations where the smuggled migrant has submitted an asylum claim or has been granted refugee status or a complementary form of protection.[102] It should be noted that State responsibility for wrongful acts such as violation of the obligation of *non-refoulement* will not be affected by the fact that the wrongful act was committed by a commercial carrier under threat of sanction.[103]

The obligation to ensure that commercial carriers are not used for purposes of transporting smuggled migrants also remains subject to the well-entrenched obligation on States, recognized in both treaties and custom, to rescue those in distress at sea.[104] This may involve, for example, providing for exemption from carrier sanctions in respect of migrants whose entry results from rescue at sea.[105] Other exemptions may be dictated by the particular geography of the State and the modus operandi of smugglers. For example, if smuggled migrants are found stranded in the desert, their rescue by passing commercial carriers should not be put in jeopardy by fear of prosecution under carrier liability provisions.[106]

[98] See examples in J. C. Hathaway, *The Rights of Refugees under International Law* (2005), at 384–385.

[99] Travaux Préparatoires *for the Organized Crime Convention and Protocols*, at 521.

[100] The *Legislative Guide* echoes the careful tone of the Interpretative Note: "States are also reminded of their discretion not to hold carriers liable in cases where they have transported undocumented refugees . . . This is not obligatory, however, and can be dealt with in the exercise of prosecutorial discretion where available and appropriate": *Legislative Guide*, at 298, para. 75.

[101] Travaux Préparatoires *for the Organized Crime Convention and Protocols*, at 521.

[102] UNODC Model Law on Migrant Smuggling, at 58.

[103] See further Chapter 4, at Section 4.3.

[104] See further Chapter 1, at Section 1.2 and Chapter 6, at Section 6.2.1.

[105] This approach is proposed in the UNODC Model Law on Migrant Smuggling, at 59–60.

[106] Ibid. at 60.

7.1.2.3. Document Security and Control

Modern immigration systems rely heavily on the integrity of travel and identity documents such as passports, visas, and national identity cards. Migrant smuggling often involves the fraudulent use and falsification of such documents along with residence or work permits and documentation needed to support fraudulent applications for business or student visas.[107] This reality is reflected in the prominence given to document security and control in both the Migrant Smuggling Protocol and relevant European instruments.[108] A review of the Protocol's drafting history confirms that the inclusion of obligations relating to security and control of travel and identity documents was relatively uncontroversial. However, modern systems and technologies are expensive to establish and maintain, and some States expressed concerns about the economic implications of ensuring appropriate document control.[109] This is reflected in the qualifier that document control obligations are to be implemented "within available means."[110]

Under the Migrant Smuggling Protocol, a State Party is obliged to take "such measures as may be necessary," within available means, to ensure that travel and identity documents issued by it are of a sufficient quality that they cannot be easily misused; readily falsified; or unlawfully altered, replicated, or issued.[111] It is clear from the relevant Interpretative Notes that the obligation is intended to encompass a broad range of situations: not only the creation of false documents but also the alteration of legitimate documents, the completion of blank documents, and even the use of validly issued documents by a person other than the lawful holder.[112]

[107] UNODC, *Toolkit to Combat Smuggling of Migrants*, Tool 9: Prevention of the Smuggling of Migrants, at 17.

[108] In the European context see, for example, Council Decision of 27 March 2000 on the improved exchange of information to combat counterfeit travel documents (2000/261/JHA), OJ L 81/1, Apr. 1, 2000, established a reporting system for detecting counterfeit documents, the purpose of which was to make it easier to detect counterfeit documents on inspection, and increase the effectiveness of the search for stolen travel documents, with particular attention being paid to the serial number of the travel document. In 2002, European policy noted the importance of uniform visa and security standards, involving in the short term, improved document security on the basis of new technologies and in the medium term, possible inclusion of biometric data: EU Comprehensive Plan to Combat Illegal Immigration and Trafficking of Human Beings, at Annex. The requirement of inclusion of biometric data in European passports and travel documents was achieved through the Council Regulation (EC) No 2252/2004 of 13 December 2004 on standards for security features and biometrics in passports and travel documents issued by Member States, OJ L 385/1, Dec. 29, 2004, as amended by Regulation (EC) No 444/2009 of the European Parliament and of the Council of 28 May 2009, OJ L 142/1, June 6, 2009.

[109] Travaux Préparatoires *for the Organized Crime Convention and Protocols*, at 524, n. 3.

[110] Migrant Smuggling Protocol, at Art. 12.

[111] Ibid. at Art. 12(a).

[112] Travaux Préparatoires *for the Organized Crime Convention and Protocols*, at 525. Although not explicitly required by the Migrant Smuggling Protocol, it is relevant to note that the International Civil

Document security is not only a matter of ensuring the technical integrity of travel and identity documents; it also concerns physical security, record keeping, and taking steps to prevent document forgery. States Parties to the Migrant Smuggling Protocol are obliged to ensure the integrity and security of travel and identity documents, and to prevent their unlawful creation, issuance, and use.[113] This would require, for example, establishing systems to ensure that blank passports are stored safely and securely and that records are kept of blank passports so that missing passports can be identified and canceled.

The Protocol's focus on international cooperation also extends to the issue of document control. States Parties are obliged, at the request of the appropriate authority or representative of another Protocol State, to verify within a reasonable time the legitimacy and validity of travel or identity documents issued or purported to have been issued in its name and are suspected of being used for the purposes of smuggling of migrants.[114] This obligation has general application, so it could be relevant as part of the return of smuggled migrants (where verification of legitimacy of documents may be in issue) but also at border points, and in the laying of criminal charges.

Some States deploy specialist personnel (often referred to as immigration liaison officers) to undertake or facilitate document checking at international airports that are considered possible embarkation points for irregular migration. Models of implementation vary: some arrangements emphasize the provision of training, advice, and assistance by visiting officials to host nation agencies and officials.[115] Others extend further, with host States granting authority to visiting officials to undertake predeparture checks, ostensibly on their behalf. In Europe, a network of immigration liaison officers has been established with the specific purpose of countering irregular migration through prevention activities carried out in the country of origin or transit.[116] Australian airline liaison officers conduct specialist document inspections

Aviation Organization (ICAO) publishes a set of standards for machine-readable passports, visas, and identity cards (Document 9303).

113 Migrant Smuggling Protocol, at Art. 12(b).

114 Ibid. at Art. 13.

115 See, for example, Department of Immigration and Citizenship, Australian Government, *Managing Australia's Borders*, available at www.immi.gov.au/managing-australias-borders/border-security/irregular-entry/combat.htm (accessed May 12, 2013) ("Airline Liaison Officers Network").

116 Airline liaison officers have been in use in Europe since 1996 at the European Union level, with the adoption of the Joint Action of 14 October 1996 adopted by the Council on the basis of Article K.3 of the Treaty on European Union providing for a common framework for the initiatives of the Member States concerning liaison officers (96/602/JHA), OJ L 268/2, Oct. 19, 1996. From this point, agreement was ultimately reached in a Council Directive in 2004 on key tasks and definition of roles: see Council Regulation (EC) No 377/2004 of 19 February 2004 on the creation of an immigration liaison officers network, OJ L 64/1, Mar. 2, 2004; and Regulation (EU) No 493/2011 of the European Parliament and of the Council of 5 April 2011 amending Council Regulation (EC) No 377/2004 on the creation of an

at major overseas airports "to prevent travel to Australia by potentially inadmissible passengers ... [and] act as a deterrent to smugglers of migrants and passengers who are inadequately documented."[117]

Irrespective of the precise parameters of a particular operation or arrangement (which are often not clear),[118] the practice raises important and complex issues of State responsibility in relation to internationally wrongful acts committed by or through deployed personnel.[119]

Once again, the principal threat is to the rights of refugees and asylum-seekers and to the broader obligation of *non-refoulement*. It is indisputable that immigration officials posted to a country of origin or transit are required to comply both with national laws (of their country of origin and host country) as well as with international human rights obligations (to which their country of origin and/or the host country are bound): in short, this form of extraterritorial migration control may not be used by a State to circumvent legal obligations to which that State is bound.[120] How responsibility is allocated (i.e., whether the sending State or the hosting State or both will be held responsible under international law for internationally wrongful acts conducted in the course of such operations) will depend on the particular facts of the case.[121]

7.1.2.4. Training and Technical Cooperation

International law and policy, as well as the practice of many States, recognizes training of immigration and other relevant officials and the provision of technical assistance as a crucial part of any comprehensive migrant smuggling prevention strategy. Training has also been recognized as a way of addressing an undifferentiated

immigration liaison officers network, OJ L141/13, May 27, 2011. The Act (Council Regulation (EC) No 377/2004) defines an "immigration liaison officer" as: "a representative of one of the Member States, posted abroad by the immigration service or other competent authorities in order to establish and maintain contacts with the authorities of the host country with a view to contributing to the prevention and combating of illegal immigration, the return of illegal immigrants and the management of legal migration" (Article 1(1)). For a discussion of the development of European instruments relevant to this issue, see further Scholten and Minderhoud, "Regulating Immigration Control," at 138–139.

117 UNODC, *Toolkit to Combat Smuggling of Migrants*, Tool 9: Prevention of the Smuggling of Migrants, at 19.

118 As Gammeltoft-Hansen has noted, such arrangements are often shrouded in secrecy and "[e]stablishing the exact authority granted to states exercising migration control inside a third country may ... be a complex and tricky endeavor": T. Gammeltoft-Hansen, "Growing Barriers: International Refugee Law," in M. Gibney and S. Skogly eds., *Universal Human Rights and Extraterritorial Obligations* 55 (2010), at 75. In this regard note the discrepancy between the descriptions of Australian practice in notes 115 and 117 above.

119 Discussed further in Chapter 2.

120 See Chapter 3, at Section 3.4, esp. Section 3.4.4.

121 See further Chapter 4, at Section 4.4.3.

approach that collapses irregular migration and migrant smuggling – thereby foregoing opportunities to target organized criminal involvement:

> Where the migrant him or herself is the target of border controls with little or no consideration given to the network that smuggled him or her, valuable criminal intelligence and evidence is lost and smugglers are able to continue their activities with impunity ... In order to avoid missed opportunities to strengthen border controls against the smuggling of migrants and related conduct, training of border officials should seek to raise awareness and build capacity specific to the crime of smuggling of migrants.[122]

Training and technical cooperation aimed at preventing migrant smuggling is commonly addressed through nonlegal means such as declarations, memoranda of understanding (MOUs), or joint policy statements.[123] Article 29 of the Organized Crime Convention imposes on States Parties a general obligation to initiate, develop, or improve training programs for personnel involved in the prevention, detection, and control of offenses falling within the ambit of the Convention. In this context and elsewhere where obligations relate to "offences covered by this Convention," this includes participating in an organized criminal group[124]; laundering proceeds of crime[125]; corruption[126]; obstruction of justice[127]; "serious crime"[128]) and, where a State has ratified or acceded to the Migrant Smuggling Protocol, the offenses of migrant smuggling[129] – an obligation that would, as discussed in Chapter 5, extend to migrant smuggling offenses in most circumstances.[130] States Parties are also required to assist each other in planning and implementing research

[122] CTOC, "Challenges and Good Practices in the Prevention of the Smuggling of Migrants," at paras. 11–12.

[123] For example, in the context of cooperation between European and African States, the Dakar Strategy (agreed at the Third Euro-African Ministerial Conference on Migration and Development) notes the importance of strengthened technical cooperation on combating irregular migration, and includes a specific action item (Action 4.1) on this point. "Third Euro-African Ministerial Conference on Migration and Development," statement by the Ministers and High of participant countries (Dakar, Nov. 23, 2011) [Third Euro-African Ministerial Conference on Migration and Development], available at www.africa-eu-partnership.org/sites/default/files/dakar_strategy_ministerial_declaration_En.pdf (accessed May 12, 2013).

[124] Organized Crime Convention, at Art. 5.

[125] Ibid. at Art. 6.

[126] Ibid. at Art. 8.

[127] Ibid. at Art. 23.

[128] "Serious crime" is defined as conduct constituting an offense punishable by a maximum deprivation of liberty of at least four years or a more serious penalty (Article 2(b)).

[129] Article 1(3) of the Migrant Smuggling Protocol provides that the offenses established in accordance with Article 6 of the Protocol shall be regarded as offenses established in accordance with the Organized Crime Convention. Article 6 requires States to criminalize migrant smuggling, document offenses, and enabling illegal stay.

[130] See further Chapter 5, at Section 5.1.3.

and training programs,[131] to promote training and technical assistance that will facilitate international legal cooperation,[132] and to maximize opportunities for bilateral and multilateral operational and training activities.[133] Article 30 of the Convention ("Implementation of the Convention through economic development and technical assistance") supplements these provisions by requiring States Parties to "make concrete efforts to the extent possible" to provide developing countries with assistance and support in combating organized crime.[134]

The Migrant Smuggling Protocol repeats much of the essence of the provisions on prevention in the Convention but makes them specific to migrant smuggling. It obliges States Parties to provide or strengthen specialized training programs for their immigration and other relevant officials involved in preventing the smuggling of migrants, and in the humane treatment of smuggled migrants.[135] States Parties are further required to cooperate with each other, with international organizations, nongovernmental organizations, other relevant organizations, and other elements of civil society as appropriate to ensure that there is adequate training in their territories to prevent, combat, and eradicate the smuggling of migrants and to protect the rights of migrants who have been smuggled.[136] This training is required to include not only that aimed at detection and investigation of the crime, but also "[t]he humane treatment of migrants and the protection of their rights as set forth in [the] Protocol."[137]

In the context of migrant smuggling, the risk that training and technical assistance by one State facilitates or makes possible the internationally wrongful acts of another State is a very real one. The secondary rules of State responsibility may, in certain circumstances, provide for such wrongful conduct to be attributed to the assisting State. This issue is considered in detail in Chapter 4.[138]

7.1.2.5. Prevention of Abuse and Exploitation of Smuggled Migrants

Not all smugglers intend to exploit their clients, and not all migrants are exploited or seriously harmed in the smuggling process. It is this single feature, more than any other, which differentiates migrant smuggling from trafficking in persons. However, although migrant smuggling is not inherently exploitative or even harmful, the risks to the well-being and security of those involved are often very serious. As illustrated

131 Organized Crime Convention, at Art. 29(2).
132 Ibid. at Art. 29(3).
133 Ibid. at Art. 29(4).
134 Ibid. at Art. 30(2).
135 Migrant Smuggling Protocol, at Art. 14(1).
136 Ibid. at Art. 14(2).
137 Ibid. at Art. 14(2)(e).
138 See further Chapter 4, at Section 4.4.

by the case studies set out in the Introduction to this book, smuggled migrants may die or be seriously injured during unsafe journeys; they may be subject to abuse, ill-treatment, and extortion by their smugglers or by public officials with whom they come into contact. Smuggled migrants may also be subject to forms of exploitation that constitute trafficking in persons: they may be subject to extortion during their journey; they may be forced into exploitative work during transit or at their final destination to pay off smuggling debts.

It is therefore relevant to consider what obligations, if any, States owe to smuggled migrants in relation to *prevention of their abuse or exploitation*. This issue is complex in comparison to human trafficking. In that case, the crime itself necessarily involves a form of abuse and exploitation. It follows that the obligation to prevent the crime of trafficking necessarily involves an obligation to prevent those harms from occurring. In contrast, migrant smuggling does not always involve abuse or exploitation, so preventative efforts could potentially be defined much more narrowly as including only a focus on preventing the actual crime from occurring, not associated harm to migrants. However, as will be discussed later on in the chapter, such a reading is unjustifiably narrow. First, it conflicts with the reality that States are obliged, under the Migrant Smuggling Protocol, to take specific steps to prevent and combat all of the conduct criminalized by Article 6 of the Protocol. This includes not just the basic offense of migrant smuggling but also aggravated offenses involving danger or death of migrants, or inhuman or degrading treatment including exploitation. Second, as was discussed in Chapter 8, States Parties to the Protocol and to other relevant instruments are obliged to protect smuggled migrants from violence, and to assist migrants whose lives or safety are in danger.[139] Finally, obligations that concern prevention of harm and exploitation will typically arise through and reference existing obligations under international human rights law. They may also implicate other areas of the relevant legal framework examined in this book such as the law of the sea. The following brief examples expand on these points.

Prevention of end-exploitation of smuggled migrants: it is well established that migrant smuggling is used to channel individuals into situations of exploitation from which they cannot escape.[140] This exploitation may involve a range of human rights violations including forced labor, debt bondage, and sexual exploitation. In many such situations, the facts of the case may give rise to conditions that would be characterized as trafficking in persons under international law. This outcome is particularly likely if it can be established that those involved in the smuggling process had an intention to exploit and secured the movement of the individual through

[139] See Migrant Smuggling Protocol, at Art. 16, and further discussion in Chapter 8, at Section 8.1.
[140] See case studies outlined in the Introduction.

deception or coercion.[141] International law recognizes certain obligations of prevention with respect to trafficking that would apply to States in these circumstances.[142] For example, States are required to take certain measures to address trafficking-related vulnerabilities associated with inequality, poverty, and discrimination. They are also required to address the special vulnerabilities of children and the increased vulnerability to exploitation that arises in situations of conflict. Although the substantive content of these obligations is unsatisfactorily vague, their existence is not in question. International law also recognizes demand reduction as an important prevention strategy in respect of trafficking-related exploitation. Under the Trafficking Protocol for example, States Parties are required to "adopt or strengthen legislative or other measures, such as educational, social or cultural measures, to discourage the demand that fosters all forms of exploitation of persons ... that leads to trafficking."[143] An equivalent provision in the European Trafficking Convention[144] is seen as placing an obligation on States to adopt or reinforce measures discouraging demand for all forms of trafficking-related exploitation, including forced labor and sexual exploitation, with the goal of achieving "effective dissuasion."[145] As with the issue of prevention through addressing vulnerability, the substantive content of the obligation to address demand is not settled. However, it certainly includes an obligation on States to recognize their role in shaping demand for the goods and services through laws and policies on a range of matters, including immigration, employment, welfare, and economic development. For example, failure to take steps to protect workers in industries known to accommodate large numbers of exploited, smuggled migrants may be characterized as a failure to exercise due diligence in preventing such unlawful exploitation from occurring.[146]

Preventing further harm to migrants in distress: as detailed in Chapters 1 and 6, international law imposes on States a duty to require masters of their flagged vessels to "proceed with all speed" [147] to assist and rescue any persons found at sea who are in danger of being lost or in some sort of distress.[148] The obligation of assistance and

[141] See Trafficking Protocol, at Art. 2(a).

[142] For a detailed consideration of these obligations see Gallagher, *The International Law of Human Trafficking*, at 414–453.

[143] Trafficking Protocol, at Art. 9(5).

[144] Council of Europe Convention on Action against Trafficking in Human Beings and Its Explanatory Report, ETS 197, 16.V.2005, done May 16, 2005, entered into force Feb. 1, 2008 [European Trafficking Convention], at Art. 6.

[145] Council of Europe, *Explanatory Report on the Convention on Action against Trafficking in Human Beings*, ETS 197, 16.V.2005, at paras. 109–110.

[146] See further Chapter 4, at Section 4.3.3.

[147] International Convention for the Safety of Life at Sea, 1974, as amended, 1184 UNTS 278, done Nov. 1, 1974, entered into force May 25, 1980 [SOLAS Convention], at Annex, Chapter V, Regulation 33(1).

[148] United Nations Convention on the Law of the Sea, 1833 UNTS 3, done Dec. 10, 1982, entered into force Nov. 16, 1994, at Art. 98. See also SOLAS Convention, at Annex, Chapter V, Regulation 33(1);

rescue is reinforced by more general human rights principles such as the right to life and the prohibition on inhuman or degrading treatment. For example, the failure of a State to come to the assistance of smuggled migrants in need of emergency medical treatment during or after being removed from a smuggling situation would almost certainly trigger the international legal responsibility of that State in relation to a number of core human rights obligations, including the obligation to protect life.[149] The discussion of State responsibility in Chapter 4 confirmed that breaches of these obligations by private persons (such as masters of fishing vessels) will be attributable to the State (thereby incurring the legal responsibility of that State) where it can be shown that the State failed to exercise due diligence in preventing those breaches. For example, the failure of a State to ensure that vessels flying its flag are aware of the obligation to assist and rescue and associated procedures may be seen as a failure of due diligence. The web of obligations around prevention of further harm to migrants in distress also renders unlawful any actions (such as threat or imposition of a penalty) that would substantially interfere with the capacity or willingness of any person or vessel – irrespective of its nationality – to provide assistance to migrants in distress.[150]

Prevention of exploitation and harm to smuggled migrants is one aspect of more general obligations of support and protection owed by States to persons who have been smuggled, whether generally or because of their special status as women, children, trafficked persons, asylum-seekers, migrant workers or refugees. Those protection and support obligations are canvassed in detail in the following chapter.

7.1.3. *Corruption and Prevention of Migrant Smuggling*

Although not precisely defined in international law, corruption is generally understood to refer to the misuse of public power for personal benefit or gain.[151]

and International Convention on Maritime Search and Rescue, 1979, with annexes, 1405 UNTS 97, done Apr. 27, 1979, entered into force June 22, 1985 [SAR Convention], at Annex, Chapter 2, para. 2.1.10. The SAR Convention defines distress as: "A situation wherein there is a reasonable certainty that a person, a vessel or other craft is threatened by grave and imminent danger and requires immediate assistance": SAR Convention (as amended by IMO Resolution MSC. 70(69), May 18, 1998), at Annex, Chapter 1, para. 1.3.13.).

149 International Covenant on Civil and Political Rights, 999 UNTS 171, done Dec. 16, 1996, entered into force Mar. 23, 1976 [ICCPR], at Art. 6(1). The relevance of the right to life in emergency medical treatment is noted in the UNODC Model Law on Migrant Smuggling, at 66.

150 See further Chapter 6, at Section 6.2.1.

151 The Oxford English Dictionary defines corruption as: "Perversion or destruction of integrity in the discharge of public duties by bribery or favour; the use or existence of corrupt practices, *esp.* in a state, public corporation, etc": "corruption": OED Online (Mar. 2013), available at www.oed.com/view/Entry/42045?redirectedFrom=corruption (accessed May 12, 2013).

As recognized in the United Nations Convention against Corruption,[152] corrupt practices take many forms including bribery of national public officials, solicitation or acceptance of a bribe by national public officials, bribery of foreign public officials and officials of public international organizations, embezzlement, misappropriation or other diversion of property by a public official, and laundering of proceeds of crime and obstruction of justice.[153] The Organized Crime Convention requires States Parties to criminalize corruption involving the promise, offering, or giving to a public official, or the solicitation or acceptance by a public official, directly or indirectly, of an undue advantage for that official him or herself or another person or entity, in order that the official act or refrain from acting in the exercise of his or her duties.[154] Complicity, a concept found in a number of international conventions,[155] denotes responsibility or liability for the actions of another that is incurred, for example, through knowledge, tacit consent, "wilful blindness," and/or acquiescence. An individual who is complicit in a migrant smuggling–related offense may or may not also be an accomplice to that same offense.[156] Complicity in migrant smuggling involving a public official will invariably fall within the definition of corruption[157] as well as potentially under one of the offenses of migrant smuggling itself.

Despite the very obvious connections it is only relatively recently that corruption has been explicitly linked to human rights violations[158] and to the capacity of States to meet their human rights obligations.[159] Available information appears to confirm that human rights violations associated with corruption disproportionately affect the poorest and most vulnerable, including women, children, migrants, and

[152] United Nations Convention against Corruption, 2349 UNTS 41, done Oct. 31, 2003, entered into force Dec. 14, 2005 [Convention against Corruption].

[153] Ibid. at Arts. 15, 16(1), 17, 23, 25.

[154] Organized Crime Convention, at Art. 8.

[155] See, for example, Convention on the Prevention and Punishment of the Crime of Genocide, 78 UNTS 227, Dec. 9, 1948, entered into force Jan. 12, 1951, at Art. 3; Convention against Torture and Other Cruel, Inhuman or Degrading Treatment or Punishment, 1465 UNTS 85, adopted Dec. 10, 1984, entered into force June 26, 1987 [Convention against Torture], at Art. 6.

[156] On obligations of criminalization relating to accomplices of migrant smuggling offenses, see the discussion in Chapter 5, at Section 5.1.3.4.

[157] Article 8(3) of the Organized Crime Convention requires States Parties to ensure "participation as an accomplice" in corruption is also itself an offense.

[158] See International Council on Human Rights Policy and Transparency International, *Corruption and Human Rights: Making the Connection* (2009) [ICHRP and Transparency International, *Corruption and Human Rights*], available at www.ichrp.org/files/reports/40/131_web.pdf (accessed May 12, 2013). The link between corruption and human rights is also noted in the Legislative Guide for the Convention against Corruption, at iv.

[159] A review of UN human rights treaty body reports (particularly reports of the Human Rights Committee and the Committee on Economic, Social and Cultural Rights) confirms a trend to increased reference to and analysis of corruption as an obstacle to the realization of human rights.

minorities.[160] Migrants, most particularly those without regular status, have been identified as particularly vulnerable to corruption-related human rights violations.[161] The link between corruption and migrant smuggling appears to be an obvious one, notwithstanding the lack of scholarly research or official data available to corroborate the widespread assumption of corruption playing a major role in migrant smuggling.[162] Put simply, smugglers will often require the active involvement or at least the acquiescence of immigration, customs, and law enforcement officials to move individuals illegally across international borders.[163] Corrupt practices range from the straightforward, one-off event (for example, payment of a small bribe to a border guard or the opportunistic theft of blank identity or travel documents) to complex and ongoing (for example, provision of advice by immigration officials on how to successfully manipulate the system, approval of visas in exchange for an unlawful fee, and direct involvement in smuggling using official protection and vehicles). Private persons who exercise authority and control over any aspect of the migration control process – such as airline and airport staff – may also be involved in smuggling-related corruption.

Corruption is intimately related to the vulnerable position of many smuggled migrants, and to the power imbalance that almost inevitably exists between the potential smuggled migrant and those who are in a position to facilitate his or her movement. The phenomenon of "rent seeking" has been noted in a number of

[160] ICHRP and Transparency International, *Corruption and Human Rights*, at 7–10. See also International Council on Human Rights Policy and Transparency International, *Integrating Human Rights in the Anti-Corruption Agenda: Challenges, Possibilities and Opportunities* (2010).

[161] ICHRP and Transparency International, *Corruption and Human Rights*, at 23–24.

[162] Although there is ample anecdotal information on corruption connected to migrant smuggling, little detailed research has been conducted to date. A report prepared for a 2009 meeting of States Parties to the UN Convention against Corruption provides a telling indication of the current poor state of knowledge in this area. That report essentially comprises a review of the limited available literature, personal information, anonymous sources, and the results of a survey completed by only eight individuals. The few studies that are available provide some limited insight. See, for example, M. Soudijn, *Chinese Human Smuggling in Transit* (2006) (detailing corruption by both Dutch and Chinese officials in the smuggling of Chinese migrants to the Netherlands as well as the involvement of an adviser on illegal migration based at an airport in Paris who used inside knowledge to advise smugglers); S. X. Zhang, *Chinese Human Smuggling Organizations: Families, Social Networks, and Cultural Imperatives* (2008) (examining the role of corruption in the smuggling of migrants from China to the United States); Human Rights Watch, *Help Wanted: Abuses against Female Migrant Domestic Workers in Indonesia and Malaysia* (Vol. 16, No. 9 (B), July 2004) (documenting involvement of official labor recruitment agencies in Indonesia in migrant smuggling–related corruption). See also United Nations Office on Drugs and Crime, *Migrant Smuggling in Asia: A Thematic Review of the Literature* (2012), where the existing (very thin) literature on the role of corruption in facilitating migrant smuggling is considered in each of the country studies.

[163] See, for example, United States Immigration and Customs Enforcement (ICE) Press Release, "2 Ex-Border Patrol Agents Convicted of Alien Smuggling and Other Federal Charges," Aug. 10, 2012, available at www.ice.gov/news/releases/1208/120810sandiego.htm (accessed May 12, 2013).

studies. In Indonesia, for example, corrupt practices influence every aspect of the migration process, distorting official labor migration channels to the point where the lines between regular and smuggled migration become difficult even for the migrants themselves to understand:

> It was almost impossible for potential migrants to know the difference between a formal, "legal" broker and the many illegal unlicensed free agents operating throughout the countryside.... Finally, even when migrants did register all of their information accurately and formally (a very difficult, expensive, time-consuming, and detailed series of tasks), there were no guarantees that government officials would treat them fairly. Rather, the rent seeking behaviour of government officials was rife at every step of the migration journey, and a completely formal set of papers did not protect migrants from those officials working through formal channels to profit from them.[164]

As noted at Section 7.1.2.5 and at various other points in this book, smuggled migrants are particularly vulnerable to exploitation and abuse, including forced labor and trafficking. Corruption can fuel such vulnerability and make exploitation much more likely. For example, public officials may own or control the factories, farms, and brothels to which smuggled migrants are channeled. They may be paid to turn a blind eye to unlawful activities in which smuggled migrants are involved, such as prostitution, child labor, and begging.

7.1.3.1. An International Obligation to Address Smuggling-Related Corruption

Identifying and dealing with smuggling-related corruption and complicity (which includes corruption aimed at facilitating smuggling *and* corruption that is directed toward facilitating exploitation of smuggled migrants) is an important aspect of the broader prevention obligation outlined previously. Certainly this is the position taken in transnational criminal law. The drafters of the Organized Crime Convention and its Protocols were aware of the strong link between organized criminal activities, such as migrant smuggling, and corruption.[165]

[164] R. Silvey, "Unequal Borders: Indonesian Transnational Migrants at Immigration Control" (2007) 12(2) *Geopolitics* 265, at 274.

[165] See the introduction to the Travaux Préparatoires *for the Organized Crime Convention and Protocols*. See also the Interpretative Note on Article 3 of the Convention ("The Ad Hoc Committee was also strongly convinced that the convention would constitute an effective tool and the necessary legal framework for international cooperation in combating, inter alia, such criminal activities as ... corruption ..."): ibid. at 32. See also UN General Assembly, "Action against Corruption," UN Doc. A/RES/54/128, Dec. 17, 1999, in which the General Assembly directed the Ad Hoc Committee to incorporate into the draft convention measures against corruption linked to organized crime, including provisions regarding the sanctioning of acts of corruption involving public officials: cited in the *Travaux Préparatoires*, at 75.

The Convention reflects that awareness, requiring States to take strong measures to criminalize all forms of corrupt practices when committed by public officials and to ensure that their laws are harmonized so as to facilitate cooperation.[166] There is no need for the criminalized conduct to be transnational in commission or effect, or to involve an organized criminal group.[167] In addition to the obligation of criminalization, States Parties are required, to the extent appropriate and consistent with their legal system, to adopt "legislative, administrative or other effective measures to promote integrity and to prevent, detect and punish corruption of public officials."[168] States Parties must also take measures to ensure effective action by domestic authorities in the prevention, detection, and punishment of corruption of public officials, including providing such authorities with adequate independence to deter the exertion of inappropriate influence on their actions.[169] In accordance with the Convention's general provisions on sanctions, the relevant corruption offenses should create liability to penalties that take into account their grave nature.[170]

The use of force, threats, and intimidation against, for example, judges, prosecutors, jurors, victims, and witnesses could be a serious obstacle to the development of an effective criminal justice response to migrant smuggling. It is also directly related to public sector corruption. As noted in the Legislative Guide,

> No justice can be done if judges, jurors, witnesses or victims are intimidated, threatened or corrupted. No effective national and international cooperation can be hoped for, if such crucial participants in the investigation and law enforcement process are not sufficiently protected to perform their roles and provide their accounts unimpeded. No serious crimes can be detected and punished, if the evidence is prevented from reaching investigators, prosecutors and the court.[171]

[166] Organized Crime Convention, at Art. 8. Note that although the Convention does not define corruption, States Parties are required to take action against three forms of conduct when committed intentionally: first, active bribery, being the "promise, offering or giving to a public official, directly or indirectly, of an undue advantage, for the official himself or herself or another person or entity, in order that the official act or refrain from acting in the exercise of his or her official duties" (Article 8(1)(a)); second, passive bribery, or the "solicitation or acceptance by a public official, directly or indirectly, of an undue advantage, for the official himself or herself or another person or entity, in order that the official act or refrain from acting in the exercise of his or her official duties" (Article 8(1)(b)); and third, participation as an accomplice to bribery (Article 8(3)). Note that States Parties are only required to "consider" criminalizing such conduct involving a foreign public official or international civil servant, or other forms of corruption (Article 8(2)).

[167] *Legislative Guide*, at 84 (para. 188).

[168] Organized Crime Convention, at Art. 9(1).

[169] Ibid. at Art. 9(2).

[170] Ibid. at Art. 11(1).

[171] *Legislative Guide*, at 91 (para. 195).

The Organized Crime Convention requires criminalization of "obstruction of justice."[172] States Parties are further required to criminalize and take steps to prevent money laundering, another form of conduct commonly associated with corruption.[173]

The sources and authorities cited earlier in the chapter are compatible with and reinforce a growing body of international law that seeks to address corruption more generally, particularly those corrupt practices with transnational reach or effect. The most important instrument in this regard is the Convention against Corruption, which was drafted several years after the Organized Crime Convention, and entered into force in 2005. The Convention against Corruption seeks to promote and strengthen measures to combat public sector and private corruption at both domestic and international levels. Its scope is wider, and its provisions, which would apply to the various forms of smuggling-related corruption identified previously, are much more detailed than those of the Organized Crime Convention. For example, States Parties are required to criminalize a range of corruption-related conduct, including bribery, embezzlement of funds, abuse of functions, trading in influence, and the concealment and "laundering" of the proceeds of corruption.[174] States Parties are further required to establish "obstruction of justice" – defined as the use of corrupt or coercive means to interfere with potential witnesses or to interfere with the actions of judicial and law enforcement officials – as a criminal offense.[175] They are also required to put in place a range of preventative measures directed at both public and private sectors. These include preventative anticorruption policies, systems, procedures, and institutions that promote the participation of society and reflect basic principles of the rule of law, proper management of public affairs and public property, integrity, transparency, and accountability.[176] States Parties are to cooperate with one another in every aspect of the fight against corruption, including prevention, investigation, and prosecution of offenders. Countries are bound to render specific forms of mutual legal assistance in gathering and transferring evidence for

[172] Organized Crime Convention, at Art. 23. The provision establishes two offenses: first, use of physical force, threats, or intimidation or the promise, offering, or giving of an undue advantage either to induce false testimony or to interfere in the giving of testimony or the production of evidence in proceedings in relation to offenses covered by the Convention (Article 23(a)); and, second, use of physical force, threats, or intimidation to interfere with the exercise of official duties by a justice or law enforcement official in relation to offenses covered by the Convention (Article 23(b)).

[173] Ibid. at Arts. 6–7.

[174] Convention against Corruption, at Arts. 16–19, 23, 24.

[175] Ibid. at Art. 25. Note that Article 23 of the Organized Crime Convention also requires criminalization of the obstruction of justice in a context that would directly cover proceedings related to migrant smuggling.

[176] Convention against Corruption, at Chapter II.

use in prosecutions, to extradite offenders, and to support the tracing, seizure, and confiscation of the assets of corruption.[177]

The UN Convention against Corruption builds on and reinforces a number of regional agreements on these issues, including the African Union Convention on Preventing and Combating Corruption,[178] the Inter-American Convention against Corruption,[179] the OECD Convention on Combating Bribery of Foreign Public Officials in International Business Transactions,[180] the Council of Europe Criminal Law Convention on Corruption (criminalizing acts of corruption),[181] and the Council of Europe Civil Law Convention on Corruption (providing for compensation for victims of corruption).[182]

7.1.3.2. Practical Application of the Due Diligence Standard

When considering the issue of State responsibility for migrant smuggling–related corruption, most particularly corruption that is directed at the exploitation of – or harm to – smuggled migrants, it is useful to summarize the main points of the relevant doctrine, previously explored in detail in Chapter 4. Legal responsibility will be incurred by a State for acts and omissions that are: (1) attributable to that State, and (2) a breach of its international legal obligations. International law is clear that the conduct of any organ of the State, such as a court or legislature, will always be regarded as an act of that State for which the State is directly responsible. Attribution for acts of officials who are part of a State organ (such as police, prosecutors, or immigration officials) will depend on whether the individual concerned is acting in an apparently official capacity or under the color of authority. Importantly, "[i]t is irrelevant for this purpose that the person concerned may have had ulterior or improper motives or may be abusing public power."[183] That the act in question was unauthorized or ultra vires is also irrelevant in determining whether it is to be characterized as an act of the State. These are both important principles in the present

177 Ibid. at Chapter IV, esp. Arts. 43–44.

178 African Union Convention on Preventing and Combating Corruption, 43 ILM 5, done July 11, 2003, entered into force Aug. 5, 2006.

179 Inter-American Convention against Corruption, OAS Treaties Register B-58, 35 ILM 724, done Mar. 29, 1996, entered into force Mar. 6, 1997.

180 OECD [Organisation for Economic Co-operation and Development] Convention on Combating Bribery of Foreign Public Officials in International Business Transactions, 37 ILM 1, done Dec. 17, 1997, entered into force Feb. 15, 1999 [OECD Convention on Combating Bribery of Foreign Officials].

181 Criminal Law Convention on Corruption, 2216 UNTS 225, ETS No. 173, done Jan. 27, 1999, entered into force July 1, 2002.

182 Civil Law Convention on Corruption, 2246 UNTS 3, ETS No. 174, done Nov. 4, 1999, entered into force Nov. 1, 2003.

183 Commentary to the ILC Draft Articles on State Responsibility, at Art. 4, para. 13.

context. As noted in Chapter 4, States may not defend themselves against allegations of public sector involvement in migrant smuggling, including exploitation of, or harm to, smuggled migrants, by pointing out that such involvement is contrary to national law and policy. Under the rules of attribution, "conduct carried out by persons cloaked by governmental authority"[184] will be attributed to the State as an act of that State. The task of distinguishing between "official" conduct and "private" conduct will, in the case of migrant smuggling–related corruption, generally be relatively straightforward: corruption by governmental authorities that is enabled by their official position – as it so often is – is necessarily imbued with the color of authority.

The due diligence standard is commonly used to identify the obligations of States in relation to acts by private entities that interfere with established human rights. The relevant principles confirm that failure to meet this standard, in terms of preventing an anticipated human rights abuse by a private entity or responding effectively to such an abuse, will invoke the international responsibility of the State. Due diligence is also the appropriate standard to be applied in considering: (1) whether the State has taken sufficient steps to prevent involvement in smuggling or smuggling-related exploitation/harm by its officials; (2) whether the State has discharged its obligation to identify, investigate, and punish public sector complicity in such conduct; and (3) whether the State has discharged its obligation to remedy violations resulting from such corruption.[185] The discussion on due diligence in Chapter 4 confirmed that deciding whether a State is meeting the due diligence standard with respect to human rights ultimately comes down to an assessment of whether that State is taking its obligations to prevent, respect, protect, and fulfill human rights seriously. In the present context, those obligations include, at a minimum, preventing and responding to public sector involvement in the human rights violations associated with migrant smuggling.

International law, including case law, provides some guidance on the actions that may be required by States to meet the due diligence standard with respect to corruption that leads to or facilitates exploitation of or harm to smuggled

184 *Petrolane Inc. v. Islamic Republic of Iran* (1991) 27 Iran-USCTR 64 (Iran–US Claims Tribunal, Aug. 14, 1991), at 92, cited in International Law Commission (ILC), *Draft Articles on Responsibility of States for Internationally Wrongful Acts with commentaries thereto*, in "Report of the International Law Commission on the Work of Its Fifty-Third Session," UN GAOR, 56th Sess, Supp. No. 10, UN Doc. A/56/10, at 59 (2001), at 102 (Art. 7, para. 7). See also the Commentary on Article 7 (at 99–103).

185 Note that some commentators have argued that the due diligence standard does not have a role to play in determining State responsibility for harm directly caused by the State and its agents; in other words, that the standard should be reserved for assessment of State responsibility for harm that originated in private acts. See further C. Benninger-Budel, "Introduction," in C. Benninger-Budel ed., *Due Diligence and Its Application to Protect Women from Violence* 1 (2008), at 14.

migrants. For example, the national legal framework should provide an appropriate framework for the identification, investigation, and prosecution of offenses involving exploitation of smuggled migrants, including those committed by or with the complicity of public officials. These may include trafficking offenses but could, as discussed in connection with aggravated offenses, conceivably be wider. States should further ensure that the involvement of public officials in migrant smuggling, trafficking, or related offenses is grounds for an aggravated offense, attracting relatively harsher penalties.[186] Procedures should be in place for receiving and effectively investigating complaints involving or implicating public officials. These procedures should aim to ensure accountability, maintain public confidence, and alleviate legitimate concerns. Investigation into corruption that involves the exploitation of smuggled migrants should commence promptly and be conducted with expedience. An investigation must not be a mere formality but must be one that is capable of leading to identification and punishment of culprits. It should also be independent and public. Effective measures should be in place to establish the truth of a victim's allegations or to obtain corroborating evidence. States should cooperate with each other to ensure that there are no safe havens for corrupt officials or their assets.[187] Due diligence also requires attention to the rights of victims of such corruption. All victims of exploitation that involves or implicates public officials, including persons who have been smuggled, should have access to justice, including remedies.[188]

186 See further the discussion of aggravated offenses in Chapter 5, at Section 5.1.4.

187 These procedural requirements are distilled from the instruments cited in Chapter 4, and a body of case law of the European Court of Human Rights, including: *Rantsev v. Cyprus and Russia*, (2010) 51 EHRR 1 (ECHR, Jan, 7, 2010), at para. 233; *Ahmet Özkan and Others v. Turkey*, [2004] ECHR 133 (ECHR, Apr. 6, 2004), at paras. 310–314; *Paul and Audrey Edwards v. United Kingdom*, (2002) 35 EHRR 487 (ECHR, Mar. 14, 2002), at paras. 69–73; *Assenov and Others v. Bulgaria*, (1999) 28 EHHR 652 (ECHR, Oct. 28, 1998), esp. at para. 102; and a series of cases involving actions of the Turkish security forces, including: *Timurtas v. Turkey*, [2000] ECHR 222 (ECHR, June 13, 2000), at paras. 87–90; *Ertak v. Turkey*, [2000] ECHR 193 (ECHR, May 9, 2000), at paras. 134–135; *Çakici v. Turkey*, [1999] ECHR 43 (ECHR, July 8, 1999), at para. 87; *Tanrikulu v. Turkey*, (2000) 30 EHRR 950 (ECHR, July 8, 1999), at paras. 101–111; *Yasa v. Turkey*, (1999) 28 EHRR 408 (ECHR, Sept. 2, 1998), at paras. 102–104; *Ergi v. Turkey*, (2001) 32 EHRR 18 (ECHR, July 28, 1998), at paras. 82–86; *Tekin v. Turkey*, [1998] ECHR 53 (ECHR, June 9, 1998), at paras. 62–69; *Kurt v. Turkey*, [1998] ECHR 44, (May 25, 1998), at paras. 135–142; *Selçuk and Asker v. Turkey*, [1998] ECHR 36 (ECHR, April 24, 1998), at paras. 93–98; *Kaya v. Turkey*, [1998] ECHR 10 (ECHR, Feb. 19, 1998), at paras. 86–92; *Aksoy v. Turkey*, (1997) 23 EHRR 553 (ECHR, Dec. 18, 1996), at paras. 95–100; and *Mentes and Others v. Turkey*, [1997] ECHR 98 (ECHR, Nov. 28, 1997), at paras. 89–92. The elements of an effective investigation have also been confirmed through several cases of the Inter-American Commission/Court of Human Rights including: *Villagrán Morales et al. v. Guatemala (The Street Children Case)*, Inter-Am Ct. of H.R. (ser. C) No. 63, Nov. 19, 1999, esp. at para. 226; *Raquel Martín de Mejía v. Peru*, Case No. 10.970, Report No. 5/96, Inter-AmCHR Doc. OEA/Ser.L/V/II.91 Doc. 7 (Inter-Am Comm. H.R., Mar. 1, 1996), at 157.

188 See the case law cited at note 187. See further the discussion of remedies in Chapter 8, at Section 8.3.2.

7.2. INTERNATIONAL COOPERATION

International law recognizes a general "duty to cooperate" in "the fight against impunity."[189] This duty is reflected in numerous international legal texts, from the Charter of the United Nations[190] to the Organized Crime Convention[191] and Migrant Smuggling Protocol.[192] The focus of the present section is on the substantive content of that duty within the specific context of migrant smuggling. The relevance of international cooperation to this crime type is readily apparent. Migrant smuggling offenses often involve criminals operating across borders: alleged offenders, victims, and evidence can be located in two or more countries, and the same

[189] See International Law Commission, "Fourth Report on the Obligation to Extradite or Prosecute (*aut dedere aut judicare*) by Zdzislaw Galicki, Special Rapporteur," UN Doc. A/CN.4/648, May 31, 2011 [Galicki, "Fourth Report on the Obligation to Extradite or Prosecute"], at paras. 26–40.

[190] Charter of the United Nations, 1 UNTS 16, done June 26, 1945, entered into force Oct. 24, 1945, at Art. 1(3) (listing one of the purposes of the United Nations as being "[t]o achieve international cooperation in solving international problems of an economic, social, cultural, or humanitarian character, and in promoting and encouraging respect for human rights and for fundamental freedoms for all without distinction as to race, sex, language, or religion"). See also the 1970 Declaration on Principles of International Law Concerning Friendly Relations and Cooperation among States in Accordance with the Charter of the United Nations (adopted by General Assembly Resolution 2625 (XXV), UN Doc. A/Res/25/2625, Oct. 24, 1970) at para. 1: "States have the duty to cooperate with one another, irrespective of the differences in their political, economic and social systems, in the various spheres of international relations, in order to maintain international peace and security and to promote international economic stability and progress, the general welfare of nations and international cooperation free from discrimination based on such differences" (both cited in Galicki, "Fourth Report on the Obligation to Extradite or Prosecute," at paras 26–27).

[191] The stated purpose of the Organized Crime Convention, at Article 1, is to "promote cooperation to prevent and combat transnational organized crime more effectively." The most specific cooperation obligations appear in Articles 13 (international cooperation for the purposes of confiscation) and the related Article 14 on disposal of confiscated proceeds of crime or property, Article 16 on extradition, Article 18 on mutual legal assistance, and Articles 26 and 27 on law enforcement cooperation. Various other references to cooperation are referenced in Article 29(2) (planning and implementing research and training programs), Article 30 (the broadly worded obligation to cooperate on "measures conducive to the optimal implementation of this Convention to the extent possible"), and Article 31(7) (prevention). States are also encouraged to cooperate on transfer of sentenced persons (Article 17), joint investigations (Article 19), use of special investigative techniques (Article 20(2)), transfer of criminal proceedings (Article 21), protection of witnesses (Article 24(3)), and the collection, exchange, and analysis of information on the nature of organized crime (Article 28).

[192] The purpose of the Migrant Smuggling Protocol, stated in Article 2, is to "prevent and combat the smuggling of migrants, as well as to promote cooperation among States Parties to that end, while protecting the rights of smuggled migrants." Further specific references to cooperation are included in Article 7 on smuggling of migrants by sea, Article 14(2) on training and technical cooperation, and Article 15(3) on prevention, and cooperation is built into the provision on cooperation at sea in Article 8, and return of smuggled migrants, in Article 18.

fact situation can justify and give rise to criminal investigations and prosecutions in multiple jurisdictions.[193] Informal cooperation mechanisms as well as more traditional legal tools are important means of eliminating safe havens for smugglers and thereby enabling States to meet their obligations with respect to criminalization, investigation, and prosecution of smuggling cases as well as cases involving the exploitation, mistreatment, or abuse of smuggled migrants. Cooperation also works to counter the displacement effects of one-sided operations against migrant smuggling.[194] The importance of cooperation between States in this area has been repeatedly emphasized.[195]

The nature and scope of States' obligations to cooperate in the investigation and prosecution of smugglers and their accomplices is considered in the following subsections in the context of the three most important vehicles for such cooperation: (1) extradition, (2) mutual legal assistance, and (3) informal cooperation. The chapter concludes with a brief consideration of several other issues that touch on international legal cooperation: joint investigations/operations, transfer of proceedings, and transfer of sentenced persons.

[193] An example is provided by a 2003 migrant smuggling incident in which the smuggling vessel sank at an unknown location between Indonesia and Australia, with the loss of 353 lives. The suspected organizer of the vessel, an Egyptian national residing in Indonesia, was located and arrested by Indonesian police shortly after the sinking. At that time, Indonesia did not have laws criminalizing migrant smuggling so was only able to detain the suspect in relation to visa irregularities. Australia sought to extradite the suspect to Australia but the extradition request failed because of a lack of dual criminality. Ultimately, the suspect was deported back to Egypt where he was charged and prosecuted for homicide through negligence and immigration offenses. See Migrant Smuggling Working Group, University of Queensland, *Migrant Smugglers: Profiles and Prosecutions* (2010), available at www.law.uq.edu.au/index.html?page=184144#Quassey (accessed May 12, 2013); M. Shaw and J. Dent, "People Smuggler Gets Seven Years," *The Age*, Dec. 29, 2003, available at www.theage.com.au/articles/2003/12/28/1072546412053.html (accessed May 12, 2013). Indonesia has since criminalized migrant smuggling and entered into an extradition agreement with Australia covering migrant smuggling. On that basis several suspects have been extradited from Indonesia to face smuggling charges in Australia, resulting in prosecutions and convictions. See Commonwealth Director of Public Prosecutions, "Annual Report 2009–2010," Sept. 30, 2011, at 60; A. Schloenhardt and L. Ezzy, "Hadi Ahmadi and the Myth of the 'People Smugglers' Business Model," (2012) 38(3) *Monash University Law Review* 1, at 7. Another illustrative example is provided by Koser: smuggled migrants who paid the smuggling fees to a jeweler in Pakistan, before transfer by plane to the United Kingdom, with smuggling fees only paid to the smuggler after the migrants arrived at their destination. K. Koser, "Why Migrant Smuggling Pays," (2008) 46(2) *International Migration* 3, at 3.

[194] Conference of the Parties to the United Nations Convention against Transnational Organized Crime, "Good Practices in Informal Cross-Border Cooperation and Information-Sharing: Background paper by the Secretariat," UN Doc. CTOC/COP/WG.7/2013/4, September 4, 2013.

[195] See ibid. at para. 13 (recalling a 2012 recommendation by the Working Group that "States should use, to the fullest extent possible, formal and informal forms of cooperation and coordination to combat the smuggling of migrants at the international, regional and national levels").

7.2.1. *Obligations Related to Extradition*

The term "extradition" refers to one of the oldest of all forms of international legal cooperation in criminal matters: a process whereby one State (the Requesting State) asks another State (the Requested State) to return an individual to face criminal charges or punishment in the Requesting State. Because of the nature of migrant smuggling, suspects wanted for prosecution in one State will often be in another State. This may be because they are nationals of that other State, because they are organizing the migrant smuggling operation from a third (usually transit) State, or because they have deliberately taken steps to avoid prosecution or sentencing by fleeing to another State. Extradition will, therefore, sometimes be essential for the successful prosecution of smuggling cases, including cases involving exploitation of and harm to smuggled migrants.

Traditionally, extradition was based on pacts, courtesy, or goodwill between heads of States. Today, the legal basis for extradition at the national level is generally domestic law and/or bilateral or multilateral treaties. Extradition based on domestic law is increasingly common, providing for extradition with countries in the absence of specific treaty-based agreements. Some States today use domestic law exclusively as their basis for extradition. Others have adopted a blended system in which extradition is permitted on a treaty basis and also on the basis of domestic law. With the emergence of international courts and tribunals exercising criminal jurisdiction, treaties also provide for extradition to these non-State bodies.[196] In the past, extradition laws and treaties would usually contain a list of offenses covered. More recent treaties and national laws are based on the principle of *dual criminality*, which allows extradition in relation to an offense if it is criminalized in both the requested and the requesting countries and the penalties provided for are above a defined threshold, for example, a defined period of imprisonment. The principle of dual criminality provides an additional, compelling reason for States to criminalize migrant smuggling as it has been defined by international law.[197]

7.2.1.1. Making Smuggling an Extraditable Offense

Key international treaties oblige States to ensure that migrant smuggling constitutes an extraditable offense under national law and relevant bilateral and regional extradition treaties.[198] Although the Migrant Smuggling Protocol does not deal with

[196] See further C. Nicholls, C. Montgomery, and J. Knowles, *The Law of Extradition and Mutual Assistance: Practice and Procedure* (2007).

[197] See further the discussion of the obligation of criminalization at Chapter 7, Section 7.1, and Chapter 5.

[198] The most specific obligations are found in Article 16 of the Organized Crime Convention, and Council Framework Decision of 13 June 2002 on the European arrest warrant and the surrender

extradition, its parent instrument, the Organized Crime Convention, sets out a basic minimum standard. The Convention provides a legal basis for extradition with regard to Convention and Protocol offenses in three ways. First, each of the offenses to which the Convention applies, including migrant smuggling, is deemed to be included as an extraditable offense in any extradition treaty already existing between States Parties. States Parties are also obliged to include such offenses as extraditable offenses in every future extradition treaty.[199] This provision has the effect of amending, as a matter of public international law, prior bilateral and multilateral extradition arrangements between States Parties to include, within their scope, offenses established in accordance with the Convention.[200] Second, if a State Party requires a treaty as a precondition to extradition, it may consider the Convention as the requisite treaty.[201] Third, if a State Party does *not* require a treaty as a precondition to extradition, it is obliged to consider the offenses in the Convention as extraditable offenses.[202]

The Organized Crime Convention provides that extradition shall be subject to the conditions provided for by the domestic law of the Requested State Party or by applicable extradition treaties, including, for example, grounds of refusal and minimum penalty requirements.[203] States Parties are obliged, subject to their domestic laws, to endeavor to expedite extradition proceedings and to simplify evidentiary requirements in respect of all Convention offenses.[204] While establishing the primacy of national law, the Convention nonetheless sets out a small number of minimum requirements that States Parties must implement as part of their extradition arrangements, including processes that should be followed when extradition of nationals is sought, limitations on the permitted grounds of refusal,[205] and human rights protections for persons who are the subject of an extradition request. These issues are all considered separately and in detail later on in the chapter. In situations where a State Party is considering refusing extradition on any ground, it should (where appropriate) consult with the Requesting State Party to provide it with ample

procedures between Member States (2002/584/JHA), OJ L 190/1, July 18, 2002 [Council Framework Decision of 2002 on the European Arrest Warrant], at Art. 2(2).

199 Organized Crime Convention, at Art. 16(3).

200 Association of Southeast Asian Nations, *ASEAN Handbook on International Legal Cooperation in Trafficking in Persons Cases* (2010), at 113; and McClean, *Transnational Organized Crime*, at 179.

201 Organized Crime Convention, at Art. 16(4). States Parties for which a treaty basis is a prerequisite for extradition are required to notify the United Nations as to whether they will permit the Organized Crime Convention to be used as a treaty basis for extradition: ibid. at Art. 16(5).

202 Ibid. at Art. 16(6).

203 Ibid. at Art. 16(7).

204 Ibid. at Art. 16(8).

205 For example, the Convention provides that extradition cannot be refused on the sole ground that the offense is also considered to involve fiscal matters (Article 16(15)). States Parties are, therefore,

opportunity to present its opinions and provide information relevant to its allegations.[206] This provision reflects the strong cooperation theme of the Convention. It recognizes that the Requesting State may well have information available to it that may result in a different outcome. Note that the obligation of prior consultation is not absolute, and the Requested State retains a measure of discretion in this regard.[207] However, there is a clear expectation of cooperation and consideration of the need to bring offenders to justice, including through extradition.[208]

The Organized Crime Convention encourages States to adopt a range of measures designed to streamline the extradition process by expediting requests and simplifying evidentiary procedures.[209] These provisions reflect an understanding that extradition is generally a very complicated and time-consuming process that is subject to numerous obstacles and restrictions. Unless States make a positive effort to streamline their extradition procedures in cases of migrant smuggling, it is unlikely that this tool of international legal cooperation will contribute greatly to ending impunity for smugglers who move across borders to escape prosecution or punishment for their crimes.

In the European context, migrant smuggling will likely fall within the categories of extraditable offenses covered by the European Convention on Extradition, provided that, under the laws of the Requesting Party and of the Requested Party, the crime is punishable by deprivation of liberty or under a detention order for a maximum period of at least one year or by a more severe penalty.[210] This is the case for similar umbrella extradition treaties referred to previously.[211] Within the European Union itself the European Arrest Warrant has generally replaced the

required to ensure that no such ground for refusal may be invoked under their extradition laws or treaties. *Legislative Guide*, at 204 (para. 434).

206 Organized Crime Convention, at Art. 16(16).

207 *Legislative Guide*, at 204 (para. 436).

208 Ibid., citing the Convention's Interpretative Notes (UN Doc. A/55/383/Add.1, at para. 35) on this point.

209 Organized Crime Convention, at Art. 16(8).

210 European Convention on Extradition, 359 UNTS 273, ETS No. 24, done Dec. 13, 1957, entered into force Apr. 18, 1960 [European Convention on Extradition], at Art. 2(1). Note the Council of Europe Convention Relating to the Simplified Extradition Procedure between Member States of the European Union, adopted March 10, 1995, to supplement the European Convention on Extradition (Convention drawn up on the basis of Article K.3 of the Treaty on European Union, on simplified extradition procedure between the Member States of the European Union, OJ C 78/1, Mar. 30, 1995). See also Council Framework Decision of 2002 on the European Arrest Warrant, at Art. 2(1).

211 For example, the Inter-American Convention on Extradition, 1752 UNTS 190, done Feb. 25, 1981, entered into force Mar. 28, 1992 [Inter-American Convention on Extradition], at Article 3, provides that an offense is extraditable provided the offense is punishable at the time of its commission, by reason of the acts that constitute it, disregarding extenuating circumstances and the denomination of the offense, by a penalty of not less than two years of deprivation of liberty under the laws of both the Requesting State and the Requested State.

extradition system by requiring the national judicial authorities in each Member State to recognize, with a minimum of formalities, requests for the surrender of a person made by the judicial authority of another Member State.[212] Such arrangements may also occur at the bilateral level through domestic legislation in both countries permitting the mutual recognition and execution of arrest warrants made in the other country.[213] In the European context, a Member State that does not extradite its nationals has an obligation to establish jurisdiction over facilitation of unauthorized entry or residence when committed by its own nationals outside of its territory.[214]

7.2.1.2. Sovereignty, Fair Treatment, and Human Rights in Extradition

As discussed in Chapter 5, an effective criminal justice response to migrant smuggling requires that the human rights of suspects and offenders are respected and protected.[215] This requirement extends to the extradition process. Chapter 5 also noted that the politicized nature of migrant smuggling, including the link made by many States between smuggling and national security, presents serious risks for suspects and their rights, and the process of extradition can be particularly fraught in this regard. The importance of fair treatment and human rights in extradition is confirmed by the Organized Crime Convention[216] as well as

[212] See Council Framework Decision of 2002 on the European Arrest Warrant. Facilitation of unauthorized entry and residence is one of the categories of crimes for which surrender procedures are possible pursuant to the European Arrest Warrant (Article 2(2)). The Framework Decision covers a number of other relevant categories including trafficking in persons, money laundering, corruption, participation in a criminal organization, and forgery of administrative documents. For a detailed consideration of the operation of the European Arrest Warrant, see F. Impala, "The European Arrest Warrant in the Italian Legal System: Between Mutual Recognition and Mutual Fear within the European Area of Freedom, Security and Justice," (2005) 1(1) *Ultrecht Law Review* 56. Note that a series of reports by the European Commission on the operation of the European Arrest Warrant system have confirmed significant improvements in efficiency but also flagged serious flaws including non-respect of procedural rights of suspected and accused persons, poor detention conditions, alleged overuse of warrants by some Member States, and failure to apply proportionality. See European Parliament, Committee on Civil Liberties, Justice and Home Affairs, *Draft Report with Recommendations to the Commission on the Review of the European Arrest Warrant*, 2013/2109(INL), Nov. 19, 2013.

[213] See, for example, *Extradition Act* (Cap 103) 1968 (Singapore), Part V; *Extradition Act* 1992 (Malaysia), Part V.

[214] Council Framework Decision of 28 November 2002 on the strengthening of the penal framework to prevent the facilitation of unauthorised entry, transit and residence (2002/946/JHA), OJ L 328/1, Dec. 5, 2002, at Art. 5.

[215] See Chapter 5, at Section 5.3.

[216] The Organized Crime Convention, at Article 16(13), provides that "[a]ny person [involved in an extradition request or process] ... shall be guaranteed fair treatment at all stages of the proceedings, including enjoyment of all the rights and guarantees provided by the domestic law of the State Party in the territory of which that person is present." Article 16(14) provides that an obligation to extradite will not

by regional extradition treaties[217] and international and regional human rights bodies.[218]

A number of principles and rules have been developed to guard against unfair treatment in extradition – as well as to protect State sovereignty.[219] For example, extradition laws and regimes including those that govern migrant smuggling require that the conduct constituting the extradition offense be recognized as a criminal offense in both the Requesting and the Requested State. This is often referred to as the principle of *dual criminality*.[220] The requirement of dual criminality in relation to migrant smuggling offenses can be satisfied by States ratifying the Organized Crime Convention and Migrant Smuggling Protocol, which stipulate and define the relevant offenses, and ensuring that domestic legislation incorporates the offenses and definitions under those treaties.[221] A Requested State may also deny cooperation if the person sought has already been tried and acquitted or punished for the conduct underlying the extradition request. This derives from the principle

exist under the Convention: "if the requested State Party has substantial grounds for believing that the request has been made for the purpose of prosecuting or punishing a person on account of that person's race, sex, religion, nationality, ethnic origin or political opinions or that compliance with the request would cause prejudice to that person's position for any of these reasons."

217 For example, the Inter-American Convention on Extradition, at Article 16(1), provides that "[t]he person sought shall enjoy in the requested State all the legal rights and guarantees granted by the laws of that State." See also the Economic Community of West African States Convention on Extradition, ECOWAS Convention A/P.1/8/94, done Aug. 6, 1994 (not yet in force) [ECOWAS Convention on Extradition], at Arts. 5, 14.

218 The European Court of Human Rights has developed a strong line of jurisprudence on this issue. The landmark judgment, in 1989, confirmed that a State's responsibility could potentially be engaged if it decided to extradite a person where there were substantial grounds for believing that the person risked being subject to ill-treatment in the Requesting State. *Soering v. United Kingdom*, (1989) 11 EHRR 439 (ECHR, July 7, 1989). For a useful summary of relevant case law see European Court of Human Rights, *Expulsions and Extraditions* (2013), available at www.echr.coe.int/NR/rdonlyres/211A6F9C-A4EC-4CF7-AB2E-42E9D49FB2EF/0/FS_Expulsions_Extraditions_ENG.pdf (accessed May 12, 2013).

219 In addition to the cited sources, the points in this paragraph draw on the UN General Assembly Model Treaty on Extradition, annexed to UN General Assembly, "Model Treaty on Extradition," UN Doc. A/RES/45/116, Dec. 14, 1990, subsequently amended by UN General Assembly, "International Cooperation in Criminal Matters," UN Doc. A/RES/52/88, Dec. 12, 1997. See also J. Dugard and C. Van den Wyngaert, "Reconciling Extradition with Human Rights" (1998) 92 *American Journal of International Law* 187.

220 See Organized Crime Convention, at Art. 16(1); European Convention on Extradition, at Art. 2 and Additional Protocol to European Convention on Extradition, ETS No. 86, done Oct. 15, 1975, entered into force Aug. 20, 1979, at Art. 2; Inter-American Convention on Extradition, at Art. 3; and ECOWAS Convention on Extradition, at Art. 3.

221 The dual criminality requirement will be automatically satisfied with respect to offenses established under Articles 6, 8, and 23 of the Organized Crime Convention (money laundering, corruption, obstruction of justice) but not necessarily in relation to offenses established under Article 5 (criminalization of participation in an organized criminal group), or "serious crime" where States Parties are not required to criminalize exactly the same conduct. *Legislative Guide*, at 200 (para. 417).

of *double jeopardy* (*ne bis in idem*) in international human rights law. Although this principle is generally restricted to double prosecution within the same jurisdiction, it has been widened to include so-called international double jeopardy under several major extradition treaties.[222] Further, under the rule of *speciality* (or specialty), a Requesting State must not, without the consent of the Requested State, try or punish the suspect for an offense not referred to in the extradition request and alleged to have been committed before the person was extradited.[223] Speciality supports the rule of double jeopardy and prevents abuse of the extradition process by States that might otherwise secure the extradition of a person for one offense and then prosecute him or her for another.

The international obligation of cooperation in the fight against impunity for serious crimes[224] is subject to serious practical challenges. One of these is the reluctance or refusal of many States to extradite their nationals. The *nationality* exception recognizes a right to decline to extradite a person who is a national of the Requested State. Refusal on these grounds is sometimes provided for in treaties and often in domestic laws. It is also enshrined within the constitutions of some countries. Depending on the relevant legal framework, the application of this principle might be mandatory or discretionary. Under some laws and treaties, if a country refuses to extradite an individual because of nationality, then the Requested State must prosecute the person in its own jurisdiction. This is known as the "extradite or prosecute" principle (*aut dedere aut judicare*). This obligation has a long history in international law, particularly international humanitarian law. It is part of all four Geneva Conventions of 1949 in relation to the commission of "grave breaches" of those Conventions.[225]

[222] See, for example, ICCPR, at Art. 14(7) ("[n]o one shall be liable to be tried or punished again for an offence for which he has already been finally convicted or acquitted in accordance with the law and penal procedure of each country"). Note that in human rights law, double jeopardy has traditionally applied only to double prosecution within the same jurisdiction. See, for example, *A.P. v. Italy*, UNHRC Comm. No. 204/1986, UN Doc. CCPR/C/31/D/204/1986, Nov. 2, 1987, decided Nov. 2, 1987, at para. 7.3: "[t]he [Human Rights] Committee observes that this provision [Art. 14(7) of the ICCPR] prohibits double jeopardy only with regard to an offence adjudicated in a given State." However, under the regime established by the major extradition treaties, an expanded double jeopardy principle can operate to exclude extradition notwithstanding that the prior adjudication occurred in a jurisdiction other than that of the Requesting State: see European Convention on Extradition, at Art. 9; Inter-American Convention on Extradition, at Art. 4(1); ECOWAS Convention on Extradition, at Art. 13. For a thorough discussion of so-called international double jeopardy, see C. Van Den Wyngaert and G. Stessens, "The International *Non Bis in Idem* Principle: Resolving Some of the Unanswered Questions" (1999) 48 *International and Comparative Law Quarterly* 779.

[223] See European Convention on Extradition, at Art. 14; Inter-American Convention on Extradition, at Art. 13; ECOWAS Convention on Extradition, at Art. 20.

[224] For a discussion of this obligation and its substantive content, see Galicki, "Fourth Report on the Obligation to Extradite or Prosecute," at paras. 26–40.

[225] For example, the Fourth Geneva Convention states that "[e]ach High Contracting Party shall be under the obligation to search for persons alleged to have committed or have ordered to be committed, such

The obligation to extradite is an important part of modern international human rights treaty law, specifically included in a range of treaties dealing with matters such as torture[226] and enforced disappearances.[227] It is also part of international criminal law[228] and transnational criminal law,[229] and is recognized in many other areas of international law including drug trafficking, currency offenses, piracy, and offenses against national and archaeological treasures.[230]

Human rights considerations impose other limits on extradition. Under the Organized Crime Convention, States are permitted to refuse an extradition request that is discriminatory in its purpose, or if the person sought for extradition might be persecuted or otherwise prejudiced because of one of the recognized grounds such as race, sex, religion, nationality, ethnic origin, or political opinion.[231] States also have a right to refuse extradition on the basis that the offense for which extradition is sought carries the death penalty, or the person would be subjected to torture, or to cruel, inhuman or degrading treatment or punishment.[232] The Organized Crime Convention further requires that all persons subject to extradition be guaranteed fair treatment in all stages of the proceedings.[233]

The Organized Crime Convention extends the principle of "extradite or prosecute" to a range of offenses falling within its scope, including migrant smuggling offenses.[234] It is possible that the obligation would apply independently of the

grave breaches, and shall bring such persons, regardless of their nationality, before its own courts. It may also, if it prefers, and in accordance with the provisions of its own legislation, hand such persons over for trial to another High Contracting Party concerned, provided such High Contracting Party has made out a *prima facie* case": Geneva Convention Relative to the Protection of Civilian Persons in Time of War, 75 UNTS 287, done Aug. 12, 1949, entered into force Oct. 21, 1950, at Art. 146.

226 Convention against Torture, at Art. 7(1): "The State Party in the territory under whose jurisdiction a person alleged to have committed any offence referred to in article 4 is found shall in the cases contemplated in article 5, if it does not extradite him, submit the case to its competent authorities for the purpose of prosecution."

227 International Convention for the Protection of All Persons from Enforced Disappearance, UN Doc. A/61/488. C.N.737.2008, done Dec. 20, 2006, entered into force Dec. 23, 2010, at Art. 13.

228 Rome Statute of the International Criminal Court, 2187 UNTS 3, done July 17, 1998, entered into force July 1, 2002, particularly at Part 2, Arts. 5, 8(1), 11, 12, 13, 17, 19, and Part 3, Art. 26.

229 Organized Crime Convention, at Art. 16(10).

230 See generally M. Bassiouni and E. Wise, *Aut Dedere Aut Judicare: The Duty to Extradite or Prosecute in International Law* (1995) [Bassiouni and Wise, *The Duty to Extradite or Prosecute in International Law*] and the list set out in Amnesty International, *Universal Jurisdiction: The Duty of States to Enact and Implement Legislation* (2001), chapter 15, at 18, cited in Galicki, "Fourth Report on the Obligation to Extradite or Prosecute," at paras. 44–51.

231 Organized Crime Convention, at Art. 16(14).

232 ICCPR, at Art. 7; Convention against Torture, at Art. 3.

233 Organized Crime Convention, at Art. 16(13).

234 Ibid. at Arts. 15(3), 16(10). Note that the *aut dedere aut judicare* rule is limited, in this Convention, to cases where the Requested State refuses extradition on the basis that the individual in question is a national of that State.

Convention (i.e., to all States on the basis of its status as a norm of customary international law) in cases where migrant smuggling involves serious violations of fundamental norms, including the right to life.[235] That position is not settled however[236] and it is certainly clear that where the relevant offense does not rise to the level of serious violations of international humanitarian law, war crimes, and crimes against humanity, the obligation is *not* customary and will apply only if imposed by treaties. Looking to the future however, it is not impossible to imagine that the identification of migrant smuggling as an issue of common international concern may eventually provide the foundation for the emergence of a customary obligation to extradite in respect of such offenses.

7.2.2. *Mutual Legal Assistance in Relation to Migrant Smuggling*

Successful investigation and prosecution of smuggling cases may require cooperation between States in securing evidence that is located in a country other than that in which the prosecution is to take place. When such cooperation relates to evidence required to be admissible in court or relates to outcomes that can only be secured through coercive means, it is generally governed by strict "mutual legal assistance" rules set out in international and domestic laws. Common types of mutual legal assistance include: taking evidence or statements from persons, locating and identifying witnesses and suspects, effecting service of judicial documents, executing searches and seizures, freezing assets, providing originals or certified copies of relevant documents and records, identifying or tracing proceeds of crime, facilitating the voluntary appearance of persons in the Requesting State, transfer of proceedings/investigation/prisoners, transfer of prisoners to give evidence, and video recording of testimony.[237]

[235] See Bassiouni and Wise, *The Duty to Extradite or Prosecute in International Law*. See also C. Enache-Brown and A. Fried, "Universal Crime, Jurisdiction and Duty: The Obligation of *Aut Dedere Aut Judicare* in International Law" (1998) 43 *McGill Law Journal* 613.

[236] For a considered overview of the debates, including insights into recent *opinio juris* see Galicki, "Fourth Report on the Obligation to Extradite or Prosecute," at paras. 74–91. As noted by Scharf, scholars asserting the customary law status of the obligation vis-à-vis crimes against humanity must contend with significant contrary State practice. They thereby, rather predictably, fall back "on resolutions by the United Nations General Assembly, hortative declarations of international conferences, and reports of the United Nations Secretary General, as evidence of an emerging rule requiring prosecution of those who commit crimes against humanity." M. P. Scharf, "*Aut Dedere Aut Judicare*," in R. Wolfrum ed., *The Max Planck Encyclopedia of Public International Law* (2008), at paras. 6 and 7, cited in Galicki, "Fourth Report on the Obligation to Extradite or Prosecute," at para. 74. On the dangers of overreliance on soft law sources to establish a customary norm, see the discussion in Chapter 1, at Section 1.4.3.

[237] See, for example, Organized Crime Convention, at Art. 18(3).

Mutual legal assistance regimes are often established through bilateral or multilateral treaties. Such regimes may cover a single issue such as terrorism, money laundering, or organized crime. Treaties can also be concluded for the purpose of providing a general framework of rules within which mutual legal assistance matters are dealt with between two or more countries. The Inter-American Convention on Mutual Legal Assistance in Criminal Matters[238] and the Treaty on Mutual Legal Assistance in Criminal Matters between Like-Minded ASEAN Member Countries[239] are examples of this latter approach.[240] Mutual legal assistance treaties generally indicate the kinds of assistance to be provided; the rights of the requesting and requested States; the rights of alleged offenders; and the procedures to be followed in making, receiving, and executing requests. States can also deal with mutual legal assistance matters through their domestic law. Many countries have passed legislation enabling them to provide various forms of assistance to other States without the need for treaty relations. The legislation usually prescribes the preconditions and the procedure for making, transmitting, and executing incoming and outgoing requests. Some laws designate the foreign States to which they will provide assistance, and some provide that assistance will be extended on a case-by-case basis.

7.2.2.1. An Obligation to Provide Mutual Legal Assistance in Smuggling Cases

The importance of mutual legal assistance in migrant smuggling cases is emphasized in international and regional policy documents and guidance materials.[241] The Organized Crime Convention, as the parent instrument to the Migrant Smuggling Protocol, obliges States Parties to afford one another the widest measure of such assistance in investigations, prosecutions, and judicial proceedings in relation to

[238] Inter-American Convention on Mutual Legal Assistance in Criminal Matters, OATS 75, done May 23, 1992, entered into force Apr. 14, 1996.

[239] Treaty on Mutual Legal Assistance in Criminal Matters between Like-Minded ASEAN Member Countries, done Nov. 29, 2004, entered into force June 1, 2005.

[240] Another example is the European Convention on Mutual Assistance in Criminal Matters, 472 UNTS 185, ETS No. 30, done Apr. 20, 1959, entered into force June 12, 1962 [European Convention on Mutual Assistance], at Article 1(1), in which the Parties undertake to afford each other, in accordance with the provisions of this Convention, the widest measure of mutual assistance in proceedings in respect of offenses the punishment of which, at the time of the request for assistance, falls within the jurisdiction of the judicial authorities of the Requesting Party. All European States are required to have criminalized facilitating unauthorized entry and residence: Council Directive 2002/90/EC of 28 November 2002 defining the facilitation of unauthorised entry, transit and residence, OJ L 328/17, Dec. 5, 2002 [Council Directive 2002/90/EC].

[241] For example, UNODC, *Toolkit to Combat Smuggling of Migrants*, Tool 6: International Criminal Justice Cooperation, at 25.

offenses covered by that instrument.[242] These provisions would therefore apply where the offenses in question involve an organized criminal group and there are reasonable grounds to suspect that victims, witnesses, proceeds, instrumentalities, or evidence of such offenses are located in the Requested State Party.[243]

The Convention sets out a detailed legal and procedural framework for mutual legal assistance between States Parties.[244] This framework is intended to complement rather than replace any mutual legal assistance regimes that already exist by virtue of any other treaty, whether bilateral or multilateral.[245] Where States Parties do not already have such a bilateral or other regime in place, the relevant paragraphs of Article 18[246] operate, in effect, as a mini-treaty. These rules address issues such as the content and form of mutual legal assistance requests, and grounds of refusal such as dual criminality.[247] Where another treaty is already in force between the States Parties concerned, then the rules of that treaty will apply instead (unless the parties specifically agree to apply the relevant provisions of the Convention).[248] Under the Convention, States Parties are strongly encouraged (but are not obliged) to apply any of the terms of the relevant articles if they facilitate cooperation to a greater extent than the terms of a mutual legal assistance treaty in force between them.[249]

The Convention also gives rise to certain obligations with regard to mutual legal assistance that apply generally. In particular, this includes the obligation on States Parties to the Convention not to decline a request for mutual legal assistance under

[242] Organized Crime Convention, at Art. 18. As noted previously, this would include all of the Convention offenses (participating in an organized criminal group, laundering proceeds of crime, corruption, obstruction of justice, "serious crime") and, where a State has ratified or acceded to the Migrant Smuggling Protocol, the offenses of migrant smuggling.

[243] Ibid. at Art. 18(1) requires the provision of mutual legal assistance where the Requesting State Party has reasonable grounds to suspect that the offense is transnational in nature and that the offense involves an organized criminal group. The *Legislative Guide* notes that the mere fact that victims, witnesses, proceeds, instrumentalities, or evidence of such offenses are located in the Requested State Party constitutes a reasonable ground to suspect that the offense is transnational. *Legislative Guide*, at 221 (para. 469).

[244] Organized Crime Convention, at Art. 18.

[245] Article 18(6) of the Organized Crime Convention provides that "[t]he provisions of this article shall not affect the obligations under any other treaty, bilateral or multilateral, that governs or will govern, in whole or in part, mutual legal assistance."

[246] Organized Crime Convention, at Art. 18(9)–(29).

[247] Article 18(9) of the Organized Crime Convention provides that States Parties that are using the mutual legal assistance provisions of that instrument (through choice or through the absence of an alternative legal basis) may decline to render mutual legal assistance on the ground of absence of dual criminality. However, the Convention also provides that the Requested State Party may, if it deems appropriate, provide assistance to the extent it decides at its discretion, even if dual criminality is not satisfied.

[248] *Legislative Guide*, at 223–224 (para. 478).

[249] Organized Crime Convention, at Art. 18(7).

the Convention on the ground of bank secrecy.[250] The mutual assistance obligations require States to provide assistance "to the fullest extent possible" under relevant laws, treaties, and other arrangements, where legal persons, such as companies or other corporate structures, are involved.[251] This may be relevant where, for example, migrant smuggling is undertaken through the cover of a recruitment company or other corporate structure.

Within Europe, migrant smuggling falls within an established mutual legal assistance regime. Under the European Convention on Mutual Assistance in Criminal Matters, the Parties undertake to afford each other, in accordance with the provisions of the Convention, "the widest measure of mutual assistance in proceedings in respect of offences the punishment of which, at the time of the request for assistance, falls within the jurisdiction of the judicial authorities of the requesting Party."[252] As all European States are required to have criminalized facilitating unauthorized entry and residence in accordance with the 2002 Directive on this issue,[253] offenses of unauthorized entry and residence would fall within the jurisdiction of all Member States. The Convention was amended by two additional Protocols, the second of which greatly modernizes the existing system of mutual assistance, and specifies that certain offenses, including "alien smuggling," can justify "cross-border observations," within specified limits.[254]

Most of the exceptions outlined earlier in the chapter in relation to extradition, including the principles of dual criminality, double jeopardy, and speciality, also apply to mutual legal assistance requests. Human rights guarantees apply as much to mutual legal assistance as they do to extradition. In this regard it should be noted that although the Organized Crime Convention is silent on the relevance of human rights standards to mutual legal assistance, there is very little doubt that human rights standards are directly applicable, not least through the savings clause contained in the Migrant Smuggling Protocol itself.[255] States must ensure that nothing in the terms of a mutual legal assistance request would constitute an actual or potential infringement of the human rights of the subject of the request or of any third parties. Particularly in relation to coercive measures, it is important to ensure that these are reasonable and necessary, taking into account the evidence sought and the

[250] Ibid. at Art. 18(8). There is an identical provision in the Convention against Corruption (Article 46) and the OECD Convention on Combating Bribery of Foreign Public Officials (Article 9).

[251] Organized Crime Convention, at Art. 18(2).

[252] European Convention on Mutual Assistance, at Art. 1(1), and Second Additional Protocol to the European Convention on Mutual Assistance in Criminal Matters, ETS No. 182, done Nov. 8, 2001, entered into force Feb. 1, 2004 [Second Additional Protocol to the European Convention on Mutual Assistance], at Art. 1(1).

[253] Council Directive 2002/90/EC.

[254] Second Additional Protocol to the European Convention on Mutual Assistance, at Art. 17.

[255] Migrant Smuggling Protocol, at Art. 19.

seriousness of the offense under investigation. Cooperation may be refused when Requesting States do not respect basic rights and procedural guarantees as set out in major human rights instruments.

7.2.2.2. Asset Recovery: Obligations to Seize, Confiscate, and Cooperate

Migrant smuggling is typically a highly lucrative crime.[256] Criminals involved in organizing and financing migrant smuggling will often distance themselves from direct involvement in the smuggling activity. This makes it difficult for investigators to gather sufficient evidence against them to secure convictions. Given the large financial interests involved and the resulting problems experienced in securing convictions against all but the lowest category of offender, it is not unsurprising that States have taken steps to ensure that smuggling does not reward its financers, organizers, and beneficiaries. A focus on confiscation of the proceeds made from migrant smuggling, and the instrumentalities used in criminal conduct, is widely considered to be vital to undermining the profit motive that drives so much of the business of migrant smuggling: to redressing the perception that "crime pays."[257]

Asset recovery for any crime is usually a three-step process: (1) investigative measures to trace the assets in question; (2) preventative measures (freezing, seizing) to immobilize the assets identified as related to the crime in question; and (3) confiscation, return, and disposal.[258] In the context of migrant smuggling it can be confidently asserted that effective asset recovery renders such an activity less lucrative and increases the risks, thereby acting as an important means of preventing future smuggling. In the context of identifying obligations, it is also relevant to note the links between asset recovery and prosecution. A strong confiscation and recovery regime can operate to support the criminal conviction of smugglers by providing evidence to substantiate and/or corroborate a case, for example by demonstrating to the court that the income of a private or legal person far exceeds that which can be explained by legitimate sources. It should be noted that asset recovery will be particularly important in smuggling that involves exploitation and abuse as such practices are inevitably tied to increasing the profits attached to the smuggling.

[256] See, for example, S. Webb and J. Burrows, "Organised Immigration Crime: A Post-Conviction Study" (Home Office, Research Report 15, July 2009), at 32. See also K. Koser, "Why Migrant Smuggling Pays" (2008) 46(2) *International Migration* 3.

[257] *Legislative Guide*, at 140 (para. 287).

[258] The term "freezing" (or "seizure") in the context of asset recovery is defined by the Organized Crime Convention as "temporarily prohibiting the transfer, conversion, disposition, or movement of property or temporarily assuming custody or control of property on the basis of an order issued by a court or other competent authority": at Art. 2(f). The term "confiscation" is defined in the same instrument as "the permanent deprivation of property by order of a court or other competent authority": ibid. at Art. 2(g).

Criminals involved in smuggling may organize their affairs so that the proceeds derived from the relevant crimes are located in a State other than the one in which they live or in which the crimes take place. The goal of ensuring that there are no safe havens for smugglers must be applied in respect of the assets accrued through the smuggling as well as through any related exploitation. International cooperation mechanisms that enable countries to give effect to foreign freezing and confiscation orders and that allow countries to work together in recovering criminal assets are a crucial part of effective asset recovery.

The legal basis of a national confiscation and recovery regime can be domestic law, bilateral or multilateral treaties, or, most commonly, a combination of the above. States generally develop their own national laws that specify a range of matters, such as: which "proceeds" can be a target of confiscation, criminal and civil evidentiary standards, institutions and tools and orders for obtaining financial information, and procedures for recovery of proceeds. In relation to cooperation with other countries, recovery of proceeds is a form of mutual legal assistance. States will, therefore, rely on provisions of their national mutual legal assistance laws as well as any treaties that may exist between them and the cooperating State. Domestic money laundering laws and extradition treaties may also contain provisions on international cooperation in the recovery of the proceeds of crime. Provision for the most appropriate use of confiscated assets is another important aspect. Some treaties specify how confiscated funds and property are to be used. Often, States have a wide discretion in this matter and regulate the disposal of confiscated proceeds or property through a combination of domestic law and administrative procedures.

The existence of an obligation on States to seize and confiscate assets of migrant smuggling is supported by relevant treaty law. The Organized Crime Convention sets out detailed rules and procedures for identification, tracing, freezing, and seizure of assets and confiscation of proceeds of designated crimes, including smuggling.[259] The term "proceeds of crime" refers to "any property derived from or obtained, directly or indirectly, through the commission of an offense."[260] Article 12 on confiscation and seizure also refers to "instrumentalities" of crime, a term not defined in the Convention but understood to refer to property used in the commission of an offense.[261] In the migrant smuggling context, assets and proceeds could

[259] Organized Crime Convention, at Arts. 12–14.

[260] Ibid. at Art. 2(e).

[261] See, for example, United Nations Office on Drugs and Crime and the International Monetary Fund, *Model Legislation on Money Laundering and Financing of Terrorism* (2005), at Art.1.3.Q, which provides that: "'Instrumentalities' shall mean any property used or intended to be used in any manner, wholly or in part, to commit one or more offenses." Article 22(4) of the Model Law on Mutual Legal Assistance in Criminal Matters defines "instrumentalities of crime" as follows: "Instrumentalities of crime mean any property: (a) used in, or in connection with, the commission of an offense or unlawful

include property and monies such as: costs paid by smuggled migrants or their families (including for passports, visas, or transport), vehicles and vessels used to transport smuggled migrants, bribes paid to public officials, profits from the services and exploitation of the smuggled migrants, and any assets connected to such exploitation.

States Parties to the Convention and to the Migrant Smuggling Protocol[262] are required to create adequate powers (relating to both substantive and procedural law) to enable and support confiscation and seizure.[263] The Convention also sets forth a number of mechanisms to enhance international cooperation with respect to confiscation, in order to eliminate advantages to criminals presented by national borders and differences in legal systems.[264] States Parties are required to comply with requests for confiscation presented by another State Party[265] in accordance with detailed rules.[266] Mutual legal assistance obligations under the Convention set out

activity; or (b) intended to be used in, or in connection with, the commission of an offense or unlawful activity; whether the property is located, or the offense or unlawful activity is committed, within or outside (name of State)": United Nations Office on Drugs and Crime, *Model Law on Mutual Legal Assistance in Criminal Matters* (2007).

262 A State that is party to the Convention and not the Protocol would be required to establish that migrant smuggling is, under its law, a "serious crime" as defined in the Convention, in order for these provisions to apply to trafficking offenses: Organized Crime Convention, at Art. 2(b); *Legislative Guide*, at 145 (para. 302).

263 Organized Crime Convention, at Art. 12. See further *Legislative Guide*, at 145–147. Note however that the UNODC Model Law on Migrant Smuggling contains only the briefest reference to asset recovery – an indication, perhaps, of a broader failure to link the Protocol with its parent Convention.

264 Organized Crime Convention, at Arts. 12–13.

265 Ibid. at Art. 13.

266 Specifically: when a State Party receives a request from another State Party having jurisdiction over an offense covered by the Convention for confiscation of proceeds of crime, property, equipment or other instrumentalities, it must, to the greatest extent possible within its domestic legal system, either submit the request to its competent authorities for the purposes of obtaining an order of confiscation; or submit to its competent authorities an order of confiscation obtained in the Requesting State (that is, seek enforcement of a foreign order) (Article 13(1)). Following such a request, the State Party is obliged to "take measures" to identify, trace and freeze or seize proceeds of crime, property, equipment or other instrumentalities of crime, for the purposes of eventual confiscation (Article 13(2)). The requirement to "take measures" does not necessarily require the enforcement in one State Party of a freezing or restraint order made in another (MacClean, *Transnational Criminal Law: A Commentary*, at 157). This obligation is subject to the general caveat in Article 13(4) of the Convention that a State Party is not obligated to do something not permitted under its domestic law. Requests for confiscation made under the Convention are required to include certain specific information. If a court order is being sought in the Requested State under the relevant provision then it must include: a description of the property to be confiscated, and a statement of the facts relied upon by the Requesting State Party sufficient to enable the Requested State Party to seek that order under its domestic law. If the Requesting State is seeking to enforce one of its orders in the Requested State then the request must include: a legally admissible copy of the order of confiscation and a statement of the facts and information as to the extent to which execution of the order is requested. If the request relates to identifying, tracing, freezing, or seizing proceeds of crime then the request must include: a statement of

earlier in the chapter are to apply to such international cooperation, including content of requests for assistance and grounds of refusal.[267]

7.2.3. *Informal Cooperation and Information Exchange*

Both mutual legal assistance and extradition are highly formalized modes of international cooperation, operating within carefully constrained rules and limitations. In practice however, much cooperation between States on the issue of migrant smuggling is likely to fall under the rubric of "informal cooperation": a term that in the present context is used to refer to a separate, less rule-bound international crime cooperation tool, which is available outside the formal mutual assistance regime. Informal cooperation enables law enforcement and regulatory agencies (such as taxation and revenue authorities or companies and financial service regulators) to directly share information and intelligence with their foreign counterparts without any requirement to make a formal mutual assistance request. In this sense, informal cooperation complements mutual legal assistance regimes. This international cooperation tool can be used prior to an investigation becoming official and prior to the commencement of court proceedings, for example to conduct surveillance or take voluntary witness statements. In circumstances where coercive measures are not required, it is usually faster, cheaper, easier, and more effective to obtain information or intelligence on an informal basis than via formal mutual assistance channels. Nonetheless, it is important to recognize the limits of information cooperation, most particularly the fact that evidence obtained through such cooperation will be inadmissible in some jurisdictions.

The Organized Crime Convention and the Migrant Smuggling Protocol both recognize the value of informal cooperation, most particularly police-to-police cooperation. The Convention lists a range of objectives for such cooperation including early identification of offenses and exchange of information and intelligence.[268] It encourages States Parties to enter into bilateral or multilateral agreements or arrangements with a view to enhancing cooperation between law enforcement agencies.[269] The Migrant Smuggling Protocol emphasizes cooperation through information exchange for purposes such as victim/perpetrator identification in transit, document verification, and proactive intelligence gathering.[270] The importance

the facts relied upon by the Requesting State Party and a description of the actions requested (Article 13(3)).

[267] Organized Crime Convention, at Art. 13(3).

[268] Ibid. at Art. 27(1).

[269] Ibid. at Art. 27(2).

[270] Migrant Smuggling Protocol, at Art. 10(1).

of law enforcement cooperation in the investigation of smuggling-related crimes has been recognized widely outside these two treaties.[271]

Although the relevance of human rights to the extradition process and to formal mutual legal assistance has long been recognized, its importance in respect of informal cooperation is not yet fully appreciated. The strong debates around joint patrols and interception operations reflected throughout this book[272] provide clear evidence that human rights are highly relevant to informal cooperation, and in fact, that the informality of cooperation arrangements may sometimes be aimed at facilitating the avoidance of human rights obligations. It is this informality that perhaps presents the greatest challenge: rules are relatively vague and flexible; political pressures can be brought more easily to bear; information about actual incidents and events can be much more difficult to track and document. A violation that would be easily foreseen and avoided in the context of mutual legal assistance or extradition can occur without oversight and under circumstances that make its impact impossible to reverse. An illustrative example is police-to-police cooperation that leads to the imposition of the death penalty in circumstances where such a situation would provide the basis for rejection of a more formal request for extradition or legal assistance.[273]

7.2.4. *Joint Investigations / Joint Operations*

Joint investigations involve cross-agency operational cooperation on real-time investigations. Such investigations could be envisaged for a case where suspects and evidence are located in more than one State (resulting in prosecutions in more than one country), but they could also be used for a case that is to be tried in a single jurisdiction if, for example, important witnesses or other evidence were located in a second jurisdiction. Joint investigations are a useful tool when more than one State has jurisdiction over the offenses involved or where a potential migrant smuggling

[271] See, for example, Agreement between the Republic of Indonesia and Australia on the Framework for Security Cooperation [2008] ATS 3, done Nov. 13, 2006, entered into force Feb. 7, 2008, at Art. 3; operational agreements between the European Police Office (Europol) and several non-EU States, including Australia, Canada, Switzerland, and the United States, available at www.europol.europa.eu/content/page/external-cooperation-31 (accessed May 12, 2013); a Moroccan-Spanish police agreement concluded in February 2012, aimed substantially at controlling irregular migration across the Strait of Gibraltar: see Frontex, *FRAN Quarterly* (Issue 2, Apr.–June 2012), at 27; UK–France Summit Declaration on Immigration, Nov. 2, 2010, available at www.ukba.homeoffice.gov.uk/sitecontent/documents/aboutus/workingwithus/uk-france-joint-declaration/ (accessed May 12, 2013); and the Integrated Border Enforcement Teams (IBET) scheme between Canada and the United States, details available at www.publicsafety.gc.ca/prg/le/bs/ibet-eng.aspx (accessed May 12, 2013).

[272] See discussion in Chapter 6, at Section 6.2.1.3.

[273] For an examination of this precise scenario see L. Finlay, "Exporting the Death Penalty? Reconciling International Police Cooperation and the Abolition of the Death Penalty in Australia" (2011) 33 *Sydney Law Review* 95, at 95.

situation is expected to have effects in more than one State. Joint investigations can be undertaken on a bilateral basis or can be coordinated through an international or regional police agency such as the International Criminal Police Organization (Interpol) or the European Police Office (Europol)[274] or a regional prosecutorial agency such as Eurojust.[275] Joint initiatives or patrols undertaken by Frontex may also be considered "joint investigations" under certain circumstances.

The Organized Crime Convention encourages (but does not require) States Parties to establish agreements or arrangements to facilitate *joint investigative bodies*. These are understood to differ from joint investigations, in that a joint investigative body is intended to be a more permanent structure, based on bilateral agreements, through which joint investigations might be facilitated.[276] In the absence of such agreements, the Convention recognizes that joint investigations may be undertaken by agreement on a case-by-case basis.[277] In either situation, States Parties are required to ensure that the sovereignty of the State Party in whose territory such investigations take place is respected.[278]

The concept of a joint investigation is not defined in the Convention, but experts have identified two main models of joint investigations, either of which will meet the requirements of the Convention.[279] Under the first model, law enforcement authorities undertake parallel, coordinated investigations with a common goal. In this model, the investigators are not physically colocated but rather undertake coordinated investigations in their respective territories, possibly assisted by a liaison officer. Where evidence needs to be transferred, this will be achieved through a mutual legal assistance request.[280] There is generally no need to establish a legal basis for these joint investigations, as these do not involve law enforcement officials operating outside of their State. The second model is referred to as "integrated" joint investigative teams, involving officers from at least two or more jurisdictions. Under this model, officers from different jurisdictions are generally colocated.

[274] The European Police Office (Europol) is the European police network created to provide a central mechanism for cooperation and communication among EU police agencies and recently upgraded to a formal entity of the European Union: Council Decision of 6 April 2009 establishing the European Police Office (Europol) (2009/371/JHA), OJ L 121/37, May 15, 2009.

[275] Established by Council Decision of 28 February 2002 setting up Eurojust with a view to reinforcing the fight against serious crime (2002/187/JHA), OJ L 63/1, Mar. 6, 2002.

[276] Conference of the Parties to the United Nations Convention against Transnational Organized Crime, "Draft Informal Expert Working Group on Joint Investigations: Conclusions and Recommendations" (document before the Conference at its Fourth Session, held in Vienna from 18 to 17 October 2008), UN Doc. CTOC/COP/2008/CRP.5, Oct. 2 2008, at 13.

[277] Ibid.

[278] Ibid. at 4.

[279] These two models are as described in the "Draft Informal Expert Working Group on Joint Investigations: Conclusions and Recommendations": ibid. at 10–11.

[280] Ibid. at 10.

Some integrated joint investigation teams involve "passive" cooperation, where for example, an officer from one State is integrated into the team of the host State but plays only an advisory role (for example, as a liaison officer or mentor). However, in other cases, the foreign operative plays a more "active" role, and is granted at least some operational powers in the territory of the host State. This latter model will typically require implementing legislation to ensure equivalence of operational powers.[281]

Integrated joint law enforcement investigations are a relatively recent development, and much of the experience in this regard is limited to the European Union.[282] In the EU context, joint investigations were specifically included in the mutual legal assistance regime by the Second Additional Protocol to the Convention on Mutual Legal Assistance.[283] However, given the slow progress on ratification of the Convention itself,[284] the Council adopted a Framework Decision on Joint Investigation Teams.[285] As a general observation however, it appears that in most States there remains a number of legal and practical impediments that limit the establishment and operational effectiveness of integrated joint investigations. For example, such investigations require a strong legal mandate (often absent) that resolves issues such as ensuring the equivalence of powers for foreign law enforcement officers, the issue of operational control and where this should lie, who can undertake evidence gathering, the civil and criminal liabilities of foreign law enforcement officers in the host country, and security and treatment of information received in the course of the investigation.[286] The debates around such matters in the context of Frontex operations[287] provide a useful indication of the range of complexities.

[281] Ibid. at 11.

[282] In 2002, the Council of Europe adopted the Council Framework Decision of 13 June 2002 on joint investigation teams (2002/465/JHA), OJ L 162/1, June 20, 2002. EU Member States have used joint investigation teams in many contexts since that time. For example, in 2011, Europol participated in seventeen joint investigation teams, and was actively involved in and supported several more joint investigative teams without a formal arrangement in place: Europol, *Europol Review: General Report on Europol Activities* (2012), at 42. For an insight into the issues that arise in respect of the operation of such teams, see Council of the European Union, Council Secretariet, "Joint Investigation Teams Manual," Doc. No. 15790/1/11 REV 1, Nov. 4, 2011 [Council of the EU, "Joint Investigation Teams Manual"].

[283] Second Additional Protocol to the European Convention on Mutual Assistance, at Art. 20.

[284] This slow progress and decision to proceed instead with a Framework Decision is noted in Council of the EU, "Joint Investigation Teams Manual," at 4.

[285] Council of Europe adopted the Council Framework Decision of 13 June 2002 on joint investigation teams (2002/465/JHA), OJ L 162/1, June 20, 2002.

[286] Conference of the Parties to the Organized Crime Convention, "Draft Informal Expert Working Group on Joint Investigations Conclusions and Recommendations," UN Doc. CTOC/COP/2008/CRP.5, Oct. 2, 2008, at 11–12.

[287] See consideration of Frontex and its mandate in Chapter 1, at Section 1.3.2.2.

7.2.5. *Transfer of Proceedings and of Sentenced Persons*

As noted previously, the transnational nature of migrant smuggling crimes means that situations will frequently arise where it is possible for more than one State to commence and maintain an investigation and prosecution of the same offense. Under such circumstances, States Parties to the Convention are required to "consider" the possibility of transferring proceedings from one country to another, where such transfer is considered in the interests of the proper administration of justice, in particular in cases where several jurisdictions are involved, with a view to concentrating the prosecution.[288] As a practical matter, the transfer of a migrant smuggling prosecution from one country to another will likely be a complex process requiring, as a first step, consultation between the two concerned States on matters such as sharing and transfer of information and evidence. This is anticipated by the Convention, which provides that where two States are involved in the investigation, prosecution, or judicial proceedings with respect to the same conduct, they shall, as appropriate, consult one another with a view to coordinating actions.[289] If the matter had already reached the courts in one country, it would be necessary to stay or suspend the prosecution, pending resolution, in another country.[290] The issue of double jeopardy may become relevant where transfer of proceedings is being considered.[291]

Situations may also arise in migrant smuggling cases where there are sound practical and policy reasons for transferring sentenced persons. For example, the convicted persons may be considered unsuited to serving their sentence in the prosecuting country because of vulnerabilities relating to age, isolation from family or community, and/or lack of communication skills. They may be subject to harsh or inhuman conditions of detention that cause the country of origin to call for their repatriation.[292] Diplomatic tensions between the country of prosecution and the country of origin may be another reason to consider such transfers.[293] Transfer of sentenced persons can have important practical law enforcement benefits, as the country of return may secure valuable information about the returning national that would not be available should the person simply serve his or her sentence

[288] Organized Crime Convention, at Art. 21.

[289] Ibid. at Art. 15(5).

[290] See further UN General Assembly, "Model Treaty on the Transfer of Proceedings in Criminal Matters," adopted by GA Res. 45/118, UN Doc. A/RES/45/118, Dec. 14, 1990, and amended by GA Res. 53/112 (UN General Assembly, "Mutual assistance and international cooperation in criminal matters," GA Res. 53/112, UN Doc. A/RES/53/112, Jan. 20, 1999).

[291] See further discussion of double jeopardy at note 222 and associated text.

[292] UNODC, *Model Legislative Provisions against Organized Crime*, at 119.

[293] United Nations Office on Drugs and Crime, *Handbook on the International Transfer of Sentenced Persons* (2012) [UNODC, *Handbook on the International Transfer of Sentenced Persons*], at 14.

overseas and then seek to return home.[294] The Organized Crime Convention encourages States Parties to consider entering into agreements and arrangements for the transfer of persons sentenced for offenses covered by the Convention.[295] More specific regimes for transfer of prisoners are in place through regional and bilateral treaties.[296]

Transfer of sentenced persons has a strong basis in international human rights law, which views imprisonment as being directed toward reformation and social rehabilitation.[297] This is echoed in the Organized Crime Convention, which affirms that States Parties are to "endeavour to promote the reintegration into society of persons convicted of offenses covered by this Convention," as part of the broader prevention obligation.[298] An effective transfer regime will generally require a detailed domestic statutory framework that "assigns authority, ensures clarity in relation to the principles behind the transfers and gives legality to the transfer process."[299] International

[294] Ibid. at 13.

[295] Organized Crime Convention, at Art. 17. In the European context, see Convention on the Transfer of Sentenced Persons, ETS No. 112, done Mar. 21, 1983, entered into force July 1, 1985; Council Framework Decision 2008/909/JHA of 27 November 2008 on the application of the principle of mutual recognition to judgments in criminal matters imposing custodial sentences or measures involving deprivation of liberty for the purpose of their enforcement in the European Union, OJ L 327/27, Dec. 5, 2008 [Council Framework Decision 2008/909/JHA]. See also Inter-American Convention on Serving Criminal Sentences Abroad, done June 9, 1993, entered into force Dec. 4, 1996 [Inter-American Convention on Serving Sentences Abroad].

[296] For example, see Council Framework Decision 2008/909/JHA. All European Member States are also States Parties to the Council of Europe Convention on the Transfer of Sentenced Persons (cited at note 295), and some are also party to the Additional Protocol to that Convention of December 18, 1997. However, as noted in the Framework Decision 2008/909/JHA, neither the Convention nor the Protocol establish a basic obligation on States to take charge of sentenced persons for enforcement of a sentence or order. This greatly undermines the usefulness of this regime. With its entry into force, the framework decision replaced the European Convention and the Additional Protocol to the European Convention in respect of transfer decisions among European Union Member States (Article 16(1)). Significantly, however, it does not replace bilateral (or other multilateral) agreements where they can contribute to the smoother transfer of prisoners between European Union Member States (Article 26(2)–(3)). Other regional mechanisms include: the Scheme for the Transfer of Convicted Offenders within the Commonwealth, open to all Commonwealth countries who accept using it as a basis for the transfer of sentenced persons; the Riyadh Arab Agreement for Judicial Cooperation endorsed by the Council of Arab Ministers of Justice in April 1983; and Inter-American Convention on Serving Sentences Abroad. See further UNODC, *Handbook on the International Transfer of Sentenced Persons*, at 19–23.

[297] See, for example, ICCPR, at Art. 10(3). See also United Nations, "Standard Minimum Rules for the Treatment of Prisoners," adopted by the First United Nations Congress on the Prevention of Crime and the Treatment of Offenders, held at Geneva in 1955, and approved by the Economic and Social Council by its resolutions 663 C (XXIV) of 31 July 1957 and 2076 (LXII) of 13 May 1977, Aug. 30, 1955, at paras. 58–60(2), 61, 62, 64–66(1), 80.

[298] Organized Crime Convention, at Art. 31(4). The purpose of social rehabilitation is noted in Article 3(1) of Council Framework Decision 2008/909/JHA.

[299] UNODC, *Handbook on the International Transfer of Sentenced Persons*, at 58.

guidance materials are available on how national laws can meet these requirements in the context of transnational criminal offenses such as migrant smuggling.[300]

7.3. CONCLUSIONS ON OBLIGATIONS OF PREVENTION AND COOPERATION

This analysis has confirmed that States Parties to the Organized Crime Convention and Migrant Smuggling Protocol, as well as Member States of the European Union, have an obligation to work to prevent migrant smuggling, including through building the capacity of national officials and ensuring the integrity of their borders and documentation processes. Critically, these instruments, along with human rights law, also impose on States a clear obligation to take steps to prevent the violence and exploitation that often accompanies the migrant smuggling process, whether that violence or exploitation is at the hands of the State or private parties. The obligation of prevention extends to public sector corruption and complicity that fuels smuggling and smuggling-related harm.

Although the existence of these obligations is beyond dispute, their substantive content is still not clear, largely because of an apparent reluctance to specify required actions in detail. Clarification of what States are actually required to do to prevent migrant smuggling will require further developments in policy and practice. At least in relation to prevention of violence and exploitation against smuggled migrants, developments in international human rights law related to responsibility for private harm, as well as the more detailed legal framework around prevention of trafficking-related harm, provide some assistance in fleshing out the nature and scope of the relevant obligations.

The duty placed on States to cooperate with each other in preventing and responding to migrant smuggling is central to the overall objectives of the international legal framework. That broader duty provides the foundation for a number

300 See, for example, the *Model Legislative Provisions against Organized Crime*, which recommend that, to ensure the efficiency of transfer of sentenced persons in this context, national laws should address: defining all critical terms, identifying and designating a central authority to receive and respond to requests, enumerating the requirements for transfer, ensuring clarity of application and other procedures, outlining the steps and procedures a country will follow in administering the program, processing applications and making transfer decisions, and noting any specific requirements that are unique to the national context (at 120). The Model Legislative Provisions further note that further relevant considerations include: whether the prisoners are entitled to be represented by counsel, and if so, at what stage of the proceeding; whether juveniles and mentally ill persons are eligible for transfer and if so, whether special procedures and protections apply; the transferability of prisoners on parole, probation, or other forms of conditional release; what impact transfer has on the civil, political, or civic rights of returning nationals and the immigration status of transferred prisoners; the identification of limitations on subsequent prosecutions of conduct forming the basis of the transferred offense; and any specific reporting requirements of the sentencing and administering countries (at 120).

of specific obligations relating to formal cooperation (mutual legal assistance and extradition) as well as informal cooperation between concerned national authorities. Although specialist treaties are the source of these obligations it is essential to note that international human rights law establishes clear rules on when and how such cooperation may lawfully occur.

8

Obligations of Protection, Assistance, and Response

Human rights are central to the issue of migrant smuggling: first because they impose important limitations on how States may respond to smuggling, but also because human rights law confers certain legal entitlements on all persons, including smuggled migrants, that States and others are obliged to protect and respect. In relation to particular fundamental rights identified in Chapter 2, the relevant entitlements are owed to all smuggled migrants, without distinction on any grounds, including race, nationality, or immigration status. Other rights may attach to a smuggled migrant by virtue of that person's membership of a group to which separate or additional obligations are owed – for example as a child, a women, a refugee, a victim of trafficking, or indeed a victim of crime or of human rights violations.

It is widely recognized that persons who have been or are being smuggled are vulnerable to ill-treatment, violence, exploitation, and life-threatening situations. For those with existing vulnerabilities, the act of smuggling may operate to enhance those vulnerabilities. Children, for example, especially those who are unaccompanied, face risks of exploitation and abuse, and smuggled migrant women are at particular risk of violence including sexual violence.[1] For all smuggled migrants, the clandestine nature of their journey; the often unscrupulous and corrupt conduct of their facilitators; and the extent to which some States will go to prevent their

[1] Reports of violence against smuggled migrants invariably indicate a strong gender dimension to such violence. See, for example, the citations attached to the Sinai and Mexican case studies in the Introduction (at notes 31 and 35–37 respectively, with accompanying text). There has been very little examination of violence against women in the specific context of smuggling although literature on violence against women in migration provides an indication of the likely scale and severity of the problem. See for example J. Freedman and B. Jamal, *Violence against Migrant and Refugee Women in the Euromed Region* (2008); and Medecins sans Frontieres, *Sexual Violence and Migration: The Hidden Reality of Sub-Saharan Women Trapped in Morocco en Route to Europe* (2010).

Sections of this chapter draw on A. T. Gallagher, *The International Law of Human Trafficking* (2010) [Gallagher, *The International Law of Human Trafficking*] (Chapters 5; 6.2 and 7.2).

departure, transit, stay, or arrival, all operate to create or exacerbate serious risks to personal security and well-being.[2]

Despite this situation, the status of "smuggled migrant" has not been elevated to a legal category to which any special or additional rights are attached. In other words, a State will not necessarily owe different or extra obligations to a person merely because that person is being, or has been, smuggled. The task of establishing the precise nature and scope of State obligations of protection and assistance toward an individual who has been smuggled will always be contextual: requiring not just a consideration of the status of the smuggled migrant but also an examination of the relationship of the State vis-à-vis the person in question. For example, is the smuggled migrant a national? Is he or she located within the territory of the State or otherwise under its control? These latter aspects have been dealt with in considerable detail in previous chapters, most particularly Chapters 2 and 3. The present section should be read in conjunction with the comprehensive discussion of human rights and refugee law, and the extraterritorial application of these regimes, contained in those chapters.

This part commences with a consideration of the deceptively simple question: Do States have a positive obligation to protect and assist smuggled migrants? That question can be answered, at least in part, with reference to the major instruments of transnational criminal law, including the Migrant Smuggling Protocol[3] as well as human rights instruments. However, it also requires consideration of the legal framework around certain situations of harm to which smuggled migrants are particularly vulnerable. For example, what obligations are owed by States to smuggled migrants who are abused or exploited by their smugglers, or to smuggled migrants who suffer from racially motivated violence in the country of transit or destination? What obligations are owed to smuggled migrants whose lives and security are in immediate danger? The chapter then considers status-related obligations of protection and support with a particular focus on ascertaining whether different or additional rights are owed to two groups of smuggled persons: children and victims of trafficking. The final part of the chapter returns to the issue of smuggled migrants who have been subject to violence and exploitation and identifies two additional obligations on States that will arise in such situations: first, an obligation to effectively investigate and prosecute such exploitation and violence to the required standard of "due diligence"; and second, an obligation to provide victims of these human rights violations with access to effective remedies.

2 See case studies in the Introduction for examples.

3 Protocol against the Smuggling of Migrants by Land, Sea and Air, supplementing the United Nations Convention against Transnational Organized Crime, 2241 UNTS 507, done Nov. 15, 2000, entered into force Jan. 28, 2004 [Migrant Smuggling Protocol].

8.1. AN OBLIGATION TO PROTECT AND ASSIST SMUGGLED MIGRANTS?

The question of whether a positive obligation of protection and assistance exists toward smuggled migrants is a complex one. It requires consideration of general rules and instruments of international and regional human rights law as well as of instruments dealing particularly with migrant smuggling and related issues such as irregular migration and border management. In relation to more general rules and instruments, reference should be made to the discussion of relevant human rights law in Chapter 2 as well as the question, addressed in Chapter 3, of when such rules will apply extraterritorially. The following discussion looks particularly at the specialist instruments before considering the main contexts within which the issue of obligations to protect and assist may arise: smuggling-related violence and exploitation, and assistance to smuggled migrants in danger.

8.1.1. *Relevant Provisions of the Specialist Instruments*

A review of the drafting history of the Migrant Smuggling Protocol, surveyed in more depth in Chapter 1, confirms that questions of assistance and protection for smuggled migrants were regularly raised throughout the drafting process, including in initial discussions.[4] However, although some States and regional groupings expressed a view that such matters should receive attention in the Protocol, most did not appear to consider this as a priority issue. The lack of attention to the rights of smuggled migrants in early drafts was picked up by, among others, the UN High Commissioner for Human Rights, who intervened to urge that States explicitly commit to preserving and protecting the fundamental rights to which all persons, including "illegal migrants," are entitled.[5] The High Commissioner noted several problematic aspects of the draft instrument, most particularly that: "Despite the acknowledgement in the preamble to the draft Protocol that 'illegal trafficking and transport of migrants is a particularly heinous form of transnational exploitation of

4 The initial draft of the Smuggling Protocol submitted by Austria and Italy referred to "illegal trafficking and transport of migrants" as "a particularly heinous form of transnational exploitation of individuals in distress" in the Preamble: "Draft elements for an international legal instrument against illegal trafficking and transport of migrants (Proposal submitted by Austria and Italy)," UN Doc. A/AC.254/4/Add.1, Dec. 15, 1998. Other discussions of the need to address the protection of smuggled migrants are noted in the *Travaux Préparatoires* with regard to the Preamble, the statement of purpose, the scope of application, the introduction of the aggravated offences, training, and the development of the specific "protection" article: United Nations Office on Drugs and Crime, Travaux Préparatoires *of the Negotiations for the Elaboration of the United Nations Convention against Transnational Organized Crime and the Protocols Thereto* (2006) [Travaux Préparatoires *for the Organized Crime Convention and Protocols*], at 453, 459, 461, 471–472, 486, 509, 520, 531–532, 537–540.

5 UN General Assembly, Ad Hoc Committee on the Elaboration of a Convention against Transnational Organized Crime, "Informal note by the United Nations High Commissioner for Human Rights," UN Doc. A/AC.254/16, June 1, 1999, at para. 5.

individuals in distress'," the draft Protocol itself contained no protection principle.[6] Her submission argued that a neglect of "victim issues" in the Protocol might compromise the effective implementation of this instrument and recommended that a provision be inserted to the effect that Member States are under an obligation to ensure respect for and protection of the rights of illegal migrants, which are owed to them under applicable international law, including the right to life; the prohibition of torture and cruel, inhumane, or degrading treatment or punishment; and the principle of non-discrimination.[7] Subsequent submissions by an informal grouping of concerned UN agencies led by the High Commissioner's office, and separately, by the UN High Commissioner for Refugees, as well as by a nongovernmental organization coalition, continued to highlight these concerns: advocating most particularly for increased attention to the potential risks to the rights of asylum-seekers posed by the new Protocol.[8]

This lobbying had a direct impact on the direction of the negotiations, particularly in its later stages.[9] The final version of the Migrant Smuggling Protocol includes a number of provisions aimed at protecting the basic rights of smuggled migrants and preventing the worst forms of exploitation that often accompany the smuggling process.[10] The most explicit recognition of the risks to human rights posed by smuggling and the obligation on States to respond to such risks is found in the stated purpose of the Protocol: to prevent and combat smuggling, and promote international cooperation, *while protecting the rights of smuggled migrants*.[11] However, the actual entitlements of smuggled migrants under the Protocol are much more equivocal and carefully circumscribed: a reflection of the fundamental tension that underlies

6 Ibid. at para. 6 (emphases omitted).

7 Ibid.

8 See, for example, "Note by the Office of the United Nations High Commissioner for Human Rights, the Office of the United Nations High Commissioner for Refugees, the United Nations Children's Fund and the International Organization for Migration on the draft protocols concerning migrant smuggling and trafficking in persons," UN Doc. A/AC.254/27, Feb. 8, 2000 (and UN Doc. A.AC.254/27/Corr.1, Feb. 22, 2000, correcting the title of that document); "Informal note by the United Nations High Commissioner for Human Rights," UN Doc. A/AC.254/16, June 1, 1999; and NGO Joint Submissions on the Protocol against the Smuggling of Migrants by Land, Air and Sea and Protocol to Prevent, Suppress and Punish Trafficking in Persons, Especially Women and Children (2000).

9 This impact is reflected in the official drafting history of the Protocol: see Travaux Préparatoires *for the Organized Crime Convention and Protocols*, at 537.

10 Specific references to "protecting" the rights of smuggled migrants are found in the Preamble ("Convinced of the need to provide migrants with humane treatment and full protection of their rights"), Article 2 ("The purpose of this Protocol is to prevent and combat the smuggling of migrants, as well as to promote cooperation among States Parties to that end, while protecting the rights of smuggled migrants"), Article 4 ("This Protocol shall apply... as well as to the protection of the rights of persons who have been the object of such offences"), Article 14(2) ("... Such training shall include... (e) The humane treatment of migrants and the protection of their rights set forth in this Protocol"), and Article 16, titled "Prevention and assistance measures."

11 Migrant Smuggling Protocol, at Art. 2.

its potentially conflicting purposes of addressing smuggling and protecting migrants. As has been explored elsewhere in this book,[12] this equivocation is reflected most starkly in the withholding of "victim" status from smuggled migrants, a status that is readily accorded to those who have been trafficked. The effect of that apparently minor differentiation is profound. Absent elements additional to the fact of having been smuggled (such as evidence of victimization through crimes of violence, abuse, or exploitation), smuggled migrants are not to be considered victims of crime or victims of human rights violations, and are thereby prima facie excluded from the special protections afforded to victims of crime and human rights violations under international law.

The substantive provisions of the Protocol on protection and assistance, although not as strong as those offered to trafficked persons under the Trafficking Protocol, are still significant. Most critically, migrants themselves are not to become liable to criminal prosecution under the Protocol for the fact of having being smuggled[13]: a direct and welcome affirmation that the purpose of the Protocol and its parent instrument, the Organized Crime Convention,[14] is not to punish irregular migration or smuggled migrants – and that they should not be used in that way. However, as discussed in Chapters 1 and 5, this concession does not provide protection to smuggled migrants from prosecution for offenses related to their smuggling. Although States may not use the Protocol to criminalize smuggled migrants, they retain full capacity to prosecute such persons under their national law for any acts that may be criminalized, such as illegal entry, illegal stay, and the possession of fraudulent travel documents.[15]

The main protection and assistance provisions of the Protocol, a version of the "protection principle" recommended by the UN High Commissioner for Human Rights,[16] are set out in Article 16,[17] which, according to the Legislative Guide, is

[12] See Chapter 1, at Section 1.1.3.2.

[13] Migrant Smuggling Protocol, at Art. 5. The noncriminalization of smuggled migrants was raised even in the earliest stages of drafting: the original draft text of the Protocol submitted by Austria and Italy refers to "Establishing a principle of penal sanctions against the perpetrators but not the victims": "Letter dated 16 September, 1997 from the Permanent Representative of Austria to the United Nations addressed to the Secretary-General," UN Doc. A/52/357, Sept. 17, 1997, at para. 3.

[14] United Nations Convention against Transnational Organized Crime, 2225 UNTS 209, done Nov. 15, 2000, entered into force Sept. 29, 2003 [Organized Crime Convention].

[15] United Nations Office on Drugs and Crime, *Legislative Guides for the Implementation of the United Nations Convention against Transnational Organized Crime and the Protocols thereto*, UN Sales No. E.05.V.2 (2004) [*Legislative Guide*], at 340 (para. 27).

[16] UN General Assembly, Ad Hoc Committee on the Elaboration of a Convention against Transnational Organized Crime, "Informal note by the United Nations High Commissioner for Human Rights," UN Doc. A/AC.254/16, June 1, 1999, at para. 6.

[17] See also note 10 above for other references to protection as found in the Preamble, Article 2, Article 4, and Article 14(2) of the Migrant Smuggling Protocol.

"intended to set an appropriate standard of conduct for officials who deal with smuggled migrants and illegal residents and to deter conduct on the part of offenders that involves danger or degradation to the migrants."[18] Article 16 subjects its various obligations to the umbrella requirement that States Parties take into account the special needs of women and children.[19] As discussed at Section 8.2.1 and at various points in Chapters 9 and 10, the existing legal framework around the rights of children provides important guidance on ascertaining "the special needs of children" and determining how those rights can be integrated into all aspects of a smuggled child's experience: from the provision of protection and assistance to questions of detention and return. The situation is less clear in respect of smuggled women migrants, and there is very little useful guidance available on how this particular obligation could be met, or indeed how its implementation could be effectively judged.[20]

The first part of Article 16 deals with the responsibility of States Parties, when implementing the Protocol, to preserve and protect the rights of smuggled migrants under international law. Specific reference is made to a number of preexisting human rights (the right to life and to freedom from torture and other inhuman or degrading treatment or punishment) and their continued applicability to smuggled migrants.[21] The *Travaux Préparatoires* confirm that "[t]he intention in listing certain rights in this paragraph was to emphasize the need to protect those rights in the case of smuggled migrants, but the provision should not be interpreted as excluding or derogating from any other rights not listed."[22] It is important to note that the responsibility of States to preserve and protect the rights of smuggled migrants is an overarching one that applies to all legislative and operational actions taken by States Parties under the Protocol. For example, the right to life and the prohibition on inhumane treatment will be paramount considerations where smuggled migrants are rescued or intercepted and found to be in urgent need of food, water, or emergency medical care, or indeed in need of protection from those who have smuggled them. The obligation to preserve the rights of smuggled migrants when implementing the Protocol is reinforced by a requirement that specialized training

[18] *Legislative Guide*, at 364 (para. 69).

[19] Migrant Smuggling Protocol, at Art. 16(4).

[20] The drafting history of the Protocol does not provide insight and the UNODC *Legislative Guide* is silent on the point of how States may implement this provision. The UNODC Model Law on Migrant Smuggling limits its commentary on this provision to proposing, as relevant considerations: "ensuring the availability of both male and female officers and authorized officers with appropriate training in the operation and ensuring the availability of basic provisions such as sanitary protection, baby food and nappies." United Nations Office on Drugs and Crime, *Model Law against the Smuggling of Migrants* (2010) [UNODC Model Law on Migrant Smuggling], at 93.

[21] Migrant Smuggling Protocol, at Art. 16(1).

[22] Travaux Préparatoires *for the Organized Crime Convention and Protocols*, at 541. The *Travaux Préparatoires* note that "[t]he words 'consistent with its obligations under international law' were included in the paragraph to clarify this point further": ibid.

in combating migrant smuggling is to focus on humane treatment of smuggled migrants and protection of their Protocol rights.[23] However, the limits of Article 16(1) are also clearly affirmed with a confirmation that this provision "should not be understood as imposing any new or additional obligations on States parties to this protocol beyond those contained in existing international instruments and customary international law."[24]

Article 16 sets out three additional obligations of protection and assistance: each of which is central to the present discussion. States Parties are required to:

- Take appropriate measures to protect smuggled migrants from smuggling-related violence "whether by individuals or groups"[25];
- Provide assistance to migrants whose lives or safety are endangered through smuggling[26];
- In respect of detained smuggled migrants, ensure their right to be informed of consular access.[27]

The Protocol's savings clause has been previously noted but deserves to be flagged again at this point. Its intention and effect is to preserve existing rights, obligations, and responsibilities of States Parties under international law, including international humanitarian law, international human rights law, and, in particular, refugee law and the principle of *non-refoulement*.[28] The savings clause also requires the Protocol to be interpreted and applied in a way that is not discriminatory to smuggled migrants and that is "consistent with internationally recognized principles of non-discrimination."[29] This provision is of direct relevance to the issues discussed in the present chapter. It would operate to prohibit, for example, discriminatory treatment with a negative intent or outcome between different groups of smuggled migrants on the basis of, for example, their national or ethnic origin or indeed their status as asylum-seekers or refugees. It could arguably also extend to prohibit discriminatory treatment of different groups of smuggled migrants, reflecting their different modes of arrival. For example, some countries have established dual systems whereby those

[23] Migrant Smuggling Protocol, at Art. 14(1), 14(2)(e).
[24] Ibid.
[25] Ibid. at Art. 16(2).
[26] Ibid. at Art 16(3). Note that States Parties are required to make smuggling offenses that involve danger to the lives of migrants or that entail degrading treatment or exploitation into aggravating circumstances. Migrant Smuggling Protocol, at Art. 6(3).
[27] Ibid. at Art. 16(5). This aspect is considered in Chapter 9, at Section 9.3.2.
[28] Ibid. at Art. 19(1). An Interpretative Note confirms that the Protocol does not cover the status of refugees. Travaux Préparatoires *for the Organized Crime Convention and Protocols*, at 555.
[29] Migrant Smuggling Protocol, at Art. 19(2).

who arrive by air are subject to different procedures than those who arrive by sea, with potentially discriminatory results.[30]

The European Union has adopted two instruments that are of direct relevance to the issue of migrant smuggling: Directive 2002/90, which provides a common definition for the facilitation of unauthorized entry, transit, and residence into EU States,[31] and a Framework Decision setting out minimum rules for penalties, liability of legal persons, and jurisdiction.[32] Directive 2002/90 contains no reference to rights, protection, or assistance. The Framework Decision does contain a savings clause but this clause is narrow in comparison to that set out in the Trafficking Protocol,[33] merely confirming that the Decision "*shall apply without prejudice to the protection afforded refugees and asylum seekers in accordance with international law on refugees or other international instruments relating to human rights.*"[34]

Operational standards of direct relevance to the issue of migrant smuggling are generally much more explicit in establishing respect for human rights as a fundamental principle and in including specific reference to protection and support obligations. The Schengen Borders Code, for example, requires due respect of fundamental rights and the appropriate training of all staff involved in its implementation,[35] as does EU Council Decision for the surveillance of the sea external

[30] See, for example, the discussion on children held by Australia in immigration detention on mainland Australia, and on those sent to Pacific Islands, with this decision resting solely on how they arrived in Australia. The Australian Human Rights Commission expressed its concern that: "The principle of non-discrimination in the CRC [Convention on the Rights of the Child] means that a child arriving in Sydney is entitled to the same level of protection from refoulement as a child arriving on Christmas Island yet the latter group is transferred to Pacific Islands where the processes are inferior. To satisfy the obligation of non-refoulement to all asylum-seeking children in Australia's jurisdiction, there must be a full and fair refugee status determination process that can properly identify whether children need that protection. Furthermore, Australia must be in a position to guarantee that children who are found to be refugees are protected from return": Australian Human Rights Commission, *A Last Resort? The National Inquiry into Children in Immigration Detention*, 2004, available at www.humanrights.gov.au/publications/last-resort (accessed May 12, 2013) [Australian Human Rights Commission, *A Last Resort?*], at Section 7.8.3.

[31] Council Directive 2002/90/EC of 28 November 2002 defining the facilitation of unauthorised entry, transit and residence, OJ L 328/17, Dec. 5, 2002.

[32] Council Framework Decision of 28 November 2002 on the strengthening of the penal framework to prevent the facilitation of unauthorised entry, transit and residence (2002/946/JHA), OJ L 328/1, Dec. 5, 2002.

[33] Protocol to Prevent, Suppress and Punish Trafficking in Persons, Especially Women and Children, supplementing the United Nations Convention against Transnational Organized Crime, 2237 UNTS 319, done Nov. 15, 2000, entered into force Dec. 25, 2003 [Trafficking Protocol].

[34] Ibid. at Art. 6 (emphasis added).

[35] Regulation (EC) No 562/2006 of the European Parliament and of the Council of 15 March 2006 establishing a Community Code on the rules governing the movement of persons across borders (Schengen Borders Code), OJ L 105/1, Apr. 13, 2006, at Recital para. 20, and Arts. 3, 6.

borders.[36] Guarantees and respect for fundamental rights are also laid down in the EU Returns Directive,[37] examined in detail in Chapter 10.

The most explicit migrant smuggling–related commitment to human rights is to be found in the 2011 Frontex Fundamental Rights Strategy,[38] which contains a detailed set of rights-based commitments to protection and assistance and sets out a number of measures to promote a rights-based approach to the work of the Agency. However, although identifying groups at particular risk (including unaccompanied children, women, and trafficked persons) the Strategy does not include references to violence. In common with the Migrant Smuggling Protocol, the Strategy also does not identify any protection or assistance obligations with respect to smuggled migrants who have been or are at risk of abuse or exploitation. A recent resolution of the Council of Europe Parliamentary Assembly, calling on Frontex, the European Union, and EU Member States to address a range of operational and structural issues in connection with Frontex and its activities, provides a useful insight into risks and shortcomings that have not been fully addressed by the Fundamental Rights Strategy.[39]

Finally, it is important to acknowledge the specialist instruments of international human rights law as a separate and substantive source of legal obligation with respect to obligations of protection and assistance owed to all smuggled migrants. Although these instruments are relevant to all engagements with smuggled migrants they will often be of most immediate relevance to those who are in danger or who experience violence and exploitation. For example, the right to life[40] will require States to take

[36] Council Decision of 26 April 2010 supplementing the Schengen Borders Code as regards the surveillance of the sea external borders in the context of operational cooperation coordinated by the European Agency for the Management of Operational Cooperation at the External Borders of the Member States of the European Union (2010/252/EU), OJ L 111/20, May 5, 2010. See particularly Recital paras. 3, 10; and Annex Part I: Rules for sea border operations coordinated by the Agency (General principles) and Part II: Guidelines for search and rescue situations and for disembarkation in the context of sea border operations coordinated by the Agency (Guideline 1.1).

[37] Directive 2008/115/EC of the European Parliament and of the Council of 16 December 2008 on common standards and procedures in Member States for returning illegally staying third-country nationals, OJ L 348/98, Dec. 24, 2008.

[38] European Agency for the Management of Operational Cooperation at the External Borders of the Member States of the European Union, *Frontex Fundamental Rights Strategy* (2011) [Frontex Fundamental Rights Strategy].

[39] Council of Europe, Parliamentary Assembly, Resolution 1932 (2013) Final version "Frontex: human rights responsibilities," adopted April 25, 2013, esp. at paras. 8–10.

[40] The right to life is enshrined in the Universal Declaration of Human Rights, adopted by GA Res. 217A (III), UN GAOR, 3rd sess, 183rd plen mtg, UN Doc. A/810, at 71, Dec. 10, 1948 [UDHR] (at Article 3); protected as a non-derogable right through International Covenant on Civil and Political Rights, 999 UNTS 171, done Dec. 16, 1996, entered into force Mar. 23, 1976 [ICCPR] (Article 6(1)), and all major regional human rights instruments. It has been the subject of extensive analysis by international human rights courts and institutions. For a review of ICCPR Article 6 for example, see M. Nowak, *U.N. Covenant on Civil and Political Rights: CCPR Commentary* (2nd revised ed. 2005), at 120–156.

positive steps to protect smuggled migrants from xenophobic violence, or from situations of extreme danger such as a threatened sinking of their vessel or risk of death following want of food, water, or medical care. Human rights instruments will also be of direct relevance with respect to particular categories of smuggled migrants such as children.[41] Of course, human rights instruments are not just relevant in these limited situations: they provide important guidance for the treatment of all smuggled migrants who come within the jurisdiction of the State. For example, the prohibition on cruel, inhuman, or degrading treatment or punishment[42] will constrain the way in which States treat smuggled migrants who have been rescued, apprehended, or detained and the way in which decisions are taken about their return.[43] The rights to food and shelter will further dictate the way in which basic needs of smuggled migrants are assessed and met by the State.[44] The right to an adequate standard of health will require States to ensure that smuggled migrants, particularly those in need of emergency assistance, are able to access medical care and treatment.[45]

8.1.2. *Protection from Smuggling-Related Violence and Exploitation*

A central question of this book – and the particular focus of the present chapter – is the extent to which States are under a legal obligation to prevent and respond to violence, abuse, and exploitation against smuggled migrants – whether at the hands of their smugglers or traffickers, officials of the State, or third persons. Violence and exploitation are not integral features of smuggling[46] but the case studies set out in the Introduction to this book provide some insight into the myriad ways in which smuggled migrants can and do experience such profound violations of their

On the equivalent provision of the Convention for the Protection of Human Rights and Fundamental Freedoms, 213 UNTS 222, done Nov. 4, 1950, entered into force Sept. 3, 1953 [European Convention on Human Rights], see D. Korff, *The Right to Life: A Guide to the Implementation of Article 2 of the European Convention on Human Rights* (Council of Europe, Human Rights Handbooks No. 8, 2006).

41 See discussion at Section 8.2.1.

42 See further discussion in Chapter 2, at Section 2.4.1 and Chapter 7, at Section 7.1.2.5.

43 See Chapter 10.

44 For a useful and detailed overview of how these rights operate in the context of asylum-seekers and refugees (a category to which many smuggled migrants will belong), see J. C. Hathaway, *The Rights of Refugees under International Law* (2005), at 471–507.

45 Ibid. at 507–514. The link between the right to life and access to lifesaving medical care is noted in the UNODC Model Law on Migrant Smuggling, at 65–67.

46 See, for example, D. Kyle and M. Scarcelli, "Migrant Smuggling and the Violence Question: Evolving Illicit Migration Markets for Cuban and Haitian Refugees," (2009) 52 *Crime, Law and Social Change* 297; and the discussion of the role of women in migrant smuggling (which does not always involve violence) in S. X. Zhang, K. Chin, and J. Miller, "Women's Participation in Chinese Transnational Human Smuggling: A Gendered Market Perspective" (2007) 45(3) *Criminology* 699.

human rights. Earlier chapters touched on various aspects of the legal obligations that may arise in such situations. For example, Chapters 2, 3, and 4 confirmed and explained the international legal obligation on States to protect persons under their jurisdiction from violations of human rights, including violations committed by private persons. Chapter 7 examined the duty on States to *prevent* smuggling-related violence and exploitation. This section briefly considers the legal framework within which such conduct is to be considered and responded to, most particularly in terms of protection and assistance. Note that Section 8.3.1 takes this discussion forward by looking at the obligation of States to investigate, prosecute, and adjudicate crimes against smuggled migrants to the required standard of due diligence.

The relevant provision of the Migrant Smuggling Protocol (obligation to protect and preserve the rights of smuggled migrants[47] as well as to take "appropriate measures to afford migrants appropriate protection against violence that may be inflicted upon them, whether by individuals or groups [under the jurisdiction of the State Party[48]], by reason of being the object of [migrant smuggling related conduct]"[49]) impose obligations of varying levels of specificity. The obligation to protect and preserve the rights of smuggled migrants for example, is a generalized one, applying to all actions taken under the Protocol: from border control to cooperation with other States Parties in dealing with smuggling by sea. Other obligations are more limited and specific in their scope of application. For example, the obligation on States Parties to take measures to afford migrants appropriate protection against violence appears to apply only in relation to violence inflicted on smuggled migrants *because of the fact of their being smuggled migrants*. Even within these narrow parameters the obligation would extend to a substantial number and range of situations: for example, the exploitation suffered by smuggled migrants in Mexico at the hands of drug cartels[50]; the kidnapping of Eritrean migrants in the Sinai[51]; and presumably also, situations involving reckless and life-endangering transportation of migrants.[52] It may also operate to prohibit the use of controlled deliveries or other covert law enforcement techniques that expose smuggled migrants at risk of violence.[53] However, despite vigorous

47 Migrant Smuggling Protocol at Art. 16(1). See also savings clause at Article 19.

48 Travaux Préparatoires *for the Organized Crime Convention and Protocols*, at 541.

49 Migrant Smuggling Protocol, at Art. 16(2). Note that in an earlier draft, the provision was broader, referring to violence "by public officials or by private individuals, groups or institutions": D. McClean, *Transnational Organized Crime: A Commentary on the UN Convention and Its Protocols* (2007), at 428.

50 See, the "United States–Mexico Border: Violence against, and Exploitation of, Smuggled Migrants" case study set out in the introduction to this book.

51 Ibid.

52 Ibid.

53 See Conference of the Parties to the United Nations Convention against Transnational Organized Crime, Working Group on the Smuggling of Migrants, "Good Practices in Special Investigative Techniques," UN Doc. CTOC/COP/WG.7/2013/2, Aug. 7, 2013, at paras. 9 and 27.

assertions to the contrary,[54] the provision may *not* extend to generalized xenophobic violence such as that experienced by irregular migrants in Greece and South Africa[55] or indeed to other manifestations of violence against smuggled migrants unless these could be shown to be directly related to the fact of the victims of the violence being smuggled. In addition, although the obligation is formulated in mandatory language ("shall"), the meaning of "appropriate measures" in the context of protecting smuggled migrants from violence is not made clear. It can be argued that broad language such as "appropriate measures" is both useful and necessary, as it allows States a degree of flexibility in how they formulate their responses in light of the particular circumstances at hand. However there is no doubt that the broad and imprecise formulation of the obligation makes it difficult to establish its substantive content and to identify how compliance could be measured, and how a breach could be objectively determined. The various sources of supplementary guidance on the Protocol are either silent on the point of how this provision could be implemented by States Parties,[56] or extremely vague.[57] Notions of reasonableness, appropriateness, and proportionality may be useful guides but in the end do not help to determine whether a State is in fact meeting its obligations.

The Protocol's weak protection provisions are ameliorated somewhat by its obligations related to prevention, discussed in detail in Chapter 7. Briefly, States Parties are subject to a range of obligations with regard to information exchange, border measures, training, and technical cooperation and other prevention measures, with respect to both the smuggling of migrants and "the conduct set forth in article 6 of

54 See for example, A. Schloenhardt and K. L. Stacey, "Assistance and Protection of Smuggled Migrants: International Law and Australian Practice" (2013) 35 *Sydney Law Review* 53, at 58 (incorrectly citing United Nations Office on Drugs and Crime, *Smuggling of Migrants by Sea* (2011) as an authority for the proposition that the reference to "individuals or groups" in Article 16(2) "is seen to draw particular 'attention to the vulnerability of migrants who may meet intense opposition from groups of people who do not wish them to enter or remain in' the country."

55 On the situation in Greece see Human Rights Watch, *Hate on the Streets: Xenophobic Violence in Greece* (2012); and United Nations Press Release, "UN Special Rapporteur on the human rights of migrants concludes the fourth and last country visit in his regional study on the human rights of migrants at the borders of the European Union: Greece" (Dec. 3, 2012), available at www.ohchr.org/en/NewsEvents/Pages/DisplayNews.aspx?NewsID=12858&LangID=E (accessed May 12, 2013). On xenophobic violence against migrants in South Africa, see generally L. B. Landau ed., *Exorcising the Demons Within: Xenophobia, Violence and Statecraft in Contemporary South Africa* (2012).

56 For example, the *Legislative Guide*.

57 See, for example, UNODC Model Law on Migrant Smuggling, at 67 ("This will need to be decided at the national level, bearing in mind the types of violence likely to be inflicted on smuggled migrants, the situations where violence may arise, the communities and individuals that may be affected, and the resources that are available to respond to these issues."). The Model Law provides examples from different countries of possible measures that could be undertaken to implement this provision, for example, development of crime prevention programs with a specific focus on engendering tolerance and community acceptance of migrants, or programs of assistance and protection for overseas nationals through embassies in major destination countries: ibid. at 67–68.

this Protocol."[58] In the latter case, the prevention obligations in the Protocol would apply not only to preventing migrant smuggling as defined in the Protocol but to all criminal conduct covered by Article 6, including aggravated forms of migrant smuggling, involving death or danger to migrants, or inhuman or degrading treatment, including exploitation.[59] Also, the Organized Crime Convention includes an obligation to "endeavor to" develop projects and policies aimed at "the prevention of transnational crime," which would include aggravated smuggling offenses, and other conduct required to be criminalized by Article 6 of the Protocol.

The Legislative Guide confirms that "inhuman or degrading treatment" as used in Article 16 of the Migrant Smuggling Protocol may include treatment inflicted for the purposes of some forms of exploitation.[60] Importantly, it also confirms that if there is no consent to the exploitation – or if consent has been vitiated through one of the accepted means (force, fraud, coercion, abuse of authority or a position of vulnerability, etc.),[61] "the presence of exploitation in what would otherwise be a smuggling case will generally make the trafficking offence applicable if the State party concerned has ratified and implemented that Protocol."[62] Exploitation of smuggled migrants accompanied by one of the means set out above would therefore generally operate to support a characterization of a particular situation as one of trafficking in persons. The following examples show how a situation of migrant smuggling can also be one of human trafficking:

- Exploitation of migrants passing through Mexico and the Sinai[63]: individuals are transported, harbored, and received (act) through force and coercion (means) into situations of exploitation, including slavery, forced labor, and exploitation through extortion (purpose);
- Migrants forced to work off excessive debts for smuggling services[64]: individuals are bought, sold, transported, harbored, received (act) through deception, abuse of a position of vulnerability (means); into situations of exploitation including debt bondage and forced labor (purpose).

58 Migrant Smuggling Protocol, at Art. 14(1).

59 Ibid. at Art. 6(3)(b).

60 *Legislative Guide*, at 347 (para. 49).

61 This reference is to the Trafficking Protocol's definition of trafficking in persons (Article 3). Note that "abuse of a position of vulnerability" may well extend to abusing vulnerability that arises through irregular migration status. See United Nations Office on Drugs and Crime, *Abuse of a Position of Vulnerability and Other "Means" within the Definition of Trafficking in Persons* (2012).

62 *Legislative Guide*, at 347 (para. 49). "The Interpretative Notes indicate that the reference to exploitation here is without prejudice to that [Trafficking] Protocol (A/55/383/Add.1, para. 96)": ibid.

63 See the "United States–Mexico Border" and "Sinai Peninsula" case studies in the Introduction.

64 See, for example, the description of fees paid by Chinese smuggled migrants, in G. Yun ed., *Concealed Chains: Labour Exploitation and Chinese Migrants in Europe* (2010), 51–52.

As explored further at Section 8.2.2, once a situation of smuggling has been identified as one of trafficking in persons, the nature of State obligations of protection and support changes substantially. Establishing a situation as one of trafficking also impacts on the nature of State obligations with regard to an effective criminal justice response, an aspect also considered at Section 8.3.1 of this chapter.

8.1.3. *Obligation to Assist Smuggled Migrants in Danger*

The lives and well-being of smuggled migrants may become endangered through the smuggling process itself. Migrants may find themselves in need of rescue through, for example, being stranded at sea, trapped in shipping containers, or subjected to harsh conditions of transport. They may be in desperate and immediate need of food, water, shelter, medical attention, and psychological assistance.

To what extent are States required to render assistance to smuggled migrants who are in danger? Although the Migrant Smuggling Protocol provides a partial answer, the various operational rules that have been developed at the European level do not directly address this question.[65] The most relevant provisions of the Migrant Smuggling Protocol are the general obligation to take all "appropriate measures" to "preserve and protect the rights of persons who have been the object of [smuggling] conduct" including "the right to life," and the requirement to "afford appropriate assistance to migrants whose lives or safety are endangered by reason of being [smuggled]."[66] A supplementary provision relating to measures against smuggling of migrants by sea requires States Parties taking measures against smuggling vessels to "[e]nsure the safety and humane treatment" of persons on board and to "[t]ake due account of the need not to endanger the security of the vessel or its cargo."[67]

As with the Article 16 provisions on protection and support discussed previously, the obligations set out above are framed around the notion of "appropriate measures." On one reading, "appropriate measures" could be understood to be referring to whatever responses and supports are objectively required, depending on the particular circumstances (and bearing in mind the savings clause referring explicitly to the right to life). Alternatively, it could be argued that States Parties have the authority and discretion to decide which measures are "appropriate" within the broader purposes of the Protocol, which includes preventing and combating smuggling of migrants, while "protecting the rights of smuggled migrants." It is unclear whether the requirement to afford appropriate protection to smuggled migrants in danger in

65 See for example the *Frontex Fundamental Rights Strategy*, which makes no mention of assistance to smuggled migrants in danger.

66 Migrant Smuggling Protocol, at Arts. 16(1), 16(3).

67 Ibid. at Art. 9(1)(a) and 9(1)(b).

fact creates anything new or different for States Parties that is not covered by their more general obligation to preserve and protect the rights of smuggled migrants. The Legislative Guide, using circuitous and rather dubious legal reasoning, argues that the provision "does not create a new right, but does establish a new obligation in that it requires States parties to provide basic assistance to migrants and illegal residents in cases where their lives or safety have been endangered by reason of [a smuggling] offence."[68] The Guide does not explain how an obligation can exist without a corresponding right and does not shed any light on the substantive content of this "new obligation." While affirming the importance of this provision to the situation of many smuggled migrants, other available supplementary materials do not satisfactorily clarify this point.[69]

Much like obligations of protection and support, fleshing out the substance of the obligation to assist endangered smuggled migrants requires recourse to other areas of law. For example, as summarized in Chapter 1 and discussed in considerable detail in Chapter 6, all States are obliged to render assistance to those lost or in peril at sea. This obligation, which is part of customary international law,[70] has been codified through the UN Convention on the Law of the Sea[71] (UNCLOS) and other widely ratified treaties.[72] UNCLOS imposes a duty on States Parties to require masters of their flagged vessels to assist and rescue any persons found at sea who are in danger of being lost or in some sort of distress.[73] The obligation extends

[68] *Legislative Guide*, at 365 (para. 71).

[69] See, for example, UNODC Model Law on Migrant Smuggling, at 93 ("[the obligation to protect against violence and provide assistance to endangered smuggled migrants] may have particular relevance in the context of smuggling of migrants by sea if, for example, simply repelling a vessel or leaving smuggling migrants on board a vessel would mean leaving the smuggled migrants effectively in the hands of members of an organized criminal group. In addition to raising serious human rights concerns, such an action would likely undermine law enforcement objectives, which may be better served by taking the smuggled migrants to a place of safety and providing the necessary facilities for debriefing with expert investigators."

[70] See generally, B. Oxman, "Human Rights and the United Nations Convention on the Law of the Sea" (1998) 36 *Columbia Journal of Transnational Law* 399.

[71] United Nations Convention on the Law of the Sea, 1833 UNTS 3, done Dec. 10, 1982, entered into force Nov. 16, 1994 [UNCLOS].

[72] International Convention for the Safety of Life at Sea, 1974, as amended, 1184 UNTS 278, done Nov. 1, 1974, entered into force May 25, 1980 [SOLAS Convention]; International Convention on Maritime Search and Rescue, 1979, with annexes, 1405 UNTS 97, done Apr. 27, 1979, entered into force June 22, 1985 [SAR Convention]. The SAR Convention was amended in 1998 by IMO Resolution MSC.70(69) ("Amendments to the International Convention on Maritime Search and Rescue, 1979"), and again in 2004 by IMO Resolution MSC.155(78) ("Adoption of Amendments to the International Convention on Maritime Search and Rescue, 1979, as amended"). References to the SAR Convention are to the consolidated text. Note that other instruments, cited and examined in Chapters 1 and 6, are also relevant to this obligation.

[73] UNCLOS, at Art. 98. This obligation is also set out in the SOLAS Convention (Annex, Chapter V, Regulation 33(1)) and the SAR Convention (Annex, Chapter 2, para. 2.1.10). The SAR Convention defines distress as: "A situation wherein there is a reasonable certainty that a person, a vessel or

to any persons regardless of their nationality or status or the circumstances in which they are found,[74] and thereby extends to smuggled migrants, including those who are or may be seeking asylum and/or are being trafficked. It applies irrespective of the number of persons involved and the maritime zone in which they are located. In discussions about its legal weight, the obligation to render assistance and rescue at sea is commonly asserted to be an expression of a elementary principle of humanity.[75] This provides ammunition for the argument that a similar obligation extends to persons in distress who are *not at sea*: for example, those who are lost or have been abandoned by their smugglers while trying to cross an inhospitable land border region. State practice provides some support for recognition of a duty of care to such persons.[76]

Of course, international human rights law is also a critical component of the obligation to assist and protect smuggled migrants in distress. For example, the right to life, which is expressly referred to in the Migrant Smuggling Protocol's provision on protection and assistance, clearly translates into an obligation on States not to ignore or abandon smuggled migrants whose lives are in danger, most particularly when the State is in a position to provide protection and assistance. The right to life, along with the prohibition on inhuman treatment, can also be used to buttress an obligation on States to provide emergency medical assistance to smuggled migrants in need. This is the view taken by the UN Office on Drugs and Crime Model Law against the Smuggling of Migrants:

> While the right of all persons, irrespective of migration status, to access emergency medical care is not clearly defined, it can be extrapolated from the right to life set out in the International Covenant on Civil and Political Rights. As the Human Rights Committee has observed, it is incumbent on States parties to the Covenant to ensure that that right is not interpreted narrowly, as protection of the right to life will frequently require positive action on the part of States parties. If that reasoning is applied, it follows that part of giving practical application

other craft is threatened by grave and imminent danger and requires immediate assistance": SAR Convention, at Annex, Chapter 1, para. 1.3.13. Further on what constitutes "distress" den Heijer, *Europe and Extraterritorial Asylum*, at 244–245.

74 SAR Convention, at Annex, Chapter 2, para. 2.1.10. See also SOLAS Convention, at Annex, Chapter V, Regulation 33(1).

75 See Chapter 6, at note 204 and accompanying text.

76 Guerette reports on the "Border Safety Initiative," a program initiated by the United States government in response to such a problem along the United States–Mexico border. The initiative includes the placement of rescue beacons in deserted locations for migrants who become stranded and need emergency assistance, and training for officials in search and rescue. See R. T. Guerette, "Immigration Policy, Border Security, and Migrant Deaths: An Impact Evaluation of Life-Saving Efforts under the Border Safety Initiative" (2007) 6(2) *Criminology and Public Policy* 245. See also UNODC Model Law on Migrant Smuggling, at 69 (reporting provisions of Belgian law that provides protections to persons subject to certain forms of aggravated smuggling).

to this right is to ensure that whenever a person (including a smuggled migrant) is in need of emergency medical care, they should be provided with such care, irrespective of considerations such as their immigration status. A denial or refusal of emergency medical care in a situation where this would have life-threatening consequences is clearly a violation of the right to life. This right has particular resonance in the smuggling of migrants context as smuggled migrants may be intercepted by the authorities after they have been locked in shipping containers without adequate air or food, or after they have undertaken long, dangerous journeys. They may be in need of the necessities of life (food, water, shelter), in addition to medical care.[77]

8.2. STATUS-RELATED PROTECTION AND ASSISTANCE

As noted previously, international law attaches different or additional rights to – and obligations in respect of – certain categories of persons. Two categories of particular relevance to the question of protection and support, children and victims of trafficking, are considered in this section. Of course it is not only children and trafficked persons who are the beneficiaries of status-related rights and protections. For example, international law (including the Migrant Smuggling Protocol)[78] recognizes that women may be especially vulnerable to violations of their human rights and that an enhanced standard of protection and assistance may be appropriate.[79] International law also recognizes the particular vulnerabilities of persons with disabilities, for example requiring that States take "all necessary measures to ensure the protection and safety of persons with disabilities in situations of risk"[80]; and "prevent all forms of exploitation, violence and abuse" against disabled persons.[81]

Refugees and asylum-seekers are another important "category" when it comes to ascertaining both obligations and rights of protection and assistance for smuggled migrants. Previous chapters have confirmed the strong link between smuggling and asylum. Put simply, a significant, if indeterminate, proportion of those seeking asylum from persecution are compelled to use the services of smugglers to leave their country and to enter transit countries as well as countries of asylum. The Migrant Smuggling Protocol implicitly recognizes this reality through its affirmation of the fact that nothing in that instrument operates to affect rights, obligations, and responsibilities of States and individuals under international law, including human rights

77 UNODC Model Law on Migrant Smuggling, at 66.

78 Migrant Smuggling Protocol, at Art. 16(4).

79 See generally, Convention on the Elimination of All Forms of Discrimination against Women, 1249 UNTS 13, done Dec. 18, 1979, entered into force Sept. 3, 1981 [CEDAW].

80 Convention on the Rights of Persons with Disabilities, 2515 UNTS 3, done Dec. 13, 2006, entered into force May 3, 2008, at Art. 11.

81 Ibid. at Art. 16(2).

and refugee law.[82] It is therefore to these areas of law that one must turn in determining the extent to which a smuggled migrant's status as an asylum-seeker or refugee affects his or her rights to protection and support under international law and, if so, in what way. Most critically, the status of being an asylum-seeker or a refugee cannot operate to exclude individuals from the protection of their fundamental human rights: rights that are owed to all persons including all those who have been smuggled, including the right to life, the prohibition on torture, the right to physical security, the right to food and shelter, and the right of access to healthcare. Many of the protection and support issues of concern to smuggled asylum-seekers and refugees relate to the question of their immediate and ultimate fate vis-à-vis the country to which they have been smuggled. Specifically: When do they have a right to enter and remain in that State, and under what circumstances and conditions may they be penalized and detained by the authorities of that State? These questions are considered in detail at various points throughout the book.[83]

8.2.1. *Smuggled Children*

There are no reliable figures available on the proportion of smuggled persons who are children. However, extrapolating from global data on general migration and asylum-seeker populations, it becomes clear that children, either traveling with their families or unaccompanied, constitute a significant proportion of people on the move.[84] There are also indications that children may be specifically recruited to play certain low level roles in the smuggling process, such as crewing migrant smuggling vessels, as children are more likely to escape prosecution and simply be returned home.[85] Despite this reality, children are rarely subject to

[82] Migrant Smuggling Protocol, at Art. 19(1). The second part of that savings clause is also relevant to smuggled asylum-seekers, confirming that in applying the Protocol, States may not discriminate between different groups of smuggled migrants (based on, for example, their ethnicity or nationality or indeed, their status as asylum-seekers or refugees). Ibid. at Art. 19(2).

[83] See Chapter 2, esp. at Section 2.3 (on the right to seek and enjoy asylum); Chapter 9 (on detention and associated rights and obligations) and Chapter 5, at Section 5.1.1.3 (on preservation of international human rights law and refugee law).

[84] In 2010, there were 33,924,476 "people of concern to UNHCR" and of these, 47 percent were under the age of eighteen: Table 13, Demographic composition of populations of concern to UNHCR, end–2010, data downloaded from www.unhcr.org/statistics/populationdatabase (accessed May 12, 2013). Note that this number includes refugees and people in refugee-like situations, asylum-seekers, internally displaced persons, stateless persons, and others.

[85] Australian Human Rights Commission, *An Age of Uncertainty: Inquiry into the Treatment of Individuals Suspected of People Smuggling Offences Who Say That They Are Children* (July 2012), available at www.humanrights.gov.au/publications/age-uncertainty-inquiry-treatment-individuals-suspected-people-smuggling-offences-who (accessed May 12, 2013) [Australian Human Rights Commission, *An Age of Uncertainty*], at 8.

special consideration in policy and practice around responses to migrant smuggling.[86] The Migrant Smuggling Protocol is vague on this point, merely requiring States Parties, when applying the Protocol's somewhat meager assistance and protection provisions, to take account of the special needs of women and children.[87] This section moves beyond the Protocol to consider the extent to which the broader international legal framework imposes different or additional obligations on States with respect to child smuggled migrants when it comes to protection and assistance.

Children are naturally included in the rules and standards governing assistance and support considered throughout the present chapter. However, international law generally recognizes the particular vulnerabilities and special needs of children and supports a relatively higher standard of protection and support. This underscores the importance of identifying when a particular smuggled migrant is a child. A smuggled child who is not identified as such is unable to access the special rights to which he or she may be entitled.[88] The impact of identification failures will be much worse if the smuggled child is also a victim of trafficking, because of the additional vulnerabilities that attach to such persons and the special legal regime that applies in cases of child trafficking.[89] Correct and timely identification of children will often require a proactive approach on the part of the relevant state. Some smuggled children may appear to be eighteen years of age or older. Their identification documents may have been destroyed or taken away from them. They may be carrying false papers that misstate their age. Smuggled children may lie about their age because this is what they have been told to do by their smugglers, or because they are afraid of being taken into care or being sent back home. The international legal framework around trafficking in persons supports a presumption of age – that a victim who *may be* a child is treated as a child unless and until another determination is made.[90] Although a similar presumption is not discernible in respect of smuggled migrants it can be convincingly argued that the existence of a regime of special rights and obligations with respect to children demands that States take active steps to identify those persons to whom this regime applies. A failure to do so could be considered an

86 See, for example, the Australian Government, *Report of the Expert Panel on Asylum Seekers* (2012) (considering the issue of asylum-seekers arriving by boat into the country, all of whom are smuggled). This extremely detailed report does not consider the situation of children at all – nor the obligations of the government in that respect – apart from a few cursory references to "the best interests of the child" and a single reference to Article 24(1) of the ICCPR. Ibid. at 82, 130.

87 Migrant Smuggling Protocol, at Art. 16(4).

88 Australian Human Rights Commission, *An Age of Uncertainty*.

89 For a detailed consideration of the applicable legal regime around trafficked children, see generally Gallagher, *The International Law of Human Trafficking*, esp. at 323–336. See also the brief discussion at Section 8.2.1.

90 Gallagher, *The International Law of Human Trafficking*, at 324–326.

internationally wrongful act to the extent that such a failure negatively impacts on the capacity of children to access the rights to which they are entitled.

"The best interests of the child" is a legal doctrine accepted in many countries that has been enshrined in international law through the Convention on the Rights of the Child (CRC).[91] Many other international and regional human rights instruments have adopted and incorporated this principle.[92] The doctrine generally requires States to prioritize or give primary consideration to the best interests of the child in relation to all actions and decisions affecting that child. A number of considerations are relevant in ascertaining what it means to prioritize the best interests of the smuggled child. First, it is in a child's best interests to enjoy the rights and freedoms provided to him or her by international law and as set out in the CRC. For example, it is in a child's best interests to maintain contact with both parents in most circumstances (Article 9(3)), and to have access to education (Article 28) and to healthcare (Article 24). Second, a child capable of forming a view on his or her best interests must be able to give it freely and it must be taken into account (Article 12). Third, parents (or, as the case may be, members of the extended family or community or legal guardians) have primary decision-making responsibility on behalf of their children (Articles 5 and 18(1)), but, if they fail to make the child's best interests a basic concern the State may intervene to protect those interests (see Article 9(1), for example). Fourth, and perhaps most important, States may not privilege other considerations, such as those related to immigration control or public order, over the best interests of the smuggled child.[93]

An important source of vulnerability for smuggled children lies in their lack of full agency – in fact and under law.[94] In the context of smuggling, a lack of agency may be made worse by the absence of a parent or legal guardian who is able to act

[91] Convention on the Rights of the Child, 1577 UNTS 3, done Nov. 20, 1989, entered into force Sept. 2, 1990 [CRC], at Art. 3(1).

[92] See, for example, the African Charter on the Rights and Welfare of the Child, OAU Doc. CAB/LEG/24.9/49, done July 11, 1990, entered into force Nov. 29, 1999 [African Children's Charter], at Art. 4; CEDAW, at Art. 5(2); Inter-American Convention on International Traffic in Minors, OAS Doc. OEA/Ser.K/XXI.5, 79 OASTS, done Mar. 18, 1994, entered into force Aug. 15, 1997, reprinted in (1994) 33 ILM 721, at Art. 1; South Asian Association for Regional Cooperation, Convention on Regional Arrangements for the Promotion of Child Welfare in South Asia, done Jan. 5, 2002, entered into force Sept. 21, 2006, at Art. III(4). Optional Protocol to the Convention on the Rights of the Child on the Sale of Children, Child Prostitution and Child Pornography, 2171 UNTS 227, done May 25, 2000, entered into force Jan. 18, 2002 [CRC Optional Protocol], at Art. 8(3), requires that the best interests of the child be "a primary consideration" in the treatment within the criminal justice system of child victims of offenses under the Protocol.

[93] UN Committee on the Rights of the Child, "General Comment No. 6: Treatment of Unaccompanied and Separated Children Outside Their Country of Origin," UN Doc. CRC/GC/2005/6, Sept. 1, 2005 [CRC General Comment No. 6], at paras. 19–22.

[94] This is acknowledged in the ICCPR, which stipulates the right of the child to "such measures of protection as are required by his status as a minor": at Art. 24.

in the child's best interests. International law recognizes that children in such situations are entitled to special measures of protection and support from the State.[95] In General Comment No. 6, the Committee on the Rights of the Child considered the application of the "best interests" principle in the context of unaccompanied or separated children.[96] In the case of a displaced child,

> the principle must be respected during all stages of the displacement cycle. At any of these stages, a best interests determination must be documented in preparation of any decision fundamentally impacting on the unaccompanied or separated child's life.[97]

Such a determination requires:

> a clear and comprehensive assessment of the child's identity, including her or his nationality, upbringing, ethnic, cultural and linguistic background, particular vulnerabilities and protection needs ... The assessment process should be carried out in a friendly and safe atmosphere by qualified professionals who are trained in age and gender-sensitive interviewing techniques.[98] Subsequent steps, such as the appointment of a competent guardian as expeditiously as possible, serves as a key procedural safeguard to ensure respect for the best interests of an unaccompanied or separated child ... In cases where separated or unaccompanied children are referred to asylum procedures or other administrative or judicial proceedings, they should also be provided with a legal representative in addition to a guardian.[99]

The Committee on the Rights of the Child has determined that: "the appointment of a competent guardian ... serves as a key procedural safeguard to ensure respect for the best interests of an unaccompanied or separated child."[100] It has recommended that States appoint a guardian as soon as an unaccompanied or separated child is identified.[101]

A number of core protections of potentially wider applicability deserve to be highlighted in the case of smuggled children. For example, every child under the

[95] See, for example, CRC, at Art. 20(1): "A child temporarily or permanently deprived of his or her family environment, or in whose own best interests cannot be allowed to remain in that environment, shall be entitled to special protection and assistance provided by the State." See also UN High Commissioner for Refugees, *Guidelines on the Applicable Criteria and Standards relating to the Detention of Asylum-Seekers and Alternatives to Detention* (2012), at Guideline 9; African Children's Charter, at Art. 25; UN Economic and Social Council, Office of the United Nations High Commissioner on Human Rights, "Recommended Principles and Guidelines on Human Rights and Human Trafficking," UN Doc E/2002/68/Add.1, May 20, 2002 [UN Trafficking Principles and Guidelines], at Principle 10.

[96] CRC General Comment No. 6, at paras. 19–22.

[97] Ibid. at para. 19.

[98] Ibid. at para. 20.

[99] Ibid. at para. 21.

[100] Ibid.

[101] Ibid. at para. 33.

jurisdiction or control of a State is entitled to care and protection on an equal basis. This means that nonnational smuggled children are to enjoy the same rights as national or resident children.[102] Their nationality, as well as their race, sex, language, religion, ethnic or social origin, birth, or other characteristic, is not to impact negatively on their rights and freedoms.[103] This should include ensuring that where needed, smuggled child migrants have full access to refugee protection systems, and national child protection systems, irrespective of their migration or other status.[104]

Although all persons have a right to privacy, this right is a particularly important aspect of providing children who have been smuggled with the care, support, and protection to which they are legally entitled. Failure to protect the privacy of children in such situations can place them in danger of intimidation and retaliation, particularly in respect of smuggled children who have also been trafficked. It can also cause humiliation and hurt to victims of trafficking and compromise their recovery. More generally, the CRC prohibits the arbitrary and unlawful interference with a child's privacy.[105] In General Comment No. 4, the Committee on the Rights of the Child elaborated on this provision, encouraging States Parties to respect strictly children's right to privacy and confidentiality, including with respect to advice and counseling on health matters.[106] In General Comment No. 6, the Committee reaffirmed a child's right to privacy in the context of separated or unaccompanied children.[107] Finally, as noted briefly in the context of "best interests," international law recognizes that a child who is capable of forming his or her own views should enjoy the right to express those views freely in all matters affecting him or her, in particular concerning decisions about his or her possible return to the family. The views of the child should be given due weight in accordance with his or her age and maturity.[108] Those views must be supported by adequate and accurate information.

[102] CRC, at Art. 2.

[103] Ibid.

[104] UN High Commissioner for Refugees, *UNHCR Guidelines on Determining Best Interests of the Child* (May 2008), at 17. See also International Committee of the Red Cross, *Inter-Agency Guiding Principles on Unaccompanied and Separated Children* (Jan. 2004). See further, CRC at Arts. 2(1), 3, 19–20, 22; CRC General Comment No. 6. See also the discussion of discrimination against different child asylum-seekers, depending on their mode of arrival, in Australian Human Rights Commission, *A Last Resort?*, at 7.8.3.

[105] CRC, at Art. 16.

[106] UN Committee on the Rights of the Child, "General Comment No. 4: Adolescent Health and Development in the Context of the Convention on the Rights of the Child," UN Doc. CRC/GC/2003/4, July 1, 2003, at para. 11.

[107] CRC General Comment No. 6, at para. 29.

[108] CRC, at Art. 12. See also African Children's Charter, at Art. 4(2); and UN Trafficking Principles and Guidelines, at Guideline 6.6.

8.2.2. *Smuggled Victims of Trafficking*

As noted above and at various other points in this book, trafficked persons are often smuggled across national borders and smuggled migrants themselves are at high risk of becoming victims of trafficking-related exploitation including through extortion, forced labor, and sexual exploitation. In both cases, the migrants fall within the international legal regime that has been developed around this phenomenon. A full description and analysis of that regime has been previously provided by one of the present authors.[109] The following paragraphs summarize that work by highlighting the most important aspects of the regime: the obligation to identify those who have been trafficked[110]; noncriminalization of victims; provision of immediate protection and support; and provision of legal assistance. The legal framework around trafficking includes special and additional protections for trafficked children, and these are also briefly summarized. Aspects of the international legal framework relating to detention and return of trafficked persons who have been smuggled are considered separately in Chapters 9 and 10 respectively.

It is relevant to note that, in addition to their status as trafficked persons, smuggled migrants who have also been trafficked are "victims of crime"[111] and "victims of human rights violations."[112] These two characterizations become important in relation to certain rights, obligations, and responsibilities that are derived from laws that have wider application than the specialist trafficking instruments. For example, victims of crime and victims of human rights violations have a right to be treated with humanity and with respect for their dignity and human rights, as well as with

[109] A. T. Gallagher, *The International Law of Human Trafficking* (2010).

[110] Guideline 2 of the UN Trafficking Principles and Guidelines specifically addresses the obligation to identify trafficked persons among smuggled migrants.

[111] The Declaration of Basic Principles for Victims of Crime and Abuse of Power defines "victims of crime" as "persons who … have suffered harm, including physical or mental injury, emotional suffering, economic loss or substantial impairment of their fundamental rights, through acts or omissions that are in violation of criminal laws": UN General Assembly, "Declaration of Basic Principles of Justice for Victims of Crime and Abuse of Power," adopted by GA Res. 40/34, UN Doc. A/RES/40/34 Annex, Nov. 29, 1985 ["Basic Principles for Victims of Crime and Abuse of Power"], at para. 1.

[112] The UN General Assembly's "Basic Principles and Guidelines on the Right to a Remedy and Reparation" defines victims of gross violations of human rights and serious violations of international humanitarian law as: "persons who individually or collectively suffered harm, including physical or mental injury, emotional suffering, economic loss or substantial impairment of their fundamental rights, through acts or omissions that constitute gross violations of international human rights law, or serious violations of international humanitarian law. Where appropriate, and in accordance with domestic law, the term 'victim' also includes the immediate family or dependants of the direct victim and persons who have suffered harm in intervening to assist victims in distress or to prevent victimization." UN General Assembly, "Basic Principles and Guidelines on the Right to a Remedy and Reparation for Victims of Gross Violations of International Human Rights Law and Serious Violation of International Humanitarian Law," UN Doc. A/RES/60/147 Annex, Dec. 16, 2005 ["Principles and Guidelines on the Right to a Remedy and Reparation"], at para. 8.

an entitlement to measures that ensure their well-being and avoid revictimization.[113] More specifically, victims of crime are entitled to receive "the necessary material, medical, psychological and social assistance through governmental, voluntary, community-based and indigenous means."[114] Victims of gross violations of human rights such as trafficking have a legal entitlement to rehabilitation, an important component of reparation, that includes medical and psychological care.[115] Certain human rights, such as the right to the highest attainable standard of physical and mental health[116] and the right to adequate food, clothing, and housing,[117] are especially relevant in this context.

8.2.2.1. Obligation to Identify Those Who Have Been Trafficked from among Smuggled Migrants

In many countries, victims of trafficking who come to the attention of the State are commonly not identified as such. Sometimes this is because the State does not

[113] Ibid. at para. 10.

[114] "Basic Principles for Victims of Crime and Abuse of Power," at para. 14. The United Nations Office on Drugs and Crime, *Model Law on Trafficking in Persons*, UN Sales No. E.09.V.11 (2009) [UNODC Model Law on Trafficking in Persons], at 43, notes that many countries already have laws and regulations in place to ensure that victims of serious crime have access to certain benefits and services and that, if necessary, such access should be explicitly extended to victims of trafficking.

[115] "Principles and Guidelines on the Right to a Remedy and Reparation," at para. 21. See further the discussion of remedies at Section 8.3.2.

[116] International Covenant on Economic, Social and Cultural Rights, 993 UNTS 3, done Dec. 16, 1966, entered into force Jan. 3, 1976 [ICESCR], at Art. 12; CEDAW, at Art. 12; International Convention on the Protection of the Rights of All Migrant Workers and Members of Their Families, UN Doc. A/RES/45/158, done Dec. 18, 1990, entered into force July 1, 2003 [Migrant Workers Convention], at Art. 28; Convention on the Elimination of All Forms of Racial Discrimination, 660 UNTS 195, done Dec. 21, 1965, entered into force Jan. 4, 1969 [CERD], at Art. 5(e)(iv); CRC, at Art. 24. The Committee on Economic, Social and Cultural Rights has asserted the obligation of States Parties to respect the right to health of all persons, including especially vulnerable groups such as asylum-seekers and illegal immigrants: UN Committee on Economic, Social and Cultural Rights, "General Comment No. 14: The Right to the Highest Attainable Standard of Health," UN Doc. E/C.12/2000/4, Aug. 11, 2000.

[117] ICESCR, at Art. 11; CERD, at Art. 5(e)(iii); Trafficking Protocol, at Art. 6(3)(a); Convention relating to the Status of Refugees, 189 UNTS 137, done July 28, 1951, entered into force Apr. 22, 1954, as amended by the Protocol relating to the Status of Refugees, 606 UNTS 267, done Jan. 31, 1967, entered into force Oct. 4, 1967, at Art. 21; Protocol to the African Charter on Human and Peoples' Rights on the Rights of Women in Africa, OAU Doc. CAB/LEG/66.6, done July 11, 2003, entered into force Nov. 25, 2005, at Arts. 15, 16; South Asian Association for Regional Cooperation, Convention on Preventing and Combating Trafficking in Women and Children for Prostitution, done Jan. 5, 2002, entered into force Dec. 1, 2005, at Art. IX(3); UN Committee on the Elimination of Discrimination against Women, "General Recommendation No. 19: Violence Against Women," UN Doc. A/47/38, Jan. 29, 1992 [CEDAW General Recommendation No. 19], at para. 24(t)(iii); "Beijing Declaration and Platform for Action," Fourth World Conference on Women, UN Doc. A/CONF.177/20 and UN Doc. A/CONF.177/20/Add.1, Sept. 15, 1995 [Beijing Declaration and Platform for Action], at para. 125(a).

wish to accept the existence of trafficked persons within its territory and the burdens that this may impose in terms of additional obligations of protection and support. More commonly, misidentification can be traced to a lack of commitment, understanding, and resources on the part of the State and its agencies. In this respect, it is relevant to note that although the additional elements, such as force, deception, coercion, etc., that distinguish trafficking from migrant smuggling may sometimes be obvious, in many cases they are difficult to prove without active investigation. In other words, many individuals trafficked across international borders, will, prima facie, be illegal/smuggled migrants, and it is this characterization that is the easiest and simplest one for national law enforcement authorities to make.

Although the Trafficking Protocol is silent on the issue of victim identification, the other major specialist instrument in this area, the European Trafficking Convention,[118] has recognized that timely and accurate identification of victims is essential for the provision of protection and assistance, and that failure to correctly identify a victim will likely lead to a denial of that person's rights as well as problems in the prosecution process.[119] States Parties to the latter instrument are required to ensure the necessary legal framework is in place as well as the availability of competent personnel for the identification process.[120] They are also required to cooperate both with one other and with victim support agencies in this process.[121] Importantly, given the complexities of victim identification, the immediate victim assistance and support provisions of the Convention are applicable, prior to formal identification, to any person who the competent authorities have "reasonable grounds to believe … has been a victim of trafficking."[122]

For those States Parties not bound by the provisions of the European Trafficking Convention, the obligation of identification can be argued to flow from the fact that any rights accorded to trafficked persons amount to nothing without a corresponding

[118] Council of Europe Convention on Action against Trafficking in Human Beings, ETS 197, 16.V.2005, done May 16, 2005, entered into force Feb. 1, 2008 [European Trafficking Convention].

[119] Council of Europe, *Explanatory Report on the Convention on Action against Trafficking in Human Beings*, ETS 197, 16.V.2005 [European Trafficking Convention Explanatory Report], at para. 127.

[120] European Trafficking Convention, at Art. 10(1).

[121] Ibid. at Art. 10(2).

[122] Ibid. As noted previously, the same Article also prevents a person in relation to whom there are reasonable grounds to suspect he or she has been trafficked, from being removed from the country prior to the completion of formal identification procedures. This provision is also reflected in the 2011 EU Directive on Trafficking, which requires Member States to: "take the necessary measures to ensure that a person is provided with assistance and support as soon as the competent authorities have a reasonable-grounds indication for believing that the person might have been subjected to any [of the stipulated] offences." Directive 2011/36/EU of the European Parliament and of the Council of 5 April 2011 on preventing and combating trafficking in human beings and protecting its victims, and replacing Council Framework Decision 2002/629/JHA, OJ L 101/1, Apr. 15, 2011, at Art. 11(2) [2011 EU Trafficking Directive].

obligation on competent authorities to identify them as such. By failing to identify trafficked persons correctly, States effectively and permanently deny victims the ability to realize the rights and protections to which they are legally entitled. Delays in the identification process can have a similarly deleterious effect. The identification of trafficked persons is never a default position and will always require a level of activity and engagement on the part of the State. Accordingly, the obligation on the State to identify trafficked persons as such can be characterized as an active one. It is also an obligation that is fundamentally linked to those related to victim protection and repatriation, as detailed further later in the chapter. International and regional policy documents confirm the connection between identification and access to rights.[123]

8.2.2.2. Noncriminalization of Smuggled Victims of Trafficking

Smuggled migrants are often criminalized for offenses such as entering or staying illegally, or possessing fraudulent documentation. Although the Migrant Smuggling Protocol is clear on the point that it cannot be used as the basis for such criminalization, States retain the right to act against smuggled migrants for offenses they may have committed under national laws.[124] The situation is different for smuggled migrants who have also been trafficked. In cases of trafficking it is now increasingly well accepted that persons who have been trafficked should *not* be criminalized or prosecuted for offenses that relate to the fact of their having been trafficked including, for example, offenses related to illegal entry, illegal stay, and illegal work. This may become relevant for example, when an apparently smuggled (but also trafficked) migrant is implicated in another crime such as drug smuggling. Although the Trafficking Protocol does not directly address this point, the 2009 Conference of the Parties to the Organized Crime Convention recommended that States Parties to the Trafficking Protocol "[c]onsider, in line with their domestic legislation, not punishing or prosecuting trafficked persons for unlawful acts committed by them as a direct consequence of their situation as trafficked persons or where they were compelled to commit such unlawful acts."[125] This recommendation identifies two potential prisms through which non-prosecution for status offenses can be viewed: the "causation model" (by which the acts in question were a result of the trafficking situation) and the "compulsion model" (by which the acts in question were carried

[123] See, for example, UN Trafficking Principles and Guidelines, at Guideline 2.

[124] See generally Chapter 1, at Section 1.1.3, and Chapter 5.

[125] Conference of the Parties to the United Nations Convention on Transnational Organized Crime, "Report on the Meeting of the Working Group on Trafficking in Persons held in Vienna on 14 and 15 April 2009," UN Doc. CTOC/COP/WG.4/2009/2, Apr. 21, 2009, at Recommendation 1(H).

out under duress).[126] Article 26 of the European Trafficking Convention follows the duress model, requiring States Parties, in accordance with the basic principles of their legal systems, to "provide for the possibility of not imposing penalties on victims for their involvement in unlawful activities, to the extent that they have been compelled to do so."[127] The notion of compulsion is linked to the "means" element of the definition of trafficking and thereby extends to include, at a minimum, involvement in unlawful activities as the result of coercion, abduction, fraud, deception, or abuse of power or of a position of vulnerability.[128] This provision does not provide complete protection from prosecution for status offenses. In other words, States Parties must only provide for the *possibility* of non-prosecution. Concern was expressed about the cautious approach taken in the European Trafficking Convention[129] and the 2011 EU Directive on Trafficking, which replaced the 2002 Framework Decision and which requires Member States in accordance with the basic principles of their legal systems, to "take the necessary measures to ensure that competent national authorities are entitled not to prosecute or impose penalties on victims of trafficking in human beings for their involvement in criminal activities which they have been compelled to commit as a direct consequence of being subjected to [trafficking-related] acts."[130] The preamble to the Directive affirms that the aim of this protection is "to safeguard the human rights of victims, to avoid further victimisation and to encourage them to act as witnesses in criminal proceedings against the perpetrators." It further notes

126 See Conference of the Parties to the United Nations Convention on Transnational Organized Crime, Working Group on Trafficking in Persons, "Non-punishment and Non-prosecution of Victims of Trafficking in Persons: Administrative and Judicial Approaches to Offences Committed in the Process of Such Trafficking," UN Doc. CTOC/COP/WG.4/2010/4, Dec. 9, 2009.

127 European Trafficking Convention, at Art. 26. See also European Trafficking Convention Explanatory Report, at paras. 272–274.

128 European Trafficking Convention Explanatory Report, at para. 273.

129 "Stakeholders have pointed out that victims of trafficking are normally detained or prosecuted or punished for minor offences which are typically connected with the victimisation process, such as violations of immigration laws, use of false documents, and prostitution, in countries where prostitution as such is criminalised. The fear of punishment and/or deportation is considered a major obstacle for victims to come forward, report the crime, and act as witnesses. Therefore the clause must be considered a major element of a successful anti-trafficking legislation. A similar non-punishment clause has been included in the CoE Convention, but the formulation is not clearly binding; moreover it does not cover all victims, since it only refers to victims who have been compelled to commit a crime, while in some cases they are trafficked by means of deception and abuse, according to the legal definition of trafficking. The added value of the new FD [Framework Decision] would be a better and binding formulation of the clause. In order to avoid an abuse of the clause, MS [Member States] could be allowed not to apply the clause in case of extreme gravity of the crime committed by the victim." "Accompanying Document to the proposal for a Council Framework Decision in preventing and combating trafficking in human beings, and protecting victims, repealing Framework Decision 2002/629/JHA, Impact Assessment," Mar. 25, 2009, SEC (2009) 358, at 24–25.

130 2011 EU Trafficking Directive, at Art. 8.

that the safeguard should not exclude prosecution or punishment for offenses that a person has voluntarily committed or participated in.[131]

Outside existing legal regulation, there is considerable and growing evidence that the policy preference for victims of trafficking not to be subject to criminalization is evolving into a widely accepted normative standard.[132] In that regard it is important to emphasize that the notion of protecting trafficked persons from criminalization for status-related offenses is not particularly innovative or radical. Rather, it reflects basic principles recognized in most national legal systems relating to responsibility and accountability for criminal offenses. The principle is not intended to confer blanket immunity on trafficked victims who may commit other non–status-related crimes with the requisite level of criminal intent. For example, if a trafficked person engages in a criminal act such as robbery or unlawful violence – or indeed migrant smuggling – then he or she should be subject to the normal criminal procedure with due attention to available lawful defenses.

8.2.2.3. Provision of Immediate Protection

Victims of trafficking almost invariably find themselves in a situation of great insecurity and vulnerability that will likely only be exacerbated by the smuggling process. Such persons may be physically injured as well as physically and/or emotionally traumatized. They may be afraid of retaliation. They are likely to have few, if any, means of subsistence. The responsibility of protecting and caring for victims lies with the State. This responsibility becomes operational when the State *knows* or *should know* that an individual within its jurisdiction is a victim of trafficking. It thereby links back to the obligation of identification discussed previously. The principle is applicable to all countries in whose territory the victim is located. It applies to all trafficked persons, whether victims of national or transnational trafficking. When considering the protection and support obligations owed to victims of trafficking, it is important to acknowledge that their experience of harm does not necessarily cease when they come to the attention of national authorities. Corruption and complicity of public officials may result in a continuation of an exploitative situation or the emergence of a new one. The harm already done to victims can be compounded by failures to provide medical and other forms of support. It may also be exacerbated by linking the provision of such services to an obligation of coopera-

[131] Ibid. at Preambular para. 14.

[132] This conclusion applies, even more strongly, to noncriminalization of child victims of trafficking. See Gallagher, *The International Law of Human Trafficking*, at chapter 5.5.3. See further Organization for Security and Co-operation in Europe, *Policy and Legislative Recommendations towards the Effective Implementation of the Non-punishment Provision with regard to Victims of Trafficking* (2013).

tion that victims may not be willing or able to meet: a practice that is now generally rejected as incompatible with the broader rights owed to victims of trafficking.[133]

The Trafficking Protocol requires each State Party to "endeavour to provide for the physical safety of victims of trafficking in persons while they are within its territory."[134] Although this provision is limited by the soft nature of the obligation and the specific reference to only physical safety, it nevertheless obliges States Parties "to actually take at least some steps that amount to an 'endeavour' to protect safety."[135] The Organized Crime Convention further requires States Parties to take appropriate measures, within their means, "to provide assistance and protection to victims [of trafficking], in particular in cases of threat of retaliation or intimidation."[136] Measures of protection may include physical protection, domestic or foreign relocation, and special arrangements for giving evidence.[137] The protection obligations of the Convention are mandatory for States Parties "but only where appropriate and within the means of the State party concerned."[138]

The European Trafficking Convention contains a general obligation on States Parties to "take due account of the victim's safety and protection needs."[139] This requirement is supplemented by a detailed provision that sets out the specific measures that must be implemented to provide "effective and appropriate protection" to victims and others (including witnesses, family members, and victim support agencies) from potential retaliation and intimidation, in particular during and after the investigation and prosecution processes.[140] Measures may include physical protection, relocation, identity change, and assistance in obtaining jobs.[141] Protection from harm is an additional aspect of the Convention's provisions on privacy and court proceedings.[142] A similar provision is found in the 2011 EU Directive on Trafficking.[143]

That instrument also makes specific reference to the protection of child victims of trafficking.[144] In this connection it should be noted that the CRC Optional Protocol

[133] See Gallagher, *The International Law of Human Trafficking*, at 298–301.

[134] Trafficking Protocol, at Art. 6(5).

[135] *Legislative Guide*, at 285 (para. 59).

[136] Organized Crime Convention, at Art. 25(1).

[137] *Legislative Guide*, at 166 (para. 350).

[138] Ibid. at 167 (para. 355).

[139] European Trafficking Convention, at Art. 12(2). Note that this provision will also apply to victims who have only been provisionally identified as such: ibid. at Art. 10(2).

[140] Ibid. at Art. 28.

[141] Ibid. at Art. 28(2).

[142] Ibid. at Arts. 11, 30.

[143] "Member States shall ensure that victims of trafficking in human beings receive appropriate protection on the basis of an individual risk assessment, inter alia, by having access to witness protection programmes or other similar measures, if appropriate and in accordance with the grounds defined by national law or procedures." 2011 EU Trafficking Directive, at Art. 12(3).

[144] Ibid. at Art. 13.

on the Sale of Children, Child Prostitution and Child Pornography also contains specific provisions on protection from further harm that would be applicable to certain child victims of trafficking.[145] Various non-treaty instruments and documents support the existence of an obligation on the part of States to protect victims of trafficking from further harm.[146]

The precise content of the obligation to protect from further harm will depend on the circumstances of each case. The standard of due diligence, discussed in detail in Chapter 4, will certainly require States to take reasonable measures to this end. In most situations, reasonable protection from harm will require a positive and immediate action on the part of the State to move the trafficked person out of the place of exploitation to a place of safety. It is also likely that protection from further harm will require attention to the immediate medical needs of the victim. As recognized in the 2011 EU Directive on Trafficking, risk assessment may be necessary to determine whether victims are under a particular risk of intimidation or retaliation.[147] Risk assessment should take into account the individual profile of the trafficked person and should also be appropriate to the situation. For example, the nature and level of any risk to a trafficked person may change if and when that person decides or declines to provide a statement, decides or declines to participate as a witness in a criminal trial, etc. Measures to protect victims from further harm should only be used with the consent of the beneficiary.[148]

8.2.2.4. Provision of Immediate Care and Support

The nature of the obligation on States to provide care and support of victims of trafficking is inextricably tied up with their status as victims of crime and victims of human rights violations – a status that, as noted previously, provides such victims with a right to be treated with humanity and with respect for their dignity and human rights, as well as with an entitlement to measures that ensure their well-being and

[145] CRC Optional Protocol, at Arts. 8(1)(f), 8(5).

[146] For example, Resolutions of the General Assembly and Human Rights Council have called on governments to ensure the "protection" of victims of trafficking and more recently identified an obligation to provide such protection. See UN Human Rights Council, "Trafficking in Persons, Especially Women and Children," UN Doc. A/HRC/RES/11/3, June 17, 2009, at Preamble ("all States have an obligation to ... rescue victims and to provide for their protection"); and UN General Assembly, "Improving the Coordination of Efforts against Trafficking in Persons," UN Doc. A/RES/61/180, Mar. 8, 2007, at Preamble ("Member States have an obligation to provide protection for the victims"). See also UN Trafficking Principles and Guidelines, at Principle 8. See also Principle 2 and Guideline 6.6.

[147] 2011 EU Directive on Trafficking, at Art. 12(3).

[148] Although the Trafficking Protocol is not specific on this point, the Explanatory Report to the European Trafficking Convention explicitly states that consent to protective measures is essential except in extreme circumstances such as an emergency where the victim is physically incapable of giving consent: European Trafficking Convention Explanatory Report, at para. 289.

avoid re-victimization.[149] Smuggled persons who have been trafficked may be entitled to additional, status-related rights of care and support. For example, as explored in Section 8.2.2.6, specific and additional obligations of care and support are owed by the State to smuggled children who have been trafficked. The prohibition on sex-based discrimination is also important when considering issues of access to support and assistance. Women victims of trafficking may also be victims of gender-based violence and thereby entitled to access help on this basis as well as on the basis of their status as victims of trafficking.[150]

The major trafficking treaties set out varying standards in relation to victim care and support. Victim protection and support is one of the three stated purposes of the Trafficking Protocol,[151] and States Parties are required to:

> *consider implementing* measures to provide for the physical, psychological and social recovery of victims … in particular the provision of (a) Appropriate housing; (b) Counseling and information, in particular as regards their legal rights, in a language that the victims … can understand; (c) Medical, psychological and material assistance; and (d) Employment, educational and training opportunities.[152]

In applying these provisions to those victims within its territory,[153] States Parties are required to take into account the age, gender, and special needs of victims of trafficking, in particular the special needs of children.[154] The requirements of the European Trafficking Convention with respect to victim support and assistance are much more specific, detailed, and substantive than those of the Trafficking

[149] "Principles and Guidelines on the Right to a Remedy and Reparation," at para. 10.

[150] See, for example, CEDAW General Recommendation No. 19, at para. 24(b) ("[a]ppropriate protective and support services should be provided for victims"). See also UN General Assembly, "Declaration on the Elimination of Violence against Women," adopted by GA Res. 48/104, UNGAOR 48th sess, 85th plen mtg, UN Doc. A/48/49 Supp. No. 49, at 217, Dec. 20, 1993, at Art. 4(g), which makes provision for specialized assistance for women subjected to violence, such as "rehabilitation, assistance in child care and maintenance, treatment, counselling, and health and social services, facilities and programmes, as well as support structures, and … other appropriate measures to promote their safety and physical and psychological rehabilitation"; Beijing Declaration and Platform for Action, at paras. 99, 106, 107, 122, 125, 130; and "Further Actions and Initiatives to Implement the Beijing Declaration and Platform for Action," UN Doc. A/RES/S-23/3, Nov. 16, 2000, at para. 97(c).

[151] Trafficking Protocol, at Art. 2(b).

[152] Ibid. at Art. 6(3) (emphasis added).

[153] An Interpretative Note relating to Art. 6(3) affirms that: "[t]he type of assistance set forth in this paragraph is applicable to both the receiving State and the State of origin of the victims of trafficking in persons, but only as regards victims who are in their respective territory. Paragraph 3 is applicable to the receiving State until the victim of trafficking in persons has returned to his or her State of origin, and to the State of origin thereafter." Travaux Préparatoires *for the Organized Crime Convention and Protocols*, at 373.

[154] Trafficking Protocol, at Art. 6(4).

Protocol. States Parties to the European Trafficking Convention are required to provide all victims within their territory or jurisdiction with a range of measures aimed to "assist victims in their physical, psychological and social recovery."[155] Such assistance is also to extend to those who have been provisionally identified as victims and, crucially, cannot be reserved only for those agreeing to act as witnesses.[156] It is to include, at least, appropriate and secure accommodation; psychological and material assistance at subsistence level; access to emergency medical treatment; translation or other services; counseling and information; assistance with legal proceedings; and, for children, access to education.[157] Additional provisions are made for victims lawfully within the territory of the State Party.[158] Obligations to provide assistance and support are linked to and reinforce the related obligation of States Parties to take due account of victims' safety and protection needs.[159] A similar level of detail characterizes the support and assistance provisions of the 2011 EU Trafficking Directive, most particularly with respect to child victims of trafficking.[160]

Non-treaty instruments developed at both the international and regional levels point to the development of an emerging consensus on the existence of certain minimum obligations on States with respect to support of trafficked persons. The Recommended Principles and Guidelines on Human Rights and Human Trafficking (UN Trafficking Principles and Guidelines), for example, require States to ensure that victims of trafficking have *access to adequate physical and psychological care*.[161] States and others are requested to consider ensuring, along with nongovernmental organizations, the availability of "safe and adequate shelter that meets the needs of trafficked persons" and "access to primary health care and counseling."[162] Regional soft law agreements and policy statements affirm the importance of ensuring that victims of trafficking are supported and assisted.[163]

155 European Trafficking Convention, at Art. 12(1). See also European Trafficking Convention Explanatory Report, at para. 148.

156 European Trafficking Convention, at Arts. 10(2), 12(6).

157 Ibid. at Art. 12(1).

158 Ibid. at Arts. 12(3)–(4). The extent to which these provisions actually impose specific obligations on States Parties or confer additional rights is unclear. See European Trafficking Convention Explanatory Report, at paras. 165–166.

159 European Trafficking Convention, at Art. 12(2). See also European Trafficking Convention Explanatory Report, at paras. 153–154 and 164.

160 2011 EU Trafficking Directive, at Article 11, and, in relation to children, Articles 13–16.

161 UN Economic and Social Council, Office of the United Nations High Commissioner on Human Rights, "Recommended Principles and Guidelines on Human Rights and Human Trafficking," UN Doc E/2002/68/Add.1, May 20, 2002 [UN Trafficking Principles and Guidelines], at Principle 8.

162 Ibid. at Guidelines 6.1 and 6.2.

163 See the extensive references at Gallagher, *The International Law of Human Trafficking*, at 308–310.

8.2.2.5. Provision of Legal Assistance

Victims of trafficking are often in a precarious legal situation and, for those who have been smuggled, this precariousness may well be exacerbated by their irregular immigration status and the fact that they may be at risk of prosecution for offenses such as illegal entry or possession and use of fraudulent documents. Victims are unlikely to have a full understanding of the rights to which they are entitled and will rarely be in a strong position to pursue those rights without help. The provision of legal assistance to such persons can best be viewed as a prerequisite to the realization of other important rights, including the right to protection, the right not to be prosecuted for status-related offenses, and the right to participate in legal proceedings against their exploiters.

The Trafficking Protocol requires that trafficked persons be provided with information on relevant court and administrative proceedings.[164] It further recognizes a duty on States to assist in making sure that victims can be present at and have their concerns and views considered during criminal proceedings against traffickers in a manner not prejudicial to the rights of the defense.[165] Both provisions are mandatory, and the latter provision echoes a similar article of the Organized Crime Convention.[166] The Protocol recognizes that the right of victims to be present and have their views known during legal proceedings is compromised by premature repatriation. It therefore requires States Parties of destination to ensure, inter alia, that such return is undertaken with "due regard ... for the status of any legal proceedings related to the fact that the person is a victim of trafficking."[167] The European Trafficking Convention, which also requires any return to be undertaken with due regard for legal proceedings,[168] establishes a range of victim assistance provisions related to the legal process, including an obligation on States Parties to ensure victims are provided counseling and information regarding their legal rights in a

164 Trafficking Protocol, at Art. 6(2)(a). Victim involvement in legal proceedings can take a number of different forms. Individuals who have been trafficked may provide evidence against their exploiters either through written statements or in person as part of a trial. Trafficked persons may also be called upon to provide a victim statement about the impact of the offense that could become part of a sentencing hearing. (This possibility is envisaged in the *Legislative Guide*, at 284 (para. 56).) In civil proceedings against their exploiters, trafficked persons may be applicants and/or witnesses. It has been noted that this should include information on the timing and progress of relevant proceedings as well as the disposition of any case in which the victim has an interest. UNODC Model Law on Trafficking in Persons, at 45.

165 Trafficking Protocol, at Art. 6(2)(b). This is an important recognition that even for a trafficked person who is unwilling or unable to testify, he or she still has a legitimate interest in relevant legal proceedings that needs to be accommodated.

166 Organized Crime Convention, at Art. 25(3): "Each State Party shall, subject to its domestic law, enable views and concerns of victims to be presented and considered at appropriate stages of criminal proceedings against offenders in a manner not prejudicial to the rights of the defence."

167 Trafficking Protocol, at Art. 8(2).

168 European Trafficking Convention, at Art. 16(2).

language they understand.[169] The 2011 EU Directive on Trafficking is much more expansive than the European Trafficking Convention, setting out a wide range of entitlements to victims of trafficking who are involved in criminal investigations and proceedings, as well as an obligation on Member States to avoid the "secondary victimization" that can occur when victims are involved in criminal proceedings.[170]

The right of victims of trafficking to receive legal information as well as legal and other assistance for the duration of any criminal proceedings against their exploiters, and the concomitant obligation on States to facilitate the provision of such assistance, are both affirmed in multiple policy documents and soft law texts.[171] Trafficked persons who are witnesses in criminal proceedings are entitled to additional measures of protection and support.[172]

8.2.2.6. Special Protections for Smuggled Children Who Have Been Trafficked

Children are naturally included in the rules and standards outlined previously. However, international law recognizes a distinction between child and adult trafficking,[173] and the need for a different response. The reasons for this are well expressed in the UN Trafficking Principles and Guidelines:

> The particular physical, psychological and psychosocial harm suffered by trafficked children and their increased vulnerability to exploitation require that they be dealt with separately from adult trafficked persons in terms of laws, policies, programmes and interventions. The best interests of the child must be a primary consideration in all actions concerning trafficked children whether undertaken by public or private welfare institutions, courts of law, administrative authorities or legislative bodies. Child victims of trafficking should be provided with appropriate assistance and protection and full account should be taken of their special rights and needs.[174]

As noted, the specialist trafficking instruments pay varying attention to the issue of protection and support for children who have been trafficked. The Trafficking Protocol's references are vague and non-substantive, particularly when compared to

[169] Ibid. at Arts. 12(1)(d)–(e).

[170] 2011 EU Trafficking Directive, at Art. 12.

[171] See, for example, the UN Trafficking Principles and Guidelines, at Principle 9 and Guidelines 4.8, 6.5. See also Basic Principles for Victims of Crime and Abuse of Power," at para. 6.

[172] See Gallagher, *The International Law of Human Trafficking*, at 317–320.

[173] Trafficking in persons comprises three elements: an act (recruitment, receipt, harboring, etc.), a means through which that act was made possible (force, fraud, coercion, abuse of a position of vulnerability), and a purpose (exploitation). The international legal offense of trafficking in children is established solely through an "act" undertaken for the purpose of exploitation. See Trafficking Protocol, at Art. 3.

[174] UN Trafficking Principles and Guidelines, at Guideline 8.

the more extensive provisions of the European Trafficking Convention and the 2011 EU Trafficking Directive. However there is general agreement States are under special and additional obligations with respect to provision of protection and support to children. It can be argued, for example, that international law recognizes certain presumptions in relation to both age and status in respect of the identification process for trafficked children. Briefly: "[i]n a case where the age of a victim is uncertain and there are reasons to believe the victim is a child, a State party may, to the extent possible under its domestic law, treat the victim as a child in accordance with the Convention on the Rights of the Child until his or her age is verified."[175] Similarly, a smuggled child (or an individual who is presumed to be a child) who *may* be a victim of trafficking is to be presumed to be a victim unless or until another determination is made.[176] More generally, the principle of the best interests of the child should guide all decision making in respect of protection and support to trafficked children. International law and policy recognizes that this requirement is even more pressing in respect of unaccompanied children who have been trafficked.[177] Many other child-specific aspects of the international legal framework around trafficking relate to matters of detention and return. These are considered further in Chapters 9 and 10.

8.3. ADDITIONAL OBLIGATIONS WITH RESPECT TO SMUGGLED MIGRANTS WHO ARE VICTIMS OF CRIME OR HUMAN RIGHTS ABUSES

As discussed earlier in this chapter and at various other points in this book, smuggled migrants are vulnerable to many different forms of criminality quite apart from trafficking, whether this is theft of their possessions, detention by smugglers in the course of being transported, physical violence, or sexual assault. Certain acts of violence, abuse, and exploitation against smuggled migrants may be characterized both as criminal acts and as abuses of human rights. The question of when a criminal act under national law becomes a human rights violation in international law (when a

[175] *Legislative Guide*, at 289 (para. 65). This provision is also inserted in the UNODC Model Law on Trafficking in Persons (at 47–48), as part of a mandatory provision relating protection and support of child victims. See also European Trafficking Convention, at Art. 10(3); European Trafficking Convention Explanatory Report, at para. 136; and United Nations Children's Fund, *Guidelines for the Protection of Child Victims of Trafficking* (Sept. 2006) [UNICEF Guidelines], at Guideline 3.1.2. The most explicit articulation of this standard is found in the 2011 EU Trafficking Directive at Article 13(2) ("Member States shall ensure that, where the age of a person subject to trafficking in human beings is uncertain and there are reasons to believe that the person is a child, that person is presumed to be a child in order to receive immediate access to assistance, support and protection").

[176] See European Trafficking Convention, at Art. 10; European Trafficking Convention Explanatory Report, at paras. 132–137, and further, Gallagher, *The International Law of Human Trafficking*, at 326.

[177] See European Trafficking Convention, at Art. 10(4)(a). See also *Legislative Guide*, at 289 (para. 65(a)); and UNICEF Guidelines, at Guideline 3.2.

victim of crime[178] becomes a victim of human rights abuse[179]) is a complicated one, requiring examination of both the primary rule (the asserted right and the obligation attached to it) and the secondary rules of State responsibility (which determine the circumstances in which an internationally wrongful act can be attributed to the State). A serious act of violence committed by a State official against a smuggled migrant will likely violate an established primary rule (e.g., the prohibition on torture or inhuman treatment) and will be readily attributable to the State under the rules of State responsibility. A similar act of violence committed by a private smuggler against a smuggled migrant will generally be a violation of the national criminal law of the State within whose jurisdiction that act takes place. Its status as a violation of international human rights law however will require an act or an omission on the part of the State that is itself a violation of that State's obligations under international law (for example, to protect smuggled migrants and to prevent offenses such as aggravated smuggling). This could occur if it were shown that the State had in some way failed to prevent the violent act, that it condoned the violent act, that it failed to seriously investigate the violent act, or that it failed to provide the victim with access to remedies. If the wrongful act cannot be attributed to the State then the State will not be held responsible.[180]

This section examines two obligations that may arise in relation to crimes committed against smuggled migrants by those who are involved in their smuggling: the obligation to investigate and prosecute such crimes, and the obligation to provide victims with access to remedies.

8.3.1. *Obligations of an Effective Criminal Justice Response*

Are States under an obligation to investigate and prosecute crimes and human rights violations committed against smuggled migrants by their facilitators or other persons with whom they come in contact? The Organized Crime Convention and Migrant Smuggling Protocol are silent on this point. However, the analysis set out in Chapter 4 confirmed that international law places a responsibility on States to

[178] For the definition of "victim of crime" see note 111 above.

[179] The UN General Assembly's "Basic Principles and Guidelines on the Right to a Remedy and Reparation" defines victims of gross violations of human rights and serious violations of international humanitarian law as: "persons who individually or collectively suffered harm, including physical or mental injury, emotional suffering, economic loss or substantial impairment of their fundamental rights, through acts or omissions that constitute gross violations of international human rights law, or serious violations of international humanitarian law. Where appropriate, and in accordance with domestic law, the term 'victim' also includes the immediate family or dependants of the direct victim and persons who have suffered harm in intervening to assist victims in distress or to prevent victimization" (at para. 8).

[180] See Chapter 4, at Section 4.2.1.

investigate, prosecute, and adjudicate serious human rights violations associated with migrant smuggling to the required standard of "due diligence." Chapter 4 also confirmed that this standard imposes a positive duty on States to ensure the effectiveness of their criminal law through investigation and prosecution. The duty to investigate and prosecute is applicable both when there is an allegation of a human rights violation by State officials and when the alleged perpetrator is a non-State actor. As noted previously, in relation to the latter case a State will become responsible under international law if it fails to seriously investigate private abuses of rights and to punish those responsible, thereby aiding in the commission of those private acts.[181] Furthermore, obligations of an effective criminal law extend to all crimes that occur against all persons within a States's jurisdiction. In other words, the fact that an assault or deprivation of liberty has been committed against persons not lawfully present does not modify the obligation on the State to investigate and prosecute that crime to the required standard of due diligence.

How does one measure whether a State is taking seriously its obligation to investigate and prosecute human rights violations associated with migrant smuggling? As has been noted in the context of human trafficking, the worst case will generally be the easiest to decide.[182] A State that disregards credible allegations of exploitation of smuggled migrants; that fails to investigate perpetrators known to be within its jurisdiction; or that arrests and deports smuggled victims of abuse, exploitation, and violence without investigating their claims will clearly not pass the due diligence test. In less egregious cases, it is necessary to evaluate whether the steps taken evidence a genuine seriousness on the part of the State to investigate and prosecute such violations.

At a general level, it is useful to look to the broad requirements of effective criminal investigation. For example, the European Court of Human Rights has, in another context, provided rudimentary indicia of an effective criminal investigation that includes factors such as whether the investigators were independent, whether the investigation was prompt, whether the investigation is capable of leading to a determination of whether the unlawful act was committed and the identification and punishment of those responsible, whether reasonable steps are taken to secure evidence concerning the incident, and whether there is a sufficient element of public scrutiny of the investigation or its results.[183] In its recent decision of *Rantsev v.*

[181] See further discussion and references in Chapter 4, at Section 4.3. Note the position of the Inter-American Court that investigations "must be undertaken in a serious manner and not as a mere formality preordained to be ineffective": *Velásquez Rodríguez v. Honduras*, Inter-Am Ct. H.R. (ser. C) No. 4, July 29, 1988 [*Velásquez Rodríguez*], at para. 177.

[182] Gallagher, *The International Law of Human Trafficking*, at 382–383.

[183] *Finucane v. United Kingdom*, (2003) 37 EHRR 29 (ECHR, July 1, 2003) [*Finucane v. UK*], at paras. 68–71. See also *McCann v. United Kingdom*, (1996) 21 EHRR 97 (ECHR, Sept. 27, 1995), at para. 161.

Cyprus and Russia, the Court reiterated these factors in the context of a human trafficking–related death.[184] The Court in that case also emphasized that investigations into trafficking must cover "all aspects of trafficking allegations *from recruitment to exploitation*,"[185] and to this end found violations by both the State of origin[186] and the State of destination.[187] Regarding the likelihood of disparate witnesses and evidence located in multiple States, the Court confirmed that "member States are also subject to a duty in cross-border trafficking cases to cooperate effectively with the relevant authorities of other States concerned in the investigation of events which occurred outside their territories."[188] These findings are directly relevant to many cases of smuggling-related exploitation including several of the case studies cited in the introduction to this book.[189]

When considering the capacity and willingness of a State to effectively investigate smuggling-related exploitation and violence to the requisite standard of due diligence, the following additional factors may be relevant:

- What procedures are in place to screen rescued or apprehended smuggled migrants in order to identify those who have been trafficked or who have otherwise suffered from criminality and human rights abuses, including exploitation and violence?
- Are there provisions for such persons, once identified, to be protected and assisted?
- Does provision of protection and assistance depend on a victim's willingness to support a criminal justice process such as an investigation or prosecution?
- Are there genuine incentives in place for victims to cooperate in investigations and prosecutions?
- How actively does the State investigate allegations of violence and exploitation against smuggled migrants? Does it rely on victims coming forward, or does it initiate its own investigations?[190]

[184] *Rantsev v. Cyprus and Russia*, (2010) 51 EHRR 1 (ECHR, Jan, 7, 2010) [*Rantsev v. Cyprus and Russia*], at para. 233 and the discussion that follows at paras. 234–242.

[185] Ibid. at para. 307 (emphasis added).

[186] Ibid. at para. 309.

[187] Ibid. at para. 300, finding the obligation to investigate trafficking allegations to be subsumed under the obligation to investigate the trafficking-related death of the deceased.

[188] Ibid. at para. 289.

[189] See also generally Chapter 7.

[190] An obligation to move beyond reactive investigations of serious human rights violations is supported by European case law as well as the pronouncements of human rights treaty-bodies. See, for example, *Sánchez v. Honduras*, Inter-Am Ct. H.R. (ser. C) No. 99, June 7, 2003, at para. 144 (an investigation "must have an objective and be assumed by the State as its own legal duty, not as a step taken by private interests that depends upon the *initiative of the victim or his family or upon their offer of proof*" (emphasis added)); *Rantsev v. Cyprus and Russia*, at para. 288 ("[t]he requirement to investigate does not depend on a complaint from the victim or next-of-kin: once the matter has come to the attention

- What is the capacity of the State to deal with such violence and exploitation? Are the appropriate laws in place? Do the relevant agencies have the knowledge, capacity, and resources to investigate and prosecute? Is there any evidence that they are discouraged from initiating or pursuing such investigations and prosecutions?
- To what extent does the criminal justice response operate to protect the rights of victims, including those who may be particularly vulnerable because of factors such as age, sex, or disability?
- To what extent does the criminal justice system guarantee free and fair trials, including respect for the rights of suspects?

Critically, for each of these points, is it even possible for States to know what is happening? In many countries, criminal justice data on violence against and exploitation of marginalized groups such as irregular migrants, including those who have been smuggled, is nonexistent, unavailable, or seriously compromised in terms of quality and/or reliability. States should be able to produce the necessary data on investigations, arrests, prosecutions, and convictions for such offenses that will either confirm or call into question their adherence to the standard of due diligence.

8.3.2. *Violence and Exploitation: The Right to a Remedy*

As with the obligations of an effective criminal justice response, the obligation to provide remedies and the right to access remedies in the context of migrant smuggling–related violence and exploitation is linked to the issue of State responsibility, discussed in detail in Chapter 4. Briefly, such an obligation can arise either directly or indirectly. In the first case, the obligation will be a consequence of the State being directly responsible for the violation of a human right or other rule that is protected under international law through either custom or treaty (for example, violence against a smuggled migrant in the course of an interdiction or during detention in violation of the prohibition on torture and inhumane treatment, or the forced return of a smuggled migrant that violates the obligation of *non-refoulement*). In the second case, the State is not directly implicated in the initial harm, but has failed to discharge its obligation to prevent the harm and/or to respond appropriately (for example, failure to investigate and prosecute smuggling-related exploitation to the required standard of due diligence). It this second case it is not the initial wrong that triggers an obligation of remedy but rather the subsequent failure of the State. In

of the authorities they must act of their own motion"); and *Finucane v. UK*, at para. 67 ("the authorities must act of their own motion, once the matter has come to their attention. They cannot leave it to the initiative of the next-of-kin either to lodge a formal complaint or to take responsibility for the conduct of any investigative procedures").

other words, the obligation on States to provide remedies for violations originating in the conduct of private persons must generally be linked to a distinct internationally wrongful act on the part of that State, such as a failure to protect or respond.

8.3.2.1. Basis of the Right to a Remedy

It is a well-established rule of international law that States have a duty to provide a domestic legal remedy to violations of human rights law that are attributable to it under the laws of State responsibility.[191] The first formal articulation of this obligation was in the Universal Declaration of Human Rights.[192] The International Covenant on Civil and Political Rights (ICCPR),[193] along with most international[194] and regional[195] human rights treaties, with the notable exceptions of the International Covenant on Economic, Social and Cultural Rights (ICESCR),[196] and the Convention on the Elimination of All Forms of Discrimination against Women (CEDAW),[197] recognizes a substantive right to remedy for violations as well as a procedural right of access to remedies. Once a treaty-based right to a remedy can be found to apply to a particular factual situation, then failure of the State to provide such remedies itself becomes an independent breach of that instrument. In the human rights context, this can mean that the State will be held responsible for a series of violations, including the individual violation that gives rise to the right to a remedy as well as the breach of that right.

The obligation to provide a remedy for human rights violations may be present even when not specifically articulated in a treaty. One approach identifies this obligation

191 See generally, D. Shelton, *Remedies in International Human Rights Law* (2nd ed. 2005). See also M. C. Bassiouni, "International Recognition of Victims' Rights" (2006) 6 *Human Rights Law Review* 203 [Bassiouni, "International Recognition of Victims' Rights"], at 213.

192 UDHR, at Art. 8: "Everyone has the right to an effective remedy by the competent national tribunals for acts violating the fundamental rights granted him by the constitution or by law."

193 ICCPR, at Art. 2(3).

194 CERD, at Art. 6; CRC, at Art. 39; Migrant Workers Convention, at Arts. 83, Art. 16(9); Convention against Torture and Other Cruel, Inhuman or Degrading Treatment or Punishment, 1465 UNTS 85, done Dec. 10, 1984, entered into force June 26, 1987, at Art. 14. In relation to violations of international humanitarian law, see Rome Statute of the International Criminal Court, 2187 UNTS 3, done July 17, 1998, entered into force July 1, 2002, at Art. 75.

195 European Convention on Human Rights, at Art. 13; American Convention on Human Rights, 1144 UNTS 123, done Nov. 22, 1969, entered into force July 18, 1978, at Art. 25; and African Charter on Human and Peoples' Rights, 1520 UNTS 217, done June 27, 1981, entered into force Oct. 21, 1986, at Art. 7(1)(a).

196 International Covenant on Economic, Social and Cultural Rights, 993 UNTS 3, done Dec. 16, 1966, entered into force Jan. 3, 1976 [ICESCR].

197 Convention on the Elimination of All Forms of Discrimination Against Women, 1249 UNTS 13, done Dec. 18, 1979, entered into force Sept. 3, 1981 [CEDAW].

as itself a norm of customary international law.[198] Cited evidence includes the above-mentioned reference in the Universal Declaration of Human Rights to the right of everyone to "an effective remedy by the competent national tribunals for acts violating the fundamental rights granted him by the constitution or by law"[199] as well as reiterations of the right to a remedy in numerous other soft law instruments;[200] conforming State practice[201]; and the decisions of international courts and tribunals.[202] Under a slightly different approach, the duty on a State Party to provide a remedy for violations "is perhaps implicit in human rights treaties which require national implementation and whose effectiveness depends on the availability of municipal remedies."[203]

A further basis of the right to a remedy may lie in the nature of the violation and/or the status of the victim. For example, it has been repeatedly asserted that, (despite the central treaty referring neither to violence against women nor to remedies), international law recognizes the right to a remedy in relation to violence against women.[204] The right to a remedy for victims of trafficking is likely on much stronger ground, having been repeatedly and emphatically asserted in both treaty and soft law, and affirmed by international jurisprudence.[205]

8.3.2.2. Standards and Forms of Remedy

The substantive content of the obligation to provide "effective remedies" has been extensively considered by international and regional treaty bodies. It is generally accepted that remedies or reparation should be proportionate to the gravity of harm suffered[206] as well as "accessible, affordable, timely and effective."[207] Other terms that

198 Bassiouni, "International Recognition of Victims' Rights," at 218.

199 UDHR, at Art. 8.

200 See, for example, "Vienna Declaration and Programme of Action," UN Doc. A/CONF.157/23, July 12, 1993, at para. 27: "Every State should provide an effective framework of remedies to redress human rights grievances or violations."

201 See Bassiouni's examination of State practice in Bassiouni, "International Recognition of Victims' Rights," at 218–223.

202 See, for example, the Inter-American Court of Human Rights in the *Velásquez Rodríguez* case at para. 174: "The State has a legal duty to take reasonable steps to prevent human rights violations and to … ensure the victim adequate compensation."

203 T. Meron, *Human Rights and Humanitarian Norms as Customary Law* (1989), at 138. It has also been contended, in the case of CEDAW, that certain of its Articles, taken together, constitute such a right. See R. J. Cook, "State Responsibility for Violations of Women's Human Rights" (1994) 7 *Harvard Human Rights Journal* 125, at 168–169.

204 See Gallagher, *The International Law of Human Trafficking*, at 360–362.

205 See ibid. at 362–369.

206 "Principles and Guidelines on the Right to a Remedy and Reparation," at para. 15.

207 UN Committee on Economic, Social and Cultural Rights, "General Comment No. 9: The Domestic Application of the Covenant," UN Doc. E/C.12/1998/24, Dec. 3, 1998 [CESCR General Comment No. 9], at para. 9.

are commonly used include "adequate" and "appropriate."[208] The precise nature of the required remedy will, of course, depend on the primary obligation and the nature of the violation. In relation to violations of the ICCPR, for example, the UN Human Rights Committee has referred to the need to take account of the special vulnerability of certain categories of persons; the importance of States Parties establishing appropriate judicial and administrative mechanisms for addressing claims of rights violations under domestic law; the key role of the judiciary in assuring rights and remedies; and the importance of administrative mechanisms giving effect to the remedies-related obligation to investigate allegations of violations promptly, thoroughly, and effectively through independent and impartial bodies.[209] Other human rights treaty bodies have affirmed the need for adequate and appropriate remedies that take into account the circumstances of the breach.[210]

As explored in detail in Chapter 4, the international law of State responsibility identifies a range of generally required actions for reparation of an international wrong, including restitution, compensation, rehabilitation, satisfaction, and guarantees of non-repetition.[211] The UN Principles and Guidelines on the Right to a Remedy and Reparation, adopted by the General Assembly in 2005, provide a soft law affirmation of the relevance of these elements for serious violations of human rights.[212] The following paragraphs define and briefly explore each of these elements

[208] This is the formulation commonly used with reference to remedies for trafficking- related violations. See further Gallagher, *The International Law of Human Trafficking*, at 364–369.

[209] UN Human Rights Committee, "General Comment No. 31: The Nature of the General Legal Obligation Imposed on States Parties to the Covenant," UN Doc. HRI/GEN.1/Rev.7, at 192, May 12, 2004, adopted Mar. 29, 2004 [HRC General Comment No. 31]. See also CESCR General Comment No. 9, at para. 9.

[210] See, for example, UN Committee on the Elimination of Racial Discrimination, "General Recommendation No. 23: Indigenous Peoples," UN Doc. A/52/18, Annex V, at 122, Aug. 18, 1997, at para. 5 (noting that restitution is the appropriate remedy for dispossession of land and that "[o] nly when this is for factual reasons not possible, the right to restitution should be substituted by the right to just, fair and prompt compensation"); and UN Committee on the Rights of the Child, "General Comment No. 5: General Measures of Implementation of the Convention on the Rights of the Child," UN Doc. CRC/GC/2003/5, Nov. 27, 2003, at para. 24 ("Children's special and dependent status creates real difficulties for them in pursuing remedies for breaches of their rights. So States need to give particular attention to ensuring that there are effective, child-sensitive procedures available to children and their representatives ... Where rights are found to have been breached, there should be appropriate reparation, including compensation, and, where needed, measures to promote physical and psychological recovery, rehabilitation and reintegration, as required by article 39."). See also CESCR General Comment No. 9, at para. 9 (the right to an effective remedy may require administrative action as well as – or instead of – judicial remedies. The selection of appropriate remedies must depend on what kind of action is required to make the relevant Convention right fully effective).

[211] See Chapter 4, at Section 4.5.

[212] UN General Assembly, "Basic Principles and Guidelines on the Right to a Remedy and Reparation for Victims of Gross Violations of International Human Rights Law and Serious Violation of International Humanitarian Law," UN Doc. A/RES/60/147 Annex, Dec. 16, 2005 ["Principles and Guidelines on

with reference to the specific situation and needs of smuggled persons who have been subject to serious violations of human rights.

Compensation is the most common form of remedy and is payable for damage caused by an internationally wrongful act to the extent that such damage is economically assessable and "not made good by restitution."[213] In other words, monetary compensation should be intended to remedy the damage caused by the breach to the extent that this is possible.[214] Compensation should be "appropriate and proportional to the gravity of the violation and the circumstances of each case."[215] It can, as acknowledged in the relevant provision of the European Trafficking Convention, cover both material losses and nonmaterial or so-called moral suffering. In the case of smuggling-related violence and exploitation, an effective, adequate, and appropriate remedy could include compensation payable (by the offender or by the State) under a range of heads identified by the Principles and Guidelines on the Right to a Remedy and Reparation, including physical and psychological harm; lost opportunities; loss of earnings; moral damage; and medical, legal, or other costs incurred as a result of the violation.[216]

Restitution involves material, judicial, or other measures aimed at restoring the situation that existed prior to the violation, as far as this is possible. Restitution can be especially important in relation to violations of a continuing character. Effective, adequate, and appropriate actions to secure restitution in cases of smuggling-related violations may include release of the victim from detention (imposed by smugglers, the State, or any other entity); recognition of legal identity and citizenship; return of property; safe return to the individual's place of residence[217]; or, in cases where the

the Right to a Remedy and Reparation"]. For a detailed analysis of the drafting history and substantive provisions of this instrument, see Bassiouni, "International Recognition of Victims' Rights," at 247–278; and Redress Trust, "Implementing Victims' Rights: A Handbook on the Basic Principles and Guidelines on the Right to a Remedy and Reparations" (Mar. 2006).

213 International Law Commission, *Draft Articles on Responsibility of States for Internationally Wrongful Acts*, in "Report of the International Law Commission on the Work of Its Fifty-Third Session," UN GAOR, 56th Sess, Supp. No. 10, UN Doc. A/56/10, at 43 (2001), at Art. 36(1). As noted previously, the compensation obligations arising from Article 25(3) of the Organized Crime Convention do not apply, prima facie, to smuggled migrants, absent additional factors such as aggravated smuggling or trafficking.

214 In *Godínez Cruz*, the Inter-American Court of Human Rights held that "it is appropriate to fix the payment of 'fair compensation' in sufficiently broad terms in order to compensate, to the extent possible, for the loss suffered": *Godínez Cruz v. Honduras, Interpretation of the Compensatory Damages*, Inter-Am Ct. H.R. (ser. C) No. 10, Aug. 17, 1990, at para. 27.

215 "Principles and Guidelines on the Right to a Remedy and Reparation," at para. 20.

216 Ibid. For a more detailed list of possible heads of compensation see UNODC Model Law on Trafficking in Persons, at 55.

217 Several of these examples are drawn from the "Principles and Guidelines on the Right to a Remedy and Reparation," at para. 19.

violation is related to the obligation of *non-refoulement*, rescindment of a decision to return a smuggled migrant. The protection and assistance measures outlined in the first part of this chapter would be another important aspect of restitution, as well as of rehabilitation.

Rehabilitation is a victim-centered notion that recognizes a need to ensure that the person who has suffered a violation of human rights has his or her status and position "restored" in the eyes of the law as well as of the wider community. Rehabilitation should include the provision of medical and psychological care as well as legal and social services.[218] Smuggled victims of serious violations of human rights such as exploitation and violence will inevitably require a range of support services. The rehabilitation element of reparation would impose an obligation on the offending State to provide such services.

Satisfaction and *guarantees of non-repetition*: Satisfaction is a remedy for injuries that are not necessarily financially assessable, but that can be addressed by ensuring that the violations of the victim's rights are properly acknowledged and dealt with. Measures aimed at cessation of violations, verification of the facts, and full and public disclosure of the truth (to the extent that this will not cause further harm) are examples of remedies aimed at providing satisfaction to the victim.[219] Measures to prevent future smuggling-related violence and exploitation, discussed in Chapter 7, would be relevant to a discharge of this aspect of the remedies obligation, as would the effective investigation, prosecution, and sanctioning of perpetrators,[220] explored in detail in the previous section.

As already noted, the form and extent of remedies required will depend on the nature and circumstances of the breach as well as the content of the relevant primary obligation. In all cases, however, the form or forms must reflect and advance the obligation on the offending State to, as far as possible, wipe out the consequences of the breach and re-establish the situation that existed prior to its occurrence.[221] It is important to note that States providing remedies do not have an unfettered discretion in deciding the appropriateness of various options. In the *LaGrand* case, for example, the International Court of Justice ruled that an apology for failure to discharge an obligation of consular notification was insufficient in a situation whereby the individual involved had been subject to prolonged detention or convicted and sentenced to severe penalties.[222] The Court has further ruled, in a different case, that an obligation to review and reconsider potential breaches of

218 Ibid. at para. 21.

219 Ibid. at paras. 22(a)–(b).

220 Bassiouni, "International Recognition of Victims' Rights," at 271.

221 *Factory at Chorzów (Germany v. Poland) (Merits)*, [1928] PCIJ Rep, Series A, No. 17, at 47.

222 *LaGrand (Germany v. United States of America)*, [2001] ICJ Rep 466, at para. 123.

the relevant treaty could not be done through informal means but must engage the judicial process.[223]

8.3.2.3. Access to Remedies

In practice it appears that the right to a remedy is very rarely made available to smuggled migrants who have suffered violence or exploitation.[224] Sometimes this is because the violations against them are not recognized (for example, through a recognition of their status as victims of crime or victims of trafficking in persons). Even if their status is correctly recognized, such individuals are often removed from the country of destination before they have a chance to seek remedies for the harm they have suffered. Sometimes national laws prevent aliens, including those unlawfully present, from accessing certain forms of remedies such as criminal compensation. Even without such restrictive laws, it is clear that in most situations, the presence of the victim in the country where the remedy is being sought is in practice an additional and important corequisite for realizing the right to a remedy. It should be noted that in the case of trafficking, the need for specific provisions enabling trafficked persons to remain safely in the country in which the remedy is being sought for the duration of any criminal, civil, or administrative proceedings has been acknowledged as a natural corollary to the right to a remedy.[225]

Smuggled migrants may be denied their rights in this area simply because they lack information on the possibilities and processes for accessing remedies.[226] A right of access to effective remedies means that in addition to making such remedies available under criminal or civil law, States should ensure that victims are provided with information and assistance that will enable them to actually secure the

[223] *Avena and Other Mexican Nationals (Mexico v. United States of America)*, [2004] ICJ Rep 12, at para. 143.

[224] One important exception is Belgium, which provides access to remedies for victims of aggravated forms of migrant smuggling. As noted in the UNODC Model Law on Migrant Smuggling (at 69) the relevant law applies to cases in which the life of the victim has been endangered deliberately or due to severe negligence, and when the offense has resulted in an incurable disease, a permanent mental or physical disability, or the full deprivation or use of an organ.

[225] European Trafficking Convention Explanatory Report, at para. 192. See also UN Trafficking Principles and Guidelines, at Guideline 9.3.

[226] The UNODC Model Law on Migrant Smuggling, at 70, recommends inclusion of a mechanism for smuggled migrants who have been victimized to seek redress, through civil proceedings. The Model Law notes "...while the criminal justice system offers the State an opportunity to pursue criminals, it may offer very little to the smuggled migrants who may merely be witnesses to a proceeding. The opportunity to take civil proceedings (which should be interpreted to include all non-criminal proceedings, such as proceedings available through labour or civil courts) against those responsible for harm or abuse in the smuggling process may provide an opportunity for the smuggled migrants to seek redress if they have been victimized in the smuggling process": ibid.

compensation or restitution to which they are entitled. Once again, it is in the area of trafficking in persons where this very practical requirement has been most explicitly recognized.[227] The Principles and Guidelines on the Right to a Remedy are even more specific in identifying the steps to be taken by States toward ensuring access to justice for victims of serious human rights violations. These include: dissemination of information about all available remedies; development of measures to minimize inconvenience to victims and their representatives; protection against unlawful interference with victims' privacy and ensuring their safety from intimidation and retaliation before, during, and after judicial, administrative, or other proceedings that affect their interests; provision of proper assistance to victims seeking access to justice; and ensuring availability of all appropriate legal, diplomatic, and consular means to ensure that victims can exercise their rights to a remedy.[228]

In conclusion, if a State is directly or indirectly involved in a violation of the human rights of a smuggled migrant then that same State must make a genuine attempt to provide the injured person with some measure of reparation or redress. In the present context, this could involve the State ensuring the possibility of compensation and actively assisting a victim to pursue a civil claim for damages and/or lost earnings. It could also require the State itself to provide compensation, particularly in situations where the State has fallen short of the due diligence standard when it comes to preventing, investigating, and prosecuting the exploitation or violence that gave rise to the violation. The obligation on States to provide remedies to victims of human rights violations requires a genuine effort, on the part of individual States, to address the legal, procedural, and attitudinal obstacles that commonly thwart access to remedies.[229]

8.4. CONCLUSIONS ON OBLIGATIONS OF PROTECTION, ASSISTANCE, AND RESPONSE

States involved in drafting the Migrant Smuggling Protocol recognized that smuggled migrants need protection from human rights violations. However, their reluctance

[227] See European Trafficking Convention Explanatory Report, at para. 192 (noting that: "[p]eople cannot claim their rights if they do not know about them"). States Parties to that Convention are required to ensure that victims are provided with both information and legal assistance for the purpose of pursuing the remedies to which they are entitled. European Trafficking Convention, at Art. 15(1)–(2).

[228] "Principles and Guidelines on the Right to a Remedy and Reparation," at para. 12.

[229] As one example of steps that States might seek to take to address the obstacles that thwart access to remedies, in the European context, the Employee Sanctions Directive reverses the onus of proof so that "illegal workers" are at a minimum owed three months wages for irregular work: Directive 2009/52/EC of the European Parliament and of the Council of 18 June 2009 providing for minimum standards on sanctions and measures against employers of illegally staying third-country nationals, OJ L 168/24, June 30, 2009. The UNODC Model Law on Migrant Smuggling, at 70, recommends inclusion of a mechanism for smuggled migrants who have been victimized to seek redress, through civil proceedings.

to embrace specific and detailed obligations of protection and support for smuggled migrants is reflected in the final text. Although important rights are affirmed, States Parties retain a significant degree of latitude in determining how they will implement the highly generalized obligations of protection and assistance.

But the Migrant Smuggling Protocol is not the first (or last) word when it comes to determining the nature and scope of State obligations of protection and support to smuggled migrants. That instrument is explicitly made subject to a web of international rules that confirm the obligation on States to provide basic and immediate protection and assistance to smuggled migrants, most particularly when such persons are in danger or distress but also when their basic needs for food, shelter, and medical care cannot otherwise be met. Special and additional obligations will arise for the State in respect of certain categories of smuggled migrants. With regard to children for example, States must be guided by the overarching principle of the best interests of the child in relation to all aspects of their response, including the provision of protection and support. Smuggled migrants who are victims of trafficking have a right to be identified as such and to be accorded the entitlements that come with that status, including the right of noncriminalization and the provision of legal assistance. Where smuggling has involved serious violations of human rights such as violence or exploitation, the State is under an obligation to exercise due diligence in investigating and prosecuting those violations. This obligation exists irrespective of whether the perpetrator is a private person or an agent or entity of the State: in this context, those who have suffered human rights violations for which the State is responsible have a right of access to effective remedies.

9

Obligations Relating to Detention of Smuggled Migrants

The detention of foreigners seeking to enter a country without authorization is a relatively recent development. For example, in the United States, it was only in the late nineteenth century that detention began to be used as a way of regulating entry at the border. Other major countries of immigration, such as the United Kingdom, only introduced immigration detention in the 1970s.[1] Today, the detention of irregular migrants – whether through the use of executive or judicial power – is a common practice in most parts of the world.[2] Immigration laws of many countries permit – and sometimes even require – the executive to detain irregular migrants, a practice commonly referred to as administrative detention, to distinguish it from judicially imposed detention. It is under such provisions that those who have been smuggled, including asylum-seekers and refugees, typically find themselves in detention. Many countries use administrative detention as a means of confining smuggled migrants for purposes of security checks or other processes, and also pending their deportation.[3] Although rarely presented as such, the detention of irregular migrants is typ-

1 The detention of migrants pursuant to immigration controls was first authorized by statute in the United States in 1891. In the main, it appears that detention was primarily used as an ancillary to border control; the period of detention was brief and most people were admitted. For a comprehensive overview of the evolution of law and practice around modern immigration detention, see further D. Wilsher, *Immigration Detention: Law, History, Politics* (2012) [Wilsher, *Immigration Detention*].

2 See the results of a mapping exercise conducted by the Global Detention Project to identify all the sites of immigration detention globally, available at www.globaldetentionproject.org/home.html (accessed May 12, 2013). This work identifies only a small number of countries that do not routinely detain irregular migrants.

3 "Specific Groups and Individuals – Migrant Workers: Report of the Special Rapporteur, Ms. Gabriela Rodríguez Pizarro," UN Doc. E/CN.4/2003/85, Dec. 30, 2002, at para. 65.

Sections of this chapter draw on A. T. Gallagher, *The International Law of Human Trafficking* (2010) [Gallagher, *The International Law of Human Trafficking*] (Chapter 5.2.2.).

ically aimed at facilitating their return, "just as it is meant to deter other migrants from a life of illegality."[4]

Although administrative detention is the principal focus of the present chapter, it is important to acknowledge that smuggled migrants may also be subject to imprisonment for breach of criminal laws, including those related to migration.[5] The rules and standards set out later in the chapter apply equally to administrative and criminal detention. However, criminal detention is subject to additional rules relating, for example, to rights on arrest and the right to a fair trial.[6] It should nevertheless be noted that the traditional distinction between administrative and criminal detention does not always hold up well in the context of immigration control, which has, in the words of one commentator, "absorb[ed] the theories, methods, perceptions, and priorities of the criminal enforcement model."[7]

Whatever its particular legal basis or focus, the practice of immigration detention – which began primarily as a temporary response to irregular movements in a time of war – has become both increasingly institutionalized and common, including in countries of transit.[8] The growing use of facilitators makes it highly likely that smuggled migrants are making up a significant proportion of persons in migration detention.[9] Available numbers have been and continue to be significant. In the United Kingdom for example, in the year ending December 2012, 28,909 persons

4 D. Broeders, "Return to Sender?: Administrative Detention of Irregular Migrants in Germany and the Netherlands" (2010) 12(2) *Punishment and Society* 169, at 179–180.

5 For example, research in the United Kingdom has pointed to a high proportion of foreign women in prisons (estimates range from 26 to 41 percent) having been arrested for offenses such as deception and fraud in relation to their immigration status and related offenses of use of false documentation to access work or benefits, or pass through customs on entry or exit from the United Kingdom: L. Hales and L. Gelsthorpe, *The Criminalisation of Migrant Women* (Institute of Criminology, University of Cambridge, 2012).

6 See, for example, International Covenant on Civil and Political Rights, 999 UNTS 171, done Dec. 16, 1996, entered into force Mar. 23, 1976 [ICCPR], at Arts. 9(2), 10(2)–10(3). For a detailed explanation of the substative content of these obligations, see M. Nowak, *U.N. Covenant on Civil and Political Rights: CCPR Commentary*, (2nd revised ed. 2005) [Nowak, *CCPR Commentary*], at 228–230 and 250–254, respectively.

7 S. H. Legomsky, "The New Path of Immigration Law: Asymmetric Incorporation of Criminal Justice Norms" (2007) 64 *Washington and Lee Law Review* 469, at 472. For a comprehensive analysis of the trend towards over-criminalization of immigration (with a focus on the situation in the United States), see J. Chacón, "Overcriminalizing Immigration" (2012) 102 *Journal of Criminal Law and Criminology* 613. Chacón cites Department of Justice statistics confirming that for 2009, about half of all federal prosecutions were for immigration-related crimes. Ibid. at 614.

8 For a thorough examination and critique of the law and politics of immigration detention with a particular focus on the situation in Europe, see G. Cornelisse, *Immigration Detention and Human Rights: Rethinking Territorial Sovereignty* (2010).

9 See note 2 above.

were placed in immigration detention.[10] In Australia at the end of December 2012, 7,237 persons, principally smuggled asylum-seekers, were being held in immigration detention,[11] and 591 of these detainees had been held for more than two years.[12] The United States detains hundreds of thousands of irregular migrants each year and those figures are increasing rapidly.[13] Countries such as Canada, which have traditionally detained relatively few irregular migrants, are shifting automatic, unreviewable detention to the center of their anti-smuggling response.[14] Inadequate and sometimes inhumane conditions of detention in many countries are regularly and reliably reported.[15]

Immigration detention of smuggled migrants can take many different forms. For example, a smuggled migrant may be deprived of his or her liberty in the "international zone" at an airport on the direction of an immigration official, or on a

10 UK Home Office, "Immigration Statistics October to December 2012," available at www.homeoffice.gov.uk/publications/science-research-statistics/research-statistics/immigration-asylum-research/immigration-tabs-q4–2012/?view=Standard&pubID=1156263 (accessed May 12, 2013).

11 Department of Immigration and Citizenship, Australian Government, "Immigration Detention Statistics Summary – 31 December 2012," available at www.immi.gov.au/managing-australias-borders/detention/facilities/statistics/ (accessed May 12, 2013), at 4.

12 Ibid. at 8.

13 Khalan reports that "[i]n 1994, officials held approximately 6,000 noncitizens in detention on any given day. That daily average had surpassed 20,000 individuals by 2001 and 33,000 by 2008. Over the same period, the overall number of individuals detained each year has swelled from approximately 81,000 to approximately 380,000": A. Kalhan, "Rethinking Immigration Detention" (2010) 110 *Columbia Law Review Sidebar* 42, at 44–45. For 2013, the Department of Homeland Security requested Congress to provide approximately $2 billion to fund a detention capacity of 32,800 on any given night. The proposed amount was increased by the House of Representatives to fund a detention capacity of 34,000 beds per night: National Immigration Forum, *The Math of Immigration Detention: Runaway Costs for Immigration Detention Do Not Add Up to Sensible Policies* (2013), at 2. See also A. Siskin, *Immigration-Related Detention: Current Legislative Issues* (Congressional Research Service Report for Congress, Jan. 12, 2012), at 12–13.

14 Global Detention Project, *Immigration Detention in Canada: A Global Detention Project Special Report* (2012), available at http://oppenheimer.mcgill.ca/Immigration-Detention-in-Canada-A,3280 (accessed May 12, 2013).

15 See, for example, on Greece, *M.S.S. v. Belgium and Greece*, (2011) 53 EHRR 2 (ECHR, Jan. 21, 2011) [*M.S.S. v. Belgium and Greece*]; UN Office of the High Commissioner for Human Rights, "UN Special Rapporteur on the human rights of migrants concludes the fourth and last country visit in his regional study on the human rights of migrants at the borders of the European Union: Greece" (Dec. 3, 2012), available at www.ohchr.org/en/NewsEvents/Pages/DisplayNews.aspx?NewsID=12858&LangID=E (accessed May 12, 2013). Conditions in Australian detention facilities for smuggled migrants have also been branded as "inhumane." See, for example, Amnesty International, "Australia: Asylum Camp Cruel and Inhumane," November 23, 2012, available at www.refworld.org/docid/50bcb6872.html (accessed May 12, 2013). For a comprehensive and nuanced examination of all aspects of immigration detention in Australia, see Australian Parliament, Joint Select Committee on Australia's Immigration Detention Network, *Final Report* (2012), available at www.aph.gov.au/Parliamentary_Business/Committees/Senate_Committees?url=immigration_detention_ctte/immigration_detention/report/index.htm (accessed May 12, 2013).

smuggling vessel following an interdiction at sea. Smuggled migrants may be confined to a camp or other designated detention facility. They may be held on offshore islands or even extraterritorially. Despite the typically administrative nature of their detention, smuggled migrants are sometimes held in public or private prisons along with convicted criminals. Apart from location and facility type, a range of other features can be used to classify the various forms of detention to which smuggled migrants may be subjected including: security level (high security, secure, semi-secure, nonsecure, and mixed regime); segregation (by age and gender); ownership and management (private or public); and custodial authority (ministries, subministries such as an immigration agency, or international organizations such as the United Nations High Commissioner for Refugees (UNHCR) or International Organization for Migration (IOM)).[16]

Despite the growing importance of its place in modern migration systems, immigration detention is not the subject of a specific, comprehensive international legal regime. This reflects the reality that, particularly over the past thirty years, diplomatic discussions over migration control and the formulation of international standards have well and truly lagged behind the development of border controls and enforcement apparatus at both national and regional levels.[17] It is therefore not surprising that the relevant legal framework is patchy and in some parts incomplete, implicating a number of different norms and standards arising from both international and regional treaties. Previous studies have helped to elucidate the essential features of the applicable legal framework[18] but many issues remain unsettled.

In attempting to isolate and examine those standards that are most relevant to the issue of detention of smuggled migrants, the following discussion adopts the approach explained in Chapter 1. In short, priority is given to the widely ratified international treaties that incorporate specific rules on detention, most particularly the International Covenant on Civil and Political Rights (ICCPR) (with guidance on interpretation provided by decisions of the UN Committee on Human Rights), as well as the regional human rights treaties including the European Convention on Human Rights[19] (along with relevant case law from the European Court of Human

[16] M. Flynn, *Immigration Detention and Proportionality* (Global Detention Project Working Paper No. 4, Feb. 2011), at 15.

[17] Wilsher, *Immigration Detention*, at 119.

[18] See, for example, A. Pacurar, "Smuggling, Detention, and Expulsion of Irregular Migrants: A Study on International Legal Norms, Standards, and Practices" (2003) 5 *European Journal of Migration and Law* 259; Amnesty International, *Migration-Related Detention: A Research Guide on Human Rights Standards relevant to the Detention of Migrants, Asylum Seekers and Refugees* (2007); I. Ricipuro and M. Flynn, *Migration and Detention: Mapping the Legal Terrain* (2009) [Ricipuro and Flynn, *Migration and Detention: Mapping the Legal Terrain*].

[19] Convention for the Protection of Human Rights and Fundamental Freedoms, 213 UNTS 222, done Nov. 4, 1950, entered into force Sept. 3, 1953 [European Convention on Human Rights].

Rights), the African Charter on Human and Peoples' Rights (African Charter),[20] and the American Convention on Human Rights.[21] The analysis also relies heavily on rules drawn from the specialist international human rights treaties including the Convention against Torture,[22] the Refugee Convention,[23] and the Convention on the Rights of the Child.[24] Instruments such as the Migrant Workers Convention[25] are included in the analysis of primary legal rules with caveats relating to their restricted applicability to a small number and narrow range of States. The issue of detention has generated substantial "soft law" in the form of standards, principles, and resolutions of international bodies. Examples considered in this chapter include pronouncements of the UN Working Group on Arbitrary Detention, the UN Rules for the Protection of Juveniles Deprived of Their Liberty,[26] the Body of Principles for the Protection of All Persons under Any Form of Detention or Imprisonment,[27] and regional standards such as the Organization of American States' (OAS) Principles and Best Practices on the Protection of Persons Deprived of Liberty in the Americas.[28] The most important soft law source in relation to detention of smuggled asylum-seekers, UNHCR's Guidelines on the Applicable Criteria and Standards Relating to the Detention of Asylum-Seekers and Alternatives to Detention,[29] is also extensively

[20] African Charter on Human and Peoples' Rights, 1520 UNTS 217, done June 27, 1981, entered into force Oct. 21, 1986) [African Charter].

[21] American Convention on Human Rights, 1144 UNTS 123, done Nov. 22, 1969, entered into force July 18, 1978 [American Convention on Human Rights].

[22] Convention against Torture and Other Cruel, Inhuman or Degrading Treatment or Punishment, 1465 UNTS 85, done Dec. 10, 1984, entered into force June 26, 1987 [Convention against Torture].

[23] Convention Relating to the Status of Refugees, 189 UNTS 137, done July 28, 1951, entered into force April 22, 1954, as amended by the Protocol relating to the Status of Refugees, 606 UNTS 267, done Jan. 31, 1967, entered into force Oct. 4, 1967 [Refugee Convention].

[24] Convention on the Rights of the Child, 1577 UNTS 3, done Nov. 20, 1989, entered into force Sept. 2, 1990 [CRC].

[25] International Convention on the Protection of the Rights of All Migrant Workers and Members of their Families, UN Doc. A/Res/45/158, done Dec. 18, 1990, entered into force July 1, 2003 [Migrant Workers Convention].

[26] UN General Assembly, "United Nations Rules for the Protection of Juveniles Deprived of their Liberty," adopted by GA Res. 45/113, UN Doc. A/RES/45/113, Dec 14, 1990. See also UN General Assembly, "United Nations Standard Minimum Rules for the Administration of Juvenile Justice (The Beijing Rules)," adopted by GA Res. 40/33, UN Doc. A/RES/40/33, Nov. 29, 1985.

[27] UN General Assembly, "Body of Principles for the Protection of All Persons under Any Form of Detention or Imprisonment," adopted by GA Res. 43/173, UN Doc. A/RES/43/173, Annex, Dec. 9, 1988 ["Body of Principles for the Protection of All Persons under Any Form of Detention or Imprisonment"].

[28] Organization of American States, Inter-American Commission on Human Rights, *Principles and Best Practices on the Protection of Persons Deprived of Liberty in the Americas*, adopted by Resolution 1/08, Inter-AmCHR Doc. OEA/Ser/L/V/II.131 Doc. 26, Mar. 13, 2008 [OAS Principles and Best Practices on the Protection of Persons Deprived of Liberty in the Americas].

[29] UN High Commissioner for Refugees, *Guidelines on the Applicable Criteria and Standards relating to the Detention of Asylum-Seekers and Alternatives to Detention* (2012) [UNHCR Guidelines on Detention of Asylum-Seekers].

referred to. In keeping with the approach to sources of law adopted by this book, those materials are examined for the possible interpretative direction or weight they can provide to rules established through treaty or custom. The authors generally adopt a conservative approach with respect to such soft law sources, particularly in view of abundant contrary State practice.

It is important to reaffirm at the outset a major theme of this book: that the sovereign power of States includes the right to control who enters their territory. As a consequence, and despite some assertions to the contrary, [30] the detention of smuggled migrants per se is not in conflict with international law.[31] However, as with every other aspect of a State's response to migrant smuggling, the fact and circumstances of such detention must be in compliance with rules of international law, most particularly rules of human rights and refugee law. This chapter seeks to establish the *basis* and *limits* of State capacity to detain persons entering irregularly. Specifically: when and under what circumstances can States lawfully justify detaining a smuggled migrant? Can States detain persons in violation of their own laws and/or with no possibility for a review of that decision? Are States prohibited from imposing arbitrary detention and, if so, what are the factors that would identify a particular situation of detention as arbitrary? What are the relevant standards relating to the conditions of detention, and what rights are detained smuggled migrants entitled to during their detention? Do different rules apply to particular categories of smuggled migrants such as children, asylum-seekers, and refugees?

[30] An illustrative example is provided by the pronouncement of the UN Working Group on Arbitrary Detention, which has stated that "criminalizing illegal entry into a country exceeds the legitimate interest of States to control and regulate illegal immigration and leads to unnecessary detention": UN Human Rights Council, "Report of the Working Group on Arbitrary Detention," UN Doc. A/HRC/7/4, Jan. 10, 2008, at para. 53. Despite the first part of this statement conflicting with the well-established principle, referred to later on in the chapter, that the right of States to control their borders includes a right to detain those entering illegally, this view has been frequently and uncritically cited as reflective of existing law. See, for example, International Organization for Migration, *International Migration Law Information Note on International Standards on Immigration Detention and Non-custodial Measures* (2011), at 4–5; and A. Edwards, "Back to Basics: The Right to Liberty and Security of Person and 'Alternatives to Detention' of Refugees, Asylum-Seekers, Stateless Persons and Other Migrants" (UNHCR, Legal and Protection Policy Research Series), Doc. PPLA/2011/01.Rev.1, April 2011 [Edwards, "Back to Basics"], at 12. Note that the view of the Working Group on this fundamental issue is inconsistent. See, for example, UN Human Rights Council, "Report of the Working Group on Arbitrary Detention," UN Doc. A/HCR/13/30, Jan. 18, 2010, at para. 58 ("The Working Group is fully aware of the sovereign right of States to regulate migration. However, it considers that immigration detention should gradually be abolished.").

[31] See, for example, *A. v. Australia*, UNHRC Comm. No. 560/1993, UN Doc. CCPR/C/59/D/560/1993, Apr. 30, 1997, decided Apr. 3, 1997 [*A. v. Australia*], at para. 9.3, discussed at Section 9.2.3.1; and *Shayan Baram Saadi v. The United Kingdom*, (2008) 47 EHRR 17 (ECHR, Jan. 29, 2008) [*Saadi v. United Kingdom*], discussed at Section 9.2.3.2 below.

One matter that deserves to be addressed upfront concerns the responsibility of States for unlawful acts that relate to the detention of smuggled migrants. The implementation of immigration detention in major countries and regions of destination for smuggled migrants including Australia, Japan, North America, South Africa, and Central/Western Europe is becoming increasingly privatized.[32] Notwithstanding the involvement of private service providers, immigration detention is quintessentially an act of the State. International law is clear on the point that wrongful acts or omissions related to that detention will be attributed to the State – irrespective of whether it was the direct agent of harm. States are therefore responsible, under international law, for any unlawful or arbitrary detention or for any other failure to protect and respect the rights of detainees.[33]

9.1. RIGHT TO LIBERTY AND FREEDOM OF MOVEMENT

The right to liberty is the starting point for any discussion on detention, including the question of whether and under what circumstances a smuggled migrant may be detained. The international legal standard in relation to liberty and the prohibition on arbitrary detention is set out in Article 9(1) of the ICCPR: "Everyone has the right to liberty and security of person. No one shall be subjected to arbitrary arrest or detention. No one shall be deprived of his liberty except on such grounds and in accordance with such procedures as are established by law."[34] Similar provisions can be found in specialist human rights instruments[35] and all major regional human rights treaties.[36] The right to liberty and other fundamental rights examined in the

[32] For a review of the issues around privatization of immigration detention see M. Flynn and C. Cannon, *The Privatization of Immigration Detention: Towards a Global View* (Global Detention Project Working Paper, 2009).

[33] See further the extensive discussion on State responsibility for acts of private persons in Chapter 4, at Section 4.3.

[34] ICCPR, at Art. 9. Note also that the Universal Declaration of Human Rights (adopted by GA Res. 217A (III), UN GAOR, 3rd sess, 183rd plen mtg, UN Doc. A/810, at 71, Dec. 10, 1948) guarantees "everyone" the right to life, liberty, and security of the person, at Art. 3.

[35] See, for example, Migrant Workers Convention, at Art. 16(1) (providing for a right to liberty for all migrant workers and members of their families). See also Article 14 of this instrument, which provides that "migrant workers and their families" shall not be subjected "individually or collectively" to arbitrary arrest or detention.

[36] European Convention on Human Rights, at Art. 5(1); African Charter, at Art. 6; American Convention on Human Rights, at Art. 7(1); Cairo Declaration on Human Rights in Islam, adopted by Organisation of the Islamic Conference Res. 41/21-P, Aug. 5, 1990, UN GAOR, World Conf. on Hum. Rts., 4th sess, Agenda Item 5, UN Doc. A/CONF.157/PC/62/Add.18, June 9, 1993 [English translation], at Art. 20; and League of Arab States, Arab Charter on Human Rights, done May 22, 2004, entered into force Mar. 15, 2008, reprinted in (2005) 12 *International Human Rights Reports* 893, at Art. 14.

present chapter apply to all persons, irrespective of their immigration status, whether they have been smuggled or whether they are asylum-seekers or refugees.[37]

A related right is freedom of movement. In terms of its substantive content, the right to freedom of movement generally refers to a set of liberal rights of the individual, including the right to move freely and to choose a place of residence within a State, the right to cross frontiers in order to both enter and leave the country, and the prohibition on arbitrary expulsion of aliens.[38] The ICCPR explicitly recognizes and protects a right to freedom of movement,[39] as do all major regional human rights treaties.[40] Under the terms of the ICCPR, freedom of movement is only guaranteed to those who are lawfully within the territory of the relevant State.[41] Smuggled migrants who are, by definition, without regular migration status are therefore unlikely to benefit from the protections afforded by this particular right. The right to freedom of movement also arises in relation to the more specific category of smuggled migrants who are asylum-seekers or refugees. Article 26 of the Refugee Convention obliges States Parties to ensure such freedom of movement for refugees lawfully in the State's territory as is accorded to aliens generally in the same circumstances.[42] The weight of commentary and case law indicates that the term "lawfully" in this context references the domestic law of the State concerned[43]: this

[37] See UN Human Rights Committee: "General Comment No. 18: Non-discrimination," UN Doc. HRI/GEN/1/Rev.7, at 146, May 12, 2004, adopted Nov. 10, 1989, at para. 1; and "General Comment No. 15: The Position of Aliens under the Covenant," UN Doc. HRI/GEN.1/Rev.7, at 140, May 12, 2004, adopted Apr. 11, 1986 [HRC General Comment No. 15]. On the application of the right to liberty to the specific situation of asylum-seekers, UNCHR argues that taken together, the right to seek asylum, the non-penalization for illegal entry, and the rights to liberty and security of persons and freedom of movement, mean that the detention of asylum-seekers should be a measure of last resort, with liberty being the default position: UNHCR Guidelines on Detention of Asylum-Seekers, at Guideline 2. See generally the discussion of nonnationals and discrimination in Chapter 2, at Section 2.1.1.

[38] Nowak, *CCPR Commentary*, at 260.

[39] ICCPR, at Art. 12.

[40] Protocol No. 4 to the Convention of 4 November 1950 for the Protection of Human Rights and Fundamental Freedoms, 1496 UNTS 263, done Sept. 16, 1963, entered into force May 2, 1968, at Arts. 2–4; Protocol No. 7 to the Convention of 4 November 1950 for the Protection of Human Rights and Fundamental Freedoms, 1525 UNTS 195, done Nov. 22, 1984, entered into force Nov. 1, 1998, at Art. 1; African Charter, at Art. 12; and American Convention on Human Rights, at Art. 22.

[41] ICCPR, at Art. 12(1).

[42] Article 26 of the Convention Relating to the Status of Stateless Persons (360 UNTS 117, done Sept. 28, 1954, entered into force June 6, 1960) includes an identical obligation but for stateless persons.

[43] See, for example, *Plaintiff M47/2012 v. Director-General of Security* [2012] HCA 46 (Aus. HC, Oct. 5, 2012) [*Plaintiff M47/2012 v. Director-General of Security*], at paras. 511–514 (per Justice Bell, citing with approval case law from other jurisdictions that support the narrow interpretation of "lawfully present"); *R. (on the application of ST (Eritrea)) v. Secretary of State for the Home Department* [2012] 3 All ER 1037 (Eng. SC, Mar. 21, 2012), at paras. 35–37. See also International Law Commission, "Second report on the expulsion of aliens, by Mr. Maurice Kamto, Special Rapporteur," UN Doc. A/CN.4/573, July 20, 2006, at paras 68–71; G. Goodwin-Gill and J. McAdam, *The Refugee in International Law*, (3rd ed. 2007), at 524 (noting that "lawful presence" implies admission in accordance with a State's

obligation would therefore not guarantee freedom of movement for asylum-seekers who have entered territory irregularly, even if such persons are refugees under the terms of the Refugee Convention. That interpretation, which appears to accord with the ordinary meaning of the provision, supports an assertion that the right to freedom of movement is not of great significance in determining the key questions related to detention of smuggled migrants considered in this chapter. However, this interpretation is not universally accepted. For example UNHCR proposes that all asylum-seekers, even those who entered irregularly, should be considered "lawfully" in the territory of the State for the purposes of benefiting from this provision.[44]

9.2. RIGHT TO LIBERTY AND THE PROHIBITION ON UNLAWFUL OR ARBITRARY DETENTION

The right to liberty is not absolute. International law recognizes that States retain the legal capacity to deprive people of their liberty. Deprivation of liberty only becomes problematic in legal terms when it is unlawful or arbitrary, or otherwise breaches the rights of the detainee.[45] This section examines the requirements of lawfulness, and the prohibition on arbitrariness. It commences however with a consideration of what is meant by "deprivation of liberty."

9.2.1. *Defining "Detention" and "Deprivation of Liberty"*

Detention has been defined at the international level as the condition of "any person deprived of personal liberty except as a result of conviction for an offence."[46]

immigration laws); and UN High Commissioner for Refugees, *"Lawfully Staying" – A Note on Interpretation* (1988), available at www.unhcr.org/refworld/pdfid/42ad93304.pdf (accessed May 12, 2013) [UNHCR, *"Lawfully Staying" – A Note on Interpretation*], at para. 8.

44 UNHCR refers to an Interpretative Note of its own, dating back to 1988, which suggests, at most, that "lawfulness" is generally to be assessed against applicable national laws and regulations, but nonetheless taking into account all of the prevailing circumstances, such as the fact that the stay in question is known and not prohibited, because of the precarious circumstances of the person. The Interpretative Note concludes that UNHCR should adopt the position that "lawfully present" includes asylum-seekers who entered irregularly, because "it is arguable on its face and it is necessary to strengthen the protection of refugee rights: UNHCR, *"Lawfully Staying" – A Note on Interpretation*, at para. 25.

45 Nowak, *CCPR Commentary*, at 211; see also UN Human Rights Committee, "General Comment No. 8: Right to Liberty and Security of Persons," UN Doc. HRI/GEN/1/Rev.7 at 130, May 12, 2004, adopted June 30, 1982 [HRC General Comment No. 8], at 130.

46 "Body of Principles for the Protection of All Persons under Any Form of Detention or Imprisonment," at Preamble, (b). UNHCR, in its Guidelines on Detention of Asylum-Seekers, notes that for the purposes of those Guidelines, "'detention' refers to the deprivation of liberty or confinement in a closed place which an asylum-seeker is not permitted to leave at will, including, though not limited to, prisons or purpose-built detention, closed reception or holding centres or facilities" (at 9 ("Terminology") (para. 5)).

Although helpful in identifying an important exclusion (restrictions on liberty following criminal conviction), the definition requires further inquiry into what constitutes deprivation of personal liberty for the purposes of international legal regulation. This may become important when States contend that certain situations do not in fact constitute detention and therefore do not amount to a deprivation of liberty. Examples where the fact of detention may be challenged by the State in the context of migrant smuggling could include the holding of a smuggled migrant in an "international zone"[47]; a situation where a smuggled migrant is technically free to leave – for example by renouncing a claim to asylum and accepting repatriation assistance[48]; or a situation in which it is argued the smuggled migrant is being "sheltered" or otherwise purportedly assisted and protected from further harm, rather than being detained.[49]

In international human rights law deprivation of liberty is assessed on the basis of practical result, with an inability to leave at will being the critical defining feature. The following definition, drawn from the OAS Principles and Best Practices on the Protection of Persons Deprived of Liberty in the Americas provides some insight into the scope of that concept:

> Deprivation of liberty means: Any form of detention, imprisonment, institutionalization, or custody of a person in a public or private institution which that person is not permitted to leave at will, by order of or under de facto control of a judicial, administrative or any other authority, for reasons of humanitarian assistance, treatment, guardianship, protection, or because of crimes or legal offenses. This category of persons includes not only those deprived of their liberty because of crimes or infringements or non compliance with the law, whether they are accused or convicted, but also those persons who are under the custody and supervision of certain institutions, such as: psychiatric hospitals and other establishments for persons with physical, mental, or sensory disabilities; institutions for children and the elderly; centers for migrants, refugees, asylum or refugee status seekers, stateless and undocumented persons;

[47] This was the situation in *Amuur v. France*, (1996) 22 EHRR 533 (ECHR, June 25, 1996) [*Amuur v. France*]. The European Court of Human Rights held the applicants in that case were in fact deprived of their liberty and detained.

[48] Ibid. The European Court noted, at paragraph 48, that "[t]he mere fact that it is possible for asylum-seekers to leave voluntarily the county where they wish to take refuge cannot exclude a restriction on liberty, the right to leave any country, including one's own, being guaranteed, moreover, by Protocol No. 4 to the Convention."

[49] See, for example, *Abdolkhani and Karimnia v. Turkey*, Application No. 30471/08 (ECHR, Sept. 22, 2009) [*Abdolkhani and Karimnia v. Turkey*], at 120, in which the government argued that individuals who claimed asylum after being arrested for illegal entry were "not detained but sheltered in foreigners' admission and accommodation centres in Turkey."

> and any other similar institution the purpose of which is to deprive persons of their liberty.[50]

The Optional Protocol to the Convention against Torture reflects a similar understanding, defining "deprivation of liberty" for the purposes of that Protocol as "any form of detention or imprisonment or the placement of a person in a public or private custodial setting which that person is not permitted to leave at will by order of any judicial, administrative or other authority."[51] In its consideration of the relevant provision of the ICCPR (Article 9, which is examined in detail below), the Human Rights Committee has generally affirmed this understanding of deprivation of liberty, making clear that: (1) The right to liberty is to be interpreted broadly in keeping with the purpose of the Article and the Convention as a whole; (2) the ambit of the relevant provision generally extends to detention that is either judicial or administrative in nature, thereby extending to immigration detention[52]; and (3) any arrest or detention that can be attributed to the State Party will likely fall to be scrutinized for compliance with the relevant provision.[53]

However there are also constraints, reflecting the potentially sweeping scope of the concept of liberty. Nowak explains that the term "liberty of the person" as used in ICCPR Article 9 is restricted to "the *freedom of bodily movement* in the narrowest sense"[54] and is not to be confused with the broader concept of liberty. He continues:

> An interference with personal liberty results only from the forceful detention of a person at a certain, narrowly bounded location, such as a prison or some other detention facility ... Only in those cases are the procedural guarantees under Art. 9 (legality, prohibition of arbitrariness, rights to information, habeas corpus and

50 OAS Principles and Best Practices on the Protection of Persons Deprived of Liberty in the Americas, General Provision.

51 Optional Protocol to the Convention against Torture and other Cruel, Inhuman or Degrading Treatment or Punishment, 2375 UNTS 237, done Dec. 18, 2002, entered into force June 22, 2006 [Optional Protocol to the Convention against Torture], at Art. 4(2).

52 HRC General Comment No. 8, at para. 1. Note that this does not extend to Article 9(3).

53 See, for example, *Sergio Euben Lopez Burgos v. Uruguay*, UNHRC Comm. No. R.12/52, UN Doc. Supp. No. 40 (A/36/40), at 176, July 29, 1981, decided June 6, 1979, where the Human Rights Committee found that the kidnapping of a Uruguayan citizen by Uruguayan security and intelligence forces on Argentinian territory constituted arbitrary arrest and detention. Similar cases included *Eduardo Bleier v. Uruguay*, UNHRC Comm. No. 30/1978, UN Doc. CCPR/C/15/D/30/1978, Mar. 29, 1982, decided Mar. 29, 1982; *María del Carmen Almeida de Quinteros et al. v. Uruguay*, UNHRC Comm. No. 107/1981, UN Doc. CCPR/C/19/D/107/1981, July, 21, 1983, decided July 21, 1983; *Elcida Arévalo Perez et al. v. Colombia*, UNHRC Comm. No. 181/1984, UN Doc. CCPR/C/37/D/181/1984, Nov. 22, 1989, decided Nov. 3, 1989.

54 Nowak, *CCPR Commentary*, at 212 (emphasis in original), citing J. L. Murdoch ed., *Article 5 of the European Convention on Human Rights: The Protection of Liberty and Security of the Person* (Council of Europe, 2002).

> compensation) applicable … All less grievous restrictions on freedom of bodily movement, such as limitations on domicile or residency … or expulsion from State territory, do not fall within the scope of the right to personal liberty but instead under freedom of movement.[55]

The Human Rights Committee has confirmed this interpretation, finding that restrictions on freedom of movement such as requiring mandatory reporting to police, placing a prohibition on change of employment without authorization, or restricting a person's movements to a small area such as a village or town do not constitute deprivation of liberty for the purposes of Article 9.[56]

The leading European case in this regard remains the decision of the European Court of Human Rights in *Amuur v. France*.[57] In that matter, the Court held that in order to determine whether someone has been "deprived of his liberty" within the meaning of Article 5 of the European Convention on Human Rights, "the starting point must be [that person's] concrete situation, and account must be taken of a whole range of criteria such as the type, duration, effects and manner of implementation of the measure in question."[58] In migrant smuggling situations States may argue (as France did in this case) that persons alleging unlawful detention are not "detained" because they can in fact choose to leave the country. In some countries of destination, for example, smuggled migrants may be offered assistance to return, on thereby abandoning a claim for asylum. However, in *Amuur v. France* the Court rejected this assertion, stating: "The mere fact that it is possible for asylum seekers to leave voluntarily the country where they wish to take refuge cannot exclude a restriction on liberty."[59] Drawing heavily on this jurisprudence, the UN Working Group on Arbitrary Detention has similarly accepted that restricting a person to international transit zones such as ports or airports can constitute detention despite the fact that they may in theory be free to leave the country, especially in cases where no other State is prepared to take them.[60]

55 Nowak, *CCPR Commentary*, at 212.

56 See, for example, *Celepli v. Sweden*, UNHRC Comm. No. 456/1991, UN Doc. CCPR/C/51/D/456/1991, Aug. 2, 1994, decided Jul. 18, 1994; and *Salah Karker v. France*, UNHRC Comm. No. 833/1998, UN Doc. CCPR/C/70/D/833/1998, Oct. 30, 2000, decided Oct. 26, 2000.

57 In this case the Court was called on to consider whether a group of four Somali nationals, who remained for twenty days in the "international zone" of a French airport, had been deprived of their liberty in breach of Article 5(1)(f) of the European Convention on Human Rights. The Court held that even though the applicants were not in French territory under national law, they were nevertheless subject to French law, including for purposes of protection: "Despite its name, the international zone does not have extraterritorial status": *Amuur v. France*, at para. 52.

58 Ibid. at para. 42.

59 Ibid. at para. 48. The Court added that this possibility becomes theoretical if no other country is available to offer protection (ibid.).

60 UN Commission on Human Rights, "Report of the Working Group on Arbitrary Detention," UN Doc. E/CN.4/1998/44, Dec. 19, 1997, at para. 41; UN Commission on Human Rights, "Report of

When does "shelter" become detention or deprivation of liberty? This question has been extensively canvassed by one of the present authors in the context of a discussion on the legality of closed shelters for victims of trafficking.[61] That study concluded that the fact of a person being unable to leave is decisive; it is ultimately irrelevant whether or not one of the purposes of that detention is to provide assistance and support. This reasoning is echoed in jurisprudence of the European Court of Human Rights in cases where States have argued that the persons involved were being sheltered and not detained. In one case, *Abdolkhani and Karimnia v. Turkey*,[62] the Court reaffirmed its previous position: "In order to determine whether someone has been 'deprived of his liberty' within the meaning of Article 5, the starting-point must be his or her concrete situation, and account must be taken of a whole range of criteria such as the type, duration, effects and manner of implementation of the measure in question."[63] Similar cases have been decided along the same lines.[64]

9.2.2. *Requirement of Lawfulness*

As noted previously, the sovereign power of States includes the right to control who enters their territory, and it follows that the detention of migrants per se is not contrary to international law.[65] However, compliance with international law requires that State-sanctioned deprivation of liberty is only permissible when it occurs "on such grounds and in accordance with such procedure as is established by law" and when it is not arbitrary.[66] The first element of this requirement is the subject of this present section.

the Working Group on Arbitrary Detention," UN Doc. E/CN.4/2000/4, Dec. 28, 1999, at Annex II, Deliberation No. 5.

61 A. Gallagher and E. Pearson, "The High Cost of Freedom: A Legal and Policy Analysis of Shelter Detention for Victims of Trafficking," (2010) 32 *Human Rights Quarterly* 73.

62 *Abdolkhani and Karimnia v. Turkey*, Application No. 30471/08 (ECHR, Sept. 22, 2009) [*Abdolkhani and Karimnia v. Turkey*].

63 Ibid. at para. 125. The Court noted that the applicants were not free to leave the police headquarters, or the Kirklareli Accommodation Centre. Furthermore, they could only access the UNHCR through permission from the Ministry of Interior, and they were only able to meet with a lawyer if the lawyer was able to present a notarized power of attorney (which the applicants could not provide because they were not permitted to meet with lawyers). The Court concluded that this situation constituted deprivation of liberty, irrespective of how it was classified under national law.

64 See, for example, *Z.N.S. v. Turkey*, (2012) 55 EHRR 11 (ECHR, Jan. 19, 2010) [*Z.N.S. v. Turkey*] where the government of Turkey argued that an Iranian national was not "detained" but rather "accommodated," pending deportation proceedings (at para. 54). The Court held that the "placement" of the applicant in the Centre amounted to a deprivation of liberty (see paras. 56–57). See also *Austin and Others v. United Kingdom*, (2012) 55 EHRR 14 (ECHR, Mar. 15, 2012), at para. 57.

65 See, for example, *A. v. Australia*, at para. 9.3.

66 ICCPR, at Art. 9(1). See also Migrant Workers Convention, at Art. 16(4) ("on such grounds and in accordance with such procedures as are established by law"); European Convention on Human Rights, at Art. 5 ("in accordance with a procedure prescribed by law"); CRC, at Art. 37(b) ("no child

The principle of legality as set out in international and regional human rights law has both substantive and procedural aspects. A person may only be deprived of his or her liberty for justifiable reasons (substantive aspect) and in accordance with procedures (procedural aspect) that are provided for by law.[67] In other words, the principle of legality is violated if someone is detained on grounds that are not clearly established, in advance, in law, or are contrary to such law.[68] The obligation relates not just to the fact of the initial detention but also to its continuation, that is, it is not sufficient that the detention was initially for reasons established by and in accordance with law: detention that continues beyond what is required or authorized by law will violate the principle of legality and thereby be a violation of the right to liberty. Failure to establish the legality of detention renders that detention arbitrary, thereby providing a second basis for its unlawfulness.[69]

The reference to "law" within the requirement of legality is generally understood as referring primarily to the domestic legal system,[70] specifically, to a "parliamentary statute or an equivalent, unwritten norm of common law, accessible to all individuals subject to the relevant jurisdiction."[71] Administrative provisions that are not based on an existing statute or norm of common law would be insufficient to satisfy the requirement of legality.[72] The European Court of

shall be deprived of his or her liberty unlawfully or arbitrarily. The arrest, detention or imprisonment of a child shall be in conformity with the law"); American Convention on Human Rights, at Arts. 7, 30; and African Charter, at Art. 6.

67 See J. Pejic, "Procedural Principles and Safeguards for Internment/Administrative Detention in Armed Conflict and Other Situations of Violence" (2005) 87 *International Review of the Red Cross* 375, at 383. [Pejic, "Procedural Principles and Safeguards for Internment/Administrative Detention"].

68 Nowak, *CCPR Commentary*, at 224; Y. Dinstein, "Right to Life, Physical Integrity, and Liberty," in L. Henkin ed., *The International Bill of Rights: The Covenant on Civil and Political Rights* 114 (1981), at 130.

69 UN Commission on Human Rights, Department of Economic and Social Affairs, "Study of the Right of Everyone to be Free from Arbitrary Arrest, Detention and Exile," UN Doc. E/CN.4/826/Rev.1, Jan. 1, 1964, at 7.

70 Nowak, *CCPR Commentary*, at 224. See also related canvassing of "lawfulness" in the context of Article 26 of the Refugee Convention (Freedom of Movement), and whether it means lawful under national law, in the Australian High Court case, *Plaintiff M47/2012 v. Director-General of Security*. In that case, two judges cited with approval a United Kingdom decision *R. (S.T.) v. Home Secretary* [2012] 2 WLR 735 at 750 [37]; [2012] 3 All ER 1037 at 1054: "It seems unlikely that the contracting states would have agreed to grant to refugees the freedom to choose their place of residence and to move freely within their territory before they themselves had decided, according to their own domestic laws, whether or not to admit them to the territory in the first place." (per Justice Heydon, at para. 288 and Justice Bell, at para. 512).

71 Nowak, *CCPR Commentary*, at 224. Note that in the context of the American Convention on Human Rights, such a law must have been "passed by democratically elected legislative bodies": *The Word "Laws" in Article 30 of the American Convention on Human Rights*, Advisory Opinion OC-6/86, Inter-American Court of Human Rights (ser. A) No. 6, May 9, 1986, at 37 (English text).

72 Nowak, *CCPR Commentary*, at 224.

Human Rights has held that unpublished decrees, circulars, and other materials intended to guide immigration officials, rather than to allow judicial review or impose limits on administrative authorities in respect of detention, do not meet this test.[73]

The question of whether international law is contemplated within the concept of "law" in this context is an important one. Some commentators appear to take for granted that the "law" in question must at least be compatible with international norms to satisfy the requirement of legality.[74] Others, such as Nowak, point to the primary focus on domestic law while also acknowledging that the lawfulness of deprivation of liberty refers to its compatibility with domestic and international law.[75] Certainly the European Court of Human Rights has expanded the concept of lawfulness in this way in its interpretation of Article 5 of the European Convention on Human Rights.[76] For example, in a 2011 case, *Lokpo and Touré v. Hungary*, the Court held that although national legislation is the primary consideration for determining the lawfulness of detention, it is "not always the decisive element in assessing the justification of deprivation of liberty."[77] In the same case the Court confirmed a link between legality and arbitrariness identified in previous jurisprudence: legality should be considered with reference to the general objective of ensuring that persons are not deprived of their liberty arbitrarily.[78] Accordingly, insufficient guarantees in law to protect against arbitrary detention (such as a lack of legal provisions establishing the procedure for ordering and extending detention, or limits on the maximum period of detention, or no access to remedies to contest detention), have resulted in findings that detention is unlawful.[79] The Human Rights Committee has also held that judicial review of the lawfulness of detention (as required by Article 9(4)) must include compatibility with international law, including the ICCPR, as well as with national law.[80] The view that the principle of

[73] *Amuur v. France*, at para. 53.

[74] See Pejic, "Procedural Principles and Safeguards for Internment/Administrative Detention," at 383.

[75] Nowak, *CCPR Commentary*, at 236.

[76] See, for example, *Riera Blume and Others v. Spain*, (2000) 30 EHRR 632 (ECHR, Oct. 14, 1999) [*Riera Blume and Others v. Spain*], at para. 31.

[77] *Lokpo and Touré v. Hungary*, Application No. 10816/10 [2011] ECHR 1348 (ECHR, Sept. 20, 2011), at para. 21.

[78] Ibid. at para. 21: "It must in addition be satisfied that detention during the period under consideration was compatible with the purpose of the relevant provision, which is to prevent persons from being deprived of their liberty in an arbitrary fashion." See also *Amuur v. France*, at para. 50.

[79] *Abdolkhani and Karimnia v. Turkey*, at paras. 134–135. See also UNHCR Guidelines on Detention of Asylum-Seekers, at Guideline 3.

[80] See, for example, *Omar Sharif Baban et al. v. Australia*, UNHRC Comm. No. 1014/2001, CCPR/C/78/D/1014/2001, Sept. 18, 2003, decided Aug. 6, 2003 [*Baban v. Australia*], at para. 7.2, and further discussion on review of detention at Section 9.2.3.3.

legality cannot be assessed solely with reference to compatibility with national law finds some additional support in soft law sources.[81] However it has met with resistance, particularly from States.[82]

International human rights bodies have identified breaches of the requirement of legality in the context of immigration detention. For example, in 2009, the UN Working Group on Arbitrary Detention found that irregular migrants arriving in Italy were being detained for periods of more than a month pending receipt of a document certifying their identity as asylum-seekers, without any legislation or procedure governing this deprivation of liberty.[83] It concluded that the practice was in violation of international law because it breached the requirement of legality.[84] The Working Group has elsewhere determined that the reasons justifying the detention of irregular migrants, such as the necessity of identification, the risk of absconding, or facilitating the expulsion of an irregular migrant who has been served with a removal order "must be clearly defined and exhaustively enumerated in legislation."[85]

As a practical matter, in many situations there may not be a substantial difference of outcome in relation to either approach because the criteria of legality and non-arbitrariness must both be satisfied. Detention that is legal under national laws that violate international norms (for example, that is directed at – and thereby discriminates against – one particular racial or ethnic group), would be unlawful because the discriminatory legal basis renders it arbitrary.[86]

[81] See, for example, OAS Principles and Best Practices on the Protection of Persons Deprived of Liberty in the Americas, at Principle IV ("No one shall be deprived of his or her physical liberty except for the reasons and under the conditions established beforehand by domestic law, and in accordance with the provisions of international human rights law. Orders of deprivation of liberty shall be duly reasoned and issued by the competent authority.").

[82] See, for example, the view of some members of the Human Rights Committee and the response of the government of Australia regarding a decision of the Human Rights Committee at notes 160–161 below and accompanying text.

[83] UN Human Rights Council, "Report of the Working Group on Arbitrary Detention, Addendum: Mission to Italy," UN Doc. A/HRC/10/21/Add.5, Jan. 26, 2009. See also UN Commission on Human Rights, "Report of the Working Group on Arbitrary Detention," UN Doc. E/CN.4/2000/4, Dec. 28, 1999.

[84] UN Human Rights Council, "Report of the Working Group on Arbitrary Detention, Addendum: Mission to Italy," UN Doc. A/HRC/10/21/Add.5, Jan. 26, 2009, at paras. 70–72.

[85] UN Human Rights Council, "Report of the Working Group on Arbitrary Detention," UN Doc. A/HCR/13/30, Jan. 18, 2010, at para. 59.

[86] The UN Committee on the Elimination of Racial Discrimination has confirmed that detention imposed on persons of a "particular nationality" may violate the prohibition on race-based discrimination: see UN Committee on the Elimination of Racial Discrimination, "General Recommendation No. 30: Discrimination against Non-Citizens," UN Doc. CERD/C/64/Misc.11/rev.3, Jan. 10, 2004 [CERD General Recommendation No. 30], at para. 19.

9.2.3. Prohibition on Arbitrariness

The *prohibition on arbitrariness* represents a second, additional requirement for States in relation to deprivation of liberty. In other words, it is not enough that the national law permits and regulates detention of smuggled migrants. That law must itself not be arbitrary and its application must not take place arbitrarily.[87] The prohibition on arbitrariness complements the requirement for lawfulness by providing a safeguard against detentions authorized by unjust laws as well as against the unjust application of those laws. It is clear therefore, that "arbitrary" is not synonymous with "unlawful." The drafting history of the ICCPR confirms an intention to ascribe a much broader meaning to the term, one that includes elements of "injustice, unpredictability, unreasonableness, capriciousness and disproportionality."[88] The Human Rights Committee has confirmed that the concept of "arbitrariness" extends beyond illegality under domestic law: "[A]n arrest or detention is arbitrary if it is (a) on grounds or in accordance with procedures other than those established by law, or (b) under the provisions of a law the purpose of which is incompatible with respect for the right to liberty and security of person."[89]

9.2.3.1. Arbitrary Detention and the ICCPR

The Human Rights Committee has provided further guidance on the concept of arbitrariness as it applies to Article 9 of the ICCPR. In *Hugo van Alphen v. The Netherlands*, for example, it confirmed that custody pursuant to lawful arrest "must not only be lawful but reasonable in all of the circumstances. Further, remand in custody must be necessary in all the circumstances, for example, to prevent flight, interference with evidence or the recurrence of crime."[90] In other words, to avoid arbitrariness, the detention must be appropriate, just, and predictable. It must also be reasonable and necessary in all of the circumstances of the individual case.[91]

The issue of immigration detention, and the question of the point at which such detention may become "arbitrary," was raised within the UN human rights system

87 Nowak, *CCPR Commentary*, at 224; S. Joseph, J. Schultz, and M. Castan, *The International Covenant on Civil and Political Rights: Cases, Materials and Commentary* (2004), at 308.

88 Nowak, *CCPR Commentary*, at 225.

89 UN Commission on Human Rights, Department of Economic and Social Affairs, "Study of the Right of Everyone to be Free from Arbitrary Arrest, Detention and Exile," UN Doc. E/CN.4/826/Rev.1, Jan. 1, 1964, at 7. See also *Hugo van Alphen v. The Netherlands, UNHRC Comm. No. 305/1988, UN Doc. CCPR/C/39/D/305/1988, Aug. 15, 1990, decided July 23, 1990* [*Hugo van Alphen v. The Netherlands*], at para. 5.6 ("The drafting history of article 9, paragraph 1, confirms that 'arbitrariness' is not to be equated with 'against the law,' but must be interpreted more broadly to include elements of inappropriateness, injustice and lack of predictability").

90 *Hugo van Alphen v. The Netherlands*, at para. 5.8.

91 See A. *v. Australia*, at para. 9.4.

in the mid-1990s in relation to the prolonged detention of Vietnamese migrants in Hong Kong by the British government.[92] However, the United Kingdom was not the only government engaging in lengthy immigration detention around that time. The Human Rights Committee had also expressed concern about the immigration detention practices of other countries, including Switzerland, Japan, and the United States.[93] In one of the Committee's earliest considerations of the lawfulness of immigration detention of irregular arrivals, it found that there had in fact been *no* breach of the prohibition of arbitrary detention. In *V.M.R.B. v. Canada*,[94] the applicant (a national of El Salvador) claimed to have been arbitrarily detained by the government of Canada, following his irregular entry to that country. The applicant had entered Canada without a visa, and had been detained on arrival, at which point he sought admission as a refugee. The detention was reviewed within two days of his arrival, and thereafter on a weekly basis. The Committee found that "the author was lawfully arrested in connection with his unauthorized entry into Canada, and the decision to detain him was not made arbitrarily, especially in view of his insistence not to leave the territory of Canada."[95]

In the communication A. *v. Australia*, the Human Rights Committee was called on to express its views about whether the detention of a Cambodian asylum-seeker, held in immigration detention by the Australian government for almost four years following his arrival by boat, constituted "arbitrary" detention under the ICCPR.[96] The applicant in this communication argued that "international treaty law and customary international law require that detention of asylum seekers be avoided as a general rule. Where such detention may become necessary, it should be strictly limited."[97] Although ultimately finding in the applicant's favor, this line of reasoning was explicitly rejected by the Committee, which stated firmly that "there is no basis for the author's claim that it is *per se* arbitrary to detain individuals requesting asylum. Nor can it find any support for the contention that there is a rule of customary international law that would render all such detention arbitrary."[98] However, the Committee did set out important basic principles for when detention can be

92 Wilsher, *Immigration Detention*, at 158.

93 Ibid.

94 *V. M. R. B. v. Canada*, UNHRC Comm No. 236/1987, CCPR/C/33/D/236/1987, July 26, 1988, decided July 18, 1988 (decision on admissibility). Canada argued in this case that the detention was not arbitrary because it was based on provisions of the Canadian Immigration Act, which permits detention of persons whose presence is considered to be detrimental to the national interest. It pointed to information it had that while in Canada, the applicant was funded by a foreign political party to carry out activities prohibited by Canadian law: at para. 4.4.

95 Ibid. at para. 6.3.

96 A. *v. Australia*, UNHRC Comm. No. 560/1993, UN Doc. CCPR/C/59/D/560/1993, Apr. 30, 1997, decided Apr. 3, 1997 [A. *v. Australia*].

97 Ibid. at para. 3.1.

98 Ibid. at para. 9.3.

considered both arbitrary and unlawful. It affirmed the principle stated in *van Alphen v. The Netherlands* that the notion of "arbitrariness" must not be equated with "against the law" but must be "interpreted more broadly to include such elements as inappropriateness and injustice."[99] The Committee also applied the concept of *necessity* as explained in *van Alphen*, and introduced the principle of *proportionality*, declaring that "remand in custody could be considered arbitrary if it is not necessary in all of the circumstances of the case, for example, to prevent flight or interference with evidence: the element of proportionality becomes relevant in this context."[100] Furthermore:

> every decision to keep a person in detention should be open to review periodically so that the grounds justifying the detention can be assessed. In any event, detention should not continue beyond the period for which the State can provide appropriate justification.[101]

In this case, Australia had argued that the applicant's detention was justified by the fact that he had entered Australia unlawfully and that he might abscond if not detained. The Committee accepted that circumstances such as these might warrant the detention of irregular entrants, stating: "[T]he fact of illegal entry may indicate a need for investigation and there may be other factors particular to the individual, such as the likelihood of absconding and lack of cooperation, which may even justify detention for a period."[102] However, the Committee emphasized that without such factors, the detention may be considered arbitrary "even if entry was illegal."[103] In this case, it noted that the government had not presented any reasons particular to this applicant's case that would justify his continued detention for a period of four years. Accordingly, the Committee concluded that the author's detention was arbitrary within the meaning of Article 9(1) of the ICCPR.[104]

The *A. v. Australia* decision prompted a series of other communications relating to irregular migrants (most of whom had been smuggled) in immigration detention in Australia.[105] The Committee's findings in relation to these communications

99 Ibid. at para. 9.2.

100 Ibid.

101 Ibid. at para. 9.4.

102 Ibid.

103 Ibid.

104 Ibid.

105 See, for example, *Baban v. Australia*. An author and his son, Iraqi nationals of Kurdish origin, were detained for two years before escaping from immigration detention. The Committee found Australia had breached Article 9(1) on similar grounds to those expressed in *A. v Australia* (at para. 7.2): "As to the claims under article 9, the Committee recalls its jurisprudence that, in order to avoid a characterization of arbitrariness, detention should not continue beyond the period for which the State party can provide appropriate justification. In the present case, the author's detention as a non-citizen without an entry permit continued, in mandatory terms, until he was removed or granted a permit.

confirmed that not only must the initial detention be justified, it must not continue past the point where those justifications cease to exist. For example, detention may be justified on the basis of a need to conduct identity and other checks. However, when it continues after such checks have been completed, the onus is on the State to demonstrate what other factors, particular to that case, suggest the need for continuing detention.[106] Further, the existence of a justification is not enough in itself; the justification must itself be valid in light of the passage of time (including the length of detention) and intervening circumstances, such as the deteriorating mental or physical health of the detainee, the impact of continuing detention on children, and whether or not return of members of that national group is in fact being practiced by the detaining State.[107] In this regard, the Committee has placed great emphasis on whether the detaining State has been able to demonstrate efforts to use less intrusive measures, such as the imposition of sureties or reporting obligations.[108] Where this or an alternative justification cannot be shown, continuing immigration detention is very likely to be found to be arbitrary.[109] More recently the Committee has assessed

While the State party advances particular reasons to justify the individual detention (para. 4.15 et seq.), the Committee observes that the State party has failed to demonstrate that those reasons justified the author's continued detention in the light of the passage of time and intervening circumstances such as the hardship of prolonged detention for his son or the fact that during the period under review the State Party apparently did not remove Iraqis from Australia (para. 4.12). In particular, the State party has not demonstrated that, in the light of the author's particular circumstances, there were not less invasive means of achieving the same ends, that is to say, compliance with the State party's immigration policies, by, for example, the imposition of reporting obligations, sureties or other conditions. The Committee also notes that in the present case the author was unable to challenge his continued detention in court."

106 See, for example, *C. v. Australia*, UNHRC Comm. No. 900/1999, CCPR/C/76/D/900/1999, Nov. 13, 2002, decided Oct. 28, 2002 [*C. v. Australia*], at para. 8.2; *Baban v. Australia*, at para. 7.2; and *Danyal Shafiq v. Australia*, UNHRC Comm. No. 1324/2004, CCPR/C/88/D/1324/2004, Nov. 13, 2006, decided Oct. 31, 2006 [*Shafiq v. Australia*], at para. 7.3.

107 See, for example, *Baban v Australia*, at 7.2; and *C. v. Australia*, at 8.2.

108 See, for example, *D. and E. v. Australia*, UNHRC Comm. No. 1050/2002, CCPR/C/87/D/1050/2002, Aug. 9, 2006, decided July 11, 2006, at para. 7.2; *Shafiq v. Australia*, at para. 7.3; *Shams and Others v. Australia*, UNHRC Comm. Nos. 1255, 1256, 1259, 1260, 1266, 1268, 1270, 1288/2004, UN Doc. CCPR/C/90/D/1255,1256,1259,1260,1266,1268,1270&1288/2004, Sept. 11, 2007, decided July 20, 2007, at para. 7.2. See also UNHCR Guidelines on Detention of Asylum-Seekers, at Guidelines 4, 4.3 (esp. paras. 18, 35, 40).

109 See, for example, *C. v. Australia*, where the Committee was asked to consider the lawfulness of the extended detention of an Iranian national. The applicant was initially detained for two years in an immigration facility. After more than six months of evidence of his severe mental health deterioration, he was released into the "detention" custody of his family. He was eventually granted a refugee visa. The applicant then went on to stalk and assault a family member in a series of burglaries and attacks, for which he pled guilty and was convicted. It appears that his mental health condition was very directly related to his criminality. As he had been in Australia for less than ten years, the Minister for Immigration made a decision to deport him back to Iran. The applicant claimed that his initial immigration detention violated Article 9(1) and (4), and the prohibition on cruel, inhuman, or degrading treatment in Article 7, and that his pending return to Iran would constitute *refoulement*

indefinite detention of refugees on security grounds to be arbitrary on the basis that failure to provide reasons for the adverse security assessment prevented the applicants from appealing their detention.[110]

In broad summary, the Human Rights Committee has found that deprivation of liberty provided by law must not be "manifestly disproportional, unjust or unpredictable."[111] The manner in which a decision is taken to deprive someone of his or her liberty must be capable of being deemed appropriate and proportionate in view of the circumstances of the case.[112] Importantly, a detention situation that was originally not arbitrary might become arbitrary if it continues over time without proper justification.[113]

9.2.3.2. Arbitrary Detention and the Regional Human Rights Systems

Under the European human rights system, a slightly different approach is taken to the issue of unlawful and arbitrary detention in the context of immigration control. As with the ICCPR, the European Convention on Human Rights enshrines a right to liberty, and requires any detention to be lawful. However, unlike the ICCPR, the Convention does not contain a blanket prohibition on arbitrary or unlawful detention, rather enumerating, in considerable detail, those situations in which the right to liberty may be restricted. In the case of irregular migrants, the Convention permits detention only where it is for the purpose of preventing a person "effecting unauthorized entry" or to facilitate deportation.[114] The European Court has confirmed

breaching Article 7. The Australian government argued that the immigration detention was necessary to ensure that persons who arrive without authorization do not enter Australia without first being properly assessed and found to justify entry. It also provides officials with effective access to those persons in order to investigate and process their claims without delay, and if those claims are unwarranted, to remove such persons as soon as possible (para. 4.26). However, the Committee held: "[T]he State party has failed to demonstrate that those reasons justify the author's continued detention in the light of the passage of time and intervening circumstances. In particular, the State party has not demonstrated that, in the light of the author's particular circumstances, there were not less invasive means of achieving the same ends, that is to say, compliance with the State party's immigration policies by, for example, the imposition of reporting obligations, sureties or other conditions which would take account of the author's deteriorating condition" (para. 8.2). The Committee found that C's detention past this point breached Article 9(1) of the ICCPR (ibid.).

110 *F.K.A.G. et al. v. Australia*, UNHRC Comm. No. 2094/2011, UN Doc. CCPR/C/108/D/2094/2011, Oct. 28, 2013, decided July 26, 2013; *M.M.M. et al v. Australia*, UNHRC Comm. No. 2136/2012, UN Doc. CCPR/C/108/D/2136/2012, October 28, 2013, decided July 25, 2013.

111 Nowak, *CCPR Commentary*, at 225.

112 Ibid.

113 Ibid. at 226.

114 European Convention on Human Rights, at Art. 5(1): "Everyone has the right to liberty and security of person. No one shall be deprived of his liberty save in the following cases and in accordance with a procedure prescribed by law ...(f) the lawful arrest or detention of a person to prevent his effecting an

that this provision of the Convention specifically permits the State to constrain the liberty of aliens in the context of immigration controls.[115]

The Court has been called upon to consider the precise meaning of detention to "prevent a person effecting unauthorized entry." In *Saadi v. United Kingdom*,[116] it confirmed that although the right to liberty is the appropriate starting point, the provision outlined above constitutes a specific exception: subject to their obligations under the Convention, States enjoy an "undeniable sovereign right to control aliens' entry into and residence in their territory ... [and] ... are permitted to detain would-be immigrants who have applied for permission to enter, whether by way of asylum or not."[117] It is clear this sovereign right would also extend to smuggled migrants who have not applied for permission to enter. The Court further noted in the same case that until the State has "authorized" the entry of a person to the country, any entry is "unauthorized." It follows that the detention of a person who wishes to effect entry to the State and who needs, but does not yet have, authorization to do so, can be considered detention to "prevent his effecting an unauthorised entry."[118] The Court rejected the argument that as soon as an asylum-seeker has surrendered him or herself to immigration authorities, he or she has in effect sought an "authorized entry," with the result that detention cannot be authorized.[119] On this point, it stated that: "To interpret the first limb of Article 5(1)(f) as permitting detention only of a person who is shown to be trying to evade entry restrictions would be to place too narrow a construction on the terms of the provision and on the power of the State to exercise its undeniable right of control."[120] The Court noted such a narrow interpretation would also be inconsistent with various policy positions of concerned organizations, which envisage the detention of asylum-seekers in certain circumstances, including

unauthorized entry into the country or of a person against whom action is being taken with a view to deportation or extradition."

115 *Abdolkhani and Karimnia v. Turkey*, at para. 128.

116 *Shayan Baram Saadi v. The United Kingdom*, (2008) 47 EHRR 17 (ECHR, Jan. 29, 2008) [*Saadi v. United Kingdom*]. This case concerned the situation of an Iraqi doctor, who fled the Kurdish Autonomous Region of Iraq when, in the course of his duties as a hospital doctor, he treated and facilitated the escape of three fellow members of the Iraqi Workers Communist Party who had been injured in an attack. He arrived at Heathrow Airport on December 20, 2000, and immediately claimed asylum. When he first arrived, the immigration officer involved contacted Oakington Reception Centre, but there was no room there, so the applicant was granted "temporary admission" with a requirement that he report to the airport the following day. He reported as required and was granted a further twenty-four hours' "temporary admission." When next reporting he was detained and transferred to Oakington on January 2, 2001. The Court was required to consider whether Mr. Saadi had been detained contrary to Article 5(1)(f) of the Convention and, specifically, the applicability of the phrase "... to prevent his effecting an unauthorised entry into the country" to the facts of the case.

117 Ibid. at para. 64.

118 Ibid. at para. 65.

119 Ibid.

120 Ibid.

while identity checks take place or elements of asylum claims are verified.[121] Aspects of the decision have attracted criticism, particularly from human rights groups and refugee advocates.[122]

In contrast with the Human Rights Committee's interpretation of Article 9 of the ICCPR, the European Court of Human Rights has found that the relevant provision of the European Convention on Human Rights does *not* imply a requirement that detention be reasonably necessary, so long as it is done "with a view to deportation."[123] In *Chahal v. United Kingdom*,[124] the Grand Chamber held that the principle of proportionality applied to detention under Article 5(1)(f) only to the extent that the detention should not continue for an unreasonable length of time. Deprivation of liberty will be justified only for as long as deportation proceedings are in progress. If such proceedings are not prosecuted with due diligence, the detention ceases to be permissible.[125] Although Article 5 of the European Convention does not explicitly

[121] Ibid. (referring specifically to UNHCR, Executive Committee, Conclusion No. 44 (Detention of Refugees and Asylum-Seekers (1986)); UNHCR Guidelines; and Committee of Ministers Recommendations). For a critical analysis of the decision see Edwards, "Back to Basics," at 30–31.

[122] Amnesty International, for example, stated that the decision "appears to give states a broad discretion to detain people who are fleeing persecution, and are often in fear for their lives, for no other reason than the administrative convenience of the state in which they have sought asylum or international protection": cited in Ricipuro and Flynn, *Migration and Detention: Mapping the Legal Terrain*, at 29. See also Edwards, "Back to Basics," at 30–31.

[123] *Abdolkhani and Karimnia v. Turkey*, at para. 129; restated in *Saadi v. United Kingdom*, at para. 45.

[124] *Chahal v. The United Kingdom*, (1997) 23 EHRR 413 (ECHR, Nov. 15, 1996) [*Chahal v. United Kingdom*].

[125] Mr. Chahal, a Sikh, had entered the United Kingdom irregularly in 1971 but was subsequently granted an indefinite stay after an amnesty in 1974. He had gone to India in 1984, taken part in Sikh political activities at a temple, and then been arrested and allegedly beaten and tortured by the Indian police. He then came back to the United Kingdom and has not returned to India since. He became an active and leading member of the Sikh community in the United Kingdom. In October 1985 he was detained under counterterrorism laws for suspected involvement in a conspiracy to assassinate the Indian prime minister while in the United Kingdom. He was released for lack of evidence, but was later arrested again on suspicion of involvement in plans to kill more moderate Sikh activists in the United Kingdom. He was served a notice of deportation in 1990 on the basis that his continued presence in the United Kingdom was not conducive to the public good, on national security grounds. He claimed asylum, although this claim was ultimately rejected. There was no question that Mr. Chahal's detention was "with a view to deportation" pursuant to Article 5(1)(f) of the European Convention on Human Rights. However, he argued that because of its lengthy duration (extending from 1990 to 1994 and then continuing until the time the case was heard in 1996), it had ceased to be "in accordance with a procedure prescribed by law" and therefore was in breach of Article 5(1). The Court noted that any deprivation of liberty under Article 5(1) will be justified only for as long as deportation proceedings are in progress. If such proceedings are not prosecuted with due diligence, the detention will cease to be permissible. In addressing Mr. Chahal's case, the Court considered factors such as the careful legal and appeals process and the substantial national security issues that were involved. It found that the requirement for due diligence had been met and that Mr. Chahal's detention was not excessive, stating: "Mr Chahal's case involves considerations of an extremely serious and weighty nature. It is neither in the interests of the individual applicant nor in the general public interest in the administration of justice that such decisions be taken hastily, without due regard to all the relevant issues and

include a prohibition on arbitrariness, the Court in *Chahal* recognized a fundamental purpose of the Article is to "protect the individual from arbitrariness."[126] It determined that certain procedures, including the establishment of an advisory panel to review the adverse security evidence against the applicant, provided "an important safeguard against arbitrariness."[127] It further found that this procedure provided an adequate guarantee that there were grounds for believing the applicant to be a security risk, and "thus that the executive had not acted arbitrarily when it ordered him to be kept in detention," even when this detention extended over six years.[128]

The concept of arbitrariness was further examined in *Amuur v. France*, discussed at Section 9.2.1. In its decision the Court confirmed that the requirement of lawfulness under the European Convention on Human Rights necessitates consideration not only of whether the detention complies with the law, but also of the "quality of the law." According to the Court: "Quality in this sense implies that where a national law authorises deprivation of liberty – especially in respect of a foreign asylum seeker – it must be sufficiently accessible and precise, in order to avoid all risk of arbitrariness."[129] In this case it was found that the relevant legal rules did not meet this standard.[130]

As with Article 9(1) of the ICCPR, the European Convention on Human Rights requires that, in addition to falling under one of the specific exceptions, any deprivation of liberty must be "lawful." On this point, the Convention refers primarily to national law, and the need to conform to the substantive and procedural rules established by national law. However, the Court has stated that compliance with national law is not sufficient. Any deprivation of liberty should also be in keeping with the purpose of protecting the individual from arbitrariness: "It is a fundamental principle that no detention which is arbitrary can be compatible with Article 5(1) and the notion of 'arbitrariness' in Article 5(1) extends beyond lack of conformity with national law, so that a deprivation of liberty may be lawful in terms of national

evidence. Against this background, and bearing in mind what was at stake for the applicant and the interest that he had in his claims being thoroughly examined by the courts, none of the periods complained of can be regarded as excessive, taken either individually or in combination" (at para. 117).

126 Ibid. at para. 118.

127 Ibid. at para. 122.

128 Ibid.

129 *Amuur v. France*, at para. 50.

130 Ibid. at para. 53. The Court found that the Decree and the (unpublished) circular relied on by the government did not offer any right of review of the conditions under which they were held, or if necessary, to impose a time limit on how long they were held for. The rules did not provide for legal, humanitarian, or social assistance, nor did they lay down procedures or time limits for access to such assistance so that the asylum-seekers such as the applicant could take steps to seek asylum. See also *Z.N.S. v. Turkey*, at para. 56 ("…in the absence of clear legal provisions establishing the procedure for ordering and extending detention with a view to deportation and setting time limits for such detention," the deprivation of liberty was not lawful").

law but still arbitrary and thus contrary to the Convention."[131] In the same case the Court noted that although there is no internationally agreed definition of what constitutes "arbitrariness" for the purposes of Article 5(1), general principles have been established by case law, including that: detention must be carried out in good faith; it must be closely connected to the purpose (either of preventing unauthorized entry of the person to the country, or of action being taken with a view to deportation or extradition); the place and conditions of detention should be appropriate, bearing in mind that detainees have committed no criminal offense and have often fled for their lives; and the length of the detention should not exceed that reasonably required for the purpose pursued.[132]

The Inter-American Court of Human Rights has also considered the issue of detention, and adopted a somewhat stronger view than the interpretations discussed previously, holding that the *only* legitimate purpose of detention is to "protect fundamental legal rights from serious attacks that may impair or endanger them" and only so far is as strictly necessary.[133] Custodial measures, the Court held, should only be applied as "necessary and proportionate in the specific case to the purposes mentioned ... [protection of fundamental legal rights from serious attacks that may impair or endanger them] and only for the shortest period of time."[134] Such measures must be preceded by an "individualized evaluation" of the necessity of detention and the possibility of alternative means if they are to avoid being characterized as arbitrary.[135]

9.2.3.3. Right to Challenge the Legality of Detention

International law requires States to ensure that necessary procedural guarantees are in place to identify and respond to situations of unlawful or arbitrary deprivation of liberty. The ICCPR specifies several of these procedural guarantees. The first is the right to judicial review of the lawfulness of one's detention. The second is an enforceable right to compensation for wrongful arrest or detention.[136] As remedies for violations of human rights are discussed in detail in the previous chapter,[137] the following paragraphs focus on the first of these key procedural guarantees, without which detention will be considered arbitrary and thereby unlawful.

[131] *Saadi v. United Kingdom*, at para. 67.

[132] Ibid. at para. 74. Note that the Court applied these principles to Mr. Saadi's case and held his detention was compatible with the listed criteria: at para. 79.

[133] *Vélez Loor v. Panama*, Inter-Am Ct. H.R. (ser. C) No. 218, Nov. 23, 2010, at para. 170.

[134] Ibid. at para. 171.

[135] Ibid.

[136] ICCPR, at Art. 9(5).

[137] See Chapter 8, at Section 8.3.2.

The ICCPR, at Article 9(4), states: "Anyone who is deprived of his liberty by arrest or detention shall be entitled to take proceedings before a court, in order that the court may decide without delay on the lawfulness of his detention and order his release if the detention is not lawful." The right to have one's detention reviewed by a domestic court without delay as set out in the ICCPR exists irrespective of the reason for the detention; States may not exclude certain types of detention (for example, detention related to migrant smuggling or immigration control or security) from review.[138] As discussed further later on in the chapter, the right to review exists regardless of whether the detention is prima facie lawful under domestic law.[139]

The European Convention on Human Rights echoes the substance of the ICCPR provision on review of detention: "Everyone who is deprived of his liberty by arrest or detention shall be entitled to take proceedings by which the lawfulness of his detention shall be decided speedily by a court and his release ordered if the detention is not lawful."[140] The Migrant Workers Convention also requires that migrant workers shall be entitled to take proceedings in court, in order that the court may decide without delay on the lawfulness of their detention, and order release if the detention is not lawful.[141] The American Convention on Human Rights states that "anyone who is deprived of his liberty shall be entitled to recourse to a competent court, in order that the court may decide without delay on the lawfulness of his arrest or detention and order his release if the arrest or detention is unlawful."[142]

[138] Svennson-McCarthy cites a pronouncement of the Human Rights Committee in arguing that the right of review as set out in the ICCPR is non-derogable: that it could not be suspended on the basis that exceptional circumstances (such as a dramatic influx of irregular migrants) constitute a "public emergency which threatens the life of the nation": A. Svennson-McCarthy, *The International Law of Human Rights and States of Exception* (1998), at 447, citing "Report of the Human Rights Committee: Volume I," UN GAOR 49th sess, UN Doc. A/49/40(VOL.I)(SUPP), Sept. 21, 1994, at para. 23. The Human Rights Committee has asserted that the right to habeas corpus as set out in the ICCPR is essential to the protection of certain non-derogable rights such as the right to life and the prohibition on torture and inhumane treatment, and that it may therefore not be derogated from: UN Human Rights Committee, "General Comment No. 29: Derogations During a State of Emergency," UN Doc. HRI/GEN.1/Rev.7, at 184, May 12, 2004, adopted July 24, 2001 [HRC General Comment No. 29], at para. 16. Note that the Committee has elsewhere concluded that prolonged administrative detention without access to judicial review, even in a situation of emergency, cannot be justified because of the risk of torture and other ill-treatment. See UN Human Rights Committee, "Concluding Observations: Israel," UN Doc. CCPR/C/78/ISR, Aug. 21, 2003, at para. 12.

[139] Nowak, *CCPR Commentary*, at 235.

[140] European Convention on Human Rights, at Art. 5(4). The European Court has reiterated that "the purpose of Article 5(4) is to guarantee to persons who are arrested and detained the right to judicial supervision of the lawfulness of the measure to which they are thereby subjected": *Abdolkhani and Karimnia v. Turkey*, at para. 40.

[141] Migrant Workers Convention, at Art. 16(8).

[142] American Convention on Human Rights, at Art. 7(6). The provision further stipulates: "In States Parties whose laws provide that anyone who believes himself to be threatened with deprivation of his

Although the African Charter on Human and Peoples' Rights does not include a right of review, such a right could be viewed as a component of the clear prohibition on arbitrary detention contained in that instrument.[143] Other human rights treaties either specify or imply a right to review of one's detention,[144] and there is ample soft law support for the existence of a right in the nature of habeas corpus.[145]

Under Article 9(4) of the ICCPR, the right to review of one's detention refers to review by a *court*. This is in contrast to related provisions, which refer to "a judge or other officer authorized by law."[146] The term "court" in Article 9(4) has been given a broad interpretation so as to include bodies such as administrative, military, or constitutional courts.[147] However, the Human Rights Committee has determined that nonjudicial decisions do not satisfy the requirement for review. In *Shafiq v. Australia*, for example, the Committee determined that the non-delegable and non-compellable power of a government minister to order the release of a detainee did not constitute a right of review for the purposes of ICCPR Article 9(4). The author of the communication in this case had not been "invited" to apply for such a review. Importantly, the Minister's power did not provide for judicial review of either the grounds or circumstances of detention.[148] The European Court has also found that an advisory panel constituted to review detention, although giving a degree of control, cannot be considered a "court" within the meaning of Article 5(4) of the European Convention.[149]

liberty is entitled to recourse to a competent court in order that it may decide on the lawfulness of such threat, this remedy may not be restricted or abolished. The interested party or another person in his behalf is entitled to seek these remedies."

143 African Charter, at Art. 6.

144 See, for example, Article 17(2) of the International Convention for the Protection of All Persons from Enforced Disappearance, done Dec. 20, 2006, GA Res. 61/77, UNGAOR, 61st Sess, Agenda Item 68, UN Doc. A/Res/61/177, entered into force Dec. 23, 2010 ("Each state party shall, in its legislation ...(f) Guarantee that any person deprived of liberty or, in the case of a suspected enforced disappearance, since the person deprived of liberty is not able to exercise this right, any persons with a legitimate interest, such as relatives of the person deprived of liberty, their representatives or their counsel, shall, in all circumstances, be entitled to take proceedings before a court, in order that the court may decide without delay on the lawfulness of the deprivation of liberty and order the person's release if such deprivation of liberty is not lawful").

145 See, for example, "Body of Principles for the Protection of All Persons under Any Form of Detention or Imprisonment," at Principle 11 ("1. A person shall not be kept in detention without being given an effective opportunity to be heard promptly by a judicial or other authority ... 3. A judicial or other authority shall be empowered to review as appropriate the continuance of detention"). See also OAS Principles and Best Practices on the Protection of Persons Deprived of Liberty in the Americas, at Principles IV, VII.

146 For example, ICCPR, at Art. 9(3).

147 Nowak, *CCPR Commentary*, at 235–236.

148 *Shafiq v. Australia*, at para. 7.4.

149 *Chahal v. United Kingdom*, at para. 130.

The Human Rights Committee has emphasized that the review decision must be one capable of actually leading, where appropriate, to a person's release.[150] Also, the right of access to a judicial body for review must be "accessible and effective" in reality not just in theory.[151] This requirement has been interpreted to mean that detainees must have access to certain procedural guarantees, including access to information about the reasons for detention and to legal representation.[152] Without these, the right to a review of the legality of detention is effectively rendered meaningless.[153] This very practical aspect of access has been picked up by the UN Special Rapporteur on the Human Rights of Migrants in his consideration of detention of irregular migrants in so-called international zones:

> Migrants and asylum-seekers are sometimes detained at airport transit zones and other points of entry, under no clear authority, either with the knowledge of government officials at the airport or simply on the instructions of airline companies before being returned to their countries. The difficulty or impossibility of reaching any outside assistance impedes the exercise of the right of the persons concerned to challenge the lawfulness of the State's decision to be detained and returned and to apply for asylum, even in the presence of legitimate claims.[154]

A highly relevant matter to be considered under this heading is the scope of a domestic court's power of review. International treaty law refers to such a review examining the "lawfulness" of the detention. Does this mean that the Court is to examine whether the detention is lawful under national law? Or does it extend to a broader examination of lawfulness, that is, whether the detention could be considered "arbitrary" or otherwise unlawful under international law? Nowak is clear on the point that the requirement of "lawfulness" must necessarily include international as well as national law:

> The decision … relates exclusively to the *lawfulness* of deprivation of liberty, i.e. the compatibility of the detention with domestic and international law. If the court finds that detention is unlawful, it is under an obligation to order the immediate release of the person concerned. This implies that the court must have the power to review the individual circumstances of the detention, above all its proportionality,

[150] *Abdolkhani and Karimnia v. Turkey*, at para. 139; *A. v. Australia*, at para. 9.5; and *C. v. Australia*, at para. 7.4 in the context of admissibility and availability of domestic remedies.

[151] *Abdolkhani and Karimnia v. Turkey*, at para. 139.

[152] Ibid. at para. 141. See also *Edgardo Dante Santullo Valcada v. Uruguay*, UNHRC Comm. No. 9/1977, UN Doc. CCPR/C/8/D/9/1977, Oct. 26, 1979, decided Oct. 26, 1979 [*Valcada v. Uruguay*], at paras.10–18.

[153] *Abdolkhani and Karimnia v. Turkey*, at para. 141.

[154] "Report of the Special Rapporteur on the Human Rights of Migrants, Mr. Jorge Bustamante," UN Doc. A/HRC/7/12, Feb. 25, 2008, at para. 47.

and the power to order the immediate release of applicants in the case of unlawful detention.[155]

This raises the question of whether mandatory detention violates the right to review of the lawfulness of one's detention and the right to be released if that detention is found to be unlawful. Nowak argues that mandatory detention schemes, which confine judicial review to the formal assessment of a stated precondition for detention (for example, whether the detainee is "a 'non-citizen' without an entry permit") "seem to be incompatible with the right to *habeas corpus*" in that they do not allow for individualized assessment of the circumstances and proportionality of the detention.[156]

This broad view of the scope of judicial review under the ICCPR's provisions on detention has been accepted by the Human Rights Committee in a series of decisions that related to immigration detention cases in Australia. In that country, the national law mandates detention of indeterminate duration for unlawful noncitizens (those without a valid visa), including smuggled asylum-seekers. Judicial review only relates to the question of whether the applicant is indeed a "designated person" (i.e., a court is not empowered to order the release from immigration detention of a "designated person").[157] In A. *v. Australia* the Committee concluded that the judicial review provision in the ICCPR "requires that the court be empowered to order release, if the detention is incompatible with the requirements [of legal and non-arbitrary detention], or with other provisions of the Covenant."[158] The Committee's interpretation, reaffirmed in similar subsequent cases,[159] was rejected by the State Party, which asserted that "lawfulness" refers only to compatibility with national

155 Nowak, *CCPR Commentary*, at 236 (emphasis in original).

156 Ibid.

157 For detailed examinations of Australian law, policy, and practice related to immigration detention see: M. Stubbs, "Arbitrary Detention in Australia: Detention of Unlawful Non-citizens under the Migration Act 1958" (2006) 25 *Australian Year Book of International Law* 273; and L. Briskman, S. Latham, and C. Goddard, *Human Rights Overboard: Seeking Asylum in Australia* (2008).

158 A. *v. Australia*, at para. 9.5. The Committee said this interpretation was supported by Article 9(5), which "obviously governs the granting of compensation for detention that is 'unlawful' either under the terms of domestic law or within the meaning of the Covenant." As the applicant's access to court review of his detention was limited to consideration of whether or not he was a "designated person" under the relevant Australian law, the Committee concluded that the applicant's right under Article 9(4) to have his detention reviewed by a court was violated.

159 In *Baban v. Australia*, the Committee held that: "[j]udicial review of the lawfulness of detention under article 9, paragraph 4, is not limited to mere compliance of the detention with domestic law but must include the possibility to order release if the detention is incompatible with the requirements of the Covenant, in particular those of article 9, paragraph 1" (at para. 7.2). See also *C. v. Australia;* and *Bakhtiyari v. Australia*, UNHRC Comm. No. 1069/2002, UN Doc. CCPR/C/79/1069/2002, Nov. 6, 2003, decided Oct. 29, 2003 [*Bakhtiyari v. Australia*], at para. 9.4.

laws.[160] Even within the Committee there was some dissent. One member expressed disapproval at the "too broad a trail" blazed by the Committee in implying that violations of the ICCPR obligations relating to legal and nonarbitrary detention meant that such detention was *ipso jure* unlawful within the meaning of the judicial review provision of the ICCPR.[161] Another Committee member noted the interpretational difficulties with the decision in A. *v. Australia*, but nevertheless considered that a broader interpretation was necessary in order to further the object and purpose of the Convention.[162] He pointed to the possibility that a State could easily pass a domestic law "negating the right under article 9, paragraph 4, and making nonsense of it. The State could, in that event, pass a domestic law validating a particular category of detentions and a detained person falling within that category would be effectively deprived of his/her right under article 9, paragraph 4."[163]

The views of the Human Rights Committee on the scope of the judicial review function are generally consistent with those of the European Court of Human Rights, which, while interpreting "lawful" in Article 5(1) of the European Convention on Human Rights to denote compliance with domestic law, has also emphasized that the domestic law in question must itself be consistent with the purpose of the

160 In *C. v. Australia*, at para. 4.34, the State Party (Australia) stated that it "rejects the suggestion by the Committee in A *v. Australia* that 'lawfulness' in this provision was not limited to compliance with domestic law and must be consistent with article 9, paragraph 1, and other provisions of the Covenant. It contends there is nothing in the terms or structure of the Covenant, or in the *Travaux Préparatoires* or the Committee's General Comments, that supports such an approach." Australia reiterated this interpretation in *Bakhtiyari v. Australia*, at para. 5.11, noting that "If article 9, paragraph 4, were to have extended meaning beyond domestic law, it would have been a simple matter for the drafters to add 'arbitrary' or 'in breach of the Covenant.'" See also Australia's dismissal of the Human Rights Committee's finding in A. *v Australia* in a press release, where it was stated: "the Government does not accept that the detention of Mr A was in contravention of the [ICCPR] ... The Committee is not a court, and does not render binding decisions or judgments. It provides views and opinions, and it is up to countries to decide whether they agree with those views and how they will respond to them," cited in D. Kinley and M. Penny, "International Human Rights Law at Home: Addressing the Politics of Denial" (2002) 26(2) *Melbourne University Law Review* 466, at 467.

161 *C. v. Australia*, separate opinion of Committee Member Mr. Nigel Rodley. Rodley went on to state that, in his view, this interpretation "was [not] justified by the text of the Covenant. 'Arbitrary' in article 9, paragraph 1, certainly covers unlawfulness. It is evident from the very notion of arbitrariness and the preparatory work. But I fail to see how the opposite is also true. Nor is there anything in the preparatory work to justify it." (at 28). Rodley reiterated this view in his dissenting judgment in *Baban v. Australia*, at 15. His judgment *in C. v. Australia* did, however, express the reservation that he did not intend to imply that every detention will be in compliance with Article 9(4) solely by reason of its legality under domestic statute, giving the example of torture of a detainee as a circumstance that would call into question the continuing legality of the detention. See also Sir Nigel Rodley's individual opinion in Human Rights Committee Communications F.K.A.G. *et al. v. Australia* and M.M.M. *et al. v. Australia*, cited at note 110 above.

162 A. *v. Australia*, individual (concurring) opinion of Committee Member Mr. Prafullachandra N. Bhagwati, at 26.

163 Ibid. at para. 9.5.

Article, which is to protect the individual from arbitrariness.[164] In considering the provision for judicial review of detention in the Convention (Article 5(4)), the Court has noted that the notion of lawfulness here has the same meaning as under Article 5(1): "so that the detained person is entitled to a review of his detention in the light not only of the requirements of domestic law but also of the text of the Convention, the general principles embodied therein and the aim of the restrictions permitted by Article 5."[165]

Although international jurisprudence clearly prefers the interpretation that review of the "lawfulness" of detention must include consideration of compliance with international legal obligations, this interpretation is not well reflected in State practice. For example, after a long line of Human Rights Committee decisions that express the view that Australia's system of immigration detention breaches Article 9(4), that State's response was not to address these concerns but to further remove the prospect of judicial review. Indeed, the Australian legislature has been so successful in tightening up the legislative framework regulating detention that the High Court has found that the relevant statute (Migration Act 1958 (Cth)) unambiguously provides for the indefinite detention of "unlawful non-citizens," and that such a law is constitutionally valid.[166]

9.2.3.4. Is Indefinite Detention Permitted?

Irregular migrants, including those who have been smuggled, are highly vulnerable to being subjected to indefinite detention.[167] The risk is particularly acute for stateless persons – persons who have no country to return to.[168] "Security" concerns are also increasingly being used to justify administrative detention of indefinite duration.[169]

[164] See, for example, *Riera Blume and Others v. Spain*, at para. 31.

[165] *Chahal v. United Kingdom*, at para. 127.

[166] M. Zagor, "Uncertainty and Exclusion: Detention of Aliens and the High Court" (2006) 34 *Federal Law Review* 127 [Zagor, "Uncertainty and Exclusion"], discussing the Australian High Court's decision in *Al-Kateb v. Godwin* (2004) 219 CLR 562 (Aus. HC, Aug. 6, 2004) [*Al-Kateb v. Godwin*]. In a 2012 case, *Plaintiff M47/2012 v. Director-General of Security*, the High Court was asked to reconsider its view on the lawfulness of indefinite detention but declined to do so, deciding the case on technical grounds and upholding the lawfulness of the plaintiff's detention on the facts.

[167] A. de Zayas, "Human Rights and Indefinite Detention" (2005) 87(857) *International Review of the Red Cross* 15 [de Zayas, "Human Rights and Indefinite Detention"].

[168] This was the situation for the applicants in *Al-Kateb v. Godwin*. Mr. Al-Kateb was a stateless Palestinian man who arrived in Australia. Having been rejected in an application for asylum, he requested to be returned to Kuwait or Gaza. Australian authorities sought – and failed – to return him to Egypt, Gaza, Jordan, Kuwait, Syria, and the Palestinian Territories. See further Zagor, "Uncertainty and Exclusion." This was also the situation for Danyal Shafiq, a stateless person detained for six years; see *Shafiq v. Australia*.

[169] For a review of Australian law, jurisprudence, and practice with regard to the indefinite detention of asylum-seekers on security grounds, see B. Saul, "Dark Justice: Australia's Indefinite Detention

Is such detention incompatible with human rights law, particularly the prohibition on arbitrary detention, and/or the prohibition on cruel, inhuman, and degrading treatment? At what point does a situation of detention become indefinite – after a set time or once all reasonable options for returning or removing a person have been exhausted?

International treaty law does not provide a ready answer to these questions. In respect of asylum-seekers UNHCR has taken the position that "indefinite detention is arbitrary and maximum limits on detention should be established in law."[170] It cites several pronouncements of the Human Rights Committee to support this position[171] and also refers to the principle of proportionality that underlies the rule against arbitrary detention. This test is noted to apply in relation to both the initial order of detention as well as any extensions: "the length of detention can render an otherwise lawful decision to detain disproportionate and, therefore, arbitrary."[172] Maximum periods of detention established by law are seen as a guard against arbitrariness.

However, the jurisprudence of the Human Rights Committee, considered in detail earlier in the chapter, suggests that the key issue from the perspective of the Article 9 prohibition on arbitrary detention is not just whether the detention is extended or extremely lengthy but whether it can be justified as nonarbitrary in the individual case, for example, to prevent flight.[173] The European Court of Human Rights has applied a similar line of reasoning to consider when very lengthy detention becomes arbitrary. For example, as noted previously, it has found that detention of an irregular migrant for six years was *not* excessive,[174] citing, among other factors, security risks presented by the detainee as well as the fact his detention was subject to regular, careful review.[175]

The length and indefinite nature of detention may raise the question of whether the prohibition on cruel, inhuman, or degrading treatment has been breached. The European Court of Human Rights has held that, although ill-treatment must attain a certain level of severity to constitute cruel, inhuman, or degrading treatment,

of Refugees on Security Grounds under International Human Rights Law" (2012) 13 *Melbourne Journal of International Law* 686. For a review of United States law and practice relevant to indefinite detention of migrants, see A. Siskin, *Immigration-Related Detention: Current Legislative Issues* (Congressional Research Service Report for Congress, Jan. 12, 2012).

170 UNHCR Guidelines on Detention of Asylum-Seekers, at Guideline 6. See also Edwards, "Back to Basics," at 23–36.

171 Edwards, "Back to Basics," at 23, citing: *A. v. Australia*, at para. 9.2; *Hugo van Alphen v. The Netherlands*, at para. 5.8; *Spakmo v. Norway*, UNHRC Comm. No. 631/1995, UN Doc. CCPR/C/67/D/631/1995, Nov. 5, 1999, at para. 6.3; and *Mukong v. Cameroon*, UNHRC Comm. No. 458/1991, UN Doc. CCPR/C/51/D/458/1991, July 21, 1994 [*Mukong v. Cameroon*], at para. 9.8.

172 Ibid.

173 *Hugo van Alphen v. The Netherlands*, at para. 5.8.

174 *Chahal v. United Kingdom*, esp. at para.117.

175 Ibid.

the assessment of this involves "all of the circumstances of the case," one of which includes "duration of the treatment" and "its physical or mental effects."[176] This argument was made in relation to eleven foreign nationals, several of whom were detained for more than three years in the United Kingdom under anti-terror laws.[177] Several of the applicants were stateless persons, and torture survivors. The Court noted that "[d]uring a large part of [their] detention, the applicants could not have foreseen when, if ever, they would be released."[178] The Court observed that the uncertainty regarding their position, and "the fear of indefinite detention must, undoubtedly, have caused the applicants great anxiety and distress, as it would any detainee in their position."[179] This, together with medical evidence of harm to the mental health of the applicants, was "one of the factors" that the court took into account when assessing whether the threshold of cruel, inhuman, or degrading treatment or punishment had been reached.[180] Ultimately however, the Court decided that the uncertain detention did not reach this threshold: that it could not be said that the applicants were without "any prospect or hope of release."[181] They were able to individually challenge the decision to certify them, and the relevant authority was required to review the continuing case for detention every six months.[182]

Are national security grounds sufficient to override the rule against arbitrary detention, and to permit indefinite detention? Temporary derogation from Article 9 of the ICCPR (and from the equivalent Article 5 in the European Convention on Human Rights) is certainly possible, including for reasons of public emergency and national security.[183] The Human Rights Committee has sought to limit the scope of this exception, asserting that "[m]easures derogating from the provisions of the Covenant must be of an exceptional and temporary nature."[184] The right to derogate from human rights obligations has been asserted by the United States in this context.[185] It was also relied upon by the government of the United Kingdom

176 *Ireland v. the United Kingdom* (1979–1980) 2 EHRR 25, (ECHR, Jan. 18, 1978), at para. 162.

177 *A. and Others v. United Kingdom*, (2009) 49 EHRR 29 (ECHR, Feb. 19, 2009) [*A. and Others v. United Kingdom*].

178 Ibid. at para. 129.

179 Ibid. at para. 130.

180 Ibid. at para. 130.

181 Ibid. at para. 131.

182 Ibid.

183 For a detailed analysis of the limits of the State's capacity to derogate both from the ICCPR and the European Convention on Human Rights, see further A. *and Others v. United Kingdom*, particularly at paras. 109, 110, 137–190.

184 HRC General Comment No. 29, at 235 (para. 2). See also the decisions of the Committee in *F.K.A.G. et al. v. Australia* and *M.M.M. et al. v. Australia*, at note 110 above.

185 In 2003, the United States Attorney General made a ruling, in regard to a Haitian immigrant, that irregular migrants, even those without known links to terrorist groups, could be detained indefinitely to address national security concerns. The attorney general framed security concerns as including "mass irregular migration" with attendant strains on national security and homeland security resources: R.

in A. *and Others v. United Kingdom*, in respect of special "emergency" domestic laws that permitted detention of persons considered to be a national security threat. Although the European Court of Human Rights in this case accepted the existence of an emergency, it ultimately held the response was disproportionate to the threat, as it unjustifiably discriminated between nationals and nonnationals.[186] This decision reinforces the considerable soft law support for a restrictive interpretation of legitimate grounds for derogation from Article 9 of the ICCPR.[187] An important additional restriction is that no derogation is permitted with regard to the prohibition on cruel, inhuman, or degrading treatment. Accordingly, there can be no justification for indefinite detention that constitutes cruel, inhuman, or degrading treatment.[188]

9.2.3.5. Indicators of Unlawful / Arbitrary Detention

International law recognizes the critical importance of individualized assessment: each situation of detention must be assessed on its merits and on the particular circumstances of the case. The previous analysis made clear that the detention of smuggled migrants could, in certain individual cases, amount to unlawful deprivation of liberty and violate the prohibition on arbitrary detention. The likelihood of detention of smuggled migrants being characterized as unlawful or arbitrary and

Swarns, "Illegal aliens Can Be Held Indefinitely, Ashcroft Says," *New York Times*, Apr. 26, 2003, cited in de Zayas, "Human Rights and Indefinite Detention," at 26.

186 A. *and Others v. United Kingdom*, at para. 190. Note that this interpretation is at odds with the far narrower interpretation of legitimate grounds for derogation from the ICCPR as asserted in the Siracusa Principles and by the UN Human Rights Committee, outlined in note 187.

187 See, for example, UN Commission on Human Rights, "The Siracusa Principles on the Limitation and Derogation Provisions in the International Covenant on Civil and Political Rights," UN Doc. E/CN.4/1985/4, Annex, Sept. 28, 1984, available at www.unhcr.org/refworld/docid/4672bc122.html (accessed May 12, 2013) (the Principles were the outcome of a 1984 high-level international conference of nongovernmental organizations; for further details see the *Note Verbale* from the Permanent Representative of the Netherlands introducing the document), at para. 39: "A State party may take measures derogating from its obligations under the International Covenant on Civil and Political Rights pursuant to article 4 (hereinafter called 'derogation measures') only when faced with a situation of exceptional and actual or imminent danger which threatens the life of the nation. A threat to the life of the nation is one that: (a) Affects the whole of the population and either the whole or part of the territory of the State, and (b) Threatens the physical integrity of the population, the political independence or the territorial integrity of the State or the existence or basic functioning of institutions indispensable to ensure and protect the rights recognized in the Covenant." Also, according to paragraph 40 of these Principles, "Internal conflict and unrest that do not constitute a grave and imminent threat to the life of the nation cannot justify derogations under article 4." Paragraph 54 notes that: "The principle of strict necessity shall be applied in an objective manner. Each measure shall be directed to an actual, clear, present, or imminent danger and may not be imposed merely because of an apprehension of potential danger."

188 See further, A. *and Others v. United Kingdom*, at paras. 109–110; and de Zayas, "Human Rights and Indefinite Detention," at 19–20.

thereby in violation of international law is particularly high if it can be shown that such detention is:

- Not specifically provided for in law;
- Imposed contrary to law;
- Provided for or imposed in a discriminatory manner (e.g., against one national or ethnic group and not another, against men but not women);
- Imposed for a prolonged, unspecified, or indefinite period;
- Unjust, unpredictable, and/or disproportionate to the aim of the detention;
- Not subject to judicial or administrative review to confirm its legality and to confirm that it continues to be necessary in the circumstances, with the possibility for release where no grounds for its continuation exist.

Additional considerations will apply with regard to groups or persons, such as children and asylum-seekers, whose special status imposes additional obligations on States. These issues are considered further later in the chapter.

9.2.4. *Detention Provisions of the EU Returns Directive*

The 2008 EU Directive on return of illegally staying third-country nationals[189] is examined in detail in the following chapter. However, the Directive contains some important provisions on detention for the purposes of effecting removal. These provisions, which generally affirm the standards set out in the previous section, may be summarized as follows:

- Return decisions should provide for a period of voluntary departure of between two and thirty days, which may be extended, shortened, or withheld if warranted by special circumstances.[190]
- A third-country national who is the subject of return procedures should *only be detained* in order to prepare the return and/or carry out the removal process, in particular when: (a) there is a risk of absconding or (b) the third-country national concerned avoids or hampers the preparation of return or the removal process.[191]
- The detention shall be maintained as long as these conditions are fulfilled and the detention continues to be necessary to ensure successful removal.[192]

[189] Directive 2008/115/EC of the European Parliament and of the Council of 16 December 2008 on common standards and procedures in Member States for returning illegally staying third-country nationals, OJ L 348/98, Dec. 24, 2008 [EU Returns Directive].

[190] Ibid. at Art. 7.

[191] Ibid. at Art. 15(1).

[192] Ibid. at Art. 15(1).

- Any detention shall be for as short a period as possible and only maintained as long as removal arrangements are in progress and executed with due diligence.[193]
- Detention shall be ordered, in writing, by administrative or judicial authorities, with reasons being given in fact and in law.[194]
- When detention has been ordered by administrative authorities, Member States shall: (a) provide for a speedy judicial review of the lawfulness of detention to be decided on as speedily as possible from the beginning of detention; or (b) grant the third-country national concerned the right to take proceedings by means of which the lawfulness of detention shall be subject to a speedy judicial review to be decided on as speedily as possible after the launch of the relevant proceedings. In such a case Member States shall immediately inform the third-country national concerned about the possibility of taking such proceedings.[195]
- The third-country national concerned shall be released immediately if the detention is not lawful.[196]
- When it appears that a reasonable prospect of removal no longer exists for legal or other considerations, detention ceases to be justified and the person concerned is to be released immediately.[197]
- Detention is to be reviewed at reasonable intervals of time and, in the case of prolonged detention, reviews are to be subject to the supervision of a judicial authority.[198]

The Directive requires each Member State to set a limited period of detention, which may not exceed six months.[199] This period can be extended by a maximum of a further twelve months (i.e., an absolute maximum of eighteen months) where this is permitted by national law and where "regardless of all ... reasonable efforts the removal operation is likely to last longer owing to: (a) a lack of cooperation by the third-country national concerned, or (b) delays in obtaining the necessary documentation from third countries."[200] The European Court of Justice has confirmed that this maximum period may not be exceeded, even if the individual concerned is not in possession of valid documents, has acted aggressively, or has no means of support or accommodation in the destination country.[201] This is in keeping with the

[193] Ibid.
[194] Ibid. at Art. 15(2).
[195] Ibid.
[196] Ibid.
[197] Ibid. at Art. 15(4).
[198] Ibid. at Art. 15(3).
[199] Ibid. at Art. 15(5).
[200] Ibid. at Art. 15(6).
[201] *Kadzoev v. Bulgaria* (Court of Justice of the European Union, C-357/09 PPU, Nov. 30, 2009), OJ C 24/17, at para. 69.

basic principle of the Directive, which foresees detention of returning third-country nationals as a "measure of last resort."[202]

The European Court of Justice has also pronounced on other aspects of the Directive of relevance to the subject of this chapter: most particularly on the question of whether and when EU Member States may impose criminal sanctions on persons for reason of their unlawful entry or stay. In the 2011 *El Dridi* case, the Court affirmed the principle of proportionality as requiring that the detention of a person subject to deportation should not continue for an unreasonable length of time.[203] In relation to the question of whether Italy could impose criminal sanctions (a term of imprisonment) on persons for not complying with an expulsion order, the Court expressed the view that a custodial penalty for such noncompliance "risks jeopardising the attainment of the objective pursued by that directive, namely, the establishment of an effective policy of removal and repatriation of illegally staying third-country nationals," as it could frustrate the application of measures aimed at enforcing the return decision, by delaying it.[204] It held that the Directive, most particularly Articles 15 and 16 "must be interpreted as precluding ... legislation ... which provides for a sentence of imprisonment to be imposed on an illegally staying third-country national on the sole ground that he remains, without valid grounds, on the territory of that State, contrary to an order to leave that territory within a given period."[205] "[This] does not preclude the possibility for the Member States to adopt, with respect for the principles and objective of Directive 2008/115, provisions regulating the situation in which coercive measures have not resulted in the removal of a third-country national staying illegally on their territory."[206] In the subsequent *Achughbabian* case,[207] the Court affirmed the right of EU Member States to criminalize illegal entry or stay and to place third-country nationals in detention in order to determine whether their stay is lawful. However, it also made clear the very narrow scope of application of criminal sanctions: EU Member States may not use custodial sentences to postpone adoption of a decision on return and thereby

202 Ibid. view of Advocate General Mazák, Nov. 10, 2009, at para. 101.

203 *El Dridi v. Italy* (Court of Justice of the European Union, C-61/11 PPU, Apr. 28, 2011), at para. 43.

204 Ibid. at para. 59.

205 Ibid. at para. 62.

206 Ibid. at para. 60. Raffaeli summarizes the essence of the judgment as follows: "while States are allowed to adopt criminal law provisions aimed at dissuading those third-country nationals against whom coercive measures were unsuccessful from remaining illegally on their territory, they cannot punish with criminal detention anyone against whom the return procedure is still ongoing; once an irregular immigrant is found, a return decision must be issued, and its enforcement must be pursued with all reasonable efforts": R. Raffaelli, "The Returns Directive in Light of the El Dridi Judgment" (2011) 3(1) *Perspectives on Federalism* N32.

207 *Alexandre Achughbabian v Préfet du Val-de-Marne* (Court of Justice of the European Union, C-329/11 (not yet published), Dec. 6, 2011) (Reference for a preliminary ruling: Cour d'appel de Paris – France).

delay the application of the EU Returns Directive. A return decision must be issued immediately when an irregular immigrant is identified as such and the procedure leading to return must commence immediately thereafter.[208]

9.3. RIGHTS OF DETAINED SMUGGLED MIGRANTS

Several rights of persons in detention (such as the right to judicial review and to release if the detention is found to be unlawful) have been dealt with earlier in the chapter in the context of the prohibition on arbitrary detention. However, as already discussed in Chapter 2, it is not sufficient that detention be lawful and nonarbitrary. The present section considers other important rights that attach to the fact of detention: the right to humane conditions of detention, and the right to legal assistance, information, and consular assistance. The section also considers whether there is an obligation on States with regard to monitoring (and inspection) of detention and places of detention.

9.3.1. *Right to Humane Conditions of Detention*

The "gold standard" with respect to the treatment of detainees is neatly encapsulated in the following provisions from the OAS Principles and Best Practices on the Protection of Persons Deprived of Liberty in the Americas:

> All persons subject to the jurisdiction of any Member State of the Organization of American States shall be treated humanely, with unconditional respect for their inherent dignity, fundamental rights and guarantees, and strictly in accordance with international human rights instruments.
>
> In particular, and taking into account the special position of the States as guarantors regarding persons deprived of liberty, their life and personal integrity shall be respected and ensured, and they shall be afforded minimum conditions compatible with their dignity.
>
> They shall be protected from any kind of threats and acts of torture, execution, forced disappearance, cruel, inhuman, or degrading treatment or punishment, sexual violence, corporal punishment, collective punishment, forced intervention or coercive treatment, from any method intended to obliterate their personality or to diminish their physical or mental capacities.
>
> Circumstances such as war, states of exception, emergency situations, internal political instability, or other national or international emergencies may not be invoked

[208] For a detailed analysis of this case see R. Raffaelli, "Case Note: The Achughbabian Case: Impact of the Return Directive on National Criminal Legislation," *Diritto Penale Contemporaneo*, February 2, 2012, available at SSRN: http://ssrn.com/abstract=1998324 (accessed May 12, 2013).

in order to evade the obligations imposed by international law to respect and ensure the right to humane treatment of all persons deprived of liberty.[209]

To what extent does this standard reflect current international law? There is no question that international law mandates certain standards of treatment for all detainees, including smuggled migrants. ICCPR Article 10(1), for example, states that "all persons deprived of their liberty shall be treated with humanity and with respect for the inherent dignity of the human person." [210] This requirement applies to all ICCPR States Parties, irrespective of resource constraints.[211] Similar provisions are contained in the major regional human rights treaties.[212] Multiple soft law sources confirm the obligation of States to ensure humane conditions of detention.[213] In the present context it is important to reiterate that the focus of the current chapter is on administrative (i.e., nonjudicial) detention of smuggled migrants. Such detention should never be of a punitive nature.[214] The rule that accused persons shall, save in exceptional circumstances, be segregated from convicted persons and shall be subjected to separate treatment appropriate to their status as unconvicted persons[215] is also relevant, as are the prohibition on torture and other cruel, inhuman, or degrading treatment or punishment[216]; and the prohibition on discrimination.

209 OAS Principles and Best Practices on the Protection of Persons Deprived of Liberty in the Americas, at Principle 1.

210 See also Human Rights Committee, "General Comment No. 21: Humane Treatment of Persons Deprived of their Liberty," UN Doc. HRI/GEN/1/Rev.7, at 153, May 12, 2004, adopted Apr. 10, 1992, at para. 2; HRC General Comment No. 15, at para. 7; CERD General Recommendation No. 30, at para. 19. See further Chapter 2 at Section 2.5.2 (on "conditions of detention").

211 *Mukong v. Cameroon*, at para. 9.

212 See, for example, European Convention on Human Rights, at Art. 3; and American Convention on Human Rights, at Art. 5(2).

213 See, for example, United Nations, "Standard Minimum Rules for the Treatment of Prisoners," adopted by the First United Nations Congress on the Prevention of Crime and the Treatment of Offenders, held at Geneva in 1955, and approved by the Economic and Social Council by its resolutions 663 C (XXIV) of 31 July 1957 and 2076 (LXII) of 13 May 1977, Aug. 30, 1955; "Body of Principles for the Protection of All Persons under Any Form of Detention or Imprisonment," at Principle 1; UN General Assembly, "Code of Conduct for Law Enforcement Officials," adopted by GA Res. 34/169, UN Doc. A/RES/34/169, Annex, Dec, 17, 1979, at Art. 2; and OAS Principles and Best Practices on the Protection of Persons Deprived of Liberty in the Americas.

214 "Specific Groups and Individuals – Migrant Workers: Report of the Special Rapporteur, Ms. Gabriela Rodríguez Pizarro," UN Doc. E/CN.4/2003/85, Dec. 30, 2002, at para. 54.

215 ICCPR, at Art. 10(2)(a). See also the EU Returns Directive, at Art. 16(1): "1. Detention shall take place as a rule in specialised detention facilities. Where a Member State cannot provide accommodation in a specialised detention facility and is obliged to resort to prison accommodation, the third-country nationals in detention shall be kept separated from ordinary prisoners."

216 See also Chapter 2, at Section 2.5.

The Human Rights Committee has considered the rights of detained persons in a detailed General Comment.[217] The points made by the Committee that are most relevant to the present discussion include the following:

- The obligation to treat detainees with respect for their humanity applies to all persons deprived of their liberty – including those who are in immigration detention;
- Persons deprived of their liberty are entitled to all ICCPR rights, "subject to the restrictions that are unavoidable in a closed environment"[218];
- All persons deprived of their liberty must be treated without discrimination[219] based on, for example, race, sex, national origin, or the fact of their being asylum-seekers;
- Conditions of detention should involve no further hardship or constraint other than that resulting from the deprivation of their liberty;
- Lack of material resources cannot be cited as a justification for failure to treat detained persons with humanity and respect for their dignity;
- All detained persons are entitled to an individualized assessment of their situation.

On several occasions the Committee has pronounced on the treatment of detained irregular migrants by States Parties. It has expressed concern about unsatisfactory conditions of detention (in terms of overcrowding, hygiene, food, and medical care), ill-treatment, failure to conduct regular inspections, and failure to protect against arbitrary expulsion.[220]

In many countries, conditions of detention for smuggled migrants can be so dire as to constitute cruel, inhumane, or degrading treatment in breach of ICCPR and regional human rights obligations. In the case of *M.S.S. v. Belgium and Greece*, the European Court of Human Rights was asked to consider the alleged violation of Article 3 of the European Convention, in respect of the applicant's detention as an asylum-seeker in Greece. The Court noted the horrifying conditions in the particular facility where the applicant had been detained:

[217] UN Human Rights Committee, "General Comment No. 21: Humane Treatment of Persons Deprived of Their Liberty," UN Doc. HRI/GEN/1/Rev.7, at 153, May 12, 2004, adopted Apr. 10, 1992.

[218] Ibid. at para. 3.

[219] Note that measures designed to protect the rights of women, detained persons with a disability, and other vulnerable groups should not be considered discriminatory. See, for example, Convention on the Elimination of All Forms of Discrimination against Women, 1249 UNTS 13, done Dec. 18, 1979, entered into force Sept. 3, 1981, at Art. 4; and Convention on the Rights of Persons with Disabilities, 2515 UNTS 3, done Dec. 13, 2006, entered into force May 3, 2008 [Convention on the Rights of Persons with Disabilities], at Art. 5(4).

[220] See, for example, UN Human Rights Committee, "Concluding Observations: Italy," UN Doc. CCPR/C/ITA/CO/5, Apr. 24, 2006, at para. 15.

> ... the sector for asylum seekers was rarely unlocked and the detainees had no access to the water fountain outside and were obliged to drink water from the toilets. In the sector for arrested persons, there were 145 detainees in a 110 sq. m space. In a number of cells there was only one bed for fourteen to seventeen people. There were not enough mattresses and a number of detainees were sleeping on the floor. There was insufficient room for all the detainees to lie down and sleep at the same time. Because of the overcrowding, there was a lack of sufficient ventilation and the cells were unbearably hot. Detainees' access to the toilets was severely restricted and they complained that the police would not let them out into the corridors. The police admitted that the detainees had to urinate into plastic bottles ... there was no soap or toilet paper, the sanitary and other facilities were dirty, the sanitary facilities had no doors and the detainees were deprived of outdoor exercise.[221]

The Court held that these conditions amounted to degrading treatment within the meaning of Article 3 of the Convention. Although some of the periods of detention were relatively brief, the Court emphasized that it did not regard these periods as insignificant. Of particular relevance was the fact that the applicant was an asylum-seeker, who was "particularly vulnerable because of everything he had been through during his migration and the traumatic experiences he was likely to have endured previously."[222] It observed that the applicant's distress was "accentuated" by "the vulnerability inherent in his situation as an asylum seeker."[223]

As noted by the European Court of Human Rights in another case, any form of detention necessarily involves a level of distress and hardship for detainees[224] and this consideration must be factored in when deciding the appropriate standard. The Court has explained that States Parties to the European Convention are required to ensure that conditions of detention do not cause distress or hardship to a degree that exceeds the inevitable suffering that is inherent in such a measure, and that an individual's health and well-being are provided for adequately.[225] It has also pronounced on the following practices, all of which have relevance to the detention of smuggled migrants in some countries.

221 *M.S.S. v. Belgium and Greece*, at para. 230.
222 Ibid. at para. 232.
223 Ibid. at para. 233. In making this finding, the Court noted that the fact that the applicants were asylum-seekers was relevant but did not explain precisely how or why. Ibid. at para. 231.
224 *Tabesh v. Greece*, App. No. 8256/07, [2009] ECHR 2224 (ECHR, Oct. 29, 2009) [*Tabesh v. Greece*], at para. 36. As noted previously, the Human Rights Committee makes a similar point in General Comment No. 21, at para. 3: "... neither may they be subjected to any hardship or constraint other than that resulting from the deprivation of liberty; respect for the dignity of such persons must be guaranteed under the same conditions as for that of free persons. Persons deprived of their liberty enjoy all the rights set forth in the Covenant, subject to the restrictions that are unavoidable in a closed environment."
225 *Tabesh v. Greece*, at para. 36.

- Solitary confinement: must not be imposed on a discriminatory basis, must not be imposed indefinitely, must be periodically reviewed; reasons must be given for any decision to continue segregation, the detainee's physical and mental condition must be monitored.[226]
- Overcrowding and poor detention conditions: degrading treatment will be found where distress and hardship caused by overcrowding exceeds the unavoidable level of suffering inherent in detention.[227] Unsanitary conditions that negatively affect a detainee's health and well-being may constitute degrading treatment.[228]
- Compulsory medical intervention such as forced feeding: forced feeding will not be considered degrading if it is medically necessary to save a person's life; procedural safeguards must be respected in relation to detainees who refuse food. The manner of forced feeding can amount to inhuman or degrading treatment or punishment.[229]

9.3.2. *Right of Access to Legal Assistance, Information, and Consular Assistance*

Persons who are held under any form of detention, including immigration detention, are entitled to certain procedural guarantees (in addition to access to judicial review), the violation of which may contribute to a finding that the detention itself is a breach of the right to personal liberty, or arbitrary and thereby unlawful.[230] One important guarantee relates to the right of access to a lawyer. On this issue, the ICCPR is silent but the Human Rights Committee has frequently referred to the existence of this right both in communications and in its monitoring of State

[226] *Ramirez Sanchez v. France*, (2007) 45 EHRR 49 (ECHR July 4, 2006). See also *Piechowicz v. Poland*, Application No. 20071/07, [2012] ECHR 689 (ECHR, Apr. 17, 2012); *Horych v. Poland*, Application No. 13621/08, [2012] ECHR 699 (ECHR, Apr. 17, 2012); and X. *v. Turkey*, Application No. 24626/09, [2012] ECHR 1950 (ECHR, Oct. 9, 2012).

[227] *Mandic and Jovic v. Slovenia*, Application Nos. 5774/10 and 5985/10 (ECHR, Jan. 20, 2012); and *Štrucl and Others v. Slovenia*, Application Nos. 5903/10, 6003/10 and 6544/10 (ECHR, Oct. 20, 2011). See also *Ananyev and Others v. Russia*, (2012) 55 EHRR 18 (ECHR, Jan. 10, 2012).

[228] *Kalashnikov v. Russia*, (2003) 36 EHRR 34 (ECHR, July 15, 2002); *Modârcă v. Moldova*, (2009) 48 EHRR 39 (ECHR, May 10, 2007); *Florea v. Romania*, Application No. 37186/03 (ECHR, Sept. 14, 2010); *Pavalache v. Romania*, Application No. 38746/03 (ECHR, Oct. 18, 2011).

[229] Hunger strikes are becoming increasingly common in immigration detention centers as a way of protesting conditions of detention. See Protest Uchodźców, "Mass Hunger Strike at Immigration Detention Centres," (undated), available at https://protestuchodzcow.wordpress.com/english/ (accessed May 12, 2013), (detailing a mass hunger strike in 2012 at a Polish immigration center); and M. Kenny, D. Salove, and Z. Steel, "Legal and Ethical Implications of Medically Enforced Feeding of Detained Asylum Seekers on Hunger Strike" (2004) 180(5) *Medical Journal of Australia* 237, at 237.

[230] See, for example, UN Commission on Human Rights, "Report of the Working Group on Arbitrary Detention," UN Doc. E/CN.4/2000/4, Dec. 28, 1999, at Annex II, Deliberation No. 5.

practice.[231] The source of this obligation is found in the right to review the lawfulness of detention, an obligation that cannot be effectively realized without access to legal counsel.[232] In the more specific context of detained asylum-seekers, the UN High Commissioner for Refugees asserts the existence of a right "to be informed of the right to legal counsel," referring to Article 16(2) of the Refugee Convention.[233]

As a practical matter, it is difficult, if not impossible, for detainees to fully realize their rights under Article 9 if they are not provided with information. On this issue, the ICCPR is ambiguous, referring not specifically to detainees but to a right of "anyone arrested" to "reasons for his arrest."[234] Nowak, however, interprets this obligation as extending to persons arrested for administrative reasons.[235]

An important clarification was provided by the International Court of Justice in the 2009 *Diallo* case in the course of the Court's consideration of the scope of the

[231] See, for example, UN Human Rights Committee, "Concluding Observations: Uzbekistan," UN Doc. CCPR/CO/71/UZB, Apr. 26, 2001. In the context of concern about torture and cruel, inhuman, or degrading treatment of detainees, the Committee notes that "[f]ree access to lawyers, doctors and family members should be guaranteed immediately after the arrest and during all stages of detention (at para. 7). See also UN Human Rights Committee, "Concluding Observations: Ireland," UN Doc. CCPR/C/IRL/CO/3, July 30, 2008, at para. 19: "The State party should amend the immigration, residence and protection bill 2008 to outlaw summary removal which is incompatible with the Covenant and ensure that asylum-seekers have full access to early and free legal representation so that their rights under the Covenant receive full protection."

[232] *Valcada v. Uruguay*, at paras. 10, 12.

[233] UNHCR Guidelines on Detention of Asylum-Seekers, at Guideline 7 (para. 47(ii)). Article 16(2) of the Refugee Convention states: "A refugee shall enjoy in the Contracting State in which he has his habitual residence the same treatment as a national in matters pertaining to access to the Courts, including legal assistance and exemption from *cautio judicatum solvi* [payment of security for legal costs]." The *Travaux Préparatoires* notes that: "Other treaties to which the Contracting State is a party may be relevant in this connection such as the International Covenant on Civil and Political Rights (Articles 14, 16), the European Convention for the Protection of Human [Rights] and Fundamental Freedoms (Articles 4, 6 paragraphs 1 and 3). That Convention provides, in particular, for the free assistance of an interpreter, if necessary. Further, the Hague Convention on Civil Procedure and the European Convention on Establishment and its Protocol are relevant. According to Article 7 of that Convention [European Convention on Establishment], nationals of the parties shall have access to the judicial and administrative authorities of the other States Parties and shall have the right to obtain the assistance of any person of their choice who is qualified by the law of the country concerned. Article 8 provides for free legal assistance in another State Party on the same basis as nationals of the State concerned. Article 9 provides for exemption from *cautio judicatum solvi* for nationals of the States Parties. It further provides that when a person has been exempted from *cautio judicatum solvi* an order to pay the expenses of proceedings shall be enforceable in the country of the person's residence": P. Weis, *The Refugee Convention, 1951, The* Travaux Preparatoires *Analysed with a Commentary by Dr Paul Weis* (posthumously published, 1995), available at www.unhcr.org/4ca34be29.pdf (accessed May 12, 2013).

[234] ICCPR, at Art. 9(2).

[235] Nowak, *ICCPR Commentary*, at 228. See also HRC General Comment No. 8, at para. 1, where the Committee notes: "It is true that some of the provisions of article 9 (part of para. 2 and the whole of para. 3) are only applicable to persons against whom criminal charges are brought."

right to be informed of the reasons for arrest under Article 9 of the ICCPR and Article 6 of the African Charter. The Court held that this obligation applies:

> in principle to any form of arrest or detention decided upon and carried out by a public authority, whatever its legal basis and the objective being pursued (...). The scope of these provisions is not, therefore, confined to criminal proceedings; they also apply, in principle, to measures which deprive individuals of their liberty that are taken in the context of an administrative procedure, such as those which may be necessary in order to effect the forcible removal of an alien from the national territory. In this latter case, it is of little importance whether the measure in question is characterized by domestic law as an "expulsion" or a "*refoulement*."[236]

Where a right to information can be established it is reasonable to maintain that such information should be provided in a language that the detainee is able to understand.[237] European treaty law is explicit on this point, providing that everyone who is detained shall be informed promptly, in a language, which he or she understands, of the reasons for the detention, and information as to his or her rights as a detainee.[238] The EU Returns Directive is also clear on obligations related to provision of information, providing that "[t]hird-country nationals kept in detention shall be systematically provided with information which explains the rules applied in the facility and sets out their rights and obligations. Such information shall include information on their entitlement under national law to contact [independent monitoring] organisations and bodies."[239]

Beyond these points, the substantive content of the right to be informed is not very well settled. Soft law sources assert that the right includes an explanation of the detained persons legal rights and information on how those rights may be asserted.[240]

[236] *Ahmadou Sadio Diallo (Republic of Guinea v. Democratic Republic of the Congo)*, [2010] ICJ Rep 639, at para. 77.

[237] This is recognized in in the 1998 "Body of Principles for the Protection of All Persons under Any Form of Detention or Imprisonment," at Principle 14; and in the OAS Principles and Best Practices on the Protection of Persons Deprived of Liberty in the Americas, at Principle V. See also Migrant Workers Convention Article 16(8), which requires that migrant workers shall be provided interpreters where necessary and without cost.

[238] European Convention on Human Rights, at Art. 5(4).

[239] EU Returns Directive, at Article 16(5).

[240] See, for example, "Body of Principles for the Protection of All Persons under Any Form of Detention or Imprisonment," at Principle 13 ("Any person shall, at the moment of arrest and at the commencement of detention or imprisonment, or promptly thereafter, be provided by the authority responsible for his arrest, detention or imprisonment, respectively, with information on and an explanation of his rights and how to avail himself of such rights."); OAS Principles and Best Practices on the Protection of Persons Deprived of Liberty in the Americas, at Principle V ("Persons deprived of liberty shall have the right to be promptly informed in a language they understand of the reasons for their deprivation of liberty and of the charges against them, as well as to be informed of their rights and guarantees; to have access to a translator or interpreter during the proceedings; and to communicate with their family.")

In relation to detained migrants and asylum-seekers the UN Working Group on Arbitrary Detention has stated that such persons must have the possibility, while in custody, of communicating with the outside world, including by telephone, fax, or electronic mail, and of contacting a lawyer, a consular representative, and relatives. According to the Working Group, such factors should be taken into account in determining whether a particular situation of detention is arbitrary.[241] UNHCR has reiterated the importance of communication and information for detained asylum-seekers.[242]

The right to consular access and support will be potentially important for many smuggled migrants who have been arrested, detained, charged with any offense, or threatened with deportation. This issue was a major concern for some States involved in the drafting of the Migrant Smuggling Protocol,[243] and the final text of that instrument affirms a right of consular access for smuggled migrants in detention.[244] Application of this provision will require that, where a smuggled migrant has been detained, arrested, or is in custody, the arresting or detaining authority should inform the smuggled migrant without delay about his or her right to communicate with consular officers. If the detainee confirms that he or she does wish to make such contact, the detaining authority should then take reasonable steps to facilitate that communication, including allowing and facilitating visits by consular officials.[245] It is essential to emphasize that the right to access consular assistance belongs to the smuggled migrant. Many smuggled migrants are escaping persecution and may have very sound reasons for not wanting their consular officials to know where they are, or the nature of the claims they are making. In this context it is relevant to note the principle of confidentiality in refugee status determination processes, including assurance by the host State not to share information about the applicant with the State of origin.[246]

241 UN Commission on Human Rights, "Report of the Working Group on Arbitrary Detention," UN Doc. E/CN.4/2000/4, Dec. 28, 1999, at Annex II, Deliberation No. 5, Principle 2.

242 UNHCR Guidelines on Detention of Asylum-Seekers, at Guideline 8 (para. 48(vii)).

243 Protocol against the Smuggling of Migrants by Land, Sea and Air, supplementing the United Nations Convention against Transnational Organized Crime, 2241 UNTS 507, done Nov. 15, 2000, entered into force Jan. 28, 2004 [Migrant Smuggling Protocol]. The drafting history confirms that although some delegates to the drafting Committee thought restating this obligation was unnecessary, others indicated they supported its inclusion, providing the wording was identical to the earlier instruments. United Nations Office on Drugs and Crime, Travaux Préparatoires *of the Negotiations for the Elaboration of the United Nations Convention against Transnational Organized Crime and the Protocols Thereto* (2006), at 538 (n. 5).

244 Migrant Smuggling Protocol, at Art. 16(5).

245 United Nations Office on Drugs and Crime, *Model Law against the Smuggling of Migrants* (2010), at 73–75.

246 See UN High Commissioner for Refugees, *Procedural Standards for Refugee Status Determination under UNHCR's Mandate* (2003).

To what extent does the right of consular access exist outside the Migrant Smuggling Protocol? Certainly other specialist instruments, such as the EU Returns Directive, do not provide for an unqualified right of access to consular assistance.[247] The extent to which general international law recognizes a right to consular assistance – and a right to timely *notification* of the right to consular assistance – is unresolved. The UN General Assembly has, in the past, recognized aliens' right of consular access as well as a right to information about this right, through a nonbinding declaration.[248] Under the Vienna Convention on Consular Relations, States Parties are required to assist noncitizens who have been detained in contacting consular officials in their country of citizenship. Specifically:

> if [the individual concerned] so requests, the competent authorities of the receiving State shall, without delay, inform the consular post of the sending State if, within the consular district, a national of that State is arrested or committed to prison or to custody pending trial, or is detained in any other manner. Any communication addressed to the consular post by the person arrested, in prison, custody or detention shall also be forwarded by the said authorities without delay. The said authorities shall inform the person concerned without delay of his rights under this sub-paragraph.[249]

The Convention further provides that "consular officers shall have the right to visit a national of the sending State who is in prison, custody or detention, to converse and correspond with him and to arrange for his legal representation."[250]

Importantly, the Vienna Convention on Consular Relations does not create an obligation on the national's State to provide assistance once it is contacted. In other words, it is up to the notified State to decide whether it will provide protection and support – and, if so, the nature and extent of that assistance. The provision on notification extracted above was subject to examination by the Inter-American Court of Human Rights in the context of an advisory opinion issued in 1999.[251]

[247] The Directive provides for third-country nationals in detention to be allowed, on request, "to establish in due time contact with legal representatives, family members and competent consular authorities." EU Returns Directive, at Art. 16(2).

[248] UN General Assembly, "Declaration on the Human Rights of Individuals Who Are Not Nationals of the Country in which They Live," GA Res. 40/144, UN GAOR, 40th sess, 116th plen mtg, UN Doc. A/RES/40/144, Dec. 13, 1985, at Art. 10.

[249] Vienna Convention on Consular Relations, 596 UNTS 261, done April 24, 1961, entered into force Mar. 19, 1967, at Art. 36(1)(b).

[250] Ibid. at Art. 36(1)(c).

[251] *The Right to Information on Consular Assistance in the Framework of the Guarantees of the Due Process of Law*, Advisory Opinion OC-16/99, Inter-American Court of Human Rights (ser. A) No. 16, Oct. 1, 1999 [*Right to Information on Consular Assistance* (Inter-Am Ct. H.R.)].

In a "surprisingly bold" and "remarkable" opinion,[252] the Court affirmed that the provision applied "to all cases in which a national of a sending State is deprived of his freedom *regardless of the reason*."[253] The Court found that whenever a foreign national is detained, that person has the fundamental right (recognized in but not created by the Vienna Convention) to be informed of his right to contact consular authorities. It further found that failure to so notify constitutes a violation of the human right to due process, recognized in Article 14 of the ICCPR.[254]

The International Court of Justice has, on several occasions, examined the implications of the relevant provision of the Vienna Convention on Consular Relations from the perspective of individual rights.[255] In the *LaGrand* case, the court identified a right to consular notification and held that the Vienna Convention does not just apply to the rights of the sending State but also to those of the detained individual.[256] Although not pronouncing directly on whether the right to consular notification was part of the right of due process, the Court did give some indication that this was something more than a treaty-based entitlement.[257] In a subsequent case, it retracted slightly on this position while still avoiding a direct conclusion on the matter of whether, as found by the Inter-American Court, the right to consular notification is a *human* right.[258]

Several other international human rights treaties contain provisions on consular assistance and protection. The Convention against Torture, for example, provides that any person in custody for a torture-related offense "shall be assisted in communicating immediately with the nearest appropriate representative of the State of which he is a national, or, if he is a stateless person, to the representative of the State where he usually resides."[259] The Migrant Workers Convention confirms that migrants falling within its provisions have a right of recourse to consular notification as well as to consular protection and assistance, including in cases of expulsion.[260] This instrument also specifies that where a migrant worker is detained, the consular

[252] C. M. Cerna, "Impact on the Right to Consular Notification," in M. T. Kamminga and M. Scheinin eds., *The Impact of Human Rights on General International Law* 171 (2009) [Cerna, "Impact on the Right to Consular Notification"], at 180, 186.

[253] *Right to Information on Consular Assistance* (Inter-Am Ct. H.R.), at para. 101 (emphasis added).

[254] For a detailed consideration and critique of the Court's advisory opinion, see Cerna, "Impact on the Right to Consular Notification," at 180–186.

[255] *Case Concerning the Vienna Convention on Consular Relations (Paraguay v. United States), Request for the Indication of Provisional Measures*, [1998] ICJ Rep 248; *LaGrand (Germany v. United States of America)*, [2001] ICJ Rep 466 [*LaGrand Case*]; *Avena and Other Mexican Nationals (Mexico v. United States of America)*, [2004] ICJ Rep 12 [*Avena and Other Mexican Nationals Case*].

[256] *LaGrand Case*, at para. 77.

[257] See Cerna, "Impact on the Right to Consular Notification," at 192.

[258] *Avena and Other Mexican Nationals Case*, at para. 124.

[259] Convention against Torture, at Art. 6.

[260] Migrant Workers Convention, at Art. 23.

or diplomatic staff of his or her State of origin shall be informed without delay of the arrest and the reasons therefore.[261] Soft law on detention affirms the importance of a right to consular access for detained foreigners.[262]

In summary, smuggled migrants who have been arrested and/or detained for any reason including unlawful entry have the right to be informed of the availability of consular assistance from their country of origin. They have the right to choose whether or not to utilize such access, to communicate freely with the consular post, and to obtain or decline consular protection and support. Failure of a State to meet its international legal obligations in this regard engages the international responsibility of that State.[263]

9.3.3. *Scrutiny and Monitoring of Detention*

Effective realization of the core international legal obligations with respect to detention requires that measures be in place to prevent the occurrence of breaches, as well as to detect and remedy violations. This will generally require the establishment and implementation of certain procedural safeguards such as: ensuring that detainees are only held in officially recognized places of detention,[264] ensuring that proper records are kept and made available to family and friends (regarding where detainees are held),[265] and ensuring that detention facilities are open to scrutiny and monitoring by independent monitoring and inspection regimes.[266]

[261] Ibid. at Art. 7(a).

[262] See, for example, the "Body of Principles for the Protection of All Persons under Any Form of Detention or Imprisonment," which provides that any detained foreigner must have the right to access consular officials of the State of which he or she is a national ("If a detained or imprisoned person is a foreigner, he shall also be promptly informed of his right to communicate by appropriate means with a consular post or the diplomatic mission of the State of which he is a national or which is otherwise entitled to receive such communication in accordance with international law or with the representative of the competent international organization, if he is a refugee or is otherwise under the protection of an intergovernmental organization": at Principle 16, para. 2).

[263] For a more detailed discussion of this aspect, see R. Perruchoud, "Consular Protection and Assistance," in R. Cholewinski, R. Perruchoud, and E. MacDonald eds., *International Migration Law: Developing Paradigms and Key Challenges* 71 (2007), at 80–81.

[264] UN Human Rights Committee, "General Comment No. 20: Replaces General Comment 7 Concerning Prohibition of Torture and Cruel Treatment or Punishment," UN Doc. HRI/GEN/1/Rev.7, at 150, May 12, 2004, adopted Oct. 3, 1992 [HRC General Comment No. 20], at para. 11. This principle is also part of international humanitarian law. See Pejic, "Procedural Principles and Safeguards for Internment/Administrative Detention," at 384–385; and J-M. Henckaerts and L. Doswald-Beck, *Customary International Humanitarian Law* (2005), Volume I, "Rules," at 442–445.

[265] HRC General Comment No. 20, at para. 11.

[266] UNHCR Guidelines on Detention of Asylum-Seekers, at Guideline 10.

With only limited exceptions, international law does not impose specific obligations on States to ensure independent monitoring of their detention facilities and practices. Where they do exist, such obligations tend to be carefully worded and provisional. An example is the EU Returns Directive, which provides that "[r]elevant and competent national, international and non-governmental organisations and bodies shall have the possibility to visit detention facilities ... to the extent that they are being used for detaining third-country nationals. Such visits may be subject to authorisation."[267] Policy statements on this issue tend to confirm the importance of such monitoring while also avoiding explicit and detailed commitment.[268]

Despite this equivocation, it is not difficult to extract an obligation related to monitoring from the broader obligations related to the rights of detainees, most particularly the prohibition on arbitrary detention. Certainly, regular and independent monitoring of closed detention facilities for smuggled migrants has been shown to bring important benefits, including: identification of existing and potential human rights violations, identification of specific vulnerabilities requiring attention, and systemic improvements across detention facilities.[269] However, in the vast majority of countries, the capacity of independent agencies to undertake adequate monitoring is severely limited. In some cases this is a matter of available resources being insufficient to meet the demand caused by a growing number of detainees and facilities. In other cases, detaining authorities directly or indirectly restrict access to detention facilities. The Optional Protocol to the Convention against Torture, which provides some guidance on how monitoring could or should take place, seeks to establish a system of regular inspection visits by independent observers to places where people are deprived of their liberty, in order to prevent torture or other cruel, inhuman, or degrading treatment or punishment.[270] The system established by the Protocol confirms that monitoring bodies should be independent; that they should be supported by adequate functions, powers and resources; that they should work in cooperation

[267] EU Returns Directive, at Art. 16(4).

[268] For example, the Parliamentary Assembly of the Council of Europe has recognized that States should "allow, *when applicable*, the monitoring of reception centres and detention centres by ombudspersons and national human rights commissions, parliamentarians and other national or international monitoring bodies. Where specialized monitoring bodies do not exist, they should be created." Council of Europe, Parliamentary Assembly, Resolution 1637 (2008) on Europe's "boat people": mixed migration flows by Sea into southern Europe, adopted Nov. 28, 2008, at para. 9.14. See also Council of Europe, Parliamentary Assembly, Resolution 1707 (2010) on Detention of asylum seekers and irregular migrants in Europe, adopted Jan. 28, 2010, at para. 9.2.

[269] C. Branson, "Applying Human Rights in Closed Environments: Practical Observations on Monitoring and Oversight," speech delivered at "Implementing Human Rights in Closed Environments" Conference, Monash University, Melbourne, Feb. 21, 2012, available at http://humanrights.gov.au/about/media/speeches/speeches_president/2012/20120221_closed_Environments.html (accessed May 12, 2013).

[270] Optional Protocol to the Convention against Torture, at Art. 1.

with detaining authorities; and that they should be able to publicly report on their work.[271] As at October 2013, the Optional Protocol has seventy Parties, including several major destination States for smuggled migrants including Germany, Italy, the United Kingdom, and Australia.[272]

9.4. SPECIAL GROUPS OF SMUGGLED MIGRANTS: ADDITIONAL RIGHTS AND OBLIGATIONS

It has been noted at various points in this book that international law attaches different or additional rights to – and obligations in respect of – certain categories of persons. The situation of women, children, and asylum-seekers/refugees is particularly important in the context of detention and is therefore subject to detailed consideration later in the chapter. Of course that list is not exhaustive, and States will be required to consider the individual situation of every smuggled migrant within their jurisdiction in order to determine whether their status requires additional or different consideration in relation to detention. For example, in relation to disabled smuggled migrants in detention, States Parties to the relevant international convention are required to make "reasonable accommodations" or changes to policies and practices to match their specific requirements and needs.[273] Similar requirements may exist in relation to the very old,[274] or to sexual minorities[275] in order to ensure that the rights of such persons are being recognized and upheld.

There is considerable soft law support for the proposition that members of particularly vulnerable groups should not be subjected to migration detention at all.[276] At a minimum, the existence of vulnerability operates to impose special or additional obligations on States. The question of whether a particular case or aspect of

[271] Ibid. esp. Part IV.

[272] United Nations Treaty Collection, available at http://treaties.un.org/Pages/ParticipationStatus.aspx (accessed November 28, 2013).

[273] Convention on the Rights of Persons with Disabilities, at Art. 14.

[274] See Council Directive 2003/9/EC of 27 January 2003 laying down minimum standards for the reception of asylum-seekers, OJ L 31/18, Feb. 6, 2003, at Art. 17(1); and UNHCR Guidelines on Detention of Asylum-Seekers, at Guideline 9.6 (para. 64).

[275] See UNHCR Guidelines on Detention of Asylum-Seekers, at Guideline 9.7 (para. 65).

[276] See, for example, ibid, at Guideline 9.1 (para. 49) (victims of trauma or torture), Guideline 9.2 (para. 51) (children), and (para. 54) (unaccompanied or separated children); Guideline 9.3 (para. 58) (pregnant women and nursing mothers), and Guideline 9.5 (para. 63) (asylum-seekers with disabilities); International Organization for Migration, *International Migration Law Information Note on International Standards on Immigration Detention and Non-custodial Measures* (2011), at 20; Council of Europe, Parliamentary Assembly, Report of the Committee on Migration, Refugees and Population, *The detention of asylum seekers and irregular migrants in Europe*, Doc. 12105, Jan. 11, 2010, at Principle IX.

detention is unlawful will depend on an assessment of the facts of the individual situation against the standards that attach to those facts.

9.4.1. *Detention of Women Smuggled Migrants*

As has been discussed previously, international law (including the Migrant Smuggling Protocol[277]) recognizes that women may be especially vulnerable to violations of their human rights and that an enhanced standard of protection and assistance may be appropriate in particular situations, such as the detention of smuggled women. Studies on the situation of women in immigration detention have confirmed the reality of compromised rights and unmet needs.[278] These problems are becoming more acute as the number of women (including women with young children) in immigration detention steadily increases in all major destination countries.[279]

The enhanced standard of protection and assistance may include measures to ensure that detained smuggled women:

- Are separated from nonfamily men;
- Are under the responsibility of, and only attended by, women officials;
- As a general rule, are not detained if they are pregnant or breast-feeding;
- Are kept with their children and otherwise able to exercise parental responsibilities;
- Have access to special facilities and services appropriate to their medical and psychological needs, including those related to pregnancy and breast-feeding;
- Are protected from all forms of gender-based violence including sexual abuse;
- Are not discriminated against on the basis of their sex or any other ground (for example, through being placed in "protective" detention in a shelter or other welfare-type facility).[280]

[277] Migrant Smuggling Protocol, at Art. 16(4).

[278] See, for example, Human Rights Watch, *Detained and Dismissed: Women's Struggles to Obtain Health Care in United States Immigration Detention* (2009); E. Cox and T. Priest, *Women in Immigration Detention: More Questions than Answers* (2005); J. Freedman and B. Jamal, *Violence against Migrant Women and Refugee in the Euromed Region – Case Studies: France, Italy, Egypt & Morocco* (2008), esp. at 37–38, 48 [Freedman and Jamal, *Violence against Migrant and Refugee Women in the Euromed Region*].

[279] Freedman and Jamal, *Violence against Migrant and Refugee Women in the Euromed Region*, at 37.

[280] These basic points are drawn from a range of soft law sources including pronouncements of the Committee on the Elimination of Discrimination against Women; the Committee against Torture; and various United Nations Special Procedures, including the Special Rapporteur on Violence against Women, its Causes and Consequence; the Special Rapporteur on the Human Rights of Migrants; and the Working Group on Arbitrary Detention. See also the United Nations Rules for the Treatment of Women Prisoners and Non-custodial Measures for Women Offenders (the Bangkok Rules), adopted by the UN General Assembly July 22, 2010 (by GA Res 2010/16, UN Doc. A/C.3/65/L.5, Oct. 6, 2010); UNHCR Guidelines on Asylum-Seeker Detention, at Guideline 9.3. For a useful overview of issues

9.4.2. Detention of Smuggled Victims of Trafficking

Detention of victims of trafficking is common in all parts of the world and can occur under a range of circumstances. As noted previously, the immigration laws of many countries permit an automatic right of detention for unauthorized migrants, and it is under such provisions that many trafficked persons end up in prison or immigration detention facilities, pending deportation. In many cases, those who are detained as illegal or smuggled migrants have not been correctly identified as having been trafficked. Trafficked persons, whether correctly identified or not, are also detained in police lockups and prisons as a result of engagement in illegal activities such as illegal entry, presentation of false documentation, or unauthorized work. Even if correctly identified as such, victims of trafficking who are unwilling or unable to cooperate in criminal investigations or to provide information that is deemed useful may be sent to immigration detention pending deportation. Finally, detention can occur when trafficking victims, including those who have been smuggled, are placed in a shelter or other welfare facility from which they are unable to leave.

The relevant international legal framework identifies trafficked persons as a group to which special and additional rights apply. This extends to the issue of their detention. The following brief overview is drawn from a much more extensive analytical summary of the relevant rules developed elsewhere by one of the present authors.[281]

In evaluating the lawfulness or otherwise of the detention of trafficked persons (including those who have been smuggled), it is important to make a distinction between *routine detention*, applied generally and as a matter of policy, law, or practice, and *case-by-case detention*. A detailed analysis of the relevant rules confirms that routine detention of victims or suspected victims of trafficking in police lockups, prisons, immigration detention centers, or shelters violates a number of fundamental principles of international law and is therefore to be considered, prima facie, unlawful.[282] Routine detention of victims of trafficking violates, in some circumstances, the right to freedom of movement, and, in most if not all circumstances, the prohibitions on unlawful deprivation of liberty and arbitrary detention. As noted previously, international law prohibits the discriminatory detention of victims, including detention that is linked to the sex of the victim. The practice of routine detention for women and girls is inherently discriminatory and therefore unlawful. Routine detention of trafficked children is also directly contrary to international law

relevant to the detention of women, see J. Ashdown and M. James, "Women in Detention" (2010) 92 *International Review of the Red Cross* 123.

[281] See Gallagher, *The International Law of Human Trafficking*, at 288–297.

[282] Ibid.

and cannot be legally justified on the basis of protection, best interests, or any other grounds.

States may, on a case-by-case basis, be able to successfully defend the detention of trafficked persons in shelters (but not in immigration detention facilities) with reference to, for example, criminal justice imperatives, public order requirements, or victim safety needs. The internationally accepted principles of *necessity*, *legality*, and *proportionality* should be used to evaluate the validity of any such defense. Application of these principles would most likely only support a claim of lawful detention in relation to a situation where detention is administered as a last resort and in response to credible and specific threats to an individual victim's safety. However, even when these basic tests are satisfied, a range of protections must be in place to ensure that the rights of the detained person are respected and protected. Such measures would include but not be limited to judicial oversight of the situation to determine its ongoing legality and necessity, as well as an enforceable right to challenge the fact of detention. Failure of the State to act to prevent unlawful victim detention by public or private agencies is an internationally wrongful act that, in accordance with the analysis presented in Chapter 4, invokes the international legal responsibility of that State. Victims may be eligible for remedies, including compensation, for this unlawful detention.

In relation to children, international law recognizes the existence of special needs and special vulnerabilities. These are explored in detail later on in the chapter. In the context of trafficked children who have been smuggled it is relevant to reiterate the underlying principle of the best interests of the child: the detaining authority must be able to demonstrate that, irrespective of the nature of the facility, the detention itself is in the child's best interests. The detaining authority must also be able to demonstrate, in relation to each and every case, that there is no reasonable option available to it other than the detention of the child. Specific protections, including the appointment of a guardian, judicial or administrative oversight, and the right of challenge must be upheld in all situations where the fact of detention can be legally justified.

9.4.3. *Detention of Smuggled Children*

No child shall be deprived of his or her liberty unlawfully or arbitrarily. The arrest, detention or imprisonment of a child shall be in conformity with the law and shall be used only as a measure of last resort and for the shortest appropriate period of time.[283]

The detention of irregular immigrant children, including those who have been smuggled, is a fraught and divisive issue. There can be no doubt that such detention is

[283] CRC, at Art. 37(b).

occurring, in significant numbers, in an increasing number of countries.[284] Children are held in formal immigration detention, either alone or with their parents or other family members. Sometimes they are subject to alternative detention regimes such as community detention facilities, transit centers, and welfare homes. Human rights advocates have protested strongly against such detention, particularly in formal facilities.[285] UNHCR states that "in principle," children should not be detained at all,[286] and that their extreme vulnerability "should take precedence over the status of 'illegal alien.'"[287] However, major States of destination that detain "unauthorized arrivals" appear highly reluctant to grant generalized exemptions from detention for smuggled children for fear that this will increase flows, including through encouraging use of children in smuggling operations.[288] It is nevertheless recognized, including by involved States, that such detention presents complex legal, operational, and ethical challenges. Multiple studies have confirmed that migrant children who are placed in immigration detention endure grave risks to their safety and physical and mental well-being, exhibiting high levels of psychopathology, much of which is

[284] See Terre des Hommes International Federation, Global Campaign to End Immigration Detention of Children and Platform for International Cooperation on Undocumented Migrants, *A Call on States to Stop Detaining Migrant Children* (Dec. 18, 2012), available at http://endchilddetention.org/wp-content/themes/end/images/uploads/Press-release-International-Migrants-Day-2012.pdf (accessed May 12, 2013) ("In Mexico, in 2011 for instance, 6.2% of migrants in detention were under 18 years of age, which means 4,172 children. In Israel, since August 2010, unaccompanied children are being sent to a separate detention facility run by prison authorities. During the first year of its operation, 169 children were detained in this center, with reports of 19 suicide attempts during this time. In Australia, asylum seeking children and children who have been refused asylum, as well as irregular migrant children awaiting removal are all detained. The latest official statistics on Australia show that 694 children were being held in secure locked facilities. Over the past year, Canada has been holding 289 children in immigration detention centers, many under the age of 10. In 2010, 356 children were detained in France, 80% less than 10 years old. In 2012 France committed to stop detaining children within mainland France, but still frequently uses detention at the border and in its overseas territories.")

[285] See, for example, J. Burnett, J. Carter, J. Evershed, M. Bell Kohli, C. Powell, and G. de Wilde, *State Sponsored Cruelty: Children in Immigration Detention* (2010); Australian Human Rights and Equal Opportunities Commission, *A Last Resort? National Inquiry into Children in Immigration Detention* (2004).

[286] UNHCR Guidelines on Detention of Asylum-Seekers, at Guideline 9.2 (para. 51).

[287] Ibid. at Guideline 9.2 (para. 52).

[288] See, for example, the statement by the Australian Minister for Immigration following calls to release smuggled children currently being held in immigration detention: "to release all children from detention in Australia would be to send a message to people smugglers that if they carry children on dangerous boats, parents and children will be released into the community very quickly" (A. Vanstone (Minister for Immigration and Multicultural and Indigenous Affairs), "Government Committed to Detention Regime," media release, Canberra, June 10, 2004, available at http://parlinfo.aph.gov.au/parlInfo/search/display/display.w3p;query=Id%3A%22media%2Fpressrel%2FAZ2D6%22 (accessed May 12, 2013). See also A. Vanstone and P. Ruddock, *HREOC Inquiry into Children in Immigration Detention Tabled*, May 13, 2004, available at http://parlinfo.aph.gov.au/parlInfo/download/media/pressrel/2TKC6/upload_binary/2tkc64.pdf;fileType=application%2Fpdf#search=%22media/pressrel/2TKC6%22 (accessed May 12, 2013).

attributable to traumatic experiences in detention and its impact on caregivers.[289] Studies also confirm the severe negative impact of prolonged detention on the emotional, educational, and social development of children involved.[290] It is also important to recall that many smuggled children may have experienced serious trauma prior to or during their journey that can be compounded by detention.

The legal framework around detention of smuggled children was discussed in Chapter 2 in the context of a broader analysis of international norms relevant to the treatment of smuggled migrants. That discussion highlighted the exacting nature of international legal rules around detention of children and their origin in an understanding of the fact that detained children are highly vulnerable to abuse, victimization, and the violation of their rights.

International law carefully stipulates the circumstances under which children can be detained. Most important is the requirement that children are not to be detained unlawfully or arbitrarily. This prohibition extends beyond penal detention to include deprivation of liberty on the basis of the child's welfare, health, and protection.[291] International law requires any form of juvenile detention to be in conformity with the law, used only as a measure of last resort, and imposed for the shortest appropriate period of time.[292] The best interests of the child are to be the primary consideration in all actions affecting smuggled children, including matters related to their detention.[293] Children deprived of their liberty also have the same rights as

289 See, for example, S. Mares and J. Jureidini, "Psychiatric Assessment of Children and Families in Immigration Detention – Clinical, Administrative and Ethical Issues" (2004) 28 *Australian and New Zealand Journal of Public Health* 520; and S. Nielsen, M. Norredam, K. L. Christiansen, C. Obel, J. Hilden, and A. Krasnik, "Mental Health among Children Seeking Asylum in Denmark – The Effect of Length of Stay and Number of Relocations: A Cross-Sectional Study" (2008) 8 *BMC Public Health* 293.

290 Ibid.

291 The "UN Rules for the Protection of Juveniles Deprived of Their Liberty," at paragraph 11(b), define a deprivation of liberty as any form of detention or imprisonment or the placement of a person in a public or private custodial setting from which a person under the age of eighteen is not permitted to leave at will, by order of any judicial, administrative, or other public authority: UN General Assembly, "United Nations Rules for the Protection of Juveniles Deprived of Their Liberty," adopted by GA Res. 45/113, UN Doc. A/RES/45/113, Dec. 14, 1990. Note that the Committee on the Rights of the Child has explicitly rejected detention of children in need of protection: "[s]uch deprivation of liberty for children who have been abandoned or abused equates to punishment for children who are victims of crimes, not the offenders." See UN Committee on the Rights of the Child, "General Comment No. 10: Children's Rights in Juvenile Justice," UN Doc., Apr. 25, 2007.

292 CRC, at Art. 37(b); "UN Rules for the Protection of Juveniles Deprived of Their Liberty," at para. 2; UN Committee on the Rights of the Child, "General Comment No. 6: Treatment of Unaccompanied and Separated Children outside Their Country of Origin," UN Doc. CRC/GC/2005/6, Sept. 1, 2005 [CRC General Comment No. 6], at para. 61. See also UN Committee on the Rights of the Child: "Concluding Observations: The Netherlands," UN Doc. CRC/C/15/Add.227, Jan. 30, 2004, at para. 54; "Concluding Observations: Canada," UN Doc. CRC/C/15/Add.215, Oct. 3, 2003, at para. 47.

293 CRC, at Art. 3. See further the discussion of the best interests principle in Chapter 2, at Section 2.4.4.

adults to challenge the legality of the deprivation of their liberty before a court or other competent, independent, and impartial authority, and to a prompt decision on any such action.[294]

The conditions under which any child is detained must be in conformity with that child's best interests and his or her right to be treated with humanity and dignity.[295] The detained child should be treated in a manner that takes into account the needs of persons of his or her age. He or she should not be discriminated against on any grounds including race, sex, national or ethnic origin, or the fact that he or she has been smuggled.

Additional entitlements of every child deprived of his or her liberty include:

- The right to prompt access to legal and other appropriate assistance[296];
- The right to be separated from adults unless it is considered not to be in the child's best interest[297];
- The right to maintain contact with his or her family through correspondence and visits, save in exceptional circumstances[298];
- The right to support for his or her physical and psychological recovery and social reintegration in an environment that fosters the health, self-respect, and dignity of the child[299]; and
- The right to have his or her case handled expeditiously without any unnecessary delay.[300]

According to UNHCR, unaccompanied or separated children should, if at all possible, be released to the care of family members who already have residency in

[294] CRC. at Art. 37(d).

[295] Ibid. at Art. 37(c). For an example of application of this principle in the context of smuggled child asylum-seekers, see UN Committee on the Rights of the Child, "Concluding Observations: Australia," UN Doc. CRC/C/15/Add.268, Oct. 20, 2005, at para. 64.

[296] Optional Protocol to the Convention on the Rights of the Child on the Sale of Children, Child Prostitution and Child Pornography, 2171 UNTS 227, done May 25, 2000, entered into force Jan. 18, 2002 [CRC Optional Protocol], at Art. 8; United Nations Children's Fund, *Guidelines for the Protection of Child Victims of Trafficking* (September 2006) [UNICEF Guidelines], at Guidelines 4.2, 7.1, 9.2.1, 10.1, 10.2; and CRC General Comment No. 6, at para. 63.

[297] CRC, at Art. 37(c): "UN Rules for the Protection of Juveniles Deprived of Their Liberty," at para. 29; and CRC General Comment No. 6, at para. 63. Note also the right to family unit that would prevent a child from being separated from his or her parents against his or her wishes: CRC, at Art. 9.

[298] CRC, at Art. 37(c); "UN Rules for the Protection of Juveniles Deprived of Their Liberty," at para. 59; and CRC General Comment No. 6, at para. 63.

[299] CRC, at Art. 39; CRC Optional Protocol, at Art. 8; and UNICEF Guidelines, at Guidelines 7.1, 7.2.

[300] CRC Optional Protocol, at Art. 8.1(g); UNICEF Guidelines, at Guideline 8.

the country. If that is not possible, alternative care such as a residential home or foster care placement should be arranged.[301]

By way of conclusion it is useful to draw together the key themes that arise around the question of detention of children who have been smuggled. (Note that the additional considerations that attach to the detention of smuggled child migrants who are also asylum-seekers are considered separately in the following section). First, although there are significant restrictions on its use, the detention of smuggled children is not, of itself, prohibited by international law. In other words, the right of States to control their own borders, which provides legitimacy for a concurrent right of States to detain persons entering or staying without authorization, does not recognize clear exceptions based on age. However, international law generally discourages the detention of children, and this extends to children who are "unlawfully present," including those who have been smuggled across an international border. The entitlement of the State to detain smuggled children is highly circumscribed, and the State is required to take a number of steps to ensure that such detention is lawful. Most importantly, States are under an obligation to try and identify alternative ways of securing necessary policy objectives. As with any other form of detention, the detaining State is required to show that the detention of smuggled children is both legal and nonarbitrary. In the case of children, there may be indicators of arbitrariness that are different from – or additional to – the indicators outlined previously in respect of all detained persons. For example, a failure to provide special protections for children (such as medical and psychological support and family unity) may render detention that is otherwise lawful arbitrary.[302] Considerations of reasonableness and proportionality will necessarily be different when the subject involved is a child. For example, it is unlikely that a State could sustain an argument that detention is a necessary and proportional response to a security threat when the individual involved is a child. Continual monitoring of children in detention and the conditions of that detention is another important aspect of ensuring that such detention is not arbitrary (or does not become so).[303]

[301] UNHCR Guidelines on Asylum-Seeker Detention, at Guideline 9.2 (para. 54).

[302] An example may be provided by the detention of children with medical issues at a remote location. See Australian Broadcasting Commission, *No Advantage* (video documentary, 2013), available at www.abc.net.au/4corners/stories/2013/04/29/3745276.htm (accessed May 12, 2013) (documenting cases of smuggled children suffering from anemia and anaphylaxis being forced to wait twenty-four hours for an "emergency evacuation").

[303] On the importance of rights-based monitoring as well as information on how it can best be conducted with special reference to countries of the Middle East and North Africa, see Penal Reform International, *Safeguarding Children in Detention: Independent Monitoring Mechanisms for Children in Detention in Mena* (2011).

9.4.4. Detention of Smuggled Asylum-Seekers

Although precise figures are unavailable, it is evident that asylum-seekers[304] constitute a significant proportion of smuggled migrants in immigration detention worldwide.[305] As with those who have been trafficked, the most important and immediately applicable obligation relates to identification. Persons with a valid claim to refugee protection will likely be indistinguishable from the larger category of detained "smuggled migrant" without further inquiry. Screening measures should therefore be in place to ensure that persons in need of international protection are identified and, if required, are able to make a claim for asylum.

Although detention is an increasingly common fate for many smuggled asylum-seekers, it should not be seen as automatic or inevitable. The European Commission for example, has clearly stated that "Member States shall not hold a person in detention for the sole reason that he or she is an applicant for asylum."[306]

It can be argued that beyond the obligation to ensure access to asylum procedures and *non-refoulement* to those identified as in need of such measures, international standards in relation to the treatment of asylum-seekers in detention are not substantially different from those that apply to all irregular migrants in administrative detention, including those who have been smuggled. Certainly the fact of the subject of detention being in need of international protection does not alter the obligation on States to ensure that such detention is both lawful and nonarbitrary. It does not alter the various procedural entitlements outlined previously, including the right of habeas corpus and the right to compensation for unlawful detention. The substantive content of the obligation to ensure humane conditions of detention similarly remains unchanged.[307] However, it has been asserted that the special situation of asylum-seekers as well as the particular needs and vulnerabilities of specific categories of asylum-seekers impose different and/or additional obligations on States. For example, persons who have suffered torture, persecution, and other serious harms are likely more vulnerable to re-traumatization through the detention process than

[304] Although the present discussion focuses on asylum-seekers, it should be noted that persons who do not fall within the international legal definition of refugee may nevertheless be considered in need of international protection and thereby entitled to benefit from the obligation of *non-refoulement*. See further discussion in Chapter 10, at Section 10.2.3.

[305] This reality is reflected in the adoption of an entire framework of guidance around "mixed migration": see further, UN High Commissioner for Refugees, *Refugee Protection and Mixed Migration: A 10-Point Plan of Action* (2007), at 1.

[306] Council Directive 2005/85/EC of 1 December 2005 on minimum standards on procedures in Member States for granting or withdrawing refugee status, OJ L 326/13, Dec. 13, 2005, at Art. 18(1). But see discussion of *Saadi v. United Kingdom* at Section 9.2.3.2.

[307] See, for example, Council Directive 2003/9/EC (laying down minimum standards for the reception of asylum-seekers).

those who have not experienced such harm.[308] The obligation on States to provide "humane" conditions of detention may thereby require special measures, such as provision of psychological support.

In 2012, UNHCR substantially revised and expanded its long-standing guidelines on detention of asylum-seekers.[309] The revision was explained as a response to the growing use of detention "sometimes for long periods and in poor conditions, including in some cases in prisons together with common criminals."[310] The new document is presented as "reflect[ing] the state of international law relating to detention – on immigration-related grounds – of asylum-seekers and other persons seeking international protection."[311] The essence of the Guidelines is encapsulated in the following introductory paragraph:

> In view of the hardship which it entails, and consistent with international refugee and human rights law and standards, detention of asylum-seekers should normally be avoided and be a measure of last resort. As seeking asylum is not an unlawful act, any restrictions on liberty imposed on persons exercising this right need to be provided for in law, carefully circumscribed and subject to prompt review. Detention can only be applied where it pursues a legitimate purpose and has been determined to be both necessary and proportionate in each individual case. Respecting the right to seek asylum entails instituting open and humane reception arrangements for asylum-seekers, including safe, dignified and human rights-compatible treatment.[312]

The substance of the document generally confirms the tentative conclusion reached previously: that the rights to which detained asylum-seekers are entitled are, in most respects, the same as those that apply to all detained persons, including all smuggled migrants who are being detained for reasons related to the unlawfulness of their entry. Special and additional rights largely relate to the obligation on States to: (1) provide access to asylum procedures – and refrain from returning persons who are in need of international protection, and (2) meet special needs. The new guidelines also assert a general presumption *against* detention of asylum-seekers.[313] This

[308] See, for example, note 109 above (on *C. v. Australia*).

[309] UN High Commissioner for Refugees, *Guidelines on the Applicable Criteria and Standards Relating to the Detention of Asylum-Seekers and Alternatives to Detention* (2012) [UNHCR Guidelines on Detention of Asylum-Seekers].

[310] UN High Commissioner for Refugees, "UNHCR Concerned at Detention of Asylum-Seekers, Releases New Guidelines," *Making a Difference*, Sept. 21, 2012, available at www.unhcr.org/505c33199.html (accessed May 12, 2013).

[311] UNHCR Guidelines on Detention of Asylum-Seekers, at 8 ("Scope") (para. 4).

[312] Ibid. at 6 ("Introduction") (para. 2).

[313] "These rights taken together – the right to seek asylum, the non-penalisation for irregular entry or stay and the rights to liberty and security of person and freedom of movement – mean that the detention of asylum-seekers should be a measure of last resort, with liberty being the default position." Ibid. at Guideline 2 (para. 14).

assumption is seen to impose additional obligations on States in relation to ensuring no arbitrary detention: for example, an obligation to ensure that detention is justified for a legitimate purpose. The document sets out, and explains in detail, ten guidelines.[314] Those elements of the guidelines that are specific to asylum-seekers are briefly considered in the next sections.

9.4.4.1. Obligation to Respect the Right to Asylum

Guideline 1 emphasizes that the internationally recognized right to seek and obtain asylum from persecution means that seeking asylum is not an unlawful act. As has been noted at various points in this book, the nature of the asylum system means that many persons seeking protection will be forced to use the services of smugglers in order to obtain unauthorized entry:

> The position of asylum-seekers may thus differ fundamentally from that of ordinary migrants in that they may not be in a position to comply with the legal formalities for entry. They may, for example, be unable to obtain the necessary documentation in advance of their flight because of their fear of persecution and/or the urgency of their departure. These factors, as well as the fact that asylum-seekers have often experienced traumatic events, need to be taken into account in determining any restrictions on freedom of movement based on irregular entry or presence.[315]

Detention should never constitute an obstacle to seeking or obtaining asylum from persecution. In practice this means that asylum-seekers in detention should be given information on accessing the relevant procedures and that timetables for lodging documentation should be appropriate to the fact of detention. Nor, as discussed in Chapter 2, should detention be used against smuggled asylum-seekers as a penalty for unlawful entry. Detention that operates to obstruct, in any way, access to asylum determination procedures would be considered punitive, as would mandatory detention that is clearly aimed at deterring future asylum-seekers.[316]

[314] 1. The right to asylum must be respected; 2. The right to liberty and security of the person and to freedom of movement apply to asylum-seekers; 3. Detention to be in accordance with and authorized by law; 4. Detention must not be arbitrary and any decision on detention must be based on an assessment of individual circumstances according to specific criteria; 5. Detention must not be discriminatory; 6. Indefinite detention is arbitrary and maximum limits should be established by law; 7. Decisions to detain or to extend detention must be subject to minimum procedural safeguards; 8. Conditions of detention should be humane and dignified; 9. The special circumstances and needs of particular asylum-seekers should be taken into account; 10. Detention should be subject to independent monitoring and inspection.

[315] UNHCR Guidelines on Detention of Asylum-Seekers, at Guideline 1 (para. 11).

[316] See further Chapter 2, at Section 2.3.2. Note that the obligation not to impose penalties for unlawful entry is considered under Guideline 2: the right to liberty and security of the person and to freedom of movement.

9.4.4.2. Obligation to Justify Detention on a Specified Ground

The Guidelines assert that, as detention of asylum-seekers is an exceptional measure, it may only be justified for a legitimate purpose: "[w]ithout such a purpose, detention will be considered arbitrary, even if entry was illegal."[317] The three grounds identified are those that are enshrined in international human rights law as lawful grounds of derogation from – or restriction on the exercise of – certain human rights: protection of public health, public order, and national security.[318] It should be noted that although the grounds of national security and public order do indeed appear in the Refugee Convention, this is not in connection with any of that instrument's provisions relating to deprivation of liberty.[319] In respect of protection of public order, the Guidelines confirm the finding of the Human Rights Committee that detention may be necessary where there are strong grounds for believing that an individual asylum-seeker is likely to abscond or otherwise to refuse to cooperate with the authorities.[320] It further asserts, largely on the basis of soft law sources, including conclusions of the UNHCR Executive Committee, that detention may also be justified on the grounds of public order if it is connected with accelerated procedures for manifestly unfounded or clearly abusive claims; where it is for purposes of initial identity and/or security verification; or for the purpose of recording, within the context of a preliminary interview, the elements of an individual's claim to international protection (where such information could not be obtained in the absence of

[317] UNHCR Guidelines on Detention of Asylum-Seekers, at Guideline 4.1 (para. 21).

[318] See, for example, ICCPR Article 12, which protects the right to freedom of movement and the right to leave any country including one's own, specifying that these rights: "shall not be subject to any restrictions except those which are provided by law, are necessary to protect national security, public order (*ordre public*), public health or morals or the rights and freedoms of others, and are consistent with the other rights recognized in the present Covenant." See also Article 13 (references to national security in the context of expulsion); Article 14 (references to "morals, public order ... or national security" in the context of exclusion of the press from trials); Article 18 (references to "protect public safety, order, health, or morals or the fundamental rights and freedoms of others" in the context of limitations on freedom to "manifest one's religion or beliefs"); Article 19 (references to "national security or of public order ... or of public health or morals" in the context of restrictions on freedom of expression); Article 21 (references to: "national security or public safety, public order ... the protection of public health or morals" in the context of restrictions on the right to peaceful assembly); and Article 22 (references to: "national security or public safety, public order ... the protection of public health or morals" in the context of restrictions on the right to freedom of association).

[319] See Refugee Convention: Article 28 (references to "compelling reasons of national security or public order" in relation to justifications for non-issue of travel documents); Article 32 (references to "grounds of national security or public order" in the context of exceptions to the obligation of non-expulsion); and Article 33 (references to "reasonable grounds for regarding [a refugee] as a danger to the security of the country" in the context of restrictions on the right to claim the benefit of the principle of *non-refoulement*). See also references to "national security" in Article 9 relating to the right of States to take provisional measures.

[320] A. *v. Australia*, at para. 9.4

detention). In respect of the ground of protection of public health, the Guidelines assert that "[c]arrying out health checks on individual asylum-seekers may be a legitimate basis for a period of confinement, provided it is justified in the individual case or, alternatively, as a preventive measure."[321]

Despite the fact that many States use variants of the "national security" grounds to justify detention of asylum-seekers, this operationally important exception to the stated principle of non-detention is only briefly considered by the Guidelines, beyond an acknowledgment that governments may need to "detain a particular individual who presents a threat to national security" and that any detention so justified must nevertheless be proportionate to the threat, be non-discriminatory, and be subject to judicial oversight.[322] In terms of purposes that are *not* permissible, the Guidelines confirm the conclusion reached previously that any detention imposed for the purpose of penalizing an asylum-seeker for unlawful entry or use of the services of a smuggler, or for deterring future asylum-seekers, would not be justified. It further confirms that detaining a person for the purposes of expulsion may occur only after an asylum claim has been finally determined and rejected.[323]

9.4.4.3. Obligation to Consider Alternatives to Detention

Guideline 4.3 asserts an obligation on States to consider alternatives to detention for asylum-seekers. This obligation is seen to arise out of the overall principle enshrined in the Guidelines of detention being exceptional and a measure of last report. The obligation to consider alternatives to detention is also seen to be an aspect of the standards of reasonableness and proportionality attached to the obligation to avoid arbitrary detention as well as of the requirement of individualized decision making.[324] The Guidelines make the important point that any alternatives to detention must themselves meet established rules and principles of human rights.

9.4.4.4. Obligation to Consider Special Needs

Guideline 9 confirms that "the experience of seeking asylum, and the often traumatic events precipitating flight" create special vulnerabilities among asylum-seekers that should be weighed in relation to assessment of the necessity to detain as well as the conditions of detention.[325] In relation to the latter, initial and periodic

[321] UNHCR Guidelines on Detention of Asylum-Seekers, at Guideline 4.1.2 (para. 29).
[322] Ibid. at Guideline 4.1.3 (para. 30).
[323] Ibid. at Guideline 4.1.4 (para. 33).
[324] Ibid. at Guideline 4.3.
[325] Ibid. at Guideline 9.1 (para. 49).

assessments of the physical and psychological health of detained asylum-seekers is necessary. Special attention must be paid to detained asylum-seekers who may have particular vulnerabilities and needs such as women and those who have been trafficked, as well as asylum-seekers with disabilities; older asylum-seekers; and those whose actual or perceived sexual orientation or gender identity exposes them to risk of violence, ill-treatment or physical, mental, or sexual abuse, or otherwise creates special needs. The Guidelines confirm that child asylum-seekers comprise a group requiring special attention, that the rights and obligations discussed previously attach to all children in detention, and that States must take special account of additional vulnerabilities that may be present in children seeking international protection.

The UNHCR Guidelines are an important contribution to the ongoing task of fleshing out the legal framework around detention of asylum-seekers. However, it would be premature to consider this document as the definitive statement of the law. At the very least it can be said that outside the core obligations related to the right to seek asylum and the prohibitions on arbitrary and inhumane detention, the legal situation is unclear. Certainly State practice in this area is highly unsettled as many countries of destination for smuggled migrants resist curbs on their capacity to detain those who have arrived without authorization, even in the face of a valid claim for international protection.

9.5. SUMMARY CONCLUSIONS ON DETENTION OF SMUGGLED MIGRANTS

The analysis in this chapter supports the following summary conclusions:

- The relevant international standards on detention apply to all situations in which a smuggled migrant is not permitted to leave at will by order of any judicial, administrative, or other authority. A place of detention can include the "international zone" of an airport, a rescue or interception vessel, and a place of shelter or rehabilitation that the migrant is unable to leave. Even when technically free to leave (for example by renouncing a claim to asylum and accepting repatriation assistance), smuggled migrants may still be considered as "detained" and thereby subject to international laws and standards governing detention.
- International law preserves the sovereign right of States to control entry into their territory. As a consequence, the detention of persons who have entered or sought entry without authorization is not, per se, unlawful. This right of control extends to all unauthorized persons including those who are or who may claim asylum. However, State-sanctioned deprivation of liberty may only occur

"on such grounds and in accordance with such procedure as is established by law"[326] and may not be arbitrary.

- The principle of legality is violated if someone is detained on grounds that are not clearly established, in advance, in law, or are contrary to such law. The reference to "law" within the requirement of legality is generally understood as referring primarily to the generally applicable law of the domestic legal system. There is some disagreement as to whether the reference to "law" also includes international law. Regional and international jurisprudence generally supports an assertion that the "law" in question must at least be compatible with international norms to satisfy the legality requirement. However, States have evidenced significant reluctance to accept conformity with international law as a necessary criterion for establishing legality.
- Any law permitting and regulating detention of smuggled migrants must itself not be arbitrary, and its application must not take place arbitrarily. The concept of arbitrariness extends beyond illegality under national law to include elements of injustice, unpredictability, unreasonableness, capriciousness. and disproportionality. To satisfy this requirement, the detention must also be reasonable and necessary in all of the circumstances of the individual case. The need to conduct identity and health checks and the need to address risk of absconding, security risks, and lack of cooperation (for example in establishing identity) may all be considered reasonable justifications for detention in the case of smuggled migrants – but only for as long as these justifications remain valid. A detention situation that was originally not arbitrary might become arbitrary if it continues over time without proper justification. In this context, indefinite or prolonged detention is not ipso facto arbitrary but must, for the entire duration, continue to satisfy the above requirements.
- Within the European system, the same general principles apply, but detention of irregular migrants must generally be aimed at either preventing unauthorized entry or be in pursuance of an effort to remove the individual concerned. EU Member States may not use custodial sentences to postpone adoption of a decision on return and thereby delay the application of the EU Returns Directive. A return decision must be issued immediately when an irregular immigrant is identified as such, and the procedure leading to return must commence immediately thereafter.
- International law requires that the necessary procedural guarantees be in place to identify and respond to situations of unlawful or arbitrary deprivation of liberty. These include the right to accessible and effective judicial review of the lawfulness of one's detention and an enforceable right to compensation for

[326] ICCPR, at Art. 9(1).

wrongful arrest or detention. It has been held that mandatory detention violates the right to review of the lawfulness of one's detention and the corresponding right to be released if that detention is found to be unlawful. Detained smuggled migrants also have a right to be informed of the reasons for their detention and to other information necessary to allow them to realize the right to review of the lawfulness of their detention. Detained smuggled migrants have the right to be informed of the availability of consular assistance from their country of origin. They have the right to choose whether to utilize such access, to communicate freely with the consular post, and to obtain or decline consular protection and support.

- All smuggled migrants deprived of their liberty have the right to be treated with humanity and with respect for the inherent dignity of the human person. They must be treated without discrimination. Conditions of detention should involve no further hardship or constraint other than that resulting from the deprivation of their liberty. All detained smuggled migrants are entitled to an individualized assessment of their situation and to having individual vulnerabilities (e.g., related to their experiences as a smuggled migrant) taken into account in relation to conditions of detention. Solitary confinement, overcrowding, and forced feeding can potentially constitute inhumane and degrading treatment and thereby be unlawful. These entitlements, together with the general prohibition on arbitrary detention, imply a corresponding obligation on the detaining State to ensure independent monitoring of its immigration detention facilities and practices.
- Detaining States are required to consider the individual situation of smuggled migrants within their jurisdiction in order to determine whether the migrants' status requires additional or different consideration in relation to detention. For example, in relation to child migrants who have been smuggled, international law carefully stipulates the circumstances under which such children can be detained: detention must be in conformity with the law, used only as a measure of last resort, and imposed for the shortest appropriate period of time. The best interests of the child are to be the primary consideration in all actions affecting smuggled children, including matters related to their detention. Separate, status-related rights attach to other groups of smuggled migrants including women, those with a disability, those who have been trafficked, and those who are seeking international protection.

10

Return of Smuggled Migrants

The concept of return generally refers to the processes and practices involved in removing a migrant from one country to another, either that person's country of origin or a transit country, or some other country with which that person may or may not have a legitimate link.[1] In the context of migrant smuggling, the main categories of return are voluntary return (assisted or spontaneous), and involuntary (forced) return. The terms "involuntary" and "forced" return tend to be used interchangeably with deportation or expulsion.[2] It is important to note that these categories do not have set definitional boundaries, and that, in reality, a particular return may fall along the continuum between voluntary and forced return.[3]

Return of irregular migrants – including those who have been smuggled – has been described as the "cornerstone" of modern national and regional migration

[1] The EU Returns Directive, for example, defines return as "the process of a third-country national going back – whether in voluntary compliance with an obligation to return, or enforced – to: his or her country of origin; or, a country of transit in accordance with Community or bilateral readmission agreements or other arrangements; or another third country, to which the third-country national concerned voluntarily decides to return and in which he or she will be accepted": Directive 2008/115/EC of the European Parliament and of the Council of 16 December 2008 on common standards and procedures in Member States for returning illegally staying third-country nationals, OJ L 348/98, Dec. 24, 2008 [EU Returns Directive], at Art. 3(3). The Directive is considered in detail at Section 10.4.

[2] I. Kruse, "EU Readmission Policy and Its Effects on Transit Countries: The Case of Albania" (2006) 8 *European Journal of Migration and Law* 115 [Kruse, "EU Readmission Policy: The Case of Albania"], at 118. Note that some commentators are highly critical of the use of the term "return," seeing it as a misleading label for what is essentially removal. See, for example, J-P. Cassarino ed., *Unbalanced Reciprocities: Cooperation on Readmission in the Euro-Mediterranean Area* (Middle East Institute Special Edition Viewpoints, Aug. 30, 2010) [Cassarino ed., *Unbalanced Reciprocities*], at 3, n. 6.

[3] For an overview of efforts to define various forms of voluntary and involuntary return, see European Migration Network, "Programs and Strategies in the EU Member States Fostering Assisted Return to and Reintegration in Third Countries," (Synthesis Report summarizing the main findings of the National Reports for the European Migration Network, Mar. 2011), at 15–19.

policies.[4] The Council of the European Union, for example, has explicitly stated that "an effective and sustainable return policy is an essential element of a well-managed migration system within the Union. The European Union and the Member States should intensify the efforts to return illegally residing third-country nationals."[5] This view seems to be widely shared by all major countries of destination for irregular migrants including those who have been smuggled.[6] However return is also one of the most vexed aspects of migration management, raising issues of the protection, safety, and dignity of the migrants, and cooperation between States. Mass expulsion or mass return of irregular migrants can raise not only human rights implications, whether through related civil disturbances or the conduct of the returns itself, but can also cause severe economic hardship for the country to which the migrants are returned.[7] In some countries, forced return of irregular migrants is practiced without even the most cursory consideration of protection needs. For example, there are credible reports of State officials forcing irregular migrants (including asylum-seekers) on to trucks, driving them to the border, and physically pushing them over, disregarding the very real risk of harm.[8] Return can also be effectively

4 A. Servent, *The European Parliament and the "Returns" Directive: The End of Radical Contestation; The Start of Consensual Constraints?* (Sussex European Institute, Working Paper No. 117, 2010), at 8–9.

5 Council of the European Union, *The Stockholm Programme – An Open and Secure Europe Serving and Protecting Citizens*, OJ C 115/1, May 4, 2010, at 30 (para. 6.1.6). See also EU Returns Directive, at Preambular para. 4 (referring to "an effective return policy as a necessary element of a well managed migration policy").

6 In relation to Australia, for example, the report of a 2012 inquiry into asylum-seekers (almost all of whom are smuggled) affirmed that "[t]he involuntary return of failed asylum-seekers is an integral part of Australia's migration and border management regime. It is also fundamental to maintaining the integrity of a properly functioning international system of protection," Australian Government, *Report of the Expert Panel on Asylum Seekers* (Aug. 2012), at 117. See also details of the International Organization for Migration's implementation of extensive State-funded Assisted Voluntary Return and Reintegration (AVRR) programs, available at www.iom.int/cms/return-assistance-migrants-governments (accessed May 12, 2013). In a regional context, see, for example, the statement on the importance of returns at paragraph 16(4) of the Co-Chair's statement from the Fourth Bali Regional Ministerial Conference on People Smuggling, Trafficking in Persons and Related Transnational Crime (Indonesia, Mar. 29–30, 2011), available at www.unodc.org/documents/southeastasiaandpacific//2011/11/som/Bali_process_FINAL_Ministerial_Co-chairs_statement_BRMC_IV-1.pdf (accessed May 12, 2013). For a domestic example of emphasis placed on removals, see United States Immigration and Customs Enforcement, "Memorandum on Civil Immigration Enforcement: Priorities for the Apprehension, Detention and Removal of Aliens," Mar. 2, 2011, available at www.ice.gov/doclib/news/releases/2011/110302washingtondc.pdf (accessed May 12, 2013), prioritizing removal of "recent illegal entrants" (immediately after "[a]liens who pose a danger to national security or a risk to public safety").

7 L. Schadomsky, "Ethiopian Workers Forced Out of Saudi Arabia," Nov. 30, 2013, available at www.dw.de/ethiopian-workers-forced-out-of-saudi-arabia/a-17263035 (accessed Nov. 30, 2013).

8 See, for example, T-A. Tekle, "Eritrea and Yemen Allegedly 'Conspire' to Deport Refugees," *Sudan Tribune*, Oct. 4, 2012, available at www.sudantribune.com/spip.php?article44102 (accessed May 12, 2012); UN High Commissioner for Refugees, "UNHCR Deeply Concerned by Deportation of

conducted prior to arrival, through "push back" practices at sea,[9] the legal implications of which have been examined in detail in Chapter 6. Even when returns take place through a properly established process, there can be little doubt that many irregular migrants, including those who have been smuggled, are returned without full and fair consideration of their legitimate claims to international protection and that some among this group are subsequently arrested, detained, tortured, or "disappeared."[10] Sometimes very practical problems relating to the need for identity verification and travel documents operate to prevent return. There are numerous examples of situations where it has become impossible to remove and return a person to his or her country of origin, because of a lack of cooperation from the person's country of origin or indeed from the individual concerned.[11]

In seeking to provide a comprehensive review of the legal framework around return of smuggled migrants, this chapter commences with an affirmation of the right of States to return nonnationals, including those who have been smuggled. It then turns to the substantial limitations that international law imposes on this right: the prohibition on arbitrary expulsion, the prohibition on collective expulsion, and the obligations of international protection and *non-refoulement*. Consideration is then given to the conduct of returns: the procedural and substantive steps necessary to ensure that a return permitted under international law does not subsequently

Eritreans from Sudan," (Press Release, July 26, 2011), available at www.unhcr.org/4e2ec8a36.html (accessed May 12, 2013).

9 See, for example, the scenario presented in *Hirsi Jamaa and Others v. Italy*, (2012) 55 EHRR 21 (ECHR, Feb. 23, 2012) [*Hirsi Jamaa v. Italy*] where Italy intercepted and returned to Libya in 2009 a group of Somalis and Eritreans without examining whether this would constitute a real risk to their lives. See also discussion of forcible pushback by the Thai military of Rohingya asylum-seekers in The Equal Rights Trust, *Unravelling Anomaly: Detention, Discrimination and the Protection Needs of Stateless Persons* (2010), at ch. 4.3.2.

10 See, for example, Amnesty International, *Eritrea: Sent Home to Detention and Torture* (2008); and C. Ramos, *Unsafe Return: Refoulement of Congolese Asylum Seekers* (2011); See also C. Tazreiter, "Between State Sovereignty and Invisibility: Monitoring the Human Rights of Returned Asylum Seekers" (2006) 12 *Australian Journal of Human Rights* 7. Tazreiter notes the difficulties of establishing the fate of returned asylum-seekers because of a gap in responsibility for international monitoring of such persons, but draws attention to the "[s]ignificant anecdotal evidence [which] exists of failed asylum-seekers and other categories of voluntary and involuntary returnees being arrested, imprisoned and tortured and 'disappearing' on return to a country of origin or to a third country" (at 14). There has been some recent effort to improve the capacity of post-deportation monitoring but this is largely a civil society initiative, and there has been little interest from reporting states or from countries receiving persons whose asylum claims have been rejected. See further L. Podeszfa and C. Manicon, "Avoiding Refoulement: The Need to Monitor Deported Failed Asylum Seekers" (2012) 2 *Oxford Monitor of Forced Migration* 10.

11 See, for example, *Mikolenko v. Estonia*, [2009] ECHR 1471 (ECHR, Sept. 8, 2009); M. Gibney and R. Hansen, "Deportation and the Liberal State: The Forcible Return of Asylum Seekers and Unlawful Migrants in Canada, Germany and the United Kingdom" (New Issues in Refugee Research, Working Paper No. 77 (UNHCR Evaluation and Policy Analysis Unit), 2003), at 11.

become unlawful or otherwise involve an unlawful act. The next part of the chapter examines the scope and substantive content of the obligation on States to accept and facilitate return of their nationals. The chapter concludes with a brief note on additional obligations related to return that arise with respect to special groups of smuggled migrants, specifically, children and those who have been trafficked.

It is important to note at the outset that there is no single instrument that comprehensively regulates the returns process either generally or in the specific context of return of smuggled migrants. In considering the applicable legal framework around return, the chapter continues the approach adopted throughout the book: prioritizing the specialist legal instruments that relate most directly to the issue at hand. In the context of returns, the Migrant Smuggling Protocol[12] is of central but narrow importance, being occupied primarily with obligations to accept and facilitate return. For States of the European Union, the Directive on common standards and procedures in Member States for returning illegally staying third-country nationals (EU Returns Directive) provides a comprehensive set of obligations regulating all aspects of the returns process. These specialist rules must be considered alongside a range of additional instruments that further define and explain both rights and obligations in this area. The most important are the major international and regional human rights and refugee treaties, which articulate key obligations such as the right of return; the obligation of *non-refoulement*; and the right to safety, dignity, and non-discrimination in the returns process. International and regional courts and tribunals (most particularly the European Court of Human Rights) have played an important role in clarifying the scope of and interplay between the various rules on return, and their judgments and pronouncements are also considered in detail at appropriate points in the chapter. In this regard it is relevant to flag a recent judgment of the International Court of Justice in the *Ahmadou Sadio Diallo* case,[13] the first decision of the Court that deals with the expulsion of aliens. Expulsion of aliens is also currently on the agenda of the International Law Commission (ILC), and its draft articles on the subject are referenced,[14] as are other "soft law" standards, principles, and resolutions of international bodies, the most prominent example of which is the Council of Europe's Twenty Guidelines on Forced Return.[15]

[12] Protocol against the Smuggling of Migrants by Land, Sea and Air, supplementing the United Nations Convention against Transnational Organized Crime, 2241 UNTS 507, done Nov. 15, 2000, entered into force Jan. 28, 2004 [Migrant Smuggling Protocol].

[13] *Ahmadou Sadio Diallo* (*Republic of Guinea v. Democratic Republic of the Congo (Judgment)*, [2010] ICJ Rep 639 [*Ahmadou Sadio Diallo Case*].

[14] International Law Commission, "Expulsion of Aliens: Texts of draft articles 1–32 provisionally adopted on first reading by the Drafting Committee at the sixty-fourth session of the International Law Commission," UN Doc. A/CN.4/L.797, May 24, 2012 [ILC Draft Articles on Expulsion of Aliens].

[15] Council of Europe, Committee of Ministers, *Twenty Guidelines on Forced Return*, CM(2005)40 final, May 9, 2005 [Council of Europe, *Twenty Guidelines on Forced Return*].

Finally, it is relevant to note that although the chapter is directed specifically at situations involving smuggled migrants, the substantive legal regime outlined and discussed below (with the exception of provisions of the Migrant Smuggling Protocol) is generally applicable to the return of all irregular migrants, irrespective of their means or mode of entry.

10.1. RIGHT OF STATES TO RETURN SMUGGLED MIGRANTS

The many objectively difficult and divisive issues around return should not operate to obscure the fact that return is widely accepted to be a core element of any effective strategy to prevent irregular migration including through migrant smuggling. One of the earliest multinational responses to flows of irregular migrants (specifically, refugees and asylum-seekers), the 1989 Comprehensive Plan of Action to respond to the mass movement of migrants from Indo-China, both anticipates and *requires* the return of those found not to be in need of protection.[16] A contemporary example of the view of States with regard to their right to return irregular migrants is provided by the EU Returns Directive, which explicitly states that "it is legitimate for Member States to return illegally staying third-country nationals, provided that fair and efficient asylum systems are in place which fully respect the principle of *non-refoulement*."[17] The Council of Europe's Twenty Guidelines on Forced Return similarly acknowledge that States may "find it necessary to forcibly return illegal residents" in the exercise of their right to control entry and residence on their territory.[18]

Equally, the United Nations High Commissioner for Refugees (UNHCR) has continued to express strong and clear policy support for the return of "persons found not to be in need of international protection."[19] As early as 1991, UNHCR affirmed the principle of return, in safety and dignity and in an orderly manner, of "persons determined not to be refugees," and of States' responsibilities toward their own citizens.[20] In declaring its support for returns, UNHCR explained that the misuse of the asylum system disadvantages those with valid claims for asylum; has a negative effect on public support for the asylum system; and results in considerable resources

[16] "International Conference on Indo-Chinese Refugees (Geneva, 13 and 14 June 1989): Declaration and Comprehensive Plan of Action" (1993) 5(4) *International Journal of Refugee Law* 617, at 623.

[17] EU Returns Directive, at Preambular para. 8.

[18] Council of Europe, *Twenty Guidelines on Forced Return*, at Preamble.

[19] This position has been reiterated by UNHCR on numerous occasions. See, for example, UN High Commissioner for Refugees, *The Return of Persons Found Not to Be in Need of International Protection to Their Countries of Origin: UNHCR's Role* (Protection Policy Paper, Nov. 2010), available at www.unhcr.org/refworld/docid/4cea23c62.html (accessed May 12, 2013), at para. 3.

[20] UN High Commissioner for Refugees, "Report of the Working Group on Solutions and Protection to the Forty-Second Session of the Executive Committee of the High Commissioner's Programme," UN Doc. EC/SCP/64, Aug. 12, 1991, at para. 39.

being wasted on manifestly unfounded claims, resources that could be better spent on averting the causes of refugee flows, enhancing protection, and searching for durable solutions to the problem of refugees.[21] More recently, UNHCR's Executive Committee has confirmed that "the efficient and expeditious return of persons found not to be in need of international protection is key to the international protection system as a whole, as well as to the control of irregular migration and prevention of smuggling and trafficking of such persons,"[22] and that the credibility of the individual asylum system is seriously affected by "the lack of prompt return of those who are found not to be in need of international protection."[23]

Previous chapters of this book, particularly Chapter 2, dealing with the rights of nonnationals, and Chapter 3, detailing States' capacity to act against migrant smuggling, have confirmed the sovereign right of States to control the entry and stay of aliens. The right to remove or deport persons who have entered their country without authorization to their State of origin, or to another State with which they have some affiliation, is a natural corollary of that sovereign right. The significant restrictions that international law places on the exercise of a State's right to remove unauthorized nonnationals should not be underestimated, and indeed are the major focus of the present chapter. However, it would be an error to disregard or minimize the legal force of the underlying rule that preserves a course of action long considered to be central to statehood.

10.2. LIMITATIONS ON THE RIGHT TO RETURN SMUGGLED MIGRANTS

Although the sovereign right of States to expel aliens remains intact, particularly with respect to those whose entry or presence is unauthorized or otherwise unlawful, it is constrained in a number of important ways. The most significant of these are: (1) a prohibition on arbitrary expulsion (applicable to persons lawfully present); (2) a related prohibition (but with a broader scope of application) on collective expulsion; and (3) the obligation not to return persons to a situation of persecution or serious human rights violations. Violation of any of these prohibitions will render return of a smuggled migrant unlawful. The international legal prohibition on arbitrary and collective expulsion has also been considered in Chapter 2,[24] as have obligations of international protection and *non-refoulement*.[25] This section summarizes the key

[21] Ibid. at paras. 37–38.

[22] UN High Commissioner for Refugees Executive Committee of the High Commissioner's Programme, *Conclusion on the Return of Persons Found Not to Be in Need of International Protection*, Doc. No. 96 (LIV) – 2003, Oct. 10, 2003, available at www.unhcr.org/refworld/docid/3f93b1ca4.html (accessed May 12, 2013), at second preambular paragraph.

[23] Ibid. at para. (b).

[24] See Chapter 2, at Section 2.4.4.

[25] See Chapter 2, at Section 2.4.

points made in that chapter while extending the analysis to the particular issue of return of smuggled migrants.

10.2.1. *Prohibition on Arbitrary Expulsion*

The prohibition on arbitrary expulsion is a central aspect of the legal framework around return. This section first examines the parameters and substantive content of the prohibition before turning to a consideration of how it may apply in the case of smuggled asylum-seekers.

10.2.1.1. Key Features of the Prohibition on Arbitrary Expulsion

The principal international legal rule on the expulsion of aliens *lawfully present* is drawn from Article 13 of the International Covenant on Civil and Political Rights[26] (ICCPR), which states:

> An alien lawfully in the territory of a State Party to the present Covenant may be expelled therefrom only in pursuance of a decision reached in accordance with law and shall, except where compelling reasons of national security otherwise require, be allowed to submit the reasons against his expulsion and to have his case reviewed by, and be represented for the purpose before, the competent authority or a person or persons especially designated by the competent authority.[27]

The UN Human Rights Committee has stated that the purpose of Article 13 is "clearly to prevent arbitrary expulsions."[28] As with the prohibition on arbitrary detention examined in the previous chapter, the rule requires that the expulsion be "in

[26] International Covenant on Civil and Political Rights, 999 UNTS 171, done Dec. 16, 1996, entered into force Mar. 23, 1976 [ICCPR].

[27] All regional human rights treaties contain similar provisions. See, for example, Protocol No. 7 to the Convention of 4 November 1950 for the Protection of Human Rights and Fundamental Freedoms, 1525 UNTS 195, done Nov. 22, 1984, entered into force Nov. 1, 1998 [Protocol No. 7 to the European Convention on Human Rights], at Art. 1 (prohibiting expulsion of aliens "lawfully resident ... except in pursuance of a decision reached in accordance with law"); American Convention on Human Rights, 1144 UNTS 123, done Nov. 22, 1969, entered into force July 18, 1978 [American Convention on Human Rights], at Art. 22(6) ("An alien lawfully in the territory of a State party may be expelled only pursuant to a decision reached in accordance with law"); African Charter on Human and Peoples' Rights, 1520 UNTS 217, done June 27, 1981, entered into force Oct. 21, 1986 [African Charter], at Art. 12(4) ("a non-national legally admitted in a territory of a State party to the ... Charter, may only be expelled from it by virtue of a decision taken in accordance with the law").

[28] UN Human Rights Committee, "General Comment No. 15: The Position of Aliens under the Covenant," UN Doc. HRI/GEN.1/Rev.7, at 140, May 12, 2004, adopted Apr. 11, 1986 [HRC General Comment No. 15], at para. 10. See also M. Nowak, *U.N. Covenant on Civil and Political Rights: CCPR Commentary* (2nd revised ed. 2005) [Nowak, *CCPR Commentary*], at 291, for discussion of the drafters' intentions to prohibit "arbitrary expulsion."

pursuance of a decision reached in accordance with law." It "entitles each alien to a decision in his own case,"[29] therefore collective expulsions will not satisfy its requirements (discussed further in Section 10.2.2).[30] The requirement of legality extends beyond national law to international law: an expulsion will be arbitrary, for example, if it violates established principles of international law such as the prohibition on discrimination.[31] In short: a decision to expel an alien who is lawfully present must have a statutory basis and not violate established human rights.[32] In relation to the relevant provision of the European Convention on Human Rights,[33] the European Court of Human Rights has confirmed that the concept of legality "concerns not only the existence of a legal basis in domestic law, but also the quality of the law in question: it must be accessible and foreseeable and also afford a measure of protection against arbitrary interferences by the public authorities with the rights secured in the Convention."[34]

The prohibition on arbitrary expulsion further requires that, barring compelling justification relating to national security and/or public order,[35] aliens lawfully present be provided certain procedural guarantees. These include a right to submit reasons against the expulsion to a competent agency and a right to have the case reviewed in a proceeding where the individual concerned can be represented.[36] These obligations attached to the prohibition on arbitrary expulsion extend to "all procedures aimed at the obligatory departure of an alien, whether described in national law

[29] HRC General Comment No. 15, at para. 10. Nowak notes that there is no express prohibition on collective expulsion in the ICCPR, and the Human Rights Committee inferred this restriction from the procedural requirements of Article 13: Nowak, *CCPR Commentary*, at 295.

[30] HRC General Comment No. 15, at para. 10.

[31] See *Anna Maroufidou v. Sweden*, UNHRC Comm. No. 58/1979, UN Doc. CCPR/C/12/D/58/1979, Apr. 8, 1981, decided Apr. 8, 1979, at para. 9.3. See also *A. and Others v. United Kingdom*, (2009) 49 EHRR 29 (ECHR, Feb. 19, 2009) [*A. and Others v. United Kingdom*], at para. 190.

[32] For an examination of the limitations imposed by the requirement that expulsion must be in accordance with the law, see J-M. Henckaerts, *Mass Expulsion in Modern International Law and Practice* (1995), at 28–30. This is the position taken by the International Law Commission in its Draft Articles on Expulsion of Aliens. Draft Article 4 states that: "An alien may be expelled only in pursuance of a decision reached in accordance with law." Draft Article 5, dealing with grounds for expulsion, affirms that "[a] state may only expel an alien on the ground that is provided for by law, including, in particular, national security and public order."

[33] Convention for the Protection of Human Rights and Fundamental Freedoms, 213 UNTS 222, done Nov. 4, 1950, entered into force Sept. 3, 1953 [European Convention on Human Rights].

[34] *Lupsa v. Romania*, (2008) 46 EHRR 36 (ECHR, June 8, 2006), at para. 55.

[35] ICCPR, at Art. 13; Protocol No. 7 to the European Convention on Human Rights, at Art. 1(2). This exception is not contained in the American Convention on Human Rights or the African Charter. See further discussion in note 36.

[36] ICCPR, at Art. 13. Note that aliens who are arrested prior to deportation are further entitled to be provided with grounds for an arrest (and therefore the expulsion itself). See, for example, Article 9(2) of the ICCPR.

as expulsion or otherwise"[37] and encompass all conduct (both acts and omissions) attributable to that State that could lead to the same result.

THE "NATIONAL SECURITY AND PUBLIC ORDER" EXCEPTION

Article 13 of the ICCPR and Article 1 of Protocol No. 7 to the European Convention on Human Rights both contain an exception to the requirement that expulsion must take place in accordance with due process of law in the case of threats to "national security" (ICCPR) and/or "public order" (Protocol No. 7). Relevant soft law suggests that the exceptions should be read narrowly,[38] and that position has received support from commentators. Nowak, for example, points to the phrase "compelling reasons" in the relevant provision of the ICCPR as indicative of its "especially narrow scope" that would permit invocation only "in serious cases of political or military threats to the entire nation."[39] However, the scope of the European provision certainly appears to be broader due to the absence of any reference to "compelling reasons" and inclusion of the potentially wider ground of "public order."[40]

The concepts of national security and public order are not defined in their respective treaties, a situation that the ILC has warned risks "giv[ing] rise to an arbitrary exercise of the power of assessing the conduct of aliens by the expelling State."[41] The ILC affirms that although international practice defers to national legal systems to determine the meaning of these grounds, States do not have absolute power of discretion in this area.[42] States must, for example, reflect the principles of reasonableness and proportionality that are integral to the concept of "non-arbitrariness." In the *Ahmadou Sadio Diallo* case, the International Court of Justice rejected an assertion of "compelling reasons of national security" (in the context of withholding

37 HRC General Comment No. 15, at para. 9.

38 See, for example, UN Commission on Human Rights, "The Siracusa Principles on the Limitation and Derogation Provisions in the International Covenant on Civil and Political Rights," UN Doc. E/CN.4/1985/4, Annex, Sept. 28, 1984, which state that "[n]ational security may be invoked to justify measures limiting certain rights only when they are taken to *protect the existence of the nation or its territorial integrity or political independence against force or threat of force*" (para. 29 (emphasis added)).

39 Nowak, *CCPR Commentary*, at 300.

40 Ibid. at 300, n. 53.

41 International Law Commission, "Sixth report on the expulsion of aliens by Mr. Maurice Kamto, Special Rapporteur," UN Doc. A/CN.4/625, Mar. 19, 2010 [International Law Commission, "Sixth Report on the Expulsion of Aliens"], at para. 99.

42 Ibid. at paras. 100–118. In *A. and Others v. United Kingdom*, the European Court of Human Rights affirmed the capacity of States to determine the nature and extent of any threat to national security, as well as the steps necessary to avert it, but nevertheless held that it is for the Court to rule on whether the States have "gone beyond the "extent strictly required by the exigencies" of the crisis" (at para. 173). Note that the Court in this case was addressing provisions enacted under Article 15 of the European Convention on Human Rights (Derogation in time of emergency), which would likely be construed more narrowly than Article 1 of Protocol No. 7, with its additional "public order" dimension.

of certain procedural rights from a person subject to expulsion) that could not be substantiated.[43]

In its work on expulsion of aliens, the ILC has proposed the following as objective criteria that should be taken into consideration in a valid invocation of public order or security grounds in this context:

- The specific circumstances and the circumstances of the factual situation contributing to or constituting a breach, or threat of breach, of public order or public safety (cited as a general principle of the law relating to the expulsion of aliens);
- The personal conduct of the individual concerned (which must represent a genuine, present, and sufficiently serious threat affecting one of the fundamental interests of society); and
- A fair balance between protecting public order and the interests of the individual.[44]

10.2.1.2. Application of the Prohibition on Arbitrary Expulsion to Asylum-Seekers

The international legal prohibition on arbitrary expulsion is restricted to persons who are "lawfully present" in the State. In relation to persons *not* lawfully present, States are generally entitled to expel such persons, subject to certain more generally applicable restrictions discussed further later in the chapter. The single treaty that extends the prohibition on arbitrary expulsion to all aliens, irrespective of the legality of their presence, is the Migrant Workers Convention,[45] an instrument that has not received support from the major countries of destination for smuggled migrants.[46] The question of who is to be considered "lawfully present" is therefore a critical one, and this "notoriously slippery expression"[47] does not lend itself to quick or definitive analysis. Nowak maintains that an alien's residence will be considered lawful for

43 *Ahmadou Sadio Diallo Case*, at para. 74.

44 International Law Commission, "Sixth Report on the Expulsion of Aliens," at para. 118.

45 International Convention on the Protection of the Rights of All Migrant Workers and Members of their Families, UN Doc. A/RES/45/158, done Dec. 18, 1990, entered into force July 1, 2003 [Migrant Workers Convention], at Art. 22. In addition to prohibiting collective and arbitrary expulsion, Article 22 of that instrument provides for extensive procedural protections in the case of expulsion.

46 As at May 2013, forty-six States were party to the Migrant Workers Convention: United Nations Treaty Collection, available at http://treaties.un.org/Pages/ParticipationStatus.aspx (accessed May 12, 2013).

47 *Kaya v. Haringey London Borough Council* (2001) EWCA, Civ 677 (Eng. CA. May 1, 2001) at para. 31, cited in J. C. Hathaway, *The Rights of Refugees under International Law* (2005) [Hathaway, *The Rights of Refugees*], at 176.

purposes of Articles 12 and 13[48] of the ICCPR "when he or she has entered the State of residence in accordance with its legal system (not necessarily a law in the formal sense) and/or is in possession of a valid residency permit (*ex lege* or by a sovereign act in the form of a visa)."[49] He further notes that the term "lawfully" refers primarily to the national legal system; however the Human Rights Committee has stated that in certain circumstances, aliens may benefit from the protection of the Covenant even in relation to entry or residence where considerations such as non-discrimination, the prohibition on inhuman treatment, or respect for family life arise.[50]

As a group, smuggled migrants will, by definition, be unlawfully present and thereby do not fall within this provision – unless they have regularized their situation through some other means. However, a key question in the present context is whether the sub-group, smuggled *asylum-seekers* (and indeed refugees), satisfy the precondition of being "lawfully present" and are thereby able to benefit from the prohibition on arbitrary expulsion that is clearly set out in both human rights and refugee law.[51]

International law certainly recognizes that asylum-seekers may be forced to seek entry into a country without securing prior permission. Article 31(1) of the Refugee Convention for example prohibits States from penalizing refugees on account of their illegal entry or presence, providing they have come directly from a territory where their life or freedom was threatened and they present themselves promptly to authorities in the receiving State. Some commentators have argued for an interpretation of this provision that would bring all asylum-seekers physically present within the prohibition on arbitrary expulsion unless and until a negative decision is made on their claim.[52] This interpretation sees protection from arbitrary expulsion as applying once an asylum application is accepted by the State for consideration and even

[48] Nowak notes that the requirement of lawfulness in Article 13 "corresponds literally to that in Article 12(1), such that the reader is referred to the comments made there in this regard": Nowak, *CCPR Commentary*, at 292.

[49] Ibid.

[50] Ibid. at 263–264.

[51] See Convention relating to the Status of Refugees, 189 UNTS 137, done July 28, 1951, entered into force Apr. 22, 1954, as amended by the Protocol relating to the Status of Refugees, 606 UNTS 267, done Jan. 31, 1967, entered into force Oct. 4, 1967 [Refugee Convention], at Art. 32: "1.... States shall not expel a refugee *lawfully in their territory* save on grounds of national security or public order. 2. The expulsion of such a refugee shall only be in pursuance of a decision reached in accordance with due process of law. Except where compelling reasons of national security otherwise require, the refugee shall be allowed to submit evidence to clear himself, and to appeal to and be represented for the purpose before competent authority or a person or persons specially designated by the competent authority" (emphasis added). Further restrictions on expulsion of refugees relate to the prohibition of *non-refoulement*, discussed at Section 10.2.3.

[52] Hathaway, for example, relies on Article 31(1) to characterize "the stage between 'irregular' presence and the recognition or denial of refugee status, including the time required for exhaustion of any appeals or reviews" as a form of "lawful presence": Hathaway, *The Rights of Refugees*, at 175.

in situations where the receiving State declines to formally verify refugee status – for example through what has been termed "temporary protection regimes."[53] UNHCR has taken a similar position, asserting that persons who enter a State's territory illegally but are permitted to stay because of circumstances "sufficiently precarious to bring into play the *non-refoulement* obligation" should be regarded as lawfully staying.[54] However, others disagree, arguing for example that the prohibition on arbitrary expulsion of refugees contained in Article 32 of the Refugee Convention "may be interpreted as a substantial limitation upon the State's power of expulsion, but with its benefits confined to lawfully resident refugees, that is, those in a State on a more or less indefinite basis."[55] The drafting history of the Convention lends some support to this more conservative view.[56] Of course, the question of arbitrary expulsion cannot be considered in isolation: even if an asylum-seeker is considered not lawfully present, expulsion of that person remains subject to the obligation of *non-refoulement*, considered further at Section 10.2.3.

States have generally not accepted the broader interpretation of the prohibition on arbitrary expulsion as extending to all asylum-seekers.[57] The consequence of such

53 See ibid. at 183–185.

54 UN High Commissioner for Refugees, *"Lawfully Staying" – A Note on Interpretation* (1988), available at www.unhcr.org/refworld/pdfid/42ad93304.pdf (accessed May 12, 2013), at para. 21. But note that UNHCR's 2012 revised guidelines on detention of asylum-seekers endorse a somewhat diluted version of this position, merely stating that difficult circumstances peculiar to asylum-seekers such as inability to produce documents because of a need for sudden flight or the experience of traumatic events "need to be taken into account in determining any restrictions on freedom of movement based on irregular entry or presence": UN High Commissioner for Refugees, *Guidelines on the Applicable Criteria and Standards Relating to the Detention of Asylum-Seekers and Alternatives to Detention* (2012), at para. 11.

55 G. Goodwin-Gill and J. McAdam, *The Refugee in International Law* (3rd ed. 2007) [Goodwin-Gill and McAdam, *The Refugee in International Law*], at 524–525.

56 An early examination of the drafting history of the Refugee Convention concluded that: "'Lawfully in the country' was understood to refer to refugees either lawfully admitted or whose illegal entry was legalized but not to refugees who, although legally admitted or legalized, have overstayed the period for which they were admitted or were authorised to stay or who have violated any other condition attached to their admission or stay." N. Robinson, *Convention Relating to the Status of Refugees, Its History, Contents and Interpretation* (1953), at 110–111, cited in *R (on the application of ST (Eritrea)) v. Secretary of State for the Home Department* [2012] UKSC 12 (UK SC, Mar. 21, 2012) [*R (Eritrea) v. Secretary of State for the Home Department*], at para. 33, per Lord Hope.

57 See, for example, the Australian High Court case of *Plaintiff M47/2012 v. Director-General of Security* [2012] HCA 46 (Aus. HC, Oct. 5, 2012) [*Plaintiff M47/2012 v. Director-General of Security*], where Justice Heydon, along with the other judges who considered the issue, held that the plaintiff (a person who had been found to be a genuine refugee but whom the Australian government was attempting to expel on national security grounds) was not "lawfully present" in the territory so long as he did not hold a visa: at paras. 293–294. It should be noted that the Australian attorney-general's website does acknowledge that the State's right to expel noncitizens may be limited beyond the requirements of Article 13 of the ICCPR where a person is a refugee within the meaning of the Refugee Convention *unless* there are "reasonable grounds for regarding the refugee as a danger to the security of Australia": Australian Government, Attorney-General's Department, "Expulsion of Aliens,"

a position is that a person with a valid claim to asylum could be removed from the country before that claim could be made or tested, provided such removal did not itself violate the separate obligation of *non-refoulement*. Arguments that this result is contrary to the spirit, if not the letter, of the Convention appear to be on solid ground. This is implicitly recognized in the International Law Commission's Draft Articles on Expulsion of Aliens, which propose a more generous approach.[58] The ILC has recognized that its position relied heavily on "judicial pronouncements and doctrinal opinions."[59] However support for the ILC's position may be emerging from more persuasive sources. For example, the Preamble to the EU Returns Directive, which indicates that "a third-country national who has applied for asylum in a Member State should not be regarded as staying illegally on the territory of that Member State until a negative decision on the application, or a decision ending his or her right of stay as asylum seeker has entered into force."[60]

In summary, the law in this area is unsettled. Relevant treaty law does not explicitly clarify whether asylum-seekers should be considered "lawfully present" for the purposes of the substantive and procedural guarantees attached to the right not to be subject to arbitrary expulsion. There is relatively strong support for the view that persons who have already made a claim for asylum may be considered "lawful" for purposes of their entitlement to international protection. It is less clear that this

available at www.ag.gov.au/RightsAndProtections/HumanRights/PublicSectorGuidanceSheets/Pages/Expulsionofaliens.aspx (accessed May 12, 2013). For other examples of States rejecting the expansive view of "lawful presence" see Hathaway, *The Rights of Refugees*, at 175–178.

58 The relevant article affirms the Refugee Convention's prohibition on expulsion of refugees lawfully on a State's territory save on grounds of national security and public order (Draft Article 6(1)). It then extends that prohibition (not just the prohibition on "*arbitrary expulsion*") to "any refugee *unlawfully present* in the territory of the State, who has applied for recognition of refugee status, while such application is pending" (Draft Article 6(2) (emphasis added)). In his introduction of the Draft Articles, the chairperson of the drafting group acknowledged the somewhat precarious legal basis of the provision but explained that it was being proposed "on the basis of judicial pronouncements and doctrinal opinions." International Law Commission, "Expulsion of Aliens: Statement of the Chairman of the Drafting Committee, Mr. Mahmoud D. Hmoud," May 29, 2012, at 8. The chairperson further noted that the draft articles would emphasize that a person "is to be regarded as a refugee if he or she meets the requirements set forth in the relevant legal instruments, *irrespective of whether or not that person has been granted refugee status*" (ibid., emphasis added). The commentary would in fact indicate that a person who does not meet the requirements of the definition of "refugee" may be expelled for other grounds, and that the Draft Article "is without prejudice to the right of a State to expel an individual whose application for refugee status is manifestly abusive" (ibid.).

59 International Law Commission, "Expulsion of Aliens: Statement of the Chairman of the Drafting Committee, Mr. Mahmoud D. Hmoud," May 29, 2012, at 8.

60 EU Returns Directive, at Preambular para. 9. The reference cites the Preamble to Council Directive 2005/85/EC of 1 December 2005 on minimum standards on procedures in Member States for granting and withdrawing refugee status (OJ L 326, Dec. 13, 2005, at 13), which contains a similar provision. It must be noted that the Preamble in EU legislation is not part of the enacting terms and is not binding.

applies to persons (such as smuggled migrants) who have not yet had a chance to make such a claim. State practice reveals a great reluctance to expand the prohibition on arbitrary expulsion to include all asylum-seekers within their territory or under their control. A more progressive position – that States are prohibited from expelling asylum-seekers except on certain very limited grounds – appears to be on the ascendancy, particularly among commentators. However, its scope is unclear and it is yet to be firmly established as a positive rule of international law.

10.2.2. *Prohibition on Collective Expulsion*

As discussed in Chapter 2, at Section 2.4.3, the term "collective expulsion" (or "mass expulsion") refers to any measures compelling nonnationals, as a group or groups, to leave a country or the territory of a country. Collective expulsion is prohibited under international law except where such a measure is taken on the basis of a reasonable and objective examination of the particular case of *each individual member* of the group.[61] This prohibition has been inferred from the procedural rights contained in Article 13 of the ICCPR[62]: the fact that expulsion must be pursuant to a lawful decision and that the subject has a right to present reasons against his or her expulsion and to have his or her case reviewed means, in effect, that any collective expulsion will be arbitrary and thereby unlawful. The Migrant Workers Convention and the major regional treaties are more direct: explicitly prohibiting collective expulsions.[63] The conclusion reached in Chapter 2 after a review of relevant authorities is worth reiterating: States may not engage in collective expulsions, even when those expulsions do not violate the prohibition on *non-refoulement* and even when the persons concerned are not "lawfully" within the territory of the State.[64]

61 See the definition and the status of the prohibition as has been reiterated by the European Court in the cases detailed in the present section, as well as by the ILC Draft Articles on Expulsion of Aliens (Draft Article 10). For additional references on the international legal prohibition of collective expulsion, see references in Chapter 2, at Section 2.4.3. "Restrictions on Collective Expulsion").

62 HRC General Comment No. 15, at para. 10.

63 Migrant Workers Convention, at Art. 22; Protocol No. 4 to the Convention of 4 November 1950 for the Protection of Human Rights and Fundamental Freedoms, 1496 UNTS 263, done Sept. 16, 1963, entered into force May 2, 1968 [Protocol No. 4 to the European Convention on Human Rights], at Art. 4 ("Collective expulsion of aliens is prohibited"); American Convention on Human Rights, at Art. 22(9) ("The collective expulsion of aliens is prohibited"); African Charter, at Art. 12(5) ("The mass expulsion of non-nationals shall be prohibited" and "Mass expulsion shall be that which is aimed at national racial, ethnic or religious groups"). Note that the ILC Special Rapporteur on the Expulsion of Aliens views the definition contained in the African Charter as unnecessarily restrictive, particularly in light of modern challenges to the prohibition of mass expulsion. See International Law Commission, "Third report on the expulsion of aliens by Mr. Maurice Kamto, Special Rapporteur," UN Doc. A/CN.4/581, Apr. 19, 2007 [International Law Commission, "Third Report on the Expulsion of Aliens"], at para. 108.

64 See further Chapter 2, at Section 2.4.3, esp. notes 252–253.

Under what circumstances, if any, would border control activities, such as interception at sea or refusal to admit at the border a group of smuggled migrants, possibly constitute collective expulsion? The emphasis of the general rule on the importance of individual determination is clearly relevant, and the rather limited case law provides some guidance. In *Čonka v. Belgium*,[65] for example, the European Court of Human Rights identified several elements of a particular expulsion procedure as relevant to its decision that the procedure was collective and thereby unlawful. These included the fact that instructions had previously been given to the relevant authority for the implementation of operations of that kind, that all aliens concerned had been required to attend the police station at the same time, that the relevant arrest and deportation orders were couched in identical terms, that asylum procedures had not been completed, and that it was very difficult for the persons concerned to seek and receive legal advice.[66] Conversely, in *Sultani v. France*,[67] the Court found that that applicant had not been part of a collective expulsion. In rejecting the asylum claim, the authorities had considered not just the situation in the country of origin but also circumstances and risks particular to that individual asylum-seeker. Importantly, the general procedural rule requiring separate consideration of individual cases does not demand that decisions relating to a group of persons need vary in their substance. As the ILC Special Rapporteur on Expulsion of Aliens has noted, a group of similar or even identical deportation orders will not be viewed as constituting collective expulsion under international law "as long as every order is preceded by specific consideration of the situation of each member of the group of persons concerned."[68]

The European Court of Human Rights has recently sharpened its approach with respect to interception-related expulsion. In its 2012 judgment *Hirsi Jamaa v. Italy*,[69] the Court was required to consider, for the first time, whether the prohibition on collective expulsion[70] applied to a case involving the removal of aliens to a third State, where the removal took place outside national territory. The Court found that Italy had violated the prohibition on collective expulsion in its interception and transfer of smuggled Eritrean and Somali asylum-seekers back to Libya because "the transfer of the applicants to Libya was carried out without any form of examination of each applicant's individual situation."[71] Italy asserted that only persons who had

65 *Čonka v. Belgium*, (2002) 34 EHRR 54 (ECHR, Feb. 5, 2002).
66 Ibid. at para. 62.
67 *Sultani v. France*, Application No. 45223/05, [2007] ECHR 2007-IV (ECHR, Sep 20, 2007).
68 International Law Commission, "Third Report on the Expulsion of Aliens," at para. 110.
69 *Hirsi Jamaa and Others v. Italy*, (2012) 55 EHRR 21 (ECHR, Feb. 23, 2012) [*Hirsi Jamaa v. Italy*].
70 Protocol No. 4 to the European Convention on Human Rights, at Art. 4 ("Collective expulsion of aliens is prohibited").
71 *Hirsi Jamaa v. Italy*, at para. 185.

reached a State's territory could be "expelled" within the ordinary meaning of that term.[72] The Court firmly rejected a territorial limitation on the prohibition on collective expulsion, in finding that:

> [T]he purpose of [the relevant article] is to prevent States being able to remove certain aliens without examining their personal circumstances and, consequently, without enabling them to put forward their arguments against the measure taken by the relevant authority. If, therefore, Article 4 of Protocol No. 4 were to apply only to collective expulsions from the national territory of the States Parties to the Convention, a significant component of contemporary migratory patterns would not fall within the ambit of that provision, notwithstanding the fact that the conduct it is intended to prohibit can occur outside national territory and in particular, as in the instant case, on the high seas.[73]

The Court further drew attention to the particular plight faced by applicants in this case if the prohibition on arbitrary expulsion were indeed found to require a territorial nexus: "migrants having taken to the sea, often risking their lives, and not having managed to reach the borders of a State, would not be entitled to an examination of their personal circumstances before being expelled, unlike those travelling by land."[74]

Similar cases are currently before the Court.[75] The extension of the right against collective expulsion beyond the territorial limits of States should be considered within the context of a wider shift toward the extraterritorial application of human rights and the international legal obligation of *non-refoulement*, discussed further at Chapter 3, Section 3.4.4.

The emphasis on individual determination as a critical element in deciding whether a situation of collective expulsion has occurred is found in the Migrant Workers Convention, which states that: "[m]igrant workers and members of their families shall not be subject to measures of collective expulsion. Each case of expulsion shall be considered and decided individually."[76] The ILC Special Rapporteur on Expulsion of Aliens has taken a similar approach in proposing the following formulation of the rule after a careful survey of custom, as well as current treaty law and practice:

72 Ibid. at para. 172.

73 Ibid. at para. 177.

74 Ibid. For further on this argument see Office of the United Nations High Commissioner for Human Rights, "Hirsi et al v. Italy: Intervener Brief Filed on Behalf of the United Nations High Commissioner for Human Rights," May 4, 2011, Application No. 27765/09, available at www.unhcr.org/refworld/docid/4f5f11a52.html (accessed May 12, 2013).

75 See, for example, *Sharifi and Others v. Italy and Greece*, Application No. 16643/09 (ECHR, June 24, 2009) (lodged on Mar. 25, 2009).

76 Migrant Workers Convention, at Art. 22(1).

Prohibition of collective expulsion

1. For the purposes of the present draft articles, collective expulsion means expulsion of aliens as a group.[77]
2. The collective expulsion of aliens, including migrant workers and members of their family, is prohibited.
3. A State may expel concomitantly the members of a group of aliens, provided that the expulsion takes place after and on the basis of a reasonable and objective examination of the particular case of each individual member of the group.[78]

In summary, international law recognizes a general prohibition on collective expulsion. This prohibition imposes a "duty of due process"[79] that can only be discharged through an examination of the individual situation of each person concerned. At least in relation to those persons lawfully within the State, the prohibition is a logical extension of the procedural safeguards required to prevent arbitrary expulsion. However, it is clear that the principle of non-discrimination, as well as the requirement on States to properly identify people entitled to special protection such as asylum-seekers and those at risk of torture, extends the obligation of individualized consideration to those who are not lawfully within the State, including smuggled migrants.[80] The decision of the European Court of Human Rights in *Hirsi Jamaa v. Italy* lends strong support to the proposition that push-backs at sea, without individualized assessment, are also a violation of the prohibition on collective expulsion and thereby unlawful.

10.2.3. *Access to International Protection and the Obligation of* Non-refoulement

Smuggled migrants will frequently be detected or identified as part of "mixed" migration flows.[81] That is, within a broader group of smuggled migrants there may well be

77 Note that the formulation of this definition differs from previous definitions proposed by the Special Rapporteur that referred to collective expulsion as "an act or behavior by which a State compels a group of aliens to leave its territory": International Law Commission, "Third Report on the Expulsion of Aliens," at para. 135.

78 ILC Draft Articles on Expulsion of Aliens, at Draft Article 10. Note further that a proposed final paragraph to this article affirms that the article is "without prejudice to the rules of international law applicable to the expulsion of aliens in the event of an armed conflict involving the expelling State."

79 J. A. Hessbruegge, "European Court of Human Rights Protects Migrants against "Push Back" Operations the High Seas" 16(14) *Insights* (American Society of International Law, Apr. 17, 2012).

80 See UN Office of the High Commissioner for Human Rights, *Expulsion of Aliens in International Human Rights Law* (2006), at 15; and W. Kälin, "Aliens, Expulsion and Deportation," in R. Wolfrum ed., *The Max Planck Encyclopedia of Public International Law* (2008–), at paras. 22–23.

81 This is acknowledged in UN High Commissioner for Refugees, *Refugee Protection and Mixed Migration: A 10-Point Plan of Action* (2007).

persons with legitimate claims to international protection, for example under the Refugee Convention, or arising from a real risk that they will be subjected to torture or other forms of cruel, inhuman, or degrading treatment or punishment on their return. As discussed separately at Section 10.5, other groups, such as children and trafficked persons, may also have particular protection needs and entitlements that must be acknowledged and met in the context of decisions relating to return.

International law requires States to provide smuggled migrants who are in need of international protection with a genuine opportunity to seek and receive that protection.[82] The obligation on States to provide protection for persons at risk of serious human rights abuses requires them to establish systems that allow the proper consideration and assessment of claims for protection, irrespective of where irregular migrants are detected or under what circumstances.[83] It is vital that any different, parallel, or "special" system created to respond to the identification and potential return of smuggled migrants is effectively connected to other systems that provide protection to persons who have a recognized claim to protection, whether under national or international law.[84] This includes claims for protection under refugee law or as victims of trafficking.[85]

The right to seek and enjoy asylum from persecution has already been canvassed extensively in this book. Reference should be made to the detailed discussion of this right in Chapter 2, at Section 2.3; the discussion of the extraterritorial application of the obligation of *non-refoulement* in Chapter 3, Section 3.4.4; and the examination of obligations of protection including those related to *non-refoulement* in the context of interdiction and rescue at sea at Chapter 6, Section 6.3.4. The present section seeks to tie this discussion together under the broader rubric of rules governing return of smuggled migrants.

[82] See further Chapter 2, at Section 2.3.

[83] The right to seek and enjoy asylum from persecution presupposes the existence of a capacity and willingness, on the part of the host State, to receive asylum-seekers and to provide the facilities that are necessary to ensure their claims are heard in an independent, fair, and efficient manner. Although the Refugee Convention does not mandate one particular approach, it is clear the legal and procedural framework should be sufficiently robust to ensure those who are entitled to refugee status actually receive it and that the risk of *refoulement* is considered. The UN High Commissioner for Refugees has identified five "core procedural standards" as being necessary for a fair and efficient asylum regime: (i) access to guidance and advice on the procedure; (ii) access to legal counsel and interpreters; (iii) the opportunity to present evidence; (iv) a written record of the decision; and (v) the opportunity to appeal against a negative decision. UN High Commissioner for Refugees, Global Consultations on International Protection, "Asylum Processes (Fair and Efficient Asylum Procedures)," UN Doc. EC/GC/01/12, May 31, 2001. Chapter 2 provides further detail of the legal and procedural framework necessary to ensure conformity with the right to seek and receive asylum.

[84] For descriptions and operation of "protection-sensitive entry systems" see UN High Commissioner for Refugees, *Refugee Protection and Mixed Migration: The 10-Point Plan in Action* (2011), available at www.unhcr.org/refworld/pdfid/4d9430ea2.pdf (accessed May 12, 2013), at 73.

[85] See Section 10.5.1.

10.2.3.1. Obligation of *Non-refoulement* in Refugee Law

International refugee law prohibits States from expelling or returning a refugee "in any manner whatsoever to the frontiers of territories where his life or freedom would be threatened on account of his race, religion, nationality, membership of a particular social group or political opinion."[86] This right places an obligation of *non-refoulement* on States with regard to asylum-seekers as well as to formally recognized refugees.[87] Outside this group, *non-refoulement* obligations may also arise with respect to others in need of international protection, as discussed at Section 10.2.3.3.

The key features of the obligation of *non-refoulement* in the specific context of asylum from persecution have been explained in detail in Chapter 2[88] and reference should be made to that chapter for additional detail and discussion. Those features can be usefully summarized for present purposes as follows:

- The obligation relates to persons within the territory or under the effective control of the State concerned.
- The obligation applies to all types of transfer and forms of forced removal irrespective of how that removal is described.
- The obligation applies to any person who may be subject to persecution if returned to that person's country of origin or to any other place, irrespective of whether he or she has been formally recognized as a refugee.
- The obligation applies only to refugees who have left their country of origin. It does not extend to allow access to asylum for persons who are still within their own State. This means that actions aimed at preventing potential refugees from

86 Refugee Convention, at Art. 33(1). Additional sources of the obligation of *non-refoulement* in the context of asylum include the Organization of African Unity Convention Governing the Specific Aspects of Refugee Problems in Africa, 1001 UNTS 45, done Sept. 10, 1969, entered into force June 20, 1974, at Art. (3); and Regulation (EC) No. 562/2006 of the European Parliament and of the Council of 15 March 2006 establishing a Community Code on the rules governing the movement of persons across borders (Schengen Borders Code), OJ L 105/1, Apr. 13, 2006, at Preambular para. 20 (the Code is to be applied "in accordance with the Member States' obligations as regards international protection and non-refoulement"), and at Art. 13(1) (the obligation to refuse entry to third-country nationals not fulfilling entry requirements "shall be without prejudice to the application of special provisions concerning the right of asylum and to international protection"). See also ILC Draft Articles on Expulsion of Aliens, at Draft Article 6(3).

87 See UN High Commissioner for Refugees Executive Committee: Conclusion No. 6: "*Non-refoulement*" (1977), No. 79: "General" (1996), No. 81: "General" (1997) and No. 82: "Conclusion on Safeguarding Asylum" (1997) reprinted in *Conclusions Adopted by the Executive Committee on International Protection of Refugees: 1975–2009 (Conclusion No. 1 – 109)* (2009). See also UN General Assembly, "Office of the United Nations High Commissioner for Refugees," adopted by GA Res. 52/103, Dec. 12, 1977, UN Doc. A/Res/52/103, Feb. 9, 1998; and Goodwin-Gill and McAdam, *The Refugee in International Law*, at 232–233.

88 See Chapter 2, at Section 2.3.1, "The Obligation of *Non-refoulement* under Refugee Law."

leaving their home State, although potentially in violation of certain human rights norms including the right to leave, are not invalidated by the obligation of *non-refoulement*.

It is critically important to establish the point – and geographical location – at which the obligation of *non-refoulement* is triggered. Chapter 3 detailed a slow but apparently inexorable expansion of the obligation to all persons subject to or within the jurisdiction of the State, (i.e., under its authority or control), irrespective of whether such persons are in the territory of that State. With regard to the existence of an obligation to admit or not reject asylum-seekers at the border, the situation is also being clarified: international law appears to accept that the obligation applies "to the moment at which asylum-seekers present themselves for entry, either within a State or at its border."[89] Commentators point to the drafting history of the Refugee Convention as evidence of a "clear commitment to [the] basic understanding that peremptory non-admittance or ejection is normally impermissible."[90] The Refugee Convention does not explicitly oblige States to admit individuals at the border for the purpose of determining their status and protection needs. However there is strong support for the existence of a limited obligation in this respect[91] – not least through the recognition that effective implementation of the *non-refoulement* principle requires that the circumstances of each case be individually assessed,[92] and necessitates "access to fair and effective procedures for determining status and protection

[89] Goodwin-Gill and McAdam, *The Refugee in International Law*, at 208, citing *R (on the application of European Roma Rights Centre et al) v. Immigration Officer at Prague Airport et al, ex parte European Roma Rights Centre et al*, [2004] UKHL 55 (UK HL, Dec. 9, 2004), at para. 26 (per Lord Bingham).

[90] Hathaway, *The Rights of Refugees*, at 316. See also Goodwin-Gill and McAdam, *The Refugee in International Law*, at 208 (arguing that *non-refoulement* now encompasses both "non-return and non-rejection"). The UNHCR Executive Committee has supported this understanding, emphasizing "the fundamental importance of the observance of the principle of *non-refoulement* – both at the border and within the territory of a State – of persons who may be subjected to persecution if returned to their country of origin irrespective of whether or not they have been formally recognized as refugees": UN High Commissioner for Refugees Executive Committee, *Conclusion No. 6 – Non-Refoulement*, adopted 28th Sess, Oct. 12, 1977, in UN General Assembly, "Addendum to the Report of the United Nations High Commissioner for Refugees," UN GAOR 32nd Sess, Supp. No. 12A, UN Doc. A/32/12/Add.1, at 13 (1977), at para. (c).

[91] UN High Commissioner for Refugees Executive Committee, *Conclusion No. 82 – Conclusion on Safeguarding Asylum*, adopted 48th Sess, Oct. 17, 1997, in UN General Assembly, "Addendum to the Report of the United Nations High Commissioner for Refugees," UN GAOR 52nd Sess, Supp. No. 12A, UN Doc. A/52/12/Add.1, at 7 (1997), at para. (d)(iii); Goodwin-Gill and McAdam, *The Refugee in International Law*, at 215.

[92] E. Lauterpacht and D. Bethlehem, "The Scope and Content of the Principle of *Non-refoulement*: Opinion," in E. Feller, V. Türk, and F. Nicholson eds., *Refugee Protection in International Law: UNHCR's Global Consultations on International Protection* 87 (2003) [Lauterpacht and Bethlehem, "The Scope and Content of the Principle of *Non-refoulement*"], at para. 100.

needs."[93] This issue is considered in more detail at Section 10.2.3.4 in the context of a discussion of anti-smuggling measures and the obligation of *non-refoulement*.

Non-refoulement obligations may also be indirectly triggered in the process of return, if State actions inadvertently create real risks for smuggled migrants. For example, the exchange between States of some personal data about smuggled migrants will generally be necessary to facilitate the return process. However, States are under an obligation to ensure that any information exchange does not put the smuggled migrants (or their family) in danger by revealing or distributing information that places them at risk of persecution or other harm.[94] In particular, no information should be shared with the country of origin regarding any asylum application made by the returnee.[95] Without these protections, States may inadvertently violate their obligation of *non-refoulement*.[96]

10.2.3.2. Exceptions to the Obligation Not to Return Refugees

The *non-refoulement* obligation in the Refugee Convention is subject to certain critical exceptions and exclusions. First, the right may not be claimed by a refugee "whom there are reasonable grounds for regarding as a danger to the security of the country in which he is, or who, having been convicted by a final judgment of a particularly serious crime, constitutes a danger to the community of that country."[97]

93 UN High Commissioner for Refugees Executive Committee, *Conclusion No. 85 – Conclusion on International Protection*, adopted 49th Sess, Oct. 9, 1998, in UN General Assembly, "Addendum to the Report of the United Nations High Commissioner for Refugees," UN GAOR 53rd Sess, Supp. No. 12A, UN Doc. A/53/12/Add.1, at 6 (1998), at para. (q). See also UN High Commissioner for Refugees, *Fair and Efficient Asylum Procedures: A Non-exhaustive Overview of Applicable International Standards* (Sept. 2, 2005).

94 United Nations Office on Drugs and Crime, *Model Law against the Smuggling of Migrants* (2010) [UNODC Model Law on Migrant Smuggling], at 101.

95 The UNODC Model Law on Migrant Smuggling recommends that this obligation be reflected in national law: see Art. 29(2) (at 101).

96 As noted in the UNODC Model Law on Migrant Smuggling, good practices on information exchange between States are captured in the Council of Europe's *Twenty Guidelines on Forced Return*, Guideline 12, in particular subparagraph (4), which provides that: "The host state shall exercise due diligence to ensure that the exchange of information between its authorities and the authorities of the state of return will not put the returnee, or his/her relatives, in danger upon return. In particular, the host state should not share information relating to the asylum application" (cited in the UNODC Model Law on Migrant Smuggling, at 101).

97 Refugee Convention, at Art. 33(2). This exception is reiterated in the ILC Draft Articles on Expulsion of Aliens, at Draft Article 6(3). See also Council Directive 2004/83/EC of 29 April 2004 on minimum standards for the qualification and status of third-country nationals or stateless persons as refugees or as persons who otherwise need international protection and the content of the protection granted, OJ L 304/12, Sept. 30, 2004) [Council Directive 2004/83/EC)], at Art. 21, which provides that where not prohibited by international obligations, Member States may *refoule* a refugee where there are "reasonable grounds for considering him or her as a danger to the security of the Member State in which

This provision does not deny or remove refugee status. However, it does allow a host State to divest itself of its *non-refoulement* obligations in instances in which that State and its citizens are seriously threatened by the presence of the refugee.[98] Second, a person who has "committed a serious non-political crime outside the country of refuge prior to his admission to that country as a refugee" is excluded from the application of the Refugee Convention in its entirety (and thereby from any protection with regard to return).[99] Both exclusions were analyzed in Chapter 2 with particular reference to the question of whether the crime of migrant smuggling could ever be used by a State to deny refugee status or to return a recognized refugee to a situation of persecution.[100] The following paragraphs summarize that analysis.

- Exclusion from refugee status: States may only exclude persons who are otherwise entitled to be recognized as refugees from this status (and therefore, potentially *refoule* them) when there are "serious reasons" for considering that the person concerned has committed a crime against peace, a war crime, a crime against humanity, or a serious nonpolitical crime, or is guilty of acts contrary to the purposes and principles of the United Nations.[101] The threshold for this exclusion is widely agreed to be very high.[102] UNHCR has confirmed that its primary purpose is "to deprive those guilty of heinous acts, and serious common crimes, of international refugee protection and to ensure that such persons do not abuse the institution of asylum in order to avoid being held legally accountable for their acts."[103] In other words, exclusion even from consideration for international protection is to be reserved for those who are essentially fugitives from justice and who are using the system of refugee protection to continue that flight.[104] UNHCR, scholars, and national courts have supported a restrictive application of the "serious crimes" category of exception.[105]

he or she is present"; or he or she, having been convicted of a "particularly serious crime, constitutes a danger to the community of that Member State." See also Article 17 on exclusion of those seeking subsidiary protection.

98 Hathaway, *The Rights of Refugees*, at 304.

99 Refugee Convention, at Art. 1F(b). See also Council Directive 2004/83/EC, at Art. 17.

100 See Chapter 2, at Section 2.3.3.

101 Refugee Convention, at Art. 1F.

102 See Chapter 2, at notes 206–214 and accompanying text.

103 UN High Commissioner for Refugees, *Guidelines on International Protection No. 5: Application of the Exclusion Clauses: Article 1F of the 1951 Convention Relating to the Status of Refugees*, UN Doc. HCR/GIP/03/05, Sept. 4, 2003, at 2.

104 For a detailed examination of all aspect of this issue including a comprehensive review of State practice (Australia, Belgium, Canada, France, Germany, the Netherlands, New Zealand, the United Kingdom, and the United States), see J. Rikhof, *The Criminal Refugee: The Treatment of Asylum Seekers with a Criminal Background in International and Domestic Law* (2012).

105 See Chapter 2, at Section 2.3.3, esp. notes 212–213 and accompanying text.

- Expulsion of recognized refugees: States may expel (and thereby *refoule*) recognized refugees on two different grounds. The first of these relates to "national security or public order."[106] The test is highly restrictive: requiring States to present evidence of a credible and serious threat to the most basic interests of the State or its citizens.[107] States may further expel refugees who have been convicted of particularly serious crimes (in the country of refuge or elsewhere) and who are considered to be a danger to the country of asylum.[108] Once again, the weight of authority leans toward a restrictive interpretation that reflects the inevitably serious consequences of *refoulement*.[109]

What is the situation with respect to mass influx: specifically, can the obligation not to return refugees to persecution be modified or rendered inapplicable in situations of mass influx that may threaten public order and/or national security? Although the Refugee Convention does not address this point, the question is provoked by the drafting history of that instrument, which revealed a clear reluctance on the part of some States to recognize an absolute duty of *non-refoulement* in the face of mass migrations or attempted mass migrations that present a grave risk to the State of refuge.[110] The issue has not been well tested and scholarly opinion is divided. Hathaway, for example, recognizes as reasonable a possibility for States to engage in peremptory *refoulement* "in truly exceptional circumstances [and] to the extent truly necessary to protect their most critical national interests."[111] Others, including UNHCR, reject the possibility outright, as being "neither supported by the text … nor by subsequent practice."[112] State responses to such situations have been highly

[106] "The Contracting States shall not expel a refugee lawfully in their territory save on grounds of national security or public order": Refugee Convention, at Art. 32(1). Note that such an expulsion is subject to certain procedural requirements.

[107] See Chapter 2, esp. at notes 216–220 and accompanying text.

[108] "The benefit of [the protection from *refoulement*] may not, however, be claimed by a refugee whom there are reasonable grounds for regarding as a danger to the security of the country in which he is, or who, having been convicted by a final judgment of a particularly serious crime, constitutes a danger to the community of that country": Refugee Convention, at Art. 33(2).

[109] See further discussion Chapter 2, esp. at notes 222–225 and accompanying text.

[110] Hathaway, *The Rights of Refugees*, at 356–357.

[111] Ibid. at 357.

[112] Lauterpacht and Bethlehem, "The Scope and Content of the Principle of *Non-refoulement*," at 103, cited in Hathaway, *The Rights of Refugees*, at 357. See also UN High Commissioner for Refugees Executive Committee, *Conclusion No. 22 – Protection of Asylum-Seekers in Situations of Large-Scale Influx*, adopted 32nd Sess, Oct. 21, 1981, in UN General Assembly, "Addendum to the Report of the United Nations High Commissioner for Refugees," UN GAOR 36th Sess, Supp. No. 12A, UN Doc. A/36/12/Add.1, at 17 (1981), at para. II(A): "In situations of large-scale influx, asylum-seekers should be admitted to the State in which they first seek refuge and if that State is unable to admit them on a durable basis, it should always admit them at least on a temporary basis and provide them with protection according to the principles set out below … In all cases the fundamental principle of *non-refoulement* – including non-rejection at the frontier – must be scrupulously observed."

varied and, as UNHCR admits, there is a "need for greater clarity concerning the scope of international protection in mass influx situations."[113]

10.2.3.3. Obligation Not to Return Persons at Risk of Torture or Other Serious Violations of Human Rights

The obligation of *non-refoulement* arises not only in relation to asylum-seekers and refugees, but also in relation to any person who is at risk of torture or other serious violations of human rights upon return. Human rights law can therefore provide an important additional ground for challenging the return of smuggled migrants including persons who are found to not have a valid claim for asylum as well as refugees whose right to protection from *refoulement* has been withdrawn on the basis of one of the exceptions cited previously. This is often referred to as a right of "complementary protection." Chapter 2, Section 2.4.1 provided a detailed examination of the sources and scope of the obligation of *non-refoulement* under international human rights law, including interpretations of the substantive content of the obligation by the human rights treaty bodies as well as the European Court of Human Rights. It is therefore necessary at this point to provide only a brief summary of the main points:

- States may not return a smuggled migrant who faces a real risk of torture, inhuman or degrading treatment, or punishment.[114] This prohibition may extend, in certain circumstances, to threats emanating from non-State actors where the relevant State is unable to provide appropriate or effective protection[115];
- This obligation is part of the broader prohibition on torture and associated practices and is thereby a norm of customary international law, binding on all States[116];
- The obligation on returning States to avoid exposing a returned smuggled migrant to torture is an active one. It cannot, for example, rely on diplomatic assurances without also monitoring the sufficiency of those assurances.[117]

These conclusions can be strongly defended with reference to treaty law as well as to the findings of international human rights mechanisms, courts, and tribunals.

[113] UN High Commissioner for Refugees, Global Consultations on International Protection, "Protection of Refugees in Mass Influx Situations: Overall Protection Framework," UN Doc. EC/GC/01/4, Feb. 19, 2001 at para. 1, cited in Hathaway, *The Rights of Refugees*, at 362. See also Goodwin-Gill and McAdam, *The Refugee in International Law*, at 335–339.

[114] See Chapter 2, at notes 227.

[115] See Chapter 2, at note 239 and accompanying text.

[116] See Chapter 2, at notes 231–232 and accompanying text.

[117] See Chapter 2, at note 235 and accompanying text.

However it is important to recognize a significant discrepancy between the generally accepted rules around international protection and State practice in this area: as noted previously, major countries of destination for irregular migrants, including those who have been smuggled, routinely return such persons to situations where their right to life and to freedom from torture is at serious risk, with inadequate or no risk assessment.[118] The failure of all States involved in return of smuggled migrants to engage in any meaningful follow-up of their situation has been well documented.

10.2.3.4. A Note on Anti-smuggling Measures and the Obligation of *Non-refoulement*

The impact of anti-smuggling measures on the obligation of *non-refoulement* has already been considered at various points and this section is limited to highlighting the key sites of vulnerability. The issue is a critical one as an assessment of State responses to irregular migration and migrant smuggling supports a conclusion that many of the measures employed (including interdiction and turn-back at sea, visa restrictions on nationals from certain countries, erection of physical barriers, placement of migration officials at foreign ports, and carrier sanctions) have the effect – and likely also the intention – of denying asylum-seekers access to adequate assessment procedures and thereby to protection. For example, in relation to smuggling by sea, responses such as interdiction and turn-back clearly seek to prevent the disembarkation that is often practically and/or legally necessary for the initiation of asylum claims.

Excision and Special Zones: The creation of special areas within which national and/or international law are said not to apply (such as an "international zone" at an airport or an "excised territory") is a common mechanism used by States to avoid considering the refugee status of persons who are, in fact, physically within that State's territory and control.[119] The lawfulness of such measures can be interrogated from a number of different angles and that is done at various points throughout the

[118] See notes 8–10 above.

[119] For an important analysis of Australian practice in relation to "zones of exclusion," particularly against standards of international refugee law, see M. Foster and J. Pobjoy, "A Failed Case of Legal Exceptionalism? Refugee Status Determination in Australia's 'Excised' Territory" (2011) 23(4) *International Journal of Refugee Law* 583. Foster and Pobjoy note that the creation of exclusion zones was explicitly justified by the Australian government as helping to "ensure that life is made as difficult as possible for those criminals engaged in the people smuggling trade": ibid. at 586. For additional government references to the connection between migrant smuggling and the Australian policy of creating zones of exclusion, see ibid. at 588, 590; 598, n. 88; 609, 618. The practice of excising migration zones was recently taken to extremes when legislation was tabled before the Australian Parliament in November 2012 proposing to excise the entire Australian mainland from Australia's migration zone: *Migration Amendment (Unauthorised Maritime Arrivals and Other Measures) Bill 2012* (Cth). As at May 12, 2013 this bill was still before the Senate.

present book. However, in the immediate context, it is most relevant to consider lawfulness with reference to the extent to which the measures obstruct or otherwise interfere with the right to seek and enjoy asylum from persecution.[120] From this perspective, Hathaway's concise conclusion on the subject is difficult to refute:

> There is ... no international legal difference between opting not to consider the refugee status of persons present in "international zones" or "excised territory" and refusing to consider the refugee status of persons clearly acknowledged to be on the state's territory. Where the refusal to process a refugee claim results, directly or indirectly, in the refugee's removal to face the risk of being persecuted, Art. 33 [of the Refugee Convention] has been contravened.[121]

Actions Constituting *Refoulement*: When considering responses to migrant smuggling from the perspective of the obligation of *non-refoulement*, it is important to consider what actions actually amount to *refoulement* within the meaning of international human rights and refugee law. For example, the central obligation in Article 33 of the Refugee Convention prohibits *refoulement* "in any manner whatsoever to the frontiers of territories where [the refugee's] life or freedom would be threatened." In the context of interdiction at sea, is denial of entry into territorial waters or return of a vessel from territorial waters to the high seas sufficient to establish a violation of this obligation? Some argue that such actions go against the duty of States Parties to avoid specific consequences – return to the risk of being persecuted.[122] Others have noted an important difference between mere denial of entry and more direct action that results in actually returning asylum-seekers to their place of persecution. Goodwin-Gill and McAdam, for example, cite the observation of the Refugee Convention's ad-hoc drafting committee that:

> [T]he obligation not to return a refugee from a country where he was persecuted did not imply an obligation to admit him to the country where he seeks entry. The return of a refugee-ship, for example, to the high seas could not be construed as a violation of this clause.[123]

The essence of the distinction here seems to be the *effect* of the action, that is, there will be *refoulement* where the interdiction actually results in the return of a refugee to the State from which he or she is fleeing – or "where removing a vessel

[120] See further Chapter 3 on the extraterritorial application of human rights law and of the obligation of *non-refoulement*.

[121] Hathaway, *The Rights of Refugees*, at 322.

[122] Ibid. at 318.

[123] UN Economic and Social Council, Ad Hoc Committee on Statelessness, "Comments of the Committee on the Draft Convention," UN Doc. E/AC.32/L.32/Add.1, Feb. 10, 1950, at 7. See also D. Guilfoyle, *Shipping Interdiction and the Law of the Sea* (2009) [Guilfoyle, *Shipping Interdiction and the Law of the Sea*], at 222–223.

to the high seas leaves it with no option but to return to the place where the refugee will face persecution."[124] But this does not necessarily lead to a clear-cut test that can be uniformly applied.[125] Certainly State practice in this area, canvassed in detail in Chapter 6, has not contributed to establishing the parameters of acceptable response with any certainty.[126] A defensible starting position, against which the particular facts and circumstances of a particular case should be assessed, is that a State will be legally responsible for *refoulement* that its own actions made possible.

Bilateral and Multilateral Transfer Arrangements[127] **and the Risk of "Chain *Refoulement*"**: Are responses to migrant smuggling that are aimed at, or result in, asylum-seekers being re-directed or sent to a third country that is deemed to present no threat of persecution, lawful? The practice of sending asylum-seekers onward or back to a country deemed safe is becoming increasingly common and well structured, often under bilateral agreements that designate one State among two or a larger group as being responsible for determination of refugee status.[128] The "first country of arrival" rule, whereby refugees are returned to the country to which they initially fled, is a variation on this theme.[129] Recent examples are numerous: under bilateral and regional arrangements, asylum-seekers from Sub-Saharan Africa arriving in or near Europe, are being sent to Libya.[130] Asylum-seekers from several countries

[124] Guilfoyle, *Shipping Interdiction and the Law of the Sea*, at 223.

[125] Mallia, for example, employs a number of different scenarios to isolate circumstances where *refoulement* would occur: merely using a megaphone to turn back a boat containing irregular migrants would, in her view not qualify. Forcibly turning back a ship would be sufficient to trigger the obligation of *non-refoulement*, but not necessarily result in its breach: for the latter to occur, the action would have had to have the effect of "returning the boat to the borders of persecution": P. Mallia, *Migrant Smuggling by Sea: Combating a Current Threat to Maritime Security through the Creation of a Cooperative Framework* (2009), at 90.

[126] See further discussion of the *Tampa* case in Chapter 6, at Section 6.2.1.3.

[127] Generally on the issues flagged in this and the following section, see UN High Commissioner for Refugees, *Guidance Note on Bilateral and/or Multilateral Transfer Arrangements of Asylum-Seekers*, May 2013, available at: www.refworld.org/docid/51af82794.html (accessed Nov. 30, 2013).

[128] "Harmonization arrangements" of this kind are most highly developed within the European Union. The first phase of a Common European Asylum System was introduced through the Treaty of Amsterdam (Treaty of Amsterdam amending the Treaty on European Union, the Treaties Establishing the European Communities and certain related acts, OJ C 340/1, done Oct. 2, 1997, entered into force May 1, 1999) in 1999 with the aim of harmonizing Member States' responses to refugee protection while enabling them to meet international legal obligations. Legislative and policy efforts to build a region-specific framework for handling asylum claims have continued to the present day. For a critical review of the harmonization arrangements from the perspective of international refugee law, see G. Gilbert, "Is Europe Living Up to Its Obligations to Refugees?" (2004) 15 *European Journal of International Law* 963. Note the European Court of Human Rights has recently found against two Member States in a judgment that asserts the incompatibility of EU law with international protection obligations: see *M.S.S. v. Belgium and Greece*, (2011) 53 EHRR 2 (ECHR, Jan. 21, 2011) [*M.S.S. v. Belgium and Greece*].

[129] On the legal implications of this policy, see Hathaway, *The Rights of Refugees*, at 293–295.

[130] See, for example, *Hirsi Jamaa v. Italy* (concerning the interception and push-back by Italian authorities of Somali and Eritrean nationals back to Libya). The Court held that Italy's actions violated

including Iran, Iraq, Sri Lanka, and Afghanistan, who seek to enter Australia by boat ("unauthorized maritime arrivals"), are being intercepted by Australian immigration officials and sent on to "regional processing countries",[131] including Papua New Guinea and Nauru where they are then pressured to return.[132] Are such practices a form of indirect *refoulement*? In exploring the *Travaux Préparatoires* to Article 33 and jurisprudence of national courts, Hathaway reasonably concludes that the real test is one of common sense and foreseeable consequences.[133] In the present context the relevant question becomes whether it is reasonably foreseeable that the return of smuggled asylum-seekers to a third State will risk their subsequent return to the frontiers of territories where they are at risk of persecution. In other words, as was concluded with respect to interdictions more generally, a State cannot avoid responsibility for indirect *refoulement* that its own actions made possible.

Bilateral and Multilateral Transfer Arrangements – "Safe Third Countries": Although asylum-seekers may have a general right to seek international protection, the Refugee Convention does not specify which State must provide such protection. Accordingly, the bilateral and regional arrangements that include concepts such as "declared country" or "safe third country" referred to previously do not,

fundamental rights, including the prohibition on torture and inhuman or degrading treatment or punishment, and the prohibition of collective expulsion of nonnationals – notwithstanding that the relevant actions occurred outside Italy's territory. See also the discussion of bilateral agreements in Chapter 1, at Section 1.3.2.2 focusing particularly on those concluded between Libya and Italy.

131 *Migration Act* 1958 (Cth) (Australia), at s. 198 AD (enabling authorities to transfer "unauthorized maritime arrivals" to a foreign country for processing of their asylum claim. Note that there is no requirement that "regional processing countries" have ratified the Refugee Convention, or even have *any* legally binding obligations with respect to refugee protection (section 198AB(4)), giving rise to the possibility of "chain *refoulement*." The only condition for the exercise of the power by the Minister is that the Minister "thinks that it is in the national interest to designate the country to be a regional processing country" (section 198AB (2)). In considering the national interest, the Minister must have regard to whether or not the country has given Australia any "assurances" to the effect that: (1) the country will not expel or return a person taken to the country to another country where his or her life or freedom would be threatened on account of his or her race, religion, nationality, membership of a particular social group or political opinion; and (2) the country will make an assessment or permit an assessment to be made, of whether or not a person taken to that country is covered by the definition of "refugee" in Article 1A of the Refugee Convention. The assurances referred to need not be legally binding (section 198AB, subsections 2, 3 and 4). Generally on the trend in "external processing" of asylum claims, see M. den Heijer, *Europe and Extraterritorial Asylum* (2012), at chapter 7.

132 UN High Commissioner for Refugees, *UNHCR Monitoring Visit to Manus Island, Papua New Guinea 23 to 25 October 2013* (Nov. 26, 2013) [*UNHCR Monitoring Visit to Manus Island, Papua New Guinea*], at para. 119 ("Pressure exerted by persons in authority to return, coupled with poor conditions, and/or the failure to correctly identify the 'voluntariness' of the asylum-seekers return, raises concerns around 'constructive *refoulement*' under Article 33 of the 1951 Refugee Convention). The same concern is raised in *UNHCR Monitoring Visit to the Republic of Nauru 7 to 9 October 2013* (Nov. 26, 2013), at para. 140.

133 Hathaway, *The Rights of Refugees*, at 322–324. See also *F.N. and Others v. Sweden*, Application No. 28774/09 (ECHR, Dec. 18, 2012), at para. 69.

of themselves, lead to an automatic breach of Article 33 triggering the responsibility of the State or States involved. The existence of such a breach will turn on whether, in their implementation, these agreements result in – or present a serious risk of – *refoulement*. The practical question of how this is to be assessed is a difficult and contested one. Some argue that assessment of the risk of persecution in the third State or subsequent *refoulement* by that State requires adequate assessment of the risk to which each individual asylum-seeker or refugee may be exposed in being returned to a given country.[134] For others, including for many States that engage in these practices, the identification of the third State as "safe" for asylum-seekers or refugees as a group is sufficient to discharge their obligation under Article 33.[135]

Capacity and Willingness of Third States: A further issue relates to the capacity and willingness of any third State to provide access to fair and efficient means to determine the status of the asylum-seekers it receives.[136] In such cases, the standard of foreseeable risk once again becomes operational. Responsibility of the returning State is engaged if that State is aware – or should have been aware – that the third State will not consider a claim to refugee protection or that its refugee determination practices are inadequate.[137] Once again, the method and criteria by which such assessments are to be made are both in dispute. Is it sufficient to make a generalized determination about a specific third country or group of returnees, or should

[134] "The prohibition on *refoulement* applies only in respect of territories where the refugee or asylum seeker would be at risk, not more generally. It does, however, require that a State proposing to remove a refugee or asylum-seeker undertake a proper assessment as to whether the third country concerned is indeed safe": Lauterpacht and Bethlehem, "The Scope and Content of the Principle of *Non-refoulement*," at para. 116. See also *UNHCR Monitoring Visit to Manus Island, Papua New Guinea*, at para. 117.

[135] See, for example, Council Directive 2005/85/EC of 1 December 2005 on minimum standards on procedures in Member States for granting or withdrawing refugee status, OJ L 326/13, Dec. 13, 2005, at para. 19 of the Preamble (creating a rebuttable presumption that a third country that meets the criteria set out in Article 27, or is on the common (Article 29) or national (Article 30) list of safe third countries, is safe for a particular applicant, with the onus on the applicant to demonstrate that it is not safe in his or her individual circumstances); Canada/United States Safe Third Country Agreement (Dec. 5, 2002), available at www.cic.gc.ca/english/department/laws-policy/safe-third.asp (accessed May 12, 2013) (providing that asylum-seekers traveling from either country to the other will be automatically returned, subject to a short list of exceptions); and *Migration Act 1958* (Cth) (Australia), at s 91D, and an example of a country being prescribed as a safe third country under that provision in the *Migration Regulations 1994* (Cth) (Australia), at reg 2.12A. See also Hathaway, *The Rights of Refugees*, at 295–296.

[136] For example, Australian authorities transfer asylum-seekers who arrive irregularly by boat to Nauru and Papua New Guinea: See reports of the UNHCR cited at note 132 above.

[137] Hathaway, *The Rights of Refugees*, at 326–327. See also *Hirsi Jamaa v. Italy*, at paras. 128–131. *UNHCR Monitoring Visit to Manus Island, Papua New Guinea*, at para. 52 ("UNHCR is of the view that Australia's responsibilities under applicable international instruments to which it is a party remain engaged and cannot be extinguished by the physical transfer of asylum-seekers to [Papua New Guinea]").

assessments be individualized? What factors are important in assessing risk? Some would argue that the third State must itself be party to the Refugee Convention and have a solid record of respecting human rights, including the rights of asylum-seekers and other nonnationals.[138] Although not explicitly prescribing so high a standard, the European Court of Human Rights has referred to the need to ascertain the existence of "sufficient guarantees" against return without "any" risk assessment.[139] However, many returning States appear satisfied to rely on diplomatic assurances, commonly provided through the bilateral or regional agreement that enables the return in the first place.[140] In considering the issue, national courts have focused strongly on outcomes: "the end result rather than the precise procedures by which the result was achieved."[141]

[138] See, for example, UN High Commissioner for Refugees, *Maritime Interception Operations and the Processing of International Protection Claims: Legal Standards and Policy Considerations with Respect to Extraterritorial Processing* (Protection Policy Paper, Nov. 2010), at para. 43. See also S. H. Legomsky, "Secondary Refugee Movements and the Return of Asylum Seekers to Third Countries: The Meaning of Effective Protection" (UNHCR, Legal and Protection Policy Research Series), Doc. PPLA/2003/01, Feb. 2003 [Legomsky, "Secondary Refugee Movements"], at 79; *Plaintiff M70/2011 and Plaintiff M106/2011 v. Minister for Immigration and Citizenship* (2011) 244 CLR 144 (Aus. HC, Aug. 31, 2011), at para. 245: "[A] positive assessment of the practical provisions which are made for refugees in a country cannot replace the requirement that the country has obliged itself, through its laws, to provide the necessary recognition and protection. That legal obligation is the minimum requirement of a country which may continue to fulfil the content of the Convention obligations earlier mentioned, of the protection of refugees from non-refoulement and from persecution" (per Justice Kiefel).

[139] *M.S.S. v. Belgium and Greece*, at para. 342.

[140] For example, s. 198A(3) (since repealed) of Australia's *Migration Act 1958* (Cth) conferred power on the relevant government Minister to declare that a particular third country "(i) provides access, for persons seeking asylum, to effective procedures for assessing their need for protection; and (ii) provides protection for persons seeking asylum, pending determination of their refugee status; and (iii) provides protection to persons who are given refugee status, pending their voluntary repatriation to their country of origin or resettlement in another country; and (iv) meets relevant human rights standards in providing that protection ..." In 2011 the Minister made such a declaration with respect to Malaysia pursuant to an informal agreement between the two governments for asylum-seeker boat arrivals to Australia to be removed to Malaysia for processing (the "Malaysian Arrangement"). Malaysia is not a party to the Refugee Convention, the ICCPR, or the Convention against Torture and, despite having agreed to respect the principle of *non-refoulement*, made no undertaking to implement this in its domestic law. The Minister had negligible evidence that Malaysia would abide by the human rights obligations that bind Australia with respect to its treatment of asylum-seekers and was apparently relying almost entirely on diplomatic assurances made in the Malaysian Arrangement. The Declaration was subsequently struck down by the Australian High Court as being inadequate to ensure Australia's compliance with its domestic and (by implication) international legal obligations. See *Plaintiff M70/2011 v. Minister for Immigration and Citizenship* (2011) 244 CLR 144 (Aus. HC, Aug. 31, 2011); and for commentary, M. Foster, "The Implications of the Failed 'Malaysian Solution': The Australian High Court and Refugee Responsibility Sharing at International Law" (2012) 13(1) *Melbourne Journal of International Law* 395.

[141] *R v. Secretary of State for the Home Department, ex parte Yogathas*, [2002] UKHL 36 (UK HL, Oct. 17, 2002), per Lord Hope, cited in Hathaway, *The Rights of Refugees*, at 330.

10.3. OBLIGATION TO ACCEPT AND FACILITATE RETURN

Establishing a legal basis for return of a smuggled migrant is only the first step in effecting a lawful return. Generally, return cannot be achieved without substantial cooperation from the country of return. Effective implementation of the right of States to return smuggled migrants, and of the right of such persons to return to their home country, both depend on a corresponding willingness on the part of the State concerned to accept returning nationals and other persons deemed to have a right of return. However this cooperation is not always straightforward or assured. Often, nationality cannot be determined without lengthy investigation. Many countries will not accept undocumented returnees alleged or claiming to be their nationals, and the process of obtaining identification documents can be complex and prolonged.

This section examines the basis, scope, substantive content, and implications of the obligation on States to accept return. The discussion begins with a consideration of the basic international legal right, accorded to all nationals, to return to their country and the related obligation of States of nationality to accept their expelled nationals. It then turns to an identification and analysis of obligations to accept and facilitate return under international agreements dealing with migrant smuggling and irregular migration. At the international level, the only directly relevant multilateral instrument on this point is the Migrant Smuggling Protocol. However, bilateral agreements governing readmission are becoming increasingly common, and these are considered in the final section of this part.

10.3.1. *Right of Nationals to Return and Obligation to Accept and Facilitate Return of Expelled Nationals*

The foundation of the obligation on States to accept return of their nationals is the right of such persons to return to their country of origin. The right of return has been briefly examined in Chapter 2.[142] That analysis confirmed the existence of an unambiguous right of all persons to return to their country – and a corresponding obligation on States not to arbitrarily deprive someone of the right to enter his or her own country.[143] There are, in the words of the Human Rights Committee, "few, if any circumstances in which deprivation of the right to enter one's own country could be reasonable."[144]

[142] See Chapter 2, at Section 2.2.2.

[143] For a review of relevant treaty provisions supporting an unambiguous right of return see Chapter 2, Section 2.2.2, at notes 146–155 and accompanying text.

[144] UN Human Rights Committee, "General Comment No. 27: Freedom of Movement," UN Doc. HRI/GEN/1/Rev.7, at 173, May 12, 2004, adopted Nov. 2, 1999 [HRC General Comment No. 27], at para. 21.

To what country does the right of return refer? It is accepted that the right relates to the country of nationality and/or citizenship of the individual concerned. It has traditionally been held that the right of return in the ICCPR referred only to a State's own nationals.[145] However, after some uneven and "restrictive" case law,[146] the Human Rights Committee confirmed that the scope of the terms "his own country" in the ICCPR is broader than the concept "country of his nationality":

> It is not limited to nationality in a formal sense, that is, nationality acquired at birth or by conferral; it embraces, at the very least, an individual who, because of his or her special ties to or claims in relation to a given country, cannot be considered to be a mere alien. This would be the case, for example, of nationals of a country who have there been stripped of their nationality in violation of international law, and of individuals whose country of nationality has been incorporated in or transferred to another national entity, whose nationality is being denied them. The language of article 12, paragraph 4, moreover, permits a broader interpretation that might embrace other categories of long-term residents, including but not limited to stateless persons arbitrarily deprived of the right to acquire the nationality of the country of such residence. Since other factors may in certain circumstances result in the establishment of close and enduring connections between a person and a country, States parties should include in their reports information on the rights of permanent residents to return to their country of residence.[147]

Factors other than nationality subsequently identified by the Committee as potentially establishing close and enduring connections between a person and a country include long-standing residence, close personal and family ties, and intentions to remain, as well as to the absence of such ties elsewhere.[148]

The individual right of return complements and reinforces an obligation on States to admit their own nationals to their territory, and to grant them residence there. This obligation has long been recognized as extending to nationals who have been expelled from another country.[149] It is seen as reinforcing and giving expression

[145] See K. Hailbronner, "Readmission Agreements and the Obligation on States under Public International Law to Readmit their Own and Foreign Nationals" (1997) 57 *Zeitschrift für ausländisches öffentliches Recht und Völkerrecht* 1 [Hailbronner, "Readmission Agreements"], at 2–5.

[146] See Nowak, *CCPR Commentary*, at 284–287 (critically analyzing the Committee's decisions in several cases, including *Charles E. Stewart v. Canada*, UNHRC Comm. No. 538/1993, UN Doc. CCPR/C/58/D/538/1993, Dec. 16, 1996, decided Nov. 1, 1996; and *Giosue Canepa v. Canada*, UNHRC Comm. No. 558/1993, UN Doc. CCPR/C/59/D/558/1993, June 20, 1997, decided Apr. 3, 1997).

[147] HRC General Comment No. 27, at para. 20.

[148] *Nystrom v. Australia*, UNHRC Comm. No. 1557/2007, UN Doc. CCPR/C/102/D/1557/2007, Sept. 1, 2011, decided July 18, 2011, at para. 7.4.

[149] See R. Jennings and A. Watts eds., *Oppenheim's International Law*, vol. I (9th ed. 1996), at 858 ("... the state of nationality of expelled persons is bound to receive them on its territory"). For a detailed survey of the relevant law from the perspective of readmission agreements, see Hailbronner, "Readmission

to the sovereign right of States to control their own borders. In other words, without an obligation on the country of origin to accept its nationals expelled from another State, the right of States to decide on access of foreign nationals to their territory would be undermined.[150] Nationality will often be easy to establish but this is not always the case. Although the question of who is a "national" is primarily one for national law, that law must reflect the true nature of nationality as it is understood in international relations: the existence of a factual connection between the State and the individual in question.[151]

The requirement to accept the return of nationals and others with a close connection to the State would be rendered ineffective without a corresponding obligation on the State to verify the identity of persons being returned and to provide them with the documentation required for return to take place. Consideration of this obligation by courts and international bodies has generally been in the context of the right to leave – and the concomitant right to obtain the necessary travel documents to allow international travel.[152] Reference should be made to the discussion of the right to leave in Chapter 2.[153]

10.3.2. *Obligation to Accept and Facilitate Return under the Migrant Smuggling Protocol*

The issue of return was a sensitive and difficult one for the drafters of the Migrant Smuggling Protocol, and the final provisions on return are very sparse: affirming little more than an obligation on States to accept and facilitate the return of their nationals. This rather dismal result was perhaps inevitable, reflecting the technical and political impossibility of dealing with the many legal issues associated with return within the constraints of a narrow instrument and a tight drafting schedule.

The initial text of the relevant article, proposed by the United States, obliged States to facilitate and accept the return of their nationals who had been smuggled, and to verify their identity.[154] This formulation was supported by a number of States

Agreements." See also N. Coleman, *European Readmission Policy: Third Country Interests and Refugee Rights* (2011) [Coleman, *European Readmission Policy*], especially at chapter 2.

150 O. Dörr, "Nationality," in R. Wolfrum ed., *The Max Planck Encyclopedia of Public International Law* (2008–), at para. 50.

151 *Nottebohm (Second Phase) (Liechtenstein v. Guatemala)*, [1955] ICJ Rep 4, at 24. See generally Hailbronner, "Readmission Agreements," at 19–25.

152 See, for example, HRC General Comment No. 27, at para. 9; and *Loubna El Ghar v. Socialist People's Libyan Arab Jamahiriya*, UNHRC Comm. No. 1107/2002, UN Doc. CCPR/C/82/D/1107/2002, Nov. 15, 2004, decided Mar. 29, 2004.

153 See Chapter 2, at Section 2.2.1.

154 Rolling text (UN Doc. A/AC.254/4/Add.1/Rev.1, May 13, 1999), cited in the United Nations Office on Drugs and Crime, Travaux Préparatoires *of the Negotiations for the Elaboration of the United Nations Convention against Transnational Organized Crime and the Protocols Thereto* (2006) [Travaux Préparatoires *for the Organized Crime Convention and Protocols*], at 547.

but others raised concerns, most particularly about its compatibility with existing human rights obligations. Some States expressed the view that return was a necessary means of deterring migrants and organized crime groups, and to ensure the right of the migrants themselves to return to their country of origin.[155] Others proposed deleting the draft article because it was beyond the mandate of the Ad Hoc Committee and "unfairly placed the burden on the migrants themselves."[156]

In its final version, the relevant provision obliges a State Party to "facilitate and accept, without undue delay," the return of a smuggled migrant who is a national of that State Party, as well as those smuggled migrants "who ha[ve] the right of permanent residence in its territory at the time of return."[157] A State Party is further required to "consider the possibility of facilitating and accepting" the return of smuggled migrants "who had the right of permanent residence in its territory at the time of entry into the receiving State in accordance with its domestic law."[158] These obligations depend on the status of the person in question, either at the time of the migrant smuggling or at the time of the return. An Interpretative Note attached to this provision confirms that it is based on the understanding that States Parties would not deprive persons of their nationality contrary to international law, thereby rendering them stateless.[159]

The obligation to accept and facilitate return, or to consider doing so, was adopted on the understanding that any return would not be undertaken before the nationality or right of permanent residence of the person in question has been duly verified.[160] Also, the Interpretative Notes indicate that the term "permanent residence" is understood as meaning "long-term, but not necessarily indefinite residence and that the article is understood not to prejudice national legislation regarding the granting of the right of residence or the duration of residence."[161] The Interpretative Notes also indicate that return should not be carried out until any relevant nationality or residency status has been ascertained.[162]

The Protocol further requires States Parties to verify the identity of smuggled nationals (and other smuggled persons falling within the provisions referred to previously), and to provide them with travel documents required for the return process. A "requested State Party" is obliged, "without undue or unreasonable delay" to verify whether a smuggled migrant "is its national or has the right of permanent residence to its territory."[163] The Protocol also responds to the situation where a smuggled

155 Ibid. at 548.
156 Ibid.
157 Migrant Smuggling Protocol, at Art. 18(1).
158 Ibid. at Art. 18(2).
159 Travaux Préparatoires *for the Organized Crime Convention and Protocols*, at 552.
160 Ibid.
161 Ibid.
162 Ibid.
163 Migrant Smuggling Protocol, at Art. 18(3).

migrant subject to return does not have travel documents, providing that in order to facilitate the return of such persons: "The State Party of which that person is a national or in which he or she has the right of permanent residence shall agree to issue, at the request of the receiving State Party, such travel documents or other authorization as may be necessary to enable the person to travel to and re-enter its territory."[164]

As with all other provisions, the Protocol's return obligations operate subject to Article 16(1), reaffirming the relevance of the right to life and the prohibition on torture, and Article 19, the savings clause, preserving the operation of international human rights and refugee law.[165] Accordingly, all actions undertaken with regard to return under the Protocol must consider and comply with the broader human rights and refugee law framework including obligations related to *non-refoulement*.

10.3.3. *Obligation to Accept Return under Bilateral Agreements*

Many countries of destination for smuggled migrants have concluded agreements with countries of origin (and sometimes third countries) specifying the way in which persons will be returned. These agreements are not a recent phenomenon and, at least within the European Union, represent some of "the oldest instruments employed by Member States to control migratory flows."[166] Return agreements (also referred to as "readmission agreements") are widely considered by countries of destination for irregular migrants as "tools of an effective return policy in order to tackle illegal immigration."[167] For critics, they are almost inevitably "repressive measures" of "pre-frontier control," which invoke the cooperation of one country in securing the borders of another.[168] Some readmission agreements are negotiated and concluded in secret and their final text is not made public.[169] Sometimes, they will extend well beyond return to include a range of support measures – typically flowing from the returning country to the country of return.[170] Incentives, aimed at "ensur[ing] the proper level of

164 Ibid. at Art. 18(4).
165 Ibid. at Art. 19.
166 A. Roig and T. Huddleston, "EC Readmission Agreements: A Re-evaluation of the Political Impasse" (2007) 9 *European Journal of Migration and Law* 363, cited in M. Panizzon, "Readmission Agreements of EU Member States: A Case for EU Subsidiarity or Dualism?" (2012) 31(4) *Refugee Survey Quarterly* 101 [Panizzon, "Readmission Agreements"], at 102. For a detailed examination of the history of readmission agreements in Europe, see Coleman, *European Readmission Policy*, at chapter 1.
167 Council of the European Union, Council conclusions defining the EU strategy on readmission, Doc. 11260/11 MIGR 118, June 8, 2011 [European Council Conclusions on Readmission], at Conclusion 1.
168 Panizzon, "Readmission Agreements," at 106.
169 On the legal implications of these secret agreements, see Chapter 1, at Section 1.3.2.2.
170 See citations at note 166 above.

cooperation by the third county concerned,"[171] can extend beyond financial and technical support to relaxation of visa requirements for travel and more favorable access to the labor market of the returning State.[172] Intergovernmental organizations can be party to return agreements that operate in respect of all Member States. Intergovernmental organizations such as the International Organization for Migration and UNHCR may also be party to return agreements in situations where they are to be involved in managing the return.[173] The central features and issues attached to return agreements are neatly captured in the following extract from a 2010 Resolution of the Parliamentary Assembly of the European Union:

> Readmission agreements reiterate and define a country's obligation to readmit its own citizens and set out the conditions under which states parties to such agreements are obliged to readmit citizens of third countries who have passed through their territory. They facilitate and expedite the enforcement of return decisions in respect of irregular migrants and may also function as an incentive for countries of origin or transit to enhance their migration control. Depending on one's viewpoint, readmission agreements can either be considered an important element in the migration management strategies of ... states, or as facilitators of questionable return decisions and part of the criticised "outsourcing of migration control."[174]

Within Europe, "readmission agreements" are a central plank of regional migration policy and practice.[175] EU Member States have concluded a large number of agreements with third States containing readmission obligations on a bilateral, often informal basis, reflecting an apparent preference for "operability" of cooperation on readmission, over formalization.[176] However, agreements concluded between the European Union and third countries ("EU Readmission Agreements") are explicitly

[171] European Council Conclusions on Readmission, at Conclusion 8.

[172] For an examination of this aspect from the perspective of the European Union and its neighboring countries, see F. Trauner and I. Kruse, *EC Visa Facilitation and Readmission Agreements: Implementing a New EU Security Approach in the Neighbourhood* (CEPS Working Document No. 290; CASE Network Studies and Analyses No. 363, Apr. 23, 2008).

[173] Although such agreements will generally not focus on the detailed modalities of return, rather dealing with support to the State of return and monitoring of returns by the international organizations. See, for example, *Memorandum of Understanding between the Government of Australia, the Government of the Islamic Republic of Afghanistan and the United Nations High Commissioner for Refugees (UNHCR) on migration and humanitarian cooperation*, Jan. 17, 2011, available at www.minister.immi.gov.au/media/media-releases/_pdf/mou-with-afghanistan-unhcr.pdf (accessed May 12, 2013).

[174] Council of Europe, Parliamentary Assembly, Resolution 1741 (2010) on Readmission agreements: a mechanism for returning irregular migrants, adopted June 22, 2010 [Council of Europe Resolution 1741 on Readmission Agreements], at para. 1.

[175] For a comprehensive analysis of all aspects of readmission agreements in the European Union context, including history, rationale, substantive content, and negotiation procedures, see Coleman, *European Readmission Policy*.

[176] On this trend toward informalization, see J-P. Cassarino, "Informalising Readmission Agreements in the EU Neighborhood" (2007) 42 *The International Spectator* 179.

provided for under the Lisbon Treaty and have emerged as an important basis for returning irregular migrants, including those who have been intercepted at or near the border. Such agreements are developed following the issuing of "negotiating directives" from the Council to the Commission in relation to a specific country. They are predicated on recognition of "the obligation of each State under customary international law to readmit its own nationals"[177] and are carefully, if somewhat disingenuously, presented as imposing strictly reciprocal obligations on all parties to readmit their nationals who are no longer authorized to remain in one of the States Parties.[178] EU Readmission Agreements generally set out detailed operational and technical criteria for the return process, including required information, evidence of nationality, and time limits for submission and response, as well as issues of data protection, costs, and some requirements for the return itself (e.g., prior notification and transportation).[179] In addition to the obligation to readmit a State Party's own nationals, all EU Readmission Agreements (and many other such agreements)[180] also require the readmission of third-country nationals and stateless persons who either hold a valid visa or permit issued by the Requested State, or who entered the Requesting State illegally through the territory of the Requested State.[181] As discussed later on in this subsection, this creates an obligation that is not part of general international law.

In principle, existing bilateral agreements or arrangements concluded between EU Member States and third countries may continue to be applied but "only … so far as they are compatible with the EU readmission agreements or they are foreseen by the EU readmission agreements."[182] In practice, however, there is potential for significant conflict between EU Readmission Agreements and bilateral migration agreements containing readmission obligations entered into by EU States with third countries, not least in relation to human rights standards.[183] As Panizzon has noted, this has led to a situation where migrant destination and source countries are able to engage in venue shopping: seeking the least restrictive human rights clauses and the broadest possible labor market access respectively: "Thus, readmission

177 European Council Conclusions on Readmission, at Preamble.

178 European Commission, Communication from the Commission to the European Parliament and the Council: Evaluation of EU Readmission Agreements, COM(2011) 76 final, Feb. 23, 2011 [European Commission 2011 Evaluation of EU Readmission Agreements], at 2. See also the EU-Pakistan agreement discussed in this sub-section.

179 European Commission, Readmission Agreements, MEMO/05/351, Oct. 5, 2005, at 2.

180 European Commission 2011 Evaluation of EU Readmission Agreements, at 8.

181 See, for example, Articles 3 and 5 of the Agreement between the European Union and Georgia on the readmission of persons residing without authorisation, OJ L 52/47, Feb. 25, 2011, done Nov. 22, 2010, entered into force Mar. 1, 2011.

182 European Council Conclusions on Readmission, at Conclusion 2.

183 See Panizzon, "Readmission Agreements," at 129.

agreements are often concluded with countries that cannot guarantee human rights protection and an asylum procedure to their own nationals, let alone third country nationals."[184]

An illustrative example of the substantive content of EU Readmission Agreements is provided by the 2010 agreement concluded between the European Union and Pakistan.[185] This instrument establishes the principle of systematic return of Pakistani nationals residing without authorization in a Member State and vice versa. It also mandates the return of third-country nationals and stateless persons under certain conditions. The principal features of the agreement, authorized on the European Union side by a Council Decision,[186] are as follows:

Readmission Obligations: Pakistan and EU Member States mutually agree to readmit their nationals who are not authorized to enter or remain in the territory of the other party. Parties are to cooperate in establishing the identity of persons proposed to be returned under the agreement. Pakistan agrees to readmit third-country nationals and stateless persons, on condition that such persons have a valid authorization to reside in Pakistan or entered the territory of an EU Member State unlawfully coming directly from Pakistan. The same provisions apply to European nationals residing without authorization in Pakistan, and to nationals of other countries who have transited via the European Union before entering Pakistan unlawfully.

Readmission Procedures: The EU State requesting return must submit a readmission application to Pakistan unless the necessary documentation for return is in place. For stateless persons and third-country nationals, the application must be submitted at the latest one year after the competent authority of the Member State wishing to expel the person has become aware of that person's unauthorized residence (extendable in special circumstances). Pakistan is required to respond within thirty days (extendable to sixty days in special circumstances). If the application is refused, reasons for the refusal must be given. The transfer of the person concerned must take place within three months following approval of the application. The Pakistani authorities and those of the Member State shall come to agreement on the transfer date, the border crossing point, and possible escorts. Pakistan further undertakes to authorize the transit of third-country nationals or stateless persons if they cannot be returned directly to the State of destination, on the basis of written evidence that

[184] Ibid. at 105.

[185] Agreement between the European Community and the Islamic Republic of Pakistan on the readmission of persons residing without authorization, OJ L 287/52, Nov. 4, 2010, done Oct. 26, 2009, entered into force Dec. 1, 2010 [Agreement between the EC and Pakistan on the readmission of persons residing without authorization].

[186] Council Decision of 7 October 2010 on the conclusion of the Agreement between the European Community and the Islamic Republic of Pakistan on the readmission of persons residing without authorization (2010/649/EU), OJ L 287/50, Nov. 4, 2010.

such State will take back that person. All transport costs incurred up to the border crossing point in the State of final destination are to be paid by the Member State requesting readmission.

Implementation: The agreement establishes a Joint Readmission Committee composed of representatives from Pakistan and the European Union, which is responsible for overseeing its implementation, strengthening cooperation and exchange of information between the parties.

Safeguards: The agreement does not make specific reference to safeguards, including the obligation of *non-refoulement*. A broad savings clause states that it "shall be without prejudice to the rights, obligations and responsibilities of the Community, the Member States and Pakistan arising from or under international law, and international treaties to which they are Parties ... [and] to the remedies and rights available to the person concerned under the laws of the host country including international law."[187]

Readmission agreements of all varieties have been heavily criticized for subjecting migrants to risks of human rights violations, in particular through failures to provide access rights such as the right to seek asylum from persecution.[188] Those agreements that provide for "accelerated procedures" (typically directed at irregular migrants, including those who have been smuggled who are apprehended at or near the border including airports) are considered particularly worrisome in this regard. It is claimed that such agreements are "frequently applied without adequate procedural safeguards" in the returning country, such as access to lawyers and information on legal rights, or opportunities to challenge return decisions.[189] Available literature appears to confirm that readmission agreements are often used as a vehicle for returning persons who have not had their protection needs determined with

187 Agreement between the EC and Pakistan on the readmission of persons residing without authorization, at Art. 15.

188 On the readmission agreements concluded between Italy and Libya see S. Klepp, "Italy and Its Libyan Cooperation Program: Pioneer of the European Union's Refugee Policy?" in Cassarino ed., *Unbalanced Reciprocities* 77. For a concise summary of human rights concerns with respect to readmission agreements concluded between EU Member States and third countries, see Council of Europe, Parliamentary Assembly, Report of the Committee on Migration, Refugees and Population, *Readmission agreements: a mechanism for returning irregular migrants, Report*, Doc. 12168, Mar. 17, 2010 [Council of Europe Parliamentary Assembly Report, *Readmission Agreements*]. For a detailed examination of readmission agreements with reference to the principle of *non-refoulement*, see Coleman, *European Readmission Policy*, at chapter 9; and Panizzon, "Readmission Agreements." For an example of the implementation of readmission agreements leading to serious human rights violations, see references to Ukraine in note 189.

189 Human Rights Watch, *Ukraine: On the Margins, Rights Violations against Migrants and Asylum Seekers at the New Eastern Border of the European Union* (2005), at 2. See also Human Rights Watch, *Ukraine: Buffeted in the Borderland, The Treatment of Migrants and Asylum Seekers in Ukraine* (2010).

reference to their own or third countries, where they may face the risk of persecution and/or severe human rights violations.[190]

Although States have an international legal obligation to admit their own nationals, they have no obligation to re-admit those who merely passed through in transit. However, readmission agreements are increasingly being used to secure agreement for readmission of third-country nationals.[191] The use of readmission agreements to return individuals to countries of which they are not nationals presents particular legal and practical challenges. As noncitizens, the returned individuals may have only limited access to necessary social assistance and may be relatively more vulnerable to violation of their rights.[192] In particular, there are grounds for genuine concern that third-country returnees will be ultimately removed to their country of origin without having had the opportunity to make claims for asylum in either the destination or transit countries.[193] This is of particular concern with regard to the conclusion of readmission agreements with countries that do not have properly functioning asylum systems and/or are not parties to the Refugee Convention,[194] or indeed to those countries that cannot offer basic human rights protections to their own citizens.[195] The lack of monitoring and evaluation of the operation of readmission agreements by Parties is another source of concern. Even within the European Union there is little reliable information available on the number of persons returned and even less information on the fate of those persons.[196] Some States are unable to provide the precise number of readmission applications made each year, or information on whether individuals were, for example, sent to their country of origin or to a transit country.[197] This lack of data and of any post-readmission monitoring makes it particularly difficult to assess the operation of the

[190] For example see Kruse, "EU Readmission Policy: The Case of Albania"; and Cassarino ed., *Unbalanced Reciprocities*.

[191] Kruse, "EU Readmission Policy: The Case of Albania," at 121.

[192] Council of Europe Parliamentary Assembly Report, *Readmission Agreements*, esp. at Summary, paras. C.2, C.28.

[193] For a more detailed summary and analysis of these concerns, see Coleman, *European Readmission Policy*, "Chapter 9: Community Readmission Agreements and the International Protection of Refugees," at 223–316. See also Council of Europe Parliamentary Assembly Report, *Readmission Agreements*, at para. A.3 (referring to "the risk that the sending or the readmitting country fails to honour their obligations under [human rights and refugee law] and then uses a readmission agreement to enforce a flawed decision").

[194] Legomsky, "Secondary Refugee Movements," at 15. See also *Plaintiff M70/2011 and Plaintiff M106/2011 v. Minister for Immigration and Citizenship* (2011) 244 CLR 144 (Aus. HC, Aug. 31, 2011).

[195] Panizzon, "Readmission Agreements."

[196] European Commission 2011 Evaluation of EU Readmission Agreements, at 3, 9–10; and Council of Europe Parliamentary Assembly Report, *Readmission Agreements*, at para. A.5.

[197] European Commission 2011 Evaluation of EU Readmission Agreements, at 3.

readmission agreements and in particular their effect on the situation of readmitted individuals.

Proponents of readmission agreements (invariably those countries wishing to return unlawful third-country nationals) view expulsion-related human rights concerns, and *non-refoulement* in particular, as issues that arise during the determination of the individual's immigration status, and thereby not directly relevant to the application of such agreements.[198] In other words, they see readmission agreements as being "neutral in terms of human rights and merely a tool for the removal of irregular migrants."[199] Yet critics argue persuasively that readmission agreements form an integral part of the return process, and contribute to the functioning of that process in particular through accelerating return procedures, which may prevent returnees from accessing legal rights and remedies.[200] In 2010, the Parliamentary Assembly of the Council of Europe recommended that both the European Union and its Member States "conclude readmission agreements only with countries that comply with relevant human rights standards and with the 1951 Geneva Convention, that have functioning asylum systems in place and that protect their citizens' right to free movement."[201] The Assembly further recommended that legal safeguards for the protection of human rights be included in any such agreements, including for example, provisions requiring Requesting States to verify that the returned person will have access to minimum social rights.[202] In addition, the Assembly directed specific recommendations to the European Union, inviting the European Union to properly consider the human rights system and the availability of a properly functioning asylum system in a country prior to forming readmission agreements with that country, and to negotiate provisions into the agreements that safeguard the human rights of readmitted persons.[203] The European Commission made similar recommendations in a 2011 evaluation of EU Readmission Agreements.[204]

198 Council of Europe Parliamentary Assembly Report, *Readmission Agreements*, at para. A.2: "Advocates of readmission agreements claim that these are neutral in terms of human rights and merely a tool for the removal of irregular migrants. The stage at which a human rights concern may arise is usually when the decision to expel the person concerned, the return decision, is taken and not when that decision is enforced by way of the readmission agreement, unless the situation in the readmitting country has changed in the meantime." See also European Commission 2011 Evaluation of EU Readmission Agreements, at 10.

199 Council of Europe Parliamentary Assembly Report, *Readmission Agreements*, at para. A.2.

200 European Council on Refugees and Exiles, *Defending Refugees' Access to Protection in Europe*, Dec. 2007, at 45; and Council of Europe Parliamentary Assembly Report, *Readmission Agreements*, at para. C.28. See also references at note 188 above.

201 Council of Europe Resolution 1741 on Readmission Agreements, at para. 6.1.

202 Ibid. at para. 6.8.

203 Ibid. at para. 7.

204 Communication from the Commission to the European Parliament and the Council: Evaluation of EU Readmission Agreements, COM(2011) 76 final, Feb. 23, 2011.

10.4. CONDUCT OF RETURNS

Establishing a legal basis for return of a smuggled migrant is only the first step in effecting a lawful return. States must also ensure that the return process itself does not violate any established obligations or rights. In other words, even if a particular expulsion is, in principle, legally justified, its legality could be compromised by the manner in which that expulsion is carried out. The principal issues relate to due process rights, pre-return detention rights, and safety and dignity in the actual process of return. Each of these aspects is considered separately in this subsection.

It is relevant at this point to formally introduce the EU Returns Directive,[205] adopted in 2008 by the European Parliament with the aim of harmonizing EU Member State responses to the voluntary and forced return of irregular migrants.[206] The Directive is intended to establish "a horizontal set of rules applicable to all third country nationals who do not or who no longer fulfill the conditions for entry, stay or residence in a Member State."[207] It also requires the establishment of a monitoring system with respect to forced returns.[208] Transposition of the Directive by EU Member States was to have been completed by December 2010.

The Directive applies to "third-country nationals staying illegally on the territory of a Member State."[209] The accompanying definitions confirm that the Directive

[205] Directive 2008/115/EC of the European Parliament and of the Council of 16 December 2008 on common standards and procedures in Member States for returning illegally staying third-country nationals, OJ L 348/98, Dec. 24, 2008 [EU Returns Directive].

[206] The Directive requires that Member States' laws and regulations are brought into compliance with the Directive, and that such measures as are necessary to bring about compliance be implemented by December 24, 2010 (at Art. 20). The Directive applies to all EU Member States, with exceptions in relation to certain countries (Denmark, United Kingdom, Ireland, Iceland, Norway, and Switzerland) as provided for in the Preamble of the Directive.

[207] EU Returns Directive, at Preambular para. 5.

[208] Under Article 8(6) of the Directive, EU Member States "shall provide for an effective forced-return monitoring system." In 2011, a comparative study providing best practice examples to support EU Member State efforts to develop an effective and transparent monitoring system of the forced-return of illegally staying third-country nationals was released. Key findings focused on the importance of ensuring that organizations entrusted with monitoring forced returns are different from the authorities enforcing those returns; that those monitoring returns are informed of pending returns in a timely manner; that the various agencies involved in conducting, supporting, and monitoring returns work more closely together; and that greater attention be paid to the return operations of Frontex. International Centre for Migration Policy and Development and European Council and Matrix, *Comparative Study for Best Practices in Forced Return Monitoring*, European Commission Directorate-General Justice, Freedom and Security, JLS/2009/RFXX/CA/1001, Nov. 10, 2011.

[209] EU Returns Directive, at Art. 2. Article 3(1) defines a "third-country national" as "any person who is not a citizen of the Union within the meaning of Article 17(1) of the Treaty and who is not a person enjoying the Community right of free movement, as defined in Article 2(5) of the Schengen Borders Code." Article 3(2) provides that: "'illegal stay' means the presence on the territory of a Member State, of a third-country national who does not fulfil, or no longer fulfils the conditions of entry as set

has wide application, covering not only migrants who have entered irregularly, but also those who may have entered through regular channels but whose right to remain in the country has ended or been withdrawn. There is however an important caveat that will operate to exclude many smuggled migrants from the operation of the Directive. This comes in the form of a provision that permits *but does not require* Member States to exclude application of the Directive to third-country nationals who are refused entry at border points, or who are apprehended or intercepted in connection with irregular crossing by land, sea, or air of the external border of a Member State and who have not subsequently obtained an authorization or a right to stay in the Member State.[210] Finalization of this provision was one of the most difficult aspects of the drafting process for the Directive. The European Parliament and the Commission had proposed that exclusion should only be permitted in respect of those who were refused entry at the border or in a transit zone respectively.[211] However, Member States wished the exclusion to be able to cover those who enter a State's territory illegally and are apprehended within a short time of the crossing,[212] and thus the broader exclusion was ultimately adopted.[213]

Although the precise scope of the exclusion remains to be clarified, it evidently has the intention of and potential to significantly reduce the range of irregular migrants to come within its ambit. On a broad reading, this exclusion could mean that, in practice, EU Member States only apply the Directive to the return of irregular migrants who have already entered and have settled to an extent in the country, and not to those smuggled and other irregular migrants apprehended at border points. This would significantly limit the scope of the harmonization achieved through this Directive and would appear to undercut the apparent purpose of the drafters. However advocates of a narrower interpretation have argued that the phrase "in connection with irregular crossing" requires that the exclusion apply only where a person is stopped at or near the border, and not later.[214]

out in Article 5 of the Schengen Borders Code or other conditions for entry, stay or residence in that Member State."

210 Ibid. at Art. 2(2)(a). Note that third-country nationals who are subject to return as a criminal law sanction or as a consequence of a criminal law sanction or who are the subject of extradition procedures are also excluded from the operation of the Directive. Ibid. at Art. 2(2)(b).

211 S. Peers, "Statewatch Analysis: The Proposed EU Returns Directive," Jan. 2008, available at www.statewatch.org/analyses/eu-ret-dir-sp.pdf (accessed May 12, 2013), at 2.

212 A. Baldaccini, "The Return and Removal of Irregular Migrants under EU Law: An Analysis of the Returns Directive" (2009) 11 *European Journal of Migration and Law* 1, at 3 [Baldaccini, "The Return and Removal of Irregular Migrants under EU Law"].

213 See discussion in European Council on Refugees and Exiles, ECRE Information note on the Directive 2008/115/EC of the European Parliament and of the Council of 16 December 2008 on common standards and procedures in Member States for returning illegally staying third-country nationals, Doc. CO7/1/2009/Ext/MDM, Jan. 7, 2009, at 7–9.

214 S. Peers, E. Guild, D. Acosta Arcarazo, and K. Groenendijk and V. Moreno-Lax eds., *EU Immigration and Asylum Law: Text and Commentary*, Volume 2: EU Immigration Law (2nd ed. 2012), at 491; and Baldaccini, "The Return and Removal of Irregular Migrants under EU Law," at 3.

EU Member States that decide to exclude certain third-country nationals from the scope of the Directive on the basis of Article 2(2)(a)[215] are nevertheless required to grant such persons certain basic rights and protections. Specifically, Member States are required to ensure their treatment is "no less favourable" than standards set out in the following Articles: Article 8(4) and (5), requiring that forced removal be "proportionate and not exceed reasonable force," with due respect for the dignity and physical integrity of the third-country national concerned; Article 9(2)(a), postponement of forced removal due to physical state or mental capacity; Article 14(1)(b), requiring provision of emergency health-care and essential treatment of illness (when removal is voluntary or postponed because of physical state or mental capacity); Article 16, specifying basic conditions of detention; and Article 17, providing additional protections for children and families. Member States are further explicitly required to respect the principle of *non-refoulement* in relation to all such persons.[216] The EU Returns Directive is considered further in Sections 10.4.1 and 10.4.2.2 in the context of due process obligations as well as pre-return detention. Importantly, States are required to "provide for an effective forced-return monitoring system."[217] A 2011 Report indicated that implementation of this provision is incomplete, most particularly in those countries with very high numbers of forced returns, including Italy, Greece, and the United Kingdom.[218]

10.4.1. Due Process Obligations under International Human Rights Law

With certain narrow exceptions, due process obligations attached to return are reserved for aliens "lawfully present." As discussed at Section 10.2.1.1 in the context of arbitrary expulsion, many smuggled migrants will not fall into this category, unless their legal status is recognized or regularized in some way. Barring a potential exception on the grounds of "compelling reasons of national security,"[219] international law requires that the following due process rights be afforded to persons lawfully present in order to render their return nonarbitrary[220]:

[215] "2. Member States may decide not to apply this Directive to third-country nationals who: (a) are subject to a refusal of entry in accordance with Article 13 of the Schengen Borders Code, or who are apprehended or intercepted by the competent authorities in connection with the irregular crossing by land, sea or air of the external border of a Member State and who have not subsequently obtained an authorisation or a right to stay in that Member State."

[216] EU Returns Directive, at Art. 4(4)(b).

[217] Ibid. at Art. 8(6).

[218] International Centre for Migration Policy and Development and European Council and Matrix, *Comparative Study for Best Practices in Forced Return Monitoring*, European Commission Directorate-General Justice, Freedom and Security, JLS/2009/RFXX/CA/1001, Nov. 10, 2011, at 43.

[219] With regard to the "national security" and "public order" exceptions, see notes 38–44 and accompanying text above.

[220] ICCPR, at Art. 13.

- Right to submit reasons: aliens lawfully present have a right, under the ICCPR, "to submit the reasons against [their] expulsion."[221] This does not amount to a right to challenge the expulsion, or indeed to a hearing in which the reasons submitted are examined.
- Right to challenge an expulsion order: aliens subject to an expulsion order have a right to appeal that decision to a higher authority. This requires States to suspend an expulsion pending the outcome of an appeal unless there are compelling reasons of national security to do otherwise.[222]
- Right of an alien to be allowed to leave for any country: as Nowak observes, the sovereign right of States to expel aliens does not necessarily include the right to decide where the person concerned is to be sent.[223] The Human Rights Committee has affirmed that an alien subject to expulsion must normally be allowed to leave for any country willing to accept him or her.[224] Subject to restrictions such as the obligation of *non-refoulement*, an alien who is not accepted by another country may be deported to the home country (or country of origin).

The International Court of Justice, in the *Ahmadou Sadio Diallo* case, confirmed the application of procedural rights to "measures which deprive individuals of their liberty that are taken in the context of an administrative procedure, such as those which may be necessary in order to effect the forcible removal of an alien from the national territory."[225] The Court noted that: "in this latter case, it is of little importance whether the measure in question is characterized by domestic law as an 'expulsion' or a '*refoulement*.'"[226] The judgment affirmed the relevant procedural rights as including a right of aliens detained pending expulsion to be informed of the reasons for their arrest and an obligation to provide grounds for the expulsion.[227] It should be noted that this aspect of the case concerned an alleged violation of Article 9 of the ICCPR and thereby an entitlement of an alien "lawfully present." However, it is clear that other restrictions on expulsion may operate to trigger a requirement for due process rights to be observed, even in respect of persons who do not satisfy the "lawfully present" requirement. For example, the International Law Commission has identified a right of States to expel, concomitantly, the members of a group of

221 Ibid.
222 Nowak, *CCPR Commentary*, at 299.
223 Ibid. at 296.
224 HRC General Comment No. 15, at para. 9.
225 Ahmadou Sadio Diallo Case, at para. 27.
226 Ibid.
227 Ibid. For an analysis of these aspects of the judgment, see International Law Commission, "Seventh report on the expulsion of aliens, by Mr. Maurice Kamto, Special Rapporteur," UN Doc. A/CN.4/642, May 4, 2011, esp. at paras. 23–27.

aliens, provided they make "a reasonable and objective examination of the particular case of each individual member of the group."[228] In the absence of such individualized assessment, the expulsion would be considered part of a "mass expulsion" and thereby unlawful.

While explicitly excluding those who have arrived at or crossed a border without authorization, the EU Returns Directive extends application of due process rights to persons who are within the European Union without authorization. In this sense, the Directive can be seen to advance the due process entitlements of irregular migrants beyond that provided for within the strict confines of existing international treaty law. EU Member States are required to ensure that return decisions and re-entry bans[229] are issued in writing and that information about available legal remedies is made available.[230] EU Member States are also required to provide an effective remedy to appeal against, or seek review of decisions related to return before a competent judicial authority or an "administrative authority or a competent body composed of members who are impartial and who enjoy safeguards of independence."[231] That authority or body must have the power to review decisions related to return, including the power to temporarily suspend their enforcement.[232] Implementing States are further required to take due account, not only of the principle of *non-refoulement*, but also the best interests of the child, family life, and the "state of health of the third-country national concerned."[233]

Can smuggled migrants, who are not "lawfully present" in the ICCPR sense, or within the coverage of the EU Returns Directive discussed previously, be summarily returned without access to any of these important due process rights? International human rights treaty law as well as regional law on returns provides little room for ascribing due process entitlements in this way. However, it is certainly possible to argue that a failure to provide basic due process to smuggled migrants who are being returned – such as the ability to have a decision reviewed – may operate to violate (or contribute to a violation of) other rights to which they are entitled, such as the right to be treated with humanity and dignity[234] and the right to family unity.[235] The right to health, the prohibition on discrimination, and the rights of the child (considered at Section 10.5.2) may also operate in a way as to render due process rights applicable to certain individuals or groups who have been smuggled.

[228] ILC Draft Articles on Expulsion of Aliens, at Draft Article 10.
[229] See further Section 10.4.4.
[230] EU Returns Directive, at Art. 12(1).
[231] Ibid. at Art. 13(1).
[232] Ibid. at Art. 13(2).
[233] Ibid. at Art. 5.
[234] As required by the ICCPR, at Art. 10(1).
[235] See Chapter 2, notes 286–290 and accompanying text ("Protection of family and private life").

This appears to be the position adopted by the International Law Commission, which makes no immediate distinction between aliens lawfully present and unauthorized aliens in its identification of procedural rights that attach to all aliens subject to expulsion. The ILC Draft Articles on Expulsion of Aliens provide that an alien subject to expulsion enjoys the following procedural rights:

- Right to receive notice of the expulsion decision;
- Right to challenge the expulsion decision;
- Right to be heard by a competent authority;
- Right of access to effective remedies to challenge the expulsion decision;
- Right to be represented before a competent authority;
- Right to have free assistance of an interpreter if he or she cannot understand or speak the language of the competent authority;
- Right to seek consular assistance.[236]

The provision contains an important caveat, echoing the EU Returns Directive concern with excluding immediate and very recent arrivals. The caveat is in the form of a "without prejudice" clause that preserves the right of States to legislate (presumably to exclude such procedural rights) "concerning the expulsion of aliens who have been unlawfully present in its territory for less than six months."[237] Although the ILC's scope of inclusion is considerably wider than international treaty law, it falls short of the EU Returns Directive, which excludes only those who are refused entry at the border or who enter a State's territory illegally and are apprehended within a short time of crossing the border. In its current draft form, it also represents a rejection of the view, expressed by some members of the drafting committee, that "a minimum core of procedural rights should apply to all aliens without any exception."[238] While international treaty law and the work of the International Law Commission point to a more conservative interpretation of the scope of the relevant obligation, there is some soft law support for an extension of procedural rights to all persons who are being returned against their will, either to their country of origin

[236] ILC Draft Articles on Expulsion of Aliens, at Draft Article 26.

[237] Ibid. at Draft Article 26(4).

[238] International Law Commission, "Expulsion of Aliens: Statement of the Chairman of the Drafting Committee, Mr. Mahmoud D. Hmoud," May 29, 2012, at 31. Members of the drafting committee further suggested that the alien's level of integration at various levels (social, economic, professional, or family) could also be taken into account in considering the extent to which the expelling State is required to grant certain procedural rights, during the expulsion process, to aliens unlawfully present in its territory. The Chairperson explained: "[t]he Drafting Committee considered, however, that a criterion referring to the level of integration of the alien concerned would have been difficult to implement, and therefore opted for an objective time-limit relating to the duration of the alien's presence in the territory of the expelling State. In this connection, a period of six months was deemed reasonable, also considering that such a time limit was found, in connection with procedural rules governing the expulsion process, in the legislation of some States." Ibid. at 31–32.

or to a third country. The most important instrument in this regard is the Council of Europe's Twenty Guidelines on Forced Return. These Guidelines are explicit in promoting a view that elementary due process rights should be afforded to "all persons subject to an expulsion measure, whichever their administrative status ("lawful resident" or not) and whether or not the proposed removal order would contravene an individual's right under the European Convention on Human Rights."[239] The Guidelines advocate that any decision to return a person is made in accordance with an established legal process that is subject to review,[240] and that any such decision should have taken into full consideration whether the proposed return would violate the individual's human rights (in particular, the right to life; the right to be free from torture or other forms of cruel, inhuman, or degrading treatment or punishment).[241] They further provide that any removal order be made on the basis of a reasonable and objective examination of the particular facts of each person's case,[242] and provide for all returning migrants the right to be are given, in a language they can understand, a copy of the removal order and any information about available review processes.[243] States are enjoined to ensure that effective remedies against the removal order are available.[244]

10.4.2. *Pre-return Detention*

For many smuggled migrants, the process of their return includes a period of detention. In an increasing number of countries, such detention is explicitly or effectively mandatory following the issuing of an expulsion order. Typically, pre-return detention is aimed at preventing the migrant from absconding prior to being returned and/or otherwise facilitating the return process. The rules set out in Chapter 9, including those attached to the prohibition on arbitrary detention, are applicable to detention that occurs in the context of return. This includes situations where it becomes no longer possible to return a person to his or her country of origin, either because of security concerns or because their country of nationality is unable or unwilling to accept them.[245] The present section does not repeat or summarize the analysis contained in Chapter 9, but focuses solely on matters that arise specifically

[239] Council of Europe, *Twenty Guidelines on Forced Return*, at 13.

[240] Ibid. at Guideline 2 (further noting that this will ensure the avoidance of arbitrariness in the decision-making process and thereby provide an essential guarantee against the risk of discrimination in the enjoyment of human rights).

[241] Ibid.

[242] Ibid. at Guideline 3.

[243] Ibid. at Guideline 4.

[244] Ibid. at Guideline 5.

[245] See further Chapter 9, esp. at Section 9.2.3.4.

in the context of pre-return detention and sources of law that are most relevant to this particular issue.

10.4.2.1. Detention in Situations Where Expulsion Cannot Be Carried Out

The period of pre-return detention is a dangerous one for smuggled migrants and their rights. As the UN Working Group on Arbitrary Detention has observed: "some national laws do not provide for detention to be ordered by a judge, or for judicial review of the detention order. Detainees often do not enjoy the right to challenge the legality of their detention. There is no maximum length of detention established by law, which leads to prolonged or, in the worst case, potentially indefinite detention in cases, for example, where the expulsion of a migrant cannot be carried out for legal or practical reasons."[246] This latter issue, detention where a removal order cannot be executed, is especially problematic. Such a situation may arise when transport to effect the removal is simply not available. It may also be the result of a bilateral cooperation failure that leads to a situation in which documentation to allow return is delayed or not issued at all. One report noted that some countries of origin sometimes refuse to admit their own citizens because of uncertainty about the person's identity.[247] Where the obstacle to removal does not lie within the detained migrant's sphere of responsibility, the Working Group has argued that the detainee should be released in order to avoid potentially indefinite detention from occurring, which would be arbitrary: "The principle of proportionality requires that detention always has a legitimate aim, which would not exist if there were no longer a real and tangible prospect of removal."[248] The International Law Commission has also recognized the importance of States' ending detention "when the expulsion cannot be carried out, except where the reasons are attributable to the alien concerned."[249]

A related issue of concern is the detention of stateless smuggled migrants. By definition, such persons do not have a country of origin to which they can be returned.[250] Many stateless persons risk prolonged detention while States of destination seek to identify a country willing to accept them – or even indefinite detention where such

[246] UN Human Rights Council, "Report of the Working Group on Arbitrary Detention," UN Doc. A/HRC/13/30, Jan. 18, 2010, at para. 62. See also A. Siskin, *Immigration-Related Detention: Current Legislative Issues* (Congressional Research Service Report for Congress, Jan. 12, 2012), at 6–8.

[247] See European Migration Network, "Programs and Strategies in the EU Member States Fostering Assisted Return to and Reintegration in Third Countries," (Synthesis Report summarizing the main findings of the National Reports for the European Migration Network, Mar. 2011), at 58.

[248] UN Human Rights Council, "Report of the Working Group on Arbitrary Detention," UN Doc. A/HRC/13/30, Jan. 18, 2010, at para. 91.

[249] ILC Draft Articles on Expulsion of Aliens, at Draft Article 19(3)(b).

[250] Generally on statelessness in international law, see Chapter 2 at Section 2.1.2.

efforts are not made or prove futile.[251] The rationale advanced previously, that detention lacking a legitimate aim is unlawful, is relevant in such cases. UNHCR has developed criteria to review the detention of stateless persons in order to determine whether it is discriminatory; undermines the right to liberty; is arbitrary; or amounts to cruel, inhuman, or degrading treatment. Relevant questions include whether the stateless persons are being detained on grounds of irregular residence or lack of identity documents, whether they are detained for prolonged periods solely because they cannot be returned to their country of habitual residence, and whether there are legally prescribed time limits for administrative detention.[252]

10.4.2.2. International Guidance on Pre-return Detention

There is scant direct treaty law on the subject of pre-return detention. The Migrant Smuggling Protocol's provisions on return are silent on the issue. The EU Returns Directive is the only instrument to pronounce explicitly on "detention for the purposes of removal."[253] It establishes that detention can only be used in the returns process if "other sufficient but less coercive measures" cannot be applied effectively in the particular case, and the subject of the return procedure presents either a risk of absconding, or is avoiding or hampering the returns process.[254] In this and other respects (e.g., in relation to determining *who* is to be removed), the provision preserves considerable discretion of the returning State and, in relation to persons who are being forcibly removed, is highly unlikely to support the emergence of a general rule establishing pre-return detention as a measure of last resort. Under the terms of the Directive pre-return detention is to be "for as short a period as possible and only maintained as long as removal arrangements are in progress and executed with due diligence,"[255] and is subject to time limits, and a range of substantive and procedural guarantees.[256]

[251] See review of State practice in The Equal Rights Trust, *Unravelling Anomaly: Detention, Discrimination and the Protection Needs of Stateless Persons* (2010), esp. at chapter 4.

[252] UN High Commissioner for Refugees, Statelessness: An Analytical Framework for Prevention, Reduction and Protection (2008), at 29–30.

[253] EU Returns Directive, at Preambular para. 16; Chapter IV.

[254] Ibid. at Art. 15(1).

[255] Ibid.

[256] Ibid. at Art. 15 ("2. Detention shall be ordered by administrative or judicial authorities. Detention shall be ordered in writing with reasons being given in fact and in law. When detention has been ordered by administrative authorities, Member States shall: (a) either provide for a speedy judicial review of the lawfulness of detention to be decided on as speedily as possible from the beginning of detention; (b) or grant the third-country national concerned the right to take proceedings by means of which the lawfulness of detention shall be subject to a speedy judicial review to be decided on as speedily as possible after the launch of he relevant proceedings. In such a case Member States shall immediately inform the third-country national concerned about the possibility of taking such

Little notice appears to have been taken of the fact that the relevance of these provisions for many smuggled migrants is seriously compromised by the Directive's scope of operation, which allows States to exclude third-country nationals who are subject to a refusal of entry or who are apprehended or intercepted in connection with the irregular crossing by land, sea, or air of the external border and who have not subsequently obtained an authorization or a right to stay in that Member State.[257] In other words, the detention of smuggled migrants intercepted before or shortly after an unauthorized arrival does *not* need to meet the test of being the only available effective measure against a migrant who may seek to avoid the return process. It does *not* need to be "for as short a period as possible" or "executed with due diligence," and it is *not* subjected to time limits or other specified procedural protections.

For this excluded group, which will include all smuggled migrants intercepted during or at the completion of their journey, the Directive's provisions on conditions of detention are preserved, including the requirement that detention shall only take place in a "specialized detention facility," with detainees kept separate from ordinary prisoners.[258] The Directive further provides that detainees shall be allowed to establish contact with legal representatives, family, and competent consular authorities, and provided information about the rules of the facility, and their rights and obligations.[259] Excluded third-country nationals in situations of pre-return detention also benefit from the requirement that States pay particular attention to the situation of vulnerable persons, including through the provision of emergency healthcare and essential treatment of illness,[260] as well as the following special protections for detained minors and their families:

proceedings. The third-country national concerned shall be released immediately if the detention is not lawful. 3. In every case, detention shall be reviewed at reasonable intervals of time either on application by the third-country national concerned or *ex officio*. In the case of prolonged detention periods, reviews shall be subject to the supervision of a judicial authority. 4. When it appears that a reasonable prospect of removal no longer exists for legal or other considerations or the conditions laid down in paragraph 1 no longer exist, detention ceases to be justified and the person concerned shall be released immediately. 5. Detention shall be maintained for as long a period as the conditions laid down in paragraph 1 are fulfilled and it is necessary to ensure successful removal. Each Member State shall set a limited period of detention, which may not exceed six months. 6. Member States may not extend the period referred to in paragraph 5 except for a limited period not exceeding a further twelve months in accordance with national law in cases where regardless of all their reasonable efforts the removal operation is likely to last longer owing to: (a) a lack of cooperation by the third-country national concerned, or (b) delays in obtaining the necessary documentation from third countries").

257 Ibid. at Art. 2(2)(a). Note that third-country nationals who are subject to return as a criminal law sanction or as a consequence of a criminal law sanction or who are the subject of extradition procedures are also excluded from the operation of the Directive. Ibid. at Art 2(2)(b).

258 Ibid. at Art. 16(1).

259 Ibid. at Arts. 16(2), 16(4)–16(5).

260 Ibid. at Art. 16(3).

- Unaccompanied minors and families with minors shall only be detained as a measure of last resort and for the shortest appropriate period of time.
- Families detained pending removal shall be provided with separate accommodation guaranteeing adequate privacy.
- Minors in detention shall have the possibility to engage in leisure activities, including play and recreational activities appropriate to their age, and shall have, depending on the length of their stay, access to education.
- Unaccompanied minors shall as far as possible be provided with accommodation in institutions provided with personnel and facilities that take into account the needs of persons of their age.
- The best interests of the child shall be a primary consideration in the context of the detention of minors pending removal.

The Directive's provisions on detention, most particularly its imposition of a maximum period of pre-return detention of six months (and up to twelve additional months in special circumstances),[261] have been subject to intense criticism by United Nations bodies,[262] nongovernmental organizations,[263] and commentators.[264] There appears to be general consensus across these different groups that the maximum period of allowable detention is excessive and that the provisions have contributed to a dangerous normalization of immigration detention.

261 Ibid. at Arts. 15(5)–15(6).

262 In a joint letter to the Presidency of the Council of the European Union, ten independent human rights experts of the Special Procedures of the United Nations Human Rights Council identified, as their major concern, "the detention regime pending removal procedures for irregular immigrants." In assessing the envisaged detention periods of up to eighteen months as excessive, the group affirmed its common position that "irregular immigrants are not criminals. As a rule they should not be subjected to detention at all. Member States are obliged to explore the availability of alternatives to detention and detention must only be for the shortest possible period of time": cited in UN Office of the High Commissioner for Human Rights, Press Release, "UN Experts Express Concern about Proposed EU Return Directive" (July 18, 2008), available at www.ohchr.org/en/NewsEvents/Pages/DisplayNews.aspx?NewsID=8440&LangID=E (accessed May 12, 2013).

263 For example, Amnesty International has expressed concern about the failure of the EU Returns Directive to guarantee the return of irregular migrants in safety and dignity, noting particularly the "excessive period of detention." Amnesty International, "EU Return Directive Affects Dignity and Security of Irregular Migrants," July 4, 2008, available at www.amnesty.org/en/news-and-updates/EU-return-directive-affects-dignity-security-irregular-migrants-20080704 (accessed May 12, 2013). See also Amnesty International and European Council on Refugees and Exiles, Press Release, "'Returns' Directive: European Parliament and Member States Risk Compromising Respect for Migrants' Rights," May 20, 2008, available at www.ecre.org/component/downloads/downloads/164.html (accessed May 12, 2013).

264 See, for example, Baldaccini, "The Return and Removal of Irregular Migrants under EU Law." For a review of the detention and other provisions of the Directive from a gender perspective, see H. Askola, "Illegal Migrants, Gender and Vulnerability: The Case of the EU's Returns Directive" (2010) 18 *Feminist Legal Studies* 159.

Case law around the EU Returns Directive was examined in Chapter 9[265] and need only be summarized at this point. Briefly, in the *El Dridi* case, the Court of Justice of the European Union affirmed the principle of proportionality as requiring that the detention of a person subject to deportation should not continue for an unreasonable length of time.[266] The Court further held that the Directive, most particularly Articles 15 (detention) and 16 (conditions of detention) "must be interpreted as precluding … legislation … which provides for a sentence of imprisonment to be imposed on an illegally staying third-country national on the sole ground that he remains, without valid grounds, on the territory of that State, contrary to an order to leave that territory within a given period."[267] "[This] does not preclude the possibility for the Member States to adopt, with respect for the principles and objective of Directive 2008/115, provisions regulating the situation in which coercive measures have not resulted in the removal of a third-country national staying illegally on their territory."[268] In a subsequent case the Court affirmed that a return decision must be issued immediately when an irregular immigrant is identified as such and the procedure leading to return must commence immediately thereafter. EU Member States may not use custodial sentences to postpone adoption of a decision on return and thereby delay the application of the Return Directive.

The ILC Draft Articles on Expulsion of Aliens implicitly recognize a right of States to engage in pre-return detention but specify conditions that should regulate the detention of any alien subject to expulsion. These include:

- Detention not to be punitive in nature;
- Aliens subject to expulsion to be detained separately from convicted persons;
- Duration of detention not to be unrestricted but "limited to such period of time as is reasonably necessary for expulsion to be carried out";
- Extension of detention to be decided upon only by a court or authorized judicial officer;
- Detention to be reviewed at regular intervals on the basis of specific criteria established by law.[269]

Available legal analysis of the issue confirms that in terms of generally applicable rules, pre-return detention of aliens subject to expulsion does not occupy a separate legal space from other forms of detention.[270] States are thereby required to

265 See Chapter 9, at Section 9.2.4.
266 *El Dridi v. Italy* (Court of Justice of the European Union, C-61/11 PPU, Apr. 28, 2011), at para. 43.
267 Ibid. at para. 62.
268 Ibid. at para. 60.
269 ILC Draft Articles on Expulsion of Aliens, at Draft Article 19.
270 See, for example, European Union Agency for Fundamental Rights, *Detention of Third-Country Nationals in Return Procedures* (Thematic Report, Sept. 2010).

ensure that such detention conforms to the legal framework applicable to detention of aliens as this has been set out in the previous chapter.

10.4.3. *Safety and Dignity in the Return Process*

As the Council of Europe and others have noted, voluntary return is to be preferred over forced return, not least because "it presents far fewer risks with respect to human rights."[271] Experience with forced returns has confirmed the existence of such risks, for example the use of disproportionate force in the return process that can rise to the level of torture or cruel, inhuman, or degrading treatment.[272] The terminology used by different instruments and actors is not always clear, and there are frequent misunderstandings about what is, in fact, "voluntary."[273] However, there does appear to be agreement that, in order for return to be truly voluntary, the returnees must be fully informed, not only of the possibilities for their return, but also of the possibilities for their staying in the destination country or a third country.[274] The return should also be *genuinely* voluntary, "based on the decision of the

[271] See Council of Europe, *Twenty Guidelines on Forced Return*, at 11 ("Voluntary return is preferable to forced return, and it presents far fewer risks with respect to human rights. Therefore it is recommended to host states to promote voluntary return, in particular by affording the returnee a reasonable time for complying voluntarily with the removal order, by offering practical assistance such as incentives or meeting the transport costs, by providing complete information to the returnee, in a language he/she can understand, about the existing programmes of voluntary return, in particular those of the International Organization for Migration (IOM) and other similar organisations, which the host states have been encouraged to set up and to develop ..."). See also EU Returns Directive, at Preambular para. 10 ("Where there are no reasons to believe that this would undermine the purpose of a return procedure, voluntary return should be preferred over forced return and a period for voluntary departure should be granted. An extension of the period for voluntary departure should be provided for when considered necessary because of the specific circumstances of an individual case. In order to promote voluntary return, Member States should provide for enhanced return assistance and counselling and make best use of the relevant funding possibilities offered under the European Return Fund").

[272] See, for example, Council of Europe, European Committee for the Prevention of Torture and Inhuman or Degrading Treatment or Punishment (CPT), "13th General Report on the CPT's activities covering the period 1 January 2002 to 31 July 2003," Doc. CPT/Inf (2003) 35, Sept. 10, 2003, at para. 31; *Agiza v. Sweden*, UNCAT Comm. No. 233/2003, UN Doc. CAT/C/34/D/233/2003, May 24, 2005, decided May 20, 2005. See further citations at note 281 below.

[273] See European Migration Network, "Programs and Strategies in the EU Member States Fostering Assisted Return to and Reintegration in Third Countries," (Synthesis Report summarizing the main findings of the National Reports for the European Migration Network, Mar. 2011), at 15.

[274] Both UNHCR and the European Union have highlighted the importance of informed consent as an essential aspect of a genuinely voluntary decision regarding return. See UN High Commissioner for Refugees, *Handbook on Voluntary Repatriation: International Protection* (1996), at 4.2; and Council of the European Union, Press Release, 2683rd Council Meeting, Justice and Home Affairs, Doc. 12645/05 (Presse 247), Oct. 12, 2005, at 23.

returnee and without use of coercive measures."[275] The Council of the European Union has recommended that information on the possibility of voluntary return should be made readily available and as early as possible. Such action may include the provision of pre-return information and counseling, including with respect to the conditions and circumstances in the country of return.[276] In the case of a child, both the child and the child's guardian should be fully informed and consulted.[277] States that are claiming to return smuggled migrants voluntarily should ensure that these basic standards are followed.

In practice however, the return of smuggled migrants will almost inevitably be *involuntary*, in the sense that the migrant does not wish to leave the country of destination but is being compelled to do so. Although such returns may be described, particularly by returning States, as "voluntary," their essentially coercive nature means that the risks referred to previously will often be present. For this reason, the issue of safety and dignity in return, explicitly articulated in the Migrant Smuggling Protocol,[278] becomes of paramount importance. That provision requires States Parties involved in the return of a smuggled migrant to "take all appropriate measures to carry out the return in an orderly manner and with due regard for the safety and dignity of the person." This general requirement should be interpreted with reference to international human rights law. Chapter 2 provided an overview of the rights to which all persons, including smuggled migrants, are entitled, and Chapter 3 considered the question of extraterritorial application of a State's human

[275] Commission of the European Communities, Green Paper on a Community Return Policy on Illegal Residents, COM(2002) 175 final, Apr. 10, 2002, at 26, cited in International Organization for Migration, *Compilation of Best Practice in Return Management in Selected EU Countries and Romania* (2005), at 25. In relation to the detention and "assisted voluntary return" of some asylum-seekers on Manus Island, Papua New Guinea, see *UNHCR Monitoring Visit to Manus Island, Papua New Guinea*, at paras. 116–117 (noting the existence of a "pervasive climate" that places emphasis on return. Relevant factors cited in the report included the harsh conditions of detention, uncertainty around processing, and response of officials to complaints about living conditions).

[276] Council of the European Union, Press Release, 2683rd Council Meeting, Justice and Home Affairs, Doc. 12645/05 (Presse 247), Oct. 12, 2005, at 24; and Matrix Insight Ltd, International Centre for Migration Policy and Development and European Council on Refugees and Exiles, European Commission Directorate-General Home Affairs Comparative Study on Best Practice to Interlink Pre-Departure Reintegration Measures carried out in Member States with Short- and Long-Term Reintegration Measures in the Countries of Return, Doc. No. JLS/2009/RF?CA/1003, Jan. 17, 2012, at 15.

[277] European Council on Refugees and Exiles and Save the Children, European Commission Directorate-General Home Comparative Study on Practices in the Field of Return of Minors, Doc. HOME/2009/RFXX/PR/1002, Dec. 2011, at 138, 151.

[278] Migrant Smuggling Protocol, at Art. 18(5).

rights obligations. That analysis supports the following points of direct relevance to the present discussion:

- The basic rights to which smuggled migrants are entitled are not affected by their circumstances or legal status. The returning State will be responsible for any violations of the right to life, the right to dignity and security of the person, and the prohibition on torture or inhuman or degrading treatment or punishment occasioned by that expulsion.[279]
- The location of the smuggled migrant at the point of return is not relevant to the nature of the obligation owed to that person by the returning State provided that State is exercising "effective control" over the return. Any violations occasioned in a return conducted through a third party (such as a private security contractor) will be attributable to the returning State.[280]

The use of excessive force in the conduct of returns has been widely documented.[281] In relation to this issue reference is made to the detailed analysis of relevant law and jurisprudence in Chapter 2.[282] This analysis confirmed the application of the prohibition on torture and cruel, inhuman, or degrading treatment or punishment to all States in respect of all stages and circumstances of return. It further confirmed that physical assault used "as a form of persuasion to board a means of transport or as a punishment for not having done so"[283] is unlawful. The European Committee for the Prevention of Torture has examined the deportation practices of European States, including conduct during preparation for departure and during the transportation itself, and has found that deportation operations by air "entail a manifest risk of inhuman and degrading treatment."[284] In particular, the Committee stated that such risk is inherent in the use of a number of individual means or methods of restraint, and is greater when such means or methods are used in combination.

[279] See further Chapter 2, at Sections 2.3.1 and 2.4.1.

[280] See further Chapter 3, at Section 3.4.

[281] See, for example, Human Rights Watch, *Pushed Back, Pushed Around Italy's Forced Return of Boat Migrants and Asylum Seekers, Libya's Mistreatment of Migrants and Asylum Seekers* (2009) (alleging beatings and use of electric shocks by Italian officials to force interdicted migrants authorities to board a Libyan vessel (at 12)). See further Council of Europe, "Report to the Italian Government on the visit to Italy carried out by the European Committee for the Prevention of Torture and Inhuman or Degrading Treatment or Punishment (CPT) from 27 to 31 July 2009," Doc. CPT/Inf (2010) 14, Apr. 28, 2010.

[282] See further Chapter 2, at Section 2.4.4.

[283] European Committee for the Prevention of Torture and Inhuman or Degrading Treatment or Punishment (CPT), "CPT Standards," Doc. CPT/Inf/E (2002) 1 – Rev. 2011, Dec. 2011, at 78 (para. 32).

[284] Ibid. at 78 (para. 31).

In this regard, the Committee has recommended that the use of force or restraint capable of causing positional asphyxia (i.e., by compression of the rib cage) should be avoided where possible, and that there be an absolute ban on use of means that obstruct the airways (nose or mouth, by tape or other means) wholly or partially.[285]

The EU Returns Directive contains a number of provisions relevant to the issue of safe and dignified returns. It anticipates the use of coercive measures in forced returns, authorizing Member States to take "all necessary measures to enforce the return decision" where either no period for voluntary departure is provided for, or that period has expired.[286] It further requires that:

> Where Member States use – as a last resort – coercive measures to carry out the removal of a third country national who resists removal, such measures shall be proportionate and shall not exceed reasonable force. They shall be implemented as provided for in national legislation in accordance with fundamental rights and with due respect for the dignity and physical integrity of the third-country national concerned.[287]

Third-country nationals who are excluded by Member States from the Directive (those who are subject to a refusal of entry or who are apprehended or intercepted in connection with the irregular crossing) are nevertheless granted certain basic protections in relation to coercive return. These include the requirement cited previously that States Parties ensure any force used in removal shall be "proportionate and not exceed reasonable force," and be undertaken "with due respect for the dignity and physical integrity" of the persons concerned.[288]

Soft law instruments provide some additional guidance on the weight and substantive content of the obligation to ensure that smuggled migrants are returned safely and with dignity. The ILC Draft Articles on Expulsion of Aliens states that "[all] aliens subject to expulsion shall be treated with humanity and with respect for the inherent dignity of the human person at all stages of the expulsion process" as well

285 Ibid. at 78–79 (paras. 34–36). The only European Court case to consider use of force in deportation did not consider force in the course of transportation, but rather use of force during arrest for deportation. See *Shchukin and others v. Cyprus*, [2010] ECHR 1210 (ECHR, July 29, 2010). In this case, a Ukrainian national alleged he had been punched, kicked, and forced to the ground by Cypriot police after being given orders for deportation. The Cypriot government denied any ill-treatment of Mr. Shchukin, and said that the police had been required to use force to arrest him because he had attacked and injured the arresting police officers. The Court in its finding noted the circumstances in which Mr. Shchukin violently resisted arrest and the police officers were injured, and subsequently found that the use of force against him was not so excessive or so extensive as to reach the threshold of treatment contrary to Article 3 of the European Convention on Human Rights.

286 EU Returns Directive, at Art. 8(1).

287 Ibid. at Art. 8(4).

288 Ibid. applicable to excluded third-country nationals through Article 4(4)(a).

as to "respect for their human rights."[289] In particular, States are to protect the right to life of an alien subject to expulsion,[290] and shall not subject an alien subject to expulsion to torture or to cruel, inhuman, or degrading treatment or punishment.[291] The Draft Articles also recognize an obligation on expelling States to provide special protections to vulnerable persons,[292] and to respect the right to family life.[293] Although voluntary departure should be facilitated, in cases of forced departure "the expelling State shall take the necessary measures to ensure, as far as possible, the safe transportation to the State of destination, of the alien subject to expulsion, in accordance with the rules of international law."[294]

The Council of Europe's Twenty Guidelines on Forced Return emphasize the importance of seeking to ensure the cooperation of returnees at all stages of the return process, to avoid or reduce the need to use any force.[295] They further note the importance of ensuring that persons in pre-return detention are given notice in advance about the removal arrangements, and any information given to the State of return. The returnees should be given an opportunity to prepare for their return, including by making necessary contacts in their host State and State of return, and if necessary, to retrieve belongings that will facilitate return in dignity.[296] The Guidelines acknowledge that safety of the returnee and others is of critical importance: "While respecting the dignity of the returnee, the safety of the other passengers, of the crew members and of the returnee himself/herself shall be paramount in the removal process The removal of a returnee may have to be interrupted where its continuation would endanger this."[297] The Guidelines further propose that persons shall not be removed if they are medically unfit to travel, and that a medical examination should be performed prior to removal where the returnee has a known medical condition, or where the use of physical restraints is foreseen.[298] Use and means of restraints are also dealt with in Guideline 19, which only permits forms of restraint that are strictly proportionate to the actual or reasonably anticipated resistance of the returnee. In order to limit the use of force, it is recommended in Guideline 15 that States provide information to, and seek the cooperation of, returnees during the removal process.

289 ILC Draft Articles on Expulsion of Aliens, at Draft Article 14.
290 Ibid. at Draft Article 17.
291 Ibid. at Draft Article 18.
292 Ibid. at Draft Article 16.
293 Ibid. at Draft Article 20.
294 Ibid. at Draft Article 21.
295 Council of Europe, *Twenty Guidelines on Forced Return*, Guideline 15.
296 Ibid.
297 Ibid. Guideline 17.
298 Ibid. Guideline 16.

10.4.4. Re-entry Bans

The immigration laws of an increasing number of countries now provide for exclusion periods (or entry/re-entry bans) during which persons who have entered or stayed without authorization, or otherwise breached immigration law, are not permitted to re-enter the country, usually for a specified period.[299] Most schemes focus on those who are forcibly returned. However, a number of countries also include those who have returned voluntarily under assistance programs.[300] The scope of such bans inevitably extends to smuggled migrants who are intercepted prior to arrival or detected at the border.

The Migrant Smuggling Protocol does not address the issue of re-entry bans. At the regional level, the application of re-entry bans is established by the EU Returns Directive, which defines them as administrative or judicial decisions or acts prohibiting entry into and stay on the territory of the Member States for a specified period,

[299] In the United Kingdom for example, paragraph 320 of the Immigration Rules sets out the general grounds for refusing entry clearance or leave to enter the United Kingdom. Some of the grounds are mandatory; others are applied at the discretion of the Entry Clearance or Immigration Officer. One of the mandatory grounds for refusal is where a person has previously breached the United Kingdom's immigration law, by either using deception in an application (whether or not successfully) (paragraph 320(7B)(d)); being an illegal entrant (paragraph 320(7B)(c)); overstaying (paragraph 320(7B)(a)); or breaching a condition attached to leave (paragraph 320(7B)(b)). *Immigration Rules* (United Kingdom) as at January 2013. Following their departure from the United Kingdom, such persons are ineligible for permission to reenter the United Kingdom for between twelve months and ten years. The length of the re-entry ban depends on whether they leave the United Kingdom at public expense (e.g., through an Assisted Return), and whether their departure is voluntary or enforced by the UK Border Agency. Persons who use deception or have an enforced removal are subject to ten-year re-entry bans (see paragraph 320(7B)(i)–(vi)). See further United Kingdom Parliament, Immigration: re-entry bans for persons who breach immigration law – Commons Library Standard Note, Sept. 28, 2012, previously available at www.parliament.uk/briefing-papers/SN06020. "Unlawful non-citizens" who are "removed" from Australia (including smuggled migrants who are not subsequently recognized as refugees or falling within the official protection program) are excluded from being granted a visa to reenter Australia for a period of twelve months after they were last removed unless compelling or compassionate circumstances are considered to justify the non-application of this otherwise mandatory provision. See J. Vrachnas, M. Bagaric, P. Dimopoulos, and A. Pathinayak, *Migration and Refugee Law: Principles and Practice in Australia* (2011), at 161.

[300] In Germany, at points in time, re-entry bans have been imposed on deported persons. Under now superceded protocols, those who returned under the IOM Return Program were required to declare their intentions about returning, and those who did return in breach of their declaration could be required to repay monies received during the return (www.iom.int/germany/de/downloads/REAG/REAG-GARP%202012%20-%20Infoblatt%20englisch%20%28Stand%20Dezember%202011%29.pdf (page no longer available)). However the 2011 guidance no longer appears on the IOM website and the above statement does not appear to be the case in the 2013 information form, available at www.iom.int/germany/en/downloads/REAG/REAG-GARP%202013%20-%20Infoblatt%20Englisch.pdf (accessed May 12, 2013), which simply states that "[t]here should be no indications for a permanent return to the Federal Republic of Germany" (at paragraph D), and does not mention repayment, suggesting there may have been a change in policy.

accompanying a return decision.[301] The Directive stipulates that return decisions *must* be accompanied by an entry ban in two situations: (1) if no period for voluntary departure has been granted, or (2) if the obligation to return has not been complied with.[302] In other cases, the Member State retains discretion to decide whether return decisions are to be accompanied by an entry ban.[303] The length of the ban is similarly left up to the discretion of the Member State making the return decision "with due regard to all relevant circumstances of the individual case."[304] In principle the ban is not to exceed five years except if the third-country national represents a serious threat to public policy, public security, or national security.[305] Member States are to consider withdrawing or suspending an entry ban where an individual who is the subject of an entry ban can demonstrate that he or she has left the territory of a Member State in full compliance with a return decision.[306]

The Directive makes some limited exceptions for trafficked persons and for smuggled migrants who satisfy certain conditions.[307] In the case of smuggled migrants, it is unlikely that any but a very small number of persons would benefit from this provision.[308] Member States also retain a discretion to refrain from issuing, withdrawing, or suspending an entry ban in individual cases for humanitarian reasons and may withdraw or suspend an entry ban in individual cases or certain categories of cases for other reasons.[309] Refugees and persons in need of international protection would not be the subject of entry bans.[310] A Member State that is considering issuing an authorization to stay to a third-country national who is the subject of an entry ban

[301] EU Returns Directive, at Art. 3(6).

[302] Ibid. at Art. 11(1).

[303] Ibid.

[304] Ibid. at Art. 11(2).

[305] Ibid.

[306] Ibid. at Art. 11(3).

[307] Ibid. ("Victims of trafficking in human beings who have been granted a residence permit pursuant to Council Directive 2004/81/EC of 29 April 2004 on the residence permit issued to third-country nationals who are victims of trafficking in human beings or who have been the subject of an action to facilitate illegal immigration, who cooperate with the competent authorities (1) shall not be subject of an entry ban without prejudice to paragraph 1, first subparagraph, point (b), and provided that the third-country national concerned does not represent a threat to public policy, public security or national security").

[308] See discussion of Council Directive 2004/81/EC of 29 April 2004 on the residence permit issued to third-country nationals who are victims of trafficking in human beings or who have been the subject of an action to facilitate illegal immigration, who decide to cooperate with the competent authorities, OJ L 261, Aug. 6, 2004, in Chapter 1, at Section 1.3.1.2.

[309] EU Returns Directive, at Art. 11(3).

[310] Ibid. at Art. 11(5) ("[The Directive's provisions on entry bans] shall apply without prejudice to the right to international protection, as defined in Article 2(a) of Council Directive 2004/83/EC of 29 April 2004 on minimum standards for the qualification and status of third country nationals or stateless persons as refugees or as persons who otherwise need international protection and the content of the protection granted (3), in the Member States").

issued by another Member State, is required to consult that State and take its interests into account.

As with so many other aspects of the migrant smuggling response, the capacity of States to impose bans or exclusion periods on the return of smuggled migrants is based in their sovereign right to control entry into their territory. However, the many restrictions on that right that have been examined throughout this book also apply in this situation. For example, even with a ban in place, States would be obliged to respect the right of the individual involved to seek and receive asylum from persecution. Access to asylum procedures could not be obstructed for reasons related to the entry ban, and the granting of a favorable decision could not be permitted to depend on whether or not such a ban is in place. The prohibition on discrimination is also highly relevant. In prescribing those who are to be made subject to such a ban, and in implementing the ban itself, States are prevented from discriminating on any of the prohibited grounds including race and nationality or indeed, it can be strongly argued, on the basis of having been smuggled. Accordingly, a scheme that imposed re-entry bans on smuggled migrants only, or on migrants from one country but not another, would not meet international standards.

10.5. RETURN OF SPECIAL GROUPS OF SMUGGLED MIGRANTS: ADDITIONAL RIGHTS AND OBLIGATIONS

An examination of the relevant legal framework around return would not be complete without a brief consideration of the additional rights and obligations attached to certain categories of persons not already considered in the previous analysis. The situation of trafficked persons and children is of particular relevance to return in the context of migrant smuggling and is therefore subject to separate and detailed consideration in this subsection. As is the case with protection, detention, and other aspects of the response to migrant smuggling, this list is not exhaustive, and States will be required to consider the situation of individual smuggled migrants within their jurisdiction in order to determine whether their status requires additional or different consideration in relation to return.

10.5.1. *Return of Trafficked Persons*

Although States are able to point to a legal entitlement to control their own borders (and the absence of an obligation to permit all persons identified as having been trafficked to stay), there can be no doubt that forced return to the country of origin or to a third country can have serious consequences for smuggled migrants who are also victims of trafficking.[311] They may be subject to punishment from national authorities for unauthorized departure or other alleged offenses; they may face social isolation or stigmatization and be rejected by their families and communities; they may be subject to violence and intimidation from traffickers – particularly if they have cooperated with criminal justice agencies or owe money that cannot be repaid. Victims of trafficking who are forcibly repatriated, particularly without the benefit of supported reintegration, are at great risk of re-trafficking. Many of the legal issues associated with repatriation of smuggled victims of trafficking are similar, or even identical to those that arise in respect of all smuggled migrants. For example, all persons being returned, irrespective of whether they have just been smuggled or whether they have been smuggled *and* trafficked have the right to return to their own country, and the right to protection of their basic human rights. The obligation of *non-refoulement* does not apply differently.

However there are also important differences based on the fact that international law recognizes special entitlements for those who have been trafficked, and a number of these relate to or are implicated in decisions about return. The Trafficking Protocol's[312] provisions on return are more detailed and more generous than those set out in its migrant smuggling counterpart. The Protocol identifies specific obligations for countries of destination and of origin. In relation to the first group, the Protocol requires repatriation to "preferably be voluntary" and to be conducted "with due regard for the safety of the person and for the status of any related legal proceedings."[313] The *Travaux Préparatoires* reveal that many States were uncomfortable with the reference to voluntary repatriation,[314] and an Interpretative Note indicates that the words "and shall preferably be voluntary" are to be understood as not placing any obligation on the repatriating State Party.[315] Countries of origin are required to accept the return of a trafficked national or resident without undue

[311] Issues around the return of trafficked persons are considered in detail in A. T. Gallagher, *The International Law of Human Trafficking* (2010) [Gallagher, *The International Law of Human Trafficking*], at chapter 6 ("Obligations Related to Repatriation and Remedies"). The present section draws on that more extensive analysis.

[312] Protocol to Prevent, Suppress and Punish Trafficking in Persons, Especially Women and Children, supplementing the United Nations Convention against Transnational Organized Crime, 2237 UNTS 319, done Nov. 15, 2000, entered into force Dec. 25, 2003 [Trafficking Protocol].

[313] Trafficking Protocol, at Art. 8(2) ("When a State Party returns a victim of trafficking in persons to a State Party of which that person is a national or in which he or she had, at the time of entry into the territory of the receiving State Party, the right of permanent residence, such return shall be with due regard for the safety of that person and for the status of any legal proceedings related to the fact that the person is a victim of trafficking and shall preferably be voluntary").

[314] Travaux Préparatoires *for the Organized Crime Convention and Protocols*, at 397, n. 19.

[315] Ibid. at 388.

delay and with due regard for their safety.[316] They are further required to cooperate in return, including through verifying victim nationality or residence and issuing necessary travel documents.[317] The Legislative Guide to the Protocol confirms the scope of application of the Protocol's requirement that repatriation must be with due regard to the safety of the victim: this provision applies to all victims, including those who have not participated in the investigation and prosecution of their exploiters. It also applies to any country to whom the victim is repatriated as a national or permanent resident, even where the victim has not testified or has done so in another country.[318] The Trafficking Protocol is careful to characterize its provisions on repatriation as supplementary to standards and agreements that may be in place within or between countries. It specifies that the repatriation provisions outlined previously are without prejudice to any right afforded to victims of trafficking by any domestic law of the receiving State Party, or to any agreement governing the return of trafficked persons,[319] including obligations under customary international law regarding the return of migrants.[320]

On the matter of return the European Trafficking Convention generally follows the lead of the Trafficking Protocol, with a stronger emphasis on both rights and dignity. States Parties to the Convention are required to facilitate and accept the return of a trafficked national or resident "with due regard for the rights, safety and dignity" of the victim and without undue delay.[321] All countries involved in repatriation are required to conduct return "with due regard for the rights, safety and dignity"

316 Trafficking Protocol, at Art. 8(1) ("The State Party of which a victim of trafficking in persons is a national or in which the person had the right of permanent residence at the time of entry into the territory of the receiving State Party shall facilitate and accept, with due regard for the safety of that person, the return of that person without undue or unreasonable delay"). An Interpretative Note states that: "[t]he words 'permanent residence' in this paragraph mean long-term residence, but not necessarily indefinite residence. The paragraph should be understood as being without prejudice to any domestic legislation regarding either the granting of the right of residence or the duration of residence." Travaux Préparatoires *for the Organized Crime Convention and Protocols*, at 388.

317 Trafficking Protocol, at Arts. 8(3), 8(4). The Legislative Guide notes that the obligation relating to the issuing of travel documents are primarily administrative, but may require legislation to ensure that the appropriate officials or agencies are both able and obliged to issue the documents when the conditions set out in Article 8 are met: United Nations Office on Drugs and Crime, *Legislative Guides for the Implementation of the United Nations Convention Against Transnational Organized Crime and the Protocols thereto*, UN Sales No. E.05.V.2 (2004) [*Legislative Guide*], at 287 (para. 61(d)). An Interpretative Note confirms the understanding of the Ad Hoc Committee that "a return under this article shall not be undertaken before the nationality or right of permanent residence of the person whose return is sought has been duly verified": Travaux Préparatoires *for the Organized Crime Convention and Protocols*, at 388.

318 *Legislative Guide*, at 287 (para. 61(c)).

319 Trafficking Protocol, at Arts. 8(5), 8(6).

320 Travaux Préparatoires *for the Organized Crime Convention and Protocols*, at 389.

321 Council of Europe Convention on Action against Trafficking in Human Beings and Its Explanatory Report, ETS 197, 16.V.2005, done May 16, 2005, entered into force Feb. 1, 2008 [European Trafficking

of the victim and for the status of any related legal proceedings.[322] States Parties are further required to ensure that such return "shall preferably be voluntary."[323] As with the Trafficking Protocol, the European Trafficking Convention requires countries of origin to cooperate in return, including through verification of victim nationality or residence and issuance of necessary travel documents.[324] Importantly, the European Trafficking Convention also imposes on States Parties an obligation to not return child victims of trafficking "if there is an indication, following a risk and security assessment, that such return would not be in the best interests of the child."[325] International and regional soft law instruments support this position and further specify the conditions under which return of a trafficked child may or may not be permissible.[326]

The core standard in relation to the return of trafficked persons, including those who have been smuggled, is "safe and preferably voluntary return." In addition to being included in the two major specialist treaties on trafficking, the standard has been reaffirmed in numerous soft law sources.[327] Its wording is of course problematic

Convention], at Art. 16(1). The Explanatory Report notes that this provision upholds the right to return that is well established in international human rights law. European Trafficking Convention Explanatory Report, at para. 210, referencing the Universal Declaration of Human Rights, adopted by GA Res. 217A (III), UN GAOR, 3rd sess, 183rd plen mtg, UN Doc. A/810, at 71, Dec. 10, 1948, at Art. 13(2); Protocol No. 4 to the European Convention on Human Rights, at Art. 3(2); and ICCPR, at Art. 12(4).

322 European Trafficking Convention, at Art. 16(2). The two references to rights of the victim would, according to the Explanatory Report, include the right not to be subject to inhuman or degrading treatment, the right to protection of private and family life, and the right to privacy: European Trafficking Convention Explanatory Report, at paras. 202–203.

323 European Trafficking Convention, at Art. 16(2).

324 Ibid. at Arts. 16(3), 16(4). The Explanatory Report clarifies these provisions as imposing a standard of due diligence on the Requested State Party. European Trafficking Convention Explanatory Report, at para. 204.

325 European Trafficking Convention, at Art. 16(7).

326 See, for example, United Nations Children's Fund, *Guidelines for the Protection of Child Victims of Trafficking* (September 2006) [UNICEF Guidelines], at Guideline 3.7; and the UNODC Model Law on Trafficking in Persons, which cites CRC General Comment No. 6 (paragraph 53) in noting that: "[c]hildren who are at risk of being re-trafficked should not be returned to their country of origin unless it is in their best interest and appropriate measures for their protection have been taken." United Nations Office on Drugs and Crime, *Model Law on Trafficking in Persons*, UN Sales No. E.09.V.11 (2009) [UNODC Model Law on Trafficking in Persons], at 65, citing UN Committee on the Rights of the Child, "General Comment No. 6: Treatment of Unaccompanied and Separated Children Outside Their Country of Origin," UN Doc. CRC/GC/2005/6, Sept. 1, 2005 [CRC General Comment No. 6]. See also Organization for Security and Co-operation in Europe, Permanent Council, OSCE Action Plan to Combat Trafficking in Human Beings (Decision No. 557/Rev.1, Doc. PC.DEC/557/Rev.1, July 7, 2005), recommending that a decision to repatriate a child victim of trafficking in human beings should only be made after all circumstances of the specific case have been taken into account and provided there is a family or special institution in the country of origin to ensure the child's safety, protection, rehabilitation, and reintegration (at 16 (para. 10.2)).

327 See further Gallagher, *The International Law of Human Trafficking*, at 341–344.

from the perspective of seeking to understand the substantive content of the obligation and the corresponding right. It could be argued, for example, that States are required to make at least some effort to avoid repatriation that goes against the will of the victim. It is equally possible to sustain an argument that the qualification "preferably" renders the notion of obligation meaningless in both practical and legal terms. One way to consider the standard is to focus on its more tangible element of "safe return." In other words, nonvoluntary return could be viewed as permissible only under circumstances where it is possible to demonstrate that the proposed repatriation is "safe."[328] This in turn implies obligations on the part of the repatriating State to secure the appropriate information and to consider that information when making decisions about repatriation.[329]

A number of other issues are also relevant to obligations and rights associated with the return of smuggled victims of trafficking. These can be briefly summarized as follows:

- **Return and legal proceedings:** The right to remain during legal proceedings, asserted in a range of soft law texts,[330] is confirmed in treaty law. The Trafficking Protocol places an obligation on countries of destination to conduct return "with due regard for … the status of any related legal proceedings."[331] This obligation should be read in light of the requirement, set out in both the Organized Crime Convention and Trafficking Protocol, that participation by victims in criminal justice proceedings against their exploiters be facilitated.[332]

[328] This interpretation finds support in the UNODC Model Law on Trafficking in Persons, which notes that although the Trafficking Protocol does envisage involuntary return, its provisions "clearly limit involuntary returns to those which are safe and are carried out with due regard for legal proceedings": at 64. See further Gallagher, *The International Law of Human Trafficking*, at 343–344.

[329] This point is made in the *Legislative Guide*, at 310 (para. 91).

[330] See, for example, UN Economic and Social Council, Office of the United Nations High Commissioner on Human Rights, "Recommended Principles and Guidelines on Human Rights and Human Trafficking," UN Doc E/2002/68/Add.1, May 20, 2002, at Principle 9. Principle 9 articulates the right of trafficked persons to remain in the country during legal proceedings against traffickers and refers to the granting of temporary residence permits for this purpose. Principle 9 is supplemented by Guideline 4.7 that requests States to consider "[p]roviding legislative protection for trafficked persons who voluntarily agree to cooperate with law enforcement authorities *including protection of their right to remain lawfully within the country of destination for the duration of any legal proceedings*" (emphasis added).

[331] Trafficking Protocol, at Art. 8(2). This provision should be read in light of the broader obligation to ensure victims are provided with an opportunity to participate in legal proceedings as set out in Article 25(3) of the Organized Crime Convention (United Nations Convention against Transnational Organized Crime, 2225 UNTS 209, done Nov. 15, 2000, entered into force Sept. 29, 2003) as well as the specific obligation in the Trafficking Protocol to provide victims with an opportunity to present their views under Article 6(2).

[332] Organized Crime Convention, at Art. 25(3); Trafficking Protocol, at Art. 6(2)(b).

The European Trafficking Convention also obliges States Parties that are countries of destination to conduct return "with due regard for ... the status of any related legal proceedings."[333] It can be convincingly argued that involuntary return that operates to deprive a victim of the opportunity to participate effectively in legal proceedings (both criminal and civil including proceedings for compensation or other remedy) violates the obligations of States Parties to these two instruments.

- **Return and asylum:** Trafficked persons may face status-related risks upon return such as reprisals, social exclusion, and re-trafficking.[334] These factors may potentially be relevant to a claim for asylum or international protection. The obligation of *non-refoulement* will apply in such cases, and States must ensure that any return measures do not violate this core obligation. States must further ensure that trafficked persons have access to fair and efficient asylum procedures.
- **Alternatives to return:** Trafficked persons may benefit from certain treaty-based rights to access alternatives to repatriation. For example, the European Trafficking Convention does not automatically assume that repatriation is the immediate or even ultimate outcome of a trafficking event. States Parties are encouraged to provide victims with residence permits "for the purpose of their cooperation with the competent authorities in investigation or criminal proceedings" *or* to do so owing to their personal situation.[335] The right to a residence period is also recognized in EU Council Directive 2004/81/EC considered in detail in Chapter 1.[336]

Finally, it is relevant to reiterate the importance of ensuring quick and accurate identification of trafficked persons. As noted at various points in this book, persons who have been trafficked may not appear as such. The State of destination

[333] European Trafficking Convention, at Art. 16(2). The Explanatory Report confirms that this is "in order not to affect the rights that the victim could exercise in the course of the proceedings as well as in the proceedings themselves": European Trafficking Convention Explanatory Report, at para. 202.

[334] See UN High Commissioner for Refugees, "Guidelines on International Protection: The application of Article 1A(2) of the 1951 Convention and/or 1967 Protocol relating to the Status of Refugees to victims of trafficking and persons at risk of being trafficked," UN Doc. HCR/GIP/06/07, Apr. 7, 2006, at paras. 17–18.

[335] European Trafficking Convention, at Art. 14(1).

[336] See further Chapter 1, at Section 1.3.1.2. See also EU Returns Directive, at Art. 11(3) ("Victims of trafficking in human beings who have been granted a residence permit pursuant to Council Directive 2004/81/EC of 29 April 2004 on the residence permit issued to third-country nationals who are victims of trafficking in human beings or who have been the subject of an action to facilitate illegal immigration, who cooperate with the competent authorities ... shall not be subject of an entry ban without prejudice to [the right of States to impose entry bans on persons not complying with an obligation to return], and provided that the third-country national concerned does not represent a threat to public policy, public security or national security" (citations omitted)).

will generally be required to take active steps to establish the identity of those who have been trafficked among a larger group of intercepted or apprehended smuggled migrants. A failure to take adequate measures to identify victims of trafficking can lead to a withholding of entitlements and to a violation of human rights, including in relation to return.

10.5.2. *Return of Children*

The rights of children have been considered at prior points in this book including in Chapter 7 (relating to obligations of prevention)[337]; Chapter 8 (relating to obligations of protection)[338]; and Chapter 9 (relating to obligations in respect of detention).[339] Reference should be made to those chapters for information on general obligations that are imposed on States involved in decisions around the return of smuggled children. Of particular relevance is the principle that in relation to all decisions affecting children, their best interests are to be prioritized. States should not put other considerations, such as those related to immigration control, before the best interests of a child, including one who has been smuggled. In the context of return, the obligation to take into account the views of the child; the right of children to privacy and to family unity; the right of children to protection from sexual exploitation and abuse; and to protection from torture and cruel, inhuman, and degrading treatment are also particularly relevant.[340]

Smuggled children are often traveling alone – or at least without immediate family members. In its General Comment on the treatment of unaccompanied children, the Committee on the Rights of the Child was clear on the point that return to the country of origin should only be arranged if such return is in the best interests of the child.[341] The General Comment identified the following factors as among those to be taken into account in making such a determination:

- Safety, security, and other conditions, including socioeconomic conditions, awaiting the child upon return, including through home study, where appropriate, conducted by social network organizations;
- Availability of care arrangements for that particular child;
- Views of the child expressed in exercise of his or her right to do so under Article 12 and those of the caretakers;

337 See Chapter 7, at Section 7.1.2.5.
338 See Chapter 8, at Section 8.2.1.
339 See Chapter 9, at Section 9.4.3.
340 For a useful summary of the relevant legal issues, see European Union Agency for Fundamental Rights, *Detention of Third-Country Nationals in Return Procedures* (Thematic Report, Sept. 2010).
341 CRC General Comment No. 6, at para. 84.

- Child's level of integration in the host country and the duration of absence from the home country;
- Child's right "to preserve his or her identity, including nationality, name and family relations" (Article 8); and
- "Desirability of continuity in a child's upbringing and to the child's ethnic, religious, cultural and linguistic background" (Article 20).[342]

The critical rule is that return to the country of origin (or indeed any other country) must not be carried out if there is a "reasonable risk" that such return would result in the violation of fundamental human rights of the child,[343] or a real risk of irreparable harm.[344] The assessment of the risk of such violations should, in the view of the Committee on the Rights of the Child, "be conducted in an age and gender-sensitive manner and should, for example, take into account the particularly serious consequences for children of the insufficient provision of food or health services."[345] Further, return should not take place in the absence of available care by parents or extended family, unless secure and concrete arrangements are made for care and custodial responsibilities for the child upon return.[346] The Committee recognizes that return may still occur but places a number of caveats on how this is to happen:

> Exceptionally, a return to the home country may be arranged, after careful balancing of the child's best interests and other considerations, if the latter are rights-based and override best interests of the child. Such may be the case in situations in which the child constitutes a serious risk to the security of the State or to the society. Non rights-based arguments, such as those relating to general migration control, cannot override best interests considerations.[347]

The EU Returns Directive explicitly addresses the particular situation of children. The Preamble of the Directive affirms "the best interests of the child" as a primary consideration of Member States when implementing the Directive, along with respect for family life.[348] The Directive makes special provisions regarding the return and removal of unaccompanied minors.[349] First, before deciding to issue a return decision in respect of an unaccompanied child, Member States must ensure that assistance is provided to that child by appropriate bodies other than the return authorities, with due consideration being given to the best interests of

[342] Ibid.
[343] Ibid.
[344] Ibid. at para. 27.
[345] Ibid.
[346] Ibid. at para. 85.
[347] Ibid. at para. 86.
[348] EU Returns Directive, at Art. 5.
[349] Ibid. at Art. 10.

the child.[350] Second, before a child is removed from the territory of a Member State, the authorities of that State "shall be satisfied that he or she will be returned to a member of his or her family, a nominated guardian or adequate reception facilities in the State of return."[351]

The European Court of Human Rights has, on a number of occasions, addressed the issue of detention and subsequent deportation of children.[352] In these cases the Court has emphasized the vulnerability of the child as the "decisive factor," taking precedence over the child's status as an illegal immigrant and giving rise to obligations on the part of the State to take adequate measures to provide care and protection.

10.6. SUMMARY CONCLUSIONS ON RETURN OF SMUGGLED MIGRANTS

The analysis in this chapter supports the following summary conclusions.

- **A general right to return:** International law preserves the right of States to return/expel irregular migrants, including those who have been smuggled. However, such return must be in conformity with certain legal obligations. Failure to observe those obligations renders the return of a smuggled migrant to his or her country of origin, or to a third country, an internationally wrongful act for which the returning State will be legally responsible.
- **Prohibition on arbitrary expulsion – lawful presence:** The right to return with respect to persons lawfully present is constrained by the prohibition on arbitrary expulsion. It will generally only be in relation to smuggled asylum-seekers that the status of "lawful presence" will have a chance of being established. Views are divided on whether persons who have sought to enter or have entered a country unlawfully for purposes of claiming asylum can be characterized as

[350] Ibid. at Art. 10(1). See further European Commission, Communication from the Commission to the European Parliament and the Council: Action Plan on Unaccompanied Minors (2010–2014), COM(2010)213 final, May 6, 2010, at 12–13.

[351] EU Returns Directive, at Art. 10(2).

[352] See, for example, *Mubilanzila Mayeka and Kaniki Mitunga v. Belgium*, (2008) 46 EHRR 23 (ECHR, Oct. 12, 2006). This case concerned a five-year-old Congolese girl who was detained in an immigration center for adults after arriving in Belgium without legal documentation. Her application for refugee status was rejected, and she was kept in detention for two months before being deported to the Democratic Republic of Congo (DRC). No arrangements were made for the proper care of the child during her deportation flight or upon her arrival in the DRC. In these circumstances the Court found this "total lack of humanity towards someone of her age and in her situation as an unaccompanied minor" amounted to inhuman treatment. Also the Court found that the Belgian State had violated its positive obligations to take requisite measures and precautions in relation to the child. See also *Muskhadzhiyeva and Others v. Belgium*, Application No. 41442/07 (ECHR, Jan. 19, 2010) (available only in French – see *Information Note on the Court case-law* No. 126 for summary).

"lawfully present" and thereby benefit from the prohibition on arbitrary expulsion. The expulsion of aliens lawfully present will be characterized as "arbitrary" and therefore unlawful if the expulsion decision is not made in accord with national law and also international law with respect, for example, to the prohibition on discrimination. The decision to return will also be arbitrary if certain procedural guarantees are not granted, such as the right of the alien to submit reasons against his or her expulsion and to have the case reviewed by a competent authority. Expulsion without such procedural guarantees may still be lawful if required by national security or public order. However this exception is to be interpreted narrowly.

- **Prohibition on collective expulsion:** Measures that compel a group of smuggled migrants to leave the territory of a State are prohibited unless they conform to a "duty of due process": a reasonable and objective examination of the particular case of each individual member of the group. Interceptions and turn-backs at sea without individualized assessment can be characterized as violating the prohibition on collective expulsion even when undertaken outside the territory of the State (for example, on the high seas or by one State in the territory of another).
- **Obligation of *non-refoulement* (refugees):** No person, including a smuggled migrant, may be expelled or returned "in any manner whatsoever to the frontiers of territories where his life or freedom would be threatened on account of his race, religion, nationality, membership of a particular social group or political opinion."[353] There are certain limited exceptions to this rule. A recognized refugee who constitutes a threat to national security or public order[354]; or in relation to whom there are reasonable grounds for regarding as a danger to security; or who, having been convicted of a serious crime, constitutes a danger to the community,[355] may not benefit from the protections against expulsion and *non-refoulement* in the Refugee Convention.
- **Obligation of *non-refoulement* (all persons):** No person, including a smuggled migrant, may be returned to a situation where he or she faces a real risk of torture or other serious violations of human rights. Smuggled migrants who are refused refugee status or excluded from the benefit of the refugee law prohibition on *refoulement* on one of the grounds stipulated previously are still entitled to this protection.
- **Anti-smuggling measures and the obligation of *non-refoulement*:** Many anti-smuggling measures, ranging from interdiction at sea, to the creation of special

353 Refugee Convention, at Art. 33(1).
354 Ibid. at Art. 32(1).
355 Ibid. at Art. 33(2).

zones at airports, to "safe third country" arrangements, have practical implications for the obligation of *non-refoulement*. There is growing recognition that the obligation of *non-refoulement* applies in any area or space where the State exercises effective control. In relation to arrangements with other countries, the test will generally be whether a return exposes the person concerned to the risk of subsequent *refoulement*.

- **Obligation to accept and facilitate return:** Smuggled migrants have the right to return home. States of origin are required to accept returning nationals and to facilitate such return without undue delay. To that end they should cooperate with the returning State in relation to both identification and the issuance of necessary travel documents. These general obligations may be extended or modified by bilateral or regional readmission agreements. However all such agreements are subject to the obligation of *non-refoulement* and related protections.
- **Conduct of returns:** An otherwise lawful return may be rendered unlawful by the manner in which it is carried out. Smuggled migrants may be entitled to certain due process rights, including the right to challenge the decision related to return. Where such entitlement exists, these procedural rights must be recognized and granted. Any pre-return detention must not be punitive and must be in conformity with established rules, including the prohibition on discrimination and on torture, cruel, or inhuman treatment. The conduct of the return itself must also not violate established rules including those same prohibitions. The use of excessive force in compelling a return is prohibited.
- **Additional entitlements:** Smuggled children and smuggled migrants who have been trafficked are entitled to special and additional rights that may preclude an otherwise lawful return or modify the way in which a return decision is taken or implemented.

Epilogue

Homo sum: humani nihil a me alienum puto
(I am human, nothing human is alien to me)

Publius Terentius Afer (Terence, 195/185–159 BCE)

In September 2013, an overcrowded fishing boat, carrying smuggled migrants from Eritrea, was set on fire to draw the attention of rescuers and capsized just off the coast of Lampedusa, Italy. Over one hundred passengers were saved by the Italian coast guard, but more than 360 women, men, and children perished. It was alleged that vessels in the area ignored distress signals and failed to come to the aid of drowning passengers, perhaps fearing criminal sanctions for assisting smugglers. Those who were rescued or made their way ashore were subsequently processed by Italian authorities and placed in shelters from which the majority quickly vanished. Investigations revealed that some of the passengers had been subject to severe exploitation and that many had been forced to pay smugglers for their freedom from a detention center in Libya and onward journey to Europe. A Somali national was subsequently arrested in connection with "trafficking" and sexual assault of passengers. The captain of the vessel was arrested on charges of manslaughter. Politicians spoke of "a European tragedy" and condemned the loss of life as a "slaughter of innocents"; Pope Francis averred to more direct responsibility in characterizing the situation as "shameful."[1] *Subsequent reporting made clear that the*

[1] M. Eckel, "Day of Tears: Will Italy Boat Sinking Change European Migration Policies?" *The Christian Science Monitor*, Oct. 4, 2013, available at www.csmonitor.com/World/2013/1004/Day-of-tears-Will-Italy-boat-sinking-change-European-migration-policies; L. Davies, "Lampedusa Boat Tragedy Is 'Slaughter of Innocents' Says Italian President," *The Guardian*, Oct. 4, 2013, available at www.theguardian.com/world/2013/oct/03/lampedusa-boat-tragedy-italy-migrants; G. Galeazzi, "Bergoglio: 'Carnage at Sea Needs to Stop, It's Shameful,'" *Vatican Insider*, Oct. 3, 2013 (all accessed Dec. 8, 2013).

tragedy was unusual only for coming to light and the level of attention it attracted.[2] *Many migrants seeking to cross the Mediterranean from Africa to Italy never arrive and their deaths remain unreported. It is impossible to know how many of hundreds of thousands of women, men, and children who have attempted the perilous crossing from East Africa to Yemen over the past several years died in the attempt. This shroud of uncertainty extends to other parts of the world: from the dangerous stretch of water between Indonesia and Australia to the vast inhospitable desert that lies between the United States and Mexico. Two months after the tragedy at Lampedusa, senior Italian immigration officials confirmed to one of the present authors that their renewed efforts to rescue migrants in distress were being successfully used by smugglers to drum up business, and that Italian authorities were being criticized by fellow EU States on that basis.*

In December 2000, the international community confirmed migrant smuggling as an issue of common concern and as a legitimate focus for legal and operational cooperation between States. New legal instruments imposed highly specific obligations on States to criminalize migrant smuggling within their domestic legal orders and to ensure that structures and processes are in place to enable interstate cooperation. As this book has shown, those rules did not emerge and do not operate in a vacuum. Other areas of international law, including law of the sea, human rights and refugee law, and general rules around jurisdiction and responsibility, provide additional substance to the specialist obligations and dictate the parameters of State capacity to act against migrant smuggling. The key tasks of the international lawyer: understanding what States must and may not do in the name of addressing "migrant smuggling"; identifying practices that are unlawful; confirming specific rights that attach to persons who have been smuggled; and calling States to account for violation of established rules, all require consideration of the full range of applicable norms. That process – ascertaining the relevant rules and ensuring they are applied correctly – is important because international law is ultimately a tool for change. As a collective expression of how things ought to be, it seeks to positively influence the

[2] See further Council of Europe, Parliamentary Assembly, *Lampedusa: Call for Investigation into Allegations That Boats Failed to Carry Out Rescue* (Oct. 4, 2013), available at http://assembly.coe.int/nw/xml/News/News-View-EN.asp?newsid=4691&lang=2&cat=134. See also F. Vietti, "Migrants in Search of Human Security: Reflections on the Lampedusa Tragedies by an Italian Red Cross Field Officer," *Center for Migration Studies*, Oct. 10, 2013; UN High Commissioner for Refugees, "Rescue Efforts Focus on Survivors of Lampedusa Boat Tragedy as Search Suspended," Oct. 4, 2013, available at www.unhcr.org/524e9b9f9.html; "Lampedusa Boat Tragedy: Migrants 'Raped and Tortured,'" *BBC News*, Nov. 8, 2013, available at www.bbc.co.uk/news/world-europe-24866338; F. V. Paleologo, "After the Lampedusa Refugee Tragedy, Exactly How 'Civilised' Was the Italian Welcome?" *Il Lavoro culturale*, Oct. 18, 2013, English translation available at http://strugglesinitaly.wordpress.com/2013/10/18/en-translation-after-the-lampedusa-refugee-tragedy-exactly-how-civilised-was-the-italian-welcome/ (all accessed Dec. 8, 2013).

behavior of States. Practitioners of international law "have power over the law, the only thing that can have power over governments."[3]

International law may be central but it is ultimately just one part of the migrant smuggling mosaic. In this area, as in all others, the relevant legal framework cannot be considered in isolation from broader political, social, and economic forces that gave rise to and shaped its development, and that will ultimately determine its future. While not a focus of the present work, the authors acknowledge that a nuanced understanding of those forces is essential to an appreciation of both the possibilities and limitations of the relevant international rules as well as to identifying opportunities for change.

Understanding the scale and nature of global migration, as well as its inevitability, is an important step in this process.[4] More than 200 million people, close to 3 percent of the world population, presently live outside their countries of birth.[5] The stories behind migration are as varied and numerous as the migrants themselves. Some people are forced to leave their countries because of war, conflict, or the threat of persecution; others migrate to escape poverty and support their families; some simply seek to take advantage of opportunities for economic or social advancement that are not available at home. Although migration is often caused by, and can cause, hardship and misery, that aspect is just one part of the picture. Migration is a central and indispensible plank of our new, globalized world. It supports national economies in countries of origin and destination. It has improved the lives of millions immeasurably, including those who stay at home.

While many migrants travel well and arrive safely, a significant proportion of those who are forced or want to move do not have access to safe and legal migration channels. Migrant smuggling, along with human trafficking, will almost inevitably be found where pressures to migrate are not matched by opportunities to do so safely and legally. The argument that migrant smuggling is a natural outcome of current global migration regimes that are continually narrowing access to the preferred destinations is difficult to refute. If borders were truly open, the market for smugglers would cease to exist. If individuals were allowed to move wherever and whenever they wanted, then the competition to be regulated would be between transport companies, not organized criminal syndicates. If international labor migration were as free as the trade in goods and services, then there would be no need to develop legal regimes to combat smuggling. In purely human rights terms, there can be no doubt that current migration regimes reinforce discrimination and inequality and

3 P. Allott, "State Responsibility and the Unmaking of International Law" (1988) 29 *Harvard International Law Journal* 1, at 25.

4 See further A. Gallagher, "Introduction," in A. T. Gallagher, ed., *Migration, Human Rights, and Development: A Global Anthology* 1 (2013).

5 World Bank, *Migration and Remittances Fact Book 2011* (2nd ed. 2011).

contribute to global suffering. A careful dismantling or reimagining of those regimes is fully compatible with the broader goals of international law: to support a just global order, to promote peace and prosperity, and to secure attainment of human rights for all persons.

But such a future remains frustratingly remote. The reality of the present international system is that States take full advantage of the carefully preserved international legal right to control their own borders. States also exploit a weak and outdated legal framework around asylum to ensure that their humanitarian obligations do not conflict with perceived national self-interest. An array of pressures and incentives encourage countries of destination to increase their control over irregular migration and to decrease or de-emphasize the legal entitlements of the individuals involved. The growing externalization of border controls and widespread criminalization of irregular migrants, trends that have been documented throughout this book, are just two manifestations of this inexorable drift. It is no coincidence that efforts to develop stronger rules around the rights of migrants have failed dismally[6]; that the entire field of what is optimistically termed "international migration law" can be so accurately described by its strongest advocates as "substance without architecture"[7]; that States negotiating the Migrant Smuggling Protocol were successful in characterizing those being smuggled as "subjects" and not as "victims"[8]; and that many of the bilateral agreements operationalizing interdiction and return of smuggled migrants are negotiated and implemented in secret.[9] It is the complex and divisive politics of irregular migration – along with a chronic "fear of bilateral disadvantage"[10] – that prevent the emergence of any credible compliance machinery around the new rules on migrant smuggling, that obstruct even the most rudimentary reforms of a failing refugee protection regime, and that serve to explain the gap between public commitment to human rights and the reality of what is occurring in border regions and on the high seas. This troubling situation is unlikely to change unless and until States, particularly the most powerful and the most desired, decide that reform to the global migration regime is in their individual and collective best interests.

An appreciation of political realities and concomitant limitations is not the same as giving up – or even accepting that international law can, at best, exercise only a moderating influence on the behavior of States. The international legal

[6] See further Chapter 2, at Section 2.1.1 and Chapter 10, Section 10.2.1.

[7] T. A. Aleinkoff, "International Legal Norms on Migration: Substance without Architecture," in R. Cholewinski, R. Perruchoud, and E. MacDonald eds., *International Migration Law: Developing Paradigms and Key Challenges* 467 (2007).

[8] See further discussion on withholding of victim status to smuggled migrants in Chapter 1, at Section 1.1.3.2.

[9] See further Chapter 1, at Section 1.3.2.

[10] J. C. Hathaway, *The Rights of Refugees under International Law* (2005), at 994.

framework described and analyzed in this book will not – and cannot be expected to – deliver the solution to a problem that extends well beyond its scope and capacities. Nevertheless, as noted in the Introduction, an approach to migrant smuggling that is firmly grounded in international law provides much-needed parameters and safeguards for the development of the national laws, policies, and actions that in the end determine much of what happens in the area of migration control. By establishing rights, obligations, and responsibilities this approach also helps to ensure that events such as occurred at Lampedusa in 2013 can never be trivialized or dismissed as senseless tragedies.

Select Bibliography

1. Books

Aust, A., *Modern Treaty Law and Practice* (2nd ed. 2007, Cambridge University Press).
Aust, H. P., *Complicity and the Law of State Responsibility* (2011, Cambridge University Press).
Bassiouni, M. C., and E. M. Wise, *Aut Dedere Aut Judicare: The Duty to Extradite or Prosecute in International Law* (1995, Martinus Nijhoff).
Battjes, H., *European Asylum Law and International Law* (2006, Martinus Nijhoff).
Benninger-Budel, C., ed., *Due Diligence and Its Application to Protect Women from Violence* (2008, Martinus Nijhoff).
Berdal, M. R., and M. Serrano eds., *Transnational Organized Crime and International Security: Business as Usual?* (2002, Lynne Rienner).
Boister, N., *An Introduction to Transnational Criminal Law* (2012, Oxford University Press).
Brierly, J. L., (H. Waldock ed.) *The Law of the Nations: An Introduction to the International Law of Peace* (6th ed. 1963, Oxford University Press).
Briskman, L., S. Latham, and C. Goddard, *Human Rights Overboard: Seeking Asylum in Australia* (2008, Scribe Publishing).
Brownlie, I., *Principles of Public International Law* (7th ed. 2008, Oxford University Press).
Cassarino, J.-P., ed., *Unbalanced Reciprocities: Cooperation on Readmission in the Euro-Mediterranean Area* (2010, Middle East Institute Special Edition Viewpoints).
Cheng, B., *General Principles of Law as Applied by International Courts and Tribunals* (1987, Cambridge University Press).
Cholewinski, R., *Migrant Workers in International Human Rights Law: Their Protection in Countries of Employment* (1997, Clarendon Press).
Churchill, R. R., and A. V. Lowe, *The Law of the Sea* (3rd ed. 1999, Manchester University Press).
Clapham, A., *Human Rights in the Private Sphere* (1996, Oxford University Press).
Human Rights Obligations of Non-State Actors (2006, Oxford University Press).
Coleman, N., *European Readmission Policy: Third Country Interests and Refugee Rights* (2011, Martinus Nijhoff).
Conklin, J., *Dialogue Mapping: Building Shared Understanding of Wicked Problems* (2006, John Wiley and Sons).

Cornelisse, G., *Immigration Detention and Human Rights: Rethinking Territorial Sovereignty* (2010, Martinus Nijoff).
da Costa, K., *The Extraterritorial Application of Selected Human Rights Treaties* (2012, Brill, Nijhoff).
Crawford, J., ed., *The International Law Commission's Articles on State Responsibility: Introduction, Text, and Commentaries* (2002, Cambridge University Press).
Brownlie's Principles of Public International Law (8th ed. 2012, Oxford University Press).
Crawford, J., and M. Koskenniemi, eds., *The Cambridge Companion to International Law* (2012, Cambridge University Press).
Crawford, J., A. Pellet and S. Olleson eds., K. Parlett assistant ed., *The Law of International Responsibility* (2010, Oxford University Press).
D'Amato, A., *The Concept of Custom in International Law* (1971, Cornell University Press).
Dauvergne, C., *Making People Illegal: What Globalization Means for Migration and Law* (2008, Cambridge University Press).
Dixon, M., *Textbook on International Law* (2007, Blackstone).
Duffy, H., *The "War on Terror" and the Framework of International Law* (2005, Cambridge University Press).
Elias, T. O., *The International Court of Justice and Some Contemporary Problems: Essays on International Law* (1983, Martinus Nijhoff).
Evans, M., ed., *International Law* (3rd ed. 2010, Oxford University Press).
Feller, E., V. Türk and F. Nicholson eds., *Refugee Protection in International Law: UNHCR's Global Consultations on International Protection* (2003, Cambridge University Press).
Gallagher, A. T., *The International Law of Human Trafficking* (2010, Cambridge University Press).
Gammeltoft-Hansen, T., *Access to Asylum: International Refugee Law and the Globalisation of Migration Control* (2011, Cambridge University Press).
Gammeltoft-Hansen, T., and N. N. Sørensen eds., *The Migration Industry and the Commercialization of International Migration* (2013, Routledge).
García-Amador, F. V., L. Sohn and R. R. Baxter, *Recent Codification of the Law of State Responsibility for Injuries to Aliens* (1974, Harvard University Press).
Gibney, M., *The Ethics and Politics of Asylum: Liberal Democracy and the Response to Refugees* (2004, Cambridge University Press).
Global Refugee Crisis: A Reference Handbook (2nd ed. 2010).
Gibney, M., and S. Skogly eds., *Universal Human Rights and Extraterritorial Obligations* (2010, University of Pennsylvania Press).
Gondek, M., *The Reach of Human Rights in a Globalising World: Extraterritorial Application of Human Rights Treaties* (2009, Antwerp Intersentia).
Goodwin-Gill, G., *International Law and the Movement of Persons between States* (1978, Clarendon Press).
Goodwin-Gill, G., and J. McAdam, *The Refugee in International Law* (3rd ed. 2007, Oxford University Press).
Guild, E., and P. Minderhoud eds., *Immigration and Criminal Law in the European Union: The Legal Measures and Social Consequences of Criminal Law in Member States on Trafficking and Smuggling in Human Beings* (2006, Martinus Nijhoff).
Guilfoyle, D., *Shipping Interdiction and the Law of the Sea* (2009, Cambridge University Press).

Hannum, H., *The Right to Leave and Return in International Law and Practice* (1987, Martinus Nijhoff).

Harris, D. J., *Cases and Materials on International Law* (7th ed. 2010, Sweet & Maxwell).

Harrison, J., *Making the Law of the Sea: A Study in the Development of International Law* (2011, Cambridge University Press).

Hathaway, J. C., *The Rights of Refugees under International Law* (2005, Cambridge University Press).

Hayes, B., *NeoConOpticon: The EU Security-Industrial Complex* (2009, Statewatch).

Henckaerts, J.-M., *Mass Expulsion in Modern International Law and Practice* (1995, Martinus Nijhoff).

den Heijer, M., *Europe and Extraterritorial Asylum* (2012, Hart).

Henckaerts, J.-M., and L. Doswald-Beck, *Customary International Humanitarian Law, Volume I: Rules* (2005, ICRC, Cambridge University Press).

Henkin, L., *International Law, Politics and Values* (1995, Martinus Nijhoff).

Higgins, R., *Problems and Process: International Law and How We Use It* (1995, Oxford University Press).

Janis, M., *An Introduction to International Law* (2003, Little Brown).

Jennings, R., and A. Watts eds., *Oppenheim's International Law: Volume I, Peace* (9th ed. 1992, Longman).

Joseph, S., J. Schultz and M. Castan, *The International Covenant on Civil and Political Rights: Cases, Materials and Commentary* (2004, Oxford University Press).

Juss, S. S. ed., *The Ashgate Research Companion to Migration Law, Theory and Policy* (2013, Ashgate).

Kamminga, M. T., *Inter-state Accountability for Violations of Human Rights* (1992, University of Pennsylvania Press).

Klein, N., *Maritime Security and the Law of the Sea* (2011, Oxford University Press).

Klein, P., and P. Sands eds., *Bowett's Law of International Institutions* (2009, Sweet & Maxwell).

Koskenniemi, M., *The Gentle Civilizer of Nations: The Rise and Fall of International Law 1870–1960* (2001, Cambridge University Press).

Kyle D., and R. Kozlowski eds., *Global Human Smuggling: Comparative Perspectives* (2nd ed. 2011, Johns Hopkins University Press).

Landau, L. B., ed., *Exorcising the Demons Within: Xenophobia, Violence and Statecraft in Contemporary South Africa* (2012, United Nations University Press).

Lauterpacht, H., ed., *Oppenheim's International Law* (7th ed. 1948, Longmans Green & Co.).

van Liempt, I. C., *Navigating Borders: Inside Perspectives on the Process of Human Smuggling into the Netherlands* (2007, Amsterdam University Press).

Lillich, R. B., *The Human Rights of Aliens in Contemporary International Law* (1984, Manchester University Press).

Lowe, A. V., *International Law* (2007, Oxford University Press).

McClean, D., *Transnational Organized Crime: A Commentary on the UN Convention and Its Protocols* (2007, Oxford University Press).

McNair, A., *International Law Opinions*, vol. 1 (1956, Cambridge University Press).

Mallia, P., *Migrant Smuggling by Sea: Combating a Current Threat to Maritime Security through the Creation of a Cooperative Framework* (2009, Martinus Nijhoff).

Mares, P., *Borderline: Australia's Response to Refugees and Asylum Seekers in the Wake of the Tampa* (2002, University of New South Wales Press).
Marr, D., and M. Wilkinson, *Dark Victory* (2003, Allen & Unwin).
Meron, T., *Human Rights and Humanitarian Norms as Customary Law* (1989, Clarendon Press).
Milanovic, M., *Extraterritorial Application of Human Rights Treaties: Law, Principles, and Policy* (2011, Oxford University Press).
Morrison, A. P., *Places of Refuge for Ships in Distress: Problems and Methods of Resolution* (2012, Martinus Nijhoff).
Nandan, S. N., and S. Rosenne eds., *United Nations Convention on the Law of the Sea, 1982: A Commentary*, Volume III (1995).
Nicholls, C., C. Montgomery and J. Knowles, *The Law of Extradition and Mutual Assistance: Practice and Procedure* (2007, Oxford University Press).
Nordquist, M. H, ed., *United Nations Convention on the Law of the Sea 1982: A Commentary*, vol. 2 (1985, Martinus Nijhoff).
Nordquist, M. H., S. Rosenne and S. N. Nandan, *United Nations Convention on the Law of the Sea 1982: A Commentary*, vol. 3 (1995, Martinus Nijhoff).
Nowak, M., *U.N. Covenant on Civil and Political Rights: CCPR Commentary* (2nd revised ed. 2005, N. P. Engel).
Nowak, M., and E. McArthur, *The United Nations Convention against Torture: A Commentary* (2008, Oxford University Press).
O'Connell, D. P., (I. A. Shearer ed.), *The International Law of the Sea*, vol. I (1982), and vol. II (1984, Clarendon Press).
Opeskin, B., R. Perruchoud and J. Redpath-Cross, eds., *Foundations of International Migration Law* (2013, Cambridge University Press).
Oppenheim, L., (H. Lauterpacht ed.), *International Law: A Treatise* (1955, Longman).
Parry, C., J. Grant and C. Barker eds., *Parry and Grant Encyclopaedic Dictionary of International Law* (3rd ed. 2009, Oxford University Press).
Pauwelyn, J., R. Wessel and J. Wouters eds., *Informal International Lawmaking* (2012, Oxford University Press).
Peers, S., *EU Justice and Home Affairs Law* (3rd ed. 2011, Longman).
Peers, S., E. Guild and J. Tomkin eds., *EU Immigration and Asylum Law (Text and Commentary): Second Revised Edition*, Volume 1: Visa and Border Controls (2012, Martinus Nijhoff).
Peers, S., E. Guild, D. Acosta Arcarazo, K. Groenendijk and V. Moreno-Lax eds., *EU Immigration and Asylum Law: Text and Commentary: Second Revised Edition*, Volume 2: EU Immigration Law (2012, Martinus Nijhoff).
Plender, R., *International Migration Law* (2nd revised ed. 1988, Martinus Nijhoff).
Price, M., *Rethinking Asylum: History, Purpose, and Limits* (2009, Cambridge University Press).
Ragazzi, M., *The Concept of International Obligations Erga Omnes* (2000, Oxford University Press).
Rikhof, J., *The Criminal Refugee: The Treatment of Asylum Seekers with a Criminal Background in International and Domestic Law* (2012, Republic of Letters).
Robinson, N., *Convention Relating to the Status of Refugees: Its History, Contents and Interpretation: A Commentary* (1953, Institute of Jewish Affairs, World Jewish Congress).
Rothwell, D., and T. Stephens, *The International Law of the Sea* (2010, Hart).

Ryan, B., and V. Mitsilegas eds., *Extraterritorial Immigration Control: Legal Challenges* (2010, Martinus Nijhoff).
Ryngaert, C., *Jurisdiction in International Law* (2008, Oxford University Press).
Schloenhardt, A., *Migrant Smuggling: Illegal Migration and Organised Crime in Australia and the Asia Pacific Region* (2003, Martinus Nijhoff).
Shaw, M. N., *International Law* (6th ed. 2008, Cambridge University Press).
Shelton, D., ed., *Commitment and Compliance: The Role of Non-binding Norms in the International Legal System* (2003, Oxford University Press).
Remedies in International Human Rights Law (2nd ed. 2005, Oxford University Press).
Smith, P. J., ed., *Human Smuggling: Chinese Migrant Trafficking and the Challenge to American's Immigration Tradition* (1997, Center for Strategic & International Studies).
Sohn, L., and T. Buergenthal eds., *The Movement of Persons across Borders, Studies in Transnational Legal Policy*, vol. 23 (1992, American Society of International Law).
Soudijn, M., *Chinese Human Smuggling in Transit* (2006, Eleven International).
Svennson-McCarthy, A-L., *The International Law of Human Rights and States of Exception* (1998, Martinus Nijhoff).
Triandafyllidou, A., and T. Maroukis, *Migrant Smuggling: Irregular Migration from Asia and Africa to Europe* (2012, Palgrave Macmillan).
Triggs, G., *International Law: Contemporary Principles and Practices* (2nd ed., 2011, LexisNexis Butterworths).
de Vattel, E., *The Law of Nations: Book III* (reprint 1974, Samuel Campbell).
Ventrella, M., *The Control of People Smuggling and Trafficking in the EU: Experiences from the UK and Italy* (2010, Ashgate).
Vrachnas, J., M. Bagaric, P. Dimopoulos, and A. Pathinayak, *Migration and Refugee Law: Principles and Practice in Australia* (2011, Cambridge University Press).
Weber, L., and S. Pickering, *Globalization and Borders: Death at the Global Forntier* (2011).
Weis, P., *The Refugee Convention, 1951, The Travaux Preparatoires Analysed with a Commentary by Dr Paul Weis* (posthumously published, 1995), available at www.unhcr.org/4ca34be29.pdf (accessed May 12, 2013).
Wilsher, D., *Immigration Detention: Law, History, Politics* (2012, Cambridge University Press).
Zhang, S. X., *Chinese Human Smuggling Organizations: Families, Social Networks, and Cultural Imperatives* (2008, Stanford University Press).
Zimmermann, A., ed., J. Dörschner and F. Machts assistant eds., *The 1951 Convention Relating to the Status of Refugees and Its 1967 Protocol* (2011, Oxford University Press).

2. Articles and Book Chapters

Ahmad, A., "Dead Men Working: Time and Space in London's ("Illegal") Migrant Economy" (2008) **22**(2) *Work, Employment and Society* 301.
Akehurst, M., "Custom as a Source of International Law" (1975) 47 *British Yearbook of International Law* 1.
Aleinkoff, T. A., "International Legal Norms on Migration: Substance without Architecture," in R. Cholewinski, R. Perruchoud, and E. MacDonald eds., *International Migration Law: Developing Paradigms and Key Challenges* 467 (2007, T.M.C. Asser Press).

Allott, P., "State Responsibility and the Unmaking of International Law," (1988) **29**(1) *Harvard International Law Journal* 1.
Altiparmak, K., "Bankovic: An Obstacle to the Application of the European Convention on Human Rights in Iraq?" (2004) **9**(2) *Journal of Conflict and Security Law* 213.
Andrade, P. G., "Extraterritorial Strategies to Tackle Irregular Migration by Sea," in B. Ryan and V. Mitsilegas eds., *Extraterritorial Immigration Control: Legal Challenges* 311 (2010, Martinus Nijhoff).
d'Aspremont, J., "Softness in International Law: A Self-Serving Quest for New Legal Materials," (2008) **19** *European Journal of International Law* 1075.
"The Articles on the Responsibility of International Organizations: Magnifying the Fissures in the Law of International Responsibility" (2012) **9** *International Organizations Law Review* 15.
Ashdown, J., and M. James, "Women in Detention" (2010) **92** *International Review of the Red Cross* 123.
Askola, H., "Illegal Migrants, Gender and Vulnerability: The Case of the EU's Returns Directive" (2010) **18** *Feminist Legal Studies* 159.
Baldaccini, A., "The EU Directive on Return: Principles and Protests" (2010) **28**(4) *Refugee Survey Quarterly* 114.
"Extraterritorial Border Controls in the EU: The Role of Frontex in Operations at Sea," in B. Ryan and V. Mitsilegas eds., *Extraterritorial Immigration Control: Legal Challenges* 229 (2010, Martinus Nijhoff).
"The Return and Removal of Irregular Migrants under EU Law: An Analysis of the Returns Directive" (2009) **11** *European Journal of Migration and Law* 1.
Barnes, R., "The International Law of the Sea and Migration Control," in B. Ryan and V. Mitsilegas eds., *Extraterritorial Immigration Control: Legal Challenges* 103 (2010, Martinus Nijhoff).
Bassiouni, M. C., "A Functional Approach to General Principles of International Law" (1990) **11** *Michigan Journal of International Law* 786.
"The History of Universal Jurisdiction and Its Place in International Law," in S. Macedo ed., *Universal Jurisdiction: National Courts and the Prosecution of Serious Crimes under International Law* 39 (2004, University of Pennsylvania Press).
"International Recognition of Victims' Rights" (2006) **6** *Human Rights Law Review* 203.
Bennett, A., "That Sinking Feeling: Stateless Ships, Universal Jurisdiction and the Drug Trafficking Vessel Interdiction Act" (2012) **37**(2) *Yale Journal of International Law* 433.
Berg, U. G. and C. Tamagno, "Migration Brokers and Document Fixers: The Making of Migrant Subjects in Urban Peru," in T. Gammeltoft-Hansen and N. N. Sørensen eds., *The Migration Industry and the Commercialization of International Migration* 190 (2013, Routledge).
Betts, A., "Towards a Soft Law Framework for the Protection of Vulnerable Irregular Migrants" (2010) **22** *International Journal of Refugee Law* 209.
"Introduction: Global Migration Governance," in A. Betts ed., *Global Migration Governance* 1 (2011, Oxford University Press).
Bialostozky, N., "Protective Jurisdiction as a Circumstance Precluding Wrongfulness" (2012), available at http://papers.ssrn.com/sol3/papers.cfm?abstract_id=2143686 (accessed May 12, 2013).
Blatt, J., "Recent Trends in the Smuggling of Chinese into the United States," (2007) **15** *Willamette Journal of International Law and Dispute Resolution* 227.

Bodansky, D., and J. R. Crook, "Symposium: The ILC's State Responsibility Articles: Introduction and Overview" (2002) **96**(4) *American Journal of International Law* 773.

Boister, N., "Transnational Criminal Law?" (2003) **14** *European Journal of International Law* 953.

Boswell, C., "The 'External Dimension' of EU Immigration and Asylum Policy" (2003) **79**(3) *International Affairs* 619.

Broeders, D., "Return to Sender?: Administrative Detention of Irregular Migrants in Germany and the Netherlands" (2010) **12**(2) *Punishment and Society* 169.

Brolan, C., "An Analysis of the Human Smuggling Trade and the Protocol against the Smuggling of Migrants by Land, Air and Sea (2000) from a Refugee Protection Perspective" (2002) **14**(4) *International Journal of Refugee Law* 561.

Brown, D., "Crooked Straits: Maritime Smuggling of Humans from Cuba to the United States" (2002) **33** *University of Miami Inter-American Law Review* 273.

Brown Weiss, E., "Invoking State Responsibility in the Twenty-First Century" (2002) **96** *American Journal of International Law* 798.

Brownlie, I., "To What Extent Are the Traditional Categories of Lex Lata and Lex Ferenda Still Viable?" in A. Cassese and J. H. Weiler eds., *Change and Stability in International Law-Making* 66 (1988, Oxford University Press).

Byers, M., "Conceptualizing the Relationship between Jus Cogens and Erga Omnes Rules" (1997) **66** *Nordic Journal of International Law* 211.

Byrne, R., "Changing Paradigms in Refugee Law," in R. Cholewinski, R. Perruchoud, and E. MacDonald eds., *International Migration Law: Developing Paradigms and Key Challenges* 163 (2007, T.M.C. Asser Press).

Cacciaguidi-Fahy, S., "The Law of the Sea and Human Rights," in S. R. Silverburg ed., *International Law: Contemporary Issues and Future Developments* (2011, Westview Press).

Carling, J., and M. Hernández-Carretero, "Protecting Europe and Protecting Migrants? Strategies for Managing Unauthorised Migration from Africa" (2011) **13** *British Journal of Politics and International Relations* 42.

Caron, D. D., "The ILC Articles on State Responsibility: The Paradoxical Relationship between Form and Authority" (2002) **96**(4) *American Journal of International Law* 857.

Cassarino, J-P., "Dealing with Unbalanced Reciprocities: Cooperation on Readmission and Implications," in J-P. Cassarino ed., *Unbalanced Reciprocities: Cooperation on Readmission in the Euro-Mediterranean Area* 1 (2010, Middle East Institute Special Edition Viewpoints).

"Informalising Readmission Agreements in the EU Neighbourhood" (2007) **42** *The International Spectator* 179.

Cassese, A., "The Character of the Violated Obligation," in J. Crawford, A. Pellet, and S. Olleson eds., K. Parlett assistant ed., *The Law of International Responsibility* 415 (2010, Oxford University Press).

Cerna, C. M., "Impact on the Right to Consular Notification," in M. T. Kamminga and M. Scheinin eds., *The Impact of Human Rights on General International Law* 171 (2009, Oxford University Press).

Cerone, J., "The Application of Regional Human Rights Law beyond Regional Frontiers: The Inter-American Commission on Human Rights and US Activities in Iraq," American Society of International Law Insights, Oct. 25, 2005, available at www.asil.org/insights051025.cfm (accessed May 12, 2013).

Chacón, J., "Overcriminalizing Immigration" (2012) **102** *Journal of Criminal Law and Criminology* 613.
Cheng, B., "On the Nature and Sources of International Law," in B. Cheng ed., *International Law, Teaching and Practice* **201** (1982, Stevens).
Cholewinski, R., "European Union Policy on Irregular Migration: Human Rights Lost?," in B. Bogusz, R. Cholewinski, A. Cygan, and E. Szyszczak eds., *Irregular Migration and Human Rights: Theoretical, European and International Perspectives* (2004, Martinus Nijhoff).
"The Criminalisation of Migration in EU Law and Policy," in A. Baldaccini, E. Guild and H. Toner eds., *Whose Freedom, Security and Justice? EU Immigration and Asylum Law and Policy* (2007, Hart).
Coleman, N., "Renewed Review of the Status of the Principle of Non-refoulement as Customary International Law" (2003) **5** *European Journal of Migration and Law* 23.
Cook, R. J., "State Responsibility for Violations of Women's Human Rights" (1994) **7** *Harvard Human Rights Journal* 125.
Coomans, F., "The Extraterritorial Scope of the International Covenant on Economic, Social and Cultural Rights in the Work of the United Nations Committee on Economic, Social and Cultural Rights" **11**(1) *Human Rights Law Review* 1.
Coppens, J., "Disembarkation of Migrants Rescued at Sea: II" (2011) *De Lloyd (Antwerpen. Nederlandse ed.)* 55.
Coppens, J., and E. Somers, "Towards New Rules on Disembarkation of Persons Rescued at Sea?" (2010) **25** *International Journal of Marine and Coastal Law* 377.
Costello, C., "Courting Access to Asylum in Europe: Recent Supranational Jurisprudence Explored" (2012) **12**(2) *Human Rights Law Review* 287.
Crawford, J., "Revising the Draft Articles on State Responsibility" (1999) **10**(2) *European Journal of International Law* 435.
"Sovereignty as a Legal Value," in J. Crawford and M. Koskenniemi eds., S. Ranganathan assistant ed., *The Cambridge Companion to International Law* 117 (2012, Cambridge University Press).
Crawford, J., J. Peel, and S. Olleson, "The ILC's Articles on Responsibility of States for Internationally Wrongful Acts: Completion of the Second Reading" (2001) **12**(5) *European Journal of International Law* 963.
Crawford, J., and S. Olleson, "The Continuing Debate on a UN Convention on State Responsibility" (2005) **54** *International and Comparative Law Quarterly* 959.
"The Nature and Forms of International Responsibility," in M. D. Evans ed., *International Law* 451 (2006, Oxford University Press).
Crépeau, F., "The Fight against Migrant Smuggling: Migration Containment over Refugee Protection," in J. van Selm, K. Kamanga, J. Morrison, A. Nadig, S. Špoljar-Vržina, and L. van Willigen eds., *The Refugee Convention at Fifty: A View from Forced Migration Studies* 173 (2003, Lexington Books).
Crock, M., "In the Wake of the Tampa: Conflicting Visions of International Refugee Law in the Management of Refugee Flows" (2004) **12** *Pacific Rim Law and Policy Journal* 49.
Crock, M., and D. Ghezelbash, "Do Loose Lips Bring Ships? The Role of Policy, Politics and Human Rights in Managing Unauthorised Boat Arrivals" (2010) **19**(2) *Griffith Law Review* 238.
De Schutter, O., A. Eide, A. Khalfan, M. Orellana, M. Salomon, and I. Seiderman, "Commentary to the Maastricht Principles on Extraterritorial Obligations of States in the Area of Economic, Social and Cultural Rights" (2012) **34** *Human Rights Quarterly* 1084.

Dehm, S., "Sovereignty, Protection and the Limits to Regional Refugee Status Determination Arrangements" (2012) **28** *Merkourios: Utrecht Journal of International and European law* 53.

Devine, D. J., "Ships in Distress – a Judicial Contribution from the South Atlantic" (1996) **20**(3) *Marine Policy* 229.

Dewhurst, E., "The Right of Irregular Immigrants to Outstanding Remuneration under the EU Sanctions Directive: Rethinking Domestic Labour Policy in a Globalised World" (2011) **13**(4) *European Journal of Migration and Law* 389.

Dinstein, Y., "Right to Life, Physical Integrity, and Liberty," in L. Henkin ed., *The International Bill of Rights: The Covenant on Civil and Political Rights* 114 (1981, Columbia University Press).

Dominicé, C., "Attribution of Conduct to Multiple States and the Implication of a State in the Act of Another State," in J. Crawford, A. Pellet, and S. Olleson eds., K. Parlett assistant ed., *The Law of International Responsibility* 281 (2010, Oxford University Press).

Dörr, O., "Nationality," in R. Wolfrum ed., *The Max Planck Encyclopedia of Public International Law* (2008, Oxford University Press).

Dugard, J., and C. Van den Wyngaert, "Reconciling Extradition with Human Rights" (1998) **92** *American Journal of International Law* 187.

Dupuy, P-M., "Relations between the International Law of Responsibility and Responsibility in Municipal Law," in J. Crawford, A. Pellet, and S. Olleson eds., K. Parlett assistant ed., *The Law of International Responsibility* 173 (2010, Oxford University Press).

Eide, A., "Economic, Social and Cultural Rights as Human Rights," in A. Eide, C. Krause, and A. Rosas eds., *Economic, Social, and Cultural Rights: A Textbook* 21 (1995, Kluwer Law International).

Enache-Brown C., and A. Fried, "Universal Crime, Jurisdiction and Duty: The Obligation of Aut Dedere Aut Judicare in International Law" (1998) **43** *McGill Law Journal* 613.

Espenilla, J-J. F., "Injustice Ignored: A Case Study of the Irregular Sea Migration of the Rohingyan Boat People" (2010) 8(1) *Asia Europe Journal* 45.

Evans, M., "The Law of the Sea," in M. D. Evans ed., *International Law* 651 (3rd ed. 2010, Oxford University Press).

Feller, E., "Carrier Sanctions and International Law" (1989) **1** *International Journal of Refugee Law* 48.

Fife, R. E., "The Duty to Render Assistance at Sea: Some Reflections after Tampa," in J. Petman and J. Klabbers eds., *Nordic Cosmopolitanism: Essays in International law for Martti Koskenniemi* 469 (2003, Martinus Nijhoff).

Fink, M. D., "The Right of Visit for Warships: Some Challenges in Applying the Law of Maritime Interdiction on the High Seas" (2010) **49** *Revue de droit militaire et de droit de la guerre* 7.

Finlay, L., "Exporting the Death Penalty? Reconciling International Police Cooperation and the Abolition of the Death Penalty in Australia" (2011) **33** *Sydney Law Review* 95.

Fischer-Lescano, A., T. Löhr, and T. Tohidipur, "Border Controls at Sea: Requirements under International Human Rights and Refugee Law" (2009) **21**(2) *International Journal of Refugee Law* 256.

Foster, M., "The Implications of the Failed 'Malaysian Solution': The Australian High Court and Refugee Responsibility Sharing at International Law" (2012) **13**(1) *Melbourne Journal of International Law* 395.

Foster, M., and J. Pobjoy, "A Failed Case of Legal Exceptionalism? Refugee Status Determination in Australia's 'Excised' Territory" (2011) **23**(4) *International Journal of Refugee Law* 583.

Francis, A., "Bringing Protection Home: Healing the Schism between International Obligations and National Safeguards Created by Extraterritorial Processing" (2008) **20** *International Journal of Refugee Law* 173.

Gallagher, A. T., "Human Rights and the New UN Protocols on Trafficking and Migrant Smuggling: A Preliminary Analysis" (2001) **23**(4) *Human Rights Quarterly* 975.

"Human Rights and Human Trafficking: Quagmire or Firm Ground? A Response to James Hathaway" (2009) **49**(4) *Virginia Journal of International Law* 789.

Submission to the Australian Parliamentary Inquiry into Slavery, Slavery-Like Conditions and People Trafficking (2013), available at http://works.bepress.com/anne_gallagher/23/ (accessed May 12, 2013).

"Article 35" in P. Alston and J. Tobin, *The UN Convention on the Rights of the Child: A Commentary* (forthcoming 2014).

Gallagher A., and E. Pearson, "The High Cost of Freedom: A Legal and Policy Analysis of Shelter Detention for Victims of Trafficking" (2010) **32** *Human Rights Quarterly* 73.

Gammeltoft-Hansen, T., "The Refugee, the Sovereign and the Sea: European Union Interdiction Policies," in R. Adler-Nissen and T. Gammeltoft-Hansen eds., *Sovereignty Games: Instrumentalizing State Sovereignty in Europe and Beyond* 171 (2008, Palgrave Macmillan).

"Growing Barriers: International Refugee Law," in M. Gibney and S. Skogly eds., *Universal Human Rights and Extraterritorial Obligations* 55 (2010, University of Pennsylvania Press).

"The Externalisation of European Migration Control and the Reach of International Refugee Law," in E. Guild and P. Minderhoud eds., *The First Decade of EU Migration and Asylum Law* (Anniversary volume of the European Journal of Migration) 273 (2011, Martinus Nijhoff).

Gammeltoft-Hansen, T., and R. Adler-Nissen, "An Introduction to Sovereignty Games," in R. Adler-Nissen and T. Gammeltoft-Hansen eds., *Sovereignty Games: Instrumentalizing State Sovereignty in Europe and Beyond* 1 (2008, Palgrave Macmillan).

Gattini, A., "Breach of the Obligation to Prevent and Reparation Thereof in the ICJ's Genocide Judgment" (2007) **18**(4) *European Journal of International Law* 695.

"Smoking/No Smoking: Some Remarks on the Current Place of Fault in the ILC Draft Articles on State Responsibility" (1999) **10**(2) *European Journal of International Law* 397.

George, B., "Extraterritorial Application of Penal Legislation" (1966) **64** *Michigan Law Review* 609.

Gibney, M., "Genocide and State Responsibility" (2007) **7** *Human Rights Law Review* 760.

Gilbert, G., "Is Europe Living Up to Its Obligations to Refugees?" (2004) **15** *European Journal of International Law* 963.

Gilboy, J., "Implications of 'Third-Party' Involvement in Enforcement: The INS, Illegal Travelers, and International Airlines" (1997) **31** *Law and Society Review* 505.

Gilmore, W. C., "Hot Pursuit: The Case of R v. Mills and Others" (1995) **44** *International and Comparative Law Quarterly* 949.

Giuffré, M., "State Responsibility beyond Borders: What Legal Basis for Italy's Push-Backs to Libya?" (2013) **24** *International Journal of Refugee Law* 692.

Gjerdingen, E., "Suffocation Inside a Cold Storage Truck and Other Problems with Trafficking as 'Exploitation' and Smuggling as 'Choice' along the Thai-Burmese Border" (2009) **26** *Arizona Journal of International and Comparative Law* 699.

Gondek, M., "Extraterritorial Application of the European Convention on Human Rights: Territorial Focus in an Age of Globalization?" (2005) **52** *Netherlands International Law Review* 349.
Goodwin-Gill, G. S, "The Right to Seek Asylum: Interception at Sea and the Principle of Non-refoulement" (2011) **23**(3) *International Journal of Refugee Law* 443.
"Article 31 of the 1951 Convention Relating to the Status of Refugees: Non-penalization, Detention, and Protection," in E. Feller, V. Türk, and F. Nicholson eds., *Refugee Protection in International Law: UNHCR's Global Consultations on International Protection* 185 (2003, Cambridge University Press).
"Forced Migration and Human Rights," paper presented at the Expert Meeting on International Legal Norms and Migration, May 23–25, 2002.
Graefrath, B, "Complicity in the Law of International Responsibility" (1996) **29** *Revue Belge de Droit International* 370.
Grewcock, M., *Border Crimes: Australia's War on Illicit Migrants* (2009, Institute of Criminology Press).
Guerette, R. T., "Immigration Policy, Border Security, and Migrant Deaths: An Impact Evaluation of Life-Saving Efforts under the Border Safety Initiative" (2007) **6**(2) *Criminology and Public Policy* 245.
Guilfoyle, D., "Maritime Interdiction of Weapons of Mass Destruction" (2007) **12**(1) *Journal of Conflict & Security Law* 1.
"Human Rights Issues and Non-flag State Boarding of Suspect Ships in International Waters," in C. R. Symmons ed., *Selected Contemporary Issues in the Law of the Sea* 83 (2011, Martinus Nijhoff).
Guiraudon, V., and G. Lahav, "A Reappraisal of the State Sovereignty Debate: The Case of Migration Control" (2000) **33**(2) *Comparative Political Studies* 163.
Guzman, A. T., and T. L. Meyer, "International Soft Law" (2010) **2** *Journal of Legal Analysis* 171.
Hailbronner, K., "Readmission Agreements and the Obligation on States under Public International Law to Readmit Their Own and Foreign Nationals" (1997) **57** *Zeitschrift für ausländisches öffentliches Recht und Völkerrecht* 1.
Harvey, C., and R. P. Barnidge, Jr., "Human Rights, Free Movement and the Right to Leave in International Law" (2007) **19** *International Journal of Refugee Law* 1.
Hathaway, J. C., "Immigration Law Is Not Refugee Law," in *U.S. Committee For Refugees World Refugee Survey 2001*, June 2001.
"The Human Rights Quagmire of 'Human Trafficking'" (2008) **49**(1)*Virginia Journal of International Law* 1.
"Leveraging Asylum" (2010) **45** *Texas International Law Journal* 503.
Hathaway, O. A., "The Promise and Limits of the International Law of Torture," in S. Levinson ed., *Torture: A Collection* 199 (2004, Oxford University Press).
Hathaway, O., P. Levitz, E. Nielsen, A. Nowlan, W. Perdue, C. Purvis, S. Solow, and J. Spiegel, "Human Rights Abroad: When Do Human Rights Treaty Obligations Apply Extraterritorially?" (2011) **43** *Arizona State Law Journal* 389.
Heckmann, F., "Illegal Migration: What Can We Know and What Can We Explain? The Case of Germany," in A. Portes and J. DeWind eds., *Rethinking Migration: New Theoretical and Empirical Perspectives* (2007, Berghahn Books).
den Heijer, M., "Europe beyond Its Borders: Refugee and Human Rights Protection in Extraterritorial Immigration Control," in B. Ryan and V. Mitsilegas eds., *Extraterritorial Immigration Control: Legal Challenges* 169 (2010, Martinus Nijhoff).

Helton, A., "The United States Government Program of Intercepting and Forcibly Returning Haitian Boat People to Haiti: Policy Implications and Prospects" (1993) **10** *New York Law School Journal of Human Rights* 325.

Henkin, L., "Interstate Responsibility for Compliance with Human Rights Obligations," in L. C. Vohrah and Antonio Cassese eds., *Man's Inhumanity to Man: Essays on International Law in Honour of Antonio Cassese* 383 (2003, Kluwer).

Hessbruegge, J. A., "European Court of Human Rights Protects Migrants against 'Push Back' Operations the High Seas" **16**(14) *Insights* (American Society of International Law, Apr. 17, 2012).

Hinrichs, X., "Measures against Smuggling of Migrants at Sea: A Law of the Sea Related Perspective" (2003) **36**(2) *Revue Belge de Droit International* 413.

Hoppe, C., "Passing the Buck: State Responsibility for Private Military Companies" (2008) **19**(5) *European Journal of International Law* 989.

Impala, F., "The European Arrest Warrant in the Italian Legal System: Between Mutual Recognition and Mutual Fear within the European Area of Freedom, Security and Justice" (2005) **1**(1) *Ultrecht Law Review* 56.

Jiménez de Arechaga, E., "International Responsibility," in M. Sorensen ed., *Manual of Public International Law* **531** (1968, Macmillan).

Jinks, D., "State Responsibility for the Acts of Private Armed Groups" (2003) **4** *Chicago Journal of International Law* 83.

Joppke, C., "Why Liberal States Accept Unwanted Immigration" (1998) **50** *World Politics* 266.

Kälin, W. "Aliens, Expulsion and Deportation" in R. Wolfrum ed., *The Max Planck Encyclopedia of Public International Law* (2008, Oxford University Press).

Kalhan, A., "Rethinking Immigration Detention" (2010) **110** *Columbia Law Review Sidebar* 42.

Kasli, K., "Criminalising and Victimising the Migrant: Reflections on the UN Protocol and UNHCR's Position against Smuggling" (2011) **1**(2) *Oxford Monitor of Forced Migration* 64.

Kelly, J., "The Twilight of Customary International Law" (2000) **40** *Virginia Journal of International Law* 449.

Kenney, F. J. and V. Tasikas, "The Tampa Incident: IMO Perspectives and Responses on the Treatment of Persons Rescued at Sea" (2003) **12**(1) *Pacific Rim Law and Policy Journal* 143.

Kenny, M., D. Salove, and Z. Steel, "Legal and Ethical Implications of Medically Enforced Feeding of Detained Asylum Seekers on Hunger Strike" (2004) **180**(5) *Medical Journal of Australia* 237.

King, H., "The Extraterritorial Human Rights Obligations of States" (2009) **9** *Human Rights Law Review* 521.

Kinley, D., and J. Tadaki, "From Talk to Walk: The Emergence of Human Rights Responsibilities for Corporations at International Law" (2004) **44** *Virginia Journal of International Law* 931.

Kirchener A., and L. Schiano di Pepe, "International Attempts to Conclude a Convention to Combat Illegal Migration" (1998) **10** *International Journal of Refugee Law* 662.

Klein, P., "Attribution of Conduct to International Organizations," in J. Crawford, A. Pellet, and S. Olleson eds., K. Parlett assistant ed., *The Law of International Responsibility* 297 (2010, Oxford University Press).

Klepp, S., "A Contested Asylum System: The European Union between Refugee Protection and Border Control in the Mediterranean Sea," (2010) **12** *European Journal of Migration and Law* 1.

"Italy and Its Libyan Cooperation Program: Pioneer of the European Union's Refugee Policy?," in Cassarino ed., *Unbalanced Reciprocities* 77 (*Middle East Institute Special Edition Viewpoints*, 2010).

"A Double Bind: Malta and the Rescue of Unwanted Migrants at Sea, a Legal Anthropological Perspective on the Humanitarian Law of the Sea" (2011) **23** *International Journal of Refugee Law* 538.

Klug, A., and T. Howe, "The Concept of State Jurisdiction and the Applicability of the Non-refoulement Principle to Extraterritorial Interception Measures," in B. Ryan and R. Mitsilegas eds., *Extraterritorial Immigration Control: Legal Challenges* 69 (2010, Martinus Nijhoff).

Kochenov, D., "The Right to Leave Any Country," in R. Plender ed., International Migration Law (forthcoming), available at http://papers.ssrn.com/sol3/papers.cfm?abstract_id=1847769 (accessed May 12, 2013).

Koh, H., "The 'Haiti Paradigm' in United States Human Rights Policy" (2004) **103** *Yale Law Journal* 2391.

Kontorovich, E., "The Piracy Analogy: Modern Universal Jurisdiction's Hollow Foundations" (2004) **45** *Harvard International Law Journal* 183.

Koser, K., "Why Migrant Smuggling Pays" (2008) **46**(2) *International Migration* 3.

Kritzman-Amir, K., and T. Spijkerboer, "On the Morality and Legality of Borders: Border Policies and Asylum Seekers" (2013) **26** *Harvard Human Rights Journal* 1.

Kruse, I., "EU Readmission Policy and Its Effects on Transit Countries: The Case of Albania" (2006) 8 *European Journal of Migration and Law* 115.

Kyle, D., and M. Scarcelli, "Migrant Smuggling and the Violence Question: Evolving Illicit Migration Markets for Cuban and Haitian Refugees" (2009) **52** *Crime, Law and Social Change* 297.

Larsen, K. M., "Attribution of Conduct in Peace Operations: The 'Ultimate Authority and Control' Test" (2008) **19**(3) *European Journal of International Law* 509.

Lauterpacht, E., and D. Bethlehem, "The Scope and Content of the Principle of Non-refoulement: Opinion," in E. Feller, V. Türk, and F. Nicholson eds., *Refugee Protection in International Law: UNHCR's Global Consultations on International Protection* 78 (2003, Cambridge University Press).

Lawson, R., "Out of Control: State Responsibility and Human Rights: Will the ILC's Definition of the 'Act of State' Meet the Challenges of the 21st Century?," in M. Castermans-Holleman, R. van Hoof, and J. Smith eds., *The Role of the Nation-State in the 21st Century: Human Rights, International Organisations and Foreign Policy: Essays in Honour of Peter Baehr* 91 (1998, Martinus Nijhoff).

"Life after Bankovic: On the Extraterritorial Application of the European Convention of Human Rights," in F. Coomans and M. Kamminga eds., *Extraterritorial Application of Human Rights Treaties* 83 (2004, Intersentia).

Legomsky, S. H., "The USA and the Caribbean Interdiction Program" **18**(3) (2006) *International Journal of Refugee Law* 677.

"Addressing Secondary Refugee Movements," in R. Cholewinski, R. Perruchoud, and E. MacDonald eds., *International Migration Law: Developing Paradigms and Key Challenges* 177 (2007, T.M.C. Asser Press).

"The New Path of Immigration Law: Asymmetric Incorporation of Criminal Justice Norms" (2007) **64** *Washington and Lee Law Review* 469.

Li, M. K., M. A. Beck, Q. Shi and R. C. Harruff, "Unexpected Hazard of Illegal Immigration: Outbreak of Viral Myocarditis Exacerbated by Confinement and Deprivation in a Shipboard Cargo Container" (2004) **25**(2) *American Journal of Forensic Medicine and Pathology* 117.

Liang, Z., and W. Ye, "From Fujian to New York: Understanding the New Chinese Immigration," in D. Kyle and R. Koslowski eds., *Global Human Smuggling: Comparative Perspectives* 187 (2001, Johns Hopkins University Press).

Lowe, V., "Uniform Interpretation of the Rules of International Law Governing Innocent Passage" (1991) **6** *International Journal of Estuarine and Coastal Law* 73.

"Responsibility for the Conduct of Other States" (2002) **101** *Japanese Journal of International Law* 1.

Lowe, A., and C. Staker, "Jurisdiction," in M. D. Evans ed., *International Law* 313 (3rd ed. 2010, Oxford University Press).

Lucht, H. "Pusher Stories: Ghanaian Connection Men and the Expansion of the EU's Border Regimes into Africa," in T. Gammeltoft-Hansen, and N. N. Sørensen eds., *The Migration Industry and the Commercialization of International Migration* 173 (2013, Routledge).

McCorquodale, R., "Impact on State Responsibility," in M. T. Kamminga and M. Scheinin eds., *The Impact of Human Rights Law on General International Law* 235 (2009, Oxford University Press).

McDougal, M. S., H. Lasswell and L. Chen, "The Protection of Aliens from Discrimination and World Public Order: Responsibility of States Conjoined with Human Rights" (1976) **70** *American Journal of International Law* 432

McGoldrick, D., "Extraterritorial Application of the International Covenant on Civil and Political Rights," in F. Coomans and M. Kamminga eds., *Extraterritorial Application of Human Rights Treaties* 41 (2004, Intersentia).

Mann, F. A., "The Doctrine of Jurisdiction in International Law," in *Hague Recueil des cours*, vol. 111 (1964, Martinus Nijhoff).

Mann, I., "Dialectic of Transnationalism: Unauthorized Migration and Human Rights, 1993–2013" (2013) **54** *Harvard International Law Journal* 315.

Mares, S., and J. Jureidini, "Psychiatric Assessment of Children and Families in Immigration Detention – Clinical, Administrative and Ethical Issues" (2004) **28** *Australian and New Zealand Journal of Public Health* 520.

Martin, D. A., "Interdiction, Intervention and the New Frontiers of Refugee Law and Policy," (1993) **33** *Virginia Journal of International Law* 473.

Mathew, P., "Australian Refugee Protection in the Wakes of the Tampa" (2002) **96** *American Journal of International Law* 661.

Meron, T., "Extraterritoriality of Human Rights Treaties" (1985) **89** *American Journal of International Law* 78.

Milanović, M., "Al-Skeini and Al-Jedda in Strasbourg" (2012) **23**(1) *European Journal of International Law* 121.

Milanović, M., and T. Papić, "As Bad as It Gets: The European Court of Human Rights' Behrami and Saramati Decision and General International Law" (2009) **58** *International and Comparative Law Quarterly* 267.

Mitsilegas, V., "From National to Global, from Empirical to Legal: The Ambivalent Concept of Transnational Organized Crime," in M. E. Beare ed., *Critical Reflections on*

Transnational Organized Crime, Money Laundering and Corruption 55 (2003, University of Toronto Press).
Monzini, P., "Sea Border Crossings: The Organisation of Irregular Migration to Italy" (2007) **12** *Mediterranean Politics* 163.
Moreno-Lax, V., "The EU Regime on Interdiction, Search and Rescue, and Disembarkation: The Frontex Guidelines for Intervention at Sea" (2010) **25**(4) *International Journal of Marine and Coastal Law* 621.
"(Extraterritorial) Entry Controls and (Extraterritorial) Non-refoulement in EU Law," in M. Maes, M.-C. Foblets, and P. De Bruycker eds., *External Dimensions of EU Migration and Asylum Law and Policy/Dimensions Externes du Droit et de la Politique d'Immigration et d'Asile de l'UE* (2011, Bruylant).
"Seeking Asylum in the Mediterranean: Against a Fragmentary Reading of EU Member States' Obligations Accruing at Sea" (2011) **23**(2) *International Journal of Refugee Law* 174.
"Must EU Borders Have Doors for Refugees? On the Compatibility of Schengen Visas and Carrier Sanctions with EU Member States' Obligations to Provide International Protection to Refugees" (2008) **10** *European Journal of Migration and Law* 315.
"The EU Regime on Interdiction, Search and Rescue, and Disembarkation: The Frontex Guidelines for Intervention at Sea" (2010) **25** *International Journal of Marine and Coastal Law* 621.
Murphy, S., "Extraterritorial Application of U.S. Law to Crimes on Foreign Vessels" (2003) **97** *American Journal of International Law* 183.
Nadelmann, E. A.,"Global Prohibition Regimes: The Evolution of Norms in International Society" (1990) **44**(4) *International Organization* 479.
Newmark, R. L., "Non-refoulement Run Afoul: The Questionable Legality of Extraterritorial Repatriation Programs" (1993) **71** *Washington University Law Quarterly* 833.
Nicholson, F., "Implementation of the Immigration (Carriers' Liability) Act 1987: Privatising Immigration Functions at the Expense of International Obligations?" (1997) **46** *International Comparative Law Quarterly* 586.
Nielsen, S., M. Norredam, K. L. Christiansen, C. Obel, J. Hilden, and A. Krasnik, "Mental Health among Children Seeking Asylum in Denmark – The Effect of Length of Stay and Number of Relocations: A Cross-Sectional Study" (2008) 8 *BMC Public Health* 293.
Noll, G., "Why Human Rights Fail to Protect Undocumented Migrants" (2010) **12** *European Journal of Migration and Law* 241.
Nolte, G. and H. P. Aust, "Equivocal Helpers – Complicit States, Mixed Messages and International Law" (2009) 58 *International and Comparative Law Quarterly* 1.
Nowak, M. "Obligations of States to Prevent and Prohibit Torture in an Extraterritorial Perspective," in M. Gibney and S. Skogly eds., *Universal Human Rights and Extraterritorial Obligations* 11 (2010, University of Pennsylvania Press).
O'Connell, R., "Only Partial Neglect? Developments in the Case-Law of the European Court on Human Rights on Socio-economic Rights of Non-nationals," in W. Benedek, W. Karl, A. Mijr, M. Nowak, and M. Kettermann eds., *European Yearbook on Human Rights 2010* **245** (2010).
O'Boyle, M., "The European Convention of Human Rights and Extraterritorial Jurisdiction: A Comment on 'Life after Bankovic'," in F. Coomans and M. Kamminga eds., *Extraterritorial Application of Human Rights Treaties* **125** (2004, Intersentia).
O'Keefe, R., "Universal Jurisdiction: Clarifying the Basic Concept" (2004) **2**(3) *Journal of International Criminal Justice* 735.

Obokata, T., "Smuggling of Human Beings from a Human Rights Perspective: Obligations of Non-state and State Actors under International Human Rights Law" (2005) **17**(2) *International Journal of Refugee Law* 394.

"The Legal Framework concerning the Smuggling of Migrants at Sea under the UN Protocol on the Smuggling of Migrants by Land, Air and Sea," in B. Ryan and M. Mitsilegas eds., *Extraterritorial Migration Control: Legal Challenges* 151 (2010, Martinus Nijhoff).

Orakhelashvili, A., "Division of Reparation between Responsible Entitles," in J. Crawford, A. Pellet and S. Olleson eds., K. Parlett assistant ed., *The Law of International Responsibility* 647 (2010, Oxford University Press).

Oxman, B. "Human Rights and the United Nations Convention on the Law of the Sea" (1998) **36** *Columbia Journal of Transnational Law* 399.

Pacurar, A., "Smuggling, Detention, and Expulsion of Irregular Migrants: A Study on International Legal Norms, Standards, and Practices" (2003) **5** *European Journal of Migration and Law* 259.

Pallis, M., "Obligations of States towards Asylum Seekers at Sea: Interactions and Conflicts between Legal Regimes" (2002) **14** *International Journal of Refugee Law* 329.

Panizzon, M., "Readmission Agreements of EU Member States: A Case for EU Subsidiarity or Dualism?" (2012) **31**(4) *Refugee Survey Quarterly* 101.

Papastavridis, E., "Interception of Human Beings on the High Seas: A Contemporary Analysis under International Law" (2009) **36** *Syracuse Journal of International Law and Commerce* 145.

"Enforcement Jurisdiction in the Mediterranean Sea: Illicit Activities and the Rule of Law on the High Seas" (2010) **25** *The International Journal of Marine and Coastal Law* 569

"'Fortress Europe' and FRONTEX: Within or without International Law?" (2010) **79** *Nordic Journal of International law* 75.

"Piracy off Somalia: The 'Emperors and the Thieves of the Oceans' in the 21st Century," in A. Abass ed., *Protecting Human Security in Africa* **122** (2010, Oxford University Press).

"Rescuing Migrants at Sea: The Responsibility of States under International Law," Sept. 27, 2011, available at http://papers.ssrn.com/sol3/papers.cfm?abstract_id=1934352 (accessed May 12, 2013).

"The Right of Visit on the High Seas in a Theoretical Perspective: Mare Liberum versus Mare Clausum Revisited" (2011) **24**(01) *Leiden Journal of International Law* 45.

di Pascale, A., "Migration Control at Sea: The Italian Case," in B. Ryan and V. Mitsilegas eds., *Extraterritorial Immigration Control: Legal Challenges* 282 (2010, Martinus Nijhoff).

Pedrozo, R. A., "International Initiatives to Combat Trafficking of Migrants by Sea," in J. N. Moore and M. H. Nordquist eds., *Current Maritime Issues and the International Maritime Organization* 53 (1999, Martinus Nijhoff).

Pejic, J., "Procedural Principles and Safeguards for Internment/Administrative Detention in Armed Conflict and Other Situations of Violence" (2005) 87 *International Review of the Red Cross* 375.

Perlmutter, T., "The Politics of Proximity: The Italian Response to the Albanian Crisis" (1998) **32** *International Migration Review* 203.

Perruchoud, R., "Consular Protection and Assistance," in R. Cholewinski, R. Perruchoud, and E. MacDonald eds., *International Migration Law: Developing Paradigms and Key Challenges* 71 (2007, T.M.C. Asser Press).

"State Sovereignty and Freedom of Movement," in B. Opeskin, R. Perruchoud, and J. Redpath-Cross, *Foundations of International Migration Law* 123 (2012, Cambridge University Press).

Petersen, N., "Customary Law without Custom? Rules Principles, and the Role of State Practice in International Norm Creation" (2008) **23** *American University International Law Review* 275.

Pobjoy, J., "Treating Like Alike: The Principle of Non-discrimination as a Tool to Mandate the Equal Treatment of Refugees and Beneficiaries of Complementary Protection" (2010) **34**(1) *Melbourne University Law Review* 181.

Podeszfa, L. and C. Manicon, "Avoiding Refoulement: The Need to Monitor Deported Failed Asylum Seekers" (2012) **2** *Oxford Monitor of Forced Migration* 10.

Pugash, J., "The Dilemma of the Sea Refugee: Rescue without Refuge" (1977) 18 *Harvard International Law Journal* 577.

Raffaelli, R., "The European Approach to the Protection of Trafficking Victims: The Council of Europe Convention, the EU Directive and the Italian Experience" (2009) **10** *German Law Journal* 205.

"Case Note: The Achughbabian Case: Impact of the Return Directive on National Criminal Legislation," Diritto Penale Contemporaneo, 2012, February 2, 2012, available at SSRN: http://ssrn.com/abstract=1998324 (accessed May 12, 2013).

"The Returns Directive in Light of the El Dridi Judgment" (2011) **3**(1) *Perspectives on Federalism* N32.

Raustiala, K., and A. M. Slaughter, "International Law, International Relations and Compliance," in W. Carlnaes, T. Risse, and B. A. Simmons eds., *The Handbook of International Relations* **538** (2002, Sage).

Roberts, A. E., "Traditional and Modern Approaches to Customary International Law: A Reconciliation" (2001) **95** *American Journal of International Law* 757.

Roig A., and T. Huddleston, "EC Readmission Agreements: A Re-evaluation of the Political Impasse" (2007) **9** *European Journal of Migration and Law* 363.

Ramji-Nogales, J., "Undocumented Migrants and the Failures of Universal Individualism" (Sept. 6, 2013), available at http://ssrn.com/abstract=2321728 (accessed Nov. 18, 2013

Rothwell, D., "The Law of the Sea and the MV Tampa Incident: Reconciling Maritime Principles with Coastal State Sovereignty" (2002) **13**(2) *Public Law Review* 118.

Rousseau, C., "L'Indépendance de l'État dans l'Ordre International" (1948) **73**(2) *Recueil des Cours* 167.

Roxstrom, E., M. Gibney, and T. Einarsen, "The NATO Bombing Case: (Banković et al. v. Belgium et al.) and the Limits of Western Human Rights Protection" (2005) **23** *Boston University International Law Journal* 55.

Ruff, A., "The Immigration (Carriers Liability) Act 1987: Its Implications for Refugees and Airlines" (1989) **1** *International Journal of Refugee Law* 481.

Ryan, B., "Extraterritorial Immigration Control: What Role for Legal Guarantees?," in B. Ryan and V. Mitsilegas eds., *Extraterritorial Immigration Control: Legal Challenges* 1 (2010, Martinus Nijhoff).

Salt, J., "A Comparative Overview of International Trends and Types, 1950–80" (1989) **23**(3) *International Migration Review* 431.

Sandoval, I. R. "Public Officials and the Migration Industry in Guatemala: Greasing the Wheels of a Corrupt Machine," in T. Gammeltoft-Hansen and N. N. Sørensen eds.,

The Migration Industry and the Commercialization of International Migration 215 (2013, Routledge).

Sari, A., "Jurisdiction and International Responsibility in Peace Support Operations: The Behrami and Saramati Cases" (2008) 8 *Human Rights Law Review* 151.

Saul, B., "Dark Justice: Australia's Indefinite Detention of Refugees on Security Grounds under International Human Rights Law" (2012) **13** *Melbourne Journal of International Law* 686.

Schaffer, R. P., "The Singular Plight of Sea-Borne Refugees," (1978–1980) 8 *Australian Yearbook of International Law* 213.

Scharf, M. P., "Aut dedere aut judicare," in R. Wolfrum ed., *The Max Planck Encyclopedia of Public International Law* (2008, Oxford University Press).

Schloenhardt, A., and C. Martin, "Prosecution and Punishment of People Smugglers in Australia 2008–2011" (2012) **40** *Federal Law Review* 111.

Schloenhardt, A., and H. Hickson, "Non-criminalization of Smuggled Migrants: Rights, Obligations, and Australian Practice under Article 5 of the Protocol against the Smuggling of Migrants by Land, Sea, and Air," *International Journal of Refugee Law* first published online March 12, 2013.

Schloenhardt, A., and K. L. Stacey, "Assistance and Protection of Smuggled Migrants: International Law and Australian Practice" (2013) **35** *Sydney Law Review* 53.

Schloenhardt, A., and L. Ezzy, "Hadi Ahmadi and the Myth of the 'People Smugglers' Business Model" (2012) **38**(3) *Monash University Law Review* 1.

Scholten, S., and P. Minderhoud, "Regulating Immigration Control: Carrier Sanctions in the Netherlands" (2008) **10**(2) *European Journal of Migration and Law* 123.

Scobbie, I., "The Invocation of Responsibility for the Breach of 'Obligations under Peremptory Norms of General International Law'" (2002) **13**(5) *European Journal of International Law* 1201.

Scott, S., "The LOS Convention as a Constitutional Regime for the Oceans," in A. Oude Elferink ed., *Stability and Change in the Law of the Sea: The Role of the LOS Convention* 9 (2006, Martinus Nijhoff).

Sein, A. J., "The Prosecution of Chinese Organized Crime Groups: The Sister Ping Case and Its Lessons" (2008) **11**(2) *Trends in Organized Crime* 157.

Shearer, I., "Problems of Jurisdiction and Law Enforcement against Delinquent Vessels" (1986) **35** *International and Comparative Law Quarterly* 320.

Shelton, D., "Private Violations, Public Wrongs and the Responsibilities of States" (1989) **13**(1) *Fordham International Law Journal* 1.

Silvey, R., "Unequal Borders: Indonesian Transnational Migrants at Immigration Control" (2007) **12** (2) *Geopolitics* 265.

Simma, B., and A. T. Müller, "Exercise and the Limits of Jurisdiction," in J. Crawford and M. Koskenniemi eds., *The Cambridge Companion to International Law* 134 (2012, Cambridge University Press).

Skogly, S., and M. Gibney, "Economic Rights and Extraterritorial Obligations," in S. Hertel and L. Minkler eds., *Economic Rights: Conceptual, Measurement, and Policy Issues* 267 (2007, Cambridge University Press).

Skulan, C., "Australia's Mandatory Detention of Unauthorized Asylum Seekers: History, Politics and Analysis under International Law" (2006) **21**(1) *Georgetown Immigration Law Journal* 61.

Slaughter, A-M. and W. Burke-White, "An International Constitutional Moment" (2002) **43** *Harvard International Law Journal* 1.

Sloane, R. D., "On the Use and Abuse of Necessity in the Law of State Responsibility" (2012) **106**(3) *American Journal of International Law* 447.

Spindler, S., "Between the Devil and the Deep Blue Sea: Anti-immigration Policies, Reckless Smugglers and Cold Commercial Calculations May Be Endangering Lives at Sea" (2007) 148(4) Refugees, available at www.unhcr.org/refmag/148/index.html (accessed May 12, 2013).

Stubbs, M., "Arbitrary Detention in Australia: Detention of Unlawful Non-citizens under the Migration Act 1958" (2006) **25** *Australian Year Book of International Law* 273.

Stumer, A., "Liability of Member States for Acts of International Organizations: Reconsidering the Policy Objections" (2007) 48 *Harvard International Law Journal* 553.

Suzuki, E., and S. Nanwani, "Responsibility of International Organizations: The Accountability Mechanisms of Multilateral Development Banks" (2006) **27** *Michigan Journal of International Law* 177.

Tanaka, Y., "Zonal and Integrated Management Approaches to Ocean Governance: Reflections on a Dual Approach in International Law of the Sea" (2004) **19**(4) *International Journal of Marine and Coastal Law* 483.

Tazreiter, C., "Between State Sovereignty and Invisibility: Monitoring the Human Rights of Returned Asylum Seekers" (2006) **12** *Australian Journal of Human Rights* 7.

Thouez, C., and F. Channac, "Shaping International Migration Policy: The Role of Regional Consultative Processes" (2006) **29**(2) *West European Politics* 370.

Thym, D., "Respect for Private and Family Life under Article 8 ECHR in Immigration Cases: A Human Right to Regularize Illegal Stay?" (2008) **57** *International and Comparative Law Quarterly* 87.

Tondini, M., "The Legality of Intercepting Boat People under Search and Rescue and Border Control Operations with Reference to Recent Italian Interventions in the Mediterranean Sea and the Ecthr Decision in the Hirsi Case" (2012) 18 *The Journal of International Maritime Law* 59.

Townsend, G., "State Responsibility for Acts of De-facto Agents" (1997) **14** *Arizona Journal of International and Comparative Law* 635.

Treves, T., "Human Rights and the Law of Sea" (2010) **28**(1) *Berkeley Journal of International Law* 1.

Van Den Wyngaert C., and G. Stessens, "The International Non Bis in Idem Principle: Resolving Some of the Unanswered Questions" (1999) 48 *International and Comparative Law Quarterly* 779.

Vlassis, D., "The UN Convention against Transnational Organized Crime," in M. R. Berdal and M. Serrano eds., *Transnational Organized Crime and International Security: Business as Usual?* 83 (Lynne Rienner).

Walker, R., "International Law of the Sea: Applying the Doctrine of Hot Pursuit in the 21st Century" (2011) **17** *Auckland University Law Review* 194.

Weil, P., "Towards Relative Normativity in International Law?" (1983) 77 *American Journal of International Law* 413.

Weissbrodt, D., "The Protection of Non-citizens in International Human Rights Law," in R. Cholewinski, R. Perruchoud, and E. MacDonald eds., *International Migration Law: Developing Paradigms and Key Challenges* 221 (2007, T.M.C. Asser Press).

Weissbrodt, D., and C. Collins, "The Human Rights of Stateless Persons" (2006) **28** *Human Rights Quarterly* 245.

de Wet, E., "The Prohibition of Torture as an International Norm of Jus Cogens and Its Implications for National and Customary Law" (2004) **15** *European Journal of International Law* 97.

White, M., "Tampa Incident: Shipping, International and Maritime Legal Issues" (2004) 78 *Australian Law Journal* 101.

Wilson, D. G., "Interdiction on the High Seas: The Role and Authority of a Master in the Boarding and Searching of His Ship by Foreign Warships" (2008) **55** *Naval Law Review* 157.

Wouters, K., and M. den Heijer, "The Marine I Case: A Comment" (2009) **22** *International Journal of Refugee Law* 1.

Zagor, M., "Uncertainty and Exclusion: Detention of Aliens and the High Court" (2006) **34** *Federal Law Review* 127.

de Zayas, A. "Human Rights and Indefinite Detention" (2005) 87(857) *International Review of the Red Cross* 15.

Zhang, S. X., K. Chin, and J. Miller, "Women's Participation in Chinese Transnational Human Smuggling: A Gendered Market Perspective" (2007) **45**(3) *Criminology* 699.

Zhang, S. X., and M. S. Gaylord, "Bound for the Golden Mountain: The Social Organization of Chinese Alien Smuggling" (1996) **25**(1) *Crime, Law, and Social Change* 1.

3. Documents and Reports of Intergovernmental Organizations

3.1. *International Maritime Organization*

International Maritime Organization, Implications of the United Nations Convention on the Law of the Sea for the International Maritime Organization, Study by the Secretariat of the International Maritime Organization (IMO), IMO Doc. LEG/MISC.6, Sept. 10, 2008.

Implications of the United Nations Convention on the Law of the Sea for the International Maritime Organization, Study by the Secretariat of the International Maritime Organization (IMO), IMO Doc. LEG/MISC.7, Jan. 19, 2012.

International Maritime Organization and Office of the UN High Commissioner for Refugees, *Rescue at Sea: A Guide to Principles and Practice as Applied to Migrants and Refugees* (2006).

International Maritime Organization, Assembly, Enhancement of Safety of Life at Sea by the Prevention and Suppression of Unsafe Practices Associated with Alien Smuggling by Ships, IMO Resolution A.773(18), Nov. 4, 1993.

Combating Unsafe Practices Associated with the Trafficking or Transport of Migrants by Sea, IMO Resolution A.867(20), Nov. 27, 1997.

Guidelines on the Allocation of Responsibilities to Seek the Successful Resolution of Stowaway Cases, IMO Resolution A.871(20), Nov. 27, 1997.

Review of Safety Measures and Procedures for the Treatment of Persons Rescued at Sea, IMO Resolution A.920(22), adopted Nov. 29, 2001, IMO Doc. A 22/Res.920, Jan. 22, 2002.

International Maritime Organization, Facilitation Committee, Principles Relating to Administrative Procedures for Disembarking Persons Rescued at Sea, IMO Doc. FAL.3/Circ.194, Jan. 22, 2009.
International Maritime Organization, Maritime Safety Committee, Interim Measures for Combating Unsafe Practices Associated with the Traffic or Transport of Migrants by Sea, IMO Doc. MSC/Circ.896, Dec. 16, 1998.
Interim Measures for Combating Unsafe Practices Associated with the Trafficking or Transport of Migrants by Sea, IMO Doc. MSC/Circ.896/Rev.1, June 12, 2001.
Guidelines on the Treatment of Persons Rescued at Sea, IMO Resolution MSC.167(78), adopted May 10, 2004, IMO Doc. MSC 78/26/Add.2 Annex 34.
Report of the Maritime Safety Committee on Its Seventy-Eight Session, IMO Docs. MSC 78/26/Add.1 and MSC 78/26/Add.2, June 4, 2004.
Unsafe Practices associated with the Trafficking or Transport of Migrants by Seas, Second Biannual Reports: IMO Doc. MSC.3/Circ.2, Oct. 31, 2001; IMO Doc. MSC.3/Circ.7, July 30, 2004; IMO Doc. MSC.3/Circ.9, July 31, 2005; IMO Doc. MSC.3/Circ.11, July 31, 2006; IMO Doc. MSC.3/Circ.13, July 31, 2007; IMO Doc. MSC.3/Circ.15, July 24, 2008; IMO Doc. MSC.3/Circ.17, Nov. 2, 2009; IMO Doc. MSC.3/Circ.20, Dec. 16, 2011.

3.2. *United Nations High Commissioner for Refugees*

Edwards, A. "Back to Basics: The Right to Liberty and Security of Person and 'Alternatives to Detention' of Refugees, Asylum-Seekers, Stateless Persons and Other Migrants" (UNHCR, Legal and Protection Policy Research Series), Doc. PPLA/2011/01.Rev.1 (April 2011).
Gibney, M., and R. Hansen, "Deportation and the Liberal State: The Forcible Return of Asylum Seekers and Unlawful Migrants in Canada, Germany and the United Kingdom" (New Issues in Refugee Research, Working Paper No. 77 (UNHCR Evaluation and Policy Analysis Unit), 2003).
Massey, H., "UNHCR and De Facto Statelessness," UNHCR Legal and Protection Policy Research Series (2010).
Legomsky, S. H., "Secondary Refugee Movements and the Return of Asylum Seekers to Third Countries: The Meaning of Effective Protection" (UNHCR, Legal and Protection Policy Research Series), Doc. PPLA/2003/01 (Feb. 2003).
UN High Commissioner for Refugees, Handbook on Procedures and Criteria for Determining Refugee Status under the 1951 Convention and the 1967 Protocol Relating to the Status of Refugees, UN Doc. HCR/IP/4/Eng/REV.1 (1979, reissued Jan. 2002).
Problems Related to the Rescue of Asylum-Seekers in Distress at Sea, EC/SCP/30 (Sept. 1, 1983).
"Lawfully Staying" – A Note on Interpretation (1988).
UNHCR Position on Conventions Recently Concluded in Europe (Dublin and Schengen Conventions) (3 European Series 2, at 385) (Aug. 16, 1991).
Refugee Children: Guidelines on Protection and Care (1994).
"The Principle of Non-refoulement as a Norm of Customary International Law: Response to the Questions Posed to UNHCR by the Federal Constitutional Court of the Federal Republic of Germany in Cases 2 BvR 1938/93, 2 BvR 1953/93, 2 BvR 1954/93" (Jan. 31, 1994).
UNHCR Position: Visa Requirements and Carrier Sanctions (1995).

Handbook on Voluntary Repatriation: International Protection (1996).
UNHCR Note on the Principle of Non-refoulement (1997).
UNHCR's Guidelines on Policies and Procedures in Dealing with Unaccompanied Children Seeking Asylum (Feb. 1997).
Global Consultations on International Protection, "Protection of Refugees in Mass Influx Situations: Overall Protection Framework," UN Doc. EC/GC/01/4 (Feb. 19, 2001).
Global Consultations on International Protection, "Asylum Processes (Fair and Efficient Asylum Procedures)," UN Doc. EC/GC/01/12 (May 31, 2001).
Procedural Standards for Refugee Status Determination under UNHCR's Mandate (2003).
Summary Conclusions on the Concept of "Effective Protection" in the Context of Secondary Movements of Refugees and Asylum-Seekers (Lisbon Expert Roundtable, 9–10 December 2002) (Feb. 2003).
Guidelines on International Protection: Application of the Exclusion Clauses: Article 1F of the 1951 Convention relating to the Status of Refugees, UN Doc. HCR/GIP/03/05 (Sept. 4, 2003).
"Summary Conclusions: The Principle of Non-refoulement: Expert Roundtable organized by the UNHCR and the Lauterpacht Research Centre for International Law, University of Cambridge, UK, 9–10 July 2001," in E. Feller, V. Türk, and F. Nicholson eds., *Refugee Protection in International Law: UNHCR's Global Consultations on International Protection* 178 (2003, Cambridge University Press).
Fair and Efficient Asylum Procedures: A Non-exhaustive Overview of Applicable International Standards (Sept. 2, 2005).
Advisory Opinion from the Office of the United Nations High Commissioner for Refugees (UNHCR) on the Scope of the National Security Exception in Article 33(2) of the 1951 Convention Relating to the Status of Refugees (Jan. 6, 2006).
"Guidelines on International Protection: The application of Article 1A(2) of the 1951 Convention and/or 1967 Protocol relating to the Status of Refugees to victims of trafficking and persons at risk of being trafficked," UN Doc. HCR/GIP/06/07 (Apr. 7, 2006).
Refugee Protection and Mixed Migration: A 10-Point Plan of Action (2007).
Advisory Opinion on the Extraterritorial Application of Non-refoulement Obligations under the 1951 Convention Relating to the Status of Refugees and Its 1967 Protocol (Jan. 26, 2007).
Statelessness: An Analytical Framework for Prevention, Reduction and Protection (2008).
UNHCR Guidelines on Determining Best Interests of the Child (May 2008).
UNHCR Statement on Article 1F of the 1951 Convention Issued in the context of the preliminary ruling references to the Court of Justice of the European Communities from the German Federal Administrative Court regarding the interpretation of Articles 12(2)(b) and (c) of the Qualification Directive (July, 2008).
Submission by the Office of the United Nations High Commissioner for Refugees in the Case of Hirsi and Others v. Italy (Application no. 27765/09) (Mar. 2010).
UNHCR Expert Meeting on the Concept of Stateless Persons under International Law ("Prato Conclusions") (May 27–28, 2010).
Maritime Interception Operations and the Processing of International Protection Claims: Legal Standards and Policy Considerations with Respect to Extraterritorial Processing, (Protection Policy Paper, Nov. 2010).

The Return of Persons Found Not to Be in Need of International Protection to Their Countries of Origin: UNHCR's Role (Protection Policy Paper, Nov. 2010).
UNHCR's Oral Intervention at the European Court of Human Rights Hearing of the Case Hirsi and Others v. Italy (Application no. 27765/09), Strasbourg (June 22, 2011).
Guidelines on the Applicable Criteria and Standards Relating to the Detention of Asylum-Seekers and Alternatives to Detention (2012).
"Expert Meeting on Refugees and Asylum-Seekers in Distress at Sea – How Best to Respond? Djibouti, 8–10 November 2011" (2012) **24**(2) *International Journal of Refugee Law* 485.
Guidance Note on Bilateral and/or Multilateral Transfer Arrangements of Asylum-Seekers (May 2013).
UN High Commissioner for Refugees Executive Committee, Conclusion No. 22 – Protection of Asylum-Seekers in Situations of Large-Scale Influx, adopted 32nd Sess, Oct. 21, 1981, in UN General Assembly, "Addendum to the Report of the United Nations High Commissioner for Refugees," UN GAOR 36th Sess, Supp. No. 12A, UN Doc. A/36/12/Add.1, at 17 (1981).
Conclusion No. 44 – Detention of Refugees and Asylum-Seekers (1986)
Conclusion No. 93 – Conclusion on the Reception of Asylum-Seekers in the Context of Individual Asylum Systems (Oct. 8, 2002).
Conclusion on the Return of Persons Found Not to be in Need of International Protection, Doc. No. 96 (LIV) – 2003 (Oct. 10, 2003).
Conclusion on Protection Safeguards in Interception Measures, Doc. No. 97 (LIV) – 2003 (Oct. 10, 2003).
Conclusion on Identification, Prevention and Reduction of Statelessness and Protection of Stateless Persons, Doc. No. 106 (LVII) – 2006 (Oct. 6, 2006).
Conclusion on Children at Risk, Doc. No. 107 (LVIII) – 2007 (Feb. 22, 2007).

3.3. *Other United Nations Documents, Standards, and Resolutions*

Conference of the Parties to the United Nations Convention against Transnational Organized Crime, "Criminalization within the scope of the United Nations Convention against Transnational Organized Crime and the Protocols thereto: Note by the Secretariat," UN Doc. CTOC/COP/2008/4 (Sept. 9, 2008).
"Report on the Meeting of the Working Group on Trafficking in Persons held in Vienna on 14 and 15 April 2009," UN Doc. CTOC/COP/WG.4/2009/2 (Apr. 21, 2009).
Working Group on Trafficking in Persons, "Non-punishment and Non-prosecution of Victims of Trafficking in Persons: Administrative and Judicial Approaches to Offences Committed in the Process of Such Trafficking" UN Doc. CTOC/COP/WG.4/2010/4 (Dec. 9, 2009).
Resolution 5/3 (2010), "Implementation of the Protocol against the Smuggling of Migrants by Land, Sea and Air, supplementing the United Nations Convention against Transnational Organized Crime," UN Doc. CTOC/COP/2010/17, at 11 (Dec. 2, 2010).
Working Group on the Smuggling of Migrants, "Challenges and Good Practices in the Prevention of the Smuggling of Migrants," UN Doc. CTOC/COP/WG.7/2012/4 (Mar. 23, 2012).

"Conclusions of the International Conference on the Smuggling of Migrants: Challenges of and Progress in Implementing the Protocol against the Smuggling of Migrants by Land, Sea and Air, held in Mexico City from 16 to 18 April 2012," UN Doc. CTOC/COP/WG.7/2012/CRP.1 (May 31, 2012).

"Report on the meeting of the Working Group on the Smuggling of Migrants held in Vienna from 30 May to 1 June 2012," UN Doc. CTOC/COP/WG.7/2012/6 (June 27, 2012).

"Report of the Conference of the Parties to the United Nations Convention against Transnational Organized Crime on its sixth session, held in Vienna from 15 to 19 October 2012," UN Doc. CTOC/COP/2012/15 (Nov. 5, 2012).

"Report of the Conference of the Parties to the United Nations Convention against Transnational Organized Crime on its sixth session, held in Vienna from 15 to 19 October 2012," UN Doc. CTOC/COP/2012/15 (Nov. 15, 2012).

Working Group on the Smuggling of Migrants, "Good Practices in Special Investigative Techniques," UN Doc. CTOC/COP/WG.7/2013/2 (Aug. 7, 2013).

"Good Practices in Informal Cross-Border Cooperation and Information-Sharing: Background Paper by the Secretariat," UN Doc. CTOC/COP/WG.7/2013/4 (Sept. 4, 2013).

Division for Ocean Affairs and the Law of the Sea, Office of Legal Affairs of the United Nations, "Table of claims to maritime jurisdiction (as at 15 July 2011)," available at www.un.org/Depts/los/LEGISLATIONANDTREATIES/claims.htm (accessed May 12, 2013).

"Documents: International Conference on Indo-Chinese Refugees (Geneva, 13 and 14 June 1989)" (1993) 5(4) *International Journal of Refugee Law* 617.

"International Conference on Indo-Chinese Refugees (Geneva, 13 and 14 June 1989): Declaration and Comprehensive Plan of Action" (1993) 5(4) *International Journal of Refugee Law* 617.

International Law Commission, "Draft Articles on the Law of Treaties with Commentaries," adopted by the International Law Commission at its 18th session, 1966, in Yearbook of the International Law Commission, 1966, vol. II, UN Doc. A/6309/Rev.1, at 231 (1996).

Draft Articles on Responsibility of States for Internationally Wrongful Acts with commentaries thereto, in "Report of the International Law Commission on the Work of Its Fifty-Third Session," UN GAOR, 56th Sess, Supp. No. 10, UN Doc. A/56/10, at 59 (2001).

"Fragmentation of International Law: Difficulties Arising from the Diversification and Expansion of International Law," UN Doc. A/CN.4/L.682, Apr. 13, 2006.

"Draft articles on the responsibility of international organizations, with commentaries," adopted by the ILC at its sixty-third session in 2011, in "Report of the International Law Commission on the Work of Its Sixty-Third Session," UN GAOR, 63rd Sess., Supp. No. 10, UN Doc. A/66/10, at 69 (2011).

Draft Articles on the Responsibility of International Organizations, adopted by the ILC at its sixty-third session in 2011, in "Report of the International Law Commission on the Work of Its Sixty-Third Session," UN GAOR, 63rd Sess., Supp. No. 10, UN Doc. A/66/10, at 54 (2011).

"Expulsion of Aliens: Texts of draft articles 1–32 provisionally adopted on first reading by the Drafting Committee at the sixty-fourth session of the International Law Commission," UN Doc. A/CN.4/L.797 (May 24, 2012).

"Seventh Report on Responsibility of International Organizations, by G. Gaja," Special Rapporteur," UN Doc A/CN.4/610 (Mar. 27, 2009).

International Law Commission, Reports on the expulsion of aliens, by the Special Rapporteur, Mr. Maurice Kamto,: "Second report," UN Doc. A/CN.4/573 (July 20, 2006); "Third report," UN Doc. A/CN.4/581 (Apr. 19, 2007); "Fifth report," UN Doc. A/CN.4/611 (Mar. 27, 2009); "Sixth report," UN Doc. A/CN.4/625 (Mar. 19, 2010); "Seventh report," UN Doc. A/CN.4/642 (May 4, 2011); and Statement of the Chairman of the Drafting Committee, Mr. Mahmoud D. Hmoud, "Expulsion of Aliens," (May 29, 2012).

International Law Commission, Reports on the obligation to extradite or prosecute (*aut dedere aut judicare*), by the Special Rapporteur, Zdzislaw Galicki: "Third report," UN Doc. A/CN.4/603 (June 10, 2008); "Fourth report," UN Doc. A/CN.4/648 (May 31, 2011).

Office of the UN High Commissioner for Human Rights, *Expulsion of Aliens in International Human Rights Law* (2006).

"*Hirsi et al v. Italy*: Intervener Brief Filed on Behalf of the United Nations High Commissioner for Human Rights," Application No. 27765/09 (May 4, 2011).

Opeskin, B., *The Influence of International Law on the International Movement of Persons*, United Nations Development Programme, Human Development Research Paper 2009/18 (2009).

UN Commission on Human Rights, "The Siracusa Principles on the Limitation and Derogation Provisions in the International Covenant on Civil and Political Rights," UN Doc. E/CN.4/1985/4, Annex, Sept. 28, 1984.

UN Economic and Social Council, Office of the United Nations High Commissioner on Human Rights, "Recommended Principles and Guidelines on Human Rights and Human Trafficking," UN Doc E/2002/68/Add.1, May 20, 2002.

"Guidelines for the Prevention of Crime," ECOSOC Res. 2002/13, Annex, July 24, 2002.

UN General Assembly, "Code of Conduct for Law Enforcement Officials," adopted by GA Res. 34/169, UN Doc. A/RES/34/169, Annex (Dec. 17, 1979).

"United Nations Standard Minimum Rules for the Administration of Juvenile Justice (The Beijing Rules)," adopted by GA Res. 40/33, UN Doc. A/RES/40/33 (Nov. 29, 1985).

"Declaration of Basic Principles of Justice for Victims of Crime and Abuse of Power," adopted by GA Res. 40/34, UN Doc. A/RES/40/34 Annex (Nov. 29, 1985).

"Declaration on the Human Rights of Individuals Who Are Not Nationals of the Country in Which They Live," GA Res. 40/144, UN GAOR, 40th sess, 116th plen mtg, UN Doc. A/RES/40/144 (Dec. 13, 1985).

"Body of Principles for the Protection of All Persons under Any Form of Detention or Imprisonment," adopted by GA Res. 43/173, UN Doc. A/RES/43/173, Annex (Dec. 9, 1988).

"United Nations Rules for the Protection of Juveniles Deprived of Their Liberty," adopted by GA Res. 45/113, UN Doc. A/RES/45/113 (Dec. 14, 1990).

"Model Treaty on Extradition," UN Doc. A/RES/45/116, Dec. 14, 1990, subsequently amended by UN General Assembly, "International Cooperation in Criminal Matters," UN Doc. A/RES/52/88 (Dec. 12, 1997).

"Model Treaty on the Transfer of Proceedings in Criminal Matters," adopted by GA Res. 45/118, UN Doc. A/RES/45/118, Dec. 14, 1990, and amended by GA Res. 53/112 (UN General Assembly, "Mutual assistance and international cooperation in criminal matters," GA Res. 53/112, UN Doc. A/RES/53/112 (Jan. 20, 1999).

"Basic Principles and Guidelines on the Right to a Remedy and Reparation for Victims of Gross Violations of International Human Rights Law and Serious Violation of International Humanitarian Law," UN Doc. A/RES/60/147 Annex (Dec. 16, 2005).
"United Nations Rules for the Treatment of Women Prisoners and Non-custodial Measures for Women Offenders (the Bangkok Rules)," adopted by the UN General Assembly July 22, 2010 (by GA Res 2010/16, UN Doc. A/C.3/65/L.5, Oct. 6, 2010).
United Nations, "Standard Minimum Rules for the Treatment of Prisoners," adopted by the First United Nations Congress on the Prevention of Crime and the Treatment of Offenders, held at Geneva in 1955, and approved by the Economic and Social Council by its resolutions 663 C (XXIV) of 31 July 1957 and 2076 (LXII) of 13 May 1977, Aug. 30, 1955.
Commentary on the United Nations Convention against Illicit Traffic in Narcotic Drugs and Psychotropic Substances 1998, UN Doc. E/CN.7/590 (Dec. 20, 1998).
"Human Rights Instruments: Compilation of General Comments and General Recommendations adopted by Human Rights Treaty Bodies," Volume I: UN Doc. HRI/GEN/Rev.9 (Vol. 1) (May 27, 2008) and Volume II: UN Doc. HRI/GEN/1/Rev.9 (Vol. II) (May 27, 2008).
United Nations Children's Fund, *Guidelines for the Protection of Child Victims of Trafficking* (September 2006).
United Nations Development Programme, *Overcoming Barriers: Human Mobility and Development* (Human Development Report, 2009).
United Nations Office on Drugs and Crime, *Legislative Guides for the Implementation of the United Nations Convention against Transnational Organized Crime and the Protocols thereto*, UN Sales No. E.05.V.2 (2004).
Legislative Guide for the Implementation of the United Nations Convention against Corruption, UN Sales No. E.06.IV.16 (2006).
Travaux Préparatoires of the Negotiations for the Elaboration of the United Nations Convention against Transnational Organized Crime and the Protocols Thereto (2006).
Model Law on Mutual Legal Assistance in Criminal Matters, (2007).
Good Practices for the Protection of Witnesses in Criminal Proceedings Involving Organized Crime (2008).
Model Law on Trafficking in Persons, UN Sales No. E.09.V.11 (2009).
Basic Training Manual on Investigating and Prosecuting the Smuggling of Migrants (2010).
Handbook on the Crime Prevention Guidelines: Making Them Work (2010).
Issue Paper: Smuggling of Migrants by Air (2010).
Model Law against the Smuggling of Migrants (2010).
Toolkit to Combat Smuggling of Migrants (2010).
International Framework for Action to Implement the Smuggling of Migrants Protocol (2011).
Issue Paper: Smuggling of Migrants by Sea (2011).
Smuggling of Migrants: A Global Review and Annotated Bibliography of Recent Publications (2011).
The Role of Organized Crime in the Smuggling of Migrants from West Africa to the European Union (2011).
Abuse of a Position of Vulnerability and Other "Means" within the Definition of Trafficking in Persons (2012).

Handbook on the International Transfer of Sentenced Persons (2012).
Migrant Smuggling in Asia: A Thematic Review of Literature (2012).
Model Legislative Provisions against Organized Crime (2012).
Transnational Organized Crime in East Asia and the Pacific: A Threat Assessment (2013)
United Nations Office on Drugs and Crime and the International Monetary Fund, *Model Legislation on Money Laundering and Financing of Terrorism* (2005).
Vlassis, D., "The Global Situation of Transnational Organized Crime, the Decision of the International Community to Develop an International Convention and the Negotiation Process," in United Nations Asia and Far East Institute for the Prevention of Crime and the Treatment of Offenders, *Annual Report for 2000 and Resource Materials* Series No. 59 475 (2002).

3.4. *European Union/Council of Europe Regulations and Policy Documents*

European Union

Commission of the European Communities, Report from the Commission based on Article 9 of the Council Framework Decision of 28 November 2002 on the strengthening of the penal framework to prevent the facilitation of unauthorised entry, transit and residence, COM(2006) 770 final, Dec. 6, 2006.
Communication from the Commission to the European Parliament and the Council: Evaluation of EU Readmission Agreements, COM(2011) 76 final, Feb. 23, 2011.
Council of the European Union, Press Release, 2683rd Council Meeting, Justice and Home Affairs, Doc. 12645/05 (Presse 247) (Oct. 12, 2005).
The Stockholm Programme – An open and secure Europe serving and protecting citizens, OJ C 115/1, May 4, 2010.
Council conclusions defining the EU strategy on readmission, Doc. 11260/11 MIGR 118, June 8, 2011.
Council Secretariet, "Joint Investigation Teams Manual," Doc. No. 15790/1/11 REV 1, Nov. 4, 2011.
Council Regulation (EC) No 377/2004 of 19 February 2004 on the creation of an immigration liaison officers network, OJ L 64/1, Mar. 2, 2004.
Council Regulation (EC) No 2007/2004 of 26 October 2004 establishing a European Agency for the Management of Operational Cooperation at the External Borders of the Member States of the European Union, OJ L 349/1, Nov. 25, 2004.
Council Regulation (EC) No 2252/2004 of 13 December 2004 on standards for security features and biometrics in passports and travel documents issued by Member States, OJ L 385/1, Dec. 29, 2004.
European Agency for the Management of Operational Cooperation at the External Borders of the Member States of the European Union, Frontex Fundamental Rights Strategy (2011).
European Commission, Readmission Agreements, MEMO/05/351 (Oct. 5, 2005).
Staff Working Document, "Study on the International Law Instruments in Relation to Illegal Immigration by Sea," SEC(2007) 691 (May 15, 2007).
Communication from the Commission to the European Parliament and the Council: Action Plan on Unaccompanied Minors (2010–2014), COM(2010)213 final (May 6, 2010).

Proposal for a Directive of the European Parliament and of the Council on the use of Passenger Name Record data for the prevention, detection, investigation and prosecution of terrorist offences and serious crime, COM(2011) 32 final (Feb. 2, 2011).
Communication from the Commission to the European Parliament and the Council: Evaluation of EU Readmission Agreements, COM(2011) 76 final (Feb. 23, 2011).
European Migration Network, "Programs and Strategies in the EU Member States Fostering Assisted Return to and Reintegration in Third Countries" (Synthesis Report summarizing the main findings of the National Reports for the European Migration Network, March 2011).
European Union Agency for Fundamental Rights, *Detention of Third-Country Nationals in Return Procedures* (Thematic Report, Sept. 2010).
Joint Africa–EU Declaration on Migration and Development (Tripoli, Nov. 22–23, 2006).
Proposal for a Comprehensive plan to combat illegal immigration and trafficking of human beings in the European Union (2002/C, 142/02), OJ C 142/23 (June 14, 2002).
Regulation (EC) No 562/2006 of the European Parliament and of the Council of 15 March 2006 establishing a Community Code on the rules governing the movement of persons across borders (Schengen Borders Code), OJ L 105/1 (Apr. 13, 2006).
Regulation (EC) No 863/2007 of the European Parliament and of the Council of 11 July 2007 establishing a mechanism for the creation of Rapid Border Intervention Teams and amending Council Regulation (EC) No 2007/2004 as regards that mechanism and regulating the tasks and powers of guest officers, OJ L 199/30 (July 31, 2007).
Regulation (EC) No 444/2009 of the European Parliament and of the Council of 28 May 2009 amending Council Regulation (EC) No 2252/2004 on standards for security features and biometrics in passports and travel documents issued by Member States, OJ L 142/1 (June 6, 2009).
Regulation (EC) No 377/2004 on the creation of an immigration liaison officers network, OJ L141/13 (May 27, 2011).
Regulation (EU) No 493/2011 of the European Parliament and of the Council of 5 April 2011 amending Council Regulation (EC) No 377/2004 on the creation of an immigration liaison officers network, OJ L141/13 (May 27, 2011).
Regulation (EU) No 1168/2011 of the European Parliament and of the Council of 25 October 2011 amending Council Regulation (EC) No 2007/2004 establishing a European Agency for the Management of Operational Cooperation at the External Borders of the Member States of the European Union, OJ L 304/1 (Nov. 22, 2011).

Council of Europe

Council of Europe, Explanatory Report on the Convention on Action against Trafficking in Human Beings, ETS **197**, **16**.V. (2005).
Council of Europe "Report to the Italian Government on the visit to Italy carried out by the European Committee for the Prevention of Torture and Inhuman or Degrading Treatment or Punishment (CPT) from 27 to 31 July 2009," Doc. CPT/Inf (2010) 14 (Apr. 28, 2010).
Council of Europe, Commissioner for Human Rights, Criminalisation of Migration in Europe: Human Rights Implications, CommDH/Issue Paper (2010)1 (Feb. 4, 2010).
Council of Europe, Committee of Ministers, Twenty Guidelines on Forced Return, CM(2005)40 final (May 9, 2005).

Council of Europe, Parliamentary Assembly, Resolution 1637 (2008) on Europe's "boat people": mixed migration flows by Sea into southern Europe, adopted Nov. 28, 2008.
Council of Europe, Report of the Committee on Migration, Refugees and Population, The detention of asylum seekers and irregular migrants in Europe, Doc. 12105 (Jan. 11, 2010).
Resolution 1707 (2010) on Detention of asylum seekers and irregular migrants in Europe, adopted Jan. 28, 2010.
Report of the Committee on Migration, Refugees and Population, Readmission agreements: a mechanism for returning irregular migrants, Report, Doc. 12168 (Mar. 17, 2010).
Resolution 1741 (2010) on Readmission agreements: a mechanism for returning irregular migrants, adopted June 22, 2010.
The interception and rescue at sea of asylum seekers, refugees and irregular migrants, Report of the Committee on Migration, Refugees and Population, Doc. 12628 (June 1, 2011).
Resolution 1821(2011) on The interception and rescue at sea of asylum seekers, refugees and irregular migrants, adopted June 21, 2011.
Lives Lost in the Mediterranean Sea: Who Is Responsible? Report of the Committee on Migration, Refugees and Displaced Persons, Doc. 12895 (Apr. 5, 2012).
Resolution 1932 (2013) Frontex: human rights responsibilities, adopted April 25, 2013.
Lambert, H., *The Position of Aliens in Relation to the European Convention on Human Rights*, Council of Europe (2007).

4. Other Materials

Albahari, M., *Death and the Moral State: Making Borders and Sovereignty at the Southern Edges of Europe* (Centre for Comparative Immigration Studies, University of California, Working Paper 136, June 2006).
American Law Institute, *Restatement (Third) of the Foreign Relations Law of the United States* (1990, ALI,).
Amnesty International, *Migration-Related Detention: A Research Guide on Human Rights Standards Relevant to the Detention of Migrants, Asylum Seekers and Refugees* (2007).
Eritrea: Sent Home to Detention and Torture (2008).
S.O.S. Europe: Human Rights and Migration Control (2012).
Association of Southeast Asian Nations, *ASEAN Handbook on International Legal Cooperation in Trafficking in Persons Cases* (2010).
ASEAN Declaration on Transnational Crime (adopted Dec. 20, 1997, 1st ASEAN Conference on Transnational Crime, Manila, Philippines).
Australian Broadcasting Commission, No Advantage (video documentary, 2013), available at www.abc.net.au/4corners/stories/2013/04/29/3745276.htm (accessed May 12, 2013).
Australian Department for Transport and Regional Services, *Guidelines for Commercial Shipping Rescuing Persons at Sea in or Adjacent to the Australian Search and Rescue Region* (June 2005), available at www.infrastructure.gov.au/maritime/safety/sea_rescue.aspx (accessed May 12, 2013).
Australian Government, *Expert Panel on Asylum Seekers, Report of the Expert Panel on Asylum Seekers* (August 2012).

Australian Government, Refugee Review Tribunal, *A Guide to Refugee Law in Australia* (2012, Commonwealth of Australia).

Australian Human Rights and Equal Opportunity Commission, *A Last Resort? The National Inquiry into Children in Immigration Detention* (2004).

Australian Human Rights Commission, *An Age of Uncertainty: Inquiry into the Treatment of Individuals Suspected of People Smuggling Offences Who Say That They Are Children* (July 2012).

Australian Parliament, Joint Select Committee on Australia's Immigration Detention Network, *Final Report* (2012), available at www.aph.gov.au/Parliamentary_Business/Committees/Senate_Committees?url=immigration_detention_ctte/immigration_detention/report/index.htm (accessed May 12, 2013).

Burnett, J., J. Carter, J. Evershed, M. Bell Kohli, C. Powell, and G. de Wilde, *State Sponsored Cruelty: Children in Immigration Detention* (2010, Medical Justice).

Canetta, E., S. Korpelainen, C. Mortera, L. Robson, V. Minkova, and K. Damianakis, "Evaluation on the Implementation and Functioning of the Obligation of Carriers to Communicate Passenger Data Set Up by Directive 2004/82" (2012, Final Report for Directorate-General for Home Affairs).

Cerone, J., *Out of Bounds? Considering the Reach of International Human Rights Law* (2006, Center for Human Rights and Global Justice Working Paper Number 5, NYU School of Law).

Carrera, S., L. den Hertog and J. Parkin, *EU Migration Policy in the Wake of the Arab Spring: What Prospects for EU-Southern Mediterranean Relations?* (MEDPRO Technical Report No. 15/August 2012).

Cox, E., and T. Priest, *Women in Immigration Detention: More Questions than Answers* (2005, University of Technology, Sydney).

Cuba–United States: Joint Statement on Normalization of Migration, Building on the Agreement of September 9, 1994, 35 ILM 327 (1996), done May 2, 1995.

David, F., *Human Smuggling and Trafficking: An Overview of the Responses at the Federal Level* (Australian Institute of Criminology Research and Public Policy Series No. 24, 2000).

Labour Trafficking (Australian Institute of Criminology, Research and Public Policy Series 108, 2010).

Dent, J. A., *Research Paper on the Social and Economic Rights of Non-nationals in Europe* (1998, European Council on Refugees and Exiles).

European Council on Refugees and Exiles, *An Overview of Proposals Addressing Migrant Smuggling and Trafficking in Persons* (European Council on Refugees and Exiles Background Paper, July 1991).

Defending Refugees' Access to Protection in Europe (Dec. 2007).

ECRE Information note on the Directive 2008/115/EC of the European Parliament and of the Council of 16 December 2008 on common standards and procedures in Member States for returning illegally staying third-country nationals, Doc. CO7/1/2009/Ext/MDM (Jan. 7, 2009).

European Council on Refugees and Exiles and Save the Children, European Commission Directorate-General Home Comparative Study on Practices in the Field of Return of Minors, Doc. HOME/2009/RFXX/PR/1002 (Dec. 2011).

European Migration Network, "Programs and Strategies in the EU Member States Fostering Assisted Return to and Reintegration in Third Countries" (Synthesis Report summarizing the main findings of the National Reports for the European Migration Network, Mar. 2011).

Federal Office for Migration (Switzerland) and International Organization for Migration, The Berne Initiative, *International Agenda for Migration Management: Common Understandings and Effective Practices for a Planned, Balanced, and Comprehensive Approach to the Management of Migration* (2004).

Flynn, M., *Immigration Detention and Proportionality* (Global Detention Project Working Paper No. 4, February 2011).

Flynn, M., and C. Cannon, *The Privatization of Immigration Detention: Towards a Global View* (Global Detention Project Working Paper, 2009).

Freedman, J., and B. Jamal, *Violence against Migrant Women and Refugee in the Euromed Region – Case Studies: France, Italy, Egypt & Morocco* (2008, Euro-Mediterranean Human Rights Network).

Gammeltoft-Hansen, T., and T. E. Aalberts, "Sovereignty at Sea: The Law and Politics of Saving Lives in the Mare Liberum," DIIS Working Paper 2010:18 (2010).

Global Commission on International Migration, *Migration in an Interconnected World: New Directions for Action* (Report of the Global Commission on International Migration, Oct. 2, 2005).

Groussot, X., T. Lock, and L. Pech, "EU Accession to the European Convention on Human Rights: A Legal Assessment of the Draft Accession Agreement of 14th October 2011" (Foundation Robert Schuman Policy Paper, European Issues No. 218, Nov. 7, 2011).

Guild, E., "Criminalisation of Migration in Europe: Human Rights Implications" (2010, Issue Paper, Council of Europe, Commissioner for Human Rights).

Hales, L., and L. Gelsthorpe, *The Criminalisation of Migrant Women* (2012, Institute of Criminology, University of Cambridge, United Kingdom).

Hansen, R., *An Assessment of Principal Regional Consultative Processes on Migration* (2010, International Organization for Migration Research Series, No. 38).

Heller, C., L. Pezzani and Situ Studio, *Report on the "Left-To-Die Boat"* (2012), available at www.forensic-architecture.org/publications/report-on-the-left-to-die-boat/ (accessed May 12, 2013).

House of Lords (United Kingdom), European Union Committee, *Frontex: The EU External Borders Agency, Report with Evidence* (9th Report of Session 2007–08).

Human Rights Watch, *Hostile Shores: Abuse and Refoulement of Asylum Seekers and Refugees in Yemen* (2009).

Pushed Back, Pushed around Italy's Forced Return of Boat Migrants and Asylum Seekers, Libya's Mistreatment of Migrants and Asylum Seekers (2009).

Fast-Tracked Unfairness: Detention and Denial of Women Asylum Seekers in the UK (2010).

Ukraine: Buffeted in the Borderland, The Treatment of Migrants and Asylum Seekers in Ukraine (2010).

The EU's Dirty Hands: Frontex Involvement in Ill-Treatment of Migrant Detainees in Greece (2011).

Hate on the Streets: Xenophobic Violence in Greece (2012).

Human Smuggling and Anti-Trafficking Center (United States), A *Report to Congress as required by Section 7202(d) of the Intelligence Reform and Terrorism Prevention Act of 2004* (2005).

International Centre for Migration Policy and Development and European Council and Matrix, Comparative Study for Best Practices in Forced Return Monitoring, European Commission Directorate-General Justice, Freedom and Security, JLS/2009/RFXX/CA/1001 (Nov. 10, 2011).

International Committee of the Red Cross, *Inter-agency Guiding Principles on Unaccompanied and Separated Children* (Jan. 2004).

International Council on Human Rights Policy and Transparency International, *Corruption and Human Rights: Making the Connection* (2009), available at www.ichrp.org/files/reports/40/131_web.pdf (accessed May 12, 2013).

International Organization for Migration, *World Migration Report* (2010).

International Migration Law: Information Note on International Standards on Immigration Detention and Non-custodial Measures (2011).

Keller, S., S. U. Luncek, B. Lochbihler, and H. Flautre, *Frontex Agency: Which Guarantees for Human Rights?* Brussels, Greens/European Free Alliance in European Parliament (2011, Migreurop).

Flynn, M., and C. Cannon, *The Privatization of Immigration Detention: Towards a Global View* (2009, Global Detention Project Working Paper).

Maccanico, Y., *The EU's Self-interested Response to Unrest in North Africa: The Meaning of Treaties and Readmission Agreements between Italy and North African States* (2012, Statewatch).

Matrix and International Centre for Migration Policy and Development and European Council on Refugees and Exiles, European Commission Directorate-General Home Affairs Comparative Study on Best Practice to Interlink Pre-Departure Reintegration Measures carried out in Member States with Short- and Long-Term Reintegration Measures in the Countries of Return, Doc. No. JLS/2009/RF?CA/1003 (Jan. 17, 2012).

Medecins Sans Frontieres, *No Choice: Somali and Ethiopian Refugees, Asylum Seekers and Migrants Crossing the Gulf of Aden* (2008).

Sexual Violence and Migration: The Hidden Reality of Sub-Saharan Women Trapped in Morocco en Route to Europe (2010).

Memorandum of Understanding between the Government of Australia, the Government of the Islamic Republic of Afghanistan and the United Nations High Commissioner for Refugees (UNHCR) on migration and humanitarian cooperation, Jan. 17, 2011, available at www.minister.immi.gov.au/media/media-releases/_pdf/mou-with-afghanistan-unhcr.pdf (accessed May 12, 2013).

Memorandum of Understanding between the Government of the Independent State of Papua New Guinea and the Government of Australia, Relating to the Transfer to and Assessment of Persons in Papua New Guinea, and Related Issues, signed Sept. 8, 2012.

Memorandum of Understanding between the Republic of Nauru and the Commonwealth of Australia, relating to the Transfer to and Assessment of Persons in Nauru, and Related Issues, signed Aug. 29, 2012.

Memorandum of Understanding between the Government of Australia, the Government of the Islamic Republic of Afghanistan and the United Nations High Commissioner for Refugees (UNHCR) on migration and humanitarian cooperation, Jan. 17, 2011, available at www.minister.immi.gov.au/media/media-releases/_pdf/mou-with-afghanistan-unhcr.pdf (accessed May 12, 2013).

Migrant Smuggling Working Group, University of Queensland, *Migrant Smugglers: Profiles and Prosecutions* (2010), available at www.law.uq.edu.au/index.html?page=184144# Quassey (accessed May 12, 2013).

Monzini, P., *Migrant Smuggling via Maritime Routes* (2004, CeSPI – Centro Studi di Politica Internazionale).

Monzini, P., F. Pastore and G. Sciortino, "Human Smuggling to/through Italy" (Research Project, The Human Smuggling and Trafficking in Migrants: Types, Origins and Dynamics in a Comparative and Interdisciplinary Perspective, April 2004).

Morehouse, C., and M. Blomfield, *Irregular Migration in Europe* (Migration Policy Institute, Dec. 2011).

Murdoch J. L., ed., *Article 5 of the European Convention on Human Rights: The Protection of Liberty and Security of the Person* (2002, Council of Europe).

National Immigration Forum, *The Math of Immigration Detention: Runaway Costs for Immigration Detention Do Not Add Up to Sensible Policies* (2013).

North, Justice A. "Extraterritorial Effect of Non-refoulement," address to the International Association of Refugee Law Judges World Conference, Bled, Slovenia, 7–9 September 2011, available at www3.austlii.edu.au/au/journals/FedJSchol/2011/19.html (accessed May 12, 2013).

Opeskin, B., *The Influence of International Law on the International Movement of Persons* (2009, United Nations Development Programme, Human Development Research Paper 2009/18).

Organisation for Economic Cooperation and Development, *International Migration Outlook 2012* (2012).

Organization for Security and Co-operation in Europe, *Policy and Legislative Recommendations Towards the Effective Implementation of the Non-Punishment Provision with regard to Victims of Trafficking* (2013).

Paoletti, E., and F. Pastore, *Sharing the Dirty Job on the Southern Front? Italian-Libyan Relations on Migration and Their Impact on the European Union* (2010, International Migration Institute Working Papers).

Penal Reform International, *Safeguarding Children in Detention: Independent Monitoring Mechanisms for Children in Detention in Mena* (2011).

Protocol between Italy and Albania to Prevent Certain Illegal Acts and Render Humanitarian Assistance to Those Leaving Albania (Apr. 2, 1997).

Ramos, C., *Unsafe Return: Refoulement of Congolese Asylum Seekers* (2011).

Ricipuro, I., and M. Flynn, *Migration and Detention: Mapping the Legal Terrain* (2009, Global Detention Project Working Paper).

Rosenblum, M., and K. Brick, *US Immigration Policy and Mexican/Central American Migration Flows: Then and Now* (2011, Migration Policy Institute).

van Reisen, M., M. Estefanos, and C. Rijken, *Human Trafficking in the Sinai: Refugees between Life and Death* (2012, Wolf Legal).

Rodier, C., "Analysis of the external dimension of the European Union's asylum and immigration policies' – summary and recommendations for the European Parliament," Doc. No. DGExPo/B/PolDep/ETUDE/2006_11 (Jun. 8, 2006).

Ronzitti, N., "The Treaty of Friendship, Partnership and Cooperation between Italy and Libya: New Prospects for Cooperation in the Mediterranean" paper presented at the Mediterranean Strategy Group Conference, May 11–12, 2009.

Servent, A., *The European Parliament and the "Returns" Directive: The End of Radical Contestation; the Start of Consensual Constraints?* (Sussex European Institute, Working Paper No. 117, 2010).

Schloenhardt, A., and J. H. Douglas, *Combatting Migrant Smuggling with Regional Diplomacy: An Examination of the Bali Process* (University of Queensland Research Paper, February 2012).

Siskin, A., *Immigration-Related Detention: Current Legislative Issues* (Congressional Research Service Report for Congress, Jan. 12, 2012).

Soucy, A., *Mixed Migration from the Horn of Africa to Yemen: Protection Risks and Challenges* (2011, Danish Refugee Council).

Story, B. *Politics as Usual: The Criminalization of Asylum Seekers in the United States* (University of Oxford Refugee Studies Centre Working Paper No. 26, Sept. 2005).

Terre des Hommes International Federation, *Global Campaign to End Immigration Detention of Children and Platform for International Cooperation on Undocumented Migrants, A Call on States to Stop Detaining Migrant Children* (Dec. 18, 2012), available at http://endchilddetention.org/wp-content/themes/end/images/uploads/Press-release-International-Migrants-Day-2012.pdf (accessed May 12, 2013).

The Equal Rights Trust, *Unravelling Anomaly: Detention, Discrimination and the Protection Needs of Stateless Persons* (2010, The Equal Rights Trust).

The White House, Washington (United States), "Memorandum: Presidential Decision Directive/NSC-9 on Alien Smuggling," June 18, 1993 available at www.fas.org/irp/offdocs/pdd/pdd-9.pdf (accessed May 12, 2013).

Trauner, F., and I. Kruse, *EC Visa Facilitation and Readmission Agreements: Implementing a New EU Security Approach in the Neighbourhood* (CEPS Working Document No. 290; CASE Network Studies and Analyses No. 363, Apr. 23, 2008).

United States Immigration and Customs Enforcement, "Memorandum on Civil Immigration Enforcement: Priorities for the Apprehension, Detention and Removal of Aliens," Mar. 2, 2011, available at www.ice.gov/doclib/news/releases/2011/110302washingtondc.pdf (accessed May 12, 2013).

United States Department of State, Office of the Legal Adviser, M. S. Pickering, S. J. Cummins and D. P. Stewart eds., *Digest of United States Practice in International Law* (1989–1990).

United States, Department of State, *Observations of the United States on the Advisory Opinion of the UN High Commissioner for Refugees on the Extraterritorial Application of Non-refoulement Obligations under the 1951 Convention Relating to the Status of Refugees and Its 1967 Protocol* (Dec. 28, 2007).

United States, *The Commander's Handbook on the Law of Naval Operations* (July 2007 ed., Department of the Navy, Department of Homeland Security and U.S. Coast Guard).

Van Criekinge, T., *The EU–Africa Migration Partnership: A Case Study of the EU's Migration Dialogue with Ghana and Senegal* (EUI Migration Working Group, Mar. 2010).

Webb, S., and J. Burrows, "Organised Immigration Crime: A Post-conviction Study" (Home Office, Research Report 15, July 2009).

Yun, G., ed., *Concealed Chains: Labour Exploitation and Chinese Migrants in Europe* (2010, International Labour Organization).

Zhang, S. X., and K. Chin, "Characteristics of Chinese Human Smugglers: A Cross National Study" (Oct. 2002).

Index

For references to treaties and other international instruments, see the Table of Treaties and Other International Instruments. For jurisprudence by case, see the Table of Cases.

Lightning Source UK Ltd.
Milton Keynes UK
UKHW012344290119
336442UK00011B/130/P

9 781107 015920